Universal Horrors

SECOND EDITION

Universal Horrors

The Studio's Classic Films, 1931–1946

Second Edition

TOM WEAVER,
MICHAEL BRUNAS *AND* JOHN BRUNAS

McFarland & Company, Inc., Publishers
Jefferson, North Carolina, and London

Other books by Tom Weaver and from McFarland: *Eye on Science Fiction: 20 Interviews with Classic SF and Horror Filmmakers* (2003; paperback 2007). *Interviews with B Science Fiction and Horror Movie Makers: Writers, Producers, Directors, Actors, Moguls and Makeup* (1988; paperback 2006). *Science Fiction Stars and Horror Heroes: Interviews with Actors, Directors, Producers and Writers of the 1940s through 1960s* (1991; paperback 2006). *Earth vs. the Sci-Fi Filmmakers: 20 Interviews* (2005). *It Came from Horrorwood: Interviews with Moviemakers in the SF and Horror Tradition* (1996; paperback 2004). *Science Fiction and Fantasy Film Flashbacks: Conversations with 24 Actors, Writers, Producers and Directors from the Golden Age* (1998; paperback 2004). *Double Feature Creature Attack: A Monster Merger of Two More Volumes of Classic Interviews* (paperback 2003; a combined edition of the two earlier Weaver titles *Attack of the Monster Movie Makers* and *They Fought in the Creature Features*). *Science Fiction Confidential: Interviews with 23 Monster Stars and Filmmakers* (2002). *I Was a Monster Movie Maker: Conversations with 22 SF and Horror Filmmakers* (2001). *Poverty Row HORRORS! Monogram, PRC and Republic Horror Films of the Forties* (1993; paperback 1999). *John Carradine: The Films* (1999)

Frontispiece: A star is born! Boris Karloff as the Monster in the 1931 *Frankenstein.*

LIBRARY OF CONGRESS CATALOGUING-IN-PUBLICATION DATA

Weaver, Tom, 1958–
Universal horrors : the studio's classic films, 1931–1946 /
Tom Weaver, Michael Brunas and John Brunas. — 2nd ed.
p. cm.
Rev. ed. of: Universal horrors / Michael Brunas. ©1990.
Includes index.

ISBN-13: 978-0-7864-2974-5
(illustrated case binding : 50# alkaline paper) ♾

1. Horror films — United States — History and criticism.
2. Universal Pictures Corporation.
I. Brunas, Michael. II. Brunas, John.
III. Brunas, Michael. Universal horrors. I. Title.
PN1995.9.H6B7 2007 791.43'616 — dc22 2006036001

British Library cataloguing data are available

On the front cover: Gloria Stuart and Boris Karloff in *The Old Dark House,* 1932 (Photofest); *on the back cover:* Rondo Hatton, mid-1940s "monster man" in a publicity pose

Manufactured in the United States of America

McFarland & Company, Inc., Publishers
Box 611, Jefferson, North Carolina 28640
www.mcfarlandpub.com

The authors gratefully dedicate this book to...
Ruth (Mrs. John Brunas) for her unconditional love, support, and stubborn belief that the authors could make lightning strike twice.
To Rich Scrivani.
And to Boris. Poor Boris.

Table of Contents

Introduction

We are presenting this updating of *Universal Horrors* with belated but sincere gratitude for the generous reception which greeted its original publication back in 1990. The surge of interest in Universal horror movies since then has been phenomenal, all the more so since it has been occurring at a time when vintage black-and-white films are fast becoming cultural relics, cinematic cast-asides for a niche audience. Yet in the last decade DVD box sets of Universal chillers have racked up impressive sales, original memorabilia sells at astronomical prices and even the U.S. Postal Service has seen fit to commemorate the studio's most famous monsters with a striking set of postage stamps — all of which hardly would have seemed likely a mere twenty years ago. This is not a phenomenon fueled only by nostalgia but it *is* another stepping stone in Universal's monsters' quest to attain some measure of critical acceptance since they first started coming on the scene back in 1931. That's not to say that historians are tripping over themselves to replace *Citizen Kane* with *Frankenstein* as The Classic American Film, but rather that the best of the Universal horror pictures are recognized as works of genuine merit as well as being popular audience favorites.

This shouldn't be surprising for the Baby Boomer generation who have always shown a natural and enthusiastic affinity for horror and science fiction in popular media. Even though writers such as Edgar Allan Poe, H.G. Wells and Bram Stoker cultivated sizable followings in their time and beyond, the critical establishment has traditionally been leery of macabre and fantastic literature as a whole. Technology, the Second World War and the dawn of the atomic age changed all this; one of its unintended consequences is the seismic impact it made on the sensibilities of those in their formative years. It wasn't a coincidence that just when it seemed that nothing was beyond the limits of modern science, the newborns of that era would find a fascination in movies and literature of the fantastic.

This makes for an intriguing comparison to the times in which the Universal thrillers were actually produced (the period starting with the early days of the Depression and ending with the dawn of the post-war era). Despite scoring an instantaneous success, their impact was measured mostly in terms of hard box office numbers. Horror movies may have sold millions of tickets but the precise demographics of those early audiences is shrouded in mystery. No doubt Universal found a thriving market in the younger set but these features also had a strong appeal for the masses, particularly the uneducated and the working classes. Of course, it was a time in which very little was written about B pictures. Except for regular newspaper reviews which tended to be rudely dismissive of monsters, the subject of genre movies was one which the mainstream press pointedly avoided. As a result, Dracula, the Wolf Man and the Frankenstein Monster simply made their rounds at the local movie houses without journalistic comment and were promptly forgotten, their celluloid adventures as disposable as other cheap entertainments such as comic books, radio shows and the Sunday funnies.

On the studio's back lot stood the legendary European Street, playground for the casts of many a classic horror film (courtesy John Antosiewicz).

It wasn't until late–'50s television audiences caught their first glimpses of Karloff, Lugosi et al. in Screen Gem's shrewdly marketed *Shock* package of feature films that these pictures began to take on some measure of cultural significance. Somehow when viewed as a collective unit rather than as a string of scattershot efforts released over a span of years, these movies ceased to be transitory cinematic fodder, especially to young audiences watching them transfixed in front of flickering, rabbit-eared television sets. Almost imperceptibly, a collective conscience was beginning to form. By the time the earliest monster movie magazines started to circulate, led by Warren Publications' *Famous Monsters of Filmland*, edited by Forrest J Ackerman, the first manifestations of a permanent fan base began to emerge. Boris Karloff's Frankenstein Monster, Bela Lugosi's Dracula and Lon Chaney, Jr.'s, Wolf Man were becoming heroic, even iconic figures as disgruntled and highly vocal parents and teachers were deriding them as being near subversive.

As the World War II generation was inevitably eclipsed by the Viet Nam–era Boomers as the major taste arbiters of pop culture, there came a rapid reordering of standards. Just as Elvis and the Beatles began sharing the spotlight with Sinatra and Crosby as legitimate artists, so did horror and science fiction movies eventually replace the traditional Western as the staple movie genre. But it was the Universal horror film which can be credited with fueling the younger crowd's passion for screen terror, eventually affecting the sensibilities of people who never even saw a Boris Karloff movie.

Wide-angle glimpse of European Street, familiar to lovers of Universal Horrors (courtesy John Antosiewicz).

It's doubtful, for instance, that *Psycho*, arguably the most influential Hollywood movie of the early '60s, would even have been made had not Alfred Hitchcock been impressed with the box office performance of low-budget horror movies, all of which owe a debt to the Universal horror films of the past. The staggering commercial success of *Psycho* more than solidified Hitchcock's position as one of the most bankable Hollywood directors. His sharply edged technique and sardonic wit, an almost seamless fusion of art and commercialism, became such an identifiable style that he would surpass such high-profile contemporaries as John Ford, Howard Hawks and William Wyler in terms of directly influencing future generations of filmmakers.

All of which brings us once again to our updated volume. We're pained to admit that in certain respects, the intervening decade and a half has made our efforts seem almost redundant. In the early '90s, we were breaking new ground by merely spotlighting these films on an individual basis. Up until then, it was standard procedure for writers and historians discussing the studio's "monster canon" to focus on a few key '30s films while giving only cursory coverage to the lesser titles. Since that time, books, magazines and websites have lovingly scrutinized most every facet of nearly every Universal horror movie, especially as more are released on home video in ever-improving formats. Consider: At the time of our first printing we were awaiting the first videotape release of *Bride of Frankenstein.* Today, even a limited-appeal potboiler such as *She-Wolf of London* has seen three video incarnations!

As we write these pages in 2006, the Universal horror pictures are enjoying a milestone with the 75th anniversary of the release of *Dracula* in 1931. While that groundbreaking movie is generally thought of as officially launching the Universal horror cycle, we must acknowledge the artists who contributed to the studio's silent genre classics. Like many of the titles covered in this book, often these weren't horror pictures in the strictest sense of the word. Certainly many of the films of Paul Leni have strong roots in the mystery thriller tradition. *The Cat and the Canary* (1927) and *The Last Warning* (1929) are typical examples of the kind of shadowy whodunits which generously employed horror conventions The last title, especially, exerted a strong influence throughout the '30s, especially in James Whale's classics.

Leni's *The Man Who Laughs* (1928), like another Victor Hugo adaptation, *The Hunchback of Notre Dame* (1923), joined the ranks of silent Universal horror classics by way of its memorably monstrous leading character. The role was played to heart-rending perfection by Conrad Veidt under makeup created by the legendary Jack P. Pierce.

But it is Lon Chaney, Sr., who can rightfully make the claim of being the screen's first horror star. Though Chaney appeared in a variety of roles in literally dozens of Universal shorts and features between the years 1913 and 1925, his *Hunchback of Notre Dame* and, especially, *The Phantom of the Opera* (1925) became signature roles which identified him with the macabre.

These early films have proven to be essential in the evolution of the all-talking Hollywood horror picture, proving to exhibitors they had commercial "legs" as they moved skittishly into the realm of the unreal and the supernatural. It was a process Universal couldn't take credit for but one which it nimbly exploited, starting in 1931. In the talkies' first decade, no other studio had the knack for producing such consistently marketable horror movies. In contrast, MGM's slate of classic chillers, including Tod Browning's *Freaks* (1932) and Karl Freund's *Mad Love* (1935), often suffered losses or were only marginally profitable.

Today, Universal looks back at its classic monster cycle as the building blocks in the formation of one of the great mega-corporations in the entertainment industry. Its early strategy of producing one sequel after another, gradually transforming horror literary properties into full-fledged monster franchises, may have been born out of a lack of imagination in developing new material. Even so, the gambit resulted in a gallery of monster characters which, over the years, amassed an enormous degree of audience sympathy and even identification. At the end of the process, these movies have become, as has often been pointed out, the cinematic equivalent of fairy tales, their elements of dread and fear turned into something reassuringly familiar, if not downright endearing.

That said, the glory days of the Universal horror movie were remarkably short-lived, their fate was so inextricably linked to the fortunes of studio founder, Carl Laemmle. His ouster as Universal's president in 1936 signaled the end of the Monsters' Golden Era even though the studio continued to crank out horror movies for another full decade, sometimes quite notably. The various management teams that succeeded him were a corps of faceless bankers and producers who, unlike the reigning moguls of the other studios, didn't have the innate instinct for picturemaking. Although the decline of the Universal horror movie is a tired subject, in fairness, it has to be placed in the context of the dwindling standards of the studio's pictures at the time. It's easy to disparage, say, *Frankenstein Meets the Wolf Man* as compared to the James Whale original but the film actually had a lot more style and craft than Universal's general run of medium-budgeted potboilers which usually featured the likes of Broderick Crawford, William Gargan and Richard Arlen; none of these films has been in official circulation for years.

Still, unlike the Laemmle era's literary approach to horror, the war years saw the cycle evolve into a series of streamlined Gothic action pieces, sustained by atmosphere and often craftsmanship. It was up to the audiences, particularly the latter Baby Boomer audiences, to furnish some of the later monster pictures with what Universal's writers and directors couldn't — the undercurrent of romanticism, the sense that the monsters were actually creatures with souls and human longings, that underneath the formula plots, these characters represented society's rejects who were trying to stake a claim in a world in which they had no place. The finite

Here's another section of the oft-used European Street (courtesy John Antosiewicz).

resources of the writers' imaginations finally petered out and, by the mid–'40s, Universal's roster of monsters not only died but stayed dead long after their final reels unspooled. It had become a moot point anyway as the war had thrust the world into the American Century, one which had little use for the European tradition of monster characters. Hollywood began to chart a new and more sophisticated menace in the dark corners and back alleys of the mind in the form of film noir and in the science fiction boom of the '50s. But, somehow, horror wasn't quite what it used to be.

As several reviewers of the original *Universal Horrors* have pointed out, we deliberately stretched the term "horror" to include a number of borderline classifications. You'll find an occasional fantasy (*Night Life of the Gods, Night in Paradise*), a couple of spooky mysteries (*Secret of the Chateau, Mystery of Edwin Drood*) and, somewhat controversially, the entire Basil Rathbone–Nigel Bruce Sherlock Holmes series, covered along with the traditional monster titles. The Holmes pictures, we felt, were a defensible inclusion in light of the fog-drenched atmosphere and latent chiller content inherent in a number of them. Also, Rathbone's association with the genre, whether fairly or unfairly, was another factor which influenced our decision to give full treatment to the series (a decision which, by the way, was not a unanimous one on the part of your authors).

Although we've noted the heartening reception which greeted our first edition, we candidly admit to having to dodge a brickbat or two, mostly thrown by rabid buffs who found some of our assessments too harsh. Frankly, we haven't always been successful in trying to strike a balance between rational criticism and a fan's enthusiasm. Like so many people, our first

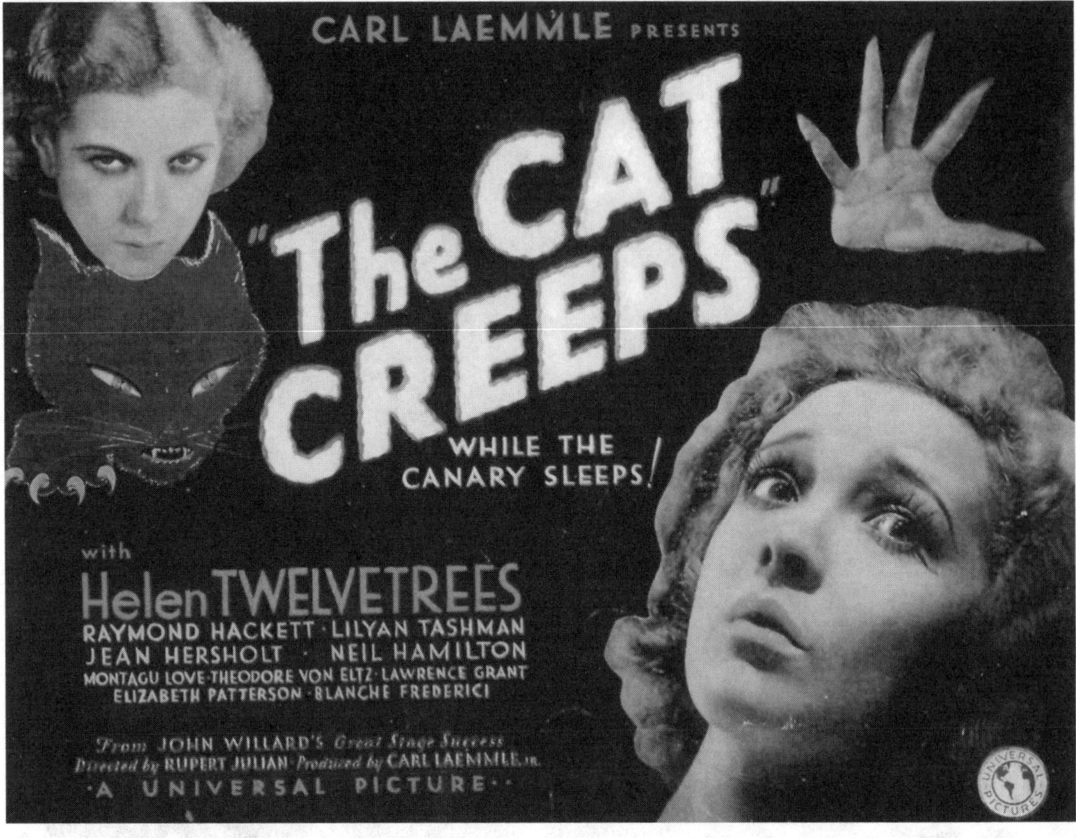

Based on the stage hit "The Cat and the Canary," ***The Cat Creeps*** **(1930) used many of the elements of the standard old-dark-house chiller.**

exposure to these movies had been as children (yes, on New York City's version of *Shock Theater*!) so we acknowledge our deep and abiding affection towards them as well as the players who acted in them. However, we feel that our decision to review these movies as objectively as possible (at least, as far as a subjective opinion can be) was the right one. If we three sane spectators come down a bit too hard on a favorite Inner Sanctum or Dracula movie, the reader is asked to consider the film in question on its particular merits rather than on some unquantifiable measure of nostalgia. Judging a horror movie, especially a grade B one, is a tricky business since so many work on the level of pure fun, in spite of their dramatic or technical deficiencies. Still, we hope we haven't entirely ruled out the entertainment value in assessing these movies and hope the reader realizes we are, after all, film fans at heart.

Anyway, we welcome you again to the new *Universal Horrors*. We think it will thrill you. It *may* shock you. It might even...

Our Great Privilege

Only the devoted film fan can fully appreciate the experience of discovering and handling original papers and documents that pertained to Universal in its heyday. Contracts, assistant directors' reports, budget sheets, scripts, memos — memorabilia such as these hold a special significance for the person who has spent countless hours in front of the television and in the darkened screening halls enjoying these movies.

To such a fan, the experience, as we three authors had, of actually meeting and interviewing some of the survivors of this bygone age is

Jack Otterson, Universal's chief art director from the mid–'30s through the mid–'40s (courtesy John Antosiewicz).

a rare privilege and a delight. Lunching with Frances Drake at the Beverly Hilton Hotel, chatting about Karloff and Lorre and Colin Clive. Discussing Lugosi's earliest days in America with Arthur Lubin. Remembering Lon Chaney, Jr., with his old-time hunting and drinking buddy Peter Coe. Learning personal details of what really went on at those polite English tea breaks from *Tower of London*'s Rose Hobart. Talking with Gloria Stuart about doing the town with James Whale. Unearthing the Mummy memories of Peggy Moran and Virginia Christine. Enjoying the running commentary of our friend Reginald LeBorg as he watched his own film *Destiny* for the first time in more than 40 years (and enjoying derisive yuks with the director as we all screen *Jungle Woman*). Swinging down memory lane with Vincent Price, Curt Siodmak, June Lockhart, John Archer, Acquanetta, Virginia Grey, Turhan Bey, Patric Knowles, Jane Wyatt, Henry Brandon, Carroll Borland, Michael A. Hoey, Henry Koster, Victoria Horne, Anne Gwynne, Susanna Foster, Anna Lee, Edward Norris, Robert Clarke, John Howard, Nell O'Day, Hillary Brooke, Donnie Dunagan, Booth Colman, Richard Davies, Don Porter, Phil Brown, Richard and Alex Gordon, Bruno, King, Corky, Moose, the cat goddess Bast, Jocko the Miracle Monkey, Diggs & Betty, Major, Brutus and Methuselah, Harry J. Essex, Edward Dein, Paul Picerni, Fritz Feld, Carey Loftin, Jane Adams, Gil Perkins, Gloria Jean, Anthony Eisley, Edward Dmytryk, Kay Linaker, Bonnie Schoonover, Bob May, Jerry Warren, Beverly Garland, Teddy Infuhr, Gloria Talbott, Howard W. Koch, Jack Pollexfen,

The *Tower of London* set on the Universal back lot (courtesy of John Antosiewicz).

Christopher Drake, Doug Benton, Harry Thomas, Robert Boyle, Gordon Hessler, Edward Bernds, Joan Weldon, Lupita Tovar, William Phipps, Shirley Ulmer, Leo Gorcey, Jr., Joanne Fulton, Patricia Morison, Jack Hill, Lloyd Bridges, Richard Denning, Frankie Thomas, and a special person whom we were honored to call our dear friend, Martin Kosleck. A great number of these fine folks have passed away since the first edition of *Universal Horrors* went to press in 1990. We will never forget the warmth and graciousness they showed us. Without their invaluable input, this book would not have been nearly as much fun to write.

A Thousand and One Thanks!

In preparing this book, we had the pleasure the generosity of such friends as Marty Baumann, Tim Lucas, Bob Burns, Glenn Damato, Greg Mank, David Colton, Tony Timpone, Bob Madison, Russell Frost, Dave McDonnell, Tony Timpone, Gary Rhodes, the folks at the Classic Horror Film Board, and John Morgan.

To those who contributed above and beyond the call of duty, we owe special thanks. Ned Comstock of the University of Southern California film department library painstakingly excavated reams of invaluable Universal production records. The late Michael Fitzgerald, author of Arlington House's *Universal Pictures* and probably the world's number one fan and authority on the subject, invited us to his annual reunions of Universal players and provided many of the anecdotes he has collected through the years. Rich Scrivani, the "Cool Ghoul" Zacherley's No. 1 fan and Universal devotee, screened numerous movies with us, pointing out the origins of familiar music cues and redressed sets. Once again, Mark Martucci came to the rescue with his staggering video-DVD collection and store of knowledge. John Antosiewicz, Bill Chase, John Cocchi, George Chastain, Dan Scapperotti and John Skillin generously shared their rare Universal stills with us. And "Jun" Lopez, Jr., provided valuable technical support and friendly, at-the-ready assistance.

Final note: The most frustrating aspect of

research is not the inability to come up with that elusive bit of data, but the difficulty in sorting out the correct information from the wrong. Release dates, running times, credits, character names, and all manner of facts are prone to all sorts of interpretations. Theater source books, interoffice memoranda, cast sheets, assistant directors' reports — even the main or end title credits on the prints themselves — are not always accurate sources of information. (Often a main title will carry the names of actors not present in the final cut, or misspell a performer's or a character's name, or attribute a role to the wrong actor or actress.) Most notorious of all are trade paper plants and ready-for-publication pressbook items, often created from whole cloth by publicity-happy studios or press agents eager to keep the names of their clients fresh in the minds of moviegoers.

It's a frustrating endeavor, this business of writing a book about films and keeping it free of error. But you have our word that ... *once again* ... we've done our best.

Tom Weaver, Michael Brunas
and John Brunas
January 2007

Milestones in the History of Universal Studios

1906: The granddaddy of Hollywood film production companies, Universal's origins may be traced back to 1905, when Carl Laemmle, 39-year-old German-Jewish immigrant manager of an Oshkosh, Wisconsin, clothing store, took a keen interest in the growing nickelodeon business while on a buying trip to Chicago. The enterprising Laemmle purchased his first nickelodeon and soon after opened up his own chain. He later advanced to movie distribution and production.

1909: In April, Laemmle pulled out of the fee-charging Motion Picture Patents Company and, in June, organized the Independent Moving Picture Company of America (IMP), based in New York (it was formerly called the Yankee Film Company). His first production was *Hiawatha*, a one-reel adaptation of the Longfellow poem. Laemmle later bought out all of his business partners. Between 1909 and 1912, the industrious tycoon produced a variety of low-budget multi-reelers.

1911: Laemmle expanded his operations to the West Coast by purchasing the Nestor Studio in Hollywood.

1912: On June 8, the IMP was incorporated into a new movie company called the Universal Film Manufacturing Company in New York. With studios now operating on both coasts, Laemmle decided to centralize all operations and bought up real estate in the Los Angeles area.

1914: In March, Laemmle's Western manager, Isadore Bernstein, purchased a 230-acre ranch (for $165,000), a short distance from the spot where Mexican General Andre Pico and U.S. Colonel John Fremont signed the Treaty of Cahuenga in 1846. Joining forces with Laemmle were Robert H. Cochrane, Charles Baumann, David Horsley, Pat Powers and W.H. Swanson. Eventually, Laemmle bought out all his partners and their various companies, thus giving him control of one major organization containing all facets of movie production, distribution and exhibition.

1915: On March 15, Laemmle held the grand opening of Universal City Studios, the world's first self-contained motion picture production community. (Actually, film production began on the lot the year before. *Damon and Pythias* was the first motion picture completed at Universal City.) The San Fernando Valley location offered movie producers an expansive area for the development of stages and a diverse terrain for exterior shooting.

In a 1943 edition of *The Hollywood Reporter*, the trade paper carried an interesting insider's view of Universal by Henry MacRae, a serial producer who, in the early days of the studio, "had the privilege of serving as general manager of the lot when most of the studio was built." In MacRae's words, "The Universal lot is the most historical one, as far as the film industry is concerned. We were the first to establish a real studio, Universal City, and incorporate, with our own mayor and council, police chief, fire department, hospital, electric lighting plant, water works and sewage system. As the tract of 230 acres which spreads out from Lankershim boulevard to the foothills was originally the battle site upon which General Pico of Mexico surrendered to [Colonel] John C. Fremont, we saved money on our sewage system simply by sinking the pipes in the former trenches dug by Pico's army! Universal developed, in those old days, many of the technical improvements still in use. It was the first studio to utilize light rays reflected by mirrors for night scenes, for heretofore NIGHT had been indicated by film tinted blue, and DAY by film colored amber.... We were also the forerunner in building a substantial, four-walled stage with movable roof for admission of daylight. Thomas Edison laid the cornerstone for this building, which now houses our mill.... When Universal put up its first 300-foot long stage, the civic dignitaries of Los Angeles turned out for a gala dance celebrating its completion."

Early '20s: Universal specialized in such popular silent film entertainments as Westerns, comedies and action-oriented films. Under the guiding genius of Wunderkind Irving Thalberg, however, such stars as Rudolph Valentino, Wallace Reid and Lon Chaney, and powerhouse director Erich von Stroheim, signed up with the studio and upgraded its image as a major contender in the industry — and a profitable one, to boot. Thalberg greatly improved the quality of the studio's output. Unlike his competitors at Paramount and MGM, Laemmle financed all his own films, thus avoiding debt. The mogul also refrained from buying his own theater chain as was the custom of the day among Hollywood's heavy hitters.

Among the studio's biggest hits of the era were *Foolish Wives* (1921), *The Hunchback of Notre Dame* (1923) and *The Phantom of the Opera* (1925).

1923: Thalberg left Laemmle's employ and accepted an offer to join Louis B. Mayer's company. After Thalberg and Universal parted ways, the studio was left without a strong, creative influence in the production department, and suffered greatly.

1924: The Music Corporation of America, or the MCA, was founded by Jules Stein. A Chicago-based agency that booked bands for dance halls, the company grew under the guidance of Lew Wasserman, who joined the MCA in 1936. His efforts built the talent agency into a multi-faceted global leader in the entertainment industry. Years later, both the MCA and Wasserman would play an important part in the future success of Universal Pictures.

1926: Laemmle organized a production unit in Germany, Deutsche Universal-Film AG. Under the direction of Joe Pasternak, it produced three to four films a year until the subsidiary's dissolution in 1936. Adolf Hitler's ascent to power compelled the unit to migrate to Hungary first and then to Austria. The productions were primarily made in the German language, but occasionally Hungarian or Polish. Universal distributed these productions in the USA via other independent foreign-language film distributors based in New York, minus English subtitles.

1928: As a twenty-first birthday gift from his father, Carl Laemmle, Jr., took over control of Universal City in 1928. Junior Laemmle got the company involved in buying and building theaters, and worked hard to upgrade its product in this post–Thalberg era. Universal released its first talkie, *Melody of Love,* and the following year, *Show Boat* (1929), the screen's first color musical.

Early '30s: Lewis Milestone's 1930 achievement *All Quiet on the Western Front* won Universal its first Academy Award for Best Picture and restored some of its prestige in the industry. With the advent of the talkies, major talents such as James Whale, John M. Stahl and William Wyler were entrusted with the studio's most valuable story properties. First-class productions such as *Waterloo Bridge* (1931), *Back Street* (1932), *Counsellor-at-Law* (1933), *Only Yesterday* (1933), *Imitation of Life* (1934), *Magnificent Obsession* (1935), *My Man Godfrey* (1936) and, of course, the early horror classics *Dracula*, *Frankenstein* and *The Invisible Man,* made an impact at box offices across the nation.

Through Mid–'30s: Universal Pictures was in dire trouble. The dynasty that "Uncle Carl" Laemmle built was slowly crumbling. The devastating effects of the Depression, an industry-wide strike that forced the studio to cease production for several months, and charges of gross nepotism (the beneficent "Uncle Carl" imported shiploads of relatives and friends from Germany and employed them in dozens of diverse positions) created turmoil and had a negative effect on the studio's profit margin. Net losses exceeded profits quarter after quarter. (The accounting department's report for the nine months ending October 31, 1932, showed a net loss of $759,646, a figure greater than the profit of the whole year 1931.)

1934: Wall Street sources predicted in January 1934 that every company in the business with the exception of Universal would show a considerable profit for 1933. This grim forecast was not refuted by the ailing film factory.

1935: Financial matters had taken a critical turn for the Laemmles by 1935. The expense of modernizing and upgrading the resources of the motion picture conglomerate in the depths of the Depression was a gamble, and the studio slipped into receivership for a period of time. The theater chain was scrapped. Universal's lavish remake of *Show Boat* had cost the studio more than had been originally anticipated; to complete the production, the studio turned to the Standard Chartered Bank for a $750,000 loan. The bank eventually foreclosed, claiming the Laemmle's family stock as collateral; consequently, Carl Laemmle and his son lost control of their own studio.

In October, Laemmle left for New York to talk with one of several groups of enterprising businessmen which expressed an interest in acquiring the studio. He flatly refused to sell out to Warner Bros. Still clinging to the slim chance that he could salvage his company, Laemmle hoped to induce former Columbia manager Sam Briskin to take charge of the lot. The deal didn't come off.

On November 1, Laemmle was forced to enter a deal with J. Cheever Cowdin's Standard Capital Corporation and tycoon Charles R. Rogers to secure emergency funds to sustain his studio. The two businessmen lent Laemmle $750,000 with the stipulation that they be given the option to buy the studio within three months at a cost of $5.5 million.

1936: Confident that the returns on his slate of pictures would stave off financial ruin, Laemmle agreed to the terms of the loan. It was a fatal mistake. Cowdin and Rogers amassed enough capital to purchase 90 percent of Universal's stock. On March 14, 1936, the Laemmle empire toppled, and the Standard Capital Corporation assumed control of the sprawling studio.

From the ashes of the Laemmle empire rose the "New Universal." Cowdin was named chairman of the board; Robert H. Cochrane, one of the studio's original founders, became the new corporation's president, and Charles R. Rogers moved into Carl Laemmle, Jr.'s, former position as vice-president in charge of production. After the release of *Dracula's Daughter* in May 1936, all horror film productions were dropped from the production schedules to make way for low-budget action subjects, innocuous musicals and comedies.

Late '30s: Twenty-eight-year-old Junior Laemmle planned to make a comeback in pictures by starting his own production company. Instead, he ended up at MGM as an associate producer but resigned shortly after, without a single film to his credit. "Uncle Carl" Laemmle retired to his palatial home in Beverly Hills and died three years later at the age of 72.

1937–38: Unlike Laemmle, Rogers ruled the lot with an iron fist. Joe Pasternak, Universal's former European production head, was brought to Hollywood. The "shining light" of the new Universal, Pasternak produced *Three Smart Girls* (1937), which brought immediate stardom to an unknown pubescent soprano named Deanna Durbin. The picture's success saved the shaky new corporation. Less than two years after the Cowdin-Rogers takeover, Universal was once again courting bankruptcy. The 1937-38 season had been a financial disaster and a rift had developed between the company's business partners; in short, the immediate future of the revamped film studio seemed bleak indeed. On November 30, 1937, Nate Blumberg, who had been in charge of theater operations at RKO, was elected president, ousting Cochrane. Six months later, on May 20, 1938, Rogers resigned, and Cliff Work, also from RKO, succeeded him as vice-president in charge of production. The new production team pulled off a miracle. The savvy reissuing of *Frankenstein* and *Dracula* pumped some much-needed coin into the company's coffers, prompting the production of the costly *Son of Frankenstein*, which reaped similar rewards.

Late '30s through Mid–'40s: Within three years, Blumberg turned a financially ailing film studio into a profit-making enterprise again. Unlike the formidable Rogers, Blumberg was a genial, benign presence. Although he had no previous experience making films, he was an adept organizer, kept up the morale of his workers, and possessed a great sense of mass entertainment, all crucial ingredients in running a successful lot. James Whale, Henry Koster, Alfred Hitchcock, Fritz Lang, Robert Siodmak and Tay Garnett were among the handful of prestige directors who toiled under the Universal banner. Among the new releases were the W.C. Fields vehicles *You Can't Cheat an Honest Man* (1939) and *The Bank Dick* (1940), *My Little Chickadee* (1940) with Fields and Mae West, Abbott and Costello's and Deanna Durbin's box office magnets, the Marlene Dietrich hits *Destry Rides Again* (1939) and *Seven Sinners* (1940), a new crop of classic horror sequels and lavish remakes (*Phantom of the Opera*), a series of Sherlock Holmes adaptations as well as a slate of Technicolor adventure extravaganzas featuring the exotic team of Maria Montez and Jon Hall.

1945: Universal's good fortunes started wearing down in the mid–'40s, as the studio's main attractions began to suffer from overexposure. On November 28, 1945, Universal joined forces with British entrepreneur J. Arthur Rank's United World Pictures, who bought a one-fourth interest in the studio. An ambitious program of modernization and improvement of the Universal City studio and the construction of added soundstages was put into effect.

1946: Rank's powerful influence instituted a merger between Universal and International Pictures on July 31, 1946. It was the biggest amalgamation since 20th Century took over Fox in the '30s. International Pictures was a struggling independent production company founded in part by William Goetz, that rare breed, a sharp businessman with aesthetic values. Goetz and Leo Spitz took charge of production, while Nate Blumberg was pushed up to the position of chairman of the board. Universal-International was born.

Mid–'40s through Early '50s: Goetz had no use for Abbott and Costello and even less for the menagerie of monsters he inherited, but was keenly aware of their box office power. So, between releasing prestige fare like *A Double Life* (1947) and such J. Arthur Rank British imports as *Great Expectations* (1946) and *Black Narcissus* (1947), Goetz begrudgingly gave the go-ahead to such box office bonanzas as *The Killers* (1946), *The Egg and I* (1947), *The Naked City* (1948), the Abbott and Costello monster matches, the rustic Ma and Pa Kettle B-comedies and the Francis the Talking Mule series. This shotgun marriage of art and popular entertainment, an uneasy compromise that Goetz was forced to live with, saved Universal-International from a premature demise.

Ronald Colman won the Oscar for Best Actor for 1947's *A Double Life*.

The production of *Hamlet* (in association with Rank of England) won the Academy Award for Best Picture of 1948 while its director-star Laurence Olivier won the Best Actor Oscar for that year.

1950: The MCA talent agency via Lew Wasserman negotiated a percentage deal between Universal and actor James Stewart on *Winchester '73* which had a major impact on the entire film industry. Stewart's action encouraged other Hollywood stars to seek out similar lucrative percentage deals in their studio contracts.

1951: In November, Decca Records acquired 28 percent of Universal-International's stock via Rank's sell-out to the recording company's president Milton Rachmil. Five months later, Goetz and Blumberg sold out their stock to Decca, thus giving the company controlling interest. By the early '50s, Universal had returned to its previous status as a purveyor of popular, low-budget fare.

1952–59: Decca Records took full control of Universal-International with Rachmil taking over the presidency in July 1953; Edward Muhl was put in charge of production. The ensuing decade saw a concentration on glossy soap operas featuring the likes of Lana Turner and Jeff Chandler, frothy bedroom farces starring Doris Day and Rock Hudson, Western shoot-'em-ups with Audie Murphy and James Stewart, and science-fiction pictures with strong horrific elements. The 1954 *Magnificent Obsession* remake, *Written on the Wind* (1956), Orson Welles' *Touch of Evil* (1958) and *Pillow Talk* (1959) were a few of the decade's most memorable Universal-International movies.

In December 1958, MCA, Inc., which had become a major player in TV production, purchased the sprawling 360-acre Universal City Studio lot for $11 million. (By 2006, the lot had expanded to 390 acres). MCA's Revue Televi-

The famous *Phantom of the Opera* stage was refurbished for the 1943 Technicolor remake (courtesy John Antosiewicz).

sion Productions relocated to Universal and Universal Pictures then leased back its property from MCA.

By the late '50s, the American motion picture business was in trouble. The rise of television and the studio-theater chain breakup were just two factors that led to a major Hollywood crisis.

1961: The Kirk Douglas–Stanley Kubrick historic spectacle *Spartacus* received four Oscars.

Another frequently filmed street set, artfully recreated on the studio's back lot (courtesy John Antosiewicz).

1962: The actual takeover of Universal-International by MCA took place in June. The name of the business reverted back to Universal Pictures, while the parent company became MCA/Universal Pictures Inc. Nearly every MCA client was signed to a Universal contract including Cary Grant, Doris Day, Lana Turner and Alfred Hitchcock.

1963: Gregory Peck copped the Best Actor Oscar for *To Kill a Mockingbird.*

1964: Universal City, a Disneyland-style complex offering the visitor to Southern California a behind-the-scenes glimpse into movie, television and video production, as well as a variety of amusement park attractions built around the studio's past successes and forthcoming pictures, was launched.

MCA purchased Alfred Hitchcock's Shamley Productions, including the rights to *Psycho* (1960) and all of the great director's TV work.

1966: Universal became the subsidiary of MCA, Inc., the feature film production division of Universal City Studios, Inc., Hollywood's busiest television series factory. MCA's Jules Stein and Lew Wasserman assumed control of the entertainment giant.

1968: With a marked reduction in motion picture production, Universal's TV ventures were expected to bring home the bacon. Around this time, Universal became closely associated with the major networks, especially the National Broadcasting Corporation (NBC), which later merged with Universal to form NBC Universal. For several seasons, the company provided up to half of all prime time programming. It was in this flourishing period that Universal created the 90-minute made-for-television movie.

Among the decade's most notable releases were *Portrait in Black* (1960), *Spartacus* (1960), *Back Street* (1961), *Lover Come Back* (1961), *To*

Regal temple set used in *Green Hell* and *The Mummy's Hand* (courtesy John Antosiewicz).

Kill a Mockingbird (1962), *Cape Fear* (1962), *A Gathering of Eagles* (1963), *The Birds* (1963), *Charade* (1963), *Marnie* (1964), *Father Goose* (1964), *The Ipcress File* (1965), *The War Lord* (1965), *Arabesque* (1966), *Thoroughly Modern Millie* (1967), *Anne of a Thousand Days* (1969) and *Topaz* (1969).

The '70s & '80s: Although TV production preoccupied Universal's time and resources during these decades, the studio affirmed its standing in the industry as an entertainment powerhouse with the box office triumphs *Airport* (1970), Best Picture Oscar–winner *The Sting* (1973), *American Graffiti* (1973), the highly successful and incredibly profitable *Jaws* (1975), *National Lampoon's Animal House* (1978), Best Picture Oscar–winner *The Deer Hunter* (1978), *Conan the Barbarian* (1981), *E.T.: The Extra-Terrestrial* (1982), *Scarface* (1983), *Sixteen Candles* (1984), Best Picture Oscar–winner *Out of Africa* (1985), *Back to the Future* (1985) and its sequels and *The Breakfast Club* (1985).

In 1980, MCA Home Entertainment Group, devoted to the burgeoning home video market, was founded.

1990: Universal Studios Florida opened in Orlando.

A fire cost the studio $20 million in damages and destroyed four acres of sets.

1991: MCA was acquired by Matsushita Electrical Industrial Co., Ltd.

1993: *Schindler's List*, directed by Steven Spielberg, won the Academy Award for Best Picture. Universal CityWalk debuted in Hollywood.

1995: In June, Matsushita sold control of MCA/Universal to the Canadian liquor distributor Joseph Seagram Company, Ltd. Ron Meyer succeeded Sidney Sheinberg as head man. It eventually acquired PolyGram, the world's largest music company.

1996: On December 10, MCA, Inc., was renamed Universal Studios, Inc.

1999: Islands of Adventure, the Portofino

Top: **The back lot collieries set utilized in *The Invisible Man Returns* and later in *The Mummy's Ghost.* *Bottom:* The European village set seen in *Son of Frankenstein* and many other movies (both courtesy John Antosiewicz).**

Top: **The familiar cliff and cave set, used in action films, serials and Westerns on the studio back lot. *Bottom:* Director James Whale (seated on right in dark suit) takes in an orchestral recording session (both courtesy John Antosiewicz).**

Resort, and Universal CityWalk opened in Orlando.

The '90s: A sampling of Universal's most resounding successes over this decade included *An American Tail: Fievel Goes West* (1990), *Kindergarten Cop* (1990), *Scent of a Woman* (1992), *Carlito's Way* (1993), the Steven Spielberg spectacular *Jurassic Park* (1993) and its first sequel *The Lost World: Jurassic Park* (1997), *Schindler's List* (1993), *The Mummy* (1999) and *American Pie* (1999).

2000: In June, Seagram announced a strategic business move—joining ventures with France's water-utility and media company Vivendi and Canal+. The new entertainment conglomerate was christened Vivendi Universal. MCA's existence came to a conclusion once it sold its music-related subsidiaries to Geffen Music.

2001: Universal Studios Japan opened. The theme park was soon followed by Universal Mediterraneo in Barcelona, Spain. Universal gained the USA Network assets including USA Films, later renamed Focus Features.

2003: Universal became the first motion picture studio with five summer releases all breaking the $100 million mark.

2004 and Beyond: Vivendi sold its majority share in Universal to General Electric, parent company of NBC. The super conglomerate was renamed NBC Universal; Universal Studios Inc. was retained as the name of the production subsidiary. NBC Universal, one of the globe's leading media and entertainment companies, officially began May 12, 2004. As of this writing, GE owned 80 percent of NBC Universal, with Vivendi Universal Entertainment controlling 20 percent.

Universal's early twenty-first century releases included *The Mummy Returns* (2001), *Jurassic Park III* (2001), *The Bourne Identity* (2002), *Seabiscuit* (2003), *The Bourne Supremacy* (2004), *Meet the Fockers* (2004), *Van Helsing* (2004), *Cinderella Man* (2005), the long-awaited remake of *King Kong* (2005), *The Producers* (2005), *Curious George* (2006) and *Miami Vice* (2006).

The studio has taken measures to protect its precious heritage by preserving original movie posters and actual film in a giant limestone mine in Pennsylvania. In addition, costumes and props of historic significance are stored in an unmarked warehouse in Sun Valley, California.

The Films

1931

Dracula

Released February 12, 1931. 75 minutes. *Associate Producer:* E.M. Asher. *Producer:* Carl Laemmle, Jr. *Director:* Tod Browning. *Screenplay:* Garrett Fort. *Continuity:* Dudley Murphy. *Based on the novel by* Bram Stoker *and the 1927 stageplay by* Hamilton Deane & John L. Balderston. *Scenario Supervisor:* Charles A. Logue. *Photographer:* Karl Freund. *Art Director:* Charles D. Hall. *Editor:* Milton Carruth. *Supervising Editor:* Maurice Pivar. *Recording Supervisor:* C. Roy Hunter. *Set Designers:* Herman Rosse & John Hoffman. *Photographic Effects:* Frank J. Booth. *Musical Conductor:* Heinz Roemheld. *Makeup:* Jack P. Pierce. *Set Decorators:* Russell A. Gausman. *Costumes:* Ed Ware & Vera West. *Casting:* Phil M. Friedman. *Research:* Nan Grant. *Art Titles:* Max Cohen.

Bela Lugosi (*Count Dracula*), Helen Chandler (*Mina Seward*), David Manners (*John Harker*), Dwight Frye (*Renfield*), Edward Van Sloan (*Prof. Van Helsing*), Herbert Bunston (*Dr. Seward*), Frances Dade (*Lucy Weston*), Joan Standing (*Maid*), Charles K. Gerrard (*Martin*), Moon Carroll (*Briggs*), Josephine Velez (*Grace, English Nurse*), Michael Visaroff (*Innkeeper*), Anna Bakacs (*Innkeeper's Daughter*), Daisy Belmore (*English Coach Passenger*), Nicholas Bela, Donald Murphy, Carla Laemmle (*Coach Passengers*), Anita Harder (*Flower Girl*), Tod Browning (*Harbor Master*), Jeraldine Dvorak, Dorothy Tree, Cornelia Thaw (*Dracula's Brides*).

> Tod Browning's *Dracula* is proving the Sensation of the Year! Wherever it is showing, it is setting new records and taking the people by storm....
> —*Carl Laemmle, Sr., "Straight from the Shoulder" trade paper column, February 18, 1931*

The vampiric vanguard of the first Universal horror cycle, *Dracula* was for years revered as perhaps the best-known of all vintage horror films, a sacred cow among buffs in general and Bela Lugosi fans in particular. Time, alas, has proved to be less kind to the film than to its ageless protagonist: It's now widely regarded as the least satisfying of the Universal originals. The film remains rich in historical importance, and its inestimable influence is felt to this day: Even in the 21st century, in the minds of many people, Bram Stoker's Count Dracula wears the face of Bela Lugosi. But while the film's reverberations are still being felt three-quarters of a century later, *Dracula* is now recognized as a film of missed opportunities. After a highly promising, much-talked-about opening, its macabre mood dissipates, leaving its viewers immersed in a lot of stagebound boudoir intrigue.

Written in 1897, the novel *Dracula* was the work of Dublin-born Bram Stoker. Sickly as a child (he could not stand or walk until age seven), Stoker grew into a red-haired giant of a man with a keen interest in writing. His first novel, a romance titled *The Snake's Pass*, didn't create much of a stir, but *Dracula* was an instant and immense success. It is written in epistolary style, with chapters comprised of a grab-bag of personal letters, diary musings, entries in a ship's log, newspaper accounts as well as a phonograph diary.

Author C.K. Hillegass rightly calls *Dracula* an example of a type of literature in which the kernel idea far transcends the execution. Stoker's later works included *The Mystery of the Sea* (1902) and *The Man* (1905) as well as the horror-mystery novels *The Jewel of Seven Stars* (1903), *The Lady of the Shroud* (1909) and *The Lair of*

Nightmarish poster art for *Dracula*, the motion picture that jump-started Hollywood's first great horror cycle.

the White Worm (1911).* Stoker's biographers didn't know (or avoided mentioning) the cause of his death in 1912 until his own grandnephew cited it in his 1975 book *The Man Who Wrote Dracula* as locomotor ataxy—also known as general paralysis of the insane—implying that Stoker had contracted syphilis.

The first film version of Stoker's novel was the 1922 German film *Nosferatu,* from the famed Expressionist director F.W. Murnau. Since the filmmakers did not secure the literary rights to *Dracula,* they made plot alterations and changed character names to camouflage their otherwise baldfaced piracy, but the Stoker estate was not fooled: They sued, won, and (unsuccessfully) sought to have all prints of the film destroyed.

Two years later, British producer Hamilton Deane (once a friend to Stoker) presented a stage version of "Dracula" at the Grand Theatre in Derby, England. A modernized retelling of the Stoker story, it was a huge success which Deane was able to take on tour for the next three years.† The play finally opened at London's Little Theatre on February 14, 1927, with a well-publicized trained nurse in attendance for the benefit of the weak-hearted; critics blasted the production, but Londoners packed the house. Horace Liveright, an American producer, bought it for Broadway, hiring John L. Balderston to streamline and further update the hoary plot. Forty-four-year-old Bela Lugosi, a stage star and screen matinee idol in his native Hungary, now an obscure political refugee scratching for work in a new country, took on the role of the undead count. The other leading roles were played by Dorothy Peterson (as Lucy Harker), Edward Van Sloan (Van Helsing), Herbert Bunston (Dr. Seward) and Bernard Jukes (Renfield).

"Dracula" opened at New York's Fulton Theatre on Wednesday, October 5, 1927, and ran for 265 performances, finally closing in New York in May of 1928. On Sunday, June 24, the Biltmore Theatre hosted the play in Los Angeles with Broadway cast members Lugosi, Van Sloan and Jukes reprising their roles. Following its L.A. run, the play moved on to San Francisco and toured in key cities around the country.

Universal had been keeping its corporate eye on "Dracula" ever since London theatergoers began queuing up outside the Little Theatre, but the difficulties of conveying the story in a silent version seemed insurmountable; interoffice communications from studio readers argued against the purchase of the property because of censorship problems. (One reader sternly reproved, "Were this story put on the screen, it would be an insult to everyone of its audiences.") But both these barriers were lifted with the near-simultaneous birth of the talkies and a lessening of the censors' clout, and treatments and continuities of various lengths were solicited from such Universal scenarists as Fritz Stephani, Louis Stevens and Louis Bromfield. In June 1930, the studio bought the rights to the book and play for $40,000, and less than a month later a completed script was turned in by Dudley Murphy. Garrett Fort contributed some finishing touches and received sole screen credit. Though the screenplay adhered closely to the American version of the play, episodes and lines of dialogue were lifted from the novel that hadn't been dramatized on the stage. (In the play, Lucy is the heroine and object of Harker's affection, and Mina is the one who falls victim to the vampire and becomes "The Woman in White.")

The title page of a fourth draft final script dated September 26, 1930, splits the credit for adaptation and dialogue between Fort and Tod Browning, who was signed to direct the picture. Lon Chaney, Sr.'s "favorite" director, Browning had his reputation as a horror specialist etched in stone for many years until, one by one, his rarest and most promising-sounding mystery films began re-emerging from the vaults; more often than not, these eagerly awaited "rediscoveries" were revealed as turgid bores, each representing one more nail in the once-fabled director's critical coffin. His best-known silents are remembered

**"The Jewel of Seven Stars" was filmed three times, by Hammer in 1972 as* Blood from the Mummy's Tomb, *in 1980 as* The Awakening, *and in 1997 as* Legend of the Mummy. *A screen version of* The Lair of the White Worm *was released in 1988. Roger Corman's* Burial of the Rats, *based on the Stoker story, came out in 1995, and the direct-to-video supernatural thriller,* Bram Stoker's Shadowbuilder, *also based on one of the writer's tales, was released three years later.*

†*Deane, who was also an actor, had initially intended to play the part of the count in the production, but circumstances forced him to accept the larger role of vampire-hunter Van Helsing. Dracula was played by Raymond Huntley, who in his later film career was strangled by Christopher Lee in Hammer's* The Mummy *(1959).*

because they star the still-popular Chaney, Sr., but they're not the best or most famous of Chaney's films; Browning's only notable sound films are again "carried" by their stars — Bela Lugosi in *Dracula* and *Mark of the Vampire* (1935), and a gang of *Freaks*.

Carroll Borland, who played Luna in *Mark of the Vampire*, told the authors she could recall almost nothing about the non-communicative Browning except that he dressed in loud sports coats and looked more than anything else like a racetrack character. "He seemed to simply stand around and puff on his cigarette, and I really didn't get much direction from him at all. He simply was not what you would expect a director of horror films to be like." Browning's apologists, whose numbers are a-dwindling, blame *Freaks* (1932) for his Hollywood decline (this "compassionate" look at the lives of circus grotesqueries created a storm of controversy and was widely banned), but the simpler truth probably was that his pedestrian, old-fashioned style and characteristically morbid themes no longer had any place in the film capital. Browning made his last film, *Miracles for Sale*, in 1939, and *Variety* published his obituary in 1944. Career-wise they were right, but Browning was actually still on this side of the grass; he lingered on this earth right up into the early '60s.

Not surprisingly, the unknown Lugosi was not Universal's initial choice for the Dracula role. The senior Chaney was of course the natural, but the star character actor had been stricken with bronchial cancer. While the Chaney name would certainly have insured box office success for the movie, the legendary "Man of a Thousand Faces" might have been a poor choice as the Transylvanian bloodsucker. The idea of Chaney skulking around ruined castles with a cape and phony accent is almost ludicrous; there's no reason to suspect that he would have fared any better than his own son did playing a well-fed middle–American count in *Son of Dracula*. Chaney died of throat cancer at St. Vincent's Hospital in Los Angeles on August 26, 1930, a month before production commenced on *Dracula*.

When it was evident, months before his death, that Chaney would not enact the role of Dracula, Universal began to field other actors for the coveted part. On April 8, 1930, Lugosi, who had gotten the thumbs down from Junior Laemmle almost two weeks before, announced that he had interested MGM in buying the rights to the Stoker novel; the deal fell through. Once the rights to the property were secured by Universal, the studio announced, on June 21 via *Variety*, that John Wray had been cast as the bloodthirsty count. Wray was fresh from his success in *All Quiet on the Western Front*, in which he played the drill sergeant with sadistic glee. (In 1932, the actor gave a memorable performance as one of Lionel Atwill's kinky colleagues in Warners' *Doctor X*.) Despite the announcement, Wray didn't get the part after all (physically, he would have been all wrong for it).

Other candidates for the title role at the time included Paul Muni, Ian Keith, William Courtenay, Joseph Schildkraut, Chester Morris and Conrad Veidt. Of these six, only Veidt seems like a viable contender; Keith eventually got the chance to play a vampire-type in a 1946 Republic cheapie, *Valley of the Zombies*, and left no scenery unchewed. Supposedly John Carradine also came under consideration; the actor later made a fine count in *House of Frankenstein* and *House of Dracula*, but at age 24 Carradine would probably have lacked the necessary gravitas. Eventually the stage Dracula prevailed: Lugosi was brought in for a screen test and, on Saturday, September 20, the Hollywood trades announced that the Hungarian thespian had been cast in the coveted role, the first in a $500-a-week, two-picture deal. The Broadway production's Van Helsing, Edward Van Sloan, joined Lugosi for the screen adaptation; Bernard Jukes, on the other hand, was bypassed in favor of stage luminary Dwight Frye. A Universal A-picture budget of $355,050 was allotted to the film with a shooting schedule planned for 36 days. Rotund German cinematographer Karl Freund's cameras began grinding on the morning of Monday, September 29 on the studio's back lot country inn set. The picture wrapped on Saturday, November 15; an additional six days were tagged onto the shooting schedule. However, on Friday, January 2, 1931, the company was reassembled for retakes. The final tally for the first film of Universal's Golden Age of Horror was $341,191.20.

The film's credits unreel to the mellifluous strains of Tchaikovsky's restful *Swan Lake*, a musical piece that Universal played behind the titles of several of their early horror thrillers. Renfield

(Dwight Frye), a British real estate salesman, has traveled to Transylvania with little luggage (and less British accent) to finalize a sale of property in England to Count Dracula. The proprietor of a local inn (Michael Visaroff) gravely warns that Dracula is a vampire, but Renfield disregards what he knows can only be peasant superstition and politely states his intention to continue on to Castle Dracula.

Boarding a coach, he journeys yet deeper into the mist and gloom of the Carpathian Mountains.

As night falls over the desolate countryside, the undead Count Dracula (Bela Lugosi) and his three undead brides rise from their coffins in the catacombs beneath his castle. "Disguised" as a coachman, the Count is waiting at midnight at a prearranged spot as the coach carrying Renfield arrives. Transferred to the vampire's coach, Renfield endures a rough ride which terminates at the door of Dracula's castle.

The vast interior hall of Castle Dracula remains the most imposing set from any of the vintage horror films, fully living up to the description in the script:

> ... a huge, square affair, in the manner of ancient feudal castles, with a long, impressive-looking staircase at the back. There is no furniture of any sort.... Dust is piled thick on every side—cobwebs—mold—broken architraves—bits of crumbling masonry which has fallen from the roof.... Across the steps a little way up from the first landing is a giant, dust-covered spider-web....

Descending the stairs, and passing (offcamera) through the still-unbroken web, comes Dracula, who welcomes Renfield to his ruined castle. Leading the solicitor into a "more inviting" upstairs chamber, Dracula finalizes the real estate deal before serving Renfield a goblet of wine.

But the drink has been drugged: After Dracula leaves, Renfield feels its effects and staggers to the nearby terrace doors, where he is accosted by a huge bat and faints. Dracula's brides appear, hovering hungrily over Renfield's prostrate body, until Dracula enters from outside and silently motions his brides away. Dracula now crouches over Renfield, moving in on his unprotected throat. (Poor continuity mars the finale of this classic vignette: A wall of fog not present in one shot appears in the next; "bat" Dracula exits to the left just before "human" Dracula enters from the right.)

The first two reels of *Dracula* are nearly perfect, packed with grim atmosphere and classic set pieces; unfortunately, from here on it's all downhill. The scene switches to a storm at sea, as the crew of the England-bound schooner *Vesta* battles to keep their boat from capsizing. In the cargo hold, which remains conveniently horizontal on the furiously pitching ship, a now-insane Renfield exhorts his "master" Dracula to rise from his coffin, and reminds the vampire of his promise to provide him with lives ("Not human lives, but *small* ones—with *blood* in them!"). Dracula ascends to the deck and watches dispassionately as the crew fights the gale. In the film the ensuing carnage is not depicted, although the original script calls for Dracula to stalk and kill the crew members in an impressionistic montage. The derelict ship eventually drifts into England's Whitby Harbor, where the sailors' deaths are conveniently attributed to the storm. Lunatic Renfield, discovered in the hold, is committed to the private lunatic asylum of a Dr. Seward.

Now at large in London, Dracula proceeds to a concert hall where he makes the acquaintance of Dr. Seward (Herbert Bunston), his daughter Mina (Helen Chandler), her fiancé John Harker (David Manners) and the Sewards' weekend houseguest Lucy Weston (Frances Dade). Dracula is attracted to the lovely Lucy, and puts the bite on her that night at the Seward home. Despite transfusions, Lucy later dies in a London hospital. Seward consults with the eminent Dutch scientist Prof. Van Helsing (Edward Van Sloan), who perceives at once that they are dealing with the undead. Van Helsing also suspects that Seward's patient Renfield, who is obsessed with the idea that he must eat flies and spiders for their blood, is in league with the vampire.

Mina falls ill and complains of strange dreams; unbeknownst to her father and fiancé, she has become Dracula's newest unsuspecting victim. Van Helsing detects that the vampire is at work again and, when Dracula pays a somewhat ill-timed visit to the Seward home, the scientist deduces that the Transylvanian count is their culprit.

All sorts of humdrum comings-and-goings

ensue, with Renfield escaping from his cell at regular intervals, Dracula making an attempt on Van Helsing's life and a worsening Mina trying to put the bite on Harker. As dawn approaches, Dracula steals into the house once again and abducts the somnambulistic Mina. Renfield makes another of his periodic escapes, unknowingly leading Van Helsing and Harker to Dracula's lair at nearby Carfax Abbey.

Sensing (wrongly) that Renfield has betrayed him, Dracula kills his slave, tossing his body down a massive staircase (another jaw-dropping set with few equals in the early horror films). The sun is rising as Van Helsing and Harker burst into the Abbey and discover Dracula abed in his coffin. Van Helsing drives a wooden stake through the vampire's heart, releasing Mina from his unearthly spell.

The flaws inherent in *Dracula* are so self-evident that they are outlined in nearly every modern-day critique; only Lugosi freaks and the nostalgically inclined still go through the motions of praising and defending the film. The main problem is that it hews too closely to the play, abandoning many potentially exciting scenes delineated in the novel. Browning is slavish in his faithfulness to the stage production, indulging in long takes and filming scenes in long and medium shots as though the audience were viewing the proceedings through the proverbial proscenium arch. Any action not seen in the stage production remains off-screen here as well (i.e., Dracula's flight from the Seward home in wolf form, Mina's midnight confrontation with the vampire Lucy, Renfield and his army of rats); later descriptions of these events add to the verbiage of an already overly conversational film.

Bela Lugosi's excruciatingly slow delivery seems to set the pace for the other players as well as for the film itself. It's a flawed, hammy, stagy performance and far from the best work that Lugosi did in films. Lugosi had an eerie magnetism and a sensually sinister presence which made him something of a screen idol for the short period when he was really in his prime. Time marches on, however, and the attributes which caused women to swoon and actresses like Carroll Borland to call him "probably the most sexually attractive male I have ever known in my life" are largely lost on modern movie-watchers. Lugosi's ashen face, slicked-back hair and bee-stung lips give him the look of a creep, not a Casanova; his accent and stiff, halting delivery add to that impression of weird decadence. (Reportedly, Lugosi insisted on applying his own makeup and hairpiece which covered his own hair.)

Undeniably Lugosi had just the right exotic "undead" look for a role like Dracula, but his broad, unnatural acting in this initial go-round leaves much to be desired. There's more humor than horror in those closeups of Lugosi looking alternately stunned, bemused, goony and stoned; the shot of Lugosi sizing up Dwight Frye with what can be described as bedroom eyes often gets a laugh. And even the staunchest Lugosi devotees would probably be hard-pressed to defend their idol while he's mangling a fairly simple line like, "Vee vill be *le-e-e-eaving ... to-morrow ...* e-e-e-e-e-veningkk!"

Lugosi remains, however, the very incarnation of suave screen evil, and portrayed vampires to near-perfection in other films. Lugosi's is a truly frightening presence in *Mark of the Vampire,* possibly because he never speaks while in his vampire guise; whatever flaws the film may have, there's something ghoulishly gratifying about the way the horror scenes are overloaded with grim atmosphere. *The Return of the Vampire* (1943) was an obvious Universal clone with a somewhat juvenile plot, but Lugosi's performance as vindictive vampire Armand Tesla (Dracula in everything but name) is effective.

Purists may howl, but Lugosi seems at or near his vampiric peak in the bastard child of the Universal horror series, *Abbott and Costello Meet Frankenstein* (1948). Smooth, articulate and at-ease despite the ravages of drugs and approaching old age, he gives one of his best '40s performances; it's one of the few comedies where Lugosi not only seems to finally be in on the jokes, but is actually enjoying himself.

Lugosi apparently had what amounts to a love-hate relationship with the Dracula character throughout his long career. Playing the role in the 1931 film eventually led to bitterness on the actor's part; Universal reaped millions from *Dracula* and its later reissues, and even from merchandising, but Lugosi never saw a nickel of it. He craved roles that were not in the Dracula/ bogeyman mold, but Hollywood bigwigs (and

Bela Lugosi has eyes only for Helen Chandler in this *Dracula* scene.

movie audiences) could picture him as little else.

Lugosi obviously was his own worst enemy: He never bothered to completely master the English language, showed a lack of judgment in his choice of film roles, and had a mulish, hard-headed streak which screwed up everything his other foibles didn't. He turned down the "undignified" role of the Monster in *Frankenstein* partly because he didn't care to be unrecognizable beneath heavy makeup, yet the following year he was caterwauling under artless clumps of facial

Bela Lugosi and Edward Van Sloan, veterans of the stage version of *Dracula*, were joined by young screen newcomers Helen Chandler and David Manners in Universal's filmization.

hair in Paramount's *Island of Lost Souls;* two short years after *Dracula* he was already lampooning the role (and himself) in a *Hollywood Parade* opposite a flesh-and-blood Betty Boop.

In actuality Count Dracula was probably the best friend Lugosi ever had; it's tough to imagine him ending up as anything more than the Paul Lukas of Poverty Row had the film role of Dracula not come his way. And probably Lugosi knew this as well. Despite his lofty pretensions and his frequent coulda-been/shoulda-been sulks, his last wish was to be buried in his Dracula cape.

While Lugosi dominates the first two reels of *Dracula*, he turns up only occasionally thereafter; the presence and menace of Dracula are felt throughout the film, but Lugosi only has three major scenes ahead of him once he leaves his Carpathian digs. The task of carrying the film now falls onto the shoulders of Helen Chandler, David Manners, Dwight Frye and Edward Van Sloan.

Van Sloan, undeservedly fifth-billed, really becomes the star of the film after the first third, at least in terms of screen time; it's a shame that this is probably one of his least enjoyable film performances. Van Sloan appears to be trying to match or outdo Lugosi's funereal delivery: He speaks too slowly and precisely, as though explaining something to a backward child. The actor also has the annoying habit of talking with his hands, gesticulating at every character to whom he talks, then never putting his hands down; many shots end with Van Sloan silently standing in what almost looks like a boxer's stance. Van Sloan is one of the best-loved character actors from the old horror films, but his baby-talk and rolling of r's in *Dracula* is atypically amateurish and irritating. (Surely it was Browning who elicited this performance; when Van Sloan reprised the Van Helsing role in *Dracula's Daughter*, he had the ratatat delivery of a Warners stock player!) Another curious faux pas in *Dracula* is that Van Sloan wears impossibly thick-lensed glasses throughout the film, and then discards them just before the finale.

Helen Chandler and David Manners are inadequate romantic leads. Chandler's much-persecuted Mina is a wistful, weak-willed heroine, far too bloodless to attract any self-respecting vampire. By all accounts, Chandler went through life with her head in the clouds, but her movie career certainly never got off the ground. Once touted as "the new Lillian Gish," her career petered out around 1937; health and emotional problems, not to mention an inordinate fondness for the grape, had her in and out of sanitariums and hospitals for many years. She died largely forgotten on April 30, 1965. In view of the fine performances the actress gave as the rich, hedonistic Nikki in *The Last Flight* (1931) and as Colin Clive's daughter in *Christopher Strong* (1933), it is perhaps unfair to judge Helen Chandler's talents solely on her wanting performance in *Dracula*.

David Manners held the distinction of starring in three of the best-known classic horror films—*Dracula*, *The Mummy* and *The Black Cat*—but the callow, lovesick characters that became his stock-in-trade have won him few fans among the horror crowd. Manners' John Harker is a particularly stuffy and petulant bore, always on the verge of bollixing up Van Helsing's meticulously laid plans. Lew Ayres, the young star of *All Quiet on the Western Front* (1930), was initially picked for the Harker role.

Bela Lugosi was typecast as a horror film star after *Dracula*, but he got off easy compared to poor Dwight Frye. Frye's unique, bizarre portrayal of Renfield remains one of the more striking performances in the movie, mostly for the wrong reasons; the one-time Broadway player was typecast as morons, ghouls and hunchbacks from that point on. "If God is good, I will be able to play comedy in which I was featured on Broadway for eight seasons and in which no producer of motion pictures will give me a chance!" Frye whined in the pressbook for *The Vampire Bat* (1933). "And please, God, may it be before I go screwy playing idiots, halfwits and lunatics on the talking screen!"

God's copy of the *Vampire Bat* pressbook must have been misdelivered, for Frye remained solidly entrenched in that ignominious little niche. Born in Kansas and raised in Colorado, Frye caught the acting bug early, worked in vaudeville and even sang and danced in something called "La La Lucille." After a few years doing stock, he began landing parts on Broadway and generally getting good notices for his work; he also owned and operated a 69th Street tearoom patronized by stage personalities. While appearing in a play on the West Coast he was spotted by a Warner Bros. representative and hired for the small role of a machine-gun–toting hood in the 1930 gangster picture *The Doorway to Hell*. This *Doorway* led to other film roles as undersized tough guys, including the part of gunsel Wilmer in 1931's *The Maltese Falcon*. But *Dracula* abruptly and permanently changed the diminutive actor's screen image.

Like other performances in *Dracula*, Frye's is mostly hammy and indulgent. Renfield seems a bit of a queen in early scenes with his effeminate look and prissy manner; he's less restrained and more effective in the later segments set in

Marked women: Helen Chandler as Mina and Frances Dade as Lucy.

London. Unfortunately, the "mad" Renfield character serves little real purpose in the film: There's never any hint of what services he would (or possibly could) render for Dracula, nor any indication why he takes an interest in Mina's well-being. He often seems on the brink of spilling his guts to Van Helsing when an abrupt mood shift turns him back into the cagey, tight-lipped Renfield once again, rendering the whole scene pointless.

Frye is at his best in the brief scenes where his character's "normal" side gleams through; the vignette of Renfield sobbing in his cell is actually rather moving, and more of a highlight than the protracted soliloquy ("Rats ... rats-s-s ... rats-s-s-s-s!") which he directs at the camera in an outdated stagebound rendition.

The remainder of the cast ranges from the competent (Herbert Bunston as Dr. Seward, Frances Dade as Lucy) to the completely inept (Charles Gerrard as a Cockney guard, Michael Visaroff as the innkeeper). Dade, whose screen time is unfortunately limited, is a strikingly pretty actress whose performance seems more realistic than those being given around her, and it's not surprising that Dracula passes over demure Mina and makes Dade's Lucy his first victim. Lucy returns from the dead in the film and goes off on her own modest vampiric spree; in the script there's a mood-crusted scene in which Van Helsing and Harker observe Lucy as she returns to the Weston family vault after one of her midnight jaunts.

A number of interesting scenes and minor visual touches are described in the *Dracula* script but do not appear in the film.* Perhaps Univer-

**The script includes several scenes of Dracula with fangs bared and also depicts his victims' neck wounds. The description of Dracula's rampage on board the storm-swept* Vesta *makes for particularly exciting reading. The script calls for a sequence filled with flash-cuts of "furiously increasing tempo": A closeup of the captain at the wheel screaming; faces of sailors wild with fear;*

sal executives had not forgotten the less-than-encouraging initial comments of the studio's readers, and sought to downplay the horror wherever they could. (The blame might rest with Browning, but considering the fact that the man gave poor taste a bad name the following year with *Freaks*, it isn't likely that he was offended by the *Dracula* script's horrific touches.) The result, after those first two magnificent Transylvania-set reels of chills and atmosphere, is a talky, thin-blooded filmed play, a tepid melodramatic exercise with tame and timorous horror embellishments.

Universal was indecisive, too, in their marketing of the film, playing it up as a Gothic romance. Whereas the play had advertised itself as "The Ultimate in Horror," Universal dubbed its new macabre feature "The Story of the Strangest Passion the World Has Ever Known."

All the flaws and limitations that get under people's skin about *Dracula* today didn't seem to faze 1931 moviegoers or critics. The movie was by all accounts a certified blockbuster. At New York City's posh Roxy Theater, according to press reports, *Dracula* attracted 50,000 paid admissions during its first two days of screenings. Browning's cinematic nightmare struck box office gold on the West Coast as well, opening at Los Angeles' Pantages Theater on Friday, May 1. The reviews for the movie were uniformly positive, some even laudatory, making the film one of the best received critically of any of the Universal horror pictures. If anything, most critical comments suggest that even a slightly stronger presentation would have proved completely unacceptable to the genteel audiences of the time. Neither Browning nor Universal was actually interested in going for the jugular of the general public as F.W. Murnau did in *Nosferatu* or, to a lesser extent, as Rouben Mamoulian did in his terrifically exciting *Dr. Jekyll and Mr. Hyde*, which was released the same year. (The Spanish-language edition of the film, directed by George Melford, at least wasn't quite so conservative in execution.) Instead, the studio and the director sought an ambiance of quiet melancholy which makes *Dracula* seem like weak tea today, but it was horrific enough at the time. Browning's aesthetic dated quickly, however, and by the time *Dracula's Daughter* was released, the studio was already well into its trademark monster movie mode. Still, *Dracula* proved to be remarkably durable and it remained a popular revival title in American theaters for at least a generation.

The judgment of time has sadly gone against *Dracula*, and most of the film's problems stem from Browning's handling. Perhaps Browning's idea was to fashion a deliberately paced, hypnotic film that would weave a spell over its audience; if so, the director was unable to sustain the required mood. Browning wasn't interested transposing the stageplay intact but he was keen on retaining the "theatrical experience." By keeping the staging and cutting rudimentary, he fulfilled his own demands. What he didn't do was fulfill the demands of future audiences who preferred their movies to be real "movies." Certainly it must be kept in mind that *Dracula* was made in 1930 while the motion picture industry was in a period of transition from silents to talkies; filmmakers were suddenly encumbered by the limitations of the microphone, and stage-bound drawing room affairs became the order of the day.

As was common in the early talkies, there is barely a note of music in *Dracula* (save for the elegant main title, the brief interlude at the opera, and the climactic ringing of celestial bells as Mina and Harker leave Carfax Abbey). This absence of a symphonic undercurrent often works to excellent advantage, especially in the early Transylvania episodes, and in several of the London sequences (particularly those involving the vampire and his transfixed female victims). Without a background score, the viewer is able to fully savor such disturbing effects as a creaking castle door, the chatter of bats in flight, and the repulsive creepy-crawly sounds made by other "children of the night"; even the lonely sounds of honking vehicles navigating their way through a chilly, fogbound night add to the aural

[continued] *a large closeup of* Dracula *with fangs bared; a sailor plunging over the rail into the surging sea; and finally a huge and impressive shot of* Dracula, *"arms upraised, dark cloak billowing in the gale, about to close in upon a screaming, helpless wretch he has cornered." None of this is seen in the film: From a shot of Lugosi in a ship's doorway, a dissolve takes us to a large closeup of a wharf pile around which a ship's hawser has been looped. The* Vesta *has arrived in Whitby, and the voice of an off-camera harbor master (actually the voice of Tod Browning) describes the tragedy.*

tapestry. What a welcome change from the obvious, horror-loaded compositions which accompanied the horror films of the silent screen. In 1999, Universal sought to "upgrade" *Dracula* by releasing a special edition of the Browning classic with a new Dolby Digital 5.1 score composed and conducted by classical music composer Philip Glass; the experiment was greeted with decidedly mixed reviews.

Like the novel and play before it, there's the germ of a great idea in Universal's *Dracula* but it's quickly sterilized by an unimaginative and impassive director. After the initial reels build expectations, the film becomes a creaky antique that seldom budges the needle on the drama meter. Not surprisingly, even the men behind *Dracula* had their reservations. John L. Balderston wrote in a studio memo that the film's last third dropped badly; Bela Lugosi apparently saw it as a bungled opportunity, and harped on the idea of one day starring in a worthier remake. Even Tod Browning, when asked in 1936 which of his own films was his favorite, bypassed *Dracula* and named the silent *The Unholy Three* (1925).

An already anemic film, *Dracula* was further emasculated prior to a mid–'30s reissue. Renfield's screams (as he is being choked by Dracula) and the count's own cries (as the stake is pounded into his heart) were removed from the soundtrack. A quaint closing curtain speech delivered by Van Helsing was also deleted. The cries of Renfield and Dracula have been restored in some home video releases; the little that remains of the badly decomposed curtain speech is on view in Universal's made-for-DVD documentary *The Road to Dracula*.

One unapologetic admirer of Browning's *Dracula* is David Colton, *USA Today* editor and creator of the ever-popular online Classic Horror Film Board. (www.monsterkid.com)

> Whereas I grew up watching the Hammer series ... I didn't see Universal's *Dracula* until I was 13. Though I'm glad [*Dracula* and *Horror of Dracula*] exist for us to enjoy, I nevertheless recognize Lugosi's Dracula as the superior characterization and Browning's *Dracula* to be the better film....
>
> Actually there is a much greater sense of Dracula's omnipresence in Universal's *Dracula* simply because he is omnipresent. When Lugosi is offscreen we can see his presence in Renfield, we see it in the great bat and we see it in Mina. And if Dracula isn't in a scene ... we find him skulking about right outside on the grounds of the Seward estate, which is why I find the criticism that there is "too much staginess" (often by the film's supporters) in Browning's *Dracula* to be an empty one and an unnecessary concession in the Hammer vs. Universal debate; too many interesting things occur during those "stagey" parts—and they're frequently punctuated by interesting visuals such as the undead Lucy perambulating in the graveyard.
>
> Truth is, Lugosi's portrayal is richer than [Christopher] Lee's, more interesting than Lee's and more believable than Lee's. The otherworldliness of the Lugosi characterization, especially when he's on his own turf in Transylvania, is an incredible performance. Lugosi imparts a genuine sense of decay and corruption ... of being undead (something lacking in the Hammer Draculas).... As for some of the great lines that Lugosi gets to speak, they are great because of the believability he gives them; Lugosi took them from Stoker and forever made them his own.

Universal more or less remade *Dracula* just one year later: Transposed to Egypt, the plot of *Dracula* was, pardon the pun, revamped into *The Mummy*, a carbon copy right down to individual scenes. Hollywood moviemakers had marched forward in seven-league boots since the production of *Dracula*, and the infinitely better *Mummy* is a film that looks years removed from Browning's stodgy piece.

A number of screen Draculas have come and gone in the decades since the Universal version: Lon Chaney Jr., John Carradine, Christopher Lee, Francis Lederer, Jack Palance, Louis Jourdan, Klaus Kinski, Frank Langella, Gary Oldman, William Marshall, Leslie Nielsen, David Niven, Udo Kier, George Hamilton, Gerard Butler, Denholm Elliott and Rutger Hauer, to name a few. For all its primitivism, crude special effects and sunlit scenes of midnight, it's still Murnau's *Nosferatu* that probably ranks as the best screen version of the Stoker tale.

Dracula's flaws are legion; its stately pace, stolid direction and overripe performances quickly betray it; the absence of a musical score is keenly felt during its many protracted stretches of complete silence. But its importance in film history and its influence on later films is tremendous. It set forth all the conventions of the archetypal vampire film, laying groundwork that would be capitalized upon in scores of latter-day follow-ups. It sparked Lugosi's unique horror career and, most importantly, spawned the classic Universal horror series of the early '30s. Its status as a movie milestone is untarnished.

Critics' Corner

Eerie, spooky, and entertaining ... Bela Lugosi does exceptionally good work in the name part.... Tod Browning's direction is his best in this one—*The Motion Picture Daily*, March 30, 1931.

What with Mr. Browning's imaginative direction and Mr. Lugosi's make-up and weird gestures, this picture succeeds to some extent in its grand guignol intentions.... Helen Chandler gives an excellent performance...—*The New York Times*, February 13, 1931, Mordaunt Hall.

[A] sublimated short story related with all surface seriousness and above all with remarkably effective background of creepy atmosphere.... It is difficult to think of anybody who could quite match the performance of Bela Lugosi...—*Variety*, 1931.

Rating: ★★★ You'll find it creepy and cruel and crazed.... Superbly photographed and presented to ... audiences at the capable movie direction of Tod Browning.... We enjoyed it!—*The New York Daily News*, February 13, 1931.

[Lugosi's] performance of the vampire is a hypnotic one.... Tod Browning has directed the picture with fine appreciation of its creepy possibilities and much praise must go to Danny Hall who created the extraordinary settings—*The Hollywood Daily Citizen*, May 1, 1931, Elizabeth Yeaman.

The settings that the stage couldn't provide for "Dracula" have all been furnished for the movie version. The effect is telling, strongly so...—*The Milwaukee Journal*, February 15, 1931.

Of all the people of the cinema, only Tod Browning ... was properly equipped to direct this grotesque, fantastic, slightly unhealthy melodrama with proper forcefulness and conviction. Yet so perverse is the motion picture that it would have surprised no one had some expert in the films who devoted himself to cowboy comedies been assigned to the task, rather than this master of shadows. Anyway, thanks to his selection and to the properly terrifying performance ... of Bela Lugosi ... *Dracula* reaches the Roxy Theater as an absorbing adventure in morbid fantasy—*The New York Herald-Tribune*, February 13, 1931, Richard Watts, Jr.

Universal and their clever technicians are to be congratulated on their adaptation of the famous Bram Stoker shocker. Especially we would commend the resourceful treatment of Tod Browning and the superb camera work of Karl Freund, for between them these two have ensured that atmosphere of brooding horror and well-nigh unbearable menace which were so characteristic of the book—*The Cinema* (GB), February 25, 1931

Where the cinema transcription falls short, it seems to me, is in its insistence of being too real, overly explicit.... [I]ts manner of storytelling is that of the stage, with imagination largely sacrificed to theatricality—*The Los Angeles Times*, March 30, 1931, Philip K. Scheuer.

One of the creepiest mystery melodramas ever screened. *Dracula* is the best talking picture of its type ever exhibited—*The N.Y. Graphic*, February 1931, Julia Shawell.

Fine melodrama of human vampire carries spooky thrills.... The screen transposition of the melodramatic stage play has been given a finished production under the expert direction of Tod Browning, who knows how to get the most of out of the weird and spooky effects.... Bela Lugosi creates one of the most unique and powerful roles of the screen in this one—*The Film Daily*, February 15, 1931.

Dracula is an exciting melodrama, not as good as it ought to be but a cut above the ordinary trapdoor-and-winding-sheet type of mystery film—*Time*, February 23, 1931.

Dracula (The Spanish Version)

Released in 1931. 104 minutes. *Associate Producer:* Paul Kohner. *Producer:* Carl Laemmle, Jr. *Director:* George Melford. *Screenplay:* Garrett Fort. *Based on the novel by* Bram Stoker, *and the play by* Hamilton Deane and John L. Balderston. *Spanish Adaptation:* B. Fernández Cué. *Photography:* George Robinson. *Dialogue Director:* Enrique Tovar Avalos. *Supervising Editor:* Maurice Pivar. *Editor:* Arturo Tavares. *Art Director:* Charles D. Hall. *Recording Supervisor:* C. Roy Hunter. *Music Supervisor:* Heinz Roemheld. *Assistant Directors:* Charles Gould & Jay Marchant. *Makeup:* Jack P. Pierce.

Carlos Villarías (*Conde Dracula*), Lupita Tovar (*Eva Seward*), Barry Norton (*Juan Harker*), Pablo Álvarez Rubio (*Renfield*), Eduardo Arozamena (*Van Helsing*) José Soriano Viosca (*Dr. Seward*), Carmen Guerrero (*Lucia*), Amelia Senisterra (*Marta*), Manuel Arbó (*Martin*), Bela Lugosi, Jeraldine Dvorak, Cornelia Thaw, Dorothy Tree (*Stock footage from the English-language version*).

> I think the Spanish is better! The other one is a little dull, it's too passive. And the Spanish ... has a little more excitement in it.
> —*Lupita Tovar, comparing both versions of Universal's* Dracula.

The opening frames are familiar but disarmingly different. A flickering candle, framed in cobwebs, is suddenly blown out, set to the murmuring strains of *Swan Lake*. It's a perfect set-up for the Spanish-language edition of *Dracula*, a film that adheres closely enough to its prototype

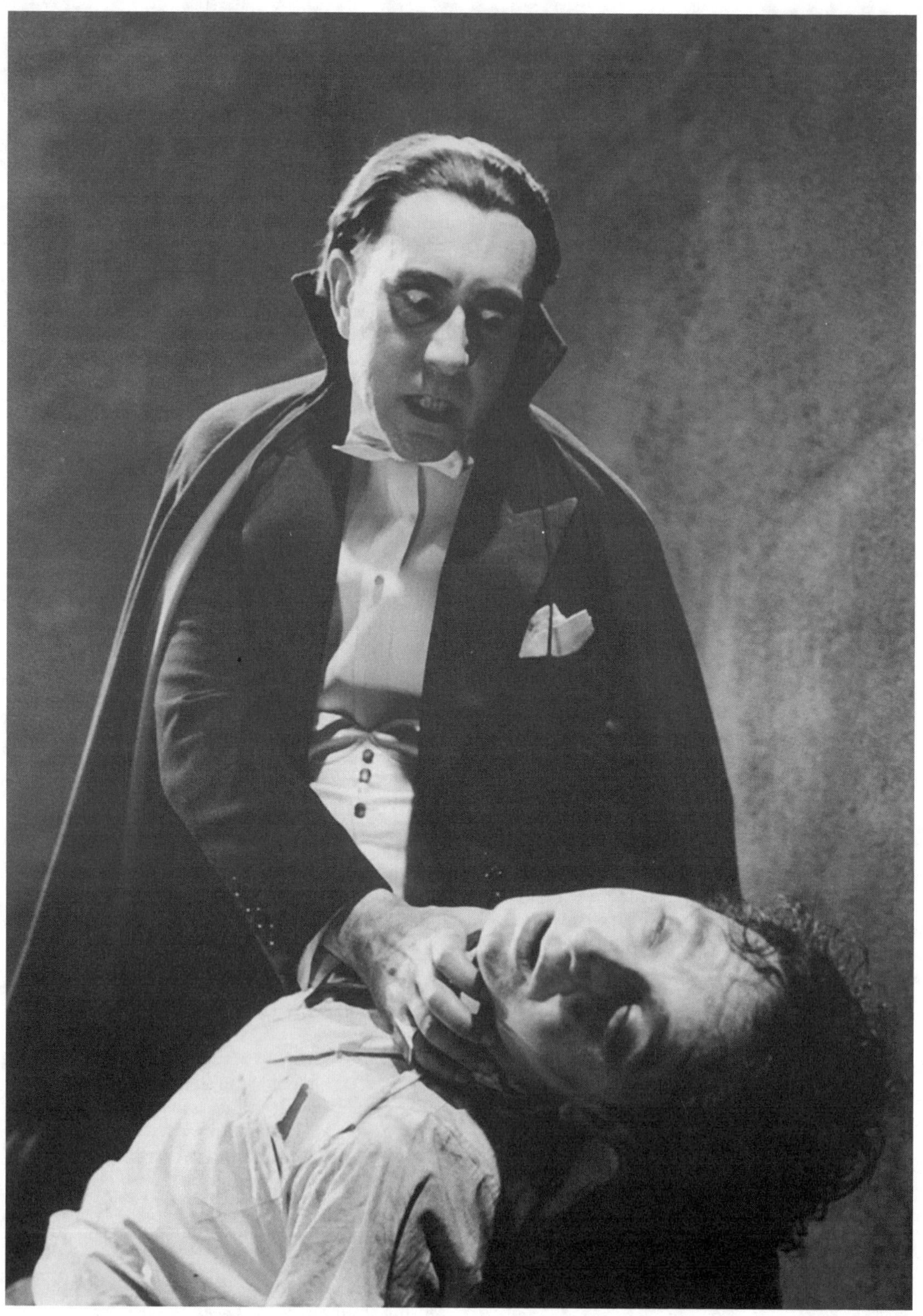

Carlos Villarías chokes the life out of Pablo Alvarez Rubio at the climax of the Spanish-language *Dracula*.

but in its subtle differences manages to find its own distinct voice. Perhaps the difference in the main title design is in itself a kind of commentary. The stately yet striking bat artwork of the original, replaced by a live action shot, suggests that this version itself is more real and immediate, something strangely more *alive*.

Notwithstanding the discovery of a print of director Rupert Julian's 1930 version of *The Cat Creeps*, the Spanish version of *Dracula* is the last great Universal horror discovery we're likely to see. Filmed on the sets of the Tod Browning version as a "graveyard shift" project with a customized script, the picture used the resources of studio craftsmen to tap into the lucrative Spanish market. For decades it remained a lost film, scarcely eliciting minimal interest from the studio which produced it. But as the home video boom took off and Universal began to embrace its monster heritage more vigorously, the film was finally given a full restoration. (Happily, the instincts of studio preservationists paid off. Videotapes of the film sold beyond expectations as a stand-alone release in the early '90s.)

Although Carl Laemmle, Jr., is the officially credited producer, the hands-on supervisor was Paul Kohner. The 27-year-old Czech-born executive had worked in various capacities at Universal, including organizing the production of the Paul Leni classic *The Man Who Laughs* (1927). There was little question who would be director Tod Browning's replacement: George Melford, a former actor who had racked up an impressive number of directorial credits, hitting the high note with the Rudolph Valentino hit, *The Sheik* (1921). After a long association with Paramount, he began a stint at Universal, often handling directorial duties on Spanish versions of studio releases. Despite the handicap of working with actors through an interpreter, Melford put his name on three of these features, including the 1930 Spanish-language version of *The Cat Creeps*. A full production crew in place, started filming Melford's *Dracula* on October 10, 1930, eleven days after the Browning company began, wrapping on November 8 for a total of 22 shooting days. The Spanish *Dracula* ultimately debuted in Cuba on March 11, 1931, and in New York City on April 24 of the same year.

The movie would prove to be the highpoint in the career of Lupita Tovar. The Mexican beauty queen with limited acting experience but screen presence to burn, more than bested Helen Chandler in her role as Dracula's heart-throb and intended victim. Although Tovar went on to wed Kohner (a marriage that lasted until his death in 1992; their daughter is actress Susan Kohner), she was actually discovered by American documentary pioneer, Robert Flaherty. Universal put her sultry Latino looks to good advantage in the Spanish *The Cat Creeps*.

Miss Tovar told the authors,

> The idea was to make the Spanish version [of *Dracula*] for as little money as possible. So they used the same sets and everything. And those [Spanish-speaking actors] were not demanding big salaries. We didn't know any better, and everybody was very happy to get a job. Most of them had been having little parts in silent films, and many of them had even played extras, even though they had a name in Spain and in Mexico. When Universal said, "The role pays so-much," you didn't argue, you said, "Fine."
>
> Also, I was always there almost an hour early, so that I would feel "at home" on the set, so that I would feel that I was secure. Many times I went in and the crew hadn't arrived yet, so I would sit there in the dark until they came and started lighting the place up. And it was very scary, the whole feeling of being there alone! If someone had come up behind me, I would have let out a scream *[laughs]*!

The resurrection of the Spanish-language version of *Dracula* proved more of a pivotal event in Universal Horrors circles than anyone could have imagined. Rather than being a mere run-through of the same script on the same sets with only the actors' faces changing, this film turned out to be a truly unique discovery. The 104-minute running time, nearly a half-hour longer than the Browning print, suggests a film more inclined to explore character and add a layer of detail to the Garrett Fort script.

For the legion of Universal fans who have virtually memorized every frame of the Lugosi film, director George Melford's modified staging is evident at once. As a few lingering bars of *Swan Lake* stray onto the opening shot, the viewer senses he's in the hands of a filmmaker less committed to recreating a theatrical event on the screen. The more natural flow of the film is seen in tiny details and Melford's general easing of the heavy, "let's not speak above a whisper" atmosphere. There's even a giggling reaction in the first scene as a coach passenger fearfully recounts the vampire legend to his fellow travelers; under Browning's direction the same speech was met with merely a stony skepticism. The comparatively relaxed tone isn't an improvement in itself. In fact, some viewers might actually prefer Browning's sense of mounting dread with his over-stylized direction of the villagers, as being more in tune to Stoker's intentions.

While the movie is, of course, of general interest to film historians and even the casual filmgoer, it's a treasure-trove to the Universal horror fanatic for whom the original film is, if not a beloved classic, then one that's etched in the memory. To savor each and every difference of each frame in both pictures is to experience the real pleasures of an unrepentant movie nerd. Scenes are restaged to an extent far exceeding the requirements of an alternate release version. Even Renfield's coach ride to Dracula's castle includes intriguing alternate footage of the wagon passing an unexplained bonfire and entirely new shots of the transport trudging through mountain passes. B. Fernández Cué's screenplay isn't a mere translation from the English, he constantly expands the dialogue, rearranges scenes and adds bits of business, including additional material for Renfield's flustered comic relief keeper, Martin (Manuel Arbó).

George Robinson's fluid, graceful camerawork is more cinematic than Karl Freund's. (The use of a fast-moving crane for Dracula's first appearance in his castle, standing, candle in hand, on the huge stone staircase, makes this the film's most commented-upon shot.) On a whole, the film seems less stymied by studio caution and is more of an all-out horror package than the American version. The downside of this approach is the sometimes heavy-handed use of shock conventions, from the creaking door sound effects of Dracula's coach (rather comically reused as the castle's weighty front door swings open for Renfield's entrance) to the vampire king's emergence from his coffin in a puff of smoke (rather like a cornball stage magician's trick). The emphasis on thrills rather than atmosphere pays off handsomely, however, during Dracula's storm-battered crossing of the inhospitable sea. A true highlight of '30s horror, the scene is closer to the spirit of Murnau's *Nosferatu* (1922) as the Count stares down the ship's terrified crew. In comparison, the original scene was badly compromised by mismatched shots of the wildly rocking ship with footage of Lugosi, shot on an even keel and unaffected by weather conditions, crudely inserted. Melford's sequence is a quantum improvement, to put in mildly.

Another advantage to the Melford version is that it leaves intact Renfield's panther-like stalking of the Seward housemaid who has fainted at the sight of him. Traditionally, the scene cuts off just as he moves in on the stricken girl, leaving her fate to the imagination of the viewer. The Spanish print reveals the actual wit of the scene as written, showing that the insect-eating Renfield's real interest was a common fly that landed on the servant; he scoops it up and promptly devours it. Hardly the most terrifying of outcomes, but it brings a pleasing sense of closure to the episode.

Apart from scene-by-scene comparisons of both productions, the more intriguing distinction is how the copycat film caters to the sensibilities of the Spanish audience. Some of these differences can be credited to the lax censorship restrictions in Europe and elsewhere: Ergo, Lupita Tovar's much-commented upon wardrobe, especially her low-cut nightgowns which would have raised more than a few eyebrows even in Hollywood's pre–Code days. While these concessions give the film a vitality lacking in the original, it wouldn't be much of a cheap shot to suggest that even the dead characters have more life to them in the Spanish edition than the live ones do in the American version. (Take a look at the ravenous expressions on Dracula's Spanish brides as they are about to pounce on the fallen Renfield.) Unfortunately, these heightened effects are also sadly disruptive to the film's sense of setting. Browning may have gone overboard in creating an embalmed atmosphere but at least it all seemed credibly British. In contrast, Melford and his troupe of actors barely acknowledge the *faux* English window-dressing and inject a good deal more earthy passion into the mix. There's little of Helen Chandler's meek and wispy Mina in Tovar's Eva (her character so rechristened) and she has a more doting and physically affectionate father in José Soriano Viosca's Dr. Seward. Tovar's fight to retain her soul is very much a struggle to the death, and unlike the passive and submissive Chandler, she seems determined to give it all she's got. With the drama and the concurrent sexual tensions far more heated, it's easier to feel more affinity for the characters in this production, especially with such a low-charisma Dracula manipulating the action.

His angular frame wrapped in the traditional cape, and with Lugosi's trademark widow's peak dutifully replicated, Carlos Villarías makes an excellent stand-in for the iconic Hungarian actor. (It's unlikely that the players were physically matched to flatter Lugosi, whose identification with the role certainly had not yet been established to 1931 movie audiences. Rather, they were made up similarly because of the practical need to occasionally cut to Bela in long shots.)

Nevertheless, Villarías' performance is the picture's most crucial weakness. As heavy and indulgent as Lugosi sometimes is, there's no denying that he almost literally comes across as the Bram Stoker character in the flesh. Villarías doesn't convey anything except what he is, an actor playing a role. The performance underscores how much a personality piece the property is; like Sherlock Holmes, all his stage or movie renditions risk utter failure by its central casting. Lugosi could convince anyone he was the King of the Vampires by simply striking a pose. For all of Villarías' mugging and facial gyrations, he looks like one of the count's foot soldiers.

The film's balance is almost offset by Pablo Álvarez Rubio's Renfield who, acting-wise, easily overpowers Villarías — not a happy circumstance in conveying the master-slave relationship. Comparing Rubio to Dwight Frye, both faithfully comply to their respective directors' conception of the part. Frye's unnerving cackle and haunting grimace generated the kind of quiet, lingering chills that stay with you like a particularly bad nightmare. Rubio is clearly relishing every nuance in an already over-the-top role, playing Renfield as The Last Word in movie madmen. There's more than a little self-conscious bravura to his playing, like an actor determined to bring home an Oscar. At times he seems to be in competition with Villarías to see who could come up with the goofiest facial expressions but, for the most part, his effective scenes outnumber his more trying ones.

The rest of the cast is a varied lot. It's not clear how large a pool of Spanish-speaking actors Universal had to draw from but Eduardo Arozamena is uncomfortably cast as a youngish, potato-nose Van Helsing. As Harker, Barry Norton comes across as a slightly vapid juvenile, a fair enough equivalent to David Manners. In all, it's an interesting assemblage of faces even in minor roles. The lack of the usual photogenic, glamour-conscious Hollywood "types" is quite noticeable among the various nurses, maids and theater usherettes, giving the film a more naturalistic edge.

The Spanish *Dracula*'s novelty value works very much in its favor. Stacked against the flawed and tired original perhaps artificially heightens its qualities a tad. Although an enthusiastic and polished work, it is not without its rough edges (some of the cuts to the original print are rather jarring). Melford cleverly works some of the "live" music from the original film to partially score a couple of scenes. Dracula's clawing hand opening the coffin lid is set to the ominous opening of Schubert's unfinished *Symphony #8* lifted from the concert scene. One surprising change is that the concert itself is turned into a ballet courtesy of a few stock shots, and Melford goes even further by having the actors read their lines while the performance is in progress. While one wonders why the other patrons are tolerating such extreme rudeness as the players yap away in their opera box, at least Dracula's highly quotable "To die, to be really dead" speech is now loftily accompanied by Wagner's *Die Meistersinger*.

In the end, it is Browning who has the last laugh with the acclaimed Melford version fated to live forever in the shadow of the official Lugosi edition with the general public. Even so, the Spanish-dialogue *Dracula* can claim to have a modest life of its own among film buffs and perhaps achieving a competitive edge over its better-known rival. A cynic, or even a realist, might say that all it had to do was to improve a movie that was deeply flawed to begin with. The film's restoration, at any rate, served to obliterate its previous status as a cinematic footnote and has paved the way for its recognition as a work of artistry.

Critics' Corner

[T]his Spanish-language version is in many ways an improvement upon the original. Whereas the English-language version ... is stylish and atmospheric only in its first two reels, the Spanish *Dracula* sustains its eerieness throughout—*All Movie Guide*, Hal Erickson.

[Carlos] Villarías does a remarkable job of duplicating Lugosi's body movements, especially the clenching of fists, and the stiff way he often walks into a scene. Villarías, unfortunately, was not much of an actor otherwise. In the closeup scenes of his face, or the closer ones just of his eyes, he becomes almost a lampoon of Lugosi, mugging to such a degree that the subtler and certainly more charismatic menace of Lugosi is never once approached—*More Classics of the Horror Film*, Citadel, 1986, William K. Everson.

[T]he film has many striking assets—first and foremost, the fact that it *isn't* the stodgy, played-out Lugosi version! But it also suffers from many of that film's nagging pitfalls.... For Universal buffs, it's fascinating to see the *Dracula* sets filled with fresh blood (that is, the different set of actors), photographed more creatively and directed with an eye toward its macabre potential rather than the way Tod Browning directed Lugosi's (i.e., to retain the stage "flavor"). But the incongruity of Slavic peasants and London blue-bloods spouting Espanol—not to mention the silent screen-style acting and overall dragginess—will certainly have many fans regarding the film merely as a curio, an object of study rather than a source of entertainment. Is it actually a better film than Lugosi's, or will it just *seem* better until the novelty wears off?—*Fangoria* #119.

Dracula's entrance is more dramatic in the Spanish, beginning with a wide shot before going to a dolly and zoom, but in general the film is far less ambitious technically with fewer dolly or tracking shots.... Versions also differ in running time. While the Browning version clocks in at a brisk 75 minutes, Melford's creeps along to 104 minutes with ponderous pausing and plodding dialog.... Villarías' Dracula lacks Lugosi's moth-to-the-flame allure and presence; his melodramatic pauses are almost comic. But the female characters ... are more concupiscent, underlining the film's basic sexuality. In any language, Renfield's role is a gift to any ham actor...—*Variety*, Paul Lenti.

[I]t follows the pattern and camera set-ups of Tod Browning's American film fairly closely—*The Museum of Modern Art Department of Film Program Notes*, 1977, Leonard Maltin.

Frankenstein

Released November 21, 1931. 71 minutes. *Producer:* Carl Laemmle, Jr. *Director:* James Whale. *Screenplay:* Garrett Fort, Francis Edwards Faragoh, John Russell (uncredited) & Robert Florey (uncredited). *Based on the composition by* John L. Balderston. *Adapted from the play by* Peggy Webling. *From the novel* Frankenstein; or, The Modern Prometheus *by* Mary Wollstonecraft Shelley. *Associate Producer:* E.M. Asher. *Scenario Editor:* Richard L. Schayer. *Continuity:* Tom Reed. *Photography:* Arthur Edeson. *Supervising Editor:* Maurice Pivar. *Editor:* Clarence Kolster. *Art Director:* Charles D. Hall. *Recording Supervisor:* C. Roy Hunter. *Set Designer:* Herman Rosse. *Makeup:* Jack P. Pierce. *Assistant Director:* Joseph A. McDonough. *Technician:* William Hedgcock. *Special Electrical Effects:* Kenneth Strickfaden, Frank Graves & Raymond Lindsay. *Technical Advisor:* Dr. Cecil Reynolds. *Music Director:* David Broekman. *Original Music:* Bernhard Kaun. *Property Master:* Eddie Keys.

Colin Clive (*Henry Frankenstein*), Mae Clarke (*Elizabeth*), John Boles (*Victor Moritz*), Boris Karloff (*The Monster*), Edward Van Sloan (*Dr. Waldman*), Frederick Kerr (*Baron Frankenstein*), Dwight Frye (*Fritz*), Lionel Belmore (*Herr Vogel, the Burgomaster*), Marilyn Harris (*Little Maria*), Michael Mark (*Ludwig*), Arletta Duncan, Pauline Moore (*Bridesmaids*), Francis Ford (*Man at Lecture/Hans, the Wounded Villager on Hill*), Robert Livingston (*Henry Frankenstein in closing scene*), Mary Sherman, Otis Harlan.

Beside it, *Dracula* is tame....
—*Mordaunt Hall,* The New York Times, *December 5, 1931*

In spite of the strong box office performance of *Dracula,* Universal Studios remained a crippled giant. The studio heads desperately sought to get the company's finances in order, often resorting to laying off its employees. Carl Laemmle, Sr., fancied his company to be one of the bulwarks of the industry but, unlike the other majors, Universal did not own a vast chain of theaters in need of a steady flow of new product. The studio's reliance on independently-owned theaters for most of its business placed it at a serious disadvantage. Less critical, but undeniably vexing, was the constant charge of nepotism leveled against the studio. Interviewed by the authors, director Henry Koster recalled working on the Universal lot in the '30s:

> Carl Laemmle brought all of his relatives over from Germany. They used to say the European comes over here not to start as a producer, but to establish a beachhead. At Laemmle's studio, everybody was a Laemmle. I remember reporting for work on one of my first days at Universal. One of the reception policemen said to me, "You're Mr. Koster?" I said, "Yes. And you're Mr. Laemmle, aren't you?" He said, "Oh, you know me?"

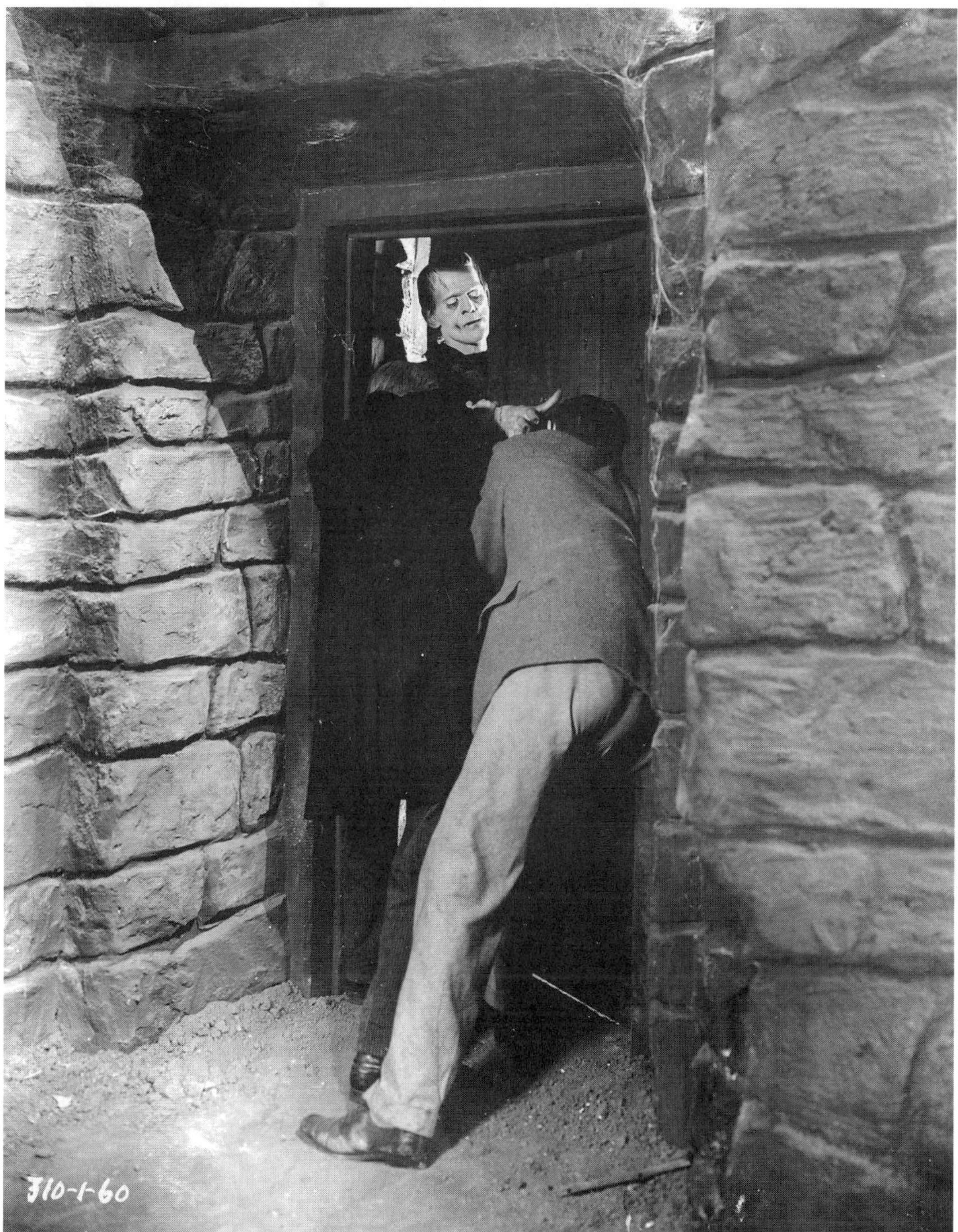

Colin Clive and Edward Van Sloan struggle to subdue Boris Karloff's Monster in *Frankenstein*.

In those more imaginative days, talk of a sequel wasn't the instant reaction to a major hit. But the disreputable horror genre was looming as a potential money-maker for the financially ailing studio. Tod Browning's retreat to his home base, MGM, did little to deter the studio's ambition to follow *Dracula* with another horror feature. Universal's real challenge was to find the right material. *Frankenstein: or, The Modern Prometheus,* Mary Wollstonecraft Shelley's sprawling Gothic nightmare of a novel, quite unfilmable without considerable pruning, was an attractive possibility. The novel was well-known and had inspired at least one earlier film, a short Thomas Edison produced in 1910, and any number of stage adaptations.

Universal's classic movie version of *Frankenstein* is recognized as the brainchild of French-born writer-director Robert Florey. Florey was invited by studio story department head Richard Schayer to work on a horror property. Edgar Allan Poe's "The Murders in the Rue Morgue" and H.G. Wells' *The Invisible Man* fit the bill but the director was pushing the idea of bringing *Frankenstein* to the screen. Stripping the novel down to its bare essentials. Florey delivered a treatment to meet Universal's rigid length and budget requirements. If Shelley's turgid plotting, meandering construction and philosophical diversions were drawbacks to the novel's appeal, Florey's streamlined, unadorned adaptation was, in contrast, simplicity itself. Florey compressed the novel's lumbering narrative into a modernistic horror mode, confining the action to a handful of sets while retaining the allegorical feel of the material. Shelley's novel was rendered all but unrecognizable, but it provided Universal with an ideal property. The go-ahead was given for a complete script.

Florey's first draft of the screenplay, written in collaboration with Garrett Fort, reveals the director's significant contribution to the finished film. Although most of the dialogue (reportedly written by Fort) would be revised, the script outlines virtually every scene in the release print, with some minor adjustments. That Florey did not receive official credit on American prints is a shameful injustice.

Florey's test reel of *Frankenstein*, virtually his audition for the studio brass who were still unsure of the director as well as the subject matter, remains one of the most sought-after of all of Hollywood's lost treasures. Photographed by Paul Ivano on the *Dracula* castle set, the footage (which lasted only 20 minutes after editing) starred Bela Lugosi in Jack Pierce's early makeup design for the Monster.

A beautiful character study of the Frankensten Monster as enacted by his greatest portrayer, Boris Karloff.

James Whale, in the meantime, was riding high in Hollywood having brought two notable stage successes to the screen, R.C. Sherriff's "Journey's End" (filmed in 1930) and, more recently, Robert E. Sherwood's play, "Waterloo Bridge" (filmed in 1931). Both were high-toned contemporary pieces recounting in their own way the devastating effects of the Great War on its participants, and marked by vivid star performances. The temptation to explore more cinematic material rather than transposing well-regarded theatrical pieces to the screen must have been great for Whale, and the *Frankenstein* script offered rich stylistic opportunities.

Whale's entry into *Frankenstein* forced out a crestfallen Florey who, to his chagrin, discovered his one-picture contract did not stipulate a specific title. Having no other recourse, he assumed directorial duties on *Murders in the Rue Morgue*. Florey, at least, picked up *Dracula* star Bela Lugosi, who, according to legend, was reportedly more than happy to forsake the non-speaking role of the Monster.

Francis Edwards Faragoh was recruited to submit a rewrite of the *Frankenstein* script, adding at Whale's insistence some mild comic touches to the decidedly downbeat material. Seizing the opportunity to inject a bit of cantankerous humor into the fully written role of old Baron Frankenstein, Whale cast British comedy player, Frederick Kerr, who had a stuffy role in *Waterloo Bridge*. For the role of Frankenstein's anguished fiancée, Bette Davis, then serving a six-month contract with the studio before moving on to Warner Bros. and Hollywood history, was briefly considered. Whale favored Mae Clarke, who played Myrna the prostitute in *Waterloo Bridge* with fierce, heart-rending persuasion.

Discussing her casting in the role, Clarke said in an interview many years later,

> When Jim was preparing *Frankenstein*, he chose me for the part of Elizabeth. Like John Ford, he had his own stock company. I was the reigning queen on the lot for a short spell and we were all treated like royalty.... I was supposed to do the part with an English accent to blend in with Colin Clive's. There was an English touch to the whole production.

The part of Victor Moritz, Henry Frankenstein's rival in love, went to Universal's up-and-coming leading man, John Boles, a fittingly uninteresting role for a singularly uninteresting actor. There was no need to look beyond the cast of *Dracula* to fill the roles of Dr. Waldman and Fritz, Frankenstein's hunchbacked laboratory assistant. Edward Van Sloan and Dwight Frye, both holdovers from Florey's test reel with Lugosi, were natural choices for the roles.

The casting of the lead role of Henry Frankenstein was a crucial decision. Leslie Howard was suggested, but Whale's first choice was Colin Clive, the neurotic young actor who had replaced Laurence Olivier in the original stage production of "Journey's End." Clive's bearing suggested learning and sensitivity, but his deep-rooted restlessness and insecurity marked him for high-strung, slightly over-the-edge characterizations. He was, in short, perfect for the part.

Interestingly, Lugosi's involvement with the project seemed to come to an end when Whale was just coming on. This has led to speculation among some that his departure wasn't the result of Lugosi's rejection of the non-speaking role, as widely reported, or merely Whale's decision to look elsewhere. Boris Karloff would claim in later decades that it was luck and a chance encounter with Whale at the studio commissary which led to his casting in the history-making role. But David Lewis, Whale's companion and lover at the time, insists that he was the one who suggested to the director that Karloff would make the ideal Monster after spotting him as the convict Ned Galloway in Howard Hawks' *The Criminal Code* (1931).

After several lean years, Karloff was beginning to establish his Hollywood career, usually playing small-time villains and crooks. He had already worked with an impressive array of top directors such as Lewis Milestone, Mervyn LeRoy, Michael Curtiz and Raoul Walsh, but always in featured roles.

To Karloff, the role of the Monster was a gamble as well as a dramatic challenge. At one point in the production, he confided to Edward Van Sloan that he felt the picture would ruin his career. He had little fear of being recognized; the grueling makeup sessions with Jack Pierce have been reported to be as brief as three and a half hours and as long as eight. Karloff's slender six-foot body was propped up to give the illusion of unnatural height.

The Monster's makeup design was once assumed to be wholly the creation of Jack Pierce, but in more recent times Whale's contribution has been recognized. That Whale's sketches of the creature's design jibes comfortably with the finished product can't be denied. The robotic appearance featuring grafted-on metallic highlights suggest a melding of science and nature. Pierce's execution is no less impressive, artistically rendered on Karloff's facial canvas to create a truly organic effect.

Pierce took credit for the Monster's square-shaped skull which supposedly came to the makeup man while he was watching a surgical operation on a man's head. The abnormal shape represented how the top of the head would look removed, with more gray matter piled in and a new cranium supplied to accommodate the oversized brain. An artificial skull was fitted over Karloff's head and his face was covered with a thick layer of gray-green greasepaint. Artificial

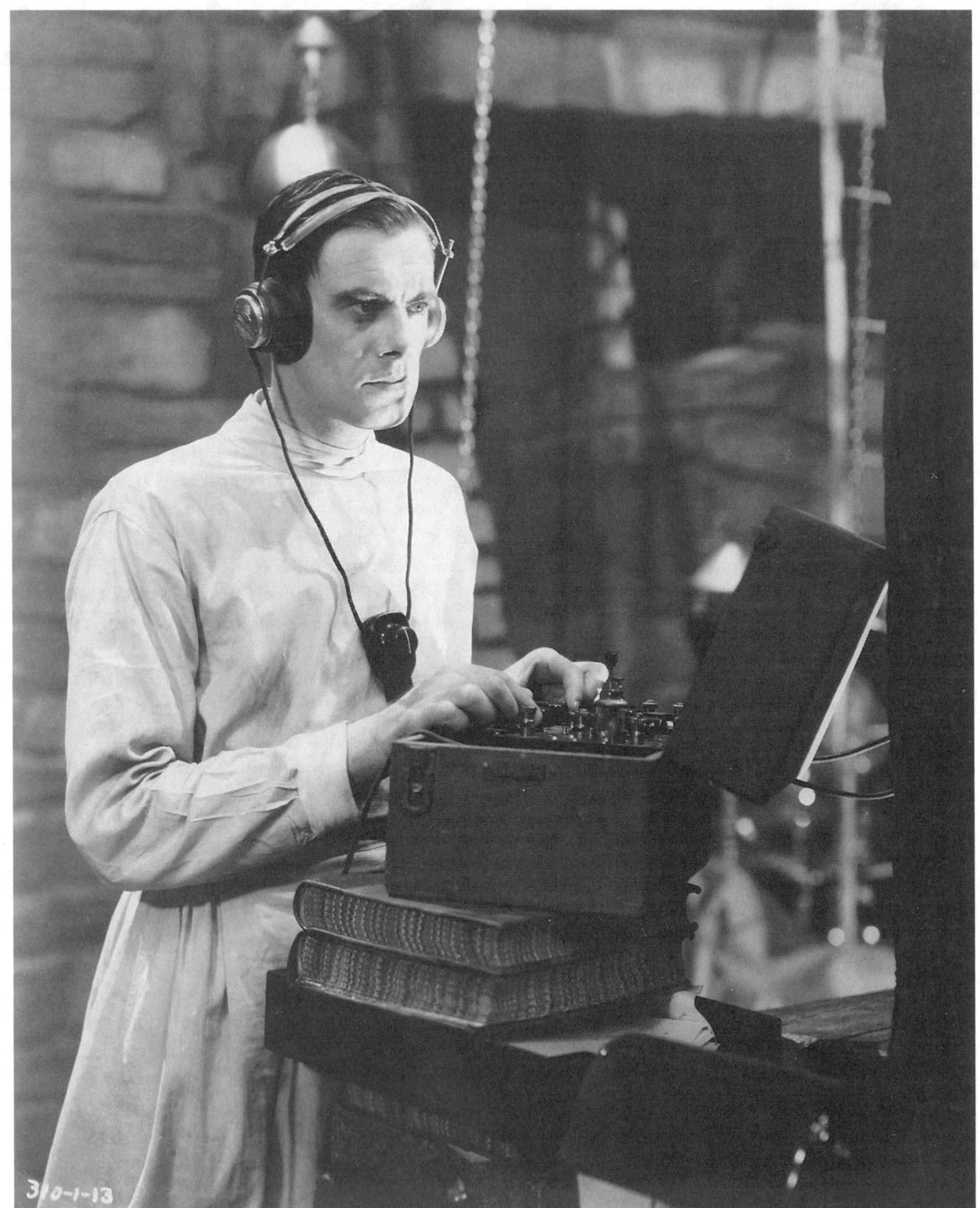

The Man Who Made a Monster: Clive as Henry Frankenstein.

veins were actually strips of cotton soaked in collodion and the actor's hands were meticulously made up. Working from James Whale's sketches, Pierce labored slowly and meticulously; even the slightest bit of makeup caused unbearable pain when caught in the actor's eyes. A 2005 issue of *MakeUp Artist* magazine listed the design as one of the fifty greatest makeups of all-time and, among the general public, it is still one of the most recognizable.

Of the $262,007 budget, $10,000 was spent on the electrical effects alone. Frank

Graves, Kenneth Strickfaden and Raymond Lindsay were in charge of the picturesque electrical gadgetry installed in Frankenstein's mountaintop laboratory. The devices were given such exotic names as a lightning bridge, bariton generator, vacuum electrolyzer and nucleus analyzer. The publicity department's claim that each device carried over a million and a half volts fooled no one but it made for the most spectacular pyrotechnics put on film up to that time.

Production started on August 24, 1931. The first scene shot, quite appropriately, was the first page of the script, on Charles D. Hall's hill and cemetery set, constructed especially for the film. The picture wrapped on October 3, five days over its allotted schedule, with a final budget of $291,000.

The pre-title teaser takes its cue from the deleted closing scene of *Dracula* with Edward Van Sloan breaking the fourth wall to directly address the audience. Supposedly speaking at the behest of Universal president Carl Laemmle, Van Sloan, in his best professorial manner but with a slight twinkle in his eye, warns the more fainthearted in the audience of the onslaught of horrors to come. It's a masterstroke of showmanship which probably did serve to brace Depression audiences for the 1931 equivalent of a Hollywood rollercoaster ride. The actor barely exits from the stage when the film cuts to the main titles superimposed over a nightmarish illustration of a partially obscured head of a humanoid creature with claw-like hands and light rays emanating from its eyes. No melancholy strains of *Swan Lake* here. Bernhard Kaun's stark, bass-heavy theme punctuates the soundtrack, suggesting a visceral, no-holds-barred shocker.

Kaun worked behind the scenes and largely without credit for a good part of his career. He served as Max Steiner's orchestrator when the legendary film composer was at RKO. He eventually scored Warners Bros.' *Doctor X* (1932), *The Walking Dead* (1936), *The Invisible Menace* (1938), *The Return of Doctor X* (1939), and *British Intelligence* (1940), as well as the main title music for Whale's *The Old Dark House.* The decision to leave the bulk of the film unscored probably was made by Whale although a full score was considered at one point in the production. The finale music, heard over the closing cast list, was an old cue composed by Giuseppe Becce. It would later be heard as the main title of the John Barrymore vehicle, *Counsellor-at-Law* (1933).

For the uninitiated: *Frankenstein* is set on the outskirts of the Tyrolean Alps. Henry Frankenstein (Colin Clive), a brilliant if erratic medical student, works in secret, assembling a human body from parts of corpses he has stolen from graveyards. Needing only a brain to complete his artificial man, he sends his hunchbacked assistant Fritz (Dwight Frye) to his old medical school. There, Dr. Waldman (Edward Van Sloan) had placed on exhibit two specimens of the human brain for his anatomy students. Accidentally dropping the glass jar containing a normal brain, Fritz grabs the other specimen, unaware that it has been removed from the body of a psychopathic killer.

Henry's fiancée, Elizabeth (Mae Clarke), his friend Victor Moritz (John Boles) and Dr. Waldman set out for Henry's mountaintop laboratory one stormy night to try to persuade the obsessed student to give up his experiments. They find the young scientist on the brink of madness. He sets his fabulous electrical apparatus in operation, sending the artificially conceived body to the rooftop where it is baptized by a powerful bolt of lightning. The body descends back into the lab, endowed with life, as Henry rejoices in his triumph.

But Frankenstein's joy is short-lived. His creation (Boris Karloff) is more monster than man, the obvious result of the abnormal brain stolen from Waldman's lecture hall. Viciously intimidated by Fritz, the Monster slays the hunchback at his first opportunity. He is overpowered by a massive dose of tranquilizer administered by Henry and Waldman. Waldman urges Frankenstein to go ahead with his wedding plans while he (Waldman) prepares to dispose of the Monster by dissection.

On the eve of Henry's wedding, Waldman is about to begin his grim task of dissecting when the Monster comes out of the anesthesia and strangles him. While roaming the countryside, the Monster comes across a little peasant girl, Maria (Marilyn Harris), who innocently befriends the brute. The encounter ends in tragedy with the Monster accidentally drowning the child in a lake.

Frankenstein's wedding is rudely interrupted by the news of the murders. The Monster crashes into Elizabeth's room, sending her into shock. Henry leads a search party after his creature as the bloodhounds track him into the mountains. Confronting the Monster, Henry is quickly overpowered and dragged to a windmill. The villagers arrive on the scene and set the structure ablaze. The Monster throws Henry's body to the ground below and becomes trapped in the inferno. Pinned under falling rafters, the pitiful creature is consumed by the flames.

The film's climax presented Whale with the vexing problem of what to do with Henry Frankenstein. As the results of his experiments culminated in several gruesome deaths, it seemed rather unfair to have him go unpunished. Florey's intention was to have the father of the little girl take advantage of the confusion at the windmill and "accidentally" shoot Henry to death while gunning for the Monster. Florey ended his script on a distinctly downbeat note, with Elizabeth, Victor and old Baron Frankenstein praying for Henry's soul in a funeral scene. Whale, too, opted for a tragic wrap-up with the deaths of the creator and his creation, but at the last moment settled on a conventional happy ending with Henry recovering from his wounds and Elizabeth sitting at his bedside. Ironically, the sequel revises the original ending, starting the story off with Henry being mistaken for dead by the villagers.

Frankenstein went on to its well-known success but only by surveying Hollywood trade papers in those last three months of 1931 can one appreciate the furor it unleashed. The picture was phenomenal, smashing box office records and igniting a storm of controversy wherever it played. Far from being regarded as the artful, literate horror classic it is now considered, *Frankenstein*, in its day, was seen as a grisly, blood-soaked example of exploitative filmmaking. Its detractors were numerous and vocal.

The picture was literally mangled by censors in Kansas City, who ordered that 32 cuts be made on all prints screened in their district. The "approved" version cut the original running time in half, rendering the film incomprehensible. Incensed editorial writers responded so loudly to this butchery that the governor was forced to take a hand, resulting in the restoration of all the missing footage. Carl Laemmle, Jr., expressed his gratitude to the newspapers for championing free speech, but inwardly the young executive was probably snickering with delight. The uproar undoubtedly sent box office grosses soaring even higher.

The Motion Picture Theatre Owners Association, feeling the pressure of civic groups, did an about-face. It urged its members to discourage producers from making horror movies, but the organization knew the plea would fall on deaf ears. The exhibitors were making a bundle on *Frankenstein* as well as Paramount's new horror release, *Dr. Jekyll and Mr. Hyde* (1931).

For years Universal continued to make a fortune off *Frankenstein*, but (predictably) very little of the spoils trickled down to the creative talents. Karloff and Whale soon found themselves clashing with the Laemmles over well-deserved pay hikes. Universal retained the rights to Jack Pierce's world-famous makeup years after they canned the genius in 1947.

Twenty years after the production of *Frankenstein*, playwright-screenwriter John L. Balderston and the estate of the late Peggy Webling were engaged a legal battle for a piece of the *Frankenstein* action. The basis for their lawsuit was an adaptation of the Webling play penned by Balderston for the Universal film shortly before Florey wrote his own version of the screenplay. (The Webling stipulated in her contract with Universal that the play was not to be staged in the United States.) The suit sought declaratory relief under a contract through which they allegedly were to receive one percent of the world gross of the film and all sequels deriving from the original picture. Universal's lawyers' contention was, of course, that the subsequent seven Frankenstein films were not based upon any of the dramatic compositions bought from Balderston and Webling. On May 25, 1953, three years almost to the day after the suit was filed, Universal settled for a sum which, the trades reported, was believed to be in excess of $100,000; in return, the studio obtained all rights to the character. The postscript to this story is that Florey later claimed he never bothered to read Balderston's adaptation in the first place!

Frankenstein, unlike *Dracula*, is a film that doesn't need apologies, and rightfully stands as Universal's first great all-talking horror movie. Countless imitations have taken a bit of the gleam off its reputation and the picture stubbornly stands in the shadow of its first sequel. To be fair, *Bride of Frankenstein* was a self-conscious attempt to outdo the original and had the advantage of far greater resources. While *Bride* certainly rates as a better movie, there's a unique appeal in the original's simplicity and lack of pretense. And *understatement.* The original is one of the few films without a score that actually *doesn't* need one (a credit to Whale's alert visual style). The long shot of Frankenstein and Waldman breaking into the Monster's chamber to find Fritz's twisted body dangling from the ceiling is just one moment that works very well without musical punctuation. Even minus orchestral accompaniment, the soundtrack is unusually rich. The climactic mountaintop pursuit of the Monster is accompanied by the mournful baying of bloodhounds and the jeers of the villagers. The windmill scene is played against the rhythmic creaking of the pump shaft. Considering that *Frankenstein* was made when film composing was a fledgling art and that most scores of this period were usually undistinguished or worse, the lack of music actually works in the movie's favor.

The grandiose, self-mocking style of the sequel is absent in the original. *Frankenstein's* stylistic indebtedness to such silent classics as *The Cabinet of Dr. Caligari* (1919) and *The Golem* (1920) have been somewhat exaggerated through the years. The influence of Fritz Lang's *Metropolis* with the creation of the female robot amid the electrical trappings is a more likely inspiration. It's not unreasonable to assume Whale might have screened a print of Rex Ingram's *The Magician* (1926) with its highly recognizable image of the dwarfish assistant doing his master's bidding. Whale opted for a starker, more naturalistic realism here than in *Bride* (no one could ever mistake *Frankenstein* for a fairy tale). It's a horror movie played for shocks, although they have been greatly diluted by time and imitation. Like the film's humor, the undercurrent of sympathy for the Monster isn't strained.

Karloff himself preferred his non-speaking but no less inventive performance in the original to his work in the sequel. After *Frankenstein's* release, the actor was instantly hailed as "The New Lon Chaney," but the typically self-effacing Boris refuted the title. "He was the master," Karloff said in early 1932. "No one suffered as he did to bring a tragic, poignant quality to his roles." Karloff went so far as to suggest that almost *any* actor could have played the role. It is true that no other actor brought the dimension that Karloff lent to the character, but it is equally true that none of these actors enjoyed the benefit of Whale's direction.

Karloff's early performances were uneven; he tended to lay it on a bit thick in pictures like *The Unholy Night* (1929), *Five Star Final* (1931) and *Behind the Mask* (released in 1932, but actually shot before *Frankenstein*). He excelled in *The Criminal Code* (1931) as the homicidal plug-ugly, a virtual warm-up for his stint as the Monster. Later producers tended to cast the Monster role for name value (Chaney Jr. and Lugosi) or physical prowess (Glenn Strange and virtually all of the Hammer players, including Christopher Lee); for decades, Whale was one of the few directors to cast the role with an eye on characterization. Whale brought out the best in Karloff, who displayed a gift for mime untapped in earlier roles.

The discovery of long-missing *Frankenstein's* footage in the late '80s, especially Little Maria's drowning scene, provides an interesting sidebar in one's appreciation of the film and Karloff's performance. In spite of Universal's best efforts to blend the new material seamlessly into the film, the viewer can't help but be distracted by the sudden loss of picture quality. This caveat aside, the Little Maria footage adds to our sense of the Monster's emotional evolution as Karloff's expression of delight gives way to his panicky reaction to her death. Desperately wringing his hands as if to separate himself from the deed, he flees into the woods in an inexplicably under-cranked shot.

Within a few years, Whale would see himself as a victim of his own success in being identified with horror films despite his eclectic output. His first foray into the genre is marked by an appropriately literary tone although flashes of his trademark humor keep slipping through. Frederick Kerr's blustery Baron Frankenstein and Lionel Belmore's Burgomaster provide the conventional geezer comedy relief. More interestingly off-center is Dwight Frye's Fritz doing a variation of his iconic Renfield performance, Frye finds himself fitted with an oversized hump on his back and a grotesque makeup only to be turned into a semi-comic figure. Whale focuses on such quirky bits of business such as Fritz's over-reaction to the suspended skeleton bouncing wildly in the medical school's operating theater or the scruffy assistant making quick adjustments to his sagging socks while scrambling around Frankenstein's tower. It's a tantalizing hint of how Whale would have handled the Renfield character had he directed *Dracula*.

It speaks rather poorly for Universal, who shunted the Monster from one sequel to another, that Whale was the only director to provide him with a fully dimensional character. Whale blocks Karloff's entrance for maximum impact. Inexplicably shuffling with his back towards the camera, he slowly turns for his memorable closeups. A series of quick cuts taken at slightly different angles underscores the Monster's cadaverous appearance, from his hollow cheeks to his heavy-lidded eyes. His stumbling, unsteady gait is the macabre parody of the first steps of a child. Indeed, the scene suggests the introduction of a new child into a family, complete with the sadistic taunts of an older sibling in the form of Fritz. The Monster stretches to grasp the streaming beams of sunlight from a skylight as if he instinctively remembers his own creation, being strapped to the elevated gurney to catch the life-giving bolts of lightning.

Colin Clive more than fulfilled the role's requirements, emerging as a Frankenstein ideally suited for its time. The sheer intensity of the character was something the actor could probably relate to, much as he did playing Stanhope in *Journey's End*. Clive's neurotic personality often came across as a form of idealized romanticism which might have proved useful in other roles as well (including his Rochester opposite Virginia Bruce's *Jane Eyre* [1934] in a typically low-rent Monogram production).

At first glance, it would appear that Clive was given the potentially star-making role. The character is carefully developed in the opening scenes. The quiet tension as he collects the numerous body parts for his experiment plays against Clive's mounting anxiety. All culminates into the grand theatrical moment before he puts the life-giving electrical apparatus into high gear. His impassioned, half-mad speech to his guests is a climactic theatrical moment and a commanding showcase for the actor. Unfortunately, after reaching this peak, Henry's character dissipates badly. His scientific curiosity evaporates at the moment of his most audacious success and he seems only too willing to retreat into the role of the submissive student to Van Sloan's knowing headmaster. In the end, the Monster's vengeance on him seems justified after the creator becomes one of the mob bent on his destruction. Henry's diminishing appeal would give Karloff a tremendous opportunity to usurp the audience's sympathy, probably even more than Whale intended.

In his biography of Whale, *James Whale: A New World of Gods and Monsters* (Faber and Faber, 1998), James Curtis hints at the director's disgruntlement at Karloff's star-making turn as the Monster. It's difficult to entirely dismiss the possibility that Whale was expecting the adulation to be showered on his old friend Clive rather than Karloff, who was not part of the director's social set. Curtis doesn't fail to note that no one even thought to invite the actor to the film's first public screening at Santa Barbara's Granada Theater in October 1931.

Except for the bland John Boles, Whale's cast selection is sound. Mae Clarke's Elizabeth is refreshingly real and unsentimental in a performance that holds up amazingly well after 75 years. Edward Van Sloan's Waldman is assured, authoritative and devoid of the stagy mannerisms that marred his Tod Browning–directed performance as Van Helsing in *Dracula*. Van Sloan so projects the stereotype of the magisterial headmaster that his momentary turn as the foil for the scowling old Baron Frankenstein is a rare example of comedy relief that actually works. Van Sloan registers a surprised, possibly real reaction in a genuinely amusing scene.

Frankenstein has long since lost its ability to frighten, but the film still exerts a hypnotic power. Technically, it's a marvel, from Arthur Edeson's atmospheric lensing to Charles D. Hall's sumptuous, Expressionistic sets. Whale's talents hadn't quite peaked, but he still towered over the average studio director and his excellent judgment is ever present. Add Karloff's milestone performance and one realizes that *Frankenstein* is still a warhorse worth viewing and re-viewing.

Critics' Corner

[A] stirring grand-guignol type of picture, one that aroused so much excitement ... yesterday that many in the audience laughed to cover their true feelings.... It is naturally a morbid, gruesome affair, but it is something to keep the spectator awake, for during its most spine-chilling periods, it exacts attention.—*The New York Times*, December 5, 1931, Mordaunt Hall

Rating: ★★★ [C]lutches at you icily and holds you until the romantic ending guarantees satisfaction after an hours [*sic*] worth of gripping, intriguing horrors.... [I]t is heartily interesting and wholly absorbing.—*The New York Daily News*, December 5, 1931, Irene Thirer

Karloff has done some excellent things in pictures, though usually in minor roles. This was his big opportunity, and whether you like the picture or not you won't deny his efficacy.—*The Motion Picture Herald*, November 14, 1931, Leo Meehan

Frankenstein looks like a *Dracula* plus... [A] new peak in horror plays.... Laboratory sequence ... is a smashing bit of theatrical effect.... Playing is perfectly paced.—*Variety*, December 8, 1931

[V]ery free and modernized adaptation. Scenes which for sheer horror were unexcelled on screen and rouse pity and fear.... [D]irection emphasizes gruesome nature of theme.... [P]owerful portrayal by Boris Karloff in one of the most difficult roles possible to imagine.—*Today's Cinema* (GB), January 21, 1932)

It touches the highest peak of sensational melodrama.... [I]ts uncompromising depiction of stark horrors and gruesome experiment are calculated to appeal to the unsqueamish.—*The Kinematograph Weekly* (GB), January 20, 1932

The most sensational motion picture ever made.—*The Sunday Times* (GB), January 1932

Brilliant to the point of genius.—*The Daily Dispatch* (GB), January 1932

You've got to admit it's good.—*The Empire News* (GB), January 1932

Universal has either the greatest shocker of all time—or a dud. It can be one or the other; there will be no in-between measures.... Whale seems to have gone far enough, but not too far.—*The Hollywood Reporter*, 1931, Billy Wilkerson

1932

Murders in the Rue Morgue

Released February 21, 1932. 62 minutes. *Producer:* Carl Laemmle, Jr. *Director:* Robert Florey. *Associate Producer:* E.M. Asher. *Screenplay:* Tom Reed & Dale Van Every. *Based on the story* "The Murders in the Rue Morgue" *by* Edgar Allan Poe. *Adaptation:* Robert Florey. *Additional Dialogue:* John Huston. *Scenario Editor:* Richard Schayer. *Photography:* Karl Freund. *Art Director:* Charles D. Hall. *Recording Supervisor:* C. Roy Hunter. *Editor:* Milton Carruth. *Supervising Editor:* Maurice Pivar. *Musical Director:* Heinz Roemheld. *Special Effects:* John P. Fulton. *Special Process Photography:* Frank Williams. *Makeup:* Jack P. Pierce. *Set Designer:* Herman Rosse. *Assistant Directors:* Scott Beal, Joseph McDonough & Charles S. Gould. *Technical Advisor:* Howard Salemson.

Sidney Fox (*Mlle. Camille L'Espanaye*), Bela Lugosi (*Dr. Mirakle*), Leon Waycoff [Ames] (*Pierre Dupin*), Bert Roach (*Paul*), Betsy Ross Clarke (*Mme. L'Espanaye*), Brandon Hurst (*Prefect of Police*), D'Arcy Corrigan (*Morgue Keeper*), Noble Johnson (*Janos, the Black One*), Arlene Francis (*Woman of the Streets*), Edna Marion (*Mignette*), Charlotte Henry, Polly Ann Young (*Girls*), Herman Bing (*Franz Odenheimer*), Agostino Borgato (*Alberto Montani*), Harry Holman (*Landlord*), Torben Meyer (*The Dane*), John T. Murray, Christian Frank (*Gendarmes*), Dorothy Vernon (*Tenant*), Michael Visaroff, Ted Billings (*Men*), Charles T. Millsfield (*Bearded Man at Sideshow*), Monte Montague (*Workman/Gendarme*), Charles Gemora (*Erik, the Ape*), Joe Bonomo (*Double for Charles Gemora*), Hamilton Green (*Barker*), Tempe Pigott (*Crone*).

Makes all other terror pictures
look like bedtime stories!
—*Ad blurb for* Murders in the Rue Morgue

For both Robert Florey and Bela Lugosi, dissociation from *Frankenstein* signaled unfortunate career turning points: Florey never again had the opportunity to direct a film with that sort of potential, and Lugosi, in backing away from the project, allowed for the emergence of a horror screen rival (Boris Karloff) who would quickly eclipse him. The studio's consolation prize to Lugosi and Florey, *Murders in the Rue Morgue*, didn't garner the critical or popular success their careers needed despite being one of the most daring of the pre–Code horror films.

The idea of adapting Poe's public domain tale to the screen occurred to Universal in the early part of 1931, while *Dracula* was in release and *Frankenstein* in preparation. A story treatment was ready by April; Lugosi was slated to star and George Melford, who had helmed the atmospheric and highly cinematic Spanish *Dracula*, was assigned to direct. But when Florey suddenly found himself shooed off of *Frankenstein*, the French director wound up in charge of *Murders in the Rue Morgue* instead. A severe slash in the film's planned budget (from $130,000 to $90,000) incensed Florey, who stalked off the picture, only to be coaxed back a short time later. The film was in production 25 days, commencing October 19, 1931, and wrapping November 13 (appropriately a Friday). Encouraged by *Frankenstein*'s grosses, Universal put the picture back into production in December, upping the budget to a total of $186,090 after seven days of retakes and added scenes.

Attending a carnival in 1845 Paris, medical student Pierre Dupin (Leon Waycoff) and his sweetheart Camille (Sidney Fox) are drawn to a unique sideshow. Dr. Mirakle (Bela Lugosi) , a strange foreign type, expounds his theory of evolution, and displays a caged ape which Mirakle announces is the ancestor of present-day man. Mirakle also tells the onlookers that his life is consecrated to one great experiment: To prove man's kinship with the apes. Pierre and Camille move forward to closely examine Mirakle's ape, Erik (Charles Gemora); the simian is attracted to the lovely Camille. Mirakle, who clearly has some sinister plot in mind, orders his servant Janos (Noble Johnson) to trail Pierre and Camille when they leave the carnival.

Later that night, after secretly following the lovers to Camille's home, Mirakle and Janos watch as two men fight over a prostitute (Arlene Francis) on a Seine embankment. The thugs kill one another, and Mirakle gently guides the sobbing prostitute into his coach. The girl winds up at Mirakle's hovel of a home-cum-laboratory in the Rue Morgue, where she is bound to an x-shaped cross while Mirakle injects her with Erik's blood. The girl is not the right experimental subject: She dies from the crude transfusion. Mirakle and Janos dispose of her body, dropping it through a trap door into the Seine below. She is Mirakle's third victim that week.

Dupin is determined to solve the riddle of the "drowned" girls who are dredged out of the river with no water in their lungs. Bribing the local morgue keeper (D'Arcy Corrigan), he is able to secure samples of the blood from the three women, and finds the same unidentifiable foreign substance (the ape blood) in each. When Paul learns that Mirakle has sent a present to Camille, he begins to sense a connection between the sideshow scientist and the Seine "suicides."

Mirakle pays a midnight call on the apartment that Camille shares with her mother (Betsy Ross Clarke); he insists on taking Camille to see Erik. ("He talks only of you. He can't forget you!" Mirakle claims.) Camille, understandably frightened, closes the door in his face but Mirakle, undeterred, sends Erik shimmying up the side of the building. The ape kills Camille's mother, shoving her broken body feet-first up a fireplace flume, and abducts Camille.

Pierre excitedly explains to the Prefect of Police (Brandon Hurst) that Dr. Mirakle and his trained ape are responsible for the recent rash of mysterious deaths, and the magistrate finally agrees to investigate. Meanwhile, at Mirakle's, the madman has determined that the unconscious Camille is the perfect subject for his ultimate experiment, but the arrival of the Prefect and his squad of gendarmes sends the scientist into a quandary. Janos is shot and killed by a gendarme while Erik, in an effort to protect Camille, suddenly turns on Mirakle, throttling him to death. The ape seizes the girl and carries her across the Paris rooftops, followed by Pierre, the gendarmes and an excited mob on the street below. Pierre, armed with a revolver, confronts Erik on a riverfront rooftop and shoots the angry beast, who somersaults off the roof into the rushing Seine. In a nice bit of climactic irony, Mirakle joins his victims in the morgue.

Though flawed and creaky, *Murders in the Rue Morgue* is very likely the most underrated of the Universal Horrors. Certainly many of the salvos that have been directed against it — the dated acting, stilted dialogue and mawkish romance, plus the fact that the picture painfully shows its age — are more-or-less deserved. The critical reception at the time was harsh (not unusual for a horror movie) and even today, its grudging praise is buried under criticism for the film's other defects. Bafflingly, the same worshipful Lugosi fans who are quick to overlook the painfully amateurish aspects of *White Zombie* (1932) and the patent absurdities of *The Raven*, are reluctant to embrace *Murders in the Rue Morgue*. Obviously, the fun factor is lacking for many.

Like *Dracula, Murders in the Rue Morgue* is best appreciated if the viewer is in a forgiving state of mind. The film's palpably European feel clashes with the English-language dialogue and American accents, only adding to an off-putting sense of strangeness and artificiality. It's not a typically movieland period-dress confection that renders even the squalor of the streets with a Hollywood sheen. Except for one or two characters, everyone in the movie is a caricature, often ghoulish (as D'Arcy Corrigan's morgue keeper) or unsavory (Tempe Pigott, who ruminates about life and death as the gendarmes pull the latest murder victim out of the Seine). Even the comedy relief figures are gargoyles.

Murders in the Rue Morgue's reputation suffers even further by the comments of some of the people who actually made it. The picture was a disappointment to the director who was counting on the film to jump-start his career. (Florey reportedly said the film would have been improved if they had written the villain out of the script.) The leading man, Leon Waycoff (better known as Leon Ames), blasted the movie in an old *Famous Monsters of Filmland* interview as "a perfectly awful film which still pops up on TV to haunt me!"

But it was John Huston who got to the heart of the matter. Employed by Universal as a staff writer (among his assignments was writing a draft of Edward Van Sloan's pre-title speech in *Frankenstein*), he was approached to tackle the screenplay. Writing in his autobiography, *An Open Book* (Knopf, 1980), he recalled,

> I tried to bring Poe's prose style into the dialogue, but the director thought it sounded stilted, so he and his assistants rewrote scenes on the set. As a result, the picture was an odd mixture of nineteenth century grammarian prose and modern colloquialisms.

The clash of styles Huston describes underscores the discordant tone of the movie as well as the strengths and weaknesses of the director. Stylistically, *Murders in the Rue Morgue* is a European horror film that happens to have been shot in Hollywood. As such, some of the Expressionistic conventions that would seem an asset in a German film, particularly a silent, seem too artificial in a Hollywood talkie, even of this vintage. The glass shots, the obvious use of painted shadows and backdrops, even the scene of the heroine being dizzily tracked by the camera as she glides through the air on a swing seem better suited to the likes of F.W. Murnau or Josef von Sternberg. Even worse are such script absurdities as Bela Lugosi talking to his pet ape in the simian's tongue. Still, one can't help but feel that if *Murders in the Rue Morgue* was shot five years earlier, these seeming defects be forgiven and the film would be ranked as one of the great silent horror masterpieces.

The horror scenes scarcely need any apologies, chiefly the triumphant Grand Guignol moment of Lugosi's live blood experiments with Arlene Francis' pitiful, bedraggled prostitute bound to an inverted cross. The scene succeeds on a number of levels, especially in providing Lugosi with one of his best opportunities to put across the character's madness as well as his motivations. The shot of the girl slumping dead on the rack as Lugosi collapses in an almost prayer-like pose is one of the highlights of pre–Code Hollywood horror. As in *Frankenstein*, the lack of a musical score helps the scene immeasurably. The film cuts to henchman Noble Johnson's axe as it individually chops through each of the girl's bonds, leading to the opening of the trap door below her as her body inevitably splashes into the river. The juxtaposition of sexual and religious images lend a faintly sacrilegious aura to the film, which no doubt enraged the censor boards of the time. It further sets a sadistic tone that the studio would use again for its later Edgar Allan Poe adaptations.

The Poe story was a departure from the writer's general run of psychological horror tales. It's widely cited as the first detective story ever published and the protagonist, Pierre Dupin, as the prototype of Conan Doyle's Sherlock Holmes. Despite the grisly premise of a middle-aged woman and her daughter slaughtered by an unknown hand, which turns out to be an escaped orangutan, the story is steeped in the stuffy atmosphere of an intellectual inquiry as Dupin coldly considers each individual clue in the case.

In typical Hollywood fashion, the Dupin character materializes in the movie as a brilliant but love-struck medical student and suitor to the younger victim in Poe's story (who emerges

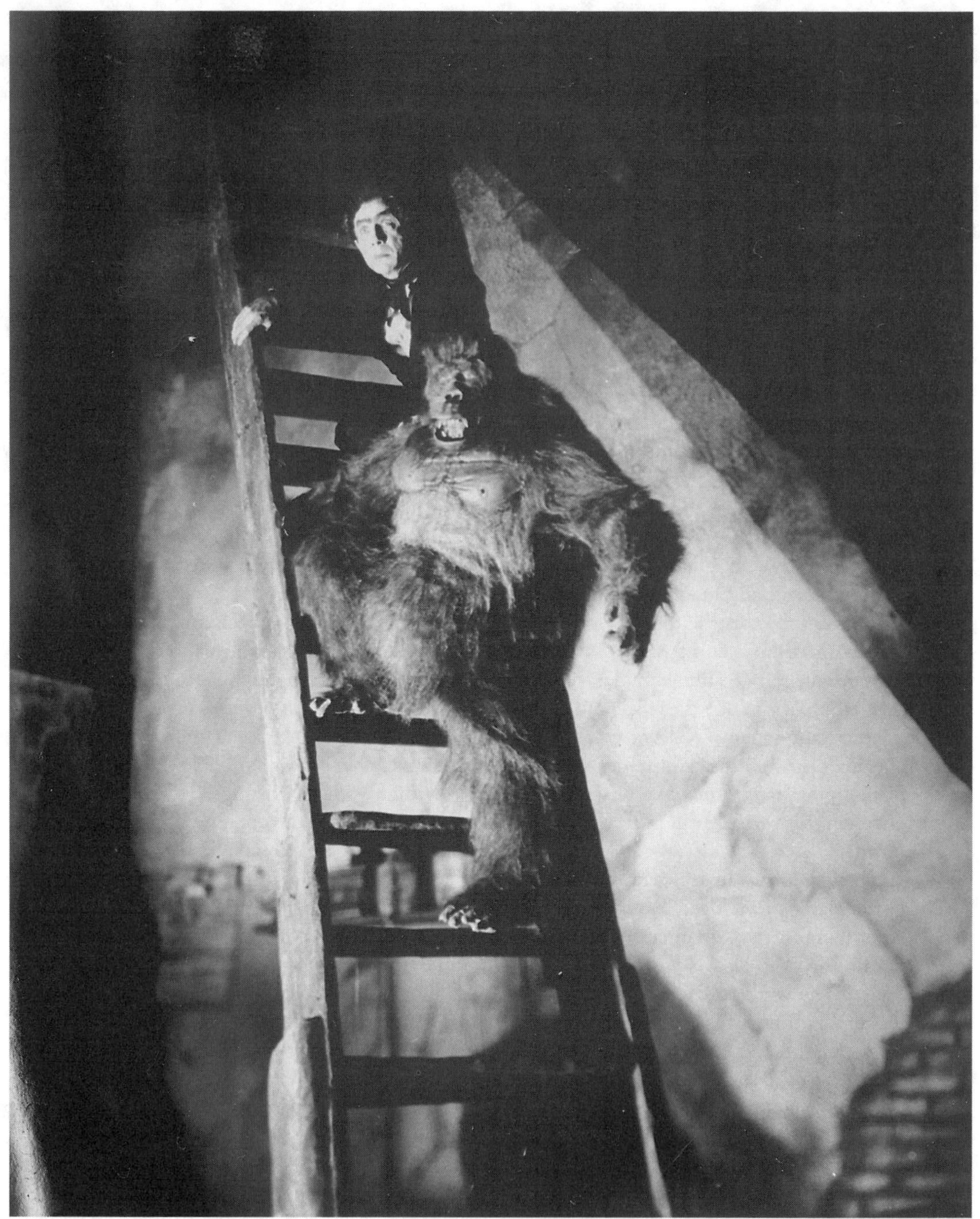

Bela Lugosi and Charles Gemora, up to no good in a scene from *Murders in the Rue Morgue* (courtesy Bill Chase).

completely unscathed as the leading female character). Later in life, director Florey was apt to ridicule his superiors at Universal for not catching on that *Murders in the Rue Morgue* was a thinly disguised variation on the Frankenstein theme. In fact, Florey's film is routinely seen as a wholesale usurping of *The Cabinet of Dr. Caligari* (1919) from its Expressionistic trappings right down its central characters. Surely, Mirakle owes much to the scientist-carnival man with

Erik the Ape a simian version of Conrad Veidt's somnambulist who snatches the leading lady from her bedroom and sends her lover in a wild rooftop pursuit at the climax.

However, the psychological implications of *Caligari* are largely lost on the writers of *Murders in the Rue Morgue*, who were apparently more interested in tapping into anti–Darwinian fears than turning the story into a cinematic soapbox for Freudian analysis. Like the later *Island of Lost Souls* (1933), the film exploits the folly of godless science and the mating of man and beast as the inevitable result of accepting an evolutionary theory of mankind. (The film was made only a few years after the inflammatory Scopes Monkey Trial.) Florey complements the theme by vesting Noble Johnson's Janos character with distinctly bestial qualities. Even the film's evocative main title art juxtaposes the theme of madness with simian imagery. But Florey, like Whale, is more of a visual stylist than a moralist with little interest in displays of outraged indignation. Indeed, his priority is delivering a good, ripping horror tale rendered in a visually rich *mise-en-scene*.

Like most '30s horror films, there's no dearth of familiar Christian symbols. Florey takes pains to spotlight a hanging cross in the heroine's bedroom and, as if this weren't enough, has her wear a choker with a miniature crucifix. Elsewhere, the placement of religious symbols seems to be used as wry commentary. The oversized wooden cross in the morgue bears witness to the shady dealings of the coroner, who flagrantly accepts the bribes of medical students as leering attendants bring in the bodies of murdered women of the night.

While Florey's artist eye for composition is on full display so, unfortunately, is his tin ear, manifesting itself in his unease with language and his handling of actors. Bela Lugosi, at least, is better suited to the material than some of his hapless co-stars. The actor follows up *Dracula* with a role that's just as fitting to his gifts, almost defying the rule of lightning never striking twice. It would seldom strike again in his career. Unlike his later performance in the modern-day setting of *The Raven*, Lugosi's florid playing finds a perfect match in Florey's stylized vision. If Bela's worst excesses aren't fully tempered, they are at least fitting for the occasion.

Lugosi's natural tendency towards grandstanding finds a perfect outlet in his carnival discourse on evolution, rich with pregnant pauses and fervent climaxes as he proclaims his pet, Erik, "the first man." Lugosi only allows a recognizably human reaction to intrude on his performance when realizing his setback upon the death of Arlene Francis. Even then, his emotions are barely held in check. Likewise, the scene where he's trying to lure Francis into his carriage with the line, "A lady ... *in distress?*" is a trenchant example of Lugosi's orchestrating his dialogue. His deep-pitched, perfectly timed, ominously slow reading leaves little doubt of his nefarious motives. Like so much of Lugosi's playing, the question isn't "is it good acting?" but "does it work?" It's vintage Bela.

Leon Waycoff as Dupin has no choice but to play his scenes broadly just to fit in but he's just another contemporary American actor ill-equipped to handle period roles. (The actor would reunite with his fellow thespian, Lugosi, playing Jonathan Harker in a West Coast production of "Dracula" in May 1932.) As directed by Florey, Sidney Fox's child-like Camille is so much the model of unblemished virginity as to make Lugosi's depraved designs on her all the more unspeakable. Bert Roach, one of the many Fatty Arbuckle clones of the period, is the stock comedy relief character, playing Waycoff's roommate in a dated "sissy-boy" fashion.

Florey encourages everyone else in the cast, down to the smallest featured actor, to play to the balcony with exaggerated gestures in the worst silent movie tradition. While even this may have comported to the director's vision, the amount of high-school quality theatrics on display is unworthy of a major studio production. Despite Florey having worked on the Marx Brothers' *The Cocoanuts* (1929), his flair for comedy seems non-existent. The film's low point is actually a comic take on an incident in the Poe story, with three foreigners bickering over what language the overheard murderer was speaking (it turns out to be Erik the Ape's yelps) during the killing. The three men get into a loud, excited argument, each of them yammering in his own language like a Euro-version of the Three Stooges.

Compounding *Murders in the Rue Morgue*'s flaws is that some of Universal's post-production tampering didn't work to the picture's ad-

"Erik! Go back in your cage!" Lugosi cries at Gemora in the Edgar Allan Poe adaptation *Murders in the Rue Morgue* (courtesy Bill Chase).

vantage. Upon the film's completion, Carl Laemmle, Jr., ordered reshoots of several key scenes. In a bid to add to the realism of Erik's scenes, closeups of an actual monkey, filmed at a zoo, were none-too-artfully edited into the final prints. In an interview with the authors, monster movie expert Bob Burns told of his 1957 meeting with Charles Gemora, who wore the gorilla costume:

> Charlie did tell me that in *Murders in the Rue Morgue*, in which he played Erik the Ape, strongman Joe Bonomo doubled him in the scenes where Erik is climbing up to the Paris rooftops. But the thing about *Murders in the Rue Morgue* that stuck in Charlie's craw a little was the fact that close-ups of an actual chimp were inserted into the movie instead of the close-ups they'd shot of Charlie in his gorilla suit. When he saw the movie, he said he was in shock because the movie would all of a sudden jump from a shot of him in his gorilla suit to a shot of that very different-looking chimp. He wasn't too pleased with that, and could never figure out why they did it. His gorilla face was perfectly mobile, it could do the expressions that were needed.

Further post-production editing resulted in the reshuffling of several scenes in the first half of the movie. The end result greatly impaired the general flow of the film, producing a choppy narrative including characters speaking of events that didn't even transpire yet. In *Video Watchdog,* editor-publisher Tim Lucas attempted to lay out a very probable version of the original cut of *Murders in the Rue Morgue* for enterprising fans interested in piecing together a more sequential print from video copies.

"The Murders in the Rue Morgue" first reached the screen in the Danish short *Sherlock Holmes and the Great Murder Mystery* (1908), which pits Poe's mischievous monkey against Conan Doyle's dauntless detective. The 1912 short *The Raven*, in which Poe dreams of scenes from some of his own tales, uses a smidgen of the story; a 1928 borderline horror film called *The Leopard Lady*, while based on some obscure play, also supposedly bears more than a passing resemblance in its story of a gorilla committing murder. At the height of the 3-D craze, Warner Brothers filmed the color-stereoscopic *Phantom of the Rue Morgue* (1954) with Karl Malden using an ape (alternately played by Charles Gemora and Nick Cravat) as an instrument of murder in nineteenth century Paris. When American International got around to adding *Murders in the Rue Morgue* to their Poe series in 1971, the resultant film owed more to Gaston Leroux's *The Phantom of the Opera* than to anything written by Poe. "The problem with the original story, which is a mystery where the *monkey* did it, was not the kind of story you could do any more," explained director Gordon Hessler to the authors. Instead of struggling to squeeze a workable screenplay out of Poe, the screenwriters developed a *Phantom*-type story of a killer terrorizing a French theater. "The Murders in the Rue Morgue" was the play within the movie. In 1986, it was George C. Scott playing Auguste Dupin in a made-for-television adaptation, directed by Jeannot Szwarc.

The disappointing box office returns for *Murders in the Rue Morgue* undoubtedly hastened Robert Florey's departure from Universal. He promptly signed on to Warner Bros. where, for a time, he maintained a four or five pictures-per-year grind, keeping his excesses in check while directing Bette Davis, Barbara Stanwyck and Mary Astor in some of their early vehicles. Despite his affinity for horror material, Florey managed to avoid the genre for most of the rest of his career although he was at his best in films with strong psychological underpinnings. One of his more macabre assignments at Warners was *The Florentine Dagger* (1935), based on a Ben Hecht novel. Set in Vienna and Italy, the plot concerns the last descendant of the Borgias who lives in terror of his inherited predisposition towards murder. When his fiancée's disapproving guardian is stabbed to death with an ancient dagger, once owned by the Borgias, the young man's fears seem justified.

Not a full-fledged horror movie, *The Florentine Dagger* recalls some of the strengths and weaknesses Florey demonstrated in *Murders in the Rue Morgue*. The picture's Continental flavor is quite convincing by Hollywood programmer standards while the characters remain curiously hollow. Florey does maintain a distinctly unnerving atmosphere, not only in the conventional horror scenes of a hooded killer on the prowl, but in some of the more unsavory implications of the plot. It was released after the Production Code took effect, but Florey still manages to hint of the psycho-sexual proclivities of the murder victim (played by the dullish, lawyer-like Henry O'Neill), who turns out to be the real villain in the piece. After setting afire a young actress who spurns his advances, he shifts his unsavory attentions to the infant daughter whom he raised. In the last reel, the hideously scarred victim, concealing herself with a wax mask, admits to the killing, and in a surprise relaxation of Production Code rules, is allowed to escape punishment by a sympathetic police inspector.

Lugosi as Dr. Mirakle and Gemora as Erik (courtesy Bill Chase).

Florey's *The Face Behind the Mask* (1941) can't shake off its identification with the horror genre despite its strong roots in film noir and, perhaps, social commentary. The picture tracks the story of Janos Szabo (Peter Lorre), literally off the boat from his native Hungary, whose plans for a new life in America are dashed when a boarding house fire leaves him horribly disfigured. The plot is inspired by the Stephen Crane short story "The Monster," except that Lorre, now a social outcast, is forced into a life of crime. That Lorre effortlessly clears the hurdles of Paul Jarrico's script, transforming from the effusive, semi-comic immigrant into a hard-bitten underworld czar, is a remarkable feat in itself. Despite the tacky Columbia B-unit look, Florey instills a sense of tragic inevitability in this grim debunking of the American Dream.

Florey's final feature-length horror picture, Warners' *The Beast with Five Fingers* (1946) was such a throwback to the gothic thrillers of the '30s one suspects it was originally intended as a psychological exercise that somehow lost its way. (Hollywood was embracing all things Freudian after the war years.) An under-appreciated effort that even the director disowned, it was the first genre outing in many seasons which had the benefit of a top-of-the-line studio production, boasting excellent camerawork and luxurious sets. Curt Siodmak's script lent the film a Universal flavor and a physical menace in the form of the disembodied hand of a murdered pianist which turns out to be the hallucinations of the guilt-wracked killer. As in *Murders in the Rue Morgue*, Florey is guided by distinct *Caligari*-like influences while allowing the film to become a vehicle for a star horror personality. Unfortunately, the director ill-serves Peter Lorre, ignoring the actor's gift for sardonic underplaying, prodding him into a self-parodying, eye-popping performance.

Florey managed to avoid the big science fiction boom of the '50s but his flair for the fantastic didn't go unnoticed by television producers in the early '60s. He made the rounds on the major genre series of the day including *The Twilight Zone* and *The Outer Limits*. One of his best-remembered works in the television arena is probably "The Incredible Doktor Markesan," an episode of *Thriller*. A true American Gothic, the Lovecraft-like tale had Boris Karloff as a cadaverous scientist who tends to a number of resurrected corpses in his crypt-like laboratory despite their pleas to return to the ranks of the dead.

The episode's producer, Doug Benton, recalled to the authors that Florey "was an interesting guy. He told me when Universal decided to make *Frankenstein*, it was assigned to him. He did all the spadework, got the script in shape, did everything." Benton described Florey's philosophical reaction to being dismissed from the movie: "He said that Whale did a hell of a job, he said it was *marvelous*. He was honest enough to say, 'He probably did it a hell of a lot better than *I* would have.'"

Murders in the Rue Morgue is a unique film for '30s Hollywood. Despite a deceptively sparse storyline, its roots cross both the horror and mystery genres with faint shadings of science fiction thrown into the mix. Entrenched in a style which condemned it as a relic before its time, Florey's experiment has come to be regarded as a cinematic barrel of spinach that even the most jaded fan finds hard to swallow. Beyond its vulgar excesses and insipid theatrics, however, lurks a daring, full-throttled, Poe-inspired thriller couched in a darkly sinister aesthetic all its own.

Critics' Corner

For pictorial and technical values the production will evoke loud praises from those who appreciate the beauty of soft artistic backgrounds in harmony with the beauty of the period and environment.... Characterization ... is near perfect as one could expect.—*The Hollywood Herald*, January 11, 1932, Bill Swigart

The crowning spectacle of the ape clambering over Paris roofs with an unconscious Camille on its arm brought some irreverent squeals from last night's audience.... The entire production suffers from an overzealous effort at terrorization, and the cast ... succumbs to the temptation to overact.—*The New York Times*, February 11, 1932, Andre Sennwald

Rating: ★★★ It's an artificial screen story.... [N]evertheless Bela Lugosi ... does make you shrink back a little in your seat.... Lugosi's suggestion of the insanely criminal doctor is effective.... [T]he excitement of the pursuit of the ape toward the end is real enough to evoke spontaneous applause from the audience when it is overtaken and killed.—*The New York Daily News*, February 11, 1932, Kate Cameron

[S]exed up to the limit.... Sidney Fox overdraws the sweet ingénue to the point of nearly distracting any audience from any fear it may have for her.—*Variety*, February 16, 1932

[S]uperior in many respects [to *Frankenstein*] in sustaining interest and convincing treatment.... Very free and greatly elaborated version of Edgar Allan Poe story.... [T]he atmosphere of creeping evil and terrifying detail will have a marked effect. Bela Lugosi plays the part of Dr. Mirakle in a most realistic fashion.—*Today's Cinema* (GB), April 16, 1932

Here is a great actor [Lugosi] who can coin new thrills.—*The Washington Post*, 1932

A horrifying and nerve-shattering motion picture.—*The Philadelphia Daily News*, 1932

The story holds one's interest throughout although the acting is not especially outstanding and the story does not take advantage of the full amount of horror that one would expect from Poe's work.—*The National Board of Review Magazine*, 1932

The Old Dark House

Released October 20, 1932. 71 minutes. *Producer:* Carl Laemmle, Jr. *Director:* James Whale. *Screenplay:* Benn W. Levy. *Based on the novel* Benighted *by* J.B. Priestley. *Additional Dialogue:* R.C. Sherriff. *Photography:* Arthur Edeson. *Editor:* Clarence Kolster. *Art Director:* Charles D. Hall. *Music:* David Broekman. *Assistant Director:* Joseph A. McDonough. *Sound Recorder:* William Hedgcock. *Makeup:* Jack P. Pierce.

Boris Karloff (*Morgan*), Melvyn Douglas (*Roger Penderel*), Charles Laughton (*Sir William Porterhouse*), Gloria Stuart (*Margaret Waverton*), Raymond Massey (*Philip Waverton*), Ernest Thesiger (*Horace Femm*), Lillian Bond (*Gladys DuCane/Perkins*), Eva Moore (*Rebecca Femm*), Brember Wills (*Saul Femm*), John Dudgeon [Elspeth Dudgeon] (*Sir Roderick Femm*).

Ten souls storm-bound in a house accursed! Murderous maniac — drink-mad monster — harpy — coward — fire fiend. Two beautiful women to be protected — three decent men not enough!

—*Ad blurb for* The Old Dark House

January 1932: The startling success of *Frankenstein* assured the Laemmles that their confidence in the studio's slightly pampered star director James Whale was justified. But Whale's next production was not a grand slam. *The Impatient Maiden* (1932) was a pedestrian affair concerning a mismatched couple, a naive intern (Lew Ayres) and a cynical secretary (Mae Clarke), who eventually fall in love. This entertaining but slight film is of interest today for what it reveals of Whale's technique with a somewhat atypical subject. Whale's gifts were obviously better suited to more flamboyant material. Hoping to strike box office lightning again, Universal steered him into another horror venture.

The suggestion of a film version of *Benighted,* a demure, ruminative thriller by the eclectic British writer J.B. Priestley, was probably Whale's. Basically, it told the story of a group of travelers, lost in a torrential rainstorm, forced to seek shelter in a gloomy mansion in the Welsh mountains. However, instead of safety, they find themselves in even more peril from the homestead's unhinged inhabitants, a bizarre family of eccentrics, including a pyromaniac bent on murder. The book probably struck an emotional chord with the director who saw past the melodramatic plot to Priestley's trenchant underlying theme of modernism encroaching on post-war Britain. (It's no accident that Priestley's novel sold poorly until his American publisher played up its penny-dreadful elements by changing the title to *The Old Dark House.*) One could well imagine Whale, likewise, pitching the project to Universal as a *Cat and the Canary*–style chiller while downplaying its inherent social subtext. It might very well be that Whale sold Universal a bill of goods but with the picture's peculiarly British underpinnings and the director's affinity for his odd lot of characters, *The Old Dark House* emerges as one of the most curious films to come out of '30s Hollywood.

Whale chose playwright Benn W. Levy to write the screenplay and solicited the assistance of "Journey's End" scribe R. C. Sherriff. The pair added a touch of whimsy utterly lacking in the novel; the result was one of the wittiest scripts ever written for a horror movie. The finished screenplay followed the novel faithfully but jettisoned Priestley's long, introspective passages which recurred with irritating frequency, even in the climactic action scenes. Priestley may have been interested in man as a social animal, but Whale envisioned the story as a mild burlesque on the Gothic thriller. The screenplay completed, *The Old Dark House* was at last ready to be cast.

Finding a follow-up role for Boris Karloff, the new king of horror, was a priority, but his range had yet to be tested. He slid into the role of Morgan, the mute, brutish butler. It was a relatively small part, but Universal wasn't taking any chances with their new star. His first lead role after *Frankenstein* wasn't very encouraging. Miscast as a nightclub owner in *Night World* (1932), Karloff didn't win many favorable notices. Universal cannily tacked a foreword onto the opening credits of *The Old Dark House* assuring the audience that this was indeed the same actor who had scared the wits out of them in *Frankenstein*; "We explain this to settle any disputes in advance, even though such disputes are a tribute to his great versatility."

For the roles of Mr. and Mrs. Waverton, the smart young English couple who needed only a shriek-filled night in a remote Victorian mansion to quell their constant bickering, there was no need to look beyond the studio's contract players. Raymond Massey, an old friend of Whale's during the director's brief acting career, had just signed with Universal, and Gloria Stuart, a theater-trained ingénue hailing from California, were selected for the roles. Whale used outside talent to fill out the cast, a shrewdly chosen assemblage of seasoned stage actors. With the exception of up-and-coming star Melvyn Douglas all of them were British: Charles Laughton, Lillian Bond, Eva Moore and Ernest Thesiger.

As usual, Whale oversaw every phase of the production, with little creative input from producer Carl Laemmle, Jr. Sets constructed from art director Charles D. Hall's specifications were erected on the soundstage, highlighted by an imposing Victorian staircase, a large fireplace and an adjoining parlor and dining room. The sets were modified for the studio's later horror movies, and even turned up in non-Universal thrillers such as Majestic's *The Vampire Bat* (also with Melvyn Douglas) and Chesterfield's *Strange People* (both 1933). The special effects crew built a miniature set for a heart-stopping trick scene in which Waverton's roadster narrowly avoids being crushed in a landslide. Huge wind machines and hoses were readied on the back lot for the spectacular nighttime storm sequence which opens the show. By April, the cameras were ready to roll.

"It was wonderful. Every morning Whale would come on the set with all the camera layouts for his script," Gloria Stuart told the authors. "He was also a brilliant cameraman besides being one of the most talented, meticulous directors I have ever worked for in films. Whale was also great with dialogue. He really knew what he was doing."

Whale followed his usual procedure of thoroughly rehearsing his cast and blocking out each scene carefully. The time-honored British tradition of tea-time was religiously observed, much to the irritation of Stuart, who felt slighted by her colleagues. She told *Films in Review*:

> The British were very clannish on that picture. They felt they were a rather superior colony and they didn't pretend otherwise. They had tea at eleven and four, the whole English cast and Whale, and they never once asked me or Melvyn or any other American to join them. It put me off. No, they were not very polite.

Despite this minor friction, the production went smoothly, finally closing in mid–March.

The Old Dark House begins in the midst of a raging thunderstorm as a lone automobile, lost in the Welsh mountains, tries to make its way along a primitive dirt road. Inside are a bickering, nerve-wracked young couple, Philip and Margaret Waverton (Raymond Massey and Gloria Stuart), and their war-disillusioned friend Roger Penderel (Melvyn Douglas). Deciding it is too dangerous to continue, the trio pull up to an imposing stone house, the only shelter in sight.

A Neanderthal-like manservant, Morgan (Boris Karloff) ushers them into a gloomy but well-upholstered room. They are met by the gaunt Horace Femm (Ernest Thesiger) who urges them to press on, and his sister, the cranky, half-deaf Rebecca (Eva Moore). The group is soon joined by another pair of lost travelers, the prosperous Sir William Porterhouse (Charles Laughton) and his unlikely companion, out-of-work chorus girl Gladys DuCane (Lillian Bond).

Rebecca Femm turns out to be a religious fanatic, while her brother Horace seems fearful of some terrible secret. A drunken Morgan gets into a brawl with Philip and is knocked unconscious. Investigating what sounds like a frail, child-like voice, Philip and Margaret come across the bedroom of the master of the house, 102-year-old Sir Roderick Femm (John [Elspeth] Dudgeon). He warns the couple that his eldest son, Saul, who is locked away in the nursery, is a madman determined to set fire to the house.

The dazed Morgan awakens and frees the dreaded Saul (Brember Wills). Philip and Porterhouse manage to subdue the brutish butler but Saul torches a staircase landing as Penderel tries to stop him. A balustrade gives way, sending both men crashing to the floor below. Saul is killed but the injured Penderel slowly regains consciousness.

The storm finally subsides. The Wavertons wearily make their way to their car, Penderel and Gladys decide to get married and the Femms, hardly turning a hair after the night's melodramatics, carry on as if nothing has happened. It's a new day.

After its reissue in the late '40s, *The Old Dark House* dropped completely from sight and was considered a lost film. Its reappearance is largely due to the tireless efforts of director Curtis Harrington, a friend of Whale's in his last years, who made an intensive search for a print in 1968. Universal claimed to have destroyed the negative and all prints when the story rights reverted back to J.B. Priestley, who, in turn, optioned the property to Columbia. Playing a hunch, Harrington contacted William Castle. The king of the gimmick horror movies, he had directed a cloddish and unwatchable color remake of *The Old Dark House* in collaboration with Hammer Pictures, released in 1963. The charismatic filmmaker, as it turned out, not only denied owning a copy of the original film, but claimed Universal couldn't even provide him with a screening while he was preparing his remake.*

Undaunted, Harrington returned to Universal, who steadfastly stuck to their story that the negative had been destroyed. At Harrington's insistence, a search of the studio vaults was made, turning up a single "lavender negative" (actually a fine grain print) still in printable condition despite shrinkage and years of neglect. The find was a real treasure, but Universal's reaction was one of indifference. Having lost the rights to the film they would be unable to market it commercially, and saw little reason to shell out the two or three thousand dollars it would cost for its restoration. Harrington came up with funding from Eastman House of Rochester, New York, for the printing of a new negative, and the film enjoyed a brief theatrical revival in the early '70s. (Further improvements were made in the mid–'90s by the Library of Congress. In addition to upgrading the visuals, the restoration team availed themselves of the original optical soundtrack which was discovered years after Harrington's discovery of the negative.)

Like *Mystery of the Wax Museum* (1933) which was also unavailable for decades, *The Old Dark House* was met with bewilderment and perhaps mild disappointment when it finally resurfaced. The oft-published stills of a ghoulish Karloff menacing Gloria Stuart in *Famous Monsters of Filmland* and the like promised unsuspecting baby boomers a horrific tour de force on the order of Whale's other horror pictures. Certainly no one could have anticipated that in rethinking the Priestley novel, Whale turned it into something of a mild lampoon of the genre. Some of the reviewers who caught the film during its limited theatrical reissue didn't get the joke either, and *The Old Dark House* accumulated more than its share of condescending notices. Initial reservations about the picture seem to have vanished with time, however, and the picture has come to take its place rightfully among the best of the Universal horror films of the period.

The Old Dark House is perhaps an acquired taste, but it's a film that grows in stature with each viewing. It has been said that only a Frenchman can fully appreciate Jean Renoir's *The Rules of the Game* (1939); likewise, William K. Everson suggests that only an Englishman can fully understand *The Old Dark House*. Perhaps. The film's wit is so dry and so gently self-mocking, a casual viewer can easily laugh the dialogue off as being ridiculous. ("Philip, this is an awful house." "It isn't very nice, is it?") The characters often indicate their disapproval of each other with a gesture or an unrelated line. In one scene, Horace shows his guests an armful of flowers his sister was intending to arrange, and then tosses them into the fireplace. In the dinner scene, Horace puts the boisterous Porterhouse in his place with a sneer and the offer of a potato. Penderel, likewise, humors his short-tempered hostess with the line, "Vinegar, Miss Femm?"

Whale paces the film carefully, portioning small increments of humor as the story progresses and then unleashing a full onslaught of mayhem in the last reel. Often he deflates his own build-up of tension with a flip remark. Karloff's creepy introduction when he responds to the travelers' frantic knocks at the door is set up with Melvyn Douglas' ominous dialogue: "Supposing the people inside were dead. All stretched out with lights quietly burning about them." When Karloff finally appears, growling

**In an interview with writer William F. Nolan in* Famous Monsters of Filmland, *Boris Karloff revealed that Castle offered him a lead role in the remake, most likely Roderick Femm, ultimately played by Robert Morley. Said Karloff, "The [script for the] new version they showed me in London was simply not to my liking. I sent back the script. Wanted no part it. After all, I've been in the acting profession for more than half a century. High time to pick and choose my vehicles. You know [*shaking his head*], I've been in some rather* awful *pictures."*

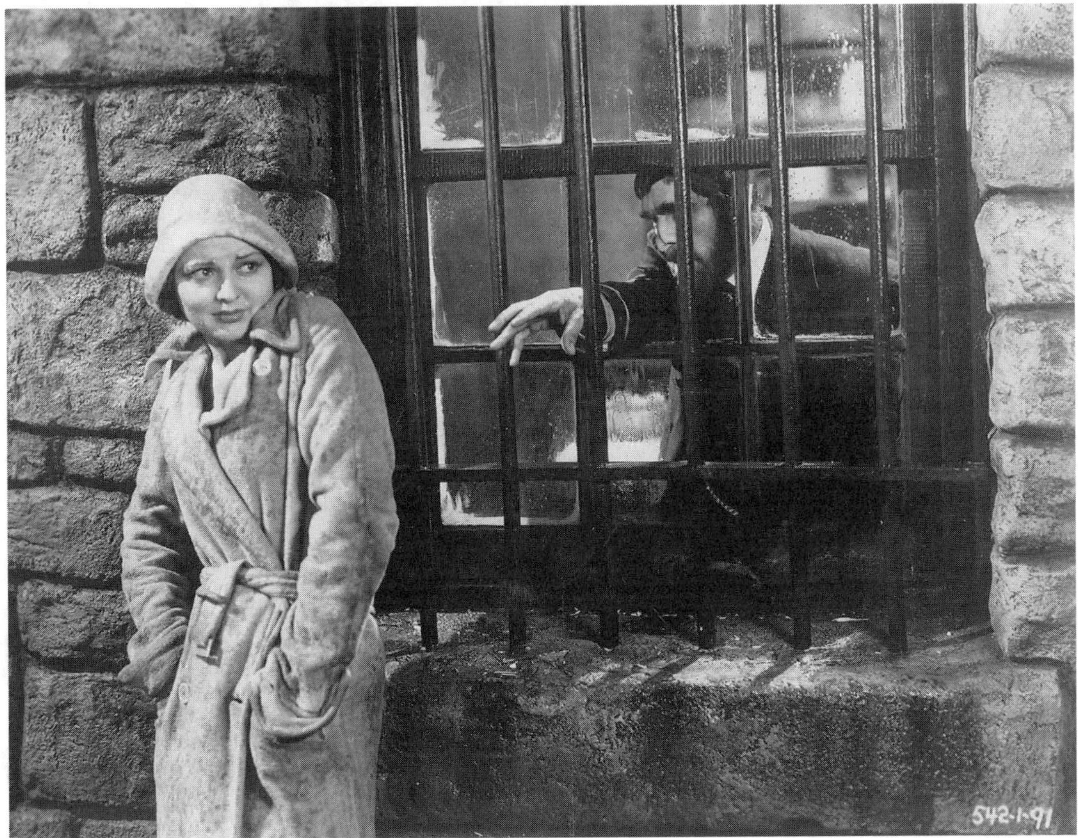

Hoping to duplicate the success of *Frankenstein*, Universal cast Boris Karloff as the brute manservant Morgan in *The Old Dark House*. Lillian Bond is the damsel in distress.

like a provoked dog, writer Benn Levy cribs Priestley's original line, "Even Welsh oughtn't sound like that." Later, an equally unruffled Charles Laughton puts the fearsome Karloff in his place with, "Looks to me like he can do with a shave!"

The introduction of Saul, too, is deliberately anticlimactic and is in startling contrast to his literary counterpart. In the book, he is both mindless and speechless, simply a raging brute bent on destruction. The Whale version finds him a far more cunning and dimensional character but no less dangerous. Again, the director seizes the opportunity to defy audience expectations. First appearing as a threatening hand on a railing, Saul is quickly revealed as a pathetic, frightened old man whose claim of being victimized by his family rings with conviction. But when the film cuts to a chilling closeup of his half-mad grin, it's obvious we've been duped. Within moments, he's living up to Father Roderick's description of him as a cackling, torch-bearing lunatic, setting the house ablaze and engaging in a fight-to-the-death struggle with Penderel. Vastly improving on his source, Levy's script insists on vesting the character with some recognizable Femm characteristics. Indeed, Saul's blather about a candle flame takes on a bit of Rebecca's obsessive tendencies and there's more of a hint of Horace's prissiness in his manner.

Whale counters the staginess of the material by digging deep into his bag of cinematic tricks. *The Old Dark House* is in fact the director's most stylized film to this date. Whale puckishly responds with his camera to Levy's funny lines. He cuts to snarling reaction shots of Eva Moore on appropriate occasions, and includes an unexpected shot of the sagging, frumpy hag quickly doing her hair after she menaces Gloria Stuart. The scene is one of Whale's boldest.

Whale photographs Moore with a dis-

Horace Femm (Ernest Thesiger) holds court for his uninvited guests (Lillian Bond, Melvyn Douglas, Gloria Stuart, Raymond Massey, Charles Laughton) (courtesy John Skillin).

torted, funhouse mirror effect as Levy's script parallels the character's religious fanaticism with her sexual repression. Handling Stuart's chic evening dress, Moore's demented, evangelistic ravings take a sinister turn: "That's fine stuff too, but it'll rot." Then placing her hand on Stuart's half-exposed breast: "That's finer stuff still, but it'll rot too in time." Moore exits but Stuart's memory of her lingers as a twisted mirror image of the hag reprises her demented speech. The dialogue is Priestley's but the style is unmistakably Whale's.

Priestley's bleak but realistic dinner scene is turned into an elaborate and hilarious feast in the movie. Whale again focuses on the peculiarities of the incompatible diners: The ritual of the passing of sliced bread, Moore wolfing down gobs of pickled onions, Massey extracting an ungodly black spot from a boiled potato.

When asked what she remembers about this marvelous scene, Gloria Stuart offered,

> My dress. I told James, "I don't understand. Everyone else changed for dinner, but I'm in this pink, bias-cut, silk velvet, practically strapless dinner dress. I just don't understand!" "Well," he said, "when Karloff chases you through the halls, I want you to be like a flame or a dancer and I want that light down the dark halls and so forth." Well, you know, you don't argue with Whale. It was pretty ridiculous but that's what he wanted and that's what he got.

Priestley's characters are neatly varied and play off one another well. The retiring Waverton, the tweed-and-pipe hero representing the thinking man, contrasts with the cynical but charming man-of-action Penderel. Likewise, Priestley carefully contrasts his female characters from the upper-crust Margaret to the common chorus girl Gladys. The Femms are introduced with a careful eye on story progression, with each character slightly madder than the last. Whatever reservations one may have about Priestley's novel, it is a marvel of construction.

Although so many Hollywood adaptations of successful novels are faithful to the spirit but not the letter of the source material, Whale turns the situation upside down. While the major incidents of the novel are transferred intact, Whale injects his own personality and humor into Priestley's often dour social ruminations. Much of the dialogue is replaced or condensed and often laced with wry humor.

All of the thriller conventions of the novel are scrupulously maintained, playing up the situation of desperate characters jumping from the frying pan into the fire. The weary travelers flee to the Femm household to escape the peril of a raging storm only to find a menace of another sort. Penderel barely escaped with his life during his war service only to lose it conducting warfare of another sort with the monstrous Saul. However, as in *Frankenstein* and, later, in *Bride of Frankenstein*, Whale opts out of the intended tragic ending (Penderel dies of a broken neck in the novel) and spares the life of his heroes. In a dramatic departure from the book, the film doesn't end mournfully but with Gladys and Penderel in a clinch while the off-camera Porterhouse snores loudly. The Femms, in the meantime, go about their usual business without seeming to notice their dead brother's body lying in the charred debris.

A major scene in the novel of the characters playing a game of "Truth" as an after-supper diversion is barely retained in the movie. Priestley used the episode to reaffirm the double meaning of his original *Benighted* title. (When it comes to how much they know about the people who are closest to them, the travelers prove just as clueless as the "benighted" Femms. Irony with a capital I.) Whale and scenarist Levy streamline the novel's stinging commentary of the British class structure with an accusing closeup of Gloria Stuart as Laughton rales against the society hostesses whom he believes drove his young wife into an early grave.

Similarly, all of Penderel's war-induced disillusionment, which goes on for pages in the novel, is dispensed with a self-depreciating witticism not found in Priestley. ("War generation slightly soiled. The study of the bittersweet. The man with a crooked smile. And *this*, Mr. Femm, is exceedingly good gin," as he toasts his host.) Throughout the movie, Whale accommodates Priestley perfunctorily while keeping focused on delivering a compact and civilized horror movie. In the end, Whale uses the original novel merely as a narrative framework in order to mold his own spoofy variation of *The Cat and the Canary* (1927), complete with visual references. The startling visual of the dark hallway flanked on both sides by ceiling-length curtains billowing in the wind is a direct lift from the Paul Leni film. (Charles D. Hall served as art director on both productions.) Happily, Whale replaces the nincompoop humor of the silent picture with his signature wit.

The Old Dark House offers a fine gallery of memorable characters and comes as close as any Universal horror film did to being an ensemble piece. The individual performances may seem dated but they're the sort that linger in the memory. In his first Hollywood film, Charles Laughton makes a grand show of it with a pronounced Yorkshire accent, slightly overdoing the *nouveau riche* vulgarity of the character. His Sir William Porterhouse is a self-made man, defined by himself and by everyone else by his money but suffers from an emotional emptiness. Laughton makes the case of how lonely it is at the top while giving equal weight to the character's fundamental decency.

The studio was more interested in building up Boris Karloff's career than Whale was. His appearance as Morgan is practically a footnote to the movie while his star billing is something of a fraud. (The grunts in his introductory scene were dubbed in by an unidentified actor during post-production.) Karloff's deaf character communicates mostly through exaggerated gestures with little sense of pantomime until his touching final scene. Cradling the body of Brember Wills' Saul gives *The Old Dark House* its only moment of genuine pathos and marks Morgan, like his Frankenstein Monster, as a tragic social outcast. Whale adds little touches such as the actor leering at the uncomfortable Gloria Stuart, who averts her gaze while the brute is serving dinner.

Stuart provided us with a charming testimonial to the cultured Englishman:

> Karloff was brilliant, beautifully educated. For his role in *The Old Dark House*, he had to come to the set at three or four in the morning so they could do his makeup. So naturally he wasn't given to a

lot of horsing around or light conversation during the day. But I thought he was a lovely man.

For the role of Sir Roderick, the ancient patriarch of the Femm clan, Whale gambled by trying to pass off stage actress Elspeth Dudgeon as a man. The deception doesn't come off but Dudgeon (listed as John Dudgeon in the credits) underscores the Femms' distinctly androgynous nature. Unbelievable as it may seem, she was still making films in the late '40s. One of her last acting roles was as a feisty lady in a retirement home in *Lust for Gold* (1949) with Glenn Ford and Ida Lupino. As the fanatical Rebecca Femm, Eva Moore is as cranky and crusty as one could hope.

The conventional characters come off well also. Gloria Stuart, who would later be saddled with too many weepy heroine roles (such as in *The Invisible Man* and, even more irritatingly, John Ford's 1936 *The Prisoner of Shark Island*), is alluring as Margaret, and Raymond Massey is competent as Waverton. The excellent Melvyn Douglas is fine as always as the acerbic, world-weary Roger Penderel (Russell Hopton was originally cast in the part). Cut from the same cloth as the post-war existential heroes, his is one of the most interesting leading men of horror movies of the '30s if one overlooks his mawkish love scenes. It's hard to believe that the hard-boiled Penderel is so easily swept away by so common a waif as Gladys, well played by Lillian Bond. In 1953, Bond would again play an uninvited guest in the British home of a strange clan with a highly unusual family member locked away in the attic; the movie was the 3-D horror mystery, *The Maze*.

But, of course, it's Ernest Thesiger who steals *The Old Dark House* as the sniffish, craven Horace Femm. He is nothing short of the ideal materialization of the Priestley character. ("A man so thin, with so little flesh and so much shining bone ought to be braver than that; he was almost a skeleton, and skeletons, jangling and defiant, are brave enough.") Jack Pierce completes the image, providing the actor with heavy eye makeup, achieving a wonderful, skull-like effect.

In 1938, Universal dipped into its story files and set Lester Cole to the task of writing a proposed remake of *The Old Dark House*. Without the talents of James Whale and R.C. Sherriff on board, the best one could expect would be a film along the lines of the *Secret of the Blue Room* remake, *The Missing Guest*: Another dreary old mansion melodrama with wiseacre characters and stock situations. In other words, everything that the 1932 film wasn't. Mercifully, it was never made.

The Old Dark House was well-received by critics upon its initial release, but it was too eccentric to match the mass popularity of *Frankenstein*. Raymond Massey, who fancied himself as going on to bigger and better things, later dismissed his role as "a long and colourless juvenile part that didn't permit much acting." He admitted in his autobiography that he never saw the movie. His co-star, Gloria Stuart, took exception:

> I think it's a wonderful film. I remember I did a seminar at Filmex on James Whale, and someone said to me, "How did it feel, Miss Stuart, making classics?" Well, we didn't know we were making classics. All we were hoping for was to make a good movie. But all of James' films are classics.

Critics' Corner

It gives Karloff another opportunity to do the thing at which he has no peer, the monster type.... [M]akes himself a shocker of no puny proportions.... [T]he whole thing has an air of genuine authenticity....—*The Hollywood Herald*, July 16, 1932

There is a wealth of talent in this production.... Mr. Karloff is, of course, thoroughly in his element as Morgan. He leaves no stone unturned to make this character thoroughly disturbing.—*The New York Times*, October 28, 1932, Mordaunt Hall

The individual performances are so excellent that the story is believable. The second half is tensely exciting.—*Harrison's Reports*, 1932

Rating: ★★★½ It is eerie and awful and logical besides.... We don't think we've ever before enjoyed a talkie of this type so immensely.—*The New York Daily News*, October 28, 1932, Irene Thirer

Let one stop and think but a few seconds about what's happened on the screen and there'd be no picture.... Melvyn Douglas is rather hit and miss under the circumstances, and that stable tête-à-tête with Lillian Bond, who is satisfactory up to that point, makes it a bit worse.—*Variety*, November 1, 1932

Universal goes British—a marvelously exceptional picture with big box office potential—should be sensational!—*The Kinematograph Weekly* (GB), 1932

Whale and Karloff have progressed since the day when they dabbled in the crude though diverting sensations of *Frankenstein*. There is a new and welcome restraint about their work.—*The Film Weekly* (GB), October 21, 1932

Evidently James Whale has a flair for pictures of this character, but he "shot his bolt" with *Frankenstein*. In fact, all studios better lay off such productions.—*The Hollywood Filmograph*, July 1932, Arthur Forde

The Mummy

Released December 22, 1932. 72 minutes. *Producer:* Carl Laemmle, Jr. *Director:* Karl Freund. *Associate Producer:* Stanley Bergerman. *Screenplay:* John L. Balderston. *Story:* Nina Wilcox Putnam & Richard Schayer. *Photography:* Charles Stumar. *Camera Operator:* James Drought. *Assistant Cameraman:* Art Glouner. *Editor:* Milton Carruth. *Art Director:* Willy Pogany. *Music Supervisor:* James Dietrich. *Special Effects:* John P. Fulton. *Sound:* Joe Lapis. *Makeup:* Jack P. Pierce.

Boris Karloff (*Imhotep/Ardath Bey*), Zita Johann (*Helen Grosvenor/Princess Anck-es-en-Amon*), David Manners (*Frank Whemple*), Edward Van Sloan (*Dr. Muller*), Arthur Byron (*Sir Joseph Whemple*), Bramwell Fletcher (*Ralph Norton*), Noble Johnson (*The Nubian*), Kathryn Byron (*Frau Muller*), Leonard Mudie (*Prof. Pearson*), James Crane (*King Amenophis*), Eddie Kane (*Dr. LeBarron*), Tony Marlow (*Inspector*), Pat Somerset (*Helen's Dance Partner*), C. Montague Shaw, Leyland Hodgson (*Small Talkers*), Gordon [Bill] Elliott (*Man on Dance Floor*). *Deleted from final print:* Henry Victor (*The Saxon Warrior*), Arnold Gray (*Knight*).

[A] delicate piece of horror crystal.
—*David Colton, Classic Horror Film Board*

The setting: A rocky area just north of the Valley of the Kings in the Egyptian desert. The year: 1921. Sir Joseph Whemple (Arthur Byron), director of an archaeological expedition sponsored by the British Museum, has made a remarkable find—a burial spot containing the mummy of Imhotep, high priest of the Temple of the Sun at Karnak, and an alabaster box which bears a forbidding inscription: "Death—Eternal punishment for anyone who opens this casket. In the name of Amon-Ra, the King of the Gods."

Ralph Norton (Bramwell Fletcher), Whemple's young assistant, is eager to open the ancient box despite the protests of Sir Joseph's friend Dr. Muller (Edward Van Sloan), a Viennese student of the occult. As Whemple and Muller are debating the issue, Norton blunders ahead. Inside, he finds the sacred Scroll of Thoth, handed down from pharaoh to pharaoh, which contains the great spell by which Isis raised Osiris from the dead. As the Oxford lad reads the magic spell aloud, the Mummy (Boris Karloff) slowly comes to life. By the time Whemple returns, he finds the Mummy and the Scroll of Thoth gone, and Norton laughing hysterically, out of his mind.

The story advances 11 years. Sir Joseph's son Frank (David Manners) and his associate Prof. Pearson (Leonard Mudie) are in the midst of breaking camp after a disappointing season in the desert when they are visited by Ardath Bey (also Karloff), a dignified Egyptian scholar. ("His face is tanned like leather," wrote scenarist John L. Balderston, "it is the face of a mummy, but not unlike that of many Orientals who have lived in the tropical sun all their lives.") The stranger generously offers to lead the two Englishmen to the site of a find of incredible magnitude: The burial spot of the Princess Anck-es-en-Amon, the daughter of Amenophis, one-time ruler of all Egypt. A treasure-trove of priceless artifacts and the mummy of the princess are recovered from the tomb and sent to the Cairo Museum.

Ardath Bey is in actually the resuscitated high priest Imhotep. Centuries before, the Egyptian was put to death for attempting to bring his beloved Anck-es-en-Amon back from the dead. With the Scroll of Thoth in his possession, he futilely attempts to raise the mummy of the princess, but discovers that her *ka* (spirit) has been reincarnated in the body of a twentieth-century woman, Helen Grosvenor (Zita Johann), a patient of Dr. Muller's.

By the time Frank and Sir Joseph learn of Bey's true identity, it is too late: The ancient Egyptian has already taken command of Helen's mind and soul. Realizing she is indeed the reincarnation of Anck-es-en-Amon, Helen is quite literally torn between two lives. Her blossoming love for Frank and the instinct to survive are tested by the omnipotent influence of Ardath Bey.

Summoning forth his ancient powers, Bey fatally strikes down Sir Joseph and makes an attempt on Frank's life. He lures Helen to the Cairo Museum and prepares her for "the great night of terror and triumph," when he will release her soul from its present incarnation and, through the power of the Scroll of Thoth, resurrect the young woman in the form of a living mummy like himself. Speaking as Anck-es-en-

Amon, Helen protests; she acknowledges the tremendous suffering Imhotep has endured in the name of love, but she cannot allow him to destroy the life of the modern-day woman that she has become.

Surrendering to Bey's influence, Helen voluntarily lies upon the altar of Anubis, the Guide of the Dead, and awaits the thrust of Bey's knife. But before Bey can administer the mortal wound, Frank and Muller intervene, bringing Helen back to her senses. She prays to the statue of Isis for salvation. Mystically, the goddess lifts her hand bearing the *crux ansata* (or symbol of eternal life) and issues forth a blinding flash of light. The Scroll of Thoth is destroyed and with it Ardath Bey.

One of Universal's most potent horror thrillers, *The Mummy* is an ingenious creation, meticulous in every detail. From its first brilliantly realized set piece, one of the most indelible of '30s horror (who could forget Bramwell Fletcher's maniacal peals of laughter?), to the final image of Ardath Bey's pitiful remains scattered across the museum's marble floor, *The Mummy* evokes an aura of wonder, romance and mystery. Eschewing the lurid and the blatantly sensational elements of the later Kharis Mummy movies, the picture modulates its chill elements with exquisite refinement. The atmosphere is almost palpable. We are ushered into a world where antiquity seamlessly melds with the modern, where ancient rituals, reincarnation of the spirit, and the all-powerful gods of Egypt are still as potent as they were millennia ago.

Blessed with a director who knew the mechanics of the camera intimately, *The Mummy*'s visual richness was assured. This quality, plus splendid performances by Boris Karloff, Zita Johann, Edward Van Sloan and Bramwell Fletcher, a masterful script by John L. Balderston, impressive sets, and one of Jack Pierce's most accomplished makeup jobs, elevate *The Mummy* to the status of an *undisputed* classic, generally untarnished by the cruelties of time.

Junior Laemmle conceived the idea of making a motion picture loosely based on the highly publicized 1922 discovery of the boy king Tutankhamen's tomb, and the alleged curse that had struck down its plunderers. (Much of the "evidence" behind the curse has since been explained away via modern scientific research.) In early 1932, Laemmle assigned Nina Wilcox Putnam, author of novels, short stories and newspaper articles, and Richard Schayer, head of Universal's scenario department, to come up with a feasible story treatment. The pair put their imaginations to work and the result was "Cagliostro," a nine-page original story.

Cagliostro was an ancient Egyptian priest who discovered the secret of eternal life: By injecting himself with nitrates, he has managed to prolong his existence for 4,000 years. He carries a similarly deathless grudge, stewing about a woman who betrayed him centuries before, and seeking out and murdering females who resemble her. Posing as the blind uncle of Helen Dorrington, a San Francisco movie cashier, Cagliostro and his Nubian servant commit a series of robberies and murders using (of all things) radio and television waves. Prof. Whemple, an eminent archaeologist, discovers the truth about the baleful holy man and plots his destruction.

Evidently satisfied with Putnam and Schayer's efforts, Laemmle announced in March his plans to feature Boris Karloff in the title role of his latest horror production, *Cagliostro*. It wasn't until summer, however, that John L. Balderston (of *Dracula* and *Frankenstein* fame) began working on the screenplay. Balderston had previously written the play "Berkeley Square" as well as the script for the 1933 screen version with Leslie Howard which also dealt with a romance that spanned the centuries.

By the time the script was submitted to the studio on September 12, it had gone through no fewer than *three* title changes: from *Cagliostro* to *The King of the Dead* to *Im-Ho-Tep*. Balderston made some refinements in the story, abandoning the scientific explanation for Cagliostro's (now Imhotep's) resurrection in favor of a purely supernatural one. By setting the story in Egypt rather than San Francisco, he buoyed the mystical elements of the tale, thus enhancing its effectiveness. (At an early stage of the script's development, actor Rollo Lloyd was credited with having provided additional dialogue; his contribution — provided that any of his material was retained — was doomed to anonymity in the picture's credit roster.)

Amply filling the director's chair on *Im-Ho-Tep* was 360-pound Karl "Papa" Freund, the brilliant German cinematographer who lensed

Zita Johann, star of *The Mummy*, enjoyed working with Boris Karloff but had a very different reaction to director Karl Freund.

Tod Browning's *Dracula*. Praised as "the Giotto of the screen," the boldly innovative cameraman was a pioneer in the development of subjective photography, devising unorthodox techniques (such as strapping the camera to his chest) to capture particular shots.

Born in Koeniginhof, Bohemia (now Czechoslovakia), in 1890, Freund began his career behind the camera as an apprentice projectionist in Berlin at the age of 15. Mastering photographic technique, he made on his own two low-budget features in 1907 and the following year signed a contract as a full-fledged cameraman at Pathé News in Berlin. By the '20s, Freund had made a name for himself in the field of cinematography. Working at Ufa and Messter studios, he "freed" the camera from its static position on the sound stage. Freund worked closely with the pioneers of the German cinema (Fritz Lang, Paul Wegener, E.A. Dupont, F.W. Murnau), creating breathtaking images for such classics as *The Golem* (1920), *The Last Laugh* (1924), *Variety* (1925) and *Metropolis* (1926). Among his technical accomplishments was the introduction of process shot techniques, the pioneering of dolly shots by placing the camera on a motorized wagon, and the development of a steel tape which would become today's magnetic film.

Freund emigrated to the United States in 1929 and immediately immersed himself in the study of American technique. He told film columnist Marguerite Tazelaar:

> I think [being a cameraman] is one of the most interesting jobs in the whole industry. The most important thing is to catch the mood of the scene in a shot. Perhaps it is only a close-up of the heroine's eyes, yet this instant can be the most significant in the entire film. Each separate scene, each setup, has a meaning to the artist. The mood of the scene is everything.

By coming to the rescue of director Lewis Milestone, Freund earned himself a directing contract at Universal. Dissatisfied with the ending of *All Quiet on the Western Front* (1930), and with only three days left before the scheduled premiere, Milestone turned to Freund for suggestions. In a burst of inspiration, the cameraman came up with the deceptively simple, unforgettable "butterfly finale." (Soldier Lew Ayres, captivated by the sight of a beautiful butterfly, absentmindedly strays into the range of enemy gunfire and is shot down; moments later, we hear an announcement that all fighting has come to a halt on the Western front.) Milestone was delighted. Universal signed Freund to direct two films a year, beginning with *Im-Ho-Tep* (the title was changed to *The Mummy* more than halfway through production).

Freund's reputation as a tireless taskmaster was certified by his industrious performance on this film. In his lecture track for the 1999 DVD release of *The Mummy*, noted film historian-author Dr. Paul Jensen speculates who deserves the greatest amount of credit for the motion picture's success, the director or the scenarist. Jensen dutifully points out that Balderston's work was so finished (with descriptions and camera angles) that Freund merely had to shoot it as written. But the artist had too strong a creative influence not to imbue the film with his own personal vision. Jensen surmises that with the month's time Freund had before *The Mummy* went before the cameras in September 1932, he may very well have had the opportunity to help develop the script in collaboration with Balderston, thus boosting Freund's contribution to the artistic merit of the film.

Seven long, hard weeks of intensive work followed; it wasn't unusual for the company to toil well past midnight. Karloff, in particular, felt the strain, as did Zita Johann. After sitting in Jack Pierce's chair for eight grueling hours, undergoing the most torturous man-into-monster makeup transformation of his career, poor Boris had to endure several hours of shooting the acclaimed resurrection scene. At 2 A.M. the following morning, after numerous retakes, the scene was in the can. By the time Pierce removed the suffocating mummy makeup and sent Karloff on his way, it was almost dawn.

Zita Johann painted a less-than-rosy picture of Papa Karl in an interview she granted Gregory Mank for his superb retrospective piece on *The Mummy* in *Films in Review*:

> Karl Freund made life very unpleasant. It was his first picture as a director, and he felt he needed a scapegoat in case he didn't come in on schedule (23 days, I believe). Well, *I* was cast as the scapegoat — and I saw through it right away!

Two weeks before the production wrapped, Freund took his company on location to picturesque Red Rock Canyon in the Mojave Desert to film some exterior shots with Karloff, David Manners and Leonard Mudie. Extensive process shots (utilizing footage taken in Egypt by staff cameramen dispatched by Universal's Berlin office), coupled with internationally renowned illustrator and artist Willy Pogany's evocative set designs and props, lent the picture an air of authenticity.

On October 30, Freund "wrapped" *The Mummy* (pun intended), his first directorial assignment, under schedule and under budget. The final cost was $196,161.

In transforming the Putnam-Schayer story into a screenplay, John L. Balderston leaned heavily upon his (and Hamilton Deane's) play "Dracula." It wouldn't be an exaggeration to call *The Mummy* a disguised remake of the Lugosi picture. Both the Count and Imhotep are immortal souls who cannot be destroyed by conventional means. They both possess hypnotic powers that can bend others to their will. Dracula preys on the weak-minded Renfield to carry out his misdeeds; Imhotep enslaves Whemple's Nubian manservant for similar purposes. Yet, in spite of their malevolent leanings and absolute powers, both are slaves to forces greater than themselves, thus arousing our pity and compassion.

Structurally, *The Mummy* follows *Dracula* very closely. Both films begin in the atmosphere-rich, ancestral homelands of the protagonists, then shift to a cosmopolitan setting. (Despite this change of scene, both creatures inhabit abodes strikingly similar to those they left behind.) At this point in both stories, a vulnerable young woman becomes the focal point in a struggle between good and evil.

As in *Dracula*, Edward Van Sloan, monster exterminator *par excellence*, wages the good fight almost singlehandedly. In both films, he is encumbered by the victim's well-meaning but ineffective fiancé (David Manners). Like Helen Chandler's Mina, Zita Johann's Helen becomes a scheming, uncontrollable pill as Imhotep makes every attempt to lure her back into his clutches. Despite Muller's safeguards, both women elude their protectors and end up in the arms of their seducers. But not for long. In *The Mummy*, as in *Dracula*, the elderly mentor and the heroine's sweetheart track the menace to his lair, arriving just in time to witness his destruction and save the heroine from a fate worse than death.

Rich in descriptive detail and fascinating Egyptian lore, Balderston's unabridged scenario makes good reading. The reincarnation motif (a concept that reached the height of fashion in the '50s with the highly publicized Bridey Murphy case) is emphasized in several scenes which went unfilmed, or, in the case of Zita Johann's trip-through-time, were shot, then discarded before the film went into release. In one such episode, Helen visits the Cairo Museum and becomes immersed in the Anck-es-en-Amon collection. Balderston painstakingly describes in glorious detail the various funerary items and toiletries that are on display. Suddenly, Ardath Bey makes his presence known. "I watched you admiring her jewels," he says. "She took the things she loved to the Kingdom of the West," Helen muses, as she stares at the mummy of Anck-es-en-Amon (which translates to "Royal Daughter of the Sun"). "Her *ka* may live today, in a body as beautiful as hers was in Old Egypt," Bey says.

The exquisite pool scene is divided into two separate episodes in Balderston's script. In the first, Bey "replays" images of Anck-es-en-Amon's death and her elaborate burial. Later, after the Mummy has lured Helen back into his sanctuary, she (and the audience) are taken on a trip through time as each of her past lives is revealed. First, we see Helen dressed in the costume of an eighteenth century French court lady, being romanced by a persistent young gallant in a setting suggesting the Garden of Versailles. Her preceding existence, set at the time of the Crusades in thirteenth century England, has Helen (again) enjoying romantic overtures, this time expressed by a handsome knight (Arnold Gray) as she stands on a dais in the hall of a medieval castle. In the midst of this time journey, the camera cuts occasionally to our heroine, lying opposite Bey's pool, writhing in mental torment.

Next, we are catapulted back to the eighth century. In the garb of a Saxon princess, Helen is seen hovering behind a blockade as a bloody battle is raging about her. With his last breath, a dying warrior (Henry Victor) reveals that all is lost. Helen picks up his dagger and stabs herself in the heart. A dungeon in the bowels of the Roman Coliseum is the grim setting of Helen's next supernatural pit stop. The valiant young woman stands amongst a band of Christian martyrs. She kisses a rough-hewn cross and fearlessly walks out into the arena with another doomed martyr. The film then cuts to a shot of hungry lions leaving their den. Awakening from her troubled sleep, Helen, her soul now fully possessed by the spirit of Anck-es-en-Amon, looks around the room with understandable confusion. "Are we in the Kingdom of Set? Are we both dead?" she asks. "We were dead, we are alive again," Bey says passionately. At this point in the script, Balderston reveals (via flashbacks framed within the pool) the terrible fate Imhotep suffered for attempting to raise Anck-es-en-Amon with the aid of the Scroll of Thoth.

Freund's direction is succinct and to the point, with little time devoted to the kind of character eccentricities beloved by such stylists as Whale, Florey and Ulmer. (Unlike the other horror films of this period, *The Mummy* contains not an ounce of humor.) As in *Dracula*, the spell that this undead being casts over his victims extends to the audience as well, suggesting Freund probably picked up a few directing pointers from Tod Browning. Freund obviously influenced his cameraman Charles Stumar (who might have felt a little intimidated working for this giant of the cinematography world). Under Freund's guidance, Stumar sets his focus on the paralyzing gaze of Imhotep and the transfixed reactions of his pawns, creating a disquieting mood. Pacing is sometimes sacrificed for this studious build-up of atmosphere and tone. Yet *The Mummy* escapes falling into the stagey, monotonous pattern of *Dracula*: Imaginative camerawork and direction make all the difference.

The dual role of Imhotep/Ardath Bey was a radical departure from Karloff's other horror assignments at Universal up to this time. Unlike his inarticulate, childlike Monster in *Frankenstein* and his lumbering brute servant in *The Old Dark House*, Karloff's Mummy is a well-spoken, all-powerful menace. He has but one purpose in

All-purpose Hollywood ethnic Noble Johnson succumbs to the ancient powers of Karloff's Imhotep.

the strange new world into which he has been reborn: To find Anck-es-en-Amon's latest reincarnation and awaken in her the sleeping spirit of his beloved.

Easily the picture's most famous (and terrifying) setpiece, the Mummy's awakening, would have been presented differently had Carl Laemmle, Jr., had his druthers. Veteran British film producer Richard Gordon got the story first-hand from Boris Karloff himself when they were shooting 1958's *The Haunted Strangler*:

> Karloff told me that Laemmle Jr. and director Karl Freund almost came to blows over the opening sequence. Laemmle wanted the Mummy to come to life and be introduced in a series of stylized close-ups like those that James Whale used in *Frankenstein*. Freund insisted that the Mummy should not be shown at all after its first stirrings of life in the sarcophagus and that audiences would be far more horrified by the specter of Fletcher's descent into madness, and his maniacal laughter, if they didn't see what drove him to it. Fortunately Freund prevailed and the sequence is one of the most revered in Universal's horror classics.

Freund may have been inspired by the German classic *The Cabinet of Dr. Caligari* (1919) in his direction of this unforgettable sequence. The ghoulish Cesare (Conrad Veidt) lies in an upright, coffin-like box. At the command of his master Dr. Caligari (Werner Krauss), Cesare slowly, painfully, opens his eyes as if from a deep sleep. It is a chillingly effective moment, the likes of which the screen would not see again until *The Mummy*.

It is difficult to despise a character with such richly romantic aspirations. Imhotep may be a cold-blooded murderer, but he doesn't belong in the same category as such blatantly evil Karloff characters as his Oriental sadist Fu Manchu (*The Mask of Fu Manchu* [1932]) or his Satan-worshipping Hjalmar Poelzig (*The Black Cat*). Because he suffered the most hideous of deaths for the woman he loved, we commiserate with Imhotep when he is spurned and even *insulted* ("I loved you once, but now you belong with the dead!") by her latter-day alter ego.

Garbed in a silk Egyptian robe, his head topped with a velvet fez, Ardath Bey's unassuming presence belies his destructive capabilities. The Egyptian's first appearance at the desert camp is delineated in celebrated James Whale fashion via a series of quick cuts of the odd-looking gentleman. Here, as well as in *Frankenstein*, *The Old Dark House* and Edgar Ulmer's *The Black Cat*, Karloff is first glimpsed framed in a doorway. The combined effect of Jack Pierce's makeup and Karloff's acting totally convince the audience that Bey is as ancient and potentially crumbly as the mummy we know him to be. By optically illuminating Karloff's eyes in key shots, John P. Fulton achieves the illusion that the omnipresent Egyptian knows all and sees all. Quietly understated and free of theatrical affectation, *The Mummy* is among the handful of Karloff's finest performances.

Only an actress of Zita Johann's talent and training could convincingly pull off the difficult role of Helen Grosvenor. (Balderston had suggested that Katharine Hepburn be screen-tested for the part but she had already left the West Coast for New York.) No shrinking violet, the Hungarian-born actress was keenly aware of her capabilities and firmly stood her ground in a world of male power-trippers. Hollywood held little fascination for the diminutive, dark-eyed actress. She turned down a lucrative five-year contract with Universal and the opportunity to star in the studio's 1929 version of *Show Boat* so that she could appear in Arthur Hopkins' play "Machinal" (opposite a young Clark Gable).

Following a headlining role in D.W. Griffith's *The Struggle* (1931), Johann signed up with MGM and later RKO. Both engagements left the actress frustrated and professionally unfulfilled. Warners cast her opposite Edward G. Robinson in *Tiger Shark* (1932) and Universal planned to feature her in their production *Laughing Boy*, scripted by a budding John Huston. When this project failed to materialize, Johann consented to appear in *The Mummy* to fulfill her contractual obligation with the studio. Long working hours and Karl Freund's chicanery soured her on Tinsel Town; she made few films following this one (making it all the more unfortunate that Johann's multi-performance reincarnation flashbacks are lost to today's film buffs).

The passage of decades had not blunted Johann's painful memories of the ordeal Freund inflicted upon her during the shoot. She told Gregory Mank,

> Late Saturday night — exhausted — I fainted — in the middle of a scene with Boris Karloff. I was out for an hour — dead. The crew, generally friendly and this time again on my side, gathered beside me. "What that son of a bitch has done to her," I heard. "You don't know the half of it," my secretary, Ruby Holloway, answered. My guardian angel was very busy. They couldn't get a doctor — it was 11 o'clock at night. So the crew prayed me back to consciousness.

But the worst was yet to come.

> I rested on Sunday. Monday morning, I was at Universal, on time. And there were lions! They

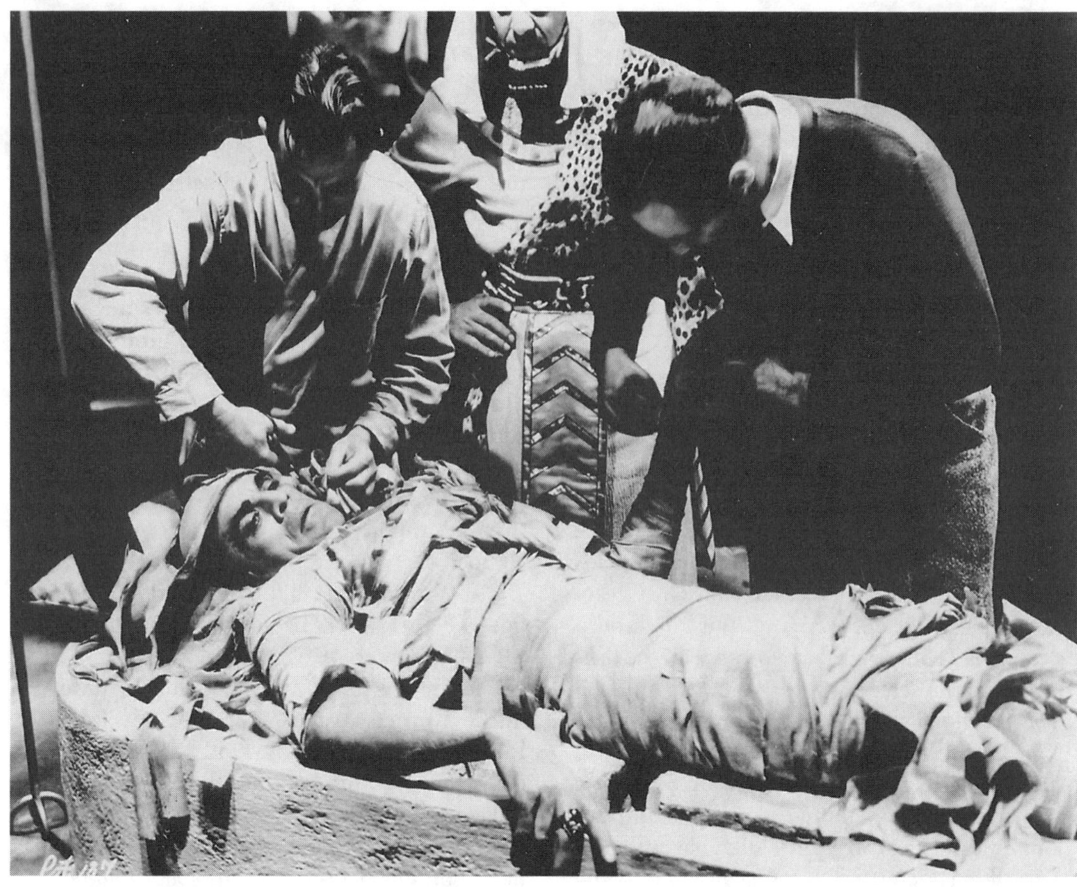

Karloff undergoes the torturous transformation of man-into-*Mummy*. In 2006, the once-terrifying Imhotep-as-mummy image was one of several Universal icons being used on a line of boxer shorts and pajama bottoms sold in Target stores.

> had this great big enormous arena outside on the back lot, and everybody was protected. Freund was in a special cage all his own (a very large one); the cameraman was safe; the whole crew was safe. No cage for me, or for Ruby. I was guided to the huge gate, leading to three enormous lions. Ruby at my side ... I took a deep breath, praying to the Holy Spirit and to my guardian angel, who were already with me. In me. "He saved this for my last day," I said. "Look, I get paid, I'm going in — I don't care. What difference...?" was all I could say. The gate was opened. I went in. That I remember. The lions were indifferent. My lack of sex appeal, perhaps. Those lions saw no fear in me — just exhausted bones! And they must have figured, "Who needs them?"

After *The Mummy* previewed, Johann got revenge on Junior Laemmle, who had big plans for her future at Universal. "Do me a favor," she told him. 'I had a lousy, rotten time at your studio. *Don't* pick up my option for another picture.' Well, he almost died! In a way I'm sorry I did that, because Junior Laemmle was an awfully nice person, a very sensitive man, and we did have great mutual respect."

Reunited for yet another brush with the undead, David Manners and Edward Van Sloan virtually repeat their performances in *Dracula*. Manners is stalwart enough in the film's early scenes in the Egyptian desert, but once he comes under Johann's spell, the actor once again reverts to a whiny schoolboy, begging her favors, and mouthing the most arcane love talk this side of Harlequin Romances. Van Sloan pursues the Mummy with the same dogged determination he did the vampire. The epitome of Old World sobriety and ironfisted will, Van Sloan has the facility to make us believe the supernatural gibberish he spouts is gospel. (The 1932 Warner

Bros. comedy-romance *Man Wanted*, starring Kay Francis, contains a priceless moment for classic horror fans: Manners and Andy Devine testing pogo sticks for stern department store manager Van Sloan.)

In supporting roles, Arthur Byron adequately fulfills the dictates of Balderston's script directive ("The actor should be able to display nerves.") while Noble Johnson, as the enslaved Nubian, exudes power without uttering a syllable. In his later years, Bramwell Fletcher balked about being remembered exclusively for *The Mummy* by film fans. He needn't have complained. Fletcher (who co-starred with John Barrymore in 1931's *Svengali* and opposite Lionel Atwill in 1932's *The Silent Witness*) has gained cinematic immortality for his relatively brief role as the Man Who Laughed. He got the part on a loanout from Goldwyn.

Jack Pierce's contribution to *The Mummy* is nothing less than extraordinary. Born in Greece in 1889, the slightly built former baseball player arrived in California in 1910. After obtaining work as a nickelodeon projectionist and later a theater manager, Pierce hooked up with Universal as a bit actor and assistant cameraman. But it was his early experiences in movie makeup work, and a striking ape guise for Fox's 1926 *The Monkey Talks*, that won Pierce the title of Universal's chief of studio makeup. (One report claims that Pierce learned his trade by studying the techniques of his mentor Lon Chaney, Sr.) Although Pierce's talents as an artist have never been doubted, the man himself has gotten some bad publicity since his death. Veteran stuntman and actor Gil Perkins, whom Pierce transformed into a hairy imbecile for the 1957 Howco-International disaster *Teenage Monster* (aka *Meteor Monster*), described Jack Pierce as "a miserable old bastard" without a moment's hesitation. In her 1983 autobiography *Elsa Lanchester, Herself*, the late actress pictured Pierce as an arrogant, self-proclaimed monarch, "meting out wrath and intolerance by the bucketful." Lanchester continued, "He had his own *sanctum sanctorum*, and as you entered (you did not go in; you entered) he said good morning first. If I spoke first, he glared and slightly showed his upper teeth."

Virginia Christine, who underwent a particularly taxing makeup job for her role as the crumbling Princess Ananka in *The Mummy's Curse*, recalled the master for us in a more favorable light: "He elevated himself to the position of top monster maker in the business. He was kind of an arrogant man, but we got along beautifully." Makeup man Harry Thomas, who inherited Pierce's reputation as a monster specialist in '50s horror cheapies, studied under him. "He was a little, feisty man that I enjoyed knowing; I respected his genius. I used to visit him over at Universal in the 1940s." Asked by the authors whether Pierce was bitter after the studio unceremoniously gave him the heave-ho in 1947, Thomas responded,

> Yes, he was kind of bitter. I believe his pride was hurt, and I don't know whether or not he resented the fact that Bud Westmore went in there and took his place. I believe that Universal mentioned that he was getting older, and they wanted somebody who would work faster, and do prosthetics; that was their excuse. I don't think anybody's ever compared with what he did. Universal was very, very ungrateful in doing this to a man whose pictures all made a lot of money.

Susanna Foster saw only the positive side of the man. "How could anyone not get along with Jack Pierce?" she asked rhetorically. "He was cantankerous but as cute as hell. I loved him. He was sharp and to the point." Gloria Jean also sang the makeup giant's praises. "Jack Pierce was just charming," she told the authors. "A delightful little man. He took such great pride. He didn't only do the monsters, but he made a lot of movie stars, Irene Dunne and a lot of others. Some of 'em wouldn't have anybody *but* Jack do them. He was just wonderful."

In a poll recently conducted by *MakeUp Artist* magazine in which the readers were asked to come up with the 50 Greatest Makeups of All Time, *The Mummy* came in thirtieth place, while Pierce's brilliant design for *Frankenstein* was selected as the first place winner.

Karl Freund directed only a handful of pictures after *The Mummy*, including musical-comedies (*Moonlight and Pretzels* [1933]), dramas (*I Give My Love* [1934]) and all-star novelties (*Gift of Gab* [also 1934]). Shortly after *The Mummy*'s release, Freund was assigned to direct Universal's elaborate and technically complex *Gulliver's Travels*. Slated for a Christmas 1934, release, the production never made it to the soundstages. He left the studio when his contract expired in the fall of 1934. Freund's most noteworthy directorial accomplishment aside from *The Mummy* was MGM's *Mad Love* (1935), a gloriously kinky mix of sadism, madness and sexual aberration.

Directing held little intrigue for Freund the cameraman. "I gave up directing because of a dull routine of stories," he said in a 1950 interview. "The camera at least gives some latitude for special creativeness." In a later interview, Freund brusquely dismissed the director's role on a film with the comment, "Anyone can make a good cake if he has the right ingredients. It all depends on story, cast and circumstances."

Returning to his position behind the camera, Freund walked away with the Oscar for his fine work on 1937's *The Good Earth*, and was nominated four times afterward. When Lucille Ball wanted audience participation in the filming of her classic television series *I Love Lucy*, Freund solved the problem with a multiple camera setup that has since become standard procedure. As a result, Lucy made Freund chief cinematographer for Desilu Productions.

At the time of his death (May 3, 1969), Freund had been enjoying a short-lived retirement from his multi-million dollar Photo Research Corporation, a firm that manufactured television and film equipment. Pooh-poohing the art of cinematography, Freund called candid camerawork "the only type of photography that is really art."

Critics' Corner

A gripping melodramatic romance and one of the best of Boris Karloff's starring pictures.... It has most of the thrills of the "shock" pictures ... without the gruesomeness of that cycle.—*The Hollywood Herald*, November 26, 1932

[M]ost of *The Mummy* is costume melodrama for the children.... Mr. Karloff acts with the restraint natural to a man whose face is hidden behind synthetic wrinkles.... The photography is superior to the dialogue.—*The New York Times*, January 7, 1933, Andre Sennwald

Karloff, whose portrayal of an unholy thing in this film aided by magnificent makeup, establishes him as not just a good character actor, but a finished character star.—*The Los Angeles Times, 1933*

The sequence in the museum with Im-Ho [*sic*] planning to kill Helen Grosvenor ... is too stagey.... Zita Johann is attractive, but always role-conscious....—*Variety*, January 10, 1933

Rating: ★★ The screams of Bramwell Fletcher ... will chill your blood, but the rest of it ... will leave you unshaken and a little too conscious of the stilted dialogue and the melodramatic workings of the plot.—*The New York Daily News*, January 7, 1933, Kate Cameron

One dinger of a thriller, with much more dramatic meat than the average.—*The Chicago Tribune*, 1933

It is weird and imaginative and at times beautiful.—*The Chicago Daily News*, 1933

Only in the startling realism of his makeup does Boris Karloff recall such [*sic*] of his terrifying earlier pictures, say as *Frankenstein*.—*The Washington Post*, 1933

The Mummy scarcely comes under the heading of an action thriller as it is almost completely devoid of the crude mechanics so long inseparable from melodrama.... Karloff's best to date.—*Today's Cinema* (GB), January 13, 1933

1933

Secret of the Blue Room

Released July 20, 1933. 66 minutes. *Producers:* Carl Laemmle, Jr., & Henry Henigson. *Director:* Kurt Neumann. *Screenplay:* William Hurlbut. *Based on the story by* Erich Philippi *and the German film* Geheimnis des Blauen Zimmers (1932). *Photography:* Charles Stumar. *Art Director:* Stanley Fleischer. *Music:* Heinz Letton. *Editor:* Philip Cahn. *Assistant Director:* Jay Marchant. *Camera Operator:* King Gray. *Assistant Camera:* Bill Richards. *Chief Electrician:* Tommy Valdez. *Chief Grip:* Fred Parkinson. *Props:* Harry Grundstrum.

Lionel Atwill (*Robert von Helldorf*), Gloria Stuart (*Irene von Helldorf*), Paul Lukas (*Capt. Walter Brink*), Edward Arnold (*Police Commissioner Forster*), Onslow Stevens (*Frank Faber*), William Janney (*Thomas Brandt*), Robert Barrat (*Paul*), Muriel Kirkland (*Betty*), Russell Hopton (*Max*), Elizabeth Patterson (*Mary*), Anders Van Haden (*The Stranger*), James Durkin (*Kruger, the Commissioner's Assistant*).

[D]ecidedly reminiscent of 365 or so similar pictures in the same category.
—The Film Weekly, *January 19, 1934*

Probably one of the best of Universal's non-horror horror films, *Secret of the Blue Room* is an engaging example of the early "spooky house" mystery at or near its best. It's a low-budget film with few pretensions, but it has the advantages of a sturdy cast, a beguiling premise and plenty of atmosphere. Most of the early Universal mysteries that masquerade as horror films are fairly dismal, but *Secret of the Blue Room* remains a charming bit of spookery.

At the lonely, storm-swept Castle Helldorf, a birthday party is in progress. Present are Robert von Helldorf (Lionel Atwill), master of the castle; his daughter Irene (Gloria Stuart), who has just turned 21; and Irene's three suitors, Capt. Walter Brink (Paul Lukas), a marine officer, Frank Faber (Onslow Stevens), a newspaper reporter, and Tommy Brandt (William Janney). Catching her alone, the boyish Tommy proposes to Irene but she doesn't take his offer seriously.

The subject of conversation turns to ghost stories and a reluctant von Helldorf is compelled by his weekend guests to tell the tragic story of the castle's "haunted" Blue Room. Twenty years before, Helldorf relates, his sister fell from the window of the blue salon and died in the moat. Four months later a houseguest was found shot to death in the room, an apparent suicide since the door was locked from the inside (although no gun was ever found). A detective seeking to unravel the riddle of the room spent a night there; there was a look of horror on his face when they found his body. All three mysterious deaths occurred at the stroke of one A.M.; the room has been locked up since. Tommy, determined to prove his courage to Irene, proposes to spend the night in the guest chamber and Walter and Frank both agree to do the same on subsequent nights. Intercut throughout this early portion are short scenes of Paul (Robert Barrat), the butler, regretfully refusing to admit a shabby stranger (Anders Van Haden) out of the storm and into the house.

Come the dawn, the Blue Room is found to be vacant: the chamber had been locked from the inside, and a window overlooking the moat is open. It appears clear that Tommy has become a victim of the room, but von Helldorf will not notify the police until the body is found. Frank is insistent upon living up to his word and sleeping in the Blue Room that night. To ease the anxiety of Irene, who is downstairs, he loudly plays a piano as the hour of one approaches; just after a clock chimes, a shot rings out. The household members rush once again to the fatal room, where Frank's dead body is found.

Summoned to the castle, police commissioner Forster (Edward Arnold) begins his inquiry. The stern, sharp-witted detective initially suspects that some of the servants may be involved in skullduggery but later sets his sights on von Helldorf, who has trouble keeping his story straight. Forster and his men apprehend the mystery stranger, and von Helldorf is forced into confessing that the man, his brother, is Irene's father. The brother had deserted his wife and baby daughter (Irene) years before; the wife died and von Helldorf raised Irene, posing as her father. Now a broken man, the brother has returned to beg for money, which von Helldorf planned to give him.

Hoping to help break the case, Walter announces his intention to stay in the Blue Room. At the stroke of one, a secret wall panel opens and a shot is fired into the room, apparently striking Walter in the head. But the "victim" is only a dummy: The real Walter now springs into action, chasing the would-be assassin into the passage. A running gunfight ensues as Walter pursues the killer into the catacombs below the house; the two men brawl, with the killer about to gain the upper hand, when Forster and his men finally arrive on the scene and nab the killer—young Tommy Brandt. Hopelessly in love with Irene, Tommy had discovered the Blue Room secret passage and hatched this plan to take advantage of the room's tragic history and bump off his romantic rivals. Walter consoles Irene as Tommy is led away by Forster's men.

Secret of the Blue Room has most of the recognizable elements of the classic Universal horror films, but never quite crosses the thin line that divides spooky "locked room" mysteries from horror thrillers. There are gales blowing and thunder roaring, an old castle with a secret room, Lionel Atwill, a hidden passage, a shadowy stranger, lots of closeups on guilty-looking pusses and even good ol' *Swan Lake* playing behind the titles (beginning *and* end), but for all this atmosphere the picture unmistakably remains a whodunit at heart. *Blue Room* is some-

29-17

629-29

times dismissed by fans who are turned off by what the picture lacks and fail to appreciate its considerable charm.

There's a quaint once-upon-a-time quality about *Secret of the Blue Room*: The castle setting, the Germanic feel of the picture, the way a ghost story told at midnight sparks the action of the film. It's the sort of story that draws a viewer into it, building steadily but without haste. It has a great cast of character stars who have not yet reached their peaks. The picture was made quickly and inexpensively ($69,000, the cheapest Universal film made that year), and admittedly it never rises above second-feature status. But despite the economics involved, it remains a strikingly good B.

As Robert von Helldorf, Atwill makes his first of 12 appearances in horror (and borderline-horror) Universal films. One of the most beloved of the old-time chiller personalities, the distinguished British stage star got stuck with the "horror" tag early in his Hollywood career, when he starred in *Doctor X* (1932) and *Mystery of the Wax Museum* (1933), and never quite shook it despite his fine work in many major pictures. Atwill generally tended to ham it up in his horror films, leaving no piece of scenery unchewed, but he's nicely reserved in *Secret of the Blue Room*, giving a realistic performance rather than his usual exuberant exhibition.

Despite his star billing, Atwill is just a red herring, with the finger of suspicion pointing directly at him throughout most of the film's unspooling. The fact that he's Gloria Stuart's father tips off a savvy audience that he couldn't have done it (in mystery films, the heroine's father is never guilty), but he's fair game again after the midpoint revelation that in reality he's only her uncle — and maybe a "funny uncle" at that; twice in the picture he gives her lingering mouth kisses. (Then again, maybe we should say *she* gives *him* lingering mouth kisses. In her debut film *Street of Women* (1932), Stuart is the daughter of Alan Crosland and instigates three flirtatious, girlfriend-ly mouth kisses ... in a single scene!)

However, Atwill becomes too obvious a suspect, especially when the skulking killer dresses like him. It is interesting to note that in early films like *Secret of the Blue Room*, Atwill is without the mustache we're all used to seeing, and it's curious how much older he looks in the earlier pictures than he does in later films where he sports that dashing little lip adornment.

Gloria Stuart reminisced for the authors:

> Lionel was what we call "an actor's actor," very much involved with one's self. He had been a fantastic matinee idol, but of course by the time he got to Universal he had a little potbelly, and he seemed old to me at the time although probably he was only in his late forties. He was a brilliant actor.

One of the most attractive and popular ingénues from the Golden Age of Universal horror films, Gloria Stuart began her stage career as an amateur in high school. While she was not a fan of motion pictures during her youth (she saw not more than a dozen pictures during her first 21 years), Stuart caught the acting bug while in college, played in various dramatic productions and ultimately worked at the famed Pasadena Community Playhouse, where she appeared in the plays "Twelfth Night" and "The Sea Gull."

Casting agents from Universal and Paramount caught her "Sea Gull" performance on opening night and both studios asked her to make a screen test. Stuart had little interest in working in films — her real ambition was to act on the New York stage — but she made the tests, both studios offered her contracts and the whole mess ended up in arbitration with the MPAA, who suggested a coin toss to settle the dispute. Universal won, and Carl Laemmle, Jr.'s, promise of a bright future at the studio convinced Stuart to sign with Universal.

In retrospect, she sees her decision as a "ghastly mistake": "I should never have gone to Universal, it was a second-rate studio and Paramount was first-rate and I was very badly advised. I really didn't have to do it, and the more I think about it [laughs], the angrier I get." Regarding Junior Laemmle and his empty promise, she recalls, "No, he didn't have great plans for me because the studio was not making great

Opposite: **What a difference a slay makes: *Secret of the Blue Room* stars Lionel Atwill, Gloria Stuart and Paul Lukas share a festive moment (top) before mayhem spoils the fun (bottom). Onslow Stevens and Robert Barrat are the newcomers in the second shot.**

films regularly. Once in a while they came up with an *Old Dark House* or a *Back Street* [1932] or something, but most of them were made by independent producers using Universal facilities. Junior Laemmle was very nice — I can't fault him — but Irving Thalberg he wasn't."

After making her movie debut as a loan-out player in Warner Bros.' *Street of Women*, replacing a recalcitrant Marian Marsh, Stuart appeared in a baker's dozen Universal pictures, including *Airmail* (1932), James Whale's *The Old Dark House, The Invisible Man* and *The Kiss Before the Mirror* (1933), *Beloved, I'll Tell the World, The Love Captive* and *Gift of Gab* (all 1934). Her dissatisfaction with Universal grew in 1934 when she went after roles in *Glamour* and *The Countess of Monte Cristo* only to see non-contract players Constance Cummings and Fay Wray, respectively, come in and play these parts.

Eventually Stuart got Universal to sell her contract to Fox, but when she ended up in the Sol Wurtzel B unit over there she knew that she was just spinning her wheels career-wise. When her Fox contract expired in 1939 she more or less quit Hollywood, returning to the stage, traveling and ultimately settling down to a normal life as wife and mother. After the death of her writer-husband Arthur Sheekman in 1978 and a decision to once again try her hand at acting, she has appeared in *Mass Appeal* (1984), *Wildcats* (1986) and, of course, the 1997 mega-hit *Titanic*, giving an Oscar- and Golden Globe–nominated performance in the modern-day framing scenes as Old Rose, the centenarian version of *Titanic* passenger Kate Winslet. She promoted the movie in Russia, spoofed her role in it in an MTV music video, got a star on the Walk of Fame, continued to reside across the street from the condo where Nicole Brown Simpson and Ron Goldman were butchered, appeared in more movies and TV series (including the genre fare *Miracles, Touched by an Angel* and of course ... of course ... the Sci Fi Channel's *The Invisible Man*) and, in her 1999 autobiography *I Just Kept Hoping*, wrote about being an advocate of free love three decades before it became fashionable, all her many lovers and even masturbation. ("I think it's probably one of the most pleasurable experiences in life. I had and have no guilt whatsoever when it comes to pleasuring myself.") "Judging from advance copies," wrote a New York Post columnist, "she might have called [the book] 'I Just Kept Humping.'"

Contractually binding herself to Universal may have been a bad career move for Stuart, but for fans of *The Old Dark House* and *Secret of the Blue Room* her presence greatly enhances these vintage productions. While chic and classy, she also had an appealing girl-next-door quality and a realness that's missing from the performances of many of her acting contemporaries. It's too bad that she considers her stint at Universal as a blunder, but for most of us that MPAA coin-toss worked out just fine.

Other *Blue Room* performances are equally professional. Paul Lukas is a smooth and likable hero, and his character clearly has the inside track with Irene throughout the film. A Hungarian with a background similar to Bela Lugosi's, Lukas is the sort of actor Lugosi might have become with a little more discipline and lot less pig-headedness; he parlayed his Continental suavity into a lucrative Hollywood career.

Onslow Stevens, who was discovered at the Pasadena Playhouse the same night as Gloria Stuart, also gives his role color, and there's a nice feeling of easy camaraderie in the scenes he shares with rival suitor Lukas. Edward Arnold is an imposing presence as the detective and William Janney plays up his boyish qualities as Tommy. Early on, Universal announced that Lillian Bond would star with Atwill and Stuart in *Blue Room*, but she was replaced by Muriel Kirkland (who later played some important Broadway roles).

Secret of the Blue Room is a remake of the 1932 German mystery film *Geheimnis des Blauen Zimmers*, starring Theodor Loos as Robert von Helldorf, Else Elster as Irene and Wolfgang Staudte (a leading German director in the post-war era) as Frank. *Blue Room* features some murky looking stock footage that probably came from the earlier production: The castle exteriors have an uncommonly authentic look to them (it doesn't look like one of Universal's back lot "castles"); stock footage looks to have been employed at other spots as well (von Helldorf's car leaving the castle grounds; a shot of the nearby forest). The film's locale is never specified but these clips, the castle setting, character names like von Helldorf and an all-around European flavor give the unmistakable impression that it's somewhere on the Continent (we'd guess Germany; William K.

Everson said it was Hungary). Unfortunately, unsuited players like Edward Arnold, Muriel Kirkland, Elizabeth Patterson and Russell Hopton spoil the ambience; too American, they don't fit in at all. It's as though Castle Helldorf magically had a front door in Europe and a servants' entrance in Jersey City, New Jersey.

Universal tried an unusual publicity tack with *Blue Room*, fashioning a pressbook that looked more like a daily newspaper. The front page told in bold headlines about the mysterious goings-on at Castle Helldorf, and various plot angles were described in the accompanying articles. The pressbook played up *Secret of the Blue Room* as "The 10 Star Picture," and while the word "star" could be, if one were in a generous mood, applied to the first five or six players, the studio was on shaky ground bestowing this title on the others. Tenth-billed James Durkin, an unheard-of actor who briefly plays the commissioner's assistant, was probably pleased as punch to be listed as a star, but it was an obvious cheat.

Some writers feel that the mystery in *Secret of the Blue Room* is embarrassingly transparent, with Janney clearly pinpointed as the killer right from the start. But critics of the day commended the picture for its surprise denouement, and none of the authors of this book pegged Janney as the killer the first time we saw the picture. Janney's plans are flimsy and poorly thought-out, but despite this forced finish the film plays nicely on its modest scale. The subplot of the mystery stranger only succeeds in muddling the plot slightly; this minor angle seems to have been lifted out of the Sherlock Holmes novel *The Hound of the Baskervilles* and adds little to the film. The footage involving von Helldorf's white-trash servants is also unrewarding, although these episodes never completely lapse into comedy relief. In another nice touch, the old Blue Room tragedies are never explained away: This may be simply an error of omission, but it enhances the picture that the eerie original mystery of the blue salon is not dispelled at the end.

Kurt Neumann's direction is just right for this type of no-frills melodrama. Neumann was brought to Hollywood from his native Germany by Junior Laemmle in the late 1920s; among his first jobs here were the directing of Spanish and German versions of Universal pictures, and then Slim Summerville comedies. Neumann had a wooden leg and liked to tell people that he lost his real leg in World War I, fighting on the German side, but Henry Koster, probably more accurately, remembers that Neumann lost it after getting nailed by a bus. He never really made his mark in Hollywood although today he's affectionately remembered by Monster Kids for some of the science fiction films he made in the 1950s: *Rocketship X-M* (1950), *She Devil*, *Kronos* (1957) and *The Fly* (1958). Probably the best review he ever got in his life, *The Hollywood Reporter*'s assessment of *The Fly*, ran on the same day, and in fact on the same page, as the announcement of his wife Irma's death. The day after *The Fly* opened, as news of its sensational grosses was coming in from many parts of the country, Neumann was at Pierce Brothers, Beverly Hills Mortuary, attending her funeral services. After almost six weeks of deep grief, the 50-year-old producer-director took his own life.

A low-budget mystery item with the added spice of mild horror touches, *Secret of the Blue Room* remains a minor gem and a fine debut vehicle for Universal first-timer Lionel Atwill. It was remade twice by the studio, in 1938 as *The Missing Guest* and in 1944 as *Murder in the Blue Room*, and both times the quaint charm of the original was replaced by lowbrow comedy hijinks.

Critics' Corner

[T]he film is better than a number of previous efforts of its school, and if it still adheres rather too pointedly to the routine formula, than it should only be added that, thanks to Miss Stuart, and a few minor virtues of casting, it is, if less than stimulating, always a pleasant enough sedative.... The acting, even in the case of Lionel Atwill, is not bad.—*The New York Herald-Tribune*, September 1933, Richard Watts. Jr.

Like its predecessor, *The Old Dark House*, the current film lopes along in quite an interesting fashion until it comes to the denouement, which is by no means as satisfactory as might be anticipated.... Mr. Atwill does well in his part and makes the most of opportunities to add to the general muddle.—*The New York Times*, September 13, 1933, Mordaunt Hall

Rating: ★★ [A]s disappointing to grown-ups as revealing the identity of Santa Claus is to a kid. In spite of the grand cast and elegant setting for a good hour's sweet misery, affording the usual thrills and chills of a murder mystery, it turns out to be too unreasonable for words.—*The New York Daily News*, September 13, 1933, Wanda Hale

Well-done, of its type... The direction, by Kurt Neumann, and the acting, especially by Paul Lukas,

Gloria Stuart and Lionel Atwill, are worthy of a stronger and less threadbare story.—*The Film Weekly*, January 19, 1934

The Invisible Man

Released November 13, 1933. 70 minutes. *Producer:* Carl Laemmle, Jr. *Director:* James Whale. *Screenplay:* R.C. Sherriff. *Based on the novel* The Invisible Man *by* H.G. Wells. *Photography:* Arthur Edeson. *Assistant Director:* Joseph A. McDonough. *Art Director:* Charles D. Hall. *Editor:* Ted Kent. *Special Effects Photography:* John P. Fulton. *Retake Photography & Miniatures:* John J. Mescall. *Visual Effects Supervisor:* Frank D. Williams. *Music:* W. Franke Harling & Heinz Roemheld. *Property Master:* Wally Kirkpatrick. *Sound Director:* William Hedgcock. *Makeup:* Jack P. Pierce.

Claude Rains (*Dr. Jack Griffin*), Gloria Stuart (*Flora Cranley*), William Harrigan (*Dr. Arthur Kemp*), Henry Travers (*Dr. Cranley*), Una O'Connor (*Jenny Hall*), Forrester Harvey (*Herbert Hall*), Holmes Herbert (*Chief of Police*), E.E. Clive (*Police Constable Jaffers*), Dudley Digges (*Chief of Detectives*), Harry Stubbs (*Police Insp. Bird*), Donald Stuart (*Insp. Lane*), Merle Tottenham (*Milly*), Walter Brennan (*Bicycle Owner*), Dwight Frye (*Reporter*), Jameson Thomas, Craufurd Kent (*Doctors*), John Peter Richmond [John Carradine] (*Informer*), John Merivale (*Newsboy*), Mary Gordon (*Terrified Woman*), Violet Kemble Cooper (*Woman*), Robert Brower (*Farmer*), Bob Reeves, Jack Richardson, Robert Adair (*Officials*), Monte Montague (*Policeman*), Ted Billings, D'Arcy Corrigan (*Villagers*), Gil Perkins (*Stunts*).

"And for five years, five years mind, I was prating to the Theater Guild about my artistic integrity. I was so cock-a-hoop about it. My artistic integrity. Then the first day at the studio, James [Whale] brought over some bandages. I asked about them, and he said, oh, yes, I was to be bandaged during most of the picture. And there I had been fighting with the Theater Guild about my artistic integrity. Oh, it served me right."
—*Claude Rains, interviewed by Eileen Creelman*

Deprive the average special effects film of its visual tricks and you rob it of its heart and soul. *The Invisible Man*, Universal's superb 1933 filmization of one of H.G. Wells' most enduring novels, is a firm exception to this rule. Its gripping narrative, masterful direction and believable performances elevate the film beyond mere novelty, and hold up alongside the unerring technical effects for the audience's attention. One of the handful of fantastic films unblemished by the ravages of time, *The Invisible Man* is a monument to the genius of four remarkable artists: Director James Whale, screenwriter R.C. Sherriff, special effects ace John P. Fulton and star Claude Rains. So brilliant is this diverse combination of talents, it's difficult to image what the film would have been like minus the participation of any one of them. And yet, in *The Invisible Man*'s earliest stages of development, three out of four of these artists weren't even considered for the project.

The phenomenal success of *Dracula* prompted Richard L. Schayer and Robert Florey to suggest the H.G. Wells novel as a suitable follow-up as early as 1931. Considering the cost and the complexities of such an undertaking, the Laemmles balked at the notion. *Frankenstein* followed the Tod Browning film, scoring an even greater success. The idea of translating the Wells novel to the screen came up again in December 1931, in the mad scramble to furnish Universal's newly crowned King of Horror, Boris Karloff, with a fitting successor to *Frankenstein*. Along with *The Wolf Man*, *The Invisible Man* was earmarked as a Karloff starrer, with both productions to be developed by Robert Florey. Garrett Fort was elected to adapt the work for the screen. But Universal, not willing to wait for Florey to iron out the considerable scriptwriting and technical difficulties, forged ahead and featured Karloff at the head of an illustrious cast in James Whale's *The Old Dark House*.

By June 1932, the production took an unexpected turn. Producer Sam Bischoff left Universal to set up his own independent studio and invited Florey to accompany him. Florey, whose relations with the Front Office were often strained, decided to jump ship. Cyril Gardner was named as the new director, while John L. Balderston joined forces with Garrett Fort to write a viable script. (In the meantime, *The Wolf Man*, Florey's second proposed horror project, was abandoned.) Within three months, Gardner, Balderston and Fort joined the casualty list in the bumpy metamorphosis of *The Invisible Man* from printed page to silver screen.

German filmmaker E.A. Dupont came on the scene for what couldn't have amounted to more than a few weeks. The celebrated director of *Variety* (1925) had been brought to Hollywood by Carl Laemmle years before but returned to his native country following a disagreement over his first American picture. Like Florey, Dupont also lost out on his share of landmark fright films. Besides *The Invisible Man*, he was announced as director of *The Black Cat* the following year, only to be replaced by Edgar G. Ulmer. When Dupont finally made his directorial bow in horror films, it was the schlocky 1953 United Artists release *The Neanderthal Man*, a sad commentary on the career of this once-esteemed filmmaker.

At long last, the man who should have been Laemmle's first choice to direct the production, James Whale, took charge of *The Invisible Man* in September 1932. No sooner did Universal sign on actor Paul Lukas (he had been at Universal for nine months and hadn't yet appeared in a picture), than the studio temporarily shelved Whale's new project, along with *The Road Back*, which was due to go before the cameras in early 1933. In their place, he was asked to direct *The Kiss Before the Mirror*, a romantic melodrama based on a Hungarian play, and starring Nancy Carroll, Frank Morgan and Lukas (whose name never came up again in conjunction with *The Invisible Man*).

Having fulfilled his obligation, Whale returned to work on *The Invisible Man*, making some immediate changes. He wasn't at all happy with Preston Sturges' free adaptation of the novel, which set the story in Czarist Russia at the time of the Revolution, turning Wells' protagonist (in R.C. Sherriff's words) into "a sort of transparent Scarlet Pimpernel." As the film was being planned as a Karloff horror vehicle, Universal purchased the rights to the Philip Wylie novel *The Murderer Invisible*, published in 1931, with the intention of lifting a few of the more gruesome elements from that work and incorporating them into the adaptation of the Wells novel.

But Whale had ideas of his own. He respected Wells and insisted on a faithful translation. Most important of all, he wanted the character of Jack Griffin to be portrayed in such a way as to elicit the audience's sympathy, not just its fear. He entrusted the job of writing the script to his friend R.C. Sherriff, who had labored long and hard on *The Road Back*, providing Whale with a screenplay faithful to the Erich Maria Remarque novel. (The film was eventually produced by the New Universal in 1937, and was all but ruined by the studio's concession to political pressures.)

Sherriff toiled on the script at his country home near London. Disregarding the studio's request that he draw his material from the Wylie book and the dozen or so failed scripts (one pictured Wells' hero as an alien who threatened to conquer the world with an invisible army of Martians!), Sherriff found his inspiration in the original source. His work completed, he returned to Hollywood in June 1933, winning Whale's instant approval with his straightforward, unaffected adaptation. (Though some sources state that Philip Wylie revised Sherriff's final draft, we have found no evidence to support this claim.)

Having won the first round in his battle to insure that *The Invisible Man* was true to his own vision, Whale next set about getting rid of Karloff, whom he always felt was wrong for the part and whose casting would further put the film in the horror category. Colin Clive's name came up as a possible alternative, but Whale had his heart set on Claude Rains, a 43-year-old fellow Briton whom Whale had befriended during the director's brief career as an actor on the stage. Rains had an admirable stage career in both London and New York, appearing on Broadway in a number of Theater Guild productions. But to motion picture audiences, he was an unknown, a fact that discouraged Junior Laemmle from following the advice of his star director. Besides, Rains had only recently tested at RKO, with disastrous results, for *A Bill of Divorcement* (1932) in the role eventually played by John Barrymore.

But Whale stuck to his guns and informed Rains' agent that he wanted the actor (who was then appearing in the Broadway play "Peace Palace") to give Hollywood another try. Rains was puzzled; after faring so poorly with his first screen test, why was he invited to make another one? "My agent said, 'I must admit there was a certain amount of laughter in your performance, but they were looking for a voice, not an actor,'" Rains later told an interviewer. The test called for the actor to enact the scene wherein Griffin boasts to his associate Dr. Kemp that he plans to rule the world.

Whale purposely kept Rains in the dark about the nature of his first Hollywood assignment and sent him over to the studio lab to have

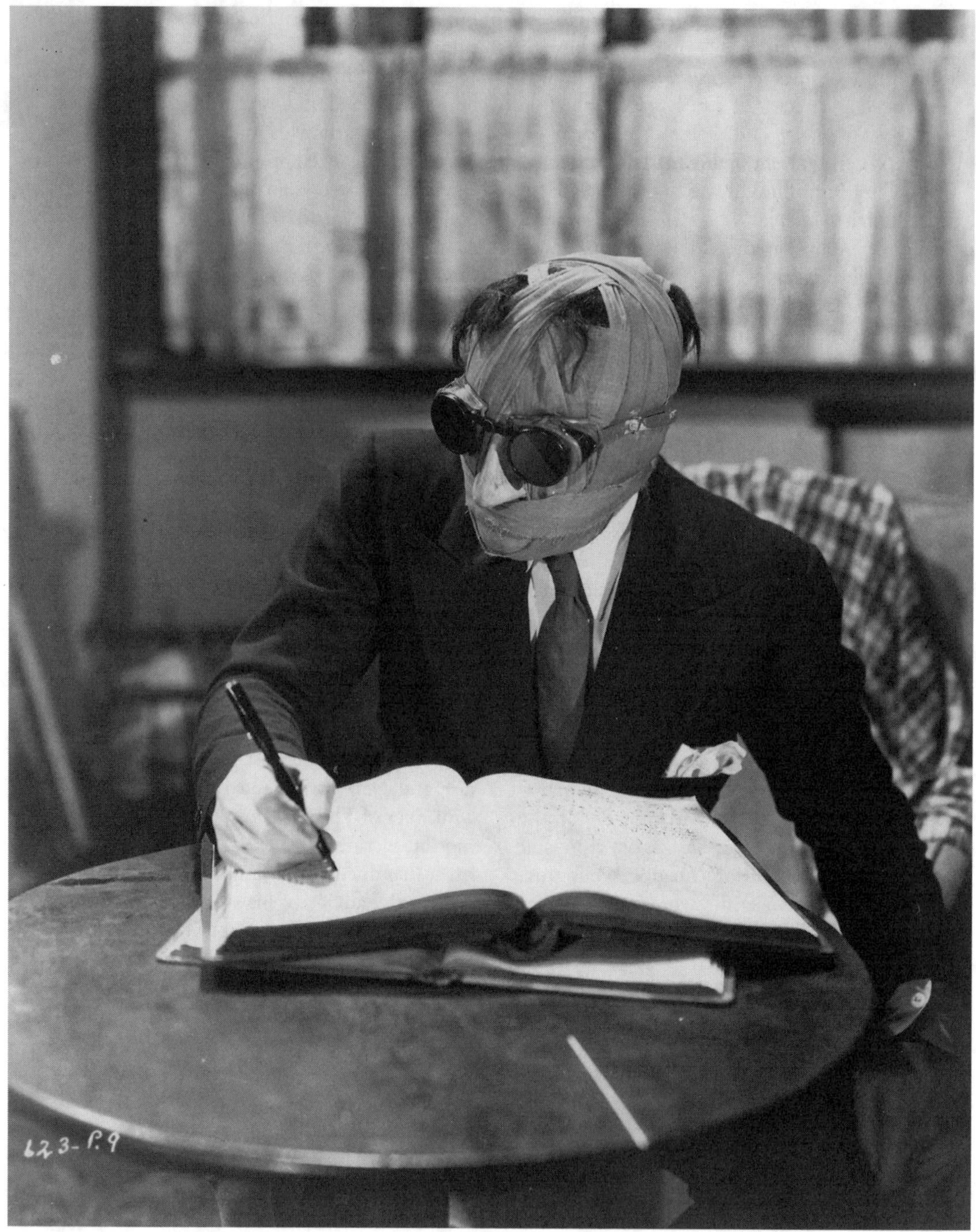

"There's a way back, you fool...." Claude Rains as the renegade scientist Jack Griffin in *The Invisible Man.*

a cast made. Rains told a *New York Times* reporter:

> The laboratory had an odd look. There were all sorts of casts about, in papier-mâché, clay and plaster. Men in white coats walked around without noise. They made a cast and nailed me in it. Just my head stuck out. They smeared me with Vaseline and then stood me off and threw plaster at my head. I thought I was going to die. Really,

I'm afraid I behaved rather badly. I went back again the next day and saw masks and half-masks of my head all over the place.

Whale wanted the stage-trained actor to get a feel for film acting. In another chat with the press, Rains related:

James kept talking about this and that in pictures, about actors and pictures of whom I'd never heard. When he learned I'd only seen about six films in my life, he told me to go right out and see pictures — to see three a day until I knew something about them.

Sherriff wisely followed the author's example by beginning his script with the arrival of the mysterious stranger (Rains) at inn in rustic Iping on a snowswept evening, at once evoking an aura of mystery and urgency. His entire head swathed in bandages, a pair of black goggles perched upon a jutting nose, the stranger cuts a striking figure, arousing the curiosity of the townspeople. Is he the victim of some horrible accident, they wonder, or perhaps an escaped criminal? Setting up shop in one of Jenny Hall's (Una O'Connor) cozy parlors, the stranger immerses himself in scientific research.

The scene switches to the home of Dr. Cranley (Henry Travers) and we are briefed on the stranger's identity and the nature of his "problem" through the conversations of Cranley; his daughter Flora (Gloria Stuart), the man's sweetheart; and Dr. Kemp (William Harrigan). The stranger is Jack Griffin. While in the midst of a crucial experiment, he packed up his belongings and left town, without a word. Going through Griffin's effects, Cranley and Kemp discovered a reference to a mysterious East Indian drug, monocane, which has the ability of bleaching the color out of living creatures, driving them mad in the process.

Unbeknownst to his friends, Griffin has rendered himself invisible, and is now struggling desperately to find the antidote to the drug. Out of his mind, he reveals his identity to the nosy villagers and, unclad and invisible, makes a mad dash through the town, eluding the police and terrorizing all in his path.

Seeking shelter at the home of Dr. Kemp, Griffin forces the astonished chemist to agree to become his "partner" and intimidates him with his insane plans to rule the world. Kemp is forced to accompany the invisible Griffin back to Iping so that he can collect the journals he left behind at the inn. Before departing, Griffin disrupts a police hearing and coldbloodedly murders an inspector (Harry Stubbs). A massive manhunt is mounted and search parties scour the countryside for the unseen killer.

At Kemp's entreaty, Flora makes a determined effort to placate Jack, but it is too late; the effects of the monocane have turned him into a power-hungry monster with a compulsion to kill. Learning Kemp has betrayed him, Griffin promises to murder him at ten o'clock the following evening. The Invisible Man escapes from the house, making a mockery of the police's efforts to track him down, and disappears into the country. Kemp is taken into protective custody as various traps are set to capture his would-be murderer.

Griffin's reign of terror begins. A speeding train is derailed, its cars sent cascading down the side of a mountain; members of a search party are picked off one by one by the invisible fiend. Disguised as a policeman, Kemp drives deep into the country to elude Griffin, but to no avail: The Invisible Man has been in the car with him all along. Bound with rope, Kemp is killed as Griffin sends his car hurtling off a cliff.

Forced to take shelter inside a barn during a blizzard, the Invisible Man's presence is detected by an old farmer (Robert Brower). He alerts the police, who surround the barn and set it afire, forcing Griffin out into the open. Racing madly across the snowy field, Griffin is felled by a policeman's bullet. He is taken to a hospital where he dies from his wound. In death, the power of the drug subsides and his body becomes visible once again.

Initial shooting on *The Invisible Man* began at the end of June 1933 and concluded in late August. Whale worked closely with John P. Fulton on the complex effects work, which consumed another two months. As Fulton had devised his own processes to pull off the feats described in the script, there was a hush-hush air about the closed set. John J. Mescall, who would later provide the wonderful camerawork for the 1934 *Black Cat* and *Bride of Frankenstein*, worked in unison with Fulton.

It was Fulton who had originally convinced Junior Laemmle that a method could be devised to bring an Invisible Man to life on the screen, thus encouraging Universal to purchase the screen rights to the property. Nicknamed "The Doctor" by his admiring colleagues and producers who required the services of a genie to pull off the miracles called for in their scripts, Fulton was a born innovator. Early on, he worked for the Frank Williams Laboratory in Hollywood, birthplace of the traveling matte system, and developed his talents in special photographic effects. Appointed head of the Universal effects department, Fulton contributed to virtually all their horror productions, from *Dracula* (he created those richly atmospheric glass shots of Castle Dracula and its environs) to *House of Dracula* (John Carradine disintegrating into a skeleton, a wonderful, surrealistic dream sequence, etc.). Fulton left Universal in the fall of 1945 and joined up with Sam Goldwyn studios, and won his first Academy Award for the Danny Kaye vehicle *Wonder Man* (1945). As head of Paramount's special effects department, he netted Oscars for *The Bridges at Toko-Ri* (1954) and *The Ten Commandments* (1956) and contributed interesting shoestring-budget effects for *I Married a Monster from Outer Space*, *The Space Children* and *The Colossus of New York* (all 1958).

Fulton's greatest challenge on *The Invisible Man* was in those instances where the partially clad Invisible One dominates the screen. In a fascinating interview Fulton granted *The American Cinematographer* (September 1934), he divulged how this trick was accomplished:

> The wire technique could not be used, for the clothes would look empty, and would hardly move naturally. So we had recourse to multiple-printing—with variations. Most of these scenes involved other, normal characters, so we photographed these scenes in the normal manner, but without any trace of the invisible man. All of the action, of course, had to be carefully timed, as in any sort of double-exposure work. This negative was then developed in the normal manner.
>
> Then the special-process work began. We used a completely black set—walled and floored with black velvet, to be as nearly non-reflective as possible. Our actor was garbed from head to foot in black velvet tights, with black gloves, and a black headpiece rather like a driver's helmet. Over this, he wore whatever clothes might be required. This gave us a picture of the unsupported clothes moving around on a dead black field. From this negative, we made a print, and a duplicate negative which we intensified to serve as mattes for printing. Then, with an ordinary printer, we proceeded to make our composite: First we printed from the positive of the background and the normal action, using the intensified, negative matte to mask off the area where our invisible man's clothing was to move. Then we printed again, using the positive matte to shield the already printed area, and printing in the moving clothes from our "trick" negative. This printing operation made our duplicate, composite negative to be used in printing the final master prints of the picture.
>
> The two principal difficulties, photographically speaking, were matching up the lighting on the visible parts of my shot with the general lighting used by Arthur Edeson, A.S.C., for the normal parts of the picture, and eliminating the various little imperfections—such as eye-holes, etc.—which were naturally picked up by the camera. This latter was done by retouching the film frame by frame with a brush and opaque dye. We photographed thousands of feet of film in the many "takes" of the different scenes, and approximately 4,000 feet of film received individual hand-work treatment in some degree....

For the shot of the Invisible Man unwrapping the bandages around his head, the same system of combining multiple printing with traveling mattes was utilized. A stand-in was used for Rains for some of the more complicated shots that called for precisely timed movements. Both the double and Rains endured stifling midsummer heat and the added ordeal of breathing through an air hose.

As Whale had promised Junior Laemmle, *The Invisible Man* was a big success at the box office. The film broke house records at New York's immense Roxy Theater for the 1932-33 season, shattering a three-year record. Eighty thousand patrons saw the film in four days; a whopping $42,000 was collected during the first week, prompting the theater to hold the film over for a second. *The Invisible Man* singlehandedly revived the fortunes of the financially ailing studio.

The Invisible Man was released at a time when the standing of H.G. Wells as a literary figure and a social commentator was at its peak. (It's a testimony to his popularity with the general public; his massive tract, *The Work, Wealth*

According to Gloria Stuart, sharing a scene with Rains was "no bed of roses."

and Happiness of Mankind, considered unreadable today, sold millions of copies when it was published in 1931.) Film reviewers, ever respectful of the distinguished man of letters, applauded Whale's good intentions with a shower of enthusiastic notices. (Actually, only the first third of the picture is truly faithful to Wells.) *The Invisible Man* instantly became one of the most acclaimed fantasy films of its day, and its reputation almost three-quarters of a century later remains intact. Seldom studied today, Wells was once admired for his lean prose style, dry wit and mastery of detail. He is remembered chiefly as a pioneer of early science fiction, a literary genre still widely regarded as pulp. Consequently, the internationally renowned author doesn't command the respect he once enjoyed. On the other hand, Whale, while rarely praised as a great director, is still ranked as one of the '30s most interesting stylists. In this age of reevaluation, it is no longer heresy to suggest that Whale's version of *The Invisible Man* is actually better than Wells' novel.

Wells' opening chapters are his best, and Whale and Sherriff wisely retained them. One literary critic described the first half of the novel as falling into the category of rural comedy; these early sequences capture the mystique of the heavily bandaged stranger, as well as the quirky humor of the local rustics. Whale's casting of the secondary characters veered the film even more in the direction of comedy, particularly the presence of Irish stage performer Una O'Connor, whose beak-like nose and ear-splitting screeches became her trademark.

Wells was so caught up in the concept of invisibility, its fascinating possibilities and excruciating drawbacks, that he is negligent in fleshing out Griffin as a literary character. In the novel he is depicted in broad strokes as an obsessive young researcher who becomes unhinged as he advances towards his goal (ultimately driving his father, whom he has robbed of his last cent, to suicide). Wells all too conveniently describes him as an albino in order to simplify his change into an invisible being. None of this served the purposes of R.C. Sherriff's script which was true to the spirit if not always the letter of the Wells novel. The screenplay transforms Griffin into a full-fledged tragic hero who succumbs to madness due to the mind-altering properties of monocane, a drug invented for the purposes of the film. The alteration reportedly did not sit well with Wells but gave the character a full measure of audience sympathy and paved the way for the prerequisite romantic subplot.

The Invisible Man is a typical James Whale production. Again, the director stubbornly avoids most of the formulaic, heavy-handed horror movie conventions. The best moments in *The Invisible Man* combine black comedy with a sense of awe (for example, the superb unmasking scene). The laughably pompous Constable Jaffers (E.E. Clive) struggles to keep his authoritative pose as Griffin disrobes. A madcap chase ensues as Jaffers and the villagers, literally tumbling over one another, try to handcuff the prancing shirt.

John Fulton's inventive technique was soon to become commonplace in pictures, but the effects here remain fresh and witty because Whale never allows *The Invisible Man* to become just a special effects picture. The director's splendid build-up in the expertly paced opening reels makes the film a dramatic as well as a technical tour de force. In another memorable confrontation with the law, Griffin pulls the trousers off a bobby. Moments later, we see a terrified woman (the future Mrs. Hudson, Mary Gordon) charging down a country lane, pursued by the same pair of trousers as they merrily skip along to a jaunty ditty sung by Griffin. One has to appreciate the shock value these episodes must have had on a 1933 audience experiencing them for the first time.

Another interesting departure from Wells was an electrical apparatus, a virtual "invisibility machine" which was used by Griffin in addition to his chemical formula to render himself invisible. Considering that Hollywood had already established the cliché of the mad scientist surrounding himself with all matter of elaborate electrically-charged gizmos, it would seem a wasted cinematic opportunity; the invisibility machine would have to wait a full seven years until Universal released *The Invisible Woman*.

The Invisible Man is that rare case when an obviously tacked-on romantic subplot actually works. Griffin's sweetheart, Flora, alas, becomes a weepy bore, but the character invented by Sherriff brings much-needed poignancy to the story. Sherriff's superb dialogue, a vast improvement over Wells,' is one of *The Invisible Man*'s greatest assets. The reunion of Griffin and Flora is, hands down, the best non-effects scene in the picture. After momentarily returning to his gentle, sensitive self, Griffin again slips into monomania, culminating in his delivery of one of Sherriff's most colorful and impassioned speeches.

Whale employs Wells' detached, impersonal style in the fairly humorless last half, which focuses on the intense police investigation. Kemp's character, like Griffin's, is greatly embellished in the screenplay. Introduced late in the novel, Kemp is an old acquaintance of Griffin who meets up with the Invisible Man (not very convincingly) by chance. He is marked for death by Griffin at the earliest hint of betrayal; only in the movie is the threat carried out. The Invisible Man's casual little speech outlining his plans for mass mayhem is still chilling in its dispassion. ("We'll start with a reign of terror. A few murders here and there. Murders of big men, murders of little men. Just to show we make no distinction. We might even wreck a train or two....") Whale and Sherriff don't soft-pedal Griffin's atrocities, yet manage to make him reasonably sympathetic. On the other hand, pains are taken to show Kemp as an unlikable weasel from the start. On screen for only a few moments, he's already making a move on Griffin's grieving girlfriend.

Whale's supporting characters are a varied lot. The army of police officials are faceless and interchangeable; clearly, the director shared Wells' affinity for the colorful rustics who mull in the background. In casting Una O'Connor as Iping innkeeper Jenny Hall, Whale found the ideal comedienne to complement his black humor; loud, cantankerous and maddeningly officious, she is the perfect candidate to send the nerve-wracked Griffin teetering over the edge. (A minor detail, not in Sherriff's script, is a

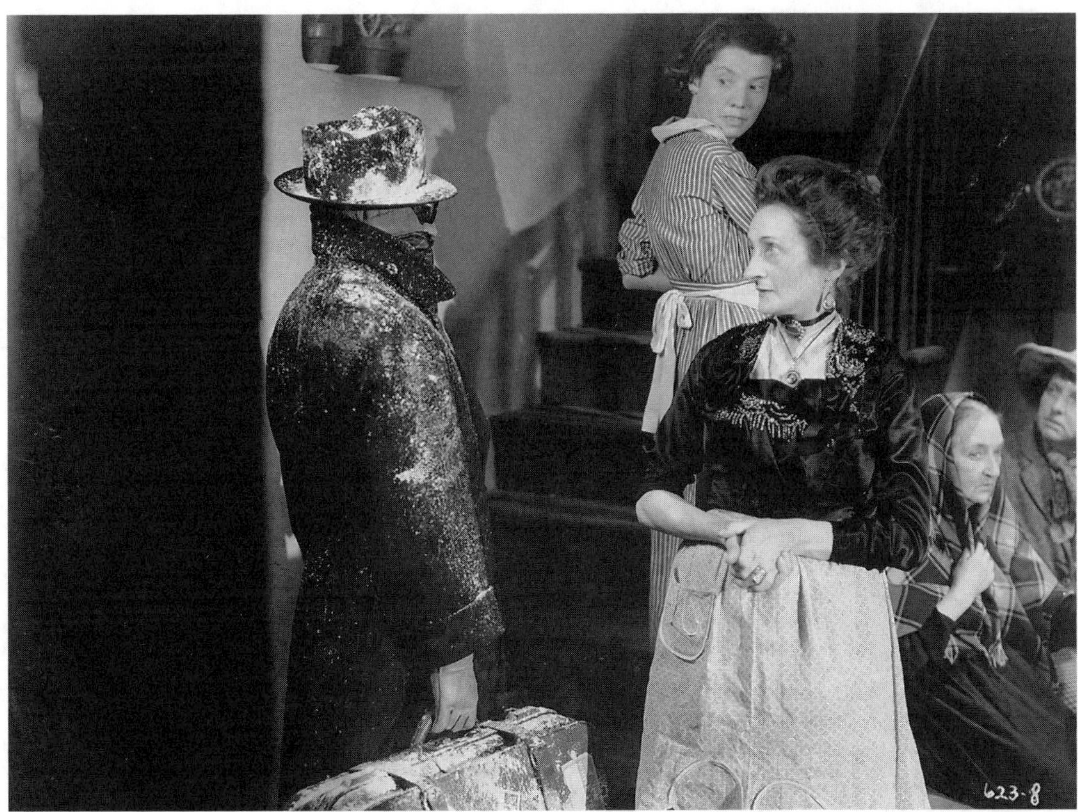

***The Invisible Man* was lauded by contemporary critics for its revolutionary special effects and fine script. Left to right: Rains, Merle Tottenham, Una O'Connor, extras.**

framed portrait of a coyly smiling Jenny hanging on the wall of the sitting room–turned-laboratory. At the height of his mad confrontation with the villagers, Griffin smashes a bottle of chemicals against the picture as though he were paying the landlady back for all those weeks he had spent under her thumb.)

Fulton's groundbreaking special effects and Sherriff's treatment of the Wells novel dominated reviews at the time but Claude Rains' performance gave them a run for their money. His wonderfully expressive voice more than fulfilled the role's requirements for a distinctive vocal presence and is, to a large extent, a centerpiece of the film. Whale had the sense to realize, even though Universal didn't, that Boris Karloff's backing out of the film was, in fact, a stroke of luck that served the production very well. Although Karloff and Rains were already in their 40s, it's difficult to imagine even a transparent Karloff satisfactorily pulling off the role of a struggling young chemist. Rains' voice, on the other hand, still possessed a youthful, flinty quality that Karloff lacked, making his scenes with Gloria Stuart all the more moving despite the fact that the actor was playing a character almost half his age. If anything, mentally casting Karloff in the Griffin role recalls the May-December relationship between the actor and Frances Drake in *The Invisible Ray*. In short, it wouldn't work.

It could be argued that Rains was essentially playing a gimmick role, merely a disembodied voice, but there's nothing gimmicky about his performance. It's probably the best of his early screen roles with his over-the-top tendencies playing neatly within the character. Rains' often humorous line readings synch perfectly with Whale's tongue-in-cheek approach to the material while evocatively conveying the character's descent into madness. The film perhaps overplays the ultimate invincibility of an invisible being in a way that the novel avoided but Rains is chillingly believable as the would-be dictator.

Gloria Stuart, so sleek and capable in *The Old Dark House* and in a small role in Whale's *The Kiss Before the Mirror* (1933), does the best she can as the maudlin heroine. Gregory Mank interviewed Stuart for his book *Women in Horror Films, 1930s,* and asked her about working with Claude Rains in *The Invisible Man.* Her response was less-than-complimentary. "Of course, it didn't help that Claude was shorter than I was, so he was always standing on a box while I was always in my stockinged feet — and in a trench!" She expressed similar displeasure working with Rains in an interview she granted the authors.

> He was *molto difficile,* he was an "actor's actor" and he didn't really *give.* One day [he tried to steal a scene] and I said to James, "James, look what he's doing." And James said, "Now, Claude — don't get *naughty.*" [*Laughs*] James said, "We can take it over and over and *over,* because we'd like half of Gloria!" But that's the kind of actor he was.

As Kemp, William Harrigan, who was chosen to replace the dull and stolid Chester Morris, is dull and stolid. Henry Travers, the British character actor who spent most of his movie career playing folksy Americans (he was Clarence the angel in Frank Capra's Christmas favorite, *It's a Wonderful Life* [1946]), is blandly efficient as Stuart's retiring scientist father. But it's Una O'Connor, Forrester Harvey and E.E. Clive who come off best in vividly etched featured roles. Walter Brennan, John Carradine, Jameson Thomas and Dwight Frye are among the walk-ons.

The Invisible Man is arguably the best H.G. Wells adaptation on film. Wells tried to top it with the British production of *Things to Come* (1936), but the passage of time has reduced this once state-of-the-art fantasy into a barely watchable bore. Admittedly it's a triumph of production design, but not even the best efforts of Raymond Massey, Cedric Hardwicke and Ralph Richardson could find the dramatic core to the pompous, thesis-like oratory which posed as a plot.

The Invisible Man is one of the few of Universal horror classics that didn't enjoy a major remake. Hammer Films, not renowned for sophisticated special effects films, passed up the opportunity to add the Wells character to its roster of Technicolored horrors. The two attempts at an *Invisible Man* television series, one produced in England in the late '50s, and the other made in the '70s by NBC with David McCallum in the title role, bore little if any resemblance to Wells.

Universal revived the Invisible Man character from time to time, but the attempt to continue a direct storyline, *à la* the Frankenstein and Mummy pictures, proved awkward. The invisibility gimmick quickly became old hat as it found its way into increasingly inferior Hollywood movies that usually employed the same crude wire effects that Fulton rejected. *The Invisible Man* remains a definitive film of its kind. Wells and Whale captured the magic and fascination of their subject in two strokes of creativity that no one has yet been able to duplicate.

Critics' Corner

The strangest character yet created by the screen.... Considering the problems involved, both from a technical and entertainment standpoint, it is in many respects astounding.— *Variety,* October 27, 1933

The story makes such superb cinematic material than one wonders that Hollywood did not film it sooner.... [I]t is a remarkable achievement. It is hardly necessary to dwell on the performances of the cast beyond saying that they all rise to the demands of their parts.— *The New York Times,* November 18, 1933, Mordaunt Hall

Rating: ★★★½ Although Rains' face is never seen, he performs his part cleverly, his voice carrying a sinister note that is very effective in this kind of horror role.... The ending is particularly good.... [A]n unusual type of picture that should not be missed.— *The New York Daily News,* November 18, 1933, Kate Cameron

A wholly distinguished thriller.... It is not, of course, merely the camera work, which accounts for the excellence of the film.... [T]he success of the picture is due as much to [the] intelligence with which R.C. Sherriff has adapted the story to the screen and the quality of awesomeness and suspense which James Whale, in his direction, has managed to inject it. The intelligence of the author has been matched by the director, and the picture stands as a testament to intelligent collaboration.... *The Invisible Man* is one of the best thrillers of the year.— *The New York Post,* November 1933, Thornton Delehanty

One of the best yet produced.— *The New York American,* November 1933

[A] stupendous thriller, remarkable, and magnificent.— *The New York Daily Mirror,* November 1933

[A] legitimate offspring of the family that produced *Frankenstein* and *Dracula,* but a lusty, healthy, willing-to-laugh youngster who can stand on his own two feet.— *The Hollywood Reporter,* October 27, 1933

1934

The Black Cat

Released May 7, 1934. Reissued by Realart as *The Vanishing Body.* 65 minutes. *Director:* Edgar G. Ulmer. *Production Supervisor:* E.M. Asher. *Screenplay:* Peter Ruric. *Story:* Edgar G. Ulmer & Peter Ruric. *Suggested by the short story* "The Black Cat" *by* Edgar Allan Poe. *Continuity:* Tom Kilpatrick. *Photography:* John J. Mescall. *Editor:* Ray Curtiss. *Camera Operator:* King Gray. *Special Photographic Effects:* John P. Fulton. *Musical Director:* Heinz Roemheld. *Art Director:* Charles D. Hall. *Assistant Directors:* W.J. Reiter & Sam Weisenthal. *Makeup:* Jack P. Pierce.

Boris Karloff (*Hjalmar Poelzig*), Bela Lugosi (*Dr. Vitus Werdegast*), David Manners (*Peter Alison*), Jacqueline Wells [Julie Bishop] (*Joan Alison*), Lucille Lund (*Karen*) Egon Brecher (*The Majordomo*), Harry Cording (*Thamal*), Albert Conti (*The Lieutenant*), Henry Armetta (*The Sergeant*), Anna Duncan (*Maid*), Andre Cheron (*Train Conductor*), Luis Alberni (*Train Steward*), George Davis (*Bus Driver*), Tony Marlow (*Border Patrolman*), Paul Weigel (*Station Master*), Peggy Terry, Lois January, Michael Mark, John George, Duskal Blane, King Baggott, John Peter Richmond [John Carradine], Harry Walker, Symona Boniface, Virginia Ainsworth, Paul Panzer (*Cultists*). *Deleted from final print:* Herman Bing (*Maitre d'Hotel*), Alphonse Martell *(Porter*), Rodney Hildebrand (*Brakeman*), Albert Polet (*Waiter*).

Karloff and Bela Lugosi, the Wampas Baby-Frighteners of 1934....
—*The Hollywood Reporter, May 4, 1934*

A work of great artistry and sinister beauty, *The Black Cat* occupies a very special niche in the history of macabre cinema. Ostensibly a showcase to exploit the mystiques of Universal's coveted Masters of Mayhem, Boris Karloff and Bela Lugosi, as well as the Edgar Allan Poe name, *The Black Cat* emerged as one of the decade's most disturbing exercises in the Grand Guignol. Boldly thumbing its nose at convention, the film is a veritable catalogue of human corruption. Sadism, shades of incest, revenge, murder, torture, voyeurism, Satan worship, ailurophobia, necrophilia, rape and (in an earlier phase) insanity are weaved into the nearly plotless story with remarkable precision. While this unsavory roll call of vice and obsession alienated many mainstream critics (who also took exception to the flagrant melodramatics and mugging of the two stars), *The Black Cat,* Depression audiences purred with approval. The picture quickly became Universal's top-grossing release of 1934.

Not only did *The Black Cat* come to symbolize the unalterable status of its star players (Lugosi would hereupon assume a subordinate position in terms of billing and salary to his professional rival, the mystically-billed KARLOFF), the production was an invaluable proving ground for its director, Edgar George Ulmer. The Austrian-born filmmaker transformed a studio property into an intensely personal work. Keeping his adaptation faithful to the "spirit" if not the word of Poe, the psychologically-scarred Ulmer integrated into the work his personal quirks, including a childhood Oedipal complex and a fascination for such larger-than-life personalities as the notorious Satanist and all-purpose degenerate, Aleister Crowley.

The Black Cat begins in a crowded, smoke-congested train depot in Budapest (stock footage from the 1933 English film *Rome Express*). Aboard the Orient Express, en route to a Carpathian resort, American novelist Peter Alison (David Manners) and his new bride Joan (Jacqueline Wells) make the acquaintance of Dr. Vitus Werdegast (Bela Lugosi), a noted Hungarian psychiatrist. Werdegast, who bears the burden of a tragic past, reveals he is planning to visit an old "friend," whom he hasn't seen since the height of the war.

Sharing a bus, Werdegast, his giant servant Thamal (Harry Cording) and the Alisons are treated by the garrulous driver (George Davis) to a vivid account of the carnage that had taken place on that very spot during the Russian invasion of Hungary. The blinding storm causes the road to give way, sending the bus hurtling into a ravine. The driver is killed instantly while Joan sustains minor injuries. Gathering their belongings, the hardy band makes its way up the side of the mountain to the cliff-top home of Werdegast's "friend," renowned Austrian engineer Hjalmar Poelzig (Boris Karloff).

Werdegast and Poelzig clash almost immediately. The doctor accuses the enigmatic Poelzig of selling their side down the river while he was in command of Fort Marmaros (Poelzig's ultra-modern fortress stands atop the fort's foundation). Werdegast was taken prisoner and sent to Kurgaal, a dreadful military prison, "where the soul is killed, *slowly*." Upon his release, Werdegast learned that the unscrupulous Poelzig spirited away his (Werdegast's) wife and child after deceiving them into believing he had been killed in action. Now, 18 years later, the vengeful doctor has returned to reclaim his family.

After the Alisons have retired, Poelzig escorts Werdegast deep into the bowels of his dark kingdom. There, encased in glass cases, rest the perfectly preserved bodies of beautiful women. One of them is Werdegast's wife, Karen (Lucille Lund). Werdegast refuses to believe she died of natural causes, as Poelzig claims, and draws a revolver. But before he can pull the trigger, a black cat enters the room and terrifies him (Werdegast suffers from ailurophobia, a fear of cats). The two rivals agree to call a truce until the Alisons have departed. Unbeknownst to Werdegast, his daughter Karen (also played by Lucille Lund), now a grown woman, has succeeded her late mother as Poelzig's wife.

The following day, Peter and Joan attempt to leave Poelzig's house but find their efforts thwarted by their strange host. A chess match between Werdegast and Poelzig determines the fate of the newlyweds: The doctor's defeat puts the couple at the mercy of the crazed architect. Peter is imprisoned and Joan is locked away in an upstairs bedroom. Encountering Karen, Joan startles the confused girl with the news that her father is alive and has come to rescue her. Poelzig overhears the conversation and murders his wife in cold blood.

In the dark of the moon, Poelzig leads his cult of modern-day Satanists in a celebration of the Rites of Lucifer. Joan, who has been selected as the sacrificial maiden, is forced to witness the ceremony. Seconds before the sacrifice is to take place, Werdegast and Thamal take advantage of the commotion, snatching Joan from Poelzig's clutches and leading her to a secret passageway in the cellars. Finding his daughter's fresh corpse awaiting preparation in the embalming room, Werdegast goes berserk. He and Poelzig attack each other like enraged animals. With the mortally-wounded Thamal's aid, Werdegast shackles Poelzig to an embalming rack and slowly peels the skin from his body. Peter, who has escaped from the dungeon, misinterprets Werdegast's intentions and fires a shot into him. Igniting the dynamite that undermines the fortress, the dying Werdegast beseeches the couple to flee. Within minutes, a series of thunderous explosions reduces the house of horrors to rubble.

Many years before he earned the reputation as the Miracle Man of Poverty Row and was courted by the *auteurist* school of film critics, Edgar Ulmer cut his teeth as an assistant stage designer, art director and (for a brief time) an actor in Berlin. F.W. Murnau hired on the ambitious young man as his assistant and art director on such productions as *Faust* (1922) and *The Last Laugh* (1924). The following year, Ulmer came to America with Austrian director-producer Max Reinhardt and offered his services to Carl Laemmle as an art director. Not content with being restricted to a single craft, Ulmer went into training as a director and, between 1923 and 1929, directed or otherwise worked on a variety of two-reel Westerns and shorts. Occasionally, whenever his services were required, Ulmer returned to the art department. When production slackened at Universal, he would be loaned out to such studios as Fox and Paramount where he toiled as a set designer and art director on Murnau's *Sunrise* (1927), *Tabu* (1931) and others. After a brief stay in Germany in 1929 (where he directed the documentarian *Menschen am Sonntag* for Ufa), Ulmer returned to Hollywood. MGM hired him for a position in the art department but found better use of his talents as a director of foreign language versions of such productions as *Anna Christie* (1930).

Back at Universal, Ulmer took a fancy to a project that had gone through several different treatments, without much success, a screen adaptation of the 1843 Edgar Allan Poe short story "The Black Cat." In December, 1932, Stanley Bergerman had co-authored a story treatment with Jack Cunningham which combined elements of Poe with a mad scientist-brain transplant plot, entitling it *The Brain Never Dies*. It was rejected. Two months later, contract writer Tom Kilpatrick and producer-writer Dale Van Every (the team responsible for 1940's *Dr. Cyclops*) submitted a story draft which contained several elements used in the ultimately filmed Peter Ruric-Edgar Ulmer treatment: a young

David Manners gets an unwelcomed visit from Boris Karloff on his wedding night in *The Black Cat* (courtesy Bill Chase).

couple trapped in a castle ruled by two madmen, the dread of cats, torture on the rack and insanity. E.A. Dupont was scheduled to direct Boris Karloff in the impending production, but the Kilpatrick–Van Every draft was never scripted. Garrett Fort also worked on the project in its infancy, drafting a more or less faithful adaptation of the Poe story; his work wasn't used either.

With his friend Carl Laemmle, Jr., squarely in his corner (and Uncle Carl conveniently out of town), Edgar Ulmer set out to create the picture of his dreams, an Expressionistic horror tale utilizing the talents of both Karloff and Lugosi. Collaborating with Peter Ruric, a minor mystery story writer, Ulmer completed his story draft on February 6, 1934. On February 17 (two days before the finished script was submitted), *The Hollywood Reporter* made the announcement that shooting on *The Black Cat* would commence on the 24th of the month, and that actress Erin O'Brien-Moore had been tested for a principal role. But it wasn't until February 28 that John J. Mescall's cameras began recording the first scenes of the Ulmer production.

As was often the case with their horror film projects, Universal maintained that the production was draped in secrecy. Budgeted at a paltry $91,125, scheduled for a 15-day shoot, Edgar Ulmer's labor of love came in on March 17, one day over schedule.

And then, a bombshell was dropped on the director's head. The studio brass deemed that *The Black Cat* was too vile for public and censorial consumption. On Sunday, March 25, Ulmer gathered together select members of his cast and technical crew for a hectic three and a half days of retakes, and the filming of at least one entirely new sequence, a real beauty: Karloff's pre-dawn prowl through his private mausoleum. The tab for these alterations amounted to an additional $6,500. The final cost amounted to $95,745.31.

Wholesale changes were made in the portrayals of Werdegast and Karen. Ruric and Ulmer's original conception had the doctor losing his mind after seeing his wife's body in Poelzig's col-

Bela Lugosi's intentions were not wholly honorable in the original screen treatment of *The Black Cat.* Lead actress Jacqueline Wells subsequently had greater Hollywood success using the name Julie Bishop (courtesy Bill Chase).

lection. Driven by vengeance and a lust for the nubile Joan Alison, Werdegast becomes a menace almost as dangerous as the Satanist himself. Much to Lugosi's satisfaction, these dark glimpses into Werdegast's psyche were eliminated.

Lucille Lund's character was also given a complete overhaul. In a role that had been initially drawn as a human counterpart (*à la* Simone Simon in *Cat People*), Karen was now reduced to a child-like innocent with an almost celestial beauty.

Ulmer was also compelled to tone down the script's graphic depiction of Poelzig's torture and other suggestive/explicit moments. During editing, Ulmer discarded a lengthy preface which followed the main title, detailing the Alisons' wedding ceremony in Vienna, and a long-winded episode which featured the Orient Express' gregarious Maitre d'Hotel (Herman Bing) tempting the newlyweds with his culinary delights. A brief scene showing an uncharacteristically abrasive Peter Alison brow-beating Poelzig's Hungarian-speaking servants was also wisely excised from the final print.

The critics were hardly impressed; the bashing that greeted *The Black Cat* was unprecedented even for a horror film. Reviewers found the picture revolting and incomprehensible; Karloff and Lugosi were cited for their endless mugging and the subject matter was branded unsavory. Even the trade papers, which tended to be kinder to the genre, pummeled the film mercilessly. The most frequent charge against *The Black Cat* is its major flaw — the lack of a clear-cut storyline. The latter-day canonization of Edgar Ulmer by the *auteurists* may have defused this charge to some degree. Today, the film is routinely praised, and praised lavishly, for its flamboyant technique. One cannot discuss *The Black Cat* without delving into the career of Edgar Ulmer but, the picture is hardly typical of the director. If anything, *The Black Cat* is an aberration in the highly erratic filmmaker's career.

The Black Cat not only towers over Ulmer's other horror-science fiction efforts, but a case can be made that it's his best film, although the highly-touted *Detour* (1945) not only cemented the director's reputation but stands as the prototype Poverty Row masterpiece. *The Black Cat* was perhaps Ulmer's last opportunity to have the facilities of a semi-major Hollywood studio at his disposal and, finding an ally in Junior Laemmle, allowed his imagination to ran rampant. A fast shooter (he once bragged about completing 80 setups in one day), the director took full advantage of his three-week shooting schedule and Charles D. Hall's extraordinary art deco sets to create a film visually as rich as anything Whale, Florey or Freund could have created. Whatever its dramatic weaknesses, *The Black Cat* displays Ulmer's talents as a designer and a stylist.

There wasn't much left of Poe in the final cut, but what little there remained is flavorful. In the original tale, Poe's typically dotty protagonist gouges out the eye of his pet black cat and later hangs the creature from a tree limb. Afterwards, he adopts another black cat as a substitute before regressing to his murderous ways. In the film, the black cat, too, serves as a recurring spectral figure. Werdegast spears the creature, but after a portentous discourse on the cat's proverbial nine lives, another black cat is seen in the Satanist's arms. Whether the creature was resurrected or just part of an endless supply is never revealed, but it's a nice, ambiguous touch.

The unrevised script contains yet another feline reference which did not make the final cut. In a postscript to the bus crash scene, a black cat suddenly materializes in the light of the moon to unnerve Werdegast as he is scrambling from the twisted wreckage. The black cat's frequent appearance serves to justify Universal's use of the Edgar Allan Poe story title, but Ulmer artfully weaves the creature's presence into the film as a lingering symbol of evil. Poelzig's black robes, evening jackets and even pajamas visually link him to his pet and they are often framed together in the same shot. The hypersensitive Werdegast isn't intent on slaying the animal in and of itself, but for what the cat stands for, adding to the supernatural aura of the picture.

The Black Cat has been hailed by such astute reviewers as William K. Everson for expertly evoking the somber spirit of Poe. Werdegast's longing for his lost love, his years of imprisonment, and his thwarted plans of vengeance, superficially at least, brand him as a typical Poe hero. But Ulmer himself down played the author's influence on his and Peter Ruric's screenplay. In a chatty, informative interview with Peter Bogdanovich, conducted in 1970, and originally appearing in *Film Culture*, Ulmer admitted that the outline of the story evolved during discussions with Gustav Meyrinck, who novelized the story of "The Golem." Meyrinck's ambition was to write a play based on the French fortress Doumont (obviously the inspiration for Fort Marmaros in the film), which was shelled by the Germans during the Great War. The freed survivors, several of whom had gone mad, were faced with the challenge of readjusting themselves after years of imprisonment. From this central idea, Ulmer added the two figures of Poelzig and Werdegast waging their sinister feud long after the war had ended.

Poe's original story was an uncompromised descent into madness but in Peter Ruric's screenplay, Werdegast's mental pathology is only slightly less jarring. The writer's choice of making him a psychiatrist adds complexity and contradiction to his character. Werdegast's madness so completely voids his scientific reasoning that he becomes an advocate for all the supernatural claims of the black cat and is moved to kill them on sight. When Joan revives from her motor accident injuries, Werdegast doesn't see her drug-induced stupor for what it is but rather cites it as evidence of the coalescing supernatural forces around her. (Of course, the psychiatrist's blatantly unbalanced behavior fails to ring alarm bells for our clueless mystery writer-hero who responds with an indifferent shrug of the shoulders and an offhand comment of what an interesting fellow Dr. Werdegast is.)

Initially, the script would seem to favor Lugosi's Werdegast, who is certainly the dominating character for the first quarter of the picture. Poelzig's delayed introduction is further marked by his unsettling lack of dialogue in his first scenes where he's a straw man to Werdegast's long and withering speeches detailing his transgressions. As the seemingly passive character of

The historic first teaming of Karloff and Lugosi.

the devil-worshipping architect is revealed, it becomes obvious he is only striking a pose, that his silence is a mere cover as he ruthlessly calculates his own position, issuing curt denials in a bid to stall for time. It's the perfect strategy of a master chess player, as the audience will soon learn. Poelzig ranks along with Charles Laughton's Dr. Moreau as one of the most fascinating of the pre–Code horror characters. Beneath his otherworldly appearance lurks a fertile if sadistic imagination. His collection of lovingly preserved, glass-encased beauties, all presumably human sacrifices in his ritualistic ceremonies, is reminiscent of Count Zaroff's trophy room of victims in *The Most Dangerous Game* (1932). The script is disturbingly casual in conveying how he bedded Werdegast's wife and child, eventually killing them both. It is doubtful that the film could have gotten a Production Code clearance had it been made only a year later.

A living dead man by his own admission, Poelzig's introduction comes in the form of a visual resurrection. Slowly rising in silhouette from his bed, with strains of Liszt on the soundtrack, Karloff's strange flat-topped hairstyle exploits the actor's identification with the Frankenstein Monster to tease the audience. However, unlike the actor's other horror roles, Poelzig makes no pleas for the viewer's sympathy. Poelzig is a true predator; like a panther in the form of a man, he is lithe, slinky, and deadly. Targeting females as his prey, this "black cat's" motivations are clearly sexual except for having to deal with the occasional meddlesome boyfriend or husband. In contrast to Werdegast, who was driven to madness, Poelzig is so unrepentantly evil that his status as a sociopath is almost beside the point.

Karloff is at his most controlled here, playing with subtlety and intelligence and a basic respect for the material. Lugosi's performance begs comparison with his other Poe roles. There is little of the sideshow boogieman of his Dr.

Mirakle in *Murders in the Rue Morgue* or the lunatic ravings of Dr. Vollin in *The Raven*. Instead, Lugosi, in fading matinee idol fashion, pours all his romantic yearnings into his characterization. Seizing the opportunity to play one of his own countrymen in a substantial role (and one in which he wasn't a vampire), Lugosi is, unsurprisingly, more dramatically generous than he needs to be, delivering a performance that was probably dated by 1934 standards. As usual, he proves to be technically adroit but, in the end, it's just too much of Bela being Bela. Which, of course, is enough to send fans of the actor into a state of rapture, leaving the rest of us to appreciate his often fascinating presence. Still, it's easy to sympathize with director Ulmer who claimed Lugosi's intensity was such that he was forced to cut away from him. Quite pointedly, Heinz Roemheld's nearly wall-to-wall score comes to a stunningly abrupt halt whenever it's time for Lugosi deliver one of his many doom-ladened speeches. For better or worse, Lugosi was so overpowering that he made the entire orchestra redundant.

The Black Cat's visual eloquence is well-matched by a lush, classically based score, a veritable work of art in itself. The actual task of transcribing the various chamber works and pieces written for solo instruments (many of the pieces selected weren't originally symphonic in nature) went to music director Roemheld but it's obviously another Ulmer concept. Although selections from the baroque to late-Romantic repertoire are represented, Liszt, with his distinctly Central European style and flair for the macabre, was the inescapable choice as *The Black Cat*'s musical godfather. The devilish *Sonata in B Flat Minor* provides the perfect leitmotif for Poelzig. Likewise, the neurotically bereaved Werdegast seems to take his cue from the subtitle of the Liszt tone poem, *Tasso: A Lament*. Not to be outdone, the newlyweds find their own musical signature in Roemheld's particularly fetching improvisation of Tchaikovsky's familiar *Romeo and Juliet* theme.

In an interview with the authors, Shirley Ulmer, who served as the script supervisor, and later became the wife of the director, provided some insights into Ulmer's working methods:

> Edgar was a very interesting director — he directed with a baton. He *timed* [Karloff and Lugosi's] speeches.... Once Edgar told Peter Bogdanovich that he was a frustrated conductor — Edgar was *very* knowledgeable.... So maybe he felt he was conducting.

The comment is useful in appreciating a key scene which highlights the film's musical inventiveness. Using a recording of Schubert's great, unfinished *Symphony #8*, not as a background cue, but as a real-time recording from Poelzig's futuristic music player, the episode is a beautifully realized melding of music, dialogue and images. Starting off pleasantly in beguiling, salon music-fashion as Karloff and David Manners exchange pleasantries, the piece unexpectedly reaches a feverish crescendo as Lugosi throws a knife at Karloff's pet black cat who saunters onto the scene. The music switches to a more *mysterioso* passage as Jacqueline Wells makes her entrance and is introduced to an ogling Karloff, who dramatically explains Lugosi's strange neurosis. The music builds to its climax as Manners passionately embraces his bride and Ulmer dramatically shifts focus to a closeup of Karloff's hand gripping the statue of a reclining nude, both aroused and enraged at the amorous display. It's timed with absolute precision, skillfully edited and rather daringly staged by Ulmer; altogether a perfect little segment that could well stand on its own.

However, *The Black Cat* shows Ulmer to be more of an artist than a craftsman. While his overall design is brilliant, his technical lapses wouldn't even pass muster in his later Poverty Row pictures. Long passages of dialogue are layered into the soundtrack even when it's painfully apparent the actors aren't speaking. Continuity lapses abound. The scene in which Lucille Lund is in bed with Karloff, she appears to be awake in one shot, asleep in the next, and again awake seconds later. In an early scene, Lugosi and the newlyweds arrive at a taxi stand in drizzly weather, only to cut to a closer angle of the actors in a torrential rainstorm.

The love interest is handled in more-or-less routine fashion. David Manners seems to be cast, in equal measure, due to his past association with the genre and for his utter lack of physical prowess. Manners was the pretty boy of Universal horror films, and the studio seemed rather cruelly disposed to humiliate him at every turn. Halfway into the film, his character is marginalized to the point of becoming a punching bag

Edgar G. Ulmer's masterpiece caught the spirit if not the essence of Poe. Here, the Black Mass is about to begin.

for brawny henchman, Harry Cording, who easily fells him with a single blow. Even the short and scrawny majordomo, Egon Brecher, makes short work of him, knocking him cold with little resistance.

As the much-coveted prize in Karloff and Lugosi's battle of wits, Jacqueline Wells certainly never looked as lovely or as vulnerable as the imperiled bride. The actress, who later changed her name to Julie Bishop, enjoyed a long career in mainstream Hollywood movies such as *Sands of Iwo Jima* (1949), often playing somewhat harder-edged characters than *The Black Cat*'s virginal Joan Alison. For the dual role of Lugosi's daughter and wife (for the latter, appearing as one of Karloff's entombed beauties), Lucille Lund has regrettably little screen time, but she makes the most of it. Beautifully photographed by John J. Mescall, she has the ethereal presence of a golden, story-book princess. Her cold-blooded murder at the hands of Karloff only served to underscore the general air of morbidity that infuriated critics at the time.

Under ordinary circumstances, the box office success of *The Black Cat* would have solidified Ulmer's position as a contract studio director. Tentative plans were made to reunite Karloff and the director to make a film based on the infamous French wife-killer, *Bluebeard*, but this never came to pass. Months after the release of *The Black Cat*, Ulmer's romantic relationship with Carl Laemmle's nephew's wife became known and the director became *persona non grata* in virtually every major Hollywood studio.

Shirley Ulmer told the authors:

> I started living with Edgar without being able to marry him because I had to wait that whole year, and we didn't get married until '35.... We were told that we'd never work in Hollywood again. He couldn't get a job — that's why we went back

to New York.... [Hollywood] just didn't want him around.

Ulmer's Hollywood film career revived in the '40s at PRC where he became the leading *auteur* of Poverty Row. Secure in his position with studio president, Leon Fromkess, the director resurrected his *Bluebeard* project, enlisting writer Pierre Gendron to write a script. Despite its bedraggled production values, the 1944 film remains a minor triumph and a key work in Ulmer's filmography. Buoyed by John Carradine's sensitive performance and Ulmer's unerring eye for composition, the picture garnered fine reviews although the passage of time has withered its impact somewhat. The director returned to the horror genre in *Daughter of Dr. Jekyll* (1957) featuring John Agar and Gloria Talbott clashing painfully with the film's turn-of-the-century English setting. Unencumbered by style or imagination, this somewhat sleazy potboiler displays none of the ingenuity that distinguishes *The Black Cat*. Even Ulmer's shoestring invasion-from-space mini-classic *The Man from Planet X* (1951) packs more atmosphere, although one suspects that its fog-shrouded landscape served to conceal the papier-mâché sets and crude studio backdrops.

In the '80s, intriguing reports surfaced about an original cut of *The Black Cat* which dealt with Werdegast's full-scale madness in the final reels and contained several tantalizing horror sequences. Supposedly included among the deleted scenes is footage of a bloodied, skin-shorn Poelzig crawling on the floor after enduring Werdegast's torture session. Horror buffs and film historians have nurtured hopes that these sequences might one day be found in Universal's vaults, however, the veracity of these claims are increasingly in doubt and now it appears that this footage never existed in the first place. Although the episode shows up in the shooting script, no production reports have been found to indicate the scenes were actually shot, nor have studio stills from the "missing scenes" ever materialized. Moreover, none of the survivors in the cast recall shooting any such scenes and Shirley Ulmer scoffed (and scoffed loudly) when the authors described the action to her. Likewise, since Edgar Ulmer himself never alluded to any of these scenes in published interviews, it appears that the entire story is the stuff of urban legends.

The Black Cat is a unique film in the Universal horror canon. It nods to Poe but its sensibilities are more closely linked stylistically to expatriate European filmmakers who were descending on American shores. Except for the presence of Karloff and Lugosi, the film seems a closer relative to the works of von Sternberg and Lang than James Whale and Tod Browning. It is certainly a contender for the title of the best of the Universal horror classics.

Critics' Corner

A dismal hocus-pocus which seems to confuse its actors as much as it fails to frighten its audience.... Silly shot: the Black Mass, with Karloff intoning Latin gibberish.—*Time*, May 25, 1934

A clammy and exceptionally ghoulish tale.... The staging is good and the camera devotes a proper amount of attention to shadows and hypnotic eyes.... But *The Black Cat* is more foolish than horrible.—*The New York Times*, May 19, 1934, Andre Sennwald

Karloff and Bela Lugosi ... fight it out for 7 reels for the mugging championship of the picture. Beyond that, there is little or no action in this so-called thriller, and the writing and directing both combine to do the almost impossible—to make an Edgar Allan Poe story dull.—*The Hollywood Reporter*, May 4, 1934

[W]ith the aid of heavily shadowed lighting and mausoleum-like architecture, a certain eerieness has been achieved.... Skinning alive is not new.... A truly horrible and nauseating bit of extreme sadism, its inclusion in a motion picture is dubious showmanship.—*Variety*, May 22, 1934

Rating: ★★ *The Black Cat* is only second-rate, as horror films go. The new story that was written to fit the title is so fantastically unreal that it is more apt to make one laugh at its absurdities than quake from its effects of horror.—*The New York Daily News*, May 19, 1934, Kate Cameron

Secret of the Chateau

Released December 3, 1934. 66 minutes. An L.L. Ostrow production. *Executive Producer:* Carl Laemmle, Jr. *Director:* Richard Thorpe. *Screenplay:* Albert DeMond & Harry Behn. *Continuity:* Harry Behn. *Additional Dialogue:* Llewellyn Hughes. *Original Story:* Lawrence G. Blochman. *Photography:* Robert Planck. *Editor:* Harry Marker. *Art Director:* Ralph Berger. *Music:* Heinz Roemheld & Oliver Wallace. *Sound Supervisor:* John A. Stransky, Jr.

Claire Dodd (*Julie Verlaine*), Alice White (*Didi*), Osgood Perkins (*Martin*), Jack La Rue (*Lucien Voltaire*), George E. Stone (*Armand*), Clark Williams (*Paul*), William Faversham (*M. Fos/Prof. Raquel Prahec*), Ferdinand Gottschalk (*Chief Insp. Marotte*), DeWitt Jennings (*Louis Bardou*), Helen Ware (*Mme.

Rombiere), Frank Reicher (*Auctioneer*), Alphonz [Alphonse] Ethier (*Commissioner*), Paul Nicholson (*Domme*), Olaf Hytten (*LaFarge*), Cecil Elliott (*Cook*), Tony Merlo (*Arthur*), Frank Thornton (*George*).

A *beautiful* murder. A *lovely* murder.
—*Ferdinand Gottschalk in* Secret of the Chateau

Who is the infamous French book thief-murderer, Prahec? Will he (or she) succeed in nabbing a priceless first edition of the Gutenberg Bible? These are the questions that haunt Chief Insp. Marotte of the Paris Surete in *Secret of the Chateau*, a creaky, dime-store whodunit that's all but forgotten today. It has little to distinguish it from the dozens of bottom-of-the-bill program mysteries that Hollywood studios cranked out with regularity in the '30s and '40s.

Surprisingly, Universal took little advantage of the story's creepy country chateau setting and invested the film with precious few eerie effects. Chills and suspense are sacrificed for a succession of low-level gags. Judging from the film's advertising, however, one would get the impression *Secret of the Chateau* was a bonafide horror film, or at least a mystery thriller with strong horrific elements. Ad lines, emblazoned above stock castle, bat and ghost artwork, cried "Shadows Come to Life!" "Traps Snare Women!" "Trunks Swallow Men!" and "Bells Toll Out Death!" Who would have thought, after reading these enticements, that the picture would be a lifeless hodgepodge about a stolen book? Those expecting the kind of florid melodrama so vividly displayed in *The Old Dark House* and *Secret of the Blue Room* were sorely disappointed.

Under the briskly efficient direction of Richard Thorpe, *Secret of the Chateau* (its early pre-release title was *Rendezvous at Midnight*, which the studio used the following year for an entirely different melodrama) went into production in late August 1934, and wrapped in early September for a scheduled December theatrical release. Universal's sunny back lot European set was redressed to resemble the cafe- and shop-dotted Montparnasse section of Paris. Rather than take advantage of Charles D. Hall's sets from the studio's past horror triumphs, the production's art director, Ralph Berger, utilized prosaic library, dining room and bedroom sets.

Richard Thorpe earned a reputation in the film colony as a "one-take director." He got his feet wet in vaudeville before coming to Hollywood in the late '20s. Graduating to the position of MGM house director, Thorpe put his workmanlike but impersonal stamp on pictures like *Night Must Fall* (1937), *Tarzan Finds a Son!* (1939) and the Joan Crawford vehicle *Above Suspicion* (1943). Evidently, someone at the Culver City super studio felt Thorpe's talent lay in high-priced costume epics. He directed, in rapid succession, *Ivanhoe* (1952), *The Prisoner of Zenda* (1952), *Knights of the Round Table* (1954), *The Prodigal* (1955) and *Quentin Durward* (1956).

When the wealthy M. Le Due de Poisse is mysteriously murdered, his collection of rare first editions is auctioned off by the respected Parisian dealer M. Fos (William Faversham). Chief Insp. Marotte (Ferdinand Gottschalk) attends the event, believing it might attract Prahec, an infamous book thief and ruthless murderer whom he has been stalking for the past ten years.

The sly old inspector spots Julie Verlaine (Claire Dodd) there and follows her. A convicted book thief who has just served six months in prison, Julie is attempting to go straight, but is blackmailed into committing further thefts by her smarmy confederate Lucien Voltaire (Jack La Rue). She befriends wealthy young Paul (Clark Williams), nephew of the late Duc, who offers to sell Julie his uncle's rare first edition of the original Gutenberg Bible, reputedly the most valuable book in existence. At Lucien's insistence, Julie accompanies the young artist to his country chateau, Aubazines.

Julie gets a hostile reception from Louis Bardou (DeWitt Jennings), the village notary and executor of the Duc's estate. The blustery old man has the Bible safely hidden in a burglar-proof cabinet. Paul's announcement that he has promised to sell the book to the hunchbacked scholar Prof. Raque of the Art Ministry irks both Bardou and Paul's aunt, Mme. Rombiere (Helen Ware), who is entitled to half the proceeds. Fearing the Bible will be stolen, Bardou has had a counterfeit produced and has placed it in the cabinet.

Late that evening, the chateau's tranquility is disrupted by the sudden toiling of a bell in the old tower. "Its ringing is always followed by a death!" Mme. Rombiere gasps. After all have retired, a shadowy figure steals into the library, shoots Bardou dead, and absconds with the tome.

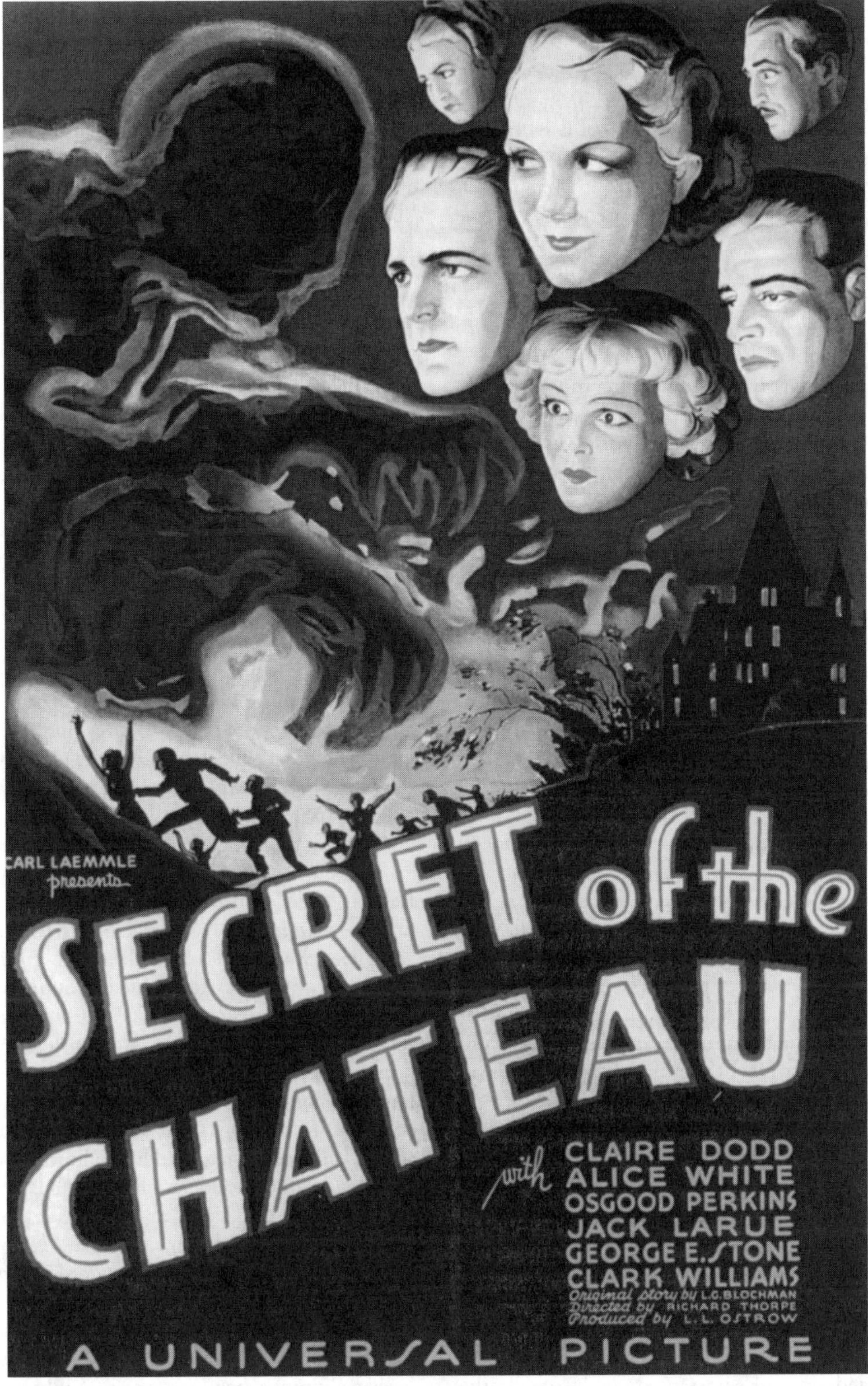

Don't let the spooked-up poster art fool you. *Secret of the Chateau* was just another murder-in-the-mansion potboiler.

Marotte and his men descend upon the chateau and question the suspects: Paul, his friend Armand (George E. Stone), Didi (Alice White), the butler Martin (Osgood Perkins) and Martin's wife, the cook (Cecil Elliott). Even the old professor comes under Marotte's sharp scrutiny. Mme. Rombiere startles the group by announcing it was the counterfeit Gutenberg, not the original, that was stolen. Her refusal to turn the book over to Marotte for safe-keeping seals her doom. Mme. Rombiere's body is found the next morning following a second tolling of the bell.

His clues assembled, Marotte gathers the house guests in the library for the inevitable showdown of the suspects. The secret hiding place of the real Gutenberg is discovered by Armand within the library's giant globe. The old professor suddenly draws a revolver. The chase is over.... Marotte and his nemesis Prahec confront each other face to face. But before the master thief can fire the fatal shot, Marotte's men break in and overpower him. The false beard falls to the floor, revealing Prahec's true identity—he is M. Fos, the rare book dealer. Martin and his wife are arrested as Prahec's accomplices and Julie is pardoned for her past transgressions by the magnanimous Marotte.

The Gutenberg Bible around which the action of the plot revolves was the first book known to have been printed with the movable metal type system invented by the German printer Johannes Gutenberg between 1450 and 1456. Two hundred copies of the two-volume Bible were printed. Originally intended to look like the work of a manuscript copyist, the Gutenberg Bible lacked page numbers, title pages and other distinguishing features; it cost the equivalent of three years' pay for the average clerk when it was sold at the 1456 Frankfurt Book Fair.

Like most films of its ilk, *Secret of the Chateau* doesn't stray far from familiar turf in fleshing out its slight story. All of the characters — from the wisecracking blonde to the bull-headed administrator — are stock-bred. Potential victims can be spotted a mile away. Here again, we have a tolling bell warning of impending doom, quick reaction shots of each suspect as particularly incriminating bits of evidence are turned up and, most predictably of all, the round-up of the surviving suspects for the final reel's "surprise" denouement.

In this case, the revelation of the master criminal's real identity is less of a surprise and more an exasperation. Why pin the murders on a character that has been out of the story (and well forgotten) since the first reel? Observant audiences must have smelled a rat when William Faversham made his initial appearance at the chateau done up in a costume shop wig and beard.

The Surete's Inspector Marotte is hardly a sleuth of the Sherlock Holmes school of deductive reasoning. For ten years he has been tracking down Prahec, yet he is still uncertain as to whether the criminal is male or female. Marotte's method of judging a person's innocence or guilt is by the amount of food left on the person's breakfast plate. ("A good appetite is a sign of a clear conscience.") Confronted with a collection of reasonably sound alibis, Marotte repeatedly grumbles, "Everyone has answers!" as though the suspects were purposely out to make his job difficult. The hiding place of the authentic Gutenberg is discovered not by Marotte or his men, but by the loutish Armand. To top it off, the detective can't be given credit even for discovering the identity of Prahec — M. Fos tips his own hand when the Bible is found in the globe. On the plus side, diminutive character actor Ferdinand Gottschalk imparts an impish charm in his portrayal of the smug but inefficient policeman.

The script by Albert DeMond and Harry Behn is loaded with witless gags, mostly insult humor between Alice White, DeWitt Jennings and Helen Ware. Little of it is the least bit funny. White, a shrill, scatterbrained blonde who played more than her share of fast-talking, sassy tootsies, gets her kicks by snitching Jennings' floppy hairpiece, much to his irritation (and ours). In an interview she granted to syndicated columnist Bob Thomas in 1958, the 49-year-old actress had recently regained her sight following a freak gardening accident which left her blind for months. White hadn't appeared in a movie since Warners' tawdry melodrama *Flamingo Road* (1949), supporting Joan Crawford, and was anxious to resume her acting career. "I never look back," the bouncy character actress revealed to Thomas. "What's past is past. I never even saved a clipping when I was a star." Sadly, when Alice White passed away in February 1983, her prayers for a comeback were still unanswered.

The biggest offender in the comic relief department, however, is George E. Stone, As Armand, Stone swats flies with rare volumes, pours salad dressing over squeaky door hinges, and ... well, you get the picture. As Dinky, a two-bit crook, Stone played opposite scar-faced Peter Lorre in Columbia's *The Face Behind the Mask* (1941) and gave an excellent performance.

As Martin, the butler, Osgood Perkins (Anthony's dad) seems above the menial mentality of those upon whom he waits. He gets to deliver the movie's single line of wry dialogue. When Alice White begs him to keep her company after DeWitt Jennings buys the farm, Perkins explains that he'd be glad to oblige, but his wife wouldn't go for the idea. "She's funny that way," he deadpans and takes his leave. Perkins was a familiar character player in early talkies; gangster Johnny Lovo in *Scarface* (1932) is probably his best-remembered role. Perkins' real forte, however, was stage acting. He made his professional debut at the age of 32 on Broadway in "Beggars on Horseback" in 1924, and scored successes in "The Front Page" as hardboiled managing editor Walter Burns, "End of Summer," and "Tovarich," among others. On September 21, 1937, just hours after the final curtain fell on the opening night performance of "Susan and God." (in which Perkins supported Gertrude Lawrence in the role of Barrie Trexel), the actor died suddenly of a heart attack at the age of 45. "I like that role," he had told his wife after they left the theater. "I hope the play never closes."

Sixth-billed Clark Williams is the vanilla-bland leading man. *Secret of the Chateau* was his first film; an inconsequential role in *Were Wolf of London* followed the next year. Warner Bros. contractee Claire Dodd appears here on a loan-out from that studio and does okay as the larcenous Julie. Jack La Rue trades on his Latin lover-gangster screen image as the swarthy Lucien, her partner-in-crime. Although she's not given an official credit, actress Binnie Barnes acted as the film's technical advisor. Her husband was renowned as one of London's best known dealers in rare books and manuscripts.

Secret of the Chateau is an ideal example of what reviewers of the day termed a "time killer." It's brief, somewhat lively, and totally predictable. Seldom revived, it richly deserves its status as a forgotten Universal picture.

Critics' Corner

Thin, creaky plot and slow movement almost negates the value of some good acting here.... Story gets off to an intolerably long premise.... It's all pretty flat.—*Variety*, February 5, 1935, Chic.

Just another of those spooky murder mysteries. Familiar in content and never rising above a mild point.... [A]ll the well-known ingredients of the spook melodrama have been thrown into this one, but the affair doesn't quite jell.... There's plenty of talent in the cast, but the story affords little opportunity.—*The Film Daily*, January 8, 1935

Highly theatricalized mystery motivates everything. As is necessary, however, the compassionate elements of romance, drama, comedy, thrill [*sic*] and suspense have their sustaining function, while it makes no attempts at pretentiousness.... See it for what it is, building a campaign that dares audiences to identify the criminal until the very end and accenting its amusing entertainment.—*The Motion Picture Herald*, September 15, 1934, McCarthy

The Man Who Reclaimed His Head

Released December 24, 1934. 80 minutes. *Associate Producer:* Henry Henigson. *Executive Producer:* F.R. Mastroly. *Producer:* Carl Laemmle, Jr. *Director:* Edward Ludwig. *Screenplay:* Jean Bart & Samuel Ornitz. *Additional Dialogue:* Barry Trivers. *From the Play by* Jean Bart. *Photography:* Merritt Gerstad. *Art Director:* Albert S. D'Agostino. *Music Director:* Heinz Roemheld. *Editor:* Murray Seldeen. *Editorial Supervisor:* Maurice Pivar. *Set Decorator:* Russell A. Gausman. *Assistant Directors:* W.J. Reiter & Fred Frank. *Second Camera:* Alan Jones. *Assistant Cameraman:* Paul Hill. *Process Photography:* John P. Fulton. *Matte Art:* Jack Cosgrove & Russell Lawson. *Wardrobe:* Vera West. *Recording Engineer:* Gilbert Kurland. *Music Recorder:* Lawrence Aicholtz. *Makeup:* Jack P. Pierce. *Hair Stylist:* Beth Langston. *Script Clerk:* Myrtle Gibson. *Child Welfare Worker:* Mary West.

Claude Rains (*Paul Verin*), Joan Bennett (*Adele Verin*), Lionel Atwill (*Henri Dumont*), Baby Jane [Juanita Quigley] (*Linette Verin*), Henry O'Neill (*Fernand De Marnay*), Henry Armetta (*Laurent*), Wallace Ford ("*Curly*"), Lawrence Grant (*Marchand*), William B. Davidson (*Charlus*), Gilbert Emery (*His Excellency*), Ferdinand Gottschalk (*Baron*), Hugh O'Connell (*Danglas*), Rollo Lloyd (*Jean, De Marnay's Butler*), Bessie Barriscale (*Louise, the Verins' Maid*), Valerie Hobson (*Mimi, the Carnival Girl*), G.P. Huntley, Jr. (*Pierre*), Doris Lloyd (*Lulu*), Noel Francis (*Chon-Chon*), Carol Coombe (*Clerk*), Phyllis Brooks (*Secretary*), Walter Walker, Edward Martindel, Craufurd Kent, Montague Shaw (*Dignitaries*), Purnell Pratt, Jameson Thomas, Edward Van Sloan (*Munitions Board Directors*), Judith Wood (*Margot*), James

Donlan (*Man in Theater Box*), Lloyd Hughes (*Andre, Dumont's Secretary*), Bryant Washburn, Sr. (*Antoine*), Boyd Irwin (*Petty Officer*), Anderson Lawler (*Jack*), Will Stanton (*Drunk Soldier*), George Davis (*Lorry Driver*), Lionel Belmore (*Train Conductor*), Emerson Treacy (*French Student/Attacked Pacifist*), John Rutherford, Hyram A. Hoover, Lee Phelps (*Soldiers*), Rudy Cameron (*Maitre D'Hotel*), Norman Ainsley (*Steward*), Russ Powell (*Station Master*), Harry Cording (*French Mechanic*), Lilyan Irene (*Woman Shopper*), William Ruhl (*Shopper's Husband*), Rolfe Sedan (*Waiter*), Ben F. Hendricks (*Chauffeur*), Maurice Murphy (*Leon*), William Gould (*Man*), Carl Stockdale (*Tradesman*), Tom Ricketts, Joseph Swickard, Billy West, Colin Kenny (*Citizens*), Ted Billings (*Newsboy*), William Worthington (*Attendant*), Nell Craig, Grace Cunard (*Women*), Wilfred North (*Bit*), Russ Clark (*French Truck Driver*), John Ince (*Speaker*), Margaret Mann (*Granny*), Charles Meacham (*Older Man*), Lois January (*Girl*).

Universal has dared to make this film story from the Broadway play because its plot affects every home, every human life, all human love!
—The Man Who Reclaimed His Head
pressbook ad

Here we go with another picture that's only in this book because of false advertising and perpetuated misconceptions. Despite the grisly promise of its title, *The Man Who Reclaimed His Head* is a straight melodrama indicting the war profiteers who made their fortunes through the slaughter of millions in World War I. It takes a little-explored theme and expands it into an effective message picture — but try explaining this to the Universal Horrors fans who, as kids, waded through it on a Saturday afternoon "Creature Features" impatiently waiting for it to "get good."

The geniuses in the Universal publicity department obviously didn't quite know what to make of this thoughtful exposé, so in addition to advertising it appropriately, as an indictment of the war breeders, they took advantage of the striking title, and a gruesome sting in the picture's tail, and designed some ads that promoted it as if it were a horror thriller. The names Claude Rains (of *The Invisible Man* fame) and Lionel Atwill (*Doctor X, Mystery of the Wax Museum, The Vampire Bat*) would also catch the eye of any self-respecting fright film aficionado.

"This isn't a horror picture," begins Char's *Variety* review, but Char's small voice couldn't outshout the roar of the Universal publicity machine. In decades to come, *Reclaimed His Head* got an all-out horror campaign during its 1949 Realart reissue; was aired in time slots reserved for shockers by local television stations; and was listed as a Universal thriller-diller in various monster magazines. And now it gets a full writeup within the pages of the book you're holding. We could have omitted it and strenuously stated our many reasons but, like the peacenik at the center of the story, we'd rather switch than fight.

The film opens on a snowy winter's night in 1915 Paris, where a German air raid has just gotten underway. Drowned out by the booming of explosions are the sounds of a brawl and a woman's scream which come from the villa of writer Paul Verin. A wild-eyed Verin (Claude Rains), dressed in a corporal's uniform, leaves the house carrying his young daughter Linette (Baby Jane) and a large valise, walking through the blizzard to the home of eminent Paris lawyer De Marnay (Henry O'Neill). De Marnay, who knew Verin in his younger days, fears that the young intellectual has gone mad — and becomes convinced of this when Verin opens the valise to reveal its gruesome (unseen) contents. As the sound of exploding bombs continues to be heard outside the darkened house, Verin, now slightly more lucid, lays out his fantastic, tragic story....

Flashbacks show us a younger, happier Verin working as an underpaid, and sometimes *un*paid political journalist, living in a poor section of pre-war Paris with wife Adele (Joan Bennett) and child Linette. (Mr. & Mrs. Verin talk as though they're poor, but live in a huge apartment in a building with a fawning doorman.) Newspaper publisher Henri Dumont (Lionel Atwill), an old acquaintance of Verin's, unexpectedly arrives and offers him a job ghostwriting pacifist editorials. Verin is reluctant because their last such association had ended with Dumont betraying him, but Adele is tired of the grind of poverty (well, *this* movie's idea of poverty) and convinces her husband to accept the high-paying job.

Verin begins to write heartfelt peacemongering editorials under Dumont's name, and soon the publisher is the toast of Paris. But unbeknownst to Verin, the politically ambitious Dumont is planning to betray the idealistic

Tycoon Lionel Atwill (at left) isn't content with just stealing Claude Rains' mind — he also has eyes for his employee's wife (Joan Bennett). A scene from *The Man Who Reclaimed His Head.*

writer once again. Selling out to the munitions manufacturers, Dumont double-crosses Verin and uses his newfound influence to abruptly sway public opinion toward patriotism — and war. Archduke Ferdinand is assassinated, armies mobilize and munitions stocks boom on all exchanges while Dumont rides to yet-greater power on the wave of war hysteria. Verin, the big dope, is inducted into the French Army, sent to the front and finally transferred to Verdun, scene of the bloodiest fighting, all through the behind-the-scenes manipulations of Dumont, who doesn't want Verin coming home. But when Verin overhears fellow soldiers discussing the false rumor that Dumont has taken up with Adele, the little egghead at last gets wise. Racing back to Paris from the front, he arrives home just in time to find Dumont forcing himself upon the unwilling Adele.

"*J'accuse*!" — Verin's mind temporarily snaps as he pulls out his bayonet* and stalks Dumont. (We're now back again at the point where the picture began.) Obsessed with the notion that Dumont has stolen his mind, Verin struggles to hack off the publisher's head. Adele faints and screams (in that order!) as the blade finds its mark. Dumont's severed noggin winds up in Verin's valise.

Just like in the movies, gendarmes arrive at the De Marnay home at the very moment that Verin finishes telling the lawyer his story. De Marnay gladly agrees to act as Verin's defense at his trial, confident that no jury will convict the man. Verin, who has found peace again at last,

**In the play, the blade Verin uses on the publisher is a Senegalese knife. Referring to his stay in Africa that resulted in his acquisition of the knife from a native, hug-thy-neighbor peacenik Verin says, "I was stationed with those black devils for some days."*

leaves in the custody of the police with Adele at his side.

The Man Who Reclaimed His Head was based on a play that opened at New York's Broadhurst Theatre on September 8, 1932. Penned by Jean Bart, the daughter of a Spanish count (and a French mother), the pseudo-historical melodrama starred Claude Rains as Verin, Jean Arthur as his wife and Stuart Casey as the wicked publisher (there named Henri Berthaud). In the play, Rains was somewhat comical in appearance, a brilliant brain and a beautiful personality in a repulsive body, *à la* Cyrano de Bergerac; *The New York Times* reported that he "has acted it with a Lon Chaney makeup and a panting of steam." In the script of the play, Verin is described as "uncommonly ugly, a painful ugliness, bordering on the grotesque. The features are coarse and funny looking. The hands and feet disproportionately large. Fan-like ears peer from under a mess of bushy hair. Only the eyes, deep and soulful, seem almost beautiful in the sincerity of their gaze. Conscious of his looks, [Verin] is hypersensitive, shyness bordering on terror. He shuns the world, and has developed an abnormal desire for seclusion." Other characters in the play comment behind his back about his looks, or even zing him right to his funny face. ("What's your hurry? The zoo don't close till six.")

Herbert Biberman, husband of character star Gale Sondergaard, directed the play through its brief run of 28 performances. Soon afterwards, making a screen test for an Eastern representative of RKO, Rains enacted for the camera scenes from "A Bill of Divorcement," Shaw's "Man of Destiny"—and "Reclaimed His Head." "And they were terrible!" he later recalled. "When I saw the test, I was shocked and frightened...."

The rights to "Reclaimed His Head" were picked up by Universal, who, per a *Hollywood Reporter* item, had George O'Neil (*Only Yesterday, Magnificent Obsession, Intermezzo: A Love Story*) write a script before putting playwright Bart on the writing team. By the time the film reached the screen, O'Neil's name was missing from the writing card, which gave credit to Bart and Samuel Ornitz. (During the House Committee on Un-American Activities era, Ornitz, one of the "Hollywood Ten," was sentenced to prison for contempt of Congress. He served nine months of his one-year term.) According to studio announcements published in Hollywood trade papers as early as January 1934, Karl Freund was assigned to direct; a different early plan called for Lowell Sherman to direct *and* play the role of Dumont—an optimistic thought on *some*body's part, since Sherman had been suffering from laryngitis for much of the year.* Eventually Russian-born director Edward Ludwig came over from Warners to occupy the director's chair. Ludwig never directed another "horror" film, although he did helm a 1950s "big bug" movie, the Mexican-made *The Black Scorpion* (1957). His other credits include *The Last Gangster* (1937) with Edward G. Robinson, the 1940 *Swiss Family Robinson* and three John Wayne movies, including (around the time Samuel Ornitz was gazing up at those high prison walls) the anti–Commie *Big Jim McLain* (1952). Ain't life funny?

The star of *The Invisible Man*, Claude Rains returned from the East aboard the *Chief*, in his pocket a contract to do two Universal pictures; he arrived on September 5, six days before *Reclaimed His Head* began production. Universal originally planned for the actor to fulfill the other half of his contract with a co-starring role in *Bride of Frankenstein*, but ultimately had him made good his obligation by starring in *Mystery of Edwin Drood.*

Horror movie fans partial to Rains and Atwill, and who have gotten over the disappointment that invariably follows that first screening ("Where's the beef??"), should find much to admire in *Reclaimed His Head.* Though the plot seems a bit long in unraveling, the picture generates strong melodrama; in 1934, there was added interest in the story because of new, eye-opening disclosures about real-life munitions kings. Articles in the pressbook played up a re-

**Throughout most of the shooting schedule of* Reclaimed His Head, *Sherman was on the Universal lot directing the fantasy-comedy* Night Life of the Gods. *At the end of 1934, after directing five days of RKO's* Becky Sharp *despite the protests of his physicians, 49-year-old Sherman collapsed at the Pathé studio and was removed to a Hollywood hospital where he succumbed to an attack of double pneumonia.*

cent Senate inquiry which turned up the fact that, during the war years (1914–18), an American munitions manufacturer filled war orders to the tune of $1,245,000,000. More topical was the news that a French armament firm had recently been accused of contributing to the war chest of Adolf Hitler, at the same time that the firm's owner was egging on France *against* Hitler through his newspapers! According to the pressbook, the world was spending six billion dollars a year for cannons, warships, tanks, airplanes, poison gas, bombs and bullets.

The production is A-1 by Universal standards, with opulent sets, throngs of extras and an overall glossy look combining to give the impression of a first-rate movie. Performances are generally good, although there's room for improvement in Rains' interpretation. Rains' Verin is perhaps too much of a doormat for the world, with VICTIM stamped all over him in big letters. In early scenes he appears tickled pink by his poorhouse lifestyle, and prefers to shower his wife with affection rather than to make an effort to improve their lot. (Tellingly, *he's* the one who has to remember their anniversary!) He makes one self-deprecating crack about his own looks, perhaps a carry-over line from the play in which he was made-up to look like a bit of a gargoyle. The movie did away with that Cyrano-like aspect of the story; in fact, in the domestic scenes, Rains with his tousled hair, aw-shucks manner and Mister Rogers sweater looks downright cuddly. In his scenes with Atwill, Rains nicely conveys his near-rabid passion for peace. Quoted in the pressbook, Rains — a World War I veteran — said,

> I detest the whole idea of warfare. As a member of the British Army I spent more than three years in France during the World War, and after the signing of the Armistice I swore that no power on earth could induce me to take part in another battle.

Atwill, of course, is his dependably roguish-reptilian self: bluff and hearty, sleek and dangerous, as situations dictate. Of Atwill's character, the film's ads cried, EACH DEATH BY BULLETS MEANT A DOLLAR FOR HIS FUN. Joan Bennett, still a blonde, gives what might have been her best performance to date as Rains' wife, who becomes a triangle point as the picture builds toward its finish.

All other roles are strictly subordinate, with Henry O'Neill and Wallace Ford faring best in their supporting assignments. If not for Ford's character, "Curly," who turns up anywhere and everywhere, nothing in the movie would happen the way it does. At the beginning he's a drunken reveler who bursts into the Verins' wrong-side-of-the-tracks apartment with a bunch of equally obnoxious friends; you get the impression this total stranger to the Verins is a local boor, and down-at-the-heels like *they* are. But at the midpoint, he's seen dressed to the nines and attending an opera with a bunch of blueblood friends; and then at the end, after the start of the war, he's a dogface lying on the floor of a railroad station! His Forrest Gump–like ability to turn up in all the best *and* worst places, every time a character is needed to do or say something that'll give the plot a small push, becomes a little ridiculous. (In the play, where he's described as "a rat at heart," he's just as ubiquitous.) Unbilled members of the supporting cast include the Monster Kid–friendly likes of 17-year-old Valerie Hobson as a carnival girl, the star of the silent *The Lost World* Lloyd Hughes as Atwill's secretary, past and future vampire hunters Edward Van Sloan and Gilbert Emery as munitions board directors, past and future Frankenstein Monster hunter Lionel Belmore as a train conductor, and past and future sourpuss Doris Lloyd as an opera patron. Phyllis Brooks, who was briefly considered for the role of the Monster's Mate in *Bride of Frankenstein*, has a bit part as a secretary.

Baby Jane, a three-year-old playing the Verins' daughter, gives a performance that makes Donnie Dunagan's *Son of Frankenstein* thesping look like the stuff of Oscar gold. She squawks her lines in an unmodulated voice and couldn't be more indecipherable if she was hollering up from the bottom of a water-filled bathtub. Film historian William K. Everson once let off steam via his typewriter by describing the moppet actress (what's in a word?) as seemingly "incapable of taking direction, ignoring necessary pauses and missing cues," and summing up, "It's a pity that Rains, given his deranged state, couldn't have performed a similar act of vengeance [decapitation] on Baby Jane"! Everson also noted that in one *Reclaimed His Head* scene, Universal's version of Paris features in the background Waterloo Bridge, the Thames and St. Paul's.

The picture tells its story in flashback, which means that the horror angle (deranged Rains toting the disembodied head) is exploited as a takeoff point as well as in the finale. The framing sequences are far from the best scenes in the picture, although Rains, going to pieces in large, dramatic chunks, is convincing in his overwrought state. Director Ludwig deftly uses lighting and shadows in an effort to build suspense in the opening scene, but a few too many silent shots of O'Neill casting apprehensive sidelong looks at the valise-in-question ultimately have a comical effect.

A far more memorable scene is set in the magnificent salon of a yacht on the Mediterranean, with Dumont and munitions barons from the four corners of the world—"men without a country"—dispassionately hatching their plans to exploit the coming war. The symbolism gets laid on a bit heavily in the sequence in which Verin decides to desert his military unit, return to Paris and settle his score with Dumont. Running recklessly across a crowded train platform, he collides with a nun who drops her crucifix while Verin drops his bayonet. Picking up both, Verin thoughtfully regards the two objects in his hands before making his unalterable choice: He returns the crucifix, retaining the weapon. It's as subtle as a sledgehammer blow, but the scene gives us the satisfying foreknowledge that the picture may be building to something other than a talk-talk-talk ending. The moral of the movie, incidentally, seems to be that in troubled times, pacifism is the thinking man's way to go, unless of course somebody really riles you up personally, in which case you're within your rights to saw off his head and take it away as a keepsake!

The shooting of the fight between Paul and Verin turned into a lengthy ordeal and the subject of a contemporary article, undated and unsourced in the files of Lincoln Center's Performing Arts Library. According to the article, the scene was the last to be shot and took eight hours distributed over three days. A real French bayonet was deemed too dangerous for use in the Rains-Atwill scuffle, so an aluminum replica was made. The collar of Atwill's dress shirt was also made of aluminum, and on the left side was a small socket to receive the point of Rains' bayonet. After a long rehearsal, the scene was shot, and "it was expected that the rushes would register gripping drama when they were screened next day." Instead, they were rather funny. The camera eye revealed Rains as too small to be a plausible victor over the burly Atwill.

To remedy the situation, the scene was reshot with Rains wearing hobnailed trench boots, their soles an inch and a half thick, and walking toward Atwill on a runway that rose from floor level to a height of four inches. Again the results were unsatisfactory: Because of the camera angle, Atwill looked to be swallowing the blade instead of being stabbed with it! On the third day, cast and crew assembled on the set at 7:30 A.M. for several more tries before director Ludwig finally got the take he wanted.

The frenzied look on Rains' face in this close-quarters struggle was partially the work of makeup man Jack Pierce, who (again according to the article) "used wax life-masks in designing makeups for both Atwill and Rains.... He based the facial expression for Rains on Japanese war-mask principles. He distended the actor's eyes by holding them open with fish skin. He deepened Rains' naturally severe vertical brow wrinkle by building a ridge on either side of it with collodion. Around the eyes he made shadows of heavy blue which photographed deep gray. With red streaks down at either side of his mouth and the edges of his teeth darkened to seem pointed, Rains looked like a painted Indian on the warpath as he stalked Atwill."

Universal wanted it both ways, hyping the movie as a condemnation of war but also, for those houses "that had unusual success with *Dracula, Invisible Man* and *Frankenstein*," suggesting a number of horror movie-style publicity ploys: dressing a man in such a way that he appeared to have no head; a Frankenstein Monster–shaped "phantom figure," cut out of compo board, with flashing red and green eyes; a plaster head of Claude Rains on a platter in a glass case in the theater lobby, illuminated by green and red baby spots and talking via a small loudspeaker in the mouth. Universal *was* honest enough, however, to stress to exhibitors that this was *not* a sequel to *The Invisible Man*, despite what well-remembered scenes from that earlier movie (Rains' "headless" Dr. Griffin cavorting about) might lead the public to assume about this new Rains film.

A handsome dramatic picture, *Reclaimed His Head* builds interest steadily and conceals its stage origins well. Bolstered by a good cast and some solid performances, it's a production in which Universal should have taken pride — perhaps even pushed as a hard-hitting successor to their 1930 Best Picture Oscar winner *All Quiet on the Western Front*. But to the surprise of probably no one, most theater managers took the horror approach in their exploitation. The result: Most folks who'd be interested in an anti-war movie probably never even heard about it.

Bizarre postscript: According to a 1942 *Saturday Evening Post* article on the past, present and future of Universal horror films, a sequel to *Invisible Agent*, the ain't-war-fun? entry in Universal's Invisible Man series, was already scripted and awaiting production. Its title: *The Invisible Man Reclaims His Head.*

Critics' Corner

Though the movies prove a more congenial medium than the stage for Jean Bart's *The Man Who Reclaimed His Head*, this rueful drama of idealism versus greed still fails, in its screen version, to probe either deeply or convincingly into its theme.... [T]he picture is a stilted harangue against war and the munitions makers, made to seem even more stilted by pompous dialogue and an exhibition of artificial acting which, in numerical strength alone, probably is unique in recent screen history. There is not a genuine performance in the cast....—*The New York Herald-Tribune*, January 9, 1935, Thornton Delehanty

As the picture comes to us from the stage, it is subject somewhat to the limitations of the theatre. That is, it is burdened with dialogue and lacking in action. Yet the dialogue is so fraught with drama and what action there is proves so dynamic, that the balance seems well maintained....—*The New York American*, January 9, 1935

The tempo of the film is slow and deliberate, but Mr. Claude Rains is there to carry it along.—*The London Times*, June 10, 1935

[H]eavy anti-war propaganda, rather clumsily expressed through the agency of old-fashioned melodrama. The French atmosphere is very poor, and the directorial touches are cheap.—*The Kinematograph Weekly* (GB), January 17, 1935

[This] is strong meat. It blithely ignores all precepts for cinema success, yet by its passion and honesty it becomes a film of vigor and singular beauty.—*Liberty*, January 19, 1935

[A] picture that is at once intelligent, thought-provoking and good entertainment.... Jean Bart and Samuel Ornitz plus the direction of Edward Ludwig ... gets such grand performances out of Claude Rains, Joan Bennett and Lionel Atwill, plus the courage of the producer ... in letting them go the whole hog to make a really important picture, deserve all the credit and backing that audiences and exhibitors have to give.—*The Hollywood Reporter*, December 24, 1934

Rating: ★★★ With his performance in *Crime Without Passion* [1934] still sharply etched in the minds of serious moviegoers, Claude Rains comes to the Rialto Theatre again to put himself over in the grandest manner.... [A] personal triumph which overshadows even the undoubted worthiness of the film of which he is star.—*The New York Daily News*, January 9, 1935, Wanda Hale

It is Mr. Rains' performance which holds the piece together, building it up to a fine frenzy of terror and suspense.—*The New York Sun*, January 9, 1935

For the type of drama that it is, this production represents a nice job of writing, directing, acting, and general production handling. Its theme and treatment, however, put it more or less in the intellectual class.... Rains, Atwill and Bennett give outstanding performances.—*The Film Daily*, January 8, 1935

Life Returns

Released late 1934(?). Re-released by Scienart Pictures in 1938. 60 minutes. *Producer:* Lou Ostrow. *Director:* Eugen [Eugene] Frenke. *Screenplay & Adaptation:* Arthur Horman & John F. Goodrich. *Dialogue:* Mary McCarthy & L. Wolfe Gilbert. *Original Story:* Eugen [Eugene] Frenke & James Hogan. *Photography:* Robert Planck. *Art Director:* Ralph Berger. *Music Score:* Oliver Wallace & Clifford Vaughan. *Editor:* Harry Marker. *Sound Recorder:* Richard Tyler.

Onslow Stevens (*Dr. John Kendrick*), George Breakston (*Danny Kenrick*), Lois Wilson (*Dr. Louise Stone*), Valerie Hobson (*Mrs. Kendrick*), Stanley Fields (*Dogcatcher*), Frank Reicher (*Dr. James*), Richard Carle (*A.K. Arnold*), Dean Benton (*Interne*), Lois January (*Nurse*), Richard Quine (*Mickey*), Maidel Turner (*Mrs. Vandergriff*), George MacQuarrie (*Judge*), Otis Harlan (*Dr. Henderson*), Robert E. Cornish (*Himself*), Mario Margutti, William Black, Ralph Celmar, Roderick Krida (*Cornish's Staff*).

Its biggest handicap is extreme dullness.
—Variety, *January 4, 1939*

We know this has happened to you, because it's happened to *all* of us: There's a genre movie you've heard about for years but never seen. It's got a horror or sci-fi angle, the plot sounds intriguing, and there are players in it that you like. You get to the point where you just *ache* to see the darn thing. Finally good fortune smiles upon you and the opportunity presents itself.

Ten minutes into the picture and your enthusiasm is starting to go. Ten more minutes: Your enthusiasm is gone and your interest is waning. You can't keep your mind from wandering, and the plot begins to get away from you. Long before the picture's over, you'd rather be in Hell with your back broken (to quote a recurring line of Billy Wilder movie dialogue).

For Universal fans, that picture is *Life Returns.*

Life Returns is a hopeless, exasperating conglomeration of events and images masquerading as a motion picture. For all the many years that it was out of circulation, fans knew only that Universal had released it and that the title and plotline suggested a borderline science fiction theme, and so hopes were raised. But the cold light of rediscovery revealed a depressingly cheap, incoherent flick built around a questionable scientific achievement.

On May 22, 1934, at the University of Southern California, a young scientist named Robert E. Cornish succeeded in surgically and chemically restoring "life" to a "dead" dog. Abetted by a team of assistants, Cornish coordinated and dominated the unusual experiment, which was captured for posterity by motion picture cameras. Dr. Eugene Frenke, a German producer-director, apparently latched onto Cornish and the filmed record of the operation and decided to make a film that would incorporate this "historic" footage. Frenke struck a deal with Universal, contracting to split costs and profits on the production.

The film opens at Hoskins University, where three young eggheads have embarked on a noble mission. John Kendrick (Onslow Stevens), Louise Stone (Lois Wilson) and Robert Cornish (as himself) are striving to develop a fluid that will restore life to the dead. Upon graduation, Kendrick proudly announces to Louise and Cornish that he has secured positions for all three at the Arnold Research Laboratory, But Louise and Cornish, puzzled and dismayed by Kendrick's action, are convinced that a commercial laboratory is no place for this type of research: for one thing, the Arnold lab would take all the credit for the eventual discovery. (So much for altruism!) Kendrick, undeterred, breaks off with Louise and Cornish and goes to work at the Arnold foundation.

A montage suggests the passage of time, and also alerts us to Kendrick's marriage to a socialite (Valerie Hobson) to whom the film doesn't even bother to give a first name. A.K. Arnold (Richard Carle), head of the foundation, loses faith in Kendrick's experiment, which he has also decided is not commercial. (Yeah, who the heck would pay money to prevent the passing of a loved one?) "We want this foundation to help the living to live better — to give them better facial creams, better nail polish, better dandruff cures — all for a nominal sum!" the crotchety Arnold announces. Arnold tries to soften the blow by assigning him to create a hair-restoring brush out of pig's bristles. Kendrick resigns.

Already the picture is beginning to come apart. Obviously the audience was expected to perceive Arnold as an exploitation-minded meddler, interfering with the work of great men and true scientists. But Kendrick comes across as such a dazed, glassy-eyed dreamer that Arnold's misgivings seem well-founded. Apparently Kendrick has been there for years and hasn't made a bit of progress; he slips into a world of his own while talking about his experiment, starts whimpering when he doesn't get his way, and finally staggers out like a zombie. Instead of resenting Arnold, the audience feels that he probably deserves a medal for putting up with Kendrick for as long as he did!

Kendrick has a private medical practice on the side, but he's in such a daze over the termination of this research work that he lets it go all to hell. Mrs. Kendrick tries to argue some sense into him — he has a wife and a little boy to support, yet all he does is mope and whine — but her pleas go unheeded. A few more years pass, and Mrs. Kendrick dies of some undisclosed ailment. Court officials want to send Kendrick's young son Danny (George Breakston) to Juvenile Hall; the irresponsible Kendrick shows up in court in his usual trance, looking like someone who sleeps in a cement mixer. To avoid being sent to Juvenile Hall, Danny and his dog Scooter run away.

A lot more film unspools without much happening. Danny finds a home with a gang of kids his own age, and brags about his genius father. Kendrick loafs around his house looking stoned. On the cheapest lab set in the history of the movies, Louise and Cornish wonder aloud what ever happened to him.

When the local dogcatcher (Stanley Fields) nabs Scooter, Danny is heartbroken. He and his gang scale the dog pound wall in an attempt to spring the mutt, but everything goes wrong and one of the kids fractures his leg during the getaway. The dogcatcher gasses Scooter.

Danny begs his dad to help the kid with the injured leg and to revive Scooter, but Kendrick moans that he can't do either. Finally fed up with his worthless dad, and rightfully so, Danny bawls him out and heads for Juvenile Hall to turn himself in. Kendrick finally snaps out of his slump, retrieves the dog's body and rushes it to a hospital. The U.S.C. film is cut into the picture at this point, with studio shots of Kendrick, Louise and other actor-doctors spliced in at intervals. Life returns to Scooter and Danny's faith in his father is restored.

Life Returns has a slapdash, slung-together quality that puts it at the level of some of the worst of that era's cheap indie productions — in fact, *below* that level. It has the low-grade look and feel of a film consisting solely of first takes, good, bad and indifferent.

As Dr. Kendrick, Onslow Stevens turns in a dreary performance. Throughout the film, he staggers about in a fog, his hair mussed and clothes disheveled. You get the feeling you're expected to be pulling for him, but he lets his ailing wife to die and permits his son to live in the streets. It's hard to think of another genre movie in which the central character sinks quite so humiliatingly low. In fact, it's also hard to think of a leading character, in *any* movie, who does less: Dr. Kendrick starts a project he can't finish, gets a job he can't hold and builds a family he can't support. He does not take part in the climactic experiment, merely standing off to one side, explaining the procedure and having the gall to take partial credit for the discovery. Throughout most of the film, he dozes on an old couch.

The entire experience must surely have been an embarrassment for Onslow Stevens, a stage and screen actor capable of better work. A native Californian, he began acting with the Pasadena Community Playhouse in 1926 and appeared in his first film (Universal's serial *Heroes of the West*) in 1932. Rebounding between film and stage work, he racked up a total of nearly 100 movie appearances between 1932 and 1962, including many films with horror or science fiction elements: Universal's *Secret of the Blue Room, House of Dracula* and the serial *The Vanishing Shadow*, plus *The Monster and the Girl* (1941), *The Creeper* (1948), *Them!* (1954), *The Couch* (1962) and others. He didn't have what it took to gain popularity as a leading man nor the panache to establish himself as a memorable movie villain (he made numerous stabs at both), and soon settled into a niche as a reliable Hollywood supporting actor. From the Too Much Information dept.: He was also a nudist who sometimes encouraged other actors to give it a try!

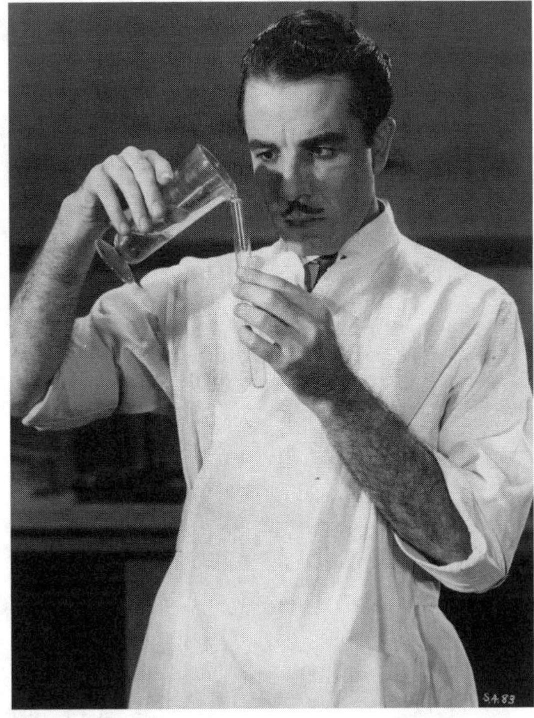

Onslow Stevens portrayed a medico searching for a method to bring back the dead in *Life Returns* (courtesy John Cocchi).

Kendrick's irritating son Danny is played by kid actor George Breakston. Breakston stuck with acting until the early '40s (he was in several Andy Hardy films), served in the Signal Corps in the Pacific Theatre during World War II, and then remained overseas after his discharge. Movie-wise he reappeared on the *other* side of the camera as a writer-producer-director of films made in Japan, Africa and Europe, including the gruesome *The Manster* (1962). At age 53, he died in the city where he was born, Paris.

No one in the rest of the cast is in the pic-

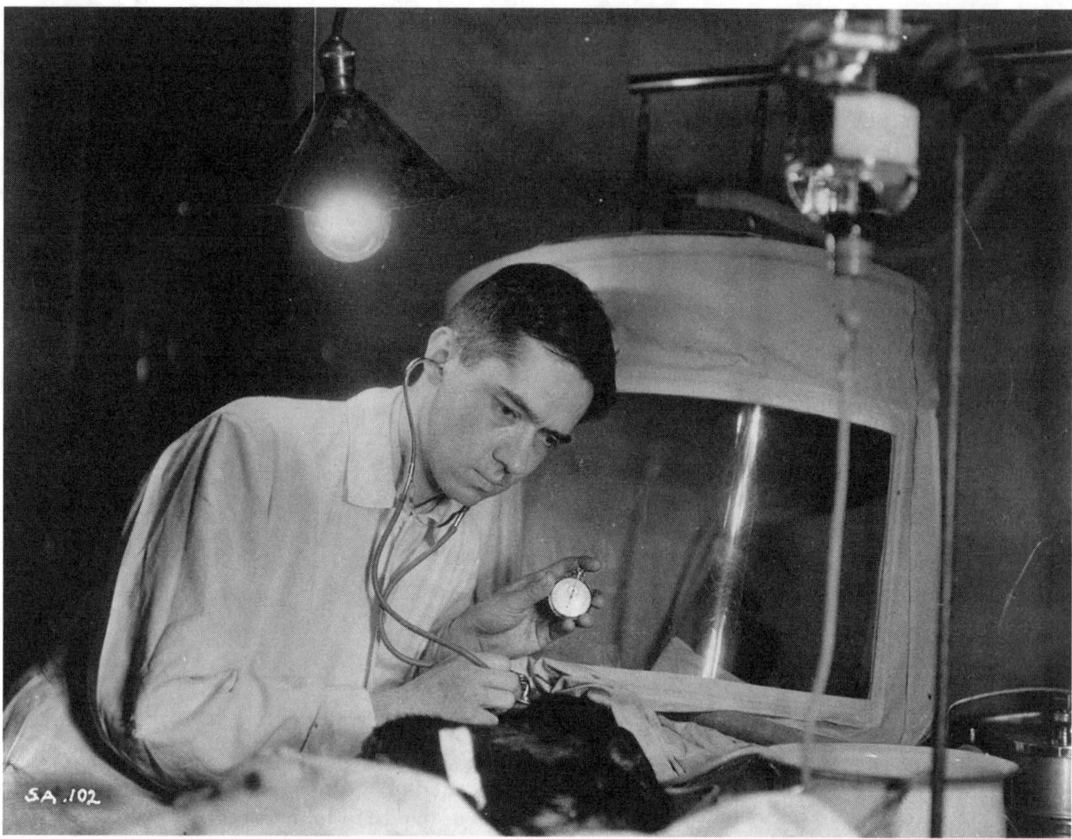

Real-life footage of Dr. Robert E. Cornish resuscitating a dead dog was incorporated into *Life Returns*. The film was banned in England for being in "bad taste" (courtesy John Cocchi).

ture long enough to make an impression. Lois Wilson (Kendrick's cohort Louise) was a silent screen star on her way down, while 17-year-old British actress Valerie Hobson (Mrs. Kendrick) was on her way up. Stanley Fields, Frank Reicher and Richard Carle are among the recognizable faces in the supporting cast. Child actor Richard Quine, who plays a member of Danny's gang, later turned director and helmed *The Solid Gold Cadillac* (1956), *Operation Mad Ball* (1957), *Bell, Book and Candle* (1958), *The World of Suzie Wong* (1960) and *W* (1974). He killed himself in 1989. Dr. Cornish, who appears as himself, hardly opens his mouth until the end — and *then* it's to give mouth-to-mouth resuscitation to the dead dog! Scooter's portrayal of the dog is highly convincing and he prances away with top acting honors.

The "money shots" in the movie are, of course, the footage of Cornish et al. working to revive the dog. They're crudely filmed and visually uninteresting: shots of the various doctors at work and of Cornish coordinating things (and giving the pooch the aforementioned mouth-to-mouth). These operation scenes are intercut with scenes of youngster Breakston tearfully hurrying toward the orphanage, accompanied through the streets by weepy violins on the soundtrack.

James Hogan was responsible (along with Frenke) for the original story of *Life Returns*, which is interesting since Hogan later directed *The Mad Ghoul*, a mediocre but infinitely more satisfying movie with the same seed idea (restoring the dead). Frenke also engaged Reginald LeBorg as a writer on *Life Returns*, but the pair had disagreements over the handling of the story and LeBorg was dropped. Since LeBorg received no screen credit, his work may have been simply discarded.

Frenke had a spotty motion picture career. He was the husband of actress Anna Sten, the Edsel of '30s Hollywood glamour girls, and most of his early pictures like *Exile Express* (1939), which he produced, and *Two Who Dared* (1937), which he produced and directed, were attempts to "return life" to her moribund acting career. Frenke later took a small step-up in class, producing "better" pictures like *Let's Live a Little* (1948), in which the ubiquitous Sten was third-billed in support of Hedy Lamarr; *Heaven Knows, Mr. Allison* (1957), *The Barbarian and the Geisha* (1958) and *The Last Sunset* (1961). In 1962 he produced *The Nun and the Sergeant*, a Korean War cheapie with (yawn) Sten again.

Frenke was apparently happy with *Life Returns* (so *he* was the one!), and he even pressed Universal to allow him to make a follow-up picture in which a dead *man* is brought back to life. Universal couldn't quite see it, and Doc Cornish was demanding too much money for his participation and the use of his name anyway. In a funny postscript, director Karl Freund contacted Frenke and asked to be allowed to view a print of *Life Returns*. Frenke had no idea why Freund wanted to see it but he probably assumed it had something to do with the proposed follow-up. Instead of using an available print, Frenke dipped into his own pocket and paid to have a new print struck, and showed the picture to Freund. After the screening, Frenke could not have been overly pleased to learn that Freund was just sniffing around for an idea or two to use in his upcoming Metro horror film *Mad Love* (1935)!

In 1937, Frenke brought a $145,424 lawsuit against Universal charging that the studio had not released *Life Returns* through regular channels with attendant publicity for his $48,000 investment. *Life Returns* was reissued in 1938 through an outfit called Scienart Pictures, at which point it garnered the bad reviews it should have gotten on the first go-round. *Life Returns* has since gone public domain, but only in recent years have purveyors of p.d. movies begun releasing it on VHS and DVD. Many of the 21st century reviewers, *and* the fans who post on horror movie-related message boards, have echoed a single comment: "The authors of *Universal Horrors* said not to bother with this movie, and I should have listened!"

Cornish and his scientific achievement appear to have slipped into near-total obscurity, which does not seem like it would be the case if Cornish had actually accomplished what the film purports he has done. The whole idea of a life-restoring serum on the real-life medical horizon is simply too far-out to accept and overlooks, for one thing, the brain's need for constant oxygenation.

But the spirit of old Doc Cornish lives on: In June 2005, a chagrined media began reporting that researchers at the University of Pittsburgh are "killing" dozens of dogs for the purpose of attempting to bring them back to life. Dogs of all breeds and sizes are drained of blood, and their veins filled with an ice-cold saline solution which drops their body temperature to near-freezing. In this state of extreme hypothermia, they are scientifically "dead" (no breathing, heartbeat or brain activity). They are then brought back to life by returning the blood to their bodies, giving them pure oxygen and applying electric shocks to restart their hearts. The maximum amount of time the dogs can lie "dead" is three hours, and many are "re-born" with physical or behavioral problems. The researchers' goal, head man Patrick Kochanek told *The New York Post*, is to be able to put humans (critically wounded soldiers, shooting victims, etc.) in suspended animation for a few hours until they can receive proper medical help.

This being the 21st century, the doctors are facing a problem which did not exist for Robert Cornish in 1935: PETA. "These experiments are indefensible nonsense," raged a spokeswoman for People for the Ethical Treatment of Animals.

Critics' Corner

The picture lends itself ideally to exploitation.... The actual production ... has been delicately handled and is not offensive or gruesome. The direction by Dr. Eugene Frenke is excellent. Onslow Stevens and George Breakston give fine performances.—*The Film Daily*, January 2, 1935

A fair human interest program entertainment.... As far as adults are concerned, the most interesting parts of the picture are the closing scenes, which show the actual experiment.... The story leading up to this situation is simple and should appeal more to juveniles than adults.... The fault lies with the director; it is slow and stilted.—*Harrison's Reports*, April 20, 1935

Every performance is plodding, colorless, and it's a pic much longer to the audience than its accredited running time would indicate. Represents small biz possibility.—*Variety*, January 4, 1939, "Barn"

[A] loser and a snoozer.... A moment, please, while life returns to my butt after watching this.—*Cult Movies* #8, 1993, Tim Murphy

1935

Mystery of Edwin Drood

Released February 4, 1935. 87 minutes. *Producer:* Carl Laemmle, Jr. *Director:* Stuart Walker. *Associate Producer:* Edmund Grainger. *Based on the unfinished novel* The Mystery of Edwin Drood *by Charles Dickens. Screenplay:* John L. Balderston & Gladys Unger. Adapted by Bradley King & Leopold Atlas. *Photography:* George Robinson. *Special Effects:* John P. Fulton. *Editor:* Edward Curtiss. *Music:* Edward Ward. *Recording Engineer:* Gilbert Kurland. *Assistant Directors:* Phil Karlstein [Karlson] & Harry Mancke. *Art Director:* Albert S. D'Agostino. *Makeup:* Otto Lederer. *Technical Advisor:* Madame Hilda Grenier. *Wardrobe:* Frank Beetson. *Hairdresser:* Margaret Donovan. *Script Clerk:* Myrtle Gibsone.

Claude Rains (*John Jasper*), Douglass Montgomery (*Neville Landless/Mr. Datchery*), Heather Angel (*Rosa Bud*), Valerie Hobson (*Helena Landless*), David Manners (*Edwin "Ned" Drood*), Francis L. Sullivan (*Rev. Mr. Septimus Crisparkle*), Zeffie Tilbury (*Opium Den Hag*), Ethel Griffies (*Mrs. Twinkleton*), E.E. Clive (*Thomas Sapsea*), Walter Kingsford (*Hiram Grewgious*), Forrester Harvey (*Durdles*), Veda Buckland (*Mrs. Tope*), Elsa Buchanan (*Mrs. Tisher*), George Ernest (*Deputy*), J.M. Kerrigan (*Chief Verger Tope*), Louise Carter (*Mrs. Crisparkle*), Harry Cording (*Turke*), D'Arcy Corrigan (*Opium Addict*), Anne O'Neal, Helena Grant, Evelyn Beresford (*Maids*), Edward Cooper (*Dean*), Corbet Morris (*Dancing Master*), Eugene Strong (*Coachman*), George Kirby (*Bailiff*), Dora Mayfield, May Beatty (*Gossips*), Gordon Douglas (*Coroner*), Will Geer (*Lamp Lighter*),Walter Brennan (*Milk Man*), Anne Darling, Rosebud Eberling, Rosita Butler, Alice Ernest, Francis Roberts, Dorothy Shearer, Bunny Beatty, Helen Parrish, Iris Moore, Violet Moore, Carla Laemmle, Anne Harrison, Barbara Perry, Lois Verner (*Girls in School*), Lloyd Whitlock, Effie Ellsler.

Not for children, adolescents, or Sundays.
—Harrison's Reports, *February 9, 1935*

When Charles Dickens died in 1870 while in the midst of writing his novel *The Mystery of Edwin Drood,* he left behind a puzzle that has fired the imaginations of literary cognoscente and armchair sleuths for many decades: What was the mysterious fate that befell young Edwin Drood? Did he take flight and disappear into the countryside during a torrential Christmas Eve storm? Did he suffer a violent death at the hands of his demented uncle, John Jasper? Or did he perhaps go into hiding, only to return to his village weeks later incognito? The last words that the celebrated author wrote in the 23rd chapter of his novel regarded the inquisitive old stranger Mr. Datchery, who came home to supper, made an elusive chalk mark on his cupboard, "and then falls to with an appetite." Was Datchery actually Edwin Drood, his youthful features buried beneath a wig and false beard?

Not content to let the matter rest unresolved, 120 authors volunteered over 100 possible conclusions to the Dickens tale over the ensuing decades. Many of the books, plays and dissertations that evolved out of this investigation asserted that Jasper was indeed guilty of killing his nephew. The furor over this tempest in a teapot peaked on the night of January 7, 1914, when John Jasper was literally put on trial in Kings Hall in Covent Garden, London. Jasper was represented by a Frederick T. Harry; the celebrated author and Dickensian Gilbert Keith Chesterton presided over the hearing as judge; the jury, composed mainly of writers, was headed by dramatist George Bernard Shaw. The result of this good-natured, entirely extemporaneous performance was that Jasper was found guilty of manslaughter, a verdict, Chesterton sarcastically contended, the jury had arrived at during lunch.* The mock trial attracted international attention and received front page coverage in the following morning's edition of *The New York Times* (evidently January 7, 1914, was a slow news day).

The idea of adapting the classic Gothic thriller by one of the giants of English literature

**British economist-humorist–Dickensian Stephen Leacock disagreed with the jury's verdict, contending that Drood had escaped from Jasper's murderous grasp and disappeared. The choirmaster, in his opium-induced delirium, believed that he had committed the murder after all. Drood eventually returns to the village to confront his guilt-stricken uncle who confesses to the attack, leaving the way open for a happy ending. Leacock based his supposition on the fact that Dickens had at one time considered titling his novel* The Flight of Edwin Drood *or* Edwin Drood in Hiding, *suggesting that the young man survives the outcome of the story.*

was an attractive proposition for a status-conscious studio like Universal. Even more tempting was the potential for exploiting a property with an open-ended finale (a marvelous built-in gimmick that begged for publicity). Unaware of the disappointing box office response that their first Dickens adaptation, *Great Expectations* (1934), would receive, Universal pulled all stops cost-wise and bolstered audience appeal of *Mystery of Edwin Drood* with a fine cast of popular players and lavish production values (the film was budgeted at $215,375). An aggressive advertising campaign naturally capitalized on the novelty of the unresolved ending. Had the public's response to *Mystery of Edwin Drood* measured up to Universal's great expectations, the studio would have more than likely produced other features based on Dickens' works. One can imagine the ire generated by the Front Office when MGM released in 1935 fabulously successful adaptations of *David Copperfield* and *A Tale of Two Cities*. When it came to creating motion picture renditions of the great classics, MGM had the resources, an enviable stable of first-rate writers and (of course) the star power to put most Hollywood studios to shame.

While it wasn't as faithful to Dickens as *Great Expectations* had been, *Mystery of Edwin Drood* won the approval of most film critics of the time. Neither an all-out horror story nor a puzzling whodunit, this Edmund Grainger production stands up today as a quaintly charming and atmospheric Victorian melodrama, handsomely outfitted and authentically detailed, though lacking in real suspense. Stuart Walker directs the period piece in a decisive manner and, with the aid of George Robinson's typically fine camerawork and Albert S. D'Agostino's evocative set design, sustains a rich Dickensian flavor. A former Cincinnati playwright and producer, Walker formed a highly successful stock company in his hometown and founded the famous Portmanteau Theatre there. After producing a series of one-act plays on Broadway, Walker became an assistant producer at Paramount, gaining valuable experience working on B films. Moving to Universal, he was put in charge of his own production unit and made such pictures as *Romance in the Rain* (1934) and the aforementioned *Great Expectations*.

Mystery of Edwin Drood is a crisper and better directed film than Walker's *WereWolf of London*, which suffers from occasional staginess and slack pacing. Headlining the cast in a role that was originally considered for Boris Karloff, Claude Rains enacts the lonely, opium-addicted John Jasper with grim conviction and his customary flair for overindulgence. His character is portrayed as the pitiful victim of the strict conventions of the era. Jasper's fatal inability to come to grips with his unrequited passion for the virginal Rosa Bud leads him to commit murder and finally resort to suicide. (Rains' dedication to his craft led to personal injury on the set: He twisted his right ankle leaping from an eight-foot roof while shooting the film's climax.)

The story is set in 1864 in the little English village of Cloisterham. Jasper, the distinguished choirmaster of Cloisterham cathedral, is hopelessly addicted to opium. His obsessive love for Rosa Bud (Heather Angel), a student whom he is teaching to sing, drives the restless churchman into deeper and deeper despair. Rosa is betrothed to Jasper's cocky young nephew Edwin Drood (David Manners), an arrangement that pleases neither party. Although Jasper loves Edwin (whom he affectionately calls Ned) like a son, he subconsciously wishes the young man dead for taking Rosa away from him.

Enter Neville Landless (Douglass Montgomery), a passionate, quick-tempered youth from Ceylon who has come to Cloisterham with his sister Helena (Valerie Hobson) to live with the Reverend Mr. Crisparkle (Francis L. Sullivan). A feud immediately develops between the argumentative Neville and the arrogant Drood, creating an uncomfortable situation that Jasper is quick to seize upon. Unbeknownst to Jasper, Rosa and Edwin have broken off their engagement, leaving her free to enjoy Neville's affections and he free to pursue the eligible Helena.

Assuming the role of peacemaker, the scheming choirmaster invites Edwin and Neville to dine with him on Christmas Eve. A furious storm erupts that evening, causing considerable damage to the surrounding area. Before they head their separate ways, the two young rivals join hands as friends.

The next morning, the village is shocked by the news that Edwin Drood has disappeared. A search of the countryside and the river turn up nothing conclusive. Jasper arouses the com-

Double life: By day, a respected choirmaster, by night, an opium-addicted killer in love with his young ward. Claude Rains (with Zeffie Tilbury) in Charles Dickens' *Mystery of Edwin Drood.*

placent constabulary to take action at once. As a result, Neville is placed under guard. Circumstantial evidence and his past history of violent behavior weigh heavily against the young man. He escapes from prison and takes off into the countryside, destination unknown.

Weeks later, a curious old man who calls himself Mr. Datchery (he's actually Neville in disguise) arrives in Cloisterham and begins making inquiries about the Drood case and John Jasper. Piecing together evidence that he obtained from several townspeople, including an opium den hag (Zeffie Tilbury) and Durdles (Forrester Harvey) the sodden stonemason, Neville concludes that Jasper murdered Edwin out of his insane love for Rosa. He then buried Drood's body in a coffin filled with quicklime in the crypt beneath the cathedral. Rosa's betrothal ring, which Drood was wearing at the time of his death, is all that remains of his former existence, but it's enough evidence to nail Jasper on a charge of murder.

Revealing his identity, Neville leads the authorities on a mad chase after Jasper through the upper reaches of the cathedral. Consumed with guilt, the tormented choirmaster throws himself from the parapet to his death on the steps below.

Banking on a winner from a critical as well as a commercial standpoint, Universal took pains to insure that *Mystery of Edwin Drood* bore the stamp of authenticity in every detail. According to studio publicity, in the summer of 1934, officials from Universal's London office shot thousands of feet of film and took numerous still shots of various Victorian-style structures in the English town of Rochester. Albert S. D'Agostino designed a replica of an English village of Dickens' time, which was erected at considerable cost on the back lot; it was the largest exterior set Universal had built since the days of *The Hunchback of Notre Dame* (1923). Mme. Hilda Grenier, a former confidante of Queen Mary of England and an authority on the mid–Victorian period, was brought to Southern California to act as technical advisor. Not only did Madame see to it that the furnishings and props were faithful to the era, she also meticulously coached the performers in the proper rules of prissy period deportment.

Delayed briefly on account of casting difficulties, shooting began on November 12, 1934, and continued into January 1935. Once again, Universal veiled a new production in a shroud of secrecy. Supposedly, only a half-dozen people on the lot knew the solution to the mystery. Playwrights John L. Balderston, Gladys Unger and Leopold Atlas and Hollywood scenarist (Miss) Bradley King were all sworn not to reveal the ending. Grainger and Walker saw to it that none of the cast members knew until the final scenes were shot how the story was going to conclude (none of the scripts had the ending attached to them). Not even the censors' office was spared; only two men other than Joseph Breen himself were privy to the picture's denouement. (Is it possible that the producers of television's *Dallas* picked up a cue from Universal when they concocted the classic "Who Shot J.R.?" episode in the early '80s?)

Many of the critics who reviewed *Mystery of Edwin Drood* in February 1935 seemed satisfied (though certainly not overwhelmed) by the predictable solution arrived at by the quartet of writers. As Dickens had left behind voluminous notes indicating that he was considering at least three possible alternatives, the scenarists simply chose the most logical one. A press release claimed that the writers drew up case histories of the characters and charted their activities from the time of the story through old age. Using these "biographies" as a guide, each author wrote an original scenario without consulting the other three. From these different accounts, a vote was taken and a decision arrived at. As might be expected, murder won out.

For all the fuss and to-do generated by Universal to stir up interest in this business, it's a mite disappointing to learn how obvious is their solution to the mystery. Right from the start of the film (the camera eavesdrops on Jasper caught in the grip of opium-induced delirium tremens), we expect the worst from the frustrated churchman. "No wretched monk who ever groaned his life away in that gloomy cathedral could have been more tired of it!" he complains bitterly to his nephew. "He could take to carving demons for relief—and did! What shall I do? Must I take to carving them out of my heart?" Here is a man whose circumstances are suffocating him; Jasper is capable of the most heinous of crimes, including snuffing out the life of a man whom he virtually worships.

By telegraphing Jasper's evil intentions so far in advance, Walker and his collaborators have left precious little to our imaginations. Jasper's descent into the cathedral's ancient crypt and his inordinate curiosity regarding such esoteric matters as locating empty tombs and the effects of quicklime on a corpse most assuredly seals Edwin's fate in the mind of the viewer. (Contrary to the claim fostered by this picture and others such as 1958's *The Haunted Strangler*, quicklime does not destroy a corpse; in fact, it is more likely to act as a preservative!) By revealing the true identity of the stranger, Mr. Datchery, three-quarters of the way into the story, the suspense factor is further dissipated.

The stifling conventions of Charles Dickens' era are observed in several telling passages. Hemmed in by the rigid behavioral codes of the churchman ("The cramped monotony of my existence grinds me away..."), Jasper dares not express his overwhelming desire for Rosa. When Neville is arrested for Edwin's murder, Jasper seizes upon it as an opportunity to claim the girl, and attempts to strike an odious bargain with her (Rosa's love for Neville's freedom). Jasper's pitiable declaration of love, passionately declared in the courtyard of Rosa's finishing school (where nary a word is whispered that isn't monitored by head mistress Miss Twinkleton [Ethel Griffies] and her network of spies), evokes our sympathies for the choirmaster if only for a moment. Racism and class status rear their ugly heads in the tense confrontation between Neville and Edwin when Drood takes offense at the Ceylonese's affections toward Rosa. ("We English don't encourage fellows with dark skins to admire our girls!")

Supporting Rains are such attractive young players as Douglass Montgomery, Heather Angel, David Manners and Valerie Hobson. Twenty-five-year-old Montgomery (who began his picture career under the name Kent Douglass) had been wearying of the long procession of juvenile roles that he was being assigned at

Showman's campaign ad for *Mystery of Edwin Drood*, Universal's filmization of the unfinished Dickens novel.

Universal, and welcomed the chance to get into old-age makeup. Montgomery's brooding, unconventional good looks made him an ideal romantic lead in such quaint dramas as *Edwin Drood* and *Little Man, What Now?* (1934). Heather Angel radiates girlhood innocence as the much-admired Rosa. Valerie Hobson, on the other hand, has little to do as Neville's loving sister Helena.

Rich, fruity portraits are etched by the minor players: Walter Kingsford's self-effacing Hiram Grewgious, Forrester Harvey's likable stonemason, Zeffie Tilbury's crusty old opium den hag and, as always, the superbly pompous E.E. Clive as magistrate Thomas Sapsea. (Actor John Howard, who co-starred with Clive in a string of '30s Bulldog Drummond mysteries, recalled the British actor with affection, and revealed to the authors that Clive claimed to have been quite the rake in his younger days.)

The epitome of the classically handsome but bland and ineffectual '30s horror leading man, David Manners fared far better in roles such as "Ned" Drood and the savvy screenwriter in 1933's *The Death Kiss* opposite *Dracula* co-stars Bela Lugosi and Edward Van Sloan. *Mystery of Edwin Drood* turned out to be the actor's final chiller credit. Born Rauff de Ryther Duan Acklom in Halifax, Nova Scotia, Canada, in 1901, Manners gained his first experience acting in a Trinity School presentation of "The Tempest." Bitten by the acting bug, he signed with Eva LeGallienne's Civic Repertory Company, and got the opportunity to act opposite Helen Hayes in "Dancing Mothers." Future horror maestro James Whale took notice of Manners' stage work and cast him in an important role (Second Lt. Raleigh) in the director's screen version of *Journey's End*, based on R.C. Sherriff's acclaimed play set during World War I.

In due time, Manners became a favorite of Hollywood's elite leading ladies. Over the next six years, he waxed romantically before the camera with such lionized stars as Katharine Hepburn, Loretta Young, Mae Clarke, Kay Francis, Claudette Colbert, Myrna Loy and Constance Bennett. Though Manners will forever be remembered for his horror film appearances, the actor gave his most deeply felt performances in such somber works as Frank Capra's 1931 *The Miracle Woman* (as a blind man under the influence of faith healer Barbara Stanwyck) and *The Last Flight* (also 1931), a moving drama delineating the trials and tribulations of the Lost Generation. He was reunited in the latter with Dracula love interest Helen Chandler; the two young stars gave earnest performances, vindicating the inadequacies of their acting in the Tod Browning classic.

Disenchanted with the film capital, Manners realized his heart's desire and built a guest ranch in the Mojave Desert, where he hosted such celebrated houseguests as Greta Garbo, Clark Gable and Albert Einstein. He devoted his time to painting and writing novels with a spiritual basis. On several occasions, he returned to performing, including an engagement on Broadway, under the direction of Elia Kazan, opposite a budding Marlon Brando. Manners clearly preferred the stage over motion pictures. In a late-in-life interview with journalist-filmmaker Rick McKay, the aged actor confided:

> I didn't like movies. You see, in a play you *become* the play, because you start in the beginning and end up at the end of the script. Movies, you do little bits and you don't know where it fits in.... It has no unity. I would advise anybody—a kid—instead of doing pictures, get experience! Do theater! Get theater in his blood!

Asked by McKay to comment on Claude Rains and *Mystery of Edwin Drood*, Manners reminisced, "Claude Rains? Oh, nice man. Very honest. Dickens would never have published it at all! It was *not* good enough. It was not a finished novel, and it was not a good movie at all." One of the last survivors of Horror's Golden Age, David Manners passed away at the ripe age of 97 on December 23, 1998.

In the summer of 1964, Tom Gries, then directing for the New York–based *East Side, West Side* TV series (and later the director of 1976's *Helter Skelter*), announced that he was going to write, produce and direct a new film version of *The Mystery of Edwin Drood* on the East Coast. The new screen adaptation never materialized.

Instead, the Dickens tale made a comeback via an immensely popular Broadway musical staged by the New York Shakespeare Festival in the 1980s. Capitalizing on the author's open-ended finis to the hilt, "Drood"'s canny producers left the solution of the mystery not to the discretion of the play's author, but to the audience itself.

Which goes to prove, as far as *The Mystery of Edwin Drood* is concerned, it isn't what Dickens wrote but what he *didn't* write that really matters.

Critics' Corner

A thoroughly entertaining, exciting and atmospherically fine screen version of the novel.—*The New York World-Telegram*, March 1935, William Boehnel

[A] gruesome melodrama with enough action and background mystery to make it go.—*The New York Sun*, Eileen Creelman

It exercises a fascination, holds complete interest.... Handsomely produced and acted.—*The New York Daily Mirror*, Bland Johaneson

[T]he combination of adroit direction and acting isn't strong enough to overcome an essentially weak narrative.... Rains imparts a wealth of weirdness and intensity to the production.—*Variety*, March 27, 1935

[E]xcellent ... Mr. Rains, who has become the devil's own brother during his brief and hair-raising screen career, is brilliantly repellant.—*The New York Times*, March 21, 1935, Andre Sennwald

If the ending concocted for Universal by four scenarists ... is somewhat obvious, the picture is nevertheless thoroughly entertaining, full of Mid-Victorian atmosphere, good acting, and Dickensian make-up.—*Time*, 1935

The individual acting is very good, and the atmosphere is faithful in detail, but neither can invest the story development with strong suspense nor preserve its secret.... Although there is no denying that Claude Rains is a brilliant actor, this does not prevent his mannerisms and inflections from becoming a trifle monotonous.—*The Kinematograph Weekly* (GB), March 7, 1935

Very good entertainment! ... [H]olds the attention well due to the interesting manner in which Douglass Montgomery solves the murder mystery.... The closing scenes are dramatic and exciting and hold the spectator in tense suspense.—*Harrison's Reports*, February 9, 1935

Belonging somewhat to the creepy type of murder melodrama, this production has the advantage of some good performances and the able direction of Stuart Walker. As a result, it should give fair satisfaction in the program houses.—*The Film Daily*, March 20, 1935

Night Life of the Gods

Released March 11, 1935. 73 minutes. A Lowell Sherman Production. *Producer:* Carl Laemmle, Jr. *Director:* Lowell Sherman. *Screenplay:* Barry Trivers. *Based on the novel* The Night Life of the Gods *by* Thorne Smith. *Photography:* John J. Mescall. *Editorial Supervisor:* Maurice Pivar. *Editor:* Ted Kent. *Art Director:* Charles D. Hall. *Music:* Arthur Morton. *Musical Director:* Edward Ward. *Special Effects:* John P. Fulton. *Makeup:* Jack P. Pierce & Otto Lederer. *Sound Supervisor:* Gilbert Kurland. *Assistant Directors:* Joseph A. McDonough & Charles Gould. *Dialogue Director:* Pat McCoy. *Assistant Camera:* William Dodds & Ross Hoffman. *Men's Wardrobe:* Frank Carr, S.B. Ware, Ed Ware, Fred Starns & Harold McCarl. *Women's Wardrobe:* Doris McCoig & Edna Simons. *Sound Mixer:* William Hedgcock. *Microphone Man:* Harry Morgan. *Technical Director:* Archie Hall. *Hair Stylist:* Gertrude Helmer. *Production Manager:* M. F. Murphy. *Script Clerk:* Grace DuBray. *Grips:* Pete Abriss, Frank Madigan & James C. Knowlton. *Props:* Harry Grundstrum. *Gaffer:* Ross Saxon. *Best Boy:* Tony Holtz.

Alan Mowbray (*Hunter Hawk*), Florine McKinney (*"Meg" Turner*), Peggy Shannon (*Daphne Lambert*), Richard Carle (*Grandpa Lambert*), Theresa Maxwell Conover (*Alice Lambert*), Phillips Smalley (*Alfred Lambert*), Wesley Barry (*Alfred Lambert, Jr.*), Gilbert Emery (*Betts*), Ferdinand Gottschalk (*Ludwig Turner*), Douglas Fowley (*Cyril Sparks*), William "Stage" Boyd (*Det. Mike Mulligan*), Henry Armetta (*Roigi*), Arlene Carroll (*Stella*), Raymond Benard [Ray Corrigan] (*Apollo*), George Hassell (*Bacchus*), Irene Ware (*Diana*), Geneva Mitchell (*Hebe*), Paul Kaye (*Mercury*), Robert Warwick (*Neptune*), Pat De Cicco (*Perseus*), Marda Deering (*Venus*), Bert Roach (*Oscar*), Fredric Santly (*Drunk*), Maidel Turner (*Burly Woman*), Maude Turner Gordon, Ruth Cherrington (*Dowagers*), Tyler Brooke (*Store Manager*), G. Pat Collins (*Times Square Policeman*), Lee Moran (*Bus Driver*), James P. Burtis (*Bit*), May Beatty (*Mrs. Betts*), Wade Boteler (*Policeman*), Larry Wheat (*Museum Guard*), Don Douglas (*Mr. Martin*), Alan Davis (*Hotel Manager*), Leo McCabe (*Assistant Hotel Manager*), Harry Cornell (*Roadhouse Manager*), Joseph Young (*Orchestra Leader*), Lois January (*Mulligan's Girl*), Kenner G. Kemp (*Man on Dance Floor*), King Baggott (*Man in Lobby*), Dick Winslow (*Student*), Harold Nelson (*Lecturer*), Beatrice Roberts, Claire Myers, Madeline Talcott (*The Three Graces*), William L. Thorne (*Detective*), Velma Gresham (*Sales Girl*), Al Hill, George Magrill (*Masseurs*), Anne Darling (*Manicurist*), Russ Clark, Jerry Frank (*Lifeguards*), Jean Fenwick, Ann Doran, Lu Ann Meredith, Ruth Page (*Girls in Pool*), Mabel Benard (*Swimmer*). Phyllis Crane, Lillian Castle, Charles Irwin.

> Once upon a time, a famous author named Thorne Smith wrote a book, conceived in a moment of delicious delirium, and written in a cuckoo clock. The first chapters convinced us *he* was crazy. The ensuing left doubt that possibly *we* were. So we leave you to enjoy this new and completely mad type of whimsical humor on the screen. Stop rattling cellophane! Take Sonny's shoes off! Park your gum under the seat where it belongs, and let's all go crazy together.
> — *On-Screen Prologue to* Night Life of the Gods

Like many of the obscure and commercially "unmarketable" Universal titles of the '30s, *Night Life of the Gods* was long thought of as a lost film. However a 35mm print of it, said to be the only one extant, was donated to the UCLA archives in the '80s, making it finally accessible to film historians and even buffs as gray market videos eventually began circulating.

The film's major drawing card is that it's one of the comparatively few cinematic adaptations of the works of Thorne Smith. A hugely popular American humorist in his day, Smith's star has faded over the decades as his novels have gone out of print. His style of combining fervent, madcap humor and fantastic storylines made him a unique literary figure. Occasional film versions of his works (all made after his death in 1934), even when produced by major studios were, likewise, considered oddities in their day. The best known of these is Hal Roach's *Topper* (1937) but Rene Clair's *I Married a Witch* (1942), based on Smith's unfinished novel *The Passionate Witch,* is no less entertaining. Even Roach's poorly received but campy sex role-reversal comedy *Turnabout* (1940) retains a certain novelty appeal as John Hubbard and Carole Landis switch their wardrobe to provide the central gimmick.

The plot of *Night Life of the Gods* is similarly offbeat. A half-mad experimenter brings a bevy of Greek gods to life only to find that, despite their worldly manner, they can't fit into the regimented, strait-laced mores of the twentieth century. It was the first of Smith's books to make it to the big screen in a feature-length venue and, as such, Universal probably regarded it as a hit-or-miss proposition. Except for slapstick, the marriage of comedy and fantasy was still a dicey proposition and the studio warily kept the project on a modest budget and used relatively inexpensive actors. The film's success depended on recreating the sass and sparkle of the novel. Unfortunately, *Night Life of the Gods* displays a tin ear for comedy even though peppered with familiar screwball elements of the day.

On March 31, 1934, *The Universal Weekly* reported that Carl Laemmle, Jr., purchased the screen rights for the Smith novel. Lowell Sherman, a leading man in silents (*Way Down East* [1920], *Monsieur Beaucaire* [1924]) and a character player in talkies (*Morning Glory* [1933]), had recently made his directorial bow and was put at the helm of *Night Life of the Gods.* Like Smith, Sherman didn't live long enough to endure his film's lukewarm critical reception. He became ill during shooting (possibly as a result of the rigorous schedule) and lost 21 pounds. Despite the protests of his physicians, Sherman contracted with RKO studios to direct the first three-strip Technicolor film *Becky Sharp* (1935), but died of double pneumonia several days after the start of production. (*Gods* star Alan Mowbray had a featured role in the *Becky Sharp* cast.)

In *Night Life of the Gods*, British-born Mowbray portrays Smith's irrepressible hero Hunter Hawk, a brilliant but wildly eccentric scientist given to periodically blowing up his workroom in the course of his experiments. The end result of these detonations is the creation of a magical ring which emits a ray that transforms living creatures into marble statues and another which reverses the process. Hawk's first successful experiment is upon his dog, Blotto, whose tail petrifies in seconds. The emboldened Hawk turns the ray on his disapproving family, sparing only his sympathetic niece Daphne (Peggy Shannon), who answers to the sobriquet "Daffy." Unfazed by the mass-elimination of her family, the girl shares a bottle of wine with her uncle before dashing off to keep a date with her dimwit boyfriend Cyril Sparks (Douglas Fowley).

Traipsing through a cornfield, the inebriated inventor runs into his gardener, Ludwig Turner (Ferdinand Gottschalk). The strange little Irishman reveals himself to be a leprechaun and invites Hunter to his home in a grotto where he lives with his daughter, "Meg" (Florine McKinney). Hunter and the girl immediately become "an item" even though she admits to being the 900-year-old descendant of one of the Three Furies, Megaera.

The couple embarks on a wild spree, petrifying all who meet with their disfavor — half of the occupants of a café, a traffic cop and a detective (William "Stage" Boyd) who attempts to arrest Hawk for disturbing the peace. They repair to New York's Metropolitan Museum of Art where Hunter decides to try his ring on an exhibit of marble statues of the Greek gods and goddesses who promptly come to life. Finally free after centuries of entombment, the affable group is anxious for Hawk and "Meg" to introduce them to the worldly pleasures of the twentieth century.

Dashing through the streets of Manhattan, the Greeks find themselves being gawked at by the various passersby. Hawk and "Meg" take the Olympians to a local department store and dress them up in modern-day fashions. A night on the town turns into a disaster. Although the gods' antics play out like a Shriners convention gone bad, they attract the attention of the police who send a fleet of motorcycle cops in a high-speed pursuit. Hawk immobilizes them with his ring before heading back to his hotel suite with his charges in tow.

The whole party retires to the so-called Roman Plunge, the oversized indoor swimming pool at the Plaza Waldorf. Stationing himself at the bottom of the pool, Neptune (Robert Warwick) playfully jabs the young women bathers with his trident. Another fracas develops before Hawk, tiring of all this excitement, transports his friends back to the museum, where they again resume their eternal poses. ("The gods can't take it!" Hawk laughs triumphantly.) With the police on their heels, Hawk realizes he'll be facing a lifelong sentence in a lunatic asylum. He and "Meg" decide their best hope of staying together is to join the gods and use the magical ring to turn themselves into marble. The story ends with Hawk awakening in an ambulance with "Meg" at his side. The opening-reel explosion resulted in a head injury for Hawk, and everything that has ensued was only with a dream.

Realizing the offbeat nature of the film, Universal's publicity machine went overboard in promoting *Night Life of the Gods,* including greatly inflating the scope of its production. One claim was that the swimming pool set was built at a cost exceeding that of any soundstage set on the lot. Pressbook copy describes how 20 studio artists created the 50 plaster statues seen in the film (each supposedly weighting 600 pounds) for a total cost of $35,000. Mounted on wheels for easy mobility, these life-size images were said to have been wheeled in by studio technicians three or four at a time on the tail of a motor dolly.

Also to be taken with a grain of salt was Universal's report that a team of horticulturists were assigned the task of growing a whole field of corn by electric light. Several months before shooting began, a section of Soundstage 14 was heaped with earth and cultivated with seed, fertilizer and castor oil. The "field" was subjected to constant artificial sunshine, produced by violet lamps and huge arc lights. The studio's sprinkler system provided the necessary "rainfall." Under these intensive methods of cultivation, the corn crop (according to the publicity department) came up in a fraction of the time it would have taken to grow the vegetables outdoors. Considering the fact that the set, which looks remarkably similar to the barren landscape utilized

Another fabulous experiment gone awry: Alan Mowbray and Peggy Shannon in *Night Life of the Gods* (courtesy John Cocchi).

in the Whale Frankenstein pictures, is only seen for a few fleeting moments, the claims are dubious.

Universal's hard-sell approach trickled down into the film itself. The pre-title scroll (see chapter header) reads as though the Laemmles were congratulating themselves on their own audacity. More likely, it was a mere strategy designed by nervous studio heads to brace ticket-buyers for the far-flung fancies of the story, in much the same manner as Edward Van Sloan's introduction to *Frankenstein* served as a consumer alert for the squeamish.

Night Life of the Gods has two strikes against it: It was made too late to take advantage of pre–Code laxity in regard to the "adult" content of the book as well as being stymied by its own lack of imagination. While Thorne Smith is often remembered for concocting his stories as modern fantasies, he was equally notorious for his daring sexual humor and for creating characters who divided their time between drinking and nursing hangovers. With the Hays Office actively cleaning up and watering down so-called objectionable content in Hollywood movies, *Night Life of the Gods* comes off as a sanitized, Code-sanctioned affair whose humor is more juvenile than knowingly sophisticated.

The novel walked a fine line between ribald humor and an almost delicate sense of whimsy which would have been tough to reproduce in the best of circumstances. Director Sherman does a fair job with the former but his handling of comedy often strains. Amusing situations are set up but there aren't enough jokes to sustain them. The film's one inspired image, the "gods" filing out of a taxi on Times Square dressed only in robes and sheets for a night out on the town, has the look of a *New Yorker* cartoon but the script doesn't provide a verbal punchline worthy of it. There are too many characters to deal with and, except for Mowbray, they have a tendency of blending together. The script tries to make funny business of the specialties of each individual god or goddess but this wears out quickly. Hebe, the cupbearer, does nothing but collect cups, Bacchus' dialogue is a succession of drunk jokes, Apollo is constantly on the make, etc. The trident-bearing Neptune's food fight with a fishmonger is an episode out of the novel but, typical of the movie, its execution is loud and clunky.

Night Life of the Gods' forced, self-conscious humor is ultimately exhausting while it barely hints at Smith's latent social commentary. Yet the film isn't without a certain charm and the script works hard to create a genial atmosphere even when the lovable hero is indiscriminately turning casual bystanders into marble caricatures. More disappointing is the way it fudges Smith's sweetly understated, romantic finale in which Hawk and "Meg" "cement" their relationship by turning into stone. The movie instead cops out with the ineffectual but commercially safe get-out clause of "it was only a dream."

According to *The Hollywood Reporter*, Lowell Sherman had aspirations to play the lead role of Hawk himself, but when his voice faltered at some point in mid–July 1934, he was confined to the director's chair. The studio set their sights on Edward Everett Horton and tried to get MGM to re-arrange the shooting schedule of the movie Horton was then making, *Biography of a Bachelor Girl* (1935), so he could be in *Night Life* but it couldn't be done. On July 25, *The Hollywood Reporter* noted that Universal had signed all-purpose actor Alan Mowbray to head the cast. Shooting officially began on August 13 and wrapped on October 15, 1934.

Mowbray isn't usually thought of as leading man material (he went on to play the comic butler in the Thorne Smith adaptations *Topper* and 1939's *Topper Takes a Trip*), but his polish and theatrical panache gives him the edge over some of his more amateurish co-stars. He and his plain-Jane leading lady Florine McKinney are a far cry from the usual Hollywood glamour couple. It's exactly the right, off-center touch the film needs although as a team, the actors have zero chemistry. In contrast, sparks seem to be flying in Mowbray's scenes with Peggy Shannon — perhaps *too* many sparks for an uncle-niece relationship in a post–Production Code Hollywood feature.

Hunter Hawk's snotty nephew is played by Wesley Barry, who had been acting in films since 1910 and had a career which extended into the '70s. As an adult, Barry switched gears and racked up numerous producer-director credits, mostly for Poverty Row features (Charlie Chan, the Bowery Boys, etc.). One of his lesser jobs was directing added scenes for the foreign version of the science fiction classic, *Invaders from Mars* (1953). 1962 found him directing and co-producing the low-budget *The Creation of the Humanoids*, a pet favorite of lovers of truly bad cinema. Eventually, he left show business to become a turkey farmer. Gilbert Emery is a standout in the supporting cast as the arch English butler. And Peggy Shannon's nincompoop suitor is an extremely callow Douglas Fowley in one of his earliest screen roles.

Shannon, a former Ziegfeld Follies girl, got her big break in pictures when Clara Bow suffered a nervous breakdown in 1931. Shannon stepped in for her in *The Secret Call* and for a time was groomed as the "It" Girl's successor. Over the next ten years, she appeared in 35 pictures including the 1933 sci-fi disaster movie *Deluge*. Through it all, she fought and eventually lost her battle with the bottle. On May 11, 1941, her husband Albert G. Roberts returned from a fishing trip to find Shannon's body slumped in a kitchen chair, her head resting on a table. A cigarette was between her lips and an empty glass was nearby. Death was attributed to acute alcoholism. Nineteen days later, Shannon's grieving husband shot himself to death right on the spot where his wife died.

There are some interesting faces scattered among the gods although most of the players give extremely broad performances. Irene Ware of *Chandu the Magician* (1932) and *The Raven* has disappointingly little to do as Diana besides shooting off an occasional arrow. As Apollo, Ray "Crash" Corrigan, appearing under his real name Raymond Benard, makes an appearance outside his familiar gorilla suit which he donned in *The Strange Case of Doctor Rx* and *Captive Wild Woman*. Brawny Pat DeCicco, playing Perseus, achieved *his* fifteen minutes of fame *off screen* for his doomed marriages to comedian Thelma Todd and "Poor Little Rich Girl" Gloria Vanderbilt. DeCicco was a cousin of James Bond movie producer Albert R. Broccoli; it was he who nicknamed his cousin "Cubby."

The all-too-human foibles of the Mount Olympus crowd was the subject of several other films following the release of *Night Life of the Gods*. Columbia's 1947 Technicolor musical *Down to Earth* had a disgruntled Terpsichore (Rita Hayworth) assume human form and take matters into her own hands when she learns that a Broadway producer (Larry Parks) is maligning the gods in his latest production. The following year, Universal-International released *One Touch of Venus*, a romantic confection which had window dresser Robert Walker bring a statue of Venus to life with a mere kiss. Curvaceous Ava Gardner falls madly in love with Walker, with predictable complications. Two of Ray Harryhausen's stop-motion animation fantasies, *Jason and the Argonauts* (1963) and *Clash of the Titans* (1981), demonstrated that even the mighty Zeus was not immune from humankind's petty jealousies. In *Argonauts*, Zeus and Hera (well-played by Niall MacGinnis and Honor Blackman respectively) guide Jason (Todd Armstrong) in his quest for the Golden Fleece. *Titans* finds Zeus (played by a sadly dissipated Laurence Olivier) acting like a doting parent in his efforts to protect his son Perseus (Harry Hamlin) from the evil machinations of his fellow Olympians.

Night Life of the Gods is likely to leave the viewer with ambiguous feelings. Its quirky potential is easy to appreciate but its raw material needed finesse and a light touch in order to pay off. It would seem that Universal snapped up the rights to the novel but skimped on the talent required to do it justice. Still, it's such a one-of-a-kind picture that even when it fails to come up to its intended levels of life-affirming enchantment or even fun, it is difficult to entirely dismiss. It's a qualified success in the way flawed movies often are, the kind that linger in the memory longer than more skilled, more conventional works often do not.

Universal released an animated spoof of *Night Life of the Gods*, entitled *Night Life of the Bugs*, an Oswald Rabbit cartoon produced by Walter Lantz, in October 1936.

Critics' Corner

[T]he screen version, though frequently side-splitting, is, on the whole, so muddled and sluggish and has failed so wantonly to make the most of its opportunities that it must be classed among the saddest of the cinema might-have-beens.—*The New York World-Telegram*, February 25, 1935, William Boehnel

There are moments when the mob direction gets beyond the director's control ... and it's noisy instead of funny.... [A]ll work toward the common end and help to create an excellent ensemble.—*Variety*, February 27, 1935, Chic.

[U]nless such a picture is brilliant it is nothing at all.—*The New York Herald-Tribune*, February 25, 1935, Richard Watts, Jr.

Rating: Good. You've either got to go for this sort of screen stuff passionately ... or else you're thoroughly cold on it. We giggled all the way through—from start to final fadeout.—*The New York Evening Post*, February 23, 1935, Irene Thirer

[O]nly mildly entertaining.... [S]omehow the petrified humans and revivified gods and goddesses are not as devastatingly mirthful as they seem under the hypnosis of Mr. Smith's antic prose.—*The New York Times*, February 23, 1935, Andre Sennwald

This may amuse class audiences but the masses will be bored.... [A]fter the first few minutes of watching these characters amuse themselves the action lags and one becomes bored.—*Harrison's Reports*, March 2, 1935

Farcical fantasy has many laughs though its basic idea is far-fetched.—*The Film Daily*, February 23, 1935

Bride of Frankenstein

Released May 6, 1935. 75 minutes. *Producer:* Carl Laemmle, Jr. *Director:* James Whale. *Screenplay:* William Hurlbut. *Adaptation:* William Hurlbut & John L. Balderston. *Suggested by the novel* Frankenstein; or, The Modern Prometheus *by* Mary Wollstonecraft Shelley. *Photography:* John J. Mescall. *Music:* Franz Waxman. *Music Director:* Mischa Bakaleinikoff. *Orchestrations:* Clifford Vaughn. *Editorial Supervisor:* Maurice Pivar. *Editor:* Ted Kent. *Art Director:* Charles D. Hall. *Special Photographic Effects:* John P. Fulton & David Horsley. *Sound Supervisor:* Gilbert Kurland. *Makeup:* Jack P. Pierce. *Assistant Directors:* Harry Menke, Joseph McDonough & Fred Frank. *Electrical Effects:* Kenneth Strickfaden, Raymond Lindsay & Frank Graves. *Second Cameraman:* Alan C. Jones. *Assistant Cameraman:* William Dodds. *Organist:* Charles Walcott. *Matte Paintings:* Russell A. Lawson & Jack Cosgrove. *Miniatures:* Charlie Baker. *Unit Sound Mixer:* William Hedgcock. *Rerecording & Sound Effects:* Ed Wetzel. *Music Recording:* Lawrence Aicholtz. *Continuity Clerk:* Flo Brummel. *Production Secretary:* Buddy Daggett.

Boris Karloff (*The Monster*), Colin Clive (*Baron Henry Frankenstein*), Valerie Hobson (*Baroness Elizabeth Frankenstein*), Ernest Thesiger (*Dr. Septimus Pretorius*), Elsa Lanchester (*Mary Wollstonecraft Shelley/The Monster's Mate*), Una O'Connor (*Minnie*), E.E. Clive (*The Burgomaster*), O.P. Heggie (*The Hermit*), Gavin Gordon (*Lord Byron*), Douglas Walton (*Percy Bysshe Shelley*), Dwight Frye (*Karl*), Lucien Prival (*Al-*

bert), Reginald Barlow (*Hans*), Mary Gordon (*Hans' Wife*), Anne Darling (*Shepherdess*), Ted Billings (*Ludwig*), Neil Fitzgerald (*Rudy*), John Carradine, Robert Adair, John Curtis, Frank Terry (*Hunters*), Walter Brennan, Rollo Lloyd, Mary Stewart (*Neighbors*), Helen Parrish (*Communion Girl*), Brenda Fowler (*A Mother*), Sarah Schwartz (*Marta*), Arthur S. Byron (*Little King*), Joan Woodbury (*Little Queen*), Norman Ainsley (*Little Archbishop*), Peter Shaw (*Little Devil*), Kansas DeForrest (*Little Ballerina*), Josephine McKim (*Little Mermaid*), Billy Barty (*Little Baby*), Frank Benson, Ed Piel, Sr., Anders Van Haden, John George, D'Arcy Corrigan, Grace Cunard, Maurice Black, Peter Shaw, Rollo Lloyd, Peter Bronte, Leah Lewis, Gene Garrick (*Villagers*), Helen Gibson (*Woman*), Murdock MacQuarrie (*Sympathetic Villager*), Elspeth Dudgeon (*Old Gypsy Woman*), Maurice Black (*Gypsy*), Marilyn Harris (*Little Girl*), Torben Meyer (*Strangled Man in Flashback Sequence*), Joseph North, Harry Northrup (*Servants*), Charles Murphy (*Guard*), Monty Montague, Peter Shaw (*Doubles for Ernest Thesiger*), George DeNormand (*Double for Reginald Barlow*). *Deleted from final print:* Gunnis Davis (*Uncle Glutz*), Tempe Pigott (*Auntie Glutz*), Edwin Mordant (*The Coroner*), Lucio Villegas (*Priest*).

The Monster Demands a Mate!
—*Poster blurb for* Bride of Frankenstein

On January 12, 1935, Hollywood trade papers reported that Carl "Junior" Laemmle was heading up his own production unit at the studio. Itching to leave his post as general manager in charge of all production, which he had held since 1929, the newly-appointed "associate producer" was scheduled to bring in six titles a year. His old job would go to an unlikely candidate: Carl Sr. In making the announcement to the press, the elder Laemmle declared that for some time his son "has been eager to pass on duties and details of complete studio direction to others that he might concentrate on an independent production unit."

The simple reason for the change was that Junior Laemmle was bored with a job he wasn't very good at in the first place. In 1988, actress Rose Hobart recalled for the authors her days as a Universal contract player in the early '30s, and her long-standing feud with the "boy wonder." "The trouble with Junior was that he had no real talent and was a lousy administrator," the feisty Miss Hobart said with disarming candor. "His father was pretty good. His father had some idea what he wanted. But Junior didn't know his ass from a shotgun! He really didn't care. He was a good Jewish boy and when Father hands you the business, you run the business. He couldn't have cared less about it."

Producer Carl Jr. could have boasted that the films made under his aegis were the most elaborate and prestigious the studio could afford. The first two of his planned six "specials" were a movie version of the Jerome Kern–Oscar Hammerstein musical *Show Boat* and *The Return of Frankenstein*, the long-awaited sequel to the 1931 horror hit, which had been in the works for some time. A major obstacle was finding the right director, since James Whale, the most logical contender, disappointingly had no interest in revisiting his past success. The assignment fell into the hands of Kurt Neumann. The competent but undistinguished director of *Secret of the Blue Room* was hardly in the same class as Whale, but at least he had some experience with Gothic subjects. An original story was written by Tom Reed, who was also selected to supervise the production; Philip McDonald was commissioned to write a treatment.

It's ironic that Whale, who directed *Frankenstein* partially to break away from the rut of war subjects, was now finding it a bit difficult to escape his identification with horror movies. A change of pace was sorely needed for the director who, since the technical rigors of *The Invisible Man*, was bemoaning his weariness with fantasy subjects to interviewers. Anxious to diversify his output, he took on the direction of *By Candlelight* (1933) when the original director, Robert Wyler (brother of William and another Laemmle!), left the film. A charming and underrated comedy of manners, *By Candlelight* starred Paul Lukas as a valet who poses as an aristocrat so that he may woo prospective paramours. It was an engaging trifle but it was dwarfed by a far more personal film for the director, *One More River* (1934), a straightforward, accomplished adaptation of John Galsworthy's novel. Surprisingly, after tackling such highbrow fare, Whale had a change of heart and agreed to return to the realm of fantasy.

In February 1934, Whale came back from a two-month holiday in London with a script by R.C. Sherriff entitled *A Trip to Mars*. It was a fanciful, H.G. Wells–type confection about Earth people abducted by the leader of an underground Martian civilization. Whale plunged

Ernest Thesiger and Colin Clive, along with creepy cohorts Dwight Frye and Ted Billings, get the watchtower lab ready for the great experiment in *Bride of Frankenstein*.

ahead with the details of the project, which was tentatively scheduled to go into production in March 1934, as soon as its proposed star Boris Karloff completed his duties on *The Black Cat*. *A Trip to Mars* would never be made. According to Whale's biographer James Curtis, Senior Laemmle didn't like the script and refused to finance it. Whale grudgingly accepted the Frankenstein sequel.

Starting from scratch, Whale drew his inspiration from the original Mary Shelley novel, focusing his attention on detailing Frankenstein's aborted attempt to create a mate for the Monster. It has also been suggested that Whale cribbed a few ideas from an early draft of Robert Florey's *Frankenstein* script. The original intention was to reunite the cast, except for John Boles, whose role of Victor Moritz was to be written out of the script.

By September 1934 Whale pressed R.C. Sherriff, who was then teaching at Oxford, into service. The writer promised to have a complete script prepared by the next semester, but he soon wearied of his new assignment and backed out of the film. By January, the reliable John L. Balderston was commissioned to write an original treatment with a finished script by William Hurlbut (who penned 1930's *The Cat Creeps*) and mystery writer Edmund Pearson. (The latter's contribution appears to be negligible as his name doesn't appear on the official credits.)

With the crucial casting of Boris Karloff and Colin Clive secure, the studio turned to Valerie Hobson, whom the studio was working heavily, for the role of Elizabeth. For a time Brigitte Helm, so mesmerizing as Maria the Robot Girl in Fritz Lang's *Metropolis* (1926), was under serious consideration for the role of the Monster's mate. The statuesque Phyllis Brooks, a well-known New York illustrator's model, was announced as the most likely candidate for the part. The final choice of Elsa Lanchester, an old friend of Whale, was probably made when the director decided to have one actress play the roles of both the Bride and Mary Wollstonecraft Shelley in the film's prologue.

In her biography, *Elsa Lanchester, Herself* (St. Martin's Press, 1983), the actress wrote, "I think James Whale felt that if this beautiful and innocent Mary Shelley could write a horror story such as *Frankenstein*, then somewhere she must have had a fiend within." The twin casting proved to be another inspired Whalesian touch.

Amazingly, the role of Dr. Pretorius was originally slated for Claude Rains, who owed Universal a film on his two-picture contract. However, Rains was bumped from the picture and reassigned the lead in *Mystery of Edwin Drood*. Whale prevailed upon Ernest Thesiger, who stole the show as Horace Femm in *The Old Dark House*, to serve as Rains' replacement.

Another key role, although a considerably smaller one, was the unnamed blind hermit who befriends and humanizes the Monster. Whale was so insistent that the Scottish stage actor O.P. Heggie play the part that he delayed production for ten days until Heggie finished another assignment, *Chasing Yesterday* (1935), at RKO.

The projected budget of $293,750 exceeded the cost of the original film by over $30,000. But even this figure was optimistic and the final cost of the production approached $400,000. Whale was paid a princely $15,000, earning even more than star Boris Karloff, who received $12,500. Colin Clive still wasn't a big name by Hollywood standards and had a $6,000 check to prove it, while Thesiger received exactly half that.

The sum of $26,000 was targeted for set construction. Art director Charles D. Hall's magnificent tower laboratory amounted to $3,600, with another $2,000 spent on various electrical props. But the big-ticket item on the art director's budget was the Castle Frankenstein set, which totaled $4,700, including the entrance and the Great Hall.

Jack Pierce went to work not only on the makeup for the Bride, but a modified design for Karloff. According to studio publicity, the actor was weighed down with 62 pounds of makeup and costuming, including a pair of 11 pound boots which propped him up to a height of just over seven and a half feet (a claim easily disputed from merely watching the movie). The worse for wear after his ordeal in the burning windmill, the Monster looked properly charred and disheveled. The mangy, newly designed wig revealed the 11 metal clamps which presumably served to hold the Monster's head together, a detail not seen in the original makeup.

The studio was strangely indecisive in regard to choosing a title. The film was alternately announced as *The Return of Frankenstein* and *Bride of Frankenstein* in the trade papers. *The Universal Weekly* of January 5, 1935, stated with finality that the title would be *Return* "since the Monster was not named Frankenstein," but by the January 19 edition, the title was changed back to *Bride*. Whale commenced shooting on January 2, 1935, and wrapped on March 7, ten days over schedule. To this day, pedants stubbornly insist that the Bride was not played by Elsa Lanchester, but by Valerie Hobson, based on the assumption that the title refers to the marriage of the doctor and not the Monster. (Ernest Thesiger triumphantly dubs Lanchester "The Bride of Frankenstein!" at the end of the creation sequence.)

The tone of the film is established with a blast of thunder and lightning as the camera prowls the rain-swept grounds of a medieval castle. But after setting up an atmosphere of dread, Whale crushes audience expectations by cutting to a charmingly baroque scene of three elegant figures luxuriating before a hearth. The company is most distinguished: Percy Bysshe Shelley (Douglas Walton), his common-law wife, Mary Wollstonecraft (Elsa Lanchester), and their friend, poet Lord Byron (Gavin Gordon). The storm prompts Lord Byron to recap the plot of Mary's new novel, *Frankenstein*, complete with film clips from the 1931 film as well as an unused take of the Monster choking the gypsy character he later encounters. The authoress confesses she never intended for her story to end the way it did and uses the occasion to reveal the rest of the story of Frankenstein and his Monster.

The story picks up at the site of the burning windmill. The Burgomaster (E.E. Clive) orders the villagers to transport the body of Henry Frankenstein (Colin Clive) to his father's castle. As the crowd disperses, Hans (Reginald Barlow), father of the drowned child Maria, pokes through the charred remains of the structure and plunges into the cistern. The Monster (Boris Karloff), alive but badly burned, emerges from the ruins and drowns the terrified villager. Making his way up to ground level, he sends Hans' wife (Mary Gordon) falling to her death and disappears into the countryside.

In the meantime, Henry regains consciousness and is reunited with Elizabeth (Valerie Hobson). Their few hours of peace are interrupted when Dr. Septimus Pretorius (Ernest Thesiger), Henry's former teacher, pays them an unexpected call. Luring the young Baron to his flat, Pretorius exhibits his collection of doll-like people housed in glass containers, a product of his strange experiments in the creation of life. Pretorius suggests they join forces to create a mate for the Monster in hopes of spawning a race of man-made beings.

Meanwhile, the Monster terrorizes the populace and then disappears back into the woods. A blind hermit (O.P. Heggie) be-

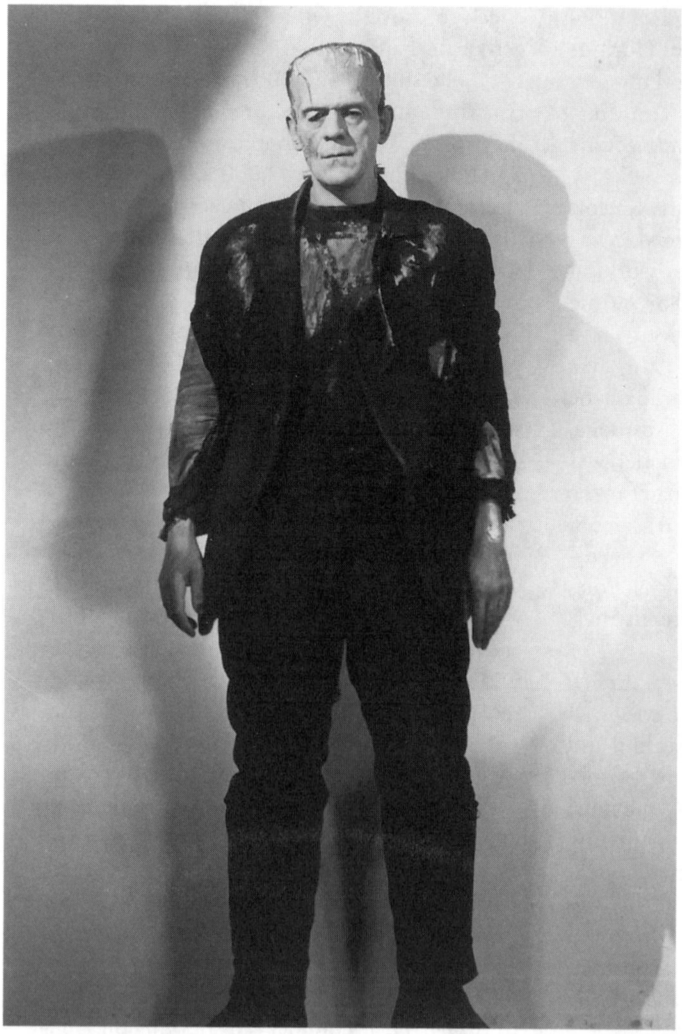

Surviving the burning of the windmill (seen at the end of *Frankenstein* and at the beginning of *Bride of Frankenstein*), the Monster looks a bit worse for wear in this publicity still.

friends the creature and even teaches him to speak a few simple words before a pair of hunters, stumbling upon the unlikely companions, sends the Monster scurrying off. Seeking refuge in an underground tomb, the Monster comes upon Pretorius, who's in the midst of snatching a body for his great experiment. The two form an alliance and confront Henry, who has reneged on his promise to work with the deranged professor. The Monster kidnaps Elizabeth, now Henry's wife, leaving Frankenstein no choice but to assist in the experiment.

A striking character study of Elsa Lanchester as the Bride.

Stitched together from body parts stolen from graveyards and a heart taken from a freshly murdered village girl, the Bride is ready to be endowed with life. In the spectacular, two-minute creation sequence, consisting of over 80 shots, she comes to life amid the blazing electrical apparatus of Frankenstein's mountaintop laboratory. Bound completely in bandages except for her head, the newly created female (Elsa Lanchester), the very image of Queen Nefertiti, expresses horror at the sight of her intended suitor. The rejection by his mate is too much for the Monster to bear. Allowing Henry and the now freed Elizabeth to escape, the Monster throws the main power lever. The laboratory is blown asunder by several massive explosions, burying the Monster, the Bride and Pretorius under tons of rubble.

Bride of Frankenstein is one of the best and least typical of the Universal horror films. In terms of acting, direction, photography, set design, editing and overall presentation, the film is close to flawless. It is another example of James Whale's back-door approach to horror. The introduction of the Monster, cruelly and pointlessly killing the parents of the drowned child, and the shock closeups of the screeching Bride, serve as stock concessions to horror. Otherwise, Whale seems hardly interested in inducing as much as a shudder from the audience. The sophisticated director was clearly bored with Universal's horror assignments and *Bride of Frankenstein* presented him with a good opportunity to poke fun at the genre with a hearty dose of parody.

The surge of interest in Whale's personal life (to a large extent triggered by Christopher Bram's speculative novel *Father of Frankenstein* and by *Gods and Monsters*, its 1998 cinematic adaptation by Bill Condon) has shed new light on his films. As the stage and screen versions of *Journey's End* tapped into the director's experiences in the trenches and POW camps of World War I, *Bride of Frankenstein* evolved from a studio assignment that the director accepted grudgingly, into a personal film which reflected the Whale humor and complicated personality.

While the original film was weighed down with all the good intentions inherent in transferring a literary classic to the screen, in *Bride of Frankenstein*, the viewer senses a director

Dwight Frye strikes a menacing pose in the role of Ludwig, Pretorius' henchman.

throwing himself with abandon into the material. Given free rein by the studio and having the luxury of a built-in audience base thanks to the first film's roaring success, Whale gave in to his somewhat overripe tastes. Screening both pictures back to back, they don't quite hold together as a unified piece (unlike, say, Coppola's *Godfather* films). In the sequel, Whale was purposefully leaving the stark, clinical atmosphere of the first film to create a far more whimsical realm starting with the purple prose scenes of Lord Byron and the Shelleys. By sending up the conventions of the Hollywood costume picture, Whale reduces the two icons of English romantic poetry into a pair of fawning, powder-puff dandies while Mary retains her alluring wit and a fiery spirit. (The disarming tongue-in-cheek approach serves to distract the audience from noticing that the film clips from the original movie are set almost a hundred years ahead of the time in which the characters are speaking.) That the story is presented not as a polished work but as an oral improvisation, casually told, allows the florid exchange between the characters to seep into the spirit of Mary's tale. It also allows the writer to embark on her boldest conceit of taking on the role of the Monster's Bride.

The change of tone required the revamping of several characters. Gone are the boring Victor Moritz and the old baron, although Pretorius' pointed addressing of Henry as *Baron* Frankenstein suggests that the aging patriarch didn't survive the wedding day ruckus. The sensible and affecting Elizabeth, so ably played by fair-haired Mae Clarke, assumes a new personality in her darker incarnation (Valerie Hobson). As the mistress of the house, she is now slightly snooty and given to operatic bursts of hysteria at the drop of a hat.

With Henry looking dissipated and forlorn, the characters seem far removed from the young couple bursting with love in the garden scene from the first film. The arrival of Pretorius, who literally plucks Henry out of his wedding bed to forge an unholy alliance, has not gone unnoticed by subtext-conscious observers. It's not surprising that the film has become increasingly examined for Whale's subtly subversive, if not frankly homosexual, humor.

Evidence of Whale's restless creativity is everywhere. In much the same way as the German Expressionists did a decade earlier, Whale creates a new world on the soundstage. Even more than he did in *The Old Dark House*, the director peoples his highly stylized sets with highly stylized players. The end result is a movie that's half-way between a fairy tale and grand opera. It's set in a European netherworld of deep forests and mountain streams. The tone is vaguely Germanic but often recognizably British in character and temperament, with a few stray American voices to complete the incongruous illusion.

Whale uses religious symbolism playfully and in stark contrast to the solemn DeMille tradition. One of *Bride of Frankenstein*'s most striking images is of the Monster trussed-up in a mock crucifixion by the jeering mob. Later, in the blind hermit's hut, Whale lingers over the image of a background crucifix during a fade-out as the Monster learns his first lesson in human love. The lesson doesn't go very far and, contrary to the audience's expectation, the creature is back blaspheming again, uprooting huge statues of the saints in a graveyard as the villagers' bloodhounds nip at his heels.

The use of religious symbolism is a facet of the director's dark strain of gallows humor, much of which focuses on Ernest Thesiger's wickedly memorable Dr. Pretorius. The scientist's arrival at the Frankenstein's homestead is another of Whale's direct visual references to Paul Leni's *The Cat and the Canary* (1927). The actor is framed exactly as Tully Marshall's character was as he as he makes his way to the mansion's entranceway. Marshall's lean build and patrician nose too closely resembles Thesiger's to be mere coincidence.

Unlike the earnest, trailblazing Henry Frankenstein, Pretorius' fascination with the dead takes on an unwholesome air. After Pretorius and his party of body snatchers complete their grim duties in a dank crypt, the scientist dawdles behind, uncorks a bottle of liquor and toasts the remains taken from a plundered coffin. When the Monster dejectedly voices his preference for the company of the dead, the necrophilic scientist glumly agrees. Thesiger delivers the goods in a rich, fruity performance that is at once pompous and slyly perverse; one wonders to what degree Pretorius' character is modeled on the actor himself.

Colin Clive is at a disadvantage in the sketchily written role of Henry Frankenstein. No longer the fervent rebel in the original, Clive appears so exhausted and dissipated that he doesn't seem to be acting. He does what he can in a diminished part but he is easily upstaged by such grandstanding gargoyles as Karloff, Lanchester and Thesiger. Understandably, Whale and his writers had higher priorities than providing a sense of continuity between Valerie Hobson's Elizabeth and Mae Clarke's. The character served a dramatic function in the earlier film by lending a sense of urgency and foreboding to the opening reels, trying to uncover her intended's dark secrets. Clarke gave Elizabeth a fresh contemporary edge but by the sequel she had somehow turned into a period character and not always an appealing one. As the lady of the House of Frankenstein, Hobson's Elizabeth is scripted to be somewhat imperious and the actress obliges at the expense of the natural charm she demonstrated in *Mystery of Edwin Drood* and *WereWolf of London*. The actress is taxed by the florid dialogue in her initial scenes and she's clearly in over her head during her big breakdown scene in Henry's bedchamber. Happily, Hobson matured into a formidable leading lady in later British films such as *Blanche Fury* (1948) and *The Rocking Horse Winner* (1950).

Bride of Frankenstein's *other* leading lady was a bit more problematic to cast. Whale needed an actress who could capture the literary, free-spirited nature of Mary Shelley as well as endow the Monster's mate with startling and imaginative nuances. Elsa Lanchester could do both masterfully. Film historian-interviewer Gregory Mank got to the root of the mystery behind the actress's curiously bird-like quality in her performance as the Bride: Her conception of the part was based partially on observing the swans in Regents Park, particularly in the way they "hissed" when provoked. Staring wide-eyed, jerkily reacting to every movement around her, it's a tightly coiled performance of sheer instinct and energy. The Bride's "look" is a classic '30s concept, more of a hairstyle than a makeup. Lanchester's natural red hair was teased up in an unworldly, fright-wig style, a wavy white streak suggesting a baptism by lightning. It's a cartoonish design, perhaps too over-the-top, but executed with Jack Pierce's usual finesse and artistry.

Understandably, it is Karloff who dominates *Bride of Frankenstein*. Promotional trailers boldly exclaimed "The Monster Talks!" but Karloff insisted that humanizing the character only detracted from his uniqueness. He steadfastly maintained this belief until his death.

Several months after the release of *Bride of Frankenstein*, *New York Sun* reporter Eileen Creelman (who had nothing but the most lavish praise for the film) was sent out to interview Karloff. But the reporter found the star, though gracious as always, surprisingly cool about his new movie. "I don't know but that that was a mistake, that build-up of so much sympathy for the Monster," Karloff opined. "I think maybe they lost the excitement of the picture." Few people are in agreement with Karloff's assessment, and *Bride* is usually ranked as one of his triumphs. Karloff again proves he is a physical actor *par excellence*, wringing a full range of emotions from the subtlest of gestures or facial expressions.

Franz Waxman's score is lush and motif-laden, although the meager 22-man studio orchestra used is hardly the last word in sonic splendor. It ranks along with Max Steiner's *King Kong* as the most re-recorded of vintage horror film scores, represented on disc at least a half dozen times since the soundtrack revival of the '70s. Encompassing as it does a remarkable variety of moods, from love themes, thrilling chases and somber processions to the crackling and triumphant Creation sequence, it makes for an incredibly rich music experience apart from the movie. Waxman went on to be one of the great Hollywood studio composers and scored such Golden Age horror movies as *The Invisible Ray* and, for MGM, *The Devil-Doll* (1936) and *Dr. Jekyll and Mr. Hyde* (1941). All were in his signature post–Romantic style but none captured the majesty of *Bride of Frankenstein*. Unfortunately, Universal saw fit to cannibalize the soundtrack, as well as those of *Dracula's Daughter*, *WereWolf of London* and others, for use as background filler in their juvenile Flash Gordon serials. (Waxman's original main title, slightly modified, would turn up under the credits of *The Black Doll*.)

It was hoped that the box office grosses on *Bride of Frankenstein* would match those of the original, making the film a hot property for theater owners. Long before the days when "saturation bookings" were commonplace, a legal battle erupted between two New York City theaters to decide which of them held the legal right to screen the movie. A settlement was reached before the case went to Federal Court, with the Roxy Theater winning the rights to exhibit the attraction. Its rival, the Rialto, picked up *Were-Wolf of London* as a consolation prize. Despite excellent notices, *Bride of Frankenstein* didn't reap quite the bonanza its predecessor did.

There have been few attempts to duplicate the fragile charm of *Bride of Frankenstein*. Hammer's *Frankenstein Created Woman* (1967) suggested something along the same lines only to fall back on a formula vengeance-driven plot. Franc Roddam's 1985 misfire, simply titled *The Bride*, was actually something of a sequel, although it did come a tad closer to the mark. Highlighted by splendid sets and a flashy laboratory sequence, the film courted disaster by casting the vapid Jennifer Beals and British rock star Sting in the leads. Even worse was a sappy and absurd upbeat ending which finds the Monster and his mate, romantically reunited, blissfully sailing down a Venetian waterway on a gondola. *Mary Shelley's Frankenstein* (1994), directed by Kenneth Branagh, went back to the novel's "Bride" sequence but it proved to be as heavy-handed as the rest of the film.

James Whale's fate was tied to the fortunes of the Laemmles to a degree that even the director would not have foreseen. When the studio president's reign ended, so did the era of Whale's creative clout. The "New" Universal saw fit to butcher what the director regarded as his masterwork, *The Road Back* (1937), a sequel to *All Quiet on the Western Front* (1930), which met with commercial and critical indifference. Whale's last film at the studio was an obvious attempt to tackle a commercial subject; *Green Hell* (1940) only proved to be a hack back lot jungle thriller.

Actress Kay Linaker, who had a small role in the picture, recalled her days working with the director for the authors:

> The further we got into the jungle, and the more the script became almost a parody, the more Whale seemed to start to enjoy it.... It didn't dawn on him that this was a horrible, horrible picture. But he seemed to have difficulty making decisions.... It was almost as though he was "on" something. You know that strange thing that happens to people when they've just taken a drug? When the pleasure and the remoteness seems to come over them? *That* was what we had with Mr. Whale.

By the time Ms. Linaker was cast in Whale's *They Dare Not Love* (1941), at Columbia, the director's erratic behavior gave way to sudden flare-ups of hostility. When Whale started berating and insulting Linaker and the film's star, Martha Scott, studio president, Harry Cohn, came on the set and dismissed him outright. Linaker said:

> Nobody on that picture developed a hate for Whale. Everybody was *sorry* for him. Before he got sick, he was a fellow who could do a fine job, as his films indicate. But then there came the breaking point. After that, he was just ... not a

whole person. He was a "part" individual functioning on ... not even two and a half cylinders.

Despite Whale's richly deserved reputation as one of the all-time great horror directors, he hasn't been a particularly influential figure. The Gothic look of his films has been slavishly duplicated, but Whale's sophisticated melding of humor and horror quickly became passé. His style was lightly mimicked in *Son of Frankenstein*, but not to the extent that has been suggested in numerous film books. The later Frankenstein movies were made by directors who appear as though they hadn't seen a Whale film. Whale's elegance and wit were perfectly in tune with the glamorous '30s and his downfall was inevitable. William K. Everson, a tireless champion of Whale, once lamented that Universal-International didn't recruit the director during the horror-science fiction boom of the '50s. Even if Whale was physically or emotionally equipped for such an undertaking, it's hard to imagine the director tailoring his talents for the drive-in market. The stock characters of '50s science fiction — the no-nonsense military types, the girl reporters, the square-jawed American hero — would no doubt seem even more alien to the director than the monsters from space and the creatures from the Amazon at the center of the action.

More than archaic museum pieces, Whale's quartet of horror classics have comfortably withstood the test of time.* *Bride of Frankenstein* is probably his finest.

Critics' Corner

The story ... has none of the hang-dog air that one expects in sequels. [The screenwriters and director] have given it the macabre intensity proper to all good horror pieces, but have substituted a queer kind of mechanistic pathos for the sheer evil that was *Frankenstein*. — *Time*, April 1935

Mr. Karloff is so splendid ... that all one can say is "he is the Monster." ... James Whale has done another excellent job.... [A] first-rate horror film. — *The New York Times*, May 11, 1935, Frank S. Nugent

[T]he "big moment" when the synthetic woman begins to breathe is duly spellbinding. — *The New York Herald-Tribune*, 1935

John Mescall at the camera managed to create a large number of unusual angles and process shots which help the film tremendously. It is this excellent camerawork coupled with an eerie but lingering musical score by Franz Waxman ... that gives a great deal of the film its real horror. — *Variety*, May 15, 1935, Kauf

[O]ne of the finest productions that come off the Universal lot for many a day.... [G]orgeously photographed ... Karloff is superb as the Monster.... — *The Hollywood Reporter*, April 6, 1935

Artistically, this surpasses *Frankenstein*.... [T]he production, direction and acting are excellent.... The most effective part of the picture ... is not the horror situations but the more human ones — those in which Karloff is befriended by O.P. Heggie.... Karloff's happy reaction to such treatment is touching. — *Harrison's Reports*, May 4, 1935

[C]arries bloodchilling, horrific incident trifle too far.... [P]rologue in execrable taste.... [S]ensation is carried a little beyond reasonable limits. — *Today's Cinema* (GB), May 30, 1935

Brilliantly set — it is wonderful! — *The Daily Herald* (GB), June 1935

Karloff is colossally fine.... [E]erie, grim, and staggering.... — *The Sunday Times* (GB), June 1935

Played, produced and directed in exactly the right spirit demanded by a thriller. — *News of the World* (GB), July 1935

An amazing spectacle. A wonderful example of cinema technique. — *The Reynolds News* (GB), July 1935

Carl Laemmle Jr.'s, initial independent production will satisfy the most solid of the thrill-seeking fans. John L. Balderston and William Hurlbut have concocted a sequel to *Frankenstein* that is a spine-tingler. Karloff as the monster is very effective.... James Whale has done a fine job of directing. John Mescall's photography is high-class. — *The Film Daily*, April 11, 1935

Were Wolf of London

Released June 3, 1935. 75 minutes. A Carl Laemmle Production. *Director:* Stuart Walker. *Associate Producer:* Robert Harris. *Executive Producer:* Stanley Bergerman. *Screenplay:* John Colton. *Original Story:* Robert Harris. *Adaptation:* Harvey Gates & Robert Harris. *Contributing Writer:* Edmund Pearson. *Contributing to Screenplay Construction:* James Mulhauser & Aben Kandel. *Photography:* Charles Stumar. *Special Photographic Effects:* John P. Fulton. *Camera Operator:* Maury Gertsman. *Assistant Cameraman:* John J. Martin. *Assistant Directors:* Phil Karlstein [Karlson] & Charles S. Gould. *Editors:* Russell Schoengarth & Milton Carruth. *Supervising Editor:* Maurice Pivar. *Art Director:* Albert S. D'Agostino. *Musical Score:* Karl Hajos. *Musical Supervisor:* Gilbert Kurland. *Sound Recorder:* Donald Conliff. *Sound Mixer:* Bob Richards. *Boom Man:* Frank Artman. *Technical Director:* Archie Hall. *Property Master:* Robert Laszlo. *Set Lighting Foreman:* Irving Smith. *Makeup:* Jack P. Pierce. *Hair Stylist:* Mary Dolor. *Script Clerk:* Jean Raymond. *Grips:* E. Brown, A.

**In 2005,* Time *magazine asked its readers to vote on the All-Time 100 Best Films;* Bride of Frankenstein *made the cut.)*

Buckley & Lester Kahn. *Production Secretaries:* Billy Moritz & Selma Platt. *Director's Secretary:* Muriel Yoemans. *Child Welfare Worker:* Mary West. *Stand-in for Warner Oland:* Alex Chivra.

Henry Hull (*Dr. Wilfred Glendon*), Warner Oland (*Dr. Yogami*), Valerie Hobson (*Lisa Glendon*), Lester Matthews (*Paul Ames*), Spring Byington (*Miss Ettie Coombes*), Lawrence Grant (*Col. Thomas Forsythe*), Clark Williams (*Hugh Renwick*), J.M. Kerrigan (*Hawkins*), Charlotte Granville (*Lady Alice Forsythe*), Ethel Griffies (*Mrs. Whack*), Zeffie Tilbury (*Mrs. Moncaster*), Jeanne Bartlett (*Daisy*), Harry Stubbs (*Constable Jenkins*), Louis Vincenot (*Head Cooley*), Reginald Barlow (*Timothy*), Eole Galli (*Mme. Ballelotte, the Prima Donna*), Joseph North (*Plimpton*), Egon Brecher (*Priest*), Boyd Irwin, Sr. (*Hotel Manager*), Helena Grant (*Mother*), Noel Kennedy (*Boy*), William Millman (*John Bull*), Tempe Pigott (*Drunk Woman*), Maude Leslie (*Mrs. Charteris*), Herbert Evans (*Scotland Yard Aide*), Gunnis Davis, George Kirby (*Detectives*), Jeffrey Hassel (*Alf*), Amber Norman (*Beggarwoman*), James May (*Bar Man*), Veda Buckland (*Mrs. Hodgeson [Yogami's Housekeeper]*), Connie Leon (*Millie [Yogami's Housemaid]*), Wong Chung, Beal Wong (*Coolies*), Roseollo Navello (*Maid*), George DeNormand (*Double for Henry Hull*), Ed Parker (*Double for Lester Matthews*). *Deleted from final print:* David Thursby (*Photographer*).

> It is a blood-curdling thing. It will give the unholy shivers to even the hardest boiled movie egg. It is as gruesome as *Dracula*— as startling as *Frankenstein*.... [I]t's a glorious change from the Pollyanna pictures which you may have been using as a steady diet. The story could never happen, and that's the very thing that will knock people somewhat goofy....
>
> —*Carl Laemmle, Sr., quoted in* The Universal Weekly, *April 20, 1935*

Were Wolf of London has gotten more than its share of hard knocks over the years. It's a film that's usually discussed in suppositions: "What if Karloff had played the Henry Hull part?" or "What if Lugosi had played the role essayed by Warner Oland?" or "Wouldn't the picture have turned out better if James Whale or Robert Florey had directed it?" These ponderings are not unjustified. Stuart Walker, the film's director, had neither the ingenuity nor the affinity for an all-out horror subject. Hull, despite his impressive theatrical track record, lacked Boris Karloff's passion as much as Oland lacked Bela Lugosi's haunting charisma.

Compared with the satanic eroticism of *The Black Cat* and the cold-blooded brutality of *Murders in the Rue Morgue*, *Were Wolf of London* is genteel indeed. It's poky, quaint and self-consciously theatrical. Although these restraints somewhat diminish the gut-wrenching human drama at the heart of the story, they don't detract from the film's considerable chills and beautifully sustained atmosphere. Setting the tone for the myriad of werewolf movies that would follow it, an air of doom and futility hangs over *Were Wolf of London* like an oppressive cloud, and the tale's unhappy conclusion is telegraphed well in advance. It is written in stone somewhere that, once one falls victim to lycanthropia, there is no hope for salvation, and nothing less than divine intervention (or a medical genius named Edlemann [see *House of Dracula*]) can rescue him from his fate.

Although the legend of the werewolf is as deeply seated in the history of mankind as the vampire, its cinematic treatment up to the '30s was, by comparison, negligible. Several short films (1913's *The Werewolf* and 1914's *The White Wolf*) featured lycanthropes of American Indian origin; there were also a number of domestic and foreign productions which bore the namesake of the supernatural creature, but whose protagonists were strictly human in nature (e.g., Reliance-Mutual's 1915 *The Wolf Man*, Fox's 1924 John Gilbert film *The Wolfman* and *Le Loup Garou* [*The Werewolf*], a 1932 German production).

Guy Endore's novel *The Were Wolf of Paris*, published in 1933, brought the mythic manimal the belated recognition it deserved. Curiously, when Universal decided to introduce the werewolf in its current horror cycle in late 1934, it ignored the Endore novel and opted for an original treatment instead. The French writer had taken up residence in Hollywood by this time, but was not invited to participate in the project. MGM obtained his services to co-author the screenplays for *Mark of the Vampire* and *Mad Love*, both released in 1935, the same year as *Were Wolf of London*.

Of the scores of prospects announced for reigning horror kings Karloff and Lugosi by Universal during this hectic period, one of the most interesting proposals was to star Boris as a lycanthrope in *The Wolf Man*. A script was prepared in early 1932, Robert Florey was slated to direct, but the production never got off the ground. Once again, poor Florey lost out on yet another major horror project.

On December 21, 1934, *The Hollywood Reporter* announced that Kurt Neumann was assigned by Universal the previous day to direct their latest horror production, *Were Wolf of London*, which Robert Harris was slated to produce upon the completion of the screenplay. Henry Hull and Bela Lugosi were the only principals assigned to the cast thus far. By mid–January of 1935, the same source revealed that Neumann had been diverted to another picture and that his replacement might be Stuart Walker, riding high after his engagements on the studio's two Dickens screen adaptations, *Great Expectations* (1934) and *Mystery of Edwin Drood*. (Eight years later, Neumann lost out on directing another werewolf movie, Columbia's *The Return of the Vampire* [1943], after providing the film's story.)

Lugosi was still being mentioned in connection with *Werewolf of London* in mid–January; however, on the 25th, *The Hollywood Reporter* revealed that Warner Oland, world-renowned for his wonderful screen incarnation of Charlie Chan, had been added to the cast (in the role previously considered for Lugosi).

Three days later, *Were Wolf of London* began production. Uncle Carl's son-in-law Stanley Bergerman served as executive producer. John Colton, once described as a world-weary homosexual playwright-scenarist, a writer whose claim to fame was adapting Somerset Maugham's short story "Miss Sadie Thompson" into the Broadway smash "Rain," authored the script. (An uncredited contributor to the screenplay was Aben Kandel, future associate of exploitation filmmaker Herman Cohen; the two co-wrote the iconic *I Was a Teenage Werewolf* [1957]).

Born in Louisville, Kentucky, on October 3, 1890, Henry Hull developed a well-earned reputation as one of Broadway's most accomplished actors, racking up an extraordinary number of successes in long-running productions over the years. Hull hailed from a theatrical family. His father, William Madison Hull, was a leading Louisville dramatic critic and also distinguished himself as a press agent for producer David Belasco. Henry's brothers Howard and Shelley were actors, and his sister-in-law was Josephine Hull, unforgettable as Abby Brewster in both the stage and screen versions of *Arsenic and Old Lace* (1944).

Abandoning a promising engineering profession for the lure of the stage, Henry Hull got his first break through Belasco in his 1911 production "The Nigger." (Hull portrayed a dual role, as a runaway slave and the county sheriff who pursued him.) Following a three-year stint in Margaret Anglin's Greek repertory company, the actor scored his first great Broadway success as the lead in the 1916 stage play "The Man Who Came Back." Another major success was scored two years later in the starring role of the popular mystery thriller "The Cat and the Canary," which ran for 42 weeks at the National Theater. While Hull was appearing in a Huntington, Long Island, production of "The Little Minister," producer-director Anthony Brown took notice of the actor and contracted him to play the part of Jeeter Lester, tobacco-chewing patriarch of a dirt-poor Southern farm family, in a theatrical adaptation of Erskine Caldwell's novel *Tobacco Road*. Debuting in 1933, the Broadway show was an instant hit and ran for over 3,000 performances.

Acting in motion pictures kept the stage star busy between theater engagements. Hull's silent film debut came in 1917's *The Volunteer*, shot in America's first film capital, Fort Lee, New Jersey. Scores of others followed, including a screen version of *The Man Who Came Back* for Fox in 1924. Hull's resonant speaking voice made him a natural in talkies. The actor said in a newspaper interview:

> You can't hypnotize the camera. You can hypnotize a [theater] audience to the point where they forget your art and react to voice and gesture. You must fall back on sheer technique, and pray to the gods that your scene is effective....

On March 24, 1934, while Hull was appearing in "Tobacco Road," Carl Laemmle signed him to a five-year contract. His first Universal assignment was of classic proportions: The actor made a strong impression as the escaped criminal Magwitch in Stuart Walker's first Charles Dickens adaptation *Great Expectations*. In July of that year, Universal announced that it was planning to feature the distinguished actor as the lead in their forthcoming adaptation of Daniel Defoe's *Robinson Crusoe*, but the picture never materialized. Instead, Hull was given a supporting part in *Transient Lady* opposite Gene Raymond and Frances Drake.

Rival doctors Wilfred Glendon (Henry Hull) and Yogami (Warner Oland) wage a life-and-death struggle for control of a cure for lycanthropy in *Were Wolf of London.*

In *Were Wolf of London*, Hull portrays eminent British botanist Dr. Wilfred Glendon, whose quest for the only known specimens of the phosphorescent moon flower, the Mariphasa lupino lumino, takes him deep into a forbidden region of Tibet. Abandoned by his native bearers and shrugging off the prophetic warnings of a holy man (Egon Brecher), Glendon and his young traveling companion Hugh Renwick (Clark Williams) enter a forbidden valley.

Suddenly, both men are overcome by unearthly sensations. Glendon reacts as though he has been struck down by a "ghostly fist" (screenwriter Colton's own words). Catching sight of the elusive Mariphasa, Glendon rushes towards it, but stops dead in his tracks. Cast against the rocks above is the shadow of a lurching figure, perched, ready to pounce. Within moments, the creature — a human being with animalistic tendencies — is upon him. The botanist wounds the beast with his knife, but not before it has inflicted a deep bite wound in his arm.

Returning to England with his specimens, Glendon is visited by the inscrutable Dr. Yogami (Warner Oland). Like Glendon, he too has searched Tibet for the rare flower. Sensing a vague familiarity about the stranger, Glendon asks Yogami if they had ever met before. "In Tibet, once, but only for a moment ... in the dark," is his disturbing reply. Yogami informs the incredulous Glendon that the Mariphasa is the only known antidote for lycanthrophobia, a strange malady in which the victim becomes a werewolf when the moon is full. Asked how these unfortunate individuals contracted "this medieval unpleasantness," Yogami, touching Glendon's scarred arm, says, "From the bite of another werewolf."

Although Glendon hasn't yet made the connection, the audience realizes it was Yogami who attacked the botanist in Tibet. The desperate conflict between two doomed men struggling to save their souls from the grip of an all-consuming power had the potential for great theater that is never fully realized. Colton's overly restrained screenplay offers the two rivals no impassioned confrontation scenes until the climax, at which point severe deletions in the scenarist's dialogue lessened the dramatic impact to a considerable degree.

Haunted by Yogami's warning that a werewolf "instinctively seeks to kill the thing it loves best," Glendon spends every waking hour coaxing the buds of the Mariphasa open with the aid of a miraculous apparatus which creates artificial moonlight. He fears for the safety of his beloved wife Lisa (Valerie Hobson), whose loneliness and despair are driving her into the welcoming arms of her dear friend and former suitor Paul Ames (Lester Matthews).

The complicated process of shooting the man-into-werewolf transformations was accomplished with deceptive grace. Cameraman Charles Stumar admitted at the time that he was scornful of shots whose beauty or power left audiences breathless; he felt they distracted the viewer from the story. Be that as it may, one cannot disregard the beauty *and* power of Hull's first full-fledged changeover, the finest sequence in the film. In a tracking shot, as the actor walks on the far side of a series of pillars, a different stage of the transformation is revealed after each pillar he passes. It was the job of John P. Fulton and his assistant David "Stan" Horsley to accomplish this feat of cinematic magic.

Horsley told *Photon*'s Paul Mandell:

> John and I pondered a lot on how this shot was actually going to get done in the pre-production stages of the film. It was obvious to us from the outset that a series of cuts would be a bit too obvious as it would entail breaks in an otherwise smooth camera movement. It was decided to photograph Hull against a black velvet background and matte his figure onto the normal background scene. The pillars were separately photographed and further matted onto this composite, making the precise instant where the alteration in makeup occurred, so that in its final stage there appeared to be no break in camera movement.

Hull's werewolf differs from Lon Chaney, Jr.'s, portrayal in *The Wolf Man* in that he's capable of reason, whereas the Chaney werewolf is motivated by pure animal instinct. Glendon hurries to the lab with the express purpose of inoculating himself with the Mariphasa fluid but discovers the blossoms have been stolen. Donning his cap and scarf *à la* Mr. Hyde, the lycanthrope seeks out Lisa, who's attending a social bash given by her flighty aunt, Ettie Coombes (Spring Byington in another of her dotty society matron roles). After lurking outside Ettie's building, The werewolf climbs up a balcony and finds a tipsy Ettie in her bedroom, sleeping off a drunk. In an eerily lit close-up, accenting the creature's satanic features, the werewolf approaches the socialite. Her full-throated scream frightens him off. On the street below, the lycanthrope snatches away the life of a prostitute.

John Colton's scenario becomes annoyingly episodic at this point. Ever desperate for the bloom of the life-saving Mariphasa, Glendon keeps dashing off to secret destinations to wait

Top: **Henry Hull in Jack Pierce's masterful WereWolf makeup.** ***Bottom:*** **The identity of the actor portraying the lycanthrope Yogami remains unknown.**

by the werewolf while on a sentimental evening outing.

Yogami, meanwhile, has his own problems. The Mariphasa blossoms he has stolen from Glendon have been used up. Unable to convince Scotland Yard that the recent rash of murders plaguing London is the work of a werewolf, and that they must secure Dr. Glendon's specimens of the Mariphasa for mass cultivation, Yogami returns to his hotel. That evening, Yogami himself becomes a werewolf and slays a chambermaid (all off-camera).

Back at Glendon's lab, the two rivals confront one another. Yogami greedily snatches the newborn Mariphasa flower right out from under Glendon's nose. "You brought this on me!" the botanist cries. "That night ... in Tibet!" "I'm sorry I can't share *this* [the flower] with you!" Yogami taunts him. The botanist attempts a getaway but Glendon seizes him by the throat and the pair struggle violently. Ironically, Yogami dies at the hands of the monster he himself had inadvertently created.

The werewolf instinctively seeks out his beloved Lisa. After overcoming Paul, the werewolf corners his wife on a staircase and stalks her like a cunning animal. This time there can be no doubt in Lisa's mind who this strange creature really is. A shot is heard and the wolf man falls to the floor, mortally wounded by a police bullet. Before he expires, the werewolf bids his grieving wife a heart-wrenching farewell, then changes back to Glendon.

By the time Stuart Walker gathered together his cast and crew for the first day's shooting of *WereWolf of London*, significant changes had already been made in Colton's talky, overwritten screenplay (dated January 26, just two days before the official start of filming). To the film's benefit, a plethora of superfluous chatter

out his next transformation, and then returns home to check on the blossom's painfully slow progress. In one of his finest moments, Hull, holed up in a seedy Whitechapel rooming house, prays to God that He intervene and prevent the botanist's awful transformation. "Dear Father in Heaven," he cries, "don't let this happen to me again! But if it must, keep me away from Lisa. Keep me away from the thing I love!"

Glendon's emotional entreaty doesn't postpone the inevitable. In a gloriously executed sequence, he becomes a werewolf in full view of the camera. Lisa almost falls victim to her husband's bestiality when she and Paul are attacked was excised and several of the major horror scenes were fine-tuned. The production's *piece de resistance*—Glendon's first transformation into a werewolf as he rushes through the column-lined corridor—doesn't even appear in the script. (Colton's version had an irate Glendon pursuing his panic-stricken cat across the estate grounds and into the laboratory, emerging moments later as a werewolf.)

Colton placed greater emphasis on the love triangle between Glendon, Lisa and Paul. Lisa is a lot more disenchanted with her marriage to the stuffy, preoccupied Dr. Glendon than the film indicates. Colton also introduced a character by the name of Dr. Phillips. (Reginald Barlow, originally cast in this part, was recast as Timothy, the groundskeeper.) The family physician is summoned by the distressed botanist after he discovers coarse hair on his forehead and a permanent five o'clock shadow. Stymied, Phillips promises to confer with an authority on hirsutism(!) before venturing a diagnosis. The decision to discard Colton's suggestion that Hull play out the remainder of his straight scenes in this ludicrous transitional stage was a wise one. A sequence which was obviously shot then later discarded featured a little boy who is grasped by the octopus-like tentacles of the giant Madagascar Carnalia while attending Glendon's botanical garden party. The botanist frees the terrified youngster by borrowing a long hat pin from a visitor and sticking it in the "mouth" of the plant.

Vigilant to a fault, the Production Code Administration (PCA) put in *their* two cents in regards to offensive material at a conference between members of their staff and Universal executives on January 15. The fear of God was alluded to in the Tibetan scenes via the old priest who warns Glendon that "there are some things it is better not to bother with." Glendon ventures forth on his mission nevertheless, thus setting the stage for a tragic yet well-deserved death (in the opinion of the PCA). The censorship board also strongly stressed that the transformation from man to beast should not dwell on the physical details. Stanley Bergerman tried to persuade the PCA (on February 7) to allow the transformation scene to remain as is; the PCA said it would withhold judgment until after a viewing of the finished film. Following the screening (on March 22), the group asked that Universal eliminate some of the graphic shots in the fight between the werewolf and Yogami. Certificate No. 714 was issued on March 23, subject to three suggested cuts. (The preview trailer for *Were Wolf of London* contains a single, gory shot, not seen in the final cut, of the werewolf inflicting deep claw marks across Yogami's face during the struggle.)

As the nosy old Mrs. Moncaster and her equally gin-sodden friend Mrs. Whack, Zeffie Tilbury and Ethel Griffies, respectively, provide *Were Wolf of London* with some flavorsome Cockney humor of the James Whale school. (Both actresses had recently been directed by Walker in *Mystery of Edwin Drood*.) Glendon poignantly describes himself to the flirtatious (and clueless) Mrs. Moncaster as "singularly single ... more single than I ever realized it possible for a human being to be." Colton would have worn out the welcome of these delightful old crones had Walker not cut a silly little scene that was evidently written for the purpose of giving the film an "upbeat" finis: Mrs. Moncaster, hailed by her fellow Whitechapelians as "the lady that lodged the werewolf," has her photo session ruined by the cantankerous Mrs. Whack, who claims that it was she who lodged Glendon first, and therefore deserves all the adoration and the six complimentary bottles of gin donated by the local pub.

Glendon's plea for salvation as he awaits the rising of the full moon in his rooming house apartment is decidedly more verbose (and consequently not as affecting) in Colton's script. However, there is one instance where a little less editing would have proven beneficial: The climactic confrontation scene between Glendon and Yogami (pared down to a few lines of dialogue for the final shoot). Colton sets up the intense exchange as the two werewolves-to-be breathlessly await the blooming of the last Mariphasa bud:

GLENDON: We meet again, Yogami ... for the last time....
YOGAMI: Between us both and doom ... there is only that....
GLENDON: The doom is yours, not mine, Yogami ... one of us must go....
YOGAMI: There is enough blood in that flower to save us both if it blooms in time—

GLENDON: No, Yogami. There isn't room on all the planet for both of us. *You* brought this thing on me.

The dialogue continues until, finally, the fragile bud begins to open. Both men rush to secure it. Glendon tears the blossom off its stem and tries to pierce his wrist with the thorn but Yogami bites him, causing the flower to fall to the floor. Glendon attacks him; Yogami, realizing he cannot secure the flower, stamps on it. The flower "dies" with an agonized cry. A ray of moonlight shoots from the dead blossom to the moon, "the soul of the flower returned to its final resting place." What had the potential to be a marvelously gripping moment was scuttled, like as not, for economic reasons.

The atmospheric, otherworldly Tibetan sequences were shot on a tract of rugged terrain in the Los Angeles area, Vasquez Rocks. Stumar claimed that since the natural shadows of the rocks were too light for the required eerie effects of the night scenes, he resorted to manufacturing his own moonlight and shadows. Sheet iron was scalloped by shears into jagged edges and set along rocks. Powerful blue-white lamps playing behind these screens threw the necessary jet black shadows and created a silvery-blue-green glow, much richer than natural moonlight.

While *Were Wolf of London* was in production, Carl Laemmle decided to perk up interest in his latest horror outing by offering a $50 reward to any studio employee who could come up with a catchy title based on the film's plot synopsis. Hundreds of suggestions were submitted, some of them reasonable, others hilariously outlandish. Here are a few of our favorites: *Moon Doom, The Relief of Death, What Price Curiosity, The Whelp from Tibet, Dr. Yogami of London, Werewolf Yogami, Beyond the Ken of Man, Kismet, The Loose Wolf* and, "best" of all, *Bloom, Flower, Bloom.* Only one submission was seriously considered, *The Unholy Hour.* But, by the time the picture was well into its final stages of post-production, the original title was reinstated. *The Unholy Hour* was employed for the film's Canadian distribution.

Completed on February 23, 1935, at a cost exceeding $195,000 (more than $36,000 over budget), *Were Wolf of London* came in four days over schedule. With a tighter script, concise continuity and sharper direction, Walker's film would have done greater justice to its fascinating subject matter. The passion and sheer cinematic artistry of a Whale or an Ulmer are lacking in the director's placid staging, and there are only a few scenes which can be termed inspired. Colton's approach to lycanthropy is more scientific than supernatural. While the scenarist makes passing references to the werewolf's mythological origins, very few of the creature's mythic elements are incorporated into the script. Glendon is slain by an ordinary bullet, not a silver one. The whole business concerning the Mariphasa and its ability to thwart lycanthropic seizures is purely the invention of Colton and Robert Harris, who authored the original story. *Were Wolf of London* shrugs off many of the Middle European influences that screenwriter Curt Siodmak so dearly embraced in his later werewolf outings.

As is often the case in the Universal horror films of this period, background music plays an all-important role in creating and sustaining dramatic tension and mood. Hungarian-born composer Karl Hajos borrowed several remarkably evocative cues heard in *The Invisible Man* and the 1934 *Black Cat*, and wrote some fine original compositions of his own, including a stirring main title theme. Ten years later, Hajos adapted a passage from the *Were Wolf of London* score to enhance the gloomy goings-on in PRC's *Fog Island* (1945).

Unanimously praised by critics of the day, Henry Hull's studious performance has come under increasing attack. Many argue that Wilfred Glendon is an arrogant, unsympathetic stuffed shirt, quite the opposite of Lon Chaney's naive and child-like Larry Talbot. Glendon's blatant jealousy of his neglected wife alienates the viewer further. Paradoxically, the deeper the scientist descends into despair, the more human he becomes. *Monsters from the Vault* magazine published a career piece on Hull, penned by writer Cortlandt Hull, in which the actor stated that he viewed the character's personality as being similar to that of Sherlock Holmes. "Glendon, being a botanist, or scientist, was not open to belief in the supernatural, as it interfered with his work."

Jack Pierce's marvelous makeup design, a subtly feline, almost satanic look, is quite a contrast from the more bestial disguise he later used on Chaney, and which was originally designed with Hull in mind.* Rumor has it that Hull protested about the prolonged application sessions, so a more modified look was created. Cortlandt Hull put the lie to this story. "Henry said his point was not vanity, but how the script was written," he wrote. "During the 'Monk's Rest' sequence, as he jumps down from the tower, Valerie Hobson and Lester Matthews were to have recognized the werewolf as being Glendon.... Jack Pierce's original design would have made this recognition impossible." Pierce disregarded Hull's suggestion that a less monstrous makeup be devised, so the actor went over the mercurial makeup master's head, directly to Junior Laemmle. "Laemmle agreed with Henry and sent a memo to Jack Pierce to make the change before filming began. After that, Pierce was rather cold toward Henry. In fact, he discovered a way to eliminate Hull from his makeup chair for two of the transformation sequences. Pierce made a life-cast of Henry and created four or five variations from Glendon to werewolf. As the change progressed, Pierce just popped a new head on the dummy body for each stage of the man-to-wolf transmutation. This allowed Pierce to film two sequences without Hull. Therefore, Pierce created the first version of 'replacement heads,' as they have been commonly referred to in recent years." These props were utilized in the Monk's Rest transformation scene and at the climax where Hull lies dying at the foot of the stairs.

A special effects technique employed by German cameraman Karl Struss on Fredric March for the 1931 version of *Dr. Jekyll and Mr. Hyde* (and previously in the 1925 silent *Ben-Hur—A Tale of the Christ*) was used by Pierce and John P. Fulton. Red makeup and a lighting shift created the first transformation of Hull's face and hands. Cortlandt Hull explained:

> A red filter on the lights hid the red makeup, then a switch to normal lighting revealed a subtle change and a darkened skin color. In the next stage, the camera panned back up from his hands to his face. Then a cut was made, and the dissolve of various makeup changes began with the camera directly on Henry.

Most of *Were Wolf of London*'s supporting cast came from the London theater world. Born in Larne, Ireland, Valerie Hobson began her acting career at the age of 14. Her charmingly ingratiating performance is a distinct improvement over her wide-eyed, weepy Elizabeth in *Bride of Frankenstein*. According to a piece in *The Hollywood Reporter* (January 28, 1935), Hobson barely finished filming her scenes in the Whale film, before she was rushed into *Were Wolf of London*, her fifth consecutive picture in five months. But, as Henry Hull remembers it, the two horror movies were shot simultaneously. The late actress shared her memories of making *Were Wolf* with Gregory Mank in his book *Women in Horror Films, 1930s*:

> *Were Wolf of London* had a rather weak ... but awfully nice director called Stuart Walker. And it had Henry Hull as the Were Wolf.... [T]hey were very hopeful that Hull ... was going to be a great star. He was, of course, a very good and powerful actor, but he didn't photograph very well—he had a snub nose, which is never good for a leading man, and he never really made it. So I think they were rather disappointed in that. I also remember the animal-eating plant.... It was a perfectly ordinary thing, in fact, made of plastic, a bird-eating thing that opens its mouth and catches a thing.... It was only there to try to be frightening, and it didn't frighten anybody! ... These boogey films, horror films, were popular in those days, and if my lot was doing one, they would pop me in, you know. I remember some of the publicity that went out—that I was the new Fay Wray. Is anything sillier than that? To begin with, she was marvelous-looking, Fay Wray, and a great star. Perhaps I could *scream* better that she could, so I did a lot of screaming!

Warner Oland seems peculiarly ill-at-ease as the sympathetic, scheming Dr. Yogami. Indeed, there are moments when it seems as though he is at odds with the dialogue. Plagued with personal demons, Oland was destined to die in three short years, on August 6, 1938, after creating a buzz when he disappeared from the set of *Charlie Chan at the Ringside* (which Fox expeditiously fashioned into a Mr. Moto movie [1938's *Mr. Moto's Gamble*] with Peter Lorre doing the sleuthing). The Swedish-born actor

**It's been suggested that the early makeup design might have made the final cut of* Were Wolf of London *after all. When Ettie awakens from her drunken stupor, she sees the shadow of the werewolf on her bedroom wall. By all appearances, the guise bears more of a resemblance to the '41 makeup than it does the streamlined version.*

was adept at playing roles of an Oriental persuasion in both serials and features, and portrayed the insidious Fu Manchu in *The Mysterious Dr. Fu Manchu* (1929), *The Return of Dr. Fu Manchu* (1930) and *Daughter of the Dragon* (1931). Oland also gave memorable performances as Al Jolson's cantor father in the screen's first talkie, *The Jazz Singer* (1927), and as the treacherous Chinese warlord lusting after Marlene Dietrich in Josef von Sternberg's *Shanghai Express* (1932). But it was the 16 Charlie Chan movies that Oland made between 1931 and 1938 that insured his place among the immortals of Hollywood's Golden Age.

Often compared to Herbert Marshall by English theater critics, Lester Matthews is smooth and thoroughly likable as Paul Ames, Lisa's old flame. Matthews hailed from a celebrated theatrical family before signing a contract with Universal. He played leading man parts on the London stage and in a variety of touring companies. His subsequent genre credits include *The Raven*, *The Mysterious Doctor* (1943), *The Invisible Man's Revenge*, *Between Two Worlds* (1944) and *The Son of Dr. Jekyll* (1951).

Henry Hull enjoyed a long and prosperous career playing a variety of character parts in over 40 movies including *The Return of Frank James* (1940), *Lifeboat* (1944), *Portrait of Jennie* (1948), *The Fountainhead* (1949), *Master of the World* (1961) and *The Chase* (1966), before retiring to his farm in Lyme, Connecticut. He passed away at the home of his daughter in Cornwall, England, on March 8, 1977.

In April 1964, Henry Hull consented to a phone interview for the Deep River, Connecticut, newspaper *New Era*. Asked by reporter Henry E. Josten if he had caught a recent airing of *Were Wolf of London* on late-night TV, the actor replied:

> I saw snatches of the film shortly after we shot it almost 30 years ago, and I saw perhaps the first 10 or 15 minutes of it on television Saturday night. Then I went to bed. Sleep means more to me than any movie, even my own. It was a pretty good get-up, wasn't it? Jack [Pierce] had a special talent for turning men into freaks. I got out of the monster mold while the getting was good. The studio liked the job I had done ... and they wanted me for similar roles, but I declined because I didn't want to be limited to work in horror films.* I'm glad I did, too, because it opened the door for me to a large variety of roles in many other films, including the very successful Jesse James series with Tyrone Power and Henry Fonda. [O]nce acting is in your blood — and I was practically born in the theater — it's hard to ever give it up completely.... I love to work in my garden — I grow a pretty good head of lettuce, if I do say so myself. And I do practically all the maintenance needed on our property. We have 'bout 40 acres here and taking proper care of that much land can be a full-time job in itself.

Were his grandchildren frightened, the reporter asked, when they first saw *Were Wolf of London* on television? "Frightened?" he chuckled. "Good Lord, no. I understand they just laughed. Probably thought it was one of the funniest comedies they had ever seen."

Critics' Corner

[D]ue to the expert cast and director, should attract those who are not 100% creep & chill fans.... [W]ill be able to hold its own with the best chillers.— *Variety*, May 15, 1935

Rightfully takes its place on the horror film roll of honor.... Beautifully photographed, well acted by a proficient cast and strikingly mounted.— *The Hollywood Reporter*, 1935

[E]xpert direction.... [O]ne of the most exciting and harrowing and pleasure-giving thrillers of the season.... [T]his writer enjoyed every moment of it.— *The New York World-Telegram*, May 1935, William Boehnel

Designed solely to amaze and horrify, the film goes about its task with commendable thoroughness, sparing no grisly detail....— *The New York Times*, May 10, 1935, Frank S. Nugent

Rating: ★★½ The suspense of the last half of the picture when the werewolf is prowling ... is very well sustained. The dialogue is good and the director ... keeps his story moving constantly.— *The New York Daily News*, May 10, 1935, Kate Cameron

This is the goods!— *The Bristol Evening Post* (GB), 1935

Grisly and gruesome, gorgeous, and enjoyable!— *The Sunday Referee* (GB), 1935

Just the kind of thing to see.— *The Birmingham Post* (GB), 1935

The actual story is too preposterous to withstand serious analysis, and the London atmosphere is marred by many inexcusable incongruities, but such is the

**It may have slipped Hull's mind that, according to a trade report, Tod Browning had begun to groom him as a successor to Lon Chaney, Sr., in 1939. An MGM series of Browning-Hull horror-mysteries was planned, although only* Miracles for Sale, *in which he plays a magician, saw the light of day.*

showmanship employed in the picture's presentation that it is able to transcend its shortcomings and take its place amongst the best of the manufactured thrillers.... Henry Hull's interpretation of the unhappy Glendon is so unpleasant that there is no marked change in his personality when he is turned to beast.—*The Kinematograph Weekly* (GB), May 23, 1935

[W]ell-acted and calculated to satisfy fans who like this sort of hoke.... Through the good work of an excellent cast, this latest of the shiver melodramas is better made than it artistically is from a story standpoint.—*The Film Daily*, May 10, 1935

[A] nasty little fantasy.... Approved by the Legion of Decency, *The Werewolf of London* is a shade sillier than *The Bride of Frankenstein*, more alarming for small children than *Mark of the Vampire*.—*Time*, 1935

The Raven

Released July 22, 1935. 61 minutes. *Director:* Louis Friedlander [Lew Landers]. *Associate Producer:* David Diamond. *Screenplay:* David Boehm. *Suggested by the poem* "The Raven" *and the short story* "The Pit and the Pendulum" *by* Edgar Allan Poe. *Photography:* Charles Stumar. *Process Photography:* John P. Fulton. *Editor:* Albert Akst. *Editorial Supervision:* Maurice Pivar. *Dialogue Director:* Florence Enright. *Art Director:* Albert S. D'Agostino. *Assistant Directors:* Scott Beal & Victor Noerdlinger. *Musical Supervisor:* Gilbert Kurland. *Music:* Clifford Vaughan, Heinz Roemheld & Y. Franke Harling. *Dance Staged by* Theodore Kosloff. *Makeup:* Jack P. Pierce & Otto Lederer. *Hair Stylist:* Hazel Rogers. *Script Clerk:* Moree Herring. *Supervising Secretary:* Ed Haskett.

Boris Karloff (*Edmond Bateman*), Bela Lugosi (*Dr. Richard Vollin*), Lester Matthews (*Dr. Jerry Halden*), Irene Ware (*Jean Thatcher*), Samuel S. Hinds (*Judge Thatcher*), Spencer Charters (*Col. Bertram Grant*), Inez Courtney (*Mary Burns*), Ian Wolfe (*Geoffrey "Pinky" Burns*), Maidel Turner (*Harriet Grant*), Arthur Hoyt (*Mr. Chapman*), Jonathan Hale (*Dr. Cook*), Walter Miller (*Dr. Hemingway*), Cyril Thornton (*Servant*), Nina Golden (*The Dancer*), Raine Bennett (*Edgar Allan Poe*), Bud Osborne (*Policeman*), Al Ferguson (*Cook*), Madeline Talcott (*Nurse*), Helen Ware (*Bit at Theater*), Monte Montague (*Double for Boris Karloff*), George DeNormand (*Double for Bela Lugosi*). *Deleted from final print:* Joe Haworth (*Drug Clerk*), Anne Darling, Mary Wallace, June Gittelson (*Autograph Hunters*).

> [B]ecause of the stark realism of numerous elements in your story, you are running the risk of excessive horror.
> —*Joseph Breen in a letter to Universal, March 1935*

Edgar Allan Poe may have been a supremely gifted writer, literary critic and all-around scholar, but as a human being, he certainly wasn't the kind of guy you'd want to hang with on a Saturday night. In the course of his 40 years (and long after his death), he's been depicted as a dypsomaniac, manic depressive, sadomasochist, sex pervert, obsessive neurotic and egomaniac. Driven to the brink of madness by private demons, unable to maintain a decent standard of living, and ridiculed by an intolerant world that did not appreciate his genius, Poe expressed his agonies in a body of work which reflected his inner torment. At least one scholar debunks the Poe myth and insists the dark side of the writer's personality was exaggerated by certain biased parties (he even claimed that Poe loved cats!). While there may be some truth to this assertion, one cannot deny the fact that the man was preoccupied with the grotesque.

A scandalously unflattering caricature of Poe, embodying many of his time-honored obsessions (plus an additional element of sadistic cruelty), emerged in the character of Dr. Richard Vollin, brilliant surgeon and proprietor of a modern-day chamber of horrors, in *The Raven*, Universal's final entry in their '30s Poe trilogy. Hoping to duplicate the success of *The Black Cat*, the studio rigorously exploited the Poe name and the reunion of costars Karloff and Lugosi. Borrowing a reference or two from the poem of the same name and the short story "The Pit and the Pendulum," a bevy of writers developed a storyline which, in its final form, was charged with exciting possibilities. Regrettably, the screenplay that emerged from this fusion of ideas didn't quite measure up to its potential. Neither did the slapdash direction of Louis Friedlander (who later changed his name to Lew Landers), a specialist in serials and Westerns, who, unlike his predecessors Robert Florey and Edgar Ulmer, failed to invest the brooding melodrama with the dark mystique and poetry of *Murders in the Rue Morgue* and the 1934 version of *The Black Cat*.

Over the ensuing decades, few of the vintage Universal shock classics (with the exception of *Dracula*) have sustained as many brickbats as this ill-conceived film. Lugosi's passionate but unbridled performance, Karloff's miscasting in a secondary role beneath his abilities, and the

Unholy alliance: Killer thug Edmond Bateman (Boris Karloff) and mad surgeon Richard Vollin (Bela Lugosi) in *The Raven*.

generally undistinguished quality of the writing and direction, are just a few of the common gripes leveled against *The Raven*. Of significance, too, was the effect that *The Raven* had on the British Board of Film Censors. By indulging in excessive, Poe-inspired sadism (this was a code-regulated feature!), the shocker hastened the ban on horror pictures in the British Isles, helping to lead to a discontinuation of Hollywood production for two years. ("[J]ust how horrible has a film to be before it is rejected?" groused one London reviewer after *The Raven*—cut to 57 minutes—was passed for distribution by the British censors by the sheerest luck.)

Admittedly, it is difficult to sit through a screening of *The Raven* and not be negatively judgmental. But, in spite of its faults, true aficionados (particularly Lugosiphiles) derive great pleasure from the film's uninhibited madness. David Boehm's dialogue is, by and large, fruity and eminently quotable, the pulse-quickening pace seldom falters, and the high-camp climax (replete with serial-style devices like swinging pendulums and bone-crushing death chambers) recreates the spirit and abandon of old chapter plays. Best of all, there's LUGOSI (billed only by his surname [as is KARLOFF]) outshining his rival at every turn and pulling all the stops in one of his greatest performances. (In another era, wouldn't Dr. Vollin have made one fantastic James Bond villain?)

Although *The Raven* originally commenced with dancer Jean Thatcher (Irene Ware) signing autographs for fans as she leaves a theater after a performance (one of the autograph hunters is Anne Darling, the shepherdess of *Bride of Frankenstein*), the release print begins with the young woman's car racing down a rain-slick highway. Encountering a detour, Jean's car spins out of control and plunges into a gully. Critically injured, the dancer is rushed to the hospital where a team of doctors, including her lover Dr. Jerry Halden (Lester Matthews), can't rouse her from a coma. Jean's only hope for survival rests with

Dr. Richard Vollin (Bela Lugosi), a gifted plastic surgeon, now in retirement. Judge Thatcher (Samuel S. Hinds), Jean's father, visits Vollin's Hillview Heights home and desperately implores the callous surgeon to save his daughter's life. At first reluctant to take on a new case (he claims that he devotes all of his time to "research"—hmmm), Vollin finally agrees to operate on Jean. She makes a miraculous recovery.

Vollin's unique abilities as a surgeon are but one facet of the man's brilliance. He is also a scholar who has devoted his life to studying the works of Edgar Allan Poe. Vollin's devotion to Poe surpasses obsession: He has furnished his home with a collection of torture devices used during the Spanish Inquisition, and has had constructed for his own edification several of the deadly implements Poe described in his stories.

Vollin's concern for Jean develops into a compulsive passion which she refuses to acknowledge. Not about to take this rebuff lightly, he plots to vent his frustrations at the expense of Jean, her father and Halden.

The crazed surgeon finds a reluctant accomplice in the person of Edmond Bateman (Boris Karloff), a San Quentin escapee who implores Vollin for a change of appearance. Bateman has a persecution complex: "Maybe if a man looks ugly, he does ugly things," he reasons. "You are saying something profound," Vollin declares, obviously inspired. "A man with a face so *hideously ugly*..." On the pretext of helping him, the surgeon performs a medical procedure on the fugitive, which leaves his face horribly disfigured. Vollin promises to restore Bateman's features if he cooperates and obeys his commands.

Vollin extends a weekend invitation to Jean, Jerry, Judge Thatcher, and their friends Geoffrey and Mary Burns (Ian Wolfe and Inez Courtney) and Col. Bertram Grant (Spencer Charters) and his wife Harriet (Maidel Turner). After his guests have retired for the night, Vollin orders Bateman to abduct Judge Thatcher and secure him to a slab in his torture chamber. Above the magistrate's body, a swinging pendulum mounted with a razor-edged blade is set into motion. In precisely 15 minutes, the blade will cut a fatal swath across Thatcher's body.

Holding Jean and Jerry at gunpoint, Vollin orders them into a chamber with walls designed to crush its occupants to death. As the pendulum descends and the moving walls close in on the lovers, Vollin breaks into a fit of hysterical laughter. "Poe!" he cries. "*You are avenged!*" Bateman, who has developed a fondness for Jean, orders Vollin to release her from the death trap. When he refuses, Bateman frees the couple himself. Vollin promptly fires a bullet into his disobedient henchman. Summoning all his strength, the mortally wounded Bateman overpowers Vollin and seals him in the death chamber. Jerry and Geoffrey rush to Judge Thatcher's aid, ignoring Vollin's cries as the walls of death close in on him.

In transferring any of Poe's tales to the screen, scenarists are generally left to their own devices to come up with a workable plotline. No two film versions of the same story or poem are identical. In 1912, Eclair Studios produced a two-reeler in which scenes from the author's most famous tales are conjured up by Poe (Guy Oliver) in a dream. An inaccurate depiction of Poe's tragic life, based on George C. Hazleton's novel and play, was depicted in the 1915 Essanay six-reeler *The Raven* (described by *Variety* as "a most pretentious effort at something artistic"). As Poe, Henry B. Walthall is confronted by the ominous raven, revealed to be his tortured mind. Another early version, filmed at Poe's cottage in the Bronx, featured silent screen star Muriel Ostriche in a role that required her to be buried in a casket. Aside from the Universal film, the most well-known version of *The Raven* is the 1963 American International Roger Corman–Richard Matheson collaboration which had that aging triumvirate of terror, Vincent Price, Peter Lorre and Boris Karloff, outwitting (and out-mugging) one another against a medieval background of magic spells and potions.

The road to the final realization of Universal's *The Raven* was a long and bumpy one. Probably the earliest mention of the production came in June 1934, when *The Universal Weekly* announced that Bela Lugosi had just signed a three-picture deal which included a screen adaptation of *The Raven*. The time was ripe for another Poe fling. *The Black Cat*, in release for just one month, was earning huge box office grosses. At the height of their popularity, Karloff and Lugosi's names popped up in the trade papers regularly (usually in regard to roles in pictures that

In this rare staged shot, Bateman (Karloff) holds Col. Grant (Spencer Charters) in a death grip.

never materialized). Universal shuffled the pair into the cast of *Gift of Gab*, an all-star potpourri, produced in the summer of 1934. Billed as the Apache (Lugosi) and the Phantom (Karloff), the stars did walk-ons in a burlesque murder sketch staged by lead Edmund Lowe for a live radio broadcast.

Between August 1934 and March 1935, no less than seven writers toiled on the shooting script of *The Raven*. On August 31, novelist Guy Endore submitted a 19-page treatment based on the poem, with elements of Poe's "The Gold-Bug" included for good measure. A week later, Universal announced that it had signed rugged leading man Chester Morris for a key role. Morris didn't make it into *The Raven*; he and the Guy Endore treatment fell by the wayside.

In October, Michael Simmons and Clarence Marks collaborated on a fuller story treatment and wrote a screenplay based upon it. After careful consideration, it too was judged unsuitable. (John Lynch and Dore Schary had their fingers in the pie, too; whether or not their contributions were used in part remains to be seen.)

Finally, David Boehm was pressed into service to come up with a reasonable script. The former Warner Bros. dialogue writer (*Gold Diggers of 1933*, *The Life of Jimmy Dolan* [1933]) turned in not one but *three* complete screenplays. One was deemed satisfactory by the Front Office and the film was at last scheduled for production.

On the surface, Boehm's approved screenplay bears a passing resemblance to *The Black Cat*. Once again, an innocent couple is held captive in the home of a madman, who wields power over his less-than-enthusiastic accomplice. As was the case of Hjalmar Poelzig's macabre digs, Dr. Vollin's home is also the devil's playground, "a monument of death" in Vitus

Werdegast's words, rigged with all sorts of lethal traps. The leading men in both films are quickly neutered by the villain, leaving the accomplice to rise to the occasion and save the day at the final moment.

Once again, Bela Lugosi was slighted in matters of finance and billing by the shrewd Laemmles. As thanks for essaying the movie's dominant role, Lugosi was given second billing and paid $5,000. Karloff, on the other hand, was awarded first billing and paid $10,000 for his subordinate assignment. For the remainder of their professional association, Lugosi would be forced to accept second-banana status to Karloff, a situation that only increased his bitterness.

Louis Friedlander took charge of directing *The Raven*, which began shooting on March 20, 1935, on a 16-day schedule. A conference was called four days prior to the start of shooting, between studio executives, Friedlander and the Production Code Administration. They came to the agreement that no detail of the operation on Bateman would be shown to the audience. It was agreed by all that Bateman's appearance would not be "unhumanly repulsive," that the instruments of torture described in the script would be passed in review as if they were museum displays, that blood would not be shown except in a flash, that the pendulum blade would not touch human flesh, and that there would be no hanky-panky in the bedroom scenes. The PCA reviewed various shots of Bateman to determine their suitability. After studying the final shooting script (dated March 19), Breen wrote, "We ... deem it necessary to remind you that, because of the stark realism of numerous elements in your story, you are running the risk of excessive horror." Nevertheless, the production proceeded as planned, and wrapped on April 5, right on schedule, but $5,000-plus over-budget (the final cost was $115,209.91). The final cut was viewed on April 15, and, the following day, Certificate No. 790 was issued.

The Raven was a decided change of pace for Friedlander, whose last few assignments for Universal had all been serials (*The Red Rider* with Buck Jones, *Tailspin Tommy* and the science fiction actioner *The Vanishing Shadow* [all 1934 releases]). The New York native began his Hollywood career in 1922 as an assistant director. By the late '20s, he had worked himself up to the rank of full-fledged director. Before his death in December 1962, Friedlander directed some 150 films. He changed his name to Lew Landers after joining up with RKO in the late '30s. Landers was destined to cross paths with his *Raven* stars again the following decade, directing Karloff (and Peter Lorre) in Columbia's wacky screwball horror comedy *The Boogie Man Will Get You* (1942) and Lugosi in the same studio's *The Return of the Vampire* (1943).

Universal's resident art director Albert S. D'Agostino followed the example of Edgar Ulmer on *The Black Cat* by adopting the axiom "less is more" in designing Vollin's torture chamber. A standing set from *Bride of Frankenstein* (the prison cell where the Monster is briefly incarcerated) serves as the entranceway leading into the stone-walled dungeon. Illuminated by candlelight, the rooms are furnished with a modest-sized collection of ancient and *outré* devices, the *piece de resistance* being a life-size replica of Poe's deadly pendulum. Taking Universal's publicity department at its word (a risky business at best), several weeks before *The Raven* began filming, D'Agostino and his crew of technicians painstakingly developed this impressive prop. (Friedlander had originally planned on shooting the sequence with the aid of trick lighting or movable prams.) A real stone room was constructed and a steel table placed in the center of it. A pendulum mounted with a 50-pound knife was created and erected above the slab. Early attempts to operate the pendulum by means of an electrical switchboard proved unsuccessful: The current caused the crescent to descend in uneven arcs. To achieve a steady swing, a huge clock with wooden innerworks was built above the set and the pendulum attached. This set-up did the trick.

Karloff himself cast doubt about a story released by Universal's publicity mavens at the time of *The Raven*'s release. While making the rounds of theaters, radio and television shows to promote AIP's *The Raven* in early 1963, Karloff and Peter Lorre did a TV guest shot on *The Hy Gardner Show*. Having done his homework, Gardner furnished Karloff with a newspaper clipping dated July 7, 1935, which reported a curious incident that allegedly happened during the filming of the Universal film. According to this article, Karloff was required to wear a 50-

Opening day ad for the Manhattan debut of *The Raven* (*New York Daily News*, July 4, 1935). Who needed a fireworks display when you could see Bela Lugosi on stage?

pound bullet-proof vest for the shooting of the climax. For some strange reason, blanks were out of the question for the scene in which Lugosi fires a fatal shot into Karloff. The plot required that the bullet go straight through his body. A studio firearms expert, using an infield rifle, stationed himself 150 feet away from the soundstage and aimed the real bullet between Karloff's left arm and his left side. Instead of hitting the designated target, the bullet grazed the actor's left side, cut through his coat and picked a chip out of the stone wall background.

An amused Karloff couldn't recall the incident. "If it happened," he laughed, "I'm sure I would have died of fright. With my experience with the chaps at the studio, they would never make mistakes and are very careful."

One would think that after spending seven months picking the brains of a half-dozen writers, Universal would have come up with a script far superior to David Boehm's. Yet it is the film's blatant extravagances that make it so much fun to watch. Most of the characters are etched in such ludicrously broad strokes, it's hard to believe they were meant to be taken seriously. While Vollin's fixation with Poe, his fascination with pain and torture, and his "longing for the lost Lenore" (personified by Jean Thatcher) account for his bizarre behavior throughout, Boehm's screenplay would have had a closer resemblance to reality had he toned down the doctor's ravings. An actor with a subtler approach to acting than Lugosi (Conrad Veidt perhaps) might also have moderated these excesses with an understated performance, but not our Bela. He forges full speed ahead, milking every line for all its worth. (We are grateful to have been spared the spectacle of Lugosi's sing-song delivery of the line, "Nevermore... Nevermore... The lost Lenore! The lost Lenore!" at the height of orgiastic frenzy.) Unlike Edgar Ulmer, Landers was incapable (or unwilling) to rein the actor in. ("You had to cut away from Lugosi continuously, to cut him down," Ulmer revealed in his 1970 landmark interview with Peter Bogdanovich.) Yet, for these very reasons, Dr. Richard Vollin remains one of Lugosi's most memorable performances, taking its place beside Count Dracula, the broken-necked Ygor and *White Zombie*'s Murder.

As for Karloff, his performance as prison escapee Edmond Bateman is ample proof that the actor was at a loss at portraying American hoodlums. ("I want you should—*fix my face*" is a line more suited to Jimmy Cagney or Humphrey Bogart.) Aside from this lapse in credibility, the actor's performance is nuanced, even heartfelt, though it isn't surprising that it should be neglected in view of Karloff's more celebrated cinematic accomplishments during this period. Anticipating Bateman's redemption at the film's climax, David Boehm furnished the sympathetic character with an alibi of sorts when it is revealed that he turned a blowtorch on the face of a guard during a bank robbery. "Sometimes you can't help things like that," he mutters apologetically.

The transformation of Karloff from bewhiskered thug to pitiful, mutilated slave is the picture's highlight. Using a nonsurgical procedure (twisting the nerve endings in the back of Bateman's neck), Vollin creates a mask of horror. "Do I look—*different?*" the fugitive asks in anticipation as Charles Stumar's camera savors the results of Vollin's gruesome handiwork. "*Y-e-s-s,*" Vollin sardonically replies. Boehm's text aptly describes the gory makeup design:

> Bateman turns so that his face is toward us. His face is a horror. Certain muscles have been paralyzed through cutting of the nerve ends. Certain others have been permitted to remain—giving life to the part of the face they control, so that here is a face—a crazy-quilt of death and life. One part of his face remains fixed in a horrible dead grimace, while the other remains alive—side by side with the corpse. One eye remains open, unblinking—staring straight ahead.

To create this ghoulish effect, Jack Pierce laid applications of cotton soaked in collodion over the right side of Karloff's face, then covered the actor's right eye with a patently false one made of beeswax and cellophane. (Leslie Banks suffered from this condition in real life.)

The Raven earns high marks in the cinematography and music departments. Charles Stumar (who died in the crash of his private plane soon after the film's completion) captured some startling closeups of his stars; a striking profile shot of Lugosi, as well as several unnerving studies of Karloff in full makeup, are particularly effective. Music supervisor Gilbert Kurland furnished the score with a liberal number of Heinz Roemheld's wonderful classic transcriptions from *The Black Cat* (including Liszt's *Hungarian Rhapsodies*) which heighten the tension of the climax and complement the film's somber atmosphere. Ballet master Theodore Kosloff conceived a surreal interpretive dance evoking the alienation of Poe. Dancer Nina Golden doubles for Irene Ware in this brief but mood-provoking set piece. (Once again, the regal stage set from *The Phantom of the Opera* is utilized to good advantage.)

It seems hardly likely that a man plotting mass murder would stick his neck out and invite over a house full of witnesses to get in his way, but that's exactly what Vollin does in *The Raven*. Of course, the real reason these partygoers are there is to provide some comic relief to lighten the gloom. It doesn't work. Strait-laced Ian Wolfe, his unlikely wife Inez Courtney (her character is described in the script as "a Gracie Allenish or Una Merkelish sort"), hefty Maidel Turner and irritatingly intrusive Spencer Charters proffer the limpest humor since the three would-be linguists in *Murders in the Rue Morgue*.

Lester Matthews, who provided Valerie Hobson with an extramarital love interest and proved thoroughly ingratiating in *WereWolf of London*, isn't quite as believable in *The Raven* (he resorts to unintentionally comic facial expressions when the going gets tough). In one amusing moment, Matthews pooh-poohs future father-in-law Samuel S. Hinds' apprehensions about spending the night under the same roof with self-professed sadist Lugosi ("There's nothing to be afraid of"), then starts at the sound of a door-knock.

A less horrific makeup devised by Jack Pierce for Karloff's character.

Irene Ware is less ethereal and more down-to-earth than the average '30s lady-in-distress and performs the role of Jean Thatcher with refreshing unaffectedness. The Pelham Bay, New York, native became a showgirl in Earl Carroll's "Sketch Book" after she had won the title of Miss America in the International Beauty Contest held in 1929 in Galveston, Texas. She replaced Lillian Roth in Carroll's ninth edition of his "Vanities" and then made a talking picture test before the show closed. Arriving in Hollywood, Ware signed a two-year contract with Fox Films: It was there she first made the acquaintance of Bela Lugosi, playing Princess Nadji to his Roxor in 1932's *Chandu the Magician*. In 1934, the young actress obtained her release from Fox and signed a contract with Universal. Her first assignment was to play the goddess Diana in *Night Life of the Gods*. Ware's motion picture career was regrettably brief. Following featured parts in such films as *Rendezvous at Midnight* (1935), *Outside the 3-Mile Limit* (1940) and a handful of British productions, she dropped out of pictures.

Giving the least affected performance in *The Raven* is Samuel S. Hinds, soon to become a pleasantly familiar fixture in '30s and '40s horror movies. Born to a well-to-do New York family (his father was president of the United States Playing Card Company), Samuel Southey Hinds enjoyed the fruits of the privileged class for the first 58 years of his life. The stock market crash of 1929 wiped out the fortune Hinds amassed as a top Los Angeles corporation lawyer. Undaunted, the businessman turned a lifelong interest in acting into a new career and enrolled at the Pasadena Community Playhouse (which he helped found in 1916) for dramatic training. Hinds' movie break came when a casting director offered him a $20-a-day job as a bit player in the ironically titled Paramount comedy *If I Had a Million* (1932). From that point on, the actor was seldom without a movie assignment and kept active until his death at age 73 in 1948.

Not surprisingly, *The Raven* caused a furor when it was released. It was banned outright in British Columbia,

China, the Netherlands, and Ontario, Canada. *The London Times* (August 4, 1935) issued a scathing report on Hollywood's preoccupation with horror films, and *The Raven* in particular.

> Every picture should have a purpose, preferably a high one. Any concentration upon Murder as Murder can only kill the films themselves. But it is difficult to speculate as to what intention, other than the stimulation of a low morbid interest, can be behind such a production as *The Raven*.... Here is a film of "horror" for "horror's" sake.... It devises shelter under the statement that it has been inspired by the genius of Edgar Allan Poe. Nonsense. Neither story nor treatment give indication of any imaginative control. To suggest that there is the slightest affinity between the creation of his powerful and extraordinary mind and this sordid and bungling work is sheer charlatanism.

Nineteen days later, the Associated Press reported that *The Raven* would be the last horror movie passed by the British Board of Censors.

The New York press roasted the film, too. *New York Times* movie critic Frank S. Nugent (on July 5, 1935) labeled it "the season's worst horror film," and griped, "[I]f *The Raven* is the best that Universal can do with one of the greatest horror story writers of all time, then it had better toss away the other two books in its library and stick to the pulpies for plot material." Echoing Nugent's distaste, Thornton Delehanty of *The New York Evening Post* wrote that "[*The Raven*] has no more bearing on the original source than a stuffed bird has to an elephant." (Independence Day celebrants who attended the premiere performances of the motion picture at Broadway's posh Roxy Theater were treated to a personal appearance by Bela Lugosi himself.) The hostile critical reaction to *The Raven* did not alter Universal's plans to co-star Karloff and Lugosi in yet another horror melodrama (with science-fiction overtones), the decidedly tamer *The Invisible Ray*.

Encouraged by a renewed interest in horror films spurred by their reissues of *Dracula* and *Frankenstein* in 1938, Universal planned a remake of *The Raven*, again pairing Karloff and Lugosi but with a "fresh angle" for the story. (Today, it sounds far-fetched that a studio would remake a movie just three years later but it was common practice in the'30s; Universal made *The Cat and the Canary* three times between 1927 and 1930, counting the Spanish-language version, and briefly considered yet a *fourth* go-round in the late '30s.) In 1951, a "disguised" version of *The Raven* reached the screen, but now ascribed to Robert Louis Stevenson! In Universal-International's *The Strange Door*, Charles Laughton starred as an English nobleman driven mad after being spurned in love; he cooks up an elaborate plot to take revenge on his beloved's daughter (Sally Forrest), her boyfriend (Richard Stapley) and her father (Paul Cavanagh). The three climactically wind up in Laughton's dungeon, sealed in a cell where the walls are coming together, as Laughton indulges in wild gloating not too far removed from Lugosi's *Raven* antics. But Forrest has shown kindness to Laughton's henchman Voltan (Karloff in an identical role), so at the decisive moment he frees the lovers and at the cost of his own life turns on Laughton, who ends up being crushed himself.

Not content with one screen version of "The Raven" to his credit, producer David Diamond launched plans to make a second movie adaptation of the poem, starring Vincent Price, in the fall of 1953. Diamond's ambition was to shoot the film in England in widescreen, Technicolor and 3-D, which was at the height of popularity at this time. Once again, David Boehm was commissioned to pen the screenplay, creating an entirely different storyline, set in England in 1845. But, like so many proposed film projects, 1953's *The Raven* never made it past the planning stage.

Quoth the Raven, "*Nevermore*" ... that is, until his 1963 encounter with Roger Corman.

Critics' Corner

A good horror flicker.... Director Louis Friedlander ... has kept the pace at a nice pitch, stripping it down to its fundamentals and letting the shock troupers ... do their worst to sock over the big punches.—*Variety*, July 10, 1935, Abel.

[S]atisfactorily fiendish fun, with something doing every instant.—*The New York American*, 1935, Regina Crewe

[S]hould have no difficulty in gaining the distinction of being the season's worst horror film. Not even the presence of [Karloff and Lugosi] can make the picture anything but a fatal mistake from beginning to end.—*The New York Times*, July 5, 1935, Frank S. Nugent

Followers of horror melodrama will get a full evening's entertainment.... [I]t has some hair-raising situations.—*Harrison's Reports,* June 15, 1935

Rating: Fair. The horrors have been piled on to such an extent that they automatically nullify each other and take on a comic hue.—*The New York Evening Post,* July 1935, Thornton Delehanty

A grim idea that is not without interest, it is here a trifle too melodramatic. Lurid entertainment for non-squeamish patrons.—*Today's Cinema* (GB), July 18, 1935

For those who thrill to horror there are thrills enough; but one audience reacted, at times, as horror was piled upon horror, with the laughter of emotional self-defense.—*Sight and Sound* (GB), August 1935

Macabre melodrama; an attempt to incorporate many of the eerie thrills to be found in Edgar Allan Poe's stories into one big thriller.... [J]ust another manufactured hair raiser with the established stooges of crime entertainment, Lugosi and Karloff, putting over the same old act.—*The Kinematograph Weekly* (GB), July 25, 1935

Author Edgar Allan Poe ... was fond of graves but he would turn in his own if he could see this Universal "masterpiece."—*The Daily Express* (GB), August 4, 1935

The Great Impersonation

Released December 9, 1935. 64 minutes. An Edmund Grainger Production. *Executive Producer:* Fred S. Meyer. *Director:* Alan Crosland. *Screenplay:* Frank Wead & Eve Greene. *Based on the novel by* E. Phillips Oppenheim. *Cinematography:* Milton Krasner. *Art Director:* Charles D. Hall. *Special Cinematography:* John P. Fulton. *Music:* Franz Waxman. *Editor:* Philip Cahn. *Supervising Editor:* Maurice Pivar. *Sound Supervisor:* Gilbert Kurland. *Sound Engineer:* Charles Carroll. *Gowns:* Brymer & Vera West. *Assistant Directors:* William Reiter & Joe Torillo. *Second Cameraman:* King Gray. *Assistant Camera:* Ross Hoffman. *Script Clerk:* Eleanor Hall. *Production Secretary:* Camille Collins.

Edmund Lowe (*Sir Everard Dominey/Baron Leopold von Ragastein*), Valerie Hobson (*Lady Eleanor Dominey*), Wera Engels (*Princess Stephanie Eiderstrom*), Murray Kinnell (*Seaman*), Henry Mollison (*Eddie Pelham*), Esther Dale (*Mrs. Unthank*), Brandon Hurst (*Middleton*), Ivan Simpson (*Dr. Harrison*), Spring Byington (*Duchess Caroline*), Lumsden Hare (*Duke Henry*), Charles Waldron (*Sir Ivan Brunn*), Leonard Mudie (*Mangan*), Claude King (*Sir Gerald Hume*), Frank Reicher (*Dr. Trenk*), Harry Allen (*Parkins*), Nan Grey (*Middleton's Daughter, the Maid*), Willy Castello (*Duval*), Priscilla Lawson (*Maid*), Pat O'Hara (*Chauffeur*), Virginia Hammond (*Lady Hume*), Thomas R. Mills (*Bartender*), Tom Ricketts, Frank Terry, Robert Bolder (*Villagers*), Lowden Adams (*Waiter*), Violet Seaton (*Nurse*), Dwight Frye (*Roger Unthank*), David Dunbar, Frank Benson (*English Farmers*), John Powers (*English Policeman*), Leonid Snegoff (*Wolff*), Harry Worth (*Hugo*), Adolph Milar (*German Bit*), Larry Steers (*Army Officer*), Douglas Wood (*Lord Allison*).

Into the open there came a dark shape...
It moved at first upon all fours, then
on two legs, then on all fours again.
—*A description of the animalistic Roger Unthank in E. Phillips Oppenheim's novel* The Great Impersonation

---

It's often difficult, looking back over more than 70 years, to figure out what was going on inside Universal's corporate head at times. Horror films were at the height of their popularity in the early to mid–'30s and Universal, which held the rights to the characters of Dracula, Frankenstein's Monster, the Invisible Man and various other bogeymen, was top dog in the horror field. So it's a little surprising to realize that the studio only made one horror film per year in 1933 and in 1934 (*The Invisible Man* and *The Black Cat,* respectively). By 1935, things were starting to pick up again (*Bride of Frankenstein, WereWolf of London* and *The Raven* all released within a three-month period), but one has to wonder whether the studio's confidence in the future of horror films had somehow been shaken.

What makes this minor riddle more curious is the fact that many Universal films of this period were promoted as full-fledged horror thrillers when they were actually mysteries or melodramas with slight, even negligible horror embellishments. If Universal feared that horror was "out," what was the good of misleading people into believing that ordinary pictures like *Secret of the Blue Room* and *The Man Who Reclaimed His Head* were red-blooded chillers? The hapless horror fan who strutted into a screening of a dreary programmer like *Secret of the Chateau* could only have exited the theater in something of a bad humor, with grave reservations about ever again taking a "horror movie" poster at its printed word.

The Great Impersonation has more going for it than most of the phony Universal horror films of this period. At heart it's a spy story set in the pre–World War I (1914) era, but incongruously slipped into the film is a horror subplot lifted right out of Arthur Conan Doyle's *The Hound of*

the Baskervilles. This melding of genres is as bizarre and distracting as it sounds; the result is a fanciful and offbeat little melodrama, oddly satisfying although it cannot possibly be taken seriously.

Everard Dominey (Edmund Lowe) staggers alone, unarmed and feverish through the East Africa jungle, stalked by stock footage clips of a lion. He is rescued and brought to a nearby encampment which, by the sheerest of coincidences, is run by Dominey's Oxford schoolmate Leopold von Ragastein, Dominey's exact twin (also played by Lowe). Both men are in Africa because of sordid events in their past lives: Von Ragastein, an Austrian, killed a man in a duel over the affections of a princess, while Dominey, now a drunkard, is suspected of having killed a onetime rival for his wife's love. Von Ragastein devises a plan to send Dominey on a safari from which he shall not come back, then to take his place and return to England. Dominey's boss, unscrupulous munitions baron Sir Ivan Brunn (Charles Waldron), endorses this scheme, as it will allow for the use of Dominey Hall as their English headquarters. War clouds are forming over Europe, and Sir Ivan needs an agent who can move in official circles.

The great impersonation seems a great success: In England, Dominey's solicitor (Leonard Mudie) and even his own cousin (Spring Byington) accept the newly arrived adventurer as the baronet. In yet another impossible coincidence, "Dominey" happens to bump into Princess Stephanie (Wera Engels), the femme fatale who caused the duel that ruined him. To prevent her from exposing "Dominey" as von Ragastein, Seaman (Murray Kinnell), another of Sir Ivan's operatives, lets the princess in on their plans.

"Dominey" returns home to ancestral Dominey Hall, now a rundown pile occupied only by Dominey's wife Eleanor (Valerie Hobson) and servants. His home life is not going to be a happy one: Eleanor has been driven batty by the suspected-murder mess, and Mrs. Unthank (Esther Dale), a servant and the mother of Roger Unthank (the man "Dominey" supposedly killed), spitefully warns him that the ghost of her son haunts nearby Black Bog. The screams of Roger's "ghost" fill the air that night as, in a scene reminiscent of *The Cat and the Canary* (1927), Eleanor's arm appears through a secret opening above the head of "Dominey"'s bed, knife in hand. "Dominey" awakens and disarms her in the nick of time — then, imprudently, goes right back to sleep!

Princess Stephanie shows up at Dominey Hall to do her part spy-wise but she's in heat, chases after "Dominey" and is more hindrance than help. Between secret conclaves and the construction of a radio transmitting room in an unused tower, "Dominey" finds time to gently woo his woozy wife; eventually he is able to get her out from under the influence of the hateful Mrs. Unthank and restore her to some degree of normalcy. To settle the question of the "ghost," "Dominey" orders the Black Bog set ablaze. As the flames spread, Roger, very much alive, bolts screaming from the bog and makes a beeline for Dominey Hall. The wild man is throttling Eleanor when Mrs. Unthank appears, shooting and killing her own son rather than to see him sent to a madhouse.

Suspicious when "Dominey" continues to resist her romantic advances, Stephanie realizes that "Dominey" might indeed *be* Dominey after all. To identify him one way or the other, she sends for von Ragastein's old associate Dr. Trenk (Frank Reicher), who arrives at the Hall. Dominey's Dominey all right; at the East African encampment, he had overheard von Ragastein discussing his plan, killed him, and has been impersonating von Ragastein-impersonating-*him* ever since. Seaman bolts toward the radio room to transmit the go-ahead order to Sir Ivan's English-based saboteurs, but despite a bullet in the shoulder Dominey remains on Seaman's heels in a chase up to the tower and puts the radio out of commission at the last instant. The authorities round up the spies and saboteurs, Sir Ivan is exposed, Dominey is hailed as a hero and England is safe to plunge ahead into the Great War.

The Great Impersonation has the look of a 1935 film but the feel of an older picture: The plot is hoary stuff and the broad acting is reminiscent of the thesping in the dawning days of talkies. For fans partial to this kind of creaky entertainment, this "makes" the picture; for the uninitiated, this spoils it. The horror scenes, intrusive as they are, are handled with old-fashioned flair, and the climactic revelation that "Dominey" really *is* Dominey comes as a genuinely surprising twist.

Edmund Lowe does a credible job in the central role(s). Early in the proceedings, both characters manage to become irritating: Dominey is an unsympathetic drunk and von Ragastein, with his monocle, phony accent and immaculate white suit in the heart of the jungle, is the kind of character found only in the movies. But as the plot begins to unfold and the locale shifts to England, Lowe becomes the smooth charmer he played to perfection in any number of films. He's most fondly remembered today for his portrayal of boisterous Sgt. Quirt in the celebrated silent *What Price Glory?* (1926), but Lowe was basically from the Waxed Mustache school of acting, and was at his best in roles that called for a cool, impeccable suaveness. Lowe was paid $16,800 for his seven weeks' work in *The Great Impersonation*, a whopping sum (for Universal) which doesn't seem commensurate with his box office worth. He had previously played a quite similar dual role in the far-out *Scotland Yard* (1930), an early Fox talkie with Lowe as a froggy-voiced crook who takes the place of a ne'er-do-well English nobleman. Among the usual complications: Once the crook begins his "great impersonation," he finds out that the aristo has got wife trouble (Joan Bennett).

Over the years it's become fashionable among fantasy film fans to take swipes at Lowe and his playing of the title role in *Chandu the Magician* opposite Bela Lugosi in 1932. Critics carp that Lowe was unsuited for the Chandu role and that he gives a hopelessly bland performance; Lugosi fans always come down on him especially hard and rhapsodize over what wonders their boy would have worked in that part. (Two years later, Lugosi did get a shot at the role in a fatiguing 12-chapter endurance test of a serial called *The Return of Chandu*. He gives the same blah performance Lowe gave — in fact, not as good — with the professional apologists among the Lugosi fans now explaining that the actor was being faithful to the character of the *radio* Chandu.) Lowe made his last picture, *Heller in Pink Tights*, in 1960 and died in 1971.

Valerie Hobson struggles with the tricky, "only-in-the-movies" character of the unbalanced Lady Dominey. In her "mad" scenes she gives a breathy, faraway performance that doesn't seem likely to have ever gotten much reaction other than laughs; she often seems on the verge of lapsing into her "Angel of Death" soliloquy from *Bride of Frankenstein*. (At one point, Lowe carries her to the very bed in which she played that scene in *Bride*!) Although Lady Dominey's mental instability is "cured" by Dominey's romantic solicitude, she remains a weak-headed wisp, always guided by the last voice she hears. When Hobson made the movie, she was 18 years old playing a girl whose husband has been away for many years.

Wera Engels fares no better as the hot-to-trot Princess Stephanie. Despite her promise to distance herself from "Dominey" and to cooperate in Sir Ivan's plan, she's constantly hounding the hapless baronet and creating scenes; at one point she stupidly yells "Leopold!" at the poor man! Stephanie becomes such an exasperating presence that you find yourself sympathizing with the spies and saboteurs she's harassing, and become impatient for one of the other characters to knock her off or at least hose her down.

Most of the rest of the leading players have insignificant roles, among them Spring Byington as Lowe's cousin, the same type of flibbertigibbet she played in *WereWolf of London*. Nan Grey, the doomed waif Lili of *Dracula's Daughter*, and Priscilla Lawson, *Flash Gordon*'s Princess Aura, here plays maids, the former briefly menaced by the mad Dwight Frye. No character in this movie is more insignificant than Henry Mollison's. Mollison's Eddie Pelham hangs around the edges of scenes with his arm in a sling; the viewer is never finds out exactly who he is, why he's around, why the character has a broken arm or why Mollison himself is fifth-billed over players with bigger and better parts. Mollison simply appears to have crashed the movie.

While *The Great Impersonation* is set in 1914, the moviemakers kept forgetting that it did not have a contemporary setting. Characters wear then-modern clothes and drive around in nearly new cars like a 1929 Ford and a 1931 Cadillac; one character sports a tobacco pouch with a zipper. In one of the picture's most curious juxtapositions, Edmund Lowe uses candles to find his way to his bedroom, but after Valerie Hobson's secret-panel attempt on his life he climbs out of bed and turns on an electric light.

The picture also has more than its share of clunker lines, plot holes and unintended funny moments. Early on, Dr. Trenk expresses disbe-

Edmund Lowe protects Valerie Hobson from lurking terrors in *The Great Impersonation* (courtesy Photofest).

lief that van Ragastein and Dominey should be exact twins who bump into each other first at Oxford and later in the middle of the African jungle; van Ragastein responds with a phlegmatic, "Lawngk odds, eh, Tr-r-renk?" Moments later, Dominey greets the regal Baron with the exuberant, "Leopold van Ragastein—'Rags'!" During a meeting with von Ragastein and Seaman, a straight-faced Sir Ivan makes the profound comment, "No one likes tragedy." The spies always seem quite pleased with the progress they've made at Dominey Hall, but all they really accomplish there is the construction of a radio room that could have been built *any*where; "Dominey" spends all his time cozying up with his nutty wife, ordering repairs to the house and going off with friends on carriage jaunts.

The best moment for Universal buffs comes at Dominey Hall, as Middleton the butler (sepulchral Brandon Hurst) escorts "Dominey" and lawyer Mangan (the equally sepulchral Leonard Mudie) to their bedrooms. "Dominey" asks where Mangan will be sleeping and Middleton solemnly responds, "The *Blue* Room, sir"—a pronouncement that causes an apprehensive over-the-shoulder reaction in the suddenly anxious solicitor!

Horror fans who gravitate to *The Great Impersonation* will find the spooky "ghost" subplot the highlight of the movie. There's never any doubt in the minds of the audience that the Roger Unthank ghost story will eventually be debunked; *Great Impersonation* is a spy story rooted in reality, and despite this bizarre detour the film basically has both feet on the ground. The entire Unthank angle has been lifted shamelessly from a subplot in the Sherlock Holmes novel *The Hound of the Baskervilles*, in which a butler and his wife surreptitiously help an escaped convict (the wife's brother) out on the moors. *Great Impersonation* bounces back and forth between its two stories and never is there any hint of one in the other: No one talks about the Unthank business any of the spy scenes, no one mentions the espionage angle during the "spooky" scenes.

The mad Roger is played by a hairy, bearded Dwight Frye, seen here in his most undignified movie role. Uncredited and unrecognizable, he scuttles across the Dominey Hall courtyard a couple of times for the benefit of Edmund Lowe, who watches from various windows; does a lot of off-camera caterwauling; and finally flees from the fiery bog and into the house, where he's shot and does a Renfield-style stair-fall into the midst of the pursuing mob of villagers. The onetime Broadway actor is seen only in long shots, and for years even diehard Universal Horrors fans didn't know it was him under all that hair and grime. *The Great Impersonation* represented one day's work for Frye, who was paid $100.

Great Impersonation gives audiences a look at sets and props from earlier Universal horror films, best of all some great, eye-opening shots of (and new angles on) *Bride of Frankenstein*'s winding watchtower staircase. Dominey's dining room is also from *Bride*; Sir Ivan's office incorporates Dr. Seward's fireplace from *Dracula*. Approximately $2,225 of the film's budget went for special effects, including trick double exposures for shots featuring both von Ragastein and Dominey; the construction and photographing of the Black Bog miniature; and matte shots of Black Bog and the exterior of Dominey Hall. Director Alan Crosland replaced the originally signed Lloyd Corrigan; the screenplay was co-written by Lt. Comdr. Frank "Spig" Wead, the famed naval hero turned screenwriter whose more typical credits include *Airmail* (1932), *West Point of the Air, Ceiling Zero* (1935), *Dive Bomber* (1941) and *They Were Expendable* (1945). Wead's life story formed the basis for a self-indulgent John Ford burlesque, *The Wings of Eagles*, 1957, with John Wayne as Wead; Edmund Lowe had a supporting role.

The film was based upon a novel by E(dward) Phillips Oppenheim, internationally popular writer of more than 150 novels, volumes of short stories and plays. Most of Oppenheim's works dealt with espionage and intrigue, and several of his tales reached the screen during the silent and early sound period. *The Great Impersonation*, published in 1920, does feature the "horror subplot" of the ghost of the Black Bog (the Black *Wood* in the novel), and we learn a good bit more about Roger Unthank in its pages. The movie *Great Impersonation* gives the impression that Dominey and Roger were romantic rivals who boldly went *mano a mano*; this is *not* the kind of backstory we expect to hear about any character played by Dwight Frye! Rest easy: In the book, Roger was a "half a madman" even in his pre–Bog days, infatuated with the future Lady Dominey, greatly annoying her with his unwanted attentions, and lunging out of the darkness in a cowardly attack on Dominey; *now* we're in Dwight Frye territory! In the movie, a fire set on an outer edge of the bog unaccountably forces Roger out into the open; in the book, more realistically, Dominey hires a gang of men to spend several weeks cutting and burning their way through the rotted woodland "until not a tree or a bush remains upright" as the means of flushing him out. In the closing pages of the book, Dominey spends a night laying in wait for Roger in a stretch of park between his house and the Black Wood; "Into the open there came a dark shape, the irregularity of its movements swiftly explained. It moved at first upon all fours, then on two legs, then on all fours again." Dominey lets Roger have his fun one last time (Roger does his screaming bit under Lady Dominey's window) and then roughly seizes him, trussing him up and ordering one of his footmen to "take this creature" to a hospital. "If Lady Dominey recovers, you and your son are forgiven," Dominey tells a sobbing Mrs. Unthank. "If she never recovers, I wish you both the blackest corner of hell."

Oppenheimer's book was first made into a movie a year after its publication, with James Kirkwood as Dominey/von Ragastein and future makeup man Cecil Holland as Roger Unthank. (In *Variety*'s write-up of the 1921 *Great Impersonation*, reviewer Fred questioned whether audiences would still buy such an old-hat spy plot!) Universal picked up the rights to the spy story and filmed it twice, first in 1935 and then again in 1942, when (naturally) the action was updated to the World War II era. In the '42 rendition, Ralph Bellamy plays Edmund Lowe's old dual role, Evelyn Ankers plays Valerie Hobson's, Henry Daniell Murray Kinnell's, and Ludwig Stossel Frank Reicher's. The real-life arrest of Rudolph Hess is worked into the plot of the 1942 *Impersonation* (in the movie, he's collared en route to the Dominey estate!) but the "ghost" business was omitted.* The story also came to TV twice: On *Dow Hour of Great Mysteries* (1960), Eva Gabor played the man-hungry Princess Stephanie—*almost*-perfect casting. On *Climax!* (1955), Michael Rennie played Dominey, Maureen O'Sullivan played Lady Dominey and *Zsa Zsa* Gabor was Princess Stephanie. *Perfect* casting!

The Great Impersonation is a well-mounted production with an attractive cast, two stories for the price of one and a just-right 64-minute running time. It's a hard-to-resist B movie ... unless, of course, you saw it for the first time on *Shock Theater* at age ten, when you didn't know what the heck munitions were, who Archduke Ferdinand was, and the only Kaiser *you* ever heard of, had poppy seeds on it!

Critics' Corner

Rating: Fair. In *The Great Impersonation* Mr. Lowe, quite properly, pretends he is some one else, and unless you are good at solving mystery stories it is possible he will fool you even as he did us. He plays a dual role ... and we couldn't for the life of us tell which was which.—*The New York Post*, December 14, 1935, Thornton Delehanty

Rating: ★★ [A]n intriguing plot that might have been made into an absorbing film story if the adapters ... and the director hadn't tried to make a penny dreadful shocker of it.... Edmund Lowe ... gives a smoothly competent performance.... [It's] attractively mounted but the story has been too loosely constructed to make it anything but a weak vehicle.—*The New York Daily News*, December 14, 1935, Kate Cameron

I am spared the humiliation of confessing my vast ignorance about the finer nuances of one of the plottiest of all the Oppenheim stories.—*The New York Times*, December 14, 1935, Andre Sennwald

This is an inadequate and unworkmanlike picture.... In trying to modernize [the plot], they only succeeded in emphasizing the creakiness of the outworn material. Edmund Lowe strives heroically with the impossible dual characterization handed him and the wonder is that he can make it seem even very remotely plausible.—*The Film Daily*, December 14, 1935

1936

The Invisible Ray

Released January 20, 1936. 79 minutes. *An Edmund Grainger Production. Presenter:* Carl Laemmle. *Executive Producer:* Fred S. Meyer. *Producer:* Edmund Grainger. *Director:* Lambert Hillyer. *Screenplay:* John Colton. *Original Story:* Howard Higgin & Douglas Hodges. *Photography:* George Robinson. *Art Director:* Albert S. D'Agostino. *Music:* Franz Waxman. *Special Cinematographer:* John P. Fulton. *Effects:* Raymond Lindsay. *Editor:* Bernard Burton. *Editorial Supervisor:* Maurice Pivar. *Gowns:* Brymer. *Sound Supervisor:* Gilbert Kurland. *Production Assistant:* Alfred Stern. *Makeup:* Otto Lederer. *Assistant Directors:* Sergei Petschnikoff & Fred Frank. *Sound Recorders:* Charles Carroll & William Hitchcock. *Script Clerk:* Myrtle Gibsone. *Technical Advisor:* Ted Behr.

Boris Karloff (*Dr. Janos Rukh*), Bela Lugosi (*Dr. Felix Benet*), Frances Drake (*Diana Rukh, later Diana Drake*), Frank Lawton (*Ronald Drake*), Violet Kemble Cooper (*Mother Rukh*), Walter Kingsford (*Sir Francis Stevens*), Beulah Bondi (*Lady Arabella Stevens*), Frank Reicher (*Prof. Meiklejohn*), Paul Weigel (*Monsieur Noyer*), Georges Renavent (*Chief of the Surete*), Nydia Westman (*Briggs*), Daniel Haynes (*Headman*), Adele St. Maur (*Mrs. Noyer*), Lawrence Stewart (*Number One Boy*), Etta McDaniel (*Zulu Woman*), Ynez Seabury (*Celeste*), Winter Hall (*Minister*), Clarence Gordon (*Boy*), Daisy Bufford, Helen Brown (*Mothers*), Jean De Briac, Francisco Maran, Robert Graves (*Gendarmes*), Ricca Allen, Isabelle La Mal (*Bystanders*), Alex Chivra (*Cook*), Lucio Villegas (*Butler*), Lloyd Whitlock, Edwards Davis, Edward Reinach (*Scientists*), Mae Beatty (*Mrs. Legendre*), Paul McAllister (*Papa LaCosta*), Ann Marie Conte (*Blind Girl*), Raymond Turner, Dudley Dickerson, Fred "Snow-

**A short time after the 1942* Great Impersonation *wrapped, its director John Rawlins helmed Universal's kick-off Sherlock Holmes entry* Sherlock Holmes and the Voice of Terror, *a whodunit in which the master detective (Basil Rathbone) uncovers a German scheme identical to the one laid out in Oppenheimer's novel and its movie adaptations.*

flake" Toones (*Natives*), Charles Fallon (*Gentleman*), Walter Miller (*Derelict*), Ernest Bowern, Charles Bastin (*French Newsboys*), Andre Cheron, Alphonse Martell (*Surete Officials*).

CONRAD BROOKS: You know which movie of yours I love, Mr. Lugosi? *The Invisible Ray.* You were great as Karloff's sidekick!
BELA LUGOSI: *Karrr*-loff? ... *Siiide*kick?? ... *Fuck* you! Karloff does not deserve to smell my shit!
—*Conrad Brooks (Brent Hinkley) incurs Bela Lugosi's (Martin Landau) wrath in* Ed Wood *(1994)*

Producer David Diamond, who reunited Karloff and Lugosi in *The Raven*, hoped to find Bela a place in the upcoming Karloff film *Bluebeard*. However, the script by Bayard Veiller, which had Karloff playing a notorious strangler in a decidedly sympathetic light, ran into problems. Anxious to have another Karloff-Lugosi shocker in release before the end of 1935, impatient studio executives put *Bluebeard* on hold and turned their attentions to an altogether different property.

In August, Universal announced that *The Invisible Ray* would commence production under the auspices of producer Edmund Grainger. The premise of the film was exciting, an effort to break away from the Old World folklore that had been the mainstay of the studio's previous horror ventures. Instead of vampires, werewolves and Poe-inspired mayhem, one of the main attractions of this new Boris-Bela vehicle would be the effects work of John P. Fulton, whose contribution to *The Invisible Man* made it a landmark trick film. *The Invisible Ray* further explored one of the genre's favorite themes, man's inability to cope with his own devices, and the corruption of science. Predictably, fragments of *Frankenstein* and most especially *The Invisible Man* crept into the script. The property wasn't based on a tested literary source, but Universal hoped to lure an audience with pseudo-science masquerading as "fact."

The Invisible Ray is cited as an example of early Hollywood science fiction with its emphasis on death rays, futuristic gadgetry and a plot that broadly hints at space travel. (Notice, in fact, that it's set in the future: In this movie, scripted and shot in 1935 and released early in 1936, the various newspapers are dated 1937.) It's still light years away from the type of science fiction–monster movies that Universal would make in the 1950s, but it's nevertheless closer in spirit to them than most of the run-of-the-graveyard Universal monster movies of the 1930s and '40s, where the scientific "explanation" for many of the monsters was, to quote Henry Frankenstein, "more like black magic." Not quite ready to totally abandon its formulaic Gothic trappings, Universal kicked off the action in an imposing Carpathian fortress cloaked in enough shadows to impress any house-hunting vampire.

Not only was *The Invisible Ray* going to re-team Universal's horror MVPs, it was also originally planned to reunite two *WereWolf of London* veterans, director Stuart Walker and scenarist John Colton, the latter engaged on June 3, 1935, to write a screenplay based on a Howard Higgin-Douglas Hodges story. Colton's *Invisible Ray* script bore a marked resemblance to the earlier film: In both, the central character is a half-cracked scientist more devoted to his work than to his much younger, long-suffering wife. When he becomes a part-time monster (a werewolf in the former, a luminous man in the latter), this worsens the domestic set-up and drives the wife into the arms of a more pleasant, age-appropriate chap, at which point the situation reaches crisis point. (Having adapted Somerset Maugham's "Miss Sadie Thompson" into the Broadway hit "Rain," Colton knew full well the dramatic value of injecting an undercurrent of sexual tension.) Both films also feature a rival doctor horning in on the first scientist's latest discovery, and even scenes where the scientist goes into hiding and takes a room in a boardinghouse with a comic-relief English landlady. Underlining the connection in a comical way, some publicity photos of *Invisible Ray*'s African scenes show Rukh expedition boxes stenciled GLENDON EXPEDITION (leftover props from *WereWolf*)!

The pre-production stage of *The Invisible Ray* was played out amid daily trade paper reports that the sale of the studio (possibly to Warner Bros.) was imminent. As news of Universal's desperate economic plight spread, there was increased pressure to get the project off the ground. Another obstacle loomed on the horizon: Misgivings on the part of director Walker. Not entirely satisfied with Colton's script (even after the writer returned to the lot to do some revisions), Walker requested a three-day delay in the start of production to iron out the deficiencies. The top brass refused to grant Walker the extension, and the director felt he had no other choice but to resign from the project.

Walker reported to the trades:

> I am very enthusiastic about the story and the cast but I did not feel that I could do the studio or myself justice under the conditions that came up suddenly. So far as I was concerned I needed more time and, as this could not be arranged, I suggested that some other director would be better for the assignment. It was not a matter of "walking out...."

Lambert Hillyer, rather surprisingly, ended up as Walker's replacement; a veteran director of action subjects and Westerns (he directed William S. Hart in 25 oaters), he was already on the lot preparing a script. Known as one of Hollywood's dependable "fill in" directors, Hillyer would later replace A. Edward Sutherland on Universal's final horror outing before the studio changed hands, *Dracula's Daughter*.

Categorizing *The Invisible Ray* as an upper-class B, the studio allotted a fairly lavish budget of $166,875. Producer Grainger took pains to create a big-picture look, camouflaging old sets, utilizing glass shots to create an illusion of spaciousness, and even resurrecting Kenneth Strickfaden's electrical hardware. The cameras began grinding on Tuesday, September 17, 1935, and on October 25, the production wrapped, over-schedule and $68,000 over-budget. Walker, who had been refused a paltry three days of extra prep time, cattily remarked, "The director who did the picture started nine or ten days after I was ordered to start and finished 25 or more days *after* I was ordered to finish."

The Invisible Ray begins with a classic Universal bromide: The camera focuses on an imposing mountaintop castle on a stormy night in the Carpathians. (An effect called for in the script would have had the castle projecting through the clouds and into a clear sky above the storm.) It is here that Dr. Janos Rukh (KARLOFF, as he is billed on-screen) summons a pair of skeptical colleagues, Belgian astro-chemist Felix Benet (Bela Lugosi) and English scientist Sir Francis Stevens (Walter Kingsford), to witness the unveiling of his greatest discovery. In his laboratory-observatory, Rukh has constructed a fabulous astronomical instrument that isolates light waves from outer space and projects age-old images of the evolutionary stages of our planet. After years of work, he has uncovered proof that a gigantic meteor crashed on the African continent eons ago, bearing a mysterious element more powerful than radium.

One man, crazy; *five* very sane spectators: Rukh's young wife Diana (Frances Drake), Benet, Stevens, Stevens' wife Lady Arabella (Beulah Bondi) and her nephew Ronald Drake (Frank Lawton) are wowed by the demonstration, and Rukh and Diana are invited to tag along on an upcoming African scientific expedition. Insanely possessive of his discovery, Rukh separates from the rest and finds the site of the fallen meteor, still a raging inferno a thousand million years later. Donning a protective outfit, the scientist descends into the blazing pit to secure an element sample. (Some of this footage was reused in Universal's 1939 serial *The Phantom Creeps*—where it's supposed to be *Lugosi* in the lead helmet and metal-cloth suit.) In a moment of carelessness, Rukh exposes himself to the extraterrestrial element and becomes contaminated. His body glows in the dark and his touch means instant death.

Desperate, Rukh confides his dilemma to Dr. Benet (Karloff strikes an awkward Frankenstein Monster-like pose when demonstrating his glow-in-the-dark condition). Benet devises a counteractive which his colleague must inject into himself all the days of his life if he is to survive. But with the antidote comes a grim condition: The surcharge of poison and antidote may have a devastating effect on Rukh's brain.

Harnessing the powers of Radium X via a ray gun-like contraption, the Concentrator, Rukh returns to his Carpathian home and pulls off a miracle, restoring the sight of his mother (Violet Kemble Cooper). (Notice in background the control panel from Dr. Vollin's chamber of horrors in *The Raven*.) Predicting tragedy, Mother Rukh implores her son to remain and perfect his discovery, but Rukh has other ideas. His brain afire and his reason gone, he heads for Paris and begins waging a campaign of terror against those whom he believes cheated him: The Stevenses and Dr. Benet for bringing Radium X

"I'll take them somewhere they've never been—back into time!" Boris Karloff and Frances Drake in *The Invisible Ray.*

to the attention of the scientific community, and Diana for leaving him for Drake.

Rukh murders Sir Francis with a touch, and Lady Arabella is #2 on his hit parade; the madman correspondingly uses his Concentrator to symbolically destroy two of the stone figures outside the Church of the Six Saints where Diana and Drake were wed. On the same sort of rainy night that started the movie, Benet and the Surete set a trap for Rukh at Benet's clinic, but the plan fails and Benet falls victim to his insane colleague. Rukh next menaces Diana in an upper-story bedroom but finds himself unable to lay his deadly hands on her. Mother Rukh arrives on the scene as Rukh, who has delayed injecting himself with the counteractive, is approaching critical mass. Realizing that her son now lives to kill, she uses her cane to strike from his hand the leather case containing the hypodermic, shattering it. "Yes, you're right," says Rukh, smoke rising from his body. "It's better this way. Goodbye, Mother." Running to a nearby window, Rukh crashes through and bursts into a ball of fire during his plunge to the street below.

Despite its status as one of the more intriguing thrillers of the period, *The Invisible Ray* belongs in the second tier of Universal's vintage horror films. Its chief asset is John Colton's intelligent, well-constructed screenplay which scrupulously avoids the excessive comedic interludes that marred *WereWolf of London*. The story is leisurely paced and sometimes remarkable in its understatement; in fact, no 1930s horror film since *Dracula* contains quite as much off-screen mayhem. Sir Francis' murder takes place offstage, and we must read about Lady Arabella's death in a newspaper front page insert shot; ditto the melting of a Church of the Six Saints statue. The movie is frontloaded with many memorable moments (the introduction of vivid characters like Rukh and his mother; the observatory "tour through time"; the descent into the Radium X pit; Rukh's first light-up scenes; Rukh using the Concentrator to liquefy a giant boulder) — but then, once the buildup is at an end and Rukh goes on his murder spree, suddenly the camera is elsewhere during nearly every major event. It's nice for us to know, courtesy of Rukh, that every event that ever took place on Earth is "recorded on nature's film," but it would have been *nicer* if a bit more of Rukh's mayhem could have been recorded on Universal's film!

An examination of the shooting script discloses the pruning, padding and subtle alterations that took place during production. Scenes are occasionally rearranged and dialogue is often added or deleted, not always to the film's advantage. In one inventive turn, after Rukh spies on the wedding ceremony of Diana and Drake (from a daringly close proximity!), he catches sight of the six marble representations of the saints near the church entrance. His mind envisages the religious figures as symbols of the six members of the African expedition. Eliminating his prey, he methodically applies his disintegrator ray on the corresponding statue. In the finished film, the frustrated viewer must read of the desecrations in yet *another* newspaper account; the original script depicts a statue melting before the horrified gaze of spectators, and a gendarme raising his sword only to have it vaporize in his hand. (One hates to think that these scenes were shot and then discarded, but the November 1935 *Universal Weekly* does mention scenes in which "statues vanish into thin air [and] steel swords disappear from the hands of their wielders" as though they were in the can.)

To avoid detection, Rukh fakes his death by killing a Parisian derelict and then planting his identification papers on the corpse. (The bit player seen as *le bum* is Walter Miller — just a few years earlier the *star* of serials in which Karloff had the smaller parts!) As originally intended, Colton had the derelict feted in Rukh's hotel room, only to be dispatched by a touch of the scientist's luminous hand. Other cuts were more judicious. In Africa, Drake saves Diana's life by bagging a charging rhino. Colton specified in his script that animal footage from the studio's library be utilized, but the use of such obvious stock shots would have only cheapened the look of the film. Also eliminated, presumably for reasons of pacing, were one or two romantic episodes as well as a prolonged conversation between Rukh's rivals en route to the Carpathian observatory.

Even the moment of Rukh's "contamination" did not make it into the movie. According to the script, Rukh was to melt the boulder in order to frighten his safari boys, then pause afterwards to admire his gooey handiwork. At that point, he absent-mindedly places an ungloved hand atop the Concentrator, and wraith-like fumes from the space rock inside curl around his fingers. Then, unknowingly making things worse, he clasps his hands together (spreading the contamination from one to the other) — and rubs *both* hands across his eyes and face!

The script called for an elaborate special effects scene in the first act at Rukh's observatory: As part of Rukh's demonstration, his guests were to be treated to a replay of a spectacular

***Porous* Karloff: Boris (right) soaks up a deadly dose of Radium X, and Bela Lugosi as Dr. Benet comes to his aid.**

"battle of the suns." According to the script, one sun would be established, and then another would loom into view.

> As the other star draws near, the surface of the sun becomes greatly agitated. Great fiery tides are raised — indeed, the sun seems to pulsate with fear and fury like a live thing. It shoots forth great fingers of fiery atmosphere as though to tear the enemy apart and the intruder responds in kind.... For a moment, it looks as though the sun were about to be absorbed but already the pull of the second sun is lessening. It is passing on its way and our sun now elongated like a pear, begins to resume its natural spherical shape.

This sequence, which would have taxed the resources of the special effects department, was completely eliminated, to be replaced by Rukh's far less elaborate "tour of the universe" set piece. Judging by the so-so effects seen in that sequence, especially the poor reproduction of the Earth (rotating at a comical rate that would result in over 8000 sunrises-sunsets every 24 hours!), the battle-of-the-suns sequence was perhaps better left unwrought. Even similar scenes in Universal's decades-later *This Island Earth* (1955) leave a great deal to be desired effects-wise in the 21st century.

Rukh's character in the unabridged text is pictured as a loving, affectionate husband at the outset, making his mental decline even more startling as the narrative progresses. The filmed version depicts the scientist as an embittered recluse from the beginning; his mental processes are glumly questioned by his own mother. He is close to raving in his introductory scene, vindictive toward his rivals, and so uncongenial that one sympathizes with his long-suffering wife. The dialogue half-heartedly blames Benet's antidote for Rukh's madness, but he was obviously a few cards short of a full deck to begin with.

Karloff truly inherited Chaney Sr.'s title of "The Man of a Thousand Faces"; his physical appearance changed radically from one movie to the next, even in straight roles. Here in the first of many films in which he plays a well-meaning scientist driven to desperation by persecutors real and/or imagined, he is capped with a curly black wig and given a mustache in order to make him "look very much Edgar Allan Poe," according to *The Universal Weekly*. Once the movie was released, *UW* predicted, Karloff would certainly "find many perfumed notes in his fan mail from feminine admirers.... [H]e is strikingly handsome all through the picture." Truth be told, Janos Rukh — socially inept, awed by women, middle-aged but still living with his mother — is the sort of Classic Horror character that many fans might regularly encounter ... in their mirrors!*

Still relatively in his prime, Bela Lugosi is uniquely mesmerizing in *The Invisible Ray*. He is saddled with most of the clunker lines, but his sinister, heavily accented delivery inserts some unintentional humor into the proceedings. During an African dinner scene, Frank Lawton flippantly inquires if the good doctor uncovered any great secrets that day. Lugosi, helping himself to a plate of antelope stew, responds matter-of-factly, "Proof that the sun is the mudder of us all." Commenting on the marriage of Drake and Diana, he offers, "I hope they vill be happy," but Lugosi imbues the line with so much deadpan foreboding, even this innocuous remark elicits chuckles (as does his mispronunciation, "The **NO**bel [pronounced like *noble*] Prize"). The script called for deeper enmity between Rukh and Benet ("I should let you die" is Benet's response to Rukh's plea for a counteractive) but it was eventually toned down. This furnished Bela with the chance to play the one and only "normal" character he *or* Boris played in the entire Karloff-Lugosi *oeuvre,* and one of Lugosi's last before his life sentence of typecasting truly began. The final Boris-Bela scene in *Invisible Ray* (the ultimate Maalox moment for Benet, as Rukh moves in for the kill) was their last good acting exchange at Universal.

A standout in the commendable supporting cast is Frances Drake. A stone fox (particularly in the opening scene when she bounces braless across the Rukh entrance hall!), the New York–born, British-trained actress had a promising career in the '30s playing opposite the likes of Cary Grant and Clark Gable. A Paramount contractee, she was on loan much of the time and was chosen as a last-minute substitute for Virginia Bruce in MGM's *Mad Love* (1935). She and costar Frank Lawton were bumped from the cast of James Whale's *Remember Last Night?* (1935) and reassigned to *The Invisible Ray*. (Gloria Stuart was originally slated to play Diana.)

Her career cut short by her marriage to a British diplomat who hated show business, Miss Drake never fulfilled her early promise. In the late 1980s, she was living the high life in Beverly Hills and sharing nothing but pleasant *Invisible Ray* memories with the authors.

She recalled:

> Boris Karloff was charming. He was such a good sport because they played a trick on him when we were on location. He went up some sort of a pole. Lunch was announced and they *left* him there! I hate those horrible tricks, they're not funny to me, but he was a darling. Bela Lugosi was an awfully nice man, too, but a dreadful thing happened. I was walking to the set one day and this young woman said, "Do you know where Mr. Lugosi is?" I said, "I suppose he's on the set." She said, "I came to drive him home," and I said, "I'll tell him if I see him." So I said to him, "Your daughter has come to drive you home." He said, "That's my *wife*!"

Supporting roles are professionally played by Beulah Bondi, purposely loud and annoying as the forceful he-woman adventurer Arabella†; Walter Kingsford in his familiar English-boob mode as Arabella's "himbo" husband; and Frank Lawton, boyishly charming as the male ingénue.

**Three decades later, in AIP's* Die, Monster, Die! *(1965), a horror–SF combo adapted from H.P. Lovecraft's novella "The Colour Out of Space," Karloff starred as a scientist living with his mother in an eerie old mansion, and experimenting with a highly radioactive meteorite. The finale finds King Karloff (or, rather his stuntman), transformed by radiation into a glowing monster, taking a second-story plunge and igniting like a matchhead. To paraphrase Dr. Benet, his luminous character "literally crumbles to an ash."*

†*In the movie, Bondi's Arabella travels to Africa and mentions bagging a leopard. In real life, at age 83, the actress did make a two-month safari to the Dark Continent, but presumably killed no cat. However, in real life, a cat killed* her*: In 1981 she fell, broke several ribs and died after tripping over her own housecat!*

Violet Kemble Cooper, playing Mother Rukh, was actually the same age as her screen son Karloff but, made up to look like George Washington in drag, the actress (a relative of British stage legend Sarah Siddons) pulls it off. Daniel Haynes, leader of the Rukh expedition safari boys, starred in director King Vidor's all-black *Hallelujah* (1929), was on Broadway and on tour with *The Green Pastures* (in two supporting roles), and graduated to the part of De Lawd in a *Green Pastures* revival. A real-life clergyman, the Reverend Dr. Haynes died in 1954. (Although the safari scenes constitute only a small portion of the movie, Universal exhorted exhibitors to ballyhoo *The Invisible Ray* by hiring blacks to dress as natives and roam the streets in the vicinity of their theaters, toting boxes stamped RADIUM X!)

Perhaps the film's most impressive set is Rukh's observatory and telescope; for a closer, *more* impressive look at it, fans can check out the Poverty Row movie *Death from a Distance* (Invincible, 1935), a murder mystery shot at Universal prior to the production of *The Invisible Ray*. The center of the publicity department's advertising campaign was, however, John P. Fulton's special effects. *The Universal Weekly* published garish full-page ads with the tag "The Luminous Man" (in such bold type one might mistake it for the title of the movie) and, not averse to distorting the facts or inventing new ones, reported that Fulton's effects process was such a closely guarded secret that the set was closed off, the cast and crew were compelled to maintain silence, and that daily production reports had been discontinued.

Immodestly extolling the studio's roster of new releases like an overbearingly proud parent, Carl Laemmle wrote in his *Universal Weekly* column, "Watch out for the technical effects, especially in a certain scene which will be discussed all over the world." Exactly *which* scene Laemmle had in mind was never revealed, though there are several that might qualify. The mesmerizing effect of Karloff's face and hands glowing from his over-exposure to Radium X, according to *The Universal Weekly*, took six weeks to perfect, and entailed a system of light filters. Veteran effects man David Horsley provided *Photon*'s Paul Mandell with a more accurate account of how this was achieved:

> Mr. Fulton had plenty of time to think this one over, and he discussed the problem with Frank Williams, who had the patents on the traveling matte processes and at the time was operating his laboratory in Hollywood. Frank suggested that John use a bi-pack film in photographing Karloff, using a suitable makeup, so that the hands and face would sort of separate out of the rest of the scene. One part of the bi-pack record would be used to print the regular scene, and the other half would be used to take off the mattes for the glowing effect. John agreed to do this, we made some tests, and they looked pretty good.... We shot two days with [the bi-pack stock] before the lab discovered they could not get enough exposure and develop enough image on the pieces to make the system work (this was *old* film, quite old) ... so we had to go ahead and photograph the film, and Fulton had to figure out a way to ink the mattes after it was finished. And that was what was done. I actually had the task of compositing all of those shots of Karloff glowing.... We had a crew of girls working around the clock, three eight-hour shifts. We had three stands, these were overhead cameras projecting down onto animation boards. The girls would pencil-in the hands and face, one frame at a time, and these would be painted onto cells so that the hands and face were black. There was well over a thousand feet of these mattes, so this involved more than 16,000 of these drawings. I was there every four hours, day and night, from the time the job started until the time all the mattes were inked and painted. [In an *Invisible Ray* thread on the Classic Horror Film Board, a poster once quipped that in the 1970s, the Aurora model company missed a bet by not including Rukh as the subject of one of their "glow" kits!]

According to the studio budget sheets, this particular effect cost a mere $250, a measly sum considering the manpower required to pull it off. Slightly more expensive were the effects scene of Rukh frightening his native bearers by focusing his Concentrator on the boulder, and the climactic shot of his plummeting body vanishing in a whoosh of flame. These tricks set the budget back a total of $700. In none of the production stills nor the promotional trailer of *The Invisible Ray* do Karloff's face or hands glow, *another* missed bet.

John P. Fulton "had a reputation of being very, very difficult to work with — and he *was*," Fulton's daughter Joanne told the authors:

> He was difficult to *live* with! He was a difficult *man*. When he was working, he was working.

> There was *no* funny business, *no* being Mr. Nice Guy, it was just, "Get the work done!" His nickname was Hard Way: That was because Dad wanted to do it *right*, and very often the *right* way is the *hard* way, and sometimes the expensive way.... My earliest memories of the movie business are of hearing about Dad fighting Carl Laemmle in the Front Office for more money to do the tricks they wanted him to do with very little money. Carl wanted him to create miracles, but he didn't want to pay for it. I think that really colored my dad's *whole view* of the movie business. My dad wasn't free to do his work in that he was *always* shackled by this money thing. Always. Always. Always.

Part of the appeal of *The Invisible Ray* is that it's an offbeat conglomeration of genres—a bridge between the studio's traditional horrors (the servants at Rukh's storm-swept castle look like they made a wrong turn at the Borgo Pass) and the breed of sci-fi films then still decades away. After the hemmed-in atmospherics of the previous Boris-Bela vehicles *The Black Cat* and *The Raven*, both of which take place primarily within the walls of a single house, it's refreshing to find *The Invisible Ray* globe-trotting like no other Universal Horror, from the Carpathians to Darkest Africa to Paris—and even taking a quick side trip to the outer edges of our solar system and beyond! The music of Franz Waxman, mostly original but incorporating some *Bride of Frankenstein* cues, is an asset as well. It's also striking, especially since the movie was made in the immediate wake of *The Raven*, that here Dear Bela is commendably restrained and Poor Boris is the one carving the ham. Amusingly, one megalomaniacal Rukh speech ("I could crumble up a city a thousand miles away. I could destroy a nation. *All* nations!") is reminiscent of a Roxor rant in Fox's 1932 *Chandu the Magician*—and here the disapproving listener is Bela, Roxor himself!

The Invisible Ray is an ingratiating addition to the Universal canon with its lively interplay between the two stars, imaginative script and journeyman direction, but it falls just short of classic status. Director Hillyer and writer Colton were talented dabblers in the genre, not first-rate stylists. The movie is too dated to be really effective science fiction and not quite Gothic enough to rank as a serious horror film, and the stiff-backed, paranoid Rukh lacks the pathos of a Jack Griffin or a Henry Frankenstein—the same complaint often lodged against Wilfred Glendon, another Colton creation.

Early makeup design for Janos Rukh (courtesy Bill Chase).

All things considered, however, *The Invisible Ray* is of more than passing interest, and essential viewing for connoisseurs of fantastic cinema.

Critics' Corner

[Y]esterday's audience, composed largely of men, gave to the picture their respectful attention, finding the laboratories especially absorbing, and the climax vastly exciting.—*The New York Herald-Tribune*, January 11, 1936, Marguerite Tazelaar

Universal, which seems to have a monopoly on films of this sort, has made its newest penny dreadful with technical ingenuity and the pious hope of frightening the children.... Boo right back at you, Mr. Laemmle!—*The New York Times*, January 11, 1936, Frank S. Nugent

It isn't as blood-curdling to the point achieved in some Hollywoodian efforts, but it is different and fairly entertaining....—*Variety*, January 15, 1936, Char

Rating: ★ Just the other day your reviewer paused to gaze with surprise at a West Side movie theatre's marquee which bore on the top line in big bright letters, "Karloff and Lugosi." On the second line, in smaller and dimmer lights, was the name of one of Metro-Goldwyn-Mayer's highest salaried stars. So, that just goes to show you that the old lady who kissed the cow was right.—*The New York Daily News*, January 11, 1936, Wanda Hale

[O]ff-beaten-track entertainment of popular pattern. Boris Karloff makes a curiously sympathetic figure of the stricken Rukh....—*Today's Cinema*, February 12, 1936

[S]ometimes amusingly dated.... [it] is also surprisingly poignant, building to a tense and dramatic climax.... [A] handsome, ambitious production in which some stilted acting and dialogue add to, rather than detract from, the fun.—*The Los Angeles Times*, August 11, 2005, Kevin Thomas

We would've preferred Bela in the demented-doc role, but this is still a strong, if downbeat, Universal outing.—*The Phantom of the Movies' VideoScope: The Ultimate Guide to the Latest, Greatest and Weirdest Genre Videos*, 2000

Dracula's Daughter

Released May 11, 1936. 71 minutes. *Presented by* Carl Laemmle. *Director:* Lambert Hillyer. *Associate Producer:* E.M. Asher. *Screenplay:* Garrett Fort. *Suggested by* Oliver Jeffries (pseudonym for David O. Selznick). *Based on the story* "Dracula's Guest" *by* Bram Stoker. *Photography:* George Robinson. *Art Director:* Albert S. D'Agostino. *Special Photography:* John P. Fulton. *Editor:* Milton Carruth. *Supervising Editor:* Maurice Pivar. *Music:* Heinz Roemheld. *Music Conductor:* Edward Ward. *Assistant Directors:* Sergei Petschnikoff & Victor Noerdlinger; *Sound Supervisor:* Gilbert Kurland. *Sound Recordist:* Joe Lapis. *Makeup:* Jack P. Pierce & Otto Lederer. *Gowns:* Brymer. *Wardrobe:* Vera West. *Hair Stylist:* Grace Boyd. *Script Clerk:* Myrtle Gibsone. *Production Secretary:* Peggy Vaughn. *Stand-in for Otto Kruger:* Fred Keck. *Stand-in for Gloria Holden:* Kathleen Deek. *Stand-in for Marguerite Churchill:* Katherine Stanley.

Otto Kruger (*Dr. Jeffrey Garth*), Gloria Holden (*Countess Marya Zaleska/Countess Dracula*), Marguerite Churchill (*Janet Blake*), Edward Van Sloan (*Prof. Von Helsing*), Irving Pichel (*Sandor*), Nan Grey (*Lili*), Gilbert Emery (*Sir Basil Humphrey*), Hedda Hopper (*Lady Esme Hammond*), E.E. Clive (*Sgt. Wilkes*), Billy Bevan (*Albert*), Halliwell Hobbes (*Constable Hawkins*), Claude Allister (*Sir Aubrey Bedford*), Edgar Norton (*Hobbs*), Eily Malyon (*Miss Peabody*), George Kirby (*Bookstore Owner*), Christian Rub (*Coachman*), Guy Kingsford (*Radio Announcer*), David Dunbar (*Motor Bobby*), Gordon Hart (*Host*), Joseph R. Tozer (*Dr. Angus Graham*), Douglas Wood (*Dr. Townsend*), Fred Walton (*Dr. Bemish*), Paul Weigel (*The Innkeeper*), George Sorel, William von Brincken (*Police Officers*), Douglas Gordon (*Attendant*), Eric Wilton, Vesey O'Davoren (*Butlers*), Agnes Anderson (*Bride*), William Schramm (*Groom*), Owen Gorin (*Friend*), Else Janssen, Bert Sprotte (*Guests*), John Blood (*Bobby*), Clive Morgan (*Desk Sergeant*), Hedwiga Reicher (*Wife*), John Power (*Police Official*), Vernon Steele (*Squires*), Edna Lyall, Sylvia Chaldecott (*Nurses*), *Deleted from final print:* Pietro Sosso (*Minister*), Paul Mitchell (*Messenger in Transylvania*).

Dracula's Daughter strikes the living with all her father's cunning!
—*Trailer blurb for* Dracula's Daughter

For a studio as economically imperiled as Universal, the sequel to the mega-hit *Dracula* had endured a remarkably long gestation period. As with their follow-up to *Frankenstein*, Universal nursed the film along meticulously, developing different ideas and contracting for several versions of the screenplay until a workable final draft that met with Production Code approval was hammered out. The mounting costs of the production did little to help Universal's struggling financial condition; the film would be released two months after the Laemmles had left the company.

Dracula's Daughter's convoluted production history dates as early as 1934 when MGM executive producer, David O. Selznick, recently arrived from RKO, entertained the idea of producing a vampire film of his own. Although Universal had a lock on the Dracula character, the producer shrewdly purchased the rights to Bram Stoker's posthumously published short story, "Dracula's Guest." Strangely, Selznick then commissioned a script from veteran Universal scribe, John L. Balderston, which was conceived as a blatant sequel to the Tod Browning picture.

As David Skal points out in *The Monster Show* (W.W. Norton & Co., 1993), the Balderston treatment was a violation of Selznick's deal with Stoker's widow regarding the rights of "Dracula's Guest." Complicating the issue was that legally, the treatment couldn't be filmed by any studio except Universal since it owed so much to the Lugosi film. All legal hurdles were cleared, however, when Selznick sold off the rights to the story to Universal in September 1934, on condition that production on the film commence by October 1935. (The deadline, as it turned out, would be extended several times.)

Balderston's 20-page treatment, dated January 1934, was prefaced with a spate of complaints. He noted that his previous horror assignments (*Dracula* and *The Mummy*) "dropped badly" in their last thirds due to scheduling and financial pressures, and insisted that this did not occur with *Dracula's Daughter*. Reasoning

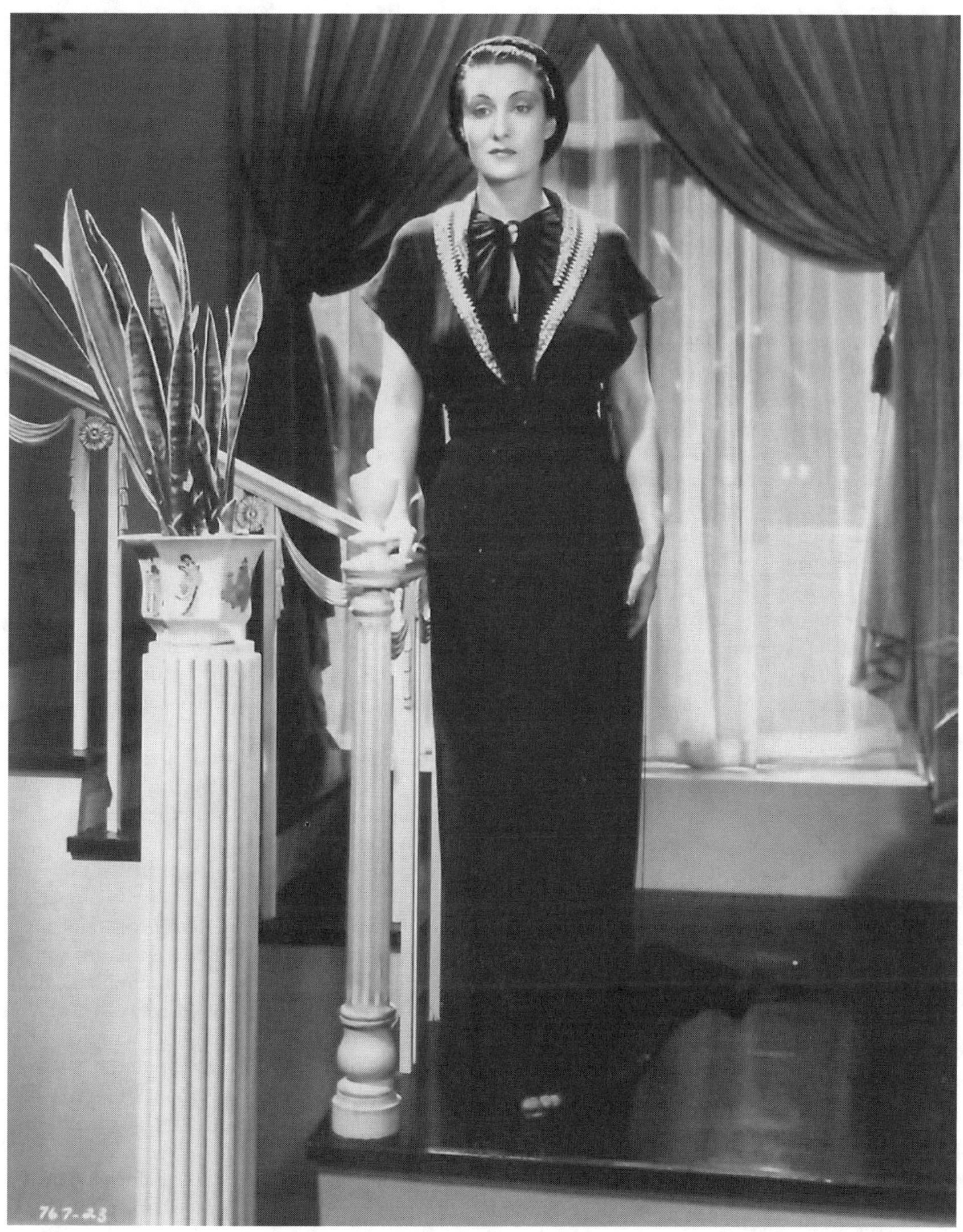

Countess Marya Zaleska (Gloria Holden) dressed for a night on the town in *Dracula's Daughter.*

that an audience might more readily accept a female vampire seducing a young man than vice versa, Balderston suggested that Universal pull all stops to create a truly *horrible* horror movie.

Queried the writer:

Why should Cecil B. DeMille have a monopoly on the great box office values of torture and cruelty in pictures about ancient Rome? I want to see her [Dracula's daughter's] loathsome deaf mute servants carry into her boudoir savage-looking whips, chains, straps, etc. and hear the cries of the tortured victims without seeing exactly what happens.... I feel sure that so long as it is a *woman* torturing *men*, the thing is not *too* unendurable as it would have been had the man Dracula so treated his female victims. [The italics are Balderston's.]

With this provocative introduction, Balderston opened his latest chiller with the final scene from *Dracula*: Van Helsing stakes the vampire in the cellars of Carfax Abbey. Realizing his work isn't quite complete, he journeys to Transylvania to destroy Dracula's brides. But Van Helsing misses the well-concealed body of Dracula's offspring. Under the assumed name Countess Szkekeley, the vampiress descends on London, setting her eyes on a young aristocrat, Edward "Ned" Wadhurst, who promptly falls under her spell. Van Helsing and Dr. Seward, aware of Ned's plight, ally themselves with the young man's friends and fiancée and confront Szkekeley on her own turf. Ned, nearly a vampire himself, finds the strength to end his ordeal by driving a stake into Dracula's daughter's heart.

Although Universal had cleared the screen rights involving the story, they apparently had little interest in the Balderston treatment as written. On May 28, 1935, *The Hollywood Reporter* announced that Carl Laemmle, Jr., "had picked his horror picture for 1935–36," and would be producing *Dracula's Daughter*. By this time, the studio had planned on having Bela Lugosi reprise his star-making role with James Whale directing. Balderston's treatment had been sent to R.C. Sherriff in London to write the script.

By December 24, Laemmle had bowed out of the film in order to concentrate on two other projects, *Lucky Baldwin* and a remake of Lon Chaney's *The Phantom of the Opera*. (Neither would be made under Laemmle.) Although E. M. Asher was named as the new producer, the next day, the studio was hinting that A. Edward Sutherland would be the studio's first producer-director and that *Dracula's Daughter* was to be his first assignment. However, two days later, Universal was reshuffling personnel yet again, confirming Asher as the producer with Sutherland confining himself to the directorial duties.

On January 6, 1936, it was apparent that production of *Dracula's Daughter* was in some disarray. Not only was the starting date postponed for the third time, a major budget cut was ordered by the studio. With the film now slated for filming on January 25, director Sutherland bowed out of the project, claiming that it would interfere with other commitments. Reliable Lambert Hillyer, who recently directed *The Invisible Ray*, was brought onto the project. Jane Wyatt, the gifted, intelligent actress who made a strong impression in a featured part in James Whale's *One More River* (1934), was cast as the romantic lead while Universal, still interested in working Lugosi into the picture, awaited the actor's clearance from the Republic production, *House of a Thousand Candles*. (As it turned out, Lugosi would not appear in the film.)

The high point of Lugosi's role was in the prologue of the R.C. Sherriff script, apparently inspired from the back story of Sir Arthur Conan Doyle's *The Hound of the Baskervilles*, which depicts the origins of the curse of Dracula. Here we see the Count in his mortal incarnation as a sadistic nobleman of the Middle Ages, who indulges his assorted vices by hosting extravagant parties, rounding up virginal village girls to supply the entertainment. At the height of the debaucheries, a "white wizard" arrives unexpectedly on the scene, showing his contempt by turning the guests into swine. Feeling that this is too kind a fate for the host, the wizard places the curse of the undead on Dracula's head.

The sequence would never be filmed as events sent the already troubled production into a tailspin. The Breen Office rejected the script outright, noting in a letter to Laemmle Jr. that it contained "countless offensive stuff" which made it impossible for Production Code approval in its present form. Even after Sherriff submitted a toned-down version, Breen considered it "not quite acceptable," objecting to the implied sex, violence and alleged debauchery. With the legal deadline for the Balderston treatment material looming on the horizon, Universal ordered a complete overhaul for the project, bringing in *Frankenstein* co-writer Garrett Fort to write a new script. Under pressure to downplay the film's horror content, the Dracula character was completely eliminated and with it, Bela Lugosi's participation in the film. How the actor greeted the news of being dealt out of the long-awaited follow-up to his greatest success isn't

With the help of her sinister servant Irving Pichel, Gloria Holden plans to use Marguerite Churchill as a bargaining chip to gain Otto Kruger's cooperation in *Dracula's Daughter*.

known. At least he probably found solace that the studio was contractually obligated to pay him $4,000. For that, Lugosi would help out in publicity and pose for production stills.

On January 14, Universal informed Breen that the first script had been shelved, and that a new script had been prepared. The next day, the censor wrote back informing the studio that the basic story met with the requirements of the Code.

The almost daily reshuffling of the picture included further cast changes. On January 28, *The Hollywood Reporter* announced that Broadway actress Gloria Holden, who was brought to the West Coast by director Clarence Brown for a screen test, signed a term contract with Universal and was assigned to the title role. Days later, it was announced that the studio was borrowing Marguerite Churchill from Warner Bros. to replace Jane Wyatt and that the well-regarded character actor Otto Kruger would substitute for Cesar Romero, who left the cast for another project.

The much-delayed production finally got underway on February 4, just in time to meet the final deadline granted in the studio agreement with Selznick. A 29-day shooting schedule was set, presumably taking into account the fact that Fort's rushed script wasn't quite finalized. By this time, *Dracula's Daughter* was shaping up as one of Universal's more expensive projects. The constant reshuffling of personnel and various production setbacks due to script problems pushed the final budget up to $278,000, one of the highest for a Universal horror picture. Sutherland, who didn't shoot a frame of film, was paid $17,500 including "retained time"— about three times the salary received by Hillyer. For all its cost overruns, *Dracula's Daughter* looks uncomfortably like the product of a studio B-unit. On April 16, the Breen Office issued a certificate for *Dracula's Daughter* in time for a preview of the film at the studio.

Picking up the action immediately after the last reel of *Dracula*, the film opens as two comic

English bobbies (Halliwell Hobbes and Billy Bevan) investigate the strange goings-on at Carfax Abbey. After first discovering the broken body of Renfield sprawled at the foot of a stone staircase, the constables happen upon Count Dracula lying in his coffin, a stake driven through his heart. Prof. Von Helsing (Edward Van Sloan), who presumably loitered behind after Mina and Harker took off, confesses to the strange crime and is immediately packed off to Scotland Yard headquarters where he is booked on a charge of murder.

Sir Basil Humphrey (Gilbert Emery), the investigating official, is understandably skeptical of Von Helsing's claim that Dracula was a vampire. He summons the man's former pupil, psychiatrist Jeffrey Garth (Otto Kruger), who reluctantly agrees to act as the professor's advocate. Garth is convinced that Von Helsing's obsession with vampires has left him somewhat unhinged.

Dracula's body disappears from the police station at Whitby and the guard is found in a paralyzed state. The corpse has been stolen by the daughter of Dracula, using the pseudonym Countess Marya Zaleska (Gloria Holden). She cremates her father's remains with the assistance of her ghoulish henchman Sandor (Irving Pichel). Confident that the curse has been broken, Zaleska hopes to lead a normal life. She finds herself unable to resist her vampiric cravings and attacks a male passerby.

Zaleska, who has gained a reputation among the London social set for her macabre paintings, meets Garth at a dinner party. She discreetly enlists his aid in combating her affliction without actually revealing its gruesome nature. At Garth's urging, she decides to put her willpower to the test. Combing the streets of Chelsea, Sandor picks up Lili (Nan Grey), a starving waif on the brink of suicide, and induces her to pose for Zaleska. The vampiress makes a staunch effort to combat her overwhelming desires, but to no avail; Lili becomes her second London victim. Hours later, Lili is found wandering the streets in a state of shock and suffering from an extreme loss of blood and is taken to a nearby hospital. There, Garth uses hypnosis to bring her back to consciousness but the girl dies under the strain, although the evidence clearly points to Zaleska.

Faced with the grim facts, Garth confronts Zaleska who kidnaps his assistant Janet Blake (Marguerite Churchill) and heads back to Transylvania. Garth follows in a private plane and traces her to Castle Dracula. Zaleska threatens to kill Janet, now in a profound trance, unless Garth joins her in the ranks of the undead. As Janet's life slowly ebbs away, Garth reluctantly agrees. Zaleska begins weaving her spell, but the jilted Sandor intervenes, shooting a wooden arrow through her heart. He then takes deadly aim at Garth but is shot down by the newly arrived Sir Basil, who has followed the psychiatrist to Transylvania with Von Helsing. Zaleska's spell is broken and Garth and Janet are reunited.

For those who can't abide the stifling staginess of *Dracula*, the art house ambiguities of Carl Dreyer's *Vampyr* (1932) or the botched ending of *Mark of the Vampire* (1935), Lambert Hillyer's solid if conventional *Dracula's Daughter* is likely to be the odds-on favorite as the best vampire movie of the '30s. Or at least the most entertaining. The film is briskly paced, nicely atmospheric by way of shadow-play photography and dollops of studio-generated fog, and is populated by engaging characters. What it doesn't have is an iconic horror personality, a crucial omission by Golden Age standards. Still, for a film that was once summarily dismissed for failing to deliver Bela Lugosi's reprise Dracula performance, *Dracula's Daughter* has been reappraised most favorably over the ensuing decades.

The film is a sad indicator of Lugosi's dwindling stature as the '30s wore on. The rationale that the added allure of a sexual twist on the classic story would attract sufficient interest to offset the actor's nonappearance was tantamount to writing Lugosi's career obituary, even though Universal still considered the actor for future horror roles. To the legion of Lugosi fans, most of whom weren't even born yet, Universal's decision was an especially bitter one for denying to actor the opportunity to cement his reputation as the quintessential screen Dracula. This is due in no small measure to Tod Browning's questionable ability to handle actors as evidenced by his work in *Dracula* which not only brought out the worst excesses of Lugosi but Edward Van Sloan and David Manners as well. Of course, that hasn't stopped Lugosi's *Dracula* from becoming the stuff of Hollywood legend. It's a testament to the ability of *Dracula's Daughter*

Bela Lugosi schmoozes with Gloria Holden and Gloria Stuart in the Universal commissary during the production of *Dracula's Daughter* (courtesy Bill Chase).

director Lambert Hillyer and writer Garrett Fort that they were able to surmount the loss of the actor most associated with Bram Stoker's classic character and produce a credible film in their own right. (If it's any consolation to Lugosi fans, a wall-sized tapestry with a rendering of Bela as the Count is briefly seen in the background as Pichel is about to use his archery skills on Otto Kruger in the exciting climax.)

As in *Bride of Frankenstein*, *Dracula's*

Daughter starts off precisely where the original film leaves off but with notable stylistic differences that distinguish it from its predecessor. While Tod Browning tried to stamp a stately Victorian look on *Dracula*, Hillyer and Fort firmly entrench *Dracula's Daughter* in the twentieth century. The pace of the film is one of a bustling modern city in which characters use telephones and radios and drive about in motorcars unlike *Dracula* in which there is rarely a modern device in sight. Commentators have made much hay of the fact that even when Count Dracula is off screen, he dominates the mood of the original movie. A case can be made that it is Helen Chandler's cloying Mina character who actually sets the tone; the midsection of the film has the woozy, precious air of a genteel, unworldly schoolgirl held in the powerful hypnotic grip of the nosferatu. So much so that the film takes on a mesmeric tone of its own and making a rather dull show of it.

Dracula's Daughter, on the other hand, is neither mannered nor affected, its characters far more rooted in everyday reality. No shrinking debutantes here; hero Jeffrey Garth functions as a psychiatrist turned detective. The accumulating evidence of the existence of the undead is filtered through a hardened, scientific mind, which not only sharpens the drama but gives the audience a commanding identification figure.

Fort's Production Code–conscious script keeps the film on a rational plane, cheating a bit by downplaying the fantasy aspect of the vampire legend. There's not a single transformation of Zaleska into a bat or wolf. Indeed, the female vampire is more reminiscent of Robert Louis Stevenson than Bram Stoker; Zaleska tries to wrest herself from the family curse in much the same way as Jekyll tried to wrest himself from Hyde's grip, at least in the various cinematic adaptations of the story. Unfortunately, likening Zaleska to a drug addict trying to kick the habit, Fort bowdlerizes some of the basic ground rules of the supernatural.

Zaleska's misguided belief that she can evolve into a normal being by sheer willpower is an outright impossibility considering she's a spiritual rather than physical entity. Likewise, her attempt to overcome her craving for blood as if it were strictly a matter of choice when, in fact, it is her only means of sustenance. Her goal to exist inconspicuously among the mortals would entail a staggering number of logistical problems such as avoiding mirrors and crucifixes, as well the embarrassment of spending the better part of her time in a coffin. Still, Fort effectively works the classic conflict of a character hopelessly at odds with her own nature into a compelling, even tragic tale, although taking more than the usual share of dramatic license. The script, unfortunately, is prone to under-plotting which gives rise to excessive comic padding in the form of Billy Bevan's stock country constable character and Claude Allister's painful turn as a high society party guest. The romantic leads, Otto Kruger and Marguerite Churchill, likewise play out their comically combative relationship in far more screen time than is required.

Lambert Hillyer's direction is unembellished and straightforward, leaving the atmospherics in the capable hands of photographer George Robinson. The stylish and alarming sequence in which Zaleska puts the bite on her first female victim, Lili (Nan Grey), has become one of the most discussed and analyzed in the entire Universal horror canon. The methodical writing and blocking of the scene, extraordinary in its detail as Zaleska directs the half-undressed girl to the fireplace, pouring her wine, requesting that her bra straps be pulled from her shoulders, would suggest a cut-and-dry study of lesbian seduction. Still, what would seem an obvious reading of the scene often provokes a reactionary response from viewers who insist on a literal reading of the situation, countering that it's a case of an animal ensnaring its prey. In fact, the distinctly homosexual tone of the scene was quite pronounced in Fort's original version of the script which had to be modified after a Breen Office ruling. In spite of this, Hillyer manages to maintain a sexually charged atmosphere and the scene remains suspenseful as well as titillating. The effect is only spoiled by an abrupt music edit as Zaleska advances on the girl, the camera quickly tilting upwards to fill the frame with a demonic stone mask, smiling approvingly.

In the plum title role, Gloria Holden is equally adept enlisting the audience's sympathy as she is at conveying the full menace of her celebrated parent. Born in London but reared in the United States, Holden was trained as an interpretive dancer and an operetta singer. The most notable items on her résumé at the time of her casting were a few bit parts and a 26-week stint on the Eddie Cantor radio program. Her motion picture career consisted of supporting roles in such productions as *Wife vs. Secretary* (1936), *The Life of Emile Zola* (1937), *Test Pilot* (1938), *Dodge City* (1939), a particularly showy role in *Behind the Rising Sun* (1943) and *The Hucksters* (1947). Perhaps Tod Browning remembered her performance in *Dracula's Daughter* when he cast her as a rather spooky psychic in MGM's *Miracles for Sale* (1939). Universal picked up Holden's option on the strength of her performance as Countess Zaleska. Strangely, she wouldn't return to the studio again until her career was winding down 16 years later. The occasion was hardly memorable. Appearing in the Douglas Sirk comedy, *Has Anyone Seen My Gal?* (1952), Holden was buried in the supporting cast well under fledgling stars Rock Hudson and Piper Laurie. Holden passed away in 1991. Her granddaughter, actress Laurie Holden, followed in her grandmother's footsteps.

With his granite jaw and patrician nose, 50-year-old Otto Kruger is a far cry from standard issue pretty boys like David Manners and Lester Matthews. His no-nonsense and often blunt personality has attracted criticism in recent commentaries. Nevertheless, Kruger's analytical approach to the character is refreshingly unsentimental and authoritative, prefiguring Peter Cushing's Van Helsing in later Hammer vampire films.

She may not exactly fit the bill as the daughter of a baroness, but Churchill provides *Dracula's Daughter* with a plucky heroine. An under-appreciated actress who was relegated to contract player status, she got her first break in Raoul Walsh's *The Big Trail* (1930). Though highly regarded today as one of the more lyrical, expressive evocations of the American West, at the time of its release the film was dismissed as an extravagant flop, being one of the first major Hollywood movies to be shot in the 70mm format. The experience proved to be an invaluable stepping stone for the star, John Wayne, but it did little to help Churchill's career which petered out in the late '30s after a string of programmers including the Boris Karloff vehicle *The Walking Dead* (1936).

Churchill was a forgotten figure until the '70s when her son, Darcy O'Brien, painted a most unflattering picture of her and his father, Western star George O'Brien, in his coming-of-age novel *A Way of Life, Like Any Other*. A thinly disguised account of his own life, the supposedly fictional story tells of growing up in a privileged Hollywood family which collapses with the end of the war. It's an alternately funny and touching novel; Churchill gets the full *Mommie Dearest* treatment, depicted as an unstable, sex-starved near-alcoholic as her beauty begins to fade. Churchill died shortly after her 90th birthday, outliving her writer-son by two years.

Edward Van Sloan's performance as Von Helsing is excellent, handily upstaging his own starchy interpretation of the character in the original under Tod Browning. His lively exchanges with Kruger in which he summons up all his zeal to make a defense attorney-like case for the supernatural, shows the actor at his persuasive best. Irving Pichel, in a cadaverous makeup, makes the most of his underwritten role as Sandor, using his rich baritone voice with effectively menacing results. (Herbert Marshall, one of the smoothest British players in all Hollywood, was considered for the role before someone at Universal's casting department came to his senses.) Pichel proved to be an actor of limited range and, frankly, limited appeal and turned his talents towards film directing. He co-directed *The Most Dangerous Game* (1932) and *She* (1935), quickly went on to getting full director's credit, eventually collaborating with legendary science fiction producer George Pal for *The Great Rupert* and *Destination Moon* (both 1950). While frequently tackling ambitious subjects, Pichel's films were marked by a stodgy earnestness and were critical near-misses.

Bride of Frankenstein is often cited as one of the few movie sequels which manage to surpass the original film but in some ways *Dracula's Daughter* could make a credible case as well. For all its striking qualities, it doesn't quite place on the "first tier" of Universal horror classics, but shares the same orbit with such notable titles as *WereWolf of London, Son of Frankenstein* and, more debatably, *Murders in the Rue Morgue*. It's checkered with marvelous scenes, but there is nothing in *Dracula's Daughter* to equal the first reels of *Dracula* in terms of weaving an almost majestic sense of horror. Lambert Hillyer at least manages to instill in his sequel some of the essence of the original film; one could almost sense Lugosi silently lingering in the shadows, prodding and wheedling his rebellious offspring over to "the dark side." (Perhaps he was casting his spell on Anne Rice, who cited *Dracula's Daughter* as the movie which inspired her to write her first vampire novel.)

Strangely enough, at the brink of the moment in Hollywood history when the howls of civic groups (both here and abroad) were about to put a temporary end to the production of horror flicks, *Dracula's Daughter* got positive reviews from some interesting quarters. The National Society of New England Women opined that "However much one may deplore the production of horror films, it is impossible to deny the artistry and finish of this version of the undying vampire superstition," but went on to add: "Audiences for this film should be strictly limited to mature persons whose nerves are steady and capable of quick comeback." Federated Church Women praised the picture for its "Thought-provoking and distinctly mature theme and development." The California Congress of Parents & Teachers' praise for the film was likewise surprising (even for California), calling it "a film outstanding of its unpleasant kind." Even Daughters of the American Revolution chimed in, lauding *Dracula's Daughter* as "An exceedingly well-produced horror film."

Critics' Corner

One of the best in its class, sustaining its eerie suspense without too much straining of credulity and weaving a spell of conviction by clever use of pseudo scientific patter, solemnly used by a just-right cast.—*The Hollywood Reporter,* May 11, 1936

Quite terrifying it all is, to be sure.... Gloria Holden is a remarkably convincing bat-woman.... [A] cute little horror picture. Be sure and bring the kiddies.—*The New York Times,* May 18, 1936, Frank S. Nugent

Rating: ★★½ Lambert Hillyer has managed to pile up a great deal of suspense ... and has gathered an excellent cast.... The excellent photography ... helps to create the weird atmosphere....—*The New York Daily News,* May 17, 1936, Kate Cameron

Rating: Good. [A] shocker deluxe.... [I]t comes to celluloid splendidly written and in plausible enough fashion as to make one believe that there really are such animals.... Really, if you go for it—and we do!—it's swell stuff.—*The New York Post,* May 18, 1936, Irene Thirer

Miss Holden does not resort to weird make-up. Nevertheless, she is sinister in appearance and manner, and at times terrifies the spectator by her actions. There is considerable comedy, relieving the tension.... The similarity of this picture to *Dracula* lessens the dramatic suspense to some degree for those who saw the first one.—*Harrison's Reports,* May 23, 1936

Murky story of vampire's daughter ... ably handled in approved horrific vein.... [F]acile revenge denouement. Not for juveniles....—*Today's Cinema* (GB), June 1, 1936

It's difficult to think that many people will be entertained by such a thoroughly morbid story.—*Films and Filming* (GB), June, 1936

1937

Night Key

Released May 2, 1937. 67 minutes. *Director:* Lloyd Corrigan. *Associate Producer:* Robert Presnell. *Screenplay:* Tristram Tupper & John C. Moffitt. *Original Story:* William A. Pierce. *Photography:* George Robinson. *Special Photographic Effects:* John P. Fulton. *Art Director:* Jack Otterson. *Associate Art Director:* Loren Patrick. *Editor:* Otis Garrett. *Musical Director:* Lou Forbes. *Sound:* Jess Moulin & Jesse T. Bastian.

Boris Karloff (*Dave Mallory*), Jean Rogers (*Joan Mallory*), J. Warren Hull (*Jimmy Travers*), Hobart Cavanaugh (*"Petty Louie"*), Samuel S. Hinds (*Stephen Ranger*), Edwin Maxwell (*Kruger*), Alan Baxter (*"The Kid"*), David Oliver (*Mike*), Ward Bond (*"Fingers"*), Frank Reicher (*Carl*), George Humbert (*Spinelli*), Charles Wilson (*Chief of Police*), Michael Fitzmaurice (*Ranger's Secretary*), George Cleveland (*Adams*), Emmett Vogan, Charles Sherlock (*Reporters*), Ethan Laidlaw, Monte Montague, Jack Cheatham, George Magrill, Frank Hagney, Ralph Dunn (*Henchmen*), Henry Rocquemore (*Boarder*), Roy Barcroft (*Office Worker*), Ruth Fallows (*Waitress*), Hal Cooke (*Manager*), Tom Hanlon (*Radio Announcer*), Nina Campana (*Mrs. Spinelli*), Charlie Sullivan (*Taxi Driver*), Johnnie Morris (*Tailor*), Jeff Corey (*Policeman*).

BORIS KARLOFF COMES OUT OF THE SHADOWS—

No more, the fear-inspiring roles that made children quake...
Now movie audiences will know Karloff, the man.
—*Studio publicity release for* Night Key

After months of denying that a sale of the studio was underway, the Laemmles found it increasingly difficult to maintain their optimistic facade before the public gaze. Financial reports detailing devastating losses made headlines in the Hollywood trade papers. Literally in its death throes, the Laemmle regime came to an end on March 14, 1936, when Carl Laemmle, Sr., announced the sale of the studio to Standard Capital Corporation. There was little left for Laemmle to do except retire gracefully. Taking advantage of his place in the spotlight, "Uncle Carl" drummed up a bit of publicity for one of the last major Universal films bearing his name, *Show Boat* (1936), directed by James Whale. The film's success came too late for the aging showman, who died in 1939.

The new owners had their work cut out for them. Bravely facing up to the grim balance sheets inherited from the Laemmles, the studio sought a fresh identity. With the words "A New Universal Picture" emblazoned on all advertising, the new regime scuttled the proud, familiar trademark of the luminous plane circling a spinning globe. In its place, art director Alexander Golitzen designed a rotating, art-deco style glass globe bearing the Universal name amid a cluster of shimmering stars to introduce each new presentation. (The original glass model used to launch the resurrected studio's latest releases was last seen in the '80s, collecting dust in a Hollywood warehouse.) If the first year's releases had anything in common, it was overwhelming mediocrity. Production values dropped appreciably as a result of budget cuts while there were fewer bankable stars under contract. Adding to the problem, the audience's appetite for horror movies (once one of the studio's most reliable sources of profits) had fallen off sharply. With an outright ban on horror movies imposed by the British Commonwealth, Hollywood turned its back on the genre altogether.

The situation undermined the value of Boris Karloff who remained under contract. Since *Night World* (1932), the studio wasn't eager to cast him in anything but horror films except for a brief cameo in a nightclub scene in *The Cohens and Kellys in Hollywood* (1932) and in a featured skit with co-star Bela Lugosi in *Gift of Gab* (1934). He was considered for a leading role in *Love Letters of a Star*, a film which, despite its title, was actually a conventional mystery dealing with blackmail, suicide and murder. It was released with a no-name cast in 1936. The title role in *The Man Who Cried Wolf* (1937) seemed more promising. Karloff was slated for the title role, a ham stage actor who confesses to murders he didn't commit in the hopes of diverting himself from suspicion after he shoots his former business partner to death. His plans go awry when his son is fingered for the crime but the police won't believe his confession. Unfortunately, the film turned out to be a turgid affair with a glum performance by Karloff's old *Mask of Fu Manchu* (1932) co-star Lewis Stone who replaced him.

Finally, the studio gave the go-ahead for a new Karloff melodrama, *Night Key*, to start production. The picture turned out to be the first in a series of parts featuring Karloff as a man of science who tends to his duties as a beautiful, devoted daughter dawdles in the background. It was the kind of role which writer Robert Bloch later categorized as "That Silver Haired Daddy of Mine." Karloff plays Dave Mallory, an aging, half-blind technical genius who invents burglar alarm systems while daughter Joan (Jean Rogers) waits on tables at the local hash-house, hoping for the day when her dad will strike it rich. After putting the finishing touches on a revolutionary new system, he approaches his former friend and associate Steve Ranger (Samuel S. Hinds), now president of a security firm, for backing. Years before, Ranger had stolen the patent rights to Mallory's old alarm system, making a fortune and leaving the inventor nearly penniless. Ever the scoundrel, Ranger hoodwinks Mallory into signing an exclusive contract, then, after the deal is sealed, reveals that he has no intention of installing the new system. Realizing he has been duped into keeping his new invention out of the hands of Ranger's competitors, Mallory leaves the executive with the bitter warning, "What I create, I can destroy!"

Mallory devises a portable device he calls

the Key, which has the ability to electronically override Ranger's alarm system. Hoping to discredit Ranger's company to the point that he will be forced to install Mallory's new system, the inventor hooks up with a small-time crook named "Petty Louie" (Hobart Cavanaugh). Together they execute a number of prankish break-ins targeting Ranger's clients in which nothing is actually stolen. Instead, the mischievous pair leave behind Mallory's calling card, a cryptic note reading, "What I create, I can destroy," and signed "Night Key." In a jewelry store, he sets all of the clocks to go off as Ranger's security team arrives on the scene. Mallory's next hit is a parasol shop where he and Louie, in a silly scene, have fun opening up all of the umbrellas.

This harmless business attracts the attention of an underworld kingpin who calls himself The Kid (Alan Baxter). Hoping to use the Key to more profitable ends, he lures Mallory to his hideout, trying to secure the inventor's cooperation at gunpoint. Mallory reluctantly goes along when the mob tries to break into a bank vault but smashes the Key before any of the loot is stolen. The gangsters retaliate by kidnapping Joan, forcing him to cobble together a replacement Key. Now armed with the new device, The Kid pulls off another heist. Mallory escapes from the gang, holding them off with an electrical booby trap, but Louie is shot dead in the melee.

Mallory manages to alert the police but soon finds himself again in the clutches of The Kid who forces him and Joan into his car. The police give chase in a high-speed pursuit on the streets of Manhattan. Mallory uses the Key to de-energize the car and it smashes into the curb. The police take the criminal into custody while Ranger arrives on the scene with the news he's going to implement Mallory's new system with the inventor finally reaping the profits of his own invention.

A studio press release described how William A. Pierce, who penned the original story for *Night Key*, came up with the plot idea. Pierce had worked as a signal checker for A.D.T., a burglary alarm protection service, back in his hometown of Memphis, Tennessee, some years before. Fortune took him westward and, eventually, he was hired as secretary to Universal studio head Charles R. Rogers. Commenting on his post at A.D.T., Pierce said,

> Those [guards] had to hurry into dark buildings to check up. They had to take their chances with crooks who might still be lurking inside the building. The suspense would be terrific until the guards called back their O.K. Sometimes they didn't call back. A thief was faster with his trigger. The exciting happenings on that job of checking alarm systems kept running through my mind years afterward. One day I made notes of the dramatic incidents and started to weave them into a continuous story. After polishing the first draft, I submitted it to the story department.

In the years following the release of *Night Key*, Pierce went on to write or co-write the stories for such movies as *Armored Car* (1937), *The Star Maker* (1939) with Bing Crosby and *The Powers Girl* (1943), among others.

A comfortable 21-day shooting schedule and a $175,000 budget did not assure a trouble-free production for *Night Key*. Any number of directors were announced to helm the project including Ralph Murphy, Arthur Lubin and Sidney Salkow. The final choice was Lloyd Corrigan, the familiar character actor who landed the assignment on the basis of having directed and co-written an Oscar-winning 1934 short, *La Cucaracha*.

For a seemingly small-scale and inauspicious undertaking, the picture was wracked with problems. The script was poorly prepared and halfway through shooting the picture an entirely different ending was devised, threatening to put the film over budget. Lloyd Corrigan proved to be an inexperienced and slow director. Karloff, one of the founders of the Screen Actors Guild, insisted that union rules be followed to the letter and declined to work more than eight hours a day. Much to the aggravation of the Front Office, the star wouldn't report to work during the day if he was required for night shooting. The production crawled along, finally wrapping on February 20, 1937, a full six days behind schedule and over $17,000 over budget.

According to studio publicity, Universal duplicated the headquarters of one of the major burglar alarm concerns. One of the features of the headquarters set was a huge control board containing 100 signals in actual operation.

Night Key is one of the more entertaining of Boris Karloff's vehicles in a generally lackluster period of his career. The actor was in the midst of fulfilling his old Warner Bros. contract which

Inventor Boris Karloff takes it on the jaw from tough guy Alan Baxter in *Night Key*.

started off promisingly with Michael Curtiz's excellent *The Walking Dead* (1936). Since then the studio was using him as a star character actor, shunting him from one low-budget film to the next. Although Karloff invariably contributed sincere, well-crafted performances, most notably as the wry Chinese warlord in *West of Shanghai* (1937) and as a surgeon wrongly accused of treason in *Devil's Island* (1940), these pictures ranked at the bottom rung of Warner's production ladder.

Production-wise, *Night Key* wasn't much of a step up but further indicated that Karloff was the rightful heir to Lon Chaney's title as "The Man of a Thousand Faces." After a decade of playing mostly morose roles in horror films and melodramas, the actor had a chance to add an almost folksy characterization to his repertoire. The story was a typical class-conscious '30s concoction concerning a down-on-his-luck character victimized by the system and ultimately exploited by crooks, white collar and otherwise. The film exudes a kind of cocky Roosevelt-era charm and optimism even when the protagonist is being pushed through the capitalist meat grinder because the audience knows he'll come out on top at the end. Like a bargain basement Frank Capra or Gregory LaCava, director Corrigan demonstrates a fresh, energetic ease with the material although obviously lacking sophistication in his camera set-ups and editing.

The film's genre trappings are peripheral aside from some eye-catching scientific gizmos. (Hardcore connoisseurs might see *Night Key* as Boris Karloff's answer to Lugosi's *Murder by Television* [1935].) An electrical ray-gun, a dead ringer to a similar weapon employed in *The Mask of Fu Manchu*, is used to ensure Karloff's escape from the gangster's hide-out. Earlier, Karloff devises a particularly nasty booby trap in which thug Ward Bond is slowly, painfully electrocuted. The " Key" itself is a particularly attractive piece of futuristic thirties hardware — an oversized handset with an array of dials and meters which hums impressively whenever Karloff switches it on. If *Night Key* was one of Universal's heavyweight horror movies, one could well imagine it becoming one of the most sought-after props from Hollywood's Golden Age.

Night Key is one of the first of many avuncular roles for Karloff whom at age 50 was playing at least 15 years his senior. Capped with a snow-white wig, Karloff is just about perfect as the kindly, seemingly doddering old man who could command both cunning and an ironclad will when the situation arises. It was very much a novelty role for the actor which came at a time when his off-camera penchants for growing flowers and reading bedtime stories for children weren't generally known outside the Hollywood community.

Despite his Santa-like portrayal, the studio wasn't hedging its bets in promoting the picture. Indeed, the poster artwork and publicity materials bury a nearly unrecognizable Karloff under a fearsome makeup and blatantly misrepresent his role as a master criminal holding a city at his mercy. An outright deception, true, but it's doubtful if it caused a ripple among moviegoers considering the picture's supporting feature status. Still, the sight of filmdom's leading Boogie Man doddering about in a paper party hat was not what audiences had in mind when they bought their tickets. The role so totally obliterates the actor's monster image, it wouldn't be out of the question to suggest Karloff in the role of Clarence, the angel looking for his wings in Frank Capra's *It's a Wonderful Life* (1946). If anything else, it would have made a terrific consolation prize for the actor's non-participation in the director's film adaptation of *Arsenic and Old Lace* (1944).

Karloff again shows his facility for handling complicated dialogue in a particularly fine example of dramatic stagecraft. After sabotaging his own security system while his daughter Jean Rogers is left to the mercy of the gangsters, Karloff blurts out the story to the police. Adroitly dispensing with a tricky, overly technical speech without missing a beat, the actor slowly savors the climactic line, "A light will go out!," referring to the huge illuminated switchboard at Samuel Hinds' corporate headquarters. It's a small moment but one that so expertly dramatizes the urgency of the situation that even the most casual viewer could not help but take note.

At 67 minutes, *Night Key* is a darn near perfect programmer, neatly constructed to go from straight drama in its opening reels, tilting towards comedy in the mid-section and then winding down into a relatively tense gangster melodrama. The bustling big city atmosphere is reasonably well-conveyed on the studio soundstage with the action culminating into a nicely-done Manhattan car chase.

Taking a break from playing Dale Arden to Buster Crabbe's Flash Gordon, Jean Rogers is a pert addition to Karloff's endless line of movieland daughters. As for working with the actor, Rogers was quoted in a press release as saying, "One swell thing about [Karloff], he never tries to hog scenes." Warren Hull, billed as J. Warren Hull here, is yet again the nominal hero, a year after performing the same function in Karloff's *The Walking Dead.* (The actor would return to Universal to play the title role in the 1941 serial *The Green Hornet Strikes Again.*) Samuel S. Hinds plays corporate thug Steve Ranger with all the ruthlessness and inner grit of a retired accountant. It's the sort of role Edward Arnold could play in his sleep but on the ever-genial Hinds, it's an uncomfortable fit. Ward Bond, still working his way into John Ford's stock company, does his usual dumb goon *shtick.* Alan Baxter is magnetic as The Kid, all the more so considering his eerie physical and vocal resemblance to a young Jack Nicholson. It's nice to see the usually wasted Frank Reicher in a small but conspicuous role as the mob's technical expert. Surrounded as he is by Bond and his fellow mugs, it's a halfway decent part with the actor exuding an air of erudition and quiet professionalism amid his unseemly compatriots.

Strictly a bread-and-butter picture, it's unlikely that *Night Key* did much to increase Universal's fortunes considering the come-and-go nature of B potboilers at the time. If anything the film probably plays better today than when it was released, its old-fashioned Hollywood spunk seeming far more inviting and far less ubiquitous. There's no apparent record of Karloff's own opinion of the film but one would like to think that the actor welcomed an opportunity for a light-steppin,' change-of-pace semi-comic role. The familiar theme of triumph and retribution would be revived in more traditional sinister shadings in his later Columbia mad scientist portrayals, particularly in *The Man They Could Not Hang* (1939) and *The Man With Nine Lives* (1940). *Night Key* serves up the same formula in an agreeable and quite irresistible fashion.

Critics' Corner

The fans who like excitement and melodrama will find the Central's newest thriller diverting and unusual. Though the cast is unsensational, it is pleasant and competent.—*The New York Daily Mirror*, April 19, 1937

The idea, with apologies to Wells and Co., is entertaining and incredible enough to be believed by persons with imagination. The amusing moments, for Karloff really has a sense of humor, are not squeezed to their last laugh, and gain from the restraint.... Karloff, in his new role, has many a welcome Hollywood part ahead of him and may eventually venture into light comedy.—*The Brooklyn Daily Eagle*, 1937, T.S.

We think you'll like the star of horror films as just a plain human being.... [R]ight intriguing though a bit on the believe-it-or-not side.... [A] pretty neat little picture.—*The New York Post*, April 19, 1937, Irene Thirer

A frequently exciting but generally disappointing thriller.... Relying more upon break-neck speed than subtlety or credibility.... [P]retty preposterous and juvenile. The acting is about par with the lines and the situations, although Alan Baxter makes "The Kid" stand out by the sinister quality of his quiet performance.—*The New York World-Telegram*, April 19, 1937

Under Lloyd Corrigan's efficient direction, *Night Key* is in the polished manner of the traditional Universal thriller, capably served throughout by enjoyable players.—*The New York Times*, April 19, 1937, John T. McManus

Rating: ★★½ Boris Karloff sheds the limitations imposed by A1 screen menace cataloguing to prove himself a top notcher in another field—versatility of performance.—*The New York Daily News*, April 19, 1937, Dorothy Masters

1938

The Black Doll

Released January 30, 1938. 66 minutes. A Crime Club Mystery. A Walter Futter Production. *Producer:* Irving Starr. *Director:* Otis Garrett. *Screenplay:* Harold Buckley. *Based on the novel by* William Edward Hayes. *Photography:* Stanley Cortez & Ira Morgan. *Editor:* Maurice Wright. *Assistant Director:* Phil Karlstein [Karlson]. *Art Director:* Ralph Berger. *Settings:* Emile Kuri. *Musical Director:* Charles Previn. *Production Manager:* Ben Hersh. *Sound Director:* Charles Carroll. *Gowns:* Vera West.

Donald Woods (*Nick Halstead*), Nan Grey (*Marian Rood*), Edgar Kennedy (*Sheriff Renick*), C. Henry Gordon (*Nelson Rood*), Doris Lloyd (*Laura Leland*), John Wray (*Walling*), Addison Richards (*Mallison*), Holmes Herbert (*Dr. Giddings*), William Lundigan (*Rex Leland*), Fred Malatesta (*Esteban*), Inez Palange (*Rosita*), Syd Saylor (*Red*), Arthur Hoyt (*Coroner*), John Harmon (*Cabbie*).

[A]n absorbing mystery story...
Wanda Hale, The New York Daily News,
February 6, 1938

The detective mystery, a Hollywood staple as popular as the horse opera, had its heyday in the '30s. Every studio, from the lofty MGM to the pennypinching Monogram, catered to fans of this genre. Gumshoes of all persuasions made the transition from page to silver screen. A few—Charlie Chan, Sherlock Holmes, Bulldog Drummond, Philo Vance, Ellery Queen, even a shrewd attorney with a detective's instincts named Perry Mason—walked off with movie series of their own.

In 1937, Universal struck a deal with the Crime Club, publishers of pulpy whodunits by such prolific writers as Jonathan Latimer. The studio was granted the right to select four of the 52 annually published novels for adaptation. Producer Irving Starr was put in charge of this unit, while former film cutter Otis Garrett frequently handled the directing chores.

Over the next couple of years, Universal released no less than ten Crime Club mysteries. According to the Universal publicity mill (always a dubious source of information), the club's legion of fans had a hand in selecting which novels or stories would be translated to celluloid.

(Unlike the Inner Sanctum series of the '40s, Universal got its material straight from the source rather than just borrowing the Crime Club banner to promote their own properties.) Advertising campaigns promoted by the studio were designed to ensnare the nation's audience of mystery and detective fiction and motion pictures. Tie-ins to the Crime Club books were a given; another gimmick dreamt up by the publicity department was to encourage filmgoers to organize their own local Crime Clubs to aid the police deter lawlessness (not to mention promote the latest series entry).

Evidently, the capers of Latimer's most popular gumshoe, the dapper Insp. Bill Crane, and his comic sidekick Doc Williams were favorites of readers, as they were the only regularly featured team of sleuths in the series. The first in the Crane-Williams "trilogy" was *The Westland Case* (based on the Jonathan Latimer novel, *Headed for a Hearse*), a formularized B with all the standard ingredients: Red herrings, brassy dames (Barbara Pepper doing a shameless Mae West rip-off), valuable witnesses dropping like flies, and the inevitable eleventh hour round-up of all the suspects. Preston Foster and Frank Jenks were cast as the wisecracking New York City investigators summoned to Chicago to save an innocent man, Robert Westland (Theodore Von Eltz), charged with murdering his wife, from the electric chair. Foster's Bill Crane seems patterned after William Powell's Nick Charles, agreeably tipsy but right on the money when it came time to charm the ladies or uncover clues that everyone else involved in solving the case overlooked. (Whoever first fostered the notion that inebriation is synonymous with suavity should have been locked up for a month with Lee Tracy and Ted Healy.) Released on October 31, 1937, *The Westland Case* was directed by Christy Cabanne. The mystery-solving duo of Crane-Williams were brought back for *The Lady*

Poster for *The Black Doll*, second entry in Universal's Crime Club series.

Thomas Jackson, Alexander Leftwich, Stephanie Howard, George Meeker and Charles Murphy are swept up in the mystery of the first Crime Club thriller, *The Westland Case*.

in the Morgue (1938) and *The Last Warning* (1938).

Whereas Universal's Inner Sanctum pictures are basically straight murder melodramas masquerading as shockers, the Crime Club mysteries made no such pretense. But, occasionally, as in the second entry, *The Black Doll*, elements of horror creep into the corners of the plot.

Based on the novel of the same name by William Edward Hayes, *The Black Doll* begins most intriguingly: Its dark-and-stormy-night setting shows genuine promise. The quiet country estate, where all of the suspects are conveniently housed under one roof, provides a striking departure from the Big City background of *The Westland Case*. Otis Garrett, making his series directorial debut, sustains an aura of apprehension in the early reels. Suspects are introduced in a slow, deliberate fashion. An element of the supernatural is brought in early on but it's quickly dismissed as it becomes obvious the mayhem is being committed by a garden variety criminal. The mystery itself is an overly-complicated business; the viewer's eyes glaze as the muddled motivations of the assorted characters are unveiled.

The victim-to-be is the misanthropic Nelson Rood (C. Henry Gordon), a ruthless businessman who gained his fortune by plundering an ore-rich Mexican mine. Rood, who literally oozes duplicity, eliminated one of his partners, Knox Barrows, at the time the mine was discovered, and double-crossed the other two.

Every member of Rood's household has good reason to hate him. He dominates his sister, Laura Leland (Doris Lloyd), and was instrumental in ruining her chance for happiness with the man she loves, Dr. Giddings (Holmes Herbert). Her son, Rex (William Lundigan), fears that his spiteful uncle will press charges against him for forging the businessman's signature on a check to cover gambling losses. Rood's Latin servants, Esteban (Fred Malatesta) and Rosita (Inez Palange), fear and despise him. His estranged business partners, Wallings (John Wray) and Mallison (Addison Richards), overnight guests at the house, don't trust him. Only Rood's daughter Marian (Nan Grey) loves him, but even she is miffed when he forbids her boyfriend Nick Halstead (Donald Woods) from invading his property.

Rood is visibly shaken when he finds a crudely made Mexican black doll lying on his desk. The last time Rood laid eyes on such a doll (the natives believe it is a portent of doom), he flung it into a ravine after disposing of Knox Barrows' body. Has Barrows come back from the dead 15 years later to avenge himself on his murderer? In one particularly well-staged scene, Rood is knifed in the back as he stands in the doorway of Marian's bedroom (the murder is glimpsed in the reflection of her vanity mirror). The killer's calling card, the black doll, is found lying opposite Rood's corpse.

Conveniently enough, Nick reveals he was once a private eye and begins to collect alibis. He is always two steps ahead of the local sheriff, Renick (Edgar Kennedy), who couldn't recognize a clue if it hit him dead on. Humor certainly has its place in mystery and horror films when it alleviates tension and suspense momentarily and then retreats into the background. When comedy oversteps its bounds and disturbs the flow of the plot, it does a film irreparable harm. *The Black Doll* is a case in point. The witless antics of Edgar Kennedy's buffoonish country sheriff shatter the film's somber mood and destroy its credibility. When Renick isn't putting his foot in his mouth, he's stumbling into furniture and upsetting any evidence Nick turns up. A veteran of both the Mack Sennett and Hal Roach schools of classic comedy, Kennedy has a field day indulging in his broadest trademark routines. One can only wonder if the script was constructed around the comedian from the get-go.

Mallison, labeled a prime suspect, is found stuffed in a closet, strangled to death; a black doll tucked in his pocket. An attempt is made on Marian's life, but Esteban intervenes and is shot through the heart for his trouble. Halstead concludes that the murderer sent Nelson Rood the doll to frighten him into thinking his two partners were planning to kill him. Both of them knew he murdered Barrows so he could marry the man's wife. When Rood later came down with jungle fever, he spilled his guts to the attending physician, whose identity is unknown.

The last-reel gathering-of-the-suspects scene is a real hoot. As Nick serves up his specialty, scrambled eggs and hash browns, he fits together the last pieces of the puzzle. Rood was not Marian's father after all, Knox Barrows was. Rood raised her as his own after marrying the dead man's widow. Nick unmasks Giddings as the mystery physician, and the killer. Giddings murdered Rood to clear the way for his marrying Laura. That act would have put the family fortune within his grasp. Only Marian stood in his way. Giddings pulls out a revolver from under the tablecloth. He fires a couple of shots, but is apprehended by Renick's men. Laura thanks Halstead profusely for getting her son off the hook. She doesn't seem the least bit disturbed that beloved has been unmasked as a murderer and a fortune hunter.

Donald Woods and Nan Grey are pleasant enough juvenile leads, while the supporting cast is bolstered by the comforting presence of such old pros as Addison Richards, Doris Lloyd and Holmes Herbert. A young William Lundigan does an adequate job as Lloyd's irresponsible son.

Though he is seen on-screen for a relatively brief amount of time, C. Henry Gordon steals the show as Nelson Rood, The Man Everyone Loves to Hate. Born in New York City (and not some exotic locale as his on-screen demeanor often seems to indicate), Gordon prospered on the stage and in over 50 pictures. The mild-manner, cultivated actor, who was once quoted as saying he didn't have the heart to go fishing because "fish have feelings," attained cinematic immortality as the mass murderer of women and children, Arab potentate Surat Khan, who is skewered by Errol Flynn's lance at the climax of *The Charge of the Light Brigade* (1936). Gordon's life and career were cut tragically short on December 3, 1940, when he died from the effects of an emergency leg amputation.

Musical director Charles Previn borrows liberally from previous scores written by Karl Hajos, Heinz Roemheld and Franz Waxman, with gratifying results. The main title is a swipe from the score of *Bride of Frankenstein*, while themes from *WereWolf of London*, *Dracula's Daughter*, *The Raven* and *The Invisible Man* are sprinkled throughout. For fans of the classic Universal horror scores, this aural embellishment is an unexpected but welcomed treat.

Evidently pleased with the box office performance of these inexpensively produced second features, Universal added eight more titles to its Crime Club series over the next two years; *The Lady in the Morgue* (1938), *Danger on the Air* (1938), *The Last Express* (1938), *The Last Warning* (1938), *Gambling Ship* (1939), *Mystery of the White Room* (1939), *Inside Information* (1939) and *The Witness Vanishes* (1939). For details on these entries, consult Appendix I at the back of this book.

Critics' Corner

Rating: ★★★ [W]ill ... stir your admiration, wrack your nerves, tickle your funny bone and, if you don't watch out, deflate your pride in your sleuthing ability.... [A]n absorbing mystery story...—*The New York Daily News*, February 6, 1938, Wanda Hale

If we were a member of the Crime Club (and we don't even know what the Crime Club is) we'd blackball any mystery story that aspired to reach our membership unless the murder or murders were committed by (1) the amateur detective himself, (2) the ingénue ... (3) the comic relief, including even Edgar Kennedy, or (4) the author, who, in most murder stories, we think, is really the guiltiest party.—*The New York Times*, February 7, 1938, B.R. Crisler

A combination of suspenseful mystery and comedy that furnishes a lot of laughs makes this an enjoyable murder picture of the regular program variety. The piece is handled in a light vein throughout and therefore too much importance cannot be given to the fact that the character of the hick sheriff, which Edgar Kennedy plays, is overdrawn. Harold Buckley's screenplay furnishes some clever dialogue and novel twists and Otto Garnett's direction gives the affair a fast-moving gait.—*The Film Daily*, January 25, 1938

This latest of the Crime Club series cannot make up its mind whether to be a mystery or a farce. Harold Buckley's screenplay is excellent, but it is difficult to understand how the presence of low comedy, which borders on actual farce, can be justified by a director in a picture dealing with murder.... [Kennedy] was obviously directed to play for laughs and did so very successfully.—*The Hollywood Reporter*, January 19, 1938

While its keynote is murder mystery, [the script] injects considerable comedy into the situations, alleviating to some degree a possible unfavorable audience reaction to the three murders whose occurrence are marked by the appearance of a black doll. Red herrings, typical of this type of story, swim throughout the unfolding of the picture, virtually every character having an opportunity to point accusing fingers at one another.—*The Motion Picture Herald*, January 22, 1938, Vance King

The Missing Guest

Released August 12, 1938. 68 minutes. *Associate Producer:* Barney A. Sarecky. *Director:* John Rawlins. *Screenplay:* Charles Martin & Paul Perez. *Based on the story* Secret of the Blue Room *by* Erich Philippi. *Photography:* Milton Krasner. *Art Director:* Jack Otterson. *Associate Art Director:* N.V. Timchenko. *Editor:* Frank Gross. *Assistant Cutter:* R. Davis. *Music Director:* Charles Previn. *Sound Supervisor:* Bernard B. Brown. *Technician:* Robert Pritchard. *Sound Mixer:* Joe Lapis. *Assistant Director:* Charles Gould. *Second Assistant Director:* Jack Bernhard. *Second Camera:* Maury Gertsman. *Assistant Cameraman:* John Mehl. *Wardrobe:* B. Macreary. *Hairdresser:* B. Preditty. *Script Clerk:* Maude Allen. *Grip:* George Schuman. *Props:* Dan Fish. *Best Boy:* S. Tenny. *Gaffer:* John Brooks. *Still Photographer:* Roman Freulich.

Paul Kelly (*"Scoop" Hanlon*), Constance Moore (*Stephanie "Steve" Kirkland*), William Lundigan (*Larry Dearden*), Edwin Stanley (*Dr. Carroll*), Selmer Jackson (*Frank Baldrich*), Billy Wayne (*"Vic"*), George Cooper (*"Jake"*), Patrick J. Kelly (*Edwards*), Florence Wix (*Linda Baldrich*), Harlan Briggs (*Frank Kendall*), Pat C. Flick (*Inventor*), Guy Usher (*Police Insp. McDonald*), Margo Yoder (*Maid*), Hooper Atchley (*Business Manager*), Michael Slade (*Kendall's Assistant*), John Harmon, George Ovey (*Gatekeepers*), Thomas Carr, Allen Fox, Billy Engle (*Men*), Myrtis Crinley (*Woman*), Frank McCarroll (*Oscar*), Leonard Sues (*Office Boy*), Ray Parker (*Wolf*).

> Every outdated [haunted house] situation and piece of business is included—not only included, but embarrassingly highlighted.—
> —Variety, *September 14, 1938*

Mile-a-minute wisecracks and inane humor stand in for atmosphere and chills in *The Missing Guest*, a dismal mystery-comedy that serves up none of either. It's one of those particularly awful little movies that almost seems to work in reverse: The scenes that are supposed to be scary are almost funny while the comedy relief interludes are so forced and appalling that the thought of people spending tens of thousands of dollars to commit this stuff to film is almost scary. A picture with nothing for everybody, *The Missing Guest* has to be one of the worst Universal mysteries of the '30s.

The Missing Guest was the first of two remakes of Universal's 1933 *Secret of the Blue Room*. Revamped, updated and Americanized, *Guest* discards the elements which made the Erich Philippi story work the first time around. Gone are the atmosphere of mystery, the European charm and the attractive roster of players; replacing them are low-brow jokes, sight gags and an offensive hero named "Scoop" Hanlon (Paul Kelly), a *Daily Blade* reporter who has been demoted to writing a column of beauty hints because of his unreliability and his penchant for mixing women with newsprint. When his boss (Harlan Briggs) learns that the Baldrich mansion on the South Shore of Long Island is being reopened, he assigns "Scoop" to inveigle his way into the house and spend a night in the haunted Blue Room where Sam Kirkland died under mysterious circumstances 20 years before. "Scoop" is reluctant since the room has a long history of mysterious deaths, but finally accepts the job.

At the Baldrich mansion, a masquerade party is in full swing. Hosting the event are Sam Kirkland's widow Linda (Florence Wix), her new husband Frank Baldrich (Selmer Jackson) and her daughter Stephanie (Constance Moore). Costumed as a ghost, Larry Dearden (William Lundigan), a would-be suitor of Stephanie's, disrupts the festivities with a ghoulishly staged entrance (duplicated in Universal's *next Secret of the Blue Room* remake, *Murder in the Blue Room*). All the party guests shake in their boots, and there are even screams, when Larry walks into the room with a sheet over his head *à la* a four-year-old's conception of a ghost, even though this is a costume party. These are the jokes, folks.

Dancing with Stephanie, Larry proposes for the umpteenth time but she has no romantic interest in him and politely turns him down once again. The party is disrupted a second time when the lights go out and a piano inexplicably plays by itself.

To gain entry to the house, "Scoop" crashes his car into the gates. Claiming to have lost control and feigning an ankle injury, he presents himself to the occupants of the house as a psychic researcher, figuring that this may get him into the Blue Room. Frank Baldrich quickly sees through the deception and "Scoop" is ejected. Later, Larry insists on spending the night in the Blue Room. Over the objections of Baldrich and longtime family physician Dr. Carroll (Edwin Stanley), the young man gets his way.

In the morning, it's discovered that Larry has vanished from the room; an open window overlooking rocky ocean surf suggests an accident or suicide. "Scoop," who sneaked back into the house during the night, is found and detained by Baldrich, who sends for private investigators to look into the mystery.

Private eyes "Vic" (Billy Wayne) and "Jake" (George Cooper) are moronic ex-jailbirds who search and rob the house while looking for clues. Dr. Carroll surprises Stephanie with the news that Larry was her half-brother; her father Sam Kirkland had fallen in love with the woman who became Larry's mother years before. Stephanie takes the news hard (too hard, considering she never knew her father and didn't love Larry anyway), and "Scoop" consoles the weeping girl.

The next morning, when the shot-dead body of Dr. Carroll is found on the Blue Room floor, Baldrich finally sends for the police. "Scoop" discovers that most of the spooky stuff that's been going on (including the self-playing piano) was engineered by Edwards, the butler (Patrick J. Kelly); Edwards confesses that the late Dr. Carroll paid him to pull the eerie pranks.

"Scoop" finds a secret entranceway in an exterior wall that leads from the garden into a hidden passage. A shadowy figure stalks "Scoop" in the passage and gunshots are exchanged. The mystery figure is Larry Dearden, who as he lies fatally wounded explains that he found the secret passage the night he slept in the Blue Room, and hoped to use it to trap his father's murderer. Dr. Carroll, a suspect in Sam Kirkland's slaying, fell into Larry's trap and confessed at gunpoint; Larry killed him. Larry himself now expires, the ghoulish legend of a "haunted" Blue Room dying with him.

In the original *Secret of the Blue Room*, the menace and the mystery were largely confined to the blue salon; there was an eerie quality to the scenes set in that quiet, frozen-in-time little room as well as a suspicion early on that perhaps supernatural forces really were in play. *Secret* also benefited from its lonely and unspecified foreign locale, the milieu in which that type of story probably works best. This is all dispensed with in *The Missing Guest*: The Baldrich mansion is the next thing to a low-end amusement park

William Lundigan is unmasked as the culprit in the Blue Room mystery *The Missing Guest.* Left to right: Guy Usher, Lundigan, Billy Wayne, Constance Moore, Paul Kelly.

funhouse for kids, with pianos and organs playing themselves, sheet-clad ghosts peeking through windows and spectral Halloween voices oo-oooo-oooo-ing in the night.

The most annoying thing about *Missing Guest* is that it's cursed with Universal's peculiar brand of painful comic relief; it pervades the picture from one end to the other, and we are never safe from it. "Scoop"'s editor is a wiseguy whose office is open to every loony inventor and his crackpot contraptions.* Most of the major characters are introduced while in their masquerade costumes (Stephanie as Bo-Peep, Dr. Carroll as the tail end of a horse, etc.); at one point there's even a big closeup of Dr. Carroll's horse's ass. "Scoop," who dominates the picture, is a cocky and self-satisfied jerk, the perfect hero for the kind of picture where a pushy manner and a wise mouth are equated with brains. But every character looks good compared to "Vic" and "Jake," the ex-cons who invade the house in the guise of private eyes. These Ritz Brothers wannabes barge in and out of rooms, boss people around and stay even after the real police have ordered them off the premises. For 21st century audiences, this is all "Oh, shoot me *now*" stuff.

The movie does at least have a legit-looking "haunted house." There's something persuasive about the look of the place: The shadowy nooks, the narrow staircases and cramped hallways and the cobwebby secret passageway. Although we never get the impression of a large house,† it's still a fine backdrop for a goosebumpy B. Now enter director John Rawlins and

**On the shelf of the editor's office is a model rocketship perhaps left over from a* Flash Gordon *serial.*

†*Like the owners of all "haunted houses" with secret passageways and hidden rooms, the Baldriches apparently never wonder why the house is so much smaller on the inside than the outside, or why whole sections of the house have no windows!*

a gang of un-lifelike smart alecks, grouches and nincompoops enacting a dud screenplay, and the mood is spoiled. *WereWolf of London* music underscores some of the Blue Room scenes; Lili's theme from *Dracula's Daughter* is also recycled.

Nothing impressive goes on in the acting department. Paul Kelly, who plays "Scoop," is the average B producer's grotesque idea of a sharp newspaperman: He sits in his office banging out stories with his hat on, treats everything like a big joke, and tries to one-up everything everybody says to him. Twice he's told (by different characters) "You're not being funny," the thought foremost in the minds of most audience members too, but he never takes the hint.

Constance Moore is pretty but unconvincing, and (like Anne Gwynne in *Murder in the Blue Room*) never gives the impression that she's really much concerned about what's going on. Selmer Jackson, usually an avuncular actor, plays an uncharacteristic hothead with a nasty disposition and a fetish for holding Paul Kelly at gunpoint throughout too much of the picture. Up-and-coming William Lundigan's best scene comes at the "big finish" of this whodunit, when he reveals that he *killed* the guy who-done-it, off-camera, and so much earlier in the movie that you've already half-forgotten that other character! As accurately reported by *Variety*'s Hobe, Harlan Briggs and Pat C. Flick ("Scoop"'s editor and a wacky inventor, respectively) are "more than necessarily objectionable," and Billy Wayne and George Cooper ("Vic" and "Jake") "are trying too hard to be actors."

Universal was no doubt happy with *The Missing Guest*: It was made on a quickie schedule and budgeted at a paltry $80,400. Production went smoothly, it wrapped up on time and, thanks to director Rawlins' strict shooting and some script changes, it came in more than ten percent under budget, at $72,000. Rawlins was from all accounts a nice, easygoing fella, but it's clear after watching several of his pictures that the man was more interested in impressing studio execs than moviegoers. *The Missing Guest* probably did find favor at the Universal Front Office, but you have to wonder if a soul alive in 1938 came home from the theater and said he was glad he saw it.

Critics' Corner

Feeble whodunit for bottom billing in the duals. It hasn't a visible selling angle.... If possible, the production and direction are worse than the writing.—*Variety*, September 14, 1938, Hobe

The cast does as little with it as it deserves, and that is little enough.—*The New York Times*, September 7, 1938, Frank S. Nugent

A high tension is maintained throughout the plot.... Not a heavy-weight mystery thriller, *The Missing Guest* is an amusing one. It has life, laughs and surprises.—*The New York Daily Mirror*, September 7, 1938, Bland Johaneson

Rating: ★★ Director John Rawlins made the mistake of trying to relieve the tension ... by injecting a lot of comedy into the proceedings. But it is such feeble fooling that it entirely destroys its purpose and merely serves to shatter whatever illusion the murder and the mystery might otherwise hold for the audience.—*The New York Daily News*, September 7, 1938, Kate Cameron

[I]f you know your mystery stories at all, you must know by now how unfunny a couple of presumably comic detectives can be when they get mixed up with spooks, sliding panels and clutching hands.... [F]or the most part, it is a feeble and fumbling attempt at being eerie and funny....—*The New York World-American*, 1938

1939

Son of Frankenstein

Released January 13, 1939. 99 minutes. A Rowland V. Lee Production. *Producer-Director:* Rowland V. Lee. *Original Screenplay:* Willis Cooper. *Suggested by the novel* Frankenstein; or the Modern Prometheus *by* Mary Wollstonecraft Shelley. *Photography:* George Robinson. *Editor:* Ted Kent. *Assistant Director:* Fred Frank. *Art Director:* Jack Otterson. *Associate Art Director:* Richard H. Riedel. *Music:* Frank Skinner. *Musical Director:* Charles Previn. *Musical Arrangement:* Hans J. Salter. *Special Photographic Effects:* John P. Fulton. *Set Decorator:* Russell A. Gausman. *Sound Supervisor:* Bernard B. Brown. *Technician:* William Hedgcock. *Makeup:* Jack P. Pierce. *Gowns:* Vera West.

Basil Rathbone (*Baron Wolf von Frankenstein*),

Boris Karloff (*The Monster*), Bela Lugosi (*Ygor*), Lionel Atwill (*Insp. Krogh*), Josephine Hutchinson (*Baroness Elsa von Frankenstein*), Donnie Dunagan (*Peter von Frankenstein*), Emma Dunn (*Amelia*), Edgar Norton (*Thomas Benson*), Perry Ivins (*Fritz*), Lawrence Grant (*Burgomaster*), Michael Mark (*Ewald Neumüller*), Lionel Belmore (*Emil Lang*), Gustav von Seyffertitz, Lorimer Johnson, Tom Ricketts, Russ Powell (*Burghers*), Caroline Cooke (*Frau Neumüller*), Clarence Wilson (*Dr. Berger*), Otto Hoffman (*Station Master*), Ward Bond, Harry Cording (*Gendarmes at Gate*), Betty Chay, Jack Harris. *Deleted from final print:* Dwight Frye (*Angry Villager*).

Movie producers attribute the public's current thirst for terror to the war scares of unsettled Europe.... Death rays, space ships, disintegration beams and other weirdly lethal instruments are being built in every property shop. "Nightmares for everybody" is Hollywood's slogan for a more horrible 1939.
—Look *magazine's New Movie Preview*

Horror film lovers could not have wished for a sweeter gift to usher in the 1939 New Year than *Son of Frankenstein*. Not only did this long-awaited second sequel to the 1931 James Whale classic boast a top-flight cast, sterling production values, and mounting on the same lavish scale as its predecessors; more importantly, *Son of Frankenstein* heralded the end of Hollywood's reluctant ban on horror pictures. All that it had taken to lift the two-year prohibition was the promise of big bucks (the only cause that ever moved Tinsel Town to do *anything*).

Wanting to get back into horror movie production again in 1938, Universal first thought about remaking *The Old Dark House*, then *The Raven* (which would reteam Karloff and Lugosi, the studio announced). Instead, the screen's top terrornauts were paired in Universal's exciting new take on the Mary Wollstonecraft Shelley warhorse.

The catalyst for this decision was the tremendous public response to a limited run, triple horror bill comprised of *Dracula, Frankenstein* and RKO's *The Son of Kong* at Los Angeles' Regina Theatre on Wilshire Boulevard. The tiny 659-seat grindhouse played the thrill-packed threesome for five solid weeks to capacity business, prompting Universal to reissue their two blockbusters on one program in theaters across the nation. The gamble paid off. Universal netted close to $500,000 as a result of rentals and percentage deals on the revivals. Shortly after the release of *Son of Frankenstein* in January 1939, Columbia, Warner Bros., Paramount and the Poverty Row penny-pinchers beefed up their own production schedules with an assortment of B-blood curdlers. Horror films were *in* once again.

Son of Frankenstein is the last of the great Frankenstein films. Grandiose in scope, magnificent in design, it supplanted the quaint romanticism and delicate fantasy flavoring of *Bride of Frankenstein* with a stark, grimly expressionistic approach to horror. (Whale's influence *is* felt, however, in the screenplay's rich vein of black humor.) The performances complement the material beautifully, from Basil Rathbone's floridly theatric baron to the impassioned portrayals of Bela Lugosi and Lionel Atwill, ranking amongst the finest of their careers. Only Boris Karloff's Monster comes up short of expectations, not through any fault of the actor, but in the manner in which the role was written. With *Son of Frankenstein*, Shelley's immortal creation began to assume the status of a supporting player whose activities took an increasingly secondary role to his human confederates.

James Whale's successor was Rowland Vance Lee. Active in the movie business since the age of 19, the 45-year-old producer-director had been enjoying the royal treatment at Universal for his expeditious handling of the frothy Constance Bennett comedy *Service de Luxe* (the 1938 film that introduced Vincent Price to moviegoers). A native of Ohio, Lee was destined for a career in Wall Street (as per his family's wishes), but his love of theater and acting lured him to Broadway and summer stock. Lee appeared in several Hollywood pictures, but it was his association with Thomas Ince that turned the tide of his career. The veteran picturemaker offered the ambitious young man a choice between acting and directing. "I decided I wanted to get on the other side, and give those directions instead of taking them," Lee revealed in an interview.

Racking up an impressive list of silent film credits (*A Thousand to One* [1920], *Alice Adams* [1923], *The Man Without a Country* [1925]), Lee made the transition to talking pictures without any difficulty. He directed Warner Oland in his

"He could have crushed me—as I would have crushed an eggshell!" Basil Rathbone and Boris Karloff in *Son of Frankenstein.*

most famous non–Charlie Chan Oriental role in Paramount's *The Mysterious Dr. Fu Manchu* (1929) and its follow-up, *The Return of Dr Fu Manchu* (1930). *Zoo in Budapest* (1933), considered one of Lee's finest films, made many of the year's Top Ten lists. With *The Count of Monte Cristo* (1934), Lee found his niche in motion pictures: Producing and directing lavish costume pictures. He followed this highly popular film adaptation of the Dumas story with screen versions of *The Three Musketeers* and *Cardinal Richelieu*, both released in 1935, and continued to make extravagant costume films well into the '40s.

Son of Frankenstein, Lee's second film for Universal, picks up the continuing saga of the Frankenstein family years after the deaths of the Monster and his Bride in the ruins of the old watchtower. Baron Heinrich (formerly Henry) von Frankenstein has died, leaving behind a legacy of hatred in the hearts of his fellow countrymen. His son Wolf (Basil Rathbone), an American college professor, becomes the victim of their contempt when he returns to the village of Frankenstein with his wife Elsa (Josephine Hutchinson) and young son Peter (Donnie Dunagan) to claim his inheritance.

Settling into the sprawling medieval castle, Wolf is visited by Insp. Krogh (Lionel Atwill) of the district police. Krogh intimates that the evidence gathered from a recent spate of hideous murders points towards the Monster. "But he was destroyed years ago," Wolf insists. "Perhaps," the policeman responds cryptically. Wolf learns the reason for Krogh's cynical attitude: As a boy, he had his arm torn from his body by the marauding Monster. A curious-looking prosthesis now takes its place.

While exploring the ruins of his father's lab (now a structure situated a stone's throw from the estate), Wolf is almost crushed to death by a boulder dislodged by a bearded hermit. The shaggy stranger identifies himself as Ygor (Bela Lugosi), a blacksmith who was hanged for body snatching years before but survived the ordeal. A twisted neck punctuated by a protruding bone is mute evidence of Ygor's fantastic story.

Learning that Wolf is a doctor, Ygor leads him to the Frankenstein family crypt. There, lying on a slab in a deep coma, lies the Frankenstein Monster (Boris Karloff). Ygor emotionally explains that his friend was struck down by lightning while "hunting." Seizing the opportunity to carry on his father's great work, and perhaps salvage his legacy, Wolf attempts to revive the Monster via electric current, but fails. The Monster slips back into his coma again.

It isn't long before another rash of brutal murders stuns the community of Frankenstein. When little Peter claims he was visited in his room by a "giant," Wolf realizes the Monster has returned to life. He confronts Ygor who confesses that he has been using the Monster to kill off the town burghers who had sentenced him to hang years before.

To quell the fury of the understandably irate villagers, Krogh promises to arrest Wolf and charge him with murder. He arrives at the castle minutes after the agitated baron has shot Ygor to death for attempting to murder him. Unfazed by Krogh's threats to extract a confession, Wolf defiantly challenges the policeman to a game of darts.

The Monster, meanwhile, has discovered Ygor's corpse. He goes berserk, wrecks the lab, and charges through a secret passageway into the castle, hell bent on revenge. He abducts Peter and leads the child into the lab, with Wolf and Krogh hot on his heels. The policeman confronts his lifelong adversary for the first time since their fateful encounter years before. Almost instinctively, the Monster grabs the inspector by his false arm and tears it from the shoulder harness, waving it madly like a club. Swinging from a ceiling chain, Wolf topples the roaring Monster into a pit of flaming sulphur. (The scream was first heard when the Monster bellows in agony over the corpse of Ygor; an echo effect was added for the same scream as he descended into the sulphur pit. The scream also "stood in" for J. Carrol Naish's at the climax of *House of Frankenstein*, the suicide's in *The Spider Woman* and possibly Jack Kelly's in 1955's *Cult of the Cobra*.)

Hailed by the villagers as a hero (rather inexplicably, as his revitalization of the Monster was directly responsible for three more deaths!), Wolf and his family return to America, deeding the castle and properties to the people of Frankenstein to do with as they please.

The earliest mention of *Son of Frankenstein* in the trades came on August 29, 1938, when *The Hollywood Reporter* revealed that Universal was negotiating a two-picture deal with Boris Karloff to appear in two new horror pictures, the first of which would be a sequel to *Frankenstein*. The Regina Theatre success story had indicated to Universal that the moviegoing public was in the mood for horror films once again.

In the September 2 edition of the *Reporter*, Universal announced that it would make *After Frankenstein* as the first of its two Karloff horror starrers. News of the casting of Rathbone and Lugosi came on October 20, and on October 24, Universal announced in the *Reporter* that its plans to team Karloff, Lugosi and Peter Lorre went overboard when the deal to borrow Lorre from Fox fell through. According to the release, Lorre turned thumbs down because of the proposed billing and because he left the horror field when he became Mr. Moto and didn't want to take a chance "on another meanie." A more unlikely candidate cannot be imagined. It's far easier to visualize Lorre in cahoots with Ygor and the Monster than to picture him as a dedicated scientist, husband and father. Claude Rains, who had previously been a candidate for the Pretorius role in *Bride of Frankenstein*, was also briefly considered for the part of Wolf.

The creator of the spooky radio show *Lights Out*, Willis Cooper submitted an original *Son of Frankenstein* script that was rejected in its initial form. Dated October 20, 1938, the screenplay began with Wolf, together with wife Else and young son Erwin, arriving at Castle Frankenstein to claim his inheritance. His father's will contains a bizarre clause which stipulates that the Monster must have remained out of commission for at least 25 years following the watchtower explosion before the inheritance may be claimed!

Cooper makes frequent reference to *Bride of Frankenstein* in this treatment. While searching through the ruins of the lab, Wolf happens upon the skeletal remains of Dr. Pretorius, the Bride and the homunculi, but not the Monster.

An excerpt Wolf reads from his father's diary on the temperament of his creation is especially telling: "We are certain that much of the Monster's evil-doing is the result of loneliness; it must be a terrible thing to be the only one of one's kind in the world."

Having survived the explosion and seeming none the worse for it, the Monster emerges from the ruins and kills a gendarme on a forest path during a violent storm. His lust for blood unfulfilled, he breaks into a peasant hut and murders its inhabitants. (Apparently the Monster's rejection by his mate and the generally despicable treatment he suffered in *Bride of Frankenstein* has vanquished any vestige of humanity left in him.)

A diabolic plans forms in his mind. He desecrates the tomb of his creator and steals the scientific records that were buried with him. Confronting Wolf in the lab, he grunts, "Now—you—make—friend—for—me." (Cooper has given the Monster ample dialogue in this draft.) He threatens to kill Else and little Erwin if Wolf doesn't obey his orders.

Wolf's antagonist in this version of the script is Insp. Neumüller, not Krogh (the Neumüller name was later swiped for Michael Mark's burgher). Neumüller didn't suffer the loss of an arm in his childhood encounter with the Monster; he lost a dad instead. The inspector understandably bears the Frankenstein family a deep-seated grudge. Learning that Wolf has been aiding the Monster, Neumüller vows, "I will pursue this Monster of the Frankensteins to the ends of the earth. I will crush it, destroy it utterly. I will have no mercy. And you, Wolf Frankenstein, listen to me. If you hinder me in any way whatsoever, if you fail for one minute to aid me when I shall call on you ... then you are a murderer yourself, and I shall see you die for it!"

The Monster attacks a military outpost, kills a gendarme, and delivers the man's corpse to Wolf. "It's useless! Worthless! You've spoiled the brain!" Wolf scolds the creature. Learning of Frankenstein's grisly intentions, Neumüller mutters in disgust, "Like father, like son."

In a fit of desperation, the Monster steals Erwin and takes him to the lab. Just as the Monster is about to perform brain surgery on the child, Wolf storms in. Neumüller and his forces polish the creature off with a round of bullets. He falls into a watery pit and drowns. For good measure, Neumüller tosses a hand grenade into the pit after him!

Cooper (or allegedly Lee himself) salvaged the principal characters from this draft and built a new plot around them. All of the alterations were for the better. Neumüller became the false-armed Krogh. His antagonism towards Wolf was toned down. Wolf was every bit as dedicated to the goal of vindicating his father's memory in the final shooting script. Elsa's (formerly Else) displeasure towards her husband's work wasn't as emphatic as the first version demonstrated. ("Would you be willing to have my weary body brought back from the grave to walk with you again?" she countered in response to Wolf's unbridled enthusiasm.)

A writer with his roots in radio, Willis Cooper flooded the first draft with superfluous talk—between the servants, between the soldiers staking out the Monster and, most irritating of all, between little Erwin and everyone else. Fortunately, the writer's revision kept the child (now called Peter) in the background. (We are spared a scene in which the little boy mimics the gendarmes marching before the castle, and another in which his nanny is dressed down for allowing her ward to vent his vivid imagination.) But the most important changes were eliminating the Monster's ability to speak and providing him with a comrade, Ygor, one of the most colorful characters in the entire Frankenstein series. (The broken-necked blacksmith comes back from the dead once again, only to suffer an ignominious demise in the third sequel, *The Ghost of Frankenstein*.)

Determined that *Son of Frankenstein* have the same lavish mounting as his earlier productions, Lee took advantage of his good standing with the studio brass and beefed the $250,000 budget up to $300,000. A generous 27-day shooting schedule was planned. At one point, he considered filming the picture in color, but this idea was ditched on account of the poor effect of Karloff's makeup in George Robinson's color tests.

No one foresaw the monumental difficulties Lee would have in getting the film completed in time for the preview. Though *Son of Frankenstein* officially began production on October 17, 1938, shooting was delayed until Wednesday, November 9, due to producer-director's dissat-

Baron Wolf von Frankenstein (Rathbone) ponders his father's legacy as butler Benson (Edgar Norton) stands by.

isfaction with Cooper's screenplay. As the cast was already on salary, the studio gave orders for Lee to forge ahead, script or no script. The budget was escalated to half a million dollars, a sure indication of the confidence that the front office had in the new horror film's box office potential. Based on Lee's sterling performance on *Service de Luxe*, Universal's top execs assumed that he would bring the production in on schedule. To put it mildly, their hopes were premature.

Son of Frankenstein's intricate special effects

slowed down the pace of the shoot. Lee worked continuously on the revised script. The actors received freshly written pages only minutes before scenes were set up to be shot. Without a complete script, it was impossible to plan a feasible schedule and come up with a realistic budget. The wrap date was pushed back from December 10 to December 17.

Up-and-coming stage and screen actress Josephine Hutchinson had the unenviable task of supporting the Titans of Terror, and acquitted herself admirably in the role of Baroness Elsa von Frankenstein. She had been discovered by MGM czar Louis B. Mayer and was signed to a contract by him. "The studio had some properties they had bought for Helen Hayes, for which they thought I was right," Hutchinson told Gregory Mank in an interview that was included in his book, *Women in Horror Films, 1930s*. Promises of a bright future and a co-starring role opposite MGM superstar Clark Gable never bore fruit; her only motion picture credit for the studio was a forgotten B-film starring George Murphy entitled *The Women Men Marry*. The disenchanted actress left MGM and tried her luck at Universal, signing a two-picture deal, appearing first in the jungle-set melodrama *The Crime of Doctor Hallet* (1938) featuring Ralph Bellamy, and then *Son of Frankenstein*.

> I had beautiful clothes in it — that was fun, as was working with Basil and Pinky [Atwill], both pros and charming men. Emma Dunn was a dear, and the little boy, Donnie, was nice. I wasn't around for most of the scenes with Karloff and Lugosi, as most of my scenes were with Basil and Pinky. Of course, doing a Frankenstein film is kind of a phony bit — you don't have to delve too deeply. Altogether, though, it was a pleasant engagement.... Mr. Lee did some rewriting on the set. We spent a lot of time in separate corners pounding new lines into our heads, which, of course, one can do, but it adds pressure.

Despite the aforementioned pressure on the cast and crew, Lee kept everyone's spirits high. Pranks and practical jokes were the order of the day. Karloff was treated to a surprise party on the occasion of his 51st birthday (November 23, 1938). He had double reason to be joyous. His wife Dorothy gave birth to his only child, Sara Jane, that same day.

Little Peter was portrayed by four-year-old San Antonio, Texas, native Donnie Dunagan, an adorable looking child actor boasting a mop of blond curls. Dunagan was obviously miscast; the part called for a refined Roddy McDowall or Freddie Bartholomew type. Unusually gifted (he became a member of the American Mensa Society), Dunagan had previously been directed by Rowland V. Lee in the 1938 RKO comedy-drama *Mother Carey's Chickens*, opposite the excellent Fay Bainter, and, following the release of *Son of Frankenstein*, acted for Lee one last time in *Tower of London*.

In an interview with the authors, the career Marine — Viet Nam vet — counterintelligence agent was right on the money in assessing his memorable performance in *Son of Frankenstein*:

> Corny. And I had a Southern accent! ... With this dignified European cast, they had this little kid in there with this loud voice. They kept saying "Speak up!," because I didn't speak that loud then.... And as you speak up, your accent is always accentuated. So here's this little curly-headed jerk runnin' around there with this *very* deep Memphis-Texas accent [*laughs*]! They had the courage to do that!

Dunagan remembered Boris Karloff with great fondness:

> I met him for the first time in the cafeteria at the studio. He was a broad-shouldered fellow in civilian attire, and very, very pleasant.... Either the first or the second time that I had time with Mr. Karloff [in the cafeteria], he gave me an ice cream cone.... Then when I first saw him in his Monster makeup, he laughed at me — "What do you think about me now?" It was just ... "easy does it." ... I had a *ball*! Boris Karloff was a wonderful man ... a real humanist.... He taught me how to play checkers, on the set.... About three or four games over a couple-day period, between scenes and rehearsals, [and] we started betting quarters.... He got to talking, having some fun with people, lost his concentration, and I double-jumped him and I had him locked up! ... When I won, he was surprised. I put my hand out. I wanted my quarter! ... He went "Rrrr! Rrrr! Rrrr" [like the Monster] and people thought he was "playing the part." I'm not sure he *was*— I don't think he liked losin' to this little runt, me!

Problems persisted as the harried production missed its completion deadline and approached the Christmas holidays. Rainfall interfered with exterior shooting and a cold forced Lee to curtail his activities. Undaunted, he vowed to get the picture finished by Christmas Eve. The dubious brass gave him the benefit of the doubt. In the November 30 edition of *The Hollywood Reporter*, Universal announced that it had doubled its staff in cutting and scoring *Son of Frankenstein* in order to meet its scheduled release date. The heads of the editorial, sound and music departments (Maurice Pivar, Bernard B. Brown and Charles Previn, respectively) alerted personnel of the day-and-night grind that would lie ahead of them, including the possibility of working through the New Year's holiday in order to meet the required shipping date on the first 20 prints.

Arguably Bela Lugosi's finest screen performance: *Son of Frankenstein*'s Ygor.

Christmas Eve arrived and Lee was still nowhere near completion of *Son of Frankenstein*. The cast and crew toiled on the sound stages till 6:15 P.M. that evening (an unusual procedure in Hollywood as work customarily finished at noon on this day). Rathbone and several other principals had their engagements extended through December 29 at considerable cost to the studio. The production *finally* wrapped, circa 1:15 A.M., on January 5, 1939, culminating a feverish 46-day shooting schedule.

But the biggest challenge in completing *Son of Frankenstein* was met and conquered by the post-production units. Only a few days before the January 7 preview date, Pivar, Brown, Previn and their various artists and craftsmen were still working industriously to prepare a finished print and to rush additional prints to showcase theaters. The first cut ran over 100 minutes and had to be pruned down to a more acceptable length. The final cost of the production tallied a whopping $420,000, almost *double* the original estimate.

Son of Frankenstein taught Universal a powerful lesson: Never embark on a production without a finished script. As Rowland V. Lee proved, it could be a costly proposition. His halo tarnished in the eyes of the studio brass, Lee undauntedly forged ahead with his next two productions, *The Sun Never Sets* (1939), a silly, dated glorification of the British realm that lucratively reteamed screen foes Rathbone and Atwill, and the handsomely mounted historic spectacle *Tower of London*. Both productions went through the roof in regard to budget and scheduling. Lee's excesses, coupled with Joe May's costly performances on *The House of Fear* (1939), *The Invisible Man Returns* and *The House of the Seven Gables*, are what probably convinced Nate Blumberg and production chief Cliff Work to scale down the ambitions of all future shockers. With few exceptions, most of the studio's subsequent horror movies were given the B treatment and were assigned to competent craftsmen who could grind 'em out on schedule within the limits of the budget. Elaborately produced, high-cost thrillers such as *Son of Frankenstein* were out, and modest programmers such as *The Mummy's Hand* and *Man Made Monster* were in.

Actually, Universal had little reason to grouse. A few weeks after *Son of Frankenstein*'s release, the studio reported that it was doing the biggest box office business in the history of horror pictures in its key city openings, with holdovers being chalked up on every play date; the all-star horror opus certainly contributed towards the studio's financial turnabout in 1939. *Son of Frankenstein* was to be the last Frankenstein film that the critical establishment treated with respect, and for good reason. Every aspect of the picture, from the acting to the technical departments, is first-rate.

There wasn't a dollar spent on the production that doesn't show on the screen. Art director Jack Otterson and his associate Richard H. Riedel fulfilled the considerable demands of the screenplay with uncanny perception. "The sets were rather an orderly array of planes and mazes which, at first glance, resembled a castle interior," Otterson commented in a press release. "But the angles and marks were calculated to force an impression of a weird locale and without intruding too strongly into the consciousness of the spectator." Otterson went on to say that the sets departed from any known style of architecture without indulging in over-stressed cubist or surreal designs.

Universal's staff art director Robert Boyle told us that it wasn't unusual for department head Jack Otterson to receive on-screen credit for films he hadn't even worked on:

> That was in the days of the studio system, when we had supervising art directors, and their name would be on everything [on every movie]. Jack Otterson didn't have anything to do with any of the Universal films that I worked on [from *The Wolf Man* on up], but he *was* the supervisor. In other words, he was the head of the department, he didn't do the work. That's true of almost all of the studios, where the supervising art director either contributed a *lot* or not *any*thing. Jack Otterson didn't contribute too much to the actual work.

When asked if Otterson was *capable* of doing that work, Boyle said with a laugh, "Well, I never found out! A lot of us felt that he was *not* capable of it, but maybe that was unfair."

With the exception of *Bride of Frankenstein*, no other film in the series contains as many striking, bizarre sets. The train transporting the Frankensteins to their new home crosses through a barren, fog-blanketed land populated by twisted, leafless trees and strange rock formations. A massive stone edifice encircled by a foreboding wooden gate (within which Ygor torments the townspeople with the mournful wailing of his crude horn), Castle Frankenstein contains cavernous foyers and living room, a dining room bedecked by two wild boar heads, bedchambers with oddly positioned beds (presumably to ward off evil sendings) and a gloomy library dominated by Baron Heinrich's life-size portrait. These are all masterpieces of concept and design and add immeasurably in creating an atmosphere of awe and foreboding.

But the most imaginative set of all is the ruined laboratory. A far cry from the old watchtower lab of the previous film, it is built on two levels and is sparsely decorated with Kenneth Strickfaden's marvelous electrical whirligigs. The central attraction is the fume-spewing, gurgling sulphur pit. (It doesn't take much foresight to predict the pit will play an important role in the plot's action. In fact, the sharp-eyed viewer can catch a glimpse of the Monster in the steamy pit when Wolf first looks down into it!) Studio set technicians toiled for two weeks creating this "lava pit." First, a layer of plaster was smeared on the walls, followed by an application of strained mud to simulate a boiling mass. Pipes, attached to a garden hose, were run under the mud in the pit. Air and steam were pumped through, making huge bubbles and heavy vapors arise from the "sulphur." Pulleys and ropes were attached to the workmen preparing the set so they could be fished out promptly if they skidded into the mud. It was feared the pool was so thick with mud that Karloff's stunt double might fracture an arm or leg in the fall.

On the day that the climactic sequence was shot, according to studio publicity, rescue parties were stationed close at hand in case of an emergency. A stunt man doubling for Rathbone swung across the lab set on a chain and struck Karloff's double head-on, pushing him into the pit. He was yanked to safety within a few seconds as he would have been unable to save himself from suffocation. First aid squads threw ropes to the double and a trapeze was lowered into the pit for him to grab onto. Studio workers hoisted him out of the dangerous predicament. Luckily, Lee got the action on film in a single take. (Dunagan provided a contrary version of the shooting of this scene, claiming that the kicked stuntman

Celebrating Boris' 51st birthday on the *Son* set are the birthday boy, Rowland V. Lee, Lugosi and Rathbone (courtesy Bill Chase).

went into a net; the sulphur pit was probably on another set.)

Shooting this intensely dramatic scene had its lighter side, according to Dunagan:

> ... I was lying on the floor and Karloff had his foot on me.... [W]e got to laughing in this scene because he was ticklin' me with his darn boot [*laughs*]! I was lying down and Karloff had his boot on me, and I could tell he was trying to keep it from pressing on me. His boot was heavy and he was very sensitive to hurting me — for which I'm grateful! But until they said, "Roll 'em!," he would wiggle his foot and *tickle* me.... He was twisting it on my back and on my side, and I'd get to laughing. Then *he'd* get to laughing. Then somebody behind the lights would get to laughing. We couldn't stop, and they had to stop for several minutes. At *this* point, I don't think Mr. Lee was too happy, because he scolded both of us.... And [scolding] wasn't his persona. He was very gentle and rather a slow talker, very deliberate, very personable.... Karloff looked down at me just sorta like "We gotta cool it." He didn't *say* that, but he had that kind of an expression on his face. Then we both smiled at each other and went back to work, and finally got that darn scene done.

As in the case of its predecessors, *Son of Frankenstein* is a reflection of the man who made it. While Whale's Frankenstein pictures inherited the erudite Englishman's poetry, grace and artistic sensibilities, Lee's film is as unaffected as the director himself. It bears the stamp of a surefooted craftsman who, unlike the tragic Whale, was in step with the dictates of the New Universal. (A gossip column bit in the January 14, 1939, *Hollywood Reporter* revealed that Whale had *paid* his way into a theater's first showing of the new Frankenstein picture on the previous day — a sad indication of the director's loss of clout with the studio.)

Donnie Dunagan was impressed by Lee's style of management:

> You didn't have to be a brain surgeon to perceive that he was in charge.... Mr. Lee had a very natural, calm, dignified presence that everybody seemed to pick up on, and after a few days on *Son of Frankenstein,* I thought he *owned* the whole place! He would move around the sound stages, very casually, checking on people, asking how people were, and I was standing pretty close by — he used to take me along with him.... They just thought the world of him.

Son of Frankenstein's narrative is, for the most part, crisp, direct and unobscured by the esoteric, stylistic little touches upon which Whale, Edgar G. Ulmer and Robert Florey thrived. Despite his subordinate role, Karloff's Monster elicits genuine chills. (Whale's films made the godforsaken creature more an object of curiosity and pity than of fear.) Never before has the Monster been photographed so imposingly. From our first glimpse of him lying in repose on the slab (George Robinson pulls his camera back so that we may appreciate the Monster's size), to his destruction of the lab after discovering Ygor's bullet-riddled body, we are reminded of Wolf's scientific deduction that the creature is "completely superhuman." Robinson's efforts are not *always* successful, however. There are a number of miscalculated group shots where Wolf and Ygor appear taller than the Monster.

The haphazard way the film was shot, with new pages of the script arriving on the set each day, probably accounts for the uneven, episodic pacing of its second half. ("The director had a theory that dialogue learned at a moment's notice would be delivered more naturally," Josephine Hutchinson recalled.) Once the resuscitated Monster renews his efforts to wipe out the last remaining jurors, the action falters, and the beautifully sustained atmosphere of dramatic tension crumbles under the weight of repetitive incidents. It's almost as though Rathbone were on a merry-go-round. He dashes madly between castle and lab, trying vainly to assuage his mounting terror (and his wife's) while avoiding the suspicious eye of Insp. Krogh. Atwill also does his share of dizzying gallivanting. Between meal courses, he's running hither and yon, collecting evidence against the Monster and Wolf at inquests, trying to keep a semblance of order in the village, and badgering the inhabitants of Castle Frankenstein for new clues. All of this rushing around dilutes suspense and creates an air of comedic chaos (quite the opposite effect Lee was hoping to achieve).

The dialogue is as rich and fruity as we've come to expect from these '30s classics. Since some of the best lines don't appear in Cooper's original draft (including all of Ygor's exchanges with Wolf), it is safe to assume that Lee, who worked on reconstructing the script, deserves the credit. The war of nerves waged between Wolf and Krogh is a delight, and their skirmishes are among the film's brightest moments. Krogh never lets his guard down for a moment. Forever probing, he studies Wolf with the hypnotic intensity of a cobra about to strike. Reduced to a bundle of raw nerves, Wolf responds to Krogh's suggestion that he show him around the lab with the sardonic comment, "I'll have you come there sometime — and *parboil* you." Momentarily stunned, Krogh counters Wolf's audacity with sardonic chuckles.

For a third-generation contender, *Son of Frankenstein* contains more than its share of great set pieces. Even Whale couldn't have improved on such bravura bits as Wolf's stirring reading of his father's letter between thunder-and-lightning claps, as an unobserved Ygor peers through the rain-streaked window; Wolf's memorable first meeting with the broken-necked blacksmith; the descent into the underground family crypt, climaxed by the discovery of the unconscious Monster; Wolf, burning with the desire to vindicate his sire, amending the graffito scratched upon his crypt to read MAKER OF MEN; the Monster's medical examination, substantiating his indestructibility ("Two bullets in his heart — and he still lives!"); the Monster comparing his grotesque features to Wolf's in the mirror, then turning away in disgust; Ygor's demonstration of his power over the Monster, who obeys him like a trained dog; and the Monster's discovery of Ygor's dead body, his mournful sobs turning into an unforgettable cry of rage and horror when his fingers are stained with blood. (This scene is reminiscent of the oddly touching moment at the climax of *The Old Dark House* when Karloff's brute servant Morgan tearfully cradles the broken body of Brember Wills' mad arsonist Saul.)

Underlining the dramatic impact of these moments is the brilliant musical score, written by Frank Skinner, orchestrated by Hans J, Salter and directed by Charles Previn. These arrangements, ranging from pensive dirges to violent action movements suggesting the Monster's outrage, are all the more admirable considering the great haste with which they were composed and orchestrated. Sliced, diced and rehashed for numerous B thrillers, this score (along with Skinner and Salter's themes for *The Wolf Man*) became as familiar to '40s audiences as *Swan Lake* was to '30s horror picturegoers.

Reconciled to the fact that his beloved Monster had outlived his dramatic potential, Karloff vowed never again to don the cumbersome makeup. (Except for the 1962 Halloween special "Lizard's Leg and Owlet's Wing" on TV's *Route 66* and a public appearance at an all-star baseball game, he kept that promise.) Inexplicably deprived of speech, the Monster becomes a mindless pawn in Ygor's campaign of terror against his persecutors, and consequently loses much of the sympathy that he had engendered in *Bride of Frankenstein*.

Dunagan vividly recalled Karloff's day-to-day ordeal during the long shoot:

> The costume was punishing him. I always felt sorry for him, because his costume was heavy and it really hurt him, he was in pain with that. But he wasn't a complainer.... The costume was extremely heavy, and it did not "breathe." It was exactly what you saw on the film, and it was *murder* on him. He must have lost weight *every day* in that darn thing. And the boots, sir, *had* to have lead in them, because when he walked, *off*-camera, between takes, it was still clunk-clunk-clunk.... When we got through with that movie, my sense was that he did not like that role. And I can *promise* you he didn't like the costume, which had to hurt him physically.... As soon as you'd go under those lights, it was just devastating. We all sweated. There was no air conditioning, and all of us were wringin' wet.... When we had a break, sometimes Mr. Karloff would take off some of that costume — he'd take off the vest, which was killing him, and those awful, heavy, lead-weighted boots. That's when I became aware that that stuff was punishing him.

In the July 25, 1948, *Sunday New York Times*, Thomas F. Brady caught up with Karloff when he visited the Big Apple at the behest of Universal-International to promote the opening of *Abbott and Costello Meet Frankenstein*. Karloff had just left Philadelphia where he attended the premiere of the studio's 1948 costume epic *Tap Roots*, in which he played Tishomingo, a 70-year-old Choctaw Indian. "[Karloff] is prepared to cooperate," reported Brady, "as long as he doesn't have to see the picture." "I'm too fond of the monster," Karloff confessed. "I'm grateful to him for all he did for me, and I wouldn't like to watch anybody make sport of him.... After *Son [of Frankenstein]*, I decided the character no longer had any potentialities — the makeup did all the work," he said. Not one to denigrate his successors in the role, the Gentle Monster added, "Anybody who can take that makeup every morning deserves respect."

Son of Frankenstein furnished Bela Lugosi with a role that enabled him to upstage his more prominent co-star. It was an opportunity he would never have again. Ygor is one of Lugosi's most vividly etched characterizations. Unlike his signature performance in *Dracula*, it hasn't aged a bit. Sacrificing his noble features to a shaggy mane, contorting his posture, and altering his melodious speaking voice to a rasp, Lugosi proved that he had the resources to do fine work as a character actor, but was seldom given the opportunity thereafter.

Not only did *Son of Frankenstein* provide Lugosi with a plum opportunity to expand his acting muscles, it made him financially solvent again after two leans years prompted by the horror ban. "[The studio heads] had branded me with the stamp of an animal." he told columnist Ed Sullivan shortly before *Son of Frankenstein*'s release. "You're a bogy-man ... and we have nothing for you today, or tomorrow, or the next day." Lugosi's only work during this period was eight weeks on the stage with the road company of "Tovarich," playing the part of the commissar. He told Sullivan that he had to stretch eight weeks' pay over one hundred and four weeks. Then, one night, he got a call from Eric Umann, the manager of the Regina Theatre. Umann wanted to know if Lugosi would make a personal appearance in conjunction with the *Dracula–Frankenstein–Son of Kong* revival. Lugosi thought it was a gag at first, but Umann finally convinced him. Shortly after, he was cast in *Son of Frankenstein*, and his bad luck streak was over. "I owe it all to that little man at the Regina Theatre. I was dead and he brought me to life."

In Ygor, the Monster finally found the ideal soul mate. Both are social outcasts and, by all accounts, both are "dead." ("I love dead! Hate living," the Monster declared in *Bride of Frankenstein.*) This mutual affection stumps Wolf, who even suggests the Monster may be under the blacksmith's hypnotic control, "or something more elemental, perhaps." Contrary to Wolf's theory, it's love, pure and simple, that motivates the Monster to do his friend's bidding. Those inclined to read deeper into these things may find elements of necrophilia, possibly even homosexuality, in this strange relationship. (In *The Ghost of Frankenstein*, Ygor is afraid of losing the Monster's affections to Ludwig, and even suggests that Frankenstein's second son unite their bodies via an operation so they'd be "together always.")

Basil Rathbone's high-strung performance, undeservedly lambasted by historians over the years, is in perfect harmony with the movie's larger-than-life melodramatics. (Compare it to Sir Cedric Hardwicke's deeply troubled, low-keyed persona as Ludwig Frankenstein in *The Ghost of Frankenstein* for a contrast in acting styles.) Rathbone had been directed by Rowland Lee in the 1937 British thriller *Love from a Stranger*, an Agatha Christie adaptation, which featured the elegant Basil as a Bluebeard-style murderer who seduces *nouveau riche* Ann Harding into marrying him. Rathbone's portrayal of Wolf von Frankenstein so closely approximates his acting style in *Love from a Stranger* (which begins on a fittingly reserved note, then rises steadily to a fever pitch), one can safely assume that Lee encouraged his star to emulate his performance in the Frankenstein film. ("Basil Rathbone was a cultured, gentle man and he was as friendly as Karloff," Dunagan told us. "He would read poems ... he was a big fan of Kipling.") In 1946, Rathbone essayed the title role in a radio dramatization of *Frankenstein* which aired on the CBS show *Stars Over Hollywood.*

Making his Frankenstein film debut (he was destined to appear in all of the remaining sequels, usually as an authority figure), Lionel Atwill, on loan from Fox, is peerless as the wholly sympathetic Insp. Krogh. Like Lugosi, he realized the potential for stylistic expression and milked the role for all its worth. Not averse to laying the ham on thick in such films as *Doctor X* (1932), *The Vampire Bat* and *Mystery of the Wax Museum* (both 1933), Atwill is the epitome of restraint here. There isn't a false note in his entire performance.

Screen veterans Emma Dunn and Edgar Norton head up the supporting cast which is peppered with such colorful Germanic types as Lionel Belmore, Michael Mark and Gustav von Seyffertitz. Ward Bond is scarcely noticeable in a bit part as a gendarme, and Dwight Frye's performance as a disgruntled villager unfortunately ended up in the cutting room's wastebasket. (Had his appearance survived the final cut, Frye would have set a record by appearing in five consecutive Frankenstein pictures!) Perry Ivins, the character player who portrayed the family servant Fritz, had previously directed at least one West Coast stage presentation of Lugosi's "Dracula." Ivins did double duty, appearing as Dracula's slave Renfield in the same stage production.

"Movie making isn't fun anymore," Rowland V. Lee beefed to an interviewer after making the decision to retire from the picture business in 1945. The day-to-day dealings with short-sighted executives and business majors who didn't know one end of a camera from the other finally got Lee's goat. It wasn't long, however, before the producer-director returned to the business he loved. Converting part of his San Fernando Valley ranch into a motion picture location, Lee played host to such long-time colleagues as Frank Borzage and Alfred Hitchcock (the climactic runaway carousel scene from Hitch's 1951 *Strangers on a Train* was shot on Lee's property). It was Borzage who agreed to direct a project Lee had long dreamed of producing, a filmization of the inspirational Lloyd C. Douglas novel *The Big Fisherman* (1959), the story of St. Peter.

On December 21, 1975, Rowland V. Lee died after suffering an apparent heart attack. The indefatigable, 84-year-old filmmaker had just completed writing a new screenplay, a mystery thriller entitled *The Belt.*

Critics' Corner

It's a knockout of its type for production, acting, and effects.... Rowland V. Lee's direction creates and keeps a chillingly sombre mood, and the grim humor that's in it, he handles very well indeed....—*The Hollywood Reporter*, January 13, 1939

[I]f Universal's *Son of Frankenstein* ... isn't the silliest picture ever made, it's a sequel to the silliest picture ever made. But its silliness is deliberate—a very shrewd silliness, perpetrated by a good director ... so that even while you laugh at its nonsense you may be struck with the notion that perhaps that's as good a way of enjoying oneself at a movie as any.—*The New York Times*, January 30, 1939, B.R. Crisler

Picture is well-mounted, nicely directed, and includes a cast of capable artists.... Universal has given "A" production layout to the thriller in all departments.—*Variety*, January 18, 1939

Artistically, *Son of Frankenstein* is a masterpiece in the demonstration of how production settings and effects can be made assets emphasizing literary melodrama.—*The Motion Picture Herald*, 1939

Rating: ★★★ Rowland V. Lee has created an eerie atmosphere for the story and he has put into the working out of the plot enough horror to send the chills and shivers racing up and down the spectators' backs.... [W]ell done.—*The New York Daily News*, January 29, 1939, Kate Cameron

A talented cast ... is aided in the delivery of believable ... performances through Rowland V. Lee....—*Box Office*, 1939

The House of Fear

Released June 30, 1939. 65 minutes. *Associate Producer:* Edmund Grainger. *Director:* Joe May. *Screenplay:* Peter Milne. *Based on the story and play* "The Last Warning" *by* Thomas F. Fallon. *Adapted from the novel* Backstage Phantom *by* Wadsworth Camp. *Photography:* Milton Krasner. *Art Directors:* Jack Otterson & John Ewing. *Editor:* Frank Gross. *Music Director:* Charles Previn. *Sound Supervisor:* Bernard B. Brown. *Technician:* Joseph Lapis. *Gowns:* Vera West. *Set Decorators:* Russell A. Gausman. *Assistant Director:* Phil Karlson.

William Gargan (*Arthur McHugh*), Irene Hervey (*Alice Tabor*), Dorothy Arnold (*Gloria DeVere*), Alan Dinehart (*Joseph Morton*), Harvey Stephens (*Richard Pierce*), Walter Woolf King (*Carleton*), Robert Coote (*Robert Morton*), El Brendel (*Jeff*), Tom Dugan (*Mike*), Jan Duggan (*Sarah Henderson*), Donald Douglas (*John Woodford*), Harry Hayden (*Coroner*), Emory Parnell, William Gould (*Policemen*), Charles C. Wilson (*Police Chief*), Milton Kibbee (*Telephone Repair Man*), Ben Lewis (*Tommy*), Stanley Hughes (*Cameraman*), Eddie Parker (*Watson*), Donald Kerr (*Cab Driver*), Tom Steele (*Stagehand*), Raymond Parker.

[A] whodunit with comedy flavor that holds sufficient edge-of-seat suspense....
—Variety, *June 7, 1939*

The House of Fear is the kind of modest-sounding Universal flick that you might put off seeing for years because it has no horror stars or monster characters—only to eventually realize, at the long-delayed hour (and five minutes) of discovery, that it's a snappy little whodunit, in some ways better than many of the monsterrific Universals you've seen repeatedly in the meantime. Breezy and compact, it's a good example of what can be done with a mildewed premise when a competent screenwriter and a spirited cast put forth their best efforts. There are even echoes of *The Phantom of the Opera* in its story of a legitimate theater reportedly haunted by a ghost who makes demands of the proprietors.

During a performance of the play "Dangerous Currents" at Broadway's Woodford Theatre, star John Woodford (Donald Douglas) collapses and dies on stage. His body is carried to a dressing room which is guarded from the outside. When police arrive and enter the dressing room, the body is gone. The theater shuts down, and remains closed once rumors about Woodford's restless ghost begin to circulate on the Great White Way.

A year passes before Arthur McHugh (William Gargan) leases the theater from owner Joseph Morton (Alan Dinehart). McHugh's audacious idea is to reassemble the cast of "Dangerous Currents" and reopen the theater with that production. Just after McHugh signs the lease, he receives a telephone call from an unearthly voice which identifies itself as John Woodford and warns him not to proceed with his plans. After the caller has rung off, McHugh discovers that he has been talking into a dead phone.

McHugh rehires many of the original players as well as the play's director, Richard Pierce (Harvey Stephens). Carleton (Walter Woolf King), a supporting player in the old production, is promoted to Woodford's role while the sole newcomer, sexy Gloria DeVere (Dorothy Arnold), is assigned the part of a secretary. Reunited for the first time since the night of Woodford's death, the members of the company begin to bicker and point accusing fingers. Handwritten warnings from "Woodford" are found inserted between the pages of the scripts. Leading lady Alice Tabor (Irene Hervey) becomes edgy over the coming production. Carleton receives more threatening notes. Comedy relief stagehands Jeff and Mike (El Brendel and Tom Dugan) observe all the standard Broadway superstitions. McHugh is nearly killed by falling scenery.

McHugh decides to spend the entire night at the theater and try to catch a glimpse of Woodford's ghost. He convinces Pierce to share his all-night vigil and the two men wait in separate corners of the darkened auditorium. In the dead of night, weird lights appear and coalesce into the glowing, mask-like visage of Woodford. McHugh fires a gun into the spectral face, which disappears in a swirl of dust. McHugh finds Pierce, bloodied from a blow on the head (or perhaps grazed by a bullet?), unconscious nearby. The two hear a crash and find a broken death mask of Woodford in the star dressing room. Investigating further, McHugh locates a secret passageway that leads to a dressing room where Alice unexpectedly appears. McHugh admits that he's a police detective posing as a producer in hopes of finally cracking the Woodford case. He extracts from Alice and Pierce a promise to keep his secret, and allows them to leave. In the secret passageway, he finds Woodford's corpse plastered up in a wall.

On the eve of the first dress rehearsal, Joseph Morton argues with his brother Robert (Robert Coote) about Robert's romantic involvement with Gloria. During a mysterious power blackout, Carleton vanishes; his dead body is later found by the bumbling Jeff. Despite another handwritten "Woodford" death threat, McHugh compels Pierce to replace Carleton in the jinxed leading role and determines to open on time. New evidence presents itself as opening night nears. A forged check against Woodford's account comes to light; McHugh conjectures that Woodford confronted the embezzler and was killed. It's also learned that Woodford was killed by a poisoned dart.

An army of cops, uniformed and plainclothes, attends the re-premiere. During a scene set at a broadcasting studio, McHugh notices a cable extending from a prop microphone down through a small hole in the stage floor; below the stage, the masked killer is waiting to give it a tug, which will fire a dart from the mike into Pierce. McHugh saves Pierce's life by disrupting the performance, then orders a search of the theater. The masked killer climbs up into the theater rafters and a frantic chase ensues before he is trapped and unmasked as Mike, the stagehand. Mike, an ex-convict, stammers that he was blackmailed into committing the murders and "haunting" the theater, and points out the real mastermind: Robert Morton. It was Morton who forged the Woodford check, and who hoped to eventually make a real-estate fortune on the theater.

With the mystery cleared up, Alice and Pierce announce their engagement; Gloria admits that she is Mrs. McHugh, an undercover policewoman; and McHugh declares that he is resigning from the force to try his hand in the theater business.

Going into production as *Backstage Phantom* (the title of the source novel), *The House of Fear* rolled on March 16, 1939, scheduled for a 15-day shoot and budgeted at just over $100,000. At the helm was director Joe May, a pioneer of German cinema who had fled to the United States when Hitler came to power. Curiously, May seems to have been unwilling or unable to master the language; it was for this reason that Universal had little faith that the veteran could bring *The House of Fear* in on time. To help him meet his deadline, studio chiefs assigned one of their most efficient crews to the production, but problems arose and the cast and crew found themselves working until ten o'clock (or later) every night. *The House of Fear* became a constant day-and-night grind, with production extending beyond the 15-day schedule into the early part of April; an April 5 memo described the picture as a terrific siege of hard work that had consumed 17 days and 13 nights. The film finally "wrapped" on April 6, considerably over schedule and $8,000 over budget. To studio insiders, the film must have seemed as much a problem child as the jinxed stageplay around which its story pivoted.

There's no hint of this production chaos in the picture itself. Despite the behind-the-scenes hubbub, *The House of Fear* emerges as an efficient and thoroughly enjoyable B. William Gargan plays his role of the undercover detective-theatrical producer like a rat-a-tat Warners stock player. The gregarious Gargan (only a year away from his Oscar-nominated emoting in RKO's *They Knew What They Wanted*) turns in a bright, glib performance, and his vigorous playing keeps

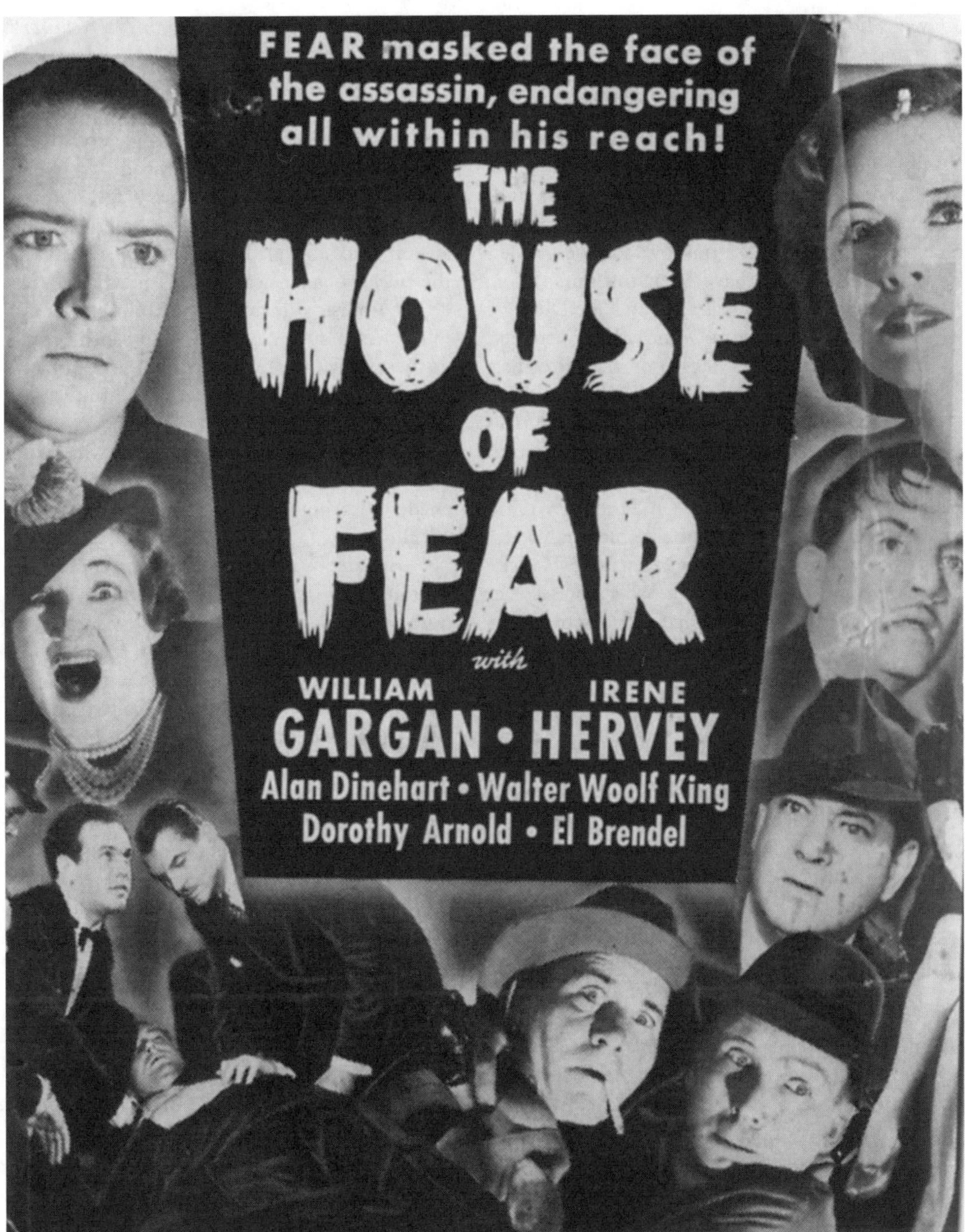

Pressbook ad for *The House of Fear*.

our interest on high even through some repetitive sequences. Irene Hervey is sober and reserved as the agitated Broadway star who reluctantly returns to the unlucky play.

Somber Alan Dinehart gets some of the best and funniest throwaway lines as the theater owner; Harvey Stephens (his last name misspelled Stevens in on-screen credits) is a personable second lead; and Robert Coote does a good job of diverting suspicion as the silly ne'er-do-well who turns out to be the killer. Although his acting scenes are restricted to the play-within-the-film, Donald Douglas has RAT written all over him as the disreputable Woodford.

On the flip side of the coin, El Brendel as the comedy-relief stagehand falls back on his usual bag of tired "Yumpin' yiminy" tricks, and Dorothy Arnold as golddigger Gloria primps and poses and sashays in a trampy Mae West style. Which might not have been too much of a stretch. "My mother was a tramp," Joe DiMaggio, Jr., said of Arnold, a Duluth native who met baseball great Joe DiMaggio on the set of her first movie, the made-in–New York *Manhattan Merry-Go-Round* (1937). They dated for two years as DiMaggio made Yankee history and Arnold made other movies, including the Bela Lugosi serial *The Phantom Creeps.* In July 1939 DiMaggio promised he'd hit a home run for her in the All-Star Game (he did). That November, before a crowd of 30,000 in San Francisco, he took her as his lawful wedded wife, for better or for worse. Mostly worse. As little as one or two drinks made her seductive around other men; DiMaggio caught her in bed with a guy three times. Even their son Joe Jr. had cause for mortification when Mom did handstands in front of him and his young friends ... *sans* panties. DiMaggio later shed Arnold and they shared custody of Joe Jr. until Arnold saw a photograph of Joey sharing a date with DiMaggio and Marilyn Monroe, which prompted her to launch a custody battle to deprive Joe Sr. of his visitation rights. Arnold died of cancer in 1984.

Producer Edmund Grainger felt that it was rather daring to climactically pin the murders on characters played by comedians (Robert Coote and Tom Dugan). He remembered the not-so-long-ago days (1930) when Universal's grim anti-war drama *All Quiet on the Western Front* was previewed, and audiences laughed at the performance of ZaSu Pitts (a comedienne slotted in an out-of-character role) as a dying mother for no reason other than that they had been conditioned to laugh at her; this unexpected, unacceptable reaction had forced the studio to reshoot the scenes with a different actress. But Grainger was annoyed by murder mysteries that wrapped with an obscure figure in the story being dragged out at the end and pinned with the rap, so he took a chance on making Coote and Dugan the culprits. According to *The New York Times*, Grainger contended that it would work in *House of Fear* "because audiences seem willing to accept anything in their murder mysteries."

The House of Fear is surprisingly well-paced for a movie that's nearly entirely confined to one setting (the Woodford Theatre's stage, auditorium and wings, a cellar, the dressing room area and an office above). The film also benefits from the *absence* of a musical score. Charles Previn receives a music director's credit, but except for music heard during the main and closing credits there's nary a note throughout the rest of *The House of Fear*'s 65-minute running time. The lack of music enhances several sequences, especially the genuinely spooky scene in which the glowing face of Woodford appears in the blackened auditorium and floats menacingly toward McHugh.

Apparently the *House of Fear* screenplay was submitted to the Breen Office while the bluenoses were napping, as there are a few surprising lines of dialogue and situations in the film. It's startling, and not entirely plausible, to learn at the end that Gloria is McHugh's policewoman-wife, as this trollop of a character has been carrying on a heavy-duty romance with suspect Robert Morton throughout the entire picture. At one point, when Gloria complains that her new hat is now minus a feather, an exasperated McHugh barks that he'd like to give her the bird. A gruesome image comes to mind when a police detective says of the local autopsy surgeon, "He's taken Woodford's body apart so many times now, he knows it like a book!" There's also some unintentionally ghoulish "retrospect" humor in a scene where the police chief (Charles C. Wilson) chides McHugh for buying cigars with police money to perpetuate his impersonation of a Broadway producer. "Eighty-five bucks for 50-cent cigars?! That makes me sick!" growls Wilson. "Oh, not half as sick as they're makin' me!" McHugh groans. "Honest, chief, they're *killing* me!" (Later in his life, William Gargan, who plays McHugh, lost his voice box to cancer of the larynx and began to campaign against smoking by speaking through an artificial voice box.)

Vienna-born Joe May, son of a wealthy Austrian merchant, was a racing driver, a businessman and a director of operettas before becoming a director of German films in 1911. May was a highly successful film pioneer in Germany, and became well-known for developing stars such as Conrad Veidt (whose first prominent role was in May's *Das Indische Grabmal*, 1922) and Emil Jannings (who first starred in May's 1922 *Tragödie der Liebe*). May fled to the United States in 1934, singing the praises of American films ("Hollywood makes far better pictures than all of Europe combined!") and making his U.S. directorial debut on Fox's *Music in the Air*. His reluctance or inability to learn English probably explains why this once-distinguished director had a spotty Hollywood career that finally petered to a halt in the mid–1940s. John Meredyth Lucas, the busy TV director, got his Hollywood start in the 1930s on the set of May's Warner Bros. picture *Confession* with Kay Francis; he wrote in his 2004 autobiography *Eighty Odd Years in Hollywood*:

> Joe May, an aging German director ... had done well in the country of his birth but here, for whatever reason, had lost confidence in his ability.... Joe had made this film in German [under the title *Mazurka*] some years before and now had a Moviola on the set to view his old picture.... Joe would run and rerun scenes from his German *Mazurka* on this machine and set up the new scene in exactly the same way, trying to recreate his prior success frame by frame, sometimes running back and forth during rehearsals to be sure he had it right. This earned him the ill-concealed laughter of the crew. It was, in retrospect, a depressing way to begin my career, watching the pitiful end of his.

Director Henry Koster and his wife, one-time Universal contract actress Peggy Moran, painted for the authors a fascinating and amusing portrait of May. According to the Kosters, May came to the United States with a big-shot attitude and was never able to humble himself. May probably would not have seemed out of place in the Universal of the Laemmles, but by 1939 Universal was well on its way to becoming apple-pie American, and May, with his fancy European manners, his penchant for pointing with a cane and his swell-headed delusions, must have seemed something of an anachronism at the studio. (It's a sad side note that he not only had trouble with English but also stuttered!) Peggy Moran was present at the Universal commissary the day that May walked in and high-handedly tossed his coat to the waitress — only to have the garment heaved back at him together with the cry, "Hang it up yourself!"

Peggy Moran Koster laughingly told us:

> He was such a temperamental man, he would lose his temper and go crazy. The story went around that he had done a picture in Germany that involved Christians and lions. The crew was all in a cage so that the lions couldn't get at them. This one lion walked out, right in front of the camera, and sat down. Joe yelled, "Get that lion out of there! Let's do it again, and don't let that lion sit down!" Well, they did it a couple more times, and the lion kept sitting down in front of the camera. Joe got so mad that he walked out of the cage, grabbed that lion by the tail and yelled, "Now, get up and behave!" Then he got back in the cage, realized what he had done, and fainted!

The House of Fear is a B-movie corker, but the stage version which preceded it sounds like it must have been even more fun. Beginning its run at Manhattan's Klaw Theater (on 45th Street, west of Broadway) in October 1922, "The Last Warning" was described by one reviewer as being "so tricked out with novelties which no 'bat' or 'cat' or 'monster' ever thought of that the result is really a most entertaining show." Part of its appeal was the showman-like gimmicks that went along with the telling of the tale, and the attempt to make the audience feel as though it was actually *in* the "haunted theater" of the story. Players went out into the auditorium and began acting in the aisles, or in one of the boxes; at one point in each performance, the house was plunged into pitch darkness (a scene retained for the movie, and reminiscent of 1959's *The Tingler*); the actor firing his gun at Woodford's ghost did so from one of the upper boxes. In the last act, as the moment of the killer's unmasking neared, a squad of "policemen" entered the auditorium, filling the center aisle or stationing themselves at every exit, as if to prevent the culprit's escape. The director orchestrating these William Castle–like antics was English-born Clifford Brooke, who by the 1940s was a Hollywood bit player (he's the gas company watchman in 1945's *Hangover Square* with Laird Cregar); Charles Trowbridge, the ill-fated Prof. Petrie in *The Mummy's Hand*, played one of the leading roles. This story was first adapted for the movies (under the title *The Last Warning*) by Universal in 1929, with *The Cat and the Canary*'s Paul Leni in the director's chair (for the last time), his camera swooping around the Phantom Stage in a style that still grabs the attention and commands respect today. That cast included Leni's former *Canary* Laura La Plante as the pretty stage star, Montagu Love as Arthur McHugh, Roy D'Arcy, a gray-at-the-temples John Boles et al. as suspects, Slim Summerville as a comic relief stagehand and D'Arcy Corrigan as Woodford.

The House of Fear is no classic by any stretch, but it's deft in its balancing of mystery, chiller and comedic elements and innovative in its frequent use of overlapping dialogue. And what fan of Universal Horrors can resist a *Phantom*-like story, shot on the Phantom Stage?

Critics' Corner

Cast has a rather tough assignment to get much out of the lines and situations provided.—*Variety*, June 7, 1939

Universal has turned out another one of those swell murder mysteries in *The House of Fear*, that sends shivers up and down the spine. Packed with plenty of good, clean comedy amid an eerie atmosphere, suspenseful action and many blood-curdling moments, [it] will give any audience a double dose of what they came to see.... [Joe May's] pace is even and builds effectively to an exciting climax.—*The Hollywood Reporter*, June 7, 1939

Rating: ★★ [A]s puzzling a murder mystery as has come along in some time. Figuring out who done it, and why, will keep you intrigued.... [T]he plot does seem to have been snatched out of thin air.—*The New York Daily News*, May 28, 1939, Wanda Hale

Tower of London

Released November 17, 1939. 92 minutes. A Rowland V. Lee Production. *Producer-Director:* Rowland V. Lee. *Original Screenplay:* Robert N. Lee. *Photography:* George Robinson. *Editor:* Edward Curtiss. *Art Director:* Jack Otterson. *Associate Art Director:* Richard H. Riedel. *Musical Director:* Charles Previn. *Orchestrations:* Frank Skinner. *Assistant Director:* Fred Frank. *Set Decorator:* Russell A. Gausman. *Technical Advisors:* Major G.O. T. Bagley & Sir Gerald Grove. *Sound Supervisor:* Bernard B. Brown. *Technician:* William Hedgcock. *Makeup:* Jack P. Pierce. *Background Photography:* Henry Shuster. *Assistant Editor:* Paul Landres. *Fencing Instructor:* Fred Cavens. *Gowns:* Vera West.

Basil Rathbone (*Richard, Duke of Gloucester/King Richard III*), Boris Karloff (*Mord*), Barbara O'Neil (*Queen Elyzabeth*), Ian Hunter (*King Edward IV*), Vincent Price (*Duke of Clarence*), Nan Grey (*Lady Alice Barton*), Ernest Cossart (*Tom Clink*), John Sutton (*John Wyatt*), Rose Hobart (*Anne Neville*), Leo G. Carroll (*Lord Hastings*), Miles Mander (*King Henry VI*), Lionel Belmore (*Beacon Chiruegeon*), Ronald Sinclair (*Boy King Edward*), Ralph Forbes (*Henry Tudor*), Frances Robinson (*Duchess Isobel*), G.P. Huntley, Jr. (*Prince of Wales*), John Rodion (*Lord DeVere*), Donnie Dunagan (*Baby Prince Richard*), John Herbert-Bond (*Young Prince Richard*), Walter Tetley (*Chimney Sweep*), Georgia Caine (*Dowager Duchess*), C. Montague Shaw (*Majordomo*), Ernie Adams (*Prisoner Begging for Water*), Ivan Simpson (*Retainer*), Nigel de Brulier (*Archbishop of St. John's Chapel*), Holmes Herbert, Charles Miller (*Councilmen*), Venecia Severn, Yvonne Severn (*Princesses*), Louise Brian, Jean Fenwick (*Ladies in Waiting*), Michael Mark (*Servant to Henry VI*), Donald Stuart (*Bunch*), Reginald Barlow (*Sheriff at Execution*), Robert Greig (*Father Olmstead*), Ivo Henderson (*Haberdeer*), Charles Peck (*Page Boy*), Harry Cording (*Tyrell*), Jack C. Smith (*Forrest*), Colin Kenny, Arthur Stenning (*Soldiers*), Evelyn Selbie, Denis Tankard, Dave Thursby (*Beggars*), Claire Whitney (*Civilian Woman*), Russ Powell (*Sexton/Bell Ringer*), Ann Todd (*Queen Elyzabeth's Daughter*), John George (*Spy*), Joan Carroll (*Lady Mowbray*), Francis Powers, Edgar Sherrod, Caroline Cooke, Ed Brady, Schuyler Standish, Harry Bailey, Murdock MacQuarrie, Claude Payton, Arthur Mulliner, Marty Faust, Howard Brooks, Margaret Fealy, Richard Alexander, Stanley Blystone.

> ...A web of intrigue veils the lives of all who know only too well that today's friends might be tomorrow's enemies....
> —*Prologue to* Tower of London

The ambitious but under-produced *Tower of London* was one of the more interesting undertakings Universal attempted in the late '30s. While Hollywood historical movies hadn't been shy about depicting various social horrors in films such as *A Tale of Two Cities* (1935) and *Marie Antoinette* (1938), *Tower of London* professed to take matters a step or two further in the depiction of more physical horrors. The film's closest antecedent is Lon Chaney's *The Hunchback of Notre Dame* (1923) which, coincidentally, producer Pandro S. Berman was remaking at RKO around the time *Tower of London* was being shot. One critic described the Universal film as "'Richard III' with all of the gore and none of the art."

Tower of London was conceived several years earlier when producer-director Rowland V. Lee journeyed to England to research an epic with a background in British history. It was then that his brother Robert N. Lee hit upon the idea of bringing the story of the notorious English monarch to the screen. "We agreed that we wanted to use the roughest, most hard-boiled period of all time," Robert explained in an interview. "Row was for the Stuart era but I held out for the time of Richard."

Lee seemed partial to British-themed projects. At Universal, he had just completed *The Sun Never Sets* (1939), a comic-book salute to The Empire which, like *Son of Frankenstein*, overshot its budget and shooting schedule (Douglas Fairbanks, Jr., Basil Rathbone and Lionel Atwill headed the cast). Rowland successfully pitched *Tower of London* to Universal and *The Hollywood Reporter* announced in June 1939 that production was imminent. The studio staked the producer to a hefty $500,000 budget and a 36-day schedule with a starting date of August 11.

Trade papers reported that Brian Donlevy was being tested for the leading role of the murderous monarch on July 27 but a week later the studio announced they were signing George Sanders. However, this failed to pan out and Lee approached Basil Rathbone for the assignment. Not only was the classically trained actor ideally suited for the part (he had played 47 Shakespearean roles in 22 plays), but he had an established working relationship with Lee. In addition to *The Sun Never Sets*, Lee also directed the actor as the notorious wife killer who finally gets the tables turned on him by Ann Harding in the Agatha Christie thriller, *Love from a Stranger* (1937).

The one snag was that Rathbone was in the midst of playing the leading role in another Universal film, the John Brahm–directed *Rio* (1939). The conflict was solved by having Rathbone divide his time between both films during the first week of production on *Tower of London*. Complicating the situation even further, RKO enticed the actor with a principal role in their remake of *The Hunchback of Notre Dame* but Universal, who had legal claim to the actor's services, refused to release him.

The role of Mord the Executioner was tailor-made for Boris Karloff who was signed on by the studio for an additional two features after *Son of Frankenstein*. Once again, the actor found himself at the tender mercies of Jack Pierce who envisaged the character with a full black beard. The concept was shelved in favor of a near-hairless look which required Karloff's head, hands and wrists to be shaved every other day during the production. Karloff's naturally dark and bushy eyebrows, which provided the only contrast, were curled and waxed. His nose was built up and hooked to throw his head out of proportion and his ears were taped back flat. The character's club foot was created with a huge shoe similar to the one the actor wore in his Frankenstein days, with his right leg built up with leather padding.

Universal and Lee were both optimistic that the schedule would be met. Getting the picture in within the budget was a different matter. The salaries of the cast as well as construction and costuming costs made economizing practically impossible. Although trade papers announced that the film would have authentic backgrounds filmed with the permission of British authorities, there's little evidence of it in the finished film. Art director Jack Otterson went to work on partially reproducing the magnificent Tower on the studio back lot, consulting historical records as well as the original blueprints of the thirteenth century edifice. The completed structure stood 75 feet high and would be used on occasion in forthcoming Universal horror and adventure pictures. With an eye for authenticity, the prop department recreated the various torture devices showcased in the script, from racks, gauntlets, Spanish collars, bilboes and brakes to an iron maiden.

The staging of the historic battles at Bosworth and Tewkesbury proved to be a disaster, dashing any hopes of keeping the production on schedule. On August 19, a 4 A.M. call was issued to over 300 extras, requiring them to travel 20 miles north of Hollywood to a ranch in Tarzana. Hoping to recreate the actual climatic conditions in which the Battle of Bosworth was waged, the crew set up fog-machines in the open terrain. But the morning winds played such havoc with the fog effects, it was impossible to continue. Lee ordered the crew to switch over to the Battle of Tewkesbury scenes, requiring the rigging-up of rain machines so that this battle, like the real one, would take place in a downpour. This time the pump broke, leaving more than 300 people to swelter in 100°-plus summer heat. When the hoses were finally turned on, the cardboard helmets worn by the "troops" fell apart. The assistant director noted in his daily

For Boris Karloff and Basil Rathbone, it's open season on the royals in Rowland V. Lee's medieval melodrama *Tower of London*.

report that "a group of unruly, uncooperative and destructive extras dressed in helmets and armor made this one of the most unsuccessful days the studio had with a large crowd of people in many years."

Lee's once-proud track record with the studio was quickly eroding. His last two films at Universal exceeded their original budgets and schedules considerably and *Tower of London* was shaping up poorly. Increasing pressure was placed on the producer to cut costs; the studio insisted on eliminating the child marriage scene at St. John's Chapel between Baby Prince Richard and Lady Mowbray. Lee fought against this decision, insisting that the scene would add immeasurably to the pageantry and color of the production. The producer finally won out, agreeing to compensate for the $10,000 expenditure by quickly finishing all the scenes with the higher-salaried players, starting with Boris Karloff.

On August 22, Lee again tried shooting battle footage, but once more the extreme California heat forced production to a halt. Undeterred, Lee decided to get around the problem by filming small groups of players against process plates of previously shot battle scenes. On September 4, *Tower of London* officially wrapped, a full ten days over schedule, exceeding its budget by almost $80,000. Serial producer Ford Beebe, moonlighting as a second unit director, was assigned to complete a few remaining shots. One of his chief challenges was rounding up cast members, many of whom had gone on to other films at other studios.

By early November, the finished film was seen by preview audiences. To the bewilderment of the studio heads, who expected the usual Hollywood symphonic pastiche on the soundtrack, studio composer Hans J. Salter used authentic period compositions for incidental music. The studio demanded new music be written, but the pressures of time necessitated cannibalizing Frank Skinner's *Son of Frankenstein* score, including a somewhat revamped main title. The results proved quite satisfactory even if the hulking, predominant brass and woodwinds seemed more to reflect the lumbering menace of Mord than the sly machinations of Richard.

Tower of London begins with Edward IV (Ian Hunter) on the throne of England, having usurped the power of King Henry VI (Miles Mander). Though the monarch faces the constant threat from Henry's supporters, he's unaware that his most sinister adversary is his brother, Richard, the Duke of Gloucester (Basil Rathbone). Although outwardly Edward's closest advisor, the malformed Richard uses his position to his best advantage, hoping eventually to seize the crown. Using Mord (Boris Karloff), the Tower of London's brutish chief executioner, as an accomplice and assassin, Richard eventually murders and conspires against those who are in the line of succession to the throne. When Edward finally succumbs to illness, Richard sees an opportunity to quickly fulfill his ambitions. After arranging for the murder of Edward's two young sons, the hunchback is named king. However, the Queen Mother, Elyzabeth (Barbara O'Neil), and her allies manage to loot the royal treasure and funnel it to Henry Tudor (Ralph Forbes) to finance an army. The opposing forces meet at Bosworth where Richard and Mord are both killed in combat. The film ends as the reign of Henry VII begins.

The star-studded gala premiere of *Tower of London* was held at the Warfield Theater in San Francisco on December 15, 1939. Emceeing the affair was Mischa Auer, who began the decade as a Boris Karloff-like movie heavy (he even dressed and walked like Karloff's Monster in *The Monster Walks* [1932]) and finished it out as screwball comedy characters! Along with personal appearances by cast members Karloff, Nan Grey and John Sutton, the studio engaged Bela Lugosi to join the line-up in an apparent bid to lure the horror trade. To emphasize the point further, large head shots of Karloff's fearsome visage were displayed on all advertisements.

Tower of London garnered its share of respectable reviews, though some of the highbrow critics disparaged what they considered Universal's tasteless approach to a valid historical subject. Today, the picture is routinely classified as a horror film, much to the bewilderment of first-time viewers. There's certainly plenty for fans of the genre to enjoy — a strong cast, wonderful sets, lots of gruesome highlights, and elaborate production values, accompanied by a Frankensteinian score. But it's borderline horror, at best.

Rowland V. Lee was, by all accounts, a producer with a lot of savvy (Vincent Price remembers him as being "fun and adventurous"), but no one ever accused him of being a first-class director. Lee's early output was eclectic. He drifted into costume pictures, a milieu for which he displayed little flair. Lee simply couldn't hack it as an action director; most of his period pieces are verbose and heavy-handed. His leaden, slightly impersonal style somehow suited *Tower of London*, and it certainly ranks as one of his best efforts.

Though he stubbornly keeps his camera immobile much of the time, Lee does display a sharp eye for composition. One of the best shots in *Tower of London* is Mord's introduction: His head shaved clean, a hawk picturesquely perched on his shoulder, he sharpens his executioner's axe with the pride of an artist. The torture scenes are slowly and deliberately staged so the audience could best savor each agonizing detail. The gratuitous gore is shoehorned into the picture to buttress the slender horror elements of the plot, but Karloff's dispassionate business-like air as he superintends his torture room adds an unexpected element of black humor.

The battle scenes, in contrast, are completely botched and are among the feeblest ever staged. Indeed, a friendly fencing bout between Richard and Edward in the first reel packs more excitement than the battles of Bosworth and Tewkesbury combined. As the Bosworth episode takes place at the climax of the picture, it makes for an abrupt and most unsatisfying conclusion. Lee's method of shooting the lead players against rear projected footage of the troops in action may have been the cheapest way out but it compromises the film's impact severely. The staging is likewise ineffectual, consisting mostly of shots of the fully armored extras milling around in the rain and fog, occasionally jabbing each other with their cardboard weapons with barely concealed indifference. After several dazzling displays of swordsmanship, Richard finally puts his skills to the test, only to be handily bested by Tudor in a perfunctory match-up. The invincible Mord, too, is finished off with only a token effort.

Tower of London's contrived storyline and baffling plot construction isn't helped by producer Lee's sloppy post-production tampering. With a raft of filmed scenes ending up on the cutting room floor and major characters mysteriously dropping from sight, the movie leaves even the most attentive viewer in a state of confusion. Rose Hobart's sensitive, engaging performance as Anne Neville is one of the more unfortunate casualties. Last seen after her betrothal to Rathbone's Richard, she disappears without a whisper of an explanation. The actress told the authors, "Some of my scenes must have been cut. I worked on *Tower of London* for almost six weeks. When I see it now, I think, 'They could have shot that in three days!'" Donnie Dunagan, in the tiny role of child-groom Prince Richard, too, recalled for us scenes that didn't make it to the final cut.

As a director, Lee wasn't aggressively stylish, but had a way of coaxing the best out of his players. Basil Rathbone's Richard, encumbered by a barely noticeable hump, is considerably less deformed than Shakespeare's misshapen rendition of the character. (Surviving portraits of the monarch show no sign of any deformity, and most scholars agree his physical imperfections were a myth.)

Admittedly a triumph of technique, Laurence Olivier's interpretation of Richard in *Richard III* (1956) so underlined the character's monstrousness, one couldn't imagine anyone being fooled by his empty gestures of good will. In contrast, Rathbone's more subtly concealed treachery made his Richard even more insidious as he plots the elimination of all who stand in his way. *Tower of London* shows off Rathbone at the peak of his talents and ranks amongst his most commanding performances.

Boris Karloff plays Mord with a sure hand on his executioner's axe and a sadistic gleam in his eye. The character is cleverly conceived, having inherited the club foot found in popular descriptions of Richard, so that the pair have a physical bond as well as a spiritual one. Mord's defining moment has him begging Richard to take him into battle in order to experience the joy of killing in "hot blood" as a change of pace from his tedious chores as the Tower's chief torturer. It's an underwritten part considering Karloff's prominent billing but the character's cruelty, so casual and memorably over-the-top, makes him a dominating force in the picture. He certainly had an effect on Mel Brooks, whose madcap western spoof *Blazing Saddles* (1974) includes a

Dog lover Karloff takes his canine companions for a stroll on the *Tower of London* set.

character named Boris the Hangman. Complete with medieval garb, gimpy gait and Karloffian delivery, the comic executioner (played by Robert Ridgely) was clearly a takeoff on Mord. Boris the Hangman made a second appearance in Brooks' *Robin Hood: Men in Tights* (1993).

Karloff's off-screen gentleness did not go unnoticed by colleague Hobart, whose acquaintance with the actor had gone back to the Laemmle years at Universal. "He was a lovely and true gentleman," Hobart told the authors. "Why he and Vinnie Price should end up as monsters when they're two of the gentlest people I've ever known is incredible." Child actor-turned-editor-director Ronald Sinclair, who played the ill-fated Boy King Edward who is murdered by Mord's henchmen, directed Karloff's scenes in the AIP 1966 production *The Ghost in the Invisible Bikini.*

Price turns the Duke of Clarence into a repulsive sop and one can sense him struggling to hold his own among his more seasoned colleagues. As usual, Price amusingly overacts but at least it's in keeping with the over-the-top tone of the film. His semi-comic drinking "duel" with Rathbone comes complete with a scene-stealing jag and is easily the film's highlight. Preparing a few comments about *Tower of London* for this book, Mr. Price offered: "I saw it again only recently and found it ponderous but interesting. The drinking match was all ad-libbed and had to be done in very few shots to heighten credibility. We shot it in one day."

For a film that has a footing in both literature and history, the characters of *Tower of London* offer little shading; they're either all good or all bad according to the needs of the script. Ian Hunter's King Edward is a jovial cutthroat; his affectionate domestic scenes with his Queen play like an old "backstage-with-the-royals" theater piece. Miles Mander, in his Universal horror debut, is perfect as the doddering "Paper Crown" King Henry. Those upholding the cause of peace and justice are disadvantaged by blandly written roles, but Barbara O'Neil, in real life the on-again, off-again fiancée of co-star Price, brings stature to the role of the Queen Mother. Nan Grey is the token juvenile lead; the nominal hero, John Sutton, has little screen time.

Hobart vividly recalled her colorful and frequently naughty co-stars on the film:

> All of those English actors were terrible womanizers and they were always telling stories about their conquests. I remember Rathbone telling me one story about Marlene [Dietrich] which really made me kind of sick. We always stopped for tea and I was the only one of the women invited to join the four guys [Rathbone, Karloff, Price and Hunter]. And their conversation was getting dirtier every day. It was really getting obscene! One day when they had just finished one really bad one and they were laughing and having a ball, I asked, "What are the three most insulting words that a woman could say to a man?" And the answer was, "Is it in?" The reaction was fantastic because I knew exactly who had been asked this question and who had not. And they were so shocked that all conversation ceased on the subject for the rest of the time I was invited back. They were trying to outdo each other, of course. The boys were showing off. They were lying through their teeth!

Donnie Dunagan remembers things a bit differently as far as Rathbone was concerned. He told the authors:

> On *Tower of London*, I saw Mr. Rathbone angry several times. He would walk around with the heavy script and talk to people who were obviously in charge ... what happened *may* have been somebody changing the storyline and/or scripting and/or dialogue as we went along. I remember very explicitly that Mr. Rathbone was very "out of character" for him, taking this big pile of typed papers and patting them in the way you do when something's wrong, and pointing here and pointing there, and big discussions that four or five people would join in on. He was unhappy with that film. *Very* unhappy. I could tell because he was always super-super-nice to me [on *Son of Frankenstein*], and on *Tower of London* he did not have the smiles on, he did not come by or pat me or invite me to ice cream or stuff like he used to do.

(Rathbone's displeasure with the film apparently became common knowledge in Hollywood. John Carradine, who worked with the actor months earlier in 20th Century–Fox's *The Hound of the Baskervilles,* once jokingly referred to *Tower of London* as *The Gripes of Rathbone.*)

Lee's persistent on-the-spot rewriting might have served him well in simple genre material such as *Son of Frankenstein* but the unwieldy storyline and complicated characters of *Tower of London* demanded the kind of sophisticated, literary writing which couldn't be hastily ground out in typical Hollywood movie-factory fashion. The film suffers accordingly and, by the last reels, it limps along B-movie style to the finale with little conviction.

When director Paul Landres, best known for *The Return of Dracula* (1958), was asked about his experiences of working on the film as an assistant editor by *Filmfax* writer Francis M. Nevins, he recalled:

> We thought we had an Academy Award picture, we really did. Each scene was remarkable. It

started low and it built to a climax, and it was sensational. And then we saw the first cut and, man, that picture died. And the reason it died was that every scene came up to its peak, and there was nothing but peaks in the whole film. There was no pacing, there was no change. Boy, did I learn. I really learned from that one.

Tower of London, surprisingly, inspired a remake in 1962 when United Artists tried to compete with Roger Corman's Poe cycle at American International with a series of literary shockers of their own. Corman himself was signed to direct *Tower of London* but became disenchanted with the project when executive producer Edward Small balked at the idea of shooting the film in color. Vincent Price graduated to the role of Richard but his shrieking, superficial performance fails to enliven even this slapdash production. The story takes on *Scrooge*-like proportions as Price is beset by one ghost after another.

Somewhere in the flawed, disjointed *Tower of London* there's the makings of a great movie but the Lee Brothers simply didn't have the finesse or resources to make a proper job of it. The talents of Basil Rathbone and art director Jack Otterson come through in full force but they are basically let down by mediocre handling. Universal's interest in historical dramas proved to be a one-film fling. The studio promptly went back to the business of producing more conventional, and affordable, thrillers.

Critics' Corner

With all its dark and sinister overtones, this is a picture of which the industry can be proud for the sheer quality in every department. Clinging to fact with extraordinary fidelity, here is history, unsoftened, made absorbing, exciting, often chilling, but at all times giving a profound sense of living reality.... Without exception the performances are superb. Basil Rathbone adds another to his great screen portraits in the role of the ruthless Richard.... As producer and director, Rowland V. Lee has turned in probably the finest effort in his career. He has executed the difficult feat of making this type of picture human and personal, building powerfully to his climaxes, injecting curiously apt touches of humor, crowning the effort with the powerful, spectacular battle scenes.—*The Hollywood Reporter*, November 17, 1939

Rating: ★★★ *Tower of London* is as sinister as Basil Rathbone, Boris Frankenstein Karloff and the rest of Universal's horror department can make it. And gruesome as it is, the story is mere child's play for a cameraman who gives every indication of having been apprenticed on Dante's Inferno.—*The New York Daily News*, December 12, 1939, Dorothy Masters

[T]his period thriller is less authentic than its elaborately spooky reproductions of London's Tower.... But the battles of Tewkesbury and Bosworth set a new high for realistic racket that should deafen the most demanding.—*Time*, 1939

Tower of London emerges as a spine-chiller with accent on gruesomeness.... As a horror picture, it's one of the most broadly etched, but it's still so strong that it may provide disturbing nightmares as aftermath.... Rathbone provides a most vivid portrayal of the ambitious Duke who schemes and muscles to achieve his ends.—*Variety*, November 16, 1939

[T]he film has a certain macabre fascination if little else.... Somehow it is all too painful and pointless.... Karloff can't be taken seriously—else he would drive one insane of fright.... Even the Rialto's audience, which no one dare accuse of hypersensitivity, grew silent after a while and stopped applauding Mr. Rathbone's villainies. He was almost too bad to be true.—*The New York Times*, December 12, 1939, Frank S. Nugent

1940

The Invisible Man Returns

Released January 12, 1940. 81 minutes. *Director:* Joe May. *Associate Producer:* Ken Goldsmith. *Screenplay:* Lester K. Cole & Kurt [Curt] Siodmak. *Original Story:* Joe May, Kurt [Curt] Siodmak & Cedric Belfrage (uncredited). *Suggested by the novel* The Invisible Man *by* H.G. Wells. *Photography:* Milton Krasner. *Art Director:* Jack Otterson. *Associate Art Director:* Martin Obzina. *Special Photographic Effects:* John P. Fulton. *Editor:* Frank Gross. *Editorial Supervisor:* Maurice Pivar. *Assistant Director:* Phil Karlstein [Karlson]. *Set Decorator:* Russell A. Gausman. *Music:* Hans J. Salter & Frank Skinner. *Musical Director:* Charles Previn. *Camera Operator:* King Gray. *Assistant Cameraman:* Jack Eagan. *Makeup:* Jack P. Pierce. *Sound Supervisor:* Bernard B. Brown. *Technician:* William Hedgcock. *Gowns:* Vera West.

Sir Cedric Hardwicke (*Richard Cobb*), Vincent

Price (*Sir Geoffrey Radcliffe*), Nan Grey (*Helen Manson*), John Sutton (*Dr. Frank Griffin*), Cecil Kellaway (*Insp. Sampson*), Alan Napier (*Willie Spears*), Forrester Harvey (*Ben Jenkins*), Harry Stubbs (*Constable Tukesberry*), Frances Robinson (*Nurse*), Ivan Simpson (*Cotton*), Edward Fielding (*Prison Governor*), Leyland Hodgson (*Chauffeur*), Mary Gordon (*Cook*), Billy Bevan (*Jim*), Dave Thursby (*Bob*), Matthew Boulton (*Policeman*), Bruce Lester (*Chaplain*), Ernie Adams (*Man*), Paul England (*Detective*), Ellis Irving, Dennis Tankard, George Lloyd, George Kirby, Harry Cording, George Hyde, Edmund MacDonald (*Miners*), Louise Brien (*Griffin's Secretary*), Frank Hagney (*Bill*), Frank O'Connor (*Policeman at Colliery*), Frank Hill (*Policeman Attending Cobb*), Rex Evans (*Constable Briggs*), Cyril Thornton, Ed Brady (*Policemen*), Clara Blore (*Woman*), Hugh Huntley (*Secretary*), Jimmy Aubrey, Colin Kenny (*Plainclothesmen*), Mary Field (*Neighbor*), Eric Wilton (*Fingerprint Expert*), Stanley Blystone, Barry Hays, William Newell, Charles Brokaw, Frank Colleti, Sidney Grayler, Boyd Irwin, Crane Whitley, Jeanne Kelly [Jean Brooks].

Leaves you pale around the gills
with its eerie shudders.
—The New York World-Telegram,
January 1940

Along with *Son of Frankenstein*, *The Invisible Man Returns* was the New Universal's most self-conscious attempt to duplicate James Whale's horror style in the post–Laemmle era with enhanced production values and a somewhat lengthier running time to give it an A-picture feel. It's a well-intentioned and, in many ways, admirable picture, especially in its attention to detail and painstaking efforts to recreate the tone of the original. Although the film often gets the critical nod in the general run of film books ("Not as stylized as Whale's original, but a very enjoyable sequel," opines the *Time Out Film Guide* in a fairly typical comment), most fan-based Baby Boomer venues regard it as a verbose or derivative effort whose major distinction is that it marked Vincent Price's official entry as a horror star. Everyone seems to agree that *The Invisible Man Returns* is somewhat lacking in verve, but one thing you can't say about it is that it's a cheap knock-off of the original.

Sir Geoffrey Radcliffe (Vincent Price), wrongly accused of the slaying of his brother, Sir Michael, is condemned to die on the gallows. When the hour of execution strikes, he vanishes from his prison cell. Scotland Yard Insp. Sampson (Cecil Kellaway) correctly deduces that the fugitive's friend and his last visitor, Dr. Frank Griffin (John Sutton), brother of the late Jack Griffin, the Invisible Man, injected the prisoner with the invisibility serum. Reunited with his fiancée, Helen Manson (Nan Grey), the now invisible Radcliffe realizes his only hope is to find the real murderer before the mind-altering effect of the drug overtakes him.

Radcliffe's suspicions are aroused when Willie Spears (Alan Napier), a slovenly and usually drunk night watchman, is promoted to a ranking position in the family mining operations. Geoffrey forces Spears' car off the road and confronts the terrified man. Spears confesses that he witnessed Radcliffe's cousin Richard Cobb (Sir Cedric Hardwicke) bludgeon Michael to death. Cobb paid Spears off with a promotion to ensure his silence. Radcliffe binds and gags Spears, and then sets out after Cobb.

Despite a heavy police guard, Geoffrey gets to Cobb and brings him face to face with Spears, who quickly incriminates him. Cobb kills Spears and escapes, but Radcliffe chases him through the teeming village streets. Making his way to the collieries, the Invisible Man pins Cobb to a moving coal cart on the mining escalator. A lucky shot, fired by Sampson, strikes Radcliffe seconds before the coal wagon releases its load, sending Cobb hurtling to the ground far below. With his dying breath, Cobb confesses to the murder of Sir Michael.

Near death from exposure and loss of blood, Geoffrey, wearing a ragged suit stolen from a farmer's scarecrow, makes his way to Griffin's clinic. Frank administers an emergency transfusion to save his friend's life only to discover that the new blood serves as the perfect antidote. His visibility restored, Geoffrey, now a free man, is reunited with Helen.

Universal first announced that *The Invisible Man Returns* was in the works in March 1939, around the time *Son of Frankenstein* was proving to "have legs" at the box office. As months wore on, pre-production tidbits began showing up in the trade papers with greater frequency. In early May, Joe May was set as the director with either Boris Karloff or Bela Lugosi hinted at to play the lead. Days later the studio was already reneging, now naming Rowland V. Lee producer-director, a natural choice considering his *Son* credentials. W.P. Lipscomb, who had such high-profile liter-

Lobby card used to promote *The Invisible Man Returns* in 1940 theaters.

ary assignments as *Les Miserables* (1935), *A Tale of Two Cities* (1935) and *Pygmalion* (1938) on his credits list, was chosen to write the screenplay. Some time later, the writing chores changed hands, now with Michael Hogan (who would later work on the adaptation of *Rebecca* [1940] and *The Blue Lagoon* [1949]) given the assignment.

On June 29, *The Hollywood Reporter* mentioned that Universal was looking for an unknown actor to fill the title role, specifying that they needed a young, good-looking contender even though he would remain invisible until the last reel. There were few doubts, however, as to who should be assigned the intricate special effects work. John P. Fulton, would be start work on his assignment as soon as he returned from filming backdrops for James Whale's *Green Hell* (1940) in Mexico.

As it turned out, three top roles of *The Invisible Man Returns* were filled with principals of the recently completed *Tower of London,* Vincent Price, Nan Grey and John Sutton. Sir Cedric Hardwicke, the distinguished British actor who slummed his way through many a Hollywood potboiler, was given star billing in what amounts to a supporting role. Ostensibly the star was Vincent Price, appearing in his third film under a long-term contract. The young actor showed a distinct flair for comedy in his first film, 1938's *Service de Luxe.* Price's slightly aristocratic bearing eliminated him from the usual run of leading man roles, and he soon drifted into character parts. His rich, theatrical voice made him an ideal choice to follow in the footsteps of Claude Rains in *The Invisible Man Returns.* Price had another unique qualification to fill the role: His ability to communicate with the film's director, Joe May. "May was difficult to understand, as he spoke no English," Price recalled for the authors. "I had something of a rapport with him because of my knowledge of German."

May unwittingly made an important contribution to the genre by hiring a writer friend he knew in Germany. His name was Curt Siodmak, and he would soon become one of the leading figures in Universal's new horror cycle.

The brother of director Robert Siodmak, Curt got sidetracked into the film business while working as a reporter for a German newspaper in the mid–'20s. He and his wife were on assignment to write a story on director Fritz Lang who was in the midst of shooting his masterwork, *Metropolis* (1926) and soon found themselves hired as extras on the production. Siodmak's initial science fiction screenwriting job was the scenario for the 1932 German picture *F.P.1 Antwortet Nicht* (*Floating Platform 1 Does Not Answer*), based on his own novel. Compelled to leave Germany when Hitler came to power, Siodmak emigrated first to England and then to Hollywood, where he met up with Joe May.

Aside from his work at Universal, Siodmak also contributed to the screenplays of shockers released by Monogram (*The Ape* [1940]), RKO (*I Walked with a Zombie* [1943]) and Warners (*The Beast with Five Fingers* [1946]). Earlier in their careers, Curt and brother Robert had an agreement that Curt would write, Robert would direct, and neither would become identified with the other's specialty. Curt broke this agreement in the early '50s when he entered the adventuresome arena of low-budget production-direction. Unhappily, his best screenwriting days were already behind him, and the films he directed from his own scripts, *Bride of the Gorilla* (1951), *Curucu, Beast of the Amazon* (1956), *Love-Slaves of the Amazons* (1957) and the silly sex comedy *Ski Fever* (1969), were uninspired and eminently forgettable.

Siodmak continued to write, lecture about horror films and travel extensively up until several years before his death in 2000. Back in the '80s, he told the authors:

> Today, nobody lives better than I do. I have an estate, fifty acres overlooking the mountains, and every night I say "Heil Hitler!" because without the son of a bitch, I wouldn't be in Three Rivers, California, I'd still be in Berlin!

Like several other Universal thrillers of this period, *The Invisible Man Returns* was plagued with production problems. A $253,750 budget and a 27-day schedule proved barely adequate for the sophisticated special effects involved and a director with May's slow, meticulous work habits. Shooting began on October 13, 1939, but within a week, trouble was brewing. Despite favorable weather conditions, exterior shooting was time-consuming and difficult. To comply with the story, the studio back lot was transformed into a northern England mining town with a full-scale reproduction of a colliery. The elaborate sets included a huge coal pile and a coal escalator, 75 feet long, running to a platform 40 feet high.

By the end of the second week of shooting, production on *The Invisible Man Returns* was slipping precariously behind schedule, even before the filming of painstaking special effects sequences; these were rescheduled for the final weeks of shooting. As was becoming the norm on a Joe May picture, the tired company worked late into the night. By early November, the cast and crew were toiling past midnight with little hope of making the deadline. A long dinner scene alone consumed three days of shooting.

May's methodical ways didn't endear him to the Front Office, nor did his temperament. According to Henry Koster, when a studio executive arrived on the soundstage one day, the blustery May snapped, "I will not work as long as you are on the set!" When the astonished executive pressed for an explanation, May presented the classic ultimatum: "Either you leave or I leave." Sticking to his guns, the executive shot back, "Well, you leave. It's okay with me." Learning a bitter lesson, the proud director found himself crawling to the studio bigwigs to get his job back!

Vincent Price, who appears in the "flesh" for less than a minute, spent most of his days on the set being groomed as a "special effect." Said the actor:

> All of the effects scenes were done with my involvement. It was terribly tedious as I had to be dressed from top to toe in black velvet and I had to work against a set draped in black velvet. John Fulton, whose ingenuity contrived it all, was the leading special effects man at that time. I enjoyed it. The tedium was ultimately more than worthwhile, and I love special effects.... Sir Cedric Hardwicke was a delightful man. He ended up being one of my best friends. He didn't like doing this film; he was facing home problems at the time. We became very close.

On November 11, 1939, the production finally wrapped. Still left to be shot were three or four days of effects footage under Fulton's supervision. In all, the crew worked 15 nights until ten or later. On the last day of shooting, May drove his exhausted company until 4:45 A.M. the following morning. The final cost, including special effects and laboratory overruns, came to $270,000, more than $15,000 over the allotted budget.

For a film that's largely the work of two German émigrés (director Joe May and writer Curt Siodmak) and a single American (co-writer Lester Cole), *The Invisible Man Returns* does an impressive job of maintaining a convincingly British ambiance. Returning to the novel's setting of northern England, the script specifically chooses a mining village as its principal locale, incorporating it as a major ingredient of the plot. The payoff comes in the form of an exciting climax as the invisible hero pursues the murderer on an elevated mining tram, finally pinning him to one of the coal carts where he ultimately plunges to his death. It's an unusual set piece for a Hollywood movie and one would be hard pressed to think of another film where such equipment was used for such dramatic use. The scene recalls Hitchcock in the way it uses a setting not particularly associated with thrillers in an entirely different context (the windmill in 1940's *Foreign Correspondent* and Mount Rushmore in 1959's *North by Northwest* are obvious examples).

Director Joe May parrots James Whale in the way he works comedy into the script, mostly by milking the broad reactions of the unsuspecting rustic characters. As in the original film, the police force seems to operate under a structured class system whereby the ranking officers diligently pursue their investigations while the uniformed constabulary are invariably depicted as lovable rubes (providing made-to-order roles for comic actors Harry Stubbs and Billy Bevan who performed similar functions in *WereWolf of London* and *Dracula's Daughter*). Forrester Harvey, Una O'Connor's henpecked husband in *The Invisible Man*, is back, this time as a scruffy gout-stricken hermit, naturally, played for laughs.

Cole and Siodmak's characters, despite superficial differences, are patterned after those in the R.C. Sherriff screenplay. With Vincent Price and Nan Grey's characters finding their dramatic equivalent in the Claude Rains and Gloria Stuart parts, likewise Sir Cedric Hardwicke's Richard Cobb counterpoints William Harrigan's Kemp nicely. Both films develop scientist figures as strong secondary characters (John Sutton substituting for the paternal Henry Travers) to provide emotional support for the leads. Taking matters further, Hardwicke and Harrigan are similar types, physically and temperamentally, who take advantage of the hero's absence to ineffectually sweet-talk his sweetheart. Both become decoys in Scotland Yard's attempt to entrap the transparent hero in elaborate scenes and ultimately pay for their sins in the last reel. There's even a scene in *The Invisible Man Returns* with Hardwicke wheedling Grey on a window seat that is composed in the same manner as a corresponding scene with Harrigan trying to birddog Gloria Stuart in the original.

If this weren't enough, *The Invisible Man Returns* employs the original's device of keeping the unseen protagonist's physical appearance under wraps until the final scene. By scrupulously avoiding flashbacks and any photographic representations of the character, the film stokes the audience's mounting curiosity about a hero they know only as a disembodied voice — a tease all the more effective considering that Rains and Price were two relative unknowns at the time their movies were released. Their "unveiling" comes with a grand build-up of John P. Fulton's materialization effects and suitably triumphant musical cues. The scene still works well for *The Invisible Man Returns* today, especially for fans who know Price mainly for his later screen and TV appearances and are unaccustomed to his youthful appearance here.

The Invisible Man Returns is somewhat let down by Joe May's rather pedantic direction. His characteristic stodgy, methodical tendencies which won his few friends at the studio are present in every frame and Frank Gross' lax editing only compounds the problem. For all the fussiness and attention to detail, there's little payoff in the way of inventiveness. Instead, May comes off as a minor-league William Wyler in his refusal to call attention to his technique but lacking his countryman Wyler's sense of stylistic precision. The film has the stateliness of a big-budget Hollywood picture in which characters go about in

Invisible Man Returns **director Joe May rehearses a scene with Vincent Price and Nan Grey.**

comfortable, well-appointed sets to over-explain every nuance of every situation in an unhurried fashion. (Two back-to-back scenes of Sutton receiving unwelcome visits from Hardwicke and then one from Kellaway seem endless.) The film's opening credits boast, "A sequel to *The Invisible Man* by H.G. Wells" prominently placed after the title card, gently prods the audience into a literary mood. In Hollywood, that too often meant a producer who was granting himself license to be at least slightly dull.

Still, overlooking *The Invisible Man Return*'s air of stuffiness, its sober, adult approach to the material is rather refreshing compared to the typically juvenile tone that was becoming *de rigueur* for horror movies. The extra little "oomph" in the production is welcome especially in an evocative early morning shot of the small mining community beginning to come to life as workers stroll and bicycle to the colliery (with the Hollywood Hills looming large on the horizon). May also deserves full marks for a lengthy, intricately timed scene of invisible Geoffrey pursuing Cobb down a village street which involved huddled clusters of extras being dispersed as the Invisible Man "charges" through them. A smart shot has the camera following Geoffrey's trail as he hoodwinks the mob into giving chase even while he's closing in Cobb who heads for the coal elevator. (Even more kudos for the unidentified stuntman who takes Hardwicke's 40-foot fall from the elevated coal platform.)

The Invisible Man Returns is disadvantaged by the fact that it's more mystery than science fiction, its plot driven by Price's perseverance to identify his brother's killer. As a result, the film lacks the original's strain of black comedy with Rains' chillingly off-handed and prankish acts of mayhem and mass murder. Price is a Boy Scout by comparison, his acts of mischief confined to the guilty parties and the gormless policemen. Allowed only a single "mad" scene,

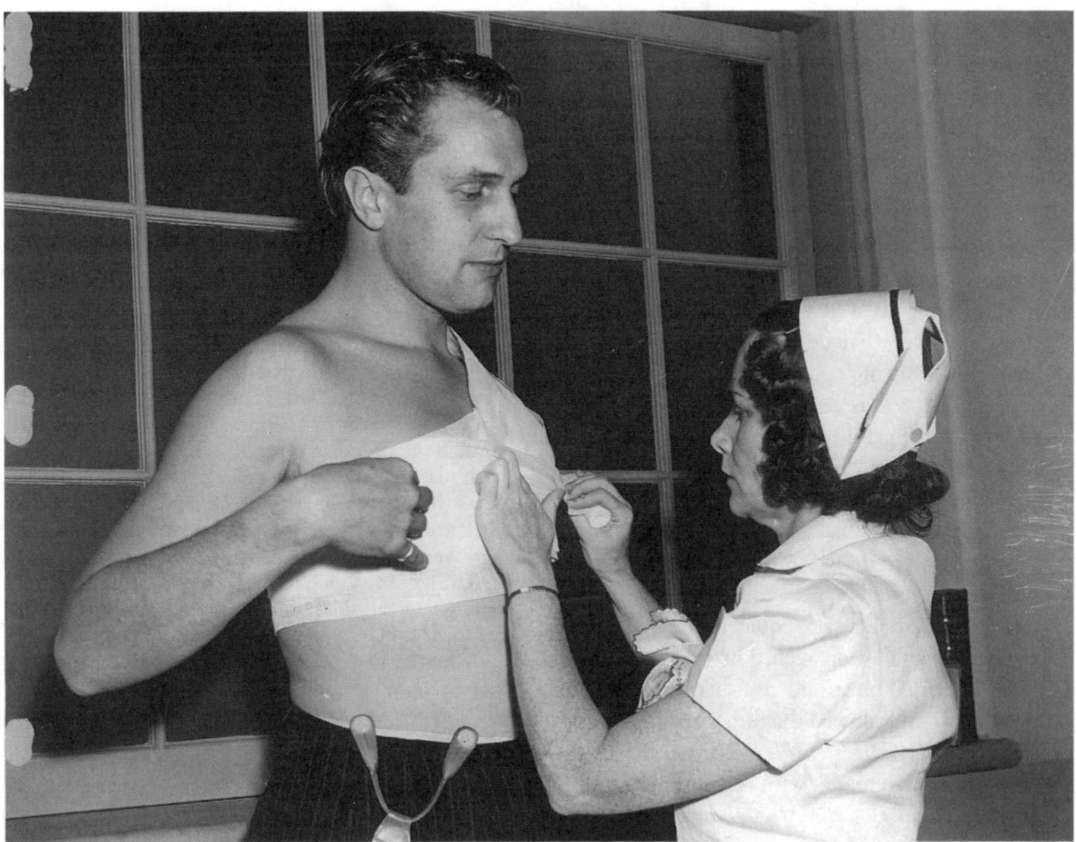

Preparing for a trick scene in *The Invisible Man Returns*, Vincent Price is bandaged by nurse Peggy Bell at the studio hospital.

Price proves to be inept as the (invisible) "man who would be king." He's barely able to blurt out his grandiose ambitions as a world dictator before he's drugged, hauled off and shackled by John Sutton, hardly the most physically imposing of actors. The incident is dismissed as "a temporary attack of insanity," however, and is promptly forgotten. There's a decided emphasis on character, and the touching, understated romantic interludes are skillfully handled. The broad, juvenile *Topper*-like antics of the sort that plagued the rest of the series, are happily kept to a minimum.

The score is among the finest of Universal horror movies though it makes excellent use of Frank Skinner's *Son of Frankenstein* in the climactic chase. Hans J. Salter's wistfully melodic main title (one of his best) would turn up in other films (*Man Made Monster*, *The Strange Case of Doctor Rx*) with a faster tempo but it never sounded better than here. The beautiful cue utilized in Price's materialization scene would be modified with the addition of a violin solo part for *Son of Dracula*.

John P. Fulton's Oscar-nominated special effects surpass his work in the original. Shots of the transparent protagonist glimpsed through rain, fog and even in the wisps of smoke from a burning cigar are executed with cunning. The matte shots of Price slowly becoming visible are more detailed than in the Whale film, as layers of muscle, sinew and blood vessels appear until the rematerialization is complete. In addition, some stop-motion animation is evident (the first and only time in a Universal horror movie of this vintage) as Price binds Napier's ankles with a rope.

Vincent Price proves to be a worthy successor to Rains, imbuing the role with a vocal presence that's at once cultured and commanding. As usual for Price, he adds more vigor than is required but that's the fun of watching the actor, who was well on his way to becoming one of Hollywood's least apologetic hams.

As in *Tower of London*, Nan Grey is far too American in these Anglo-Saxon settings, but is appealing if somewhat mousy. Sir Cedric Hardwicke is believable in what is essentially a walk-through performance. "Solid support," that overworked phrase, is entirely fitting for Cecil Kellaway and John Sutton. But the real surprise is Alan Napier as Willie Spears. Although Napier later confessed that he regarded his part as the smooth, reassuring country doctor in *The Uninvited* (1944) as his only good Hollywood role, his turn as the grimy, underhanded night watchman is a highlight in his career.

Fueled by receptive reviews, box office grosses for *The Invisible Man Returns* were healthy: It netted $815,100 in domestic and international rentals. New York's Rialto Theater reported that ticket sales equaled that of *Tower of London*, their all-time record breaker of the previous season. The studio couldn't resist the opportunity and followed the film up with the outright comedy, *The Invisible Woman*. In 1951, the film was semi-remade (with obvious alterations) as *Abbott and Costello Meet the Invisible Man*. With the title character rewritten as a boxer framed for murder, lengthy passages of Siodmak and Cole's dialogue were lifted almost verbatim, as well as a couple of Fulton's trick shots. Well past their prime, Bud and Lou's antics were growing tiresome and Arthur Franz, a limited, unappealing actor to begin with, made a glum and obnoxious protagonist.

Not to be outdone, in 1958, a Mexican outfit shamelessly availed themselves of sizable portions of the storyline for an unauthorized semi-remake, *El Hombre Que Logro' ser Invisible* (released here as *The New Invisible Man*) with Arturo de Cordova. The South of the Border production lifted the ending of Philip Wylie's novel *The Murderer Invisible*, which Universal owned the rights to, and may have used to some small extent in writing the script for *The Invisible Man*. At the climax of Wylie's book, his Invisible Man prepares to dump deadly bacilli into a major city's water supply. *The New Invisible Man* used that ending; the rest of the plot was stolen from *The Invisible Man Returns*. It's interesting that a Mexican movie from the '50s would also turn to the Wylie book to augment what they had already swiped from H.G. Wells and Universal.

The 1940 *The Invisible Man Returns* never looked better.

Critics' Corner

It is a picture that will be enjoyed thoroughly by kids as well as grown-ups and is sure-fire entertainment for the Saturday matinee crowd.—*The Hollywood Reporter*, January 10, 1940

[N]either so horrendous nor so humorous as [*The Invisible Man*]. Blame that on time and Topper.... [T]he script is annoyingly unoriginal.—*The New York Times*, January 16, 1940, Frank S. Nugent

Rating: ★★★ [S]ome of the novelty of the strange situation has worn off. [The plot is] ... filled with suspense and at times take[s] on the comedy aspects that made *Topper* such an amusing film.... Sir Cedric Hardwicke is an effective menace....—*The New York Daily News*, January 16, 1940, Kate Cameron

Rating: Very Good to Excellent. The suspense, accruing from all sides, mounts to an impressive total. Sir Cedric Hardwicke accomplishes his shift from early suavity to gibbering fear with a conviction rarely seen in unimportant or trick effect films. He is splendid.—*The New York Post*, January 16, 1940, Archer Winsten

[T]he new invisible man is up, and his invisibility ... is the source of drama, comedy and an eeriness which may strain the credulity but which never fails to be highly diverting.—*The Hollywood Citizen-News*, 1940

Black Friday

Released April 12, 1940. 70 minutes. *Associate Producer:* Burt Kelly. *Director:* Arthur Lubin. *Original Screenplay:* Kurt [Curt] Siodmak & Eric Taylor. *Photography:* Elwood Bredell. *Art Director:* Jack Otterson. *Associate Art Director:* Harold MacArthur. *Editor:* Philip Cahn. *Music Director:* Hans J. Salter. *Assistant Director:* Fred Frank. *Gowns:* Vera West. *Set Decorator:* Russell A. Gausman. *Sound Supervisor:* Bernard B. Brown. *Technician:* Charles Carroll. *Special Effects:* John P. Fulton. *Makeup:* Jack P. Pierce.

Boris Karloff (*Dr. Ernest Sovac*), Bela Lugosi (*Eric Marnay*), Stanley Ridges (*Prof. George Kingsley/Red Cannon*), Anne Nagel (*Sunny Rogers*), Anne Gwynne (*Jean Sovac*), Virginia Brissac (*Margaret Kingsley*), Edmund MacDonald (*Frank Miller*), Paul Fix (*William Kane*), Murray Alper (*Bellhop*), Jack Mulhall (*Bartender*), Joe King (*Chief of Police*), John Kelly (*Taxi Driver*), James Craig (*Reporter*), Jerry Marlowe (*Clerk*), Edward McWade (*Newspaper File Attendant*), Eddie Dunn (*Detective Farnow*), Emmett Vogan (*Detective Carpenter*), Edward Earle, Kernan Cripps (*Detectives*), Edwin Stanley (*Dr. Warner*), Frank Sheridan (*Chaplain*), Harry Hayden (*Prison Doctor*), Dave Oliver, Harry Tenbrook (*Cab Drivers*), Raymond Bailey

(*Louis Devore*), Ellen Lowe (*Maid*), Franco Corsaro (*Headwaiter*), Frank Jaquet (*Fat Man at Bar*), Dave Willock, Tommy Conlon, Wallace Reid, Jr. (*Students*), William Ruhl (*Man*), Victor Zimmerman (*G-Man*), Jessie Arnold, Doris Borodin (*Nurses*).

By day a man of culture ... by night a monster let loose by a mad scientist who gave him two brains....
—*Ad blurb for* Black Friday

A then-unique blend of science fiction, horror and gangster elements, *Black Friday* marked the fifth and final teaming of genre giants Boris Karloff and Bela Lugosi in a Universal horror vehicle. Unfortunately, it's a film that fails to take proper advantage of its lead players, the horror equivalent of an Astaire-Rogers musical in which the two stars do not dance together or even meet. This, coupled with the fact that Lugosi plays a demeaning minor role, has soured many fans, while still others complain that the film's juiciest role is squandered on a character actor that no one cared to see. Rarely mentioned is the fact that this character actor, Stanley Ridges, does a superb job that Lugosi, and perhaps Karloff, could not have matched.

Black Friday was at least partly the brainchild (pun intended) of Curt Siodmak, the talented German-born screenwriter whose efforts went a long way toward shaping the '40s horror film scene. Its theme of brain-switching became an *idee fixe* with Siodmak, who fell back on the device many times during his long career. Aside from co-writing *Black Friday*, the single-minded Siodmak also wrote the novel *Donovan's Brain*, its sequel *Hauser's Memory*, the screen stories for *House of Frankenstein*, *Creature with the Atom Brain* and *Earth vs. the Flying Saucers* (multiple brain transplants, remote-controlled brains and brain-draining, respectively) and the teleplay for the failed 1958 pilot *Tales of Frankenstein* (more brain juggling).

December 28, 1939, marked the first day of *Black Friday* shooting, with work progressing more than two weeks into the New Year. Director Arthur Lubin was forced to contend with an extremely tight schedule and the added onus of frequent stage moves (to take advantage of standing sets). Production was further hampered by rain delays and by union-happy Karloff, who steadfastly refused to work more than eight hours a day. By January 12, *Black Friday* had been branded a problem picture in a studio memo which cited Karloff's hard-line attitude and director Lubin's "erratic pacing." Despite the delays, Lubin wrapped *Black Friday* on January 18, right on schedule and nearly $5,000 under the $130,750 budget originally earmarked for the film.

Dr. Ernest Sovac (Boris Karloff), sentenced to die in the electric chair, walks the last mile, pausing to hand his medical diary to one of the reporters (James Craig) who has come to witness the execution. Sovac is led away as the reporter thumbs through the journal....

Flashbacks take us to Newcastle (a small town in "the sticks," according to dialogue), where George Kingsley (Stanley Ridges), a professor at the local university, is preparing to take the train east. Driving Kingsley to the depot is his friend Sovac, accompanied by his (Sovac's) daughter Jean (Anne Gwynne). Kingsley is just stepping out of the car when the sound of gunfire is heard and two cars appear from around a bend in the road: Gangster Red Cannon (also Ridges, in a different makeup), driving one of the cars, is embroiled in a high-speed gun battle with the occupants of the second car. Cannon's car runs down Kingsley and crashes while the other car, occupied by rival gangsters Marnay (Bela Lugosi), Miller (Edmund MacDonald), Kane (Paul Fix) and Devore (Raymond Bailey), makes its getaway.

Kingsley suffers head injuries and slips into a coma; Cannon sustains a broken spine. Apparently left alone with the two men at the local hospital for many hours, Sovac secretly performs an illegal operation, transplanting part of Cannon's brain into the crushed cranium of his dying friend. Cannon dies while Kingsley rallies.

When Sovac learns that Cannon had hidden $500,000 in stolen cash shortly before his death, he becomes obsessed with the idea of reactivating the Cannon brain and locating the loot. Sovac invites Kingsley to accompany him on a trip to New York City: He tells the unsuspecting scholar that the trip will hasten his recovery while in reality he hopes that a visit to Cannon's stamping grounds will rouse the dormant Cannon brain.

Sovac and Kingsley check into the Manhattan hotel where Cannon hid out from police.

Stanley Ridges in the role of his screen career in *Black Friday*.

That night the scheming Sovac takes Kingsley to the Club Royale where Cannon's old sweetheart Sunny Rogers (Anne Nagel) is a singer. When Kane — one of Cannon's killers — passes near their table, Kingsley spots him and instantly develops a blinding headache. Sovac rushes him back to the hotel where, as Kingsley sleeps, Sovac taunts him with Cannon's name; Kingsley writhes in agony as the music rises and images of Cannon's killers dance in his aching noggin. When Kingsley raises his head, we see that his face has taken on a slightly different look. The Cannon brain has been awakened!

Sovac explains the situation to "Cannon," who catches on quickly and, behind Sovac's back, hurries out of the hotel. In a montage-style series of nighttime shots, we see "Cannon" at large in Manhattan, stealing into a vacant building where he throttles Louis Devore.

By morning, Kingsley is himself again, with no memory of the previous night's dirty work. That night, however, the sound of a siren triggers a second transformation. "Cannon" catches up with Kane and strangles him, then pays a visit to Sunny Rogers. Sunny is initially angry with the stranger who claims to be Cannon, but as he moves confidently around her apartment, opening secret panels that only Cannon knew about, the girl is dumbfounded.

Sunny betrays "Cannon," setting him up to be killed by Marnay and Miller. The two gangsters trail "Cannon" as he drives to the city reservoir and descends into the underground control room where his $500,000 is hidden in a metal box. Returning to the surface, he is confronted by Marnay and Miller, who hold him at gunpoint and demand the money. In the brawl that ensues, "Cannon" chokes Miller to death while Marnay escapes with the box. "Cannon" later catches up with Marnay at Sunny's apartment and seals him in a broom closet by blocking the door with a heavy freezer. Amidst the frantic cries of the suffocating Marnay, "Cannon" strangles Sunny.*

"Cannon" falls asleep during a taxi ride to the airport, reawakens as Kingsley and asks the frustrated driver to take him to his hotel. Absent-mindedly carrying "Cannon"'s metal box, Kingsley retires to his room and collapses into bed. Sovac finds and keeps the money.

Sovac and Kingsley return to Newcastle, Kingsley goes back to teaching and the Cannon brain is dormant. Kingsley is addressing his students one day when the wail of a siren fills the air. Kingsley becomes frantic as the transformation begins; in a nice macabre touch, he envisions the ghosts of Marnay, Miller, Kane, Devore and Sunny rising up from between the rows of seated students and menacingly moving closer. "Cannon" bolts from the classroom and hurries to the Sovac home, bursts in and attacks Jean. Responding to his daughter's screams, Sovac appears with gun in hand and fires. "Cannon" slumps to the floor where, in death, he reverts for the last time to Kingsley.

With the flashbacks at an end, we return to the death house where the reporter (evidently a speed reader) has just finished perusing Sovac's diary. Sovac dies in the electric chair at the appointed hour, the tenth casualty of this 70-minute movie. On the last page of his diary he expresses the hope that, in better hands than his, these notes can be used for the benefit of mankind.

Because of the New York-gangster milieu, *Black Friday* doesn't even look like a horror or sci-fi film except during the surgical scene and the Kingsley-into–Cannon transformations, perhaps two minutes of screen time out of 70. And yet it might be Universal's best no-monster horror movie of the 1940s. The opening sequence, with Karloff walking the last mile,† gets the picture off to an appropriately downbeat start, and the flashback scenes quickly establish every major character and create strong interest in the unusual story that is building. The movie lurches into crime-drama territory after the action moves to Manhattan, but even here, the Kinglsey-Cannon transformations, cinematographer Elwood Bredell's use of light and ominous shadows, and Frank Skinner's *Son of Frankenstein* music in the murder scenes are frequent reminders that it's also a horror movie. The clever writing, high death rate, staccato Warners-style pacing and Ridges' outstanding performance add up to a fast, lively and rather impressive B thriller.

Nevertheless, it continues to be held in somewhat low esteem by some fans who know what Universal's initial plans for the film were, and continue to complain decades later about the studio's change of heart. In *Black Friday*'s pre-production stage, it was planned that Lugosi would play the surgeon Sovac and that Karloff would play the dual role of the professor-gangster. As the first day of production neared, however, the cast was suddenly shuffled: Karloff became Sovac, Bela Lugosi landed with a deafening crash in the film's supporting cast as the rival gangster, and Stanley Ridges was signed up to play Kingsley-Cannon. (Signed up and put to work quite quickly, it seems; the day before production began, *The Hollywood Reporter*'s gossip columnist announced that "New York legiter" Ridges was in town being tested by director Arthur Lubin for the Kingsley role.) Some modifications had to be made in order to accommodate all this role-swapping, although the veddy British Karloff was still hung with a Slavic-sounding character name (one reference to Sovac's European roots, and his Jewishness, was deleted from the script; a second implication remained).

In a *Fangoria* interview, Curt Siodmak told the authors that it was Karloff himself who had prompted Universal to recast the picture:

> Karloff didn't want to play the dual role in *Black Friday*. He was afraid of it; there was too much acting in it, it was too intricate. So they took Stanley Ridges, who was a stage actor, and he filled the part. Karloff was smart enough to know that he might not come off too well in the role.

Then Siodmak suddenly got on Poor Bela's case:

**In the night club scene in which Sunny sings, it sounds like Anne Nagel is doing the warbling herself— but in her death scene, the scream that comes out of Nagel is Anne Gwynne's! "Whenever a girl couldn't get [a scream] out, they always called on me," Gwynne later recalled.*

†*Incorporated into these scenes is Death Row footage from James Whale's* Wives Under Suspicion *(1938). It later turned up again in* Man Made Monster.

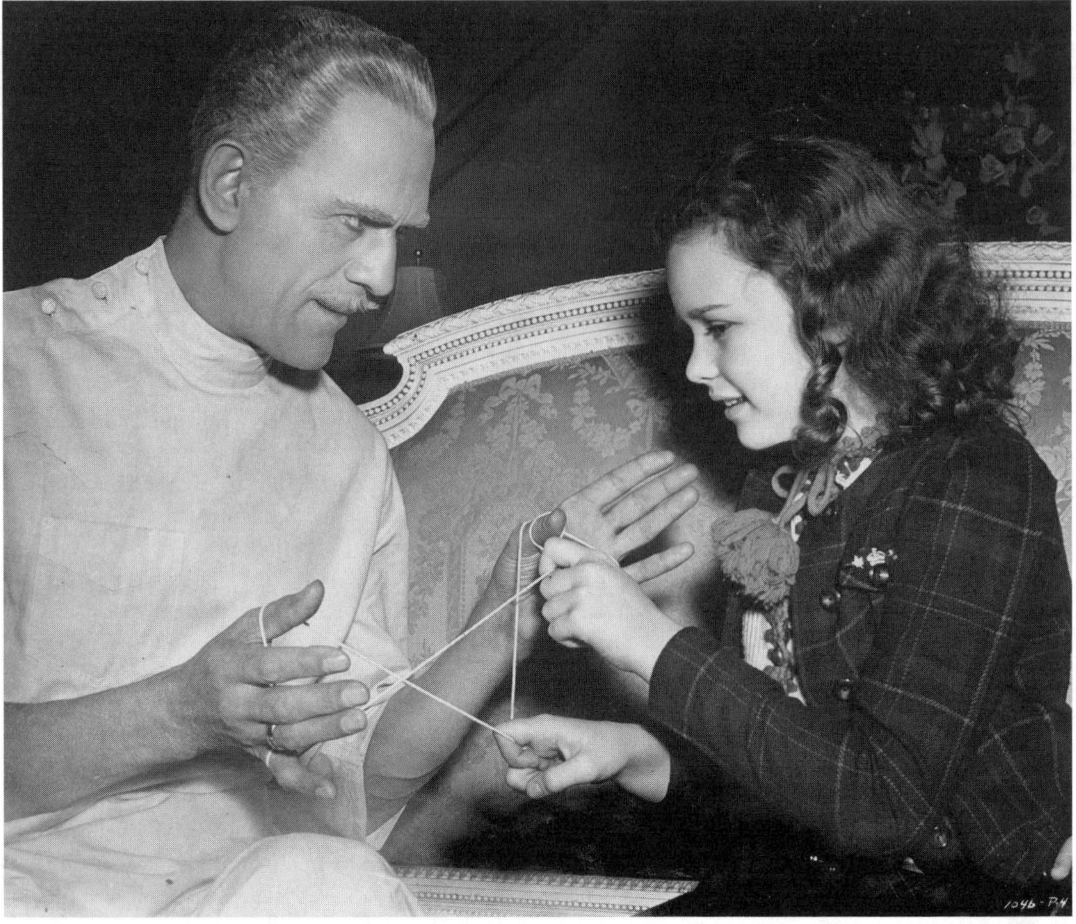

Child star Gloria Jean pays Boris Karloff a visit on the *Black Friday* set (photograph courtesy Rich Scrivani).

> Bela Lugosi ended up playing a gangster in *Black Friday*, and that didn't turn out well at all. Bela never could act his way out of a paper bag. He could only be Mee-ster Drac-u-la, with that accent and those Hungarian movements of his.

Fangoria's mailbox soon bulged with missives from offended fans wanting to debate Siodmak's comments in the magazine's letter column. Richard Gordon, the New York–based producer of the English-made Karloff films *The Haunted Strangler* (1958) and *Corridors of Blood* (1962), got in the best licks at Siodmak. He dismissed the man's comments about Karloff as "rubbish," bringing up several interesting and valid points, and also rose to the defense of Lugosi. Of Siodmak himself, Gordon wrote:

> Regrettably he proves that he can no longer be taken seriously, and belongs inside the paper bag out of which Bela Lugosi had acted his way when Curt Siodmak was still a child.

His points are well-taken, but his inference that Karloff would have done full justice to the gangster role in *Black Friday* is arguable. In the early '30s, Karloff played gangland characters in a number of Hollywood films, with mixed results. It's fun to see Karloff as a mug or a racketeer in pictures like *Smart Money* (1931), *Scarface* (1932) and others, but he's a convincing gangster like Edward G. Robinson would have made a convincing Imhotep. If *Black Friday* had been filmed as planned, there's little doubt that Karloff's Red Cannon would have held his own in nose-to-nose encounters with Lugosi's Dr. Sovac, and probably at other points as well. But it's a little embarrassing trying to picture a 1940 Karloff using gangland slang, jumping around urban rooftops, playing kissy-face with Anne Nagel or brawling in the waterfront dirt with burly Edmund MacDonald.

Although the slightly demented Dr. Sovac is a character right out of stock, Karloff was correct in opting for this more standard role (reminiscent of some in his concurrent Columbia Mad Doctor series), and leaving Cannon to an actor who seems younger and less British. ("*Seems*" younger and less British — in reality, Ridges was about the same age as Boris, and English-born!)

Like Kingsley-Cannon, Sovac undergoes a change during the course of the picture as well. In early scenes set in Newcastle, Sovac is an affable, decent fellow, but once he learns about the Cannon cache, the dark side of his personality manifests itself. Conspiring to lay his hands on Cannon's "500 Gs," he drags Kingsley along to New York and mercilessly badgers his sick friend. Finally achieving his goal of restoring Cannon to "life," he amuses the gangster by belittling Kingsley as "a professor of literature"; he does not seem concerned when the newly reborn killer goes off on his revenge kick, even though Kingsley's life is obviously at stake as well. Even when "Cannon" comes back from one of his forays with a bullet in his arm, Sovac allows the situation to continue. Karloff is ice-cold in the role, all sidelong avaricious leers and sly innuendo.

Sovac is a somewhat different character in an earlier script draft. Here it's scientific curiosity and not the stolen money which prompts the New York trip (Sovac doesn't learn about the hidden half-million until after their arrival in Manhattan). There's also a bizarre, wisely deleted scene in which Sovac rants at his daughter about his ultimate goal. He explains that the human brain requires 300 years of life to reach full development; if the brain of an old man is transplanted into the head of a child, time and again over the space of those centuries, it will eventually solve the riddles of the cosmos and bring happiness to all mankind.

Karloff benefited from the switch while Lugosi, as usual, found himself holding the short end of the stick. The minor role of Eric Marnay is a thankless one, and Lugosi is completely wrong for the part. Some rewriting was required to expand the role for Lugosi: In the first draft of the script, the head of the gang is killed in the fight at the reservoir, and a lesser gangster is smothered to death in Sunny Rogers' broom closet. By having Lugosi's Marnay survive the reservoir fight to become the closet victim, Lugosi's screen time is extended.

But Lugosi is a complete washout: He's silly rather than sinister, and the gang members he bosses around look as though they could chew him up and spit him out. Lugosi also muffs several lines during the course of the picture ("He's leading us to half million dollars"; "Red's been dead since two month"), and on *Black Friday*'s tight schedule there was little time for retakes that were not entirely necessary. And why being locked in a closet causes him to suffocate is anybody's guess. Lugosi should have turned down the assignment when he learned about the cast shake-up, but the actor, a forgotten man during the horror ban, was probably just glad to be working.

In casting Lugosi as Marnay, Universal gypped audiences out to Karloff-Lugosi encounters that first-time viewers of *Black Friday* naturally anticipate. Although behind-the-scenes still photographs depict Karloff and Lugosi on the set together, in the film itself the actors' paths never once cross. Expectedly, horror film fans felt cheated by a Karloff-Lugosi film in which the two premier bogeymen shared no scenes. Probably the most disappointed fans were the folks from Richmond, Virginia, who attended the movie after reading in their local paper *The News Leader* that Lugosi played the dual role of Kingsley-Cannon "with artful makeup"!

Stanley Ridges does a superb job of acting in his dual role. His Kingsley is a gentle and instantly likable chap, much beloved by his students and a staunch friend to the Sovacs. He's equally fine as Cannon, first as Cannon himself (there's a fake nose and mustache on Ridges for the ambulance and hospital scenes) and then when he's playing "Kingsley-Cannon." Several years prior to the debut of Universal's horror character The Creeper, back-breaking is the murder method of choice for Cannon, getting even with the gangsters who (by causing the car crash) broke *Cannon's* back.

As is the case with most far-out films, there are some holes in the plot. There's no explanation for why Kingsley's face takes on a different image when he becomes "Cannon." His hair

Anne Nagel and Bela Lugosi are about to get caught red-handed by murderous thug Stanley Ridges in *Black Friday* (courtesy Bill Chase).

color also changes, and he can see without his glasses. It's difficult, too, to believe that Kingsley has the strength or endurance to do the things that "Cannon" must do, like breaking the backs of the toughest of New York gangsters or outrunning police across rooftops. At the height of his fight with Frank Miller at the reservoir landing, "Cannon" snarls, "You never saw the day I couldn't break you apart!"; it's a sad commentary on tough-guy Miller that he apparently *also* never saw the day that English literature professor Kingsley couldn't break him in two!

The earlier draft of the script outlines an entirely different set of framing scenes. It opens at the State Hospital for the Criminal [*sic*] Insane, where Sovac has been sent for observation. Dr. Small, head of the institute, reads Sovac's diary aloud to three other alienists; here, *that* is the "frame" for the flashbacks. When the flashbacks end with Cannon-Kingsley's death, we cut back to the mental hospital where Small has just stopped reading from the journal; none of the doctors believe Sovac's incredible account. Sovac is waiting outside with Jean; "his whole bearing radiates the egotistic superiority of the insane." He goes in to hear the panel's verdict while Jean, bleak and hopeless, rightly convinced that her father has gone mad and will be permanently confined, leaves without hearing the official decision.

The original script underwent several other alterations, mostly minor. In the first draft, Sovac outlines his brain-transplanting plan to Dr. Warner in the hospital where Kingsley lies dying. Despite Sovac's impassioned plea, Warner highhandedly reminds him that he (Sovac) is only an interne and not a surgeon, and has no right to operate in the United States. (In the finished film Dr. Warner, played by Edwin Stanley, is on screen only long enough to wearily describe the extent of Kingsley's injuries, and does not clash with Sovac.) The name of the gangster in this early draft is Red Banning, and we learn that he used a two-by-four to smash Devore's spine.

Universal evidently felt that *Black Friday* had come up somewhat short in the horror department and the Lugosi department, and came up with a two-in-one solution. An imaginative publicity stunt centered on Lugosi and a hypnotist engaged to put the actor in a trance for the filming of his death scene. Douglas W. Churchill was a columnist who viewed the publicity stunt in its proper light and described the event in a *New York Times* article. Lugosi, "looking like a benign Irish cop," was seated in a chair and placed in a "spell" by hypnotist (and long-time Lugosi pal) Dr. Manly Hall. The "hypnotized" Lugosi was then directed to a nearby two-sided set representing the fatal broom closet. Hall went over the script one last time with Lugosi before "action" was called. Hall whispered, "Now you're suffocating," and Lugosi began sniffing the cracks in the door. Lugosi's voice became shrill as the scene progressed; he finally began putting his shoulder to the door, the set started to give and the actor slumped to the floor. (Karloff, who was also on hand, said he was positive that Lugosi had been hypnotized because he had never seen his fellow actor keep his back to the camera so long!)

After a doctor determined that Lugosi's pulse rate had increased from normal to 160, Lugosi was carried to a chair and Hall awakened him from the trance. Director Lubin stepped forward and claimed that the scene was 100 percent better than it had been in the afternoon, when it was enacted without benefit of hypnosis. "The one flaw in the experiment," Churchill concluded, "was revealed when the cameraman said that he had run out of film when the thing was half over." The stunt gets a big play in the *Black Friday* trailer, where we get to see more of this closet footage than the few short snippets that are in the film itself.

In later years, not surprisingly, participants came clean about this corny hoax (as if fans ever really believed it!). Anne Gwynne told interviewers Michael Fitzgerald and Tom Weaver (in *Fangoria*) that it was all "a put-on for the camera and the press," and Lubin dismissed the silly stunt as well. "There was no truth to that at all, that was only publicity," he told us. The veteran director had known Lugosi since the actor first came to America: Lubin was assistant stage manager on Lugosi's first American play, and helped him with his English between rehearsals and at night. "I was very, very close to both Boris and Bela. They were charming, wonderful people to work with," Lubin reminisced.

On the subject of Karloff, Gwynne told *Fangoria*:

> What an actor; what a *man*! I had a key scene with Boris [and they] shot the entire scene with the camera on Boris. Arthur Lubin was the director, and for some reason I've always felt that he didn't like me. He said, "Wrap!," but Boris came to my rescue and said, "*Don't do this to her*. Give Anne a closeup." Which is exactly what Lubin had to do, and it's in the picture. Now that is a really terrific guy. Most actors wouldn't think of it, or do it if they *did* think of it, but Boris Karloff I'll always admire. He was not only a fine actor who could play just about anything, but a really terrific human being.

Black Friday's theme of brain switching was not new to films, nor even to Karloff films. In one of Karloff's best B productions, the Gaumont-British *The Man Who Lived Again* (1936), he plays an eccentric brain specialist who has perfected a method of electronically transferring the consciousness from one human brain to another. When Karloff's financial benefactor (Frank Cellier) turns against him, Karloff swaps Cellier's mind with that of a bitter cripple (Donald Calthrop) and allows Calthrop (with Cellier's mind) to die. Witty and striking, *The Man Who Lived Again* is a cut above most of Karloff's better-known "mad doctor" excursions, including *Black Friday*. It's interesting to note that Curt Siodmak was working for Gaumont-British around the time of this film's production, and may possibly have been inspired or influenced by this earlier Karloff film.

Elements of *Black Friday* turned up in several subsequent horror films. In Paramount's *The Monster and the Girl* (1941), the brain of an executed man (Phillip Terry) is transplanted into the head of a gorilla which begins knocking off the gangsters who had framed him. *The Man with Two Lives* (1942) went a step further, clearly echoing *Black Friday* in its story of a man (Edward Norris) killed in a car crash but resuscitated at the exact moment that a gangster dies in the electric chair; the revived Norris, of course, now has the personality and memory of the gangster and goes back to his old moll and his gang life. *Man with Two Lives* barely conceals its indebtedness to *Black Friday*; Republic's *The Phantom Speaks* (1945) is simply shameless, again using the basic idea of *Black Friday* and giving the role of the scientist-turned-gangster to Stanley Ridges! *Creature with the Atom Brain* (1955) features a gangster who's *not* the hands-on, do-it-yourself type; he has a mad scientist operate on the brains of *other* men so that he (the gangster) can send them out by "remote control" and break the backs of fellow gangsters and other enemies. This "*Black Friday* for the Push-Button Age" was scripted by Curt Siodmak. Of course, *Donovan's Brain* and all the other aforementioned Siodmak efforts also expand on ideas he first used moviewise in *Black Friday*.

Karloff and Lugosi had other pairings ahead of them at RKO (*You'll Find Out* [1940] and *The Body Snatcher* [1945]), but *Black Friday* was their last time together at the studio which made them household names.* In recent years, some horror aficionados have made much of their professional rivalry, and even many general movie fans know about it from an expletive-filled tirade (by Martin Landau in the role of Lugosi) in Tim Burton's *Ed Wood* (1994)— a movie that Alex Gordon, producer of many early AIP films and a friend to Lugosi, categorizes as "grossly inaccurate." He told the authors that in *Ed Wood*, Landau's Lugosi

> is constantly using terrible language, especially in relation to Boris Karloff, denigrating him with all kinds of four-letter words — which [Lugosi] *never* did. He and Karloff were very good friends — they worked in a number of pictures together, and although they didn't see each other socially, I never heard one say a bad word about the other.

Alex's brother Richard agrees that Boris and Bela coexisted harmoniously. He told the authors that, on one of the occasions that Lugosi spoke to him about Karloff, Lugosi's comments "dispelled the myth" that he and Karloff feuded. (The idea of a feud, Richard maintains, was something that Universal's Carl Laemmle, Jr., cooked up in the 1930s as a publicity stunt.)

> Boris always respected Lugosi and felt sorry [about] Bela's personal demons that destroyed his career. Lugosi respected Karloff's virtuosity as an actor although he envied him for his greater success. Both men shared certain qualities, among them their great loyalty to those who had helped them — which was also reflected in their willingness to help others. We experienced this personally when Bela gave my brother and me the opportunity to represent him. A few years later, Boris was instrumental in launching my career as a producer by giving me a script [*The Haunted Strangler*] that he owned and offering to come to England to star in it if I succeeded in setting it up.

The Haunted Strangler, incidentally, features Karloff in a stand-out performance as a gentle novelist who Kingsley-Cannon–ishly transforms into a depraved killer — a close cousin to the type of role that *Black Friday*'s Curt Siodmak maintained that Karloff could not play.

Critics' Corner

Stanley Ridges' dual role is exceptionally executed.— American Legion Auxiliary, 1940

[*Black Friday*] has all the elements of appeal for a sadist.... By no means does this leave "a good taste in the mouth." — Daughters of the American Revolution, 1940

Mr. Karloff is properly frightening in the role of a scientist whose interest in his theory of brain transplantation takes precedence over human values. Mr. Lugosi is equally sinister as a gangster, while Stanley Ridges provides an outstanding performance.... Previewed at the Alexander Theatre, Glendale, Cal., where it met with a tense and favorable response.— *The Motion Picture Herald*, March 9, 1940, Walter Selden

A highly imaginative story.... Stanley Ridges gives a splendid performance.... Karloff is generally good.... Suspense and interest is maintained throughout....— *The Hollywood Reporter*, February 29, 1940

Lugosi's terrifying talents are wasted in the role of a mere gangster ... but Karloff is in artistic form as a surgeon....— *The New York Times*, March 22, 1940, B.R. Crisler

Rating: Good. Stanley Ridges ... turns in a really remarkable performance.... It's improbable (or is it?) and impressive.— *The New York Post*, March 22, 1940, Irene Thirer

Rating: ★★ The picture has a few exciting scenes, but the story is too incredible to be a good

**In 1941, Universal announced the upcoming horror production* The Monster of Zombor, *which was to star Karloff and Lugosi, but it was never made. In all probability it never got past the wishful-planning stage.*

hair-raiser.—*The New York Daily News*, March 22, 1940, Kate Cameron

The music is dramatically effective, especially in the silent moments. [Huh??]—General Federation of Women's Clubs, 1940

The House of the Seven Gables

Released April 12, 1940. 89 minutes. *Associate Producer:* Burt Kelly. *Director:* Joe May. *Screenplay:* Lester Cole. *Based on the novel by* Nathaniel Hawthorne. *Adaptation:* Harold Greene. *Photography:* Milton Krasner. *Art Director:* Jack Otterson. *Associate Art Director:* Richard H. Riedel. *Editor:* Frank Gross. *Set Decorator:* Russell A. Gausman. *Gowns:* Vera West. *Dialogue Director:* Lester Cole. *Music Director:* Charles Previn. *Music:* Frank Skinner. *Song:* "The Color of Your Eyes," *Music & Lyrics by* Frank Skinner & Ralph Freed. *Sound Supervisor:* Bernard B. Brown. *Technician:* William Hedgcock. *Assistant Director:* Phil Karlson.

George Sanders (*Jaffrey Pyncheon*), Margaret Lindsay (*Hepzibah Pyncheon*), Vincent Price (*Clifford Pyncheon*), Dick Foran (*Matthew Maule*), Nan Grey (*Phoebe Pyncheon*), Cecil Kellaway (*Philip Barton*), Alan Napier (*Mr. Fuller*), Gilbert Emery (*Gerald Pyncheon*), Miles Mander (*Deacon Arnold Foster*), Charles Trowbridge (*Judge*), Harry Woods (*Wainwright*), Margaret Fealy, Caroline Cooke, John K. Loofbourrow, Marty Faust, Murdock MacQuarrie (*Town Gossips*), Hugh Sothern (*Rev. Smith*), Edgar Norton (*Phineas Weed*), Mira McKinney (*Mrs. Reynold*), Ellis Irving (*Man*), Harry Stubbs (*Jeremiah*), Harry Cording (*Mr. Hawkins*), Kernan Cripps (*Workman*), Colin Kenny (*Foreman*), Robert Dudley (*Bailiff*), Etta McDaniel (*Black Woman*), Nelson McDowell (*Courtroom Spectator*), Hal Budlong (*Driver*), Ed Brady (*Man with Blacksmith*), Russ Powell (*Grocer*), Leigh De Lacy (*Laundress*), Claire Whitney (*Woman*), Michael Mark (*Man*), Ruth Rickaby, Patrick J. Kelly, Lois Ransom, Jack C. Smith.

God hath given him blood to drink!
—*Clifford Pyncheon (Vincent Price) in* The House of the Seven Gables

---

Nathaniel Hawthorne (1804–64), one of the great names from New England's Golden Age of Literature, dipped into his own family history for the plot of *The House of the Seven Gables* (1851), a relatively early work. According to a family legend (probably apocryphal), Hawthorne's great-great-grandfather was John Hathorne (*sic*), one of the judges at the 1692 Salem witchcraft trials, and the judge's family was cursed by two of his victims, Rebecka Nourse and Philip English. Later, supposedly, the daughter of English married a son of Hathorne, mingling the blood of accuser and accused, and the fortunes of the Hathorne declined for nearly a century. Hawthorne's story elements of romance, intrigue and horror are reworked and interwoven in Universal's *The House of the Seven Gables*, a well-mounted melodrama.

On a side street in New England stands a seven-gabled mansion with a dark past. In the mid–seventeenth century, Col. Pyncheon accused carpenter Matthew Maule of practicing witchcraft; Maule was condemned to hang and Pyncheon claimed the man's land. From the scaffold Maule hurled out the curse, "God hath given him blood to drink!" Pyncheon built Seven Gables on the dead man's land, but on the day the house was completed he was found dead in the library. The strange seizure which killed Pyncheon became known as Maule's Curse, and the legend that the spirit of Maule dwells in the house was born.

The film opens (in 1828) with Boston lawyer Jaffrey Pyncheon (George Sanders) returning home to Seven Gables in response to an urgent summons from his father Gerald (Gilbert Emery). A series of bad investments has left the Pyncheon family penniless, and Gerald is preparing to sell the house before it falls in the hands of creditors. Jaffrey's older brother Clifford (Vincent Price) and distant cousin Hepzibah (Margaret Lindsay) are eagerly looking forward to the sale; using Clifford's share of the proceeds they can marry and live in New York, where Clifford will pursue a living as a musician. Both Gerald and Jaffrey are appalled at the idea of losing their home, but Clifford, bright and forward-thinking, has no love for the decaying house nor respect for his scurrilous and disreputable ancestors. Clifford catches the money-grubbing Jaffrey searching the house in the middle of the night and realizes that he still clings to his belief in the rumor that a valuable land grant has been well hidden somewhere within its walls.

Gerald and Jaffrey maneuver to find a way to retain the house while Clifford continues to look forward to a sale. In private, Clifford gets into a vehement argument with his father, who suffers a sudden seizure and strikes his head as he falls. Jaffrey realizes that Gerald has succumbed to Maule's Curse but he seizes the opportunity to charge Clifford with the old man's murder. Clifford's day in court is a travesty reminiscent of the old Salem witch trials; the jury decides on a verdict of guilty without leaving the box. He is sentenced to life imprisonment.

The dead father's insurance money pays off the debt on the house but, unbeknownst to Jaffrey, Gerald had signed the deed over to Hepzibah, to prevent creditors from seizing Seven Gables. Ordering Jaffrey to leave the house forever, Hepzibah seals up the place and begins to lead a dismal, solitary existence pining for her lost Clifford. Many years pass, the house falls into disrepair and Hepzibah becomes a drawn, middle-aged spinster. In the State Prison, a brash young abolitionist who briefly shares a cell with Clifford turns out to be Matthew Maule (Dick Foran), descendant of the original landowner.

Living in poverty, Hepzibah is forced to take in a boarder and to turn her front parlor into a one-cent shop which is tended by Phoebe Pyncheon (Nan Grey), a newly arrived relative. (The boarder is Maule, who lives there under the assumed name "Matthew Holgrave.") Clifford's sentence is commuted and he returns to Seven Gables, but he has been stripped of his civil rights: He cannot leave the property or marry Hepzibah until he proves his innocence. Romance blooms between Phoebe and Matthew.

The legend of the hidden land grant resurfaces and Matthew spreads the word that Clifford has lost his reason and is searching the house for the document. This news intrigues Jaffrey, who becomes determined to take possession of Seven Gables and find the document himself. On the side, the sly Jaffrey has also duped the local deacon (Miles Mander), treasurer for the local Anti-Slave Society, into investing $5,000 of Society money in an illegal venture.

Jaffrey shows up at Seven Gables, unaware that he is being played for a sucker: This revival of the land grant rumor has been cooked up by Clifford and Matthew. Clifford will allow Jaffrey to search the house only if he (Jaffrey) signs a paper exonerating Clifford. The deacon arrives on the scene, frantic: The abolitionists he has cheated are right at his heels. When Jaffrey coldly turns him away, the deacon shoots himself. Realizing that Clifford is in a perfect position to frame him, Jaffrey becomes understandably apoplectic. He signs the confession but then suffers one of the hereditary Pyncheon attacks, collapsing and dying before witnesses. Clifford is now cleared and the "curse" at an end. Clifford and Hepzibah as well as Matthew and Phoebe are joined in a double wedding.

As is invariably the case when Hollywood undertakes to film a classic story, changes were required for the sake of greater dramatic interest. The Hawthorne novel is set up quite differently from the Universal film: Most of the action seen in this film transpired before the novel's page one.

After laying out the story of Matthew Maule and his curse, the book begins with Hepzibah already a scowling, sixtyish spinster living at Seven Gables with "Holgrave" inhabiting a remote gable upstairs. Phoebe arrives early on, and Hepzibah's brother Clifford comes back to Seven Gables a broken man with the intellect of a child; there's no explanation (that is, his years in prison) for his partly demented condition until late in the story. Clifford dislikes Hepzibah's ugliness, and the task of caring for him falls to Phoebe. Judge Jaffrey Pyncheon, a wealthy cousin, shows up and warns that unless Clifford reveals to him the location of hidden land grant documents, he will have Clifford institutionalized. But the judge has a seizure and dies quietly in the parlor. After a lot more comings and goings, everything is resolved with the late judge revealed as the murderer of a rich uncle (for whose death Clifford has been jailed). The land grants, now useless, are found in a recess behind a portrait. "Holgrave," pledged to wed Phoebe, reveals that he is a Maule just before the entire family packs up and leaves for Judge Jaffrey's country place.

Universal's changes made for a tidy, streamlined drama with more incident and less wordy detours than Hawthorne's original. Harold Greene (credited with "Adaptation") and screenwriter Lester Cole (of Hollywood Ten fame) do a good job of adding conflict and romantic flourishes—although, deep down, it *is* still just the story of a frame-up, a quest for justice, the last-minute confession and death of the baddie, and a romantic happy ending. The movie *Seven Gables* dresses up this rather rudimentary plotline by putting the players in the required Colonial drag and emphasizing the legend of the

Maule's Curse strikes down Gilbert Emery as Vincent Price and Margaret Lindsay look on in *The House of the Seven Gables* (courtesy John Cocchi).

curse. Perhaps coincidentally, perhaps not, the previous film written by Cole and directed by Joe May, *The Invisible Man Returns*, had at its core the same basic story, *that* one dressed up in science fiction drag, and even had many of the same cast members (Vincent Price as the framed man, Nan Grey, Cecil Kellaway, Alan Napier, a number of bit players). According to Universal publicity, initial preparations for the production of *Seven Gables* were made long before the film was officially announced, as Universal feared that other studios might try to beat them to the screen with the classic Hawthorne tale. This could mean that the *Seven Gables* screenplay was written first, and that *Invisible Man Returns*, while released first, could be Cole-May's heavily disguised sci-fi remake!

The flaws in Cole's screenplay are its inclination toward talk and an over-reliance on coincidence. The film benefits from its deliberate pacing, but occasionally mistakes "pokey" for "stately." Most of the highlights are featured in the opening reels, and the drop-off in drama is felt during some uninteresting midpoint scenes. *Seven Gables* drops badly in the final third; the plan that Clifford and Matthew concoct to entrap Jaffrey is silly and transparent, and the two men carry out their scheme with a mischievous twinkle that's not in keeping with the seriousness of the situation. The ending, too, is a disappointing copout, with the frazzled deacon forcing his way into Seven Gables, committing a discreet off-screen suicide and inducing a too-convenient seizure in Jaffrey. It's a forced, *deus ex machina* wrap-up to an otherwise respectable film.

Some of the acting in *Seven Gables* is first-rate. George Sanders does a typically fine job as the blackguard whose false accusation of his brother sparks the film's action. "I always felt he was embarrassed playing that part," Vincent Price told the authors, but Sanders' reported unease never shows through; Sanders' Jaffrey is a dark, brooding cloud that hangs portentously over the heads of the other characters.

Margaret Lindsay, one of the more talented '30s leading ladies, contributes a mature performance that might be the best, certainly the most striking in the picture. In early scenes as young Hepzibah, she's ingenuous, intelligent and appealing; later disguised in middle-age makeup, she becomes quite the bundle of (kill)joy, skillfully conveying the inner suffering of her character with some masterful little bits of acting. *Seven Gables* might well be the closest thing to a major picture in which Lindsay enjoyed a meaty part; she meets with flying colors the challenge of what practically amounts to a dual role. Had a Bette Davis played Hepzibah, this same performance would be hailed as a classic, but it's Margaret Lindsay and so-what? as far as snob-appeal critics are concerned. "Margaret Lindsay was a delight to work with and a very good actress," Price added.

Price, 28 when *Seven Gables* was made, is also effective as Clifford, tragic victim of Jaffrey's evil machinations. Exuberant and impulsive — but with more than a trace of repressed bitterness seething beneath the surface — Price is also at his best in early scenes: Wooing Hepzibah, tinkering away at his harpsichord, matching wits with his sardonic brother, and challenging his father's authority in a crackling dialogue exchange. Price's rendition of the song "The Color of Your Eyes" (music by Frank Skinner, lyrics by Ralph Freed) is a highpoint of the film, as is his emotional condemnation of perjurer Jaffrey in the courtroom. Most of Price's best acting opportunities are already behind him by the time his greatly aged character returns from prison, but there's still the touching, near-brilliant scene of Clifford's middle-of-the-night reappearance at Seven Gables: Catching sight of himself in a mirror for the first time in years, finding that the clothes he wore as a young man have been ruined by moths, quietly playing the harpsichord to draw Hepzibah into the room.

There's another good scene for Price in the opening reel, rattling off the crimes of his ancestors as he stands beneath their various portraits. It's a good, fervently acted, appropriately hammy monologue and a forerunner to similar Price scenes in the Roger Corman Poe films of the '60s, particularly *House of Usher*. (In the original Hawthorne novel, the character of Clifford Pyncheon is often reminiscent of Poe's Roderick Usher, although few of these similarities are carried over into the Universal film.) For Price it was a substantial, sympathetic part, the kind that would later be denied him once Hollywood typecasters stuck their labels on him; here he even gets his first screen kiss (from Margaret Lindsay).*

It probably didn't take a lot of rehearsal for Price and George Sanders to act like they didn't get along; according to actress Kay Linaker, who had worked with both in Universal's *Green Hell* a few months earlier, Sanders was a bastard — "he *majored* in bastardry!" she laughingly told the authors:

> On *Green Hell*, he managed to sort of alienate *every*body, everybody from the board boy right straight up.... *Green Hell* was made at a time when King George VI was getting ready to make a speech to the world — it had to have been his announcement of England's declaration of war on Germany. Mr. Sanders came and stood and said to all of us sitting in the chairs around the radio, "You are not going to be such *asses* as to pay attention to this fool, *are* you?" Remember, the "fool" to whom he was referring was the king of some of these people — there were some Britishers on that set. When Sanders made that remark, Vinnie [Price] said, "Well, if you don't want to hear it, why don't you just step outside?"
>
> Well, that set things off. Sanders began talking about the king and what an ass he was, and laying bets what the king was going to say. All of a sudden, the radio announcer introduced His Majesty. With that, Sanders kind of drew himself up and said, "And *now*, I will interpret...." At that point, [Douglas Fairbanks, Jr.] came forward and stood nose-to-nose with him, and said, "*You* will keep your mouth shut, or I will beat the *hell* out of you." Sanders kind of stepped back, and put that typical Sanders smirk on, and said [with a nervous laugh], "Oh, well, now reeeally..." Fairbanks said, "I mean it ... with *everything in my soul*." At which point, Vinnie got up and moved in, and said, "If you disrupt *my* listening, *I* will *hold* you." At that moment, the king began to

**Robert Cummings, originally pencilled in for the part of Clifford, had to pass up the assignment because of illness. It's hard to picture him in the embittered role.*

The double-wedding ending of *Seven Gables*: Dick Foran, Nan Grey, Vincent Price, Cecil Kellaway, Margaret Lindsay, Alan Napier and Hugh Sothern are posed (courtesy John Cocchi).

> speak and everybody sort of froze. Fairbanks and Vinnie and Sanders held their poses — believe me — through the entire speech. They stood through that entire speech, and Fairbanks was nose-to-nose with Sanders.

Cowboy star Dick Foran seems altogether the wrong type of actor for this kind of movie but after a boisterous opening scene he's more modulated and in tune. The novel's depiction of Maule as a part-time mesmerist is wisely dropped; instead the screenwriters make him an abolitionist. Cecil Kellaway, Alan Napier, Miles Mander and Charles Trowbridge, in more minor roles, add to the local color. Perhaps no two actors in Hollywood were *less* suited to play abolitionists (or any *other* kind of do-gooder) than Harry Woods and Harry Cording, whose combined number of ruthless, land-grabbin,' head-bashin,' hornswogglin' roles in Westerns, serials and other dramas must be in the hundreds!

Jack Otterson was sent to the actual House of the Seven Gables on Turner Street in Salem, Massachusetts, where the art director inspected, photographed and drew plans which were used by Universal in their reconstruction of the famous edifice. (The house still stands on the Universal lot — now looking a great deal more modern, of course — and is on the end of the street where TV's *Desperate Housewives* is shot.) Three stages were crowded with sets representing the Seven Gables interiors, including replicas of the main living rooms and of the upper and lower hallways. More than 500 pieces of authentic early American kitchenware and tableware were used to dress the sets. Cues from Frank Skinner's Oscar-nominated score later enlivened a number of Universal's more conventional chillers, among them *The Mummy's Hand, Man Made Monster, Horror Island,* the 1941 *The Black Cat, The Wolf Man, The Mad Ghoul* and *The Scarlet Claw.*

Being a Joe May production, *The House of the Seven Gables* hit more than its share of production delays, snags and snafus. In a December 29, 1939, memo came the announcement that the start of production was being delayed due to casting difficulties. At this point the set for the lower floor of the house had been finished but other sets were still under construction. Production got underway on the third day of the new year, with 21 days' shooting and a budget of $161,625 allotted. But by January 5 a studio memo was already describing the film as a difficult production, with time-consuming elements like aging characters, period costumes, special lighting effects, etc., making progress slow. Rain plagued the picturemakers, prompting a re-arrangement of the scheduling in order to keep everyone working.

By January 19 the memo-writers were complaining that May was working too slowly. More difficulties, like airplane noises ruining exterior takes, caused additional delays. Pressure was put on May to speed up production, and by January 26 it began to pay off. *Seven Gables* finally wrapped two days over schedule with a final budget of $178,000; the company had worked ten nights until 10 o'clock or later.

Henry and Peggy Moran Koster, who were friendly with May and his wife Mia, remembered him best for his impulsiveness and temper. "I remember that he and his wife used to come over at night and we'd play a game," Peggy told the authors. "It was a game they played in Germany, it's like Parcheesi, when you move the game pieces around and if you land on somebody else's, he has to go home again. Joe would play, and if you'd send his piece home, sometimes he'd get so mad he'd take the whole board and throw it across the room!"

Seven Gables was one of the final Universal films for May, whose once-great career was on its last legs. After his Hollywood days ended, he and his wife opened a restaurant called the Blue Danube. But May was never one to leave well enough alone: He would sit down at the table with customers, read to them from the menu and then tell them what they wanted. Which apparently was the kiss of death for the Blue Danube. May died in 1954, his wife Mia in 1980. In its Mia May obituary, *Variety* wrote that her husband "died in Hollywood more than twenty years ago after making *one or two films* in this country" (italics ours), which suggests rather plainly that Joe May was already a forgotten figure.

In 1963 Price starred in the anthology *Twice-Told Tales*, United Artists' schlocky cash-in on Price's popularity in the Poe pictures. The third and final sequence was a loosely adapted version of *The House of the Seven Gables* with Price as a money-grubbing Pyncheon who returns home to Seven Gables and his devil-worshipping sister (Jacqueline de Wit) to search for the missing land grant. Beverly Garland and Richard Denning co-starred in this lurid, garishly colored exploitation item.

Universal's *The House of the Seven Gables* seems like the sort of "Shaky A" that the studio could and should have made a big deal out of, but instead they stuck it on the bottom rung of a double bill with the cheaper, shorter *Black Friday* and let it go at that. Is the film an effective treatment of Hawthorne's novel? Vincent Price told us no, although he allowed that it was an interesting picture to make. But the cinema isn't the place for a dry, heavy and intricately symbolic work like *Seven Gables*; this commercialized film version is largely faithful and often seems to capture the spirit of Hawthorne, which is about as much as any viewer should hope for. *Seven Gables* and *Black Friday* world-premiered at Chicago's Palace Theatre, with Vincent Price and Bela Lugosi in attendance. For the West Coast premiere at San Francisco's Orpheum, Price and Lugosi were joined by George Sanders, Boris Karloff et al.

One previous version of *Seven Gables* had been shot, by Edison's company in 1910; that same year, its writer-director and star also made the Edison *Frankenstein*. Republic announced plans to make a version in 1935, but never got around to it. TV-wise, there was a 1951 *Robert Montgomery Presents* adaptation with Gene Lockhart, his daughter June Lockhart and Leslie Nielsen; a 1956 *Matinee Theater* with John Carradine, Marshall Thompson and Carolyn Craig; and a 1960 *Shirley Temple's Storybook* with Temple, Agnes Moorehead, Robert Culp, Jonathan Harris, Martin Landau and John Abbott.

An impressive collaborative effort of director, stars, camera and set design, Universal's *The House of the Seven Gables* is a well-carpentered period piece endowed with good pictorial values. Despite its contrived finale, it's a strong drama flavored with dashes of spookery and stands as one of Universal's most respectable semi-horror films.

Critics' Corner

[A] grim and sinister drama.... [W]atered-down treatment of a nineteenth century shocker. [I]t is likely to prove dull business with its costumed refinements, its tenebrous deliberations and its slow, heavily mannered pace.... As the sorely oppressed lovers, Vincent Price and Margaret Lindsay perform in the perfect lavender-and-old-lace tradition, with much sighing and misting of eyes.—*The New York Times*, April 15, 1940, Bosley Crowther

[A] worthy contribution to the screen.... Universal started this almost as a quickie but a combination of fine performances, good scripting and noteworthy direction make it into a picture considerably more worthwhile.—*The Hollywood Reporter*, March 1, 1940

Rating: ★★½ [A] pretty stuffy affair made almost laughable by melodramatics and painfully stilted language. Goodness knows how the Rialto Theatre's regular customers are going to take it.—*The New York Daily News*, April 14, 1940, Wanda Hale

[T]houghtfully and effectively presented.... Jack Otterson rates special mention for providing settings and backgrounds which add much to the realism.... [I]ntricately plotted narrative moves smoothly to a gratifying climax. George Sanders and Margaret Lindsay give powerful performances....—*The Motion Picture Herald*, March 9, 1940

The Mummy's Hand

Released September 20, 1940. 67 minutes. *Director:* Christy Cabanne. *Producer:* Ben Pivar. *Screenplay:* Griffin Jay & Maxwell Shane. *Original Story:* Griffin Jay. *Photography:* Elwood Bredell. *Editor:* Philip Cahn. *Art Director:* Jack Otterson. *Associate Art Director:* Ralph M. DeLacy. *Music:* Frank Skinner & Hans J. Salter. *Musical Director:* Hans J. Salter. *Assistant Director:* Vaughn Paul. *Set Decorator:* Russell A. Gausman. *Sound Supervisor:* Bernard B. Brown. *Technician:* Charles Carroll. *Makeup:* Jack P. Pierce. *Gowns:* Vera West.

Dick Foran (*Steve Banning*), Peggy Moran (*Marta Solvani*), Wallace Ford (*Babe Jenson*), Eduardo Ciannelli (*High Priest*), George Zucco (*Prof. Andoheb*), Cecil Kellaway (*Tim Sullivan, a.k.a. The Great Solvani*), Charles Trowbridge (*Dr. Petrie*), Tom Tyler (*Kharis*), Siegfried Arno (*The Beggar*), Eddie Foster (*Egyptian*), Harry Stubbs (*Bartender*), Michael Mark (*Bazaar Owner*), Mara Tartar (*Girl*), Leon Belasco (*Ali*), Frank Lackteen, Murdock MacQuarrie (*Priests*), Jerry Frank, Kenneth Terrell (*Egyptian Thugs*).

Terror That Waited 3000 Years...
Stalks the Earth Again!
—*Trailer blurb for* The Mummy's Hand

Eight years had passed since the Egyptian goddess Isis unleashed the lightning bolt that transformed Imhotep into a pile of dust and dried bones. The star-crossed romance between the accursed Egyptian and the Princess Anck-es-en-Amon, a love that bridged the centuries, had come to a bitter end. But it would take a whole lot more than the fury of the ancient gods to squelch a Hollywood formula as potent as this one.

Having recently revived (with glowing box office results) two icons of the Laemmle era, Frankenstein's Monster and the Invisible Man, the top brass at the New Universal felt the time was ripe to resurrect the Egyptian heartthrobs, furnish them with new identities, and retread the Karl Freund classic as a streamlined B, catering less to connoisseurs of pure cinematic horror and more to thrill seekers.

The result was *The Mummy's Hand*, a slick, competently produced chiller, tailor-made for the action house trade. Its title menace, the withered Kharis, supplanted Karloff's urbane and articulate Imhotep as the Hollywood personification of the killer mummy, and the series of films in which he featured made tana leaves and the Curse of Amon-Ra a part of our American pop culture.

The resurrected Egyptian prince had none of the grace nor the otherworldly omniscience of his wizened predecessor. The forbidden love affair that Kharis and Ananka shared would not be resuscitated via a twentieth century reincarnation until another sequel was in the can. For the time being, at least, Kharis' mission in this strange, modern world was to serve as Ananka's bodyguard, to protect her mummy against desecration by archaeologists and native plunderers. Gone were the pitiful declarations of love, the "troubled pool" revealing reincarnations of past lives, and the heart attack–inducing incantations: Kharis had only to reach out his hand and clasp it around the throats of his enemies to make his point.

With a budget set at a modest $80,000, *The Mummy's Hand* went before "Woody" Bredell's cameras at the end of May 1940. (*Man*

"Please—five more minutes!" The centuries-long sleep of Kharis (Tom Tyler) is disturbed by archaeologists (Cecil Kellaway, Charles Trowbridge, Wallace Ford, and Dick Foran) in *The Mummy's Hand.*

Made Monster, which began production seven months later, also felt the belt-tightening bite of the accounting office.) Rampant cost-cutting is evidenced by the film's utilization of stock shots (chiefly from *The Mummy*), hand-me-down sets (most notably the extravagant temple left over from James Whale's *Green Hell*), a musical score lifted almost entirely from *Son of Frankenstein*, a cast headlined by no major horror players (fifth-billed George Zucco hadn't made his mark on the genre yet), and a grueling shooting schedule that left little time for aesthetic nuance. Lines of dialogue are obviously redubbed, and the whir of the camera can be heard in the background of a scene or two.

A former film editor turned producer, Ben Pivar was put in charge of production on *The Mummy's Hand*. The British moviemaker piloted more B-chillers chillers for Universal during this period than any of his peers. According to director Reginald LeBorg, who worked under Pivar on *The Mummy's Ghost*, Pivar was the epitome of the artless, noncreative studio executive. He holed himself up in his office, was often crude, and occasionally seemed illiterate. Any resemblance between the filmmaking aesthetics of Ben Pivar and RKO's maven of malice Val Lewton was strictly coincidental.

Christy Cabanne, who handled the directing chores on *The Mummy's Hand*, was a former associate of D.W. Griffith and Douglas Fairbanks whose reputable career soured with the advent of sound. Cabanne's considerable list of credits dates back to 1910 and includes various engagements at Columbia, Goldwyn studios, and such defunct outfits as FBO and Tiffany-Stahl. Undistinguished programmers such as *Mutiny on the Blackhawk* (1939) and *Scattergood Baines* (1941) kept the director active until his death in 1950. Cabanne's only other fantastic film credit is a dismal one: The indescribably bad 1947 Bela Lugosi–George Zucco starrer *Scared to Death*.

Production on *The Mummy's Hand* continued through mid–June. In order to maintain the picture's (approximate) two-week shooting schedule, Cabanne and Company had no choice but to put in plenty of overtime. Though her memory of the film was a bit fuzzy, Peggy Moran vividly recalled for us the arduous shooting schedule: "I had to be there at six to do hair and makeup, and we started shooting at eight. We had to do those late-night shots in the caves. They were all done on the back lot at Universal, and we would work sometimes from eight in the morning until four the next morning. They could do that with people like me because we were under contract. The law requires that outside talent only work for X-number of hours, but me they could work all the time!"

Despite the harried efforts of the overdriven production team, *The Mummy's Hand* ran slightly over schedule and $4,000 over budget. Universal's editorial department, which had been working to capacity on a full schedule of features, made a final cut of the film before the end of June, and the picture was set for its East Coast premiere in September. (In the print screened for *Variety*, certain scenes of the movie were tinted an eerie green.)

Establishing a pattern that would be followed for all of its sequels, *The Mummy's Hand* commences with a sacred indoctrination. Answering a sacred summons, Andoheb (George Zucco), noted Egyptologist and member of the secret religious sect of Karnak, arrives at the Temple of Karnak on the Hill of the Seven Jackals. The resident high priest (Eduardo Ciannelli), his life rapidly ebbing away, passes on to his successor a secret guarded for centuries by their royal den. Three thousand years ago, the Princess Ananka, daughter of King Amenophis, grew ill and died. She was worshipped by Kharis (Tom Tyler), a prince of the Royal House. Daring the anger of the ancient guards, Kharis snatched a quantity of forbidden tana leaves. With a brew distilled from the leaves, Kharis knew he could bring his beloved Ananka back to life. But before the sacrilegious act could be consummated, Kharis was seized by palace guards. For the sin he had committed, he was condemned to be buried alive. First, his tongue was cut out so his protests wouldn't assail the ears of the gods. Then, he was wrapped in gauze and buried in an unmarked grave. Later, his coffin was unearthed by disciples of Ananka and sealed in a secret mountain location.

To Andoheb's amazement, the withered priest reveals that Kharis never really died, that he still rests in his tomb waiting to bring death to any who would defile Ananka's resting place. Turning over a supply tana leaves to Andoheb, the high priest instructs him to brew three tana leaves during the cycle of the full moon and feed the fluid to Kharis. But under no circumstance is Andoheb to feed Kharis more than nine leaves. "Should Kharis obtain a large amount of the fluid, he will become an uncontrollable monster, a soulless demon with the desire to kill and kill." His mission completed, the holy man quietly expires.

In Cairo, Steve Banning (Dick Foran), an accomplished young archaeologist who has recently fallen on hard times, discovers a piece of pottery which bears a clue to the location of Ananka's tomb. He and his doubting sidekick Babe Jenson (Wallace Ford) take the find to Dr. Petrie* (Charles Trowbridge) of the Cairo Museum. The exuberant prof verifies the pottery's authenticity but insists on conferring with a colleague for a third opinion. Petrie's associate is none other than Andoheb. The saturnine scientist dismisses the relic as a worthless imitation. According to Andoheb, two expeditions had already penetrated the forbidden region; they were never heard from again.

Steve isn't discouraged. With the financial backing of a Brooklyn magician named Solvani (Cecil Kellaway), Banning organizes an expedition into the desert. Accompanying him and Babe on the quest to uncover Ananka's tomb are Solvani, Solvani's cautiously cynical daughter Marta (Peggy Moran) and Petrie. Unbeknownst to them, Andoheb and his underling (Siegfried Arno) are several steps ahead of them, anticipating their every move.

A freak explosion uncovers a sealed entranceway in the side of the mountain which, Steve believes, may lead to the resting place of the princess. Instead, the party discovers the

**It is very likely that the screenwriters named this character after renowned British archaeologist and Egyptologist Sir Flinders Petrie (1853–1942), one of the great innovators of scientific methods in excavation.*

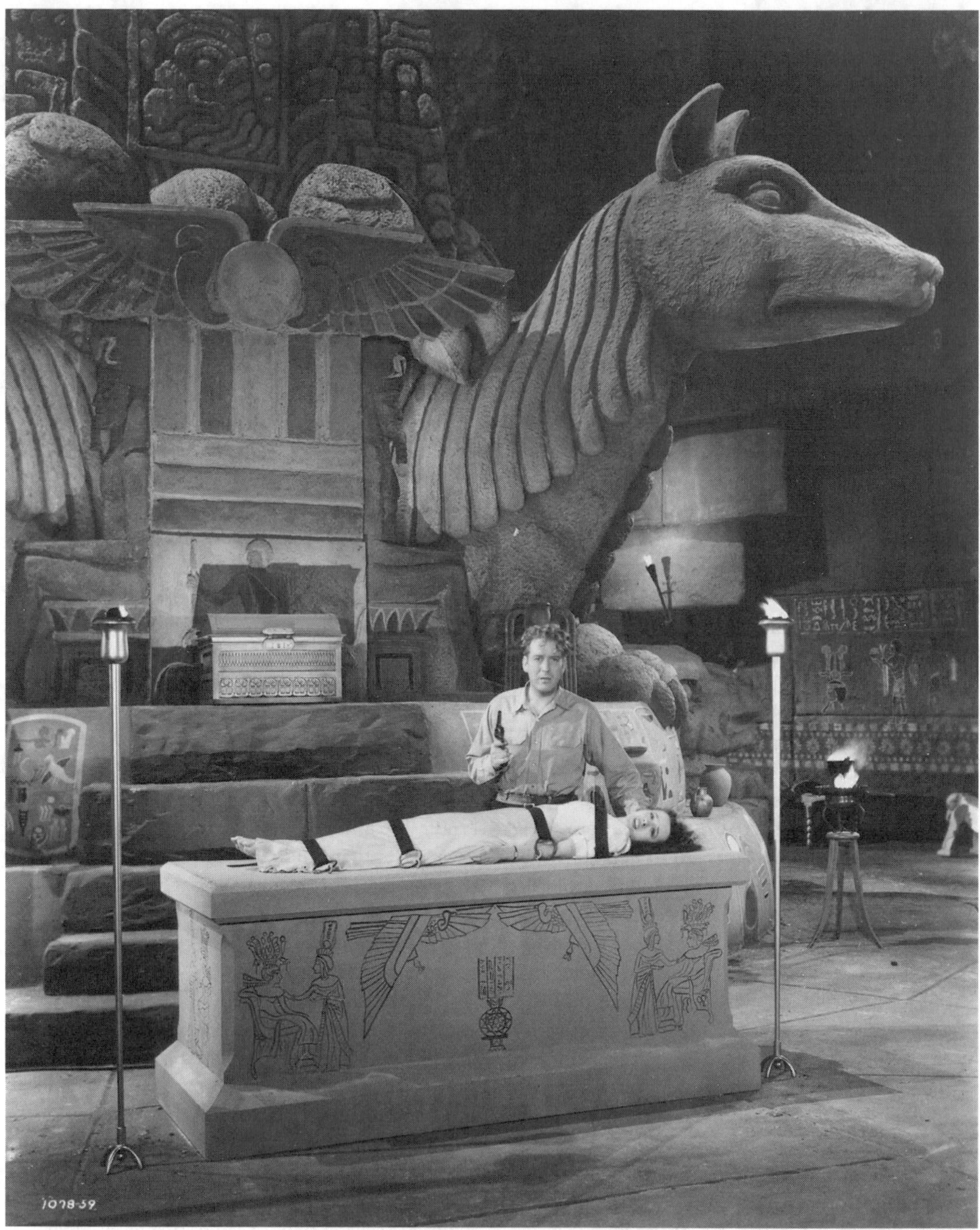

Art director Jack Otterson and his staff redesigned the *Green Hell* temple set for use in *The Mummy's Hand.*

mummy of Kharis in a remarkable state of preservation.

After the others have retired, Dr. Petrie is making a minute examination of the mummy when he is confronted by Andoheb, garbed in a priestly robe. With a dosage of tana brew, Andoheb brings Kharis back to life. The resuscitated ancient Egyptian promptly strangles to death the horror-stricken professor.

Plotting to do away with the rest of the unbelievers, Andoheb orders his henchman to place vials of tana brew in each of their tents. Steve's native overseer Ali (Leon Belasco) is the second member of the expedition to fall victim to the Mummy. Solvani is nearly killed by the tana-seeking Kharis, who carries Marta away, disappearing with her through a hidden passageway in the mountain.

Splitting up in two different directions, Steve and Babe search for the Mummy. In a bravura setpiece, Kharis (with Marta in his arms) enters the altar room, where Andoheb awaits them. As a reorchestrated cue from *Son of Frankenstein* plays ominously on the soundtrack, the camera gradually reveals the full scope of the magnificently decorated set, bedecked with huge carvings of jackal heads. With Marta as his captive, Andoheb forsakes his mission and prepares an injection of the immortalizing tana fluid for himself and the young woman. Babe arrives in the nick of time and engages the high priest in a gun battle. Riddled with bullets, Andoheb is sent hurtling down the temple steps.

Discovering the entranceway into the temple through a tunnel, Steve frees Marta and attempts to escape with her but finds their path blocked by the Mummy. The archaeologist crashes a flaming urn over Kharis, destroying him before he can obtain an overdose of the mind-bending tana brew. The Banning expedition tracks down the tomb of Ananka and prepares to return to America with its treasure-trove of riches.

Lacking the brooding atmosphere and poetic beauty of the 1932 Karloff classic, *The Mummy's Hand* substitutes old-fashioned thrills and serial-flavored action, making for 67 minutes of brisk entertainment. Its conviviality and boisterous spirit (there's even a gratuitous *Seven Sinners*–style barroom brawl to keep the proceedings moving at a lively clip) reminds one of Universal's B action-adventure programmers of the period, starring the likes of Richard Arlen and Charles Bickford. Despite the somber, pseudomystical opening scenes and the eerie Mummy passages, Griffin Jay and Maxwell Shane have kept the tone of their script light. The so-called scientific expedition into the forbidden Egyptian hills comes off as little more than an adventuresome treasure hunt. (*Variety*'s Hobe is right on the money when he describes Dick Foran and Wallace Ford as "a couple of Rover Boy archaeologists.")

While many horror buffs begrudgingly concede that *The Mummy's Hand* is the best of the Kharis series, they are quick to point out that the jovial mood damages the film's intentions. Fortunately, Foran and company are such immensely likable players, we are inclined to overlook this misplaced frivolity in a picture about ancient curses and an avenging mummy. The actors *appear* to be having a good time, and this attitude carries over to the viewer. Peggy Moran found her co-stars a pleasure to work with, describing Dick Foran as "very nice and friendly" and Wallace Ford as "very funny always."

The most amusing bit in a film already packed with humor is supplied not by Ford's Brooklynite buddy nor Kellaway's bumbling magician, but by the hero Dick Foran himself. The

Adept at playing underworld lowlifes, Eduardo Ciannelli essays the role of the high priest of Karnak in *The Mummy's Hand.*

celebrated archaeologist, lauded for having played an important role in the discoveries of such wonders as the Temple of the Sun in the Gobi Desert, the ancient Mayan cities, and the Inca ruins in Mexico, is so down on his luck he can't even land a halfway decent staff job at the Scripps Museum.

All of the elements of the Mummy films that had become stale by the time *The Mummy's Curse* rolled around in 1944 were fresh and exciting in 1940. The extended flashback sequence from *The Mummy* depicting Imhotep's sacrilege was cleverly re-edited by Philip Cahn, who inserted new close-ups of Tom Tyler in place of Karloff's. (Boris can still be seen in the long shots.) This impressively mounted montage has become so ingrained in the minds of horror fans, one immediately assumes it was revived in every sequel, when in fact it made just one more appearance (in *The Mummy's Curse*).

The Mummy's key to eternal life, tana leaves, was the invention of screenwriters Jay and Shane (who claimed the ancient Egyptians used them for embalming purposes). With the introduction of the leaves into the series came a whole set of ludicrous laws governing their use. For some unfathomable reason, the leaves must be brewed during the cycle of the full moon. Three leaves keep Kharis' heart beating; additional fixes sustain his strength and correct such physical malformations as a paralyzed arm and a lame leg (neither of which was ever healed despite ample slugs of the stuff over the course of four movies). *The Mummy's Hand* toys with the threat of the Mummy's becoming an uncontrollable and indestructible monster should he obtain a dosage exceeding nine brewed tana leaves. This state of sublime menace never came to pass in the Kharis pictures, nor did it need to. Nourished with the recommended serving of tana fluid, the Mummy is nasty enough. Any further enhancement of his homicidal disposition would just be gilding the lily.

Christy Cabanne draws more eerie chills out of the Mummy than any of the directors who followed in his footsteps. Slipping in and out of the shadowy passageways, stalking through moonlit forests, the 3,000-year-old dead man assumes the form of an ancient Grim Reaper meting out punishment to trespassers. In the film's most satisfying moment, Zucco demonstrates the power of tana fluid by dribbling a small amount on the dormant creature's lips, and then asks Charles Trowbridge to check his pulse. The rhythmic beating of the Mummy's heart increases in intensity on the soundtrack; it culminates as Kharis opens his eyes. Locked in the Mummy's powerful grip, Trowbridge is choked (and frightened) to death as the camera closes in on the monster's Sphinx-like stare.

In his intriguing analysis of the original screenplays of the Kharis films, *The Mummy Unwrapped* (McFarland, 2003), author Thomas M. Feramisco details one particularly bloodthirsty sequence which, unfortunately, ended up on the cutting room floor. As Andoheb contemplates Marta's fate as she lies unconscious on the marble slab, he is approached by two priests (Frank Lackteen and Murdock MacQuarrie). "You must destroy the girl. This is sacrilege. The wrath of Isis will fall on our heads!" one of them exclaims. Undeterred, Andoheb orders Kharis to dispatch the terrified holy men. One of them falls to his death from the temple staircase, while the other is sent crashing to the floor by the blindly obedient mummy. Horror film buffs can only decry the decision of the creative minds behind *The Mummy's Hand* who saw fit to cut this exciting scene, whole retaining not one but two episodes of Babe Jenson practicing his rock trick!

Rugged B-Western star Tom Tyler was a fine choice to play Kharis. Tyler was the first of three cowboy stars — the others were Ray Corrigan and Glenn Strange — to play Universal monsters. One of Republic's popular Three Mesquiteers and the star of the 1941 serial *Adventures of Captain Marvel*, the darkly handsome actor surpassed the portly Lon Chaney, Jr., in the role. Tyler's expressive eyes do wonders in bringing life and emotion to the one-dimensional part. Jack Pierce made up Tyler only for the close-ups, which were shot in one day, according to reports. The rest of the time the actor wore a rubber mask.

In real life, Tyler, despite his athletic build, was a large, clumsy individual, who in later life was reportedly plagued by the ravages of arthritis. Kharis was probably the only role where his reputed awkwardness actually benefited his performance. In our 1988 meeting with Peggy Moran Koster, she shared these reminiscences of the late actor:

> I never met Tom Tyler without his makeup. I think he had to be at the studio at four in the morning. I never did meet Tyler otherwise, and he couldn't talk with that makeup on, so I never heard his voice. So as far as I was concerned, he *was* the Mummy! And I was really a little afraid of him, especially at night, on the back lot, when he'd creep up on us. When he picked me up and started carrying me around, I had the eeriest feeling.

The Iowa-born ingénue was one of Universal's brightest (and busiest) contract players, appearing in no less than 22 productions over a period of just four years. Her wholesome, girl-next-door looks and sprightly charm invigorated a variety of pictures including comedies (*One Night in the Tropics* [1940], *Hello, Sucker* [1941]), Westerns (*West of Carson City*, *Trail of the Vigilantes* [both 1940]) and homespun musicals (the Deanna Durbin vehicles *First Love* [1939] and *Spring Parade* [1940], both of which were directed by future husband Henry Koster). Their marriage in October 1942 signaled the end of the starlet's brief but productive screen career.

Moran delivers an ingratiating performance in *The Mummy's Hand*: Her no-nonsense attitude is in sharp contrast to that of her gullible father, well-played the always delightful Cecil Kellaway, who falls for Banning's buried treasure sales pitch lock, stock and barrel. Tragically, the actress died as a result of injuries she sustained in an automobile accident on the Ventura Freeway on October 24, 2002 (she outlived her husband by 14 years). In a *Los Angeles Times* obituary, Peggy was quoted as saying that *The Mummy's Hand* was "probably the worst picture I ever made ... a lousy picture." It is to the lovely lady's credit that she withheld her personal disdain towards the film from enthusiastic horror fans whom she met at nostalgia conventions in the last years of her life.

George Zucco was assigned the most interesting character in the film. Andoheb is introduced to the audience with almost the same aura of mystery as Kharis himself. Bespectacled, dark complected, and wearing a native fez, the aloof, professorial-looking gentleman is first glimpsed disembarking from a train in a bustling Cairo depot, oblivious to the throngs milling about him. Riding camelback through the desert and back country, Andoheb arrives at the imposing Temple of Karnak to lay claim to his holy position. It isn't until later that we learn that Andoheb is affiliated with the Cairo Museum, for the chief purpose, it seems, of dissuading expeditions from venturing into the forbidden valley. Less than a week before *The Mummy's Hand* went into production, Universal sought the services of Peter Lorre for the film, presumably for the Andoheb role.

For every *Dead Men Walk* and *The Flying Serpent* on George Zucco's filmography, there are three or four movies in the *Joan of Arc* and *Arise, My Love* class. But it's his B horrors that have earned the actor cinematic immortality. Born in Manchester, England, in 1886, Zucco traveled to Canada in his teen years and signed up with a Winnipeg touring company. His travels with the group took him to New York in 1913 where he played in a vaudeville sketch entitled "The Suffragette." Answering the call to duty, the young man returned to England and fought in the Great War. Gravely wounded in combat (Zucco lost the use of his right arm and was forced to conceal the disfigurement of his two fingers), he returned to London to resume his stage career. Then came a role which won Zucco critical acclaim: Lt. Osborne in R.C. Sherriff's "Journey's End," directed by James Whale. Zucco enacted the role of Osborne for over 500 performances. Other stage successes followed, and eventually the rising actor made his debut in British pictures.

During a summer break of the hit Broadway play, "Victoria Regina," in the summer of 1936, Zucco received an offer from MGM to try his luck in Hollywood. His American screen debut in *After the Thin Man* (1936) led to featured roles in a bevy of MGM movies, as well as loanouts to Paramount and 20th Century-Fox. It was on the Fox lot that Zucco scored his greatest success to date in the realm of screen villainy by portraying Sir Arthur Conan Doyle's nefarious Professor Moriarty to Basil Rathbone's Baker Street super-sleuth in *The Adventures of Sherlock Holmes* (1939). A screen icon was born. For the rest of his life, for better or worse, George Zucco would be firmly associated with the dark side of the cinema.

Following an appearance in 20th Century–Fox's *David and Bathsheba* (1951), Zucco's career came to a halt. He suffered a stroke during the filming of *The Desert Fox* the same year, and was eventually committed to a sanitarium in South San Gabriel, California, where he died at age 74 on May 27, 1960. Author–*avant garde* filmmaker Kenneth Anger's grossly fraudulent account of the actor's final days in *Hollywood Babylon II* claims that Zucco had become a raving lunatic and spent the last phase of his life in the proverbial padded cell. Tragically, Zucco's daughter Frances died within two years of her father. She had a brief run in pictures, appearing in *Never Wave at a WAC* (1952) and a few others.

Actors like George Zucco, Lionel Atwill, Dwight Frye and Conrad Veidt have a certain mystique. They all passed on long before the galvanized forces of fantastic fandom could have had the chance to interview them firsthand. Consequently, we must content ourselves with the reminiscences of survivors of the Golden Age of Hollywood (and their memory-challenged offspring) to ascertain what these people were like off-camera. As Bulldog Drummond, John Howard waged an on-screen battle with an especially dastardly George Zucco in Paramount's *Arrest Bulldog Drummond* (1939). Almost half a century later, Howard had this to say about his co-star:

> George Zucco was a strange fellow but awfully nice. Completely different from the characters he always played. He wasn't the slightest bit menacing at all. He was a pussycat. It was as though he had a dark secret he didn't want anyone to know about.

Fifties exploitation film producer Alex Gordon recalled the day he visited George Zucco in his room at the sanitarium and offered the ailing actor the mad scientist role (eventually played by Tom Conway) in American International's *Voodoo Woman* (1957). Gordon had previously been told by Zucco's agent that the old trouper's career was over, but the prospect of returning to work might cheer him up. Zucco graciously declined Gordon's offer, explaining that he didn't wish to appear in any more horror pictures. Perhaps old George was hoping for a vehicle worthier of his time and talents than the tawdry AIP film.

Motion picture and television veteran Paul Picerni, the romantic lead in Warners' 1953 3-D classic *House of Wax* and Robert Stack's sidekick on TV's long-running series *The Untouchables*, shared with us this vivid recollection of meeting George Zucco in his twilight years:

> I brought a guest onto *The Untouchables* set on one occasion, and I still feel bad about what happened. Back in my Warner Brothers days, I did screen tests opposite a lot of actresses, and I never forgot one gal, a beautiful brunette who couldn't have been more than 21. The screen test we did was a beautiful love scene from *Force of Arms* [1951]. The girl in that test was Frances Zucco, the daughter of George Zucco, the famous monster movie guy from all of those old Mummy films. Well, several years later, she called me, I think to see if I could get a part for her father in an episode of [the show]. I'm Italian, I thought he was Italian (the name Zucco is Italian), so I invited him to the set. I always enjoyed helping out-of-work actors. I didn't specify that I was going to get George a job, or that I was going to be able to entertain him or anything, I just said, "Come by the set and I'll introduce you to Bob Stack and to some of the other people, and maybe something will happen." I was doing it as a favor to Frances. George arrived around 11:30 or 12. For a man his age, he looked pretty strong, and I thought he was in good shape. I introduced him to Bob and to the director, and to whoever else was on the set. He sat down in a director's chair and I spent as much time with him as I could. But when it came time for lunch, I guess I wasn't even thinking about Zucco at that moment, because when Bob said, "Let's go to lunch," I jumped into Bob's car with him and we took off for Tracton's—leaving George Zucco behind on the set! About an hour later we came back and there he was—and he was angry! He was steaming! "How dare you do this to me! You invite me here and then you leave me stranded, you don't even invite me to lunch!" I began to stammer out an apology—what I did was terrible, and I felt so bad about it. Of course I would have invited him to lunch if it hadn't slipped my mind that he was there, but it did slip my mind. It's been more than 40 years since that happened and I'm still embarrassed about it!

Stella Zucco, who outlived her husband by 35 years, knew only too well his frustration at being typecast in dastardly roles. In Gregory Mank's groundbreaking interview with Mrs. Zucco (*Hollywood's Maddest Doctors*, Midnight Marquee Press, 1998), she frankly stated,

> They really overdid it here—I really don't think Hollywood did the best they might have done with George. And when they started making him do horror movies, then I think it was a big mis-

take—a *big* mistake. I hated those Mummy movies—they weren't good enough for him! Always, no matter what role he was doing, George was a real professional. I don't think he could go on and give a bad performance. He loved what he did—which is one of the reasons why he was so very good.

When Universal got around to producing the first Kharis sequel, *The Mummy's Tomb*, it not only carried over the storyline and two of the key characters from *The Mummy's Hand*, but several minutes of that film's footage for flashback purposes. By spicing up *The Mummy's Tomb* with some of the best moments from the 1940 film, horror buffs of the postwar decade got a taste of a movie ultimately deprived them: *The Mummy's Hand* (as well as a handful of other Universal releases) were passed by when the studio sold its library to Film Classics and Realart for theatrical reissue in the late '40s–early '50s.

Critics' Corner

[S]tacks up as good horror stuff of the spine-chilling variety.... [H]as just enough hoke and mystery to satisfy addicts....—*The Hollywood Reporter*, August 23, 1940

A scare a minute.... [M]uch of the plot is sheer nonsense.... [M]anages to raise a few more goose pimples than other recent horror movies.—*The Philadelphia Record*, 1940

[M]uddled in the writing and clumsy in the production. Direction and photography are bush league. Acting varies from violent mugging to smooth underplaying.—*Variety*, September 25, 1940, Hobe.

[T]he usual mumbo-jumbo.... Once or twice Miss Moran makes a grimace—as if she had caught an unpleasant odor—and screams.... Frightening or funny, take your choice.—*The New York Times*, September 20, 1940, Theodore Strauss

Rating: ★★½ (out of 4 stars): [A] second-rate thriller....—*The New York Daily News*, September 20, 1940, Kate Cameron

The Invisible Woman

Released December 27, 1940. 70 minutes. *Director:* A. Edward Sutherland. *Associate Producer:* Burt Kelly. *Screenplay:* Robert Lees, Frederic I. Rinaldo & Gertrude Purcell. *Original Story:* Kurt [Curt] Siodmak & Joe May. *Suggested by the character created by* H.G. Wells. *Photography:* Elwood Bredell. *Special Photographic Effects:* John P. Fulton & John Hall. *Art Director:* Jack Otterson. *Associate Art Director:* Richard H. Riedel. *Editor:* Frank Gross. *Musical Director:* Charles Previn. *Sound Supervisor:* Bernard B. Brown. *Technician:* Joe Lapis. *Set Decorator:* Russell A. Gausman. *Assistant Director:* Joseph McDonough. *Gowns:* Vera West.

Virginia Bruce (*Kitty Carroll*), John Barrymore (*Prof. Gibbs*), John Howard (*Dick Russell*), Charlie Ruggles (*George*), Oscar Homolka (*Blackie Cole*), Edward Brophy (*Bill*), Donald MacBride (*Foghorn*), Charles Lane (*Growley*), Thurston Hall (*John Hudson*), Margaret Hamilton (*Mrs. Jackson*), Mary Gordon (*Mrs. Bates*), Anne Nagel (*Jean*), Maria Montez (*Marie*), Shemp Howard (*Hammerhead/Frankie*), Kathryn Adams (*Peggy*), Kitty O'Neil (*Mrs. Patton*), Eddie Conrad (*Hernandez*), Kay Leslie (*Model*), Kay Linaker, Sarah Edwards (*Fashion Show Buyers*), Harry C. Bradley (*Want Ad Man*), Kernan Cripps (*Postman*).

At Last! A Woman You Can See Through!
—*Ad blurb for* The Invisible Woman

The success of *The Invisible Man Returns* encouraged Universal to take further advantage of their screen rights to the H.G. Wells novel. In 1933, James Whale had flirted with the comic possibilities of the Invisible Man; Hal Roach pressed invisibility gags to their limit in United Artists' 1937 comedy-fantasy *Topper* with Cary Grant. After the fairly humorless *The Invisible Man Returns*, the time seemed right for an all-out farce, especially given the studio's inclination towards lowbrow, lightweight fare at this time. With the added titillation of a sex role reversal thrown in, *The Invisible Woman* was eagerly announced.

Curt Siodmak was signed to develop the idea in 1940, but veteran comedy writers Frederic I. Rinaldo and Robert Lees were brought in to write a more conventional, slapstick-heavy script. After being burned by the costly budget overruns of the last *Invisible* sequel, Universal allotted a more realistic budget of $300,000 for the production. By Universal's standards, *The Invisible Woman* was a major attraction calling for a name cast.

For the title role, the studio decided on Margaret Sullavan. Although proving to be a most affecting dramatic actress at MGM, Sullavan was no stranger to comedy, having appeared in the Broadway productions of "Dinner at Eight" and "Stage Door" as well as recently starring opposite James Stewart in the Ernst Lubitsch comedy, *The Shop Around the Corner* (1940). She still owed Universal a picture under her contract stemming back to the Laemmle days when she was directed by the likes of Frank Borzage

(*Little Man, What Now?* [1934]) and William Wyler (*The Good Fairy* [1935]). *The Invisible Woman* might have been the new management's idea of a major release, but Sullavan saw little glory in appearing in a baggy-pants burlesque, especially with more enticing roles in the offing from other studios.

Sullavan had been approached by director John Cromwell to play the lead in *So Ends Our Night* (1941), an adaptation of the Erich Maria Remarque novel, *Flotsam.* The film couldn't be more timely, a stirring tale of Nazi refugees and their vain attempt to find sanctuary in war-torn Europe. The combination of a top director, a story from the author of *All Quiet on the Western Front*, and working opposite leading man Fredric March, was too much for the actress to resist. When Sullavan failed to report to Universal for *The Invisible Woman*, she was served with a restraining order preventing her from working elsewhere. The legalities were finally ironed out with the actress agreeing to appear in two films for Universal if they would free her to continue with the Cromwell picture. (Sullavan honored her Universal commitments by starring in a remake of the Fannie Hurst soap opera, *Back Street* and the forgettable *Appointment for Love* [both 1941 releases and both co-starring Charles Boyer]). Universal tapped Virginia Bruce as her replacement on *The Invisible Woman*, signing the former MGM contractee on September 12, 1940.

John Barrymore, selected for the role of Prof. Gibbs, a batty old geezer of a genius who tinkers together an invisibility machine, couldn't afford to be choosy. The once-legendary actor, now a sad parody of himself, had become *persona non grata* at most Hollywood studios and was exploited by B picture-makers to give their product a touch of respectability.

Adding to Barrymore's misfortune was his worsening inability to memorize dialogue. John Howard, the romantic lead of *The Invisible Woman* and Barrymore's co-star in Paramount's Bulldog Drummond series of the '30s, remembered a few tricks the actor used to remedy his problem:

> He developed, with my help, a system of cutting up the script and putting it down on the set: Behind vases, behind phones, on the backs of other actors, whatever. This way he could just look around and find the lines. And of course he was such a superlative actor, it looked as though this was an inspirational way to say the lines! It worked very well, but it must have driven him nuts—he must have realized what was happening to him and I felt terribly sorry about that.
>
> Barrymore was an ordinary fellow. He wasn't stuffy and he had no pretense whatsoever. Even in pictures that you felt weren't up to snuff, I don't think he showed any disdain. We knew perfectly well *The Invisible Woman* wasn't going to be an award-winning picture, but it was fun to do. No one took it seriously; we took it seriously as a picture, but it was obviously designed to entertain rather than to make people think.

The Looney Tunes mood of the film is established from the first scene as an elegantly attired butler (Charlie Ruggles), tray in hand, plummets down the full length of a grand staircase after tripping over a champagne bottle. With this easy laugh out of the way, *The Invisible Woman* embarks on its dubious way.

Prof. Gibbs (John Barrymore) is a dotty inventor who perfects an invisibility machine, financed by millionaire playboy Dick Russell (John Howard). He selects fashion model Kitty Carroll (Virginia Bruce) to be his first guinea pig. The experiment is an unqualified success but Kitty has plans of her own. Wasting no time, she gives her miserly, slave-driving boss Mr. Growley (Charles Lane) his well-deserved comeuppance.

While Prof. Gibbs and the invisible Kitty pay a visit to Dick's lodge, Blackie Cole (Oscar Homolka), a gangster on the lam in Mexico, sends his battery of dim-witted thugs after the scientist's invention. Reassembling the apparatus at the hideaway, the fumbling fools can't get it to work. The gang kidnaps the now-visible Kitty and Gibbs, as Dick follows hot on their trail. Kitty, who has learned that alcohol will restore her visibility, manages to sneak a drink and, with Dick's aid, overpowers her abductors.

A clever postscript shows us the characters a year or two later. Now married, Dick and Kitty are fawning over their newborn son when the tot begins to fade. Gibbs suspiciously eyes the kid's rubbing alcohol and knowingly concludes, "Hereditary!"

The Invisible Woman is a typical low-brow comedy of the period. What it lacks in wit and sophistication, it makes up for with spirit, a galloping, madcap pace, a game cast, and an occa-

Virginia Bruce never revealed *this* much flesh in *The Invisible Woman* with John Barrymore and Margaret Hamilton.

sional funny line. The film was obviously geared for mass consumption by a working class audiences who got their money's worth. The picture plays out the middle-class fantasies of a rags-to-riches Cinderella of a heroine who uses her new-found power to exact a playful revenge on snobs and bullies. Snooty butlers, petty crooks and a monstrous caricature of a sadistic boss fall victim to her pranks. Times have changed but it's hard to believe that this trifle was considered mildly risqué when it was released. *The Invisible Woman* now seems more cartoonish than anything else.

Virginia Bruce is a pretty package of charm and energy in the title role. Although rarely materializing on the screen, her wonderfully melodious diction marks well her presence. John Howard smoothly plays the amiable Dick Russell, a role he found particularly challenging. He told the authors:

> The thing that was difficult for me was that I had to work opposite nobody, to talk to a non-existent person. The first time I mentioned this to a reporter, he said, "Well, that's no different from just doing a scene with anybody who's not there and that happens all the time in pictures." But it's not the same, it really isn't. There's a kind of funny transition that you have to make, and I think it's a different technique in a sense.
>
> For instance, how can I kiss an invisible hand if it isn't there? Am I going to look as though I'm pretending to kiss an invisible hand? That would throw the whole picture out of kilter. I have no experience in life that deals with this sort of thing. Of course, the director is no help with it 'cuz he doesn't know, either!

John Barrymore was near the end of his life and at the nadir of his career, though Universal's publicity mill continued to play him up as the Great Matinee Idol and his hamming was reverently cited as "a notable acting triumph."

Once America's most distinguished actor, Barrymore overplays like mad, but one can guiltily enjoy the audaciousness of his performance.

A studio press release insisted that Barrymore was delighted with his role and quotes him as telling the director, "It's a relief to play a straight role for a change" after playing so many madcap comedy parts. Obviously, the author of this publicity quip never bothered to see the film.

The actor hadn't had a good role since Mitchell Leisen's *Midnight* (1939), a frothy Lubitsch-styled confection about a down-on-her-luck American chorus girl loose among the swells of Monte Carlo. Playing the world-weary, cuckolded husband of socialite Mary Astor, Barrymore received third billing under Claudette Colbert and Don Ameche. Barrymore's somewhat dissipated appearance notwithstanding, his was an assured and graceful performance that never misses a beat. Still, the actor's erratic behavior coupled with his legendary bouts with the bottle didn't endear him to the major studios and his career slide seemed inevitable.

Although Barrymore's doddering Prof. Gibbs is a long way from his bravura performance as Oscar Jaffe, the manic Broadway impresario in Howard Hawks' *Twentieth Century* (1934), he elevates *The Invisible Woman* slightly from Universal's usual run of comedies. It's the kind of role that would have been a breeze for any perfectly competent Hollywood comic such as Edward Everett Horton or Franklin Pangborn. But Barrymore's decline was such a public spectacle, his mere presence makes him the centerpiece of the film, lending it an extravagant decadence that couldn't be written into the script. Barrymore has a few good lines in addition to the ones he makes up himself. His amusing dressing-down of his pet cat, with Barrymore down on all-fours, was about to segue into a Shakespearean tangent before it was regrettably cut short by the merciless film editor.

The supporting cast abounds with familiar faces. Charlie Ruggles, playing the much put-upon butler, comes off as the funniest in the film's roster of comedy actors. Oscar Homolka huffs and puffs as the homesick underworld kingpin. Shemp Howard, Edward Brophy (the guillotined murderer from *Mad Love* [1935]) and Donald MacBride are the hapless members of the gang. *The Wizard of Oz*'s (1939) Wicked Witch, Margaret Hamilton, gets in a few choice lines in the scanty part of Barrymore's housekeeper. Only the sharpest eye will be able to spot Maria Montez (on her way up) and Anne Nagel (on her way down) in bit parts. Crack stunt work adds to the fun and includes some skillfully executed pratfalls and tumbles off ladders and down staircases.

John Howard recalled a particularly hazardous feat during the climactic rescue scene:

> One stunt that blew my mind was when the stunt man dove into the fish pond which actually was a fish pond. That thing was only about three feet deep! I used to do a lot of shallow diving but I wouldn't have done that one for the love of money.

[The stunt man looks like it might be Dave Sharpe.]

Technically, *The Invisible Woman* is expertly handled with John P. Fulton's now-familiar special effects once more providing the visual interest. (Fulton was again nominated for an Academy Award.) The largely original score, as usual, went directly into the Universal's music library and would resurface in typical studio cut-and-dice fashion in many a genre picture to come. The score was used prominently in Abbott and Costello's *Hold That Ghost* and a good deal less appropriately in *Mystery of Marie Roget,* whose exciting rooftop chase was all but ruined by the jaunty action cue cribbed from *The Invisible Woman*'s climax. The picture has enjoyed a prolonged circulation on video, thanks to being a part of Universal's official *Invisible Man* series; it's often packaged along with more desirable titles (at least as far as horror fans are concerned). The movie continues to be a good bet for aficionados of vintage comedy (Leonard Maltin rates it quite highly) who'll appreciate the roster of veteran laugh-getters going through their paces.

For those who cherish the memory of the James Whale classic, *The Invisible Woman* is a minor desecration. As a lampoon, it's harmless enough and actually stands up better than the over-the-hill *Abbott and Costello Meet the Invisible Man* (1951). H.G. Wells, who was generously paid for the rights to his story, again receives screen credit for being the inspiration of this confection. His sole contribution was to sit back and watch one of his most renowned novels being shoved through the Hollywood meat grinder. Despite the film's novelty value, it proved to be less of a moneymaker than the studio's straight Invisible Man pictures, racking up a total gross of just under $660,000.

Not quite ready to take the Invisible Man theme out of the province of clowns, comedians and aging vaudevillians, Universal used it as a throw-away gag in Olsen and Johnson's relentlessly overstuffed *Hellzapoppin'*, released in 1941. The same year, Warner Bros. gave movie audiences their *second* Invisible Woman: Jane Wyman in the B-comedy *The Body Disappears* with a similarly see-through Jeffrey Lynn.

Critics' Corner

We think Universal's *The Invisible Woman* is one heck of a funny show.... There isn't a dull spot in the swell comedy script ... and it is a thoroughly excellent production which Burt Kelly has put together. There are a number of hilarious sequences and several situations which border on the sex danger-line but the latter are so apropos and fall so neatly into the story that they add to the general merriment.... John Barrymore is immense. He plays Hamlet, brother Lionel, Richard III and Little Eva — all in the garb of John Barrymore, 1940, taking time out twice to comment on his front page "activities." — *The Hollywood Reporter*, December 30, 1940

Rating: ★★½ It's a farcical piece, often amusing and sometimes downright funny, but rather too engrossed in slapstick to be an entirely successful comedy. — *The New York Daily News*, January 9, 1941, Dorothy Masters

As far as the trick photography is concerned, it is handled well; but it does not offer anything new to those who saw the other pictures in which the characters became invisible. — *Harrison's Reports*, January 11, 1941

Because everyone concerned with *The Invisible Woman* apparently (and in hiding) had so much fun taking daffy direction from Eddie Sutherland, who's at his best on unconventional cinema, the Rialto's audience has a good time, too.... It's a mighty merry movie, and it won't do anybody any harm to chuckle along with it, as a respite from the worries of the world.... Of course, the goofy comedy climaxes in a happy ending — but even the fadeout, is a gag, a cute one, too.... It's giggle fare that satisfies. — *The New York Post*, January 1941, Irene Thirer

The current calendar year is unlikely to disclose a rival — from the standpoint of story originality — of this new Universal comedy meller, and, further, there will not be many features released which will boast more solid and skillful casts.... It is laugh-packed, brightly directed, and the spirit of the yarn is fully captured by the players and director.... [A] lot of fun and decidedly off the beaten track of celluloid production. — *The Film Daily*, January 7, 1941

1941

Man Made Monster

Released March 28, 1941. Reissued by Realart as *The Atomic Monster*. 60 minutes. *Director:* George Waggner. *Associate Producer:* Jack Bernhard. *Screenplay:* Joseph West (George Waggner). *Based on the story* "The Electric Man" *by* Harry J. Essex, Sid Schwartz and Len Golos. *Photography:* Elwood Bredell. *Art Director:* Jack Otterson. *Associate Art Director:* Harold H. MacArthur. *Editor:* Arthur Hilton. *Music Director:* Hans J. Salter. *Special Photographic Effects:* John P. Fulton. *Set Decorator:* Russell A. Gausman. *Sound Supervisor:* Bernard B. Brown. *Technician:* Charles Carroll. *Makeup:* Jack P. Pierce. *Gowns:* Vera West. *Assistant Director:* Fred Frank. *Electrical Properties:* Kenneth Strickfaden.

Lionel Atwill (*Dr. Paul Rigas*), Lon Chaney, Jr. (*"Dynamo" Dan McCormick*), Anne Nagel (*June Lawrence*), Frank Albertson (*Mark Adams*), Samuel S. Hinds (*Dr. John Lawrence*), William B. Davidson (*D.A. Ralph D. Stanley*), John Dilson (*Medical Examiner*), Frank O'Connor (*Detective*), Ben Taggart (*Det. Sgt. Regan*), Russell Hicks (*Warden Harris*), Connie Bergen (*Nurse*), George Meader (*Dr. Bruno*), Chester Gan (*Wong*), Ivan Miller (*Doctor*), Douglas Evans (*Police Radio Announcer*), Byron Foulger (*Second Alienist*), William Hall (*Mike*), Victor Zimmerman (*Dynamo Operator*), Gary Breckner (*Radio Announcer*), John Ellis (*Assistant D.A.*), Wright Kramer (*Judge*), Mel Ruick (*Defense Attorney*), Paul Scott (*Minister*), David Sharpe (*Man on Haywagon*), Francis Sayles (*Frank Davis*), Jessie Arnold (*Mrs. Davis*), Jack Gardner (*Reporter*), James Blaine (*Charlie*), Lowell Drew (*Foreman of Jury*), Bob Reeves (*Guard*).

The sock shocker of them all ... the story of a voltage vampire!
—*Ad blurb for* Man Made Monster

Man Made Monster is a pivotal Universal horror film. It's not especially well-produced; in fact, it's far from the best that the studio was capable of making. But it introduced two of the most important figures to emerge from Universal in the '40s, Lon Chaney, Jr., and George Waggner.

A former pre-med student, George Waggner came to Hollywood in 1920 as an actor and writer. He landed a role in *The Sheik* (1921) starring Rudolph Valentino and played Buffalo Bill in John Ford's *The Iron Horse* (1924). His acting career floundered but he plugged away at various writing assignments and tried his hand at songwriting when the talkies came in. Frequently using the name Joseph West, he penned several long-forgotten potboilers at Monogram with titles like *Laughing at Danger*, *Son of the Navy* and *Phantom of Chinatown* (all 1940). He turned to directing in the late '30s and amassed over two dozen credits (mostly cheap Westerns), six of which were made for Universal in 1938.

After an eight-year stint in Hollywood, recognition if not stardom came to Lon Chaney, Jr., with his deeply affecting performance as Lennie Small, the ironically named gentle giant in John Steinbeck's *Of Mice and Men* (1939). Universal saw the actor's potential to replace Boris Karloff as their leading horror star mainly in the form of name recognition. Except for the recent Steinbeck adaptation, Chaney's hadn't distinguished himself in either A or B pictures. Even though he played his share of heavies, his acting style was closer to brawny Dick Foran than the sort of *mysterioso* Europeans who were usually associated with the genre. This seemed to matter very little to the studio which was abandoning the Laemmle's literary approach to horror films in favor of a juvenile, actionful take on the genre. If Chaney lacked the dark charisma of a Lugosi or the protean dramatic skills of a Karloff, he at least was a formidable physical presence even without the help of the studio makeup and costuming department.

That Chaney's services could be had relatively cheaply (*Of Mice and Men* was too downbeat to be commercially successful) was an added allure to the studio, which wasn't interested in squandering a great deal of capital on their latest investment. Indeed, Chaney's horror career was launched with a paltry estimated budget of only $86,000, making *The Mysterious Dr. R* (*Man Made Monster*'s original shooting title) one of the cheapest films then being shot on the lot despite a three-week shooting schedule and intricate special effects work.

Man Made Monster arose from the ashes of the unmade Karloff-Lugosi starrer *The Man in the Cab*, based on the story "The Electric Man" which Universal bought on August 1, 1935. The studio had lost interest in that project; it was possibly shelved in favor of the somewhat similar *The Invisible Ray*. The original yarn was cowritten by Harry J. Essex who intended it as a movie treatment while he was still a reporter on *The New York Daily Mirror*.

Essex told the authors:

> Sidney Schwartz, who also wrote for the paper, and Len Golos, a press agent, and I were bouncing story ideas around, and I came up with the notion to do a thing called "The Electric Man." It was based on a true story I read about: A government organization was performing tests on electricity and the human body, how much we use up throughout the day and how we "recharge the batteries" by sleep at night. Out of that was born the idea of "The Electric Man"—if there was some way to recharge the body's electricity, we wouldn't have to eat or sleep. The story was submitted to an agency, and sold to Universal. We didn't get much money for it at the time, I think we got something like $3,300, but it was my first big sale.

When Universal revived the project in 1940, it assigned George Waggner to direct the film and rewrite the script. Using his pseudonym Joseph West, Waggner changed the title to *The Human Robot*, smoothed over the rough edges, and submitted the finished screenplay for approval. In November 1940, he was signed to direct the film.

Lionel Atwill was a natural choice for what was essentially the lead role as the loony Dr. Rigas. The portly actor had just left 20th Century–Fox and was about to enter the field of independent production, having bought the rights to the novel *The Dark River*; Atwill was eager to sign up his old friend and neighbor James Whale to direct. In the meantime, he picked up whatever fast money he could by appearing in Universal's penny dreadfuls, unaware that this type of fare would soon be his main source of income. Atwill's infamous Christmas

Eve orgy took place at his Pacific Palisades home just as *Man Made Monster* was wrapping up production. The scandal that erupted permanently short-circuited his acting career and cancelled his aspirations of becoming an independent producer.

Man Made Monster benefits from a well-constructed plot that wastes little time in getting underway. A bus speeding across a rainswept highway veers out of control and crashes into a high-voltage tower. The accident leaves five people electrocuted. The lone survivor is "Dynamo" Dan McCormick (Lon Chaney, Jr.), a carnival performer who, in his act, shows himself to be impervious to electrical shocks. Dr. John Lawrence (Samuel S. Hinds), a noted "electro-biologist," suggests to Dan that he may now, in fact, be impervious to high voltage current. The scientist invites Dan to his country estate for observation. There Dan meets Lawrence's lovely niece June (Anne Nagel) and his obsessive associate, Dr. Rigas (Lionel Atwill).

Rigas sees Dan as the perfect guinea pig in his efforts to spawn a race of electrically automated supermen, a pet project that has been a source of derision to his colleagues, including Lawrence. Secretly, Rigas experiments on Dan, sending tremendous surges of current into his body until he begins pulsating with light and becomes dependent on electricity for strength. Lawrence learns what has been going on in the lab and threatens to call the police. On Rigas' order, Dan, now a monster completely subject to Rigas' will, pounces upon the scientist, breaking his neck in the struggle. Returning back to normal, Dan is charged and convicted of the crime and condemned to die.

Strapped in the electric chair, Dan is "re-charged" by the high voltage and once again becomes a human dynamo. He kills the warden (Russell Hicks) during his flight and heads for Rigas' lab. Finding the crazed scientist about to try out his electrical apparatus on June, Dan kills Rigas with his deadly grasp and, donning an insulating rubber suit, disappears into the woods with June unconscious in his arms. The electrical man tries to tear through a barbed-wire fence, but the razors rip through his protective suit. As the power races out of his body through the metal wires on which he is snared, Dan's life slowly ebbs away and he collapses dead.

Clocking in at an hour, *Man Made Monster* is an extremely well-structured little picture which belies its low budget to showcase the prodigious talents of a top technical team. From the first scene, special effects ace John P. Fulton takes center stage with a superb display of studio miniatures as the speeding bus crashes into the electrical pylon. Chaney's luminescent effects are a variation on the technique Fulton devised for *The Invisible Ray*; in fact, *Man Made Monster* owes a considerable debt to the earlier picture in its premise of an energized creature whose touch brings death.

The similarities end there, however, for the George Waggner film is a far more streamlined affair that's fast-moving, unpretentious and entirely predictable. There isn't a single character who isn't a cliché, from the brash newspaper reporter-hero to the lunatic scientist. It's the kind of (pardon the pun) shocker that Monogram and PRC regularly churned out, yet the style is distinctly Universal. *Man Made Monster* has a drive and crispness sorely lacking in the drab, fleabag Poverty Row quickies. In fact, it has the cocky charm of a '30s Warner Bros. programmer with its slam-bang opening scene and the instant introduction of all the main characters within the first few minutes. The groundwork of the story is carefully laid out in a deliberately paced first half with Chaney's gradual transformation into a super-charged creature punctuated by photographer Elwood Bredell's increased use of low-keyed lighting, complimenting the script's ever-darkening mood.

The script has the wit not give in to romantic distractions, unlike *The Invisible Man Returns* or the later *The Mad Ghoul*, dismissing a potential triangle between Chaney, Nagel and Albertson in a couple of terse lines. The prioritized horror scenes are over the top in comic-book style, in keeping with the crisp, hard-sell tone of the film. *Man Made Monster* rides roughshod over logic to the point of becoming over-generous in its horror effects (it's not enough that Chaney becomes a glow-in-the-dark fiend, his electrocuted victims succumb in a similarly gruesome fashion). The mayhem reaches its zenith as Chaney is dragged off to the electric chair for the unsuspecting world to bear witness to Atwill's triumph. Unfortunately, the film lapses into squeamishness, probably in a

Man Made Monster was Lon Chaney, Jr.'s, official entrée into horror movies.

concession to the Production Code, which no doubt looked askance at the morbid details of Chaney being strapped into the chair and the juice applied. (As in *Black Friday,* the tasteful shadow shots of the device were lifted from 1938's *Wives Under Suspicion.*)

For a pre-war film, *Man Made Monster* is surprisingly prescient in addressing some of the issues that would be placed front-and-center in the months ahead. Atwill's dream of social "non-entities" transformed into a race of electrified robots controlled by a "superior intelligence" (his, of course) is the sort of Hitlerian dogma that would be written into the scripts of cheap horror movies the instant that war was declared. To find this in a film as early as 1940 is unusual enough for us to surmise that writer George Waggner, who was of German extraction, may have been capitalizing on the European situation, imbuing a low-rent genre piece with hints of a cautionary tale.

Atwill's mad doctor Rigas, like so many of the Hollywood mad scientists of the period, foreshadowed the grim handiwork of notorious Nazi scientist Dr. Mengele (although writer Essex claimed the story was a takeoff of *American* researchers of the period). The character is so obviously unhinged that it's hard to believe he could so easily hoodwink the investigating authorities, especially after offering a bovine police captain a demonstration of his pulsating "electrothermostatic" table, which he shows off with drooling delight. Nevertheless, Atwill's casting is exactly right; his slightly off-kilter personality and hardwired manner mark him as an intrusive presence in Samuel S. Hinds' well-ordered "American apple pie" household. In contrast to Sir Cedric Hardwicke, George Zucco or even Karloff, who could barely conceal their own self-loathing by acting in movies they felt were beneath them, Atwill takes to career slumming with an unwholesome glee. It would seem that horror movies provided Atwill with the perfect outlet to bare the dark recesses of his soul, standing in sharp contrast to his conventional, sometimes slightly dull performances in respectable MGM or Fox projects. Unlike Vincent Price whose trademark ham became a signature style in later horror pictures, Atwill never gave the impression he was sending up the material. Instead, he always fully committed himself to the project at hand, grounding his excesses in a solid theatrical technique. Atwill is usually classed in the "second tier" of Hollywood boogie men, but he's a fascinating actor to watch, perhaps even more so than any of the horror kingpins.

Samuel S. Hinds contributes another of his smoothly avuncular performances as the scientist who's willing to overlook his associate's disturbing fascist tendencies in the interest of the greater good only to find too late he's made a fatal mistake (continuing the film's strain of political subtext). Anne Nagel's performance is one of the better in the run of prim, pretty girl heroines who end up being carried off by the mon-

Dan McCormick (Chaney Jr.) struggles in a barbed wire fence in the *Man Made Monster* finale (courtesy Rich Scrivani).

ster in the last reel. It's a limiting, Sunday schoolmarm role but the actress plays up the character's intuition very well, seeming more attuned to the monstrous conspiracy afoot than her benevolent-to-a-fault uncle or her affably dim newspaper reporter boyfriend (Frank Albertson).

Lon Chaney is fine in the title role, a part which at first glance wouldn't seem to demand much of his talents. His Dan McCormick may not be the book learnin' type but he's a big lug with a big heart who likes dogs and girls ("Immunity? What's *that?*" he queries his scientist employer). Chaney delivers a solid performance, sealing the deal with a spectacular death scene staged as an electrified crucifixion, as a barbed wire fence cuts through his insulated suit, sapping his life-force. The actor, getting the benefit of being framed in Fulton's glow effects, silently expresses all the emotions of an animal caught in a trap, finally accepting his sad fate before dying, all in dramatic closeup. Chaney couldn't ask for a better platform, especially with Hans J. Salter's taut chase music segueing into saccharine strings as Corky, the family dog, snuggles up to his lifeless body.

Chaney's horror debut was a comparative throwaway compared to the box office bonanzas which launched Karloff or Lugosi's. Nevertheless, Universal saw young Lon's potential not only as a horror star but as a useful addition to their roster of contract players and rewarded him with an exclusive long-term contract. For his services, Chaney would be paid a modest $500 per week for a one-year period; however, it wasn't long before his salary escalated. Director-writer Waggner didn't fare badly with Universal, either. On the basis of *Man Made Monster* and its companion feature *Horror Island*, Waggner secured a seven-year contract with the studio and went on to produce some of their most lavish pictures. But that was in the future. For the moment, the studio needed to cement Chaney's identification with horror movies with a success worthy of *Dracula* and *Frankenstein* and put their faith in Waggner to deliver the goods. The producer's efforts would succeed beyond anyone's wildest expectations with *The Wolf Man*, which would be in pre-production in a matter of months.

Harry Essex eventually drifted back to Universal as their '50s science fiction boom took off in grand fashion with *It Came from Outer Space*, adapting Ray Bradbury's elaborate treatment into a screenplay. A curious postscript to *Man Made Monster* came in the form of an ad placed by Essex in an October 1953 edition of *The Hollywood Reporter*. Included on a list of his "pictures in preparation" at Universal was the title *Electric Man*. Whether the project was intended as a remake of *Man Made Monster*, or merely a film with a similar theme, could not be determined.

Critics' Corner

As long as the fans continue to demand this type of horror mystery film ... *Man Made Monster* is a notable example of how they should be made. Waggner's screenplay makes the fantastic premise of the original story almost believable.... Lon Chaney, Jr. makes a place for himself on the screen in the footsteps of his late great father. Skillfully, he handles the character changes as he becomes more and more dependent on the doses of electricity administered him by Lionel Atwill.... There are some genuinely spine-tingling scenes as the monster runs berserk....—*The Hollywood Reporter*, March 24, 1941

Rating: ★★ Chaney is a curious looking sight on the screen, but is not as frightening as his creators tried to make him.... [A] synthetic screen story.—*The New York Daily News*, March 19, 1941, Kate Cameron

[W]e grew rather fond of Dan. Silly? Of course he's silly and the picture is low-grade shocker fare.... [H]e's always good for a laugh.—*The New York Times*, March 19, 1941, Bosley Crowther

The story is extremely far-fetched; for that reason, an adult audience will find it difficult to take it seriously or be shocked by the action; it may, however, prove thrilling to the youngsters.... One has sympathy for the killer, a victim himself of a madman, but on occasion, his actions, resulting from his predicament, are somewhat sickening.—*Harrison's Reports*, March 29, 1941

Since the production of the so-called horror film is predicated upon spine-chilling, *Man Made Monster* cleaves to its function and gets by as a program meller.... There's good menace and suspense. George Waggner's direction is okay and ditto the photography.—*The Film Daily*, March 21, 1941

Horror Island

Released March 28, 1941. 60 minutes. A Ben Pivar Production. *Director:* George Waggner. *Associate Producer:* Jack Bernhard. *Screenplay:* Maurice Tombragel & Victor McLeod. *Based on the story* "Terror of the South Seas" *by* Alex Gottlieb. *Photography:* Elwood Bredell. *Camera Operator:* Walter Strenge. *Assistant*

Director: Seward Webb. *Editor:* Otto Ludwig. *Art Director:* Jack Otterson. *Associate Art Director:* Ralph M. DeLacy. *Musical Director:* Hans J. Salter. *Set Decorator:* Russell A. Gausman. *Sound Supervisor:* Bernard B. Brown. *Technician:* Jess Moulin. *Gowns:* Vera West.

Dick Foran (*Bill Martin*), Leo Carrillo (*Tobias Clump*), Peggy Moran (*Wendy Crayton*), Fuzzy Knight (*Stuff Oliver*), John Eldredge (*George Martin*), Lewis Howard (*Thurman Coldwater*), Hobart Cavanaugh (*Prof. Jasper Quinley*), Walter Catlett (*Sgt. McGoon*), Ralf Harolde (*Rod "Killer" Grady*), Iris Adrian (*Arleen Grady*), Foy Van Dolsen (*The Phantom/Panama Pete*), Emmett Vogan (*The Stranger*), Walter Tetley (*Delivery Boy*), Eddy Chandler (*Policeman*), Robert Barron (*Wreck Spectator*), Ed Parker, Dale Van Sickel (*Stunts*).

Is this party goin' on all night? Radios playin' and dames screamin'!
—*Iris Adrian in* Horror Island

Devised to support *Man Made Monster* on the second half of an all-horror double bill, *Horror Island* is the quintessential kids' matinee crowd-pleaser, concocted according to a foolproof formula: Combine one part mysterious chills, one part adventure, a dash of romance, season it with humor, and simmer for an hour. Depending on your tolerance for over-the-top mugging, *Horror Island* is guaranteed to go down easy and leave no unpleasant after taste.

Produced on a meager budget of $93,000, *Horror Island* is a modest, undemanding entertainment that just misses the mark. We are inclined to set aside our critical sensibilities and play along with this good-natured romp for half of its length before the whole affair wears thin and becomes too silly and repetitious for its own good. Many of the daily news critics and trade reviewers shrugged *Horror Island* off as a mere trifle, no more, no less; any criticism that it yielded stronger than this was just plain overkill.

Starring in his second thriller in less than a year, Western favorite Dick Foran plays Bill Martin, a Princeton grad who can't seem to pass muster in the business world. (Foran seems a bit too mature to be playing an out-of-work college grad, but his easygoing, affable personality compensates for the miscasting.) Searching for the perfect get-rich-quick scheme, Bill and his partner Stuff Oliver (Fuzzy Knight) join forces with peg-legged Spanish seaman Tobias Clump (Leo Carrillo), affectionately known as the Skipper. The salty mariner owns half of an ancient map which, he claims, pinpoints the location of a $20,000,000 treasure in Spanish gold and royal jewels. The other half of the map was stolen by a black-caped figure whom the Skipper refers to as the Phantom (Foy Van Dolsen).

Although Bill doesn't really believe in the existence of the treasure, he sees gold dust on the horizon anyway. Why not arrange touristy treasure hunts on Morgan's Island off the Florida coast? (The property was left to Bill by his grandfather.) After rigging up the island's 400-year-old pirate castle with a variety of spook trappings, Bill leaves port with his first boatload of eager weekenders. The guest list includes heiress Wendy Crayton (Peggy Moran), her fortune-hunting suitor Thurman Coldwater (Lewis Howard), escaped con Rod Grady (Ralf Harolde) and his blowzy wife Arleen (Iris Adrian), Sgt. McGoon (Walter Catlett), mousy map expert Jasper Quinley (Hobart Cavanaugh) and Bill's greedy cousin George (John Eldredge), who wants the island for himself.

Mayhem erupts almost immediately. The Skipper is nearly skewered by an arrow fired off by an ancient suit of armor; Wendy has a similar close call of her own. Later, she is visited in her room by the Phantom himself. "This castle belongs to the spirits of the past!" the stranger bellows. "Death waits for those who *dare* spend the night here!" Ace photographer Elwood "Woody" Bredell has a field day capturing actor Foy Van Dolsen's angular, deeply shadowed face and bat-like figure darting across staircases and the ship's decks or peering through lattices and window panes.

When Rod is shot dead while attempting to leave the island, the party realizes that the Phantom means business. Tracing the alleged location of the treasure to an old torture chamber, Bill and his partners discover a jewel box with a gold coin inside. The Phantom, hidden behind a drape, is about to strike again when yet *another* suit of armor discharges an arrow, piercing the mystery man's heart. The Skipper identifies the dead man as Panama Pete, a former shipmate who was there when Clump first discovered the map.

With the complete map in their possession, Bill, Stuff and the Skipper resume the search but are interrupted by Wendy's disappearance. George is found shot to death, his body stuffed inside (what else?) a suit of armor. Bill gets wise to Quinley, whom he has discovered "sleepwalking" through the castle's corridors (real sleepwalkers don't stop to put on slippers). Unmasked, Quinley admits that he killed both the Phantom and George. Holding the group at gunpoint, the professor slips the coin into the axe handle mounted above the door of the treasure chamber. "Now you're going to see *my* treasure," he gloats. His triumph is short-lived. The axe blade dislodges and crushes Quinley's skull.

As might be expected, the treasure turns out to be a fraud. But all ends well when the U.S. Coast Guard shows up unexpectedly and offers to buy the island from Bill for a naval defense base.

Horror Island had an incredibly hectic production schedule. It was originally slated to begin shooting on February 20, 1941, but was delayed until March 3. Faced with a previously arranged preview date, George Waggner had just three weeks to get his picture shot, edited and scored.

Although Peggy Moran's memories are dim concerning the particulars of the shooting, she did recall for the authors that making the film was an exhausting experience:

> Most of my pictures I felt they raced through! They were two-week pictures, but this was really two weeks day and night. I remember going home and being so exhausted I couldn't eat dinner. My mother would rub my back and I would start crying just from being so exhausted.

Keeping a close eye on the tight budget, art directors Jack Otterson and Ralph M. DeLacy dusted off old *Tower of London* sets and put them back into action. A fine miniature of Morgan's Castle was devised. (PRC borrowed the castle image under *Horror Island*'s main title for the opening scene of the 1945 Lionel Atwill-versus-George Zucco retribution chiller *Fog Island.*) Misty, atmospheric night scenes were shot along briny Waterfront Street and in and around the studio tank. Poor weather conditions hampered exterior shooting and only increased pressure on the company. As an emergency measure, tarpaulins were set up to shield the cameras and sets from rain, but this precaution did little or no good.

Waggner worked his cast and crew until midnight on some nights in an effort to stay within the 12-day shooting schedule. Otto Ludwig screened and edited the footage *during* production to save time. Dick Foran came down with a cold and had to miss a day's work. Consequently, his last scene was cut out of the script altogether in order to bring the film in — on schedule — at 11 P.M. on the night of March 15. Hans J. Salter swiped the rousing main title theme from *Seven Sinners* (1940) and several comfortably familiar cues from past scores to expedite the completion of his assignment.

Everyone's hard work paid off. *Horror Island* was ready for trade previews just 23 days after the start of production. The frenetic shooting schedule didn't appreciably damage the quality of the movie from a technical standpoint. Despite a reliance on stock music and standing sets, it is a slick, good-looking picture with especially fine camerawork. Where greater attention should have been paid was in the writing. Once the basic situation is set up, the adventurers are nestled in the castle, and the treasure hunt begins in earnest, the plot flounders under the weight of its own devices. Maurice Tombragel and Victor McLeod dusted off their handbook of trite haunted house and pirate lore gimmicks with predictable, uninspired results. Sliding panels, torture chambers, cryptic treasure map messages and chalked-up victim countdowns are but a few of the half-baked elements they stirred into the potpourri.

Horror Island owes a debt to the classic Bob Hope comic chiller *The Ghost Breakers*, released the previous year. In this handsomely mounted Paramount film, the comedian accompanies Paulette Goddard to the island she has inherited (located off the coast of Cuba), which is reputedly hagridden with zombies and voodoo practitioners. All of the basic elements — a foreboding ancestral castle, red herrings, elusive clues pointing to the whereabouts of a treasure (in this case, a rich vein of silver), a fiendish character (Noble Johnson, memorable as the island's resident zombie), right down to the revelation that the most innocent-appearing cast member (Richard Carlson) is actually the villain — were nabbed, by design or coincidence, by the writers of *Horror Island.* What they could not emulate was *Ghost Breakers*' witty script nor the Bob Hope brand of humor. (In 1942, yet *another Ghost Breakers* rip-off, this one even more brazen, reached movie screens, 20th Century–

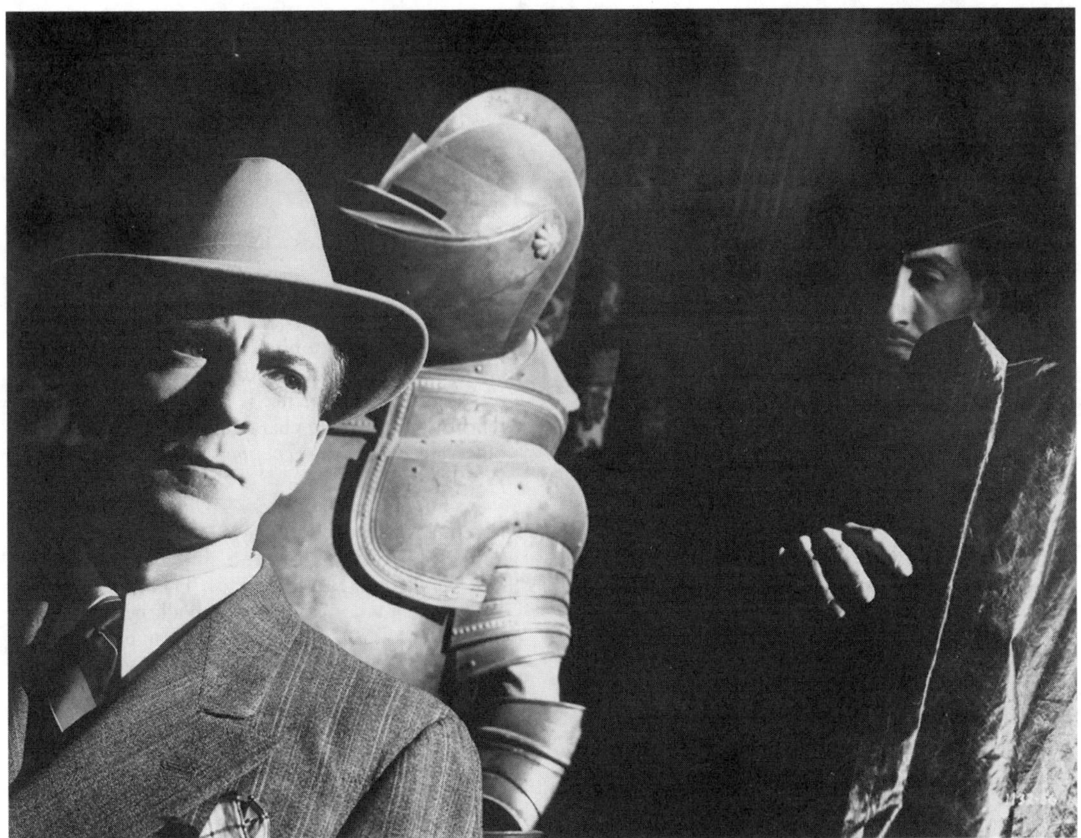

Caped Phantom Foy Van Dolsen is about to add gangster Ralf Harolde to his list of victims on *Horror Island.*

Fox's *Whispering Ghosts* with Milton Berle and Willie Best.)

Befitting the material, the *Horror Island* characters are mostly caricatures brought to life by an amiable cast. Foran and Moran are as ingratiating here as they had been in *The Mummy's Hand.* In his first assignment for Universal under a new term contract, Leo Carrillo gives a flavorsome account as the Skipper, looking as though he had just stepped out of the pages of Robert Louis Stevenson. Considered (in the minds of the studio publicity people) a master dialectician, Carrillo lent an appealing Latin piquancy to his roles. Foy Van Dolsen (in a role originally assigned to Philip Sleeman) is physically imposing as the Phantom, and Iris Adrian, saucy as ever, gets off a few well-timed cracks.

The most poorly written role in *Horror Island* is Hobart Cavanaugh's Jasper Quinley. He is so unbelievably timorous that his last reel revelation as the story's *other* villain shouldn't have provoked any cries of disbelief. Whether he's passing out on cue or doing a burlesque comic's imitation of a sleepwalker, Cavanaugh strikes a false note at all times. Surprisingly, the scrawny little man gets the best of burly Dick Foran in a climactic donnybrook. Cavanaugh began his career in motion pictures in the late '20s and appeared in over 180 movies before his death in April 1950. Like Arthur Hoyt, Chester Clute and Milton Parsons, Cavanaugh got more than his share of "Casper Milquetoast" parts; horror fans remember him chiefly as Petty Louie, Boris Karloff's partner-in-crime in *Night Key. Horror Island* reunited Cavanaugh with his partner from his vaudeville days, Walter Catlett. In 1899, Cavanaugh and Catlett appeared together as boys in a juvenile operetta at a San Francisco theater. Afterwards, they started a juvenile vaudeville act known as the Irish Boy Comedians, and played up and down the West Coast.

Andy Devine was originally chosen for the

role of Dick Foran's sidekick, Stuff. Reportedly, he and his screen partner had a falling-out prior to the start of shooting, and Fuzzy Knight was assigned the role instead. (With his low-comedy acting style and fingernails-across-the-blackboard voice, Devine would have undoubtedly scored higher on the viewer irritation scale than Knight.) For fans who delight in gutter trivia (don't we all?), there's the bizarre death of Rex Reed look-alike Lewis Howard, Peggy Moran's sleepy-eyed suitor. In the late '40s or early '50s, the actor walked into a Times Square shooting gallery, rented a rifle, fired several shots at moving targets and then turned the rifle around and put a bullet through his brain. He miraculously managed not to die right away, and began begging onlookers to finish him off. (Howard's picture adorned the wall of Holocaust diarist Anne Frank.)

Another *Horror Island* cast member whose personal life was marred by tragedy was Ralf Harolde. Serial director William Witney told us that young stunt man Jimmy Fawcett was killed in a motorcycle accident caused by Harolde. Witney recalled:

> We all rode motorcycles just before the War, and we'd all stopped after work and had a couple of drinks.... There were about six or eight of us, and Jimmy and some others took off for home in one direction and I took off the other way ... 'cause I lived in the *other* direction. And when I got home, there was a phone call and my wife said, "He was killed!" A god-damned drunken actor named Ralf Harolde came out of a motel [in his car], and all of the guys cut in back of him. And I guess Jimmy thought he could make the front, but he ran into the car and it killed him.

In his other genre credit, Harolde plays the man running from the maddened dinosaur in the surviving footage from Willis O'Brien's unrealized project *Creation* (1931).

Horror Island bears a passing resemblance to another Ben Pivar production also released in 1941, *A Dangerous Game*. One of several action-mystery thrillers co-starring the unlikely screen team of Richard Arlen and Andy Devine, this raucous little film features a treasure hunt of another kind. Andrew Tombes portrays a seemingly wacky insurance beneficiary who conceals his loot somewhere in a shady sanitarium, prompting an off-kilter assortment of cops, gangsters and lunatics to mount a merry hunt after the hidden cache. Seldom has a movie tried so hard for laughs and failed so miserably. As in *Horror Island*, Pivar mixed murder with merriment, but this time the results were disastrous.

Critics' Corner

The screenplay ... is a loose affair, the mysterious goings-on never quite believable nor sufficiently funny to be farce.... Waggner gets all the action possible from the script in hand.... [His] direction is first-rate throughout as is the photography of Elwood Bredell.... [The cast] all do justice to their assignments but the brightest performance is that of Lewis Howard, repeating his drowsy characterization. He sleeps as others are murdered.—*The Hollywood Reporter*, March 27, 1941

It's not much fun nor very frightening, but it's innocent and any one can play.... It is also suitable for kiddies' birthday parties and church socials.—*The New York Times*, March 31, 1941, Theodore Strauss

Rating: ★★½ [R]eplete with all the claptrap of the mystery film.... Pretty Peggy Moran plays Wendy nicely and Dick Foran is the gullible Bill Martin to the life.—*The New York Daily News*, March 30, 1941, Kate Cameron

The story is silly, and the direction is stilted; even the performances lack conviction. Situations presumably meant to be eerie and frightening turn out to be just ridiculous. As entertainment, its appeal will be directed mostly to juveniles.—*Harrison's Reports*, April 5, 1941

[T]his is a nicely paced quickie that throws all the elements together, hopes for the best, and is contented with considerably less than that because, after all, how much did it cost to make anyway? ... The trouble with the picture is that it tries so hard to be scary, funny and mysterious that the component parts never come together. The frightening parts tend to be funny, and the funny parts are just a little frightening and the mystification is just plain subterfuge on the part of the plot maker....—*The New York Post*, March 31, 1941, Archer Winsten

The Black Cat

Released May 2, 1941. 70 minutes. *Director:* Albert S. Rogell. *Associate Producer:* Burt Kelly. *Screenplay:* Robert Lees, Frederic I. Rinaldo, Eric Taylor & Robert Neville. *Suggested by the short story* "The Black Cat" *by* Edgar Allan Poe. *Photography:* Stanley Cortez. *Art Director:* Jack Otterson. *Associate Art Director:* Ralph M. DeLacy. *Editor:* Ted Kent. *Musical Director:* Hans J. Salter. *Special Photographic Effects:* John P. Fulton. *Assistant Director:* Howard Christie. *Set Decorator:* Russell A. Gausman. *Sound Supervisor:* Bernard B. Brown. *Technician:* Hal Bumbaugh. *Gowns:* Vera West. *Makeup:* Jack P. Pierce.

Basil Rathbone (*Montague Hartley*), Hugh Herbert (*Mr. Penny*), Broderick Crawford (*Gilbert Smith*), Bela Lugosi (*Eduardo Vitos*), Gale Sondergaard (*Abigail Doone*), Anne Gwynne (*Elaine Winslow*), Gladys Cooper (*Myrna Hartley*), Cecilia Loftus (*Henrietta Winslow*), Claire Dodd (*Margaret Gordon*), John Eldredge (*Stanley Grable*), Alan Ladd (*Richard Hartley*), Erville Alderson (*Doctor*), Harry C. Bradley (*Coroner*), Jack Cheatham (*Moving Man*).

I hated doing the thing. It was beneath me.
— *Gale Sondergaard on* The Black Cat

From the beginning, the limitations of the creaky old mansion thriller, from their stock situations to their almost painful staginess, were so obvious that they quickly fell into the hands of Hollywood gagmen and comedy writers. With a few notable exceptions, such as the highly Germanic *Secret of the Blue Room*, the bromide-ridden formula was rarely played straight except in minor pictures, mostly by minor studios. The subgenre was revitalized somewhat by Paramount's surprise 1939 hit *The Cat and the Canary* which added a jarring note of brash American humor as supplied by Bob Hope, who was making a name for himself as a leading comedy star.

Universal was watching with interest and, perhaps, a little envy. The studio already scored impressively with their own adaptation of the John Willard stage play in 1927 and remade it as an early talkie under the title *The Cat Creeps* in 1930. With the tenuous link between spooky homesteads and cat-killers on the prowl now seemingly established, Universal's brainstorm to use the Edgar Allan Poe short story "The Black Cat" to reshuffle the moldy ingredients was, depending on your point of view, either ingenious or mildly outrageous. That the studio had a big hit using the same title in 1934, which also used a forbidding and isolated mansion as its central locale, undoubtedly was a factor in the studio giving the project the go-ahead.

Eric Taylor and Robert Neville were commissioned to produce the script, but a rewrite was called for, presumably because neither writer had much background in slapstick. As he did on *The Invisible Woman*, associate producer Burt Kelly brought in *Hold That Ghost* writers Robert Lees and Frederic I. Rinaldo to punch up the material with the sort of broad, fast-clipped humor that was the hallmark of Universal comedies of the period. The "new and improved" script easily won approval and Kelly was given a $176,000 budget to bring the film in.

Albert S. Rogell was signed to direct *The Black Cat* on January 22, 1941, five days before the scheduled starting date, but production delays demanded a postponement to February 24. Casting proved to be a problem, necessitating the usual last-minute substitutions. Richard Carlson, who was maturing as a smooth, romantic lead, was dropped from the cast and was replaced by the burly, street-wise Broderick Crawford. Kelly negotiated with urbane British character player Paul Cavanagh for a leading role, but eventually signed Basil Rathbone, obviously a much bigger name and was, accordingly, given star billing. Claire Dodd, returning from a short-lived retirement, was pegged for a supporting part in her first assignment under a newly negotiated long-term contract. Tying up the loose ends in short order, the starting date was pushed ahead to February 17 with production wrapping on March 10.

The curtains open to the ominous strains of Frank Skinner's main title for *Tower of London* followed by an appropriate but amusing shot of a black cat slinking down a tree branch; its electronically distorted "meows" add a spooky touch. (This brief clip turned up several years later in the 1948 indie, *The Creeper*.) The mood is sustained as the scene shifts to the living room of a sprawling estate where the relatives of ailing Henrietta Winslow (Cecilia Loftus) await the news of the dowager's latest brush with death from the family doctor. As young Richard Harley (Alan Ladd) hammers out a mock-funeral dirge on the piano, the rest of the greedy group, dressed to the nines as if they were at the wake of a head of state, can hardly conceal their disappointment when it is reported that Henrietta is well on the road to recovery.

Henrietta assembles the group and relieves them of their anxieties by reading her last will and testament. Granddaughter Elaine (Anne Gwynne) is heavily favored in the legacy but Henrietta fails to mention a strange stipulation in her will. No monies are to be dispersed until after the death of her housekeeper, Abigail Doone (Gale Sondergaard), to whom Henrietta leaves the responsibility of caring for her pet cats,

Basil Rathbone and Gale Sondergaard were just two of the fine players whose talents were squandered on 1941's *The Black Cat.*

who saunter about the estate by the dozens.

Antique dealers Gil Smith (Broderick Crawford) and Mr. Penny (Hugh Herbert) arrive at the estate at the request of Henrietta's son-in-law Montague Hartley (Basil Rathbone) to appraise the furnishings. Gil discovers in the nick of time that someone has poisoned the dowager's milk. Soon after, Henrietta is found murdered in the estate's private crematorium, stabbed to death with a knitting needle.

Much to their dismay, the family learns of Henrietta's provision for Abigail and the cats, and Monty moves to have the will contested. A storm strands the entire group in the house. An attempt is made on Abigail's life; later, her body is found dangling from the end of a rope, an apparent suicide. But Gil proves she was murdered.

A cloaked figure is seen prowling through the corridors of the estate, leaving a trail of crematory ashes. Henrietta's daughter Myrna (Gladys Cooper) is nearly hanged in her room but is rescued by Gil. When she regains consciousness, she accuses the gardener, Eduardo Vitos (Bela Lugosi), of being the assailant. As the others search the grounds for the culprit, Eduardo enters Myrna's room and insists she accused him unjustly. Myrna pulls out a gun and shoots the gardener dead.

Myrna soon realizes Elaine has guessed the truth, quickly overpowers her and manages to carry her off to the crematorium. Gil intervenes as Myrna is about to plunge Elaine into the inferno. However, a fallen candle sets Myrna's flowing nightgown ablaze, sending her screaming into the night, engulfed in flames.

Its allusions to Poe and *The Cat and the Canary* notwithstanding, *The Black Cat* is mainly notable for squandering a fine cast and the considerable skills of a top technical crew on bottom-drawer material. That such a patchwork script ever made it out of the story department in the first place to become the most polished genre piece Universal produced in 1941 (including *The Wolf Man*) is amazing. Despite its impressive cast, the real star is photographer Stanley Cortez. The distinguished technician whose puzzling career included working from the heights of Orson Welles' *The Magnificent Ambersons* (1942) and Charles Laughton's *The Night of the Hunter* (1955) to the dizzying depths of *The Madmen of Mandoras* (1963) and *The Navy vs. the Night Monsters* (1966) gives this sow's ear of a movie the look of a silk purse. Universal's familiar mansion sets, from the imposing staircase to the cavernous, sumptuously appointed living room, never looked as handsome and the photographer provides some striking images of the cloaked murderer skulking through the dimly lit secret passageways.

The script was cobbled together by two separate teams of writers with no one taking it upon themselves to conceal the seams. The viewer can easily see how the screenplay evolved in early drafts as a standard gloomy old house melodrama before being passed on to gag writers to provide the finishing touches. As a result, the supposed humor doesn't flow naturally out of the material, as if the writers didn't have a clue how to make the basic situation seem funny. Instead, they merely plied on disjointed gags by the truckload and hoped for the best.

The lack of cohesion is compounded by the lack of a central comic personality. Although *The Cat and the Canary* served as the template, it was ludicrous that the producers thought they could get by without the equivalent of a Bob Hope as the hero. The former vaudevillian not only wrote the book on comedy delivery but had the faculty to turn a humorous role into a fully dimensional character, complete with nuance, nervous tics and one of the best "scared takes" in the business. *The Black Cat*'s Broderick Crawford was merely a lovable lug with little of the fine-honed comedic and improvisation skills that were required to take a bum script and run with it.

To make things worse, Crawford's buffoonery is supposedly bolstered by Hugh Herbert, another in Universal's pool of comic actors which included, at various times, Shemp Howard, Olsen and Johnson and Leon Errol. Playing the role of the archetypal scatterbrained best friend of the hero, Herbert's one-joke routine has him demolishing every stick of furniture in sight in order that he could better pass them off as antiques. Writers Lees and Rinaldo had so much confidence in this lame shtick, they had the meek comic perform endless variations on it until his mere presence becomes painful. It's no credit to this alleged laugh-getter that he was actually upstaged by Bela Lugosi, who pulls off the funniest scene in the movie. Carting away a sack full of live cats in a driving rainstorm, Lugosi's task is interrupted by Crawford who blunders on to the scene, thinking the gardener is kidnapping his sweetheart. Predictably, Lugosi is left to haplessly round up the scattering pets on all-fours in a torrent, crying "Here, kitty, kitty, kitty" in his typically s-l-o-w, theatrical delivery. No credit to the writers here; it's only funny because it's Bela.

The Black Cat whiles away its running time with the usual quota of predictable mayhem. There are a couple of murders, but the characters only seem to exist to look as guilty as possible so, surprise!, the most innocent looking among them is revealed as the killer. The underdeveloped plot gives rise to the kind of stale secret passage comedy routines that should have gone out with the silents. In the meantime, Lugosi lurches meaninglessly around corners or peeps through windows.

Most of the time, though, Broderick Crawford takes center stage, heroically charging through the spacious halls at the slightest sign of trouble, usually to discover that there is nothing actually wrong in the first place. A scream in the night is nothing more than a whistling tea kettle; Anne Gwynne's disappearance is a false alarm (she was downstairs looking for a book). The phantom killer leaves behind a trail of crematory ash for no apparent reason and risks exposure in order to indulge in pointless mischief, such as stealing into the sleeping heroine's room to place a black cat on her bed. And, no, the writers didn't miss the cliché of characters forced to stay in the family homestead because a thunderstorm washed out the roadway.

At least the script doesn't entirely neglect

Sondergaard, Bela Lugosi and Anne Gwynne enjoy a light moment during a shooting break.

Poe (remember him?). The tip-off of a wailing cat sealed in the crematorium, alerting Crawford to Gwynne's peril, is a direct lift from the original story in which the cries of an imprisoned animal reveal the location of the entombed victim. Although the ending doesn't come soon enough, it's far too abrupt as Gladys Cooper goes up in flames and races off screaming into the night. Considering the lightweight atmosphere of the film, it's an unexpected and gruesome closing act until Herbert & Co. return for the usual romantic wrap-up.

Receiving eleventh billing, a young Alan Ladd, just on the brink of stardom, was still honing his hard-bitten, romantic persona. Minus his famous shoelifts, he comes off more as a diminutive sorehead than a charismatic tough guy and clearly seems flustered by his thankless role and the more experienced stage actors he's surrounded with.

The "almost" all-star cast is largely wasted, their main function being to pump up the marquee value of a movie that had no business being anything other than a cheap filler feature. Even worse than the relentlessly unfunny comedy is watching the slumming actors trying to keep their dignity in their shameless pursuit of a paycheck. Gladys Cooper brings a believable, sullen desperation in the one or two moments she's allowed to use her acting skills.

In Gregory Mank's *Women in Horror Films, 1940s* (McFarland, 1999), Gale Sondergaard bluntly recalled, "I hated doing the thing. It was beneath me." It was no doubt a sentiment shared by many of her colleagues but at least Sondergaard keeps busy in a comparatively substantial role as the "Mrs. Danvers" clone, Abigail Doone. Once or twice the actress can be glimpsed suppressing a smile in spite of her public comments. Her startling "mad laughter" (the highlight of the performance) might sound foolish coming from anyone else but a seasoned pro like Sondergaard gives it a dotty, goose-bumpy conviction.

Lugosi's Eduardo Vitos seems based on the actor's Ygor persona but the part is basically a throwaway. (The name Vitos may have been a homage to Bela's character Vitus in the 1934 version of the Poe story.) Photographer Cortez favors the actor with an arresting introduction, as the camera zooms in for a closeup, then tilts downward so the lantern he's carrying dissolves into the headlights of Broderick Crawford's auto. Unfortunately, the big visual build-up comes to naught and what might have been an interesting opportunity for the actor to play comedy is squandered.

Still, Lugosi gets off relatively lightly compared to the indignities suffered by his *Son of Frankenstein* costar, Basil Rathbone. Watching the proud actor continually bested or bullied by the bovine Crawford is almost too painful to endure and, for good measure, the script tosses in a few impolite digs at his expense. Cecilia Loftus' comment, "He should have been an actor," is delivered as a private aside to the audience. Likewise, Crawford's line, "He thinks he's Sherlock Holmes" comes off less than a good-natured barb.

Cecilia Loftus brings an unforced likeability to her role as Henrietta Winslow and, unlike some of her better-known colleagues, never seems to be above the material. In his book *Women Vaudeville Headliners* (McFarland, 2006), Armond Fields reveals that the Scottish actress was the illegitimate daughter of music hall headliners. Growing up, she developed a knack for mimicking popular stage personalities of the day. Loftus gained her acting experience on the stage in England and America in comedic and dramatic roles. In 1905, the young actress appeared as Peter in a production of her friend J.M. Barrie's "Peter Pan." Her career continued through the '20s and into the '40s despite bouts with alcohol and drugs and at least one drug arrest. *The Black Cat* was the veteran performer's last picture: She died in 1943 of a heart attack and the debilitating effects of alcoholism.

Universal planned to continue Basil Rathbone's association with writers Lees and Rinaldo for at least one more project. In their excellent book *Abbott and Costello in Hollywood* (Perigee-Putnam, 1991), Bob Furmanek and Ron Palumbo's research indicate that Rathbone was in line for a role in one of the team's comedies. The script, which was submitted under the title *By Candlelight* (no relation to the earlier James Whale film) in early 1942, has Rathbone as a mad scientist whose invention taps into the surgically removed brains of his former patients, which are kept in a state of preservation in his laboratory. The project was retitled *You Hypnotize Me* but was eventually shelved, although a couple of the story points found their way into the screenplay of *Abbott and Costello Meet Frankenstein* (1948) years later.

While an intended comedy, Universal sold *The Black Cat* as an all-out horror movie in its trailers and advertising. The studio didn't fail to notice that Alan Ladd had rocketed to stardom months later in Paramount's film noir classic *This Gun for Hire* (1942). Quick to cash-in, *The Black Cat* was promptly placed back into circulation with the Paramount star given prominent billing despite his brief appearance.

Critics' Corner

Al Rogell directed with a keen eye toward giving the play all possible comedy in the piece, and he misses no trick in underscoring the laughs.... The writers purposely confuse the audience, but manage in its finale to explain most of their dodges.—*The Hollywood Reporter*, April 28, 1941

The cast is fine, the horror element in the story is sufficient.... Direction and screenplay are both good.—*The Film Daily*, 1941

Rating: ★★½ [A] synthetic chiller ... a reasonably satisfactory climax ... enlivened by occasional comedy....—*The New York Daily News*, April 26, 1941, Dorothy Masters

It is somewhat slow in getting started; as a matter of fact, it is not until the closing scenes when the murderer's identity becomes known and the heroine's life is endangered that the action is really exciting.—*Harrison's Reports*, May 3, 1941

The proper eerie touch is given to the character portrayed by Rathbone, a sinister relative.—*Variety*, April 30, 1941

All the best mystery props known to the film business have been whipped out for this story, and in addition, a nice flavoring of farce is worked in for good measure.... The cast is fine, the horror element in the story is sufficient, with a full complement of secret passages, yowling cats and sinister characters, and the direction is able.—*The Film Daily*, July 28, 1941

Hold That Ghost

Released August 6, 1941. 85 minutes. *Director:* Arthur Lubin. *Producer:* Alex Gottlieb. *Associate Producers:* Burt Kelly & Glenn Tryon. *Screenplay:* Robert Lees, Frederic I. Rinaldo & John Grant. *Original Story:* Robert Lees & Frederic I. Rinaldo. *Photography:* Elwood Bredell. *Editor:* Philip Cahn. *Art Director:* Jack Otterson. *Associate Art Director:* Harold H. MacArthur. *Musical Director:* Hans J. Salter. *Musical Numbers Staged by* Nick Castle. *Set Decorator:* Russell A. Gausman. *Assistant Director:* Gilbert J. Valle. *Dialogue Director:* Joan Hathaway. *Sound Supervisor:* Bernard B. Brown. *Technician:* William Fox. *Gowns:* Vera West.

Bud Abbott (*Chuck Murray*), Lou Costello (*Ferdinand Jones*), Richard Carlson (*Dr. Jackson*), Joan Davis (*Camille Brewster*), Mischa Auer (*Gregory*), Evelyn Ankers (*Norma Lind*), Marc Lawrence (*Charlie Smith*), The Andrews Sisters (*Themselves*), Ted Lewis and his Orchestra (*Themselves*), Milton Parsons (*Harry Hoskins*), Russell Hicks (*Bannister*), William Davidson (*Sidney "Moose" Matson*), Frank Penny (*Snake-Eyes*), Edgar Dearing (*Irondome*), Don Terry (*Strangler*), Edward Pawley (*High Collar*), Nestor Paiva (*Glum*), Thurston Hall (*Alderman*), Janet Shaw (*Alderman's Girl*), Harry Hayden (*Mr. Jenkins*), Shemp Howard (*Soda Jerk*), William Ruhl (*Gas Station Customer*), Frank Richards (*Gunman*), William Forrest (*State Trooper*), Bobby Barber, Ronald R. Rondell (*Waiters*), Harry Wilson (*Harry*), Jeanne Blanche (*Pretty Thing*), Kay, Kay & Katya (*Dancers*), Chuck Hamilton (*Police Car Driver*), Ralph Brooks (*Nightclub Extra*), Hans Herbert. *Deleted from final print:* Paul Fix (*Lefty*), Howard Hickman (*Judge*), Paul Newlan (*Big Fink*), Joe LaCava (*Little Fink*), Spencer Charters (*Storekeeper*), Charles B. Smith (*Kid*), Stanley Smith (*Clerk of Court*), Mrs. Gardner Crane (*Mrs. Giltedge*).

Look, from now on, keep one eye on that candle, another eye on that one, and with the other eye, watch me.
—*Lou Costello in* Hold That Ghost

In January 1941, that lean, fast-talking, double-dealing, comic straight man Bud Abbott and his partner Lou Costello, baby-faced, roly-poly top banana from Paterson, New Jersey, entered the fifth year of their show business association riding on the crest of a tremendous box office success, *Buck Privates* (1941), Universal's biggest moneymaker to that date. Both men gained their reputations as first-class clowns on the burlesque circuit, teaming for the first time in a road show entitled "Life Begins at Minsky's" in 1936, just months before the risqué art form was outlawed in the Big Apple. Most of the team's great routines were devised for this showcase. Their astounding success in vaudeville theaters and nightclubs led to Kate Smith's offering them a regular spot on her immensely popular radio show. Bud and Lou added Broadway to their growing list of conquests with the extravagant musical revue "The Streets of Paris," which ran over a year.

Hollywood was the next frontier. Universal signed up the skyrocketing comics to a one-picture deal, but instead of providing them with their own vehicle, the studio awarded the burlesque kings supporting slots in the musical comedy *One Night in the Tropics* (1940) co-starring Allan Jones and Robert Cummings. Generally considered a flop, the picture nevertheless garnered Abbott and Costello the attention of movie audiences and paved the way for *Buck Privates* and the great Hollywood success that followed.

A creepy spook-haunted house, the playground of a good many comics since the advent of pictures, provided the perfect setting for Bud and Lou's next vehicle, *Oh, Charlie!* (the title was eventually changed to the more salable *Hold That Ghost*). Hoping to duplicate the success of *Buck Privates*, Universal assigned that film's director, Arthur Lubin, to helm the team's new comedy, which began shooting on January 21, 1941, with a budget that exceeded $200,000 after all was said and done. (Up-and-coming director John Rawlins was put in charge of shooting second unit material.) An efficient no-frills craftsman with a long list of Bs to his credit, Lubin developed a good rapport with "the boys" and ended up directing a total of four of their most popular pictures. The director told us:

> I was the first director that [studio head] Charlie Rogers signed up. I had finished *Where Did You Get That Girl?* [1941] and *Buck Privates* was the only thing that was open. They didn't think it would amount to anything. The minute it was previewed, they called me in and said, "We're going to give you $5,000 if you don't mind starting tomorrow on another picture." And that was *Oh, Charlie!*

As work progressed steadily on *Hold That Ghost*, the box office revenues from *Buck Privates* increased daily; it soon became the motion picture hit of the country. Universal's top brass rushed Lubin and Abbott and Costello into another service comedy, *In the Navy*, which they rightly felt would be a more appropriate follow-up to *Buck Privates*, and booked it into theaters across the nation.

In May (three months after production was halted), *Hold That Ghost* went back before the cameras. Pumping more greenbacks into the budget, Universal omitted a number of lengthy comedy scenes already in the can, and replaced them with several elaborate production numbers featuring the Andrews Sisters and showman Ted Lewis and his Orchestra. This practice of sprucing up the team's comedies with glitzy, gratuitous musical numbers became a routine for a while (as it had in the Marx Brothers comedies). One could never predict when the zany antics of the comics would come to a screeching halt to make way for a kitschy production number featuring the likes of the Merry Macs or the Saronga Dancing Girls.

Like every other Abbott and Costello vehicle, the plot of *Hold That Ghost* is a mere framework upon which the comics hang their routines. Chuck Murray (Bud Abbott) and Ferdinand Jones (Lou Costello), two virtually unemployable jacks-of-no-trades, inherit the fortune of big-time gangster Sidney "Moose" Matson (William Davidson), a total stranger, who was gunned down by the police in the presence of the two men. Bannister (Russell Hicks), the late gangster's mouthpiece, informs Chuck and Ferdie that the whereabouts of Matson's loot is a mystery; "Moose" always boasted that he kept his money "in my head." The best Bannister can do for them is turn over the keys to Matson's abandoned Forrester's Club, a dilapidated tavern on a desolate stretch of road which was a speakeasy during Prohibition.

Bannister's associate, a slimy hood named Charlie Smith (Marc Lawrence, the "Charlie" of the film's original title), arranges to have Chuck and Ferdie driven to the club by coach operator Harry Hoskins (Milton Parsons, who was born to portray undertakers in movies). Hoskins picks up a few extra passengers: the bookworm Dr. Jackson (Richard Carlson), lovely Norma Lind (Evelyn Ankers), and radio actress/"sound effect" Camille Brewster (Joan Davis). No sooner do the passengers disembark than the shifty bus driver takes off, leaving them stranded at the crumbling watering hole in the midst of a storm.

From this point on, every predictable weird situation that could possibly occur within the confines of a haunted old house takes place. Charlie Smith is strangled by a mysterious figure as he ransacks the cellar looking for Matson's loot. Later, the gangster's corpse keeps turning up in the least likely places, sending Ferdie into fits of hysterics. Camille encounters a "ghost" (Nestor Paiva) which takes refuge in Ferdie's bedroom. A pair of men, identifying themselves as detectives, show up at the tavern and soon disappear, leaving no trace.

After endless cavorting, Chuck and Ferdie stumble across Matson's bankroll, stuffed inside the mounted head of a moose! (Much of Costello's dialogue in this scene was ad-libbed by the comedian.) But before the boys can take stock of their fortune, the tavern is besieged by gangsters. Grabbing the bag containing the money, Ferdie leads the hoods on a frantic chase through the hotel, finally scaring them off by emitting a loud wailing cry which they foolishly mistake for a police siren.

Heartened by Dr. Jackson's discovery that the water in the area is a health tonic, Chuck and Ferdie raze the tavern and erect a glamorous resort, complete with (you guessed it) live musical entertainment.

In *Abbott and Costello in Hollywood*, A&C historians Bob Furmanek and Ron Palumbo interviewed co-scripter Robert Lees. Lees and Frederic I. Rinaldo were veterans of the MGM shorts department in the '30s, writing for Robert Benchley, Pete Smith and the *Crime Doesn't Pay* series. Universal signed the pair up in 1940; their first feature credit for the studio was the zany script for *The Invisible Woman*. Lees told Furmanek and Palumbo:

> [Producer] Burt [Kelly] liked us, and he was producing *Hold That Ghost*, so that's how we got our first Abbott and Costello assignment. As I recall, the whole reason for the haunted house thing was that they wanted to use the "Moving Candle" routine. That was something that they did in burlesque. But *Hold That Ghost* started with a very strong idea — which was Fred's — that there's this gangster who's so distrustful of those around him, he wills everything to whoever is with him when he dies. And, of course, that's where we had Abbott and Costello come in. Fred and I were

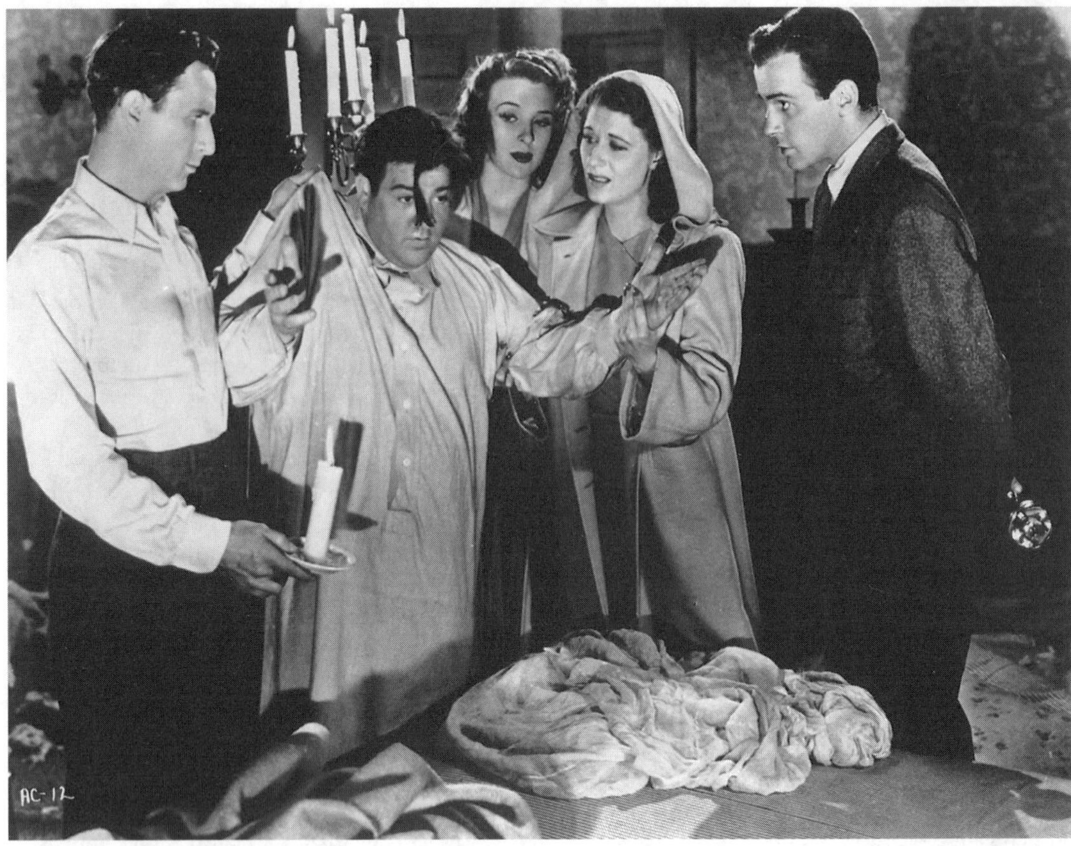

Bud Abbott, Lou Costello and Joan Davis (with hood) keep the hilarity level at a high pitch in *Hold That Ghost*, also featuring Evelyn Ankers and Richard Carlson.

screenwriters, not gag writers. We wanted to write stories that held up, had character, and developed.

As trite and hackneyed as the old-dark-house gags were at the time of *Hold That Ghost*'s release, it didn't make a bit of difference to fans of classic comedy, back then nor today, more than a half-century later. *Hold That Ghost* has so much vitality and spirit, any attempt to criticize its considerable excesses pales in light of the picture's uninhibited joys. Simply put, it's one of the best horror farces ever made and, arguably, A & C's funniest film. Though *Abbott and Costello Meet Frankenstein* (1948) surpasses it in terms of novelty, star names and production values, *Hold That Ghost* has the edge in several respects: The boys were younger and more agile in 1941 and their old burlesque routines (which were constantly revitalized by chief writer John Grant, an ex-vaudevillian himself) hadn't yet grown stale from overuse.

Hold That Ghost is essentially a one-joke picture: The old scare-'em gag wherein the comic is menaced by a variety of monsters or evil presences yet cannot convince anyone he's on the level. As stale as it is, this old routine dominates Abbott and Costello's series of lackluster monster farces released between 1949 and 1955. In *Hold That Ghost*, the exasperated Costello is always a second or two short of proving to the others that the candle *did* move, or that his bedroom *has* changed into a casino. The pudgy comedian's repertoire of wails, stammers and convulsive reactions to these strange phenomena qualifies him as the screen's most outrageously entertaining patsy. Bud Abbott is at his obnoxious best, bossing his chubby partner around and putting him in his place with an occasional slap or two (one slapping scene is so nasty it makes this viewer cringe).

Although he cheerfully admitted that working with the pair was often a trying experience, Arthur Lubin's memories of them were, nevertheless, warm and affectionate:

> They were both generous men. When they first arrived, Bud gave the first party for me. What astonished me was, they brought out pictures of their wives, who were strippers, completely nude. Bud was the brighter of the two. Lou hated to memorize his lines. Whenever we had any of their tricks to do, John Grant usually came on the set. If Lou went off the script, Bud would bring him back. They took direction and always added a little more.

There are enough mysterious goings-on in *Hold That Ghost* (sliding panels, clutching hands, falling bodies, shrouded figures dashing in and out of rooms, etc.) for two straight melodramas. The queasy haunted house atmosphere, sustained by Elwood Bredell's fine camerawork and Hans J. Salter's kinetic scoring (many of the cues were lifted from *Black Friday*), effectively offsets the film's humorous situations. Of course, the whole set-up is a sham: It's gangsters, not goblins, that are driving the boys mad. The audience is in on the gag, but that doesn't diminish the fun a bit.

Seeing *Hold That Ghost* for the first time was a disheartening experience for Lees and Rinaldo. Lees told Furmanek and Palumbo:

> When we saw the first cut ... in the projection room, we were almost so upset that we considered taking our names off it. You see, in writing it, you visualize it, and you visualize it much funnier or much better than what they did. I said to Fred, "Damn it, if we were on the set, we would have done this, we'd do that." ... But when we saw the picture with an audience, we were rolling in the aisles along with everyone else. You see, it was all in their timing. Something absolutely happens with an audience and Abbott and Costello. So Fred and I said to ourselves, "We must have been crazy. We didn't realize how funny this thing really is!'

Indeed, *Hold That Ghost* turned out to be one of the studio's top-grossers of the 1940–41 season.

In *Hold That Ghost*, the pair got plenty of competition in the laughs department from Joan Davis. Active in show biz since infancy, the klutzy comedienne's broad antics provided a welcome respite from the moonlight-and roses-schmaltz of the Sonja Henie vehicles *Thin Ice* (1937), *Lucky Star* (1938) and *Sun Valley Serenade* (1941). Complementing each other's uninhibited lunacy, Davis and Costello share some great moments. The couple perform a fractured rendition of the "Blue Danube" waltz; Joan also contributes to the amusement of the famous floating candle routine (used again in *Abbott and Costello Meet Frankenstein* and on their television show). Although Davis' character is conspicuously absent from the picture's wrap-up, she was written into the original ending. (Chuck and Ferdie hire her on as staff dietician of their deluxe spa.) This sequence was ditched in favor of a tuneful finale which had the Andrews Sisters performing a catchy Latin number, "Aurora."

It's a shame that Lou Costello and Joan Davis never worked together again. That may have been the decision of Costello, who, like other insecure show biz clowns, didn't like anyone else getting too many laughs while he was on-stage. In an interview Robert Lees granted *Filmfax*'s Jeff Miller, the writer shed light on Costello's personal insecurities:

> I'll tell you an interesting story about that one, showing you what kind of character Costello was. We didn't see them too much because we were working like crazy on a million pictures. What they were doing was releasing them like crazy because Universal was making a fortune. They were the top box office draw for two or three years and they saved the studio's neck. Now this was that dancing on the water on the floor, which was puddles and skidding and stuff, and [Joan Davis] was wonderful. Later, we happened to be in the projection room when they were showing the rushes. From the back of the room I hear a voice saying, "Who's the star of this picture?" And it was Costello. He was wanting this thing to be cut out with her, and that thing cut out with her, because he wanted to be the focus. He had no concept of a good picture being anything more than Abbott and Costello. He was the ego guy, he didn't see that. He was really a shortsighted character.

A sad postscript to the Robert Lees story: He was blacklisted in Hollywood during the McCarthy Era witch hunts and, throughout the '50s and '60s, contributed numerous scripts to network television under the pen name "J.E. Selby." On June 13, 2004, Lees was decapitated by a crazed individual (Kevin Lee Graff, age 27), who also killed the retired writer's neighbor.

Two of fantastic filmdom's all-time favorites, Evelyn Ankers and Richard Carlson, do a commendable job in the romance department (a thankless task in this kind of film). *Hold That Ghost* was Ankers' first exposure to a genre with which she'd have a more than passing acquaintance over the next few years. Born to British parents in Valparaiso, Chile, Evelyn spent most of her childhood in South America. It was there that she developed her interest in acting. She studied theater at the Royal Academy of Dramatic Art in England and eventually won small roles in such British films as *Belles of St. Mary's* (1936), *Rembrandt* (1936), *Fire Over England* (1937) and *Knight Without Armour* (1937).

Arriving in the States in 1940, Evelyn Ankers' talents (and some canny connections) got her the plum role of the maid in the 1940 Broadway hit "Ladies in Retirement" with Flora Robson. While on tour with the play in Los Angeles, Ankers was offered long-term contracts at 20th Century–Fox, Warner Bros. and Universal. She signed with Fox and was scheduled to appear in the film *Scotland Yard* (1941), but the studio ultimately felt the actress was not well-known enough for the top part in so expensive a production, and she was replaced by Nancy Kelly. On January 8, 1941, she signed a seven-year contract with Universal. The rest is horror film history. Although she worked at Universal for three of those seven years (she left the studio in 1944 after giving birth to a daughter by husband Richard Denning, himself no slouch in the *cinefantastique* department), Evelyn Ankers brightened the casts of no fewer than 27 of their B horror films, comedies, musicals and wartime propaganda efforts.

Even the usually-serious Richard Carlson gets a few laughs in *Hold That Ghost* as the stereotypical absent-minded professor, Dr. Jackson. The writers neglected to provide the character with a first name, leaving even love interest Evelyn Ankers no choice but to address him as "Doctor" throughout the film. *Hold That Ghost* was Carlson's second haunted house comedy; the previous year, he supported Bob Hope and Paulette Goddard in Paramount's *The Ghost Breakers* (1940). In that film, it was Carlson's seemingly innocent character who-done-it.

Destined to become the dean of sci-fi movie heroes in the '50s, Richard Carlson invested his performances with intelligence and conviction, and lent credence to the far-fetched premises of *It Came From Outer Space, The Maze* (both 1953) and *Creature from the Black Lagoon* (1954), among others. "I'm one of the few actors who look the academic type," he told syndicated columnist Bob Thomas in 1953. "People believe that I might have just stepped out of a laboratory." A native of Albert Lea, Minnesota, he wrote, acted in and directed his own plays while studying at the University of Minnesota. Upon graduating summa cum laude, the Phi Beta Kappa honoree opened his own repertory company in St. Paul. When this venture failed, Carlson packed his bags and settled in New York City in the mid–'30s.

Scoring a modest success playing juvenile roles on Broadway, he tried his luck in Hollywood, making his motion picture debut in United Artists' *The Young in Heart* (1938), featuring Janet Gaynor and Douglas Fairbanks, Jr. His thriving film career lost momentum after the war, and Carlson turned to writing fiction and human interest stories for *The Saturday Evening Post, Collier's* and other popular magazines. TV came to the rescue in the early '50s when he garnered the part of Herbert A. Philbrick, a counterspy for the F.B.I., in the fact-based series *I Led Three Lives*. "Examine the men who have been successful in television," he once told an interviewer. "They're almost always people whose careers have gone down or, like myself, whose careers are not likely to get any bigger ... I was not going any higher." Carlson even tried his hand at directing (1954's *Riders to the Stars* and others). Richard Carlson died in Encino, California, on November 27, 1977, at the age of 65, ten days after suffering a cerebral hemorrhage.

Rating a high seismograph reading in riotous entertainment, *Hold That Ghost* is Abbott and Costello at the height of hilarity. With Joan Davis on hand to buoy the merriment, the Andrews Sisters providing a touch of camp, the enjoyable contributions of Evelyn Ankers and Richard Carlson, and a higher-than-average number of well-wrought thrills, it remains one of the best films of that rarely successful subgenre, the horror farce.

Critics' Corner

Rating: ★★★ Seems to me it's funnier than [*Buck Privates* and *In the Navy*]. Better lines and bits of business plus something laughable in the way of a plot.—*The New York Daily News*, August 8, 1941, Dorothy Masters

Yes, Ladies and Gentlemen, they've done it again. In fact, by count and with witnesses, the Messrs. Abbott and Costello got more, louder, and longer laughs in *Hold That Ghost* at its Hollywood preview than they did in *Buck Privates* or *In the Navy*. Veritably, it is to be doubted if any two comedians ever got so many laughs in one picture any time anywhere.—*The Motion Picture Herald*, 1941

On the evidence provided by a capacity preview audience, this is the screamingest riot the boys have turned in—and I mean screams, not just guffaws, blurts or haw-haws, but screams!—*The Motion Picture Daily*, 1941

To an impartial observer ... it does seem that the boys are running short on material.... *Hold That Ghost* only occasionally has the two boys firing the question and answer business at each other, with much more of the sliding door business thrown in than we really need.... [G]ood, rowdy, risible slapstick.—*The New York World Morning Telegraph*, 1941

A sure-fire riotous comedy is a cinch to please and it should ring the bell at the box office.... Lou Costello has never been funnier. At times his comedy is so fast that lines of dialogue are ignored and the audience roars at the pantomime he uses with his lines.... Producers Burt Kelly and Glenn Tryon ... have plenty of production here.... [The script] is topnotch material for the funny men.—*The Film Daily*, July 30, 1941

The Wolf Man

Released December 12, 1941. 70 minutes. *Producer-Director:* George Waggner. *Original Screenplay:* Curt Siodmak. *Photography:* Joseph Valentine. *Special Effects:* John P. Fulton. *Art Director:* Jack Otterson. *Associate Art Director:* Robert Boyle. *Editor:* Ted Kent. *Musical Director:* Charles Previn. *Music:* Hans J. Salter & Frank Skinner. *Assistant Director:* Vernon Keays. *Set Decorator:* Russell A. Gausman. *Director of Sound:* Bernard B. Brown. *Technician:* Joe Lapis. *Makeup:* Jack P. Pierce. *Gowns:* Vera West.

Claude Rains (*Sir John Talbot*), Lon Chaney, Jr. (*Lawrence Stewart Talbot, The Wolf Man*), Warren William (*Dr. Lloyd*), Ralph Bellamy (*Capt. Paul Montford*), Patric Knowles (*Frank Andrews*), Bela Lugosi (*Bela*), Maria Ouspenskaya (*Maleva*), Evelyn Ankers (*Gwen Conliffe*), Fay Helm (*Jenny Williams*), Leyland Hodgson (*Kendall*), Forrester Harvey (*Victor Twiddle*), J.M. Kerrigan (*Charles Conliffe*), Doris Lloyd (*Mrs. Williams*), Olaf Hytten (*Villager*), Harry Stubbs (*Rev. Norman*), Tom Stevenson (*Richardson*), Eric Wilton (*Chauffeur*), Harry Cording (*Wykes*), Ernie Stanton (*Phillips*), Ottola Nesmith (*Mrs. Bally*), Connie Leon (*Mrs. Wykes*), La Riana (*Gypsy Dancer*), Caroline Cooke, Margaret Fealy (*Women*), Jessie Arnold (*Gypsy Woman*), Eddie Polo (*Churchgoer*), Gibson Gowland (*Villager*). Deleted from final print: Kurt Katch (*Gypsy with Bear*).

> [At Universal] ... the prevailing idea of horror was a werewolf chasing a girl in a nightgown up a tree.
> —*Director Mark Robson*

The last of the great Universal horror films, *The Wolf Man* proved that the new management could produce a first-rate shocker without a first-rate director on the payroll. Lon Chaney, Jr., may not have been a top-tier talent but his stint as "Dynamo Dan" in *Man Made Monster* demonstrated a physical prowess that would show him to fearsome advantage, especially under heavy makeup. All that Chaney now needed was a proper launching with a four-star vehicle to establish him as a major horror star. As far as Universal was concerned, the Chaney name was a potential gold mine.

There wasn't much else the studio could do with Lon. Chaney was kept busy in the months following the release of *Man Made Monster*, but his roles were uninspired. The burly actor was a natural at playing thugs and dimwits and drifted to supporting roles. He appeared in *San Antonio Rose* with Robert Paige and Jane Frazee and in a Rudy Vallee vehicle, *Too Many Blondes* (both 1941). Universal showed little interest in grooming him as a Western star (they already had several) so he was again low-billed in *Badlands of Dakota* and the serial *Riders of Death Valley* (both 1941). Apparently forgetting that Chaney's greatest success was playing a *sympathetic* giant in *Of Mice and Men* (1939), Universal insisted on casting him as a one-dimensional heavy.

This would all change with *The Wolf Man* and Chaney's enduring portrayal of one of horror film's most tragic figures, the doomed Larry Talbot. The studio made millions off the picture and Chaney reportedly received more fan mail than any other star on the lot.

Universal entrusted the picture to George Waggner, whose stock with the studio was climbing quickly. Now a producer, Waggner's hectic days as a down-to-the-wire fast-buck director on pictures like *Horror Island* were drawing to a close. Making sure all Hollywood knew Universal was back in the horror market in grand style, Waggner assembled a name cast, concentrating on well-regarded but reasonably priced players to draw the public's attention. Waggner undertook the direction himself, recruiting the dependable Curt Siodmak to author the original screenplay. Unlike *WereWolf of London,* which combined lycanthropy with modern science, Siodmak rooted his story in European folklore.

According to Siodmak, he wrote the film from scratch without being influenced by the 1935 picture or the unfilmed werewolf script prepared for Boris Karloff in the '30s. Producer Waggner provided little inspiration.

Siodmak told the authors:

> I never talked to George, except on Thursdays. I'd go into his office and gave him all the honey I could think of— I told him how big a man he was — and I figured, "This guy must know I'm kidding." He never found out. I couldn't sit down and talk about these pictures because he'd say, "I don't want *my* ideas, I want *your* ideas!" So, he never talked to me. But he was a nice man, and we had a good relationship.
>
> They told me who would be in the pictures before I would even start to write them. On *The Wolf Man,* for instance, I was told, "We have $180,000, we have Lon Chaney, Jr., Claude Rains, Ralph Bellamy, Warren William, Maria Ouspenskya, Bela Lugosi, a title called *The Wolf Man* and we shoot in ten weeks. Get going!"

Unexpected delays pushed the original starting date from September 8 to October 27, 1941. Dick Foran was announced as one of the film's stars right up until a week before the start of shooting, only to be replaced by Warner Bros. contractee Patric Knowles. The film was shot under the title, *Destiny*, although it's doubtful that anyone seriously thought it would be released as anything but *The Wolf Man.*

As with *Son of Frankenstein*, art director Jack Otterson gets the credit for the film's visual style although most of the creative heavy lifting was done by his associate, Robert Boyle. The film turned out to be a major stepping stone in the career of the young artist who would eventually rack up four Oscar nominations, including those for *North by Northwest* (1959), *Fiddler on the Roof* (1971) and *The Shootist* (1976). Boyle claims Alfred Hitchcock decided to hire him on the basis of his work on *The Wolf Man* after Universal screened a print for the director.

Boyle told the authors:

> I think Universal was quite varied, with a large amount of their output being in these so-called "horror" pictures, but they were also doing a lot of comedies — cheap ones, like Abbott and Costello. The *Wolf Man* mansion was for the most part a standing set, but it had to be rearranged for the needs of this particular project. They gave us Stage 12 — a huge area to cover — but very little money. I was looking for material for this forest, and someone had told me that in the San Fernando Valley there was this grove of walnut trees being torn down to make room for a subdivision.

After arranging for the studio to buy the lot of torn-down trees:

> We trucked them in to Universal and on the stage. They were all bare of foliage, so I painted them black to make them stand out and look ominous. Then I put a shine on them. We must have had at least 30 trees. It was Universal's largest stage. The forest covered an area of maybe 100 by 200 feet. It was *big*! I decided to use a lot of fog, sort of a ground fog cover, to cover up a lot of the inadequacies of the actual built stuff.
>
> We built the gypsy camp on the same set as the forest. We built the gypsy wagon, and then others we rented and found. But we built a lot of that gypsy camp ... a traveling carnival really.

It had to have been a proud day for young Lon when the production unit shot a scene on the Notre Dame set from his father's classic *The Hunchback of Notre Dame* (1923). Sensing that the edifice appeared a bit too imposing a structure for a small country church in Wales, film editor Ted Kent cunningly eliminated all long shots of the exteriors in *The Wolf Man*'s final cut. Most of the remaining exteriors were shot on the studio's familiar European Street.

A version of Jack Pierce's famous Wolf Man makeup was originally created for Henry Hull's *WereWolf of London.* The publicity department laid it on a bit thick, claiming that Pierce traveled to Europe and spent five years combing countless histories of England to come up with a description or illustration of a werewolf. Baring his soul to a visiting reporter on the set, Pierce described how tough it is when a producer tells you to create a monster: "Or when he tells you to come up with a *couple* of werewolves. So you try to do some research. And all you learn about werewolves is that they're supposed to howl in the light of the moon in the deserted castles of Scotland. Nobody's ever seen one. So, you sit down and try to figure out how a werewolf ought to look. And then you go to work with hair and putty and glue and paint."

Pierce's design, made from hard-to-find yak hair and a set of sharp, jutting teeth, took four hours to apply; that includes making up Chaney's hands and feet. The script called for two full transformations. For one scene, Chaney was forced to lie prostrate on the ground while the makeup was removed, changing him from a wolf back to a man. Chaney thought that taking the makeup off was even worse than putting it on:

> What gets me is after work when I'm all hot and itchy and tired, and I've got to sit in that chair for 45 minutes while Pierce just about kills me, ripping off the stuff he put on me in the morning.

***The Wolf Man*: Lon Chaney, Jr., in his most famous role.**

In her chatty and oft-quoted introduction to Doug McClelland's book, *The Golden Age of "B" Movies* (Charter House, 1978), Evelyn Ankers admitted there was little love lost between her and Chaney, who delighted in creeping up behind the actress in his full makeup and scaring the wits out of her. Even more harrowing was the time a huge bear (appearing in the famous deleted wrestling match scene) broke loose from its chains and chased the actress straight up into the rafters of the soundstage.

Another delay in the less-than-harmonious production came during the shooting of the finale. Claude Rains, getting a bit carried away bludgeoning his werewolf son to death, whacked Chaney full force with the prop ten-pound silver-headed cane. Chaney, suffering from a black eye and considerable swelling, was sent home after an ice-pack treatment proved useless. As a result, his afternoon scenes, *sans* makeup, were postponed.

Falling just short of a one-month shooting schedule, *The Wolf Man* wrapped on November 25, followed by a hasty post-production period. By early December, the first prints were being screened for an unenthusiastic press while the studio readied the picture for its national release, topping a double-bill with *The Mad Doctor of Market Street* in many situations. But Universal's confidence in its new gala horror show would soon be badly shaken. The attack on Pearl Harbor sent shock waves across the country, and it was feared that the public's appetite for Hollywood's manufactured horrors would suffer. Taking the hard line, *Variety* branded *The Wolf Man* a dubious entertainment in light of grim world events. Happily for the studio, their reservations proved unfounded as *The Wolf Man* became a top grosser despite the critics' middling reception.

The opening scenes are routinely handled. Lawrence Talbot (Lon Chaney, Jr.), the second son of a titled European family, returns to his ancestral estate nestled on the outskirts of a small Welsh village. With the death of an elder brother, young Talbot stands to claim his rightful place in the family hierarchy. This sad state of affairs does not go unnoticed by his father Sir

John (Claude Rains), who nevertheless greets his son warmly after his 15-year absence.

Larry takes a liking to a village girl, Gwen Conliffe (Evelyn Ankers). Despite her engagement to Frank Andrews (Patric Knowles), Gwen keeps a date with Talbot. Taking along her friend, Jenny Williams (Fay Helm), Gwen accompanies Larry to a nearby gypsy camp. Jenny volunteers to have her fortune told by Bela the gypsy (Bela Lugosi), who reacts violently to the woman's bouquet of wolfsbane. Peering into the palm of Jenny's right hand, Bela sees the pentagram, the five-pointed star, marking her for death at the hands of a werewolf (a device abandoned for the rest of the series). Bela's transformation from man into beast takes place off-camera.

Jenny's screams fill the air as Larry, charging to her rescue, desperately tries to pull away the wolf hovering hungrily over her body. Using his newly purchased silver-tipped walking stick, Larry clubs the beast to death but is bitten in the struggle.

Investigating officer Capt. Paul Montford (Ralph Bellamy) fails to turn up the carcass of the wolf, instead finding Bela's bludgeoned body at the scene. Paul questions Larry, whose wounds suffered in his fight with the beast have strangely disappeared. Soon, word that Larry has killed Bela sweeps through the village; his relationship with Gwen, too, raises eyebrows.

In keeping with gypsy tradition, Bela's funeral is a festive one, attracting crowds to the gypsy campgrounds. Larry confronts the dead gypsy's mother, Maleva (Maria Ouspenskaya). She warns him that the curse of the werewolf has been passed on to him. Disturbed, Larry flees as the power of the full moon exerts its terrible effect. Venturing out into the forest, Larry, now a werewolf, kills a gravedigger (Tom Stevenson).

Larry awakens the next morning dimly aware of his ordeal. The villagers set traps to ensnare what they believe to be a murderous wolf. That night, Larry transforms again into the werewolf and steps into one of the traps. After transforming back into Larry, he frees himself with Maleva's help and returns to Talbot Castle.

In a determined effort to prove to his son that his fears about becoming a werewolf are a figment of his overworked imagination, Sir John binds him to a chair facing a window before dutifully joining in the hunt to slay the wolf. Meanwhile Gwen, hopelessly in love with Larry, combs the woods to find him. A werewolf once more, Larry tears himself free and picks up Gwen's trail. He attacks Gwen, whose screams alert Sir John. Armed with his son's cane, Sir John beats the creature mercilessly, finally killing it. Maleva happens upon the grim scene and recites an ancient gypsy prayer over the monster's body, which slowly returns to human form. Montford and the other hunters, seeking Gwen, find Sir John, dumbstruck, leaning over the body of his son.

In spite of the popularity of *The Wolf Man*, it still hasn't received its due in certain critical quarters. To many, the '40s was the decade of Val Lewton and, compared to his highly imaginative thrillers wherein the focus was on the unseen presence of terror, *The Wolf Man* seems extremely conventional. It's a rather unfair assessment, considering the fact that RKO didn't jump on the horror bandwagon until *The Wolf Man* drew record crowds. It's worth noting, too, that Lewton's first horror *Cat People* (1942), while excellent, smacks of imitation. Curt Siodmak's unrevised original script clearly anticipated Lewton's subtle approach, keeping the monster out of camera range throughout most of the movie. But concealed horrors just didn't fit in with Universal's formula; shortly after shooting commenced, it was decided that the werewolf bare his hair, fangs and claws in loving closeups in the final cut. It's not the most sophisticated approach, and yet *The Wolf Man* remains an intelligent film that works on almost every level.

Also added on was a hallucinatory sequence (apparently inspired by a similar scene in Victor Fleming's 1941 *Dr. Jekyll and Mr. Hyde*) which takes place after the gypsy festival episode. Special effects ace John P. Fulton provided this dizzying, somewhat pretentious montage, representing Chaney's nightmarish visions before his physical change. The transformation scenes were also added as well as the scene of the werewolf stalking the gravedigger. Unseen, suggested horrors have their place but it's tough to make a case that the werewolf scenes don't improve the film.

Not counting *I Walked with a Zombie* (1943), co-written by Ardel Wray and undoubt-

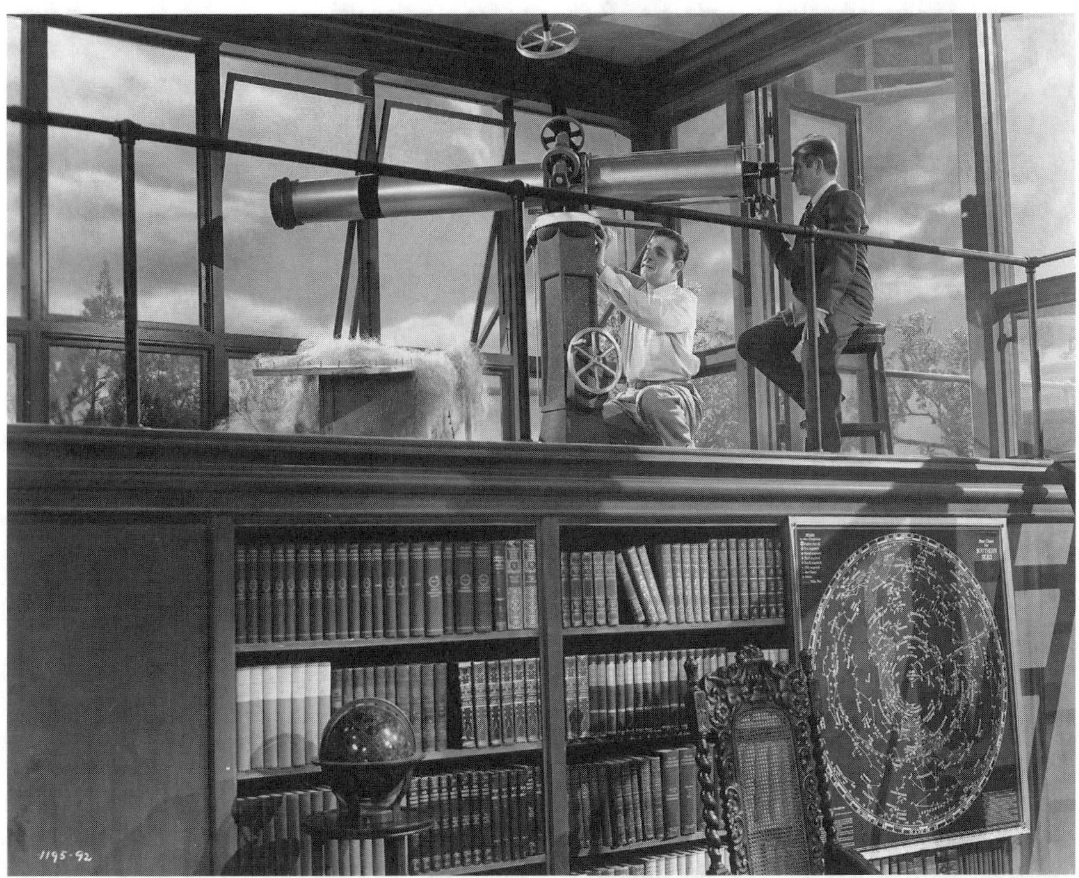

Chaney Jr. and Claude Rains made an unlikely father and son in *The Wolf Man.* Note the beautifully designed set.

edly touched up by Val Lewton, *The Wolf Man* is Curt Siodmak's finest script; his then-upcoming *Frankenstein Meets the Wolf Man* is hackwork in comparison. Siodmak's intriguing ditty ("Even a man who is pure in heart...") is so apt and original that it's routinely ascribed to folklore. One may complain about the skimpily drawn characters and the uneven dialogue, but Siodmak's screenplay is beautifully constructed and a model of simplicity. In later years, Siodmak admitted that he unconsciously duplicated the structure of Greek drama in his script by featuring a hero who cannot escape his fate; the Sir John character classically represents the ever-dominant Greek gods.

And then there's Larry's dual personality to consider. Claiming his legacy under somber circumstances, Talbot bears the pain of estrangement. Neglected by his aristocratic family as a child (the old "an heir and a spare" syndrome), Larry's uneasy reconciliation with his father soon splinters. ("Does the prestige of your family name mean more to you than your son's life?" family physician Dr. Lloyd [Warren William] pointedly asks Sir John.) Larry is a true outcast, there's nary one among the suspicious townfolk who doesn't brand him a murderer; their cold stares even freeze him out of a church service. Larry's boyhood friend Montford eyes him icily and cruelly ridicules him after Talbot, obviously in a frazzled state, suggests that a werewolf is responsible for the killings. The festering resentment of the outwardly kindly Larry comes out in his wolf-self, a marauding "id" terrorizing the populace. Siodmak spells this out in Sir John's thumbnail definition of lycanthropy: "It's the technical term for something very simple: The good and evil in every man's soul."

Like Rowland V. Lee, George Waggner's talents as a director only serve to remind you that

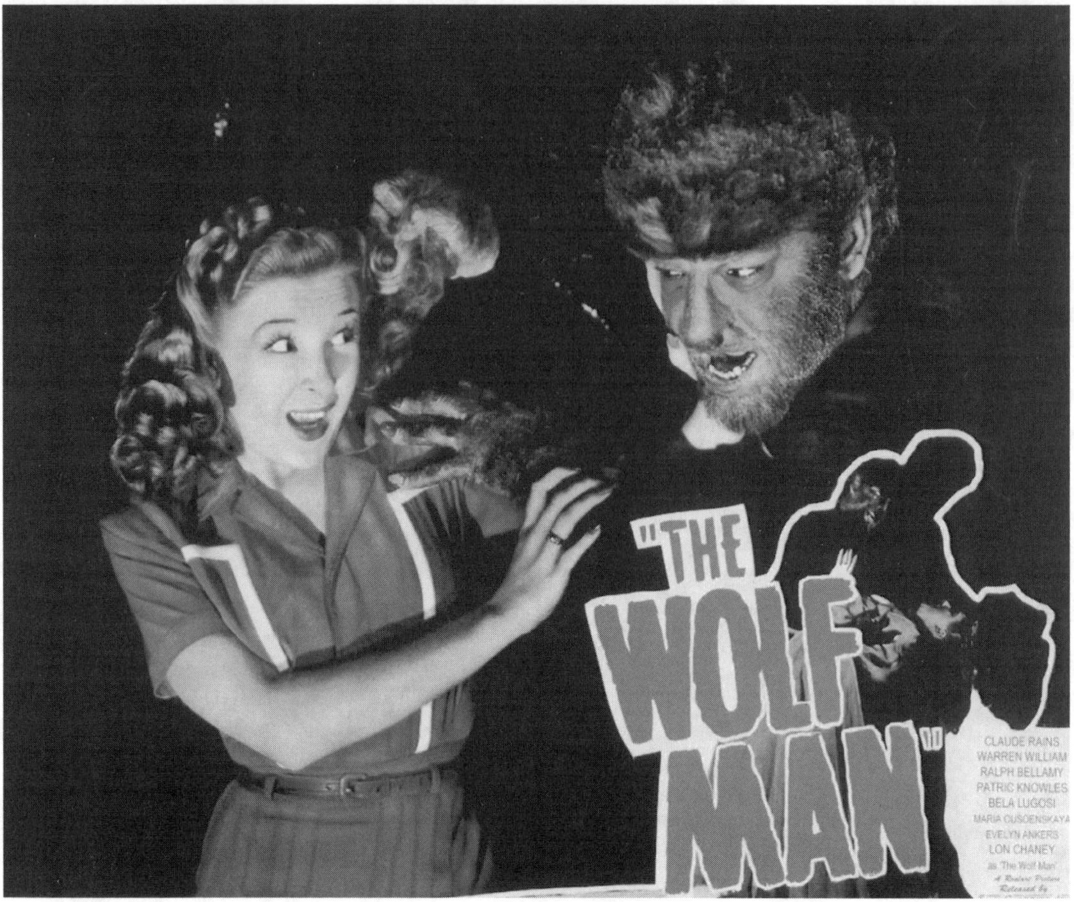

***The Wolf Man* was the first of five Universal shockers which teamed Chaney Jr. with Evelyn Ankers.**

his real gifts lied in producing, although he does a satisfactory, if not particularly imaginative, job. He can't quite overcome the film's clash of styles and, like the studio's Frankenstein movies, the sense of locales seem vague at best. British commentators have been particularly sensitive to *The Wolf Man*'s back lot rendering of the small Welsh community, shot on Universal's one-size-fits-all European Street. To be fair, Waggner was no more Welsh than James Whale was German when he was shooting his Frankenstein assignments. Whale, however, was a stylist who could more easily get away with creating a never-neverland atmosphere even when he was adding quaint British touches to his supposedly German trappings. While Whale was more akin to an artist working on canvas, Waggner's approach was more photographic, literal and altogether more "Hollywood." As such, *The Wolf Man* charts a tentative departure from the fairy tale quality of the Universal monster movies of the '30s and seems more vaguely aware of its psychological implications. Chaney's Talbot evolves from a brash young American-on-the-make to a tortured soul heavy with sexual self-loathing and Christian guilt.

Top-billed Claude Rains made great professional strides since his debut in *The Invisible Man*. At age 51, he was the top character man at Warner Bros. and at the peak of his talents. There isn't a false moment in Rains' sturdy portrayal of the proud Sir John Talbot, whose determination to cure his son of his "obsession" tragically backfires.

The challenging role of Sir John required him to fill in the gaps for, what appears on paper, a rather sketchily written part. More than a lord of the manor, Rains is given such deference that

King of the gypsies: Bela Lugosi as Bela, the ill-fated fortune-teller.

the small community is his own fiefdom. Rains exudes his easy, slightly aristocratic charm in his opening scenes, his dialogue hinting at the uneasy relations between him and his son. As the film unfolds, Rains tempers his character's basic amiability with measured doses of stern, stiff-upper-lip pride which occasionally breaks through the surface. By the denouement, Rains plumbs the depths of Sir John's soul well beyond Siodmak's script with the character's benign but domineering intractability bringing on the death of his son and, with it, his family lineage. The sequel, *Frankenstein Meets the Wolf Man*, reveals that Sir John soon died of grief. That this was inspired by Rains' look of stunned realization in his closing scene in *The Wolf Man* is an interesting speculation.

Larry Talbot became Lon Chaney's most famous role, even supplanting his acclaimed Lennie in 1939's *Of Mice and Men*, and is among his handful of exceptional performances. His open, outgoing nature in the first reel and his dramatic intensity in the later scenes sharply contrast with his dreary monotone in the Inner Sanctum pictures, making one wonder what became of Chaney's talents in a few short years. Unlike his Mummy performances, the Wolf Man was so uniquely Chaney, no one ever doubted it really was him under the yak hair and not a stunt man. Leering through the twisted timbers of the eerie misty forest set, Chaney's werewolf, now a familiar sight, must have been a real jaw-dropper to audiences in the early '40s. Chaney's most affecting scenes with Evelyn Ankers (never more beautiful or vulnerable as Gwen Conliffe) contain not a hint of their off-camera friction. The couple's mutual attraction is believable and unencumbered by the presence of Patric Knowles as Ankers' humorless suitor. The romantic triangle adds tension to *The Wolf Man*, though Knowles' character was probably added to the plot simply to furnish Ankers with a marriageable alternative to the ill-starred Chaney in the downbeat ending.

Maria Ouspenskaya's Maleva is a classic portrayal. In what might have been a stock role or a showy, high-camp performance, Ouspenskaya, with obvious respect for her character, lends the part intensity and dignity. Robert Boyle has particularly fond memories of the actress. "I met all the people on that film," he told the authors:

> I was on the set constantly. It didn't receive much in the way of a budget but what an excellent cast! We were particularly fascinated by the work of Ouspenskaya. We had all heard of her and known of her legitimate work in the theater, so she was the one that we thought was the most interesting. Lon Chaney and Claude Rains were the real stars, but we were all most interested in Ouspenskaya! She was a very lovely lady. This was a very expensive cast by today's standards.

Bela Lugosi, who unrealistically sought the Larry Talbot role early in the production, makes the most of his limited opportunities. Playing one of his best and least heralded roles as the doomed gypsy, the actor registers a memorable, haunted pathos in the few scenes in which he appears.

Ralph Bellamy and Warren William, both rather poor, provided exhibitors with bankable names but very little else. Like Chaney, Bellamy seems to emphasize rather than downplay his Yankee origins, working against the ambiance of the script. His old-before-his-time character seems unduly harsh and unwelcoming to Chaney's Talbot, and a distinct departure from his usually smooth, nonabrasive screen persona. Warren William's career hit its stride in the pre–Code days, often playing cads, crooks and private eyes with panache. His carousing, man-about-town take on Perry Mason in a short-lived Warner Bros. series stands in contrast with Erle Stanley Gardner's staid conception of the character and Raymond Burr's classic portrayal in the '50s–'60s television series. In his heyday, the actor was sometimes compared to John Barrymore but, by the '40s, his star was fading. He ran the last lap of his career in forgettable B-pictures and on Poverty Row but his performance as a twisted wife-killer with pedophilic tendencies in Edgar G. Ulmer's noir *Strange Illusion* [*Out of the Night*] (1945) is a memorable one.

Like Lugosi, Fay Helm makes a strong impression despite her limited screen time as the ill-fated Jenny Williams. Playing the rather thankless part of the plain, suitor-less best friend of the much prettier heroine, Helm communicates the character's humor, loyalty and, ultimately, sheer terror in a compact, well-honed performance. Silent film buffs might have difficulty spotting Gibson Gowland as one of the villagers pursuing the hirsute hero; the star of Erich von Stroheim's masterwork *Greed* (1923) was reduced to playing bits by this time.

Also contributing to the effectiveness of the film is its exciting score by Hans J. Salter and Frank Skinner. Rich in evocative gypsy melodies, melancholy processions and searing action cues, it's a benchmark horror movie score, fated to be recycled dozens of times in upcoming films. (Actually, the score is not a wholly original composition; at least one cue was cribbed from Skinner's *The House of the Seven Gables*.) Siodmak had his own ideas how the film should be scored, suggesting in his script that the Welsh folksong "Men of the Halleck" be played over the titles.

The early draft of Siodmak's script is filled with curious and interesting deviations from the film that was to be. The protagonist here is Larry Gill, an American engineer who travels to Wales to install a telescope at Talbot Castle for amateur astrologer Sir John Talbot. The names of the chief constable (Capt. Montford in the finished film) is Insp. Kendall and his assistant (Mr. Twiddle in the film) is Mr. Cotton. Larry proposes to Gwen the morning after he is attacked by the wolf (and even offers to take her old man along on the honeymoon!); Gwen declines.

Bela is seen in his coffin with head bandaged, eyes open, the dark imprint of the pentagram on his forehead and a malevolent grin on his lips; as pallbearers carry his coffin from the church to the crypt, there's the description of a trucking shot (from Bela's point of view) to give the impression that Bela is alive but is unable to move. The murder of the gravedigger is heard but not seen. The script has an abundance of religious references, crosses, hymn music, church bells and stained-glass tableaux; the Reverend Norman has a beefed-up role; there's even a prominent picture of Christ in a hunting lodge.

The tension between Larry and Frank Andrews is thicker, and Frank even threatens to "shoot [Larry] down like a dog"; later, Larry gives wolf-hunting Frank the silver bullet which he himself has forged from Maleva's charm. The script's one transformation scene (Larry turning into the Wolf Man) is seen in a reflection in a dark pool, through Larry's eyes, so that the audience will get the impression that Larry only imagines himself to be a monster. A four-legged wolf attacks Gwen, but Frank arrives in time to shoot it with a silver bullet; wounded, the beast runs off. Moments later, Larry, shot, his face unseen by the camera, staggers once again to the edge of the pool and sees a monstrous wolf's face in the water before dying.

The script's final shot is an extended low-angle one (from the dead Larry's point of view) with various characters huddled around Larry, whose face (we're told) is contorted and fiendish. Maleva hands Gwen a spring of wolf bane and instructs her to touch Larry with it — his heart, his cheeks, his lips, his eyes. "Look! He's smiling!" Gwen exults through her tears as the wolfsbane fills the camera lens, the music rises to a majestic hymn and the script ends.

In another early script, it's Sir John who slays Larry with a silver bullet just as he's about to attack Gwen. The film's superior, revised ending in which Larry is killed by the same weapon that dispatched Bela, is more thrilling and even lends a poetic touch to the mayhem.

Despite the raft of script changes, Siodmak was never quite able to lick the problem of the central Wolf Man character. Locked in with the casting of Lon Chaney, Jr., the writer's first instinct was to write him as a visiting American, yet the storyline seem to require him to have far deeper ties to Rains' Sir John than those of a contracted workman. Upgrading Larry to the heir to the Talbot title, Siodmak vested the film with a more affecting dramatic resonance. The downside to this crucial revision was that we're left with the improbable image of Chaney as a born-to-the-purple Englishman. (The situation gets the finished film off on the wrong foot as the diminutive Rains warmly welcomes the big, strapping Chaney to the family homestead; Lon's line is, "The old place hasn't changed much"—a particularly cringe-worthy moment.)

Both scripts of *The Wolf Man* contain a fully detailed account of the famous, deleted bear scene. At the gypsy festival, Larry, Gwen and Frank come upon a gypsy (played by Kurt Katch) with a trained bear, and Frank goads Larry into accepting the gypsy's challenge to wrestle with the beast. Talbot confronts the bear, who backs off in fear. Taking a boxer's stance, Larry vents his rage, pummeling the animal to the ground before Gwen stops him. Regaining his composure, Larry walks off as the stunned Frank remarks that Larry "looked like a wolf" during the bout.

Ten years later, Siodmak, apparently fresh out of material, plundered the script of *The Wolf Man* to little effect in *Bride of the Gorilla* (1951), which he wrote and directed for Jack Broder's Realart Pictures. The film is weirdly fascinating in the manner which Siodmak transposes his brother Robert's noir style onto a cheap soundstage jungle, keeping the familiar Universal horror bromides close at hand and even throwing a bit of Val Lewton into the mix. Siodmak returns to the idea of an unseen menace (in this case, Raymond Burr who imagines himself to be a mythical ape-like creature), and includes a thinly disguised Maleva counterpart and a wolfsbane-like plant bearing a name approximating the pentagram; the film even features Chaney in the cast. Once again, Siodmak had to bow to the wishes of the producers by including non-subjective shots of the rampaging gorilla. "They forced me to do that—sometimes you can't fight 'em," he told us.

The Wolf Man's influence in Hollywood was almost immediate, greatly surpassing the studio's previous exercise in lycanthropy, *Were-Wolf of London*. The film's success directly inspired Val Lewton's cycle of horror films at RKO. In the meantime, other studios were taking note with werewolf characters turning up in 20th Century-Fox's Sherlock Holmes-inspired mystery *The Undying Monster* (1942) and Columbia's Bela Lugosi vehicle *The Return of the Vampire* (1943). While Hollywood sporadically revived werewolves in various incarnations since Larry Talbot first bayed at the full moon, *The Wolf Man* takes credit for catapulting the creature into the popular culture. Though it may lack the richness of style found in the best of Whale, Freund and Ulmer, *The Wolf Man* makes a powerful appeal to our imagination. The tragic story of Lawrence Talbot is basic yet compelling, and so classically structured it almost transcends its often unexceptional execution. Critics may be reluctant to place it on the list of definitive horror classics, but its popularity and influence demand its inclusion.

Critics' Corner

Many of the elements found most effectively for producing goose pimples and spine chills are found in this yarn of murder, psychiatry, superstition, and romance. It's pretty fantastic, but none the less stirring stuff which will have the horror seekers on chair edge. Cast is capable, as are the direction and photography.—*The Film Daily*, December 10, 1941

This horror melodrama ... is suitable mostly for theaters catering to audiences that enjoy entertainment of this kind. It is a little too harrowing and somewhat depressing for the general run of picture-goer, for the hero ... is a pitiful creature for whom one feels sympathy. There are a few scenes that are properly frightening. And the production values are good, particularly the photography, which gives the picture an eerie atmosphere.—*Harrison's Reports*, December 20, 1941

Rating: ★★ *The Wolf Man* will have to do ... until a better shocker comes along.... None of the performances is outstanding. Chaney is all right but his work in the picture won't get him anything better to do.—*The New York Daily News*, December 21, 1941, Wanda Hale

Embellished by a cast of well-known players and having a fairly dressy production, it is one of the more successful of this type of film....—*The New York Herald-Tribune*, December 1941

Perhaps in deference to a Grade-B budget it has tried to make a little go a long way ... nobody is going to go on believing in werewolves or Santa Clauses if the custodians of these legends don't tell them with a more convincing imaginative touch.—*The New York Times*, December 22, 1941, Theodore Strauss

It is a little too harrowing and somewhat depressing for the general run of picture-goer....—*Harrison's Reports*, 1941

1942

The Mad Doctor of Market Street

Released February 27, 1942. 61 minutes. *Director:* Joseph H. Lewis. *Associate Producer:* Paul Malvern. *Original Screenplay:* Al Martin. *Photography:* Jerome Ash. *Art Director:* Jack Otterson. *Associate Art Director:* Ralph M. DeLacy. *Editor:* Ralph Dixon. *Musical Director:* Hans J. Salter. *Set Decorator:* Russell A. Gausman. *Sound Supervisor:* Bernard B. Brown. *Technician:* Jess Moulin. *Assistant Director:* Melville Shyer. *Gowns:* Vera West.

Una Merkel (*Margaret Wentworth*), Lionel Atwill (*Dr. Ralph Benson/Graham*), Nat Pendleton (*Red Hogan*), Claire Dodd (*Patricia Wentworth*), Hardie Albright (*R.B. Saunders*), Richard Davies (*Jim*), Anne Nagel (*Mrs. Saunders*), John Eldredge (*Dwight*), Noble Johnson (*Elon*), Al Kikume (*Kalo*), Milton Kibbee (*Hadley*), Ray Mala (*Barab*), Rosina Galli (*Tanao*), Byron Shores (*Crandall*), Tani Marsh, Tavia [Billy] Bunkley (*Tahitian Dancers*), Boyd Davis (*Ship's Captain*), Alan Bridge (*First Mate*), Charlotte Treadway (*Dowager*), Clara Blore (*Stout Lady*), Claire Whitney, Vangie Beilby (*Spinsters*), Charles Sherlock (*Radio Engineer*), Eric Lonsdale, Douglas Gordon (*Radio Operators*), Guy Kingsford, Barry Bernard (*Pilots*), Paul Parry (*Ship's Officer*), Bess Flowers (*Dance Extra*), Tom Steele (*Policeman*).

Just as the natives worship me ... call me the God of Life ... so shall all the people of the earth.
—*Lionel Atwill in* The Mad Doctor of Market Street

This mad scientist thriller drops the familiar laboratory environs for an exotic (but equally cheap) backdrop of the South Sea islands. The film is so threadbare and haphazard it has a lot more in common with a Poverty Row product than the Hollywood B-unit sausage factory. That said, *The Mad Doctor of Market Street* isn't lacking in verve thanks to Lionel Atwill's irrepressible hamming and a director who has more on the ball than the average Monogram hack. The picture looks so much like a rush job that one could be forgiven for assuming it was simply tossed out as a second feature to play with *The Wolf Man* (both made a popular double bill on the neighborhood theater circuit in the early months of 1942). This doesn't seem to be the case, however, as *The Mad Doctor of Market Street* was already in the can long before its distinguished companion piece went before the cameras.

Unlike *The Wolf Man*, the film was an extremely minor studio project that hardly taxed the company's resources. The "suspended animation" plot gimmick had a strong budgetary appeal in that it didn't require any special, time-consuming makeup or effects. Even the South Sea island setting was another concession to the green eyeshades in Universal's accounting department. With the success of John Ford's *The Hurricane* (1937), Universal took a sudden interest in romance under the palm trees and readied Maria Montez as their answer to Dorothy Lamour, via George Waggner's *South of Tahiti* (1941).

The original script of *The Mad Doctor of Market Street* was written by Al Martin under the title *Terror of the South Seas*, but by the time the cameras rolled in July 1941, it became *Terror of the Islands*. Purportedly shot in under three weeks (quite a bit under three weeks considering what's evident on the screen) with a cast composed of studio contract players and low-salaried pick-ups. *The Mad Doctor of Market Street* is a foolish but occasionally entertaining little time-killer if viewed with low expectations.

Character study of Lionel Atwill, the short-sighted, delusional "genius" of *The Mad Doctor of Market Street.*

The storyline is pure hokum. Dr. Ralph Benson (Lionel Atwill), a self-proclaimed "professor of research" (he's later referred to as a chemist), enthusiastically pursues his experiments in suspended animation. Not satisfied with laboratory animals as subjects, Benson lures Saunders (Hardie Albright), a down-on-his-luck family man, to his San Francisco office. The scientist promises a cash payment of $1,000, which he removes from his wallet, if the man will consent to be a living guinea pig in his first experiment with a human subject. Saunders accepts the offer even though Benson puts the wad of bills the scientist was dangling in front of him *back* into his wallet. Saunders' wife (Anne Nagel), learning of her husband's intentions, alerts the police. As a squad car approaches Benson's office, the alarmed scientist discovers that Saunders has died; the mad medico escapes through the window.

Dubbed "The Mad Doctor of Market Street," Benson dodges a police dragnet and boards a luxury liner destined for Australia, passing himself off as an antiques dealer. Although undercover cop Crandall (Byron Shores) is hot on his heels, Benson has little to fear: His adversary proves so inept, he can't even identify his man upon meeting him face to face. Blowing his cover, Crandall announces to all within earshot that he's out to nail the fugitive scientist. In spite of his receding hairline and unmistakable build, Benson easily eludes detection merely by shaving off his beard and tosses Crandall overboard at the first opportunity.

A flash fire engulfs the S.S. *Paradise*. Benson, along with a handful of his fellow passengers, board a lifeboat which beaches on a nearby island. The ship steward, Jim (Richard Davies), makes the announcement that there's not a soul on the island and, within moments, the harried group is rounded by a mob of headhunters determined to sacrifice them in a ceremonial fire. Benson convinces the tribe he is the "God of Life" and proves it by reviving the comatose wife of the native chief with a shot of adrenalin.

Surrounded by a throng of admiring savages who spout lines like, "Anything you want, you ask," Benson lusts after his fellow castaway Patricia Wentworth (Claire Dodd). To pressure her into consenting to marriage, Benson places the girl's sweetheart, Jim, into a cataleptic state. Patricia reluctantly agrees and Benson grudgingly revives Jim to appease the superstitious natives. Dwight (John Eldredge), the cowardly ship's officer, tries to escape from the island in a stolen canoe, but gets into an underwater fight with Barab (Ray Mala, native star of 1933's *Eskimo*). Both men drown in the struggle. The body of the islander washes up on shore and native chief Elon (Noble Johnson) threatens Benson with execution unless he can bring the dead young man back to life by sunrise.

Atwill puts his all into the last scene, trembling with fear and sweating bullets as the nerve-wracked scientist feverishly works on the body, knowing the fate that awaits him. As the morning sun peeks over the horizon, Elon orders the lighting of the ceremonial fire and Benson torched alive. The blaze attracts a rescue plane which picks up the remaining castaways just as the enraged natives were about to close in on them.

The Mad Doctor of Market Street was directed by Joseph H. Lewis, a longtime favorite among *auteur*-minded critics with a reputation for delivering accomplished, high-powered B-pictures with style and economy. His first of several "breakthrough" pictures was Columbia's much-imitated *My Name Is Julia Ross* (1945), a Hitchcockian story of a young woman who takes a job as a live-in secretary only to discover she's being set up as a "suicide" by her demented employers. Studios took notice of Lewis, and he went on to an interesting career highlighted by the benchmark 1949 film noir thriller *Gun Crazy*. Despite working at a number of major studios, including MGM and Warner Bros., the director never made a movie that struck lightning at the box office. Not surprisingly, considering Lewis' penchant for grim plots and shadowy, non-traditional characters who often went against the Hollywood grain. In the late '50s, he finally gave up on the movies to ply his trade on standard television programs.

The Mad Doctor of Market Street came at a time when he was still honing his technical skills on low-end productions and but not quite ready to break from the pack of contract directors stuck in the B-movie grind. His earlier Bela Lugosi vehicle, *Invisible Ghost* (1941) stood out a bit from the actor's other Monogram assignments with a slightly unsettling atmosphere and occasionally interesting use of the camera (at least, compared to, say, 1943's *The Ape Man*). *The Mad Doctor of Market Street* is a somewhat slicker production although his *Invisible Ghost* writer, Al Martin, could only come up with a barely sustained storyline. Realizing the hopelessness of the situation, Lewis keeps the film on such a tongue-in-cheek level that it only stops being funny when the official comedy relief takes over. It's a terrible movie but a non-stop delight on its own terms.

Lewis' luxury liner fire sequence is an exciting little montage composed mostly of stock shots (culled mainly from the 1935 Fox film, *Dante's Inferno*) and miniatures. The director makes fine use of photographer Jerome Ash's atmospheric low-keyed lighting in the opening scenes and spices up the picture with some excellent, startlingly tight shots of Atwill in action. Subjective photography is used to chilling effect as Atwill meticulously prepares his victims, descending on the camera with an ether-soaked swath of cotton (a device later purloined by Erle C. Kenton for a scene in *The Ghost of Frankenstein*).

But it is Atwill who dominates the film with another over-the-top performance. As in *Man Made Monster*, Atwill goes for the jugular, unsuccessfully trying to boost the morale of his understandably reticent subjects. ("Disease, the scourge of humanity, will be cast out.... Think of it, man! The span of human life will be prolonged indefinitely!") Not even such latter-day hams as Vincent Price and Michael Gough could match the sadistic glee in Atwill's eye as he is turning up the juice or coaxing his latest human guinea pig into submission. Whether he is greedily sampling a native fruit basket or beaming with sexual anticipation at the suggestion of a tryst with the leading lady, Atwill could always be counted on to play it to the hilt.

The only problem is that Atwill's character just isn't much of a menace. In fact, he might be the dimmest mad scientist this side of Hollywood and Vine. Easily hoodwinking the natives into thinking he is the "God of Life," Atwill doesn't have the wit to realize that his bluff will be called the minute the first one of them actually *dies*. Atwill has unshakable confidence in his experiments in spite of his dismal track record. He just can't seem to do *any*thing right, starting with his first human subject who predictably expires on the operating table. What he lacks in achievement he makes up for in bravura, occasionally looking up from his maze of test tubes to make a ridiculous, self-serving pronouncement such as, "Just as the natives worship me ... so shall all the people of the earth."

Pressbook ad.

The rest of the cast has a tough time competing for the audience's attention. Amazingly, Una Merkel gets top-billing in the cast credits, even nudging out Atwill, for a supporting role as Claire Dodd's slightly dotty, underaged aunt. The diminutive, wide-eyed actress, with her clucking, bird-like delivery, manages to rise above some extremely asinine dialogue. ("I just love the Chinese. They're so *Oriental.*") A natural at light comedy, her talents were put to good use by Universal in pictures like *Destry Rides Again* (1939) and *The Bank Dick* (1940), in which she played W.C. Fields' daughter.

On the other hand, the amateurish, painfully unfunny Nat Pendleton nearly sinks the show as the cloddish boxer. The spunky Claire Dodd, who was winding down her film career, is likable as always as the subject of Atwill's affections. Anne Nagel, who was finishing up her Universal contract, is barely visible in the negligible role of the weepy wife of Atwill's first victim. The enigmatic Noble Johnson, alas, probably has more dialogue than he was given in any of his other genre roles. With a commanding presence, the actor manages to keep his dignity intact under trying circumstances and actually lives up to his first name.

The film's nominal hero, Richard Davies, does a reasonable job. The role was something of a coup for the actor, who spent most of his career at Universal playing inconsequential juvenile parts in lightweight fare. When asked about *The Mad Doctor of Market Street* in 1988, he remembered little and even less about Atwill: "He was the star of the picture and we just had a speaking acquaintance. He was a good enough actor so that his personal problems did not affect his performance. In my opinion, the picture was not as good as the picture I made with Fred Astaire called *The Sky's the Limit* [1943] for RKO." (The late Mr. Davies had a persuasive gift for understatement.)

A picture like *The Mad Doctor of Market Street* could be picked apart endlessly. There are those ersatz South Pacific locales, complete with a rear-projected beach and patently Caucasian extras haplessly posing as islanders. Moreover, the film's choppy continuity leave gaping holes in the action as if major scenes were left on the cutting room floor or, more likely, weren't filmed at all. There are no scenes in the lifeboat, nor are there any of the castaways arriving on the island. A single cut finds the players imprisoned by the natives without explanation.

Film historian John Cocchi has, very plausibly, made the case that the opening scenes set on the mainland were added to the script as an afterthought. According to Cocchi, the Call Bureau Cast Sheet, issued in August 1941, lists neither Anne Nagel nor Hardie Albright (both seen solely in the stateside scenes) among the cast members. Since, at the time, the film was registered under its shooting title *Terror of the Islands,* it's possible that the title change was prompted by the inclusion of the San Francisco scenes.

The film is so small-scale and disposable that it was virtually sequel-proof even by Universal standards. (The studio, ever anxious to capitalize on its backlog of horror titles, to this day hasn't released this title on any home video format.) Nonetheless, *The Mad Doctor of Market Street* spawned a follow-up of sorts several months later, the typically madcap Abbott and Costello romp, *Pardon My Sarong* (1942). One of the comedy team's funniest, if disjointed, pictures, it starts off with a nightclub routine by The Ink Spots and ends up in the South Seas with smuggler Lionel Atwill fleecing the indigenous population. The redoubtable actor gets into the spirit of the slapstick and proves to be an excellent straight-man to the baby-faced Costello. When the comic innocently asks who is next in line to be the human sacrifice in the island tribal ritual, Atwill makes the most of his line, "*You* are!" The actor didn't even require a change of wardrobe from his stint as the loco scientist.

The Mad Doctor of Market Street is poorly produced, to be sure, but the viewer can reap minor dividends. If you're willing to play along with Joseph Lewis' lark, there's more fun to be had than one has a right to expect, as long as Lionel Atwill is center stage.

Critics' Corner

[Atwill's] performance, as well as that of the rest of the cast, is on a par with the film—which is on a par with all the other mad doctor mellers which have been shown on the Rialto screen.—*The New York Daily Mirror*, January 5, 1942, Lee Mortimer

If you want to see what a really bad piece of workmanship Hollywood can produce when it sets its mind to it, I would refer you to *The Mad Doctor of Market Street*.... The story is so bogus, so labored, so dreary, the dialogue so unfunny and the acting so embarrassing that the whole thing is in a class by itself. Rarely has anything more ponderous or tasteless come out of the film capitol.—*The New York World-Telegram*, January 5, 1942, William Boehnel

Although this is supposed to be in the thriller class, it is doubtful if it will have a frightening effect on anyone. So ridiculous is the story, and so slow-moving the action, that patrons will be bored instead of excited. There is nothing that the players can do to enliven the proceedings, for they are up against trite material and stilted dialogue. The romance is routine.—*Harrison's Reports*, January 10, 1942

Rating: ★★ Lionel Atwill, who isn't the worst actor in Hollywood, although he is darned near it, gives one of his standard performances....—*The New York Daily News*, January 4, 1942, Kate Cameron

The Ghost of Frankenstein

Released March 13, 1942. 67 minutes. *Producer:* George Waggner. *Director:* Erle C. Kenton. *Screenplay:* W. Scott Darling. *Original Story:* Eric Taylor. *Photography:* Milton Krasner and Elwood Bredell. *Art Director:* Jack Otterson. *Associate Art Director:* Harold H. MacArthur. *Editor:* Ted Kent. *Musical Director:* Hans J. Salter. *Set Decorator:* Russell A. Gausman. *Sound Director:* Bernard B. Brown. *Technician:* Charles Carroll. *Assistant Director:* Charles S. Gould. *Makeup:* Jack P. Pierce. *Gowns:* Vera West.

Sir Cedric Hardwicke (*Dr. Ludwig Frankenstein*), Lon Chaney, Jr. (*The Monster*), Ralph Bellamy (*Erik Ernst*), Lionel Atwill (*Dr. Theodor Bohmer*), Bela Lugosi (*Ygor*), Evelyn Ankers (*Elsa Frankenstein*), Janet Ann Gallow (*Cloestine Hussman*), Barton Yarborough (*Dr. Kettering*), Olaf Hytten (*Hussman*), Doris Lloyd (*Martha*), Leyland Hodgson (*Chief Constable*), Holmes Herbert (*Magistrate*), Lawrence Grant (*Mayor*), Brandon Hurst (*Hans*), Otto Hoffman, Dwight Frye (*Villagers*), Julius Tannen (*Sektal*), Lionel Belmore, Michael Mark (*Councillors*), Harry Cording (*Frone*), Dick Alexander (*Vision*), Ernie Stanton, George Eldredge (*Constables*), Jimmy Phillips (*Indian*), William Smith (*Village Boy*), Eddie Parker (*Stunts*), Harry Tenbrook, Glen Walters.

> [Horror movies] help people to get away from the horror of realism. A Chinese baby crying in the midst of a bomb-blasted station is heart-rending, but a monster strangling Sir Cedric Hardwicke is entertainment.
>
> —The Saturday Evening Post, *May 23, 1942, on the future of Universal horror flicks*

The Ghost of Frankenstein is as much a product of Universal's management of the '40s as the initial two Frankenstein films reflected the Laemmles' upscale aspirations of the '30s. The movie is consistently exciting but it is, at the same time, slick, streamlined and artless. Sadly, *The Ghost of Frankenstein* would be the last solo appearance of the Monster.

The fourth installment of the ever-profitable Frankenstein series was a foregone conclusion. On November 13, 1941, Universal made the formal announcement and unveiled the title of their new production. A press release indicated that the major hurdle facing the project was to find a suitable replacement for Boris Karloff in the Monster role. Undaunted, the studio assured all that the search was well underway.

On November 14, the very next day, the "search" came to an end. According to a new announcement, producer George Waggner was instructed to order the same makeup that Karloff wore for the new Monster out of fear that changing his appearance would "kill the interest of Frankenstein followers." Unsurprisingly, Lon Chaney, Jr., who was toiling on the set of *The Wolf Man*, was picked as Karloff's successor and it was reported that he would presently be fitted for "wigs, greasepaint and other gadgets" by makeup man Jack Pierce.

Universal publicly admitted it was taking a box office risk by replacing Karloff, but it had no intentions of waiting a year for the actor to fulfill his stage commitments. In fact, the studio was pressing for a starting date before Christmas. This announcement, of course, was bunk. Karloff was no longer under contract and hadn't even appeared in a Universal film for nearly two years. Since then he had carved quite a niche for himself in the Broadway production of "Arsenic and Old Lace" and personally felt that the Monster role was played out.

Curiously, Universal submitted its script to the Production Code Association under the title *There's Always Tomorrow*. As usual, the Breen people warned against excessive violence and reminded the studio that scenes set in Frankenstein's operating room and insanity ward would be deleted in England. (The film would be banned outright in Denmark when Universal tried to release it there in 1948.)

The Ghost of Frankenstein is set four years

after the events of the last sequel. The ever-complaining townspeople of Frankenstein blame the Monster's "curse" for everything from a bad harvest to the town's lackluster tourist trade. They implore the Mayor (Lawrence Grant, former Burgomaster in *Son of Frankenstein*; the Americanized title was probably an attempt to downplay the German setting, a sensitive issue during the war years) to grant them the right to destroy Frankenstein's castle. The Mayor reluctantly gives his consent and the mob converges on the crumbling edifice.

The villagers' attempts to detonate the structure are temporarily thwarted by Ygor (Bela Lugosi), scarcely affected by the bullets that Wolf von Frankenstein fired into him in the previous film. As the first blasts of dynamite rock the castle, Ygor flees to the catacombs below. Dumbstruck, he sees the Monster's hand emerging from a wall of hardened sulphur. Ygor frantically unearths the Monster (Lon Chaney, Jr.) from his strange tomb and the pair make their way into the woods as the last standing walls of the castle crumble.

A fierce thunderstorm breaks out and the Monster is struck by a tremendous bolt of lightning, but instead of killing him, the jolt only seems to renew his tremendous strength. Realizing that electricity is the only means to restore the Monster's power, Ygor and his friend head for the village of Vasaria to enlist the aid of Dr. Ludwig Frankenstein (Sir Cedric Hardwicke).

The second son of the outlaw scientist, Ludwig, a prominent brain surgeon, has managed to keep his family history a secret from his daughter, Elsa (Evelyn Ankers), as well as from the community. When Ygor threatens to tell all, Frankenstein grudgingly agrees to take custody of the Monster (who has been apprehended by the constabulary for killing a villager). When Frankenstein arrives at the courthouse, the Monster goes berserk and escapes with Ygor at his side.

That night, Ygor and the Monster make their way back to Ludwig's estate. The Monster crashes through the door, kills Frankenstein's assistant, Dr. Kettering (Barton Yarborough), and attempts to carry off Elsa. Ludwig manages to subdue Ygor and the Monster with an anesthetizing gas pumped in through the ventilator ducts. Determining that the only way to destroy the Monster is by dissection, Ludwig seeks the aid of his associate, Dr. Bohmer (Lionel Atwill). Bohmer balks, suggesting that it would be murder. Ludwig himself has second thoughts; while he is preparing his instruments, the "ghost" of his father, Henry Frankenstein (also played by Hardwicke), implores his son to vindicate his great experiment by replacing the Monster's demented brain with a sound one. Realizing he has a perfect specimen in the dead body of Kettering, Frankenstein becomes obsessed with restoring the Monster to his full power.

The crafty Ygor decides that his own brain should be the one to go into the Monster's head and enlists Dr. Bohmer's aid to carry out the scheme. The surgeon, who has been discredited by the medical profession for a past experiment that had gone awry, seizes this opportunity to regain his standing and consents. But the Monster has his own ideas. He steals into the village and abducts Cloestine (Janet Ann Gallow), a little girl who has befriended him. He takes the child back to the laboratory with the notion of having Ludwig use her brain for the operation. Ludwig intervenes, takes the child away, and prepares the Monster for surgery. The operation proceeds with Frankenstein unknowingly placing Ygor's brain into the skull of the Monster.

The townspeople, meanwhile, have become frustrated with the constabulary's inability to find the Monster and the missing Cloestine. Certain that Frankenstein is responsible, they storm the estate. Elsa's fiancé, town prosecutor Erik Ernst (Ralph Bellamy), alerts Ludwig of the brewing crisis. Frankenstein admits that he has been harboring the Monster and has, in effect, rehabilitated him by giving him the brain of the kindly Kettering. To prove his point, he unveils the "new" Monster, only to discover Bohmer's treachery. Speaking in Ygor's crackling voice, the Monster revels in his power but soon finds himself going blind (the result of Ygor and the Monster's incompatible blood types). As the villagers descend upon the estate, the enraged Monster flings Bohmer into an electrical panel which sends a lethal charge through his body. Groping sightlessly around the lab, the Monster topples a rack of chemicals to the floor, touching off an

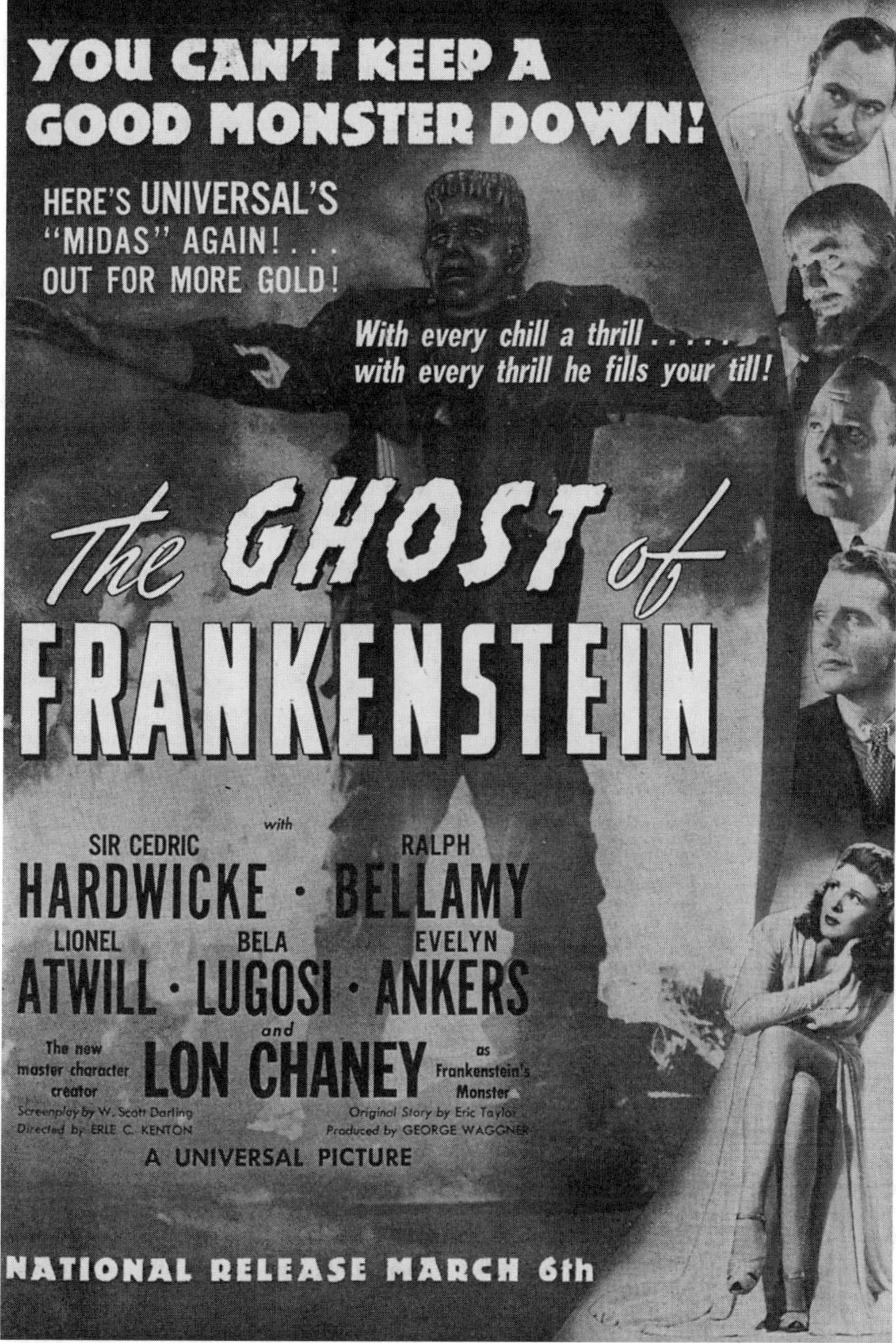

After a three-year hiatus, the Monster returned to the silver screen with a new impersonator, Lon Chaney, Jr., in *The Ghost of Frankenstein*.

inferno. Ludwig and the Monster perish in the flames as Elsa and Erik flee to safety.

The Ghost of Frankenstein, like *The Mummy's Hand*, made it plain that Universal was less interested in producing horror films than it was in churning out mere "monster movies." While horror films, at their best, offer a wide palette of interesting possibilities (nuance of character, hints of subtext, echoes of the folklore or literature that inspired it), the "monster movie" blithely tosses away the subtlety to serve hard-sell horror in the form of grotesque makeup, swooning heroines and/or rip-roaring action. *The Ghost of Frankenstein* offers monster moviemaking at its classy best which is the reason why it has been embraced by fans in a way that *Son of Frankenstein,* a better film by any standard, has not. As such, *The Ghost of Frankenstein* is a tricky film to critique. Any criticism directed against it is deflected by the fact that it's so much fun to watch.

The film's 67-minute running time, over a full half-hour shorter than its predecessor, would suggest a bottom-of-the-bill filler feature. The studio, however, wasn't quite ready to downgrade its prize horror franchise, enhancing the film with decent production values and a strong B cast. As it was the fourth film in the popular horror series, Universal undoubtedly realized that it wouldn't likely win plaudits from the critics and concentrated instead on making an actionful, crowd-pleasing film devoid of pretensions.

Originally, Universal intended to have Basil Rathbone's Wolf von Frankenstein character resume his adventures with the Monster and Ygor after being driven into exile after the events in *Son of Frankenstein.* This early version of the script, by Eric Taylor, proved to be a bizarre, downbeat affair in which Ygor makes a pact with Wolf's hunchbacked assistant and attempts to organize the village cripples to take over the town with the Monster as their leader. This unpleasant and ludicrous diversion, possibly influenced by Tod Browning's *Freaks* (1932), was closer in spirit to pre–Code excesses of the '30s than it was to the comparatively bland tastes of the war years and didn't quite strike the tone that Universal wanted.

Taylor had obviously immersed himself in the earlier Frankenstein films to come up with a pool of ideas: The Monster's bond with children, the cliché of the villagers storming the castle, and of course the Monster's fiery demise, all of which were retained in W. Scott Darling's final draft. Conspicuously absent in Darling's script is the slow build-up of character and atmosphere so effectively rendered in *Son of Frankenstein* and *The Wolf Man.* The formula of introducing a couple of American or Americanized audience "identification characters" who slowly acclimate themselves to a Gothic netherworld, a device which served to make the horror elements more palatable, is nowhere to be found in this sequel. In *The Ghost of Frankenstein*, the audience is in a take-it-or-leave-it position from the first frame as the villagers growl over "the curse of Frankenstein." Within moments, the crowd is at their torch-bearing best, descending on the castle with armloads of dynamite to blast their last remaining ties with the Frankenstein clan to smithereens. It's a terrifically exciting curtain-raiser and it's probably not an accident that the next few films in the series also began with bold opening acts.

The siege of the castle sequence is very well put together, with shots of the villagers fleeing from the explosive charges seamlessly interspersed with special effects footage of the stone edifice shattering into ruins. It's another feather in the cap of John P. Fulton, under whose guidance Universal's effects department could rival any major Hollywood studio. The striking images of the exploding structure served as a grim reminder of the bombs that were falling over Europe and lent a timeliness to the film's fantasy-like air.

Erle C. Kenton directs the film in a brash, distinctly American style. A former Keystone Cop and Mack Sennett director, his approach to horror was as direct and uncluttered as it was for comedy. Kenton directed some of Universal's better Abbott and Costello efforts but also got more than his share of horror assignments probably as a result of his work on Paramount's *Island of Lost Souls* (1933). An efficient technician with little apparent use for the time-tested horror conventions, Kenton keeps *The Ghost of Frankenstein* moving briskly, preferring sunny exteriors and brightly-lit scenes to the usual deep shadows and stylized lighting associated with the genre. As with Kenton's later monster rallies, the viewer gets a sense that the director is presiding over an elaborate charade, allowing neither character nor subtext to seep too deeply into the narrative. In other words, he's Mack Sennett directing a horror movie. (More than one commentator has noted that *Island of Lost Souls* owes its reputation more to Charles Laughton's perversely sinister performance and Karl Struss' photography than Kenton's prosaic staging.)

The Ghost of Frankenstein is not let down by Universal's technical crew. Jack Otterson's production design lacks the experimental, psychologically oppressive qualities of *Son of Frankenstein*, but his sets are spacious and well-appointed. There's commendable work, too, by photographers Milton Krasner and Elwood Bredell, who accent the Monster's height via point-of-view shots of the little girl. Throughout there are interesting angles such as framing Lugosi through the open lid of a grand piano and shooting Lionel Atwill through an oversized ring atop a piece of laboratory apparatus. Hans J. Salter serves up an orchestral *Sturm und Drang*, every bit as compelling (and actually more sophisticated) than Frank Skinner's landmark score for *Son of Frankenstein*, providing Universal's B film producers with an abundance of horrific musical cues that would be tapped well into the next decade.

W. Scott Darling doesn't have the same flair for dialogue as previous writers in the series and, unfortunately, retains the brain transplantation angle that was left over from Eric Taylor's original draft. That plot twist shows the unmistakable influence of Taylor's *Black Friday* collaborator, Curt Siodmak, whose fixation with the subject was also mined in his highly successful novel *Donovan's Brain*. The concept would reach new heights of absurdity in the forthcoming *House of Frankenstein* (with an original story by Siodmak) with Boris Karloff as a Frankenstein-like scientist who can't decide which brain he wants to pop into the poor creature's head.

Having the Monster harbor Ygor's brain could have been a witty and novel way of wrapping up the entire series. But as Universal expected to get a lot more mileage out of their most popular horror character, the ending only served to confuse the Monster's identity in future sequels. It seemed to confuse the scriptwriters, too, since there is no mention of Ygor's brain for the rest of the series except for the deleted scenes from *Frankenstein Meets the Wolf Man*.

Where *The Ghost of Frankenstein* scores impressively is its splendid cast. Bela Lugosi's encore performance as a somewhat better-groomed Ygor (at least by Ygor's standards) is welcome, and he has a spate of first-rate scenes. (His coercion of Hardwicke in the latter's study is a potent reminder of how good an actor Lugosi can be.) The actor also rates high marks in the scene where he conspires with Atwill in regards to the brain transplantation. For once, Lugosi's slow theatrical delivery pays off and he manages to undercut the silliness of the business at hand ("We would rule the state, and even the whole country!"), conveniently forgetting that the Monster was handily rounded up by a handful of Vasarian constables a few reels earlier.

Sir Cedric Hardwicke is somewhat at a disadvantage as the rather colorless descendant of Henry Frankenstein. Whereas Basil Rathbone's Wolf von Frankenstein captured Clive's sang-froid in the original film, Hardwicke, on the other hand, is more akin to the morose and fluctuating Clive in *Bride of Frankenstein*. A smug and distant gentleman surgeon, Ludwig Frankenstein caves in to Ygor's blackmail threats as readily as Henry weakened under Pretorius' pressure. Far from being the driven, half-mad genius, this Dr. Frankenstein is a rather monk-like steward of the family name who needs the coaxing of a "ghost" to move him into action. (Hardwicke himself plays the spirit of his father in a makeup more reminiscent of the aging Thomas Edison than Colin Clive.)

Hardwicke proves to be an uncomfortable horror personality as befitting a titled, classically trained British actor slumming it in a project which he probably felt was beneath him. ("God felt sorry for actors," he once offered in a gently damning testimonial to Hollywood, "so he gave them a place in the sun and a swimming pool. The price they had to pay was to surrender their talent.")

Compared to his Inspector Krogh, Atwill's role as Bohmer is a step down but he attacks the part with customary relish, even managing to add a layer of dimension to a rather limited character. Bohmer's fate is telegraphed in his first scene at the operating table where he's the subject of a rude dressing-down by Frankenstein

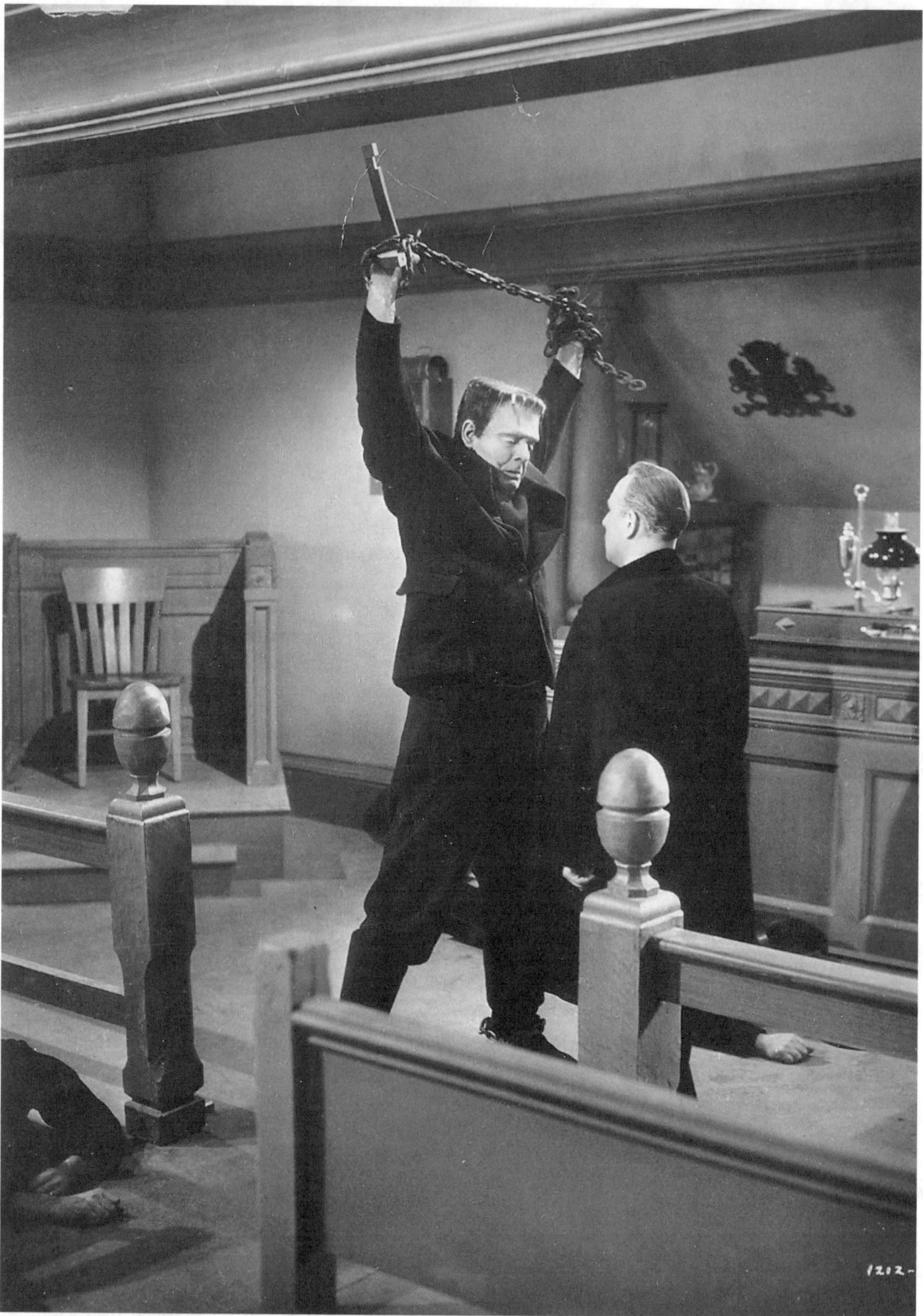

The Monster (Chaney Jr.) proves that he can't handle familial rejection. Cedric Hardwicke is the uncaring "stepbrother."

Chaney Jr.'s Monster posed no threat to the Karloff legacy.

after the pair perform an apparent miracle of brain surgery. Their respective roles of master and pupil are now reversed, and Frankenstein's reminder to Bohmer of his butterfingers reputation (years earlier, an experimental surgery ended in an unspecified tragedy) is gratuitous at best. The incident sows the seeds of Bohmer's treachery but until then Atwill catches the character's principled decency before traipsing over to the dark side. Atwill can't help but upstage his colleagues at every opportunity, packing his performance with plenty of dramatic flourishes. Note his squirming, uncomfortable reaction as Frankenstein triumphantly announces to Ernst that he has replaced the Monster's brain with Kettering's. Later, as Ygor reveals himself in his new body, it is neither the Monster's ravings or Frankenstein's horrified reaction that commands attention but Atwill, deep in the background, indulging in his trademark mad doctor expressions.

Chaney is victimized by a poor makeup (the result of an allergic reaction to Jack Pierce's materials), so the full-faced actor is a far cry from the emaciated, corpse-like image of Boris Karloff in the original film; Chaney capitalizes instead on the Monster's towering dimensions in much the same way his predecessor did in *Son of Frankenstein. The Ghost of Frankenstein* gave the son of "The Man of a Thousand Faces" a unique chance to compete directly in his father's arena with a makeup-heavy role where he could attempt to present a range of emotions without dialogue. Instead of seizing the opening and running with it, Chaney shambles through the role mechanically with limited facial expressions and little apparent interest in pantomime. Chaney's best moment is in the courtroom scene as the Monster's recognition of Frankenstein turns into rage when the scientist boldly forsakes him. The scene as originally written offered Chaney a made-to-order chance to convey some of the pathos of his father's classic performances, particularly when little Cloestine tries to communicate with the creature. (The script's stage directions indicate that the Monster should become "hysterical with joy" as the little girl climbs on his knee.) Under Kenton's direction, a minimum of joy, or *any* recognizable emotion, is allowed to seep through the greasepaint; this was probably a bid to keep the film moving along. *The Ghost of Frankenstein* may be a fast-paced film but its impressive tally of thrills and excitement comes at no small price.

More's the pity since Chaney and little Janet Ann Gallow shared some touching moments of bonding off-camera. In a 2005 interview with author Michael Fitzgerald, she said, "I spent a lot of time with Lon. I was always riding his legs, his knees, sitting on his lap. He was nice, gentle with me and easy to work with — better than anyone else!"

Recalling her scenes with Chaney's Monster, Gallow recalled,

> I approached him like I was going to a favorite uncle, not a monster. The director yelled that maybe I should be frightened, but I wasn't — Chaney even told me, "You won't be scared of me — just watch every day as they put on the makeup and change my looks." And he was right — it didn't scare me at all, and it worked better that way.

When Gallow's mother died in 1946, Chaney was eager to adopt the little girl and her brother, an idea which understandably didn't sit very well with her father. "He asked my father, but of course, he wouldn't consent.... This was, of course, before [*sic*] he adopted his two sons."

Ralph Bellamy and Evelyn Ankers do their professional best but seem oddly incongruous in their surroundings. Bellamy looks every bit the Connecticut Yankee amid the British accents and European accoutrements. Ankers goes through her paces in an eye-straining array of Vera West gowns.

It isn't likely that *The Ghost of Frankenstein* can be appreciated by general audiences as anything but a camp horror movie. But for those select film fans who've memorized Lugosi's credits, who attend monster conventions and regularly devour all the genre fanzines, it doesn't need apologies. If the film is marred with less than iconic performances by Chaney and Hardwicke, there are compensating values in just about every technical department. All told, *The Ghost of Frankenstein* is a heartily entertaining monster movie.

Critics' Corner

[I]nventively stands on an imaginative par with all of its interest-gripping, quasi-scientific predecessors.... Erle C. Kenton's direction makes magnificent use of every element of suspense ... The cast is definitely above average.... — *The Hollywood Reporter*, March 2, 1942

Rating: ★½ The new monster picture is horrid, not horrendous and horribly boring even though a lot of good players ... do the best they can with the dreadful material. — *The New York Daily News*, April 4, 1942, Wanda Hale

The current installment in the continued adventures of the Frankenstein Monster maintains a standard of performance, effectiveness and quality exceeding the average for horror films by a considerable margin.... — *The Motion Picture Herald*, March 7, 1942

[T]he replenished monster is being consumed by

fire when we see him last, but the thought that he may yet return ... fills us with mortal terror. That is the most fearful prospect which the picture manages to convey.—*The New York Times*, April 4, 1942, Bosley Crowther

Mystery of Marie Roget

Released April 3, 1942; 60 minutes; Re-released by Realart as *Phantom of Paris*; *Associate Producer:* Paul Malvern. *Director:* Philip Rosen. *Screenplay:* Michel Jacoby. *Based on the short story* "The Mystery of Marie Roget" *by* Edgar Allan Poe. *Photography:* Elwood Bredell. *Art Director:* Jack Otterson. *Associate:* Richard H. Riedel. *Editor:* Milton Carruth. *Music Director:* Hans J. Salter. *Sound Director:* Bernard B. Brown. *Technician:* Robert Pritchard. *Set Decorator:* Russell A. Gausman. *Assistant Director:* Seward Webb. *Songs:* Everett Carter & Milton Rosen. *Gowns:* Vera West.

Patric Knowles (*Dr. Paul Dupin*), Maria Montez (*Marie Roget*), Maria Ouspenskaya (*Mme. Cecile Roget*), John Litel (*Henri Beauvais*), Edward Norris (*Marcel Vigneaux*), Lloyd Corrigan (*Prefect of Police Gobelin*), Nell O'Day (*Camille Roget*), Frank Reicher (*Magistrate*), Clyde Fillmore (*M. De Luc*), Paul E. Burns (*Gardener*), Norma Drury (*Mme. De Luc*), Charles Middleton (*Zoo Curator*), Bill Ruhl (*Detective*), Reed Hadley (*Naval Officer*), John Maxwell, Paul Bryar (*Detectives*), Paul Dubov (*Pierre, News Vendor*), Joe Bernard, Frank O'Connor (*Men*), Raymond Bailey (*Gendarme*), Charles Wagenheim, Lester Dorr (*Subordinates to Prefect*), Alphonse Martell (*Vegetable Cart Driver*), Francis Sayles, Jimmie Lucas (*Parisians*), Beatrice Roberts (*Wife on Street*), Caroline Cooke (*Woman*), Dorothy Triden (*Singing Voice of Maria Montez*)

Phantom Girl Walks Streets

Get over the strange appeal of your picture with a feminine bally ... girl dressed all in black ... with added black flowing cape and hat that comes well down over her face. Veil the head and face entirely with black gauze wrapped around face bandit style (to get away from any appearance of mourning). High-heeled jeweled slippers and sheer black hose should accentuate the lure of this strange creature. Letter on her cape:
WHO IS THE PHANTOM MANGLER OF PARIS?
See—Thrill—Scream to
EDGAR ALLAN POE'S
classic of horror
"THE MYSTERY OF MARIE ROGET"
RIVOLI NOW

Mystery of Marie Roget is another instance of a slick Universal mystery dressed up in ersatz "chiller" trappings to attract the horror trade. "Who is the Phantom Mangler of Paris?" demanded the poster, suggesting something of a Gallic Jack the Ripper which the picture itself scarcely delivers. But the Edgar Allan Poe brand name and a few gratuitously gruesome touches within the film gave the studio press boys all the excuse they required to promote it as a full-blooded thriller. *Marie Roget* is brisk and entertaining, but it isn't horror and it isn't even good mystery.

The famous horror author's 1842 "The Mystery of Marie Roget" was a follow-up to his earlier (1841) work "The Murders in the Rue Morgue." A continuation of the exploits of the celebrated amateur detective C. Auguste Dupin, "Marie Roget" was based on the real-life murder of a young New York girl, Mary Cecilia Rogers, whose body had been found floating in the Hudson River near Weehawken, New Jersey. The Poe story mirrored the particulars of the Rogers case, changing only the names of the principals, the locale and a few additional minor points. Poe transposed the scene of the crime to Paris, centering his story on Dupin and his ruminations on the murder of Marie Roget, counter-girl at a perfumery in the Palais Hotel.

Poe's "The Mystery of Marie Roget" was a lugubrious and long-winded account, with the garrulous Dupin merely scrutinizing newspaper descriptions of the atrocity and drawing various conclusions without conducting an inquiry of his own. (Poe, like Dupin, never investigated personally nor did he visit the murder scene.) It's interesting to note, however, that the confessions of two individuals, made subsequent to the 1842 publication of "Marie Roget," confirmed the conclusion that Poe arrived at in his story as well as *all* of the chief hypothetical details by which his conclusion was reached.

In adapting Poe's century-old story to the screen, scenarist Michel Jacoby updated the story to 1889 (allowing for a scene involving diving equipment) and changed the profession of Marie Roget from shopgirl to musical comedy star to better suit the talents of up-and-coming Universal attraction Maria Montez. Montez receives star billing in the film's opening credits but in the closing cast list she is listed second, below Patric Knowles (as Dr. Dupin). Jacoby also beefed up the insubstantial original tale, adding a veritable Poe-pourri of extra story elements and the usual B-film gallery of red herrings required to muddy the plot waters for the redoubtable Dupin.

The story opens in Paris, at the height of public commotion over the unexplained disappearance of Comédie Française star Marie Roget. Henri Beauvais (John Litel), a friend of the Roget family, is in the office of Police Prefect Gobelin (Lloyd Corrigan) haranguing the diminutive detective, when news of the discovery of a woman's body in the Seine arrives. Accompanied by Paul Dupin (Patric Knowles), the department's chief medical officer, Gobelin and Beauvais hasten to the waterfront to examine the corpse. Although the dead woman's face has been torn to a pulp, the distressed Beauvais identifies the body as that of Marie Roget.

Gobelin and Beauvais appear at the home of Marie's imperious grandmother Mme. Cecile Roget (Maria Ouspenskaya) and are about to break the grim news to the old woman when Marie (Maria Montez) sweeps into the room. When Gobelin asks her about her mysterious behavior, Marie high-handedly dresses him down and Beauvais asks the inspector to leave the house.

Camille (Nell O'Day), Marie's sister, becomes engaged to Marcel Vigneaux (Edward Norris), a young man attached to the Ministry of Naval Affairs. Secretly Marie and Marcel are lovers plotting to murder Camille (she is about to come of age and receive her late grandfather's 1.5 million franc fortune). Mme. Roget overhears Marie and Marcel planning to kill Camille at an upcoming soiree and sends for Dupin. Without divulging what she has overheard, Mme. Roget offers him 50,000 francs to act as Camille's bodyguard at the party. Dupin resists the offer until Camille enters the room, at which point the suddenly smitten scientist-sleuth graciously accepts the position. In a surprising twist, it's Marie, not Camille, who disappears from the party. Like the unfortunate mystery girl of the opening reel, her body is later dredged out of the river, face horribly mangled.

After another reel or two of mystery-laden exposition, Vigneaux confesses to the murder of Marie, claiming to have killed her to protect Camille. Dupin, convinced that Vigneaux is banking on a verdict of justifiable homicide, imposes on Gobelin to drop the charges until they can prove premeditation on Vigneaux's part. The discovery of the identity of the initial mutilation-murder victim — Vigneaux's first wife — provides the evidence which Dupin needs. He and Gobelin race to the Roget home just as Vigneaux is attacking Camille. A running gunfight across the Paris rooftops ensues, and Vigneaux is shot and killed.

A galloping pace and an appealing roster of players help *Mystery of Marie Roget* over the hurdles and overall the 60-minute film sizes up as one of Universal's more attractive B mystery-adventures of the '40s. As a horror thriller, however, the film comes up distressingly short. All the Poe story provided the film were title, Paris setting, Gallicized character names and the basic premise of a woman's body being fished out of the drink. Otherwise writer Jacoby was on his own to embellish the thin story to the best of his abilities. Jacoby adds the mutilated-face angle, and leads audiences to believe that the women may have been mauled by Mme. Roget's pet leopard. (As in the later Universal film *The Scarlet Claw*, a garden weeder was actually used to commit the crimes.)

The film's horror high point is an effective sequence where a Phantom-like cloaked figure (Dupin, as it turns out) slips into the Rue Morgue by night to steal the brain of Marie Roget. (The scene is highly reminiscent of Warners' 1933 *Mystery of the Wax Museum*, in which burn-faced Lionel Atwill raids the New York City morgue to filch a cadaver.) Late in the film, Vigneaux wears similar black raiment during his attempt on Camille's life and in the subsequent rooftop chase. These half-hearted horrific touches add nicely to the atmosphere of gaslit gloom, but they were probably inadequate compensation for paying customers rightfully expecting a whole-hog horror show.

Patric Knowles' Dupin is a far cry from the analytical bookworm of Poe's stories and from Leon Ames' affected and excitable medical student of the '32 *Murders in the Rue Morgue*. The Dupin of *Marie Roget* is a glib yet basically serious-minded chemist attached to the Paris police force; Knowles brings his usual genial charm to the role, and wrings a good bit of dry humor out of the dialogue. Jacoby's script also bestows upon Dupin a modest measure of fame (he has become something of a household name throughout Paris for unraveling the Rue Morgue mystery), although the inordinate emphasis placed on this long-past triumph leaves us with the impression that as a detective he's quite the one-hit wonder.

Knowles' interplay with Lloyd Corrigan (as the prefect of police) is a highlight of the film, with Knowles' nimble analytical mind always keeping him several steps ahead of the unimaginative, often flustered inspector. The two men make a good screen team; other B-films with Knowles and Corrigan as the Paris version of Holmes and Watson might have enlivened Universal's release schedule. Knowles told the authors that he would have been delighted to star in a string of Dupin films.

Actor Edward Norris told the authors:

> On that Edgar Allan Poe picture [*Marie Roget*], Pat Knowles and I had a wonderful time and became longtime friends, very good friends. We got along so beautifully [on *Marie Roget*] that soon we were spending a couple weekends a month playing around with motorcycles and our campers and stuff. We used to take a few martinis, and then we'd ride our motorcycles and we'd go hunting. He and his wife Enid, and my wife Sharon and I, sometimes we'd all get together, all four.

Up-and-coming "camp" star Maria Montez gives her usual lacking performance as the doomed Marie: The character is dead before the movie is half over, and her top-billed status (in the opening credits, anyway) is undeserved. Her one song, "Mama Dit Moi," is mouthed by Montez but was actually sung by vocalist Dorothy Triden.

The film's Camille, actress Nell O'Day, told the authors:

> Maria Montez was quite new to films at the time. She was from an affluent Spanish family — at one time her father had been Spain's ambassador to France. I never learned how or why she came to the U.S. and signed a contract with Universal.
>
> She was not popular with the staff and crew because she thought of them almost as servants. She treated the dressers and other people from the wardrobe department as though they were maids! I tried to tactfully tell her that *all* the people on films were members of a guild or union, that the U.S. was somewhat different from many other countries. But she was intelligent and charming, and we got on very well. She told me I was a *real* professional, probably because I had played in the New York theater. She said more than once that she didn't want to be an actress, "I want to be a *pair-sone-ality*." She was very effective in the films she played in — beautiful and original.

Peter Coe told the authors:

> Everybody says Maria was a bitch but I loved her. She was temperamental, but we were great pals. She was a firm believer in astrology, and she wouldn't do without consulting Carroll Righter, who writes for *The L.A. Times*. One day on *Gypsy Wildcat* [1944] we had about 600 horsemen, gypsy villagers and so on all set to be photographed in one spectacular shot which would eventually move into a closeup of just Maria and me. We rehearsed it until about 11 o'clock, and then the director Roy William Neill said, "Okay, let's shoot." Maria snapped, "No." Roy said, "What do you mean, *no*? Come on, we rehearsed it, everything is set, let's shoot the thing!" She said, "No. I do not look good."
>
> Roy was puzzled. "What the hell do you mean, you don't look good? Maria, you look beautiful, you are the most beautiful woman in Hollywood, in the world! Come on, let's take the goddamned shot!" Maria said, "No. No. No," and started to cry — there went the fucking makeup and everything! Roy said, "Why not?" and she said, "My astrologer told me I will not look good until one o'clock in the afternoon!"

Asked about Montez's "star temperament," Edward Norris told the authors:

> I saw some of it, and I *heard* a lot about it. I know that she had a dog that she kept in her dressing room, and they didn't like *that* idea, of cleaning *that* up. She had the idea that she was a big star. The people on the lot resented her. Because of her holding things up. That's when they finally got rid of her. But she and I got along very well, I liked her very much, I thought she was underrated. It was tragic, the way she died.

In 1951, Montez, just 31 years old, died after suffering a heart attack in the bathtub of her Paris home.

Mystery of Marie Roget was one of three Universal Horrors to employ the talents of Maria Ouspenskaya during her stint as a Hollywood character actress. Born in 1887 (if you want to be the first to believe the date on her grave marker), Ouspenskaya had hopes of becoming a coloratura singer in her native Russia before turning her attention to the theater. As a stock company player she toured the Russian provinces and later fell in with the method actors of Stanislavsky's Moscow Art Theater. She appeared

Movie director turned actor Lloyd Corrigan as the bumbling Prefect Gobelin in *Mystery of Marie Roget* (courtesy John Cocchi).

in scores of stage plays and in a half-dozen silent Russian films before making her American stage debut in the mid-1920s. Remaining in America, she continued to work in the theater and founded her own acting school in 1929.* Ouspenskaya made her American film debut in 1936's *Dodsworth* (reprising her stage role) and was Oscar-nominated for her performance, although she lost out to another screen newcomer, Gale Sondergaard, who won the Best Supporting Actress award for *Anthony Adverse*.

Dodsworth was the first of 20 Hollywood film roles for the 90-pound Ouspenskaya, who went back and forth between prestige pictures (*Conquest*, *Love Affair*, *Waterloo Bridge*, *Kings Row*) and B flicks (*Judge Hardy and Son*, *Tarzan and the Amazons*— the latter featuring Madame as the world's shortest Amazon). She is not used to good advantage in *Marie Roget*: As Mme. Roget she alternates between annoyingly cagey and annoyingly cranky, and her infirm appearance and mannerisms rule her out as a suspect. Then there's that face that only Mother could love, and *then* only if Mother was blind in one eye and couldn't see out of the other. In November 1949 Ouspenskaya fell asleep with a lit cigarette, and died from the burns and a subsequent stroke three days later. Nell O'Day reminisced for us:

> Mme. Ouspenskaya was a *real* actress — she had been acting and teaching all her long life. She and I had those scenes with Lisa, the leopard, on the hearth rug beside us. I think we were the only people on the set who were not nervous about that. I was asked more than once if I was nervous, and I quite truthfully said that I *liked* all animals — they could see that I was not afraid. Mme. Ouspenskaya appeared so tiny and vulnerable in her wheelchair, the entire crew looked worried. After all, Lisa *was* a real leopard! The assistant cameraman came to the edge of the set and said quietly, "Madame, are you afraid?" In her deep contralto voice, Maria Ouspenskaya replied in a fashion that settled the entire question: "I am not afraid of *any-sing*!"

A polished B production, *Mystery of Marie Roget* achieves a more expensive look through the liberal use of handsome standing sets. Lighting and camerawork combine to create a convincing nineteenth century ambience, while director Philip Rosen keeps his players moving and talking at a fast clip. Rosen had helmed some major productions during the silent era, but spent most of his talkie career heading up cheapies for Poverty Row studios like Chesterfield, Liberty, Invincible, Mascot and (especially) Monogram. His other horror credits include *Spooks Run Wild* (1941) with Bela Lugosi and *Return of the Ape Man* (1944) with Lugosi and John

**"Oh, the old lady," Edward Norris scoffed when we asked about working with Ouspenskaya. "Very difficult to understand. She was a dramatic teacher, and [*laughs*] I thought, 'My God. How the hell could anybody understand what she was telling 'em?' How could she teach when you couldn't even understand her English? Terrible! She was very 'important' to herself, and I didn't cotton to that. I thought [*dismissively*], 'Well, so what? She's important to herself. That's good. She's not to me!'" [*Laughs*]*

Carradine. "Rosen was a good director — very good," Edward Norris told the authors. "First I did *Mystery of Marie Roget* with him, and then I did three or four with him *after* that, he kept requesting me. So he was a very nice guy, and he had a lot of talent, *I* thought." (Norris' next picture for Rosen, begun just a few weeks after *Marie Roget* wrapped, was *The Man with Two Lives*, Monogram's *Black Friday* rip-off, with Norris starring as the Jekyll-Hyde killer.)

For a low-budget picture, *Roget* does a good job of pulling you into its time and place; Elwood Bredell's photography and lighting (and *lack* of lighting) go a long way toward giving the proceedings that aura of authenticity. Bredell has an interesting "let the shadows fall where they may" attitude (even across faces), there are eye-catching shafts of light in a garden scene, some backlighting, and a number of interesting compositions; the courtroom and Mme. Roget's living room appear to have been lit for an audience of bats. Insuring that you never forget for a moment that you're watching a Universal B, we see pre-existing sets (and European Street) and hear music written for other pictures (Franz Waxman's *The Invisible Ray* Paris music establishes the Paris setting, the waltz music in the party scene is from the '41 *Back Street*, etc.).

Although fans rarely think to call *Marie Roget* a sequel to Universal's *Murders in the Rue Morgue*, it surely is; in fact, *Roget's Rue Morgue*–like beginning (a woman's body found in the Seine), middle (Dupin investigates) and end (a Paris rooftop chase) raise the possibility that writer Jacoby screened the Lugosi flick before tackling the new script. Here, however, a lot of the horror stuff has an unfortunate out-of-left-field quality. It's never explained why Vigneaux murders Marie, nor why he disfigures her face before dumping her body in the river. Although it makes sense that he mutilated the face of the first victim (his wife), his indulging in this sadistic excess a second time with Marie seems ill-advised, and would serve only to eventually link him with the *earlier* murder. Vigneaux hopes to win a courtroom acquittal by maintaining that, in order to protect Camille, he murdered Marie, ripped off her face and chucked her corpse in the river, a courtroom strategy than sounds like it'd be a non-starter anywhere but California.

The fact that Dupin is able to ascertain that the late Marie had a criminal nature through an examination of her brain sounds quaint and preposterous, but modern research shows that Dupin may have been ahead of his time. In a recent study, it was determined that 21 men with violent criminal histories all had the same brain defect, a reduced amount of gray matter in the prefrontal lobe, just behind the eyes. This part of the brain is known to be involved in judgment and impulse control. Held up as the poster boy for the "blame the brain" crowd: Texas mass murderer Charles Whitman, who killed 16 people during a 1966 sniper attack at the University of Texas in Austin (the basis for the 1968 Boris Karloff movie *Targets*). Following Whitman's death by police bullets, an autopsy revealed a tumor deep in an area of the brain associated with rage.

Mystery of Marie Roget is not a horror film, despite Universal's campaign to palm it off as such, and it tips its hand far too soon to cut muster as a solid whodunit. But judged strictly for what it does deliver — 60 minutes of adventuresome sleuthing, flavored with mystery and mild horror embellishments — it's a good example of Universal's B-unit working at peak efficiency.

As a closing "aside": Edward Norris never made a movie with Maria Montez's frequent sword-and-sandal co-star Jon Hall but, according to Norris, he and Hall were friends — and he may have saved Hall's life. Late one night in 1944, after first wetting their whistles at the Macombo, a group of well-lubricated actors, actresses and other Hollywood types (including Norris and bandleader Tommy Dorsey) weren't yet ready for beddy when the nightclub closed, and so they moved the party to Dorsey's apartment. There, after many *more* adult beverages had been dispensed, Norris was startled to see Dorsey bending Hall backwards over the third-floor balcony rail, trying to drop him to the cement below!

The fight had begun in the kitchen, when Dorsey thought he overheard Hall making a pass at his (Dorsey's) actress-wife Patricia Dane — when what Dorsey had *actually* heard was Hall talking on the telephone to *his* wife, Frances Langford. Shockingly, Dorsey came up with a knife and attacked Hall. As Dorsey tried to pitch Hall off the balcony, Norris joined the fray. Norris told the authors:

Mystery of Marie Roget **(the on-screen title does not have the *The* in front) was inspired by a Poe story which was inspired by a real-life 1841 murder — the latter recently examined in depth in the book *The Beautiful Cigar Girl* by Daniel Stashower.**

I pulled Dorsey off of him, but now I saw that the tip of Hall's nose had been cut off, and it was hanging on the side of his cheek. And so [*laughs*] — so I beat up Dorsey! Then I took Hall downstairs, so that he could get to the hospital, to take care of his face. I shouldn't have gone back up ... I could have just gone away and everything would have been fine [*laughs*] ... but I figured Dorsey had destroyed him, I thought Hall's features would never be the same. You don't cut a man up who's working in the motion picture business. So I went back up, and when the doors opened I got hit with brass knuckles by ... oh, I'm trying to think of his name ... he was a gangster, he was that Vegas gangster ... [*Bugsy Siegel?*] That's the guy.

Then Bugsy Siegel stood back, and Dorsey jumped on top of me, 'cause I was flat [on the floor] in the hallway. But as we wrestled around, I got my consciousness, and we rolled down the staircase ... and then I went on top and luckily was bangin' *his* head [*laughs*], so *he* was going unconscious. By this time everybody was saying "Call the police!" and they were calling the police and [*laughs*] calling the firemen — they called *every*body! Three of 'em took me out to my car and told me to get the hell out. Quick. They wanted me to get out of there, because they thought Bugsy Siegel was gonna kill me. And he probably would have. Oh [*laughs*], it was a ... [*More laughs*] Oh, it was a mess [*laughs*]!

And here *we* thought that Movies Are Your Best Entertainment...!

Critics' Corner

Rating: Fair. [T]here has been no original thought expended on lines and direction. Thus, both conversationally and in business, [the picture] moves with the pat assurance of a routine quickie. In point of fact, despite the famous author, the better-than-average cast and the singing of Maria Montez, that is exactly what it is. — *The New York Post*, May 5, 1942, Archer Winsten

[B]utchered retelling of [Poe].... [A] dreary, aimless film, devoid of logic or excitement or even a shadow of suspense. Vaguely it leaves an impression of wretched futility. — *The New York Times*, May 5, 1942, Bosley Crowther

Rating: ★★½ [A] fair-middling mystery thriller.... With a little more care spent on the script to clear up the reasons for the second murder and with a tighter hand on the directorial reins to keep the mystery running smoothly and suspensefully through the film, this story of Poe's might have been built into a first class thriller. — *The New York Daily News*, May 5, 1942, Kate Cameron

[I]t is done with a modern flavor to play down much of the mustry [*sic*] tang of the 19th Century. Even in the sequences involving horse-drawn cabriolets, the pace is in the Hollywood manner, swift and melodramatic.... [A] considerably better than average murder mystery.... — *The Film Daily*, April 3, 1942

Outside of a brief horse-and-carriage chase and some last-minute gunplay, there's little action in the piece, which doesn't contain much mystery, either, since the identity of the murderer is obvious all along. — *The New York Journal-American*, May 5, 1942, Rose Pelswick

[A] creaky piece. The acting is as old-fashioned as the screenplay. [It] has sound, but otherwise it might be guessed to date from silent days.... [A]s dull a piece of trash as has hit Broadway for quite a while. — *The New York Sun*, May 5, 1942, Eileen Creelman

Since Edgar Allan Poe is considered the peer of all mystery story writers, doubtless it seemed like a good idea to film his "The Mystery of Marie Roget." But what may have seemed like a great idea in theory is something else again in practice. [The movie] is dull and static and almost entirely lacking in suspense. — *The New York World-Telegram*, May 5, 1942, William Boehnel

The Strange Case of Doctor Rx

Released April 17, 1942. 66 minutes. *Director:* William Nigh. *Associate Producer:* Jack Bernhard. *Original Screenplay:* Clarence Upson Young. *Photography:* Elwood Bredell. *Assistant Director:* Vernon Keays. *Art Director:* Jack Otterson. *Associate Art Director:* Martin Obzina. *Editor:* Bernard W. Burton. *Musical Director:* Hans J. Salter. *Set Decorator:* Russell A. Gausman. *Sound Director:* Bernard B. Brown. *Technician:* Charles Carroll. *Gowns:* Vera West.

Patric Knowles (*Jerry Church*), Lionel Atwill (*Dr. Fish*), Anne Gwynne (*Kit Logan Church*), Samuel S. Hinds (*Dudley Crispin*), Mona Barrie (*Eileen Crispin*), Shemp Howard (*Det. Sgt. Sweeney*), Paul Cavanagh (*John Crispin*), Edmund MacDonald (*Det. Capt. Bill Hurd*), Mantan Moreland (*Horatio B. Fitzwashington*), John Gallaudet (*Ernie Paul*), William Gould (*D.A. Nason*), Leyland Hodgson (*Thomas*), Mary Gordon (*Mrs. Scott*), Jan Wiley (*Lily*), Boyd Davis (*Police Commissioner*), Gary Breckner (*Radio Announcer*), Matty Fain (*Tony Zarini*), Eddy Chandler (*Policeman*), Ray "Crash" Corrigan (*Inbongo*), Victor Zimmerman (*Kirk*), Harry Harvey (*Night Club Manager*), Selmer Jackson (*Judge*), Paul Bryar (*Bailiff*), Joe Recht, Leonard Sues (*Newsboys*), Drew Demarest (*Club Waiter*), Leonard Sues (*Second Newsboy*), Jack Kennedy, Jack C. Smith (*Policemen*), Frank Austin (*Jury Foreman*).

... Couldn't Scare a Baby
— *Wanda Hale,* The New York Daily News, *March 28, 1942*

The Strange Case of Doctor Rx is a movie with an identity problem: It can't quite make up its mind whether it is a detective mystery or a horror film. It has all the basic ingredients of your standard B mystery — flip private eye, hardboiled dame, the usual sideline comic relief, and enough red herrings for two pictures. But, being a Universal picture, released in the midst of its second great horror cycle, its producers couldn't resist tossing in some misplaced chiller effects for a healthier box office return. There's a megacriminal who polishes off his adversaries with poisoned darts, a captive ape awaiting a brain transplant, and the threat of a terror so great it turns men's hair white from fright. And, it has Lionel Atwill creeping around the corners of the plot looking sinister in thick-lensed glasses, but doing very little else. Even the ad campaign, highlighted by a huge head shot of Lionel in a grimacing pose, was deliberately aimed at the shock trade.

Clocking in at a little over an hour, *The Strange Case of Doctor Rx* is too inconsequential to be considered anything more than a minor miscalculation. It's far-fetched and preposterous, in the affable way *The Mummy's Hand* and *Man Made Monster* are. On the other hand, the whole affair strikes a ludicrous pose. We get the impression that no one, from the actors to those behind the cameras, believed in it for a minute.

The Strange Case of Doctor Rx went before the cameras on October 6, 1941. Jack Bernhard, who had done a competent job mounting *Man Made Monster* the year before, was put in charge of production, and William Nigh was assigned to direct. Nigh certainly knew the motion picture business inside and out. During the course of his long Hollywood career, he edited, produced and directed, wrote scripts, and even acted. Nigh was at the director's helm on the fine Lon Chaney vehicle, *Mr. Wu* (1927). In addition, he guided Karloff through the entire series of Mr. Wong detective mysteries at Monogram, as well as directing the slumming horror star in the same studio's tepid 1940 thriller, *The Ape*. *Doctor Rx* reunited Nigh and gorilla impersonator Ray "Crash" Corrigan for a second go at simian shenanigans. Corrigan was the proud possessor of one of the best ape suits in the business (for proof of this, just check out Emil Van Horn's pitiful costume/ape impersonations in such films as *Keep 'Em Flying* [1941] and Lugosi's criminally abysmal *The Ape Man* [1943]).

Originally entitled *Dr. RX*, the picture underwent a title change in short order, possibly so it wouldn't be confused with the 1932 Warner Bros. classic, *Doctor X*. Bernhard signed Patric Knowles and Anne Gwynne as the amiable (and photogenic) leads and secured the services of Lionel Atwill for the part of Dr. Fish, the film's reddest herring. His insultingly brief role amounts to little more than a cameo, wasting his wonderful facility for screen mayhem.

As the picture opens, the police are investigating the fifth in a series of baffling murders in which the victims, all previously acquitted of various felony charges, have been struck down by an unknown avenger who calls himself Dr. Rx. Capt. Bill Hurd of Homicide (Edmund MacDonald) tries to enlist the aid of his close friend and former partner Jerry Church (Patric Knowles), now working as a private investigator. Church turns Hurd down cold.... He has decided to quit the racket once and for all and join his family's bond business ("Did you say blonde business?" interjects Hurd).

Church is summoned to the Long Island estate of wealthy criminal lawyer Dudley Crispin (Samuel S. Hinds). Crispin had defended three of the murdered men in court, and is upset by his current shortage of clients.

Church's on again-off again fiancée, Kit Logan (Anne Gwynne), a mystery writer-amateur sleuth, reappears after a long absence, and immediately takes charge of Jerry's affairs. After a quickie marriage (tossed in, no doubt, to appease the Breen Office watchdogs), Kit uses her influence to get Jerry to drop the case. (Dr. Rx has just claimed his sixth victim, right in the middle of a crowded courtroom.) Kit's fears are compounded after she visits the home of a former detective who has become a jibbering, white-haired idiot following a face-to-face encounter with the crazed medico. All of this beautiful exposition only increases our displeasure with the disappointments to come.

After much ado, Jerry finally agrees to Kit's demands. But, before the newlyweds can hop a train to Boston, Church is kidnapped by a gang of thugs led by Ernie Paul (John Gallaudet). Ernie is irate because the police have tagged him Suspect #1 for the last Rx murder (the victim was a gangland rival of his). He forces Jerry to resume his investigation and exonerate him ... or else.

Jerry and his valet, Horatio (Mantan Moreland), are abducted by a cowled stranger, Dr. Rx himself. Knocked unconscious, Church awakens to find himself strapped to an operating table opposite a restless caged ape (Ray Corrigan). Dr. Rx, his identity concealed behind a surgical smock and hood, details the motive behind his bizarre homicides. "For every crime there is a punishment. Men who sin must pay a just penalty." And then, in his best bedside manner, he adds, "You see Inbongo — he is very stupid but he will be very smart. And you will be, well, not so smart. In other words, I am going to transfer your brains."

The good doctor attaches one end of the ape's chain to Jerry's table, then watches with grim satisfaction as the curious Inbongo pulls the helpless detective closer to his cage. Church blacks out. The next morning, the police discover Church and Horatio wandering aimlessly around the waterfront, their hair turned dead white.

The District Attorney (William Gould) gathers everyone connected with the case around the unconscious detective's hospital bed. Dr. Fish (Lionel Atwill), a stranger who has been seen following Jerry around town, is called forth to provide medical testimony. He turns to Crispin and requests the use of his pen. Visibly shaken, the attorney removes the pen from his pocket, points it towards his chest, then drops dead. Church leaps out of his bed (dropping his phony white hairpiece), but he is too late to prevent the suicide.

Don't let the evil glare fool you; Lionel Atwill is a mere red herring in the horror-mystery *The Strange Case of Doctor Rx.*

Later, Jerry and Doc Fish (who, we learn, had been working with Church all along) explain the foggy details of the case to the bewildered Hurd. "The man had two phobias," Fish states. "Number one, he was an egomaniac with a desire to mesmerize a jury and get his client acquitted. Number two, he wanted to punish the criminal himself." (May we please have a hand count of those readers who think a Dr. Rx–type should be posted in California courtrooms whenever a high-profile celebrity criminal trial is conducted?) Crispin's instrument of murder was a pen that projected poisonous darts which left no trace on the victim's body. Jerry noticed the strange-looking pen amongst Dr. Rx's lab instruments. Another tip-off was the manner in which the lawyer signed his name — Dudley Crispin. The misplaced capital "R" matched that appearing in the Rx murder notes tagged on each victim's corpse.

With a more coherent script, a plausible denouement, and less ham-fisted humor by fourth Stooge Shemp Howard, *The Strange Case of Doctor Rx* might have amounted to something more than just a barely passable time killer. The germ of a good idea is there, but Clarence Upson Young disinfects it by overloading his screenplay with irritating detours and extraneous details. The story's horror elements are, to put it charitably, patently absurd. Poison dart-throwing pens have never numbered amongst Hollywood's more credible murder weapons. (The 1939 *The House of Fear* featured a similar gizmo; so did the 1943 serial *The Adventures of Smilin' Jack.* A poison dart serial killer also figured prominently in the plot of the Universal's 1945 comedy-mystery *She Gets Her Man* with Joan Davis.) The poison that Crispin used "strangled" the victim after it had entered the bloodstream. Granted, this method proved to be successful, but wouldn't it have been more practical for the deranged advocate to eliminate his foes in a dozen more convenient ways? It also seems highly unlikely that Crispin would go to such outlandish lengths to silence savvy investigators when a simple bullet in the brain would have been just as effective (not to mention saving him the cost of maintaining Kenneth Strickfaden's electrical apparatus and a live gorilla!). Casting the venera-

That's Ray "Crash" Corrigan in the ape costume, menacing Anne Gwynne.

ble Samuel S. Hinds as the "surprise" villain was a smart move though it's doubtful the actor actually played Dr. Rx in the abduction and laboratory sequences. (In 1949's *Abbott and Costello Meet the Killer, Boris Karloff*, the *real* villain of the piece, Alan Mowbray — or more likely a stuntman — pursues Lou through the underground caverns dressed in a similar white lab smock and hood as that worn by Dr. Rx.)

Patric Knowles and Anne Gwynne turn in

their usual amiable performances as the comfortably laid-back detective and his inquisitive wife (their friends call the bickering pair the "Battling Churches"). Knowles, Gwynne and costar Edmund MacDonald have such a good chemistry going here it's quite probable that with better scripts and directors, a Jerry Church mystery-thriller series might have caught on. In an interview, the late actress enthused to the authors, "I loved working with Patric Knowles. So very tall and handsome. A Britisher and very nice — but married. He and I also worked together in *Sin Town* [1942]."

Knowles, who was on a Royal Canadian Air Force furlough when he made *The Strange Case of Doctor Rx*, had the kind of easy-does-it, unassuming charm that made him perfectly suited as the second lead or the hero's best friend. A former member of Dublin's Abbey Players, he was put under contract at Warner Bros., RKO, Republic, Paramount, and of course Universal (where he enjoyed working despite the fact he was once suspended by the studio after they refused to allow him to do a Broadway play). Knowles confirmed to the authors a claim made by Anne Gwynne that a good share of the dialogue in *The Strange Case of Doctor Rx* was improvised by the actors who were forced to work with an incomplete script. ("Yes, we all contributed," he told us.)

Anne Gwynne found working on *The Strange Case of Doctor Rx* a pleasantly unique experience:

> [Making the film was] fun, fun, fun ... it was done off-the-cuff. I would go home at night and study my lines, only to arrive the next morning to learn that everything was thrown out! It didn't take me too many nights to know to just go home and relax — there was no telling what to expect the next day — but it was an anxious-to-get-to-the-studio feeling, that was for sure. Like in *The Black Cat* [1941], the ad-libs were used, only much more so. Each of us would suggest things, and the director, William Nigh, would use them. That was just great, an experience I never had before or since. Of course, as a result, there are some plot loopholes in the finished product, but who cares? It was an hour of laughs and chills, a real crowd-pleaser.

"Working with Anne was a great joy," Knowles fondly reminisced. "Lionel Atwill and I shared dirty stories! I retired fifteen years ago. Nowadays people ask me, 'Didn't you use to be Patric Knowles?' They nearly always add, 'Never got the girl, did you?'!" Knowles passed away in Woodland Hills, California, from a brain hemorrhage on December 23, 1995.

In the tradition of the period's great detective series, Clarence Upson Young abuses that frequently misused ingredient known as "comedy relief." Black comic Mantan Moreland is made the butt of the kind of racist humor so prevalent at this time. His valet-servant-gofer Horatio is presumably so dense, he's forced to resort to "thought association" tricks in order to keep track of his menial duties. ("Airport ... airplane ... clouds ... birds ... nest ... eggs ... *breakfast!*") This good-natured degradation has an unpleasant, rather sinister pay-off: Poor Horatio suffers the fate intended for Church. Cackling like a madman, his hair turned white from fright, Moreland has the dubious honor of closing the film just before the final credits flash across the screen. Unlike the insufferable antics minority actors such as Stepin Fetchit and Willie Best were forced to endure during their movie careers, Moreland's bug-eyed, scaredy-cat shtick in *The Strange Case of Doctor Rx*, Monogram's *King of the Zombies* (1941), *Revenge of the Zombies* (1943) and the Poverty Row outfit's Charlie Chan B-programmers of the mid-to-late '40s, is often quite funny. Moreland effectively "sends up" the material he is saddled with rather than being victimized by it; his comedic contributions to these movies help to relieve the tedium of some pretty dreary scripts.

Slickly made, nominally entertaining, but at the core erratic and absurd, *The Strange Case of Doctor Rx* is a decidedly lesser light in Universal's galaxy of horror.

Critics' Corner

The film [is] a better than average B from Universal.... William Nigh's direction is fast paced, in the accepted whodunit tempo.—*The New York Post*, March 28, 1942, Irene Thirer

Every studio has its favorite B-picture recipe. Here is Universal's: one penthouse set, preserved from *Top of the Town*; one eerie Long Island estate, complete with mastiff; one Karloff-model metaphysio-diathermy apparatus, with automatic brain-changer; one gorilla, in good fur; one dumb cop (Shemp Howard); one smart cop (Pat Knowles); one blonde (Anne Gwynne). Add corpses to taste.—*PM New York*, March 31, 1942, John T. McManus

I don't know who played the gorilla, but he was the most convincing actor in the cast.—*The New York Sun*, March 28, 1942

Rating: ★★ It's gory, but unreasonable and disconnected—like a nightmare. The comedy is flat, the direction choppy, and what the story proves is beyond us. Maybe you can get it; we didn't.—*The New York Daily News*, March 28, 1942, Wanda Hale

[A] collection of babbled clues, butlers at windows and gloomy manses, mysterious messages, stupid policemen, leers by Lionel Atwill and matrimonial badinage ... most of which is beside the point.—*The New York Times*, March 28, 1942, Theodore Strauss

This is a horrible example of a horror picture, or whatever it was meant to be, but a good example of a production that should not have been made in the first place. The story is unintelligible, it leads nowhere, and ends in the same place.—*Harrison's Reports*, April 4, 1942

The tortuous course of the plot is so complicated and muddled [the audience] will be lucky if they can unravel the whole mess at all. As per formula, one of the mildest in the parade of characters turns out to be the louse.—*The Film Daily*, April 2, 1942

Invisible Agent

Released July 31, 1942. 79 minutes. A Frank Lloyd Production. *Director:* Edwin L. Marin. *Associate Producer:* George Waggner. *Screenplay:* Curt Siodmak. *Suggested by the novel* The Invisible Man *by* H.G. Wells. *Photography:* Les White. *Special Photographic Effects:* John P. Fulton. *Editor:* Edward Curtiss. *Art Director:* Jack Otterson. *Associate Art Director:* Robert Boyle. *Assistant Director:* Vernon Keays. *Musical Director:* Hans J. Salter. *Set Decorator:* Russell A. Gausman. *Associate Set Decorator:* Edward R. Robinson. *Director of Sound:* Bernard B. Brown. *Technician:* William Hedgcock. *Gowns:* Vera West.

Ilona Massey (*Maria Sorenson/Maria Goodrich*), Jon Hall (*Frank Raymond/Frank Griffin*), Peter Lorre (*Baron Ikito*), Sir Cedric Hardwicke (*Conrad Stauffer*), J. Edward Bromberg (*Karl Heiser*), Albert Basserman (*Arnold Schmidt*). John Litel (*John Gardiner*), Holmes Herbert (*Sir Alfred Spencer*), Keye Luke (*Surgeon*), Philip Van Zandt (*Nazi S.S. Man*), Matt Willis (*Nazi Assassin*), Mabel Colcord (*Maid*), John Holland (*Spencer's Secretary*), Marty Faust (*Killer*), Alberto Morin (*Free Frenchman*), Wolfgang Zilzer (*van Porten*), Ferdinand Munier (*Bartender*), Eddie Dunn, Hans Schumm (*S.S. Men*), John Burton (*RAF Flier*), Lee Tung-Foo (*General Chin Lee*), Milburn Stone (*German Sergeant*), Michael Visaroff (*Verichen*), Walter Tetley (*Newsboy*), Pat West (*German Taxi Driver*), Leslie Denison (*British Radio Operator*), William Ruhl, Otto Reichow (*Gestapo Agents*), Pat McVey (*German*), Wally Scott, Bobby Hale (*English Tommies*), Charles Flynn, Phil Warren, Paul Bryar, John Merton (*German Soldiers*), Lee Shumway (*Brigadier General*), Henry Zynda (*Colonel Kelenski*), Ferdinand Schumann-Heink (*German Telephone Operator*), Victor Zimmerman, Bill Pagan, Henry Guttman (*Storm Troopers*), Lane Chandler, Duke York, Donald Curtis (*German Sentries*), Charles Regan (*Ordnance Car Driver*), Sven Hugo-Borg (*German Captain*), James Craven (*Ship's Radio Man*), Eddie Parker (*Stunts*).

The Phantom Commando—Striking Terror
Into the Very Heart of Germany
—*Ad blurb for* Invisible Agent

By 1942, Hollywood was swept into the war in earnest with each studio pitching in to boost morale at home with a spate of slick propaganda pieces. Overnight, the cynicism of the '30s was replaced by the flag-waving of the '40s. Poverty Row outfits began to inject war-related themes into their action pictures and it wasn't long before horror and propaganda merged into an uncomfortable hybrid. The result was a subgenre of wartime horror flicks. These dubious exercises in patriotism thrived at Monogram where such clinkers as *King of the Zombies* (1941), *Black Dragons* (1942) and *Revenge of the Zombies* (1943) established the formula of a mad scientist who moonlights for the Third Reich. A bit of war talk was ineffectually shoehorned into PRC's *The Mad Monster* (1942) featuring George Zucco as a batty doctor working for *our* side who tries to convince his peers that the way to win the war is to breed an army of werewolves! Even Warner Bros. got into the act with a borderline horror opus, *The Gorilla Man* (1943) and the atmospheric *The Mysterious Doctor* (1943), which had a Nazi agent stirring up trouble in the disguise of a headless ghost.

On the whole, these features were a pretty poor lot but Universal's contribution to the subgenre was a cut above average. Announced as *The Invisible Spy* early in 1942, the picture was released under the slightly modified title *Invisible Agent.* Frank Lloyd and Jack Skirball, the team responsible for Alfred Hitchcock's *Saboteur,* one of the studio's few prestige releases that year, were the picture's original producers. But Skirball dropped out of the project and George Waggner was assigned the title associate producer.

The Scottish-born Lloyd (whose name was misspelled *Llloyd* in the main titles) was a big-time director with a decidedly elusive style. Although a polished craftsman, most of his films are best remembered for the contributions of others. He won an Oscar in 1933 for *Cavalcade*, a straightforward adaptation of a hit Noël Coward play. *Mutiny on the Bounty* (1935) is noted for the flinty chemistry of Charles Laughton and Clark Gable, and *If I Were King* (1938) for Preston Sturges' witty dialogue. Lloyd, if nothing else, had to his credit an unflinching eye for talent and uncommonly good taste until this inexplicable lapse. In 1942, he produced a couple of Universal's more ambitious features, including the John Wayne–Marlene Dietrich vehicle *The Spoilers*. How his participation in a follow-up to *The Invisible Woman* came about is anyone's guess.

Although *Invisible Agent* was promoted as a straight-faced war melodrama, the film is very much a tongue-in-cheek affair. With a plot out of a Saturday matinee serial, the film's major character is an invisible commando who parachutes over enemy lines to fight the Nazis in typical superhero fashion. The studio's decision to upgrade the potboiler storyline into a minor A production with a prominent producer and a strong cast might have been owing to the fact that H.G. Wells was still a literary figure to be reckoned with and that Universal's contract with the author's estate was still in effect. The film proved to be the most successful of the studio's Invisible Man sequels with profits surpassing the $1,000,000 mark.

Unlike the last two films in the Invisible Man franchise whose main titles unfold in rather gimmicky fashion (dissolving animation lettering in *The Invisible Man Returns*, a disappearing shadow of a girl in *The Invisible Woman*), the credits of *Invisible Agent* are merely functional with titles superimposed over bland cityscape artwork. Frank Griffin (Jon Hall), grandson of the Invisible Man, runs a modest Manhattan print shop under an assumed name. The first scene is a good one. Four suspicious-looking men enter the shop on the premise of conducting routine business. A confrontation ensues as one of the men produces a pistol, informing Griffin he is aware of his true identity. The gentleman is Conrad Stauffer (Sir Cedric Hardwicke), a top dog in Hitler's S.S. (The film has a curious aversion to awarding ranks to its military characters, but Stauffer appears to be a general.) Stauffer explains that he and his Japanese companion, Baron Ikito (Peter Lorre), are seeking Griffin's invisibility formula and are prepared to use force in order to obtain it. Griffin barely avoids having his fingers lopped off in a paper cropper by Stauffer's strong-arm men and manages to escape with the secret formula still in his grasp.

His cover blown, Griffin is implored by government officials to turn the invisibility drug over to the military, but he refuses. With the bombing of Pearl Harbor, Griffin has a change of heart and volunteers to become an invisible spy for the Allies and parachutes over German lines.

The now-transparent Griffin locates his contact, carpenter Arnold Schmidt (Albert Basserman), who reveals that Frank's mission is to obtain a list of Japanese spies operating in the United States, now in the possession of Stauffer. Griffin dashes off to the home of Maria Sorenson (Ilona Massey), a British spy posing as a German agent and Stauffer's paramour. (The number of coincidences in the film amount to an impressive total.) With Stauffer away on government business, Maria entertains his immediate subordinate Karl Heiser (J. Edward Bromberg), who makes no secret of his affections for Maria. Griffin, who has been imbibing Heiser's champagne, takes advantage of his invisibility to harass the Nazi. Stauffer unexpectedly turns up and, sensing disloyalty, orders Heiser arrested.

Hoping to pinch the prized list of Japanese spies, Griffin arrives at Stauffer's office only to find the German officer ready and waiting for him. Frank outfoxes his adversaries, steals the list and heads for Schmidt's shop to have the invaluable information sent to England.

Griffin's next stop is Heiser's prison cell, where he forces the condemned ex-officer to reveal the date of Germany's planned bomber attack on New York. Heiser confesses that the attack is scheduled for that very night and in return is sprung from the jail. Unaware that Schmidt has been arrested by the S.S., Frank steals into the shop and is captured by Baron Ikito, who ensnares him in a net lined with razor-sharp fishhooks. Frank and Maria are whisked away to the Japanese embassy, which is soon overrun with Stauffer's men. Griffin and the girl escape in the melee as Stauffer and Ikito clash. The Japanese stabs Stauffer to death, then, realizing the depth of his failure, is honor-bound to commit hara-kiri.

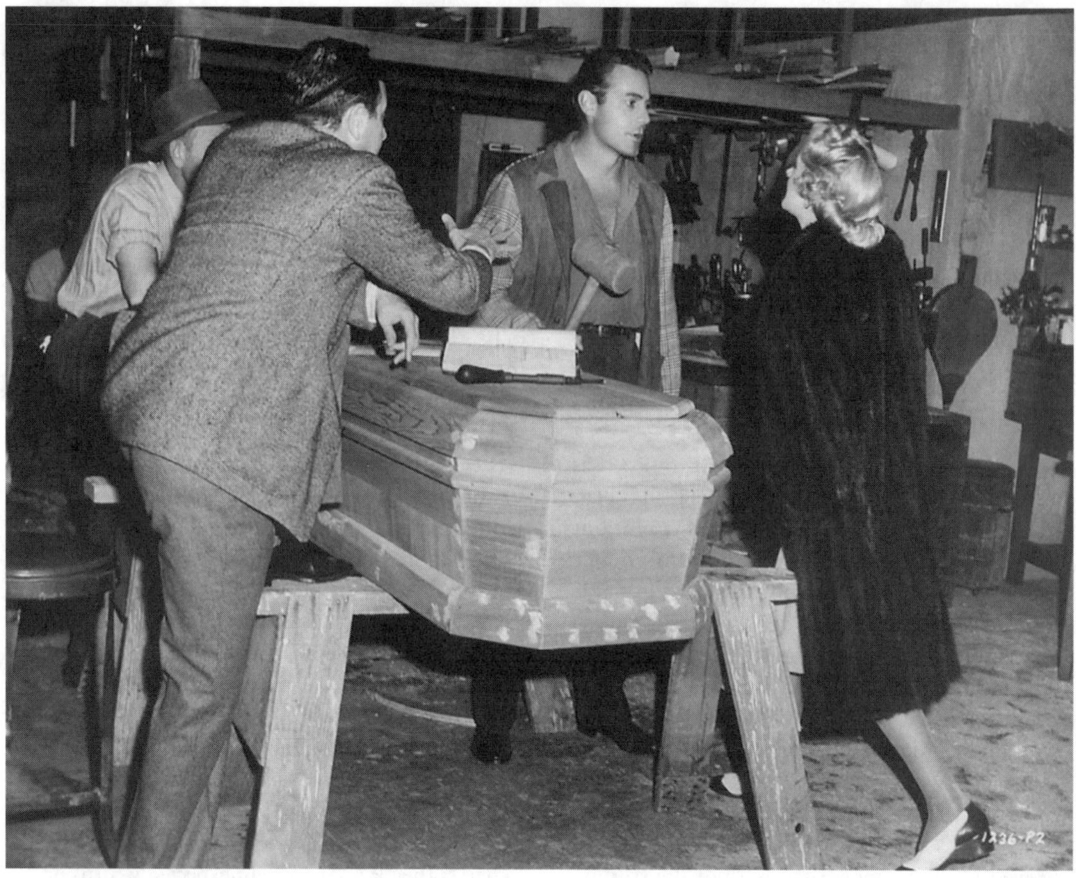

Jon Hall, the *Invisible Agent* himself, is dressed in casual street wear as he rehearses a scene with mink-clad Ilona Massey.

Making their way to the airfield, Griffin and Maria commandeer one of the bombers earmarked for the New York air raid. They drop a load of explosives on the rest of the fleet, as Heiser is cut down by Stauffer's assassins. In a romantic wrap-up, Griffin is restored to visibility and is reunited with Maria.

H.G. Wells was officially credited as the inspiration for this film, but the real auteur of *Invisible Agent* is scenarist Curt Siodmak. For a writer who had recently fled from his native Germany, Siodmak takes a rather cavalier attitude towards his foes. Most of the time, the German military are sadly reminiscent of the bumbling Nazi buffoons of television's infamous *Hogan's Heroes.* At least one reviewer questioned the wisdom of downplaying the diabolical nature of the enemy even though Ernst Lubitsch was doing much the same thing at the same time in *To Be or Not to Be* (1942). Siodmak contributes a decent, action-oriented script with occasional patches of good dialogue. In a dinner scene, Bromberg fetes Massey with the culinary delicacies from countries recently plundered by the Fatherland. "Every country we conquer feeds us," he boasts, though wincing painfully at a tin of Russian caviar. "Very hard to get!" he pointedly comments in an obvious reference to the Russian resistance.

Siodmak's humor, unfortunately, is more often than not heavy-handed although one doesn't quite know what to make of a highly dubious pressbook claim which refers to a scene in which Griffin plants his foot into the seat of Hitler's pants. (Supposedly, the episode was cut owing to a Hollywood edict that forbade making enemy dictators the target of personal attacks.)

Still, the anti–Nazi sentiments run deeply and, in some cases, forcefully. The longest speech in the film comes when the invisible Hall taunts Bromberg in his prison cell with a blistering tirade (which somehow escapes the notice of roaming German prison guards stationed within earshot). More to the point is a scene in which Hardwicke insists that the battered Albert Basserman sign a release form after an official interrogation (in real life, he no doubt would have been shot). Hardly in a position to handle a pen, Basserman declines, holding up to Hardwicke the gnarled, broken fingers he incurred in his brutal session with German guards. Interestingly, for all the blatant propaganda present in the film, Siodmak was perhaps too cynical to indulge in a lot of mawkish, jingoistic flag-waving for the Allies, preferring to keep the blistering anti–Nazi tract front and center.

Surprisingly, Griffin proves on many occasions to be a less-than-ideal hero. An amateur spy, he isn't particularly resourceful and is downright boorish in his groundless suspicion of Maria's loyalty. Indeed, he seems more interested in stomping on toes, kicking ass and pulling chairs out from under ever-fumbling Nazi stooges than in getting down to the serious business of undercover work. The script seesaws precariously between Griffin's prankish behavior and scenes of casual cruelty, such as when he's ensnared by Ikito in a net lined with monstrously oversized fish hooks. By the climax, the film almost totters into farce as Maria, clad in furs, is whisked away in midair by the invisible Griffin amid a rabble of dumbstruck German soldiers.

Far and away the best thing about *Invisible Agent* is the casting of Sir Cedric Hardwicke and Peter Lorre as representatives of the Axis. Their scenes are a casebook example of how a bit of stylish acting can transcend routinely written roles. Siodmak couches both characters well within the guidelines of wartime stereotypes: Hardwicke, the steely, ruthless German; Lorre, the insidious, cat-like Japanese with a sadistic streak a mile wide. While Hardwicke never seemed engaged in his horror assignments, here, perhaps because he found a soul mate in Lorre, he gives an almost relaxed performance that's attuned to the humor of the script. Together, they nimbly go through their scenes as if sharing a private joke, invariably sending up the material. At one point, Hardwicke momentarily drops his dignity, answering Lorre with an exaggerated, almost asinine grin, probably thinking it would never make the final cut. Lorre projects an amused detachment to all the "Heil, Hitler!" business surrounding him, at last responding with a comic half-hearted "Heil" himself which may or may not have been in the script. He acts under a pasty Asian facial makeup reminiscent of his Mr. Moto get-up in the 20th Century–Fox series in the late '30s, but the similarities are only skin-deep. Lorre gives in to his ironic sense of humor instead of his usual cute and condescending turn as the gap-toothed detective.

A partnership of convenience, Stauffer and Ikito's alliance is an uneasy one at best, roughly parallel to actual German-Japanese relations at the time. At every opportunity, Siodmak depicts them as cutthroats plotting against each other whenever the other's back is turned, their feigned politeness hinting at the mutual contempt lurking beneath the surface. When both rivals fail to deliver the Invisible Man to their governments, Ikito is bound by custom to do the only "honorable thing," disemboweling Stauffer with a hara-kiri knife before turning it on himself. The camera lingers on both their bodies in a bitter political statement that's easily the strongest scene in the film.

Ilona Massey is well cast as Maria and Jon Hall is adequate in the title role. Hall would soon prove to be one of Universal's most valuable players. The second film under his contract, *Invisible Agent* was completed a few weeks prior to the shooting of *Arabian Nights* (1942), the movie that kicked off his teaming with Maria Montez. It was an association that lasted four years and encompassed a half-dozen movies; their gloriously garish Technicolor adventures were popular escapist fare in their day and are still considered milestones of camp by those who have the endurance to sit through them. Hall was set to join the Diplomatic Corps before being spotted by a talent scout, and later claimed he became an actor mostly for the money. Like most stars who built their careers on how well they looked in a bathing suit, Hall was hardly a major talent but proved to be a likable if somewhat wooden leading man.

Hungarian-born J. Edward Bromberg had a background in New York's Group Theater before going Hollywood, where he found himself

Secret agent Hall creates a cold cream mask to make himself more presentable to Massey in this series of shots.

playing mostly smarmy Europeans. As the weaseling, mustachioed Heiser (for whatever peculiar reason, Universal seemed to think that exact physical type was ideal to serve as the Invisible Man's chief foil every time), Bromberg mugs excessively but captures the character's swinishness. The supporting cast is thronging with bit players in Nazi uniforms, separated into three basic groups: American actors employing *faux* German accents (Donald Curtis, Matt Willis), European actors using their own dialects (Philip Van Zandt, Otto Reichow) and Eddie Dunn, who doesn't give a damn, barking through his role as an S.S. man as if he was just another Chicago cop.

Invisible Agent is directed with larkish verve by Edwin L. Marin, who doesn't allow the horrifying reality of the World War get in the way of anyone's fun. A prolific Hollywood hack of the Lew Landers school, Marin's career was checkered with more missed opportunities than most. In 1933, he directed Reginald Owen as a pre-Basil Rathbone Sherlock Holmes in *A Study in Scarlet,* a one-shot programmer best remembered as a curiosity. Marin's version of *A Christmas Carol* (1938) for MGM reaffirms the classic status of the popular 1951 Alastair Sim version. He's best remembered by horror fans for having directed Bela Lugosi in an innocuous red-herring role in 1933's *The Death Kiss.* The director pulls the film off with verve, without taking it too seriously.

John P. Fulton's Oscar-nominated special effects aren't quite up to the series' standards Scuttling the usual bandages-and-goggles look established in previous pictures, Fulton materializes Hall in a bathrobe, sunglasses and a heavy application of cold cream. The effect is less than awe-inspiring and rather carelessly concocted since the inside of Hall's mouth including his teeth is inexplicably visible. Hall's image is frequently silhouetted in a few of his transparent appearances (a glitch which rarely occurred in the earlier films), suggesting that Fulton was probably rushed more than usual. Hall planting an invisible kiss on Ilona Massey's lips was probably one of his more daunting challenges. Again, Universal's expertise in special effects miniatures is on full display, with the bombing of an airfield scene being particularly effective.

Invisible Agent may be a maddeningly uneven film but it's still a fast-moving and entertaining package. One is swept along by its enthusiasm and pacing and some occasional powerful passages. But the picture is built on a silly premise and there are juvenile digressions to spare. The film doesn't do any great service to H.G. Wells but could be enjoyed as an interesting artifact of the war years.

Critics' Corner

[T]he studio has assembled a cast that is much too good for the nonsense on the agenda. The film's authors can be funny when they try to be, though sometimes funnier when they don't.—*Newsweek*, August 17, 1942

[F]airly entertaining.... The trick photography is handled well, but it doesn't offer anything new....—*Harrison's Reports*, August 15, 1942

Rating: ★★½ [A]musing and exciting.... [The actors] play their supporting roles capably, although none of them tries to be convincing.—*The New York Daily News*, August 6, 1942, Kate Cameron

H.G. Wells doubtless would be extremely pleased to learn that the character he imaginatively created is now engaged in confounding the Axis.... The show is all in fun and absolutely guaranteed not to give information to the enemy.... Possibly, the smartest thing about the picture is its consistent refusal to underrate the intelligence of the Gestapo and Rising Sun operatives. They are as hep to the plot as you are, this being one of the first times such [villains] have been shown as capable of adding two and two to reach a correct answer.—*The Hollywood Reporter*, July 30, 1942

All in all, this is the ordinary peace-time meller translated into wartime pattern.... The Nazis are made to look pretty stupid and beset with official rivalry, while the Japs appear like slippery villains of the old serial days.—*The Film Daily*, August 7, 1942

Sherlock Holmes and the Voice of Terror

Released September 18, 1942. 65 minutes. *Director:* John Rawlins. *Associate Producer:* Howard Benedict. *Screenplay:* Lynn Riggs & John Bright. *Adaptation:* Robert D. Andrews. *Based on the story* "The Last Bow" *by* Sir Arthur Conan Doyle. *Photography:* Elwood Bredell. *Art Director:* Jack Otterson. *Associate Art Director:* Martin Obzina. *Editor:* Russell Schoengarth. *Music:* Frank Skinner. *Music Director:* Charles Previn. *Set Decorators:* Russell A. Gausman & Edward R. Robinson. *Sound Director:* Bernard B. Brown. *Technician:* Robert Pritchard. *Technical Advisor:* Tom McKnight. *Gowns:* Vera West.

Basil Rathbone (*Sherlock Holmes*), Nigel Bruce (*Dr. John H. Watson*), Evelyn Ankers (*Kitty*), Reginald Denny (*Sir Evan Barham*), Thomas Gomez (*R.F. Meade*), Henry Daniell (*Anthony Lloyd*), Montagu Love (*Gen. Jerome Lawford*), Hillary Brooke (*Jill Grandis*), Mary Gordon (*Mrs. Hudson*), Arthur Blake (*Crosbie*), Leyland Hodgson (*Capt. Roland Shore*), Olaf Hytten (*Adm. Sir John Prentiss*), Harry Stubbs (*Taxi Driver*), Harry Cording (*Camberwell*), Robert O. Davis [Rudolph Anders] (*Schieler*), Donald Stuart (*Grady*), Leslie Denison (*London Bobby*), Robert Barron (*Gavin*), Alec Harford (*Grimes*), John Rogers (*Duggan*), Charles Jordan (*Man*), Herbert Evans (*Smithson*), John Wilde (*Heinrich*), Arthur Stenning (*English Officer*), George Sherwood (*London Cab Driver*), Gavin Muir (*BBC Radio Announcer*), Edgar Barrier (*The Voice of Terror*), Ted Billings.

People of Britain, greetings from the Third Reich. This is the voice you have learned to fear—this is the Voice of Terror.
—*Edgar Barrier in* Sherlock Holmes and the Voice of Terror

The late '30s and early '40s were the true heyday of the detective film in Hollywood, with almost every studio begetting at least one series based on a popular fictional detective. Cheap and popular entertainments, the genre thrived at second tier and Poverty Row outfits as well as at the B units of the major studios (as well as A-picture treatment at MGM for the Thin Man pictures). For years, Universal was producing a bumper crop of mysteries but their entry into the detective series sweepstakes had been a long time coming.

Sir Arthur Conan Doyle's master detective certainly had the makings of a stylish series star. Several screen versions of the enduring character had already been attempted, climaxed by 20th Century–Fox's pedigree pair of Holmes features (both released in 1939). By any standard, *The Hound of the Baskervilles* and *The Adventures of Sherlock Holmes* were top-drawer productions, marked by good casts, fine sets and journeyman direction. But it is the pairing of Basil Rathbone and Nigel Bruce as Sherlock Holmes and Dr. Watson that gives the films genuine historic interest.

The team was a popular success, but critical reservations persist to this day. Basil Rathbone brought a commanding screen presence to the role and became intractably identified with the character for decades. Dr. Watson as written by Conan Doyle was unflappable, studious and unerringly competent, so much so the story department felt there was insufficient contrast between the members of the somewhat stuffy duo. Watson's basic humanity and good humor was stressed but with the casting of the endearingly comic Nigel Bruce in the role, the character was increasingly drawn to buffoonish humor. As a result, the chemistry of the pair became significantly altered, at least with this teaming of actors. As Watson seemed more and more a bumbling fool, it became difficult to believe that the characters could maintain a temperamentally compatible relationship, especially with Holmes' formidable intellect on constant display. Inevitably, the latent feelings of condescension Holmes always had for his devoted sidekick became part of the pair's chemistry. Many critics were appalled but audiences loved it. Rathbone himself went so far as to say that the fans' attraction to Sherlock Holmes begins with Watson.

Flush with the success of two Sherlock Holmes films, 20th Century–Fox was anxious exercise their options on the Conan Doyle novels. Their plan called for producing one film a year for an indefinite period with Rathbone and Bruce continuing in their roles. Sadly, negotiations broke down with a major sticking point: The Conan Doyle estate insisted that all future scripts must remain faithful to the original stories instead of contriving new adventures built around the detective. Not long after, Warner Bros. expressed interest in announcing their intention to bring "The Speckled Band," one of the more popular Holmes stories, to the screen with Rathbone and Bruce reprising their roles. This, too, came to naught due to what *The Hollywood Reporter* claimed were "difficulties encountered in clearing all rights in the complicated copyright setup covering the Holmes yarns."

It would seem that Universal would have little success in their bid to secure the rights to the celebrated literary detective. But in an apparent turnaround from their stringent demands on Fox, the Conan Doyle estate entered into a contract with the studio in early 1942. Universal agreed to pay $300,000 for the screen rights to the Sherlock Holmes character, as well as the rights to 21 of the author's short stories, for a seven-year period. Universal promptly secured the services of Rathbone and Bruce, who were cementing their identification with the roles by starring in a Sherlock Holmes radio program. With all of the legal hurdles cleared, the studio turned the series over to Howard Benedict, the newly hired associate producer, recently recruited from RKO.

With the exception of MGM's swank Thin Man films, Hollywood's detective movie series were almost always relegated to second features status. Universal didn't intend to break the mold. The Sherlock Holmes movies were given adequate budgets and less hectic production schedules than the usual 12-day cheapies, but Universal wasn't about to match 20th Century–Fox's princely expenditure on the detective. Fortunately, the studio's standing sets, even if they were becoming increasingly familiar, could be counted on to give the pictures a richness which transcended their budgets.

Universal's decision to update the Holmes character no doubt provoked the ire of more than a few of the hardcore disciples of the Conan Doyle "canon," despite Arthur Wontner's already having played the detective in contemporary settings in a slate of British films of the early '30s. Somehow the concept of the iconic character enlisting in Great Britain's monumental struggle with the Axis powers seemed incongruous, possibly because the detective's adventures, on film, stage, radio or in print, seemed to exist in an alternate universe, unblemished by the unpleasant realities of the day. The charm and universal appeal of Holmes was that he provided perfect escapist entertainment no matter what medium he appeared in. However, Universal's tinkering with the character's situation had some basis in the canon itself. In the short story "His Last Bow," written in 1917, the author himself took a graying Holmes out of retirement to nab a German spy at the behest of the government. It would seem, then, that advancing the timeline a mere 25 years or so and presenting Holmes at the peak of his powers wasn't an entirely outlandish proposition, especially since "His Last Bow" was the first of the Conan Doyle stories Universal chose to adapt for the screen.

The ink had barely dried on the studio's contract with the Conan Doyle estate when the studio plunged into production on the series' initial offering. Filming commenced on May 5, 1942, under the working title *Sherlock Holmes Saves London*. In what would become a standard practice, a tentative title was assigned each picture, only to be changed well before its release date. In this case, *Sherlock Holmes and the Voice of Terror* was finally chosen as the official title.

The film begins with a short, introductory card which loftily expounds on the "timelessness" of the Sherlock Holmes stories and the inherent "ageless, invincible and unchanging" qualities of the character himself. It's clearly a

Sherlock Holmes (Basil Rathbone) enlists the aid of Cockney girl Kitty (Evelyn Ankers) to help crack a Nazi ring in *Sherlock Holmes and the Voice of Terror* (courtesy Dan Scapperotti).

precautionary gambit designed to address Holmes' sudden materialization in the middle of the twentieth century. The point couldn't be more dramatically made than with the next shot as the camera sharply frames Germany's position on a map of Europe and Frank Skinner's music swells with militaristic menace. With this, a cruel, strident voice, identifying itself as the Voice of Terror (Edgar Barrier), goads British radio listeners while the film cuts to disaster footage of ships and dams being blown up and munitions factories bursting into flames, all perpetrated by agents of the Third Reich. (The "Voice" was probably based on Germany's notorious "Lord Haw Haw," who was heard on the British airwaves during the war, mocking the Allies' attempts to defeat the "invincible" Nazi enemy.)

As the Voice continues to break into radio transmissions with news of further military disasters and acts of sabotage, Sir Evan Barham (Reginald Denny) of the Intelligence Inner Council enlists the assistance of Sherlock Holmes and Dr. Watson (Basil Rathbone and Nigel Bruce) to unmask the identity of the "Voice," who seems to be privy to military secrets known only to the top heads of government. Later that evening, Gavin (Robert Barron), one of Holmes' operatives working on the case, crashes into the detective's flat with a dagger buried in his back. He utters only one word, "Christopher," before dying. The urgency of the message compels Holmes and Watson to enlist the aid of Gavin's wife, Kitty (Evelyn Ankers), a barmaid at a seedy waterfront pub, to learn the meaning of her late husband's message. Kitty appeals to the patriotism of the rowdy patrons and urges them to help Holmes learn the meaning of Gavin's cryptic message.

Kitty comes through and tips off the detective that Gavin was referring to the Christopher Docks. Holmes, Watson and Anthony Lloyd (Henry Daniell) of the Inner Council arrive at the site and uncover a nest of enemy spies led by Meade (Thomas Gomez), who holds them at gunpoint. Kitty's gang intervenes and rescues the trio but Meade manages to escape in a speedboat.

Doing a bit of undercover work of her own, Kitty manages to locate Meade and become his mistress while discreetly advising Holmes of the Nazi's clandestine activities. In the meantime, the Voice of Terror takes to the airwaves once again, announcing that a German air strike against the North Coast will take place the following night. Barham orders an alert to counter the attack. But Holmes insists that the Voice's message is only a ruse and the South Coast will be the place of attack.

Inducing the Inner Council to accompany him to the South Coast the next evening, Holmes and his forces round up Meade and a band of German soldiers, hiding out in a crumbling cathedral. Holmes, in his most grandiose manner, announces to the stunned members of the Council that the Voice of Terror is none other than Sir Evan Barham. The minister, it turns out, is actually Heinrich Von Bork, a member of the German Secret Police, posing as Barham for the last 20 years after the real Barham was executed while a prisoner of war. Holmes discloses that the Council was deliberately misinformed; the RAF's defense planes are fully prepared to meet the German attack on the South Coast.

Taking advantage of the understandable confusion, Meade draws a pistol, fatally shoots Kitty and is himself killed while attempting to escape. Holmes mournfully salutes the girl's extraordinary service to her country and the humbled Council assures the detective that her sacrifice will not be forgotten.

From Universal's point of view, *Sherlock Holmes and the Voice of Terror* was an ideal entry to launch the new series. In his opening volley, the greatest of all fictional detectives wouldn't be squandering his skills on some mundane matter of homicide but on a case with staggering international ramifications. This wasn't the strategy of a literary-minded steward of the Holmes legacy, but of a studio trying to make the most of its new investment. In other words, it was a producer's choice and, no matter how misguided it might have seemed to some, it was one that was designed to attract the attention of an audience that was gradually acclimating itself to the cold, hard realities of wartime.

Once you accept the incongruity of a character so intractably identified with the late nineteenth century matching wits with Nazis and fifth columnists, *Sherlock Holmes and the Voice of Terror* emerges as an entertaining, even underrated movie that isn't lacking Sherlockian flavor and generally remains true to the spirit of Conan Doyle. Production-wise the film isn't on a par with the 20th Century–Fox pictures but it's extremely well-mounted by programmer standards, photographed with style, and effectively uses the studio's back lot European and waterfront settings as well as matte shots to hide its limited budget. On the debit side, there's an abundance of disaster footage culled from newsreels and familiar stock shots from previous movies (including the impressive train wreck scene from *The Invisible Man*). Despite the updated characters, there's probably more in the way of the detective's trademark deductive reasoning at work here than in some of the later, more esteemed entries in the series.

This is in no way better demonstrated than in Holmes' introduction as he and Watson deal with their cold reception from the Inner Council. Deep footprints in the carpet tellingly indicate one member's heated disapproval of Holmes' invitation to join the group. Holmes calculates that Barham had just arrived from his country estate by identifying the type of clay smeared on his boots. It's reassuring that this updated version of the detective isn't much different from his Victorian counterpart, even if his modernized wardrobe is a bit disconcerting.

The first item to go when Holmes was updated to the '40s was his famous double-visored hunting cap. The script rather deftly handles the problem as the detective is about to charge out of his Baker Street flat hot on the trail of a fresh lead. Instinctively picking up the familiar cap, he is stopped cold by Watson, who sternly reminds him, "Ah-ah! You promised!" Obligingly, Holmes selects a turned-down fedora. Strangely, Holmes' coiffure is stubbornly stuck in the pre-

Down time: Rathbone, Nigel Bruce and Evelyn Ankers share a laugh on the *Voice of Terror* set (courtesy Dan Scapperotti).

vious century. His much commented-upon swept-from-the-sides haircut is a throwback to the Victorian era's Yellow '90s crowd where it was most famously seen on Wilde, Whistler, Swinbourne, and others. Still, Universal's insistence on such an odd hair design doesn't have precedence in Sidney Paget's original illustrations of the character.

The art department was careful not to risk offending Holmes fans by modernizing the detective's rooms at 221-B Baker Street. As director Roy William Neill, who would take over for John Rawlins for the rest of the series, would later explain, "[Sherlock Holmes'] fans seem to love [the room's] musty clutter. The setting is decorated exactly as suggested in the Doyle descriptions, except that we have substituted electric lights for gas, and have added a telephone. So far, the fans haven't kicked on this score."

The political drumbeating sometimes gets the better of the script but not the actors. Evelyn Ankers has one of her rare dramatic opportunities as the plucky streetwalker, Kitty. Breaking away from her Scream Queen image, she delivers an impassioned Rule Britannia speech, rallying a pub-full of drifters and barflies into Holmes' underground army of patriots. Thomas Gomez responds in kind. Making his film debut, the actor sounds off in a speech rife with heavy-handed symbolism as he recalls a boyhood dream in which he's a knight on horseback trampling ruthlessly over the swarming masses. "What if it were no dream?" he ponders. "What if it were prophesy?" (Gomez's participation didn't go unnoticed by Universal executives and the actor made a long string of films for the studio in upcoming months, and went on to a notable career.)

In between the occasional bursts of theatrical oratory, Holmes and Watson steer their way through the waterfront dives of Limehouse and the high-domed headquarters of the British monarchy, melding the elements of mystery with a plea for unity into a compelling and highly watchable example of Hollywood wartime propaganda. And since it's all for a good cause, the lack of humor and subtlety is forgivable. Both Ankers and Gomez's speeches were probably the work of scenarist Lynn Riggs, best remembered for having authored the play "Green Grow the Rushes," out of which the Rodgers and Hammerstein mega-musical "Oklahoma!" was adapted.

Rathbone's portrayal of Holmes is indeed of classic stature and *Sherlock Holmes and the Voice of Terror* finds him at the top of his game. The script is sufficiently weighty in that there's little time for comic padding, especially since Nigel Bruce's Watson hadn't yet reached his peak of buffoonery. As a result, Rathbone is less condescending and far more appealing than he would be later in the series. Rathbone's performance actually improves on repeated screenings after the viewer has the advantage of knowing the film's outcome. Re-examining scenes in which Holmes is required to sham a reaction, such as after facing Barham/Von Bork after the spy fires on the German plane, one can more easily see subtleties in Rathbone's performance as Holmes hoodwinks the unsuspecting villain, who is unaware that the detective is on to him.

In the rest of the cast, Henry Daniell is certainly notable. Although seemingly wasted in a non-villainous role, he is a marvelous, snarling red herring, snapping at Holmes at every opportunity. On the other hand, the usually smooth and affable Reginald Denny makes an uncomfortable transformation into the heel-clicking Von Bork, spewing Nazi boilerplate with fervent intensity. It's nice to see Universal regulars (and soon-to-be Sherlock Holmes series regulars) Olaf Hytten and Leyland Hodgson in slightly more substantial roles than their usual one- or two-line walk-ons. Edgar Barrier affects a German accent for his off-camera role as the insidious "Voice of Terror"; he's also the English-sounding radio voice announcing that there'll *be* no more Voice of Terror broadcasts at film's end! Making her Sherlock Holmes film debut, Hillary Brooke replaced Marjorie Lord as chauffeur Jill Grandis, a nothing part that looks as if it might have been the subject of trimming.

Voice of Terror is the only Universal Holmes film not directed by the talented Roy William Neill but contract director John Rawlins rises to the occasion. Visually, the film is a distant cousin of the others in the series, mostly because of Rawlins' fondness for long, intimate closeups. Conan Doyle's "His Last Bow" provided the basis of the Riggs-Bright screenplay, retaining the basic situation of Holmes on the trail of a German spy (named Von Bork) as well as a stirring closing speech, beautifully read by Rathbone. More than Conan Doyle, *Voice of Terror* owes perhaps an even greater debt to Universal's *The Great Impersonation* (1942) with Ralph Bellamy, which completed shooting weeks before the Sherlock Holmes film went before the cameras. Both World War II films share the storyline of a Nazi plot to murder a titled Englishman and replace him with a German who is his exact double, the latter now able to infiltrate the War Department in London. If that weren't enough, both films were helmed by director John Rawlins and co-starred Evelyn Ankers and Henry Daniell!

For viewers inclined to overlook what many consider to be a compromised vision of the character, *Sherlock Holmes and the Voice of Terror* can be enjoyed as a relatively lavish and engrossing curtain-raiser to what would prove to be one of the most enduring of Hollywood's movie detective series. Universal sent the film out to many theaters with the raucous, very funny *Pardon My Sarong* with Abbott and Costello, inadvertently burying the political platitudes of the Holmes-Watson picture in a welter of broadly-played belly laughs. A more inappropriate co-feature couldn't be imagined but somehow the comedy team *and* the detectives managed to endure.

Critics' Corner

Rating: ★★★ The picture is competently directed by John Rawlins, who has created an atmosphere of suspense and terror.... Rathbone and Bruce are an ideal team for the Holmes and Watson roles.—*The New York Daily News*, September 19, 1942, Kate Cameron

John Rawlins maintains the air of excitement in his

direction, a first-rate job. The mood of the piece is enormously aided by the artful photography of Woody Bredell, in an especially low-key.—*The Hollywood Reporter*, September 4, 1942

Holmes ... is so up-to-the-minute, that he no longer wears his peaked cap.... [L]ess a conflict than a rat hunt with a foregone conclusion. It is to be feared that neither the Holmes series nor the war effort are greatly aided by this ambitious but uneffective attempt to merge the two.—*The New York Post*, September 1942, Archer Winsten

The plot cannot be taken too seriously, in spite of director John Rawlins' use of striking photography in relating it. The screenplay is decidedly dated.... [T]he Rialto thriller is too far from reality to keep up suspense.—*The New York Sun*, September 1942, Eileen Creelman

Rathbone carries the Sherlock Holmes role in great style, getting able assistance from the flustery Bruce as Dr. Watson.—*Variety*, September 9, 1942

Though routine and undistinguished, this melodrama ... has a fair amount of thrilling action and much speed.... The acting is generally good.—*The Film Daily*, September 16, 1942

The Mummy's Tomb

Released October 23, 1942. 60 minutes. *Associate Producer:* Ben Pivar. *Director:* Harold Young. *Screenplay:* Griffin Jay & Henry Sucher. *Original Story:* Neil P. Varnick. *Photography:* George Robinson. *Art Director:* Jack Otterson. *Associate Art Director:* Ralph M. DeLacy. *Editor:* Milton Carruth. *Musical Director:* Hans J. Salter. *Sound Director:* Bernard B. Brown. *Technician:* William Schwartz. *Set Decorator:* Russell A. Gausman. *Associate Set Decorator:* J. Andrew Gilmore. *Assistant Director:* Charles S. Gould. *Makeup:* Jack P. Pierce. *Gowns:* Vera West.

Lon Chaney, Jr. (*Kharis*), Dick Foran (*Prof. Stephen A. Banning*), John Hubbard (*Dr. John Banning*), Elyse Knox (*Isobel Evans*), Wallace Ford (*Babe Hanson*), Turhan Bey (*Mehemet Bey*), George Zucco (*Andoheb*), Mary Gordon (*Jane Banning*), Cliff Clark (*Sheriff*), Virginia Brissac (*Ella Evans*), Paul E. Burns (*Jim*), Frank Reicher (*Prof. Matthew Norman*), Eddy C. Waller (*Chemist*), Frank Darien (*Old Man*), Harry Cording (*Vic*), Myra McKinney (*Vic's Wife*), John Rogers (*Ship's Steward*), Otto Hoffman (*Caretaker*), Emmett Vogan (*Coroner*), Fern Emmett (*Laura*), Janet Shaw (*Girl*), Dick Hogan (*Boy*), Bill Ruhl (*Nick*), Guy Usher (*Doctor*), Pat McVey (*Jake Lovell*), Jack Arnold [Vinton Haworth] (*Frank [Reporter]*), Glenn Strange (*Farmer*), Rex Lease (*Al*), Grace Cunard (*Farmer's Wife*), Lew Kelly (*Bartender*), Charles Marsh (*Man*), Walter Byron (*Searcher*).

> Spawned from the depths of doom comes the most fearful monster of the ages....
> —*Trailer blurb for* The Mummy's Tomb

The joviality which marked the finale of *The Mummy's Hand* was, in retrospect, premature indeed. Released only two years after its predecessor, but picking up the plot 30 years later, *The Mummy's Tomb* brought back some of the cast members of the first film for a bleak reunion as the Mummy, now played by Lon Chaney, Jr., returns with a vengeance, stalking down our favorite players in one of Universal's nastiest sequels.

Chaney had renewed his contract in February 1942, and already his horror vehicles were slipping in quality. Unlike the Laemmles, who nurtured Boris Karloff's horror career with literate scripts and generally accomplished directors, the current management was primarily interested in getting Chaney into as many monster makeups as possible. The care and talent that was lavished upon *The Wolf Man* is sorely lacking in *The Mummy's Tomb*.

As with the other films in the post–Karloff Mummy series, this movie gets by as entertainment for hardcore Universal enthusiasts by its cozy familiarity alone. All of the bromides, from the changing of the guard in the opening Egyptian scenes to the ritualistic brewing of the tana leaves, are here but these are dubious charms for the uninitiated. Praise for the later Mummy sequels is rare in film books although they are affectionately regarded by film buffs willing to overlook their glaring shortcomings.

George Zucco returns in the role of Andoheb, now one of the old guard of high priests of Karnak, who apparently has inherited Eduardo Ciannelli's job of doling out thankless tasks to new recruits. Mehemet Bey (Turhan Bey) pulls the plum assignment of transporting Kharis (Chaney), alive but dormant, to America. Setting up shop in a cemetery caretaker's cottage in Mapleton, Massachusetts, Bey is ordered to periodically unleash the Mummy to polish off the surviving members of the accursed Banning expedition. (It is never explained how Zucco occupied his time during the ensuing decades, or why he has waited so long to wreak vengeance. The hail of bullets fired into him by Wallace Ford, he tepidly explains, merely "shattered my arm.")

Stephen Banning (Dick Foran), virile hero of the 1940 film, is now a lovable old codger who entertains his dinner guests by challenging them to checkers and recounting his adventures in

Egypt (thus giving the writers a chance to recap the plot of *The Mummy's Hand* via some well-chosen excerpts). Banning and Babe Hanson (Wallace Ford) are the sole survivors of the now-famous expedition; the camera pans to a framed head shot of Peggy Moran, artlessly and unflatteringly touched up with penciled-in wrinkles and hints of gray in her hair.

Bey administers the sacred tana fluid and restores Kharis to life. Slinking through the forest, the Mummy arrives at the Banning estate and chokes the life out of Stephen, leaving a streak of grayish mold on his throat. When Stephen's sister Jane (Mary Gordon) falls victim to the Mummy soon after, it becomes apparent that the whole Banning family has been marked for death. Babe Hanson arrives on the scene and insists the Mummy is back in business. His claims are shrugged off by the local sheriff (Cliff Clark), who sticks to his theory the killings are the work of a maniac. Undeterred, Babe tips off the press to the murderer's identity, but is soon silenced by the vengeful Kharis.

Impressed by the mounting death toll, Banning's son John (John Hubbard) reckons that the mysterious Egyptian caretaker at the local cemetery is the likeliest suspect, but before he can investigate, his pretty fiancée, Isobel Evans (Elyse Knox), is carried off by the bandaged baddie. Bey is shot down in a confrontation with the sheriff and his posse, who track Kharis to the Banning estate. John manages to wrest Isobel away from Kharis as the townspeople set the house ablaze and the Mummy perishes in the flames.

While *The Mummy's Hand* bears the flavorful, high-spirited charm of some of the better Hollywood comic-action pictures, *The Mummy's Tomb* is a more conventionally-toned sequel. Characters are introduced only to be dispatched in the creature's stranglehold with little sense of pain or loss under Harold Young's flat, homogenized direction. The movie underscores the importance of setting in any version of the classic Universal horror characters. Transporting the Mummy to the U.S.A., turning him into a monster in our backyard so to speak, puts the film on a par with some of the PRC and Monogram features, many of which were set in backwoods locations to avoid the expense of set construction. Likewise, the plot of a fanatic who unleashes a killer-monster to settle an old score is reminiscent of such Poverty Row favorites as *The Devil Bat* (1940) and *The Mad Monster* (1942). Even with its excessive humor and a back lot desert location, *The Mummy's Hand* more effectively conveys the terror of the situation than its sequel for all its straight-faced underpinnings.

Young was a former editor who, in the '30s, went to England to work under Alexander Korda. His most prestigious credit was *The Scarlet Pimpernel* (1934) with Leslie Howard and Merle Oberon. His subsequent Hollywood career consisted of an uninterrupted string of virtually forgotten B programmers. *The Mummy's Tomb* is probably his best remembered film.

The Mummy's Tomb is unique in the series in that it directly references World War II in its script. (At one point, John Hubbard receives a telegram informing him of his draft induction accompanied by a roaring, patriotic Hans J. Salter musical cue that would be enough to send the great God Amon-Ra packing.) Such atmosphere-killing distractions may have played well at the time, but seen today, they're more likely to denote the film's subtle exploitation of the American distrust of foreign nationals during wartime. The solution, predictably, comes in the form of a call-to-arms as the sheriff's posse confronts the high priest in a showdown. As in *The Mummy's Hand*, the enemy conceals a pistol in the sleeve of his robe (the characteristic sneak attack), but he proves too slow on the draw for the trigger-happy sheriff.

Photographer George Robinson lifts the picture a couple notches above the latter series entries with his fluid camerawork, providing some striking night-for-night shots of the Mummy prowling through the windswept countryside. Hans Salter's mostly retread score doesn't serve the film particularly well especially with inappropriate lightweight "mood" music written for *The Invisible Woman* thrown into the mix. Sadly typical of the series after *The Mummy's Hand*, the monster's resurrection scene is a throwaway. After being fed the brewed tana leaves (reducing the process from a supernatural one into a silly matter of biology), the Mummy lackadaisically shambles out of the coffin without any sense of suspense or mounting terror.

For a film that pads a good portion of its abbreviated running time with cannibalized

Two generations of high priests are represented in this image: George Zucco as Andoheb and Turhan Bey as Mehemet Bey in *The Mummy's Tomb.*

footage from *The Mummy's Hand*, one could at least appreciate the relative care and detail which is lavished on the climax. Taking its inspiration from *Frankenstein* (lifting some crudely matched shots of the torch-bearing villagers in the bargain), the sequence has the hero going one on one with the creature on the balcony of the palatial home as the angry mob below torches the building. Crisply edited by Milton Carruth with a generous number of camera set-ups, the ending is the best and most excitingly mounted in the entire series, notwithstanding the glaring use of stuntmen and doubles who alternately fill in for Hubbard and Chaney.

The Mummy's Tomb makes excellent use of the familiar Shelby House for the Banning residence. Originally built on the studio back lot for *Uncle Tom's Cabin* (1927), the façade was in constant use for decades. Called The Moors in *Man Made Monster*, Dark Oaks in *Son of Dracula*, and seen in such genre pictures as *The Spider Woman Strikes Back* and *The Brute Man*, the home continues to be a part of the famous Universal City tour. The structure was set afire in many a film; in *The Mummy's Tomb*, one could see the uniform flames emanating from the concealed gas jets along the railings during the fiery climax.

The Mummy's Tomb is so perfunctory, so small scale in ambition and execution, it seemed destined for the bottom-of-the-bill slot. Yet Universal, who was playing up Chaney big at the time, offered it as a main attraction, heading a double bill with Ford Beebe's worthier *Night Monster*.

The cast is a mostly colorless bunch, especially John Hubbard whose Ivy League persona made him unsuitable for anything except fluff comedy and second banana roles. Eight years after *The Mummy's Tomb*, he had a supporting

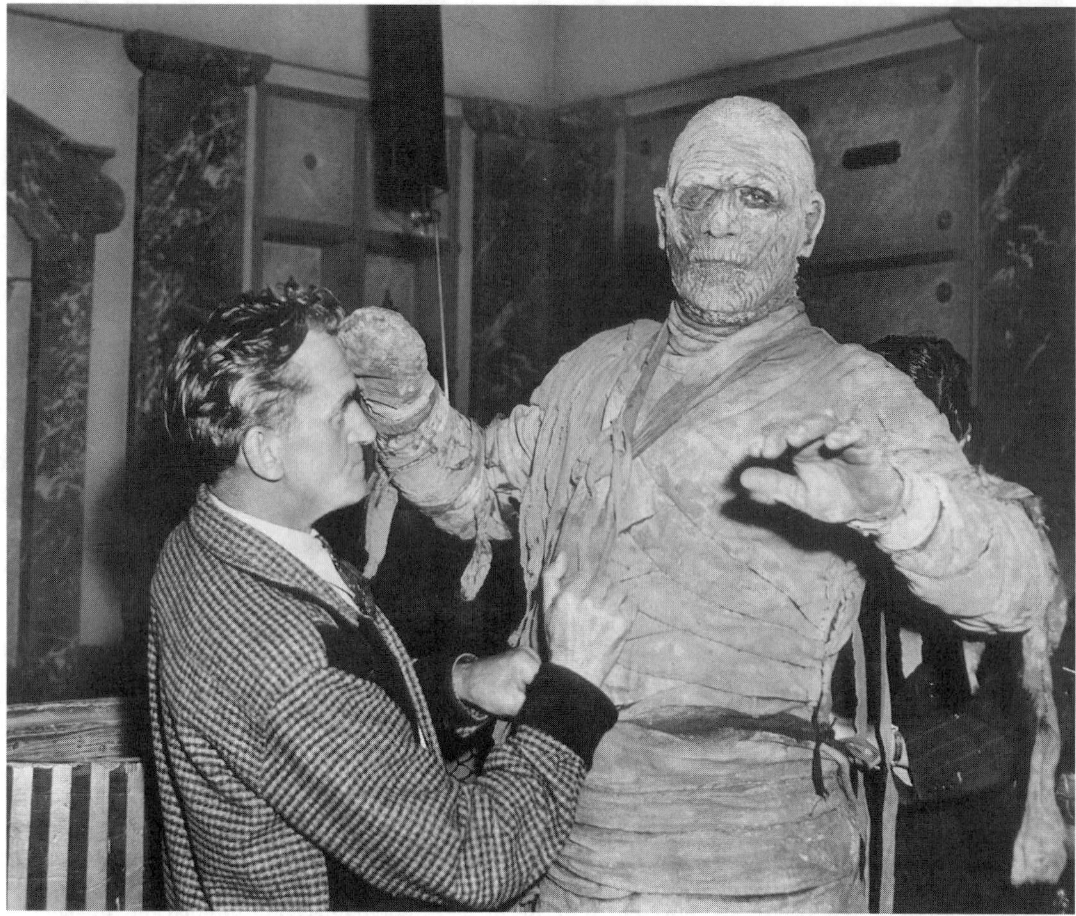

Lon Chaney, Jr., gets a last-minute makeup adjustment on the *Mummy's Tomb* mausoleum set. Note the carrying belt around his waist.

part in a Hal Roach–produced, Robert Clarke–starring TV production of *The Three Musketeers.* Clarke told the authors:

> John Hubbard was a very smooth, professional actor, and also a pleasant guy. He was a light leading man type who had been under contract to Roach, Sr., years before, and had starred for Roach in a movie with Carole Landis called *Turnabout* (1940).... It was meant to help John's career but it actually didn't do *anything* for his career [except to hurt it], because it gave the effect of his being effeminate. When we were doing *Three Musketeers,* John pointed to a sizable dressing room there on the Roach lot and said, "That was built for me"—and now there he was, back on that very lot, doing this little TV thing for just $55 a day. Like many actors who find it necessary to make a transition to other jobs during the course of their careers, John later became a maitre-d' at a well-known Hollywood restaurant called the Tail o' the Cock, and then following that he worked as a dialogue director.

Elyse Knox is a fetchingly beautiful ingénue of almost unbearable wholesomeness whose role as the bland heroine was well within her range. Dick Foran expresses mostly discomfort in an unconvincing old age makeup but does his best to give Steve Banning dignity. He still comes out ahead of the game compared to Wallace Ford, the former quick-with-a-quip Brooklynite Babe Jenson, who looks uncharacteristically senatorial with a pince-nez and a boutonniere. His name change to Babe Hanson is more than likely a flub on the part of the three writers involved in the film. Turhan Bey, playing "the last of a strange race of high priests," according to the dialogue, has, for a change, the right physical appearance for a Middle-Eastern fanatic.

Stranger in a strange land: Kharis (Chaney Jr.) haunts the New England town of Mapleton.

Born in Vienna in 1922 as Turhan Selahettin Schultavey, Bey's early years can best be described as "comfortable" (his mother's family owned large glass factories and, allegedly, a film studio in Czechoslovakia while his father was the Turkish military attaché in Austria). Bey arrived in Hollywood with his mother and grandmother and a letter of introduction from a lawyer-friend of Arthur Lubin. The director told the authors:

> When he arrived, Bey had little spit curls that the Turkish people had in those days. He really was something! Ernie Westmore was the makeup man at Universal at the time and we cut all of this out. We restyled his hair and made a test of him. The women were *crazy* about him.

Knowing little English, Bey was sent by Lubin to the Ben Bard School of Speech. Warner Bros. offered him a screen test after seeing him play a suave young heavy in one of Bard's productions and debuted him in a small part in *Footsteps in the Dark* (1941) with Errol Flynn. Lubin showed the young man's screen test to Universal and Bey was signed on as a contract player. At first, the studio cast him in minor roles in programmers like *Burma Convoy* (1941), *Bombay Clipper* (1942) and *The Unseen Enemy* (1942), eventually finding him useful playing second leads in Maria Montez's Technicolor vehicles. The actor got a taste of the "big time" when MGM signed him to play the husband of Katharine Hepburn (playing a Chinese peasant) in 1944's *Dragon Seed.* Bey's greatest successes, however, were offscreen as he became known as one of Hollywood's most celebrated, and busiest, heartthrobs.

Bey's smooth, exotic romanticism became passé after the war years. Released from Universal after its merger with International Pictures in 1946, he was signed at Eagle Lion while freelancing in B pictures like Columbia's *Song of India* (1949). Usually dismissed as another of the '40s "camp" actors, the exotic star was nonetheless an engaging presence and delivered a fine performance as a phony medium in *The Amazing Mr. X* (1948). He eventually moved to Vienna where he worked as a freelance photographer for soft-porn magazines, including *Penthouse*.

Although he's quick to admit he's never seen *The Mummy's Tomb*, Bey rates it as his favorite screen role. He told the others:

> I guess it's my favorite because it was a part closest to my own nationality — it was a young Egyptian who believed in something which we couldn't comprehend with our five senses.... If I could have picked my roles, I would have played these kinds of heavies, people who have a mental quirk or who, for some reason or another, are acting against the positive side of the plot of the picture.

Lon Chaney's Kharis summons more rage than Tom Tyler's with a physique that made him the sort of Mummy you wouldn't want to meet up with in an alley; he's a quarterback under wraps. Jack Pierce's revised mummy design incorporated a charred look as befitting the monster's fiery demise in the last episode. A blackened facial mask covered the actor's face, leaving only a single eye slit, and his left hand was reduced to a burned-out stump. Still, Chaney doesn't have the quietly chilling, blank-eyed presence of the lean, angular cowboy star.

Bey told the authors:

> I felt terribly sorry for this excellent actor Lon Chaney, who had to wrap himself every day, even in the greatest heat, in that fabulous costume of his. Except to speak with his body, he couldn't do anything.... He was a real professional. He may have felt that he couldn't do any acting [as the Mummy], but when you watched the way he moved, the rhythm of his various movements, he *did* do some acting with his body, as his father did.

To Chaney's dismay, the studio dropped the "Jr." from his billing and from then on officially listed him as "Lon Chaney."

The rest of the characters in *The Mummy's Tomb* consist of a tiresome array of skeptical sheriffs and dumb-looking sidekicks. These hick types would become the Mummy's unlikely sparring partners for the rest of the series and therein lies the fatal error in judgment from which the Mummy films never recovered. The monster's relocation to America may have been a necessary ploy to inject variety into the increasingly hackneyed plots, but the idea of a mummy slinking through the back alleys of New England was so ludicrously inappropriate, it engendered little fright or intrigue. Removed from the mystical trappings of Egypt, the Mummy seemed more of an anachronism than a monster, more of a curiosity than a threat. The hopelessly banal dialogue spouted by the country bumpkins in this film and *The Mummy's Ghost* only demystified the most enigmatic and balefully romantic of all of Universal's classic monsters. Poor Kharis deserved a better fate!

Critics' Corner

For all we know [the Mummy] will bop up again as Bela Lugosi. No wonder the Mummy lasted for 3,000 years. In that tandem fashion, he may go on for another 3,000 — heaven forbid! — *The New York Times*, October 26, 1942, Theodore Strauss

Much happens, but nothing that will surprise the horror fans. — *Harrison's Reports*, October 17, 1942

Lon Chaney as the villain carries a movie calculated to scare you out of your wits. Most of the rest of the cast is scared to death. — *The New York Herald-Tribune*, October 1942, Joseph Pihodna

[S]uch shows have a habit of paying off for Universal, and [the fact that the Mummy] seemingly is consumed in a roaring fire at the finale does not necessarily mean that it is dead. [If this] offering catches on at the box office, as well it may, you can expect a second chorus of "My Mummy Done Told Me." — *The Hollywood Reporter*, October 13, 1942

Night Monster

Released October 23, 1942. 73 minutes. *Associate Producer:* Donald H. Brown. *Producer-Director:* Ford Beebe. *Original Screenplay:* Clarence Upson Young. *Photography:* Charles Van Enger. *Art Directors:* Jack Otterson & Richard H. Riedel. *Editor:* Milton Carruth. *Sound Director:* Bernard B. Brown. *Technician:* Robert Pritchard. *Musical Director:* Hans J. Salter. *Gowns:* Vera West. *Set Decorators:* Russell A. Gausman & Andrew J. Gilmore.

Bela Lugosi (*Rolf*), Lionel Atwill (*Dr. King*), Leif Erikson [Erickson] (Laurie), Irene Hervey (*Dr. Lynn Harper*), Ralph Morgan (*Kurt Ingston*), Don Porter (*Dick Baldwin*), Nils Asther (*Agor Singh*), Fay Helm (*Margaret Ingston*), Frank Reicher (*Dr. Timmons*), Doris Lloyd (*Sarah Judd*), Francis Pierlot (*Dr. Phipps*), Robert Homans (*Cap Beggs*), Janet Shaw (*Millie Carson*), Eddy Waller (*Jeb Harmon*), Cyril Delevanti (*Torque*).

What Kind of a Thing Is It?
— *Ad blurb for* Night Monster

One of the most macabre horror characters of the 1940s stalks the halls and grounds of a walled country estate in *Night Monster*, an original and imaginative low-budget horror who-done-it ... or, more descriptively, a *what*-done-it. This lively mix of mystery, mysticism and monster menace boasts a well-mounted eeriness, a striking and unusual plot, a handsome B cast and capable direction by Ford Beebe. Relegated to the bottom of a double-bill with *The Mummy's Tomb*, *Night Monster* stands a full head-and-shoulders over its by-the-numbers co-feature, and sizes up as one of Universal's better Bs from the war years.

Long before Yogism became the province of TV entrepreneurs and girls in uncomfortable sitting positions, the ancient science enjoyed nearly 2,000 years of reasonable respectability. An orthodox system of Indian philosophy, it's an eight-stage process with the purpose of establishing identity of consciousness with the object of concentration. The age-old practice still held plenty of intrigue for '40s audiences, and writer Clarence Upson Young uses it as the hub of his *Night Monster* screenplay.

Young's plot revolves specifically around mantra yoga, involving sound vibration and prayer. (Believers in Hindu mysticism teach that the world evolved from the essence of sound, through the diversity and intricacy of vibration and utterance.) *Night Monster*'s yogi in resident, Nils Asther, uses the ancient secret practice to materialize objects which he has mystically transported from distant places. This astounding achievement is reduced to mere parlor trickery, however, measured against the more ambitious stunt of magically restoring the limbs of a twisted paraplegic lusting for revenge against the physicians who failed him. The premise, and the movie built around it, are both outrageously bizarre, and it requires the best efforts of cast and crew to put the weird story over. Shot as *House of Mystery*, the film was completed on July 18, 1942, and reached theaters just over three months later.

In the foyer of the desolate Ingston Towers estate, Margaret Ingston (Fay Helm) catches housekeeper Sarah Judd (Doris Lloyd) in the act of sopping up bloodstains from a carpet. Margaret's not sure if she's nuts or if everybody else in the house is, and to solve this riddle she has sent for a woman psychiatrist, Dr. Lynn Harper. Judd angrily tells Margaret that Kurt Ingston, Margaret's crippled and reclusive brother, has summoned his own personal physicians, who are due to arrive shortly. After the two exit, Millie the maid (Janet Shaw), who has been eavesdropping, phones the local sheriff to apprise him of mysterious goings-on. Rolf the butler (Bela Lugosi) disconnects her and insists on knowing what "gossip" she is planning to spread. His interrogation is interrupted by the appearance of Laurie (Leif Erickson), a loutish chauffeur who "rescues" the girl from the suddenly aggressive Rolf. Millie quits.

Laurie drives to the railroad depot to pick up the newly arrived Dr.'s King (Lionel Atwill), Timmons (Frank Reicher) and Phipps (Francis Pierlot), the physicians who attended Kurt Ingston in his major illness. Timmons is guilt-ridden about Ingston's disability but the pompous King seems unconcerned and the dotty Phipps prattles on and on about glands.

In town, Millie tries to inveigle one of the townsmen, Jeb Harmon (Eddy Waller), to drive her to the Towers so that she can collect her belongings. Harmon is reluctant because of the Towers' proximity to Pollard Slough, the fog-bound marsh where a local physician was recently strangled by a killer so horrible that in his presence the frogs stop croaking. Millie gets her way, Harmon drives her in his horse-drawn buggy to the Towers at nightfall and waits at the main gate as she walks up to the house. Minutes later, gatekeeper Torque (Cyril Delevanti) relays to Harmon the false phone message that Millie has decided to spend the night, and Harmon departs.

When the croaking of the frogs abruptly ceases, the frightened Harmon whips his horse into a gallop, racing down the lonely road past psychiatrist Lynn Harper (Irene Hervey) and her disabled car. Millie has just begun the long walk back to town when a sinister *some*thing attacks her in the fog. Lynn hears Millie's scream and dimly spots the killer through the mists. She flags down an approaching car which, conveniently, is headed for Ingston Towers. The driver is Dick Baldwin (Don Porter), mystery writer and friend of Kurt Ingston.

Lynn and Dick arrive at the Towers where Kurt Ingston (Ralph Morgan) greets the new-

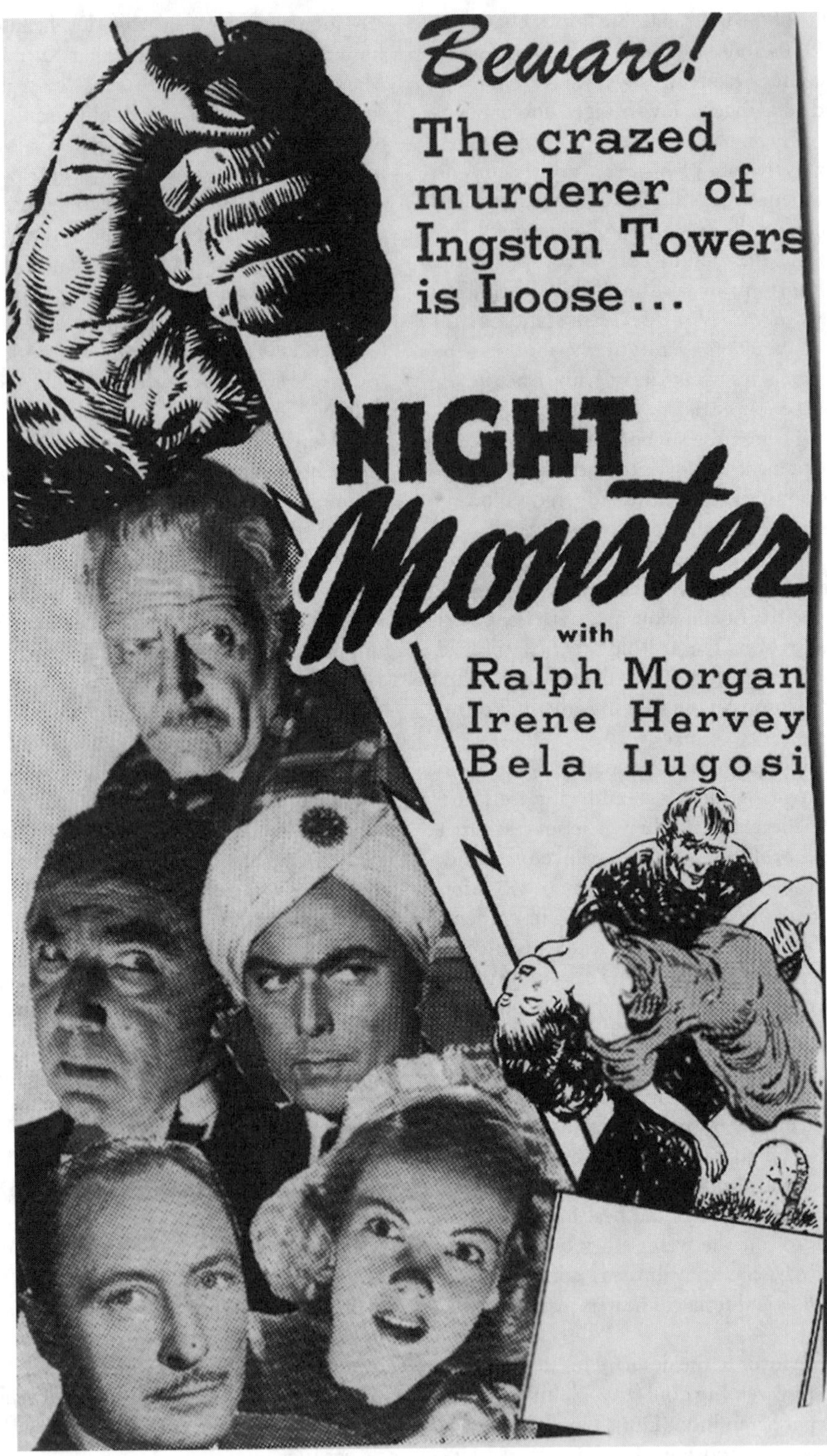

When frogs stop croaking, characters start *getting* croaked in *Night Monster*, one of the studio's best B horrors.

comers. After dinner, Agor Singh (Nils Asther) lectures on a new healing process. Much the same way that a lobster can regenerate a new claw, man can grow new tissues at will through an understanding of the nature of cosmic substance, Singh declares. To demonstrate, he goes into a deep trance and the assembled party watches in astonishment as a kneeling skeleton materializes in the room. In the ensuing commotion, Singh is startled back to consciousness and the skeleton vanishes. Blood which had dripped from the skeleton's hands fails to disappear from the library rug. Rolf, run and get the Stain-Be-Gone. Quick like a bunny!

Investigating Millie's murder, local lawman Cap Beggs (Robert Homans) begins to question the occupants of the house, but his inquiry is interrupted by the discovery of the dead body of Dr. King. King has been strangled but not wounded and, par for the *corpse* (sorry!), there's a small pool of blood nearby.

From this point on, *Night Monster* is in a great hurry to kill off as many characters as possible in the remaining running time. Dr. Timmons is murdered in his room by the "night monster" (seen only in shadow). Dr. Phipps, certain that he (Phipps) will be next, agrees to let Laurie smuggle him out of the house to safety that night. But the killer strikes first, stalking the terrified Phipps in a striking subjective shot. Another trail of blood leads to the body of Laurie, hung in a closet.

Wisely deciding to clear out, Dick and Lynn are confronted by an irate Miss Judd, who feels they know too much and must remain. Margaret tussles with Judd and subdues her as Dick and Lynn flee. The unbalanced Margaret knows that Miss Judd has been a silent accomplice to the killer, and decides to burn the house. To Judd's horror, Margaret sets fire to the drapes and the two women die in the conflagration.

Outside, Dick and have left the grounds when the frogs become silent and the two become aware of a pursuer. Crossing a rotted footbridge, Lynn's foot becomes wedged in a break and Dick is forced to engage in a hand-to-hand struggle with the killer — a fully ambulatory Kurt Ingston, with regenerated limbs and supernatural strength. Ingston chokes Dick into unconsciousness and is advancing toward Lynn when a shot rings out and he topples over dead. Singh, who fired the fatal shot, appears on the scene together with Beggs, and the four watch as Ingston's limbs vanish before their eyes. Singh explains that he had taught Ingston the secrets of matter materialization so that he could restore himself to normalcy, but the warped mind of Ingston planned only to use the mystical process to wreak vengeance on his doctors. In the distance, Ingston Towers is burning to the ground.

For many fans, *Night Monster* has become a sitting target as they bemoan the fact that Lugosi and Atwill play such minor roles. But for the more open-minded, there's plenty of compensation. Ford Beebe's direction catches just the right feel of mystery and suspense, and while the plot can perhaps most charitably be described as improbable, the unusual aspects of the story place the picture a rung above many of the completely standardized and formulized B Universal chillers. There's genuine atmosphere in the scenes on the marsh, and in general a creepy aura surrounding the whole production that too many other Universal films miss. Despite the modest budget, the usual short schedule and a confined setting (we hardly get beyond the house and grounds), *Night Monster* conveys a feeling of dread far more effectively than many of its better-known contemporaries.

The acting in *Night Monster* is on the whole better than that found in the usual Universal meller. Irene Hervey and Don Porter give good, lifelike performances, and the always-dependable Fay Helm delivers another strong portrayal as the neurotic Margaret. There's plenty of the usual loud, confrontational acting, but it's nicely offset by scenes more realistically enacted in hushed tones. *Night Monster* boasts a certain amount of this type of underplaying, and there's a quiet quality about some of these scenes that makes the situations seem more true to life.

Where the picture falls down is in its whodunit aspects. The script goes to a great deal of trouble to divert the finger of suspicion from Kurt Ingston, but with no success. Although the character's paraplegic condition would instantly remove him from consideration in any conventional movie, audiences know that in a horror film, anything goes, and that some explanation for Ingston's nocturnal perambulations will eventually be forthcoming.

A flaw common to Universal's horror whodunits is that there aren't enough suspects, and ordinary logic quickly points to the inevitable killer. The only victims are Ingston's doctors and servants who have betrayed him; there isn't any attempt to establish a motive for red herrings Rolf, Singh or Laurie. The women in the story never become suspects, and the string of murders begins before the three doctors arrive. The pools of blood found near the bodies are also a tip-off that paranormal forces are coming into play, and once again Ingston is the only suspect who would require "supernatural" assistance to dispose of these people.

Ralph Morgan works overtime on his innocent act: In his first scene, his character is a benign and personable host who engages in glib repartee with Lynn and Dick, and hardly seems the misshapen creature discussed in dialogue. It's only later that Ingston begins to project a sly drollness and we detect a cryptic quality and a cold streak.

Just as Ingston-the-man hardly lives up to his "misshapen creature" image, Ingston-the-monster fails to come up to the descriptions laid on him throughout the film. After viewers hear for an hour-plus about the horrible, twisted fiend of Pollard Slough, it comes as a letdown to see that it's Ingston with one eyebrow raised and nostrils flared. (Perhaps, like Henry Hull and the latter-day Chaney Jr., Morgan disliked being unrecognizable beneath heavy makeup: In the 1935 cheapie *Condemned to Live*, he had played a ghoulish vampire-type, again *sans* the expected cosmetic embellishments.) In a nice touch that almost compensates for this disappointment, Morgan's legs and feet are hair-covered, with animal-like claws and toes reminiscent of the Wolf Man. To stretch the suspense of the final confrontation scene, Ingston walks at a slow, Kharis-like pace, the moviemakers banking on the audience not remembering that, earlier in the movie, he ran at top speed to kill Dr Timmons.

Despite the fact that, as a paraplegic, Ingston "couldn't-a done it," almost everyone in the film has an inkling that he's the killer—and probably everybody in the audience, too, after Agor Singh's speech about man's latent ability to grow new tissues at will. (Major-league multi-movie spoiler: Ralph Morgan played in a large number of murder mysteries and, according to the experts, there isn't a single one in which he turns out *not* to be the killer.) As preposterous as its denouement turns out to be, *Night Monster* had at least one forebear in the horror field: 1932's *Doctor X*, a murder story again set at an estate filled with strange doctors (including Atwill!) and sinister servants, where one-armed doctor Preston Foster, above suspicion because of his handicap, turns out to be the monstrous killer, regenerating a grotesque new limb via secret electrical equipment and "living manufactured flesh."

Ingston is at the center of one of the film's oddest and most memorable scenes. Convinced that Ingston is only pretending to be para-

Janet Shaw recoils in horror from the *Night Monster*.

lyzed, Dick and Beggs go to his bedroom and confront him. Ingston, lying in bed, listens politely to their accusations and then quietly asks them to pull back the blanket. Dick complies, revealing pajama-clad legs that end (above the knees) in stumps. Ingston then reaches across with his right hand and draws a mechanical left arm out of the sleeve of his nightshirt. It's a bizarre, disquieting and almost distasteful little vignette, hearkening back again to that pre–Code horror *Doctor X*, and it boggles the mind that the Breen Office, constantly inveighing against excessive grisliness, should allow the character to casually dismantle himself in this fashion. It also seems in bad taste, during the World War II era when on a daily basis young soldiers were coming home to America minus arms or legs (or both), that an individual like Ingston should be described, amidst shudders, as a "misshapen creature."

Supporting performances are also capably handled by Leif Erickson, Nils Asther and Doris Lloyd. Erickson chews up a lot of toothpicks in the alternately ominous-comical role of the boorish chauffeur and makes with a number of genuinely funny one-liners; talking to interviewers Jim and Tom Goldrup, Erickson called *Night Monster* "a dandy." Although Erickson is a minor delight in the role, it's fun to picture Lon Chaney, Jr., in the part and to derive equal delight from that sight-unseen performance. Swedish-born Asther, a silent screen heartthrob whose type began going out of style after the advent of sound, became a solid character actor whose one-time star status gave added dignity to B pictures like *Night Monster*. As the enigmatic yogi, the type of role that many actors (you know who) would have invested with lot of mysterioso and ham, Asther gives a relaxed and assured performance. Doris Lloyd is the housekeeper who lays out the un-welcome mat for Irene Hervey; there are no acting opportunities for the British actress in the film, but her familiar frozen face adds to the gloom in this Mrs. Danvers-type role. Pretty Janet Shaw replaced Elyse Knox as Millie the maid, and Cyril Delevanti is made-up to look a bit like *Bride of Frankenstein*'s Karl (Dwight Frye) in his role as the grotesque gatekeeper with a Ygor-esque humped back. Delevanti was in real life the father-in-law of *Night Monster* producer-director Beebe.

For the second and last time (after *Dracula*), Bela Lugosi is top-billed in a Universal film, which may have been good for his oft-battered ego. The star billing, however, probably raised false expectations in *Night Monster* for a lot of his fans: As Rolf, his scenes are few, and nothing he does affects the plot. Early scenes give the impression that Rolf may be in on the villainy, but once the film shifts into gear the character recedes into the background. There's also an attempt to play Lugosi for laughs: Rolf's squeamish side shows through when the killer begins to strike within the house, and from then on Lugosi plays it like a milquetoast. This is a refreshing change, one supposes, from the familiarly cold and supercilious butler Lugosi started out playing, but the actor cannot play this type of comedy, and what should have been a stereotypical role becomes yet another slightly demeaning one. Also, even though Lugosi is well-dressed and appears quite healthy, he's described in dialogue as looking "like something you'd find under a wet rock." The picture doesn't even bother to let us know if Rolf survives the fiery finish.

Lugosi's in the film strictly for name value, as is Lionel Atwill, who plays Dr. King. Atwill makes the most of his limited screen time as the puffed-up, self-satisfied medico, and is particularly amusing in his scenes of exasperation with Francis Pierlot's gland-happy Dr. Phipps. Atwill seizes every opportunity to silently "comment" on other cast members' dialogue with sometimes hilarious facial expressions. Second only to *Man Made Monster* in the horror field, *Night Monster* finds Atwill at his material-spoofing best.

Don Porter reminisced for the authors:

> *Night Monster* was great fun for me, one of the reasons being I'd been nuts about Irene Hervey for years. Nils Asther was aging at that point, but in his young days was one of the handsomest men in Hollywood, with a marvelous aquiline nose. I remembered seeing him in films, and the ladies adoring him. I was just getting started and to work with Irene and some of these people was a thrill.... The big thing I remember about *Night Monster* was the reading of the line, "It's blood!" [in the skeleton scene]. It's a hokey thing to do [*laughs*], but things like that have to be played dead seriously, so we had to stifle our amusement and do our best!

One of the more memorable supporting performances comes from reliable Frank Reicher. Although Reicher's scenes are few and his dialogue is limited, the actor works to convey a sense of unease as the mild-mannered Dr. Timmons. Timmons visits Ingston Towers with a premonition of foreboding: His is the only character that appreciates the horror of the fate that has befallen Ingston, and Timmons remains almost visibly edgy throughout most of his scenes. Reicher's palpable agitation contrasts nicely with the smug, arrogant assurance of Atwill, and adds subtly to the eerie atmosphere.

Like many of the better character actors of that era, Reicher could be relied upon to contribute effectively to any film. A native of Germany, he was educated in Berlin, Wiesbaden and Hamburg, during which time he learned the English language. He was active on the German stage before he emigrated to the United States in 1899 and began to work on Broadway. In 1914, Cecil B. DeMille lured him west to appear in films, but he returned to Broadway two years later, resuming his stage acting career and joining the New York Theatre Guild as a director. Reicher went back to Hollywood again in 1926 as an actor, director and dialogue director, racking up scores of motion picture credits before his apparent retirement in 1951. In addition to his Universal genre credits, the big-nosed, baggy-eyed actor appeared in other studios' *The Return of the Terror* (1934), *Dr. Cyclops* (1940), *The Face Behind the Mask* (1941), *The Canterville Ghost* (1944) and *Superman and the Mole-Men* (1951), which may have been his last film. Fantasy film fans remember him best for his portrayal of Capt. Englehorn in the classic *King Kong* and the sequel *The Son of Kong* (both 1933). The pioneer film actor died in Playa del Rey, California, in 1964 at the age of 89.

From a technical standpoint *Night Monster* is a handsome film, with a far more polished look than bigger, "better" Universal B titles. Superbly shaded camerawork gives a uniquely cold look to the imposing sets, formerly seen in *The Wolf Man* and *The Ghost of Frankenstein*. It's hard not to keep thinking of *The Wolf Man* as you watch the first reel of *Night Monster*: The opening credits use the misty *Wolf Man* forest as background, *Wolf Man*'s main title music plays, the first interior is the Talbot Castle set, and three of the characters we see *on* that set are *Wolf Man* alumni Doris Lloyd, Fay Helm and Bela Lugosi (underscored by yet more *Wolf Man* music)! The movie also ends on a too-familiar note, with *Wolf Man*'s end title music and reused footage of the burning *Ghost of Frankenstein* sanitarium. Sound effects (the croaking of the frogs, the creaking of a door in one of the estate's walls) provide more chills than the familiar music cues from *Wolf Man* and *Son* and *Ghost of Frankenstein*.

There are a few striking "bridges" in the film, like a shot of the skeleton's blood on the library rug dissolving to a blood splotch on the ground near Millie's body on the foggy marsh, and another clever moment when a shot of black smoke from Margaret's blazing drapes cuts to a shot of prowling fog out of which Lynn and Dick appear. Just as Western director Lambert Hillyer made the most out of *Dracula's Daughter* and *The Invisible Ray* during the Laemmle era, former serial ace Beebe appears to have lavished as much care and imagination on *Night Monster* as time and budget allowed. This was his first feature after his promotion from the Universal chapter plays.

Universal rightly recognized *Night Monster* as an above-par thriller, and promptly assigned Beebe to the post of producer on *Son of Dracula* on the basis of his work. Decades later, Beebe told Richard Bojarski (in *The Films of Bela Lugosi*, Citadel, 1980), "Though it was a quickie, I always was kind of proud of it. Hitchcock, who was also making a picture on the lot [1943's *Shadow of a Doubt*], screened a rough cut because he was interested in Janet Shaw for a part in his film, was impressed with *Night Monster* and seemed to think it was a much more important picture than the studio thought. He couldn't believe the picture was shot in 11 days." (Shaw did get a part as a waitress in *Shadow of a Doubt*.)

From 1949 to 1955, Beebe was the director of Johnny Sheffield's entire Bomba the Jungle Boy movie series. Of the last Bomba movie, 1955's *Lord of the Jungle* with Sheffield and Wayne Morris, co-star Paul Picerni told the authors:

> Ford Beebe the writer-director was a typical old-timer *à la* Cecil B. DeMille, with the boots and the jodhpurs, and even a pith helmet! He was a sweet man, but his script for *Lord of the Jungle* was as corny as you could possibly imagine. Every lunchtime while we were shooting at Allied

Artists, Wayne Morris and I would go across the street to a bar-restaurant and have lunch, and he would have about six martinis. Wayne loved his drinks, and by the time we'd get back to work, he was feeling pretty good. We came back from lunch one day and sat down in a couple of director's chairs with scripts, rehearsing the next scene with Beebe. Wayne said to him, "Ford, you were telling me the other day that you don't drink."

Beebe said, "I haven't had a drink in my life. I've *never* had a drink."

Wayne looked at him for a long moment, serious and straight-faced. Then, holding up the script, he asked, "How the hell can you write this *shit* and not *drink*?" I can still picture in my mind the shocked look on Ford Beebe's face when Wayne said that!

Night Monster is one of those movies which, strangely, could have been improved by a little *less* effort — or, at least, less repetition. Several of the discovery-of-the-body scenes are almost identical (the same *Ghost of Frankenstein* music is played as Our Heroes bound up the staircase, rush to a room and find a victim; the audience usually gets to see only an outstretched hand). These scenes, obviously meant to be *Night Monster's* highpoints, go from effective to repetitious to comically repetitious, proving that movies of this sort *can* often go a corpse (or two or three) too far.

If it had run a reel or two less, *Night Monster* might almost begin to resemble a deluxe, mood-drenched *Thriller* episode as it would have been made in the '40s with all the resources and some of the stars of the Universal Fright Factory of that era. Fans of Universal Horrors might have been better off with a few less sequels featuring the studio's flagship monsters, and a few *more* movies like *Night Monster*.

Critics' Corner

Rating: ★★½ The explanation for the multiple murders comes at the end of the picture but not as too great a surprise to the audience as the author has seen fit to drop a number of obvious hints.— *The New York Daily News*, November 29, 1942, Kate Cameron

Old hands at the game like Bela Lugosi and Lionel Atwill are simply present for atmospheric purposes.— *The New York Herald-Tribune*, 1942

Night Monster is a horror film, as lurid as any that home of thrillers [New York's Rialto Theater] has ever shown.... It's not good; but it is crowded with killings.— *The New York Sun*, November 30, 1942, Eileen Creelman

You would think that such a picture, brimming with gore, could be seen only by the most stout of heart. But that is not true in this case. Despite the presence of Bela Lugosi and Lionel Atwill, veteran horror men [and others], the effect is not too much to be borne. Perhaps the reason for one's persistent calm can be found in the remark of one of the characters who said plaintively, "It still doesn't add up."— *The New York Post*, November 30, 1942, Archer Winsten

Before this potpourri of occult mumbo-jumbo runs its tedious and fantastic course no less than eight ... actors wind up as corpses.— *The New York Times*, November 30, 1942, Thomas M. Pryor

One of the most fantastic melodramas that defy all fact and reason and only serve to bore people whose taste in melodramatic entertainment are closer to reality. Devotees of spine-chillers will find the action in this film suspenseful and exciting. The way people are bumped off should be a real treat for them.... Charles Van Enger's camera work helps to build up the melodramatic tone of the film.— *The Film Daily*, October 20, 1942

1943

Sherlock Holmes and the Secret Weapon

Released February 12, 1943. 68 minutes. *Associate Producer:* Howard Benedict. *Director:* Roy William Neill. *Screenplay:* Edward T. Lowe, W. Scott Darling & Edmund L. Hartmann. *Adaptation by* W. Scott Darling & Edward T. Lowe. *Based on the story* "The Adventure of the Dancing Men" by Sir Arthur Conan Doyle. *Photography:* Les White. *Art Director:* Jack Otterson. *Associate Art Director:* Martin Obzina. *Editor:* Otto Ludwig. *Music:* Frank Skinner. *Musical Director:* Charles Previn. *Set Decorator:* Russell A. Gausman. *Associate Set Decorator:* Edward R. Robinson. *Sound Director:* Bernard B. Brown. *Technician:* Paul Neal. *Technical Advisor:* Tom McKnight. *Makeup:* Jack P. Pierce. *Gowns:* Vera West.

Basil Rathbone (*Sherlock Holmes*), Nigel Bruce (*Dr. John H. Watson*), Lionel Atwill (*Prof. Moriarity*), Kaaren Verne (*Charlotte Eberli*), Dennis Hoey (*Insp. Lestrade*), William Post, Jr. (*Dr. Franz Tobel*), Mary Gordon (*Mrs. Hudson*), Henry Victor (*Prof. Frederick Hoffner*), Paul Fix (*Mueller*), Robert O. Davis [Rudolph Anders] (*Braun*), Holmes Herbert (*Sir Reginald Bailey*), Harry Cording (*Jack Brady*), Harold DeBecker (*Peg Leg*), Paul Bryar (*Waiter*), Guy Kingsford (*London Bobby*), George Eldredge (*Policeman*), Vicki Campbell (*Aviatrix*), Gerard Cavin (*Scotland Yard Man*), Harry Woods (*Kurt*), George Burr MacAnnan (*Gottfried*), James Craven, Leyland Hodgson (*Officers*), Michael Mark (*George*), Leslie Denison, John Burton, Philip Van Zandt.

What shall it be, Holmes? The gas chamber, the cup of hemlock, or a simple bullet through the brain?
—*Lionel Atwill in* Sherlock Holmes and the Secret Weapon

Universal wasted little time getting their second Sherlock Holmes film off the ground. *Sherlock Holmes and the Secret Weapon*, filmed almost back-to-back with *Sherlock Holmes and the Voice of Terror*, continued the exploits of the master detective in war-torn England. The cameras rolled on June 21, 1942, under the working title *Sherlock Holmes Fights Back.*

Howard Benedict continued to function as the series' associate producer but there was a major personnel change which would affect the rest of the series. Taking over the directorial chores from John Rawlins was veteran director Roy William Neill, who had recently come to Universal after a string of interesting B pictures at various studios. Born Roland de Gostrie in Dublin Harbor on a ship commanded by his father, Neill was a former war correspondent who eventually drifted into the theater. He toured in stock companies, and became a stage manager with David Belasco for ten years.

Neill first tried his hand at film work in England and eventually came stateside as a contract director at the Columbia B unit in the '30s. His relatively obscure voodoo thriller *Black Moon* (1934) is both stylish and fascinating, having much in common with the classic Fritz Leiber story "Conjure Wife" which it predates by a decade. With a cast headed by Jack Holt and Fay Wray, the film involves a modern American woman haunted by her past associations with Haitian black arts. Far better known, however, is his excellent Boris Karloff vehicle *The Black Room* (1935) which, though intended as a programmer, ranks among the actor's best pictures of the decade.

Sound man-turned-director Edward Bernds, who worked with Neill in his Columbia days, told the authors:

> In appearance, Neill was dark, had jet black hair and plenty of it. Roy's speech was that of an educated Irishman, somewhat British-sounding, but with just a hint of the Irish lilt or brogue. Roy had some fingers missing on one hand, I'm sure it was his right hand.
>
> Some of the crew called him "Rocking Chair" Neill. The prop man had to have a rocking chair on the set for him when he directed. Eventually, they fixed up a director's chair with rockers, with a big canvas pocket hanging onto one arm of the chair to hold the director's script.

Neill's career at Universal was launched in 1942 with *Eyes of the Underworld*, a minor Richard Dix crime meller. The studio promoted the picture as a shocker, emphasizing the publicity tag line "Lon Chaney in His Most Fearsome Role!" and featuring lurid poster art of the actor in ghoulish gray tints. It was a typical tease; horror fans found to their dismay that Chaney Jr. was wasted in a conventional thug part, and a pretty small one at that.

Neill, affectionately called "Mousey" by his co-workers, was the ideal choice as director of the Holmes series with his sure eye for atmosphere and his crisp, straightforward style. He worked well with modest budgets and conveyed a convincingly British tone. No mean feat considering that years later the director explained the difficulty in shooting an entire run of Sherlock Holmes features.

The studio story department set "The Adventure of the Dancing Men" as the next of Conan Doyle's tales to be transposed to the screen. Associate producer Benedict told author Michael B. Druxman in his book *Basil Rathbone: His Life and His Films* (A.S. Barnes and Company, 1975):

> [The Holmes series] was a very enjoyable project to work on.... All of the plots in the films were basically original, as we were unable to utilize more than an element or two from any of the Doyle stories. For example, we borrowed the idea of the stick figures from "The Adventure of the

Dancing Men" and built a new story around it to make *Sherlock Holmes and the Secret Weapon.*

In Edward T. Lowe and W. Scott Darling's freewheeling adaptation, Holmes is enlisted to provide security for a scientist who is in fear of falling into the clutches of the Nazis only to find him abducted by Prof. Moriarity.

A far cry from Conan Doyle, *Sherlock Holmes and the Secret Weapon* forges a familiar cloak-and-dagger atmosphere from the first frame. The movie opens in Zurich as Holmes (Basil Rathbone) engineers a plan to prevent Dr. Franz Tobel (William Post, Jr.) from being nabbed by German agents who are hot on his trail. Tobel has invented a revolutionary bombsite of uncanny accuracy which he intends to offer to England for her defenses.

Holmes manages to smuggle Tobel into London; it isn't long before the scientist is abducted by Prof. Moriarity (Lionel Atwill), who plans to strike a deal with Germany for the secret weapon. Taking extreme security precautions, Tobel has divided up the bombsite into three separate components which he has entrusted to various scientists. As a further safeguard, Tobel has inscribed the names and addresses of the three men in a memo, written in code, using stick figures of dancing men. Working against time, both Holmes and Moriarity deduce that it's an alphabet substitution code. When two prominent scientists are found murdered, it becomes apparent that Moriarity has two-thirds of the bombsite in his possession.

Frantically competing with Holmes to break the code on the last cipher, Moriarity discovers Tobel's secret: The last name has been coded in *reverse.* Paying a call on the scientist on the list, the Professor finds instead a heavily disguised Holmes. The sleuth has beaten his adversary to the punch. Realizing he can no longer offer the bombsite to Germany, Moriarity decides to sell Tobel himself, but first he must eliminate Holmes. Stalling for time, the detective suggests his own method of execution: Being bound to an operating table and slowly drained of blood. Moriarity happily obliges, but before Holmes lapses into unconsciousness, Watson (Nigel Bruce) and Insp. Lestrade (Dennis Hoey) burst on the scene with a team of agents. Tobel is rescued and Moriarity, fleeing through a secret passageway booby-trapped by Holmes, plunges to his death.

Like *Sherlock Holmes and the Voice of Terror,* this follow-up adventure presents the war as the great inescapable crisis from its first frame. In the opening scene, even supposedly neutral Zurich is depicted as a hotbed of intrigue with German operatives at work in every corner. The action promptly moves to London, now a besieged fortress with sandbag fortifications around every building, forcing Holmes to traipse through Baker Street's rubble ruins in order to get to the sanctity of his flat. The earnest, stiff-upper-lip tone dissipates long before the "saved in the nick of time" ending in which Holmes barely escapes having his lifeblood drained in Moriarity's operating theater. (The staging of the scene forecasts James Bond's near-death-by-laser-beam as *Goldfinger*'s [1964] Moriarity-like villain gloats menacingly.) Despite *Secret Weapon*'s comic-book airs, Neill and his writers weave the life-and-death reality of the war and the Allies' unswerving struggle for victory compellingly into the narrative. The charged, call-to-arms spirit energizes the film's pace under Neill's strong direction.

There are a few clunky moments. At one point, Holmes instantly cobbles together an impromptu device which, presumably, was meant to invoke the same "gee-whiz" reaction from the audience as the character Q's gimmicky hardware did in James Bond's adventures 20 years later. However, the only function Holmes' "hi-tech" apparatus would serve is to splatter a trail of luminous paint from the car of Moriarity's henchmen, which is en route to the master criminal's lair. Of course, with such infamous bunglers as Watson and Lestrade leading the charge, Holmes' plan nearly leads to disaster, as the pair are sidetracked when another car picks up the paint, leading to a double trail on the road. The heroic detective does a fair bit of bungling himself. His security measures for the highly vulnerable Tobel are slapdash in the extreme with Moriarity easily managing to abduct him twice in the course of a 68-minute movie.

The script makes a passing reference to the original story in order to expedite the plot. In Conan Doyle's tale, Holmes is summoned to the aid of a well-to-do country squire whose young American wife is driven to near-madness upon

On the lookout for danger: Basil Rathbone, Kaaren Verne and Nigel Bruce in *Sherlock Holmes and the Secret Weapon* (courtesy Dan Scapperotti).

receiving a series of anonymous messages bearing only random stick figures. The detective deduces that the figures, actually pencil drawings resembling dancing men, are a message written with an ingenious alphabet substitution code. In an unlikely wrap-up, Holmes reveals the culprit to be the wife's spurned lover, a Chicago mobster determined to make things difficult for the woman in her adopted country. In the film, Holmes immediately grasps the meaning of

Lionel Atwill as Holmes' greatest adversary Prof. Moriarity (the studio's preferred spelling in their Holmes-Moriarity adventures).

Tobel's coded figures with the "earlier case" in mind and proceeds to decode the message. Universal claimed that director Neill employed the services of the studio's dance director, Johnny Mattison, to actually work out the code, designing a separate body position for each letter, creating an alternate alphabet for the film's purposes.

Last seen hurtling to his death from London Tower in 20th Century–Fox's *The Adventures of Sherlock Holmes* (1939), Prof. Moriarity makes his Universal debut graduating from master criminal to wholesaler of government secrets. (The studio inexplicably altered the character's name from the traditional "Moriarty" in all the films and publicity materials for the run of the series.) The scientist's collusion with the Nazis provided a reasonable updating of the character with Lionel Atwill playing the role a bit broadly but in his customary grand manner. Taking a cue from the dialogue which refers to Moriarity's snake-like eyes, the makeup department gives Atwill a dull gray pallor and a pair of eyebrows which peculiarly slope upwards.

But it was Holmes' disguises which provided the studio with most of the publicity opportunities. The film's pressbook claims that rubber shortages incurred during the war forced Jack Pierce to stretch his supply by using reclaimed rubber sponges in a base solution of alcohol and liquid glass. The first results of the process are seen in *Sherlock Holmes and the Secret Weapon* as the detective disguises himself as a doddering old book-seller and as a native seaman.

The repetition of the Sherlock Holmes role had not yet taken its toll on Rathbone, who gives one of his most incisive performances in the series. Rathbone and Atwill were a good match over the years and in this, their final teaming, the stars are in top form, delivering the ripe dialogue flawlessly. Cozily perched on Moriarity's overstuffed divan, the rivals hurl salvoes at each other with unerring accuracy, the arch-villain scoring points by undiplomatically reminding his rival of his addiction to morphine.

Kaaren Verne, then the wife of Peter Lorre, is fine in the female lead. William Post, Jr., as Dr. Tobel, reads his lines with distracting elocutionary precision, contributing to a hollow, unnatural performance. Far more notable in the cast is Dennis Hoey, making his series debut as the dull-witted Insp. Lestrade with endearing comic flair.

The actor's son, Michael A. Hoey, a longtime director whose pictures include the 1966 cult favorite, *The Navy vs. the Night Monsters,* discussed his father's most memorable role with the authors:

> In 1942, my father was hired by Universal to play the character of Scotland Yard Insp. Lestrade in *Sherlock Holmes and the Secret Weapon*, the second of the Holmes films and the first in which the character Lestrade appears. My father created

the role and ultimately did six of the 12 Holmeses.... My father's hair was a light red, a "blondeish" red color—what there was of it. He lost his hair fairly early, so in most of his films he was wearing the marvelous toupee that he owned. *Except* when he was playing Lestrade. In real life, he grew his hair long on one side and combed it over the bald spot on top, and so as Lestrade you see him as he actually looked, with his own hair.

In the course of the series, the Lestrade character is always seen through Holmes' eyes, which is to say, he's a caricature of bureaucratic bungling at its unimaginative worst. As such, he could be depended on to be at least two steps behind Holmes (and possibly even one behind Dr. Watson), while serving as the official representative of Scotland Yard.

Universal was so unsure about the public's reaction to the classic detective character appearing in tales of espionage rather than musty mysteries, the publicity department circulated a signed letter from the author's son, Denis P.S. Conan Doyle, for theater owners to post in their lobbies. Very likely bogus, the missive congratulates the studio for their "subtle and effective handling of the character and material," adding, "Truly genius has no age." Mr. Conan Doyle went on to opine that Universal's new film "is fully as good as *Sherlock Holmes and the Voice of Terror*, which I consider the best Sherlock Holmes film that has ever been made." Nonetheless, Universal was still using its new franchise as a bottom slot attraction, combining the film with Abbott and Costello's *It Ain't Hay* (1943) in some situations.

While Sherlockians still consider Universal's efforts to turn the detective into one of Churchill's foot soldiers a major misstep, *Sherlock Holmes and the Secret Weapon* is a more entertaining film than it's usually given credit for. In terms of content, its horror elements may be slight, but the irresistible teaming of Rathbone and Atwill make it more genre-friendly than some of Neill's more atmospheric offerings.

Critics' Corner

This second in the series of modernized Sherlock Holmes detective stories should satisfy the followers of this type of entertainment. The picture offers a substantial portion of action, and should prove to be an acceptable supporting feature.—*Harrison's Reports*, January 2, 1943

Rating: ★★ Holmes' various deductions and escapades on behalf of the valuable mechanism don't add up to much of a picture. Through no fault of Basil Rathbone ... nor any lack in Nigel Bruce ... Rialto's new film has too many dull moments and too many fantastic ones to rate with the previous chapter, *Sherlock Holmes and the Voice of Terror*. Script trouble is largely to blame, although some of the discredit falls to director Roy William Neill.—*The New York Daily News*, January 5, 1943, Dorothy Masters

Sherlock Holmes and the Secret Weapon is far from Conan Doyle's days. The story is much like one he might have written ... Basil Rathbone and Nigel Bruce are still perfectly cast....—*The New York Sun*, January 1943, Eileen Creelman

Plenty of suspense, lots of punch-packed action, glib direction ... and right neat performances.... If you're a Sherlock Holmes fan, this one won't let you down.—*The New York Post*, January 1943, Irene Thirer

[G]ood fare for mystery movie addicts.... Picture is well acted and ably directed and should go a long way towards satisfying the ghoulish appetites of the members of the Rialto Murder Club.—*The New York Daily Mirror*, January 1943

Basil Rathbone assumes the part of Sherlock Holmes with the suavity that is his stock in trade.—*The Hollywood Reporter*, December 23, 1942

A film that should do well on the bottom of a double bill despite its mildness.... Basil Rathbone does another of his smooth jobs in the role of the sleuth.... The director Roy William Neill sustains the mood of the film capably. Good acting does much to put the film over for the type of audience for which it is intended.—*The Film Daily*, December 28, 1942

Frankenstein Meets the Wolf Man

Released March 5, 1943. 72 minutes. *Producer:* George Waggner. *Director:* Roy William Neill. *Original Screenplay:* Curt Siodmak. *Photography:* George Robinson. *Art Director:* John B. Goodman. *Associate Art Director:* Martin Obzina. *Sound Director:* Bernard B. Brown. *Technician:* William Fox. *Set Decorator:* Russell A. Gausman. *Associate Set Decorator:* Edward R. Robinson. *Editor:* Edward Curtiss. *Gowns:* Vera West. *Musical Director:* Hans J. Salter. *Makeup:* Jack P. Pierce. *Assistant Director:* Melville Shyer. *Special Photographic Effects:* John P. Fulton.

Lon Chaney, Jr. (*Lawrence Stewart Talbot, the Wolf Man*), Ilona Massey (*Baroness Elsa Frankenstein*), Patric Knowles (*Dr. Frank Mannering*), Lionel Atwill (*Mayor*), Bela Lugosi (*The Frankenstein Monster*), Maria Ouspenskaya (*Maleva*), Dennis Hoey (*Police Inspector Owen*), Don Barclay (*Franzec*), Rex Evans (*Vazec*), Dwight Frye (*Rudi*), Harry Stubbs (*Guno*), Beatrice Roberts (*Varja*), Adia Kuznetzoff (*Singer*), Torben Meyer (*Erno*), Doris Lloyd (*Nurse*), Jeff Corey

(*Grave Digger*), David Clyde (*Police Sergeant*), Tom Stevenson (*Grave Robber*), Cyril Delevanti (*Freddy Jolly, Grave Robber*), Martha MacVicar [Vickers] (*Margareta*), Charles Irwin (*Constable*), Eddie Parker (*Lon Chaney's Stunt Double*), Gil Perkins (*Bela Lugosi's Stunt Double*).

> [W]e're partners, aren't we? And what a combination —*Frankenstein Meets the Wolf Man* up there on the marquees all over the country. The cash customers pilin' in and we're slayin' 'em.
>
> —*The Wolf Man to Old Doc Frankenstein in "Where Do We Go from Here, Boys?," a humorous essay written by Lon Chaney, Jr., for the twelfth anniversary issue of* The Hollywood Reporter, *January 1943*

"Never make a joke in the studio," warns writer Curt Siodmak:

> I was sitting down at the Universal commissary having lunch with George Waggner and I said, "George, why don't we make a picture *Frankenstein Wolfs the Meat Man*— er, *Meets the Wolf Man*?" He didn't laugh. This was during wartime; I wanted to buy an automobile and I needed a new writing job so I would be able to afford it. George would see me every day and ask me if I had bought the car yet. I said, "George, can I get a job?" He said, "Sure, you'll get a job, buy the car." Well, the day finally came when I had to pay for the car. George asked me that day, "Did you buy the car?" and I said, "Yes, I bought it." George said, "Good! Your new assignment is *Frankenstein Wolfs the Meat Man* —er, *Meets the Wolf Man*! I'll give you two hours to accept!

There may be just a whiff of apocrypha in Siodmak's priceless anecdote, but the end result remains *Frankenstein Meets the Wolf Man*, fifth installment in the ongoing Frankenstein soap opera and the dawn of what would come to be known as the "monster rally" films. While Val Lewton and his coterie at RKO continued to titillate audiences with unseen horrors, Universal began to redouble their efforts in the opposite direction, assembling their name-brand movie monsters in *Frankenstein Meets the Wolf Man* (two monsters), *House of Frankenstein* (five) and *House of Dracula* (four).

It took a deal of imagination, and a little cheating, to bring the Monster and Wolf Man franchises together in a single picture. *The Wolf Man* was set in the present day but this sequel, which takes four years later, is set in the much earlier era of the Frankenstein series. But *Frankenstein Meets the Wolf Man* was not designed to stand up to this sort of scrutiny. Probably almost no one noticed or cared about details like this when the film was released; by this point Universal had begun tailoring most of their pictures to the younger set anyway.

In an article on the future of Universal horror films in a 1942 *Saturday Evening Post*, writer Richard G. Hubler revealed that production of the then-upcoming *Frankenstein Meets the Wolf Man* was prompted by the nearly one million dollar gross of *The Wolf Man* and wrote that it was going to be *the* "supercolossal horror picture ... to scare addicts." Hubler continued, "It is a cinch that the fans who like horror films — estimated at 60,000,000— will [enjoy it]. The only way Universal can top that one is to produce *Frankenstein Marries the Cobra Woman with the Wolf Man as Best Man*."*

The idea of combining monsters in one picture was the shot in the arm these series (especially the Frankensteins) needed at this late date. These ghoulfests are often blamed for the decline and demise of the classic Dracula and Frankenstein series, but by the mid–'40s they were on their last legs anyway. The monster rally films may be juvenilia but they're slick and enjoyable, and a welcome opportunity for many of the best-loved horror stars to congregate in a single picture. *Frankenstein Meets the Wolf Man* went into production in October 1942, with George Waggner producing and Roy William Neill directing.

One windy night at the Llanwelly Cemetery, grave robbers (Cyril Delevanti and Tom Stevenson) break into the Talbot family vault intending to steal a valuable ring from the dead Larry Talbot (Lon Chaney, Jr.). Opening Talbot's coffin reveals his body in perfect condition despite the passage of years; the corpse is covered with a blanket of wolfsbane sprigs. As the full moon shines in through a window, Talbot's Wolf Man side is restored to life. He kills one of the would-be defilers while the other flees in terror.

**According to Hubler, "Metro-Goldwyn-Mayer reputedly offered Universal a cool $250,000 for the rights to the Frankenstein productions. The offer was disdainfully turned down."*

Deadly clash: Lon Chaney, Jr.'s, Wolf Man and Bela Lugosi's Monster come to grips while Ilona Massey pretends not to notice in *Frankenstein Meets the Wolf Man.*

In nearby Cardiff some time later, a constable finds Talbot unconscious in the street, blood trickling from a forehead wound. (The opening of *Abbott and Costello Meet Frankenstein* uses footage of the constable filmed for this scene — in fact, more than is seen in *FMtWM.*) Hospitalized, a greatly agitated Talbot tells Dr. Mannering (Patric Knowles) and Police Inspector Owen (Dennis Hoey) about his lupine alter ego, a story the two men are quick to dismiss. That night's full moon triggers another transformation, and the Wolf Man leaves the hospital and kills a bobby. (As in *The Wolf Man*, the werewolf makes an off-camera change into his familiar "prowl clothes" before going out, again to the point of buttoning his shirt and tucking in his shirttails!)

Talbot, desperate, searches Europe for Maleva (Maria Ouspenskaya), mother of the werewolf whose bite cursed him. Maleva, sympathetic to his plight, promises to guard and protect him. Convinced that Dr. Frankenstein can end his existence, Maleva sets out with Talbot in a horse-drawn cart for the Bohemian Alps and the little town of Vasaria. When they spot it in the distance, the stock footage insert shot is of the Western town of Greasewood from the Mae West-W.C. Fields comedy *My Little Chickadee* (1940)!

Talbot and Maleva receive a chilly welcome in Vasaria, and are disheartened to hear that Dr. Frankenstein, along with the Frankenstein Monster, perished in a fire at the doctor's sanitarium. (*The Ghost of Frankenstein* sanitarium and the burned-out castle seen in this film look nothing alike.) There's a full moon that night, and the Wolf Man kills young Margareta (Martha Vickers); in a scene recalling the "Ludwig–Little Maria walk" in *Frankenstein*, her dazed tavern-owner father Vazec (Rex Evans), a crowd in tow, carries her body down a Vasarian street. Angry townspeople form a hunting party and chase the Wolf Man into the darkened ruins of Frankenstein's sanitarium, where the man beast plummets through a hole in the floor and into an underground ice cave. Later, as Talbot, he explores the frosty catacomb and discovers the body of the Monster (Bela Lugosi) embedded in a wall of ice. (Notice the rubber icicle which bends as Talbot backs into it.) Talbot frees the Monster from the ice (in a scene reminiscent of Ygor rescuing the Monster from the wall of dried sulfur in *Ghost*) and asks him for Dr. Frankenstein's diary, which contains the secrets of life and, more importantly to Talbot, death. The Monster leads Talbot to the hiding place of the diary, but the book is not there.

Sartorially splendid in Dr. Frankenstein's clothes (Lon Chaney and Cedric Hardwicke wear the same size?), Talbot poses as "Mr. Taylor," a potential buyer for the ruined castle, in order to make the acquaintance of Baroness (?!) Elsa Frankenstein (Ilona Massey), Dr. Frankenstein's lovely daughter. Grimly he now admits that he wants only to locate Dr. Frankenstein's diary, and Elsa refuses to help. The mayor (Lionel Atwill) invites Elsa and "Taylor" to be guests of honor at Vasaria's Festival of the New Wine that evening.

The Festival is in full swing when Dr. Mannering unexpectedly arrives on the scene and corners Talbot. Mannering has followed Talbot across Europe via newspaper accounts of the Wolf Man murders, and is determined to see him institutionalized. The Monster blunders into town and creates a panic before Talbot is able to round up his new friend and escape in a wagon.

United in their desire to help Talbot escape his curse and to destroy the Monster, Mannering and Elsa make their way to the castle and convince Talbot of their good intentions. Elsa produces her father's diary and turns it over to Mannering, who decides that he can repair the charred electrical equipment in Frankenstein's laboratory and use it to drain the life energies from both Talbot and the Monster.

Mannering puts the lab back into working order and prepares for the ultimate experiment with both Talbot and the Monster strapped to adjacent operating tables. But in an uncharacteristic moment of mad doctor-style zeal he decides that it would be more interesting, or more fun, or some damn thing, to see the Monster at its full power, which he accomplishes by reversing the polarity, or some damn thing. Ungrateful for his new lease on life, the Monster menaces Mannering and Elsa just as the full moon begins to rise and Talbot undergoes his familiar change.

What the scripts calls "the fight of the Titans" commences: As Mannering and Elsa flee the castle, the Monster and the Wolf Man engage in an exciting brawl complete with furious strangleholds, spectacular tackles, flying lab equipment and a combination of *Wolf Man* and *Ghost of Frankenstein* music cues. By a well-timed coincidence, Vazec blows up a nearby dam in order to destroy the Frankenstein castle and the monsters within. Still locked in their life-and-death struggle, the Monster and the Wolf Man are swept away in the raging torrent.

Poor Bela Lugosi. In 1931, he turned up his

nose at the notion of playing the Monster in the original *Frankenstein* and inadvertently created a monster of his own in the person of Boris Karloff, who quickly and easily outpaced Lugosi as the screen's premier bogeyman. Hollywood in general and Universal in particular were never overly kind to Lugosi in the years following that career blunder, and by late 1942, when *Frankenstein Meets the Wolf Man* was filmed, the actor was in no position to turn down the Monster role, or any other. In fact, at the time he made *Frankenstein Meets the Wolf Man*, Bela was between stanzas #5 and #6 (*Bowery at Midnight* and *The Ape Man*) of his infamous Monogram nonet. (According to Bela's fellow Monogram contract player Gabriel Dell of the East Side Kids, "When you landed [at Monogram], even the unemployed actors at Schwab's Drug Store wouldn't talk to you.")

In keeping with the finale of *The Ghost of Frankenstein*, in which the brain of Ygor is transplanted into the head of the Monster, the script of *Frankenstein Meets the Wolf Man* called for a nearly blind Monster who still spoke and still nurtured Ygor's mad plan to subjugate the world. (Since the Monster was no match for a mob in *Bride of Frankenstein*, or even a handful of Vasarian constables in *Ghost of Frankenstein*, it seems fair to say his mouth was writing checks his body couldn't cash.) Three scenes in which the Monster had dialogue were shot.

The first, the longest and most elaborate, was set right after the Monster's rescue from the ice wall. The Monster and Talbot are sitting in the catacomb, where the Monster is warming his hands over a small fire. The Monster bemoans the loss of his sight and strength, and tells the story of how he came to be trapped in the ice, conscious for years, unable to move. The unholy pair now make their way back up into Dr. Frankenstein's old lab, ravaged by fire and festooned with cobwebs, where the Monster brags about his immortal body.

Superb character shot of Chaney Jr.'s lycanthrope as he appears in *Frankenstein Meets the Wolf Man*.

"Dr. Frankenstein created this body to be immortal! His son gave me a new brain, a clever brain. I shall use it for the benefit of the miserable people who inhabit the world, cheating each other, killing each other, without a thought but their own petty gain. I will rule the world!" (A *faux pas* for the brain-happy Siodmak: The Monster talks as though his old brain *and* Ygor's newly installed brain are both at work in his head.) Interested not in life but in death, Talbot eagerly asks the Monster for Frankenstein's diary; the Monster leads him into Frankenstein's study, but the book cannot be located.

More Monster dialogue followed the scene of the Monster's unexpected guest appearance at the Festival of the New Wine. Propped up with pillows in the castle study, the Monster explains that he had come into town because he feared that Talbot had deserted him. "I was afraid you'd left me — I thought you'd found that diary — and run away," the Monster mopes; Talbot calls him dumb. Later in the scene, after Dr. Mannering has arrived, the Monster belly-aches about his eyesight. The third and final scene is set once again in the study, with the Monster (clad in a white operating gown) sitting motionless "like a Tibetan god" while Talbot paces the floor in anticipation of the coming lab procedure. The Monster brags that his strength will soon be renewed, then rises and tells Talbot, "Then I shall see again — and be fit to rule the world!"

The inevitable happened only a few short weeks later, when the *Frankenstein Meets the Wolf Man* production staff gathered in a studio screening room to view the finished product. The film worked well until Lugosi's Monster first opened his mouth, and the sheer ludicrousness of a talkative monster finally struck the picture-makers. The screening turned into a shambles, with the little audience nearly convulsed with laughter over Lugosi's performance.

"Lugosi couldn't talk!" Curt Siodmak told the authors. "They had left the dialogue I wrote for the Monster in the picture when they shot it, but with Lugosi it sounded so Hungarian funny that they had to take it out!" Take it out they did; producer George Waggner, suddenly running scared, ordered all of the Monster's dialogue scenes removed from the film, not realizing (or not caring) that every reference to the Monster's near-blindness was being deleted as well.

The effect on Lugosi's already shaky performance was disastrous. Now the uncertain way in which the Monster gropes his way around, bumping into things, becomes inexplicable, as does a shot where he opens and closes his mouth like a goldfish (the line he spoke now unheard); it's a performance closer to Fred Gwynne's Herman Munster than to the Monster as played by Karloff (or Chaney or Glenn Strange — or Kiwi Kingston!). At one point in the climactic fight scene, he even spreads and raises his arms like Dracula about to turn into a bat. How ironic that the frail Lugosi, who turned 60 during the shooting of *FMtWM,* should be padded-up to play the Monster in this action-filled film whereas the next actor to play the role, burly Western tough guy Strange, hardly ever gets up off his rear!

But even though the Monster looks like "he's perpetually drunk and searching desperately for the nearest men's room" (The Phantom of the Movies), it's Bela's Monster with its arms outstretched and eyes half-closed, not Karloff's, that people down through the years are imitating when they "do" the Monster; Bela's Monster, not Karloff's, that the Aurora model kit seems to be based on; Bela's Monster, not Karloff's that Brendan Fraser mimics as he stomps around in the rain in the closing scenes of *Gods and Monsters* (1998). It's even Bela's Monster, not Karloff's, that Glenn Strange plays in the *House* films and *Abbott and Costello Meet Frankenstein,* despite being tutored on how to play the Monster *by* Karloff. Poor Boris!

It seems odd, in retrospect, that no one seemed to guess in advance the effect a speech-making Monster would have. Aside from being funny, these scenes had to have slowed the action. (Even with them cut, the movie still takes a dip entertainment-wise once the Monster is part of the story.) Siodmak admits that he wrote in at least one intentionally humorous line: Responding to Talbot's claim that he turns into a wolf, the Monster frowns, "Are you kidding?" But this bit is not much less risible than most of the other Talbot-Monster exchanges.

Edward Bernds, sound man on many a Roy William Neill Columbia B film, offers what may be an explanation as to why the director failed to recognize the comic potential of these dialogue scenes. Bernds remembers Neill as a man with "absolutely no sense of humor. I'm pretty sure that at Columbia he never directed a comedy, and if he did or if he had pictures perhaps with some lighter moments, I'm sure the humor got to the screen without much help from him."

In a Neill picture called *Wall Street* (1929), Ralph Ince plays a ruthless tycoon whose manipulations are ruining a number of other Wall Street characters. One of them comes to Ince in his office, pleading for mercy: If Ince doesn't back off, doesn't him a break, he will be bankrupt and he will kill himself. Ince tells him to get lost. Cut to the outer office. The man dashes through, over to a window and out he goes. Ince hears the commotion, comes out of *his* office and looks down out of the window. Ed Bernds was on the set:

> At this point, Ince said to his secretary, "And I said he didn't have the guts!' Well, there was an ab-

Hungarian thespians Ilona Massey and Lugosi share a tense moment in this staged scene.

solute spontaneous roar of laughter from the crew — it just hit everybody at once. And Neill was bewildered, he wanted to know what the hell it was all about. The gruesome incongruity of looking down at a man with his insides splattered on the sidewalk, it caused what I guess would be called a black humor laugh. Yet, Neill just couldn't seem to comprehend why it got that crazy, ghoulish laugh.

On a later Neill film, 1935's *Mills of the Gods*, Bernds' wisecracking assistant kiddingly renamed the picture *Oh, God, the Mills Brothers.* "Not funny, you might say, and maybe you're right," Bernds told us, "but it tickled the crew and a lot of people started calling it by that title. And Roy Neill, a nice man, no sense of humor, couldn't fathom why the cast and crew was getting the title of his film wrong!"

Contributing in large part to the success and popularity of *Frankenstein Meets the Wolf Man* is Lon Chaney's portrayal. Chaney gives a pent-up performance that is as good or better than the one he gave in *The Wolf Man.* The role this time is less demanding, with Talbot fully aware of his werewolf side from his first scene.

Chaney now seems more seasoned, more at ease with the character he was later proud to call his "baby." Chaney dominates the film: Forlorn but no longer whiny, desperate but not as panic-stricken, his Larry Talbot evokes greater sympathy as he searches for the secret of death. In one of Chaney's best moments, frustration moves him nearly to tears at Llanwelly Hospital. ("Lon Chaney always liked to have a scene where he could cry, which he had done very effectively in *Of Mice and Men* [1939]," actor Don Porter told the authors.) *Frankenstein Meets the Wolf Man* also boasts some of the best Wolf Man scenes from any of the character's five movies: The opening scene in the crypt, his attack on the Cardiff bobby, the posse scene in Vasaria and ultimately the roof-raising brawl with Lugosi's Frankenstein Monster. Universal's initial plan, at a time when the pre-production title was *Wolf Man Meets Frankenstein*, called for Chaney to play *both* monsters. That idea was dropped just days later when George Waggner decided it wasn't feasible because of the intricate makeups and the physical strain of playing two such parts.

Ilona Massey and Patric Knowles make for better-than-adequate leads. Massey, a former Metro star, brings a touch of class to the picture; occasionally her rolling r's and halting delivery get to be a bit much, but for the most part she fills the bill nicely (perhaps better than Evelyn Ankers) and she's an eye-opening treat in her long blond braids and low-cut nightgown.

Patric Knowles, as polished and professional a young leading man as ever drew a Universal paycheck, also acquits himself well, although his character wears perhaps a few too many different "hats" in the course of the film's 72 minutes (first he's a pill-pusher in a little Welsh town, then he turns amateur detective and bloodhound, and finally electrical engineer and "mad scientist"). It seems fitting that Knowles' character — the first non–Frankenstein to revive the Monster — should have the first name of Frank, an alias later used by the mad doctors in *Frankenstein's Daughter, The Revenge of Frankenstein* (both 1958) et al.

Good character support is provided by Lionel Atwill, Maria Ouspenskaya and Dennis Hoey. Atwill, in his third of five Frankenstein films, plays a minor role as the unnamed mayor of Vasaria. Although the script doesn't call for it, Atwill brings a few self-spoofing touches to the role, playing the part in the pompous, sputtering style of Nigel Bruce as Dr. Watson. The messy sex scandal that threatened to ruin his career was perhaps at its height at this time; on October 15, 1942, just a few days into production on *Frankenstein Meets the Wolf Man*, Atwill was sentenced to five years probation for perjury. Bred in England, the Toast of Broadway, but now just another Hollywood crumb, Atwill may have thought that *Frankenstein Meets the Wolf Man* would be his last film.

Maria Ouspenskaya is as hard on the eyes and ears as ever but, true to her vaunted rep, brings the same dignity to this meshugena monster movie that she brought to A-studios' A-productions. Annoyingly, the film neglects to let viewers know if Maleva survives the climactic castle destruction. Asked by the authors whether we were supposed to think that Maleva lived or died at film's end, Curt Siodmak simply laughed, "She died in the meantime!"* As Inspector Owen, Dennis Hoey plays, and even *dresses*, in a too-familiar fashion; it's as though his Inspector Lestrade had committed the ultimate blunder and wandered into the wrong film! Dennis' son Michael Hoey told the authors:

**In the script, as the flood waters are starting to reach the castle, Dr. Harley (Dr. Mannering), Elsa and Maleva hurry to Maleva's carriage and ride off. Perhaps Ouspenskaya was not able to appear in the finale because of an on-set injury (a coach ran over her foot and chipped a bone in her ankle) and her subsequent hospitalization (four days at Cedars of Lebanon).*

> My dad was under a non-exclusive contract to Universal, playing Lestrade. They only used him in two or three other [non–Holmes] pictures—but they seemed to see him playing only one role, Lestrade, even though they might have called his character by another name! In *Frankenstein Meets the Wolf Man*, he plays a Scotland Yard inspector and even wore the same bloody wardrobe—Lestrade's bowler hat and the raincoat! Then he did a film called *She-Wolf of London* and it was the same thing, a Scotland Yard inspector, only at least he was not wearing the same clothes in *that* one. So my father was very typecast at Universal.

In smaller parts, future Warners star Martha Vickers, seen as the girl killed (off-camera) by the Wolf Man, makes her film debut here under her real name, Martha MacVicar; Lance Fuller, co-star of such '50s fright flicks as *The She-Creature*, *Voodoo Woman* and *The Bride and the Beast*, once said in an interview that he was an extra in *FMtWM* and one of the *House* movies. Moose, Lon Chaney's dog since the days of *The Wolf Man*, turns up in a gypsy camp scene. This was perhaps his last film: Moose was road-killed on the back lot during the shooting of *Cobra Woman* (1944).

Frankenstein Meets the Wolf Man was the final Universal film for Dwight Frye, that stalwart of the ghouls 'n' geeks circuit, who died several months after its release. Plugging away day and night (by day as an actor, by night as a tool designer in a Los Angeles aircraft plant), Frye succumbed to a heart attack in November 1943, his dream of breaking with his screen image of a graveyard rat unrealized. That said, it *would* have been a nice touch if instead of playing Rudi, a Vasarian villager with a line here and there, he'd played one of the opening scene's grave robbers *à la Frankenstein* and *Bride*. The script describes Frye's character in this film as a blushing newlywed; in the script, it's he, not the mayor, who dances with Elsa at the Festival.

Among the stuntmen seen in the movie is Australian-born stuntman Gil Perkins, whose many other *cinemafantastique* credits include the 1933 *King Kong* (doubling Bruce Cabot), the 1941 *Dr. Jekyll and Mr. Hyde* (doubling Spencer Tracy as Hyde) and 1958's *Teenage Monster* (in the title role!). Perkins told the authors:

> The beautiful Hungarian actress Ilona Massey was the girl in [*Frankenstein Meets the Wolf Man*], and [stunt-doubling Bela Lugosi as the Monster] I had to carry her all around this basement with all this broken-down stuff in it. All she had on was a very pale blue, see-through negligee kind of thing and I think she had a pair of shorts, but she had no bra or anything like that. She was almost stark naked! I can remember somebody saying, "Jeez, I'd like to get this dame somewhere where I can *do* somethin' with her!"—I think that was a guy named Wes Hopper, a stuntman in those days.

As for the filming of the climactic brawl (in which Perkins portrayed an almost comically robotic, stiff-armed Monster), the stuntman continued:

> Roy William Neill just told Eddie Parker [Chaney's double as the Wolf Man] and myself to work out a fight and let him see it. We worked out the thing, then we just walked through it [for Neill], went through the motions, and said, "This is what we'll do here," "This is what we'll do there." He told us what he wanted, where he wanted us to start and where he wanted us to finish and what kind of a fight he wanted it to be. Apart from that, he left us pretty well alone.*

Many minor changes were made to Siodmak's script before cameras rolled. In the original script, the grave robbers who find Talbot's body in a state of perfect preservation notice that his fingernails have grown quite long in death. (Explaining the undecayed condition of Talbot's corpse, one grave robber nervously sputters, "The air in here—it's kept him like that!") At the hospital, when Dr. Harley (Dr. Mannering's name in this draft) and Inspector Owen examine Talbot's clothes for clues, they find them rotten and moldy as though they had been buried for years; Talbot's shirt falls apart at a touch "as if it were woven of spider's thread." Maleva is initially unsympathetic to Talbot when he appears at her camp, firmly telling him, "Go away! And don't cross my path again!" before she takes pity on the suffering lycanthrope. Pursued by a mob after the murder of Margareta, the Wolf

**In October 2005, the burning question of what stuntmen played the Monster in the various Universal films was raised on the Classic Horror Film Boards (www.monsterkid.com) by moderator David Colton (Taraco). Scores of CHFB members joined in the discussion, hundreds of photos and frame grabs of Monsters and stuntmen were posted, and as of June 2006, the number of posts in the thread had risen to over 2000!*

Man hurls rocks and even a crumbling wall downhill onto the heads of the villagers. And in the finale, just before the monsters clash, it's the Wolf Man who first breaks free from his bonds and menaces Harley and Elsa, and the Monster who comes to the rescue. In the script, the film's last image is of a page of Frankenstein's diary bobbing along on the waves of flood water: "And when I succeed in creating life, I shall be as great as God!"

On the list of Good Things about *Frankenstein Meets the Wolf Man*, Siodmak's screenplay probably lands somewhere near the bottom, if it deserves to be on the list at *all*. Movie-to-movie continuity gaffes had been made in the past, but here for the first time is a script which makes it apparent that the writer didn't remember, or never knew, or didn't care about accurately recapping events of previous Franken-films. Characters refer to Ludwig Frankenstein, Cedric Hardwicke's *Ghost* character, as the original creator of the Monster. The people of Vasaria, whose lives have hardly been touched by the Monster (his only innocent victims in *Ghost* were two villagers and Dr. Kettering), talk as though he was their Pearl Harbor and 9/11 rolled into one. Talbot, chatting with Maleva, says they met in England rather than Wales, and the Llanwelly police sergeant says the Wolf Man drained the blood of his victims. Elsa recalls with a shudder that Ludwig became "obsessed by his power," something that never happened. At this point in the series, generic spook talk about past events became the rule rather than the exception.

Mannering, quite suddenly and implausibly deranged, talks out loud to himself to let the audience know what's going on in his head, and makes the death-wish decision to conduct his Frankenstein-Talbot experiment at two minutes before moonrise even though he's fully aware that Talbot is the Wolf Man. In Vazec's tavern, Talbot and Maleva look like they're in danger of being tarred and feathered just for asking about Dr. Frankenstein, Vasaria's Most Hated Man, but one reel later the villagers open their arms for the returning Elsa Frankenstein and make her guest of honor at the Festival of the New Wine.

Combining the two monster characters in one movie points up the almost comically small size of the talent pool from which Universal drew its horror picture players. Chaney was the last actor to play both the Monster and the Wolf Man, so Universal was in a pickle right from the get-go. The part of Elsa should have been assigned to Evelyn Ankers because she played the role in *Ghost*, but she'd also played Talbot's girlfriend in *The Wolf Man* and having her now turn up as a different starring role in a new Wolf Man movie set in another country would have been awkward. *Ghost of Frankenstein* mad scientist Lionel Atwill is now the mayor of Vasaria. In Queens Hospital, Talbot is attended by a doctor and a nurse played by Patric Knowles and Doris Lloyd, also left over from *The Wolf Man* but here playing different characters. Lloyd, Chaney, Jr., and Lugosi were in all *three* movies (*Wolf Man, Ghost, FMtWM*). Harry Stubbs, a *Wolf Man* priest, is now a grumpy law officer; agitated Frankenstein villager Dwight Frye (*Ghost of Frankenstein*) is now an agitated Vasarian; and Tom Stevenson, a grave digger (and the Wolf Man's first victim) in *The Wolf Man*, is now a grave *robber*, breaking into the crypt of the man who killed his previous character! Unbecoming of a major studio, this endless, sometimes bewildering recycling of the same few faces is like something out of *Monster Kid Home Movies*.

October 5, 1942, was an unlucky day on the *FMtWM* set: In addition to Maria Ouspenskaya suffering an ankle injury, Bela Lugosi collapsed and was ordered home by a physician. The cause was diagnosed as exhaustion brought on the 35 pounds worth of Monster get-up the actor was packing around.

In an unusual move, Universal "pushed" *Frankenstein Meets the Wolf Man* in some of their *other* 1943 movies. In *He's My Guy*, Dick Foran and Irene Hervey work in a vaudeville-movie house where *FMtWM* is playing. In one scene, Joan Davis comes into the auditorium, looks up at the screen and sees the Wolf Man growl, she growls back, and (in a redubbed bit of footage) the Wolf Man runs away whining! Then in *Top Man*, Peggy Ryan jumps into the back seat of a convertible with Donald O'Connor, and for no reason at all blurts out "Frankenstein meets the Wolf Man!"

Of the three straight monster rallies, *Frankenstein Meets the Wolf Man* is easily the best. Taking a break from the Sherlock Holmes series, Roy William Neill puts forth what seems a sincere effort, injecting some mood and style into a film whose baldly exploitative title and premise set it down as routine even before a frame of film was exposed. Unlike director Erie C. Kenton, who was more of a ringmaster than a craftsman on the two *House* pictures, Neill puts his familiar stamp on the film. It's atmospheric, almost noirish in spots, and is enhanced by good performances as well as some excellent technical credits.

Photography by George Robinson is particularly good. The film opens with an ambitious shot of the windswept Llanwelly Cemetery; Robinson's camera fixes first on the graveyard sign, glides over a high wall taking in the bleak landscape, focuses on the approaching grave robbers and accompanies them up to the door of the Talbot crypt. While there are few of the curious, striking camera compositions that crop up in *The Ghost of Frankenstein*, Robinson's camerawork and lighting remain a plus factor throughout, helping to endow the picture with some handsome pictorial values. The sets, miniatures and special effects are also high quality.

The Festival of the New Wine sequence is a pleasant interlude that breaks up the atmosphere of grimness and gives the picture a nice splash of color and pageantry. Adia Kuznetzoff, a toothy, big-eyed Russian baritone, makes the most of his minor role as the Festival singer, belting out "Faro-La, Faro-Li" (lyrics by Siodmak!) and adding appreciably to the Oktoberfest, oom-pah-pah feel of the film. (Actually, the whole movie gives off a chilly atmosphere, from the wind and blowing leaves of the opening scene, and bundled-up characters throughout, to the ice- and snow-filled cave beneath the Frankenstein sanitarium — where you can actually see Lon Chaney's breath!)

Critical reaction to *Frankenstein Meets the Wolf Man* was generally lukewarm, with many writers treating the film as a joke, which was perhaps to be expected. But it's a far better film than its audience required. What should have been a mere exploitation horror film with its accent on monsters and action is also a well-crafted production with fine attention to detail. The film that led the classic series permanently astray does so in handsome style: It has what might be the most effective opening scene in the entire Universal Horrors canon; it boasts the best Wolf Man scenes; it gives us one last real look at the Monster before he becomes a lowly prop in *House of Frankenstein* and *House of Dracula*; it has atmospheric as well as action highlights, a game cast and, of course, that terrific last-reel donnybrook. *Frankenstein Meets the Wolf Man* teeters atop a rickety pedestal as a milestone in monster movie history.

Critics' Corner

Not very horrible. Universal will have to try again.... Why not unite with Monogram and turn out a horror to end all horrors — *Wolf Man and Monster Meet the East Side Kids*...?—*The New York Times*, March 6, 1943, Bosley Crowther

As lurid, as wild and as screwy as it sounds on paper, it's magnificent melodrama —*if* you like your movies that way — and there are plenty who do to make it a whale of a hit.... [A] special bow to the camera and special effects. — *The Hollywood Reporter*, February 19, 1943

[Curt Siodmak] delivers a good job of fantastic writing to weave the necessary thriller ingredients into the piece.... Eerie atmosphere generates right at the start.... — *Variety*, February 19, 1943, "Walt"

[A] horror feast in which devotees of the weird and the fantastic will gorge themselves to bursting. The opportunities for screams are offered with unparalleled generosity. Heaven knows what so rich a diet of scariness will do to the kids.—*Film Daily*, March 1, 1943

Rating: ★★½ The producers have spent time and money on the production and have gone to considerable trouble to give it the proper atmospheric touches.... — *The New York Daily News*, March 6, 1943, Kate Cameron

Sherlock Holmes in Washington

Released April 30, 1943. 71 minutes. *Director:* Roy William Neill. *Associate Producer:* Howard Benedict. *Screenplay:* Bertram Millhauser & Lynn Riggs. *Original Story:* Bertram Millhauser. *Based on the characters created by* Sir Arthur Conan Doyle. *Photography:* Les White. *Editor:* Otto Ludwig. *Art Director:* Jack Otterson. *Associate Art Director:* Martin Obzina. *Assistant Directors:* William Tummel & Gilbert Valle. *Music:* Frank Skinner. *Musical Director:* Charles Previn. *Set Decorator:* Russell A. Gausman. *Associate Set Decorator:* Edward R. Robinson. *Sound Director:* Bernard B. Brown. *Technician:* James Masterson. *Technical Adviser:* Tom McKnight. *Gowns:* Vera West.

Basil Rathbone (*Sherlock Holmes*), Nigel Bruce (*Dr. John H. Watson*), Marjorie Lord (*Nancy Partridge*), John Archer (*Lt. Peter Merriam*), George Zucco

(*Richard Stanley/Heinrich Hinkle*), Henry Daniell (*William Easter*), Gavin Muir (*Bart Lang*), Edmund MacDonald (*Detective Lt. Grogan*), Don Terry (*Howe*), Bradley Page (*Cady*), Holmes Herbert (*Mr. Ahrens*), Thurston Hall (*Sen. Henry Babcock*), Gilbert Emery (*Sir Henry Marchmont*), Ian Wolfe (*Clerk*), Mary Forbes (*Beryl Pettibone*), Gerald Hamer (*John Grayson/Alfred Pettibone*), John Burton (*Army Inspector/Commentator "Voice of London"*), Regina Wallace (*Mrs. Bryce Partridge*), Mary Gordon (*Mrs. Hudson*), Margaret Seddon (*Miss Pringle*), Alice Fleming (*Mrs. Jellison*), Clarence Muse (*George*), Leyland Hodgson (*Airport Official*), Evelyn Cooke (*Girlfriend*), Charles Marsh, Gene O'Donnell, Alexander Lockwood (*Reporters*), Eddie Coke (*Steward*), Paul Scott, Lee Shumway (*Army Majors*), Irving Mitchell (*Laboratory Assistant*), Leslie Denison (*Bomber Pilot*), Jason Robards (*Doorman*), Phil Warren (*Young Officer*), Tom Martin (*Waiter*), Caroline Cooke (*Mrs. Ruxton*), Kernan Cripps (*Hotel Porter*).

A big country, Watson, and a small match folder.
—*Basil Rathbone in* Sherlock Holmes in Washington

Well on his way to becoming England's most illustrious freedom fighter (an image Sir Arthur Conan Doyle couldn't possibly have anticipated), Sherlock Holmes fought against enemy forces on American soil in *Sherlock Holmes in Washington* (original title: *Sherlock Holmes in U.S.A.*), produced at Universal City in the fall of 1942. The first Universal Holmes entry not directly inspired by one of Conan Doyle's stories, *Sherlock Holmes in Washington* doesn't fare well with thrill-seekers. It hasn't the verve or the color of *Sherlock Holmes and the Voice of Terror* or *Sherlock Holmes and the Secret Weapon*, nor does it boast the macabre elements that made *The Scarlet Claw* and *The Pearl of Death* so memorable. Nevertheless, the film succeeds on its own modest terms.

Marking the series debut of screenwriter Bertram Millhauser (who cowrote the script with Lynn Riggs, who, in turn, coauthored the script of *Sherlock Holmes and the Voice of Terror*), *Sherlock Holmes in Washington* benefits greatly from solid characterizations, an interest-holding tale couched in smart dialogue, and snappy direction by the adept Roy William Neill.

Unlike the more highly regarded entries in the series, *Sherlock Holmes in Washington* conspicuously lacks bravura set pieces that encourage revisits. Instead, the film is filled with little moments, inventive bits of business which, while they may not quicken the pulse, work effectively on a less audacious level. Its slow, methodical tempo and low-keyed excitement notwithstanding, *Sherlock Holmes in Washington* is still an enjoyable caper, undeserving of the second-class treatment it sometimes receives.

A secret government document of "great international importance" (that's the only clue we are given regarding its contents throughout) is (presumably) entrusted to ace British diplomat Sir Henry Marchmont (Gilbert Emery) on its journey to Washington, D.C. A gang of Axis agents led by William Easter (Henry Daniell) follows the diplomat to New York, and then aboard the Washington Express.

Easter rifles through Sir Henry's baggage and concludes that he is only a decoy employed by the British. The real courier is Alfred Pettibone (Gerald Hamer), alias John Grayson, a meek senior clerk working undercover for the British Secret Service. Pettibone had the foresight to transfer the bulky document to a minuscule piece of microfilm, and then glued it inside the cover of a matchbook. Minutes before he is seized by Easter's men, Pettibone passes the matchbook to socialite Nancy Partridge (Marjorie Lord), who leaves the train unaware she is carrying a "time bomb."

Back in London, Sherlock Holmes (Basil Rathbone) and Dr. Watson (Nigel Bruce) receive an urgent visit from Mr. Ahrens (Holmes Herbert) of the Home Office. Pettibone has undoubtedly been kidnapped and, chances are, the document is now in the hands of enemy agents. With all due haste, Holmes and Watson are whisked off on their first trip to America.

A grim discovery awaits the Britons immediately upon their arrival: a trunk containing Pettibone's corpse. Holmes is convinced that the enemy agents have not yet recovered the document (which he has already deduced had been transferred to microfilm). Although the Washington, D.C., police have made a thorough search of the club car in which Pettibone was abducted, Holmes conducts his own investigation. He quickly deduces the identity of Pettibone's unwitting accomplice, Nancy Partridge.

The scene shifts to a festive afternoon reception celebrating Nancy's forthcoming marriage to

Master spy George Zucco confronts Marjorie Lord and Basil Rathbone in *Sherlock Holmes in Washington* (courtesy Dan Scapperotti).

Lt. Peter Merriam (John Archer). Disguised as caterers, two of Easter's men, Cady and Howe (Bradley Page and Don Terry), separate Nancy and Peter from their guests. Merriam is knocked out and Nancy is anesthetized, rolled up in a carpet, and carried off in full view of the celebrants. (After making the rounds of the guests, the "traveling" matchbook has fortuitously found its way back Nancy's handbag again.)

Based on a minute investigation of the scrapings taken from the blanket used to conceal Pettibone's body, Holmes concludes that the agents operate out of an antique shop. Impersonating an eccentric collector, Holmes wrangles his way into the office of the shop's proprietor, the respected Richard Stanley (George Zucco). The detective's guise doesn't fool Stanley, nor does Stanley's veneer of reputability throw Holmes, who recognizes him to be none other than Heinrich Hinkle, ex-secret agent of the German Kaiser, now head of the world's most insidious international spy ring.

Searching Nancy's purse, Stanley comes across the matchbook and, unaware of the treasure it conceals, blithely uses it to light his own pipe. Holmes taunts his adversary, who has obviously come to a dead end in his quest for the document, with the remark, "The man who has it doesn't know he has it." Throwing Stanley off course, Holmes suggests the possibility that the document might have been transferred to microfilm and hidden behind something as minute as a postage stamp.

Confident he now knows the whereabouts of the document, Stanley is about to murder Holmes and Nancy when the police, alerted by Watson, converge on the shop and round up Easter and his cohorts. Stanley escapes the raid by disappearing into a secret passageway hidden behind an Egyptian sarcophagus. He heads straight for the home of Senator Henry Babcock (Thurston Hall), whom Pettibone had given a stamped envelope bearing his mailing address on the train ride to Washington. But Stanley is too late: Holmes has beaten him there. Holding the men at gunpoint, Stanley is about to flee with the envelope when the police nab him. Unable to resist the temptation to mortify his opponent, Holmes sets the envelope on fire. Removing a bit of microfilm from the matchbook, he reminds the livid master spy of the clue he threw his way earlier — that the man who had the document *didn't know he had it!*

Of all the Sherlock Holmes adventures written by Sir Arthur Conan Doyle, none of them were set in America. The author confined the activities of his immortal detective to the British Isles exclusively. Holmes' only connection with the U. S. of A in Conan Doyle's stories were occasional references to the gumshoe's "trips" to that wild country on the other side of the pond.

Bertram Millhauser's first encounter with Conan Doyle's legendary detective took place in 1932, when the New York–born stenographer-turned-writer penned the screenplay for the Fox release *Sherlock Holmes*, inspired by the Conan Doyle short stories and the William Gillette play. Millhauser distinguished himself as one of Universal's most literate writers, specializing in motion pictures with British backgrounds (he scripted a total of five Sherlock Holmes adventures for the studio). Gaining his early cinematic experience writing Pearl White serials, Millhauser came to Hollywood in the '20s as a writer-producer for Cecil B. DeMille, then worked as an associate producer for such studios as Radio, RKO and Fox. Tough-edged urban dramas of the kind that built Warner Bros.' reputation kept the writer busy. These included *The Life of Jimmy Dolan* (1933), which Millhauser adapted from his own play, *Jimmy the Gent* (1934), *They Made Me a Criminal* (1939) with John Garfield, Claude Rains and the Dead End Kids, and *The Big Shot* (1942), a lesser Humphrey Bogart gangster outing.

Finely-etched characterizations and pungent dialogue were Millhauser's strong suits. With the exception of *The Pearl of Death*, probably his best work, the writer's genre pictures (*Sherlock Holmes Faces Death*, *The Spider Woman*, *The Woman in Green*, *The Invisible Man's Revenge*) occasionally suffer from flaccid pacing. Although *Sherlock Holmes in Washington* doesn't pack a wallop, it does maintain a direct narrative course, builds tension, and doesn't get too preoccupied with tangential plotlines.

Neill and the screenwriters have taken a tongue-in-cheek approach to the deadly serious business of tracking down missing top security documents. One could accuse them of aping Alfred Hitchcock in one of his more mischievous moods. The document is, after all, nothing more than one of the master's beloved "MacGuffins" (i.e., an object of great desirability — usually a secret code, a weapon, or a valuable formula — which sets the plot in motion but gradually takes a back seat in terms of relevance to the characters and their adventures). The suspenseful cat-and-mouse scene played out in the club car also recalls Hitchcock. As in *The Lady Vanishes* (1938), the club car is inhabited by colorful character types, all of whom are blissfully unaware of the dramatic situation unfolding around them.

Ironically, the document constantly ends up in the palms of its pursuers. "You have a document I must have," Zucco says with grim determination to Marjorie Lord as he holds the matchbook between his fingers. She, of course, hasn't the slightest inkling of what he's talking about. Having deduced that the document has been transferred to microfilm, Holmes points up the absurdity of the chase with the line, "A big country, Watson, and a small match folder."

A dour side to the detective's personality is revealed this time out. Unlike Watson, who revels in such Americanisms as chewing gum, ice cream sodas and the Sunday comics, Holmes is unfazed by his first trip to the States and is totally preoccupied with the business at hand. Sitting stone-faced in the back seat of the car en route to the hotel, he spouts an obligatory "most impressive" and "magnificent" as Detective Lt. Grogan (Edmund MacDonald) points out such landmarks as the Lincoln Memorial and the Capitol Building. A short time later, Holmes ruffles the detective's feathers when he authoritatively directs the investigation of an essential piece of evidence. Realizing he's hit a nerve, Holmes softens his approach with an apologetic,

"I sometimes forget the more modern scientific methods *so particularly effective* here in America." Naturally, the remarkable sleuth uncovers evidence (some of it quite extraordinary) that the D.C. police lab never dreamed existed.

But most unpleasant of all is Holmes' condescending treatment of Watson, a habit that he retains for the rest of the series. He snaps at the old man as if to an unloved spouse. On more than one occasion, Holmes makes a fool of the doctor in front of strangers. While his brilliance as an investigator is beyond reproach, this offensive new character trait hardly endears us to Holmes the man.

Rathbone's climactic confrontation with George Zucco harks back to their battle of wits in the superior *The Adventures of Sherlock Holmes* (1939). It's always a pleasure to see these old pros play off each other, even though their scenes together in this film lack the fire of their earlier encounter, and are also a notch below the verbal fencing match Rathbone and Lionel Atwill waged in *Sherlock Holmes and the Secret Weapon*. Rathbone's impression of a prissy antique connoisseur who questions the authenticity of Zucco's wares ("Ming for T'ang, indeed!") is a joy.

Zucco is up to his old tricks. He has rigged a Moorish chest with a deadly booby trap, a bow and arrow device which is set to fire the second the lid is opened. Searching the office for clues, Rathbone curiously fiddles with the lid as Zucco stands by with studied calm. Sensing something foul is afoot, he places a vase before the chest, stands off to the side and opens the lid. The vase is demolished. ("The Moors were an incredibly inventive people, weren't they?" he chides Zucco.) The serial-like rescue of Rathbone and Marjorie Lord by the police a moment before Zucco pulls the trigger on them is, to put it charitably, unbelievable.

In the supporting cast, Marjorie Lord (in a role the studio originally announced for Evelyn Ankers) is fine as the debutante suddenly thrust into a world of international intrigue. She and love interest John Archer met while appearing in a stage production of "The Male Animal," and were already husband and wife when they were cast in *Sherlock Holmes in Washington*. (Robert Paige was the original choice for Archer's part; he was removed for another role in a different picture.) John Archer (who passed away on December 3, 1999, after a battle with lung cancer) warmly recalled for us the making of this picture:

> I enjoyed that movie, even though the part was minimal. Basil Rathbone and Nigel Bruce were both consummate pros, and a pleasure and a delight to work with. They were wonderful people to be around, and very helpful. They each had a subtle sense of humor, which was always kind of fun. Marjorie and I had a scene together where I said goodbye to her, and I did the usual thing, I patted her on the butt, "See ya later"—you know what I mean. And the director [Neill] said "Cut! Cut! Oh, come on, John. What are you *doing*?" You can do those kinds of things in the movies today, but not *then*. Those Sherlock Holmes fans—by God, they are rabid. They want everything to be just the way it was. But Universal was producing pictures to make money, and this was a question of making a buck. I'm sure that was their feeling—"Let's update it or change it in some way, and see if we can make a little bit more money." *That's* when all of the diehards got on them.

Marjorie Lord also had positive things to say about her Holmes experience, as she told Michael Fitzgerald in a May 2005 *Classic Images* interview:

> I was pleased with [the picture]. It had a mostly British cast, and every afternoon at 4:00, we stopped for tea and cookies. I liked that. It was very English, and when I'm around people with an accent, I tend to pick it up. So, I thought I spoke with a slight English accent in the film, even though I was supposed to be an American, not English!

The Archers had two children; one of them, Anne, went on to enjoy a successful Hollywood career of her own. She was nominated for a Best Supporting Actress Oscar as Michael Douglas' betrayed wife in the 1987 mega-hit, *Fatal Attraction*.

Once again, Henry Daniell is slighted in an insignificant role not worthy of his gifts. Not until *The Woman in Green*, his third Sherlock Holmes caper, was the actor was finally given the opportunity to share the spotlight with Rathbone. British character actor Gerald Hamer makes his series debut as the ill-fated Alfred Pettibone, while Clarence Muse, the prolific black actor whose dry wit enhanced dozens of Hollywood features (he was one of the few bright spots in the 1941 Lugosi Monogram cheapie, *Invisible Ghost*), makes the most of his small role as George, the keen-eyed club car barman. A sad commentary on the state of race relations in the United States at the time *Sherlock Holmes in Washington* was made, the name "George" was routinely designated to the low-paid African-Americans who most often labored in menial railway jobs; the source of the name was the inventor of the Pullman railroad coach, George Pullman.

Rounding out Bertram Millhauser's screenwriting career is a mixed bag of melodramas and action pictures including *The Web* (1947), *Walk a Crooked Mile* (1948) and *Tokyo Joe* (1949). He branched off into television in the '50s and worked as a story editor on two popular series, *The Adventures of Jim Bowie* and *The Lone Ranger*. The erudite screenwriter, who put Conan Doyle's hero through some of his most intriguing adventures and introduced two of the macabre cinema's beloved menaces, the Spider Woman and the Creeper, died of a heart attack at the age of 66 on December 1, 1958.

A studio publicity release reported that Rathbone and Bruce "hurried to finish their roles in *Sherlock Holmes in Washington* in order to take part in a bond-selling rally throughout Texas and New Mexico and parts of Arizona. At one rally, the two stars conducted an auction which resulted in the sale of $4,000,000 in bonds in less than an hour."

As the British say, "Full marks, gentlemen!"

Critics' Corner

Rating: Fair–Good. This picture is a pleasure, in its small way.—*The New York Post*, May 28, 1943, Archer Winsten

Basil Rathbone gives his usual good portrayal of "Holmes," and Nigel Bruce, as "Dr. Watson," his aide, provokes many laughs with bright bits of dialogue.—*Harrison's Reports*, April 3, 1943

It is done in a manner that the Baker Street Irregulars will relish, except for one minor point. It is difficult to believe even an up-to-date Holmes would forego his famous pipe for cigarettes. [Producer Howard] Benedict may hear from the Baker Street gang about such an unnecessary liberty. Ordinary audiences will not notice it.—*The Hollywood Reporter*, March 26, 1943

This one looks like the best of Universal's Sherlock Holmes series. The screenplay ... is one that permits of many effective moments of melodrama and action in generous quantities.... [T]he film sustains the suspense rather well under the directorial guidance of Ray [*sic*] William Neill.—*The Film Daily*, March 31, 1943

Captive Wild Woman

Released June 4, 1943. 60 minutes. *Director:* Edward Dmytryk. *Associate Producer:* Ben Pivar. *Executive Producer:* Jack Gross. *Screenplay:* Griffin Jay & Henry Sucher. *Original Story:* Ted Fithian, Neil P. Varnick & Maurice Pivar. *Photography:* George Robinson. *Assistant Director:* Melville Shyer. *Editor:* Milton Carruth. *Art Directors:* John B. Goodman & Ralph M. DeLacy. *Musical Director:* Hans J. Salter. *Set Decorators:* Russell A. Gausman & Ira S. Webb. *Sound Director:* Bernard B. Brown. *Technician:* William Hedgcock. *Makeup:* Jack P. Pierce. *Gowns:* Vera West.

John Carradine (*Dr. Sigmund Walters*), Evelyn Ankers (*Beth Colman*), Milburn Stone (*Fred Mason*), Lloyd Corrigan (*John Whipple*), Martha MacVicar [Vickers] (*Dorothy Colman*), Vince Barnett (*Curley Barret*), Fay Helm (*Miss Strand*), Paul Fix (*Gruen*), Ray "Crash" Corrigan (*Cheela*), Ed Peil, Sr. (*Jake*), Ray Walker (*Ringmaster*), Gus Glassmire (*Coroner*), Fern Emmett (*Neighbor*), William Gould (*Sheriff*), Grant Withers (*Vet*), Joey Ray (*Attendant*), Frank Mitchell (*Handler*), Anthony Warde (*Tony*), Harry Holman (*Clerk*), Alexander Gill (*Waiter*), Charles McAvoy (*Policeman*), Virginia Engels (*Trapeze Artist*), Turhan Bey (*Closing Narration*), Clyde Beatty, Tom London (featured in footage from *The Big Cage*). *Deleted from final print:* Joel Goodkind (*Boy*).

And introducing Acquanetta as *Paula Dupree*.
"A New Sensation in Savagery"
—*Ad blurb for* Captive Wild Woman

Universal's most erotic offspring of ungodly scientific experimentation — a woman fashioned from the body of an ape through the injection of sex hormones — was the creation of writers Ted Fithian, Neil P. Varnick and Maurice Pivar. Christened Paula Dupree, the exotic menace was the center-ring attraction of a three-picture miniseries began by producer Ben Pivar. The best of the trio, *Captive Wild Woman*, is a brisk action-melodrama for the juvenile trade which made little attempt to underplay the sensationalistic aspects of its unappetizing premise.

The concept of scientifically transforming animals into humans (and vice versa) was hardly new. Charles Laughton created a nightmarish menagerie of "manimals" (including an alluring Panther Woman [Kathleen Burke], an ancestor of Paula Dupree) in Paramount's vivid adaptation of H.G. Wells' *The Island of Dr. Moreau*, *Island of Lost Souls* (1933). The previous year, Bela Lugosi vainly attempted to establish a link between man and beast in Universal's own *Murders in the Rue Morgue*. Stuart Heisler's stylish *The Monster and the Girl*, released by Paramount in 1941, featured a vengeful ape with the mind of an executed murderer, while Monogram's 1943 *The Ape Man* had Poor Bela strutting around a cheap Poverty Row lab in a hilarious half-man/half-ape get-up. But it was 20th Century–Fox's *Dr. Renault's Secret*, released a year before *Captive Wild Woman*, that came closest to the Universal thriller in concept. In this minor but surprisingly well-mounted B, George Zucco transforms an ape that he had acquired on a jungle expedition into a pathetic imbecile with simian-like mannerisms (sympathetically played by J. Carrol Naish).

Less thoughtful but a lot more provocative than the Fox picture, *Captive Wild Woman* wears better with today's thrill-seeking horror fans. The angle of creating a *female* hybrid brought to the film an element of sensuality missing from the staid *Dr. Renault's Secret*.

A Canadian-born film editor turned director, Edward Dmytryk does an efficient job, keeping the story moving at a fast clip. After several years of working in B programmers (including the chilling 1941 Karloff vehicle *The Devil Commands* for Columbia), Dmytryk struck pay dirt with *Hitler's Children* (RKO, 1943). He made *Captive Wild Woman* while on loan-out from RKO, then returned to the studio and established himself as a first-rank talent via pictures like *Tender Comrade* (1943), *Murder, My Sweet* (1944) and *Crossfire* (1947). The McCarthy witch hunts forced Dmytryk to seek temporary employment in Britain, but he returned to Hollywood in the early '50s and directed such critically acclaimed and/or commercially successful pictures as *The Caine Mutiny* (1954), *Soldier of Fortune* (1955), *Raintree County* (1957), *The Young Lions* (1958) and *The Carpetbaggers* (1964).

More than two years before its release, Universal announced its intentions to produce *Captive Wild Woman* in *The Hollywood Reporter*. August 8, 1941, was the designated starting date, yet the studio was still undecided as to who should play their newest horror creation, "The Wild Woman." (According to one source, Maria Montez was considered for the role.) Two distinctly different concepts of this character appeared in preview ads planted in the trade paper: A July 29 ad featured a furiously leering female, while a second ad showed an exotic woman, knife in hand, running through the jungle (suggesting a *Jungle Girl* or *Tiger Woman*-like character). Neither rendition even hinted at the half-woman/half-ape hybrid that eventually surfaced.

Although January 2, 1942, was designated as the kick-off date of the new George Waggner production, *Captive Wild Woman* didn't go into production until December 10, 1942, nearly a year-and-a-half after it was first announced. By then, Waggner had dropped out of the project and Ben Pivar had taken over. Shooting picked up again after the Christmas holidays and post-production work began at the start of the New Year. Universal held up the theatrical release of *Captive Wild Woman* until June 1943, qualifying it as an exciting summer attraction for the kids and adults seeking escapist entertainment.

Griffin Jay and Henry Sucher's screenplay shifts effortlessly between laboratory and Big Top. Ace wild animal trainer Fred Mason (Milburn Stone) returns to the States following an African expedition with a cargo of killer cats and a remarkably genial female ape named Cheela (Ray Corrigan in his customary gorilla costume). The animal attracts the fancy of renowned endocrinologist Dr. Sigmund Walters (John Carradine), who has been treating Dorothy Colman (Martha MacVicar), the ailing sister of Fred's fiancée, Beth (Evelyn Ankers). Walters, a pioneer in his field, has succeeded in changing the sex and breed of lower animals through glandular transplants and has performed miracles of surgery on deformed humans.

But the doctor's scientific aspirations have a dark side. In the basement of his Crestview Sanitorium, Walters is attempting to create a race of superior beings through the biological interpolation of man and beast (an idea purportedly advanced by the Nazis at this time). The doctor's jittery nurse, Miss Strand (Fay Helm, giving another convincing performance), offers up the old cliché that Walters mustn't "tamper with things no man or woman should ever touch." Naturally, he turns a deaf ear to her warning.

Drawing off sufficient amounts of excessive

Acquanetta's Ape Woman was another triumph of Jack Pierce's makeup wizardry. Here she is in mid-transformation in her debut film *Captive Wild Woman.*

sex hormones from Dorothy and injecting the fluid into Cheela (whom he has nabbed from the circus), Walters hopes to create an entirely different species of life. To achieve mental stability in his creation, he sacrifices the life of his rebellious nurse and transplants her cerebrum into Cheela's shaggy noggin. The repugnant clinical details of this bloody procedure are merely suggested through a neat montage of operating room actions. Our first glimpse of the newborn

Paula Dupree (Acquanetta) is eerily underscored by Hans J. Salter's awe-inspiring musical cue. George Robinson focuses his camera on the she-beast's vacant stare as Fay Helm's earlier dialogue ("What will you have? A human form with animal instincts!") is played on the soundtrack.

Walters escorts Paula to Fred's circus performance, where she is introduced to her (Cheela's) former mentor. She is immediately attracted to the animal trainer while bearing a jealous grudge against Beth. The sexual ramifications of this romantic "triangle" are discreetly side-stepped. It would take a writer of Edward D. Wood, Jr.'s persuasion (1958's *The Bride and the Beast*) to mine the kinkier aspects of such a situation.

Paula saves Fred's life when he is knocked unconscious during a rehearsal and almost attacked by a lion. Her influence over the jungle beasts is uncanny. Ecstatic over this exciting show-biz discovery, Fred hires Paula as his assistant; she quickly becomes the rage of the circus world.

But Paula's seething passions take a toll on her physical appearance. Her glands trigger an excessive amount of animal secretions, causing the girl to degenerate into a clawed, hirsute creature (one of Jack Pierce's most brilliant yet least heralded creations). Donning a cape (*à la* Henry Hull in *WereWolf of London*) and sneaking off to Beth's rooming house, Paula makes an attempt on the young woman's life but resorts to throttling an innocent neighbor (Fern Emmett) instead. Later, Beth confides to Fred that she suspects the dark stranger who tried to attack her that night was Paula, and even suggests a link between Paula and Cheela. Fred quickly dismisses her admittedly far-fetched theory.

When Paula reverts back to Cheela completely, Walters prepares Dorothy for further surgery. Beth, who has just arrived at the sanatorium, is elected to sacrifice her cerebrum this time out. But before the procedure can begin, Beth unleashes the furious Cheela from her cage. She stomps through the lab after Walters and strangles the lunatic scientist to death.

Fred, meanwhile, has his own problems. While doing his lion-and-tiger taming act, he loses control of the wild cats during a bellowing storm. Sensing her master's danger, Cheela beats it over to the circus grounds and carries the mauled trainer to safety. The ape's good intentions are mistaken by a zealous police officer who shoots Cheela to death.

John Carradine is *Captive Wild Woman*'s strongest asset. Unlike a Lionel Atwill or a George Zucco, Carradine performs the part of the crazed scientist with a minimum of ham. Dr. Walters is a stock genre character; dedicated beyond reason to advancing the cause of science, he raises nary an eyebrow when compelled to sacrifice his nurse of 13 years to further his experiments. His character's icy demeanor is first established in a scene where he stoically stands by as Cheela chokes the life out of an abusive animal handler (Paul Fix). *Captive Wild Woman* was Carradine's first starring role in a Universal horror film; in a sense, this lively but inconsequential B was primarily responsible for changing the course of the talented actor's motion picture career.

The late director Edward Dmytryk shared his thoughts on John Carradine with us:

> He had always been kind of a ham. I hadn't known him *personally*, but I had [known *of* him] when he used to walk the streets of Hollywood, even in summertime, with a topcoat thrown over his shoulders Barrymore-style and wearing his Barrymore-style hat. He used to go down and try to get the attention of Doug Fairbanks and Charlie Chaplin at the Cinegrill, the little downstairs café at the Roosevelt Hotel. And the [movie] parts he did do, like *The Hurricane* (1937), where Carradine played a cruel guard — he was a *ham*.
>
> So I was really afraid of what he would do in *Captive Wild Woman*, but I had a little talk with him and I think we got a very controlled performance out of him for a mad scientist!

A healthy portion of *Captive Wild Woman*'s already brief running time is devoted to the derring-do exploits of Milburn Stone in the circus ring. What should have been a pleasant diversion from the story's horror elements becomes more of an irritation as virtually all of the animal footage used in the film was lifted from the 1933 Universal production *The Big Cage* featuring the legendary animal trainer Clyde Beatty. Beatty is acknowledged by the producers for his "cooperation and inimitable talent" in the picture's title credits, but all the world-class circus performer did was to give the okay for Universal to use snippets of his *Big Cage* performance in their new film ... that is, if he had any say in the matter at all. Film editor Milton Carruth had his work cut out for him in mating the stock footage with the new film's live action shots. The results are generally satisfactory, although it's easy to spot Beatty filling in for Stone, despite their physical similarities. (Film historian Michael Fitzgerald noted that Universal never gave Stone a big star build-up due to his below-average height, and usually shuffled him around in second lead parts, small featured roles, and even voice-overs! The only reason he was given such a prominent role in *Captive Wild Woman* was his resemblance to Clyde Beatty.)

In the long run, this blatant misrepresentation works against the picture; it's difficult to muster up much enthusiasm over action scenes originally staged for another film with an entirely different storyline. Even more insulting are shots of advancing jungle cats printed in reverse to give the impression of the animals in retreat. (A university audience once howled over this *un*-special effect at a revival of the film.)

Amazingly, the sordid premise of *Captive Wild Woman* seems to have gone over the head of chief censor Joseph Breen, who made no mention of the sex angle in correspondence in which he complained about Paula's skimpy outfits and the excessively gruesome animal fights. Breen also took umbrage at the scene in which Dr. Walters transfuses some of Dorothy's blood into the body of the gorilla. Breen pointed out that a *direct* blood transfusion would offend audiences and suggested that the scene be broken up in such a way that Dorothy's blood would go into some container; only in a later step, after Dorothy had been removed from the scene, could the blood be transfused into Cheela. He also asked for some dialogue changes, "to obviate any objections from religious groups who would object to any idea of transferring a human soul into an animal body" (as if society's leaders hadn't more important things to worry about in wartorn 1943). Ultimately, the film received a February 19, 1943, Certificate of Approval from the Motion Picture Producers & Distributors of America, issued on the understanding "that the picture of the nude baby [seen in the medical journal] will be blown up to a chest and head shot only...." Surprisingly, the photo of the full-frontal nude baby is still in the movie. Those vigilant watchdogs of national morality, the Catholic Legion of Decency, hit *Captive Wild Woman* up with a cautionary "B" rating, objecting to "its allusions to sex and its horror synthesis."

Once again, B-Western star–stuntman Ray "Crash" Corrigan donned his custom-made gorilla costume for a Universal horror film. The brawny 6'6" actor was born Ray Benard in Milwaukee, Wisconsin, on Valentine's Day 1902. When Corrigan was 18, his family moved to Los Angeles, where the teenager was put in charge of the gym at MGM studios in Culver City. Through client Dolores Del Rio's husband, art department head Cedric Gibbons, Corrigan began his career as a motion picture stuntman; he allegedly doubled for Johnny Weissmuller in an early Tarzan movie. Corrigan's first big break came in 1936 when he got the lead role in the Republic sci-fi serial *Undersea Kingdom*. B-Western stardom soon followed when he was cast in two popular series, The Three Mesquiteers and The Range Busters.

To supplement his income, Corrigan had several gorilla costumes created and soon became one of Hollywood's most renowned ape impersonators. Film historian *extraordinaire* Bob Burns met the aging actor when he (Corrigan) played the role of the vampire alien in 1958's *It! The Terror from Beyond Space*. By that time, Corrigan had perfected his gorilla act in such low-budget programmers as *Murder in the Private Car* (1934), *The Ape* (1940), *Nabonga* (1944), *The White Gorilla* (1945), *White Pongo* (1945) and *Unknown Island* (1948). Burns told us:

> I thought Corrigan's gorilla's "dying scenes" were great. When a Corrigan gorilla died, he always fell on his back and kicked one leg up in the air, and then let that leg *sloowly* fall as he died. In most everything he did gorilla-wise, he had a definite style.

Tiring of the arduous role, Ray Corrigan sold two of his ape suits to movie extra Steve Calvert, and devoted his time to maintaining Corriganville, a sprawling 1611-acre piece of property in the San Fernando Valley, which he hired out to movie companies shooting outdoor location scenes. (Calvert went on to play Corrigan-style apes in *Bride of the Gorilla* [1951], *Bela Lugosi Meets a Brooklyn Gorilla* [1952], *The Bowery Boys Meet the Monsters* [1954], and the aforementioned *The Bride and the Beast*.) Ray Corrigan sold Corriganville, which by this time

Pressbook ad.

had grown into a popular tourist attraction, in 1965, and spent a quiet retirement in Brookings Harbor, Oregon, where he passed away at the age of 73 in 1976.

Proclaimed the "Venezuelan Volcano" by her friend William Randolph Hearst, Acquanetta's alleged origins were decidedly less exotic. Acquanetta revealed to us:

My mother was Arapaho, and I was born on the Arapaho Reservation in Wyoming. I was given away to my father when I was approximately three years old. He took me to Pennsylvania and gave me to his then-wife. And I grew up in Norristown, Pennsylvania, where I went to school. Somehow a bit of my background came out, that my father was a descendant of the Royal House of England — be it legitimate or not! My dad was English and French, and from what I'm told, his grandmother, who was French-Jewish, was a lady-in-waiting or something in the Royal House and she became pregnant, and out of that union came my father! That's why the background is shaded in mystery....

Edward Dmytryk cited a different set of facts concerning Acquanetta's origins:

> Acquanetta was a little insecure because she hadn't done much, and she was in the middle of a thing there. [Universal] was beginning to find out where she came from [the fact that she was part-black]—which eventually ruined her career, of course. Acquanetta and her agent had hidden that from Universal. She was called the "Venezuelan Volcano," and then she had to go someplace out of the country, she had to get a passport, and they found out she was born in Philadelphia! After that, rather quickly, they found out she was part-black—which today wouldn't mean a damn thing. But in those days it still did.

After graduating high school, Acquanetta went to New York, became a John Powers model and lived at the Barbizon Women's Hotel. She told us:

> Louis Sobol and Walter Winchell and all the scribes were writing about me. When they found out that I was an Indian in New York, they said, "Oh, nobody cares about Indians." But Roosevelt was President, and the big South American Hands Across the Border policy was on. It was almost like "Pygmalion"—they fabricated for me this story that I came from Venezuela. And I looked the part—I was dark and exotic, and I wore these big scarves and a big gardenia, three-quarter length flowered skirts, collars and capes and those kinds of things!

On her way to South America to perform at the Copacabana, Acquanetta made a stop-over in Hollywood and ended up at the Beverly Hills Hotel:

> We went out to the Mocambo—the head of MGM was there, the head of Warner Bros., Dan Kelley from Universal studios and Walter Wanger. He was the one that really went ape over me. He tried to get me for *Arabian Nights* [1942] but unfortunately they had already signed Maria Montez. That started the big, so-called "feud" between the two of us.

Although she was cast in a small speaking role as one of the harem girls in *Arabian Nights*, and was featured in *Rhythm of the Islands* (1943) in a fairly good part, Universal insisted on "introducing" their exotic attraction to movie audiences all over again in *Captive Wild Woman*:

> I know that they were testing various actresses at the studio; I think Yvonne de Carlo was one under consideration. They were always threatening me with her, and again, like with Maria Montez, she got the big Technicolors. I think she was tested for *Captive Wild Woman*, but I'm not absolutely certain. But in any event I tested, and they said I was perfect for the role.

As with Rondo Hatton, a novelty personality in his own right, Acquanetta was far more effective in movies like *Captive Wild Woman* where she wasn't called upon to recite dialogue. Without uttering a word, the olive-skinned beauty conveyed a raw, primitive sensuality that made her the ideal Paula Dupree:

> There was no preparation on my part, but I sat sometimes for two and a half hours being made up by a makeup artist. I think I had more emotional feeling, being made up for that, than anything that I ever did, because it was exhausting. Edward Dmytryk and I had great rapport—we dated briefly. I thought he was tremendous. Eddie gave me more freedom, I think, than other directors. I've always felt that I was never "me" in movies—do you know there was never a film where I was allowed to smile? John Carradine was great—he was always acting, you know! Even when we were off the set, there was John being John! Milburn Stone was a gentleman, a real nice person, and Evelyn Ankers, too. Evelyn and I were never really close, like close girlfriends, but that could have been partly because of me. I was somewhat withdrawn.... Nothing I ever did in Hollywood was exciting to the degree where I felt, "This is going to be my life." It was wonderful and surprising, but I just seem to have taken everything in stride. It was just another part of my destiny, and I somehow knew that, always. I did my very best, but it wasn't something that was so meaningful to me that I would give up something else for it. That's why I ended up walking away from Universal.

Acquanetta abandoned her Hollywood career in the early '50s and moved to Phoenix, Arizona, where marriage, motherhood and charitable causes occupied her time. She made a brief comeback in 1990 via the movie *The Legend of Grizzly Adams*. Tragically, she became afflicted with Alzheimer's Disease and passed away on August 16, 2004.

The ultimate Saturday-afternoon-at-the-Bijou crowd-pleaser, *Captive Wild Woman* is 60

A couldn't-have-happened shot of Cheela the female gorilla (Ray Corrigan) *and* Paula (Acquanetta), two sides of the same character in *Captive Wild Woman.*

minutes of chills, thrills and good old-fashioned B-movie entertainment. Neither of its sequels — the pseudo-stylistic *Jungle Woman* nor the uninspired *The Jungle Captive*—came close to capturing the wanton spirit of this beloved camp classic.

Critics' Corner

The production by Ben Pivar is an all-around good job, and its direction by Edward Dmytryk packs more conviction than is average in such subjects.... John Carradine gives an exceptionally smooth performance....—*The Hollywood Reporter*, 1943

[S]hould not let the thrill-seekers down.... Either you decide to meet this bit of scientific hocus-pocus at its own inane level or you are likely to get hopping mad, since there is nothing to recommend in the story or the performances.... The picture as a whole is in decidedly bad taste.—*The New York Times*, July 6, 1943, Thomas M. Pryor

While much of the plot is strictly off the cob, the film has enough excitement and strange elements to appease the thrill patrons.—*Variety*, April 28, 1943

Rating: ★★½ [A] thing of horror.... Unless you like pictures of this type, we won't recommend *Captive Wild Woman*. If you do, you'll get your money's worth in thrills.—*The New York Daily News*, July 6, 1943, Wanda Hale

This is another one of those implausible horror melodramas, suitable as a supporting feature in situations where this type of entertainment is acceptable.... A good deal of footage is given to stock shots.... [I]t has been skillfully blended in with the action. Acquanetta, a new screen personality, is effective as the ape woman. The action provides plenty of thrills and suspense.—*Harrison's Reports*, May 1, 1943

Phantom of the Opera

Released August 27, 1943. 92 minutes. *Producer:* George Waggner. *Director:* Arthur Lubin. *Executive Producer:* Jack Gross. *Screenplay:* Eric Taylor & Samuel Hoffenstein. *Adaptation:* John Jacoby. *Based on the composition* The Phantom of the Opera *by* Gaston Leroux. *Photography:* Hal Mohr & W. Howard Greene (Technicolor). *Technicolor Color Director:* Natalie Kalmus. *Art Directors:* John B. Goodman & Alexander Golitzen. *Editor:* Russell Schoengarth. *Assistant Director:* Charles Gould. *Set Decorators:* Russell A. Gausman & Ira S. Webb. *Dialogue Director:* Joan Hathaway. *Sound Director:* Bernard B. Brown. *Technician:* Joe Lapis. *Music Score & Direction:* Edward Ward. *Opera Sequences Staged by* William Von Wymetal & Lester Horton. *Choral Director:* William Tyroler. *Orchestrations:* Harold Zweifel & Arthur Schutt. *Makeup:* Jack P. Pierce. *Makeup Technician:* Samuel Kaufman. *Hair Stylist:* Emily Moore. *Costumes:* Vera West.

Nelson Eddy (*Anatole Garron*), Susanna Foster (*Christine DuBois*), Claude Rains (*Erique Claudin/The Phantom*), Edgar Barrier (*Police Insp. Raoul Daubert*), Leo Carrillo (*Signor Ferretti*), Jane Farrar (*Mme. Biancarolli*), J. Edward Bromberg (*Amiot*), Fritz Feld (*Lecours*), Frank Puglia (*Villeneuve*), Steven Geray (*Vercheres*), Barbara Everest (*Christine's Aunt*), Hume Cronyn (*Gerard*), Fritz Leiber (*Franz Liszt*), Nicki Andre (*Mme. Lorenzi*), Miles Mander (*M. Pleyel*), Gladys Blake (*Jeanne*), Elvira Curci (*Yvette*), Hans Herbert (*Marcel*), Kate Lawson (*Landlady*), Rosina Galli (*Celeste*), Walter Stahl (*Dr. Le Fort*), Paul Marion (*Desjardines*), Tudor Williams, Tony Marlow, Francis White (*Opera Singers*), Beatrice Roberts (*Nurse*), Marek Windheim (*Renfrit*), Muni Seroff, Dick Bartell, Jim Mitchell, Wheaton Chambers (*Reporters*), Belle Mitchell (*Ferretti's Maid*), Ernest Golm (*Office Manager*), Renee Carson (*Georgette*), Lane Chandler, Stanley Blystone (*Officers*), Cyril Delevanti (*Bookkeeper*), John Walsh (*Office Boy*), Alphonse Martell (*Policeman*), Edward Clark (*Usher*), William Desmond, Hank Mann (*Stagehands*), Sally Sweetland (*Singing Voice of Jane Farrar*).

Who is afraid of a Phantom that is billed beneath Mr. [Nelson] Eddy in the cast?
—*Bosley Crowther,* The New York Times, *October 15, 1943*

Written in 1910, Gaston Leroux's *The Phantom of the Opera* is one of the more mishandled classics of horror literature adapted for the screen. The French writer fancied himself as creating a no-holds-barred Gothic spine-tingler. One can only guess at what the writer would make of the various cinematic and theatrical versions that have emerged since. The property has become, more often than not, an easy mark for producers eager to turn his shocker into a vulgarized romance with the Phantom a tragic, misunderstood hero eternally vying for the hand of the virginal diva, Christine. Leroux's tale invariably suffers under the weight of the operatic style with which it has become associated; the very title, *The Phantom of the Opera*, conjures in the mind a sense of dated, purple prose romanticism as much as it does thrills and chills.

From the early days of the silent cinema (Germany's 1916 *Das Phantom der Oper*), there seems to have been a prominent Phantom for every generation in a variety of media. He first catapulted to cinematic immortality in the person of the brilliant Lon Chaney in Universal's pioneering 1925 silent film, which has never been equaled for unadulterated chills. Archaic plot devices and hopelessly overdramatized performances notwithstanding (leading lady Mary Philbin is especially difficult to take), Chaney's *The Phantom of the Opera* is still a compelling, thrilling work, aided immeasurably by the flamboyance of Rupert Julian's direction.

Carl Laemmle, Jr., was announced as producer of a *Phantom* remake in December 1935; Charles Rogers planned a full-scale production with Anatole Litvak earmarked as director almost immediately after the New Universal production head moved into the Front Office in

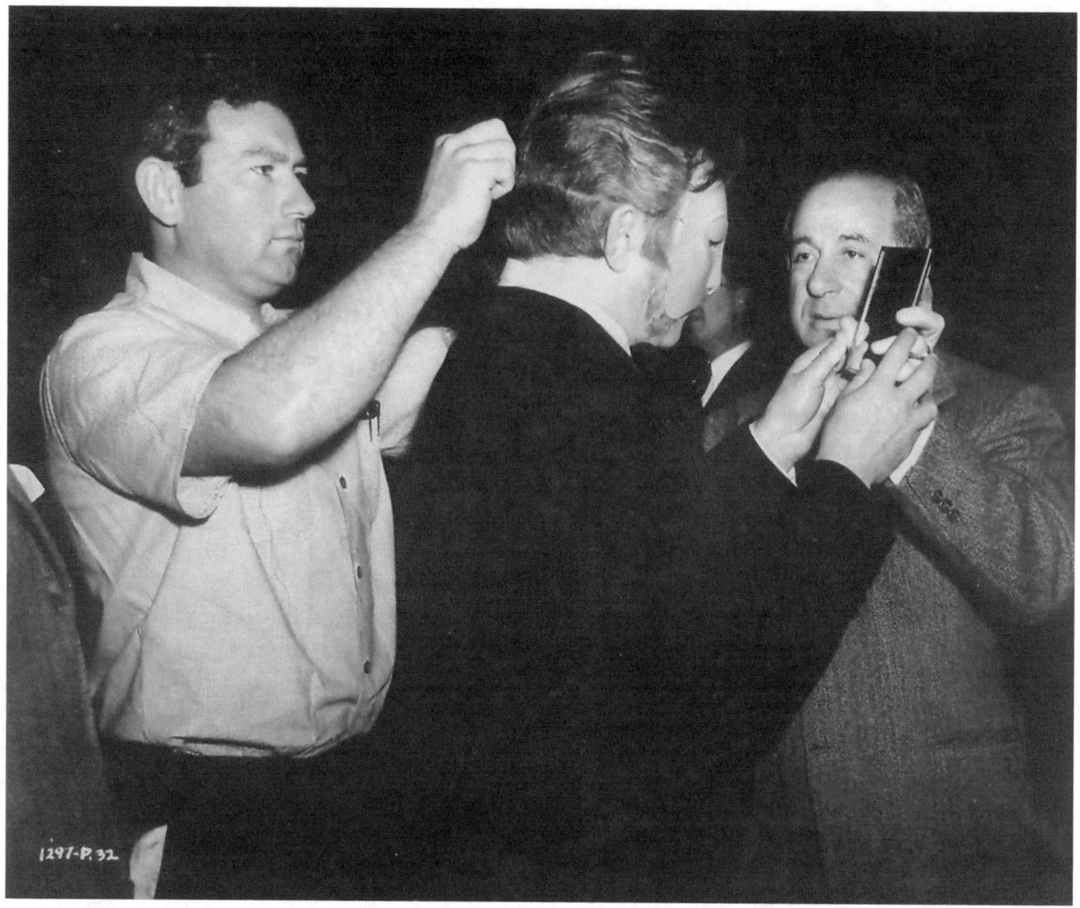

Claude Rains, following in the footsteps of silent star Lon Chaney, prepares for the shooting of the climax of the 1943 *Phantom of the Opera*.

1936. Lon Chaney's successor was to be none other than Boris Karloff. William P. Lipscomb devised a script in which Universal's King of Horror would portray the Music Master, a mysterious figure who wears a mask to conceal combat injuries he received during World War I. Meeting Christine, the Music Master becomes obsessed with making her a great star of the opera. The unmasking scene in this version yields surprising results: The Music Master isn't disfigured after all; his combat wounds are all psychological, not physical. Although this version never got off the ground, interestingly, Karloff went on to play a crazed but ultimately innocent Phantom-like character the same year in 20th Century–Fox's *Charlie Chan at the Opera, and* starred in the 1943 *Phantom*'s follow-up film *The Climax.*

It wasn't until the early days of Hollywood's second great horror cycle that Universal resuscitated plans to make a new version of the Leroux classic. In October 1940, the studio made the announcement in a *Hollywood Reporter* news item. The new production was put under the supervision of producer Joseph Pasternak, Henry Koster was signed on as director, Deanna Durbin, Queen of the New Universal, would star and Broderick Crawford (of all people) would play the title role. Months later, the same trade source revealed that, with the temperamental Durbin under suspension at the time, Universal had decided to rewrite *The Phantom of the Opera* as a spoof for Abbott and Costello! Even with producer Pasternak and "good luck" director Koster on board, Durbin balked at the idea of singing duets in one of her vehicles.

By September 1941, plans for the remake were put into high gear. The new *Phantom of the Opera* (the studio dropped the article *The* from the title) was conceived as a deluxe Technicolor production and would be shot on the same Opera House stage that had been built for the Chaney original. The remake seemed to have everything going for it except timing. The cold reality of a second World War had softened American tastes in escapist entertainment considerably. Leroux's ornate penny-dreadful with its rococo characters, deliriously overwrought plot twists, and puzzling stretches of narrative that alternated between the surreal to the serial-like, seemed hopelessly artificial in those dark days of battling Adolf Hitler. Perhaps the dark, stylized tones of Grand Guignol were just the ticket for Lon Chaney but Universal opted for a more up-to-date Hollywood costume-movie sensibility with just enough ersatz opera thrown in to lure the carriage trade.

On September 28, 1942, nearly two years after Universal first announced plans to get the new production rolling, *The Hollywood Reporter* revealed that shooting would be further delayed pending an availability date from Technicolor. The plant was tied up with war work and bookings for studio productions had to be arranged a considerable time in advance. Koster was also cited as another reason for the delay: The director was busy working on a musical-comedy at the time.

By November, Pasternak was out and George Waggner was in. A news item in the November 4, 1942, edition of *The Hollywood Reporter* stated that Waggner had been visiting the Shrine Auditorium where the San Francisco Opera Company was presenting a series of operas in order to get a first-hand impression of how the musicals are staged. Henry Koster was replaced by house director Arthur Lubin. Charles Laughton was initially considered for the role of Erique Claudin, based on his fine work in RKO's 1939 sound remake of *The Hunchback of Notre Dame* (another remake of a Chaney classic). And, for a time, Lon Chaney, Jr., was also announced for the coveted part. It would have been the fulfillment of a dream for Chaney, but good sense prevailed, and he was denied the role. In typical fashion, the emotionally unstable Chaney stewed over this perceived injustice for years.

As further proof that Universal desired to downplay the story's horror angle, handsome blonde baritone Nelson Eddy, the romantic lead, was given top billing. (A December 1942 *Hollywood Reporter* piece indicated that Jon Hall was considered for the male lead but Lubin told us he had no memory of this.) The personable Eddy, who had just completed his final picture with Jeanette MacDonald (1942's *I Married an Angel*), his singing partner of eight box office smashes for MGM, complained about having his blond hair dyed brown. "Don't forget, Nelson," Lubin told him, "if it doesn't look good on you, we can always wash it out."

A January 1943 *Hollywood Reporter* news item revealed that golden-voiced Chicago native Susanna Foster, an attractive 18 year old and formerly a Paramount contract player, had been hired to take over the part Durbin abandoned, the inexperienced understudy who becomes an overnight sensation at the Paris Opera House. Foster told the authors:

> There was a man named Charles Spears who was in the publicity department. He went to Universal and worked in the casting area in an executive position. When they were looking for someone for *Phantom*, he suggested me. I met Arthur Lubin by accident at a mutual friend's home and he became interested in me because I sang. [Composer] Eddie Ward remembered me from MGM.... So when I went out for the audition for George Waggner, they right away wanted me. Boom! That was it.

At long last, in the January 7 *Hollywood Reporter*, Universal announced that Claude Rains had been signed to play the title role in *Phantom of the Opera*. Lubin told us:

> Claude Rains was my only choice, and he was wonderful. He was a very difficult actor, very precise. He wanted to be correct. Weeks before we photographed his scenes, he practiced the piano and the violin. He was really perfect. And he was very difficult to direct. But he was worth listening to; most of his suggestions were very valuable. I would say to him, "Well, Claude, I don't agree with you, but we'll shoot it your way, then we'll shoot it my way and see." He forgot that the director in those days had the final cut!

Susanna Foster had no qualms whatsoever about Rains: "I thought Rains was wonderful. He was a little reserved but he had that vicious little twinkle in his eye that was so cute. You got back so much working with him."

After a long gestation period, *Phantom of the Opera* finally began production on January 17,

Lon Chaney, Jr., chats with Susanna Foster on the set of the remake of his dad's greatest film vehicle.

1943. The decision to shoot it in gorgeous Technicolor (the studio's second color film in the past year) was a smart one, greatly increasing the film's value. By the time the picture was ready for exhibition, Universal had pumped over a million dollars into it. Fortunately, the Opera House set from the Chaney version (located on Stage 28) had been well maintained through the years. It had originally cost the studio $500,000 to construct, plus an additional $100,000 was spent for sound-proofing. (The then-current wartime restrictions on set building would have had a detrimental effect on the creation of an entirely new structure.) All that was left for acclaimed art director Alexander Golitzen to do was to have the set repainted, regilded and strung with new curtains.

According to studio publicity, the gigantic crystal chandelier used in the Chaney version was actually dropped and splintered during the filming of that famous scene. For the remake, Universal purchased Czech crystal and had the glittering fragments duplicated in a local glass factory. Twenty-thousand pieces were used in constructing the new 11' × 14' lighting fixture. Because of a "no waste" policy, it was attached to a wire when it dropped, stopping short of the soundstage floor. The chandelier was then carefully taken apart and the pieces scattered. After completing the elaborate shot, the glass fragments were reassembled and stored for future use.

The story of *Phantom of the Opera* is set in Paris in the late nineteenth century. Erique Claudin (Rains), a Paris Opera House violinist for 20 years, suffers a mental breakdown after he's discharged on account of an arthritic condition that has adversely affected his performance. Claudin has spent his last nickel advancing the singing career of operatic understudy Christine

DuBois (Susanna Foster). Christine has no idea that the shy, reclusive Claudin is her benefactor. Except for exchanging an occasional pleasantry, they are virtual strangers to each other.

In desperate need of money, Claudin drops in on the music publishing house of M. Pleyel (Miles Mander), with whom he has left his crowning achievement, a piano concerto, for eventual publication. Mistakenly believing his work has been stolen, Claudin flies into an insane rage and strangles the publisher. In retribution, Pleyel's assistant (Renee Carson) throws acid into Claudin's face, sending the violinist rushing out into the street screaming in agony. (Though the acid hits Erique dead on, only half his face is burned, and the hands he holds to his face are unaffected.) Pursued by the police, he takes refuge in the sewers.

Months later, the Opera House is haunted by the presence of an uninvited guest. His petty thefts drive the opera's directors, Amiot (J. Edward Bromberg) and Lecours (Fritz Feld), to distraction. Christine also feels the stranger's presence, but his influence on her has always been of a positive nature.

When the tempestuous Madame Biancarolli (Jane Farrar [niece of opera great Geraldine Farrar], whose singing voice was dubbed) suddenly falls ill on the midst of a performance of *Amour et Gloire*, Christine takes her place and is an overnight success. Suspecting she has been drugged, Biancarolli charges Anatole Garron (Nelson Eddy), the star baritone and Christine's admirer, with attempted murder. The crafty prima donna promises to withdraw the charge providing that the understudy go back to the chorus permanently.

The next night, Biancarolli discovers the Opera House phantom hiding in her dressing room. It is Claudin, dressed in a flowing cape and hat, his face hidden behind a stage mask. He warns the singer against standing in the way of Christine's success. When she defies him, the Phantom murders her and her maid.

Hoping to draw Claudin out into the open, Amiot and Lecours stage a fabulous new opera, *Le prince masque de caucasie*. They refuse to heed the caped terrorist's warnings and cast Madame Lorenzi (Nicki Andre) opposite Anatole. Midway through the performance, the crazed Claudin severs the chain supporting the massive chandelier, sending it hurtling down on the heads of the hapless audience.

In the ensuing melee, Claudin spirits Christine away and takes her deep down through the bowels of the theater to his hideaway in the sewers. Learning that his sweetheart has been kidnapped, Anatole prevails upon Franz Liszt (Fritz Leiber) to play a passage from Claudin's belatedly appreciated piano concerto in the hope of attracting his attention. Anatole and his rival for Christine's affections, Police Inspector Raoul Daubert (Edgar Barrier), trace the sound of Claudin's piano-playing through the sewers. Catching her kidnapper off guard, Christine tears off his mask, revealing hideous scars left by the chemicals. Anatole and Raoul rescue her before the crumbling sewer ceiling and walls gives way. Claudin is buried under tons of rubble.

The movie concludes with Christine becoming the rage of all Paris. Though she is heartened by her success, the young star is haunted by memories of the kindly Claudin, whom she believes played an important part in her past life.

Phantom of the Opera is a textbook example of a class-conscious grade-B studio hell bent on turning out a prestige product that could rival the output of its more respected competitors. The film's style can best be described as imitation MGM, infected with the short-of-awe-inspiring blandness and overblown production values that Louis B. Mayer mistook for taste. Audiences who thrilled to the Lon Chaney version were apt to find this version strikingly tame. There are simply no equivalents to the hair-raising moment when Mary Philbin tears the mask off the Phantom, revealing the skeletal ugliness of Chaney's ingenious makeup. Or the fabulous Grand Ball sequence in which Erik, in a flowing crimson robe and his blood-freezing Grim Reaper mask, shadows the girl and her lover to the Opera House rooftop.

That said, Lubin's *Phantom* is a visual knockout with superb sets intermingling with glass shots to create some jaw-dropping effects even if rationality frequently becomes a casualty. A case in point, the cavernous underground catacombs of the opera house with its "secret lake" and music chamber, complete with piano. Photographers Hal Mohr and W. Howard Greene provide the picture with an elegant sheen, with graceful crane shots which do full justice to Universal's famous Phantom Stage as well as calling attention to the massive crystal chandelier which serves as its centerpiece. The downside of such admirable craftsmanship is that it makes the film's flaws all the more jarring. This is especially evident in the tacked-on, mismatched silhouetted shots of the Phantom which seem to appear at random, as if to remind the audience there really is a bad guy lurking in the shadows (if only he would appear).

Producer George Waggner's insistence on a "rational Phantom," one driven by motivations that audiences could readily accept, was a sound idea sabotaged by a dysfunctional script. The final script has its roots in 1941 adaptation of the Leroux work by John Jacoby. In this treatment, the Claudin character is actually Christine's father; he abandons his home, leaving the child to be raised by his late wife's family. When the grown Christine finally encounters Claudin, she quickly falls under his spell and is coached by him to be a world-class opera star. The Phantom finally reveals his identity to his daughter, and is shot to death by police on the stage of the Opera House.

By the time the production went before the cameras, Samuel Hoffenstein and Eric Taylor had put to paper their own visions for the new *Phantom of the Opera*. Taylor so loaded the script with the family history of Claudin and Christine that Waggner and Lubin were forced to make drastic cuts, leaving only an inference that they were father and daughter. "They never could make up their minds during the whole making of the picture," Susanna Foster told us.

The Phantom's makeup proved to be an issue for Rains. He didn't want to play the part with his face completely covered; it was decided that he'd wear a half-mask. "He thought that his image as a leading man would be hurt," Lubin stated. "He didn't want to follow in the footsteps of Lon Chaney."

Susanna Foster shed more light on the makeup issue. "We had been in the war for just over a year and they were worried about boys coming back with terrible injuries on their faces. So they decided not to make a fantastically horrible makeup." Jack Pierce's compromised design consists of ragged scar tissue on one side of Rains' face. According to publicity, this highly anticipated scene was shot on a closed set under rigid studio security. The final (mild) results hardly warranted all of the fuss.

The ever-vigilant Breen Office was less concerned with the gruesome elements of the film and more with Susanna Foster's cleavage. On May 21, 1943, the censors rejected *Phantom of the Opera* due to a number of unacceptable breast shots of Christine in her dressing room. Universal made the suggested alterations and Universal's super production was released three months later with PCA approval.

Rains plays the Phantom effectively, lending stature to an unexpectedly diminished role. (The actor had just scored a great personal success at Warners portraying the conniving but convivial Capt. Renault in the 1942 classic *Casablanca*, for which he was nominated for a Best Supporting Actor Oscar.) Claudin is neither as enigmatic as Erik in the novel nor as monstrous as in Chaney's interpretation. But whereas Chaney hinted at the pathos lurking beneath the surface, Rains is faced with a script that piles it on from the first scene. The actor has the distinctive voice and erudite demeanor to be a first-class intellectual villain but his height made him a poor choice as a physically intimidating adversary. (Rains often found himself being propped up in order to stand eye-to-eye with his various female co-stars. Ingrid Bergman recalled having to walk in an out-of-camera-range ditch while shooting a scene with the actor in 1946's *Notorious*.) Director Lubin gets around the problem in one key scene by having Rains attack the statuesque Jane Farrar by positioning him a step or two above his victim.

For the most part, Lubin lavished far less imagination on the rest of the film, which glistens with old-fashioned Hollywood professionalism despite the rather prosaic staging. The director admitted in later years that his knack for meeting tough production schedules and keeping budgets under control made him a favorite of Universal executives. But Lubin's low-profile style is a little too low, too literal for the material at hand. The build-up to the chandelier scene is well-handled (the Phantom is courteous enough to wait for the diva to wrap up her aria before dropping the huge fixture on the unsuspecting audience). True to the spirit of the Breen Office, no one even seems scratched for his efforts. The unmasking scene is awkward with a merrily singing Foster trying to position herself to best advantage before pouncing on Rains. Even the acid scene is shot without a cut in a boring long shot.

The musical scenes, on the other hand, are played up for all their worth with the big showstopper saved for last. Using Tchaikovsky's entrancingly lyrical, folk song-based *Fourth Symphony* (with a tacked-on libretto) as a musical backdrop, the production number is nothing if not spectacular. It's basically a full-scale Radio City Music Hall romp complete with galloping horses, peasant dances, acrobats and, of course, Eddy garbed in full Cossack regalia.

Rains as Erique Claudin, pre-acid facial.

As in the *Phantom* follow-up, *The Climax*, little real opera is actually heard in the film. A studio press release insisted war conditions made it impossible to get copyright clearances from legitimate operas, a baffling claim since most major operas were in the public domain. Although the film opens with an authentic opera segment (the third act of Von Flotow's *Marta*), what follows are Edward Ward transcriptions of popular light classical themes with producer Waggner providing the librettos. Universal enlisted the services of expert William Von Wymetal to authenticate the operatic selections, while William Tyroler maintained the integrity of the choral passages. Both had previously labored on the staging of the Charles Gounod opera *Faust* in the Lon Chaney version.

The leitmotif of the score, a beautiful refrain written by Ward and passed off in the movie as a French folk song, became the basis of the Phantom's piano concerto. Titled "Lullaby of the Bells," the composition was released as an arrangement for piano by the Robbins Music Company while the film was in its first run. Pop conductor Mantovani recorded the piece in 1948 in time for the film's re-release by Realart.

The performances in *Phantom of the Opera* range from the conditionally satisfactory (Rains) to the modest (Foster, Eddy) to the hammy (Edgar Barrier, Leo Carrillo, J. Edward Bromberg). Bromberg, Fritz Feld and Steven Geray are amusing in their comic interplay as keepers of the Paris Opera House. Nelson Eddy's talents as a singer compensate for the occasional stiffness of his performance. (It is mildly depressing to see the youthful Susanna courted by such overripe suitors *as* Eddy and Barrier.) Frank Puglia, Miles Mander and the distinguished-looking Fritz Leiber (made up to resemble Franz Liszt) do good work in minor roles. If you pay close attention, you will catch sight of Hume Cronyn in the thankless part of a gendarme.

The care that Universal lavished on *Phantom of the Opera* paid off handsomely: It was the studio's most heralded attraction of the season. The film's world premiere was held in Cincinnati, Ohio, on August 19, 1943. In New York City and across the nation, it broke records at the box office. *Phantom of the Opera* also had the distinction of netting five nominations in the 1944 Oscar sweepstakes: John B. Goodman and Alexander Golitzen for Best Color Art Direction, Hal Mohr and W. Howard Greene for Best Color Photography, Russell A. Gausman and Ira S. Webb for Best Set Decoration, Bernard B. Brown for Best Sound Recording and Edward Ward for Best Scoring of a Musical Picture. Goodman, Golitzen, Mohr, Greene, Gausman and Webb walked away with Oscars tucked under their arms that night.

Almost immediately, Universal set about making plans to contrive a sequel to their operatic blockbuster. Claude Rains wanted no part of it; he returned to Warners, signed a lucrative new contract, and resumed his distinguished career playing opposite the likes of Bette Davis and Humphrey Bogart. By the time November came around, the proposed follow-up to *Phantom of the Opera* wasn't a sequel at all, but a thinly disguised remake—*The Climax*, with Boris Karloff (at long last) doing the opera house haunting.

Gaston Leroux's deathless creation has sustained a number of wildly diverse resurrections since the tale's inception (including four Chinese motion picture adaptations). On September 13, 1943, *Lux Radio Theater* presented their version of the fright classic on the airwaves. Hosted by Cecil B. DeMille, the radiocast featured Susanna Foster reprising her Christine role and, as the Phantom, Basil Rathbone (at his hammiest and in bad voice besides). James Cagney donned the hideous guise in a poor recreation of the great unmasking scene in 1957's *Man of a Thousand Faces*, Universal-International's highly fictionalized account of the life of Lon Chaney. On November 23, 1959, *Boxoffice* magazine reported that European filmmakers were preparing a new version of *The Phantom of the Opera* starring Kathryn Grayson, but nothing ever came of it. Hammer's inevitable remake in 1962 starring Herbert Lom in the title role owes more to the 1943 than to the 1925 production for its inspiration.

There have been Argentinian and Mexican versions (1954 and 1960 respectively), as well as television adaptations. A Latin-style Phantom-of-sorts makes an appearance in Mexico's *Santo contra el Estrangulador* (1966). Masquerading as an entry in the Edgar Allan Poe sweepstakes, American International's *Murders in the Rue Morgue* (1971) is a blatant Phantom rip-off with Herbert Lom once again featured as a disfigured killer terrorizing a theater. The 1974 20th Century–Fox rock opera *Phantom of the Paradise*, directed by promising young director Brian De Palma, features a zonked-out rock musician (William Finley) who loses it all after he is double-crossed. That same year, Skye Aubrey and Jack Cassidy co-starred in a made-for-television version of the classic entitled *The Phantom of Hollywood*. In 1983, Robert Markowitz put Maximilian Schell and Jane Seymour through their paces in a second television adaptation, while Tony Richardson directed Burt Lancaster in a 1990 US-British TV mini-series. Robert Englund (*A Nightmare on Elm Street*'s Freddy Krueger) added his name to the list of Phantom portrayers in a 1989 British version while gore cinema's godfather Dario Argento guided Julian Sands through 1998's *Il Fantasma dell'opera* from Italy.

Leroux's story didn't get another workout until 2004 with the screen version of the Andrew Lloyd Webber stage musical. With director Joel Schumacher providing the dazzling eye candy to accompany the infectious but saccharine melodies, the over-the-top production courted condescending notices and yet another round of speculation about the death of the movie musical. But, it's doubtful that we've seen the last of the genre or Leroux's classic horror character.

Critics' Corner

[I]n every way it is a vastly superior entertainment.... You can call it a rare musical treat, an arrestingly beautiful spectacle in the magnificence of its Technicolor photography, or a handsomely performed psychological melodrama.—*The Hollywood Reporter*, 1943

Phantom of the Opera is essentially great theatre and here it gets magnificent treatment to set it up as one of the foremost money-making film entertainments of the year.... [F]rom adroit showmanship and highest skills from all ... production departments to back up the superb performances.—*Variety*, August 13, 1943

[B]ereft of much of the terror and macabre quality of the original.... Together, they [Nelson Eddy and Edgar Barrier] make about as boring a pair of rival suitors as we dread to see.—*The New York Times*, October 15, 1943, Bosley Crowther

[A] good entertainment, the sort that will direct an

appeal to all types of audiences.... Unlike the original version, which was a thriller of the horror type ... this version has been altered in a way that makes it more of a musical than a thriller. It does, however, retain the horrific flavor of the original, but to a lesser degree.—*Harrison's Reports*, August 21, 1943

[T]his remake of a screen classic has both sound and fury. The music selections are pleasant, if a bit loud. The violence, with Claude Rains in the original Chaney role, is first-rate.—*The New York Herald-Tribune*, October 15, 1943, Howard Barnes

Sherlock Holmes Faces Death

Released September 17, 1943. 68 minutes. *Producer-Director:* Roy William Neill. *Executive Producer:* Howard Benedict. *Screenplay:* Bertram Millhauser. *Based on the story* "The Adventures of the Musgrave Ritual" *by* Sir Arthur Conan Doyle. *Photography:* Charles Van Enger. *Art Directors:* John B. Goodman & Harold H. MacArthur. *Editor:* Fred R. Feitshans, Jr. *Set Decorators:* Russell A. Gausman & Edward R. Robinson. *Musical Director:* Hans J. Salter. *Assistant Director:* Melville Shyer. *Sound Director:* Bernard B. Brown. *Technician:* Paul Neal. *Lightning Effects:* Kenneth Strickfaden. *Gowns:* Vera West.

Basil Rathbone (*Sherlock Holmes*), Nigel Bruce (*Dr. John H. Watson*), Dennis Hoey (*Insp. Lestrade*), Arthur Margetson (*Dr. Bob Sexton*), Hillary Brooke (*Sally Musgrave*), Halliwell Hobbes (*Alfred Brunton*), Milburn Stone (*Capt. Pat Vickery*), Gavin Muir (*Phillip Musgrave*), Frederic Worlock (*Geoffrey Musgrave*), Olaf Hytten (*Capt. MacIntosh*), Gerald Hamer (*Maj. Langford*), Vernon Downing (*Lt. Clavering*), Minna Phillips (*Mrs. Howells*), Mary Gordon (*Mrs. Hudson*), Heather Wilde (*Jenny*), Harold De Becker (*Pub Proprietor*), Norma Varden (*Gracie*), Joan Blair (*Nora*), Charles Coleman, Dick Rush (*Constables*), Eric Snowden, Peter Lawford (*Sailors*), Martin Ashe (*Slinking Figure*), Joseph North.

Some were murderers and some worse, but they all knew how to keep a secret and so do *I*.
—*Halliwell Hobbes in* Sherlock Holmes Faces Death

In *Sherlock Holmes Faces Death*, Universal transported Conan Doyle's immortal sleuth back to the classic trappings of the original stories. Although the plot's time frame is still Britain at the height of World War II, politics takes a back seat to a good old-fashioned murder mystery. Gone are the scheming Axis agents, complex enemy codes and eleventh-hour spy bashes of the first three films of the series. Instead, a cunning killer lurking about a ghost-infested manor challenges the detective's remarkable powers of deductive reasoning. As promised in the title, Holmes does indeed come face to face with Death in the last reel, and uses his keen knowledge of the criminal mind to cheat the Reaper once again.

Bertram Millhauser wrote an original screenplay using Conan Doyle's "The Adventures of the Musgrave Ritual" as his inspiration. In the story, aristocrat Reginald Musgrave enlists Holmes' aid after his butler, Brunton, mysteriously disappears following his dismissal for insubordination. It seems the family retainer was something of a lech. His latest conquest, Rachel Howells, a maid at Musgrave's estate, has also vanished without leaving a trace.

Holmes makes a careful study of an old family document, The Musgrave Ritual, which Musgrave found in Brunton's possession. On the surface, the ritual is a meaningless collection of odd verses. Holmes deduces that its vague references to locations in and around Hurlstone, the old family manor, point the way to something of great value.

During the investigation, the detective discovers Brunton's corpse, hunched over a chest containing a "battered and shapeless diadem"—the ancient crown of the kings of England. Evidently Brunton broke the secret code in the ritual and, with Rachel's help, discovered the chest in a hiding spot. Rachel's fury proved greater than her greed. She murdered Brunton for having rejected her and then fled the country, possibly for America.

In Millhauser's script, Musgrave Manor, formerly Hurlstone Towers in Northumberland, is turned into a haven for convalescing military officers by the Musgraves. Despite this altruistic gesture, only younger sister Sally (Hillary Brooke) appears to exhibit any compassion toward her fellow man. Her brothers, Geoffrey (Frederic Worlock) and Phillip (Gavin Muir), are scheming, disagreeable men. The older Geoffrey heartily disapproves of his sister's affections for recuperating American pilot Pat Vickery (Milburn Stone), which, in a picture of this sort, makes it a sure bet that Geoffrey's fate is sealed.

Soon both he and Phillip are found dead. Their bodies bear tiny puncture wounds in the backs of their skulls. The supremely inept Insp.

Lestrade (Dennis Hoey) and his Scotland Yard men arrive on the scene and immediately put the cuffs on the least likely but most highly motivated suspect, Capt. Vickery. Thanks to the shrewd detective work of Sherlock Holmes (Basil Rathbone), who has come to Hurlstone after Dr. Watson (Nigel Bruce) tips him off to the threat of danger there, suspicion is shifted from Vickery to Alfred Brunton (Halliwell Hobbes), the butler. The character of Brunton has metamorphosed from the middle-aged Lothario of the Conan Doyle piece to an alcoholic old man with a penchant for spouting verse.

In one of the film's showiest set pieces, Sally recites The Musgrave Ritual before the entire household during a furious storm (the pointless duty has been passed down to her after her brothers' deaths). It comes as no great surprise that a threatening bolt of lightning (courtesy of Kenneth Strickfaden) crashes through the window at the height of the recital and demolishes a suit of armor.

In keeping with Conan Doyle's tale, Holmes learns that the ritual itself is the key to solving the murder mystery. Realizing the floor of the Main Hall has the appearance of a giant chessboard, the cagey detective maneuvers each member of the household around the giant "board" as though they were chessmen according to the directions in the litany. This novel invention is Millhauser's; Conan Doyle's story contains no such scene. "Film-goers who know the proper position of 'White King's Bishop Three' at the proper time," according to the movie's pressbook, "may be able to solve the string of strange slayings." According to the studio publicity machine, Rathbone, Bruce and producer-director Roy William Neill all possessed ratings as chess experts and each had participated in Hollywood chess tournaments.

An ancient wine cellar, reached via a maze of secret passageways, is discovered under the Main Hall. Brunton's body is found on the floor of a gloomy burial chamber beneath the cellar. Falling back on a timeworn ruse, Holmes discloses that Brunton scrawled a message in his own blood before expiring. But before it can be deciphered, the message must be treated with chemicals.

After giving everyone the impression he's gone to Newcastle to collect the chemicals, Holmes stations himself in the crypt and awaits the inevitable arrival of the guilty party. It is Watson's associate, Dr. Bob Sexton (Arthur Margetson). (Once again, we have a case where the culprit is revealed to be a friend or associate of the dear doctor — a sad commentary on the company he keeps, perhaps.) The treasure alluded to in the ritual is not a king's crown but a forgotten land grant entitling the Musgraves to thousands of acres of local countryside. Sexton discovered the secret, murdered the two brothers and incriminated Vickery. With them out of the way, the scheming doctor planned to woo Sally, who stood in line to inherit the riches. During a drunken binge, Brunton witnessed Phillip's killing, proved to be an uncooperative accessory and was eliminated by the desperate Sexton.

Having foolishly spilled the beans to the trapped detective, Sexton pulls the trigger but finds the gun has been loaded with blanks. Lestrade and his men converge on the crypt and haul Sexton away, but not before the killer sarcastically compliments Holmes on his prowess.

Arthur Margetson's Dr. Sexton proves himself to be one of the sleuth's most colorless adversaries. He contributes so little to the plot that when Holmes unmasks him as the killer, our reaction is understandably mild. Sexton's confident boast that he'll win Sally's affections after Vickery is out of the picture is a great conceit even for an egomaniac like him; Sally doesn't give the mild-mannered doctor a second glance throughout the whole film. Holmes, we later learn, was onto the sly fox almost from the outset. In examining Sexton's carry case, the detective spotted a surgical needle, which he suspected may have been used in the murders of Geoffrey and Phillip. Sexton gave himself away during the human chess game. At first professing little knowledge of chess, the young doctor stepped into the correct square on the "board" without direction after Holmes noticed he was in the wrong position.

Sherlock Holmes Faces Death was not the first film based on the Conan Doyle short story. *The Musgrave Ritual* (1922), one of a series of 47 silent two-reelers released by Great Britain's Stoll Picture Productions, and featuring Eillie Norwood and Hubert Willis as Sherlock Holmes and Dr. Watson respectively, was more faithful to the source material than the Universal production.

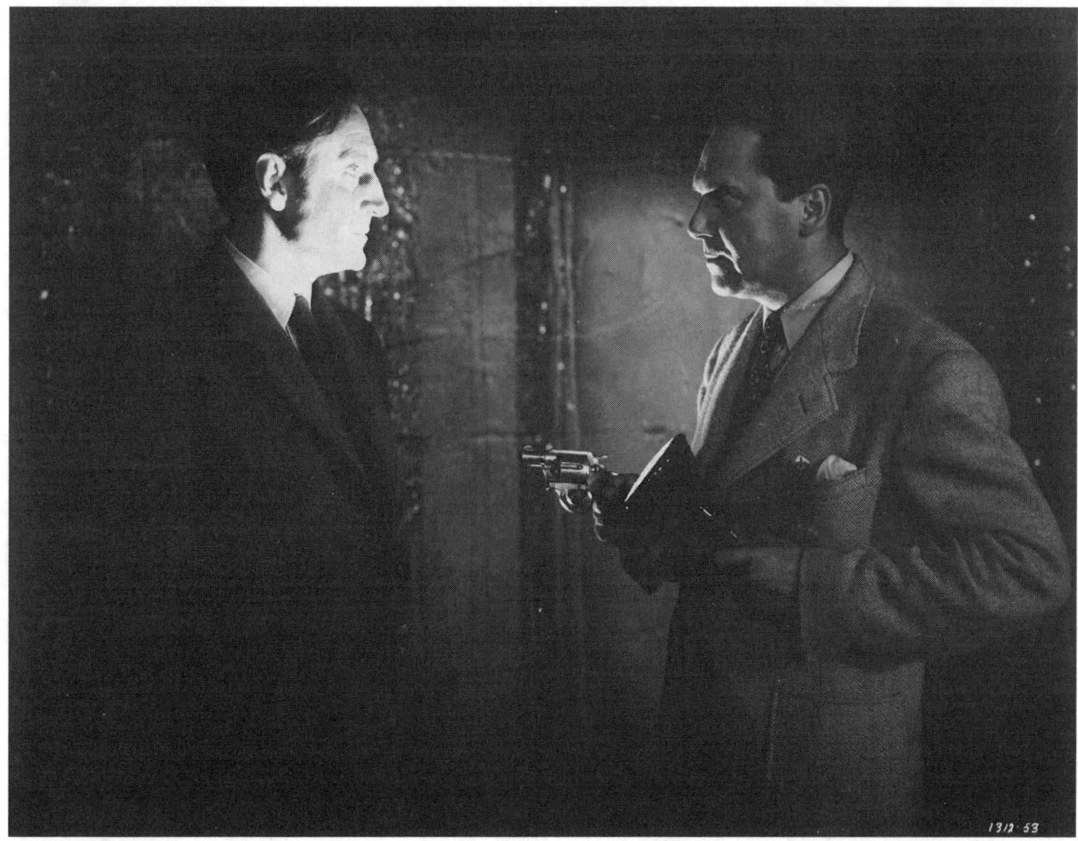

Basil Rathbone comes close to meeting his Maker in *Sherlock Holmes Faces Death* with Arthur Margetson.

Many of these British adaptations were updated from the Victorian era to the '20s, for much the same reason the Universal films were set during World War II — audience identification. Just as in the Conan Doyle original, one of the keys to the solution of the mystery is knowing that a particular tree on the estate (now cut down) was exactly 64 feet tall! Holmes uses his knowledge of trigonometry and other tools of his trade following the instructions set down in The Musgrave Ritual. At the end of his convoluted search, the detective finds himself standing in the cellar over a huge trap door with a pull ring that, in hundreds of years, nobody ever bothered to open and peek in!

As the first Sherlock Holmes picture to feature the master detective in a Gothic setting since Fox's 1939 *The Hound of the Baskervilles*, *Sherlock Holmes Faces Death* is a breath of fresh air. All of the right elements have been mixed into the brew for an outstanding whodunit, but the results just barely hit the mark. Roy William Neill's adeptness at sustaining mood-provoking atmosphere was proven in Columbia's 1935 Boris Karloff vehicle, *The Black Room*, as well as the *Frankenstein Meets the Wolf Man*, released several months earlier. *Sherlock Holmes Faces Death* is proof positive that the underrated director hadn't lost his touch. From the first sequence (a gossipy pub proprietor speaks of the evil Musgraves in hushed tones as the camera takes in the shadowy candlelit corridors of the windswept manor) to the closing reels set in the Musgrave burial crypt, an aura of doom and despair is evoked, aided in no small measure by the fine low-keyed camerawork of Charles Van Enger.

In the thrills and suspense department, however, *Sherlock Holmes Faces Death* comes up decidedly short. The problem lies in Millhauser's rather eccentric script. It's talky and stagebound. The murders of the Musgrave brothers (both of whom richly deserve their grisly demise if only for being so obnoxious) and poor old Brunton are committed off-camera, thus spoiling the potential for some sorely needed suspense. Red herrings lurk around every corner. The most obvious are three convalescing officers all suffering from combat fatigue — one is a compulsive knitter, another is shell-shocked, and the third has a nervous tic. This peculiar trio, conceived by Millhauser to muddy the waters of the murder investigation, is too dotty to be taken seriously as suspects. They impart a self-conscious theatricality that is grating. A bell tower that sounds 13 chimes as a warning of impending doom doesn't win the screenwriter any accolades for plausibility or originality, neither.

The recent promotion of Howard Benedict to the status of executive producer of the series prompted the studio brass to elevate Roy William Neill into the vacant post of associate producer. Neill utilized two impressive sets when shooting commenced on April 12, 1943 — the familiar European Street set (better known as Vasaria in the Frankenstein films) and a bleak burial crypt set that is reminiscent of Carfax Abbey in *Dracula*.

Once again, we find Holmes in the same churlish mood as we last saw him. When Watson remarks that even a child could make a particular observation, Holmes sarcastically counters, "Not *your* child, Watson." He is uncharacteristically abrupt to a hysterical Sally and downright rude to drunken old Brunton. Later, however, Holmes *is* impressed by Sally's unselfish decision to destroy the land grant rather than take away the homes of thousands of farmers and villagers. "There's a new spirit abroad in the land. The old days of grab and greed are on their way out," the naively optimistic detective declares with confidence.

The supporting cast boasts a number of reliable players (Dennis Hoey, Hillary Brooke, Gavin Muir, Frederic Worlock, Olaf Hytten, Gerald Hamer, Vernon Downing and Mary Gordon) whose frequent appearances in the Sherlock Holmes films qualify them as members of a rapidly growing repertory company. Hillary Brooke, who made her series bow in the first entry, *Sherlock Holmes and the Voice of Terror*, as a lady chauffeur, and three years later made a fine impression as Professor Moriarity's seductive accomplice, *The Woman in Green*, is uncharacteristically demonstrative as Sally. The aloof, regal-mannered blonde was the kind of actress Alfred Hitchcock felt best personified cool, calculating sexuality on the screen. (She had a small, insignificant role in the director's 1956 remake of *The Man Who Knew Too Much*.)

In describing her character to Matthew Boulton in *The Woman in Green* ("a very handsome woman, not born to the purple, but giving an excellent imitation"), Rathbone accurately appraises the actress herself. An icon of sophistication in B pictures of the '40s and '50s, Hillary Brooke affected an impression of British gentility, when in reality she hailed from Long Island (her real name was Beatrice Peterson). The actress told the authors:

> Working at Universal at the time that the Sherlock Holmes pics were made was delightful. The Holmes pics made so much money that we were more or less on our own. Nigel Bruce became a dear friend and Basil was a darling. We both loved animals and ice cream. When we were not working, we would get ice cream cones and stroll to the back of the lot to see and visit with the animals. Roy Neill was a dear person. Very easy to work with and very kind.

Contract player Milburn Stone had few opportunities to play the leading man in the movies that he made at his home studio on account of his stature. *Sherlock Holmes Faces Death* was an exception, though his height was the cause for some special accommodations. "Everybody in the picture was taller than me," he told Michael B. Druxman in *Basil Rathbone, His Life and His Films*. "There was this shot where Basil and I had to walk across the room together. He walked on the floor, but they built a special platform for me, so I'd look taller. I had a love scene with Hillary Brooke, which was even worse. We were sitting on the sofa and I looked almost like a midget next to her. The property man supplied me with some pillows to prop me up."

Veteran British stage and screen actor Halliwell Hobbes, the quintessential English butler in scores of pictures, plays yet another old family retainer in *Sherlock Holmes Faces Death* although this time his role has more substance than usual. Hobbes' "Alf" Brunton knows where all the Musgrave family skeletons are hidden and he's not talking, even though the weight of this responsibility has driven him to drink. Hobbes had the opportunity to play the great Sherlock Holmes himself in the 1909 London stage production of "The Speckled Band" at the Adelphi Theatre, and again on tour. Born at Stratford-on-Avon in 1877, Hobbes' extensive stage career began in Glasgow, Scotland, in 1898. Among his leading ladies on the British stage were such legendary grande dames as Ellen Terry and Mrs. Patrick Campbell. Settling in Hollywood in 1929, Hobbes supported Jeanne Eagels in *Jealousy*, and lent strong support to Fredric March in *Dr. Jekyll and Mr. Hyde* (1931). His subsequent movie credits include *The Menace* (1932), *Payment Deferred* (1932), *Lady for a Day* (1933), *British Agent* (1934), *Charlie Chan in Shanghai* (1935), *Captain Blood* (1935), *The Story of Louis Pasteur* (1935), *A Christmas Carol* (1938), *The Undying Monster* (1942), *Gaslight* (1944), *If Winter Comes* (1947) and *Miracle in the Rain* (1956). Hobbes died of heart failure at the age of 84 in Santa Monica, California, on February 20, 1962.

The great detective's welcome return to the Gothic milieu in *Sherlock Holmes Faces Death* was regrettably brief. In his next caper, *The Spider Woman*, the sleuth is, alas, once again firmly entrenched in the dangers and intrigues of a more timely nature.

Critics' Corner

In *Sherlock Holmes Faces Death* ... Axis spies and saboteurs are not his antagonists, and probably will not be again for the duration. As a matter of fact, the latest feature ... returns Holmes to Doyle, or at least its story is less streamlined and closer to the "Musgrave Manor" original.... Some loose ends are left unexplained in the solution, and the yarn doesn't move quite as fast as several of its predecessors. Yet *Sherlock Holmes Faces Death* should make a very good showing at the box office.—*The Hollywood Reporter*, September 2, 1943

Rating: ★★ [N]ot one of the better Holmes mysteries.... We suspect, almost from the beginning [the identity of the murderer]. And, we were right.—*The New York Daily News*, October 8, 1943, Wanda Hale

Universal, which likes to shoot the works on a bloody tale, has done just that in *Sherlock Holmes Faces Death*.... Mr. Holmes moves with absolutely mathematical precision and the clipped peremptory tones of Basil Rathbone; and ... Nigel Bruce ... carries on nobly.—*The New York Times*, October 8, 1943, Theodore Strauss

[M]easures up well with the best of the three turned out last season.... Producer-director Roy William Neill left nothing to be desired in suspense, action, and portrayal of the true Holmes and Watson characters in his direction....—*The Motion Picture Herald*, September 11, 1943, Jack Cartwright

Flesh and Fantasy

Released October 29, 1943. 94 minutes. *Producers:* Charles Boyer & Julien Duvivier. *Director:* Julien Duvivier. *Screenplay:* Ernest Pascal, Samuel Hoffenstein & Ellis St. Joseph. *Based on stories by* Laslo Vadnay, Oscar Wilde & Ellis St. Joseph. *Photography:* Paul Ivano & Stanley Cortez. *Camera Operators:* William Dodds, Len Powers & Carl Webster. *Special Effects:* John P. Fulton & Willis R. Cook. *Art Directors:* John B. Goodman, Richard H. Riedel & Robert Boyle. *Editor:* Arthur Hilton. *Music:* Alexander Tansman. *Musical Director:* Charles Previn. *Assistant Directors:* Joseph A. McDonough, Seward Webb & Phil Bowles. *Set Decorators:* Russell A. Gausman & Edward R. Robinson. *Dialogue Director:* Don Brodie. *Sound Director:* Bernard B. Brown. *Technicians:* Joe Lapis, Bill Fox & Jack Bolger. *Properties:* Leigh Carson & Robert Laszlo. *Makeup:* Jack P. Pierce. *Miss Stanwyck's Gowns:* Edith Head. *Gowns:* Vera West.

Framing Scenes: Robert Benchley (*Doakes*), David Hoffman (*Davis*).

Episode One: Betty Field (*Henrietta*), Robert Cummings (*Michael*), Edgar Barrier (*Stranger*), Marjorie Lord (*Justine*), Charles Halton (*Old Proprietor*), Lane Chandler (*Satan*), Gil Patric (*Death*), Paul Bryar, George J. Lewis (*Harlequins*), Clinton Rosemond (*Old Negro*), Jacqueline Dalya (*Angel*), Peter Lawford (*Pierrot*), Eddie Acuff (*Policeman*), Sandra Morgan, Phil Warren, Carl Vernell (*Neighbors*).

Episode Two: Edward G. Robinson (*Marshall Tyler*), Thomas Mitchell (*Septimus Podgers*), Anna Lee (*Rowena*), Dame May Whitty (*Lady Pamela Hardwick*), C. Aubrey Smith (*Dean of Norwalk*), Ian Wolfe (*Librarian*), Mary Forbes (*Lady Thomas*), Doris Lloyd (*Mrs. Roger Carrington*), Heather Thatcher (*Lady Flora*), Edward Fielding (*Sir Thomas*), Bruce Lester, Geoffrey Steele (*Party Guests*), Leyland Hodgson (*Bobby*), Olaf Hytten (*Chemist*), Harry Stubbs (*Desk Clerk*), Harold De Becker (*Clerk*), Anita Sharp-Bolster, Ferdinand Munier (*Relatives*), Sailor Vincent, George Suzanne, Carey Loftin (*Stunts*), Constance Purdy, Laurence Grossmith, Anne Shoemaker, Paul Scott, Pat O'Hara.

Episode Three: Charles Boyer (*Paul Gaspar*), Barbara Stanwyck (*Joan Stanley*), Charles Winninger (*King Lamarr*), Clarence Muse (*Jeff*), June Lang (*Angela*), Joseph Crehan, Arthur Loft, Lee Phelps (*Detectives*), Frank Mitchell, Lane Chandler (*Acrobats*), Jerry Maren, Jannette Fern, Fern Formica (*Midgets*), Marcel Dalio, Frank Arnold (*Clowns*), Mary Ann Hyde (*Gaspar's Assistant*), Nedra Sanders, Beatrice Barrett (*Chorus Girls*), Marian Novikova, Yvette Bentley, Anita Venge, Marion de Sydow (*Circus Girls*), Bess Flowers (*Circus Crowd Extra*), Jack Gardner (*Gunman*), Eddie Kane (*Immigration Officer*), Con Colleano (*Wirewalker Double for Charles Boyer*), John Burton, William Gould, Ted Jacques, Bob Scheerer, Charles Sherlock, Nolan Leary, Silvay Chaldicott, Eddie Coke. *Scenes may have been deleted from final print*: Grace McDonald (*Equestrienne*).

You are going to kill someone, Mr. Tyler.
—*Thomas Mitchell in* Flesh and Fantasy

The prolific director of such stylish French films as *Le Golem* (1936), *Pepe Le Moko* (1937) and *La Fin du jour* (1939), Julien Duvivier leaned towards the omnibus style of storytelling during his wartime sabbatical in Hollywood. *Tales of Manhattan*, released by 20th Century–Fox in 1942, is a five-episode amalgam of stories threaded together by a single theme: The profound effect a dress tailcoat has on the lives of its wide range of owners. Sporting an all-star cast (Charles Boyer, Rita Hayworth, Edward G. Robinson, Charles Laughton, W.C. Fields, Ginger Rogers, Paul Robeson, Thomas Mitchell, Cesar Romero, Ethel Waters), this offbeat but unevenly effective comedy-drama garnered respectable reviews, encouraging the Gallic *auteur* to attempt a second such project with the supernatural as its central theme, *Flesh and Fantasy*.

Forming a co-production partnership with his friend (and *Tales of Manhattan* star) Charles Boyer, Duvivier sealed a deal with Universal in the spring of 1942. Boyer agreed to play a major role in the film aside from his producing duties for a flat $125,000. Barbara Stanwyck and Edward G. Robinson, another *Tales of Manhattan* carry-over, were signed up at $50,000 apiece. In the course of the production's erratic shooting schedule (lasting a little over a year), such popular players as Betty Field, Thomas Mitchell (also from *Tales*), Robert Cummings, Gloria Jean and Alan Curtis were added to the cast. The player roster didn't have the status of *Tales of Manhattan*'s but it came close. Other actors that Universal sought but did not get included Adolphe Menjou, Deanna Durbin, *Tales*' co-star Charles Laughton and, incredibly, Greta Garbo.

Algonquin Round Table wit Robert Benchley (a sparkling addition to any cast) was enlisted to play a comedic role in *Flesh and Fantasy*'s delightful framing scenes. As Mr. Doakes, a jittery businessman, Benchley confides the details of a disturbing dream and a recent experience with a fortune-teller to impish bookworm Mr. Davis (David Hoffman), whom he meets in the library of the Gentleman's Club. With the fervor of a salesman, Davis sets out to teach Doakes a moral lesson. He reads him three fanciful tales about ordinary people caught up in extraordinary circumstances who ultimately learn that man is the master of his own fate, and that by believing in ourselves, we may attain inner peace.

Flesh and Fantasy is (at least two-thirds) cinematic storytelling at its best. Stylish, witty and urbane, it just falls short of being a minor classic. Duvivier's European influence and subtle touch are ever present. He has a powerful, rich visual sense. Characters are artfully positioned within the frame. There's an abundance of striking close-ups and spirited montages. Bizarre camera angles impart a surreal, dreamlike quality. Evocative sound effects work wonders in establishing a palpable, otherworldly mood. *Flesh and Fantasy* is the creation of a master filmmaker who uses the vocabulary of the cinema with expertise and assurance.

Ernest Pascal, Samuel Hoffenstein and Ellis St. Joseph (who also authored one of the three original tales) wrote a polished, generally sophisticated script containing a trio of morality plays. Though each story has a built-in message (the more worldly viewer may resent their unadulterated naïveté), the accent is squarely on fanciful entertainment.

Flesh and Fantasy originally contained a fourth vignette. Co-starring Alan Curtis and Gloria Jean, it told the story of an unregenerate hoodlum and a blind girl (the latter gifted with spiritual powers) whose encounter in a pastoral never-neverland ends in tragedy. After the movie was previewed, Universal determined that it ran approximately a half-hour over what they considered acceptable theater running time. Following the example set by 20th Century–Fox, who deleted a wearisome W.C. Fields vignette from *Tales of Manhattan*, Universal pulled this episode out of *Flesh and Fantasy*. A year later, Curtis and Jean, now under the direction of Reginald LeBorg, shot more scenes, expanding the vignette into the feature-length release *Destiny*.

The second episode of *Flesh and Fantasy*, an indictment against prognostication, was the first to go before the cameras (it was shot over a

Hands-on producer Charles Boyer helped make some of the masks seen in *Flesh and Fantasy*'s opening segment. Pictured: Edgar Barrier as the mysterious Stranger (courtesy Photofest).

three-week period, from July 21 to August 11, 1942). Based on Oscar Wilde's "Lord Arthur Saville's Crime," this vignette ranks as the best in the trilogy. Edward G. Robinson, Thomas Mitchell and a fine supporting cast complement the story's sardonic wit and rich black humor.

Robinson plays Marshall Tyler, an American lawyer visiting London. Attending a frivolous social hosted by his friend Lady Pamela Hardwick (Dame May Whitty), Tyler incredulously agrees to have his palm read by Septimus Podgers (Thomas Mitchell), a renowned forecaster. (Podgers' uncanny abilities are dramatically proven when he foresaw the reappearance of Roger Carrington, who was presumably killed while on an expedition in Antarctica. In typical Hollywood fashion, an announcement heralding the explorer's rescue is heard over the radio just minutes after the seer predicts his return.)

Examining Tyler's palm, Podgers suddenly grows somber. Later, he reveals to the lawyer what he had seen: "You are going to kill someone, Mr. Tyler." Dismissing the prediction as utter nonsense, Tyler attempts to put it out of his mind, but to no avail. Haunted by portentous images, he struggles with the dark side of his conscience (amusingly depicted as a leering, wicked version of himself), who reminds Tyler that he cannot escape his destiny.

Tyler finally succumbs to this unrelieved pressure and selects Lady Pamela as his victim. He presents her with a charming seventeenth century box containing a piece of poison-laced chocolate, then goes into hiding to await news of her passing. Much to his chagrin, Tyler learns the dowager has indeed died, but from *natural* causes.

Now more desperate than ever, Tyler attempts to set up the garrulous Dean of Norwalk

(C. Aubrey Smith) as a victim, but the scheme backfires when the clergyman guesses his intentions. Rushing out into the night, Tyler providentially encounters Podgers strolling across London Bridge (the old *Phantom of the Opera* set). Fearing for his life, the forecaster unconvincingly disclaims his prediction, but it is too late. The madman strangles him and dumps his body into the Thames. Spotted by two bobbies, Tyler escapes to the grounds of the Lamarr Circus, but is quickly captured. As the police take him away, the lawyer insists that he was forced to commit murder by an uncontrollable force within himself. Acrobatic star Paul Gaspar (Charles Boyer) witnesses the tragic scene; his presence leads us into the next episode.

As ever, the Breen watchdogs kept a keen eye on the Universal production. The Code dictated that so-called predictions of future events from palm reading, dreams, etc., must be handled in such a way that only evil results; a person is really in control of his own destiny. To quell any apprehensions, Duvivier and Boyer met with Breen officials to reassure them that the edict would be followed.

Robinson, as always, is a joy to watch. His pompous Yankee lawyer regards the act of murder as a mere inconvenience — something to be done with immediately so he may resume his daily activities. With all the painstaking care he takes to set up Dame May Whitty, we almost feel sorry for the man when Providence intervenes and cheats him of his victim. Robinson's increased paranoia is skillfully suggested via weird montages and clever camera effects, as his mocking "other self" unexpectedly materializes in eyeglass lenses, etc.

Robinson once again played a character (ironically named Chris Cross) whose tragic fate is similarly preordained after a chance social encounter (this time with a heartless prostitute) in Fritz Lang's unrelentingly cynical noir classic *Scarlet Street,* produced by Walter Wanger for a 1945 Universal release. Unaware that his efforts as a Sunday afternoon painter are the work of genius, the blissfully naïve Chris is victimized not only by Kitty (Joan Bennett) but by her bullying pimp, Johnny Prince (Dan Duryea). Prince passes off Chris' unsigned masterpieces as Kitty's work, attracting the attention of art critics and wealthy collectors. Realizing at last that he has been playing the fool, Chris brutally stabs Kitty to death, then stands by with grim satisfaction as Prince is arrested, convicted and executed for the young woman's murder. As might be expected, the Breen Office had the last laugh. Jobless and homeless, Chris ends up in the gutter; he cannot convince the authorities that he was responsible for two deaths and should be tried and put to death. Our last glimpse of this pathetic figure, wandering aimlessly amid throngs of Christmas celebrants, the spectral "voices" of his two victims mercilessly taunting his conscience, is unforgettable.

Anna Lee, Robinson's *Flesh and Fantasy* love interest, told us what it was like acting under Duvivier's guidance. "It was a little odd working with him, as all his directions were in French and had to be translated by somebody else. I remember wearing a lovely green and silver gown which I took with me overseas when I was entertaining the troops — and it was stolen by the Arabs!"

On August 26, Duvivier began production on *Flesh and Fantasy*'s most elaborate episode, a sentimental, romantic vignette co-starring Barbara Stanwyck and the oh-so-debonair Boyer as a pair of lovers whose meeting and ultimate separation were predestined.* The screen adaptation of Laslo Vadnay's story is strong on mood (there's an aura of impending doom hovering over the entire episode), but it lacks the acerbic wit and sense of the unreal imparted by the other vignettes. The slim metaphysical element (predicting the future through dreams) is diluted by the schmaltzy trappings of a Hollywoodish soap opera. By comparison, it is the weakest episode in the package.

Billed as the Drunken Gentleman of the Tight Rope (a rather silly concept), Paul Gaspar is haunted by a recurring nightmare in which he imagines himself plummeting to the ground while performing his specialty act. The dream has an interesting sidelight: Gaspar envisions an attractive woman, wearing a pair of curious earrings, sitting in the audience, screaming in horror as he falls to earth.

**In 1952, the circus sequence was re-done for television on* CBS Screen Guild Players, *with one of Universal-International's top stars of the '50s, Jeff Chandler, in the lead.*

Mardi Gras demons and devils (also seen in the first sequence) line up for a spooky posed shot (courtesy Photofest).

Taking a rest cure, Gaspar is awestruck when he recognizes his "dream lady" amongst the passengers on board a transatlantic ship en route to New York. She is Joan Stanley (Stanwyck), a recluse with a dark secret. Joan pooh-poohs Paul's suggestion that they have met before, but starts taking him seriously when he describes in detail the pair of earrings she was wearing in his dream (two bejeweled lyres). She suggests that Gaspar avoid her ("I might bring you bad luck") but Paul isn't dissuaded. When a fellow passenger addresses the young woman as Miss Templeton, Gaspar becomes even more fascinated.

During the course of the voyage, the couple fall in love. In an eerily portentous dream sequence, filled with distorted images and exaggerated sound effects, Paul "witnesses" Joan's arrest after the ship arrives in New York Harbor.

His confidence restored, Paul plans on performing his act on opening night. At his request, Joan dons the earrings and sits in the audience. The performance is a success. But before Joan can reach Paul, she is stopped by a pair of detectives. Weary of fleeing the law and her jewel thief confederates, Joan had alerted the police of her whereabouts, scheduling her own date with destiny. In the tearful finis, she reveals all to the knowing Gaspar. She walks off with the policemen, just as Paul had dreamed she would.

It took Duvivier nearly three weeks to complete this episode. He suddenly fell ill in early September, causing the production to close down for two days. Henry Koster was called in on September 4 to fill in for the ailing Frenchman when he couldn't return to work. Another day was lost on account of the Labor Day holiday. Filming was finally completed on Tuesday, September 15 (or September 21, according to a second source). But nearly a month later, Boyer and Stanwyck were called back to the studio for retakes after flaws were discovered while the episode was being edited.

The Stanwyck-Boyer story's languid pacing is somewhat alleviated by the colorful circus-shipboard backgrounds. Duvivier takes advantage of these settings and creates some stunning visuals. Most of the aerial feats were performed by Con Colleano (of the world-famous family of high-wire walkers); the rest were shot on a process stage. Acquanetta was slated to appear as equestrienne Grace McDonald's assistant, but had to bow out on account of illness.

Cinematographer Stanley Cortez had a reputation in Hollywood as a perfectionist (which also meant he was painstakingly slow in his methods). He started shooting *Flesh and Fantasy*, but left after a few weeks following a disagreement with Duvivier. The director hired fellow countryman Paul Ivano to finish the film. Their chats (in French) drove Stanwyck to distraction. Ivano finally won Barbara's respect by taking the trouble to insure that the actress wouldn't be injured in the execution of a particularly dangerous crane shot.

Slated to start production in late October (according to *The Hollywood Reporter*) but begun shortly after the Thanksgiving recess, the ultimately discarded Alan Curtis-Gloria Jean vignette was originally set to feature Warner Bros. star John Garfield and Teresa Wright in the lead roles. The tempermental Garfield balked at being loaned out to Universal, and was placed on suspension by his home studio. Wright, on the other hand, was forced to turn down the role on account of health reasons. (Perky juvenile star Bonita Granville was also considered for the part.) The same trade paper also reported that Duvivier and his company had intended to shoot the entire episode outdoors in the picturesque Lake Malibu area, but a fire destroyed the planned location spot.

The director pushed his cast and crew right up until late afternoon on Christmas Eve (a rare practice in Hollywood). Special effects men Willis R. Cook and John P. Fulton performed their intricate tasks after the holiday recess, bringing the project into its sixth month of production.

Gloria Jean bitterly regrets Universal's decision to can her episode of *Flesh and Fantasy*. The actress told us that she had seen the movie intact at a theater right on the Universal lot:

> [T]hey had a preview at a theater in Hollywood, and what was *really* something was that everybody's favorite was *my* episode. I *saw* all the [audience response] cards, and it was wonderful. Those cards were just incredible. A lot of them said, "Gloria Jean's episode was the best." "Oh," I thought, "this is gonna be a whole new career for me." Well, I was so disappointed when it was cut out. I was devastated! I understand that there were some people who had stock in Universal, and had a *lot* to do with what **I** did, personally, and they had it cut out. I think Edward G. Robinson ... was more upset than *any*body, because he thought the one with me and Alan Curtis was the best in the whole movie! He was quite an art collector and he had a big party at his home, shortly after the preview, and I was invited. He said to me, "I will *nnnever* get over the fact that they cut the best sequence in the whole movie—*yours*." I was quite impressed with that. And he said, "There's *some*thing wrong here...!"

The last *Flesh and Fantasy* vignette shot can be called a modern Cinderella story. On a temporary loanout from her home studio, Paramount, Betty Field shared top billing with Robert Cummings, who was on leave while serving in the Civil Air Patrol's anti-submarine force. A precursor of the 1959 French-Portuguese classic *Black Orpheus*, this enchanting fairy tale is the purest example of fantasy in the film; there's even an old-fashioned moral at the end. The action takes place in the last hours of Mardi Gras, that magical time when the yearly celebration is at its most frenzied, when carnival masks are discarded to reveal the true identities of the revelers. Duvivier wisely positioned this moody adaptation of Ellis St. Joseph's story at the head of the others in the final cut. It captures the spirit of *Flesh and Fantasy* best, and puts the audience into a receptive mood to "accept" the paranormal elements of the forthcoming playlets.

Plain, unappealing Henrietta (Field), a New Orleans dressmaker, is an embittered shell of a woman. Friendless and loveless, she is attracted to Michael (Cummings), a disillusioned law student who is about to chuck it all and become a stoker on a departing freighter. Contemplating suicide, Henrietta is approached by a bearded old man (Edgar Barrier) who dissuades her from leaping into the murky river. "Something miraculous might occur to change your whole life!" he comforts her.

In *Flesh and Fantasy*'s second segment, Tyler (Edward G. Robinson) cracks under pressure and confronts Septimus Podgers (Thomas Mitchell), who predicted that Tyler was fated to commit murder (courtesy John Cocchi).

The stranger escorts Henrietta to a closed costume shop, and implores her to choose a desirable mask and costume. "For a few hours, it is still possible for you to be beautiful!" He makes her promise to return the mask before the hour of midnight.

Bedecked in the alluring disguise, Henrietta melts into the throng of cavorting celebrators. Michael "rescues" her from a would-be admirer and the couple settles into a cafe. Putting her desires and self-interests in check, Henrietta builds Michael's confidence, convincing him to believe in himself. She at last learns the true meaning of love: Giving of oneself and expecting nothing in return.

The clock strikes 12. The time has come for everyone to unmask. Henrietta rushes back to the shop with Michael in close pursuit. She cannot bear for him to see her as she really is. "I know your face is beautiful because you are," Michael says reassuringly. Removing the disguise, Henrietta is ecstatic as she sees her features have changed to resemble those of the mask. By being selfless, Henrietta has altered her own visage of selfishness and envy. As she and Michael depart from the shop, the camera focuses on a mask with the face of the bearded old stranger on display in the window.

With a sharp eye for the beautiful and the grotesque, Duvivier creates in the Mardi Gras footage an extraordinary tableaux of haunting images resembling an orgiastic feast before the coming of the Apocalypse. Enigmatic faces are reflected in sparkling pools. Rockets and firecrackers light up the night sky. Swirling clouds of confetti choke the air. A bizarre group of curiosity seekers (including a pair of harlequins, Satan, Death and an angel, looking as though they had stepped out of the pages of Dante) philosophize around the body of a drowned man (Alan Curtis' ill-fated hoodlum from the unused episode). It is within this surreal landscape that Henrietta and Michael seek out their destinies and find peace and happiness.

Duvivier shot the episode between the 8th and 24th of March 1943, utilizing Soundstage 12 (for the river bank) and the old *Phantom of the Opera* set. Robert Cummings and the underrated Betty Field marked their second screen teaming as lovers (Warners' 1942 *Kings Row* was the first). Never very convincing in heavy, dramatic roles, Cummings' baby-face looks and unimposing presence were more suited to homespun comedy. Alfred Hitchcock resented his casting as the man-on-the-run in *Saboteur* (1942), but the great director was forced to use him on account of the actor's contractual obligations.

Field, on the other hand, was a strong asset to *any* film in which she appeared. The American Academy of Dramatic Arts graduate came to the attention of producer George Abbott who cast her in a succession of Broadway shows. The screen version of the play "What a Life!" was Field's ticket to the movie capital. She made a lasting impression in the role of Mae, Bob Steele's bad-lucky-penny spouse in the moving 1939 screen version of John Steinbeck's *Of Mice and Men*. The actress' style — gutsy, honest and unadorned — won her major roles in *Victory* (1940), the aforementioned *Kings Row*, *Tomorrow the World* (1943) and *The Southerner* (1945). In 1946, Field won the New York Drama Critics Award for Best Performance by an Actress in the play "Dream Girl," written by Elmer Rice, her husband at the time. In Paramount's 1949 film version of F. Scott Fitzgerald's *The Great Gatsby*, Field enacted the role of Daisy Buchanan opposite Alan Ladd as Gatsby. On September 13, 1973, the day before she was scheduled to leave Hollywood to enact a role in director John Schlesinger's *The Day of the Locust* (1975), Field was stricken with a cerebral hemorrhage and passed away.

According to a press report, Walter Huston could not meet the schedule to play the kind old stranger in this episode, so Universal assigned Edgar Barrier. As soon as Boyer saw the first day's rushes, he assigned Barrier further duties as narrator of a Samuel Hoffenstein poem that was originally planned to open the film.

But *Flesh and Fantasy* art director Robert Boyle had a different version as to why the great character actor was not in the film. Boyle told us:

> Walter was getting a little older, and he couldn't always remember his lines, he was having a hard time with them. The mask shop had a low ceiling with beams and all sorts of nooks and crannies, and I said, "Look, it'll be very easy, we'll have his lines printed and we'll paste them on masks and on jars and other places on the set, so that he can refresh his memory by looking at 'em." Well, Duvivier would have none of that. I remember this happened at lunchtime, 'cause when I came back from lunch, they said, "Duvivier just fired Walter Huston." I said, "You can't fire Walter Huston, he's one of our great actors!" But he *did*, and I was sort-of against Duvivier from that moment on!
>
> Duvivier was a very interesting director who had done films *like* this before, where you follow a certain thing, like a dress suit, from one owner to another. It was kind of a fad, particularly with the French at that point. And Duvivier, being French, followed the tradition. [He was a] very meticulous, very strict, very hard-nosed guy. I must say that, for me, everything [Duvivier-connected] was colored by the fact that he was the man who fired Walter Huston [*laughs*]!

Boyle had fonder memories of working with Boyer:

> Charles Boyer was a wonderful gentleman, and I loved him. I had trouble getting the masks made — the sculptor or sculptors that we hired didn't seem to understand [what was required], they weren't able to get the grotesque features of the masks. So I said to Boyer, "I'm going to make those masks myself. I'll be in the staff shop, making the masks tonight." I had planned to work all night. Well, Boyer came over and said, "I'll *help* you." So he and I worked all night on those masks.... Moviemaking, to most of us, has always been a collaborative effort anyway. So that was not unusual. What *was* unusual was that someone of the stature of Boyer would be able to come down and get his hands dirty working in the staff shop. We made all these dozens of masks. He just wanted to be part of it.

On August 18, 1943, after more than a year in on-and-off production, *Flesh and Fantasy* wrapped following a day's shooting of the Benchley framing scenes. (Lenore Aubert and

Milburn Stone tested for small roles in these scenes, but they were written out of the script.) Just days before Duvivier began work on the Field-Cummings episode, Universal decided to retitle their film *For All We Know*, a tag more suggestive of a wistful love story than a surreal fantasy. But on August 24, 1943 (a week after the last scene was shot), the studio had a change of heart and wisely restored the picture's original, more appropriate title.

Universal set aside $250,000 to promote *Flesh and Fantasy*, the largest advertising expenditure any feature attraction in the studio's recent history. Released on October 29, 1943, the film wasn't an unqualified critical success. (*The Hollywood Reporter* ran a compendium of reviews — some of them unfavorable — in their November 22 edition.) A French-language version was prepared for overseas in the spring of 1944, followed by a Spanish-language edition that summer.

Duvivier remained in Hollywood for the duration of the war, directing his long-time star Jean Gabin in 1944's *The Imposter*. Traveling to Great Britain in 1948, he directed Vivien Leigh and Ralph Richardson in an adaptation of Tolstoy's *Anna Karenina* before returning to France. Over the next two decades, the celebrated filmmaker directed a variety of French and French-Italian co-productions including *Don Camillo* (1952) with French comedian Fernandel, *The Man in the Raincoat* (1957), also starring Fernandel, *Marie Octobre* (1959), *La Chambre Ardente* (*The Burning Court*) (1962), an occult thriller, set in a castle in Germany's Black Forest, which combines elements of mystery, witchcraft and the supernatural, *Chair de Poule* (1963) and *Diaboliquement Votre* (1967). An automobile accident claimed the life of the 71-year-old writer-director that same year.

Critics' Corner

[A] decidedly novel and unusual picture.... — *Variety*, September 22, 1943

Rating: ★★★½ [L]ike all Julien Duvivier creations, an extraordinary production and a remarkable picture.... [I]mmensely entertaining.... [A]ll the performances are as good as you'd expect from ... splendid players. — *The New York Daily News*, November 18, 1943, Wanda Hale

The production is beautifully mounted and certainly imaginatively directed by Duvivier.... Duvivier's direction is notable for its holding mood without undue emphasis upon the unexplainable. What he has done is to treat of [*sic*] fantasy in not too uncommon denominators. — *The Hollywood Reporter*, September 17, 1943

The picture has been produced artistically, and it should direct a particular appeal to class audiences, as well as to those who seek something different in screen entertainment. Whether or not it will appeal to the masses is questionable.... — *Harrison's Reports*, September 18, 1943

[I]f your interest in dreams and the predictions of fortune-tellers is as indifferent as this observer's, then the chances are you will regard this three-episode Universal production as just so much palaver. For at best *Flesh and Fantasy*, notwithstanding its novelty, is an uneven entertainment. It starts lamely, and ends in the same condition.... — *The New York Times*, November 18, 1943

[A] distinctly novel enterprise, recalling Duvivier's *Tales of Manhattan* in its episodic treatment but entering fresh fields in its subject matter.... There is no single impression. The film stands on the merits of its three separate acts, each on the appeal of its theme and on the strength of its cast. — *The Motion Picture Herald*, September 18, 1943, E.A. Cunningham

Son of Dracula

Released November 5, 1943. 78 minutes. *Associate Producer:* Donald H. Brown. *Executive Producer:* Jack Gross. *Producer:* Ford Beebe. *Director:* Robert Siodmak. *Screenplay:* Eric Taylor. *Original Story:* Curt Siodmak. *Photography:* George Robinson. *Editor:* Saul A. Goodkind. *Art Directors:* John B. Goodman & Martin Obzina. *Musical Director:* Hans J. Salter. *Set Decorators:* Russell A. Gausman & Edward R. Robinson. *Assistant Director:* Melville Shyer. *Second Unit Director:* Ford Beebe. *Sound Director:* Bernard B. Brown. *Technician:* Charles Carroll. *Special Effects:* John P. Fulton. *Makeup:* Jack P. Pierce. *Assistant Cutter:* Carl Himm. *Script Clerk:* Mary Chaffee. *Property Man:* Wally Kirkpatric. *Camera Operator:* Eddie Cohen. *Assistant Camera:* Walter Bluemel. *Stills:* Bill Fildew. *Gaffer:* Max Nippell. *Grip:* Roland Smith. *Floorman:* Roger Parrish. *Recorder:* John Kemp. *Women's Wardrobe:* Ann Fielder. *Men's Wardrobe:* Tom Clark. *Hairdresser:* Emmy Eckhardt, *Gowns:* Vera West.

Lon Chaney, Jr. (*Count Anthony Alucard/Count Dracula*), Louise Allbritton (*Katherine Caldwell*), Robert Paige (*Frank Stanley*), Evelyn Ankers (*Claire Caldwell*), Frank Craven (*Dr. Harry Brewster*), J. Edward Bromberg (*Prof. Lazlo*), Samuel S. Hinds (*Judge Simmons*), Adeline de Walt Reynolds (*Queen Zimba*), George Irving (*Col. Caldwell*), Etta McDaniel (*Sarah*), Patrick Moriarity (*Sheriff Dawes*), Walter Sande (Matt), Cyril Delevanti (*Dr. Peters*), Joan Blair (*Mrs. Land*), Charles Bates (*Tommy Land*), Jess Lee Brooks (*Steven*), Sam McDaniel (*Andy*), Charles R. Moore (*Matthew*), Emmett Smith (*Servant*), Robert Dudley (*Jonathan Kirby*), Jack Rockwell, Ben Erway, Robert Hill (*Deputies*).

"Prepare for New Horror ... so real ... You'll Believe Every Chilling Scene!"
—*Trailer blurb for* Son of Dracula

Universal's horror film output of the '40s is so intertwined with the career of Lon Chaney, Jr., that it's almost impossible to separate them. Unlike Karloff and Lugosi, who more or less stumbled upon the genre they became most identified with, Chaney was launched as a horror star for no other reason than because of his highly recognizable name. While Lon certainly had limitations as an actor, he was often very good when a role suited him, but in the case of *Son of Dracula*, one could only feel sympathy for his being so cynically miscast by his studio. One gets the feeling that if Ward Bond, Broderick Crawford or Barton MacLane (all successful studio players in the same approximate range as Lon) were born with the name Chaney, Universal would be fitting them into a Dracula cape as well.

George Waggner was originally set to produce the film, but was sidetracked by Universal's lavish remake of *Phantom of the Opera*. He was replaced by serial ace Ford Beebe, who landed the assignment on the strength of his impressive *Night Monster*. Curt Siodmak was commissioned to write a script in May 1942. The studio kept the writer busy with a glut of horror assignments, but he wasn't getting any richer. He told us:

> I never got a raise at Universal, never. "You get a raise outside, then we pay you more," they told me. Basically I never pushed it because, this may sound silly, money doesn't mean as much to me as an objective in life. I'm a writer, and to write the right things is more important than getting a lot of dough for it.

But things were looking up for Siodmak at the time. *Adventure Magazine* was set to publish the writer's eagerly anticipated *Donovan's Brain*, for which several studios were already bidding. In the end, it was Republic that got the screen rights to the novel, which was filmed as *The Lady and the Monster* (1944).

Universal's choice of a director spelled trouble for the writer: His brother, Robert. Born in Dresden, Germany, in 1900, he had some early experience an actor, writer, film cutter and assistant director, and collaborated with future Hollywood émigrés Edgar G. Ulmer, Billy Wilder, Fred Zinnemann and brother Curt on the groundbreaking documentary *Menschen am Sonntag* (1929). Made for $5,000, the film gave these artists their first taste of recognition. Siodmak soon joined Germany's prestigious Ufa Studios and cemented his reputation with *The Tempest* (1931) featuring Emil Jannings. Hitler's rise to power compelled Siodmak to flee to France, where he scored a success directing the acclaimed musical *La Crise est Finie* (1934). Just one day prior to the Nazi occupation of France, Siodmak fled to America.

Siodmak's impressive European credentials meant nothing in Hollywood and he soon found himself, like Joe May, faced with the impossible task of trying to rebuild his reputation on second-rate pictures at Paramount, Republic and 20th Century–Fox. Brother Curt reflected:

> They forced him to do this shot and that shot. Robert didn't want to do it. One day an assistant said to him, "I thought you were such a big director! Why don't you fight to do it your way?" Robert said, "Because this is Paramount shit, this is not a Siodmak picture!" So they fired him.

It was at Universal where his career eventually took off with a remarkable streak of highly stylized thrillers: *Phantom Lady*, *Christmas Holiday*, *The Suspect* (all 1944) and *The Strange Affair of Uncle Harry* (1945). Previously, the director bided his time with the Maria Montez-Jon Hall kitsch classic *Cobra Woman* (1944), which was preceded by his first Universal assignment, *Son of Dracula*. An option for a term deal was injected into Siodmak's contract so there was pressure on the director to make good fast. The first thing he did was to have his brother Curt thrown off the picture. (Eric Taylor wrote the screenplay. The Siodmaks would never make another movie together.)

Curt told us:

> We had a sibling rivalry. When we were in Germany, Robert had a magazine and when I wrote for it, I had to change my name. He only wanted one Siodmak around. This lasted 71 years, until he died.

The second follow-up to *Dracula* had been a long time coming. Universal enthusiastically

Lon Chaney, Jr.'s, interpretation of the famed bloodsucker in *Son of Dracula* still arouses strong opinions, both pro and con.

churned out Frankenstein, Mummy and Invisible Man pictures, but was oddly hesitant about reviving the Bram Stoker character, even though the original film was one of their biggest grossers. It seemed an ideal time to turn again to the Count now that they had a contracted actor they had groomed for just such a role. And even if it did seem that Lon Chaney would make an unlikely Hungarian, even an undead one, makeup genius Jack Pierce would at least make him look the part. This was quite a blow for the career-challenged Bela Lugosi, who was cooling his heels at Monogram until Universal's inevitable resurrection of Dracula, only to lose the part to a young rival. His grudge against Chaney would last for years. (According to Reginald LeBorg, Lugosi was still stewing over *Son of Dracula* when he costarred with Chaney in *The Black Sleep* in 1956.)

The embittered Lugosi ended up with a consolation prize, playing a Dracula-like vampire in Columbia's *The Return the Vampire* (1943), a shameless Universal imitation if ever there was one. There were even hopes for a *Return* follow-up with Lugosi's Armand Tesla character, but the studio had second thoughts and the proposed sequel (*Bride of the Vampire*) was reworked as a werewolf film, *Cry of the Werewolf* (1944), a resounding dud.

Son of Dracula's credits unfold as a gloved hand wipes away a swath of cobwebs, revealing the film's title painted on a black surface in sweeping white letters. The device was used 16 years earlier in Paul Leni's *The Cat and the Canary* (1927) but Hans J. Salter's dynamic score adds an appropriate measure of menace and urgency. As the final credit fades, we are presented with a leisurely, sun-drenched scene in a small-town American train depot. The accents and manner of dress of the characters suggest the Midwest but the setting is actually somewhere in the Deep South.

Two men, Frank Stanley (Robert Paige) and Dr. Harry Brewster (Frank Craven), impatiently await the arrival of Count Alucard, a nobleman from Central Europe, who has been invited to Dark Oaks, the plantation home of Stanley's fiancée Kay Caldwell (Louise Allbritton). When the Count doesn't appear, the pair leave.

Kay's reception party proceeds despite the absence of its guest of honor. The festivities are cut short when Kay's father Col. Caldwell (George Irving) is found in his bed, seemingly dead from shock (he was actually a victim of Alucard). Count Alucard (Lon Chaney, Jr.) makes a belated arrival. When the suspicious Dr. Brewster notices the name Alucard is actually Dracula spelled backwards, he implores Kay's sister Claire (Evelyn Ankers) to leave the plantation, and consults Prof. Lazlo (J. Edward Bromberg), an authority on the occult.

Leery of Alucard's motives, and jealous over his attentions to Kay, Frank shadows Alucard and Kay. Confronting the pair, Frank is appalled to learn Kay and the Count were just married. Frank and Alucard clash. Frank empties his revolver into the Count but the bullets pass through his body and kill Kay.

The next morning, Frank confesses his crime to Sheriff Dawes (Patrick Moriarity). Brewster is quick to intervene, insisting that he spoke to Kay hours after the alleged murder took place. Combing the grounds of the plantation, the sheriff discovers Kay's body in the family crypt and promptly books Frank on a charge of murder.

Barely escaping being charged as an accessory, Brewster fills Lazlo in on the case. Convinced that Alucard is a descendant of Count Dracula, the professor theorizes that Kay deliberately courted the vampire in order to attain eternal life, and is now plotting to initiate Frank into the ranks of the undead.

Meanwhile, the bat-form of Kay appears in Frank's jail cell and draws a small quantity of blood while he sleeps. Kay rematerializes, awakens Frank and reveals to him her fantastic scheme. Escaping from jail, he heads for Dracula's coffin, hidden in the underbrush of a swamp drainage tunnel. Frank sets fire to the coffin and is about to make his getaway when the Count appears. The enraged vampire desperately attempts to extinguish the flames but is caught in the rays of the new day's sun and perishes.

Frank makes his way to Dark Oaks, keeping his promise to Kay to meet her in the attic nursery. Finding her body lying in a casket, he gently places his ring on her finger. Moments later, Brewster, Lazlo and Sheriff Dawes arrive to find Frank calmly standing by as the fire he set engulfs the nursery and the undead Kay, freeing her soul forever.

Although *Son of Dracula* was often lumped together with the rest of the Universal monster pictures of the '40s in the early years of horror movie scholarship, it has incrementally been seen as the product of a more sophisticated mindset. Even so, its reputation generally still lags behind *Dracula's Daughter*, especially by commentators who overstress the erotic underpinnings of the earlier Lambert Hillyer film rather than its artistic or technical merits. Still, in the canon of Robert Siodmak's career, *Son of Dracula* is still re-

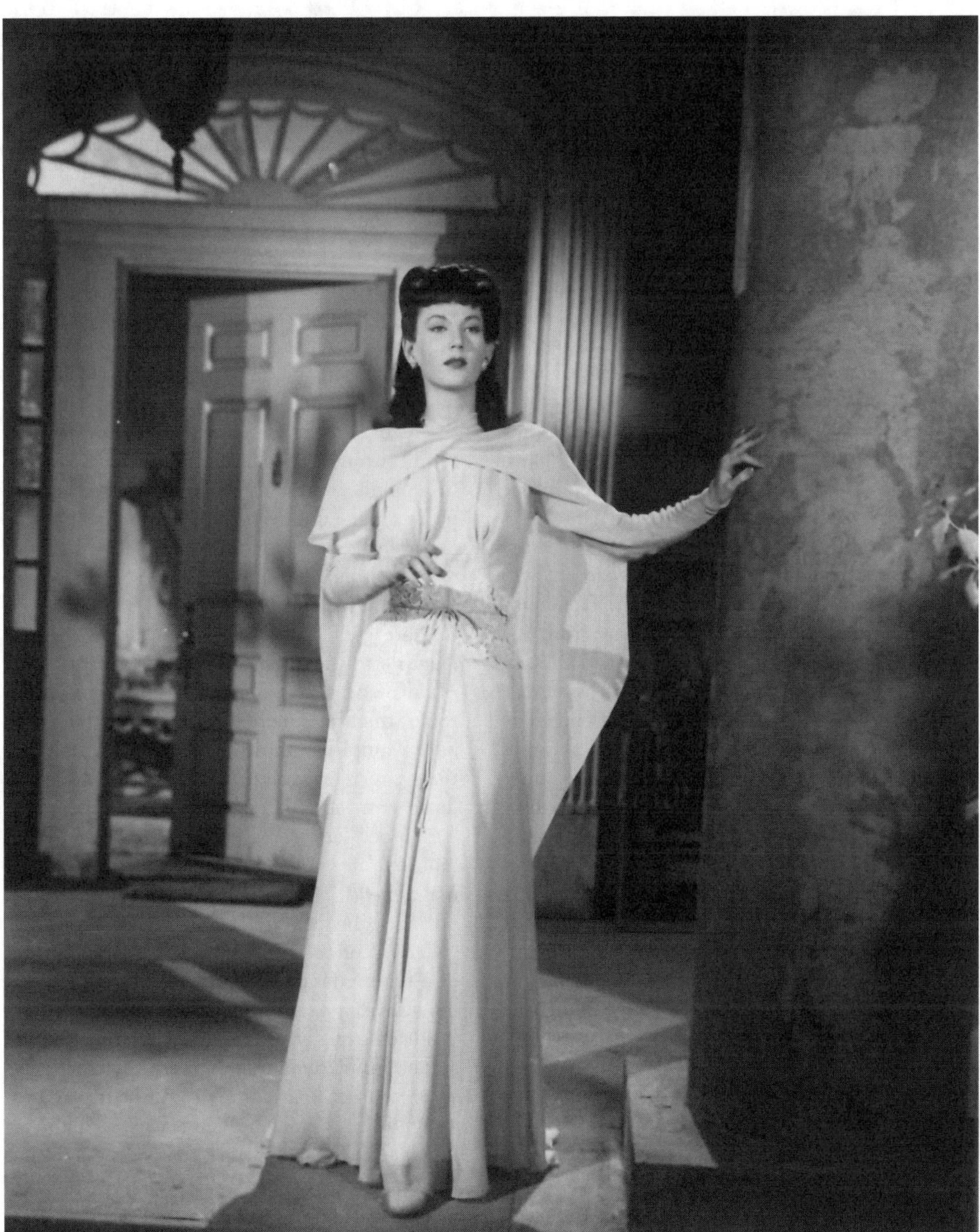

Married to the Macabre: Katherine (Louise Allbritton) destroys the lives of many around her, *and* her own, in her quest for immortality.

garded as a footnote, a stepping stone to his later, highly regarded film noir works.

Eric Taylor deserves as much credit as Siodmak for elevating *Son of Dracula* above the standard B level, working an adult sensibility into the material and underscoring character development and motivation to a greater extent than the recent run of Universal shockers. Indeed, Siodmak's most important contribution to the film, along with his polished direction, might very well be his dismissal of his brother Curt from the movie. While there may have been a family dynamic at play, as Curt suggested, it's possible it could have been a case of Robert being underwhelmed by some of his sibling's recent horror assignments. Surely if the script of *Frankenstein Meets the Wolf Man*, with its action-driven plot and comic book ruminations on the nature of life and death, were any indication of how Curt would have handled the Bram Stoker character, who could blame him? In comparison, Taylor's brew of film noir, Gothic romance and traditional horror was probably a lot closer to Robert's temperament.

Transmigrating the Count to America imparts to the film a crisp, modernized look, though it is a pity Universal didn't attempt one last truly Gothic vampire bash with Dracula as a solo menace. (The often disguised *Tower of London* set could have provided the vampire with handsome accommodations indeed.) The small-town American setting is a far cry from the Gothic flavor of the first two Universal Dracula films, yet Siodmak, with excellent assistance from art directors John B. Goodman and Martin Obzina and photographer George Robinson, manages to turn this atmospheric disadvantage into an asset by concentrating on the misty swamplands, expertly realized on the studio soundstages. The stylized sets are every bit as chillingly effective as *The Wolf Man*'s foggy forest or *Frankenstein Meets the Wolf Man*'s windswept cemetery.

The director, sad to say, doesn't bring any of the underlying carnality which highlighted his film noir classics such as *The Killers* (1946) and *Criss Cross* (1949). Indeed, *Son of Dracula* is closer in spirit to the prim, rather genteel characters of *The Strange Affair of Uncle Harry* (1945) and *The Spiral Staircase* (1946). Though lovers, straitlaced Frank and Kay fail to generate any smoldering passion; indeed, they seem more like kissing cousins. Adding Chaney's low-libido Count Dracula into the mix makes a romantic triangle that barely simmers. Strong undercurrents of Universal's recently released *Shadow of a Doubt* (1943) abound; in fact, *Son of Dracula* may be the first of dozens of Hollywood movies to be directly influenced by the Hitchcock classic, especially in its attempt to capture the details of small-town American life and the central premise of a family playing host to a force of evil.

Son of Dracula divides itself between brightly lit daytime scenes of incredulous lawmen and no-nonsense country doctors embroiled in a headlong encounter with the supernatural, and the shadowy, twilight world of Dracula. It's in these latter episodes that Siodmak puts his Expressionist training to work. The crowning imaginative moment has Dracula's casket surfacing in a misty bog with Chaney materializing in a wisp of vapor above it, then commandeering the float-like coffin to land. It adds a momentary touch of fantasy to the film which reverts back to standard horror in the next scene as Allbritton and Chaney arrive at the doorstep of an understandably flustered justice of the peace. As the unlikely couple enter the house, a "Heaven Protests!" lightning storm breaks suddenly shatters the midnight calm.

Another fine, understated shock comes a bit later when Frank Craven, investigating Paige's story, arrives at the gloomy plantation. After Chaney ushers Craven into the master bedroom, the film cuts to a long shot of the obviously vampiric Allbritton. It's a quietly unsettling shot, her waxen makeup giving her a death-like pallor, her lips fuller and darker with her fur bed-jacket covering her throat. It's all the more effective in the way it eerily recalls the original *Dracula* in its lack of music.

Eric Taylor provides *Son of Dracula* with a gallery of offbeat, interesting characters. More of a femme fatale than a conventional horror movie heroine, the wily, cold-blooded Katherine Caldwell casually arranges for her father's death and has similarly murderous designs on her own sister in order to attain immortality. It's far and away the best female role in a Universal horror movie since the sad, sinister Countless Zaleska in *Dracula's Daughter* but Allbritton seems as ill-equipped to play a neurotic as Lon Chaney was to play a vampire. The part was a change of pace for the Universal contractee, who specialized in playing sunny, strong-willed roles in their comedies. She was the standard-issue love interest in *Who Done It?* (1942) with Abbott and Costello, a surrogate mother to a pixilated family in *San Diego I Love You* (1944), and a society girl on the make in *That Night with You* (1945). Allbritton is never less than poised and proficient

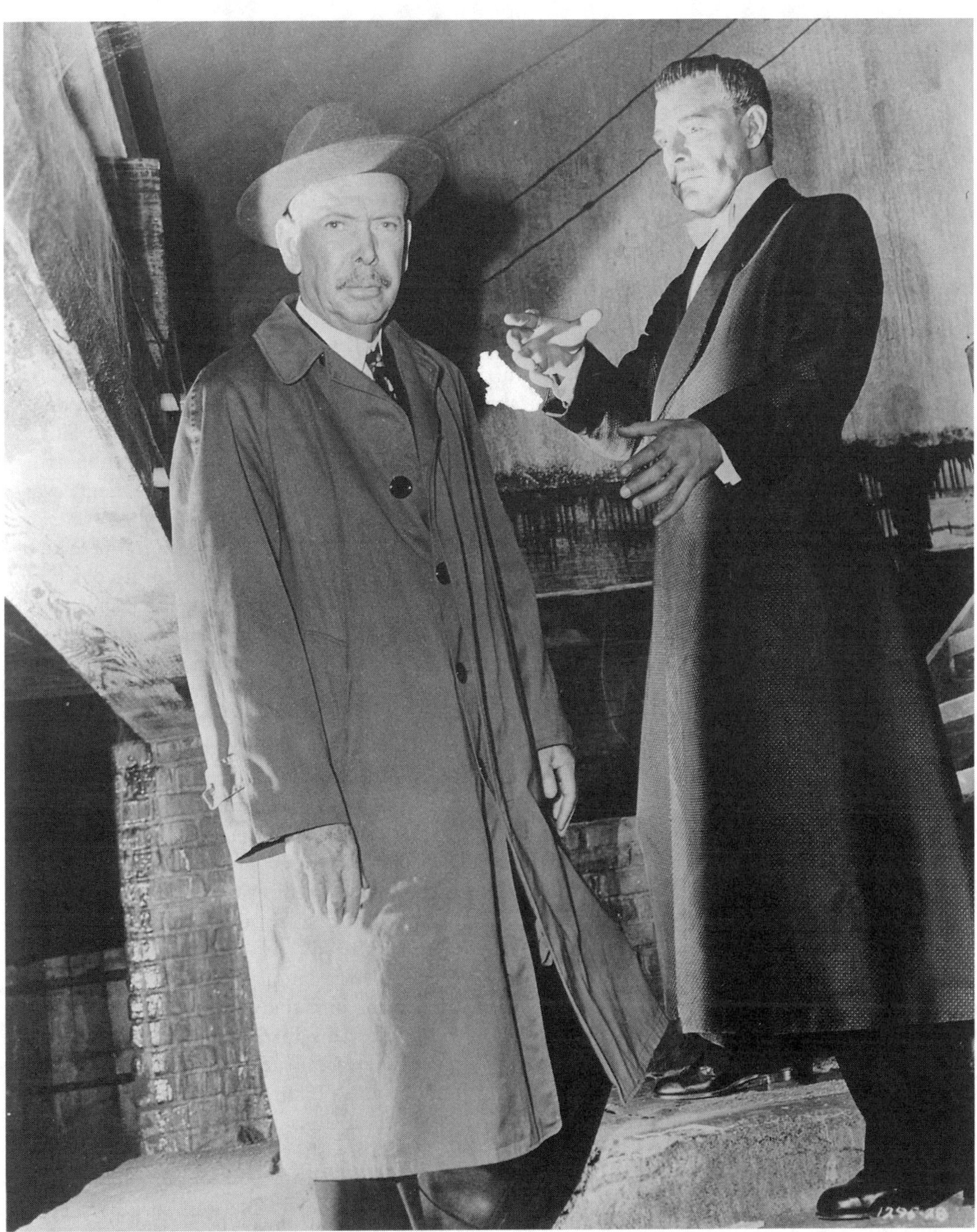

Chaney Jr. gives trespasser Frank Craven the evil eye.

but she comes across as exactly what Louise Allbritton was, a blonde in a black wig. The obviously uncomfortable actress struggles for an elusive, mysterious effect, but she summons little of the dark sensuality that the role demands.

The Frank Stanley character is also a refreshing break from the run-of-the-mill horror movie hero. Vulnerable to the punishing turns of the plot, Robert Paige comes off rather unsympathetically as a comfortably over-privileged boor but, layer by layer, he is stripped of his defenses *and* his reason and is finally left a broken man. It's a nuanced, rather courageous performance that never got its due and is easily the best in the movie.

Paige, who worked in movies in the mid-'30s under the name David Carlyle, came to Universal after a stint at Paramount. "I made four screen tests at Universal studios and was kicked out every time. I kept coming back until they couldn't stand the sight of me," he revealed in an interview. Paige became a familiar leading man in the '40s; the studio claimed *Son of Dracula* was his first dramatic role (it wasn't). When Universal decided to groom him as a musical star, teaming him with Jane Frazee, the studio called it his first major assignment. Paige's acting career sputtered out in the '50s. He was seen as a graying, heavy-set romantic lead in the senile *Abbott and Costello Go to Mars* (1953), and shortly afterward became a game show emcee and a newscaster. Years later, he insisted that he missed out on the big time because of Universal's refusal to loan him out to other studios to play what he claimed were star-making roles.

Universal coronated Lon Chaney, Jr., as the King of Horror of the '40s but he never wore his crown more uncomfortably than he did in *Son of Dracula*. While Chaney, with his lumberjack physique and Midwestern bearing, could pass himself off as the Count's country cousin, casting him as the cultured descendant of a titled Transylvanian family hardly showed the actor to his best advantage. His brawny, outdoorsy personality would serve him in well in various roles over the years but, as a creature of the night, he was hardly in the same league as Lugosi, Max Schreck or even his own father. To his credit, Chaney puts out a damned good effort though his best moments are, unsurprisingly, non-verbal, flinging Robert Paige across a room or whisking Louise Allbritton into her freshly prepared coffin. Chaney, apparently, didn't have any Method Actor predilections towards keeping in character when off-camera, even when playing a role as challenging as Count Dracula. The story goes that the prankish actor smashed a vase over the head of director Siodmak, yet it would seem that Lon had a degree of respect, and possibly affection for him. When the director had all the cast members sign his script that he was keeping as a memento, Chaney offered, "I can't wish all foreigners luck but I do you."

Frank Craven comes off best in the supporting cast. A former playwright and librettist, Craven became inextricably identified with his role as Narrator in the stage and motion picture versions of Thornton Wilder's *Our Town*. He was the sort of actor one would least expect to see in a horror movie but his homespun, plain-speaking, common sense-spouting, middle-aged American persona filled the bill perfectly as Dr. Brewster. J. Edward Bromberg's Prof. Lazlo is an apparent European refugee, but he's Van Helsing in every respect except in name, down to his white hairpiece and Edward Van Sloan's pebble eyeglasses. Evelyn Ankers' supporting performance as Allbritton's ever-patient, ever-practical sister is a nice bonus.

Son of Dracula has come in for its share of critical barbs over the years but if it's deserving of any of them it is for its sluggish pacing about mid-section as Bromberg details the fatiguingly familiar legend of Dracula to a disbelieving Craven. By Universal B-horror standards, its 78 minute running time is actually generous but, if Eric Taylor's final unabridged shooting script was shot as written, the film would probably exceed the length of the studio's deluxe horror attraction, the Claude Rains *Phantom of the Opera* or even *Son of Frankenstein*. The jail cell and jail office scenes, already overlong in the movie, consume almost 20 script pages, nearly one-fifth of the entire story. Taylor included a scene of Dracula's incarnation as a huge wolf-dog which transforms into the vampire bat that pursues Frank after his Dark Oaks confrontation. A scene that was apparently filmed has the plantation servants packin' up and runnin' scared after the death of Col. Caldwell while a vampire bat circles ominously above. The one amusing detail the uncut script offers is Count Alucard's announced reason for his visit to Dixie: Duck hunting!

The wisest cut of all!

Critics' Corner

In the shocker horror field, *Son of Dracula* is a topline entry. [It's] well made, its intelligent direction by Robert Siodmak ... one of the more substantial contributions to the chiller-diller market.... Chaney's Dracula is an outstanding job, accomplished without the gobs of makeup with which he is generally smeared. As a matter of fact, his performance takes on an almost romantic flavor.—*The Hollywood Reporter*, October 29, 1943

[O]ften as unintentionally funny as it is chilling.... [A] pretty pallid offering.—*The New York Times*, November 6, 1943, A.H. Weiler

Rating: Fair to Good. The script is neatly turned out ... and is certainly guaranteed for goose-pimples—and, we might add, laughs. The Rialto's audience yesterday took it with good-natured, audible shrieks and the usual grain of salt.—*The New York Post*, November 6, 1943, Irene Thirer

Rating: ★★ [U]nearthly hokum and spoofing.... It's entirely up to you whether you can enter into the spirit of the thing.... Or whether you're so practical as to think the whole thing is crazy and that you're just plain nuts for watching it.—*The New York Daily News*, November 6, 1943, Wanda Hale

[E]xtremely weird, fantastic, and morbid, but, because the theme has been done many times, it fails to attain the terrifying impact of the original [*Dracula*].—*Harrison's Reports*, November 13, 1943

The Mad Ghoul

Released November 12, 1943. 65 minutes. *Associate Producer:* Ben Pivar. *Executive Producer:* Joseph Gershenson. *Director:* James Hogan. *Screenplay:* Brenda Weisberg & Paul Gangelin. *Original Story:* Hans Kraly. *Photography:* Milton Krasner. *Editor:* Milton Carruth. *Art Directors:* John B. Goodman & Martin Obzina. *Assistant Director:* William Holland. *Musical Director:* Hans J. Salter. *Songs:* "All for Love," *Adapted from* "Minuet in G" by Milton Rosen, *Lyrics by* Everett Carter; "Our Love Will Live," *From the Concerto by* Tchaikovsky, *Lyrics:* Everett Carter; "I Dreamt I Dwelt in Marble Halls," *From the Operetta,* The Bohemian Girl, *Music:* M.W. Balfe. *Set Decorators:* Russell A. Gausman & Andrew J. Gilmore. *Sound Director:* Bernard B. Brown. *Technician:* Jess Moulin. *Makeup:* Jack P. Pierce. *Gowns:* Vera West.

David Bruce (*Ted Allison*), Evelyn Ankers (*Isabel Lewis*), George Zucco (*Dr. Alfred Morris*), Turhan Bey (*Eric Iverson*), Robert Armstrong (*Ken McClure*), Milburn Stone (*Police Sgt. Macklin*), Rose Hobart (*Della Elliott*), Charles McGraw (*Detective Garrity*), Andrew Tombes (*Mr. Eagan*), Addison Richards (*Gavigan*), Gus Glassmire (*Caretaker*), Gene O'Donnell (*Radio Announcer*), Isabelle La Mal (*Maid*), Lew Kelly, Bill Ruhl (*Stagehands*), Hans Herbert (*Attendant*), Bess Flowers, Cyril Ring (*Audience Members*), Lillian Cornell (*Vocalist for Evelyn Ankers*), Mike Lally (*Reporter*).

What am I? Alive or dead? Man or beast?
What have you done to me?
—*David Bruce in* The Mad Ghoul

Like Lionel Atwill, George Zucco approached most of his horror movie roles with his tongue planted firmly in his cheek. To this cultured stage actor, breathing life into such poorly written parts as the delusional scientist in PRC's *The Mad Monster* (1942) and the white witch doctor in Monogram's *Voodoo Man* (1944) must have been the height of indignity. *The Mad Ghoul* provided Zucco with yet *another* mad scientist role, but this time the stock character was conceived with more sensitivity and shading than usual. Zucco himself must have felt that the part was worthwhile as he performs it with atypical restraint and perception.

The Mad Ghoul is that rarity, a successful Universal horror film that didn't spawn a series. Designed to support *Son of Dracula* on an all-horror double bill, *The Mad Ghoul* deserves more credit than it is usually given. It's a slick, competently done B with a new twist on the old body-snatching theme: Instead of stealing the whole corpse, this fiend is only interested in the deceased's heart.

His career as a purveyor of shock fests on the rise, Ben Pivar put *The Mystery of the Mad Ghoul* on the drawing board in February 1943. Brenda Weisberg and Paul Gangelin contributed a reasonably intelligent script based on a story by Hans Kraly (the recipient of the 1928/29 Academy Award for Best Screenplay for *The Patriot*; Kraly was also nominated for the 1937 Deanna Durbin musical comedy *One Hundred Men and a Girl*).

Studio contract player David Bruce suddenly found himself cast as a walking corpse, a far cry from the bland second lead parts that dominated his career. Born Marden Andrew McBroom in Kankakee, Illinois, on January 6, c. 1914, Bruce was discovered by a talent scout while attending Northwestern University. The budding young actor was groomed for stardom at Warner Bros. in the late '30s–early '40s, and got minor roles in such prestige productions as *A Dispatch from Reuters* (1940), *The Sea Hawk* (1940), and *The Sea Wolf* (1941), as well as the comedy-thrillers *The Smiling Ghost* (1941) and *The Body Disappears* (1941). Leaving Warners, Bruce landed a small part in Republic's World War II combat drama *Flying Tigers* (1942) with John Wayne; soon after, he signed a three-year contract with Universal. When America entered the war, Bruce joined the Navy Air Service School at St. Mary's. The Air Service understandably discharged him when he showed a tendency to lose consciousness during pull-outs!

Assigned to direct the new chiller was James Hogan, who had joined the studio in April after a seven-year stint at Paramount. Around the time he made *The Mad Ghoul,* Hogan directed the compelling drama *The Strange Death of Adolf Hitler* (1943), then completed the script for the Maria Montez–Jon Hall adventure *Gypsy Wildcat* (1944); poor health forced him to withdraw as director of the latter. The 52-year-old filmmaker died of a heart attack on November 4, 1943, just one week before *The Mad Ghoul* went into national release.

After years of research, Dr. Alfred Morris (George Zucco) has recreated an insidious poison gas which the ancient Mayans used in their religious rites. The gas has a diabolical power, causing a "state of death in life." Exposed to the odorless vapors, a sacrificial victim would slip into a living dead state. Morris came to the conclusion that the Mayan ritual of removing the hearts from living men was performed not to appease their gods as was commonly believed, but to restore life to the gassed victims. His goal is to discover a method of reversing the action of the gas.

Other than to satisfy his scientific curiosity, one is hard-pressed to come up with a good reason why the doc would devote his time and energy to such a purposeless pursuit. Considering the time period in which *The Mad Ghoul* was made, it's surprising (and even refreshing) that the writers didn't think to utilize this novel gimmick as a potent new super-weapon against the Axis powers (much as Zucco had devised in the aforementioned *The Mad Monster*, i.e., turning combat soldiers into wolf men with the aid of his secret formula).

Morris enlists the aid of promising medical student Ted Allison (David Bruce). Using a combination of crystals and ancient herbs, Morris gasses a monkey, then revives the dead animal successfully with a shot of heart fluid taken from another simian.

That evening, Ted and his fiancée, Isabel Lewis (Evelyn Ankers), drop in on Dr. Morris for a nightcap. Isabel, a concert singer, is about to embark on a multiple city tour yet seems uncharacteristically disturbed. Morris guesses the problem immediately: "You're no longer in love with Ted." For some reason known only to him, the aging intellectual comes to the baseless conclusion that the attractive young woman has fallen in love with *him.* "It's only natural that you should turn to an older man," Morris coos solicitously. "Someone who knows the book of life, and can teach you to read it." In the context of what we know about their relationship thus far, this assumption on his part is quite preposterous. Isabel is understandably oblivious to the doctor's attentions, mistaking the moves he puts on her for fatherly concern.

Ted is easy prey for the death trap that Morris sets for him. Falling under the influence of the vapor, the young surgeon becomes an emaciated automaton. Jack Pierce didn't have much to go on when he was ordered to create David Bruce's gruesome makeup: "All they told me was that they wanted Bruce to look like a reasonably fresh cadaver," Pierce said in an interview. "'How fresh?' They said a couple or three weeks buried. This was not much to go on but I did my best. They seemed satisfied."

The makeup procedure was based on Pierce's brilliant guise for Karloff's Imhotep. In his first scenes as the Ghoul, the actor appears pale, wizened and fish-eyed. But as the movie proceeds and the degenerative effect of the gas reaches an advanced stage, his features become parchment-like, resembling a corpse in an accelerated state of decomposition.

Bruce described his ordeal in Pierce's makeup chair in an interview that he granted *Famous Monsters* magazine shortly before his death:

> My makeup was green and it made my hair look red for some reason — bright red. They tinted me green and combed my hair over my eyes and for the later thing they put the false skin on, which was absolute murder. I wore it for three days and the third time I took it off my skin was bleeding because you had to peel the makeup off. They put on spirit gum and then a layer of cotton and then another layer of gum so this created an entirely false face on top of mine. Then they'd wrinkle it up and the wrinkles would stay in....

With Ted entirely in his control, Morris plants in the young man's subconscious mind the notion that Isabel no longer wants him. Handing Ted a scalpel, Morris escorts him to the town cemetery, orders him to despoil the

"First Eric ... then myself!": Walking corpse David Bruce is sent on a mission of murder by mad scientist George Zucco in *The Mad Ghoul.*

grave of a recently interred businessman, and then perform a cardiectomy on the corpse. The heart substance is used by Morris to bring Ted out of his terminal state; the student is entirely oblivious to the ordeal he has gone through.

When the doctor's "miracle monkey" has a sudden relapse, Morris realizes the fatal consequences of his act. An emotional confrontation with Isabel during one of her concert tour stops takes its toll on Ted's fragile condition. Once again, he reverts back into a zombified state without the benefit of exposure to the gas. This time, the pair's visit to the local cemetery has tragic results. Morris is forced to kill a caretaker (Gus Glassmire) who catches them unearthing a grave. The man's heart is used to restore Ted to temporary normalcy.

Unable to conceal her secret any longer, Isabel unburdens herself to an understandably mortified Dr. Morris. It seems that another man is occupying his corner of the triangle — Isabel's handsome accompanist, Eric Iverson (Turhan Bey). Now saddled with two rivals, the desperate doctor drives Ted into having another seizure, then orders him to make arrangements to meet Eric later that night after the concert.

At the stroke of midnight, Ted, loaded pistol in hand, silently approaches Iverson as he paces the deserted alley behind the concert hall. Hans J. Salter's pounding score builds to a dramatic crescendo as Ted's menacing shadow closes in on his best friend. But before the Ghoul can pull the trigger, Isabel arrives on the scene and upsets his preprogrammed command with a piercing scream. Unseen by the couple, Ted escapes to Morris' waiting car.

Acting on a hot tip provided by a colleague, ace reporter Ken McClure (Robert Armstrong) has a hunch that there's a connection between the graveyard atrocities and Isabel's concert appearances. Planting a phony obit in the local paper of the town in which the singer is next scheduled to appear, McClure sets a trap for the killer: He stations himself inside a coffin in a funeral parlor and waits patiently for the murderer's arrival. But McClure makes a fatal blunder. Covering Morris with his gun, the reporter fails to notice Ted creeping up behind him. The pair easily overcome McClure and use his heart for the life-saving procedure.

Convinced that McClure's hunch was on-target, Police Sgt. Macklin (Milburn Stone) and his partner Garrity (Charles McGraw) pay Isabel a visit on the eve of her last concert appearance. They suspect Eric might be their man. Aghast at their accusations, Isabel confides in Ted. Her tearful admission of love for Eric and full disclosure of the evidence presented to her against Eric puts everything in perspective for Ted. "What am I? Alive or dead? Man or beast? What have you done to me?" he beseeches his mentor.

Getting hold of himself, Ted plans a devilish revenge. He writes a suicide note, prepares a mixture of the deadly gas, and lures Morris into the lab. Suddenly seized by the effects of the gas, Ted becomes Morris' blindly obedient slave once more. Morris hands him the revolver and orders him to kill Eric and then himself.

To his horror, Morris realizes that he, too, has been exposed to the gas. Seizing the surgeon's scalpel, he implores Ted to help him, but it is too late. His initial command has already been programmed into the zombie's mind. Ted blunders onto the stage as Isabel is in mid-performance and aims the gun at Eric. But before he can fire, the Ghoul is cut down by Macklin's bullets.

In a grimly ironic postscript, Morris, his features distorted, attempts to dig up a grave to obtain heart substance for himself, but collapses and dies, scalpel in hand.

There's no shortage of carnage, either visualized or implied, in *The Mad Ghoul*, yet the film manages to stay within the guidelines of accepted standards for the period it was made. Considering its morbid preoccupation with death (cemeteries, funeral parlors, blood sacrifices, desecration of the dead and murder), co-writers Weisberg and Gangelin have done a commendable job in appeasing those watchdogs of the Production Code, the Breen Office. They've somehow managed to soft-pedal yet not render sterile the story's abundant indelicacies. Director Hogan is simpatico with their efforts: During the potentially graphic murder and mutilation scenes, the director focuses on Bruce's deadpan face, discreetly cutting away from the bloodbath.

The stifling restrictions of the Breen Office no doubt influenced the writers to tone down the love interest element as well. Isabel spends almost the entire picture in a guilt-ridden pout over her betrayal of Ted. Eric's attitude is more moderate and realistic. Although he is not proud that he has "stolen" his best friend's

As the Ghoul, Bruce made for a sympathetic victim in this well-crafted B thriller.

girl, the suave accompanist isn't about to let this impede romance. By the time the last reel unwinds, Isabel has suffered enough and deserves vindication, while Eric comes away from the tragedy smelling like a rose. None but the most conservative of viewers is bound to hold the couple in contempt, even as they stand over Ted's bullet-riddled body.

Saddled with a title that must have kept sophisticated moviegoers away in droves, and promoted by Universal with all of the usual shock-it-to-'em campaign gimmicks, *The Mad Ghoul* nonetheless ranks as one of Universal's more mature thrillers. As often happens in horror films, an innocent person's life is destroyed by the far-flung ambitions of a renegade scientist. Along with a desire to vindicate himself to a doubting world, the scientist often has an ulterior motive: More often than not, to avenge himself on his oppressors, but occasionally to reap financial reward or to gain the love of a woman. Universal had exploited this formula in *Captive Wild Woman*, and before that in *Black Friday* and *Man Made Monster*. Fifties exploitation producer Herman Cohen had the formula down to a science in such classic drive-in shockers as *I Was a Teenage Werewolf* (1957), *Blood of Dracula* (1957), *How to Make a Monster* (1958) and *Horrors of the Black Museum* (1959).

The first two reels of *The Mad Ghoul* are of necessity slow and talky. The storyline regarding Zucco's experiments is established, as is the multi-sided romantic dilemma. Once these plot elements are revealed, the picture travels a steady course, handling its shock sequences with enthusiasm. The inclusion of Robert Armstrong's comic reporter-*cum*-investigator is a jarring note, but it isn't long before even he becomes grist for the gore mill. Armstrong's unbridled enthusiasm and show-bizzy tactics bring back warm memories of Kong-stalking Carl Denham. It comes as something of a shock — and a suspense highlight — to first-time viewers that the comic relief character is so gruesomely killed off.

James Hogan does a competent, craftsmanlike job of directing and elicits very good performances from the sturdy cast. The director draws a maximum amount of suspense out of the major shock sequences and pulls off a couple of particularly arresting bits (i.e., Bruce as the Ghoul walking directly into the camera, blocking out the lens; Bruce, standing behind Armstrong, holding the scalpel inches away from his neck, as the movie lights cast an effectively menacing gleam on its smooth surface). Only at the film's climax does Hogan fail to generate the prerequisite suspense when Bruce staggers across the old *Phantom of the Opera* Stage and points the pistol at Bey in front of the panic-stricken audience.

George Zucco and Bruce take top honors in the acting department. Zucco tempers his stock villain mad scientist with an affecting vulnerability. Discovering the antidote is effective only temporarily, he earnestly warns Bruce of this dire situation without revealing to his victim what he has done to him. ("Ted, we've got to find a permanent cure!") Later, learning that the "other man" in Ankers' life isn't he but Turhan Bey, Zucco says with touching remorse, "We see what we want to see most of the time, Isabel. Even I, a scientist, have such moments of weakness."

Bruce is the ideal victim, a naive child-man who is blissfully unaware of the deceptions in operation around him. He is appropriately devoid of emotion as the Ghoul, and seems to operate on automatic pilot while under Zucco's influence. His state of mental oblivion is especially chilling while he is committing his heinous deeds.

Bruce's acting assignments at Universal were a mixed bag of lightweight musical comedies (*Allergic to Love* [1944], *Can't Help Singing* [1944]), wartime propaganda pictures (*Gung Ho!* [1943]) and thrillers (*Calling Dr. Death*, *Christmas Holiday* [1944], *Lady on a Train* [1945]). After the war, Bruce found himself seeking movie parts in such cheapjack productions as *Young Daniel Boone* (1950), *Cannibal Attack* (1954) and *Jungle Hell* (1956). Following a stint playing the head of the house in TV's *Beulah* opposite Louise Beavers, the actor, disillusioned with Hollywood, changed careers and entered the advertising field. He resumed acting in the '70s and was on the verge of making a comeback in feature films when he dropped dead on the set of *Moving Violation* on May 3, 1976. The cause: His heart!

Gregory Mank sat down with Bruce's daughter, Amanda McBroom, in June 1995 to reminisce about her late father's life and career. McBroom, a successful stage, film and TV actress as well as a popular concert singer, recalled her Dad's experience making *The Mad Ghoul*:

> He had so much fun on that film. I remember him telling me about coming home from the studio — we lived on the poor end of Toluca Lake, where the ducks were, as opposed to the rich end of the lake, where Bob Hope and the swans were — and one time he came home for lunch in full Mad Ghoul makeup. Well, he walked behind my mother, she saw his face in the mirror — and he scared her so terribly that she passed out in the bathroom! That was a very serious makeup. And that was back in the days before they knew how to protect somebody's face. Your face was bare, and they just did what they did to it. He had a lot of fun with it. He really liked George Zucco a lot — they became quite good friends. And he loved Evelyn Ankers; they were great pals. He called her "Moo"— don't ask why! *The Mad Ghoul* was evidently a very pleasant experience for him; he really enjoyed it.

Evelyn Ankers lends beauty, grace and intelligence to the role of the emotionally torn Isabel. At first, Universal planned to have the actress record the classic pieces in her own voice, but the idea was scrapped at the last moment. Library recordings of Lillian Cornell were ineffectively substituted. The supporting cast is peopled by such old reliables as Robert Armstrong, Rose Hobart, Addison Richards and a wryly amusing Andrew Tombes as an overzealous funeral parlor director.

There was little Turhan Bey could do with the colorless role of Eric, Ankers' lover, but to act suave and Continental, yet remain sympathetic. In retrospect, Eric Iverson was a dry run for Bey's more prominent role of Franz (the romantic support of yet another beautiful singer, Susanna Foster) in 1944's *The Climax*. Yet, the actor spoke well of his experience making *The Mad Ghoul* and had high regard for his costars. He told the authors:

> [George] Zucco was one of the finest gentlemen I have ever worked with, and the last person in the world I would suspect to play horror parts. Except for his fantastic, menacing eyes and his voice, which he could manage so well, there was nothing horrible about him at all.

His memories of Evelyn Ankers were also warm:

> [She was] a very pleasant, wonderful girl with whom I had lunch once. We were talking about romance and things like that, and she said to me, "Turhan, you're the kind of a man I'd like to have an affair with, but I'd hate to be married to." [*Laughs*] That was her definition of Turhan Bey!
>
> [David Bruce was] the sort of pleasant young man that was under contract to Universal at the time, a fellow who tried to make life as agreeable as possible for everybody. I think that at Universal, that was the tendency. We all got along fine and I don't remember ever having a serious clash with anybody.... [James] Hogan was very matter-of-fact, but an excellent craftsman. And a craftsman was what you had to be when you directed B pictures. You could be an artist at the same time, but mainly you had to be a craftsman, because you had X number of scenes to shoot every day and you had to keep on schedule. And Ben Pivar was a wonderful man.

An offbeat, macabre tale generously plied with morbid effects, unusually good performances and adept writing and direction, *The Mad Ghoul* is a cut or two above the average chiller released by Universal during this period of gradual decline.

Critics' Corner

Rating: ★★½ If you're willing to enter into the spirit of the horror in this Rialto Theatre offering, you'll get your creeps and chills in abundance at what George Zucco, making with his evil eyes, does to corpses and a human being.... Enough occurs to prevent the chills from leaving you until it's over.—*The New York Daily News*, December 11, 1943, Wanda Hale

This ghoul, handicapped by a severe case of schizophrenia and at the same time carrying mental burdens of sex and science, proves a dangerous fellow. Note the old adage: mad ghouls are bad ghouls.—*The New York Post*, December 11, 1943, Archer Winsten

James Hogan directs the yarn in a straightforward manner which reflects his knowledge that the tale is spine-chilling enough without dwelling on the most horrible details.... David Bruce plays the medical student for a sizeable personal hit.—*The Hollywood Reporter*, October 29, 1943

It's remarkable how Hollywood can limit itself to a scant half-dozen basic plots, yet come up with variations and combinations thereof for original screenplays. Current chiller is a rehash of Frankenstein and the romance triangle formulas. Incredible, impossible, but interesting enough to whet the appetite.—*The New York Daily Mirror*, December 11, 1943, Frank Quinn

The crystal[s] from which [Zucco's gas] is produced are supposedly all destroyed in the last reel ... but obviously not soon enough. It is my personal conviction that this gas has been floating around Universal Pictures for some time, inducing such ghastly affairs as *Captive Wild Woman*, *Son of Dracula*, [the remake of] *Phantom of the Opera* and other hitherto unaccountable cinemisdeeds.—*PM New York*, 1943, John T. McManus

[W]e would call him a definitely second-rate ghoul. And if anyone is privileged to be crazy, it's us poor folks who have to look at such things.—*The New York Times*, December 11, 1943, Bosley Crowther

A routine program horror melodrama.... The theme has been done many times, and this version offers little in the way of originality. It should, nevertheless, satisfy horror picture fans.... Discriminating audiences will probably find it tiresome.—*Harrison's Reports*, December 5, 1943

It is another Universal "horror" thriller, well done, but just that. Zucco's performance is the only one which will command audience attention.—*The Motion Picture Herald*, October 23, 1943, Floyd Stone

Calling Dr. Death

Released December 17, 1943. 63 minutes. An Inner Sanctum Mystery, produced by arrangement with Simon and Schuster, Inc., Publishers. *Associate Producer:* Ben Pivar. *Director:* Reginald LeBorg. *Original Screenplay:* Edward Dein. *Photography:* Virgil Miller. *Special Photography:* John P. Fulton. *Editor:* Norman A. Cerf. *Art Directors:* John B. Goodman & Ralph M. DeLacy. *Set Decorators:* Russell A. Gausman & Andrew J. Gilmore. *Assistant Director:* Charles S. Gould. *Musical Director:* Paul Sawtell. *Sound Director:* Bernard B. Brown. *Technician:* William Hedgcock. *Gowns:* Vera West.

Lon Chaney, Jr. (*Dr. Mark Steele*), Patricia Morison (*Stella Madden*), J. Carrol Naish (*Insp. Gregg*), Ramsay Ames (*Maria Steele*), David Bruce (*Robert Duval*), Fay Helm (*Mrs. Duval*), Holmes Herbert (*Bryant*), Alec Craig (*Bill*), Mary Hale (*Marion*), Fred Gierman (*Father*), Lisa Golm (*Mother*), George Eldredge (*District Attorney*), Charles Wagenheim (*Coroner*), John Elliott (*Priest*), David Hoffman (*Inner Sanctum*), Frank Marlowe (*Newspaper Reporter*), Keith Ferguson (*Telephone Operator*), Rex Lease, Paul Phillips, Perc Launders, Jack Rockwell (*Detectives*), Robert Hill (*Judge*), Jack C. Smith, Al Ferguson (*Death House Guards*), Kernan Cripps (*Officer*). *Deleted from final print:* Isabel Jewell (*Peggy Morton, Night Club Singer*).

This is the Inner Sanctum.... A strange, fantastic world, controlled by a mass of living, pulsating flesh ... *the mind!* It destroys ...distorts ... creates monsters ... commits *murder*! Yes, even you, without knowing, can commit murder!

—*David Hoffman, the Master of the Inner Sanctum*

Reaping the financial rewards of Hollywood's second great horror cycle, Universal turned to popular literature for a fresh source of filmable material. In June 1943, the studio struck a deal with Simon and Schuster, publishers of the popular Inner Sanctum mysteries, obtaining the screen rights to the Inner Sanctum name (though, curiously, not the pulps nor the Inner Sanctum radio plays themselves) for a brand new series of murder mysteries starring their hottest horror property, Lon Chaney, Jr.

By installing Ben Pivar as the guiding mentor, Universal inadvertently revealed their modest ambitions towards the project immediately. Instead of pulling the financial stops and producing a slate of classy little B's (or minor A's) with first-rate talent, the cost-conscious studio heads decided (once again) to take the safe route. The result: A half-dozen feeble melodramas with little to recommend them beyond their camp qualities and the morose spectacle of seeing the badly miscast Chaney struggle his way through acting assignments that were painfully beyond his depth.

Having grown disenchanted with the way Universal was shuffling him from one uncomfortable monster disguise to another, Chaney hoped that the Inner Sanctum films would provide the diversity he craved. Evidently, Universal still hadn't grasped the fact that this was an actor of limited talent and appeal, who simply did not fit the mode of the archetypical Inner Sanctum hero: The suave mustachioed professional man who is all the rage with the ladies.

Searching for a suitable property as the series' kickoff entry, Pivar purchased an original screenplay penned by freelancer Edward Dein entitled *Calling Dr. Death*. A former bit player who turned to writing and later to directing, Dein was proficient at writing whodunits; at various times, he wrote for RKO's Falcon series and worked on Columbia's Lone Wolf and Boston Blackie pictures. More importantly, Dein was a part-time member of Val Lewton's RKO production unit, contributing to the screenplay of one of 1942's most acclaimed sleepers, *Cat People*, and (according to Dein) writing the script for *The Leopard Man* (1943), although sole screen credit was given to novice Ardel Wray. (Dein's other genre credits include the Faustian 1944 Columbia shocker *The Soul of a Monster*; Universal-International's preposterous 1959 vampire Western *Curse of the Undead*; and their 1960 release *The Leech Woman*.) As these latter credits indicate, Dein never lived up to the promise shown by his early work in the genre.

In a 1984 interview, the late writer-director recalled for the authors the start of his brief career at Universal, where he also wrote the screenplays for *Jungle Woman* and the 1946 *The Cat Creeps*:

> I recall having a job at Universal as a reader for a few weeks, which was another horror story. We called this the Snake Pit. In those days, we were not considered to be prolific writers; we were hacks.

At the outset of the series, Ben Pivar planned to produce two Inner Sanctum mysteries a year, each featuring Chaney and Gale Sondergaard in starring roles. Reginald LeBorg, who had done an admirable job directing *The Mummy's Ghost,* was selected by Pivar to direct *Calling Dr. Death*. LeBorg told us:

> Pivar had confidence in me because I was a fighter who tried to get better and better material. Pivar was sometimes afraid that I would go over budget, but whenever he saw that I was on budget, he didn't worry any more—he stayed in his office and played gin rummy.

Calling Dr. Death went into production on October 25, 1943, and was completed within 20 days. Just a few days prior to the start of filming, Sondergaard was dropped from the cast. Her role was substantially rewritten and given to Patricia Morison. Despite the studio's original intent, Sondergaard would never appear in an Inner Sanctum mystery.

LeBorg had his own theory as to why the controversial actress got the boot. He told the authors:

> I don't know whether this was the real cause of it or not, but she was a leftist and she and her husband [filmmaker Herbert J. Biberman] were shooting their mouths off quite often. The war was still going on, of course. Executives there at Universal may have decided to recast it—but I can't be sure. I was not in on any such conference. I just heard one day that she was out, and that they were going to cast somebody else—that's all. They didn't say why, you could only speculate. It happened later on that she *did* find it difficult to get work, and then it *was* due to that situation.

In *Calling Dr. Death,* Chaney portrays neurologist Mark Steele, whose professional success is eclipsed by a miserable home life: Steele's beautiful but unfaithful wife Maria (Ramsay Ames) refuses to grant him a divorce. He confides his problems to his adoring nurse, Stella (Patricia Morison); although they're evidently attracted to one another, Steele's marital status dictates that they keep their desires in check.

Distraught over Maria's philandering, Steele suffers a mental blackout. When he awakens, it's Monday morning. The doctor finds himself seated behind his office desk unshaven and his clothing disheveled. Two police detectives of the *Dragnet* school of criminal interrogation, tell the understandably baffled neurologist that his wife has been brutally murdered at some point during his "lost weekend."

Dr. Steele's nagging suspicions concerning his culpability are fueled by the suspicious Insp. Gregg (J. Carrol Naish) of the Homicide Department. "You're big game, doctor," Gregg taunts Steele. "Makes the chase interesting." Momentarily relieved when the police put the cuffs on Maria's last paramour, businessman Robert Duval (David Bruce), Steele's devilish doubts return to plague him after he speaks with Duval's paralyzed wife (Fay Helm). Stella's futile attempts to prove Steele's innocence only muddy the waters further.

On the eve of Duval's execution, the desperate doctor places Stella in a deep hypnotic trance. In a surrealistic flashback, Stella's "subconscious voice" betrays her: She confesses to having murdered Maria and implicated Duval in the crime. The inspector arrives at Steele's office in time to hear her unintended confession and places the hysterical murderess under arrest.

Calling Dr. Death set the standard for the other melodramas in the Inner Sanctum series by introducing several intriguing devices and recurring plot motifs. With the exception of *Pillow of Death* (the final installment), each picture is prefaced by a brief sequence in which the bobbing head of a wizened seer (David Hoffman), staring out of a crystal ball, forewarns the audience (*à la The Twilight Zone*) that we are about to enter a realm where even the most innocent

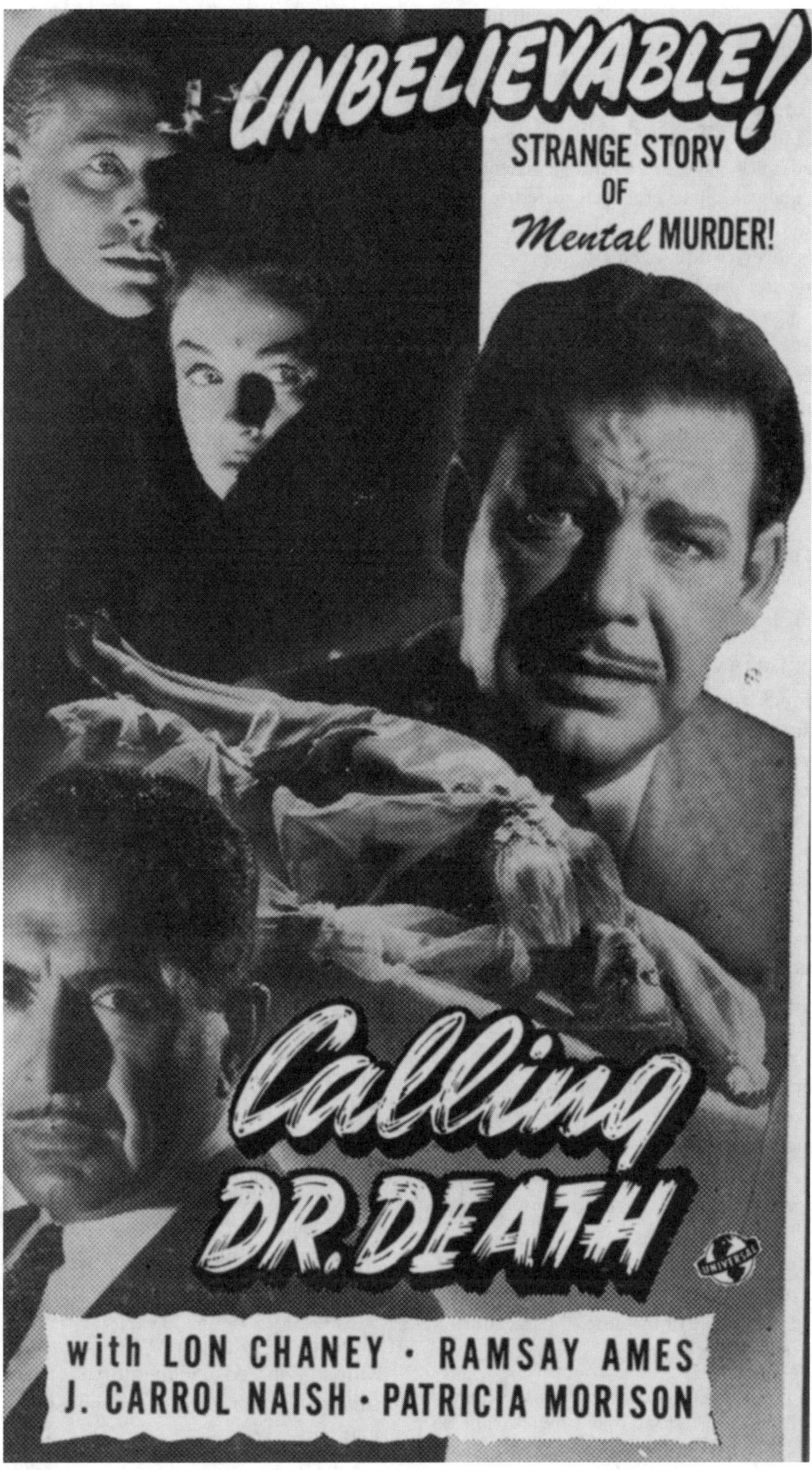

Pressbook ad for the first of Universal's Inner Sanctum mysteries.

among us is capable of murder. In all but two entries (*Strange Confession* and *Pillow of Death*), an innocent man (Chaney) is accused of committing or instigating one or more murders. He may find at himself at odds with the evidence presented, and may even doubt his own innocence. Finally, after several reels of tedious self-flagellation, our hero learns he has been duped by a jealous lover, a dear friend or a greedy business associate.

Another recurrent device peculiar to the Inner Sanctum mysteries is the "stream of consciousness" voiceover. Effective at times, laughably intrusive at others, this gimmick might have been better received had it been used more judiciously. Edward Dein maintained that he incorporated these monologues into his script for *Calling Dr. Death* at Chaney's behest: "Lon Chaney, Jr., begged me to put the dialogue on the soundtrack because it was too technical, and although he played a doctor in it, he just couldn't say the words."

Reginald LeBorg insisted that Ben Pivar was as much the reason for Dein's use of this gimmick as Chaney, and for not very complimentary reasons: "We had to do a little bit of simplification, that's true, but I think it was not only Chaney but also Pivar. Pivar was very, very crude, not very intelligent, and he couldn't read very well."

Calling Dr. Death's unevenly paced story is somewhat enlivened by LeBorg's impressive stylistic touches. In one scene, Chaney, looking like he's got murder on his mind, quietly creeps up to a sleeping Ramsay Ames, but is stopped in his tracks by the sudden screech of a pet cockatoo. Emphasizing Ames' devious nature, Virgil Miller's camera zooms into a tight close-up of the woman's cruel eyes in an oil portrait. Patricia Morison's climactic, hypnosis-induced "confession" is highlighted by tilted camera angles and eerie sound effects.

One of the film's most memorable sequences has the camera standing in for Chaney as he visits the scene of his wife's brutal murder. As LeBorg explained it to the authors:

> I put a few different visual effects in there which were absolutely fresh at that time. In one sequence, I had the camera *become* Lon Chaney, with everybody else looking *into* the camera. That's the sequence where Chaney is brought to the house where his wife was murdered — the reporters look into the camera as it moves forward into the house; then J. Carrol Naish, playing the detective, also addresses the camera. Then, the camera pans down to the floor where the coroner is examining the body. The whole sequence was shot this way until Lon Chaney is accused, and *then* you see his face. That was one sequence in the whole film which I thought was a novelty at that time. It was so fresh and new that when Robert Montgomery, who was also directing at that time, saw *Calling Dr. Death*, he made a whole picture this way —*Lady in the Lake* [1946] — and that was a *flop!* For one sequence that was all right, but it couldn't sustain an entire film. One critic wrote about *Lady in the Lake* that it was a copy of *Calling Dr. Death* but Montgomery made the mistake of doing the whole picture that way.

Nearly all the characters Chaney portrays in the Inner Sanctum mysteries are undeserving of our sympathies because they are so weak and naive. In *Calling Dr. Death*, Dr. Steele and his nurse are attracted to one another, yet neither is capable of expressing any gesture more passionate than an innocent peck or a reassuring pat. This reticence (obviously encouraged by the Breen bluenoses) is all the more absurd in light of the fact that Stella committed coldblooded murder in an effort to win the doctor for herself.

Patricia Morison and J. Carrol Naish head a particularly strong supporting cast. Morison, a one-time contender for Paramount stardom, was often cast as a lethal lady or "other woman" in '40s B's. Her cool, deliberate emoting in *Calling Dr. Death* gives every indication she isn't as innocent as she pretends to be. Morison's unsettlingly detached demeanor is especially revealing in the flashback scene in which she beats Ramsay Ames to death with a fire poker, then, in a surprising touch of gratuitous gore, disfigures the corpse's face with acid. Though shown only in shadows (a favorite LeBorg device), the sequence's horrific impact comes across undiminished.

Interviewed by Gregory Mank in the December 2004 edition of *Classic Images*, Patricia Morison shared her memories of working on *Calling Dr. Death* and with Lon Chaney, in particular:

> I didn't get to know him terribly well — he was a rather shy man, but I enjoyed working with him

Lon Chaney, Jr., uses hypnotism to crack a murder case in *Calling Dr. Death.* Patricia Morison is his unwilling subject.

> very much. He was very nice to me. He was always nice, always helpful, and a very warm man.

Regarding the actor's oft-reported problems with alcohol, Morison pooh-poohed, "No. You never saw it in his performance. No, Lon Chaney was a very gentle man...." Her memories of Reginald LeBorg? "Well, he was a lovely man to work for. I know he wanted to keep going late in his life. He was a creative man—your body might fade, but your creativity shouldn't."

J. Carrol Naish's persistent policeman, given to turning up at the oddest moments, stalks Chaney with the zeal of a predatory cat. (Naish has a similar role in William Castle's 1944 Columbia thriller *The Whistler*, playing a hit man "shadowing" Richard Dix, plotting to scare him to death simply by staying on his heels.) His subtle underplaying and confidence contrasts with Chaney's instability. Only in the film's final moments does the detective reveal that he never suspected the neurologist of murder in the first place, but was using him as bait in order to flush out the real killer. In a 1944 interview, Naish established what was to eventually become a trend among horror stars by denying that *Calling Dr. Death* was a "horror" picture: "That's what a lot of people call it, though ... it's strictly a psychological study in crime."

Edward Dein proudly recalled a compliment paid to him by the excellent character player:

> J. Carrol Naish read the script and thought it was one of the best examples of screenplay writing he had ever read, which was a great compliment coming from this wonderful actor. He wanted me to direct it, but Universal preferred Reggie LeBorg.

Fresh from his memorable performance in *The Mad Ghoul*, David Bruce arouses compassion as the wrongly accused Duval. Bruce replaced George Dolenz in the role after shooting began; Dolenz was forced to forfeit the part on account of a studio cross-scheduling error. Fay Helm once again demonstrates her talents at playing distraught victims, and invests her brief part with sensitivity and dignity. Ramsay Ames, on the other hand, is pathetically amateurish as Chaney's fulsome mate. (Ames was proof that all the looks in the world couldn't *really* compensate for a woeful lack of talent.) Her battle royale with husband Chaney is so badly acted and staged, it seldom fails to elicit giggles. Although Isabel Jewell (one of our favorite character actresses) is given official billing, her performance as a night club singer didn't make it into the final cut. Many published *Calling Dr. Death* castlists credit Norman Rainey with the role of "Governor," but the movie features no such character, and Patricia Morison told the authors that she has no memory of her father Rainey, a Pasadena Playhouse stage and occasional movie actor, being in the film.

New York stage actor David Hoffman had the honor of introducing this and other Inner Sanctum mysteries in the series' eerie preface. (A close examination reveals that the actor doesn't blink once during the entire 23 second sequence.) The diminutive thespian fulfilled a similar function in *Flesh and Fantasy* and, three years later, played the part of the shifty attorney who is throttled by *The Beast with Five Fingers* (1946). Hoffman's brother was Al Hoffman, a songwriter of some renown. He was Oscar-nominated for the Walt Disney 1950 *Cinderella*'s "Bibbidy-Bobbidi-Boo," and contributed musical numbers to such films as *She Shall Have Music* (1935), *Listen, Darling* (1938), *Stage Door Canteen* (1943), *Alice in Wonderland* (1951), *Singin' in the Rain* (1952), Disney's 1954 classic *20000 Leagues Under the Sea* ("A Whale of a Tale," sung by Kirk Douglas), and the 1961 Elvis Presley hit, *Blue Hawaii* ("Hawaiian Wedding Song").

Universal's Inner Sanctum mysteries are generally regarded by buffs and film historians as a missed cinematic opportunity. Had the studio lavished more time and expense on these productions in terms of sharper writing, directing and performing, the series might have attained the quality standards set by a similar series of B mystery thrillers produced around the same time, the Columbia Whistler films. (Television had its own series of *Inner Sanctum* mysteries in 1952, narrated by Paul McGrath.)

Critics' Corner

This item ... is mildly interesting but not thrilling. [I]t has a dreary habit of talking itself out of promising situations. What suspense is attained occasionally is dissipated by Mr. Chaney's sepulchral "voice" breaking in on the murder investigation.... The intrigue in *Calling Dr. Death* ends with its title.—*The New York Times*, February 12, 1944, A.H. Weiler

Accustomed to arising early and having nothing to do in the morning, none of the soldiers or children at the opening of *Calling Dr. Death* at the Rialto yesterday walked out on the show, but their audible comments were quite expressive of their attitude, which was one of utter boredom and occasional irritation.—*The New York Herald-Tribune*, February 12, 1944, Bert McCord

Rating: ★★½ Had Director Reginald LeBorg been as masterful with his cast as he was with the script, *Calling Dr. Death* could have been a most promising introduction to Universal's new "Inner Sanctum" series.... [P]lenty good enough for everyday consumption, and likely to encourage an appreciable following.—*The New York Daily News*, February 12, 1944, Dorothy Masters

It should prove a treat for the followers of this type of entertainment, for the identity of the murderer is concealed so well that when it is finally divulged it comes as a complete surprise.—*Harrison's Reports*, December 18, 1943

Reginald LeBorg's direction ... is filled with imaginative touches and extracts a maximum of suspense from the psychological plot.... Lon Chaney gives an arresting portrayal of the doctor.—*The Hollywood Reporter*, December 10, 1943

1944

The Spider Woman

Released January 21, 1944. 61 minutes. *Producer-Director:* Roy William Neill. *Screenplay:* Bertram Millhauser. *Based on a story by* Sir Arthur Conan Doyle. *Photography:* Charles Van Enger. *Art Directors:* John B. Goodman & Martin Obzina. *Editor:* William Austin. *Set Decorators:* Russell A. Gausman & Edward R. Robinson. *Musical Director:* Hans J. Salter. *Sound Director:* Bernard B. Brown. *Technician:* Paul Neal. *Gowns:* Vera West.

Basil Rathbone (*Sherlock Holmes*), Nigel Bruce (*Dr. John H. Watson*), Gale Sondergaard (*Adrea Spedding*), Dennis Hoey (*Insp. Lestrade*), Vernon Downing (*Norman Locke*), Alec Craig (*Radlik*), Arthur Hohl (*Adam Gilflower*), Mary Gordon (*Mrs. Hudson*), Teddy Infuhr (*Larry*), Stanley Logan (*Robert* [*Colonel*]), Lydia Bilbrook (*Susan* [*Colonel's Wife*]), Donald Stuart (*Artie*), John Burton (*Announcer*), Belle Mitchell (*Fortune Teller*), Harry Cording (*Fred Garvin*), John Roche (*Croupier*), John Rogers (*Clerk*), George Kirby, Jimmy Aubrey (*News Vendors*), Marie de Becker, Sylvia Andrews (*Charwomen*), Angelo Rossitto (*Pygmy*), Arthur Stenning (*Plainclothesman*), Frank Benson (*Attendant*), Gene Stutenroth [Roth] (*Taylor*), Wilson Benge (*Clerk*).

Trapped in the Deadly Web of a Silken Killer!
—*Ad blurb for* The Spider Woman

Sherlock Holmes' fifth Universal visitation was a brief one, making a gag appearance in the Olsen and Johnson free-for-all *Crazy House* (1943). It's a typically disjointed opus for the stuck-on-overdrive comedy team, but of minor interest. For one thing, it was actually set on the Universal back lot, which the comics turn upside down on the pretense of shooting a musical. Recruiting just about every contract player on hand (Lon Chaney, Jr., Andy Devine, Leo Carrillo and Shemp Howard are among the familiar faces), the picture contains several guest shots, including Rathbone and Bruce in their Holmes and Watson garb. It was a sly piece of self-promotion, giving the two Britons the welcome opportunity to poke fun at themselves in their well-established roles.

The bit was actually shot during a break in shooting on the upcoming adventure tentatively titled *Sherlock Holmes in Peril* but soon rechristened *The Spider Woman*. It was Holmes' first of several entanglements with various femmes fatale and possibly the best. Bertram Millhauser wrote a lively, original script with only a suggestion of the Conan Doyle story "The Adventure of the Dying Detective," in which Holmes feigns having a fatal condition in order to solve a case.

Universal was pleased with the popular reception of their detective and began to get curious about who comprised the Holmes audience. As director Roy William Neill wrote:

> By consistent observation, we have discovered that [Sherlock Holmes fans] predominate in two age brackets. He has a tremendous audience among people over 40, and a rabid following among those under 25.... The in-between span presumably prefers more sophisticated movie fare.

The Spider Woman was most likely geared for the detective's younger fans with a wildly melodramatic plot and a super-villainess with a name more attuned to a Saturday matinee serial than the pages of Conan Doyle. In an attention-grabbing opening, the dim figure of a man crashes through a high window and plunges to the street below. It is the latest in a rash of "pajama suicides" that has gripped London. Noting that none of the victims left suicide notes, Holmes (Basil Rathbone) is convinced of foul play. Hoping to lure the killer (whom he suspects is a woman) out into the open, he fakes his own death while vacationing in Scotland.

Upon the discovery that all of the victims were known gamblers, Holmes takes the name Raghni Singh and disguises himself as an East Indian diplomat and heads for London's posh gambling parlors. In short order, he befriends the glamorous Adrea Spedding (Gale Sondergaard) who consoles the "Indian" who claims to have lost his fortune. She then persuades him to cash in his insurance policy, making her the beneficiary. Holmes is now certain he has found the culprit, but Spedding catches on to the detective's game.

Holmes learns that Spedding is using a deadly breed of spiders to do her dirty work, a species so poisonous that its venom drives victims to self-destruction. When tiny footprints are found at a crime scene, Holmes deduces that Spedding is using a child to deliver the spiders to her intended victims.

Holmes and Dr. Watson (Nigel Bruce) visit the home of a well-known entomologist whom the sleuth suspects is supplying Spedding with her lethal pets, but finds the scientist murdered in his study. Rifling through the dead man's notes, Holmes turns up proof that the Spider Woman's accomplice is not a child but an African pygmy whose immunity to the venom makes him an ideal candidate to transport the spiders.

Playing a hunch, the detective locates Spedding's hideout, the back room of a bustling carnival shooting stand, and finds himself entrapped by the Spider Woman and her gang. Propping the bound-and-gagged detective behind a shooting stand mock-up of Hitler, Adrea and her cohorts watch from the sidelines as Holmes is nearly shot by an unsuspecting Watson, idly trying his hand at target practice. The detective manages to free himself and delivers Spedding and company into the hands of Scotland Yard.

The Spider Woman was another important step in the Sherlock Holmes series' break from war-related plots to something approaching the sensibilities of the Hollywood horror movie. Nothing remotely supernatural occurs in the film or its follow-ups and Holmes' adversaries are never anything less than mortal, even if they are criminals. Yet, as the hard-edge political realities of the day began to fade, more and more standard horror movie dialogue began creeping into the scripts with Holmes typically characterizing his opponents and their misdeeds as sinister and evil, even monstrous. The tonal shift from topical terrors to a slightly macabre literariness agreed with the series which was now entering its glory years. *Sherlock Holmes Faces Death* treaded lightly into genre conventions with its medieval castle and ancestral curses but, in the end, it was a case of a gentleman killer finishing off his rivals (and even their butler) in a bid to marry into money. Next to Adrea Spedding and her activities as *The Spider Woman*; it all seemed very civilized indeed. The lurid nature of the latter picture is closer in spirit to a pulp novel than to Conan Doyle, especially as the grim details of the "pajama murders" come to light. It's only with the appearance of its strutting, high camp villainess does the film regain its bearings as a relatively lightweight thriller.

It's typical of the series that no one in the film is quite whom they appear to be as Holmes and his adversaries continually try to outdo one another by affecting different disguises. Amazingly, the detective saves his cruelest ruse for poor Watson, who is about to engage in fisticuffs with an insolent postman only to discover it's the resurrected Holmes in makeup. The Spider Woman responds in kind, trying to throw the detective off track by arriving at his Baker Street flat with her "nephew" (Teddy Infuhr).

An apparent mute, the odd, scrawny youngster makes an uneasy impression, swatting at passing flies and moving about with sudden jerks. Easily hoodwinking Holmes into believing he is the child who's been planting the spiders on her victims, Spedding casually exits, leaving behind a cache of poison gas powder to do its work.

Infuhr recalled to the authors how he happened to be cast in the role:

> A few weeks before I went on the interview for that movie, I was up for a part in a movie called *The North Star* [1943]. I was supposed to work for six weeks, which was a big deal. The only problem was that I had to have my head shaved bald. So, they shaved my head but I only worked three days! That's the reason why I got the part in *The Spider Woman.* I had no hair so it worked out perfect for the part.

The ensuing air of mistrust provides Watson with one of his funnier blunders. Holmes arranges a consultation with a noted entomologist. When a coarsely bearded stranger in dark glasses arrives at the doorstep, Watson is convinced it's the detective buried under another disguise. Backing his caller into a corner with a blast of ridicule, the doctor is about to try to yank off the befuddled scientist's whiskers when Holmes saunters onto the scene and sternly rebukes his red-faced friend. Arthur Hohl was cast as the put-upon scientist, presumably because of his mild resemblance to the similarly built Rathbone. Hohl would perform the same function again in the upcoming *The Scarlet Claw*, which included a situation of the detective disguising himself as one of the characters at a particular point in the plot.

Adrea Spedding (Gale Sondergaard) was one of Sherlock Holmes' (Basil Rathbone) most formidable adversaries in *The Spider Woman.*

The staged death of Holmes results in one of the film's more appealing scenes. As Watson packs up the "dead" detective's personal effects, he is joined by Lestrade who lets down his guard to offer a slightly emotional tribute to his rival. The scene is a treat for audiences, giving the familiar characters a chance to respond to each other as people and momentarily dropping the central situation. It works because the scene doesn't get mired in excess sentiment and is balanced with enough humor to keep it unforced and basically honest.

It's interesting to note that there seems to have been more of a bond between the characters of Holmes and Lestrade than there was between Rathbone and Hoey off-screen. Hoey's son, Michael, recalled his father's relationship with the Rathbone-Bruce team to the authors:

> My father was very good friends with Nigel Bruce — "Willie" Bruce — a lovely, lovely man. I was on the Holmes sets on a number of occasions, and one time Basil Rathbone and Nigel Bruce signed pictures for me. From Willie, I got a photograph of him by himself, and he signed it, "To Michael, who is a nice boy in spite of his father!" I had that picture pinned to my bedroom wall for some time, and then suddenly one day it "mysteriously" disappeared. I think my father must have gotten tired of seeing that particular comment on there!
>
> Rathbone was somewhat of an aloof person, and I didn't really warm up to him. Willie and my father were good friends; Rathbone and my father probably respected one another, I don't think they *dis*liked one another, but they never got close.

The highlight of *The Spider Woman* is the malignant presence of Gale Sondergaard in the title role, described by Holmes as a "female Moriarity." Rathbone more than meets his match in the Dragon Lady of screen terror although she was even more frequently typecast as the dour, distinctly creepy housekeeper. At her scene-stealing best, Sondergaard puts on a grand show, but it's difficult to put a finger on the actress' talents. She won an Academy Award for Best Supporting Actress for her very first screen role, in Warner Bros.' pedigree production of *Anthony Adverse* (1936). She quickly became one of Hollywood's favorite period-dress actresses, often playing calculating characters in the sort of heavy-handed historical dramas the studios were passing off as art. Sondergaard became well-regarded by the critics on the basis of her solid, theater-quality performances, playing Mme. Dreyfuss in *The Life of Emile Zola* (1937), and brought a dated, disconcerting "mysteries of the Orient" flavor to her role in William Wyler's *The Letter* (1940).

When cast as villainesses, Sondergaard responded with her characteristically intransigent demeanor and her trademark frozen smile; she would be most everyone's ideal of the schoolmarm from hell and quite a lethal one at that, especially when delivering stock horror movie dialogue. Sondergaard was beyond vulnerability, even sexuality, but when she was going full blast like a female Lionel Atwill, her oozing campiness seemed slightly comic although she never seemed to be in on the joke. As a result, Sondergaard went from straight horror movies such as *The Climax* and *The Spider Woman Strikes Back* to broad Abbott and Costello (*The Time of Their Lives*) and Bob Hope comedies (*Never Say Die* [1939]) without missing a beat.

Sondergaard's cat-and-mouse game with Rathbone is a delectable display of one-upmanship although it provides the series with its few instances of unintended humor. Sizing up Holmes' "Raghni Singh" as a possible victim, Spedding turns to her epicene partner-in-crime Norman Locke (Vernon Downing) and inquires, "What do they do in India, Norman?" "Ride elephants," he fatuously replies. In the next scene, Adrea, who has obviously boned up on Eastern culture, gallantly tries to evoke the spirit of "Mother India" for her tea-time companion. Draped in an Indian sari, emerging from a mist of burning incense, she's a startling sight as Holmes discreetly examines rental company labels on her bogus Asian decorations. The silly charade reaches a climax of sorts when Holmes examines a photograph of what Spedding identifies as "The Shrine of the Sacred Cow." The film cuts to a "Sun Valley" banner billowing on a flagpole as the detective examines it under a magnifying glass.

The sparring match, at least, delivers a neat payoff a few scenes later. Angling for a sample of his adversary's fingerprints, "Singh" entices Adrea with a silver cigarette case. After she eagerly snatches up her new trinket, he abruptly takes it back, promising to have it personally inscribed. In their next encounter, at Baker Street, Holmes returns her case, not bearing Adrea's monogram, but a striking etching of a black widow spider.

The Spider Woman works up a considerable head of steam as the final pieces of the puzzle fall into place but the amusement park wrap-up is something of a letdown. The episode of Watson plying his shooting range skills unaware that Holmes is the actual target is just an old-hat suspense gimmick with the bumbling character

Sondergaard uses little Teddy Infuhr to throw Rathbone off-track in *The Spider Woman.* That's Infuhr's autograph in the upper right hand corner.

conveniently fumbling every time the Hitler figure passes. Spedding bows out in style, at least. In our last glimpse of her, she is cozying up to Inspector Lestrade with thoughts of escape obviously looming in her mind.

With such overpowering leads as Rathbone and Sondergaard, the supporting players vanish into the woodwork. Vernon Downing, who twitched his way through *Sherlock Holmes Faces Death* as a shell-shocked soldier, is outclassed as Spedding's brother and right-hand man. Nigel Bruce and Dennis Hoey share some quietly touching scenes reminiscing about the supposedly dead detective. Startlingly, the enigmatic pygmy accomplice turns out to be famous Hollywood dwarf, Angelo Rossitto, in dark body makeup.

The Spider Woman, at least, provided Sondergaard with a worthy showpiece that earned her a special niche in Hollywood history. (Director Mike Nichols once admitted in the course of a radio interview that, in his early years, he would set his alarm clock to catch a late-night airing of *The Spider Woman Strikes Back.*) The critics were receptive to her colorful villainy and showered the actress with notices even better than Rathbone's. Realizing they really had something, Universal signed Sondergaard to a long-term contract before *The Spider Woman* wrapped in May 1943.

In a 1971 interview with Leonard Maltin in *Film Fan Monthly*, Sondergaard had mixed feelings about her tenure at Universal:

> It was a period when they weren't making things like *Zola*s anyway, and they were making more run-of-the-mill things. They weren't always things I enjoyed, particularly *The Spider Woman Strikes Back*. I liked *The Spider Woman* ... that was fun playing with Basil and Nigel Bruce. The set was always really fun ... those guys were marvelous, so adept, and we had a wonderful time.

Except for the aforementioned silly missteps, Roy William Neill's direction is spare and efficient, with an evident focus on pacing. In some situations, Universal used *The Spider Woman* as bottom-of-the-bill fodder, pairing it with the lavish and heavily promoted *Ali Baba and the Forty Thieves*, which actually was one of the studio's better Technicolor-saturated forays into exotica. Sherlock Holmes' touch of class was a welcome addition to the program — especially with Gale Sondergaard doing the menacing.

Critics' Corner

[Hollywood] is running the great Baker Street detective into the ground.... Even with such props as poisonous spiders and murderous African pygmies, *The Spider Woman* is a yawning show.—*The New York Herald-Tribune*, January 15, 1944, Howard Barnes

Neat direction, atmosphere and adequate acting.... The story, if analyzed, hasn't a leg to stand on.... Gale Sondergaard makes a delightful meanie.—*The New York Daily News*, January 15, 1944, Wanda Hale

Fans of Basil Rathbone will find him at his best ... for he employs a minimum of histrionics and lets a good story pretty well tell itself. Nigel Bruce ... also curtails the huffing and puffing and trails admirably after Holmes.... How Miss Sondergaard can screen so beautifully and yet so menacingly is one of the delights of the film.—*The Hollywood Reporter*, January 6, 1944

I honestly believe this current episode is better plotted in many ways than "The Speckled Band," the Conan Doyle story it resembles most.—*PM New York*, John T. McManus

[T]he current installment of the master sleuth serial is above the average in plausibility, suspense and interest and has been really quite well presented.—*The New York Journal-American*, January 1944, G.E. Blackford

[Rathbone and Bruce] push their expert portrayals to new heights in this number, best of the series, in part because the screenplay by Bertram Millhauser provides solid material with which to work and in part because Gale Sondergaard's performance as "the spider woman" of the title is of quality and merit matching theirs.... [T]he film stacks up as tops in its field.—*The Motion Picture Herald*, January 15, 1944, William R. Weaver

Weird Woman

Released April 14, 1944. 63 minutes. An Inner Sanctum Mystery, produced by arrangement with Simon and Schuster, Inc., Publishers. *Associate Producer:* Oliver Drake. *Executive Producer:* Ben Pivar. *Director:* Reginald LeBorg. *Screenplay:* Brenda Weisberg. *Based on the story* "Conjure Wife" *by* Fritz Leiber, Jr. *Adaptation:* W. Scott Darling. *Photography:* Virgil Miller. *Special Photography:* John P. Fulton. *Assistant Director:* William Tummel. *Editor:* Milton Carruth. *Musical Director:* Paul Sawtell. *Art Directors:* John B. Goodman & Richard H. Riedel. *Set Decorators:* Russell A. Gausman & Andrew J. Gilmore. *Sound Director:* Bernard B. Brown. *Technician:* William Hedgcock. *Gowns:* Vera West.

Lon Chaney, Jr. (*Prof. Norman Reed*), Anne Gwynne (*Paula Clayton Reed*), Evelyn Ankers (*Ilona Carr*), Ralph Morgan (*Prof. Millard Sawtelle*), Elisabeth Risdon (*Grace Gunnison*), Lois Collier (*Margaret Mercer*), Elizabeth Russell (*Evelyn Sawtelle*), Harry Hayden (*Prof. Septimus Carr*), Phil Brown (*David Jennings*), Jackie Lou [Kay] Harding, William Hudson (*Students*), Hanna Kaapa (*Laraua*), Chuck Hamilton (*Carpenter*), David Hoffman (*Inner Sanctum*), Milburn Stone (*Voice of Radio Announcer*).

I believe that voodoo merely is the
untutored savage's realization of
the power of auto-suggestion.
—*Lon Chaney, Jr., quoted in publicity piece for* Weird Woman

---

The second installment of the Inner Sanctum series, *Weird Woman* is regarded with contempt by those who hold the Fritz Leiber, Jr., story upon which it is based ("Conjure Wife") and its second screen adaptation (the British thriller *Night of the Eagle*, released in the U.S. in 1962 as *Burn, Witch, Burn*) in high esteem. For those willing to place their critical faculties in reserve and approach the movie with their tongues firmly planted in their cheeks, *Weird Woman* is an absolute joy, outclassing the other films in the tepid series for its sheer audaciousness alone. Brenda Weisberg's mildly hysterical screenplay has all the sobriety of a Hollywood lampoon and is almost as funny.

Once again, Lon Chaney, Jr., is laughably miscast as a brooding intellectual. One of his character's legion of female admirers describes him as a "mental giant," though he's incapable of solving the slightest social disorder. Lon gets fine support from an uncharacteistically venomous Evelyn Ankers as the proverbial "woman scorned"; Anne Gwynne, who's quite excellent as Chaney's neurotic island bride; Lois Collier and Phil Brown as a pair of naive romantics; and RKO's Empress of Menace Elizabeth Russell, once again cutting a striking figure in the role of a vindictive widow. This canny combination of overwrought writing and spirited performances makes *Weird Woman* a high camp classic. Indeed, it's more entertainingly funny than *Burn, Witch, Burn* is entertainingly eerie.

It is difficult to believe that the source material for this romp was Fritz Leiber, Jr.'s, "Conjure Wife," a heady brew of modern-day witchcraft which first appeared in serialized form in the pages of *Unknown Worlds Magazine*. Much of the story takes place in the mind of college professor hero Norman Saylor (changed to Norman Reed in the movie), whose scientific reasoning is stripped away as an onslaught of supernatural forces converge on him and his black arts-practicing wife. Leiber's story is a no-holds-barred horror melodrama that ends on a note on ambiguity; the last line reveals that the protagonist himself doesn't rule out the possibility that the unreal occurrences are the result of mental suggestion. Unfortunately, little of Leiber's distinctly macabre tone or his sense of mounting, white-knuckle terror filters down into the *Weird Woman* script, which comes off instead as a spooky soap opera.

By the time shooting was completed on *Calling Dr. Death*, Universal had a change of heart and decided to follow up their first Inner Sanctum mystery with *The Frozen Ghost* instead of *Conjure Wife* (*Weird Woman*'s original title). This decision was short-lived; *Ghost* had seven more months of labor pains before its multi-author script was deemed suitable for filming. And by then, it followed yet *another* Inner Sanctum entry, *Dead Man's Eyes*.

By early December 1943, Universal began production in earnest on *Weird Woman*. (A trade paper write-up at the time revealed that the studio had established a precedent by hiring a publicist whose sole function was to coin catchy titles, "to insure the most effective way of publicizing each film.")

Having done such an efficient job directing *Calling Dr. Death*, Reginald LeBorg was rewarded with the job of directing *Weird Woman*. LeBorg offered us this insight on what it was like working on a typical B movie at Universal:

> I got the script on a Friday and was told to start shooting a week from Monday. So I had to read it over the weekend and then come in and prepare. That was the norm at Universal. Sometimes you'd get two or three weeks in between, if they had no script, but sometimes they had to rush these things out. Of course, me being a hard worker and a fast worker, they gave me the *dirt*. When they had something they wanted done fast, they rushed me in.

LeBorg admitted that he didn't even have the time to study the Leiber story.

Just prior to the December 6 start date, Anne Gwynne was chosen to portray Paula, probably the most demanding role of her career, thus sparing her the indignity of appearing in yet another of the studio's featherweight farces (1944's *Hi, Good Lookin'!*). Lois Collier, a pretty newcomer from radio, and Phil Brown (later an occasional dialogue director), landed key roles. Brown's Hollywood career came to a screeching halt during the McCarthy Era. Settling in England, the young man picked up a few directing and acting assignments (most notably, Edward Dmytryk's 1949 suspense-melodrama *The Hidden Room* with Robert Newton). In 1977, a

Between his superstitious bride (Anne Gwynne) and a jealous ex-flame (Evelyn Ankers), Lon Chaney, Jr., has his hands full in *Weird Woman.*

grayer, plumper Brown popped up as Luke Skywalker's (Mark Hamill) uncle in George Lucas' *Star Wars*.

Monroe College sociology professor Norman Reed (Lon Chaney, Jr.) has his hands full. Instead of celebrating the success of his new book *Superstition Versus Reason and Fact*, and looking forward to the day when he'll most assuredly win his department's chairmanship, Reed nervously paces the floor of his study, chain-smoking, and staring questioningly into the grotesque faces of the native ceremonial masks he has collected while exploring the South Seas. It was on one of those lush tropical islands that Reed met his childlike future bride Paula (Anne Gwynne), the source of all his current troubles. The daughter of American missionaries, Paula was raised by Laraua (Hanna Kaapa), the high priestess of Kauna-Ana-Ana, who taught the impressionable girl to place her faith in voodoo gods and follow her people's superstitions.

Norman struggles vainly to free his new wife from her island heritage. He gets little support from his old flame, college librarian Ilona Carr (Evelyn Ankers). When Norman rejects Ilona's generous offer of a little extramarital monkey business, Ilona, not one to take rejection lightly, sets out to poison the minds of the gullible against the troubled couple. She tells everyone within earshot that Paula is a "witch wife" and has been using her magical powers to insure Norman's recent success.

Ilona finds a ready audience in Evelyn Sawtelle (Elizabeth Russell); her henpecked husband Millard (Ralph Morgan) is Norman's only rival for the coveted sociology chair. With Evelyn in tow, Ilona works on Margaret Mercer (Lois Collier), a starry-eyed minx who regards the prof with the kind of adoration now reserved for rock stars. ("He's the most brilliant man on the campus!" she swoons.) Banking on the insecurities of Margaret's Dobie Gillis-like boyfriend David Jennings (Phil Brown), Ilona lasciviously suggests that something's been going on between Reed and Margaret during those late nights at the office.

Ilona's biggest coup, however, is discovering that a dead student's brilliant thesis was filched by Millard Sawtelle to form the basis for his new book. She misinforms the timorous old man that Reed plans on using this scandalous information as a means of getting him to withdraw from the chairmanship campaign.

Fed up with Paula's nightly disappearances, Norman follows her to a local cemetery. Aghast, he watches her light a ceremonial candle, don a native headpiece, and perform a rite over an effigy of Ilona. Enraged, Norman interrupts the ceremony and destroys his wife's collection of tourist-trap voodoo paraphernalia. The "circle of immunity" that she had created to protect herself and Norman from the forces of evil has been broken.

It isn't long before the couple is beset with all manner of troubles. Prof. Sawtelle commits suicide; Evelyn accuses Norman of "murder." Reed is forced to discharge Margaret as his student secretary after she makes a play for him. As a consequence, word spreads around the campus that he's a philanderer. Paula is tormented by an anonymous caller who plays a voodoo death chant over the phone. An insanely jealous David has two violent confrontations with Norman. The second one ends in disaster: David's gun goes off in a struggle with the professor and the student is killed. Norman is jailed and released on bail pending a court case. Understandably, Norman himself begins to believe that maybe there's something to Paula's babblings about protective medallions and circles of immunity. Life hasn't exactly been a bed of roses since he destroyed her collection of voodoo artifacts.

Reed finally gets to the bottom of this mess when Evelyn admits that it was Ilona who had warned Millard of impending disaster and then filled Margaret and David's minds with vicious lies. Realizing the only way he can clear himself of the murder charge is through Ilona's confession, Reed hatches a plan and enlists Evelyn's cooperation.

Late that evening, Evelyn summons Ilona to her home and pretends to be shaken up over a nightmare she's just had. "Millard came and stood over me.... He said, 'I am dead because a woman lied. A woman lied!'" The widow produces a hideous effigy which, she claims, represents the woman who lied. According to Millard, unless this woman confesses (in 13 days, one minute after midnight), she will die.

The ruse works. Ilona rushes from Evelyn's home in hysterics. In a wonderful series of quick cuts, we see glimpses of Ilona over the next two weeks, slowly going out of her mind. On the night of the appointed hour, the hagridden librarian storms into Evelyn's house and demands the effigy. As the clock strikes the hour of midnight, Ilona blurts out a confession. Surprise! Norman, Paula and Margaret emerge from the next room and confront her. "You tricked me!" Ilona cries, and dashes for an open window. Racing across a second-story catwalk, she slips through the slats and is choked to death by the entwining vines ... just as Evelyn's dream predicted she would.

The premise of "Conjure Wife," a smug, self-satisfied academic clinging desperately to his scientific skepticism as dark forces overtake his life, seems like ready-made movie material although a scene-for-scene adaptation of the story would be rather unworkable. (Leiber didn't novelize the story until 1953 when he apparently expanded the text, even adding references to atom bomb jitters to reflect the unnerving political anxieties of the day.)

Leiber makes it clear that the Saylors are battling against the Sawtelle and Carr characters who are full-fledged sorceresses in their own right. By the final chapter, the evil Carr (depicted as a sex-starved, youth-obsessed old crone) manages to switch her soul with Saylor's wife in order to bed the husband; her scheme fatally backfires. Leiber overworks the soul-transference angle in the course of the story and, of course, it is completely dropped in the movie versions. By the last chapter, Saylor manages to isolate the soul of a third sorceress (a character who has no counterpart in the film) to hold as "hostage," unaware that the evil Carr has already switched her soul with the professor's wife. The confusing cross-current of various individual souls becomes a cumbersome and ludicrous plot device almost reminiscent of the silly brain-switching activity in the later *House of Frankenstein*. It diminishes what is until then a classic of horror literature.

In comparison to the source material, the simplicities of *Weird Woman* go beyond the pale. While the Inner Sanctum movie retains Leiber's concept of using institutional rivalries as a backdrop to the college campus-set story, it jettisons most of the supernatural content in favor of a gimmicky denouement in which everything is logically explained. In true Inner Sanctum fashion, *Weird Woman* sidesteps being a full-blooded horror chiller and instead exploits the supernatural elements of Leiber's work merely to set up a standard melodrama. Its approach is heavy-handed, inadvertently offering viewers more titters than thrills. *Weird Woman*'s lunacy is contagious as the plot takes on the dimensions of a comic opera with crisis upon crisis piling up on Norman Reed's doorstep.

Structurally, *Weird Woman* suffers from episodic pacing. The opening scenes of Gwynne arriving at home in the middle of the night from a secret rendezvous as Chaney, alone in his study, tries to make sense of his bride's puzzling behavior, create an instant mood of mystery and intrigue. This aura is quickly shattered, however, by flashbacks depicting the risible chance encounter of Norman and Paula at a South Seas ceremonial dance. An apparent bid to "open up" the film with the *faux* exotica of dancing native girls, a voodoo high priestess and pulsating rhythms, the ploy only serves to add a campy touch to a movie already brimming with them. (In the Leiber story, we learn that "conjure wife" Tansy Saylor's obsession started from watching the descendants of African slaves practice black magic in the Deep South.)

Seldom have so many neurotic characters been crammed into one picture. It's amazing how easily this presumably educated bunch fall prey to Ilona's schemes. Only wise, sardonic Grace, nicely played by Elisabeth Risdon, displays any semblance of rationality. ("Ilona, there's something about your smile that makes me think of Jack the Ripper.") Surprisingly, Evelyn Ankers didn't relish the challenge of portraying a miscreant for a change. LeBorg told the authors:

> Evelyn Ankers was a very sweet girl and a very good actress, but she wasn't very happy about her part. She was a very good friend of Anne Gwynne's, and she had to play Gwynne's enemy, to torment her. When Ankers had a scene with Gwynne that was rather macabre, she *couldn't* do it very well because she loved Gwynne so much; she *couldn't* be mean to her. I gave her a few pointers, and after three or four takes, she did it very well.

The women remained friends right up until Ankers' death from cancer in 1985. In light of the characters they portray in *Weird Woman*, it is amusing to note that Gwynne acted as Ankers' character witness when the actress obtained her United States citizenship in August 1946.

Anne Gwynne's response to Michael Fitzgerald's *Fangoria* inquiry about Lon Chaney bears out remarks made about the horror great by other co-workers:

> I have nothing but glowing things to say about Boris Karloff, and only praise for Bela Lugosi, but Lon Chaney was something else, although we actually got along fine together. But he would pull practical jokes on people—and they did become quite cruel. He never bothered me at all—it was Evelyn who incurred his wrath. They worked together more often, and yet they couldn't stand each other, sort of like the way Jon Hall and Maria Montez never got along....

Phil Brown, who passed away while this edition of *Universal Horrors* was in production, looked back on his early filmmaking experiences at the studio with distaste. In a conversation with the authors, Brown revealed:

> I had a strange relationship to Universal. I was hired on two or three Chaney pictures, because Chaney had mainly played monsters, and now Universal wanted him to play doctors and other intellectual types. So they hired me to help him learn his lines and develop characters. The first morning when I showed up at his dressing room about ten o'clock to start work, he handed me a large glass of whiskey. Now [*laughs*], I'm not a prude, I like to drink with the best of them, but that was not my idea of the best preparation for a hard day's work! It was crazy working with him, really quite crazy, but he was a very nice guy and we got on well.
>
> In *Weird Woman*, Chaney and I had a fight scene. I took a poke at him and he knocked me down, and we were down there on the floor when the director called "cut." In the course of this fake fight, he tore the sleeve of my jacket. Our faces were close together, and he whispered, "Look, kid, don't worry about that jacket. I'll getcha a new one." And ripped it some more. What he didn't know was, it was *my* jacket—my own!—and the studio was not going to buy me another. [*laughs*]! And it was a good jacket, a *damn* good tweed jacket of my own wardrobe! Somebody there sewed it up and gave it back to me.

One player who didn't have qualms about playing dark characters was Elizabeth Russell. The statuesque ash blonde (christened the Houri

Sociologist Norman Reed (Chaney Jr.) inadvertently breaks a native taboo.

of Horror by *The Hollywood Reporter*) got the showy part of Evelyn Sawtelle through her agent, veteran director E.A. Dupont. Earlier in her life, Russell enjoyed a lucrative career as a top New York fashion model for John Robert Powers and fostered no ambitions toward becoming an actress. She submitted to a screen test in 1936 and was signed up to a long-term contract with Paramount. After appearing in a trio of undistinguished programmers, Russell returned to modeling after the studio dropped her option.

Russell's friend ZaSu Pitts convinced her to give the picture business another whirl and that she did, appearing in two of ZaSu's comedies. This led to her first horror film appearance as Bela Lugosi's remarkably preserved 80-year-old wife in Monogram's riotous *The Corpse Vanishes* (1942). Then came *Cat People* (1942) and a long and fruitful association with Val Lewton. The producer's superb *Curse of the Cat People* (1944) was the actress' finest hour. Jokingly calling herself "a female Bela Lugosi in a constant zombie state," Russell had no regrets concerning the brevity of her acting career. ("I made a lot of mistakes because I wasn't aware of the opportunities involved.")

In Gregory Mank's interview with her for his book *Women in Horror Films, 1940s*, Russell recalled how the whole crazy business of making *Weird Woman* came to a head one night during shooting:

> [W]e were working overtime, late—and we got hysterical laughing. Lon Chaney would say a line, we would all laugh—the cast, the crew, the director, Reginald LeBorg—and we could not speak! We were trying to save time late at night, but the whole unit was in tears, laughing!

Retired from acting since 1960, Elizabeth Russell passed away on May 4, 2002, at the age of 95.

Burn, Witch, Burn is rightfully regarded as the definitive screen treatment of the Leiber tale, though even here, the narrative is greatly simplified to accommodate the requirements of the medium. (The screenplay by Richard Matheson and Charles Beaumont was reportedly reworked by George Baxt when the producers deemed their effort "unfilmable.") While it may not be 100 percent faithful to its source, *Burn, Witch, Burn* is the definitive version of the Leiber story. (Like Reginald LeBorg, Baxt didn't bother to read the Leiber original either!)

Prior to the U.S. release of *Burn, Witch, Burn*, "Conjure Wife" was dramatized on the live TV anthology series *Moment of Fear* on July 8, 1960, with Larry Blyden in the lead role. In 1980, the Fritz Leiber classic underwent a fourth adaptation, a TV movie-like feature called *Witches' Brew*. In this uncomfortable melding of light comedy and suspense-horror, Richard Benjamin is cast as the hapless professor saddled with an oddball wife (Teri Garr). Lana Turner has a featured role as a smug, devious doyenne of an informal coven of suburban witches. Co-directed by Richard Shorr and Herbert L. Strock, *Witches' Brew* follows the general plotline of *Burn, Witch, Burn*, right down to Benjamin's professor being breathlessly pursued by a winged, demonic creature. (Leiber isn't given a word of credit!) Garr's method of winning her husband the psychology seat at the university — smearing his bare back and belly with bat guano, cat urine and lamb's blood and leaving him out on the front lawn overnight — is indicative of the film's sense of humor.

Weird Woman is a heck of a lot more amusing.

Critics' Corner

[A] violent but well-told story.... [W]ith the exception of occasional lines of extraordinary dialog, the picture conveys the impression of plausibility.— *The Hollywood Reporter*, March 31, 1944

Deliberately fashioned to capture attention of the suspense-minded customers.... [A]chieves that purpose to rate as a standard programmer.... Direction ... accentuates the suspense.... Chaney does well in top spot....— *Variety*, March 31, 1944

It certainly is weird what some women — and some film studios will do in a fit of desperation.... Weird, isn't it? And, boy, is it dull!— *The New York Times*, April 1, 1944, Bosley Crowther

The story ... is far-fetched and lacks excitement. Discriminating audiences will find it tiresome, and even the most ardent followers of this type of entertainment may find it but mildly interesting.— *Harrison's Reports*, April 8, 1944

This is another in the Inner Sanctum series, which is beginning to serve as outlet for interesting suspenseful fare. Chaney, Gwynne and Ankers handle their assignments ably as does director LeBorg.— *The Motion Picture Exhibitor*, 1944

The Scarlet Claw

Released May 26, 1944. 74 minutes. *Producer-Director:* Roy William Neill. *Screenplay:* Edmund L. Hartmann & Roy William Neill. *Original Story:* Paul Gangelin & Brenda Weisberg. *Based on the characters created by* Sir Arthur Conan Doyle. *Photography:* George Robinson. *Art Director:* John B. Goodman. *Associate Art Director:* Ralph M. DeLacy. *Musical Director:* Paul Sawtell. *Editor:* Paul Landres. *Special Photography:* John P. Fulton. *Set Decorators:* Russell A. Gausman & Ira S. Webb. *Sound Director:* Bernard B. Brown. *Technician:* Robert Pritchard. *Dialogue Director:* Stacy Keach. *Assistant Director:* Melville Shyer. *Camera Operator:* Eddie Cohen. *Properties:* Henry Gundstrom.

Basil Rathbone (*Sherlock Holmes*), Nigel Bruce (*Dr. John H. Watson*), Gerald Hamer (*Potts/Jack Tanner/ Alastair Ramson*), Paul Cavanagh (*Lord William Penrose*), Arthur Hohl (*Emile Journet*), Miles Mander (*Judge Brisson*), Kay Harding (*Marie Journet*), David Clyde (*Sgt. Thompson*), Ian Wolfe (*Drake*), Victoria Horne (*Nora*), George Kirby (*Father Pierre*), Harry Allen (*Taylor*), Frank O'Connor (*Cab Driver*), Olaf Hytten (*Hotel Desk Clerk*), Gertrude Astor (*Lady Penrose*), Tony Travers (*Musician*), Charles Francis (*Sir John*), Norbert Muller (*Page Boy*), Al Ferguson (*Attendant*), Eric Wilton (*Night Clerk*), Pietro Sosso (*Trent*), Clyde Fillmore (*Inspector*), Charles Knight (*Inspector's Assistant*), Bill Cartledge (*Hotel Bellhop*), Ted Billings (*Villager*), Gil Perkins, Charles Morton (*Stunts/Doubles*), William Allen.

The Red-Death Strikes
— *Poster blurb for* The Scarlet Claw

As Universal's horror line was quickly eroding with one rehashed plot after another, the Sherlock Holmes series was, conversely, reaching its peak. With all references to the war abandoned, except for a quick tip of the hat to Winston Churchill, the studio embarked on the detective's darkest, grimmest and bloodiest adventure.

The Scarlet Claw is, hands down, the perennial favorite among the Universal Holmes pictures, although most Conan Doyle buffs still rate the film a notch below the two 20th Century–Fox features which inspired the series. *The Scarlet Claw* is, first and foremost, a mystery, yet the film can pretty well stand on its own as a genuine horror movie, arguably the best that Universal released in 1944.

Pictorially, this back-to-basics feature harks back to *The Hound of the Baskervilles* with a plot set on the foggy marshlands (the Canadian wilderness substitutes for the north of England). Much of *The Scarlet Claw*'s success is attributable to Roy William Neill. The director's uncanny ability for creating a rich, horrific atmosphere hadn't been tapped since the opening scene of *Frankenstein Meets the Wolf Man*. He found the ideal cameraman in George Robinson, whose fine work was the saving grace of the '40s Frankenstein romps (*The Scarlet Claw* was Robinson's only Holmes film). It was the first time that Neill received official writing credit on the series, sharing billing with Edmund L. Hartmann. (Tom McKnight worked without credit on the script but, whimsically, his name only appears on the registry when Holmes and Watson check into their hotel.)

The *Scarlet Claw* screenplay is, in the final analysis, serviceable but unexceptional; the film's real merit lies in its brooding sense of evil and madness. The plot maintains interest by offering a spate of reliable horror bromides (a legendary monster on the prowl, a psychopath with the unique ability to adopt an array of disguises, huddled throngs of superstitious townsfolk who fearfully retreat to the village inn). Wringing every ounce of atmosphere from this catalogue of clichés, Neill produced the series' undisputed gem.

The third Holmes film in the 1943-44 production year, the project was tentatively titled *Sherlock Holmes Versus Moriarity,* from a story by contract writers Paul Gangelin and Brenda Weisberg. By the time the script was rewritten by Hartmann and Neill, Moriarity was dropped and the project was blandly re-titled *Sherlock Holmes in Canada*. By the first day of shooting, January 12, 1944, the film underwent its final title change to *The Scarlet Claw*. Neill overshot his 16-day schedule by three days, bringing the picture in on February 3. He went to the southeast corner of the back lot to take advantage of nearby Nagana Rocks, a reasonable substitute for the Canadian marshlands, at least with the artificial fog machines operating at full capacity. Additional exterior shooting was done on the European Street, which was rendered nearly unrecognizable by Robinson's dark, moody photography.

It's apparent the film got underway with no small degree of confidence on the part of those behind the cameras. Film editor Paul Landres told Michael B. Druxman in his book, *Basil Rathbone: His Life and His Films*: "Everybody involved was very excited about this film because we all knew that it was far superior to anything else in the series." Roy William Neill would hyperbolically write a few years later:

> We launched the Universal series with the naïve notion that he would make an entertaining screen character. Instead, we lifted him to a plane of immortality beyond the imagination even of his creator, Sir Arthur Conan Doyle.
>
> Holmes has become legendary. He doesn't have to be sold to audiences.... They're his friends; they go to the theater prepared to spend a pleasant evening at 221-B Baker Street. If the picture fails to take them inside his cozy rooms, they're let down — a feeling they're not loath to express in critical letters to the studio.

The Scarlet Claw gets right down to business with the eerie pealing of a church bell on the misty moors of La Morte Rouge, a small hamlet nestled on the outskirts of Quebec. The patrons of the local inn, run by Emile Journet (Arthur Hohl), fear that the bell is a harbinger of doom. The local farmers report that their sheep have been found dead with their throats cut, and a glowing "phantom" has been seen stalking the marshlands. Father Pierre (George Kirby) induces the local postman, Potts (Gerald Hamer), to drive him out to the village church to investigate. There, clutching the bell-rope, is the body of Lady Penrose (Gertrude Astor), her throat slashed.

Sherlock Holmes (Basil Rathbone) and Dr. Watson (Nigel Bruce), in Quebec to address the Canadian Occult Society, receive an urgent letter written by Lady Penrose shortly before her death; in fear for her life, she had implored the pair to come to her aid. Holmes and Watson arrive at the village and waste little time formulating a list of suspects: Journet the innkeeper; Judge Brisson (Miles Mander), the retired, wheelchair-bound magistrate whose paralysis the detective discovers to be a hoax; and Lord William Penrose (Paul Cavanagh), the husband of the slain woman, who seems more than willing to pin the crime on supernatural forces.

As the reports of the legendary monster of

the moors grow more widespread, Holmes sets out to investigate. A luminescent figure emerges from the fog but Holmes misses him when he opens fire with his pistol. However, the detective finds a fragment of glowing matter caught on a tree and, upon examination, finds it is only a scrap of clothing treated with phosphorescent paint. As he suspected, a human agent is at work.

Focusing his investigation on Lady Penrose's past, Holmes uncovers evidence that she was formerly an actress who years before witnessed the murder of one of her colleagues by another actor, the psychopathic Alastair Ramson. The detective is convinced that Ramson, who was believed to be killed in a subsequent prison break, is the marsh killer. Learning that Judge Brisson passed sentence on Ramson, and that Journet was a former prison guard where the murderer was incarcerated, Holmes suspects that they, too, are marked for death.

The detective dashes to Brisson's home but it is too late. The jurist has been slain by the madman, disguised as the housekeeper. When Journet's daughter Marie (Kay Harding) is found with her throat slashed, Holmes enlists the innkeeper to help him trap the murderer. Using himself as bait, Holmes, disguised as Journet, walks along the lonely trail through the foggy marshlands. Potts, concealing a blood-stained garden weeder, suddenly appears on the path. A struggle ensues and Holmes reveals his true identity. Ramson/Potts attempts to escape but finds himself hemmed in by the local police and villagers. He spots Journet in the group and wrestles him to the ground. The innkeeper slays his daughter's murderer with the man's own instrument of death. *The Scarlet Claw* concludes as Holmes salutes Canada with a well-chosen quote from Churchill. (Holmes closing line, "God bless him!" referring to the great British statesman, was deleted from the release print.)

As enjoyable as *The Scarlet Claw* is, it doesn't escape the occasional flaws and gaps in logic that mark the rest of the series. It seems highly unlikely, for instance, that Ramson's complete roster of enemies, all of vastly different backgrounds and social positions, should all settle in a small backwater town populated mostly, it would seem, by poor farmers and trappers (especially one as dreary as this one and whose name happens to translate to The Red Death!).

Holmes is not at his most likable, often seeming arrogant and condescending. In his first scene, he's snootily putting "the superstitious peasants" in their place in a discussion with members of the Occult Society. Yet rarely has the character appeared as bungling as he does in this episode. Ramson outfoxes Holmes at every turn, and has little difficulty in dispatching almost all of his intended victims while the master detective looks on in frustration. Holmes can't even protect the leading female character from the killer's butchery, a startling development for this kind of film. Confronted by a gun-toting Ramson, Holmes only manages to save his skin after the ever-klutzy Watson creates a diversion by plummeting down a flight of stairs at the crucial moment. Not even the sleuth's celebrated powers of deduction serve him well enough to catch the killer. When his investigation hits a dead end, Holmes simply dresses up as the next likely victim, and patiently waits to be pounced upon by the guilty party. The climax of *The Scarlet Claw*, too, is somewhat anticlimactic, as the murderer turns out to be a character so incidental to the plot that a less observant viewer can be forgiven for not recognizing him immediately. The script throws a bone to the armchair sleuths in the audience by tipping them off to the killer's identity in the form of a barroom conversation about writer G.K. Chesterton, who carried on the tradition of British detective fiction with his popular Father Brown stories.

Neill may have been thinking of this particular film when he wrote of his involvement with the Sherlock Holmes series in 1946: "The sustained merit of these productions is due in a large measure to story situations and atmosphere. I feel that the atmosphere created provides fifty percent of the picture value." With this, the director turns up the fog to saturation levels, determined that the town of La Morte Rouge live up to its name; the place never seems to get any sunnier than the dark side of the moon. The characters are guarded and morose, speaking in hushed tones. Neill often closes scenes with an anguished close-up of a prospective suspect, with Rathbone's looped-in voice repeating an ominous line as if it were a portent of doom.

Kay Harding and Gerald Hamer in a publicity still for *The Scarlet Claw* (courtesy Dan Scapperotti).

The somewhat morbid subject matter of *The Scarlet Claw* sets it apart from the usual Sherlock Holmes confections. The film doesn't deal with the gentlemanly art of murder or some Moriarity-like mastermind of crime. Instead, the culprit seems to be not only an unredeemed psychopath, but a malignant presence that justifies his victim's premonitions of their own deaths. The unsavory tone edges the film closer to the sensibilities of *The Spiral Staircase* (1946) with all its psychopathic underpinnings than the typical Sherlock Holmes adventure. In fact, *The Scarlet Claw* succeeds less well as a mystery than as a thriller that bows to its horror elements. In this, Neill might have taken pride that the horror episodes are more genuinely chilling and are more imaginatively staged than those in any of the routine monster films that were currently shooting on the lot.

The "monster on the moors" scenes get the benefit from Neill's flavorful direction as well as John P. Fulton's ingenious photographic effects, as the phosphorescent creature darts amidst the twisted trees of the craggy landscape. But it is in the murder of Judge Brisson that Neill goes for the jugular, in more ways than one. Though not a drop of blood is shed on screen, the scene foreshadows the grisly "shock" moments of the *Psycho* spin-offs of the '60s. With Hans J. Salter's graveyard dirge from *Frankenstein Meets the Wolf Man* droning appropriately in the background, the director shoots the murderer, now disguised as the housekeeper, methodically pulling each window shade in the judge's study. (This is a cheat since it is obvious that actress Victoria Horne is on-camera for that particular shot.) The low-key photography catches the murderer slowly descending on the unsuspecting jurist, cutting to a startling silhouetted closeup of the killer posed with the claw-like garden tool, ready to strike. It's one of the most potent "sleeper" horror scenes of the '40s, buried as it is in a film usually classified as a mystery.

Horne offered the authors her recollections of making the film:

> The Sherlock Holmes pictures were a joy to do. It was like working in a stock company: All the actors knew each other and worked so well together. Mr. Hamer and I both shared that darkly lighted scene. I remember admiring the great strength of Basil Rathbone when he lifted me from the floor of the closet easily.

The Scarlet Claw is, predictably, top-heavy with red herrings, all smoothly played by familiar Holmes regulars. Paul Cavanagh is the icy Lord Penrose, who shows an unnatural disposition toward keeping his wife's murder unsolved. The excellent Miles Mander is the judge who fakes his own paralysis. Arthur Hohl plays Journet rather too stolidly and unsympathetically while Ian Wolfe is amusing as Cavanagh's slightly batty family retainer. The weakest link acting-wise is Kay (formerly Jackie Lou) Harding; as the doomed Marie, her bogus French accent is as awkward as her acting.

As the demented and rather inventive murderer, Gerald Hamer very probably got the best role of his career, playing a host of characters in different makeup and disguises. His best scene is shot in shadows, confronting Rathbone at gunpoint, which required him to employ a flat, unemotional reading of his lines so as not to rule out any of the other leading suspects. (The device doesn't especially work since it's clear that he's neither Cavanagh, Hohl, or any of the other suspects.) But the actor rises to the occasion, conveying a strain of undiluted evil with the chilling detachment of a full-fledged sociopath. While there's little room for psychoanalyzing in the relatively uncomplicated world of Sherlock Holmes, Hamer tells us all we need to know about the character's deteriorating mental condition in the starkest terms possible.

With *The Scarlet Claw*, Neill proved himself to be the most dependable and interesting of Universal's contract directors, but the studio seemed unwilling to relocate him from Baker Street. For the time being, his only break from the lucrative Holmes series was to helm one of the studio's Technicolor extravaganzas, *Gypsy Wildcat* (1944). A typically high-spirited Maria Montez romp, this improbable movie has the actress giving up her sarong for traditional gypsy garb, blissfully unaware that she's actually a long-lost countess. Nigel Bruce bravely troops through the proceedings in a supporting role.

Although often cited as the best in Universal's Sherlock Holmes series in film books and critical guides, *The Scarlet Claw*'s indebtedness to *The Hound of the Baskervilles* rarely goes unmentioned. However, a more direct similarity may be found in the little known *London by Night* (1937). A lightweight MGM whodunit with George Murphy and Virginia Field, the film features Leo G. Carroll as a murderer who adopts a long series of disguises. Among the characters is a whistling postman who carries the tune "British Grenadiers," which later turns up as a favorite of *Scarlet Claw*'s whistling postman Potts.

Critics' Corner

Rating: ★★★ Basil Rathbone and Nigel Bruce ... are exceptionally good ... and they are supported by a first-rate cast....—*The New York Daily News*, May 20, 1944, Kate Cameron

The Scarlet Claw makes much of Sir Arthur Conan Doyle's celebrated sleuth and puts a clown cap again on Doctor Watson.... When Holmes bores one and Watson is not even faintly amusing, it is high time to switch to something more substantial in the way of melodrama.... It is time, I think, that the whole cycle [the Holmes series] should be dropped.—*The New York Herald-Tribune*, May 20, 1944, Howard Barnes

[O]ne of the most intriguing, fastest-moving Sherlock Holmes features to date.... The story, again employing with marked success the background of fog and marshland so characteristic of the Sherlock Holmes tales, is exceptionally well conceived....—*The Hollywood Reporter*, April 24, 1944

Basil Rathbone plays Holmes with a rather tired approach.... Nigel Bruce, whose fine talents are rapidly being buried under the weight of this assignment, does almost nothing to enliven the proceedings.—*The New York Herald-Tribune*, May 20, 1944, Howard Barnes

[R]outine.... [A]nother in a series of mystery yarns so inferior to Conan Doyle's originals that it isn't even mentionable any more.—*The New York Times*, May 19, 1944, Bosley Crowther

The Invisible Man's Revenge

Released June 9, 1944. 77 minutes. *Producer-Director:* Ford Beebe. *Executive Producer:* Howard Benedict. *Suggested the novel* The Invisible Man *by* H.G. Wells. *Screenplay:* Bertram Millhauser. *Photog-*

raphy: Milton Krasner. *Special Photographic Effects:* John P. Fulton. *Editor:* Saul A. Goodkind. *Camera Operator:* Maury Gertsman. *Assistant Director:* Fred Frank. *Music Score & Director:* Hans J. Salter. *Art Directors:* John B. Goodman & Harold H. MacArthur. *Set Decorators:* Russell A. Gausman & Andrew J. Gilmore. *Sound Director:* Bernard B. Brown. *Technician:* William Hedgcock. *Property Master:* Eddie Keyes. *Gowns:* Vera West.

Jon Hall (*Robert Griffin*), Leon Errol (*Herbert Higgins*), John Carradine (*Dr. Peter Drury*), Alan Curtis (*Mark Foster*), Evelyn Ankers (*Julie Herrick*), Gale Sondergaard (*Lady Irene Herrick*), Lester Matthews (*Sir Jasper Herrick*), Halliwell Hobbes (*Cleghorn*), Leyland Hodgson (*Sir Frederick Travers*), Ian Wolfe (*Jim Feeney*), Billy Bevan (*Police Sergeant*), Doris Lloyd (*Maud*), Cyril Delevanti (*Malty Bill*), Skelton Knaggs (*Alf Parry*), Olaf Hytten (*Grey*), Leonard Carey (*Police Constable*), Yorke Sherwood (*Jim Yarrow*), Tom P. Dillon (*Ned Towle*), Guy Kingsford (*Bill*), Jim Aubrey (*Wedderburn*), Arthur Gould-Porter (*Tom Meadows*), Lillian Bronson (*Norma*), Janna DeLoos (*Nellie*), Ted Billings (*Pub Patron*), Beatrice Roberts (*Nurse*), Grey Shadow (*Brutus*).

[O]ne of the best and most entertaining of the series....
The Hollywood Reporter, *1944*

The least ambitious but hardly the least entertaining of Universal's widely varying series, *The Invisible Man's Revenge* boasts a direct, no-frills approach to its subject matter which is refreshing after the excesses of *The Invisible Woman* and *Invisible Agent*. While the film's attempt to capture the spirit of H.G. Wells seems half-hearted, at least it brings the action back to the author's home turf, the heart of the English countryside, while keeping its horror elements intact in the bargain. *The Invisible Man's Revenge* seems too small-scale to be anything but a standard genre piece, but there are enough off-kilter ingredients to keep it from being a strictly by-the-numbers programmer.

Just as blood had been the antidote that restored Vincent Price to visibility in the last moments of *The Invisible Man Returns*, that precious fluid performs a similar service here. Only the invisible protagonist this go-round happens to be a homicidal maniac who doesn't flinch at the prospect of draining men dry in order to obtain it. Bertram Millhauser's screenplay gleefully thumbs its nose at the Hollywood convention that, as in the original *The Invisible Man*, the audience needs as its major character a personality it can identify with. Millhauser offers a central figure that isn't a mere social dysfunctional anti-hero, but a full-fledged psychopath who doesn't summon forth a glimmer of audience sympathy. Unlike other Hollywood charm school psychos (such as Robert Montgomery in 1937's *Night Must Fall* and Joseph Cotten in 1943's *Shadow of a Doubt*), Griffin's instability is communicated at once and he rarely lets the viewer forget it (we first see him slashing his way out of a cargo delivery after escaping from a Capetown madhouse).

As was his custom, Ford Beebe invested his Universal horror films with exceptionally strong values and solid casts, but, in the case of *The Invisible Man's Revenge*, the producer-director failed to overcome the malaise that affects all late bloomers. Once-startling camera tricks — a cigarette puffing away in midair, a talking headless body, household objects darting about the room with a life of their own — fail to arouse the same sense of wonder as they had only a few movies before.

In shaping his screenplay, Millhauser tossed out a few of the plot contrivances established in the earlier films of the series. Following the example set by *The Invisible Woman* and *Invisible Agent*, Millhauser eliminated any reference to monocane (or duocane), thus eliminating the Invisible One's facility for total madness in the grip of the insidious drug. Instead, the screenwriter created in the story's antihero, Robert Griffin (no relation to the Griffins of the previous films), a character who doesn't require the degenerative effects of a serum to corrupt his personality. Griffin harbors none of the lofty pretenses of his invisible predecessors. He cares nothing about advancing scientific progress, and isn't seeking vindication for a crime he didn't commit. Nor is he interested in using his newly acquired powers to promote world peace. At first, Griffin isn't even tempted by the real possibility of world domination. His only (rather trivial goal) is to avenge himself on the titled British family whom he believes has done him wrong.

When Universal first announced its plan (on June 10, 1943) to produce another Invisible Man movie, it had hopes of obtaining the services of Claude Rains in the starring part. (It seems highly unlikely that the British actor would have accepted such a role at this stage of

Psychopathic killer Robert Griffin (Jon Hall), soon to become invisible and haunt his enemies in *The Invisible Man's Revenge.*

his film career.) When this plan failed, the studio drafted Jon Hall to play the part. Since his first appearance as a heroic transparent man, Hall had become firmly entrenched in Universal's campy Technicolored Maria Montez mini-epics, so portraying a homicidal invisible man was a real change of pace. Surprisingly, the nominally talented star brings to the part a healthy dose of melodramatic zest heretofore untapped in his screen career.

Harboring a persecution complex, "Rob" Griffin escapes from the psychopathic ward of a Capetown asylum (a newspaper clipping informs us that he's left behind a trail of murder and mayhem). After making his way to England. Griffin pays a surprise visit to his former friends and business partners, Sir Jasper Herrick (Lester Matthews) and his wife Irene (Gale Sondergaard). Griffin accuses the couple of trying to murder him while the trio was on safari in search of a diamond field in Tanganyika five years before. Although the Herricks are innocent (presumably), the ambiguous tone of Millhauser's dialogue in the stormy confrontation scene suggests otherwise. Matthews is the epitome of the pampered English aristocrat who lives comfortably off the fruits of his ancestors' labors. In her aloof, coolly sophisticated manner, Sondergaard can't help but exude wickedness. A line like, "Don't worry, Rob, you'll get all that's coming to you," carries a malevolent charge when spoken by the marvelously malicious Gale.

Accusing the couple of drugging him, Griffin is escorted off the estate. He seeks shelter in the home of a reclusive scientist, Dr. Peter Drury (John Carradine in a delightfully fruity performance). Introducing Griffin to his invisible pets, a parrot named Methuselah and a German shepherd called Brutus, the eccentric Drury states, "In this house, you've got to believe what you *can't* see!"

Drury explains that after years of tireless research, he has developed a formula capable of rendering any living creature transparent. More eccentric than mad, Drury is the sort of obsessive researcher so consumed by his own brilliance that he fails to notice that the "guinea pig" he has chosen for his first experiment with a human being is a certified sociopath. For Carradine, it is a subtle yet colorful part, in stark contrast to the by-the-numbers mad scientist roles the actor played in *Captive Wild Woman* and *Revenge of the Zombies* (1943). Except for a single, cliché-packed outburst in which the actor really lets it rip ("I've outstripped the immortals of science..."), he generally doesn't stray from his relatively low-keyed, almost folksy mode in the manner of an English country doctor. It's an interesting take on the usual out-of-control Hollywood stereotype.

The Invisible Man's Revenge contains few of the elaborate effects that distinguished the earlier Wells adaptations. As in *Invisible Agent*, several effects sequences (particularly those shots of Hall walking around *sans* head and hands) have a careless, slapdash quality. Still, John P. Fulton pulls off a few startlingly effective tricks: A beautifully composed shot of Hall dashing down a corridor as his hands and face rapidly fade from sight, a chilling bit wherein the actor dips his invisible hand into an aquarium and dabs water on his invisible face, creating a ghostly visage that frightens Sondergaard into hysterics, and the always-fascinating effect in which the Invisible Man removes his goggles, thus allowing the audience to see clear through to the inside-back of his gauze-wrapped head.

An undeveloped element of the story deals with Griffin's passion for the Herricks' daughter, Julie (Evelyn Ankers). Though he has never encountered her in the flesh, Griffin falls in love with the willowy girl strictly on the basis of seeing her photograph (shades of Otto Preminger's *Laura*). Realizing he doesn't stand a ghost of a chance of winning Julie away from her present beau, newspaperman Mark Foster (Alan Curtis), in his present translucent state, the determined suitor returns to Drury's lab and demands to be changed back to his normal self again.

At this point in the story, Millhauser's most interesting deviation from the Wells classic, the "vampire" gimmick, is introduced. Drury informs his rebellious creation that the only way in which he may attain a *temporary* state of visibility is through an infusion of all the blood from another human being. How he's supposed to store all this excess fluid in his body is a trifling detail Millhauser doesn't bother to address (individual blood types are seldom a matter of great concern to movie monsters, neither). In *The Invisible Man Returns*, Lester Cole and Curt Siodmak introduced the idea of a blood transfusion being instrumental in bringing Geoffrey Radcliffe (Vincent Price) back to visibility, but in that case, he had already lost a great deal of blood due to a bullet wound, so the idea is more acceptable. Also, in Radcliffe's case, we are to assume the "cure" is permanent.

When Drury foils Griffin's plot to trick Mark Foster into becoming an unwilling blood donor, the Invisible Man knocks the scientist out cold and drains him dry. Griffin sets the

The Invisible Man (in invisible clothes, and wielding an invisible gun!) threatens Alan Curtis and Evelyn Ankers in a fun but foolish staged shot.

house ablaze and beats a path to the Herrick estate Drury's as now-visible dog Brutus trails him.

Using an assumed name, Griffin worms his way into Julie's good graces and, during breakfast, he gives one of those repetitious power trip speeches about how ego-boosting it must be to be invisible — until his features begin to fade away. The exciting climax takes place in the wine cellar where Griffin has successfully lured Mark, beaten him unconscious, and prepared him for a massive blood transfusion. Midway through the procedure, Drury's vengeful dog claws his way into the wine cellar, attacks Griffin, and mauls him to death.

Although the final cut of *The Invisible Man's Revenge* leaves no doubt that Robert Griffin is bonkers ("A man fighting shadows," is how one character describes him), there *does* exist hard evidence that indicates he might not have been so far out in left field in regards to the motives of his "old friends," Jasper and Irene. At least one scene still released by the publicity department features Griffin lying unconscious on a river bank as the Herricks hover over him. (In the film, we only see Jasper dragging Griffin off the premises; later, he regains consciousness and stumbles into the water). It is quite possible that a different version of the script held the Herricks accountable for Griffin's "accident" in Africa and for his near-fatal plunge into the river.

According to the pressbook synopsis, the story opens in Africa where Griffin discovers a diamond field. Shortly afterward, he is injured by a falling tree branch. The Herricks leave him to die, hurrying off to register the claim in their name. A native comes to Griffin's rescue. As a result of the blow from the branch, he can remember nothing. From there, the story picks up five years later, with Griffin's memory fully restored. Presumably, the person who wrote the synopsis worked with a script or perhaps a cut of the movie the public never saw. A last-minute rewrite may have exonerated the Herricks, if only to save their daughter the indignity of having two such unsympathetic parents in the finale.

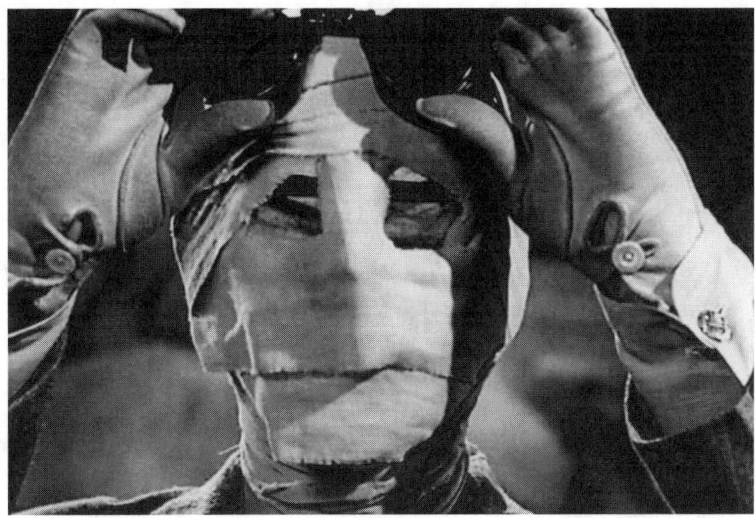

One of John P. Fulton's most startling special effects.

Prior to the first day of shooting on *The Invisible Man's Revenge*, Universal's attorneys struck a deal with H.G. Wells for the rights to make two more Invisible Man sequels between July 1943, and October 1951, remunerating the author with a sum of $7,500. In a letter dated December 14, 1943, the Breen Office notified Maurice Pivar that Millhauser's screenplay needed the usual amount of revisions, including a hold on all excessive gruesomeness, deletion of the offensive word "shyster," and one or two changes in dialogue. (Julie's line "He says the chambermaids are so obliging" was deemed unacceptable.)

Actual production on *The Invisible Man's Revenge* began on January 10, 1944, and continued for five weeks and three days, wrapping in mid-February with John P. Fulton taking over to complete the special effects sequences. Pollard Lake on the Universal back lot was used in some of the outdoor shots with the exterior of the Hacienda set doubling for the Herrick estate, Shortlands. Soundstage 17 became the Herrick wine cellar and saw extra duty when Fulton's effects crew took over on the 17th of February.

Character player-second lead Edgar Barrier was lined up for a key role in *The Invisible Man's Revenge* (probably that of Sir Jasper), but bowed out on January 6, four days before the start of production. Barrier, who had important roles in *Phantom of the Opera* and *Cobra Woman* (1944), had grown disenchanted with the kind of roles the studio was offering him and requested an amicable discharge. On a happier note, Universal retained the services of five-year-old German shepherd Grey Shadow, great-grandson of the silent-picture canine luminary, Strongheart, to play Dr. Drury's faithful dog.

Unquestionably, the weakest aspect of *The Invisible Man's Revenge* is comic relief Leon Errol's village shoe mender-turned-petty blackmailer. As Hall's cohort, Errol offers some mild amusement but his role consumes too much screen time and detracts from the horror element. (Millhauser very likely modeled this character on the tramp Marvel from the H.G. Wells novel.) Errol's Herbert Higgins is reminiscent of the Cowardly Lion from *The Wizard of Oz* (1939), blustery on the outside but a shivering heap within. The comic's seemingly endless dart-throwing match at the Running Nag Inn* (with the invisible Griffin piloting the darts to the bull's-eye) stops the plot's action dead in its tracks. A vaudeville and Broadway headliner for over 40 years, Australian-born Errol broke into films in 1924 and achieved modest fame as the star of countless two-reel comedies and a running

**This scene is brilliantly sent up in a bawdy comedy skit entitled "Son of the Invisible Man," which was included in the cult classic* Amazon Women on the Moon *(1987). Ed Begley, Jr., plays a delusional Griffin relative who* thinks *he's found the secret of achieving invisibility. The last time we see him, he's prancing about a village pub stark naked, driving darts into the bull's-eye of a dartboard before a chagrined crowd.*

part as Lord Epping in RKO's Mexican Spitfire series with Lupe Velez. He died in 1951 at the age of 70.

Throughout his prolific career, John Carradine felt nothing but contempt for the horror films that put food on his table, financed his Shakespearean company, and helped him pay his alimony. On one occasion, a writer for the British fanzine, *House of Hammer*, caught up with the aging actor at a London hotel and asked him if he liked *any* of the horror films he claimed to loathe. Carradine thought for awhile and then said that he had enjoyed *The Invisible Man's Revenge*. He had fun making the picture and clearly tended to remember and like those films where this had been the case. Carradine and Jon Hall were sailing buddies at one time and had already acted together in John Ford's *The Hurricane* (1937), as brutal jailer and Polynesian prisoner, respectively.

While it's hardly in the same league as *The Invisible Man*, nor *The Invisible Man Returns*, for that matter, *The Invisible Man's Revenge* is a distinct improvement over Universal's previous two bastardizations of the H.G. Wells character, from a horrific point of view at least. Enjoyable performances, smart dialogue and a high caliber B look give this Ford Beebe production that touch of class which many of its contemporaries lack.

Critics' Corner

[This] has a complicated plot, the usual occult physical mumbo-jumbo and more than one touch of violence. For all of that, it is singularly unexciting.... John Fulton's special photography is the most striking aspect of the picture [but] the tricks have been done too often before by the camera to make them particularly effective by themselves.—*The New York Herald-Tribune*, June 10, 1944, Howard Barnes

A fairly good program melodrama.... It has been produced well and has enough novelty, excitement and even comedy to satisfy melodrama-loving audiences.—*Harrison's Reports*, 1944

Some of the earlier variations of H.G. Wells' invisible man idea were filmed with an idea that the story should make good sense. That policy has been abandoned this time.... Jon Hall in his invisibility is [a] much more effective actor than he has been in some of his recent adventures in gaudy Technicolor.—*The New York World-Telegram*, June 1944

A mild exercise in trick photography.... [J]ust plain old-fashioned ham.—*The New York Times*, June 10, 1944, Bosley Crowther

Rating: ★★½ By now, the frightening creature ... is no novelty. Like most seconds, *The Invisible Man's Revenge* is not the stimulating thriller that *The Invisible Man* was. It's just an average thriller....—*The New York Daily News*, June 10, 1944, Wanda Hale

Ghost Catchers

Released June 16, 1944. 67 minutes. *Executive Producer:* Milton Feld; *Writer-Producer:* Edmund L. Hartmann. *Director:* Eddie Cline. *Based on the story* "High Spirits" *by* Milt Gross & Eddie Cline. *Photography:* Charles Van Enger. *Music Director:* Edward Ward. *Musical Numbers Devised & Staged by* Louis DePron. *Songs:* "Blue Candlelight," "Three Cheers for the Customer," "Quoth the Raven" (by Paul F. Webster & Harry Revel), "I'm Old Enough to Dream" (by Everett Carter & Edward Ward). *Art Directors:* John B. Goodman & Richard H. Riedel. *Director of Sound:* Bernard B. Brown. *Technician:* Joe Lapis. *Recorder:* Ralph Brown. *Set Decorators:* Russell A. Gausman & A.J. Gilmore. *Editor:* Arthur Hilton. *Gowns:* Vera West. *Assistant Director:* Howard Christie. *Special Photography:* John P. Fulton. *Special Effects:* Carl Lee & Eddie Robinson. *Assistant Directors:* Howard Christie & Judson Cox. *Dialogue Director:* Stacy Keach. *Assistant Camera:* Arthur Gerstle. *Camera Operator:* Harold I. Smith. *Gaffer:* Ross Saxon. *Stills:* Sherman Clark. *Painter:* W.A. Graham. *Props:* Bill Tapp & Harry Gunstrom. *Wardrobe Woman:* Olive Koenitz. *Wardrobe Man:* Albert Deano. *Boom Operator:* Jack Bolger. *Makeup:* Eddie Zimmer. *Hairdresser:* Emmy Eckhardt. *Script Supervisor:* Dorothy Hughes. *Grip:* Fred Buckley. *Best Boy:* Bill Harmon. *Cable:* Ernie Pierson. *Construction Foreman:* Lloyd Merrill. *Production Secretary:* Bee Edlund.

Ole Olsen (*Himself*), Chic Johnson (*Himself*), Gloria Jean (*Melinda Marshall*), Martha O'Driscoll (*Susanna Marshall*), Leo Carrillo (*Jerry*), Andy Devine (*Horsehead*), Lon Chaney, Jr. (*Bear*), Kirby Grant (*Clay Edwards*), Walter Catlett (*Col. Breckinridge Marshall*), Ella Mae Morse (*Virginia Bennett*), Morton Downey (*Himself*), Henry Armetta (*Signatelli*), Walter Kingsford (*Chambers*), Tom Dugan (*Bricklayer*), Edgar Dearing (*Police Sergeant*), Ralph Peters, Wee Willie Davis, Frank Mitchell, Sammy Stein, Tor Johnson, Joe Kirk (*Mugs*), Mel Torme (*Drummer*), Leonard Sues (*Trumpet Player*), Al Mirkin, Harry Monty, Billy Curtis (*Midgets*), Mary Louise Houk, Marie E. Wagner, Cornelia Bona, Miriam R. Lickert (*Four Harpists*), Christine Forsyth (*Tired Blonde*), Armando & Lita (*Specialty Act*), Barbara Blain, Bill Alcorn, Genevieve Grazis, John Duncan, Venna Archer, Jack Archer, Betty Story, Don L. Gallaher, June Williams, Jerry Warren, Jean Davis, Bobby Scheerer, Bill Raymond, Joy Vahl, Betty Marie, Tim Taylor, Sheila Roberts, Gil Dennis, Patti Lacey, Nancy Marlowe, Jack Arkin, Jean Marlowe, Mike Termini, Lennie Smith, Marion Musso, Nickie Reed, Alice Scott, Barbara Hall, Mike Musso, Walter Lee

Doerr, Laurie Sherman (*Jitterbugs*), Jack Norton (*Wilbur Duffington*), Larry Steers (*Man*), Ken Broeker, Perc Launders (*Cops*), Bess Flowers (*Woman in Nightclub*), Forrest Taylor (*Passerby*), Alec Craig (*Diggs*), Edward Earle (*Ticket Seller*), Larry Steers, Buddy Wilkerson, Carey Harrison, Lee Bennett (*Men*), Cyril Ring (*Man in Tuxedo*), Isabelle LaMal (*Woman*), Belle Mitchell (*Mrs. Signatelli*), Robin Raymond (*Gag Specialty*), Kay Harding (*Girl*), Irene Thomas, June Horne, Eleanor Welz, Sarah Swartz, Mary Jane Hodge, Luce Potter.

If you can laugh convincingly [at your own jokes], you'll fool the public into thinking that what you've said is really funny.
— *Chic Johnson, 1944*

Ghost Catchers is a conglomeration of everything that Universal thought was necessary in a haunted house comedy. In the style of their moneymaking *Hold That Ghost*, they included a ghost, a murder, a body in a closet, gangsters, even the same cartoon (behind the opening credits) as in *Hold That Ghost*. So far, so good.

Then, to provide the laughs, Olsen and Johnson. And it all went to Hell in a handbasket.

Ole Olsen and Chic Johnson were vaudeville buffoons who teamed in 1914 and enjoyed a long career on stage, in radio and (sporadically) in Hollywood films. They were never a hit with critics, but their bizarre antics caught the fancy of some audiences, especially in the sticks, and the two men remained a team with never a thought of splitting, right up until Johnson's death in 1962.

It's hard to knock a comedy duo that collaborated *that* long and *that* successfully, and starred in one of Broadway's longest-running shows ("Hellzapoppin'")—but we're sure gonna try. To the innocent, uninitiated viewer who stumbles upon *Ghost Catchers*, the Olsen and Johnson shtick can be a painful thing to behold. Their forte was wild sight gags, hoary jokes and puns and what film historian Leonard Maltin lovingly calls "a flair for the ridiculous that has never been duplicated." Time, however, has passed them by: There's no longer any humor in seeing these loudmouths cavorting in women's clothes or zoot suits, no pleasure left in the dreamworld plots left over from their vaudeville pastiches. Fans of Olsen and Johnson complain about the big band musical numbers and romantic subplots which bog down some of their pictures, but others may find these added elements a welcome respite from O&J. Universal lost interest in them after their fourth film for the studio (1945's *See My Lawyer*) and sent them packing. They never worked in pictures again.

In *Ghost Catchers*, Col. Marshall (Walter Catlett), a pauper still posing as the moneyed Southern gentleman he once was, brings his daughters Melinda (Gloria Jean) and Susanna (Martha O'Driscoll) to New York to make their Carnegie Hall concert debut. The trio moves into a candlelit Manhattan brownstone which Chambers (Walter Kingsford), the lawyer who leased them the property, and Diggs (Alec Craig), the cleaning man, have failed to mention is haunted. When strange nocturnal noises awaken the Marshalls, Susanna runs next door to find help.

The neighboring house, unfortunately for her (and for us), is the Olsen and Johnson nightclub, a three-ring madhouse. Susanna is seized by headwaiter Jerry (Leo Carrillo) and other stooges, strapped into an "electric chair" and forced to watch the "fun": Acrobats fling themselves and each other around, Olsen throws knives at Johnson (who's in drag), the chefs parade through the dining area, and songstress Virginia Bennett (Ella Mae Morse) belts out "Three Cheers for the Customer." Susanna has been dropped through a trap door before O&J realize that the girl may have been in real trouble; once they do, they hurry next door to investigate.

Grateful for company—even Olsen and Johnson's—the Marshalls offer to put them up for the night, and Ole and Chic retire to their room. They are undressed by invisible hands and spun like tops by a supernatural force which now dresses them in pajamas; neither one of them realizes that anything unusual is happening until they're both in bed, at which point they sit up and scream. Tee-hee.

Col. Marshall wants to break the lease and move out but Chambers insists that he live up to their signed agreement. Chambers reveals that the ghost is that of Wilbur Duffington, a millionaire who plummeted from a third-story window during a turn-of-the-century New Year's Eve bash; Wilbur now haunts the house because he never got to enjoy his own party. Olsen and

Johnson hope to satisfy and exorcise Wilbur's ghost by throwing a new party with Wilbur as the guest of honor. The festivities degenerate into the usual Olsen and Johnson brawl with raucous music and jitterbugs dancing up and down the stairs and through the entire house. Toting a white flag, the invisible Wilbur pinches Melinda's behind and leaves. Ho, ho, ho.

Susanna is sweet on bandleader Clay Edwards (Kirby Grant), but bitchy Virginia is also attached to him and won't let go. Even though the house has been exorcised, Melinda and the colonel are seized and abducted in a mysterious fashion, and Susanna finds the body of the cleaning man in a closet. Olsen and Johnson investigate and find a bizarre assortment of idiots overrunning the house: Midgets in Santa Claus costumes, a guy wearing a horse costume (Andy Devine), another one dressed as a bear (Lon Chaney, Jr.), and a motley collection of gangster-types. It turns out that there's a secret cellar full of valuable pre–Prohibition era liquor and, this being an Olsen & Johnson movie, these crooks have decided that *this* (buying costumes, hiring midgets, etc.) is the way to scare away the Marshalls and steal the hootch. Olsen and Johnson, mistaken for gangsters, are ordered to help move the stuff out, but eventually the real gangsters catch on and a chase ensues. Olsen (or Johnson, who gives a damn?) puts on Devine's horsehead and pretends to be dead while the other jerk kneels over him, bemoaning the death of his horse; the assembled gangsters actually start crying as they watch this scene. O&J are almost able to get away using this ruse, but then one of the brighter gangsters finally catches on ("Wait a minute — he ain't no horse!"). Ha ha ha.

Chic and Ole are caught and walled up, "Cask of Amontillado"–style, together with Melinda and the colonel. Luckily the ghost of Wilbur (Jack Norton) appears and gives them the idea to break through a wall into the basement of their own next-door nightclub. Johnson (or Olsen, who gives a damn?) just happens to have the necessary tools on his person, and they makes their escape. After a series of chases and brawls, the gangsters are apprehended along with their secret leader, who turns out to be Jerry, O&J's headwaiter. The Melinda-Susanna Carnegie Hall concert is cancelled because only one ticket was sold, so they put on their show at the O&J nightclub and are a hit.

Olsen and Johnson buffs give *Ghost Catchers* high marks; Leonard Maltin, clearly a fan, wrote that it comes closer to O&J's original conception of insane humor than any of their other movies. But in the new millennium, even the most open-minded newcomer to the film will probably have trouble finding the qualities that made the comedians such favorites. It doesn't matter *how* hard Chic and Ole laugh at their own jokes, they're still not funny; and it's madness without humor to see them (for example) needlessly blow up a wall in order to enter a lawyer's office, or to watch one pulling a pick, an ax and a jackhammer out of his pockets. There's no rhyme or reason, just a couple of hollering old men acting like eight-year-olds, doing and saying things so unfunny as to seem like desperation-time ad libs.

An appalled Reginald LeBorg, a second-unit director on the first Universal O&J *Hellzapoppin'* (1941), told the authors:

> They weren't funny. They were not as good as Abbott and Costello, they were not even as good as the Bowery Boys — at least the Bowery Boys had some élan, and there was some characterization! These guys were like the Three Stooges, they were just stupid.

Different strokes for different folks: "Olsen and Johnson were *delightful*," Gloria Jean told the authors. "Both of those men were *so* nice, and very funny. Just the best!"

Not according to *Ghost Catchers*' writer-producer Edmund L. Hartmann. He told *Filmfax* interviewer Robert Nott:

> Olsen and Johnson had gotten too old by the time I worked with them. They had been a big hit on Broadway with "Hellzapoppin'," and were at their best in that. But [by 1944] the camera picked up the fact that these were two old men. Chic Johnson, a wonderful guy, had false teeth. He had nine pairs and not one fitted him! ... We'd be making a picture, and he would work his teeth out of his mouth with his tongue in the middle of a shot! Sometimes he would even take his teeth out and gesture with them! You'd have to throw it out and shoot it again.
>
> The first picture I did with them was *Ghost Catchers*. We took it for a preview and the theater was jammed. I think the audience thought they were going to see an Abbott and Costello film.

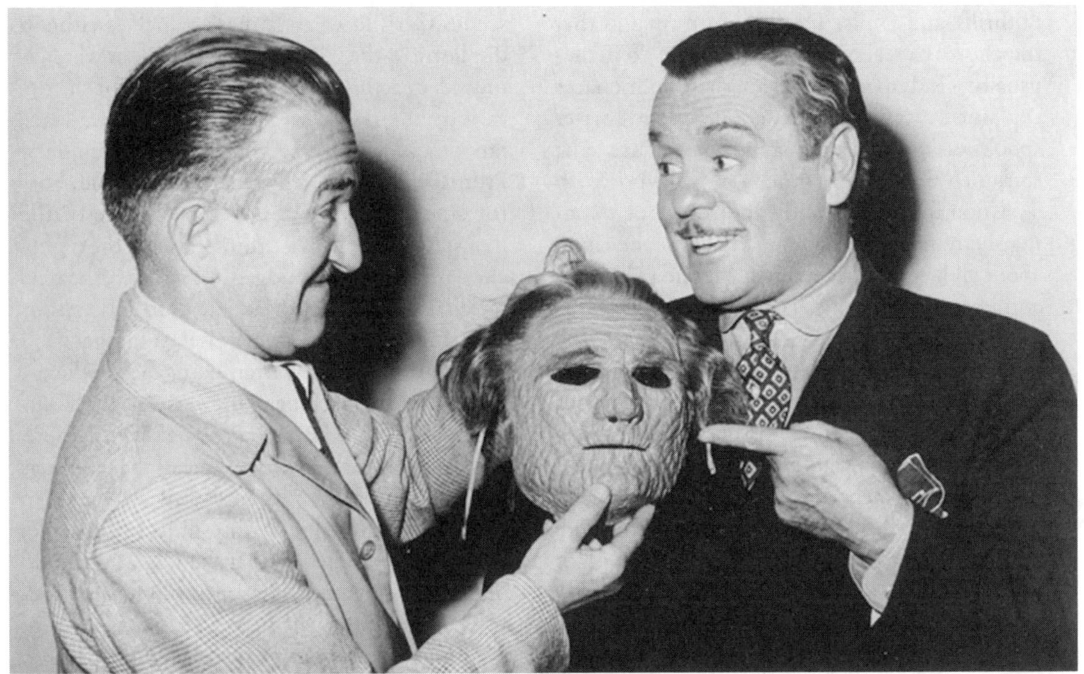

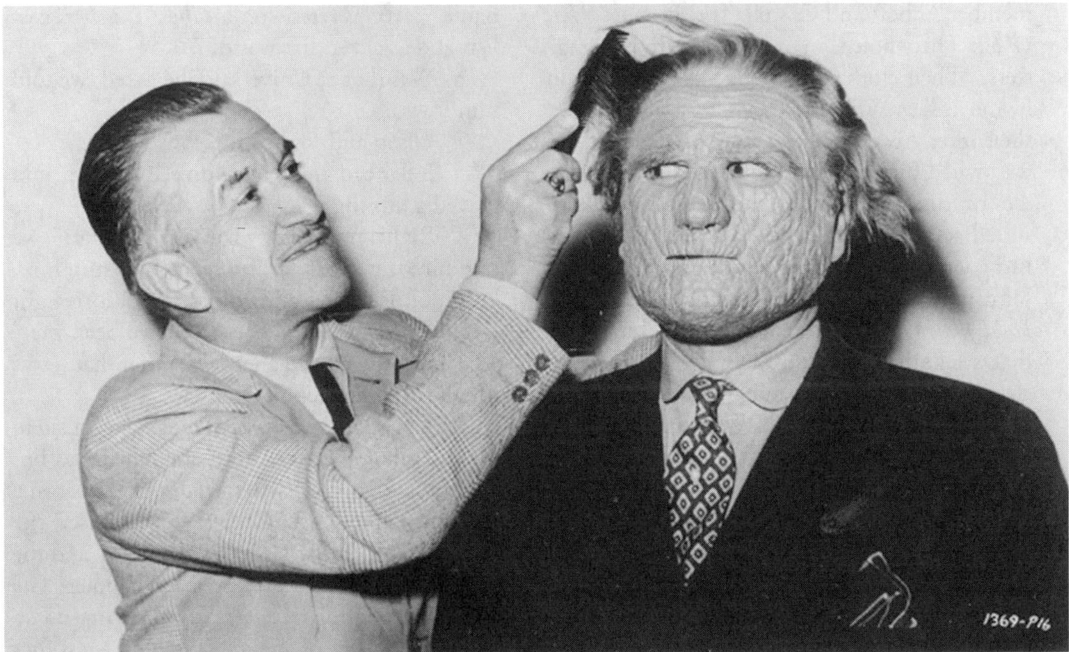

Jack Pierce applies a Kharis mask to *Ghost Catchers* supporting player Leo Carrillo in these backstage shots (courtesy Bob Burns).

The titles read "Universal Presents — Olsen and Johnson in *Ghost Catchers*," and before the titles were over, half the audience was in the aisle, leaving. They didn't even wait for the first sequence. That was sad, because they were decent gentlemen. It was just that their best years were behind them.

Ghost Catchers comes up short in the comedy department, and falls even flatter in the area of thrills-and-chills. The film is unusual in that the ghost is a real one (haunted house comedies usually wind up with the supernatural menaces explained away), but this is one of the sorrier spooks ever to turn up in a motion picture. The spirit of Wilbur Duffington, a silly playboy with a passion for plum brandy and soft-shoe dancing, he remains invisible nearly all of the time; about all he ever does is pinch Melinda's bottom and leave senseless messages on the walls. Simple special effects (floating props) indicate the apparition's unseen presence throughout most of the film, although toward the end he does make a brief appearance in the person of Jack Norton, the actor who made a one-note career out of playing inebriates. Wilbur is never scary, just a nuisance; the film's one killing is committed by the "gangster-ghosts," and it takes place off-screen.

One of the few fun moments comes early on, as Olsen and Johnson are preparing for bed in the haunted brownstone. Olsen asks, "Remember Abbott and Costella [*sic*] in *Hold That Ghost*? The whole thing turned out to be gangsters." Their clothes are being yanked off them by the unseen Wilbur as they talk casually about the earlier A&C film and how preposterous it was; when Bud and Lou's famous "moving candle" routine is mentioned, their candle begins to slide back and forth across a table. The scene isn't good, and isn't funny, but hearing Olsen and Johnson discussing Abbott and Costel*la* and *Hold That Ghost* makes for an unusual moment that sticks in the mind after everything else about *Ghost Catchers* has faded. (O&J also mention A&C in their 1943 Universal comedy *Crazy House*.)

A good supporting cast is squandered. Gloria Jean and Martha O'Driscoll are pleasant and easy on the eyes, and up-and-coming Kirby Grant, who plays the romantic interest, is agreeable but has nothing to do in the film. Andy Devine and Lon Chaney are utterly wasted (Chaney plays his small role straight, despite the ignominy of a bear costume, while Devine plays his usual dolt). Leo Carrillo, who is seen as Olsen and Johnson's headwaiter, doesn't get much more than a minute's worth of footage in the entire film; it never crosses your mind that he might be the mystery villain because you've forgotten that he's even in the picture! In his "monster" scenes Carrillo wears a mask which is either a duplicate of the Chaney Kharis mask or which is indeed an actual Kharis mask, cut up for the occasion; one reviewer, apparently a Dick Tracy fan, described him as "a frightening facsimile of Pruneface." Also briefly seen: Tor Johnson, horror star of '50s low-budgeters, as one of the mugs; Mel Torme as a drum player in the nightclub orchestra; and midget Luce Potter, the tentacled, disembodied Martian head in *Invaders from Mars* (1953), as (what else?) a midget.

The late Jerry Warren, later the producer-director of such schlocky films as *Teenage Zombies* and *The Incredible Petrified World* (both 1957), also appears briefly, as one of the jitterbugs ... or does he? When we interviewed Warren in 1984, he was touchy on the subject of his age; he wanted us to believe that he was 21 years old in the mid-50s when he turned out his first picture, *Man Beast*. But he made the mistake of telling us that he had played some bit parts "a short time" prior to that. We had spotted the name "Jerry Warren" on a *Ghost Catchers* cast list, and asked if that was him.

"Was that at Universal?" he asked; we told him it was.

"Olsen and Johnson, right?"; right.

"I danced in that, didn't I?"; yeah, you played a jitterbug.

"Right, right! Say, what year was that?"; we told him it was 1944. *That* seemed to stun him; he shook his head and told us with a straight face, "Then, no, that couldn't have been me." The interview moved ahead, but after that it was tough for *us* to keep straight faces.

Diana Barrymore was originally pencilled in for the role of Susanna, but she felt it was beneath the dignity of a Barrymore to appear in a burlesque like *Ghost Catchers* and refused the role. This killed her Universal contract, and the studio probably couldn't have been happier: The effects of alcohol were already showing up so badly on the face of the 23-year-old actress that even makeup failed to hide it.

Ghost Catchers began production (under the title *High Spirits*) on February 22, 1944, and wrapped at the end of March after 32 days of filming. (According to Universal expert Michael Fitzgerald, several musical numbers were filmed and later cut from the picture, which would at least partially explain the longish schedule.) At 67 minutes it's no longer than the average Universal quickie, although director Eddie Cline, a former Keystone Cop whose best days were also behind *him*, manages at least to make it *seem* longer.

In the twenty-first century, *Ghost Catchers* is the kind of movie that you'd be embarrassed to have someone walk in and catch you watching — but watch it we Universal devotees must, at least once, because it's a Universal "haunted house" movie, and because it features Lon Chaney, Jr. "Lon was quite a cut-up — he was always kidding people, and playing tricks on them," Gloria Jean told the authors. She and Chaney, Jr., later appeared together in another movie, a 1950 Monogram musical comedy called *There's a Girl in My Heart.* "They had a big party after that movie was over, and my sister Bonnie was there. Lon Chaney took Bonnie's shoe and filled it with champagne and drank ... and then threw it up in the rafters! He was *that* kind of a man. We never got over that!"

"I was only 15 years old at the time but I remember it as if it was last night," says Bonnie Schoonover, Gloria's sister. "Lon Chaney was a real goofball. After he finished with my shoe, he flung it up on the catwalk and a prop man had to go up and get it for me. We had lots of fun at that party. Everyone was drunk and especially Lon Chaney!"

"Lon kidded us about [the shoe incident] for a long time afterwards," Gloria adds. "I liked him. He was a lot of fun, and he worked very hard." He wasn't too much of a pain in the neck, with his drinking and pranks and all?, we asked.

"Well, don't forget," Gloria says with a laugh, "I also worked with W.C. Fields!"

* * *

Chic Johnson died in 1962 and was buried in Las Vegas. When Ole Olsen died 11 months later, the plan was to bury him alongside Johnson. Bob May, Johnson's grandson (and the Robot on TV's *Lost in Space*), told the authors:

> But the only plot that was open was on the right side of my grandfather and the plaques would have read JOHNSON and OLSEN, which would have been wrong. So I went down to Palms Mortuary in Las Vegas and I had to witness that they opened up the crypt my grandfather was in, and moved him *over*, so Ole could be buried on the *left* side of him, so it would read OLSEN and JOHNSON.

Now, *that's* funny!

Critics' Corner

It's getting so when you see an Olsen and Johnson picture you have the feeling that you've seen all this before, more than once, and didn't like it very much the first few times.... The confusion, as the plot stumbles on, defies description. Olsen and Johnson, who aim to be a couple of funny fellows, miss their goal by a mile.—*The Brooklyn Daily Eagle*, 1944

If you giggle right off at lunacies and you're strong for absurd slapstick, you're apt to find the business amusing. There's not an iota of sense in the whole pictorial package.—*The New York Post*, Irene Thirer, May 31, 1944

The comedy is rough-and-tumble, the laughs frequent. Nothing makes any sense; but then no one is trying to make any sense. The whole picture is like a Coney Island funhouse translated into movie farce.—*The New York Sun,* May 31, 1944

[A] tedious lot of hocus-pocus.... Since *Hellzapoppin'* of a few years back the boys have become less and less funny in successive appearances on the screen, according to this department's laugh meter.—*The New York Times*, May 31, 1944, Thomas M. Pryor

The Olsen and Johnson technique of slapping one gag onto another until customer resistance wears thin would seem about right for the haunted house routine if a minimum of sanity were maintained for contrast. As it is, the difference between ghosts in bear suits and horse heads flitting through walls and tapping to "Swanee River" and Olsen and Johnson making their way out of tight spots by donning magicians' garb and causing the proper tools to materialize, is scarcely perceptible.... Seen at Loew's Criteron theatre in New York where a sparse, early morning audience was slow to catch the spirit.—*The Motion Picture Herald*, June 3, 1944, E.A. Cunningham

Olsen and Johnson seem to have learned after two unfettered film flights ... that not even such bounding genius as theirs can only endure without rhyme, reason and a certain attention to production. Hence, *Ghost Catchers* has all these, as well as a characteristic portion of the irrepressible and unpredictable Olsen and Johnson fun-making.—*PM New York*, May 31, 1944, John T. McManus

The slapstick is laid on with a heavy hand, as visual gags of the most obvious type are substituted for clever lines and situations.... At best, it's just a streamlined custard pie comedy.—*The New York Herald-Tribune*, May 30, 1944, Otis L. Guernsey, Jr.

Jungle Woman

Released July 7, 1944. 60 minutes. *Associate Producer:* Will Cowan. *Executive Producer:* Ben Pivar. *Director:* Reginald LeBorg. *Screenplay:* Bernard L. Schubert, Henry Sucher & Edward Dein. *Original Story:* Henry Sucher. *Photography:* Jack Mackenzie. *Musical Director:* Paul Sawtell. *Art Directors:* John B. Goodman & Abraham Grossman. *Editor:* Ray Snyder. *Set Decorators:* Russell A. Gausman & Edward R. Robinson. *Dialogue Director:* Emory Horger. *Director of Sound:* Bernard B. Brown. *Technician:* Jess Moulin. *Makeup:* Jack P. Pierce. *Assistant Director:* Melville Shyer. *Camera Operator:* Dick Towers. *Special Effects:* Red Guthrie. *Properties:* Dan Fish. *Gowns:* Vera West.

Evelyn Ankers (*Beth Mason*), J. Carrol Naish (*Dr. Carl Fletcher*), Acquanetta (*Paula Dupree*), Samuel S. Hinds (*Coroner*), Lois Collier (*Joan Fletcher*), Milburn Stone (*Fred Mason*), Douglass Dumbrille (*District Attorney*), Richard Davis (*Bob Whitney*), Edward M. Hyans, Jr. (*Willie*), Christian Rub (*George*), Pierre Watkin (*Dr. Meredith*), Nana Bryant (*Miss Gray*), Alec Craig (*Morgue Attendant*), Richard Powers [Tom Keene] (*Joe*), Heinie Conklin, Nolan Leary, Charles Marsh, Edward Clark, Diane Carroll, Beatrice Roberts, Kernan Cripps (*Members of the Jury*), Wilson Benge (*Court Stenographer*).

Aw-w-w, it's a *gyp*!
—*Edward M. Hyans, Jr., in* Jungle Woman

The Universal horror mill was in full bloom in 1944, churning out thrillers at a furious rate but with increasing indifference to quality. With creativity at a comparatively low ebb, the studio was content to merely to add chapter upon chapter to its established monster series rather than developing original material; even the lavishly produced Technicolor bauble, *The Climax*, was merely a warmed-over version of *Phantom of the Opera*. *Captive Wild Woman*'s formula, combining sex-appeal with tepid thrills, though in questionable taste, had sufficient box office legs that a follow-up seemed like a sound venture.

With programmer stalwart Ben Pivar now promoted to the lofty title executive producer, Will Cowan assumed associate producer duties on the project, which was initially titled *Jungle Queen*. The Scottish-born, former song-and-dance man had been with the studio for a few years, producing musical shorts such as *South Sea Rhythms* and *Dancing on the Stars* (both 1943). Finally elevated into the ranks of feature film producers, Cowan would remain at the studio as house producer for minor projects well into the next decade.

The film's production had a shaky start, in no small measure due to the Breen Office which cited Edward Dein's script as being "unacceptable under the provisions of the Production Code by reason of a flavor of bestiality." A conference between the Breen Office, Cowan and Maurice Pivar was set up to tone down the lurid implications of the screenplay in addition to making other modifications. The character of the District Attorney (played in the film by Douglass Dumbrille) was altered so as not to appear undignified or unsympathetic. Also, the script had to make it plain that the Paula Dupree character wasn't naked when changing from her animal to human form. In a letter dated February 8, 1944, Breen accepted the changes in the script (now titled *Jungle Woman*), although the censors stressed that great restraint must be exercised in suggesting that Paula is in love with the leading man.

Despite the romantic restrictions placed on the film, shooting began on Valentine's Day 1944 at Pollard Lake for a day of pre-production with Acquanetta. J. Carrol Naish, who barely had enough time to recover from a typical mad scientist role in the middling PRC cheapie *The Monster Maker*, was signed on to play a far more benevolent disciple of science. The versatile character actor was slumming between Academy Award-nominated performances in *Sahara* (1943) and *A Medal for Benny* (1945). This latest indignity had, at least, a mercifully brief shooting schedule. Milburn Stone and Evelyn Ankers, both still under contract, slid back into their old roles as did Acquanetta, whose frail talents were now challenged by the considerably beefed-up part of Paula, the Ape Woman.

In the opening scene, a dim figure of a man is seen prowling the wooded grounds of a private sanitarium at night. Photographed in shadow, what appears to be a creature, half-woman and half-ape, charges out of the shrubbery. The two clash and a violent struggle ensues. The snarling, clawing creature appears to have the upper hand when the man reaches into his pocket, produces a hypodermic needle and plunges it into his adversary's body. Within seconds, the beast falls to the ground, apparently dead.

Having spent its most exciting sequence at the starting gate, *Jungle Woman* quickly descends into unrelieved tedium. After the inevitable flash of newspaper headlines announcing that Dr. Carl Fletcher (J. Carrol Naish) is under suspicion of murder, the scene shifts to a coroner's inquest.

Pressed by the coroner (Samuel S. Hinds) to reveal all that he knows of the case, and faced with a snarling District Attorney (Douglass Dumbrille), Fletcher reluctantly agrees to recount what he assures the court will be a fantastic story.

Fletcher recalls attending a performance of the Whipple Circus on the night that the ape Cheela saved animal trainer Fred Mason (Milburn Stone) from being mauled to death by a cat. (The film neatly segues into flashbacks to the finale of *Captive Wild Woman*, supplemented by new footage of Naish nestled in the bleachers among a popcorn-munching crowd.) After a trigger-happy cop shoots Cheela dead, Fletcher secures permission to bring the ape's carcass to his laboratory for experimentation.

Fletcher detects a faint heartbeat and successfully nurses the creature back to health (Universal economized by conveying the incident verbally via a dull courtroom scene, thus saving the rental costs of an ape suit). So obsessed does the doctor become with his furry pet, that he runs out and purchases Dr. Walters' old sanatorium just so that he may have access to the late medico's notes. Cheela escapes from the laboratory off-camera (another bit of economizing). Later, Fletcher's dim-witted houseboy Willie (Edward M. Hyans, Jr.) drags a sultry brunette from out of the bushes. Fletcher diagnoses that the strange girl (Acquanetta) is suffering from shock and seems to have super-human strength.

Snapping out of her trance, the girl identifies herself as Paula Dupree and immediately sets her sights on Bob Whitney (Richard Davis), the naive fiancé of Fletcher's daughter Joan (Lois Collier). When Bob and Joan take a moonlit canoe ride, an unseen creature topples their boat and tries to drown Joan. Later, Joan sees a strange, animal-like face staring at her through her bedroom window. When Willie's mangled body is found on the grounds of the sanatorium, Fletcher, now well-versed in Walters' work, correctly concludes that Paula and Cheela are one and the same. Armed with a syringe containing a knockout drug, Fletcher follows Paula into the forest. She emerges as the Ape Woman and attacks him. He plunges the needle into her body, accidentally killing her with an overdose.

Back in court, the D.A. scoffs at Fletcher's story and insists that an examination of Paula's corpse be made. The entire jury troops over to the city morgue where the half-human monster is unveiled, confirming Fletcher's story. The judge and prosecutor limply shake the doctor's hand and Fletcher leaves the scene, cleared of all criminal charges. The film fades with a Lewtonesque closing quotation: "The evil man has wrought shall in the end destroy itself."

Often cited as among the worst, if not *the* worst of Universal's horror movies, *Jungle Woman* is a cynical studio hack-job that reaches almost bizarre levels of incompetence. That Universal was bent on using this deliriously poor movie to capitalize on its new screen siren, Acquanetta, as well as nurturing what they considered a promising horror franchise, is a sad commentary on the studio mentality at the time. The management may not have had the filmmaking savvy of the other studio heads but, to their credit, they at least knew how to market their wares. As such, the movie's poster and advertising art prominently featured cheesecake poses of Acquanetta in a low-cut leopard skin, although she spends the entire movie in street clothes. A suitably deceptive campaign for a *faux* jungle thriller that hardly ever gets out of the woods.

A mere 60 minutes long, *Jungle Woman* is a contrived farrago of unseen terrors and old film clips. Its narrative is easily divided into two distinct segments, the first, a garbled recapping of *Captive Wild Woman*, and the second, a foolish and uneventful continuation of the tale. *Jungle Woman* begins and ends at a coroner's inquest with all of the action unreeling in a clumsy flashback format. To make matters even more taxing, there are flashbacks within flashbacks. All of this expended energy for a lame horror story about an ape who transforms herself into a girl and then back again. *Jungle Woman* is a miscalculation from start to finish.

Although only ten minutes' worth of footage from *Captive Wild Woman* is used, it seems endless, especially with all those mismatched animal shots from Clyde Beatty's *The Big Cage* thrown into the mix. (Beatty is again given token credit in the titles.) With the added reaction shots of J. Carrol Naish cut into the climactic moments of *Captive Wild Woman*, the viewer is actually watching footage from three different movies! Film editor Ray Snyder didn't even bother to correct the cutting room foibles of the first Ape Woman film. At one point, Milburn

Poster for the second installment of the Paula Dupree trilogy.

Stone peers into a cage and sees himself (actually Beatty) battling the ferocious cats. The next shot has Stone just about to enter the cage. This hopeless clutter of film does little to clarify the muddled storyline and, unless one has seen *Captive Wild Woman*, its sequel is all but incomprehensible.

Jungle Woman's "let's-get-it-over-with" attitude creeps into every phase of the production. In our 1984 interview, Edward Dein, who cowrote the script, barely could recall any of the features he worked on, including this one. As he told to the authors:

> I don't remember much about *Jungle Woman*, but the economy ... was commonplace. We always used old sets from other films. These jungle pictures and horror films were exploitable, so we did them. Sixty minutes was about right for a B film because they were used as filler, like a newsreel.

Jungle Woman's director Reginald LeBorg had little regard for the film:

> I think we made it in one week. Most of these were done in ten days and this one was practically done in seven. It was an atrocious script and a silly idea anyway. But again, I was under contract. If I had refused it, I would have been suspended without pay, and I wouldn't have gotten anything any more. You had to play ball with the Front Office.

Despite Mr. LeBorg's claims, studio paperwork indicates that the film took a full 12 days to shoot. It's apparent also that Universal had sufficient confidence in *Jungle Woman*'s potential, placing it top-of-the-bill on an all-horror program with *The Mummy's Ghost.* Artistically, though, the film went against the established Universal fang-and-claw formula in favor of a more subtle approach that emphasized psychological terror in much the same manner as Columbia's *Cry of the Werewolf* (1944) and, more pointedly, Val Lewton's highly successful series of horror films at RKO. In retrospect, it was a strategy born of desperation rather than any aesthetic conviction. LeBorg admitted as much to the authors in our chat with him:

> I think that was the only way to make the script palatable. I tried that especially because I think you have suspense that way. If you'd seen the Ape Woman immediately, you wouldn't care about it any more. The story was so bad, I felt I had to do *something*. If I gave it away in the first reel, I would have no more picture.

Jungle Woman is a disguised attempt to rewrite *Cat People* with the Simone Simon character turning into an ape instead of a leopard. Not inappropriately since *Captive Wild Woman* also treaded lightly in Lewton territory, lifting the premise of a beautiful but emotionally stunted woman who reverts to animal form at the moment of sexual arousal. But revamping the Lewton formula wholesale, taking what was essentially a style and turning into a gimmick, was a failed ploy. The Lewton films had a solid grounding in fine-honed, carefully developed screenplays in which the normal characters are incrementally drawn into a fantastic situation. It's a level of sophistication that the writers of *Jungle Woman* don't even aspire to; there's no mystery to unravel or characters to explore, and, unfortunately, even less logic. Since Acquanetta's full monster makeup is shown in the film clips from *Captive Wild Woman*, holding off our next view of the creature until the last reel hardly makes an impact on the viewer.

Although the J. Carrol Naish character is now the custodian of John Carradine's research from the first film, he blithely accepts the fact that his pet ape has merely sauntered off at the exact time that Acquanetta arrives on the scene. Even given that she identifies herself by name, demonstrates super-human strength, and that a strange, subhuman creature is seen lurking about, he hasn't the wit to figure out what's going on until late in the action.

The script makes little sense of what was already established in *Captive Wild Woman*. In that film, Acquanetta's transformation from ape to human was undone by the character's jealous reaction which turned her into an anthropoid hybrid. While the change in the first film was understood to be permanent, in *Jungle Woman*, she shunts back and forth between her various transformations in typical movie monster fashion, cavalierly ignoring the writer's own ground rules. The film goes so far as to recreate *Cat People*'s famous scene of Simone Simon's stalking of Jane Randolph down a quiet New York City street, this time with Lois Collier being pursued in the woods by a blank-faced Acquanetta who, for no discernable reason, takes to walking like Frankenstein. The results are ludicrous and, without any hint of *Cat People*'s imaginative "bus" trick (the sound of the supposed giant cat turns out to be the airbrakes of a stopping bus) as a payoff, it simply falls flat.

Yet, it doesn't fall nearly as flat as the dialogue, which combined with the sub-par acting, makes *Jungle Woman* a chore to sit through even for hardcore Universal horror buffs. After learning of Paula's monstrous nature, Collier warns boyfriend Richard Davis, "She's no ordinary girl! She's a horrible creature!" To which our insipid hero dumbly replies, "She isn't *that* bad!" Milburn Stone suggests to Naish that Cheela the Ape (whom he describes as "the smartest and most affectionate creature I ever took out of the jungle") was, according to the natives, a human being transformed into an animal by black magic. Naish, supposedly a redoubtable scientist, nods and says, "Yes. There have been many efforts made in that direction." (He was undoubtedly referring to the mad scientist antics of 20th Century–Fox's *Dr. Renault's Secret* [1942] wherein George Zucco transforms a simian into *Naish!*)

Dein's script seems grimly determined to keep melodramatic incident to an absolute minimum and, as a result, much of the film is spent merely marking time with one dull talking-heads scene after another. A consulting physician gives Paula a medical once-over, only to tell her to go back to Naish. One of the film's daffier episodes has Naish submitting samples of Paula and Cheela's fingerprints to a police consultant. The awestruck fingerprint man (played by popular cowboy star and future Ed Wood alumnus Tom Keene, here acting under the name Richard Powers) declares, "There's something unholy about these prints," simply because both prints match. (The fact that one of the prints is as big as a golf ball barely stirs his scientific interest.)

Evelyn Ankers' walk-on undeservedly earned her top billing; she reads her few lines with little conviction. Though a noted scientist,

J. Carrol Naish's Dr. Fletcher comes off more like a simpleton; even an actor as versatile as Naish can't rise above the simplistic dialogue. As the juvenile lead, Lois Collier alternates between swooning over the stars in a romantic haze or screaming her head off at the slightest provocation.

Acquanetta again proves she's unequipped to handle a basic line-reading (her sobs when she's romantically spurned by Davis were obviously dubbed in by another actress). In an interview with the authors, she reflected on her role:

> I just did *Jungle Woman* because I was assigned to it. But once I accepted it, I did it to the best of my ability. It made money because Acquanetta was in it. I came to realize that I was the property, not the film. That's why I left Universal. I felt that I was being used.
>
> J. Carrol Naish helped me more than any actor or actress that I ever worked with. I thought he was a fabulous actor, one of the greatest. I think he accepted *Jungle Woman* in order to work with me. He always had visions of the two of us working together in something fabulous. I had met him at Universal prior to *Jungle Woman*, and we became friends; he was like a mentor.

On the subject of why she left Universal, the actress recalled:

> I went to Mexico at the instigation of the President, Mr. Roosevelt, as one of the emissaries from Hollywood. I made lots of contacts with some of the producers, and they wanted me to come to Mexico and do films. When I came back, I asked for a release from my contract. Universal never forgave me for that. They had this *Jungle Woman* series on the boards. They tried desperately to find someone else, and in fact they did get a girl who did one film [Vicky Lane in *The Jungle Captive*] and it bombed, and that was the end of that.

Nothing in *Jungle Woman* makes sense, from the opening titles (inexplicably written in Egyptian-style script) to its feeble attempts to emulate the famous Lewton style. While admittedly a juvenile potboiler, *Captive Wild Woman* is at least enthusiastically acted and has the crisp, spirited direction of young firebrand Edward Dmytryk to its credit. *Jungle Woman* is just a glum, boring misfire.

A curious postscript to the movie: Universal's *Skullduggery* (1970) ends with a lengthy trial in which a character is implicated in the killing of a half-woman, half-ape creature, raising the legal question of whether a person could be charged with the killing of an apparent non-human. Shades of *Jungle Woman*, but whether or not the filmmakers were actually influenced by the earlier movie is an open question. One thing we do know: the writer of *Skullduggery* asked that his name be taken off the credits, something the authors of *Jungle Woman* should have considered.

Critics' Corner

[S]ome murderous high spots [of *Captive Wild Woman*] are rerun to give zip to the opening of this one. Once you get through with those man-eating lion and tiger scenes, you can just settle back for a quiet session. People talk about murders and mayhem but vaguely. For excitement, they rely on shots of a girl named Acquanetta walking through the woods.... After *Jungle Woman* is over you may have a furtive desire to turn yourself into a gorilla just once — and wreck the theater.—*The New York World-Telegram*, July 14, 1944

For so fantastic a conception, the story is told reasonably enough. Naish turns in the most convincing performance as the puzzled medico.—*The New York Daily Mirror*, July 1944, Frank Quinn

We are given the thrills second-hand, except for a couple of flashes of Burnu [Acquanetta] in an intermediate phase in which she resembles the Wolf Man in burnt cork.—*The New York Post*, July 15, 1944, Archer Winsten

Rating: ★★ Universal produced the sequel on an economic scale, since director Reginald LeBorg has unashamedly made use of discarded film from the first picture... Acquanetta plays the role ... with a stilted air, while the other members of the cast go through their parts ... with assurance, trying to give the absurd story a semblance of reality.—*The New York Daily News*, July 15, 1944, Kate Cameron

And again [Universal] is cloaking the whole thing in a blather of scientific bunk.... What's Universal doing to us — trying to make monkeys of us all?—*The New York Times*, July 15, 1944, Bosley Crowther

[P]ermits little, pictorially, of Acquanetta's primitive sex appeal to filter on the screen but conveys with powerful suggestion the emotional unbalance driving her to murderously insane jealousy when about to be thwarted in her desires.... As a chiller ... it ranks well up with others of its ilk. Reginald LeBorg directed a capable cast ... smoothly through a series of tense situations climaxed with a crowning horror slaying averted in the nick of time by Naish.—*The Motion Picture Herald*, May 27, 1944

The Mummy's Ghost

Released July 7, 1944. 60 minutes. *Associate Producer:* Ben Pivar. *Executive Producer:* Joseph Gershenson. *Director:* Reginald LeBorg. *Screenplay:* Griffin Jay, Henry Sucher & Brenda Weisberg. *Original Story:* Griffin Jay & Henry Sucher. *Photography:* William Sickner. *Art Directors:* John B. Goodman & Abraham Grossman. *Editor:* Saul Goodkind. *Music Director:* Hans J. Salter. *Sound Director:* Bernard B. Brown. *Technician:* Jess Moulin. *Set Decorators:* Russell A. Gausman & L. R. Smith. *Makeup:* Jack P. Pierce. *Gowns:* Vera West. *Assistant Director:* Melville Shyer.

Lon Chaney, Jr. (*Kharis*), John Carradine (*Yousef Bey*), Robert Lowery (*Tom Hervey*), Ramsay Ames (*Amina Mansouri*), Barton MacLane (*Police Insp. Walgreen*), George Zucco (*High Priest*), Frank Reicher (*Prof. Matthew Norman*), Harry Shannon (*Sheriff Elwood*), Emmett Vogan (*Coroner*), Lester Sharpe (*Dr. Ayad*), Claire Whitney (*Ella Norman*), Oscar O'Shea (*Night Watchman*), Jack C. Smith, Jack Rockwell (*Deputies*), Carl Vernell (*Student*), Stephen Barclay (*Harrison*), Dorothy Vaughan (*Ada Blake*), Mira McKinney (*Martha Evans*), Bess Flowers, Caroline Cooke (*Townswomen*), Eddy Waller (*Ben Evans*), Fay Holderness (*Woman*), Ivan Triesault (*Scripps Museum Guide*), Anthony Warde (*Detective*), Pietro Sosso (*Temple Priest*), Martha MacVicar [Vickers] (*Girl Student*), David Bruce (*voice only; Radio Actor*).

No Chains Can Hold It! No Tomb Can Seal It!
—*Ad blurb for* The Mummy's Ghost

Shambling stiffly out of the silent world of out-of-work movie monsters, Kharis the Mummy terrorizes the townsfolk of sleepy Mapleton a second and last time in *The Mummy's Ghost*, third installment in Universal's Kharis saga. Arguably the best of *The Mummy's Hand*'s three sequels, this entry reintroduces the theme of reincarnation, taking a (tana) leaf from the book of Karl Freund's evergreen 1932 *The Mummy*. It took some creative thinking, not all of it sound, to add this angle, but the new approach, coupled with okay production values and capable handling on the part of first-time horror director Reginald LeBorg, make up for the film's lapses.

Ghost was only the second feature film for director LeBorg, who went on to make horror flicks something of a specialty. His later genre credits include three Inner Sanctums and *The Black Sleep* (1956), all with *Mummy's Ghost* star Lon Chaney, Jr., *Voodoo Island* (1957), *Diary of a Madman* (1963) and others; probably no director worked with more players associated with the genre (Karloff, Lugosi, Chaney, Carradine, Rathbone, Price, Acquanetta, Evelyn Ankers, Anne Gwynne, Elizabeth Russell—even Tor Johnson!). LeBorg began his film career in the mid–'30s as an extra at Paramount and MGM before moving up the Hollywood ladder. He staged the opera sequences for a number of early musicals; worked on second units for Metro, Goldwyn and Selznick; and eventually began grinding out band shorts for Universal.

LeBorg told the authors:

> The first feature I made at Universal was an overgrown short musical, *She's for Me* [1943]. It had no stars in it, just their stock players. I was supposed to get a comedy afterwards, because I had some comedy in *She's for Me* and Universal liked it very much. Ben Pivar, an associate producer at Universal, had a director assigned to *The Mummy's Ghost*—I don't know who the man was—but I think he had an accident or something, and they had nobody there right then to take his place. Pivar seemed to like me and he said, "How 'bout reading the script?"

The Mummy's Ghost went before William Sickner's camera on August 23, 1943, with Acquanetta in the co-starring role of Amina. Production hit an unexpected snag that very morning when according to LeBorg the actress suffered a fainting spell and collapsed, striking her head. Unconscious for half an hour, she was taken to the Universal dispensary with a slight concussion while producer Pivar pulled actress Ramsay Ames from Universal's bullpen of curvy contract actresses to take over the role.

Acquanetta had her own, quite different version of that day's sequence of events. The actress told us, "We had scabs [non-union workers] on the set. We had a scene where I had to fall, and these scabs had put real rocks down on the path. They were supposed to have papier-mâché rocks but they didn't—these scabs painted real rocks white. I fell and struck my head, and that's all I remember. I woke up in the hospital. I have the effects of that to this day; I struck my arm, too, when I fell, and when I had my second son, my elbow swelled up like a ball. They said that was still from that accident because it crushed a little bone in my elbow."

The film begins with confusion: Stock footage of Egyptian tourist spots give way to a

Mummy's Hand clip of George Zucco as Andoheb (seen only from the back) mounting the wide outdoor staircase to the temple atop the Hill of the Seven Jackals. In *this* movie, however, the stair-climber is supposed to be Yousef Bey (John Carradine), en route to an appointment with the current High Priest (Zucco), formerly Andoheb. But in a way, it's Zucco going up the stairs to meet Zucco. Things get worse once Yousef is inside: Nicely recovered from his death at the beginning of *The Mummy's Tomb* (his second demise of the Kharis series), the High Priest misidentifies their cult as Arkam instead of Karnak and garbles up the story of Kharis and Ananka. In this new account, it was the Princess Ananka who was cursed by the gods (hardly); Kharis was buried with her (*not*!); and now the gods of Egypt are determined to see the ancient lovers reunited (huh?). The swarthy Yousef, wearing a no-tassel, shapeless fez that looks like it's been through the wash too many times, absorbs every detail of the error-filled recap. The smallish, torch-lit temple appears more Aztec than Egyptian. Occasionally seen in the foreground is the instantly recognizable "magic flashback pool," complete with rising mist, but it's not utilized or even referenced.

The scene switches to a Mapleton college classroom where Egyptologist Matthew Norman (Frank Reicher) is regaling his students with the same Kharis-Ananka yarn, probably a good bit more accurately than the High Priest is spinning it for Yousef. (Reicher as Prof. Norman is a *Mummy's Tomb* cast carry-over, as are Chaney as Kharis, Zucco as the High Priest and Emmett Vogan as the Mapleton coroner.) After class, student Tom Hervey (Robert Lowery) meets with his girlfriend, Egyptian exchange student Amina (Ramsay Ames). When Tom brings up Prof. Norman's lecture, Amina becomes upset. Any mention of Egypt agitates the girl, and holding a book on the subject nearly causes her to swoon. She must have been a real lulu when she lived there.

That night, in the library of Prof. Norman's home, the antiquarian conducts an experiment that involves brewing tana leaves (different-looking ones than in previous Kharis movies) in a ceremonial urn. Kharis, lurking in the nearby woods, picks up a tana-talizing whiff and begins following his withered nose in the direction of the Norman residence. Kharis has apparently spent all his time since the Banning house fire hiding out in the woods. One wonders how he filled the days.

As Kharis shuffles past the house where Amina lives, the sleeping girl sits up in bed and, in a trance, begins to follow the Mummy at a distance. In the film's best scene, Kharis crosses the lawn of Norman's house to an exterior door leading to the library. Sensing another presence, Norman turns and sees Kharis framed in the entranceway. Norman rises from his chair and staggers backward in shock and disbelief as Kharis lurches into the room. The camera now alternates between subjective shots of Norman, backing away in terror, and of the Mummy, his face livid with hate, strangling arm extended. Kharis pins the startled scientist against a wall, chokes him to death and then quaffs the steaming tana fluid. Amina, sleepwalking onto the grim scene, falls to the lawn in a dead faint at the sight of the departing Mummy.

The next morning, Sheriff Elwood (Harry Shannon) and his men begin the murder investigation. Even though the mold on Norman's throat indicates the return of Kharis, the Sheriff wrongly believes that Amina (found on the scene) is somehow involved or is holding back some clue. Amina has also developed a Bride of Frankenstein-ish streak of silver white in her hair — spotlighted in a grainy optical close-up — which no one ever comments upon.

Yousef Bey arrives in Mapleton (paging Homeland Security!) and, setting up a tana leaf-brewing station in a clearing in the woods, lures Kharis to him. As Kharis savors the first cup of the day, Yousef explains that his (Yousef's) mission is to reunite him with Ananka. Fortunately for them, at the Scripps Museum in New York, security is as low as the institution's regard for their exhibits: The bandage-wrapped mummy of Ananka is on open-air display in a no-lid sarcophagus surrounded on only three sides with stanchions and velvet rope. Yousef secretes himself until after closing time, when Kharis (who's apparently been "laying low" for hours in a Manhattan alley) breaks into the building and joins him at sarcophagus-side. They've come to steal the body of Ananka, but as Kharis reaches into the sarcophagus, about to cop his first feel since Amenophis ruled the roost, the bandaged corpse

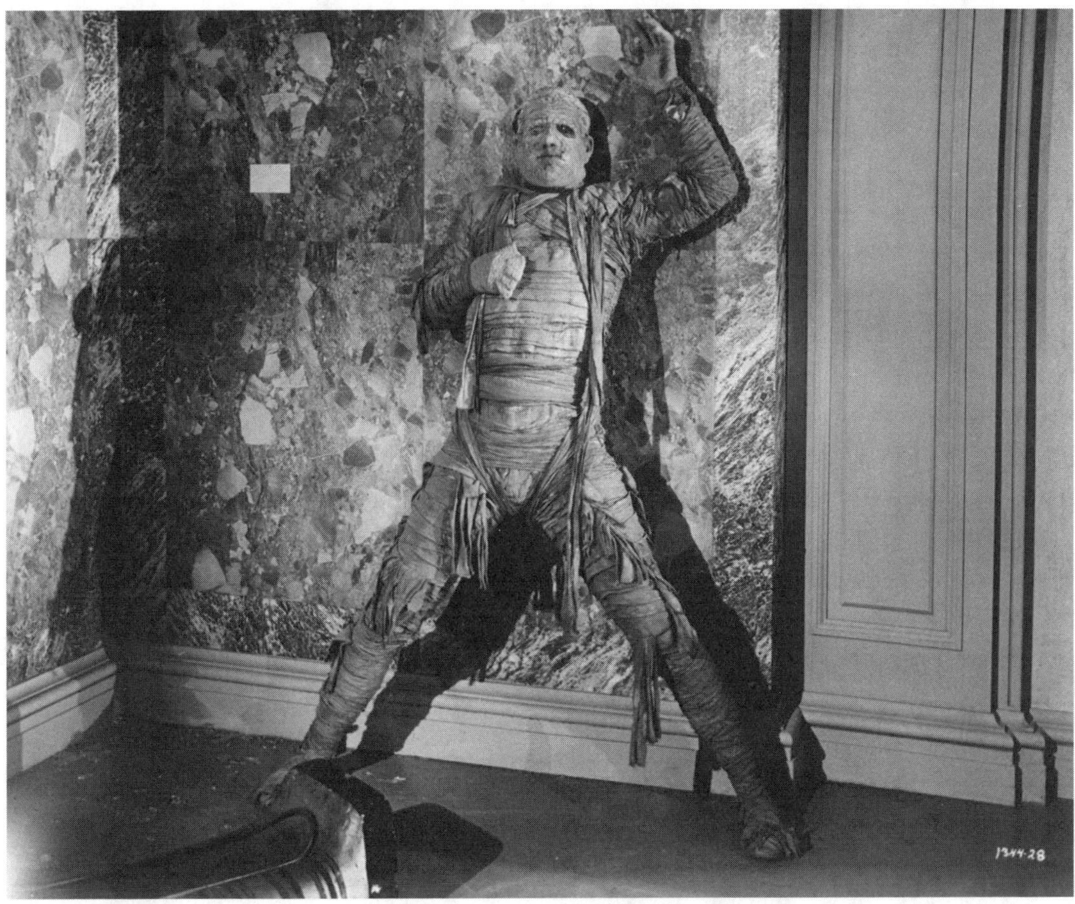

Kharis (Lon Chaney, Jr.) attempts a split in *The Mummy's Ghost.*

vanishes before his astonished eye, leaving only the collapsed wrappings. Bey announces that Ananka's soul must have entered another form, and that their task now is to find that reincarnation. A furious Kharis smashes many of the other exhibits, which brings the elderly night watchman (Oscar O'Shea) a-running. As Yousef looks on with a satisfied smile, Kharis adds the old man to his list of victims.

Returning to their hideout in an elevated mining shack outside Mapleton, Yousef and Kharis pray for a sign that will lead them to the reincarnation of Ananka. A gust of wind blows open window shutters and a shaft of light appears. Guided by the light, Kharis trudges to Amina's home, abducts the fainting girl and carries her to the shack. Yousef starts acting like he never saw a girl before: Instantly developing a case of the hots for the curvaceous coed, he and his "inner voice" get into an argument about whether he should complete his sacred mission, or forsake it and take Amina for himself. Succumbing to temptation, Bey cooks up a cupful of immortalizing tana fluid (insatiable tana leaf bloodhound Kharis doesn't notice even though he's standing right outside the door!). Preparing to bring the cup to the unconscious girl's lips, Yousef makes the mistake of talking aloud about what he's doing and Kharis, overhearing, shuffles back into the room and fatally knocks him out the window.

With Tom and a mob of townsmen in pursuit, the Mummy carries Amina into the nearby swamp. Kharis retreats into a pool and becomes mired in quicksand. Wading into the water in a futile rescue attempt, Tom sees that Amina has mystically turned into a white-haired, withered hag. He turns away in revulsion as Kharis and the reincarnated princess are swallowed up by the swamp.

Elevating *The Mummy's Ghost* are the effective Chaney and Carradine performances, the welcome albeit inexplicable "Egyptian gods as matchmakers" slant, and some well-staged Mummy murder scenes. For the first and only time, Chaney brings some color to his Mummy role: In the scene at the Scripps Museum, where Kharis reaches out with trembling hand to touch the cheek of Ananka, and in a scene at the mining shack where the monster lowers his head praying for guidance from the gods, we see a new and quite different side of Kharis. (In the fourth and final Kharis film, *The Mummy's Curse*, Chaney is once again on the trail of his reincarnated sweetheart, but is again is playing the mindless wind-up Mummy of *Hand* and *Tomb*.)

Chaney and actor William Phipps (*Five*, *Cat-Women of the Moon*, *The Snow Creature*, more) both appeared in the 1955 Kirk Douglas Western *The Indian Fighter* and in an episode of TV's *Rawhide*. According to Phipps, Chaney once talked to him about the Mummy movies and revealed that he had a container (presumably a hip flask) of vodka tucked away inside his Mummy outfit. "He told me how he had a tube that went [from the container] all the way up through those bandages, up to his mouth. And he just sucked on that vodka all day long [*laughs*]! Isn't that funny? He could just push that tube out of the way, to one side, when they were working, and then when they weren't, he'd pull it out and suck on it! Later on, I did the TV show with him and he was drinking all day—dry vermouth. I made the mistake of joining him. He could hold it, but I was getting plastered!"

LeBorg and cinematographer William Sickner make the most of their moldering monster, giving fans some of the series' most memorable shots of Chaney's Kharis:

- One of our first glimpses of the Mummy is a low-angle exterior night shot in which he oomphs his way through the splintering boards of a split-rail fence.
- Kharis is eerily lit as he fills the screen in striking subjective shots while stalking Prof. Norman.
- He's the subject of another low-angle shot, and has the shadow of a wagon wheel cast upon him, in a barn interior as he awaits the arrival of a new victim.
- We get a good profile shot of him in the Scripps Museum as he stands over the sarcophagus of the Princess, his face lit by the flickering flames of off-camera ceremonial lamps.

The outstanding picture quality of recent Universal Studios Home Video DVD releases of *Ghost* (2001 and 2004) even affords us the opportunity to get a distant look at the "Evelyn Ankers strap," the harness-like device that helped Chaney (in his various monster roles) carry his female victims. Look at the back of Kharis' neck in the shot where he first goes "off-road" alongside a countryside bridge with the unconscious Amina in his arms.

Also visible, especially in the Scripps Museum scene, is the zipper up the left side of Chaney's "Mummy shirt." Bob Burns met makeup man Jack Pierce at a Hollywood TV station in 1962 and got the full story of the Mummy costume and makeup: According to Pierce, the Mummy suit was in two sections, "pants" and "shirt." The pants went on Chaney like regular pants. The "shirt" (with side zipper open) went over Chaney's head like a T-shirt and then, once it was on him, it was zipped up to make it snug. (That technique has been used for years to show off actors' builds; notice the form-fitting shirts on serial superheroes like Flash Gordon and Captain Marvel and on Clayton Moore, TV's Lone Ranger.) Chaney would also have Mummy feet, which were very much like thick socks.

Chaney would next be wrapped from neck to feet with gauze (dyed with earth tones), with special care taken to hide "seams" (for instance, between the shirt and pants). Then the suit was painted with liquid clay (also called "slip"), applied with a paintbrush. The next step was the application of fuller's earth, which is like clay in a powdered form. (Whenever Chaney's Kharis is struck on-camera, notice the dried liquid clay and fuller's earth flying off of him, looking like mummy dust.) In *Ghost*, he wore a complete over-the-head mask with the "hair" and detail already on it (plus "Mummy color earth tone" around the open eye). Pierce made up the mask after it was put on Chaney: He painted the mask with makeup and liquid clay to duplicate the color and texture of the gauze bandages. He also

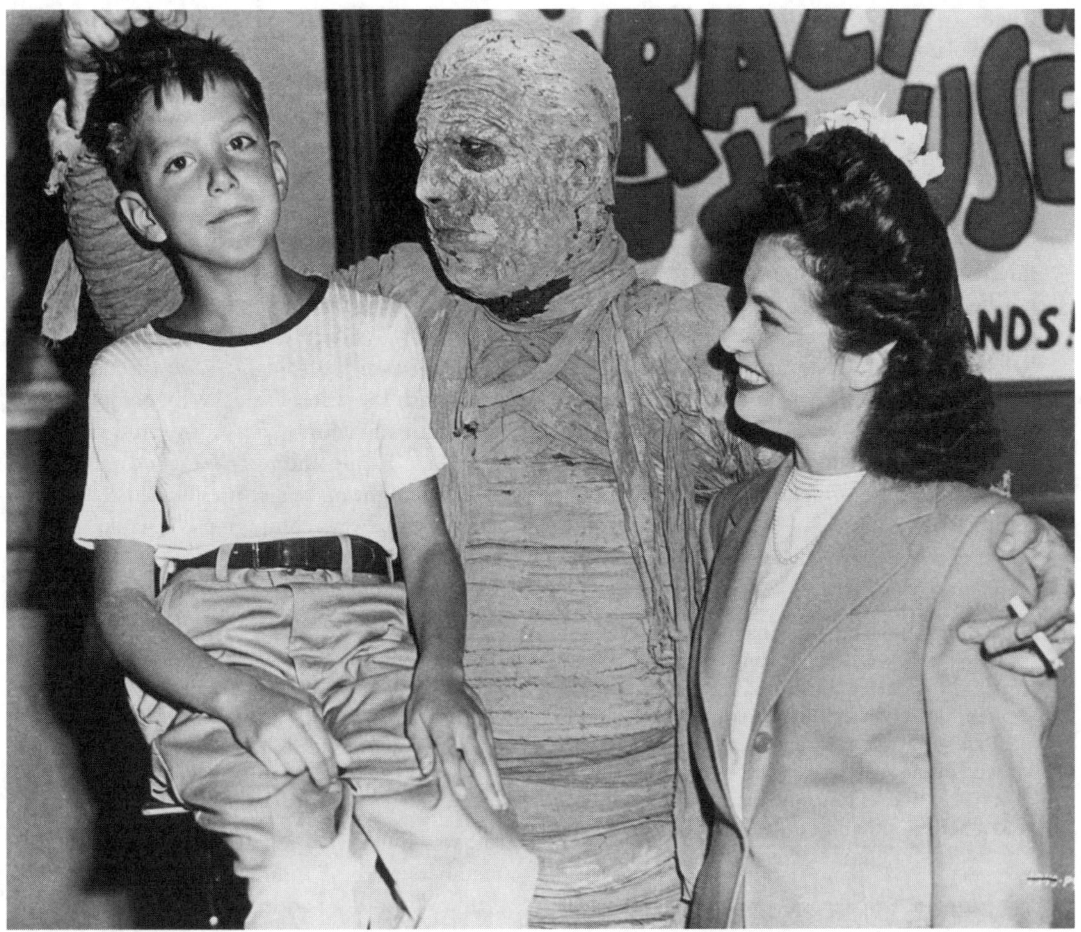

Chaney Jr. is visited by his wife Patsy and son Ronald in this *Mummy's Ghost* candid shot.

painted Lon's mouth and lips black and glued the mask to his lips to give him some movement of the mask's mouth. His rubber Mummy gloves went on last just so that Chaney would be able to use his hands up until that point, throughout the long process. When the procedure was finished, everything matched perfectly.

After strenuous takes, the 6'4", 220-pound actor would be partially unwrapped, the zipper would be opened (to let out some of the built-up heat) and he would allowed to sit in the shade for a few minutes before being zipped and wrapped up once again. "You can kind of see why it wasn't Lon's favorite role," Burns laughs.

When United Press reporter Frederick C. Othman visited the *Mummy's Ghost* set, Chaney was indulging in his second favorite pastime: Bellyaching. Kharis was his least favorite horror role, and not without justification. "I sweat and I can't wipe it away. I itch and I can't scratch," a steam-cooked Chaney grumbled to the U.P. reporter as makeup men sprinkled him with more fuller's earth. Chaney also told the writer that movie audiences were nuts for spending their money to see Mummy films. On *Ghost*, the actor got his usual bottom-of-the-castlist "and" billing.*

Director LeBorg recalled that he "bribed"

**Othman's 13-paragraph story seems to be very much on the level, with a short but accurate description of the wrapping-unwrapping process, quotes from others on the set, and even a word picture of producer Ben Pivar's sweater ("striped like a convict's suit in blue and yellow"). But it also raises a question: According to the U.P. reporter, one scene he watched involved the Mummy carrying the princess to the top of the "coal mine tower" and then tossing a dummy of the princess ("skirts fluttering") off of it. Nothing like this does,* or *could, happen in the movie.*

Chaney a bit, hinting at the likelihood of the actor's playing a dapper gentleman-type role in their next picture together (which in fact he *did*— their next was *Calling Dr. Death*). What LeBorg apparently didn't know was that a little bit of Chaney went a long, long way. In shooting the scene where the Mummy strangles Prof. Norman, Chaney seized actor Frank Reicher's throat "and squeezed so forcefully that Reicher nearly fainted," LeBorg told us. "Reicher was an old man, and frail, and Chaney got carried away. Reicher cried out, 'He nearly killed me! He took my breath away!'" There is evidence of this in the film itself: In the few frames where Reicher's face is visible as Chaney chokes him, the pinched expression on the older actor's face looks uncomfortably real.

LeBorg told Greg Mank in *Cinefantastique*:

> Reicher very nearly was unconscious! He was moaning on the floor.... Chaney had just become carried away — he was putting everything he had into the monster. Luckily, Reicher didn't complain. He was an older man, nice; he knew Chaney was the star, and he let it go. We massaged his neck and gave him some water. But the next day, when I saw him again, I spied a look at Reicher's neck, and you could see he had spots there, from the strangling!

Sympathy for Reicher aside, the idea of one of the *Mummy's Ghost* actors sporting *real-life* throat bruises from a *real-life* "Mummy" attack ("A grayish mark...!") is amusingly weird.

The Scripps Museum scene, as originally planned, involved the Mummy shattering a pane of plate glass, but when cast and crew converged on the museum set, it was discovered that the breakaway glass had not yet been installed. Not wishing to hold up production, LeBorg told Chaney that the window glass was still real and to forget the idea of crashing through it. But when cameras rolled and Chaney attacked the watchman (Oscar O'Shea), Lon went ahead and recklessly shattered the glass. Nursing a gashed hand, the actor told LeBorg, "I wanted to show you that I had the courage." Actually, a frame-by-frame examination of the scene makes it look as though Chaney may have only mustered up enough courage to break the glass with the back of O'Shea's head!

LeBorg's direction makes the most of scenes like these and other, more modest highlights. Despite an excess of extraneous passages and a few silly scenes (Chaney trying to give the false impression he's descending the mining shack ramp by just bending over more and more; Carradine entering into an out-loud debate with his inner voice), *The Mummy's Ghost* is easily the director's best horror film, possibly his best film, period. LeBorg took credit for the unusual downbeat finale, although he admitted without any prompting that he was inspired by the climax of Frank Capra's 1937 romantic-fantasy classic *Lost Horizon*. He told us, "We discussed the finale with Pivar and I said, 'Why not let Amina sink with the Mummy? Why should there always be a happy ending?' Somebody else said, 'No, we might make a sequel.' I told him, 'The Mummy is always coming up — Ananka doesn't have to!'"

LeBorg's handling of *The Mummy's Ghost* rises above the level of the sloppy script turned in by scenarists Griffin Jay, Henry Sucher and Brenda Weisberg. Apparently they saw little purpose in building upon the groundwork laid by the earlier Kharis films and branched off on their own. Admittedly, the series was in dire need of rejuvenation; *The Mummy's Tomb*, while eventful, was filled with repetitive episodes, and all members of the Banning expedition were now dead. Without an added twist, the Kharis saga clearly had nowhere to go. Making the imperious Egyptian gods frustrated matchmakers didn't jive with the first two movies, but did give the writers a clean slate and a chance to start anew. (Actually, there *is* one possible explanation: Talking to Yousef Bey, the now-daffy High Priest bollixed up the old story and gave him the wrong mission, which would neatly explain why the gods of Egypt subsequently step in to *thwart* Yousef and Kharis!)

Where has the Mummy been hiding out since the Banning house fire? Why did an incineration at the end of *Mummy's Hand* make Kharis look burned in *Tomb*, but a second incineration (at the end of *Tomb*) clean him up again? Has he been living on nuts and berries (and then *more* nuts and *more* berries, judging by that expanded waistline) during those lonely hours in the woods? Why is Amina upset by references to Egypt *before* she is possessed by the spirit of Ananka? There are more loose ends in the *Mummy's Ghost* script than in Kharis' ancient wrappings.

Besides being too old (thirty-ish) to play a college student, Robert Lowery is the most disagreeable "hero" of any Universal horror film. Lowery's Tom Hervey has the patience of *two* saints with the hypochondriac Amina, then takes his frustrations out on others (a fellow student who points out that Amina is Egyptian, the roommate who brings him the news of Prof. Norman's murder, etc.). While all able-bodied men are being urged to help in the search for the Mummy, he goes out on a date with Amina. A farmer tells Hervey that he tripped and fell while on patrol, but instead of expressing sympathy Hervey more or less tells him to beat it. At the end of *Son of Dracula*, as Frank Stanley (Robert Paige) watches his girl die, we "feel his pain"; at the end of *Mummy's Ghost*, when Lowery's Tom Hervey watches *his* girl die, we don't give this hair-trigger-temper boor a second thought.

A Kansas City, Missouri, native and a direct descendant of Abraham Lincoln, Lowery got his start as a singer with orchestras and as an actor in little theater groups. Shortly after making his film debut in 1936's *Come and Get It*, he was placed under contract by 20th Century–Fox, where he played many bit roles while being groomed in the Fox studio training school. (Another Fox contractee was Chaney Jr.; the two young actors were in at least 12 of the same movies.) Lowery's early publicity made much of his supposed resemblance to Clark Gable, but Lowery didn't even remotely resemble Gable until he was much older and *both* actors had lost their looks. Lowery played a succession of seedy villains in a number of 1950s B films, and eventually ended up in forgettable '60s fare like Paramount producer A.C. Lyles' low-budget oaters and in Universal-TV's Western sitcom *Pistols 'n' Petticoats*— both of the latter again putting Lowery and Chaney on the same soundstages. Lowery's other horror film credits include Monogram's *Revenge of the Zombies* (1943) and Universal's *House of Horrors*, in which he played yet another bilious and belligerent "hero." The 57-year-old Lowery was in the middle of a phone conversation with his mother when he died at his Hollywood apartment in 1971.

A former rumba band leader in Miami and Chicago and a singer at New York's Stork Club, 24-year-old Universal contract player Ramsay Ames (*née* Ramsay Philips) is handicapped by slapdash screenwriting: In every scene she comes across as a whining, woozy wet blanket, and we never get any hint of what Lowery sees in her. In a night scene with Lowery in a parked convertible, her mood swings constantly until the scenes verges on the comical. (The *Harrison's Reports* reviewer caught *Mummy's Ghost* at New York's Rialto Theatre, where "the audience greeted the actions of the characters with derisive laughter.") In the final reel, Ames wears the same satin nightgown as Peggy Moran in *Mummy's Hand* and is loosely bound to a table as Yousef, his hormones unexpectedly reaching critical mass, is preparing a hypodermic injection. Like so much in this movie, it's a remake of a scene in an *earlier* movie, in this case, the Zucco-Moran scene in *Mummy's Hand*. The sight of a bra-less Ames nipping up through her nightgown, however, is generous compensation for the redundancy. Asked about Chaney Jr. by autograph hound Paul Parla, Ames demurred, "I'd rather not discuss [it]. Overall, he was a nice guy to work with, but he did have his problems." She died in 1998.

Barton MacLane seems quite disinterested in his role as a Manhattan police inspector who assists in the Mummy manhunt. Except for the finale, all of the scenes in which MacLane is featured are just padding. The inspector hatches a banal plan to lure the Mummy back to the proverbial scene of the crime (Prof. Norman's house) by brewing tana fluid, and has a ten-foot pit dug and camouflaged in hopes of then capturing the monster. All of this effort, and the audience's attention to these dull scenes, turns out to be wasted: The pay-off is that when his plan is put into operation, Kharis (busy elsewhere) responds only with a quick, uninterested glance in the general direction of the far-off Norman house, and then moves on!

Carradine brings his customary blend of cold authority, commanding screen presence and the usual slice of ham to his role of Yousef Bey, the newest addition to Karnak/Arkam's New England–based sleeper cell. He under-acts in his early scenes with Zucco but the blustery stage actor in him comes through at other points, resulting in a slightly uneven but entertaining performance. Chaney's Kharis puts an end to Carradine's hot-and-cold thesping with a neck-breaking karate blow. Check out the *Mummy's Ghost* trailer to see a shot of Kharis' attack on

Yousef not included in the movie. Additionally, the trailer editor allowed the shot of the plummeting Yousef dummy to go a few frames longer so that we see it hit the ground.

LeBorg agreed with us that Carradine hammed it up as the High Priest,

> but considering the character he played it wasn't too much of a fault. There were no heavies in that picture other than him — Chaney was no heavy, playing that poor mummy — so we had to have somebody to fill that slot. Carradine's voice was sonorous and excellent, much better than the average actor's, so I let him go on. In a picture like that, you can be a little hammy — it was usually kids and teenagers that went to see that kind of a picture.

It's a little hard to believe that at the time of his death in 1988, at the end of a 60-year Hollywood career which consisted largely of horror films, Carradine's best starring or co-starring genre credits might be four of the '40s thrillers (*The Mummy's Ghost*, *Captive Wild Woman*, *House of Frankenstein* and *House of Dracula*) that he did for Universal. They're enjoyable but, in "the big picture," basically mediocre titles, and yet probably represent his best work in the field. (Carradine gave a particularly restrained and sensible performance as the tormented strangler in director Edgar Ulmer's 1944 *Bluebeard*, a stylish cheapie which falls just short of being a horror film.)

Beyond some striking shots of the Mummy and a couple exciting murder scenes, the main attraction of *Mummy's Ghost* are the comfortable, "old shoe" elements that Universal horror nuts expect and appreciate: The familiar faces in the cast, recognizable sets and/or exteriors from other movies (the *Weird Woman* library, the *Son of Dracula* courthouse, etc.), the usual Kharis scare tactics (his shadow moving over people sleeping in bed, and over lovers in a parked car), etc. Then, too, there are the music cues, "reincarnated" in one Universal Horror after another until they wore permanent grooves in the heads of the diehard fans. The examining-the-Monster violin music from *Son of Frankenstein* is played in *Mummy's Ghost* on organ as the High Priest boils up tana leaf tea; the music chanted by a male chorus over *The Mummy's Hand*'s flashback burial scene is also now played on organ as Yousef stands by Ananka's sarcophagus; there are also riffs from *Frankenstein Meets the Wolf Man*, *Man Made Monster* and an abundance from *The Wolf Man*. Enacting small supporting roles in *Ghost* are Martha Vickers (a future Warners contractee, memorable as the sexoholic sister of Lauren Bacall in *The Big Sleep*), Stephen Barclay (producer of the 1960 schlock classic *Macumba Love*), Eddy Waller (a chemist in *The Mummy's Tomb*, a farmer here), Mira McKinney (a farmer's wife in *Mummy's Tomb*, a *different* farmer's wife here), Anthony Warde (Republic serial "dog heavy" extraordinaire) and David Bruce (the Mad Ghoul himself, heard over a radio as the star of a spooky airwave murder mystery program).

Despite all its shortcomings, *The Mummy's Ghost* shapes up as one of Universal's better Bs from this era of decline. By imbuing Kharis with some sympathetic qualities, new dimensions were added to the spavined series, and the road for a final sequel, 1944's *The Mummy's Curse*, was neatly paved.

Critics' Corner

Rating: ★★½ As a sop for logic, the movie falls back on such mind-taker-offers as can be managed with gruesome makeup, stalking monstrosities, reincarnated spirits, sepulchral incantations and attendant hocus-pocus. — *The New York Daily News*, July 1, 1944, Dorothy Masters

The Mummy always has been the least impressive of movie monsters and he is doing nothing to enhance his reputation in his latest incarnation.... He is just repulsive without being picturesque or even particularly frightening. — *The New York World-Telegram*, July 1, 1944

Mediocre! It is the fourth in Universal's "Mummy" series [and] also the weakest of the lot.... [T]he audience greeted the actions of the characters with derisive laughter, and one cannot blame them.... — *Harrison's Reports*, July 8, 1944

Kharis carries [Amina Mansouri] off and they sink blissfully ... into the murky depths. Oh! please, Universal, do not disturb their rest. — *The New York Times*, July 1, 1944, Thomas M. Pryor

Chaney's performance in the film advances his claim to a large following.... [P]icture has considerable professional polish.... [I]t sticks to its premise well enough. Only in the finale, which lacks spectacular incident, does the picture depart from the proven pattern developed by Universal. — *The Motion Picture Herald*, May 13, 1944, William R. Weaver

The incredible situations are well handled by a clever director and the suspense is carefully sustained to the end. — Daughters of the American Revolution (Eastern Committee), 1944

The Pearl of Death

Released September 22, 1944. 68 minutes. *Executive Producer:* Howard Benedict. *Producer-Director:* Roy William Neill. *Screenplay:* Bertram Millhauser. *Based on the short story* "The Adventure of the Six Napoleons" *by* Sir Arthur Conan Doyle. *Photography:* Virgil Miller. *Music Director:* Paul Sawtell. *Art Directors:* John B. Goodman & Martin Obzina. *Sound Director:* Bernard B. Brown. *Technician:* Joe Lapis. *Set Decorators:* Russell A. Gausman & Edward R. Robinson. *Editor:* Ray Snyder. *Gowns:* Vera West. *Dialogue Director:* Ray Kessler.

Basil Rathbone (*Sherlock Holmes*), Nigel Bruce (*Dr. John H. Watson*), Dennis Hoey (*Inspector Lestrade*), Evelyn Ankers (*Naomi Drake*), Miles Mander (*Giles Conover*), Ian Wolfe (*Amos Hodder*), Charles Francis (*Francis Digby*), Holmes Herbert (*James Goodram*), Richard Nugent (*Bates*), Mary Gordon (*Mrs. Hudson*), Rondo Hatton (*The Hoxton Creeper*), J. Welsh Austin (*Sgt. Bleeker*), Connie Leon (*Ellen Carey*), Charles Knight (*Bearded Man*), Al Ferguson, Colin Kelly (*Guards*), Audrey Manners (*Teacher*), Billy Bevan (*Constable*), Lillian Bronson (*Housekeeper*), Leslie Denison (*Constable Murdock*), John Merkyl (*Dr. Julian Boncourt*), Harry Cording (*George Gelder*), Eric Wilton (*Chauffeur*), Harold DeBecker (*Boss*), Arthur Mulliner (*Thomas Sandeford*), Wilson Benge, Arthur Stenning (*Stewards*), Leyland Hodgson (*Customs Officer*), Diana Beresford (*Bit Woman*).

Twice a hand of The Creeper is viewed, which is more hideous than the full-face view of him at the end of the picture. Rathbone and Bruce fans will not appreciate a "monster" being added to one of their pictures.
—*American Legion Auxiliary, 1944*

The movie-producing career of Howard Benedict was consistent in its improbability: During much of his early–'40s tenure at RKO, he alternated B-musicals with B-mysteries featuring that studio's resident sleuths, The Saint and The Falcon. Then he moved to Universal and did the exact same thing, making innocuous song-filled entertainments (typical titles: *Hi' Ya, Chum* and *Larceny with Music,* both 1943) between installments of the Sherlock Holmes series.

His final RKO credit, before leaving that studio for Universal, was the detective drama *The Falcon Takes Over* (1942), based on Raymond Chandler's novel *Farewell My Lovely.* Of course Chandler's hardboiled tale was vastly changed: In *Takes Over,* instead of Marlowe's iconic private eye Philip Marlowe, it's the Falcon (George Sanders), an amateur detective, on the trail of a priceless stolen jade necklace, accompanied on his adventure by "Goldy" (Allen Jenkins), his comedy-relief sidekick, and O'Hara (James Gleason), a comically gruff police inspector. Also figuring into the plot of Benedict's movie are a criminal mastermind, pulling the strings from behind the scenes; his dual-identity partner-in-crime, the beautiful Velma; and the 6'5", 265-pound Moose Malloy (played, *sans* screen credit, by Ward Bond), a man-mountain recently escaped from prison, and now searching for Velma, with whom he has long been obsessed. The monstrous Moose's method of murder: He uses his hands to snap the necks of his victims.

Two years later (April 1944, to be exact), RKO was counting down the days to the start of production of *Murder, My Sweet,* an A-budget rendering of *Farewell My Lovely* with Dick Powell as Philip Marlowe. Meanwhile, at Universal, Benedict was busy shooting his newest Holmes stanza, *The Pearl of Death*—which plays like *Farewell My Lovely* re-jiggered to fit into the Holmes series the same way it was done for the Falcon film. The gumshoe here is of course Holmes (Basil Rathbone), joined by a comic sidekick (Nigel Bruce's Dr. Watson) and police inspector (Dennis Hoey's Lestrade) on the trail of a priceless stolen pearl. Other plot links include the criminal mastermind (Miles Mander as Giles Conover), his female associate of many identities (Evelyn Ankers as Naomi Drake) and, most conspicuously, the Moose Malloy counterpart: Rondo Hatton as "The Hoxton Creeper," a Devil's Island escapee long obsessed with Naomi ... a man-mountain whose method of murder is snapping the *spines* of his victims.

The film opens at night aboard the boat to Dover. Goodram (Holmes Herbert), a museum agent entrusted to deliver the Borgia Pearl (value: £50,000) to the Royal Regent Museum, is lured out of his stateroom with the false news of an urgent message. Nefarious Naomi Drake (Evelyn Ankers) seizes the opportunity to break into the stateroom and steal the pearl, which she conceals inside a camera. Fearing that Dover customs agents will find it, she dupes an elderly clergyman into carrying the camera ashore for her, and retrieves it from him later. Naomi presents the camera to her boss, international criminal Giles Conover (Miles Mander), who opens it and discovers only a note. The clergyman was Sherlock Holmes in disguise, and the note informs Conover that the pearl has been recovered by the famous detective.

The Borgia Pearl is placed on display in the Royal Museum, but Holmes fears for its safety with Conover on the loose. Museum curator Digby (Charles Francis) smugly explains to Holmes, Watson and Lestrade that the pearl cannot be removed from its case without triggering alarm bells and activating steel shutters that would trap the would-be thief, but Holmes perceives a flaw in museum security: He secretly cuts off the electricity, demonstrating that the pearl *can* be stolen during a power failure. Conover, disguised as a workman, has overheard the conversation, filches the pearl from its deactivated case and escapes through a window. He is apprehended after a chase, but the master criminal no longer has the jewel. While Conover is released from police custody for lack of evidence, Holmes is condemned by the press for his unwitting part in the affair.

Holmes' attention is caught by a series of broken-back murders, each victim found in their London home amidst mounds of smashed plaster and china. Since Conover's right-hand man in murder has always been the spine-snapping Hoxton Creeper, Holmes is convinced that these killings are connected to the theft of the pearl.

Through an examination of shattered bric-a-brac taken from all the murder houses, Holmes deduces that the common denominator is a plaster bust of Napoleon; further inquiry leads him to the manufacturer, whose workshop is near the museum. Using his deductive reasoning, Holmes determines that Conover, during his flight from the museum, dashed into the plasterer's shop and inserted the pearl into one of six still-wet plaster Napoleons; Conover and the Creeper are now tracking down the people who bought the busts in order to find the one that contains the pearl. (The extra breakage conceals the true object of their search.) At the art shop of Amos Hodder (Ian Wolfe), Holmes learns the address of Dr. Boncourt, the sixth and final buyer; Naomi, who has infiltrated the shop, also finds this information and passes it along to Conover before Holmes spots and apprehends her.

Conover and the Creeper (Rondo Hatton) drive to Boncourt's and break in, but Holmes has beaten them there and disguised himself as the physician. Getting the upper hand over Holmes after a struggle, Conover holds him at gunpoint while the Creeper begins to search the house for the bust. Quick-thinking Holmes tells Conover, in a voice loud enough to be overheard by the Creeper, that Naomi has been arrested and will be hanged; the Creeper, who worships the girl, goes berserk and kills Conover. The Creeper then advances on Holmes, who is forced to shoot and kill him. After Watson, Lestrade and Lestrade's men arrive at the scene, Holmes smashes open the last of the six Napoleons and finds the Borgia Pearl amidst the plaster fragments.

The Pearl of Death is a model example of "the Holmes unit" working at peak efficiency. Bertram Millhauser's screenplay, blending *Farewell My Lovely* with Conan Doyle's "The Adventure of the Six Napoleons," is an ingenious amalgam of mystery, horror and humor, and director Roy William Neill succeeds in extracting the full measure of suspense from Millhauser's work. Rathbone and Bruce are also in top form, perhaps at their best, with excellent support from Mander, Ankers and series regular Hoey.

Failing to fall prey to the usual movie clichés, Giles Conover comes across as a unique and offbeat Holmes antagonist. Seedy and perverse, he's a criminal with none of the silky charm or Machiavellian cunning that generally mark the Baker Street detective's big-brained arch-nemeses. The only problem with Conover is that Holmes gives him perhaps too big a buildup. In an early scene, Holmes says that Conover "pervades England like a plague. No one had heard of him. That's what puts him on the pinnacle in the records of crime." Later he adds, "If I could free society of this sinister creature, I should feel that my own career had reached its summit."

Based on what we see in *Pearl of Death*, however, Holmes has over-hyped his adversary: Conover operates like a small-timer with aspirations toward grandeur. He takes on menial jobs that a Moriarity would leave to confederates, needs Holmes' unwitting help to steal the pearl, and never finds the easy way to do *any*thing (he has Naomi take a job in an art shop so that she can break two Napoleons that he or she could have just walked in and bought).

***The Pearl of Death* introduced movie audiences — and Sherlock Holmes (Basil Rathbone) — to the character of "The Creeper" (Rondo Hatton) (courtesy Dan Scapperotti).**

But it's Conover's foibles, and his sordid side, that make him an interesting, lifelike villain. Between the unsavory dialogue descriptions and Mander's fine performance, we get the distinct impression that *The Pearl of Death* scarcely scratches the surface of this slippery sadist. (Instead of making time with lovely Naomi, who looks to be more than willing, he chooses instead to taunt her with news of the Creeper, whose company he seems to prefer; this unhealthy situation brings all sorts of new possibilities to mind!) Mander was probably a sweetheart of guy in real life but here he's got a seedy, debauched look that probably lost him a lot of babysitting jobs in his day.

Mander led the sort of colorful life that sounds like a Hollywood publicist's wacky concoction: New Zealand sheep rancher, auto racer, pioneer aviator, novelist and playwright, prizefight promoter, radio news commentator, owner of British movie studios, film actor, writer and director. The son of an affluent varnish manufacturer in Staffordshire, England, Mander had a knack for getting kicked out of school and a genius for going broke. Early on, the young and wealthy Mander pursued his horse racing and auto racing enthusiasms (in 1910 he set the Monte Carlo–Nice racing record and reached the finals for the Prix at Paris) before losing all his money and joining the Army. Later he formed several of his own motion picture firms but eventually they all collapsed despite the fact that he turned out the most successful of all British silent films, 1928's *The First Born*, which he produced, directed, acted in and co-wrote (based on his own novel and play!).

He had also produced a number of talking short features in 1925, and is credited with discovering screen stars Merle Oberon and Madeleine Carroll. Apart from the films he wrote, produced or directed, and apart from the Swedish, German, Danish, Italian and French films in which he appeared in the late '20s, he also turns up in British pictures like Hitchcock's *The Pleasure Garden* (1926) and *Murder* (1930), as well as *The Private Life of Henry VIII* (1933). After an unsuccessful 1934 campaign for a seat in Parliament, he gravitated to Hollywood and played a long string of character parts in costume pictures and historical epics. Dead in Hollywood of a heart ailment in February 1946, the 57-year-old actor left a will that read in part,

> I wish to take this last opportunity to express my gratitude to the American people and their Government for permitting me to spend the last years of my life in their marvelous country, enjoying the American way of life.

Rathbone and Bruce are in rare form in *The Pearl of Death*, thanks to a good, dramatic story that also puts Holmes' reputation in danger. Implicated in the Borgia Pearl theft, Rathbone's Holmes seems more harried and intense, and takes out his frustration on poor Lestrade; it's an interesting bit of character development, Holmes with a new, frazzled attitude now that it's *his* ass in the sling. Bruce is also somewhat more serious and generally helpful, although there are of course the expected comedy relief moments for the bumbling Watson. Dennis Hoey gets a bigger than usual part, and enjoys several of the film's funnier bits. (For a change, Hoey wears a toupee as Lestrade in this entry.)

As usual, disguises and false identities play a large part in the story, with Rathbone, Mander and Evelyn Ankers donning a variety of facial makeups and outfits. Holmes' impersonation of a clergyman on the Dover boat is particularly ineffective: The character's face is kept in darkness and his voice sounds dubbed, so audiences instantly suspect that this guy isn't what he seems. Mander impersonates a museum workman and an elderly, nearsighted visitor to Holmes' Baker Street digs. Ankers spends so much of her screen time imitating others (a tourist, a dishwasher, a match girl, a prim shop clerk) that we don't get to see much of her as Naomi Drake. The disguise-a-thon reaches its zenith when Holmes disguises his voice, impersonating Conover, while on the phone with a disguised Naomi!

Making his Universal horror film debut in *The Pearl of Death* is Rondo Hatton, the real-life victim of acromegaly, playing Mander's strong-arm man "The Hoxton Creeper."* Universal saw horror movie star potential in Hatton, but apparently not enough to give him the sort of buildup he really needed. Hatton was no Titan of Terror, like Karloff or Lugosi, or a Master of Menace like Chaney Jr.; he wasn't even on a level with Elizabeth Russell, the Houri of Horror, or Acquanetta, the Venezuelan Volcano. A lowly Glutton of Glands, Hatton remained a minor-league player, added to the Universal lineup at the bottom of the horror cycle's final inning. As a starring or featured actor he went to bat four times for the studio after making his bow in *Pearl of Death*, and went down swinging every time. Hatton was a formidable physical presence, and in the right vehicle, like *Pearl*, he could be an imposing asset to the picture. Universal felt that Hatton would catch the public's fancy, and plug-ugly roles for the one-time bit player were written into the desultory *The Jungle Captive* and *The Spider Woman Strikes Back*. It might not have been dignified work but at least it eventually paid well: Hatton's paychecks grew, from the $408.35 he raked in for his work on *Pearl* to the $3,500 he earned for starring in 1946's *The Brute Man* (he was that film's highest-salaried player).

Suspense builds nicely around Hatton's Creeper character in *The Pearl of Death*. Early dialogue references to the back-breaking killer whet our curiosity ("A monster ... with the chest of a buffalo [not a Moose?] and the arms of a gorilla"); later we get short glimpses of the Creeper in silhouette or in shadow. Swaying side to side in wind-up toy fashion, his lethal hands concealed in tight surgical gloves, the character seems more monstrous than human; there's no

**The Creeper's ability to stand out as a horror even in Hoxton, London's most notorious slum area, rates a tip of the hat to the ol' back-bruiser. According to the 2003 book* Clouds of Glory: A Hoxton Childhood *by former member of Parliament Bryan Magee, who lived there the first nine years of his life, Hoxton was called "the leading criminal quarter of London, and indeed of all England" in a report written at the turn of the twentieth century. It was known for its poverty and crime, and for being London's busiest market for stolen goods; its main thoroughfare Hoxton Street had the reputation of being Britain's roughest. "The old Hoxton" was eradicated by the German blitz and by slum clearance programs. The new one is now among inner London's most fashionable areas.*

mention of his facial deformity, making the first close-up of Hatton (in Boncourt's foyer, at the very end of the film) a genuine eye-opener. The Breen Office recommended that Holmes only shoot the Creeper once, but a unique and terrifying menace like this needed more than just a single bullet; ignoring the censors' mandate, Holmes plugs him three times. The Breen Office additionally suggested the removal of a scene of Naomi (as the dishwasher), after being slapped by her boss, kicking him in the groin.

The score is one of the Holmes series' best; the slow and eerie "Creeper motif" was later heard in *The Mummy's Curse* and perfectly suited that vehicle for Kharis, another low-velocity Universal monster. Sounding ahead-of-its-time is the genuinely scary musical cue heard in the final reel as the Creeper stalks an uncharacteristically panicked Holmes in the Boncourt home; director Neill sets this scene in a comparatively small, low-ceilinged room, adding to the sense of hemmed-in terror. Working wonders with sets was one of the many talents of director Roy William Neill, according to Dennis Hoey's son Michael A. Hoey, nine years old when his father invited him to watch some of the shooting of *The Pearl of Death*. Michael told the authors:

> I asked if my friend Neville Jason could come along, and my dad was agreeable to that, and so the two of us went with him over to Universal and watched the shooting of the museum scene where the villain steals the pearl, runs across the room and up some stairs, crashes out through a stained-glass window and escapes. In the movie, the villain was played by Miles Mander, but it was a stunt double, naturally, who went out through the window. At the time I thought, "My *God*, it's real glass!," but of course in those days it was actually candy glass — plates of "glass" which could be broken without injury. After the scene was shot, Roy William Neill gave Neville and me, as a souvenir, a fairly large piece of this broken "glass." Of course, when Neville and I went home, we began to turn my garage into a "soundstage" and put together a "camera" out of cardboard boxes and immediately began to "re-film" the whole sequence with our imagination. That was how I first began to really become fascinated with film, by watching the making of films with my father.

(Michael went on to become an editor, writer, producer and director.)

Michael continues:

> I met Roy William Neill on a couple of occasions. He was an Irishman, a very nice man, and an *amazing* director. You know how everything looks large to you when you're small? Well, I remember that when I went on that museum set, at that time, at *that* age, my thought was, "My goodness, it's much smaller than I imagined it would be." But when I saw the movie on the screen, that set looked fabulous. Those Sherlock Holmes films were basically B-movies, they didn't spend a lot of money on sets and things like that, but Neill could take a set and make it look incredible with the way he had it lit. He was a marvelously talented man. Another set that comes to mind is the one they used for the hospital ward in the opening reel of Neill's *Frankenstein Meets the Wolf Man*, where Patric Knowles and my father come in to talk to Lon Chaney, Jr. It's just this large, kind-of strange-looking arrangement with a couple of walls, a couple of pillars in the foreground, and then a big opening in one wall and a splash of light representing a window. That's all there was, but on-screen it *looks* incredible. Neill had an amazing ability to take all of these modest sets and make them look absolutely fascinating.

The Pearl of Death, the third homerun in nine months for the Holmes series (after *The Spider Woman* and *The Scarlet Claw*), helped make 1944 the franchise's best year. But one wonders how Rathbone would have felt about the movie, remarkable for its lineup of grisly, sadistically motivated murders and for its "monster," when/if he later revisited it. In the 1950s, he wrote that he deplored the rise of violence in the world of mystery fiction:

> I regret the passing of an era both in novel writing and in dramatic offerings. It seems almost as if the age of charm, of delicate humor and drawing room conversation, is gone for good. I greatly doubt whether some of our immortals of the stage could even find employment today.

A gem of a B mystery, suspense-filled and excitingly mounted, *The Pearl of Death* features an unholy *three* villains for the price of one and furnishes a fine debut vehicle for Rondo Hatton's Creeper. Executive producer Benedict rated it as his personal favorite among the Holmeses ... and perhaps also enjoyed getting his disguised version of *Farewell My Lovely* "in the can" (it wrapped on May 1, 1944) exactly one week before the start of production on RKO's sanctioned *Farewell My Lovely* adaptation *Murder, My Sweet*.

Miles Mander, a member of the cast of

Murder, My Sweet, no doubt went directly into that picture after finishing *Pearl of Death*. And so, a few weeks after his *Pearl* character was killed by the Creeper, his *Murder* character was killed ... by Moose Malloy.

Critics' Corner

Rating: ★★½ [O]ne of the best.... [A] workmanlike baffler and therefore intriguing! ... [E]xceptionally good Universal murder mystery.—*The New York Daily News*, August 26, 1944, Wanda Hale

Although the picture is one of the weaker numbers of the Sherlock Holmes series, thus giving rise to hope that it is tapering off to an unprofitable conclusion, it cannot be said that Mr. Rathbone seems tired of his chore.... It succeeds in impressing one with the fact that the picture is better made and acted more competently than the material deserves.—*The New York Post*, August 1944, Archer Winsten

The pace set by Roy William Neill ... is brisk and suspenseful, never faltering. A further element of realism is lent to the film by the work of Virgil Miller and Paul Sawtell, director of photography and music, respectively.—*The Motion Picture Herald*, September 2, 1944, Mandel Herbtsman

The picture builds up suspense and, of course, holds a good share of thrills and horror-chills. The Rathbone-Bruce team turns in a good, solid performance....—*The New York Times*, August 26, 1944, Paul P. Kennedy

[*The Pearl of Death*] will succeed in diverting most murder mystery addicts.... Rondo Hatton plays [the Creeper] and if he goes to the right Hollywood parties with the right people, Boris Karloff had better look to his horrors.—*The New York Herald Tribune*, August 26, 1944, Bert McCord

Too tense and horrible for children.—General Federation of Women's Clubs (Western Committee), 1944

Run-of-the-mill mystery of interest chiefly to *Sherlock Holmes* fans and any others who can overlook the fact that a great detective is capable of committing an act of such stupidity that it costs three people their lives....—National Film Music Council, 1944

The Climax

Released October 20, 1944. 86 minutes. *Executive Producer:* Joseph Gershenson. *Producer-Director:* George Waggner. *Screenplay:* Curt Siodmak & Lynn Starling. *Adapted by* Curt Siodmak *from the play by* Edward J. Locke. *Photography:* Hal Mohr & W. Howard Greene (*Technicolor*). *Technicolor Color Director:* Natalie Kalmus. *Associate:* William Fritzsche. *Music Score & Direction:* Edward Ward. *Librettos:* George Waggner. *Operettas Stager:* Lester Horton. *Vocal Director:* William Tyroler. *Orchestrator:* Harold Zweifel. *Art Directors:* John B. Goodman & Alexander Golitzen. *Director of Sound:* Bernard B. Brown. *Technician:* William Fox. *Set Decorators:* Russell A. Gausman & Ira S. Webb. *Editor:* Russell Schoengarth. *Dialogue Director:* Gene Lewis. *Makeup:* Jack P. Pierce. *Costumes:* Vera West. *Assistant Directors:* Charles S. Gould & Harry O. Jones. *Special Effects:* John P. Fulton.

Boris Karloff (*Dr. Fredrick Hohner*), Susanna Foster (*Angela Klatt*), Turhan Bey (*Franz Munzer*), Gale Sondergaard (*Luise*), Thomas Gomez (*Count Seebruck*), June Vincent (*Marcellina*), George Dolenz (*Amato Roselli*), Ludwig Stossel (*Carl Bauman*), Jane Farrar (*Jarmila Vadek*), Erno Verebes (*Brunn*), Lotte Stein (*Mama Hinzl*), Scotty Beckett (*King*), William Edmunds (*Leon*), Maxwell Hayes, Stuart Holmes (*King's Aides*), Dorothy Lawrence (*Miss Metzger*), Cyril Delevanti (*Sweeper*), Rex Lease, George Eldredge, Joe Kirk (*Reporters*), Roy Darmour (*Secretary*), Polly Bailey (*Cleaning Woman*), Ernie Adams (*Man in Audience*), Genevieve Bell (Dowager), Francis Ford (*Man*), Lee Sweetland (*Singing Voice for George Dolenz*), Grace Cunard, Maurice Costello, William Desmond, Eddie Polo, Jack Richardson, Ann Cornwall, Harry Mayo, Gertrude Astor, Helen Gibson, Fred Curtis, Homer Dickerson, Barry Regan.

I would welcome a tall glass of buttermilk and some butter cookies.
—*Boris Karloff to an assistant director after "killing" June Vincent on the set of* The Climax

---

With *Phantom of the Opera* cleaning up at box offices nationwide and well on its way to becoming one of Universal's top grossers, it was probably inevitable that the studio would announce that they were planning a sequel. In August 1943, while *Phantom* was still in general release, Universal broadcast their intention to film a *Phantom* follow-up which would be the most expensive picture on the 1943-44 schedule. The new film would team Nelson Eddy and Susanna Foster under the supervision of *Phantom* producer George Waggner.

By November, however, Universal's plans had been overhauled. *The Climax* would no longer be a sequel to *Phantom* (even though it would reunite Waggner, Foster and now *Phantom* director Arthur Lubin) but would be based on the 1909 Edward Locke play "The Climax." (Why the *Phantom* sequel had the title of the Locke play practically from the first day of planning is not clear; perhaps the initial plan was to shoehorn the Phantom character into Locke's story.) Locke's play, previously filmed by Universal in 1930, underwent a change in setting, with the story now taking place in an opera house in 1870s Vienna. At this point, George Waggner had hopes of adding Claude Rains to his cast, but ultimately it was Boris Karloff who took the top spot; Universal-wise it was his comeback after 18 months on Broadway and a 66-week national tour in "Arsenic and Old Lace." More reverses lay ahead: In January 1944, because of a last-minute change in starting dates, Arthur Lubin was diverted to another project, and producer Waggner now took on the added responsibilities of director.

Scheduled for a 47-day shoot, *The Climax* commenced on Friday, January 28, with three days' pre-production activity on the Phantom Stage and on Stages 14 and 21. Cameras rolled for the first time on Tuesday, February 1, on the Phantom Stage. At 11:10 on the evening of April 1, at the end of a 14-hour day for players Foster and Turhan Bey, production wrapped up on *The Climax*, which had run six days over schedule. A dour Arthur Lubin remembers the project well: "It was the picture that finished off George Waggner's career."

Again, as with the Rains *Phantom of the Opera*, there's no studio logo at the beginning, Universal obviously putting off the expense of shooting a color logo for as long as they possibly could. The credits are superimposed over a shot of a dark street, accompanied by cloying, string-laden romantic music — but as soon as the credits end, we see Karloff exit a house and do a measured, melodramatic "scary guy" walk down a flight of stairs and into the street, and the music instantly segues into a bombastic "Heeeeere's the bad guy" cue, like something a silent-movie theater organist would play every time the black-hatted villain came on screen.* Savvy fans in 1944 would have been able to predict, based on examining the castlist and then watching these first five seconds of the movie, that Karloff was quite obviously going to be the baddie, that he would therefore menace the boy-girl team of Turhan Bey and Susanna Foster, and that he would die at the end. And that's what happens. Feel free to skip the following, now redundant synopsis:

Fredrick Hohner (Karloff), resident physician at the Royal Theatre, carries a dark secret which is not long withheld from the audience: He walks to the theater, goes into a dressing room, plops down in a chair and indulges in ten-year-old Vaseline-edged daydreams† of the day when he realized that his sweetheart, young opera star Marcellina (June Vincent), was drifting away from him, partly because of the success of her starring vehicle "The Magic Voice." Being the selfish sort, he doesn't want theatergoers to be able to hear her voice or look at her for the price of a ticket, so when she refuses to give up her career, he strangles her. (Since that day, her embalmed body has been hidden in a shrine-like room in Hohner's palatial home.)

Music student Angela Klatt (Susanna Foster) and her fiancé Franz Munzer (Turhan Bey) are rehearsing "The Magic Voice" in the Royal Theatre's music library when Angela's golden voice is overheard by Hohner and Count Seebruck (Thomas Gomez), the theater impresario. Hohner is outraged that Angela should give voice to this "sacred" music, but Seebruck is impressed by her talent and offers her a singing role in the theater's current production. Angela is a smash and Seebruck now plans to revive "The Magic Voice" as a vehicle for the pretty newcomer.

The mad Hohner is determined to thwart Seebruck's plan. He lures Angela to his home under false pretenses, then hypnotizes the girl and plants in her mind the notion that she will never again wish to sing. Hohner also makes her a present of an atomizer which will remind the girl, even in her posthypnotic state, of his control.

Count Seebruck gathers members of the press at the Royal Theatre to announce his plans for Angela. But when she attempts to sing an aria for them, she is helpless but to obey the subconscious command Hohner planted in her mind; her voice breaks and the mystified girl rushes to her dressing room in tears. Plans for the "Magic Voice" revival progress but Seebruck now intends to star bitchy prima donna Jarmila

**In one Karloff interview, he said that one of his pet peeves was horror movies' heavy, sinister "Heeeeere's the bad guy" background music.*

†*According to Harold Heffernan of* The Detroit News, *who visited the set during the shooting of this scene, "[T]he cameraman has a cobwebby screen and other mystic gadgets attached to the lens to give the thing an eerie complexion on the screen." Whoever reviewed* The Climax *for the National Board of Review thought Susanna Foster also played the part of Marcellina.*

(Jane Farrar, playing exactly the same kind of character she did in *Phantom of the Opera*) in the production.

Hohner insists that Angela requires professional care and convinces the girl to stay in his home, where the hypnosis treatments secretly continue. Luise (Gale Sondergaard), once a maid and friend to Marcellina, works as Hohner's housekeeper because she is convinced that someday she will find evidence that links him to Marcellina's "disappearance." Luise tricks Hohner into leaving the house, which gives Franz an opening to rush in and carry Angela off to safety.

Franz feels that if Angela has an opportunity to sing "The Magic Voice" in front of a live audience, she will be cured of her mysterious malady. Seebruck balks at the notion, but Franz and his uncle Carl (Ludwig Stossel) are able to convince the country's boy-king (Scotty Beckett) to command a performance. On opening night, Angela is apprehensive until Franz smashes the atomizer, releasing her from Hohner's spell. Hohner abducts Angela and takes her to his house, where he is preparing to slit her vocal cords when Franz and Carl arrive on the scene; Franz rushes her back to the theater while Carl holds Hohner at gunpoint. Angela appears on stage and, after a false start, finds her voice and her confidence once again.

Back at Hohner's, the mad sawbones clubs Carl and rushes upstairs to the shrine just as police arrive at the house. Hohner accidentally knocks over a brazier, setting fire to the room's curtains. As the policemen look on, Hohner perishes in the flames.

It's difficult, in dissecting a muddle of a movie like *The Climax*, to know just where to start and to stop. It's some poor fool of a studio executive's idea of a work of art with its gaslit sets, gaudy costumes, stiff acting and stretches of pseudo-classical music. George Waggner's intention had to have been to create a plushy, "artful" costume melodrama with an added accent on operatic themes. But *The Climax*, a piece of costume jewelry posing as the real thing, comes no closer to art than a 60-minute horse opera.

The Climax has all of the weaknesses and none of the virtues of *Phantom of the Opera*. Here again, as in *Phantom*, the horror elements which ought to be the main thrust of the film are subordinated. The plot pivots around a young soprano and her boyfriend while the menace is reduced to a secondary character. The *Climax* trailer features screen-filling ad lines like MANIA RISING TO FLAMING HEIGHTS OF TERROR! and calls Karloff "the terrifying star of *Arsenic and Old Lace*," when the movie is actually just the story of a Gloomy Gus (Karloff) throwing cold water on Vienna's version of Mickey and Judy (Bey and Foster) when they try to put on a show. Lengthy musical interludes break up the picture and would have diluted the suspense had there actually *been* any suspense. In the role of the king of Austria, we

Boris Karloff as the obsessed murderer Dr. Hohner in *The Climax*, Universal's follow-up to *Phantom of the Opera*.

get Scotty Beckett of the *Our Gang* series. Nearly everything that could possibly be wrong with this sort of picture afflicts *The Climax*, seemingly beyond the laws of chance.

The film's few "horrific" moments are appallingly tame. Dr. Hohner sweeps Marcellina off her feet and strangles her (with one hand) in a matter of only a few seconds; never once does the gloomy expression on his face change. His frequent references to the dead diva begin to sound like a broken record; he must also set a record for the number of times he calls another character (Angela) "my dear." The dreaded atomizer has its own ominous two-note motif, identical to one repeatedly heard in 1932's *The Most Dangerous Game*(!), and the effect becomes comical. Hohner's "attack" on Luise is especially badly written and staged. Alone with Hohner, the woman, at last triumphant after ten years spent trying to link him to Marcellina's disappearance, calls him a murderer and gleefully announces she's going to call the police — and yet she just stands there as Hohner menacingly saunters toward her. When he finally gets kissing close and reaches up to squeeze her throat, her face takes on a very mild look of surprise.

Probably intended as the horror highlights of the film are the short scenes set in Hohner's shrine to Marcellina (called the Blue Beard Room in a set construction memo). Here in a canopied bed lies the embalmed (stuffed?) body of Marcellina, untouched by decay despite the passage of years; there's just a hint of necrophilia here, although no objections were raised by the Breen Office brigade. Breen did object to an early script's implication that Hohner commits suicide by throwing himself upon Marcellina's burning bier; Universal adopted his suggestion that Hohner attempt to escape before collapsing onto the bed. (The fiery finish is a lazy copout, although one disgruntled critic pointed out that the scene illuminates a movie theater nicely and permits a smart viewer to make a hasty exit ahead of the crowd!)

No one ever explains why Hohner is still employed at the opera house when everybody right down to the doorman knows he's nuts. No one ever explains why he lives in a veritable palace when his only visible means of support is as the theater's "Say *ah*" guy. No one ever explains why, after ten years, Marcellina's old dressing room is still permanently closed off, the contents preserved like it was Abe Lincoln's log cabin. No one ever explains how in the *world* Luise the housekeeper could spend ten years in Hohner's house searching for evidence and *not* find the enormous shrine room. But none of this matters because, out in movie theater and TV audiences, no one has ever really cared!

Horror also took a backseat to music in the 1943 *Phantom*, but at least that film had some atmosphere and a few action highlights (the acid-throwing, several murders, the falling chandelier and the climactic unmasking and cave-in). The closest thing to "suspense" in *The Climax* are the scenes of Susanna Foster starting to sing and then doing an el foldo; what would today be an *American Idol* outtake was advertised in 1944 as a MASTERPIECE OF HORROR (again from the trailer). Perhaps the creepiest thing in the movie is the flashback scene of Karloff, pushing 60, trying to make lovey-dovey with college-age June Vincent. Had *The Climax* been made with someone other than a Karloff type in the Gloomy Gus role, it probably wouldn't have been promoted as a horror film and probably wouldn't have made this book.

Karloff gives the sort of performance which makes it clear that either he considered the film beneath him, or that "Arsenic and Old Lace" had gotten him to the point where his natural instinct was to constantly try to project "Don't forget, I'm the Villain!" to the back row of the theater. Some of the actor's fans don't care to admit it, but it's fairly obvious from watching *The Climax, House of Frankenstein, Voodoo Island* (1957), *Frankenstein 1970* (1958), etc., that Karloff had a take-the-money-and-run policy when it came to some assignments; just as clearly as you can see the actor "going the extra mile" *one* way (*The Body Snatcher* being perhaps the best example), you can *also* tell when he's doing the reverse. Edward Bernds, sound man on some of Karloff's starring vehicles at Columbia, saw him go in both directions:

> Because of Karloff's standing, [director] Roy William Neill had a pretty decent budget and schedule on *The Black Room* [1935], and Roy took real pains with the picture. He didn't have to work long hours to meet a quickie schedule and I believe the film turned out well. I had the feeling that Neill and Karloff had a lot of respect for one

another, and Karloff seemed well-satisfied with the film and his performance in it. That certainly wasn't true of some other films he made for Columbia with other directors. Karloff on them was more aloof and seemed a lot less happy with the material.

Karloff plumbs new depths of detachment in *The Climax*, where he's so cold he has arctic circles under his eyes. In this 86-minute movie, his performance has more than enough time to go from disappointing to downright irritating. Remembering *The Climax* for the authors, Susanna Foster has no fond memories of her costar:

> Boris Karloff was ice cold, and I never had any kind of a relationship with him. On *Phantom*, Claude Rains was reserved but he had that little vicious twinkle, so cute—you could understand why he had four wives! He and I had a friendship that was kind of quiet. I loved him and I loved working with him. Working with Karloff was like working with a slab of ice.

Turhan Bey was surprised to learn from us about Foster's reaction to Karloff:

> He was an Englishman, and Englishmen are not as outgoing as Americans are on the set. But, my God, he was a very pleasant, wonderful partner whom you could rely on to give you every cue—so disciplined! I didn't know Susie felt that way about him. Boris was a very shy man who I don't think associated really in what I would call a palsy-walsy form with anybody on the set.

Of his own role in the picture, he continued,

> I enjoyed that part very much. It wasn't a very large role, but it was very interesting and quite different from what I had done before.... To me, it was a great pleasure playing it. George Waggner was a wonderful, sensitive man, one of the most enthusiastic people I'd ever known. I think you could have given him a Mickey Mouse picture to do—no offense to Mickey Mouse [*laughs*]—and he would have put as much of his efforts and excitement and enthusiasm into that. I had one big row with him, and it was my own fault. It was a scene where he needed the camera to stay very long on me, for a dissolve, and I had to hold still. Then suddenly I said, "This is too long for me. I just can't stand it any more." Poor George, he had to do something much different from what he had planned. That was our only row and it was my own doing.

Lovely Susanna Foster gives a good performance, easily the best in the picture. While the studio's nightingale-in-residence allows that Universal did talk about making a sequel to *Phantom of the Opera*, she maintains that no real plans for a sequel were actually ever laid.

> They just took me and Karloff and Turhan Bey and did *The Climax*, which was a kind of sequel. I loved working with Turhan, the color was beautiful and I loved working with Hal Mohr, the cameraman. I enjoyed it very much. What I didn't like were those hypnosis scenes—I was sick for days after watching that damned hypnosis gizmo winding around. Nauseating! They kept going back, shot after shot. And the title *The Climax* was terrible—it should have been called *The Magic Voice*.

Remembering producer-director George Waggner, Foster recalls good times and bad.

> George Waggner was a very stoic, stiff-upper-lip kind of person—he hid his emotions. I was always very good about being on time, but I came back late from lunch one day on *Frisco Sal* [1945] and he bawled me out unmercifully. He broke me up completely, and I cried one whole afternoon—they couldn't work the whole day! I didn't do it on purpose, I just couldn't believe that George would do a thing like that.

Waggner again shocked Foster by discharging her musical director-friend Edward Ward.

> George fired Eddie from the lot because of drinking and I felt just everything went for me because Eddie and I bloomed together. That just killed me. And I thought, how could George, after all of those years of being associated with Eddie, cut him off like that? I didn't care if Eddie did sometimes come in shaking, he still did his job.
>
> George Waggner was like a soldier and his idea was to discipline you. And I meant a lot to George; he told me that recently, just before he passed away. He said, "I'll never forget you coming down the stairs in *Phantom*." He was a warmhearted man, basically, but he had this military thing about him.

Waggner was back to Universal Bs following the *Climax* debacle. He directed only five films after leaving Universal (*The Gunfighters* [1947], *The Fighting Kentuckian, Operation Pacific* [both 1951, both with John Wayne], *Destination 60,000* and *Pawnee* [both 1957]) although he also worked extensively in television, where he whimsically billed himself george

Susanna Foster poses for the camera with producer-director George Waggner on the *Climax* set (courtesy Photofest).

waGGner. He died at the Motion Picture Home in 1984.

Every other performance in *The Climax* is a disappointment, usually because of the writing. Turhan Bey, more animated than usual, again plays the piano (after *The Mad Ghoul*) but this time also plays the *fool* as Franz. Nervously watching Foster's stage debut, Bey absent-mindedly takes bites out of his program like a billy goat, sings along from the audience and

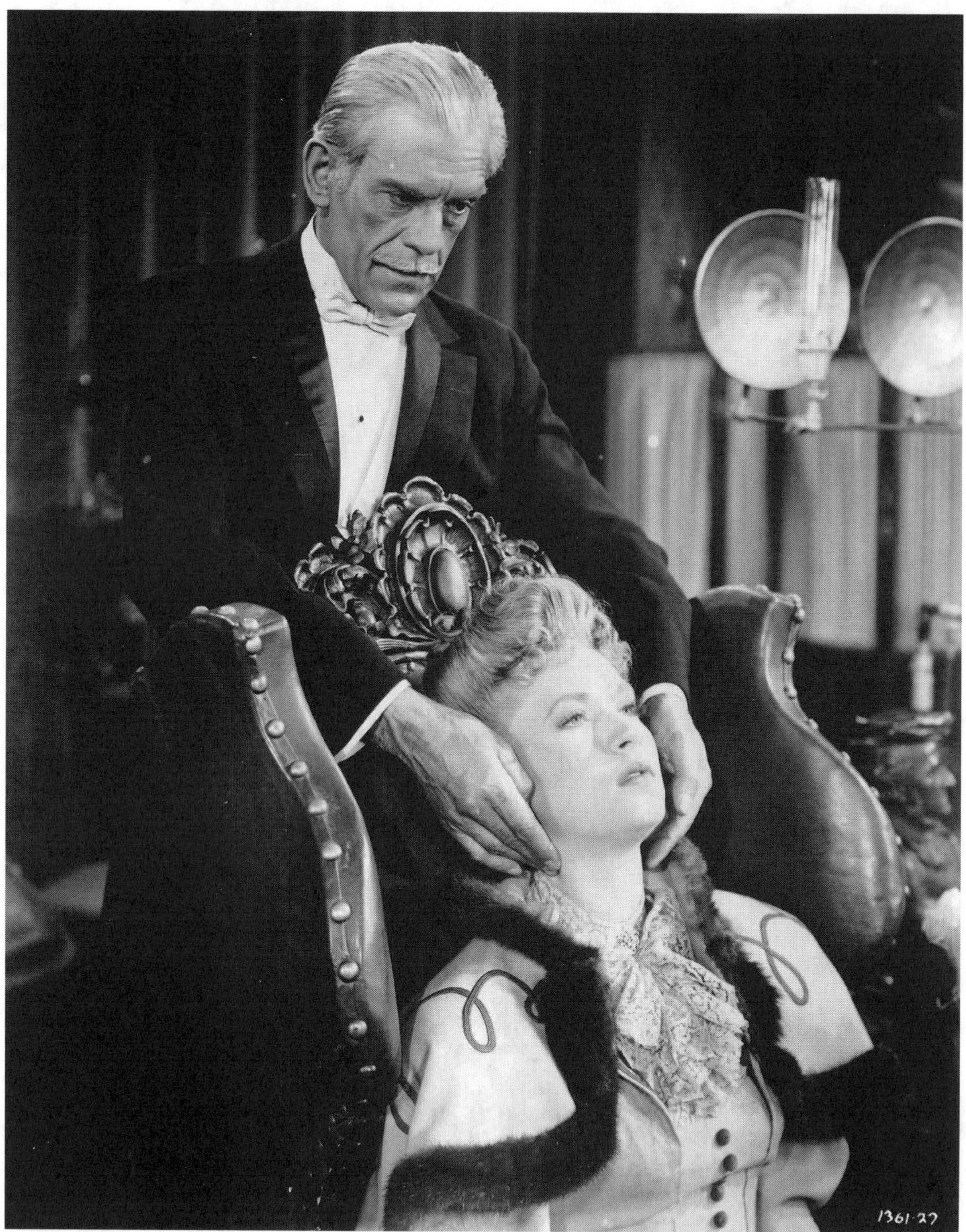

Demented opera house physician Karloff works his black magic on Foster.

joins the standing ovation with the little that's left of the program hanging out of his mouth; during a later appearance, he claps long and loud after everyone else has stopped and until every eye in the place is upon him. (Bey had just returned from a loanout to MGM, where he made his one major film, *Dragon Seed*, with Katharine Hepburn; the *Climax* poster played him up as *Dragon Seed*'s "Romantic Hit.") All of *The Climax*'s "humor" is equally forced, from the bickering of rival opera stars Jane Farrar and George (father of Mickey) Dolenz, to the frumpy low-jinks of Ludwig Stossel and the cutesy posturing of boy king Scotty Beckett. Maria Ouspenskaya met with George Waggner on the fourth day of shooting to discuss a role (probably the part of Mama Hinzl, ultimately played by Lotte Stein), but obviously came away empty-handed.

The cost for *The Climax*'s tired-blood script ran up to a surprising total. A $650-a-week writer, Curt Siodmak worked on the project for nearly 20 weeks, raking in $12,891.65. Lynn Starling, whose list of credits otherwise leans heavily toward comedies (including the 1939 *The Cat and the Canary*), worked four and a half weeks at a weekly rate of $1250. Dialogue director Gene Lewis worked on the script as well, earning $700-plus for his contribution. "Stenos and miscellaneous" were paid over $1,200. The total script cost amounted to $20,500. The movie itself ended up costing $750,000.

On the night of March 2, 1944, 27th day of production of *The Climax*, the 17th Annual Academy Awards were held at Grauman's Chinese Theatre, hosted by Jack Benny; *Climax* cinematographers Hal Mohr and W. Howard Greene won an Oscar for their work on *Phantom of the Opera* (presented by Rosalind Russell), as did its art-set directors Alexander Golitzen, John B. Goodman, Russell A. Gausman and Ira S. Webb (presented by Carole Landis). The same art-set directors would later be nominated for *The Climax*.

The Climax was the first color film for Karloff, who worked on the picture from February 1 to March 29. The actor had signed a two-picture, $60,000 contract with Universal, with two-thirds of his salary earmarked for *The Climax* and the remaining third designated for a second picture (which turned out to be *House of Frankenstein*). On screen he gets top billing but on the posters he's *third*-billed(!).

"It was not a great picture as far as I was concerned," says Susanna Foster, in a textbook example of understatement. Evening clothes, a cape and a silk hat do not make a class act out of a bored Karloff and an unimaginative reverse-twist on the Trilby theme can't sustain interest for 86 minutes — or even close. *The Climax* sizes up as one of Universal's more outstanding horror disappointments.

Critics' Corner

Rating: ★★½ [A] poor imitation of the Gaston Leroux thriller. — *The New York Daily News*, December 14, 1944, Kate Cameron

[S]tarts off on a fine ghoulish tangent, but soon wanders off the straight, narrow and creepy path onto a sidetrack of conventional boy-girl doings.... It has too much difficulty deciding whether to keep its mind on music or murder. — *The New York Herald-Tribune*, December 14, 1944

Having hit a successful pattern for a musical-horror film with its *Phantom of the Opera* a year or so ago, Universal is repeating the process in an almost identical film.... [T]he brooding malevolence of Mr. Karloff ... and the vocal displays of Susanna Foster ... have their entertaining points.... The staging of these lively numbers, with fancy choruses and corps de ballet, is more in the Radio City fashion than in that of an old opera house. But who is going to cite anachronisms when the whole film is one whopping hoax? — *The New York Times*, December 14, 1944, Bosley Crowther

George Waggner's contributions to the enterprise are multiple and competent.... While action and comedy are subordinated to suspense, music and spectacle, the production is high in popular entertainment values. — *The Motion Picture Herald*, September 30, 1944, E.A. Cunningham

It has been seldom indeed that Hollywood has produced a picture of an artistic stature equal to ... *The Climax*. The occasions have been rarer still when a picture successful artistically has been able to boast a balancing commercial and man-in-the-street appeal to insure its being one of the top money films in its studio's history. But the laurel of artistry and the same prediction of boxoffice acceptance undeniably belongs to this thrilling George Waggner production. — *The Hollywood Reporter*, 1944

Karloff excellently handles the heavy spot of the maniacal physician.... — *Variety*, September 21, 1944, "Walt"

The story ... is theatrical and full of artificial situations but the period decors and costumes, together with a fine cast, create a pleasant enough illusion which is further enhanced by Technicolor. — National Board of Review, 1944

A sparkling musical mystery of such ingenuity of plot that the audience is held spellbound. — American Legion Auxiliary, 1944

Numbers and arias are stylized for a bygone time — a period and treatment reminiscent of Anthony Hope. The Chopin "Minute Waltz" is cleverly adapted for coloratura and the Schubert "Marche Militaire" is ideal for the men's choruses. The Viennese lilt, the fanfare for the King — all are delightful.... Miss Foster sings with charm, simplicity and good style and her manner of attacking her phenomenal high notes is improving. — National Film Music Council, 1944

The Climax is a film that gave me a new appreciation for the fast forward button on my remote.... Boris

Karloff turns in a fascinating performance against nearly insurmountable odds.—Nathalie Yafet, *Boris Karloff*, MidMar Press, 1996

In 1944, after 13 years of star performances in horror thrillers, Boris Karloff could play villains in his sleep. In *The Climax*, unfortunately, he does just that.... [H]is dull, gloomy portrayal is the sourest note in a symphony of dramatic slip-ups.—"Dr. Cyclops," *Fangoria* #157, October 1996

Dead Man's Eyes

Released November 10, 1944. 64 minutes. An Inner Sanctum Mystery, produced by arrangement with Simon & Schuster, Inc., Publishers. *Associate Producer:* Will Cowan. *Executive Producer:* Ben Pivar. *Director:* Reginald LeBorg. *Original Screenplay:* Dwight V. Babcock. *Photography:* Paul Ivano. *Editor:* Milton Carruth. *Musical Director:* Paul Sawtell. *Art Directors:* John B. Goodman & Martin Obzina. *Dialogue Directors:* Stacy Keach & Phil Brown. *Set Decorators:* Russell A. Gausman & Leigh Smith. *Special Photography:* John P. Fulton. *Sound Director:* Bernard B. Brown. *Technician:* William Hedgcock. *Assistant Director:* Seward Webb. *Camera Operator:* William Dodds. *Properties:* Ernie Smith. *Gowns:* Vera West.

Lon Chaney, Jr. (*Dave Stuart*), Jean Parker (*Heather Hayden*), Paul Kelly (*Dr. Alan Bittaker*), Acquanetta (*Tanya Czoraki*), Thomas Gomez (*Police Capt. Drury*), Jonathan Hale (*Dr. Samuel Welles*), George Meeker (*Nick Phillips*), Edward Fielding (*Stanley "Dad" Hayden*), Eddie Dunn (*Policeman Moriarity*), Pierre Watkin (*Attorney*), Beatrice Roberts, Gwen Kenyon (*Nurses*), John Elliott (*Trevers*), Rex Lease (*Taxi Driver*), Allen Fox (*Waiter*), Leslie O'Pace (*Headwaiter*), David Hoffman (*Inner Sanctum*), Gil Perkins (*Stunts*).

All of this is brought to a high point of ineptness by a sloe-eyed lady known as Acquanetta who seems to have run a talent for inarticulateness into professional recognition. —*Paul P. Kennedy,* The New York Times, *October 7, 1944*

The individual Inner Sanctum films have gotten their critical lumps, at the time they were released as well as today, usually deservedly. Taking the series as a piece, however, placing them in the context of their time and the circumstances in which they were made, the franchise proved to be a viable concept that paid off commercially.

After directing the first two films in the series, Reginald LeBorg reluctantly returned to the director's chair yet again for *Dead Man's Eyes*, although itching for a change of pace and better assignments: "The Inner Sanctum pictures made a lot of money. They only cost $125,000 to $150,000 each. That was the trouble. I was good with these. I couldn't get any better." LeBorg, who admitted to liking stories that had some basis in medical fact, was attracted to the Dwight V. Babcock script.

Dead Man's Eyes is basically a variation on the theme of a blind man trying to solve a murder (in much the same manner as Edward Arnold's blind detective character, Duncan Maclain, who was featured in two MGM mystery thrillers, *Eyes in the Night* [1942] and *The Hidden Eye* [1945]). Universal added the macabre twist of the blind man inheriting the "eyes" of the victim and setting out to find the murderer. The premise not only had a gimmicky appeal but added the ham-fisted irony of a dime-store novel. Quite appropriately since the Simon and Schuster literary series *were* dime-store novels. Introducing new medical techniques into the script probably added an interesting slant for audiences at the time who patiently sat through such programmer features in order to get to the main attraction.

The Inner Sanctum films are often compared to the studio's Crime Club pictures of the '30s although they were the product of a slightly more advanced imagination. Unlike the Crime Clubs, which were relatively happy-go-lucky affairs with amiable investigators (professionals such as Preston Foster in *The Last Warning* or *Lady in the Morgue*, or enthused dilettantes such as Donald Woods in *The Black Doll* or *Danger on the Air*) sifting through the obscure clues and even more obscure motivations, the Inner Sanctum films were cut from a different cloth. Crude and angst-ridden as these pictures were, they seemed dimly aware of the dark psychology of the situations at hand despite their boilerplate dialogue and barely fleshed-out characters. What the series unfortunately lacked was the sophistication, insight and raw talent to cobble together these elements into a cohesive whole as Robert Siodmak and other directors began to do at Universal and other studios in their early forays into film noir.

Dead Man's Eyes was afforded the usual shoestring budget and quickie 12-day schedule, with contract players Lon Chaney, Jr., and Acquanetta commanding the top salaries in the

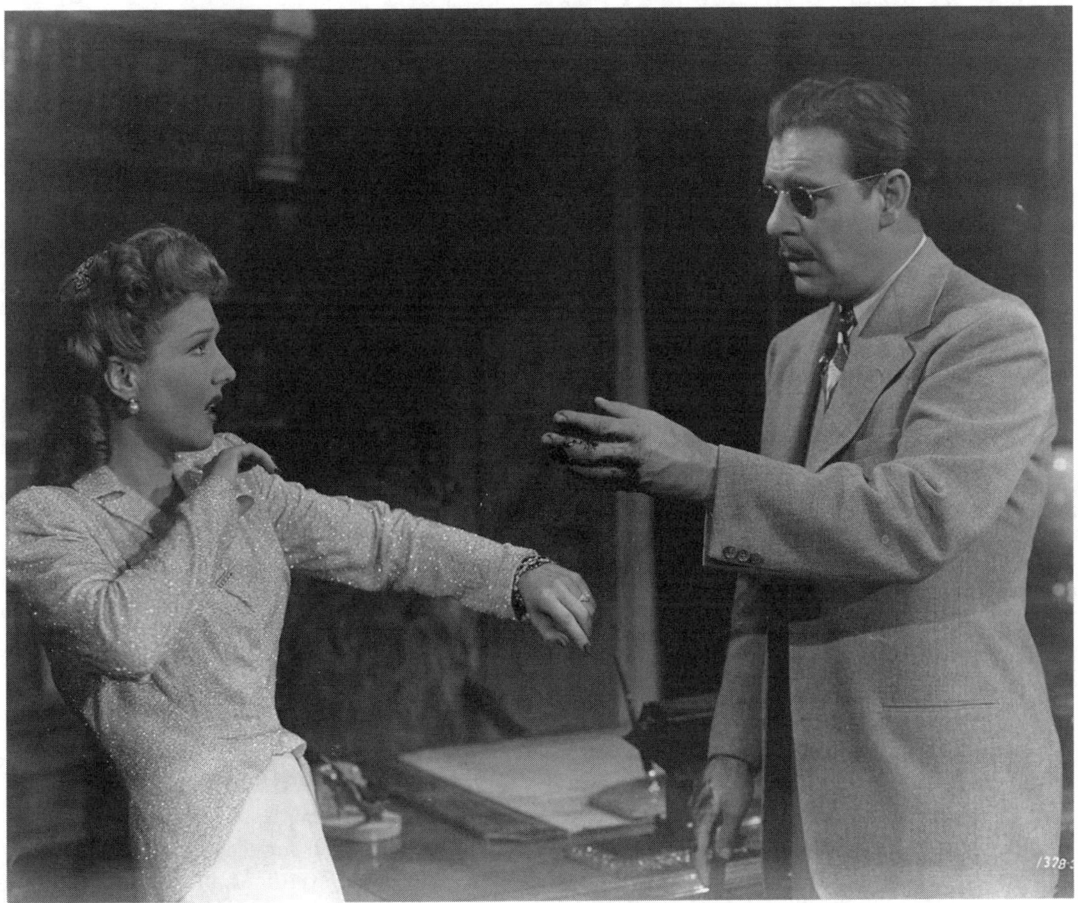

Blind artist Lon Chaney, Jr., stumbles upon a murder scene as Jean Parker reacts appropriately in *Dead Man's Eyes.*

cast: $10,000 and $4,000 respectively. Supporting actor Paul Kelly walked off with $2,750 for his labors, even nosing out leading lady Jean Parker who was only paid $2,500. Directors came considerably cheaper, with a $1,500 paycheck earmarked for Mr. LeBorg.

On March 14, 1944, Chaney, Acquanetta and Parker gathered on Stage 20 for the first shot (appropriately, the first scene in the film). Art directors John B. Goodman and Martin Obzina had created a set which was a reasonable representation of an artist's studio. The plush Hacienda set was used for the palatial digs of heiress Jean Parker in several scenes.

Dave Stuart (Lon Chaney, Jr.), a promising but not-much-in-demand artist, is confident that when his latest (an oil canvas of an exotic gypsy dancer) is completed, he'll at least be able to call his own shots in the art world. It might even earn him enough to maintain his rich fiancée Heather Hayden (Jean Parker) in the style to which she has become accustomed. But a freak accident cuts the artist's plans short. After his model, sultry Tanya Czoraki (Acquanetta), rearranges a few items on his work shelf, Dave picks up a bottle of acetic acid, thinking it's eyewash. Gripped by pain and shock, the artist desperately calls for an ambulance as his world is plunged into darkness.

Heather responds to an emergency call from the hospital, flanked by her father, Stanley Hayden (Edward Fielding), and former beau Nick Phillips (George Meeker). Eye specialist Dr. Samuel Welles (Jonathan Hale) confirms that Dave's condition is permanent unless the artist undergoes a corneal transplant to replace the damaged eye tissue.

Dave's adjustment to his new life is uneasy

at best. His career in a shambles, he spends most of his days in an alcoholic haze. "Dad" Hayden arrives to console his future son-in-law and breaks the news that he has made legal arrangements to "will" his eye tissue to Dave. Stuart rejects the offer and the pair clash over Tanya's culpability for the mishap.

Dave arrives at Hayden's estate to make amends only to find the old man's bludgeoned body lying on the floor of his study. Heather stumbles on the scene and, after seeing Dave's bloodied hands, accuses him of the crime. Capt. Drury (Thomas Gomez) of Homicide investigates but postpones putting the cuffs on Dave until he can get more evidence.

In spite of Dave's status as a murder suspect, the corneal transplant proceeds. Apparently, the graft doesn't take, leaving the artist to contemplate the hard fact that his blindness is permanent. Back at his studio, Dave shows Tanya a tiny threaded nail which he found at the murder scene. When the model reacts suspiciously, the artist is convinced she knows the identity of the murderer. Tanya is soon found clubbed to death.

An urgent call brings Tanya's beau, psychiatrist Alan Bittaker (Paul Kelly), to Dave's apartment. Accusing him point blank of being the murderer, Dave shows him that the tiny nail fits perfectly in the silver top of Bittaker's walking stick; it had become dislodged when the psychiatrist bludgeoned Hayden to death. The old man's fate was sealed when Bittaker deduced that winning Tanya's affections hinged on Dave's recovery as Tanya was in love with the artist. When Tanya discovered that the missing nail came from Alan's stick, the psychiatrist was forced to eliminate her, too. Bittaker is about to smash in Dave's skull but the artist foils him. Dave reveals that he feigned blindness after the operation in order to trap the murderer. Drury arrives on the scene and takes Bittaker into custody.

The third in the Inner Sanctum series, *Dead Man's Eyes* shows that producer Ben Pivar and Company were at least trying to vary the content, if not the style, of the franchise. *Calling Dr. Death* effectively launched the series with director LeBorg's adding idiosyncratic touches to a conventional murder story. *Weird Woman* glumly kept the formula going, introducing a strain of voodooism only to explain it away as mental suggestion at the wrap-up. With *Dead Man's Eyes*, LeBorg keeps the stylistic flourishes in check, creating a film that's less psychologically self-conscious and more in line with the traditional Hollywood whodunit. The movie is cheerfully overlit, starkly contrasting with the world of darkness that the hapless hero is thrust into. Except for a couple of brief montages, *Dead Man's Eyes* doesn't have any particular visual interest and its razor-thin plot limits its appeal to B movie buffs and hardcore Universal enthusiasts. *Dead Man's Eyes* may not be the worst of the series but it's the most conventional.

As a mystery, *Dead Man's Eyes* proves to be sadly unsubstantial, telegraphing virtually every turn of the plot long before it transpires on the screen. Starting with the murder of "Dad" Hayden, the ensuing story complications become increasingly obvious. We are to assume that the murder weapon, "the well-known blunt instrument," is Dave's walking stick, but Bittaker's own cane is a dead giveaway, especially since he dutifully totes the thing around with him in every scene. The mystery revolves solely around a small, threaded nail that the blind Stuart stumbled upon at the crime scene, far too trifling a plot contrivance even for a 64-minute feature, leaving the armchair sleuths in the audience with nothing to occupy themselves with except the murky motivations of the vacuous characters.

The narrow field of suspects doesn't leave much room for speculation. The calculating Tanya is knocked off well before the finale. Nick Phillips, Heather's simpering boor of a suitor, has red herring written all over him and is almost beneath consideration. Stuart earnestly pursues the only shred of physical evidence found on the crime scene. This leaves only Bittaker, although the script is hard-pressed to contrive the feeblest of motives for his acts of cold-blooded murder.

The "surprise" revelation that Stuart was faking blindness in the last half of the movie is given away long before the climax. He virtually flaunts his restored sight, dabbling with his paint brushes and easel yet tapping all over the place with his walking stick even when he isn't being observed by other characters. Writer Dwight V. Babcock, unsure whether to give the game away completely, seems to have wanted it both ways.

Babcock's storyline, incidentally, is similar enough to a plot twist used in the Crime Club thriller, *Mystery of the White Room* (1939), that it might have been the direct inspiration for the film. In the earlier picture, a hospital janitor (Frank Puglia) is blinded by acid by an attacker who ends up receiving the grafted corneas of an earlier victim (Frank Reicher). In the wrap-up, Puglia, using the "eyes" of his dead benefactor, is able to finger the culprit, and she's whisked away by the investigating detective.

Even allowing for the script's deficiencies (actually, most B mysteries at this time were no better than this one), *Dead Man's Eyes* is a movie that rises and falls on the appeal of its characters and the strengths of its cast, which can only be described as weak and weaker. The characters are a disagreeable lot who spend an inordinate amount of time drinking, bickering and nightclubbing. Everyone seems convinced that Dave's canvas of Tanya, a barely competent studio knock-off, will skyrocket the fledgling artist to fame, calling everyone's intelligence (as well as their eyesight) into question. The borderline comic dialogue attributes enigmatic qualities to Tanya which she clearly does not possess. "There's something primitive and passionate about her. She intrigues me!" swoons Bittaker as the camera cuts to the girl, who can only register an expression of pained indifference. Stuart, no stranger to inconsistency himself, entertains his rich girlfriend in glitzy nightspots, unmindful that he's supposed to be a struggling artist.

Chaney isn't an actor who can easily summon the sensibilities of an artist to begin with and the script doesn't make his job any easier. It's a typical Inner Sanctum performance; his role as the anguished artist is barely different from his previous roles as an anguished neurologist (*Calling Dr. Death*) or an anguished sociologist (*Weird Woman*), except *Dead Man's Eyes* finds his character fighting off the effects of a hangover most of the time. Although he doesn't appear in the movie, actor Phil Brown, Chaney's co-star in *Weird Woman*, was on the set, functioning as his colleague's dialogue director. "I came on the set the first day, and as I walked in from the outdoors, the whole stage was empty, except for Chaney sitting waaaay on the opposite side talking to somebody," Brown told the authors. "And as I walked across, I said, in a very loud voice, 'Look, Chaney, who the *fuck* wrote this hunk of shit?' Chaney turned casually, indicating the man he had been talking to, and said, 'Meet the author!' Well, what could I say? I think it's a hunk of shit and I'm sorry! I'm sorry for you and I'm sorry for all of us!"

Jean Parker, one of the classiest and most likable of B leading ladies, exudes '40s glamour as Heather. ("Jean Parker was excellent. She was very chic and amiable," recalled LeBorg.) Thomas Gomez lays it on a bit thick, as usual, as the undeterred policeman and George Meeker is saddled with the part of Parker's whiny suitor. Paul Kelly, always at his best in introspective roles, doesn't quite come across as the dapper, devil-may-care psychiatrist. Kelly was one of those actors who didn't seem to make much of an impression on audiences while unfailingly winning the admiration of his colleagues; even LeBorg lavishly praised his performance in the film. In 1948, Kelly's stage performance as the stalwart bomber unit commander in the play "Command Decision" was up against Marlon Brando's legendary Stanley Kowalski in "A Streetcar Named Desire" for the coveted Tony Award. Most of the traditional voters preferred Kelly over the upstart Brando in one of the more egregious injustices in the history of the award.

Acquanetta once again proves she's no volcano, Venezuelan or otherwise, and her monotone performance as the supposedly fiery model belongs in the annals of wretched movie acting.

Acquanetta told the authors:

> I got along with Lon Chaney beautifully. He was a good friend. I finally had some dramatic scenes, but they still would not allow me to come out. Everything was kind of capped; they wanted me to hold it to a low key. Emotions inside that were building, I had to hold down. [*Were you happy with your performance?*] Pleased, let's say. When you're new and never had the experience, as they call it, the directors are in charge. And they like that because they project themselves through you. Reginald LeBorg was a gentleman — with the accent on the gentle.

LeBorg seemed to have his hands full not only with the girl's hopeless emoting but with the antics of his producer: "Acquanetta was doing a scene and she was terrible and I wanted to rewrite it," he told the authors. "Ben Pivar wanted to know of any changes. I changed it so it would be easier for her to act it. I called him from the stage and said, 'Ben, I want to rewrite this,' and he said, 'Don't rewrite! Don't rewrite!' So I said, 'Let's talk it over first.' He said, 'I'm busy. Do it as it is and we can see it in the rushes and then see what is no good.'"

Annoyed, LeBorg sent his second assistant director to see what Pivar was doing that was so important that prevented him from coming on the set for a few moments. The assistant presently returned to report: 'He's playing gin rummy!'"

LeBorg tried valiantly to bring a bit of style to the material. He recalled:

> I did one shot that was never done before. Simultaneously, I did two close-ups. I had two cameras on the stage, one on each actor. I thought it was better acting; they could talk to each other, and they didn't have somebody behind the camera. I wanted to see photographically what it would look like if they lit it this way, and it came out beautifully.

Such technical delicacies largely go unnoticed and *Dead Man's Eyes* is generally regarded as an indifferent film at best. LeBorg finally got fed up with his assignments at Universal and what he considered to be factory-like conditions. He got a worthwhile opportunity in *Destiny* and found a comedy script to his liking, the well-regarded but rarely seen *San Diego I Love You* (1945) with Jon Hall, Louise Allbritton and, in a small role, Buster Keaton. LeBorg considered both of these films to be his personal favorites, but it wasn't enough to keep him happy. He was released from his studio contract, at his own request, in February 1945. It was a decision the director would later regret in light of the studio merger with International Pictures and their commitment to upscale entertainment. Even as a freelance director LeBorg couldn't escape the grind of B picturemaking and found himself directing Joe Palooka and Bowery Boys quickies. By the mid-'50s, he was back to directing Universal's former bogeymen in low-budget indie productions (Chaney, Lugosi, Carradine and Rathbone in the 1956 *The Black Sleep* and Karloff in 1957's *Voodoo Island*). Ironically, Reginald LeBorg's best-remembered movies were released by the studio from which he tried so hard to break away.

An odd postscript to the film. In 1961, horror-science fiction leading lady, Kathleen Crowley, suffered nearly the same fate as the Lon Chaney character in *Dead Man's Eyes*. She wanted to rinse her eyes but instead of reaching for boric acid she picked up a bottle of cleaning fluid. She was blinded and, for a time, didn't know if she would see again but eventually recovered.

Critics' Corner

Universal has another class stanza in its Inner Sanctum series with *Dead Man's Eyes*. It is a superior whodunit.... The players, headed by Lon Chaney, who appears to have inherited a great deal more than a likeness from his talented father, are all above par.... LeBorg has injected sense and good judgment into a script that in the hands of a less capable director might have been just another kid frightener.—*The Hollywood Reporter*, September 13, 1944

The acting, if, indeed, that's what one would call those gyrations and speeches by Lon Chaney, Jean Parker et al., was apparently hampered by the significant absence of anything to act about.—*The New York Times*, October 7, 1944, Paul P. Kennedy

[T]he proceedings add up to a great big yawn. The direction might have been handled by a script girl.... There are one or two moments in which [Chaney] makes you think that the show is about to generate some suspense and terror. They go out like his eyes when he accidentally washes them in a bottle of acid.—*The New York Herald-Tribune*, October 1944

Rating: ★★½ The mystery is well worked out ... but, unfortunately, the acting of some of the members of the cast is so inept and stilted and the direction lacking in spontaneity that the interest of the audience is distracted occasionally from the mysterious and dramatic doings on the screen.... Acquanetta invariably walks through her part like a somnambulist.—*The New York Daily News*, October 6, 1944, Kate Cameron

[E]ven though the identity of the murderer is not revealed until the closing scenes, one guesses early in the picture just who he is. Lon Chaney, as the blind artist, and Thomas Gomez, as the detective, are good, but the other members of the cast are unimpressive.—*Harrison's Reports*, September 16, 1944

Dead Man's Eyes is somewhat out of the pattern. It is, in spite of its thriller title, a tight crime puzzle dealing quite as much with the personalities and motives involved as with murder and clues. Unfortunately, the pace is too slow and the dialogue too trite to hold the serious attention of the audience at all times.—*The Motion Picture Herald*, September 16, 1944, E.A. Cunningham

Murder in the Blue Room

Released December 1, 1944. 61 minutes. *Associate Producer:* Frank Gross. *Executive Producer:* Edward Dodds. *Director:* Leslie Goodwins. *Screenplay:* I.A.L. Diamond & Stanley Davis. *Based on the short story* "Secret of the Blue Room" *by* Erich Philippi. *Photography:* George Robinson. *Music Director:* Sam Freed, Jr. *Art Directors:* John B. Goodman & Harold H. MacArthur. *Director of Sound:* Bernard B. Brown. *Technician:* Charles Carroll. *Set Decorators:* Russell A. Gausman & Edward R. Robinson. *Editor:* Charles Maynard. *Dance Director:* Carlos Romero. *Gowns:* Vera West. *Dialogue Director:* Howard Banks. *Special Photography:* John P. Fulton. *Songs:* "The Boogie Woogie Boogie Man" (Milton Rosen & Everett Carter), "A-Do-Dee-Doo-Doo" (Lew Porter, F.J. Tableporter & Ted Erdody), "One Starry Night" (Dave Franklin & Don George). *Assistant Directors:* Fred Frank & Mort Singer, Jr. *Camera Operator:* Eddie Cohen. *Assistant Cameraman:* Phil Lathrop.

Anne Gwynne (*Nan Kirkland*), Donald Cook (*Steve Randall*), John Litel (*Frank Baldridge*), Grace McDonald (*Peggy*), Betty Kean (*Betty*), June Preisser (*Jerry*), Regis Toomey (*Police Insp. McDonald*), Nella Walker (*Linda Baldridge*), Andrew Tombes (*Dr. Carroll*), Ian Wolfe (*Edwards*), Emmett Vogan (*Hannagan*), Bill MacWilliams [Williams] (*Larry Dearden*), Frank Marlowe (*Curtin*), Grace Hayle (*Dowager*), Alice Draper, Victoria Horne (*Maids*), Milton Parsons (*Driver*), Jack Gardner (*Booking Agent*), Robert Cherry (*Ghost*).

It's Murder to Music....
—*Trailer blurb for* Murder in the Blue Room

This fourth go-round for the Erich Philippi short story "Secret of the Blue Room" (counting the original German version) is a silly but watchable 61 minutes of B comedy, mystery and music. It doesn't come near the quality of the original *Secret of the Blue Room* (a picture that seems to improve with every insipid remake), but neither is it an insufferable stiff like the first Americanized rehash, *The Missing Guest. Murder in the Blue Room* falls prey to many of the same problems that plagued *Guest*— the mystery isn't mysterious and the comedy isn't funny — but at least the comedy isn't also obnoxious. *Murder* has new problems all its own, but it also has a better cast, a lighter approach and, best of all, a shorter running time.

A seaside country house ("played" by the Shelby House at Universal) is rumored to be haunted after the death of owner Sam Kirkland in its "Blue Room." Twenty years after Sam's death, the place is reopened by his widow Linda (Nella Walker), her new husband Frank Baldridge (John Litel) and Linda's daughter (by her first marriage) Nan (Anne Gwynne). Determined to dispel the rumors of ghosts, the Baldridges throw a housewarming party complete with an orchestra and dancing. Larry Dearden (Bill Williams), one of Nan's most ardent admirers, proposes to her as they dance, but she declines; she likes, not loves him. Nan asks another guest, debonair mystery writer Steve Randall (Donald Cook), to use his talents to solve the mystery of the Blue Room. A sudden blackout and a self-playing piano pounding out "Moonlight Sonata" get the guests to wondering whether ghosts still occupy the house. When order is restored, the Three Jazzybelles (Grace McDonald, Betty Kean, June Preisser), entertainer friends of Nan's, do one of their dancing-singing numbers, which is a hit. As the girls are leaving, they are accosted by a nerdy-looking, derby-wearing ghost (Robert Cherry) who asks for a match.

Larry, invited to spend the night, announces his intention to sleep in the Blue Room. Baldridge raises objections but Larry persists. In the morning, the room is found empty and Larry is presumed to have fallen out of a window into the sea far below.

Inspector McDonald (Regis Toomey) and his men begin their investigation. The Jazzybelles are brought back to the house to answer questions, and end up being detained there by the suspicious McDonald. The dizzy dolls want out so badly that they determine to solve the case themselves. When they sleep in the Blue Room, a hand reaches out through a secret opening in the wall at the head of the girls' bed *à la The Cat and the Canary*, touching their faces, with the expected results.

Randall becomes convinced that Sam Kirkland's murder and Larry Dearden's disappearance are linked; the only people involved in both cases are Frank Baldridge, the family physician Dr. Carroll (Andrew Tombes) and the butler (Ian Wolfe). In a too-long comedy relief sequence, the Jazzybelles truss up Edwards and grill him before lapsing into a singing-dancing rendition of the spooky novelty number "The

Boogie Woogie Boogie Man." Somewhere along the line, the comic ghost turns up again and scares one of the girls.

Steve decides to spend a night in the Blue Room; this results in *his* disappearance and the discovery of *Larry's* dead body in the room. Dr. Carroll tells Nan that Larry was her half-brother; Sam Kirkland had had an extramarital affair with a woman who became Larry's mother. The Jazzybelles find the gun which killed Larry, and Frank Baldridge, the gun's owner, is arrested.

Acting mighty suspicious, Dr. Carroll opens a panel leading into a secret passageway and steps inside. An unseen figure, gun in hand, is already in the passageway, and a gunfight between the two men ensues; Carroll is hit. McDonald arrives on the scene and finds that Randall, no worse for wear from his Blue Room experience, has done the shooting (in self-defense) as well as cracked the case. Randall explains that Dr. Carroll had found out about Sam Kirkland's little fling and threatened him with blackmail; Kirkland balked and Carroll killed him in the Blue Room. When Larry found out that Kirkland was his dad, he eventually put the facts together and began to suspect Carroll, so he had to go, too.

During his night in the Blue Room, Randall continues, he discovered an entrance to the secret passage where Larry's body was hidden; he placed the corpse in the Blue Room where it could be found so that the killer would know that he (Steve) was on to him. Dr. Carroll, dying, congratulates Steve on his fine detective work. Romance blooms between Steve and Nan, and the comedy ghost scares the Jazzybelles one last time as the curtain closes.

Murder in the Blue Room was originally written with Universal's resident clowns the Ritz Brothers slated for the comedy relief roles. (Perhaps a screening of *The Missing Guest*, in which Billy Wayne and George Cooper do an upsettingly accurate Ritz Brothers imitation, gave some studio exec the notion.) But the Ritzes apparently had become disenchanted with Universal's quickie schedules and hour-long Bs and left the studio after completing the misleadingly titled *Never a Dull Moment* (1943); they began to work the nightclub circuit and television and, as a full team, never made another film.

The departure of the Brothers Ritz prompted some rethinking, and a decision was made to replace them with a trio of *female* bumblers. According to Universal expert Michael Fitzgerald, very few changes were made to the existing (Ritz Brothers–centric) script; actress Betty Kean told Fitzgerald that the script used in shooting still called for the Ritzes, and that she read the dialogue ascribed in her script to "Harry" (Ritz). Among the small modifications made was a change for the name of the trio, from the Mad Hatters to the Three Jazzybelles. The story cost ultimately ran up to a total of $3,200; I.A.L. Diamond, later the writer of the Billy Wilder hits *Some Like It Hot* (1959), *The Apartment* (1960), *One, Two, Three* (1961) and *Kiss Me, Stupid* (1964), pocketed $2,400 while co-writer Stanley Davis, stenos and miscellaneous walked off with the rest.

With or without the Ritz Brothers, *Murder in the Blue Room* is a thoroughly unexceptional B; there's more emphasis on the humor and the musical numbers than on the event promised in its title. The story of the Blue Room itself had held center stage in *Secret* but was slightly subordinated in *The Missing Guest*; here it gets bulldozed under by comedy scenes, dance numbers and acrobatic routines. The original Blue Room story also underwent some more modifications, some for the better, others not. The reporter character played by Paul Kelly in *The Missing Guest* is dumped, with a clever mystery writer taking his place. "Vic" and "Jake," the comic goons in *Guest*, are replaced by the Jazzybelles, whose roles are expanded. And Larry, the poor bastard, is no longer a killer but a victim while Dr. Carroll extends his homicidal streak.

No one in the cast seems overly affected by the tragic goings-on in the house. Anne Gwynne, here nearing the end of her Universal tenure, wrings her hands and frets most prettily, but doesn't convey a sense of real anxiety. Donald Cook looks upon the whole business as an interesting challenge while John Litel regards it as a nuisance; McDonald, Kean and Preisser, playing the type of scared characters who exist only in movies, use the spooky situations as an excuse to pop off with one-liners. *Murder in the Blue Room* is silly only when the Jazzybelles are on screen; otherwise, everything is played straight. The trio also does some acrobatic dancing and lets loose with a few songs during the course of its 61 minutes, although it's "One Starry Night,"

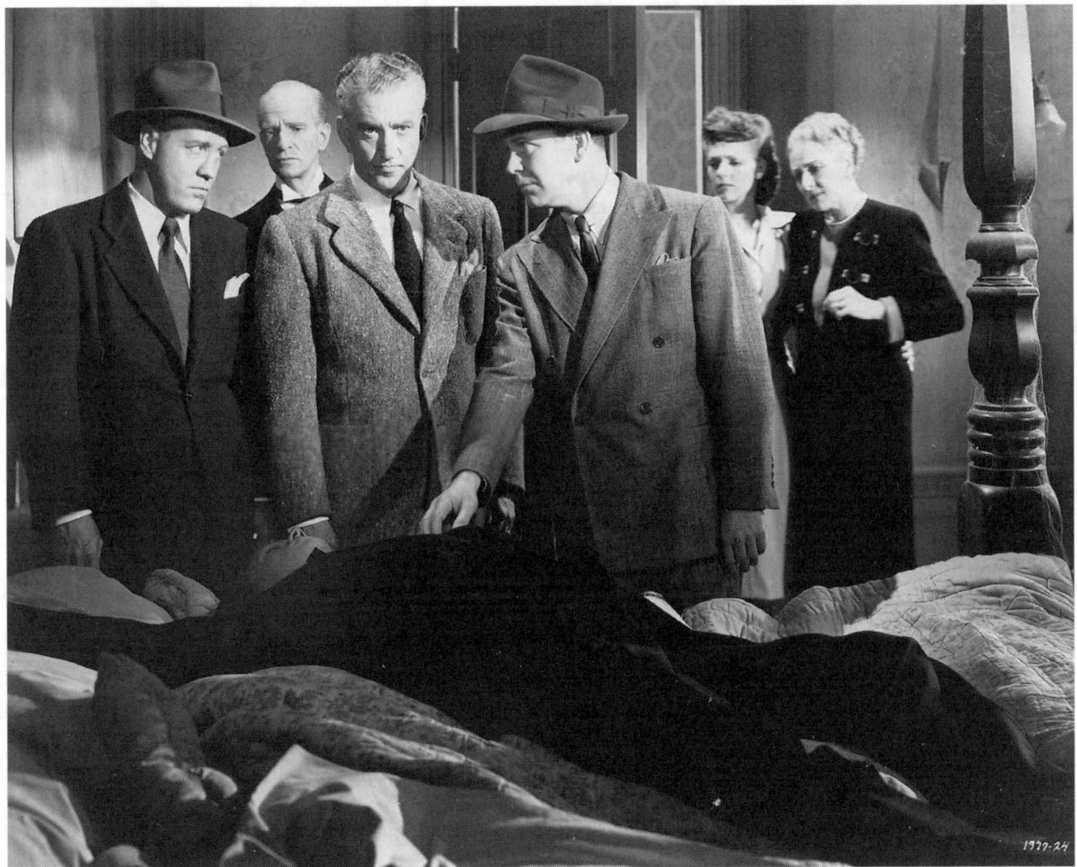

Frank Marlowe, Ian Wolfe, John Litel, Regis Toomey, Anne Gwynne, Nella Walker and (on bed) Bill Williams in the tuneful whodunit *Murder in the Blue Room* (courtesy John Cocchi).

mouthed by Anne Gwynne, that comes off as the best number in the film. "I am not always pleased with myself [on screen], but I did especially like my 'singing' of the song in the opening party scene," Anne Gwynne told Michael Fitzgerald in *Fangoria*. "[Big Band vocalist] Martha Tilton sang for me, but it really sounded and looked like I was doing it. It comes across on film when the cast is having a good time, and we certainly did on [*Murder in the Blue Room*]."

Since the Ritz Brothers were the same in every picture, it's not hard to imagine what the picture would have been like *with* them. So it's also not hard to come to the conclusion that their replacements Grace McDonald, Betty Kean and June Preisser, teaming for the first and only time in this one movie, are arguably an improvement in every way—*inarguably* in the looks department, since the Ritzes had faces only a radio audience could love.

- Grace McDonald started dance training at eight but by 11 was bedridden with an illness (alternately given in studio bios as arthritis and rheumatic fever) "which seemed to mark 'finish' to her dancing." Her brother Ray practiced *his* intricate steps beside her bed, and Grace was inspired to try to keep up with him; this may have speeded her miraculous recovery. Grace and Ray became dance partners performing in vaudeville and nightclubs and even in Broadway's "Babes in Arms." They came to Hollywood but never appeared together in a film, Ray finding a home at MGM and Grace at Universal; her genre films there were *Flesh and Fantasy* (from which she must have been cut), *Murder in the Blue Room* and *Destiny*, the latter finding the dance star playing her entire role sitting down! She died in 1999.
- Betty Kean, who plays *Murder in the Blue Room*'s Betty in a very "Joan Davis style," once

called herself "the original hard-luck girl": She became a comedienne because she was fired as a chorus girl for tripping and knocking down other girls in the line; then, in Republic's *Yokel Boy* (1942), her first Hollywood break, she worked two weeks before she slipped and fractured her ankle. Better things were in her future, like a popular sister act with Jane Kean (Walter Winchell called the comics "the female Martin and Lewis"), a stint on Broadway with Jane in the musical comedy "Ankles Aweigh" and much more. While Jane became Trixie on TV's "The Honeymooners" (during its Miami Beach–"Awaaaaay we go!" era), Betty also continued acting, right up to the 1984 SF-fantasy film *Dreamscape* with Dennis Quaid. The widow of actor Lew Parker (the father on TV's *That Girl*), Kean died in 1986.

- June Preisser danced on street corners in her native New Orleans prior to work as an acrobatic dancer, touring with her sister Cherry Blossom. She worked in the Ziegfeld Follies and then shared the screen with Mickey Rooney and Judy Garland in films at MGM; she also worked at Paramount, Universal and Monogram in a movie career that lasted up through the late 1940s. Preisser was long-retired, living in Boca Raton, Florida, and working at an office supply company in 1984 when she and her 41-year-old son lost their lives in a head-on car crash.

A viewer attracted to *Murder in the Blue Room* by its mystery angles is bound to feel cheated, as there's not the slightest attempt to build atmosphere. Contrary to the title of the classic James Whale film, the Baldridge mansion ought to be called the New Bright House; the place is relatively small and modern, overcrowded with family, friends, police and servants, and you never get the impression that anything scary or supernatural could happen here. A ghost does show up several times, but in keeping with the film's sometimes-ridiculous tone he's a white-faced goofball in white sheet and derby hat with his own cutesy-funny musical motif; all he does whenever he comes on is frighten one (or more) of the Jazzybelles. The process of elimination indicates that this would have to be the ghost of Sam Kirkland, the only person known to have died in the house, but it's difficult to imagine that this goon of a ghost could be Anne Gwynne's father. Of course we're not supposed to make that assumption: He's just another zany character in a movie that's already brimming with inane lowjinks.

Joseph Breen, the Czar of All the Rushes, offered up his usual comments and objections, recommending restraint in the gruesomeness and horror angles and insisting that, in the climactic secret passage gunfight, Dr. Carroll fire first. Breen also objected to the speech in which Dr. Carroll implies that Larry was an illegitimate child. Breen suggested a change in the dialogue and even turned screenwriter, proposing a convoluted line ("Your father was secretly married to Larry's mother before he married your mother") to use in its place. Associate producer Frank Gross stuck to his guns, however, and in a discussion with Breen Office rep Mr. Metzger, Gross pointed out that the identical situation and dialogue had been passed by the censors for *The Missing Guest.* Apparently deciding that two wrongs make a right, the Breen Office okayed the speech but continued to insist on great restraint in the romantic scenes between Nan and Larry (shades of incest!).

In mid–March, 1944, when *Murder in the Blue Room* was made, every Universal film being shot was horror, horror-related or science fiction-related: *Murder in the Blue Room, The Climax, Ghost Catchers, Dead Man's Eyes* and the serial *The Great Alaskan Mystery* (see the serial appendix at the back of this book). Even at horror-happy Universal, this situation had to have been unique, and it says a lot about the studio's confidence in the genre and their continuing perception of themselves as leaders in that field. It's just too bad that none of these films is really much good.

Director Leslie Goodwins, who finished the film on schedule March 22, 1944, was paid \$2,000; "outside talent" (non-contractees) Betty Kean and June Preisser earned \$1,875 apiece for their two and a half weeks of work. An early wardrobe estimate indicates that several of the smaller parts were reassigned: This memo lists Samuel S. Hinds as Dr. Carroll, Andrew Tombes as the inspector and Edward Gargan as Curtin. While *Murder in the Blue Room* was in production, Universal announced that associate producer Gross' next assignment would be another musical "chiller," *Night Life*. The resultant film reached the screen as *Night Club Girl* (1944); a musical comedy with Vivian Austin and Edward Norris, it's well beyond the scope of this book despite the initial false alarm.

Despite its silly excesses, *Murder in the Blue Room* is still fun for the dying breed of fans who enjoy this type of escapism. McDonald, Kean and Preisser are talented dancers who put on a good show, Anne Gwynne and Donald Cook make a handsome couple, veteran players John Litel, Regis Toomey, Andrew Tombes, Ian Wolfe and Milton Parsons (the latter as a creepy driver, *à la Hold That Ghost*) provide good back-up, and Universal's favorite "locked room" mystery story gets its last workout. And when the going does get rough, all you have to do is to remind yourself that in a crueler world this would be a Ritz Brothers movie, and suddenly everything will be all right again.

Critics' Corner

[T]he new Rialto film makes almost no sense as a whodunit or a comedy. Its one redeeming feature is the presence of Betty Kean, an extremely versatile young performer.... [A] piece of claptrap.—*The New York Herald-Tribune*, October 28, 1944, Howard Barnes

Although there is small likelihood of *Murder in the Blue Room* ever playing the Radio City Music Hall, the film is a creditable entry on the Universal release schedule.... Three hoofer-singers ... provide plenty of comedy as they romp through dangerous situations with some very cute cracks.—*The Hollywood Reporter*, 1944

[P]ackaged in light wrappings of hilarity.... [R]outine story.... [A]ll the time honored devices are used to heighten the atmosphere.... Seen at the Rialto theatre, New York, where some of the comedy scenes produced audible reactions.—*The Motion Picture Herald*, November 4, 1944, Mandel Herbtsman

Rating: ★★ [A] routine murder story.—*The New York Daily News*, October 28, 1944, Wanda Hale

[T]his one has nothing more to offer than Grace McDonald, June Preisser and Betty Kean behaving as one might expect the Andrews [Sisters] to behave in a haunted house. And if that warning isn't enough to scare you out of going to see it, go ahead—and squirm.—*The New York Times*, October 28, 1944, Bosley Crowther

A puerile adventure in imitative criminology....—L.A. Sec. National Council of Jewish Women, 1944

An hour of light, often hilarious, diversion is offered by this "gag" film on the Red Skelton pattern.... No attempt is made to create a mood of horror or of genuine suspense.—General Federation of Women's Clubs (Western Committee), 1944

Story is thin and laughs and situations too widely spaced to amount on sock comedy score. Direction and cast do well by the thin story.—*Variety*, November 1, 1944, Edba

There is mystery surrounding the murder, but the story is so inane that it fails to hold the spectator's attention. Moreover, the comedy situations fall flat because they are forced. The musical interpolations are dragged in by the ear, but even so they are a welcome relief from the rest of the proceedings.... [T]he general effect is boredom.—*Harrison's Reports*, October 28, 1944

House of Frankenstein

Released December 15, 1944. 70 minutes. *Executive Producer:* Joseph Gershenson. *Producer:* Paul Malvern. *Director:* Erle C. Kenton. *Screenplay:* Edward T. Lowe. *Based on the story* "The Devil's Brood" *by* Curt Siodmak. *Photography:* George Robinson. *Camera Operator:* Eddie Cohen. *Special Photography:* John P. Fulton. *Editor:* Philip Cahn. *Special Effects:* Carl Elmendorf. *Assistant Director:* William Tummel. *Art Directors:* John B. Goodman & Martin Obzina. *Music:* Hans J. Salter, Paul Dessau, Charles Previn. *Musical Director:* Hans J. Salter. *Music Mixer:* Paul Neal. *Re-Recording & Special Effects Mixer:* Edwin L. Wetzel. *Set Decorators:* Russell A. Gausman & Andrew J. Gilmore. *Sound Director:* Bernard B. Brown. *Technician:* William Hedgcock. *Sound Recorder:* John Kemp. *Properties:* Eddie Keys. *Dance Director:* Carlos Romero. *Makeup:* Jack P. Pierce & Otto Lederer. *Gowns:* Vera West.

Boris Karloff (*Dr. Gustav Niemann*), Lon Chaney, Jr. (*Lawrence Stewart Talbot, the Wolf Man*), John Carradine (*Count Dracula*), J. Carrol Naish (*Daniel*), Anne Gwynne (*Rita Hussman*), Peter Coe (*Carl Hussman*), Lionel Atwill (*Insp. Arnz*), George Zucco (*Prof. Bruno Lampini*), Elena Verdugo (*Ilonka*), Sig Ruman (*Burgomaster Hussman*), William Edmunds (*Fejos*), Charles Miller (*Toberman*), Julius Tannen (*Hertz*), Philip Van Zandt (*Insp. Muller*), Hans Herbert (*Meier*), Dick Dickinson (*Born*), George Lynn (*Gerlach*), Michael Mark (*Frederick Strauss*), Olaf Hytten (*Hoffman*), Frank Reicher (*Ullman*), Brandon Hurst (*Dr. Geissler*), Glenn Strange (*The Monster*), Joe Kirk (*Schwartz*), Belle Mitchell (*Urla*), Edmund Cobb (*Driver*), Charles Wagenheim (*Prison Guard*), Gino Corrado (*Man at Horror Show*), Gil Perkins, Carey Loftin, Billy Jones (*Stunts*), George Plues, Babe De Freest.

Glenn Strange wasn't as lucky as I was. I got the cream of it, being the first [to play the Monster]. I know I wished him lots of luck ... hoping it would do as much for him as it did for me, but...

—*Boris Karloff,* Castle of Frankenstein *interview*

Val Lewton could *have* his artsy camera angles, ominous silhouettes and psychologically induced chills. Universal had *monsters* and made no apologies about flaunting the greatest of them in the 1944 horror spectacular *House of Frankenstein.* The enthusiastic box office reaction to *Frankenstein Meets the Wolf Man* was proof enough to the big thinkers in the Front Office that monsters were more potent in numbers. With plotlines rapidly deteriorating and gimmicks growing stale, Universal hoped that quantity would compensate for lack of originality. With the exceptions of the Mummy and the Invisible Man, the studio's major league horrors were destined to co-habit with one another for the next few years of the '40s horror wave.

House of Frankenstein had a rather tentative genesis. On June 7, 1943, *The Hollywood Reporter* announced that Universal was developing a new shocker entitled *Chamber of Horrors* with an all-star cast of goons including the Invisible Man, the Mad Ghoul, the Mummy and "other assorted monsters." George Waggner was named as the ringleader of this three-ring circus of horrors. The cast read like a Who's Who of cinemacabre: Karloff, Chaney Jr., Lugosi, Lorre, Rains, Zucco, Hull and ... James Barton (!). *Chamber of Horrors* never saw the light of day.*

Preparations for *The Devil's Brood* (the shooting title of *House of Frankenstein*) began in August 1943, although it wasn't until February of 1944 that the cast was assembled. Paul Malvern took charge of the production, assigning prominent roles to Boris Karloff (fulfilling the second half of his two-picture deal with Universal and receiving $20,000 for his efforts), Lon Chaney, Jr. (paid a flat $10,000 for his third appearance as the Wolf Man), John Carradine and J. Carrol Naish (paid $7,000 apiece). Lionel Atwill and George Zucco were paid $1,750 and $1,500 respectively for their "cameo" appearances while Western regular Glenn Strange picked up an easy $500 for his nominal efforts as the Monster.

Curt Siodmak, who was given a story credit on *House of Frankenstein,* was decidedly terse on the subject of this particular film. He told us, "The idea was to put all the horror characters into one picture. I only wrote the story. I didn't write the script. I never saw the picture."

The unenviable task of writing a screenplay melding together so many different plotlines and personal dramas required a magician, not a Hollywood writer. Edward T. Lowe, whose previous horror credits included the 1923's *The Hunchback of Notre Dame* and the 1933 Majestic quickie *The Vampire Bat,* accepted the challenge. Bearing that tiresome generic title *Destiny,* Lowe's completed script was subjected to the scrutiny of the Breen Office, who passed it under the condition that a cap was put on undue gruesomeness, emphatic religious references, suggestive gypsy dance gyrations and the usual incendiary subjects. (The studio was instructed to handle the strangling of Prof. Lampini with restraint, avoiding or toning down the character's "choking cry and dying groan.")

A $354,000 budget plus a generous 30-day shooting schedule were arranged. Initial shooting began on Tuesday, April 4, 1944, on the old *Green Hell* and *Pittsburgh* sets, now doing duty as a medieval prison and an underground tunnel, respectively. Art directors John B. Goodman and Martin Obzina took full advantage of leftover sets from *Gung Ho!* and *Tower of London* in designing the production while extensive outdoor shooting was done on the studio's spacious back lot. Director Erie C. Kenton and his company contended with inclement weather while filming the flavorsome gypsy camp scenes on the grounds of the Shelby Home and a campfire scene at Nagana Rocks. A set from *Green Hell* was utilized for the Frankenstein ruins.

Kenton's schedule called for the early Dracula sequences to be shot last. John Carradine, Anne Gwynne and Peter Coe had to report to

*The Hollywood Reporter *also noted that Karloff, Lugosi and Lorre had been assigned leading roles in an RKO farce called* Star Strangled Rhythm *with Boris and Bela portraying movie actors whose bodies are taken over by the bogey-men characters they played on the screen. An even more outrageous* Hollywood Reporter *"scoop" was the October 13, 1943, announcement that RKO had just handed over to Val Lewton a property entitled* They Creep by Night, *boasting a cast of characters that included Dracula, the Monster, the Invisible Man, Cat People, plus a variety of werewolves and zombies. Anyone in the industry having even a passing acquaintance with the Lewton brand of screen horror would have immediately seen through this bit of tomfoolery.*

work one hour earlier than usual to makeup for the time lost in transporting them to Sherwood Forest near Malibu, a spot frequently used by movie studios for pastoral location shoots. With the final scenes in the can, the production came to a close on Monday, May 8.

In August, Universal announced in the Hollywood trades that the title of their monster fest had been changed from *The Devil's Brood* to the more bankable *House of Frankenstein.* (Evidently, the studio had long since forgotten Laemmle Jr.'s 1932 edict discouraging multiple title changes which, he rightly believed, translated into a loss of valuable publicity dollars.) In teaming the new feature with the final installment of the Kharis series, *The Mummy's Curse,* for nationwide distribution, Universal racked up high box office grosses while at the same time willfully orchestrating the decline and fall of its once great monster series.

The episodic story of *House of Frankenstein* begins in the slimy dungeon of Neustadt Prison. Serving a long sentence for following in the blood-stained footsteps of the renegade scientist Frankenstein, Dr. Gustav Niemann (Boris Karloff) is driven by two obsessions: To secure Frankenstein's journals so that he may perfect his own experiments in brain transplantation, and to gain vengeance on the three men who sent him to Neustadt 15 years before. Daniel (J. Carrol Naish), his hunchbacked prison mate, promises the doctor his allegiance in return for a "perfect body" once the Frankenstein records have been secured.

In an expertly executed, thrillingly scored sequence, a lightning bolt demolishes the cellblock. Escaping into the storm, Niemann and Daniel are given shelter by the bombastic Prof. Bruno Lampini (played with *savoir-faire* by George Zucco). The proprietor of a traveling "Chamber of Horrors," Lampini boasts about the most prized item in his grisly collection: The skeleton of Count Dracula. Having conveniently rattled off a talking points memo of the vampire's powers and foibles, Lampini is choked to death by the hunchback.

Passing himself off as the late showman, Niemann travels to the village of Burgomaster Hussman (Sig Ruman), one of his nemeses. Withdrawing the stake from Dracula's ribs in a fit of rage, Niemann watches in amazement as the vampire's flesh and blood (and eveningwear) take form again. Count Dracula (John Carradine) has been restored to life. (When *House of Frankenstein* was aired on Philadelphia TV's *Dr. Shock* in the '70s, guest star Carradine claimed that it was his idea to have the Count "gasp" as life returned to his skeletal remains.)

Using the alias "Baron Latos," Dracula charms his way into the Hussman household. In one of the film's finest moments, the vampire changes himself into a bat, hypnotizes Hussman and, in a nightmarish silhouette, feeds on his throat. He then spirits away the dead man's granddaughter Rita (Anne Gwynne) in his coach. In hot pursuit are her husband Carl (Peter Coe) and Insp. Arnz (Lionel Atwill) and his gendarmes. The horses break loose, causing the coach to careen down a hillside. Racing up the side of the hill, Dracula is cut down in his tracks by the first rays of dawn. Resembling a huge prostrate bat, his caped arms like black wings, the vampire struggles to lift open the lid of his coffin (conveniently provided by Niemann). By the time his pursuers arrive on the scene, the Count has been reduced to a skeleton again. Kenton directs this sequence with panache, and is afforded strong support by Hans J. Salter's surging score.

Arriving on the outskirts of the village of Frankenstein, Niemann and Daniel make preparations to penetrate the flooded Frankenstein ruins. (Inexplicably, the location of the late Ludwig Frankenstein's burnt-out sanitarium has been changed from Vasaria [now called *Visaria*] to the accursed scientist's hometown.) Visiting a gypsy camp, Daniel saves a young gypsy dancer from a vicious thrashing. In the film's most touching moment, the hunchback shyly romances the girl, Ilonka (Elena Verdugo), as she recuperates from her experience in the berth beneath the coach driver's seat. She can only see the man's kindly face. Her gratitude towards her knight is tinged with sexual curiosity and she playfully invites him to come closer. In a moment worthy of Victor Hugo (and *Notre Dame* scriptwriter Lowe), the hunchback stands triumphantly over the girl, only to see her shrink in disgust at his physical grotesqueness. Filled with compassion, Ilonka assures Daniel of her friendship and gratitude.

Within the ruins of the castle, Niemann

Boris Karloff leers menacingly at someone for whom he has "unloving memories" in *House of Frankenstein.*

dictably, Ilonka falls in love with Talbot. After two lifetimes worth of suffering, the doom-laden man is immune to emotion, but he doesn't discourage her attentions. Daniel understandably takes offense at Talbot's ill-timed intrusion and a triangle-of-sorts develops.

Restoring his lab to working order, Niemann becomes immediately immersed in nursing the Monster back to health. Late that night, the doctor and Daniel steal into town and kidnap Niemann's last two persecutors, Ullman (Frank Reicher) and Strauss (Michael Mark). The brain transplant subplot that made *The Ghost of Frankenstein* so ridiculous was a minor distraction in comparison to the wholesale organ switching that goes on here. For starters, Niemann plans to transplant Ullman's brain into the Monster's skull and give his former assistant Strauss the brain of Talbot (thus passing on to him the curse of the werewolf). Niemann dismisses Daniel's impassioned plea for Talbot's strong, healthy body. "Talbot's body is the perfect home for the Monster's brain!" the scientist insists.

and Daniel discover the frozen bodies of the Monster (Glenn Strange) and Lawrence Talbot, the Wolf Man (Lon Chaney, Jr.). A roaring fire frees the two monsters from the ice tomb. (Hammer Films borrowed this idea for the third entry in their Frankenstein series, 1964's *The Evil of Frankenstein.*) Talbot emerges from it all unscathed but the Monster has suffered internal damage and requires constant medical attention. Banking on Niemann's promise that he will free him of his affliction once they reach their destination, Talbot furnishes the doctor with the Frankenstein records.

The bizarre party heads for Niemann's abandoned estate in Visaria. Lowe seems to have taken his inspiration from *The Wizard of Oz* at this point in the story, with Niemann assuming the role of the Great and Powerful Oz, promising his followers new brains and/or bodies. Pre-

In a jealous fit, Daniel reveals the tragic truth about Talbot to Ilonka. She is determined to free the man she loves from his unspeakable torment. Armed with a revolver containing the required silver bullets, the gypsy girl stands outside Talbot's bedroom window. She raises her hand to fire but cannot bring herself to pull the trigger. In a beautifully executed transformation scene, Talbot becomes a snarling werewolf. He attacks Ilonka and murders her but not before she fatally fires two bullets into his body.

The grief-stricken hunchback has had his fill of Niemann's treachery. Daniel seizes the doctor by the throat and snaps his spine. The Monster, infused with renewed strength, sends the hunchback hurtling through the skylight to his death. (Naish's scream as he plummets off the roof is actually Karloff's from the sulphur pit plunge in *Son of Frankenstein.*) In a scene fraught with irony, the Monster picks up the mortally injured Niemann and cradles him in his arms. It's a special moment in Universal horror film history: The originator of the role and his final successor bonding before the final conflagration.

Bearing flaming torches, the irate villagers storm the castle and chase the pair into the adjoining marshes. As the brush around them is set ablaze, the terrified Monster and his benefactor are driven back into a quicksand bog. Within moments, they are swallowed up by the slime.

High-keyed, aggressive and shrewdly calculated, *House of Frankenstein* is horror filmmaking at its slick, superficial best, with all the subtlety of a carnival freak show. The abundance of thrills is logged in with clockwork precision. Cherished clichés are dusted off and polished to a shine. That the whole picture tastes of yesterday's leftovers is rather beside the point and in this instance, almost forgivable.

What isn't quite so forgivable is the shameful manner in which the Monster is shunted aside as though he were an inconsequential bit player (and even billed at the bottom of the onscreen cast list). The territory that the Monster yielded to Chaney's Wolf Man in the previous film was but an omen of the degradation that was ahead for Frankenstein's notorious creation. One could almost make the point that Universal didn't think any of its three monster heavyweights had enough star power left to carry a film squarely on its own shoulders. Since *Son of Frankenstein,* the Monster had been reduced to playing second fiddle to Frankenstein's sons, Ygor, Larry Talbot and, in *House of Frankenstein,* a cast full of competing menaces. While the Frankenstein legacy fuels the plot of the film, the Monster is in and of itself negligible.

Glenn Strange, a great big teddy bear of a man, very graciously credited Boris Karloff for taking the time and energy to coach him in the fine art of Monster playing. Sadly, precious little of Karloff's guiding influence comes through in Strange's performance. The lion's share of the blame rests on the shoulders of Kenton and Lowe, whose concept of the creature is an imbecilic brute, acting on pure animal instinct. What Strange's portrayal lacks in characterization, it makes up for in sheer physical presence. The actor's stark features and imposing physique give the part an added dimension of strength and gruesomeness (his is a Monster that's truly frightening to behold). The actor brought these same physical qualities to his werewolf character in PRC's vapid *The Mad Monster* in 1942.

Although he could never be accused of being a stylist in the strict sense of the word, Erle C. Kenton was nevertheless an efficient house director. *House of Frankenstein,* like his earlier series entry *The Ghost of Frankenstein,* demonstrates the director's flair for breathless action and thrill sequences. The film has flamboyance to spare: The storm-swept jail break, Dracula's pursuit and ultimate destruction, and the fiery climax (in which five leading characters are killed off in rapid succession) are trenchantly realized. Kenton (and photographer George Robinson) had a knack for composing vivid images: The subjective shot of Naish lurching forth to strangle Zucco, the vampire bat dining on Sig Ruman's jugular, Elena Verdugo's brutal flogging (discreetly blocked off by extras standing in the foreground), Chaney's first werewolf transformation, and Naish's long-overdue throttling of Karloff, visualized as giant shadows cast against the laboratory wall, to name just a few. (Kenton created similarly chilling images for *Island of Lost Souls,* which he directed for Paramount in 1933.) The collaborative efforts of musical director Hans J. Salter, Paul Dessau and the tireless Charles Previn underscore these memorable images and give the picture a dramatic aural richness. Most of the music was written specifically for *House of Frankenstein* and is not the usual collection of oft-heard musical cues dating back to 1938.

For such a well-mounted production, it's rather disconcerting how many gaffes got past the director and his company and wound up in the final print. After Dracula's coach careens down the embankment and the vampire recovers from the ensuing tumble, sharp-eyed viewers will notice that Carradine has lost half his mustache! Chaney's otherwise finely realized werewolf transformation before the mirror is flawed in that his hands remain unchanged. In the scene inside the wagon where Karloff, Naish and Chaney are tending to the Monster, Karloff orders Chaney to take the reins. Chaney leaves through the back door. If you look closely

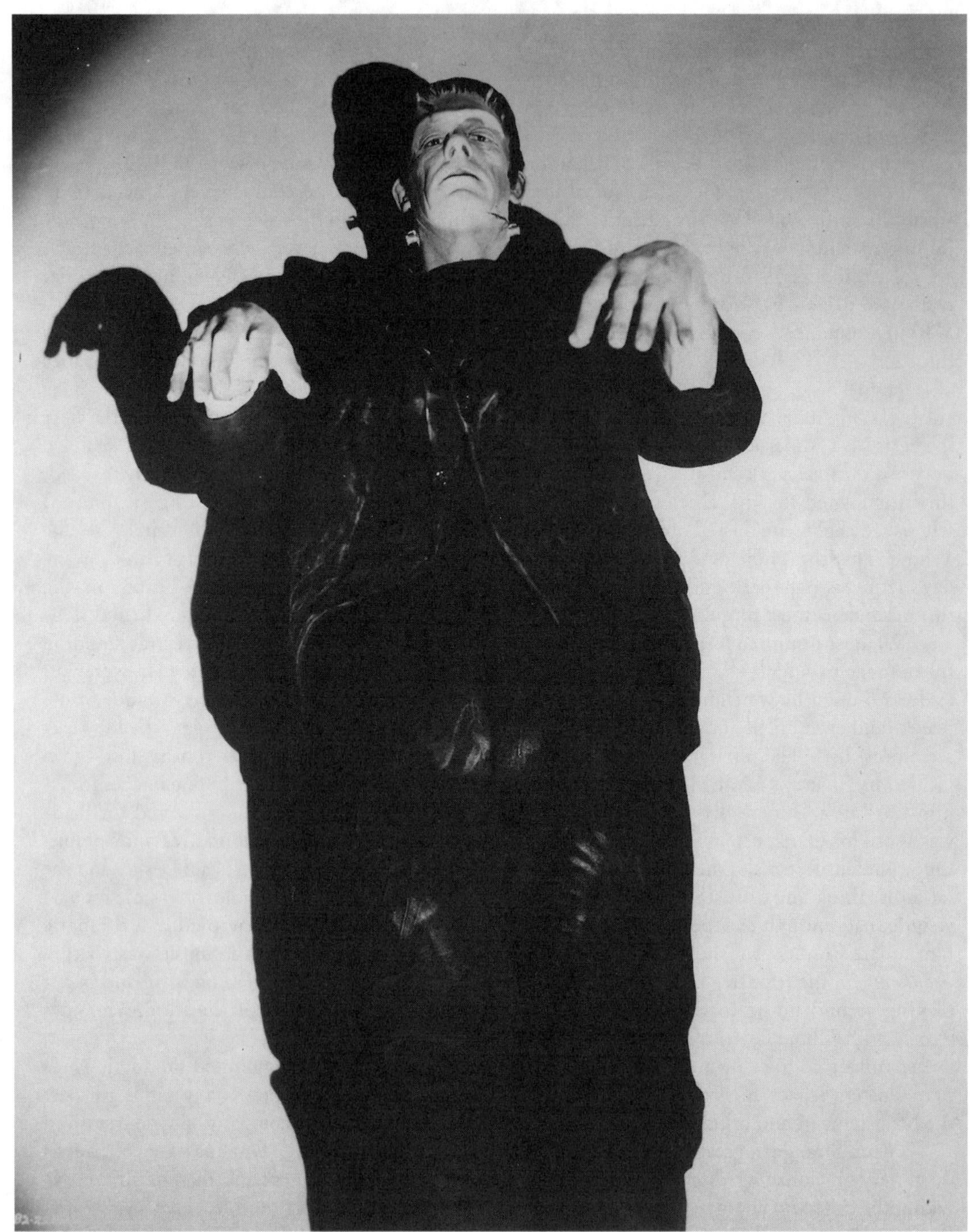

Glenn Strange in his debut performance as the Monster.

through the window in the door, you'll spot the actor loitering outside to watch Karloff and Naish complete their dialogue. The Wolf Man transforms back into Talbot after he is thawed out of the ice block by Niemann; suddenly, the presence of moonlight (or the lack of it) has nothing to do with the man-into-wolf (and vice versa) process. To cap it off, Sig Ruman's Burgomaster Hussman is misspelled "Russman" in the end credits.

On the verge of beginning his career-resuscitating association with Val Lewton, Karloff gives the impression of marking time here. His performance is in the same mode as the one he contributed in *The Climax*— stolid and detached, with an occasional touch of condescending hamminess. No doubt, it aggravated Karloff to see just how much his beloved Monster had degenerated in 13 years. That he himself was a party to this sacrilege must have been doubly painful for him. In any event, the character of Dr. Niemann is so unsympathetic and one-dimensional, even a heartfelt reading wouldn't have alleviated the taint of the familiar here. ("I don't think [Boris Karloff] was happy with his mad scientist part," Anne Gwynne confided to interviewer Michael Fitzgerald.)

Although Lon Chaney's gloom-and-doom routine was quickly reaching the point of parody by now, the actor does infuse qualities of sincerity and dignity into his performance. Providing Talbot with a gypsy love interest, however brief, is a bittersweet touch, particularly in light of the fact it was a (male) gypsy who passed the curse of the lycanthrope onto him.

John Carradine has gotten a well-deserved share of applause over the years for his classy performance as Count Dracula. There are those of us who prefer Carradine's enactment to Lugosi's, even though the eccentric Shakespearean lacks those elements of loneliness and tragic resignation that Lugosi brought to the part. (Supposedly, Lugosi was considered for the Dracula role in *House of Frankenstein* but was forced to bow out on account of other commitments.) Carradine's Count is the devil incarnate — seductive, ruthless, without conscience. His subtle underplaying and impeccable appearance give the character a genuine air of distinction.

"Do it real, do it honestly, and don't worry about being big." That was the credo J. Carrol Naish followed throughout the course of his wonderful screen career. The Irish-American actor whose stock in trade was all manner of humanity from Latins and Orientals to blacks and Hindus had a reputation for studying his stage and movie roles meticulously, using real-life subjects whenever he could find them. According to studio publicity, the diligent Naish discovered a hunchback derelict living in a poverty-stricken area of Los Angeles and observed the man's mannerisms in preparation for his role in *House of Frankenstein* (Naish is given special billing).

"It's interesting ... to put yourself into the character of this psychopathic deformity," he told a reporter who was visiting the set in late April 1944. "It [the costume] doesn't fit too well, but it takes five-and-a-half hours to get into this makeup. I have to get up at half past two so I can get here on time."

Naish's performance in *House of Frankenstein* is unquestionably his best work in the horror genre. In the film's early reels, Daniel is personified as a homicidal misfit and a puppet of the nefarious Niemann, just another single-sided stock horror film character. With the introduction of Ilonka (a barely disguised imitation of Esmeralda), the hunchback's loneliness and overwhelming desire for love surfaces. By giving Daniel a vulnerable disposition, Lowe puts us squarely in his corner in spite of the fact he's left behind more broken bodies than any other character in the film. Decades later, Naish would end his movie career playing a Niemann-like character (a mad scientist-Chamber of Horrors operator) in the drecky drive-in chiller *Dracula Vs. Frankenstein* (1971) — with his murderous henchman played by Lon Chaney, Jr.

Heading up the supporting cast is an impressive lineup of seasoned troupers and talented second leads. Frank Reicher, Michael Mark, Brandon Hurst, William Edmunds, Sig Ruman, and of course Lionel Atwill and George Zucco add a sweet, nostalgic "old home week" flavor to the film. Topped with a curly black wig, vivacious Elena Verdugo acts up a storm as the ill-fated Ilonka though Anne Gwynne seems a bit out of place as the saucy American bride who's swept off her feet by the flirtatious vampire.

"The part was nice but not great," Gwynne admitted in the Fitzgerald interview. "I had fun with it, but I'm only in the first 25 minutes and then zap, I'm off for the rest of the film! I felt that my scenes with [John] Carradine were some of the best acting I ever did...." Disillusioned with the countless B films Universal had assigned to her, Gwynne asked for and got a release from her contract following her work in *House of Frankenstein*. But instead of moving on to greener pastures, as her new agent had predicted, the actress found herself toiling on Poverty Row.

The Wolf Man (Lon Chaney, Jr.) awakens from his frozen sleep in the catacombs of the ruined castle. The character was referred to in dialogue as "The Wolf Man" for the first time in this movie.

A welcome guest at autograph shows and reunions in her later years, Anne Gwynne succumbed from the complications of surgery following a stroke on March 31, 2003. She was 84 years old.

Gwynne wasn't the only contract player in the film dissatisfied with the way Universal had managed their career. Yugoslavian-born actor Peter Coe abandoned a budding career on the Broadway stage at the behest of the studio with the promise he'd be groomed as the next Charles Boyer. In *Gung Ho!* (1943), his first Universal movie, Coe played a member of Carlson's Raiders, a special division of the Marines selected for the 1942 raid on Japanese-held Makin Island. The Technicolored Maria Montez–Jon Hall spectacle *Gypsy Wildcat* (1944) was just one of a number of undistinguished program pictures the studio cast him in. Coe responded favorably to the studio's offer to co-star him as Anne Gwynne's husband in *House of Frankenstein* because it gave him the opportunity to perform opposite Karloff and Chaney.

Recalling *House of Frankenstein,* the genial Coe painted a less-than-flattering portrait of co-star John Carradine. He told the authors:

> In my first encounter with John Carradine, we had a scene where he's dressed up in tails and hat and is on a coach. My wife Annie Gwynne and I are walking at night. And he [Carradine] stops and in his very Shakespearean way says [Coe impersonated the ham-fisted actor], "I beg your pardon but if you happen to be going my way, I'll be delighted to you a lift." I said to myself, "Jesus Christ! What did I get myself into?" So he went up and I went down. I underplayed it. He looked so ridiculous when they saw it the next day in the rushes, they had to reshoot it. So I told John, "Are you going to be on the level with me or am I

going to pull the same shit? Don't try to fuck with me!" He liked that, and we became good friends afterward.

Although Coe and Lon Chaney, Jr., only ran into each other fleetingly during the filming of *House of Frankenstein*, it was on their next movie they struck up a lasting friendship.

I met him [*sic*] when we did *The Mummy's Curse*, and we really became friends. He had a ranch up in the northern part of California, the pheasant season had just opened and we went hunting. We were so drunk, I mean *drunk*— it's a wonder we didn't shoot each *other*! We had a case of booze as we drove up to his ranch — a seven- or eight-hour drive and we drank like crazy. Lon was a good drinker, an excellent drinker. We got to the ranch about 9:00 at night as we had to get up early, about two or three in the morning, to go hunting. Lon shook me and woke me up, and in his hand he was holding a glass. I thought to myself, "Oh, tomato juice or orange juice, how wonderful!" I took a sip and choked — it was straight booze! *That* was an eye-opener!

Coe continued:

We did a horrible thing on this trip. We were in the rice fields up north, it was about 10:00 in the morning and the sun was shining on us, when all of a sudden, *boom*, it was dark. We looked up and there was a flock, a whole *sky* of Canadian geese. They landed in the rice field, and Lon said, "We're gonna get some geese, baby!" So we crawled on our bellies holding our rifles, just like in the Army — we got up close and started firing, *pow pow pow pow pow pow*. Lon turned around to leave — "Come with me, run!" he said. I asked, "What about the geese?" and he said, "Tonight!" I asked, "Why?" and he held up a single finger: "*One goose* per hunter!" We had killed 47! We had to come back at night with a truck and load it up!

Veteran stuntman Carey Loftin substituted for Boris Karloff as the Monster carries the dying Niemann out of the castle and into the swamp. Loftin told the authors:

They set the tumbleweeds on fire, and they thought they had it set so that just the tumbleweeds alone would burn. But instead of just the tumbleweeds around us burning, the whole *thing* lit up! We just *barely* got out of there! We both got scorched! It just went *boom* and, instead of just a triangle [of burning tumbleweeds] lightin' up, the whole thing went up!

Stuntman Billy Jones doubled for J. Carrol Naish for the death plunge from the lab skylight window. Jones was a slightly built man who doubled mostly for actresses. Loftin, who was through filming for the day, accompanied Jones to the roof as he prepared for the stunt. The roof was at a steep angle, and there were nails sticking out of the wood, some as much as a quarter-inch or a half-inch. "Billy, I'll get a hammer and knock those nails down for you," Loftin suggested. "No, no, no, no, you just wait, I'll show you the 'scientific way' to get over those," Jones insisted, assuming he would be able to harmlessly roll over them. But when Jones performed the stunt, he *slid* across the surface of the roof before dropping down into the off-camera net. Afterwards, as Jones went to change his clothes to go home, he ran into Loftin, and said to him, "Did ya *learn* anything? Aren't ya glad you stayed?" But as Jones disrobed, Loftin spotted many cuts and scrapes on the stuntman's stomach and legs. "But he didn't want to admit it, he was that type of guy!" Loftin chuckled.

With its top-flight cast and excitement-packed narrative, *House of Frankenstein* would have been a more fitting final tribute to Universal's fabled monster series than the low-keyed, anticlimactic *House of Dracula*, the film it directly inspired.

Critics' Corner

[A] thriller deluxe.... [T]hrill-packed and spine-tickling. It's a film guaranteed to provide an acute case of the jitters....—*The Hollywood Citizen-News*, December 23, 1944

It's like a baseball team with nine Babe Ruths. But this grisly congress doesn't hit hard; it merely has speed and a change of pace.... [I]t is bound to garner as many chuckles as it does chills.—*The New York Times*, December 16, 1944, A.H. Weiler

Aimed entirely for suspense and weird dramatics, picture is a solid entry for the attentions of the Horror addicts ... Erle Kenton generates plenty of creeps and suspense....—*Variety*, December 20, 1944, Walt

Don't take it seriously, and you'll have yourself a whale of an amusing time.—*The New York Post*, December 16, 1944

There's enough gore to satisfy even the most avid reveler in vicarious bloodshed.—*The New York Daily Mirror*, December 1944

Rating: ★★½ Be sure and check your credulity outside or you won't believe what your eyes are seeing. Fortunately, settings, lightings and costumes, impressively eerie and horrendous, will help you enter into the sinister proceedings....—*The New York Daily News*, December 16, 1944, Wanda Hale

In this excellent horror film, each member of the

cast portrays his part effectively. Skilled makeup, clever photography, lighting effects and musical background all add to the weird and striking effect.... Seen at the Rialto theatre, New York, where a matinee audience was more than satisfied. — *The Motion Picture Herald*, December 23, 1944, M.R.Y.

The Mummy's Curse

Released December 22, 1944. 62 minutes. *Associate Producer:* Oliver Drake. *Executive Producer:* Ben Pivar. *Director:* Leslie Goodwins. *Screenplay:* Bernard L. Schubert. *Original Story and Adaptation:* Leon Abrams, Dwight V. Babcock, Bernard L. Schubert & T.H. Richmond. *Photography:* Virgil Miller. *Camera Operator:* William Dodds. *Special Photographic Effects:* John P. Fulton. *Editor:* Fred R. Feitshans, Jr. *Assistant Director:* Mack Wright. *Art Directors:* John B. Goodman & Martin Obzina. *Musical Director:* Paul Sawtell. *Song:* "Hey, You," *Music:* Oliver Drake, *Lyrics:* Frank Orth. *Music Mixer:* Paul Neal. *Dialogue Director:* Louis Herman. *Set Decorators:* Russell A. Gausman & Victor A. Gangelin. *Sound Director:* Bernard B. Brown. *Technician:* Robert Pritchard. *Properties:* Ernie Smith & Eddie Case. *Recording & Effects Mixer:* Edwin L. Wetzel. *Makeup:* Jack P. Pierce. *Hair Stylist:* Millissa Irwin. *Gowns:* Vera West.

Lon Chaney, Jr. (*Kharis*), Peter Coe (*Dr. Ilzor Zandaab*), Virginia Christine (*Princess Ananka*), Kay Harding (*Betty Walsh*), Dennis Moore (*Dr. James Halsey*), Martin Kosleck (*Ragheb*), Kurt Katch (*Cajun Joe*), Addison Richards (*Pat Walsh*), Holmes Herbert (*Dr. Cooper*), Charles Stevens (*Achilles*), William Farnum (*Michael*), Napoleon Simpson (*Goobie*), Ann Codee (*Tante Berthe*), Herbert Heywood (*Hill*), Nina Bara (*Cajun Girl*), Eddie Abdo (*Pierre*), Tony Santoro (*Ulysses*), Budd Buster, Hector Sarno (*Cajuns*), Carey Loftin, Teddy Mangean (*Stunts*), Heenan Elliott, Al Ferguson.

[Kharis claws] his way through the swamp, dragging a bad case of athlete's foot in his right pedal, at the speed of a guy pushing a Cadillac up hill.
—The Hollywood Reporter, *December 20, 1944*

The last chapter of a long-running horror series rarely offers anything fresh or particularly innovative. Generally, it's a tired rehash of all the tried-and-true elements that have worked before. While *The Mummy's Curse* doesn't break any new ground in regards to plot, it does offer a few pleasant surprises — a welcome change in locale, a strong performance by Virginia Christine, the most beautifully executed sequence in the entire series, plus lots of eagerly anticipated Mummy murders (in fact, more than in any of the other series entries).

The marshy grave that consumed Kharis and his reincarnated lover Princess Ananka in *The Mummy's Ghost* was just a temporary resting place for the indefatigable pair. Even before the Reginald LeBorg film was released, Universal announced plans (in early spring 1944) to produce a fourth sequel, *The Mummy's Return*. It could be made quickly, at a nominal cost, and be released in time to support the studio's all-star horror spectacular, *House of Frankenstein* (then called *The Devil's Brood*) on a double bill.

No less than four writers had a hand in cobbling together the original story and shooting script for *The Mummy's Return*. Leon Abrams concocted a 23-page treatment. Few of Abrams' unorthodox plot devices made it into Bernard L. Schubert's shooting script, and for that, fans who have a soft spot in their hearts for these ragtag epics can be eternally grateful.

Film buffs and historians who have studied a motion picture's story treatment or early draft of a script often come away with the feeling that what eventually ended up on the screen was a vast improvement in terms of plot and dialogue. Though no one can ever accuse *The Mummy's Curse* of being great art, it is certainly preferable to Abrams' absurd concepts. There *are* fleeting similarities: The outdoorsy *milieu*, the renewed quest for the reincarnated Princess Ananka (first introduced in *The Mummy's Ghost*), uncovering the mummies during swamp excavations, an unusually high murder count, as well as the typical stock elements familiar to this series — a fanatic high priest, a mild comic relief figure, more tana leaf mumbo-jumbo, etc.

In Abrams' treatment for *The Mummy's Return,* Kharis wastes little time in getting down to the business of throttling defenseless bystanders. We soon learn that these killings are flashbacks to the Mummy's earlier crime sprees. The authorities believe Kharis has disappeared forever in the primordial ooze of the swamp.

The first hint of the treatment's in-your-face lunacy occurs shortly afterward. A work crew of Italian migrant workers, in the midst of dredging up the disease-breeding swamp, stumble upon the dormant body of Kharis. The project foreman mistakes the mummy for a dummy! A farmer making a delivery offers to take the thing off their hands; the corpse is unceremoniously dumped in the back of a pick-up truck,

Kay Harding and Lon Chaney, Jr., in a staged scene from *The Mummy's Curse*.

driven back to the farm, dressed up in an old overcoat and hat, and propped up like a scarecrow in the field.

But this is only the beginning of the gross indignities foisted upon Kharis in this go-round. The proprietor of a traveling carnival buys the interesting-looking "scarecrow" from the farmer for a measly five bucks. "A grand prop. We can use it in the act," he tells his handsome young assistant, ultimately the hero figure. During the carnival act, the "exhibit" is continually struck across the puss with a bamboo cane.

Enter two more characters, a foxy newspaper reporter and Abdullah Bey, the latest High Priest of Karnak, passing himself off as an Egyptian scholar. From this point on, the treatment confines itself to the comparatively sober plot machinations of past sequels. The mummy of the Princess Ananka is recovered from a riverbed, where it ended up after being stolen from the Scripps Museum. Bey is determined to return the mummy to its rightful resting place in Egypt. He brings Kharis to life using tana fluid. The revived mummy kills the proprietor, escapes from the carnival and disappears into the darkness. Back at the museum, Bey injects Ananka's corpse with a dose of tana fluid; she emerges from the mummified heap as a beautiful young woman once again. Inexplicably, Bey tries to stop the exuberant Kharis from claiming his beloved, and has his neck broken by the creature in return. But the reunion of Kharis and Ananka is short-lived: A twister strikes the museum, literally carrying off the pair of ancient lovers.

With Bernard L. Schubert's script adaptation of the Abrams treatment in hand, Ben Pivar assigned Leslie Goodwins to the task of directing *The Mummy's Curse* a week before it went into production on July 26, 1944; 12 days were allotted to get the quickie in the can. Goodwins took full advantage of standing sets and back lot locations. The *Tower of London* set stood in as the lower level of the monastery where Kharis is brought back to life. For the exterior [*sic*] of the monastery, the old *Gung Ho!* and *Phantom of the Opera* stages were put back into action. The *Green Hell* steps were revamped for Kharis' ascent to the monastery. The Singapore Street (used in many a lusty action programmer) served as the rear entrance to Tante Berthe's cafe. Such familiar locales as the *Gung Ho!* jungle, Lubin Lake and Pollard Lake did extra duty for the eerie swamp shots.

On August 8, after hours of toiling in the stifling mid-summer heat, the production drew to a close. (All of the Kharis movies had the misfortune of being produced during the often unbearably uncomfortable Southern California spring-summer seasons, much to the displeasure of Chaney and presumably Tom Tyler.) There still remained, however, additional pages of script to be shot, most of which focused on the picture's most elaborate sequence, the rebirth of Ananka in the mire. After careful consideration, the producers decided to shoot this scene straight and eliminate the complicated camera effects originally called for. Apparently, the higher-ups feared Virginia Christine's health would be in jeopardy from the prolonged effects of the makeup she wore and the conditions under which the scene would be shot. In short, Universal didn't want a lawsuit on their hands.

While it does not follow the continuity of the past two sequels, the choice of the Louisiana bayous, land of the dreaded *loup garou*, forsaken by all but the superstitious Cajuns, is a vast improvement over hick-infested Mapleton. Twenty-five years after the disappearance of Kharis and Ananka in the swamplands, a team of excavators, commissioned by the U.S. government to drain the marshes, unwittingly uncovers the mummies. Two representatives from the Scripps Museum, Dr. James Halsey (Dennis Moore) and Dr. Ilzor Zandaab (Peter Coe), arrive on the scene. Zandaab, secretly a high priest of Egypt, has recruited Ragheb (Martin Kosleck), one of the workmen, to assist him in his sacred mission: To recover the mummies and return them to their Egyptian tomb.

Under cover of night, Zandaab and Ragheb (referred to in an early stage of the script by their Egyptian names, Ismail and Abbas, respectively) sneak away to an abandoned monastery at the edge of the swamp. There, Zandaab initiates his new recruit into the Royal Den of High Priests. (Those old clips from *The Mummy* and *The Mummy's Hand* are trotted out once again to refresh our memories of Kharis and Ananka's forbidden tryst.) Kharis (Lon Chaney, Jr.) is brought back to life with tana brew and, after permanently silencing the monastery's sacristan (William Farnum), sets out to claim his bride.

In what ranks as one of the most arresting sequences of '40s cinemacabre, the withered Princess Ananka (Virginia Christine) emerges from her swamp tomb. One clawing, muddy hand breaks the slimy surface, then the other. A Sphinx-like face, encrusted with mud, follows. Moments later, a woman painfully struggles to her feet. She draws strength from the rays of the late afternoon sun. (Later, at Halsey's camp, Ananka turns to the sun again for sustenance.) The age-old princess slips into a pond and steps out in all her twentieth century glory (coiffured black tresses and mascara-lined brows).

Discovered wandering aimlessly through the swamp like a sleepwalker, Ananka is taken to Halsey's campsite. The archaeologist is astonished by her uncanny knowledge of the ancient Egyptians. Zandaab is even more impressed. Returning to the monastery, he commands a visibly weary Kharis to track her down.

This quest results in a string of murders. Two of them are particularly well-staged. Cafe singer Tante Berthe (Ann Codee) is strangled to death by Kharis as a jaunty Cajun folksong is heard from the next room. Later, Virgil Miller's camera stands directly behind Cajun Joe (Kurt Katch) as he pumps bullets into the indestructible fiend.

Haunted by feelings that she is being dragged back to a world of which she has only fleeting recollections, Ananka confides her fears to Dr. Cooper (Holmes Herbert), who is understandably confused. Kharis suddenly bursts into the tent. Ananka escapes from his clutches once again. Cooper is not so lucky.

Ananka's luck finally runs out. Kharis takes her to the monastery where a triumphant Zandaab feeds her tana brew. Ragheb, meanwhile, has grown tired of the chaste life of a disciple of Amon-Ra, and lures Betty Walsh (Kay Harding), niece of the swamp project manager, to the secret hideaway. Zandaab is furious. "The vultures will pick the flesh from your bones when Kharis learns of your treachery!" he threatens. The unrepentant laborer plants a dagger in the priest's back. Enraged over the murder of his mentor, the Mummy corners Ragheb in a cell and literally brings the house down trying to reach him. Both are buried under tons of rubble. Halsey arrives on the scene and identifies the mummified remains as those of the strange young woman they had sheltered.

Suffering from a plodding, repetitive script (the movie is essentially one prolonged chase), *The Mummy's Curse* redeems itself with a generous share of cheap thrills. It lacks the polish of the previous Kharis pictures, but this actually works to its advantage. The plot wastes little time in getting down to the business at hand. We are spared those ponderous police investigation scenes that dragged down the previous two sequels. And, unlike *The Mummy's Hand*, it has minimal comedy relief.

Probably no one was happier than Lon Chaney that Universal dumped the Mummy series after this film. He hated the role with a passion and goes through the familiar paces with little heart. Virtually none of his tortured character's centuries-old passions are conveyed in the screenplay or in Chaney's performance. For years, it was rumored that Chaney *never* played the part of Kharis in this film or any of the other sequels, that only his name was used for publicity purposes. A teenage (or younger) Joe Dante was the first to hatch this theory in a 1962 edition of *Famous Monsters*; William K. Everson seconded it years later in his book, *More Classics of the Horror Film*. Although the horror star had various stand-ins and stunt doubles during the shooting of these pictures, the fact that he did indeed don the wrappings was attested to by Reginald LeBorg, Elyse Knox, Peter Coe, Martin Kosleck, Virginia Christine and a backlog of studio production reports.

Chaney walked off with a cool $8,000 for his uninspired performance. Peter Coe came in second with $3,500, followed by Martin Kosleck ($1,200) and Dennis Moore ($1,000). Second female lead Kay Harding received a total of $750 for her services, while seventh-billed Kurt Katch made that same figure on a per week basis. Considering she was third-billed, gave the best performance in the picture, and endured immeasurable discomfort during shooting, Virginia Christine ended up with the poorest salary — a total of $541.67 for a bit over two weeks' work (that comes out to $250 per week!). Even black comic relief Napoleon Simpson ($500 per week) and Charles Stevens ($525 total for a week and a half of service) fared better. Christine improved her purse when she received an extra $250 to cover the intervening time between completion of her role and her recall for shooting the arduous rebirth-of-Ananka sequence.

A few intriguing budget tidbits: Tom Tyler received a $60 check for the use of his clips from *The Mummy's Hand*; a $100 salary allowance was reserved for a narrator (this part was scrapped); and, most fascinating of all, the mummy suit set Universal back $100.* The producers also paid a fee, one dollar each, for the songs "Hey, You" and "Monsieur Le Good for Nothin'" (the latter was not recorded). Frank Orth, who wrote the lyrics for "Hey, You," (sung by Ann Codee in the first scene), was the real-life husband of the actress. Billed as "Codee and Orth," the couple had appeared in vaudeville and in a series of musical shorts released between 1929 and 1931.

Although she had made hundreds of motion picture and television appearances, Virginia Christine was most frequently recognized as "Mrs. Olson," the amiable Swedish woman of the old Folger's Coffee TV commercials. (It is a part she essayed for 21 years.) Born in Iowa, the actress came to Hollywood as an accomplished pianist. There, she met and married comic actor Fritz Feld. "Fritzie," as he was affectionately called by his friends and family, took charge of his young wife's career. She received critical recognition when she appeared on the Los Angeles stage in a 1942 revival of Ibsen's "Hedda Gabler." Fox and Warner Bros. offered Virginia short-term contracts. She chose Warners. Her

*Monster Kid Memories *author Bob Burns is the proud owner of one of the Kharis masks worn by Chaney in* The Mummy's Curse, *given to him by Jack Pierce himself. It is possibly the only remaining piece of the makeup master's work in existence. Pierce told Burns that his nephew used to wear the mask at Halloween. (To make it fit more comfortably on the boy [a consideration he didn't have for Chaney], Pierce cut the mask's right eye open and put a slit in the mouth.)*

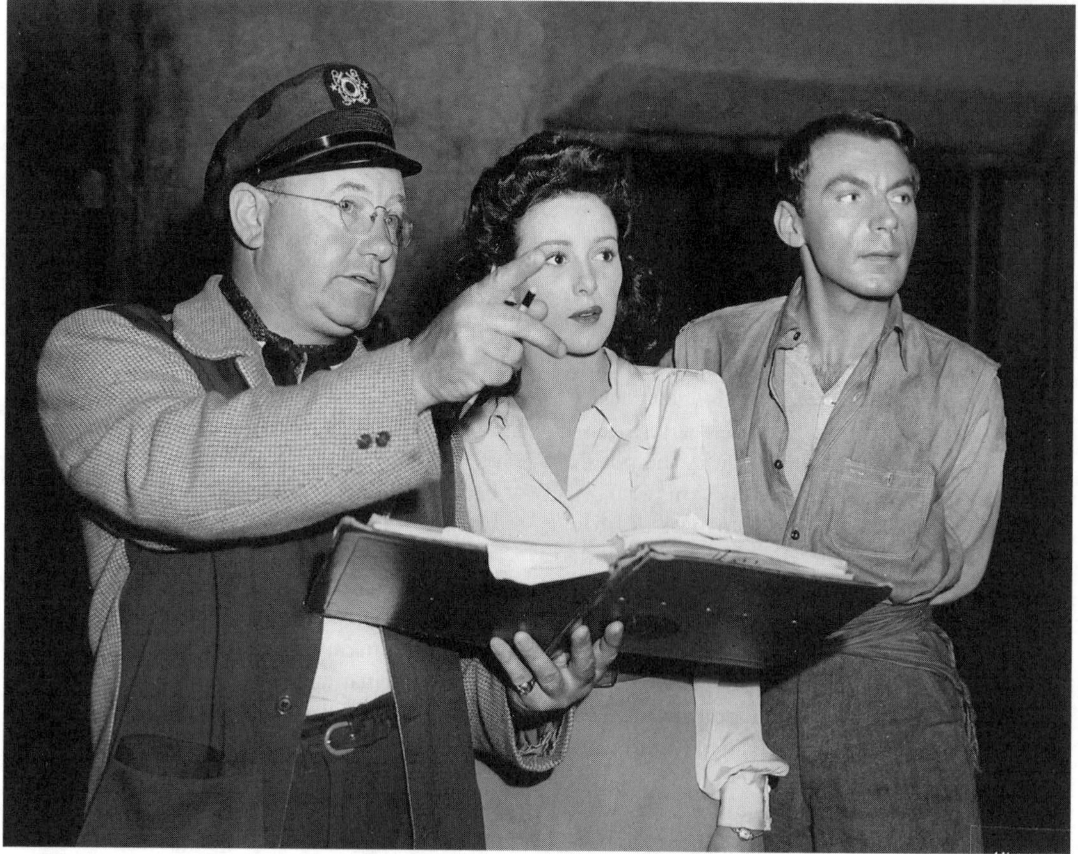

Director Leslie Goodwins issues instructions to Kay Harding and Martin Kosleck for a scene in *The Mummy's Curse.*

stay there was not particularly lucrative, but she had warm memories of working with Errol Flynn in the anti–Nazi drama *Edge of Darkness* (1943).

The actress signed up with Universal, and was cast as Lionel Atwill's partner-in-crime in the 1944 western serial, *Raiders of Ghost City*. ("He was a wonderfully pompous old ham. I kind of stood in awe of him," she told the authors. "We got along very nicely, but he was the kind of man that you would call 'Mr. Atwill.' He was this wonderful matinee idol-type ham.") *The Mummy's Curse* marked the horror film debut of the 27-year-old blonde actress. Her performance as the tormented Ananka is the finest in the entire Kharis series.

With great humor, Christine recalled for us her bizarre experience shooting the resurrection scene:

> I had to be okayed by Jack Pierce in order to get the part. He elevated himself to the position of top monster maker in the business. He was an arrogant man, but we got along beautifully. He said my cheekbones were fine, so I got the part.
>
> We shot the film, and then came the last day of shooting when I change from a mummy to a lovely Egyptian princess. All through the picture, Jack kept coming on the set, saying, "I'm using something new on you, Virginia. It's going to be terrific. *Don't worry*, it won't hurt your skin." I was very young and "It won't hurt your skin" began to ring in my ears. I was a basket case the night before shooting. So, "Fritzie" called Jack on the phone late that night and said, "Jack, what are you going to put on Virginia's face? She's as nervous as a cat!" Jack laughed and said, "Oh, it's nothing — it's a Denver mudpack!"
>
> I was there at four or five in the morning, and sat in the makeup chair for five-and-one-half hours. He started with pieces of cotton dipped in witch hazel to fill in all the youthful lines. Then, he lined it with an orange stick to make the wrinkles. That had to be dried. And then came the Denver mudpack, and that had to be dried. He

> worked a little patch at a time. Unfortunately, we made a mistake in wardrobe because we left the arms bare, which meant that the arms had to be done, too, and the hands ... every place the skin was exposed. It was a tedious, long process. And, of course, the natural thing happened ... I had to go to the bathroom. The body makeup lady was Jack's wife. She took me in like a baby because if I spoiled the hands we'd have to start all over again as they would crack. It was hardened now. I couldn't smile, I couldn't laugh. I couldn't talk. And I got the giggles in the john. It was so ridiculous! We got through that and I got hungry. I would have stolen for food. And so they spoiled the lips a bit and got me a malted milk.
>
> After the full session, they put me in a cart and took me out to the back lot. Very carefully, they dug a hole, my height, right in the dirt. For any big star, they would have sifted the sand and done it on the stage, and had it cleaned. They laid me down in the thing and covered me with burnt cork which photographs like dirt. They turned the hose on so the dried cork got wet and looked like the earth around it. I laid there with this much of me exposed and thought, "Oh, God, how many creepy, crawly things are in this with me?" And just before they shot, they covered my face. So I emerged — and you have to do a little acting along with this ... and how do you act like a mummy? They had built steps in this murky, ugly, swampy, greenish lake. I'm supposed to take two or three steps.... I took one look and said, "I can't do it, I simply can't do it." And then you psyche yourself up and say, "You wanted to be an actress, do it! This time tomorrow, it'll be over."

Ingrid Bergman happened to be on an the lot shooting the railway station exteriors for Hitchcock's 1945 thriller *Spellbound* when the Ananka resurrection scene was shot.

> They all heard about this episode that was being shot, and everybody came out to watch the sequence. We got through it in only one take.
>
> Les Goodwins was one of the sweetest guys on earth. He didn't help *at all.* He could get a picture finished on time, was good-natured, but you never really got any direction from him. You were pretty much on your own in those films. Ben Pivar was very good to me all through the years. I played in several of his films. I never regretted making *The Mummy's Curse.*

As Christine's film career escalated, so did her list of fantastic film credits. She appeared briefly but memorably in *House of Horrors* and *Invasion of the Body Snatchers* (1956), as well as *Billy the Kid Versus Dracula* (1966) and television's *Daughter of the Mind* (1969). Valued as one of Hollywood's "dependables" by such producers as Stanley Kramer (who cast her in a number of his major productions), Virginia came within a hair's-breadth of achieving stardom when she was a leading contender for the Pat Kroll role opposite Ronald Colman in the 1947 Universal-International melodrama *A Double Life*—but lost to Shelley Winters. Virginia Christine died of a heart ailment on July 24, 1996, nearly three years after the death of her beloved "Fritzie."

The supporting cast of *The Mummy's Curse* includes Kay (formerly Jackie Lou) Harding and Dennis Moore as the nominal romantic leads. Moore had previously portrayed the whiskered, bespectacled professor who commits a series of "vampire killings" for which stage magician Bela Lugosi is blamed in Monogram's 1941 East Side Kids farce, *Spooks Run Wild.* Peter Coe's Ilzor Zandaab proves himself to be the Egyptian gods' staunchest disciple. Unlike his predecessors Zucco, Bey and Carradine, Coe zealously sticks to his game plan and doesn't succumb to weaknesses of the flesh. That transgression is committed by acolyte Martin Kosleck, who literally oozes treachery with every grimace. Coe overacts his part. He's as inscrutable and coolly aloof as Turhan Bey is in the same role, but he lacks Bey's assurance and his velvety delivery.

Coe told the authors about one particular incident during shooting which tested his mettle as a professional. He was in the midst of a lunch break interview with columnist Hedda Hopper, when an assistant director informed him he'd have to prepare for an extra scene the company planned on shooting within the hour. "I looked at the script — thirteen pages of soliloquy — solid dialogue. Nobody would believe it but I did it in one take! The whole crew stood up and cheered."

The late actor painted a different picture of Chaney than many of his co-workers did during this phase of his career. Aging silent picture star William Farnum was cast as the sacristan, the Mummy's first victim. Apparently, Farnum had problems remembering his few lines and caused Leslie Goodwins a lot of grief. Coe recalled, "He was a friend of Chaney's father — a big star. Both Chaney and I said, 'Lee — get him a star's chair, otherwise we're going to walk off the set.' Chaney didn't have to do that for the old man." According to Coe, Chaney never showed any discontent playing Kharis under such oppressive conditions.

Both Virginia Christine and Martin Kosleck recalled that Chaney was almost constantly fortified during the filming of *The Mummy's Curse*. Christine told us:

> They had this old shrine built at Universal, and the steps leading up to it were kind of worn. Chaney got into that mummy suit. He was a *very* big guy. Evelyn Ankers had played the leading lady before that, in other monster movies opposite Lon. She was big and tall, and heavy, so Chaney had a canvas strap that went around the back of his neck and then attached to her waist so that his arms wouldn't have to support her whole weight. I inherited that. Chaney had to carry me up these steps — all uneven surfaces. Lon was weaving a little bit and I had to play limp. And I'm *attached* to this big guy, so there's no way to get loose if he falls. Thank God Les Goodwins said, "Hold it a second!" and he got a stand-in to go into the mummy suit.

Chaney retired his tattered mummy outfit after making *The Mummy's Curse*, never dreaming he would reprise the role twice more in the future. In the 1959 Mexican film *La Casa del Terror* (*The House of Terror*), Chaney plays a mummy who also turns out to be a werewolf. (This poor film was finally released in the United States in 1965 by notorious exploitation film mogul Jerry Warren under the title *Face of the Screaming Werewolf.*) And in 1962, the Mummy was one of three great horror characters (the other two were the Hunchback and the Wolf Man) Chaney recreated for the all-star *Route 66* Halloween episode entitled "Lizard's Leg and Owlet's Wing."

The crumbling, 3000-year-old Kharis returned to the screen ten years after the release of *The Mummy's Curse* to face perhaps his greatest challenge — upstaging a sadly aging and painfully unfunny comedy team in 1955's *Abbott and Costello Meet the Mummy*. The screenwriters inexplicably changed his moniker to *Klaris*; this time the role was assigned to stunt veteran Ed Parker, who goosesteps about some interesting Egyptian temple sets looking more like a bandaged Creature from the Black Lagoon.

Having raided the Universal monster cast of characters to come up with their own ragtag versions of the classic monsters, it was only inevitable that the Mexicans would create their own version of Kharis — the Aztec Mummy — and feature him in such laughably overcooked schlock classics as *La Momia azteca* and *La Maldición de la Momia azteca* (both 1957). It was *also* a sure bet that England's Hammer Films would take the plunge and add the Mummy to its roster of classic horror updates. Terence Fisher's 1959 *The Mummy* is hands-down the best version of the enduring yarn since the Karloff original. Christopher Lee's physically imposing yet touchingly soulful portrayal blew Lon Chaney's one-note portrayals of the withered ghoul out of the water. Interestingly enough, the script's author Jimmy Sangster may have gotten his inspiration not only from the Kharis classics, but from Leon Abrams' discarded *The Mummy Returns* treatment as well, particularly in the climax, when the high priest Mehemet Bey (George Pastell) comes between Kharis and Ananka look-alike Isobel Banning (Yvonne Furneaux), and is brutally killed by the hotheaded Egyptian. *The Mummy* spawned two sequels, 1964's *The Curse of the Mummy's Tomb* and 1967's *The Mummy's Shroud*, both of which were a notch or two above the substandard product that the British company was churning out in this period of decline.

The late '90s saw a resurgence of interest in the Mummy mythos. Bringing things full circle, *The Mummy Lives* (1993) featured characters who broke three cardinal mummy movie rules: You don't excavate in the Valley of the Kings, you don't desecrate a tomb marked with the hieroglyphic equivalent of a DO NOT DISTURB sign and you don't — repeat, *don't*— update and remake the 1932 *The Mummy* with Tony Curtis in the old Karloff role! Scripted by Nelson (*The Haunting*) Gidding, the Cannon release depicts archaeologists uncovering the tomb of an ancient Egyptian who, we learn via flashbacks featuring Curtis in the role, was buried alive for the sin of trifling with a sacred concubine (Leslie Hardy). Hardy also plays a modern woman who is the reincarnation of Curtis' lost love. The resuscitated mummy, once again resembling his old self (Curtis), adopts a new identity and is alternately charming and menacing as he knocks off the tomb desecrators and makes bedroom eyes at the not-unreceptive Hardy, for whom he has unholy plans. Location photography of pyramids and desert plains give the proceedings a nice feeling of authenticity, but Curtis' presence soon dispels it; with his smoky voice and Brooklynese delivery, he seems every bit as out-of-place in these settings as he did 40-odd years prior, during the "desert swashbuckler" phase of his early career.

Though rooted in the classics, Russell Mulcahy's offbeat *Tale of the Mummy* (aka *Talos the Mummy*) boasts more than its share of unique touches, including a bizarre CG effect of a cloud of swirling mummy wrappings snuffing out unsuspecting victims' lives. Christopher Lee, Jason Scott Lee and Honor Blackman head the cast of this 1998 curiosity. And, finally, Stephen Sommers ushered the Mummy into the twenty-first century, exploiting the Imhotep-Kharis legends for two pleasantly nostalgic, Indiana Jones-flavored adventure-horror stories, *The Mummy* (1999) and *The Mummy Returns* (2001), both featuring *Gods and Monsters* star Brendan Fraser.

Critics' Corner

Rating: Fair. It's all very gruesome, menacing in a slow way and old hat. A thirteen-headed dragon could be no more preposterous, but people who gobble up this sort of thing are not students of possibilities.—*The New York Post*, March 31, 1945, Archer Winsten

Rating: ★★ Lon Chaney ... plays the mummy effectively....—*The New York Daily News*, March 31, 1945, Kate Cameron

[A] wretched little shocker.... It's all very juvenile and silly and, except for a few hollow laughs, is as dull as Uncle Henry's old jack-knife.—*The New York Times*, March 31, 1945, Bosley Crowther

Since what transpires is, in the main, repetitious of the weird, fantastic dramatics that were used in the previous "Mummy" pictures, its chief appeal will be to those to whom the series is new, as well as to the avid horror picture fans.... The bayou country of Louisiana and a deserted monastery provide an effective eerie background....—*Harrison's Reports*, December 30, 1944

[The Mummy,] who looks like Tom Tyler at first and might be Deanna Durbin after that for all you see of Lon Chaney, comes to life mad as hell and begins knocking off the cast. This is not a bad idea....—*The Hollywood Reporter*, December 20, 1944

Destiny

Released December 22, 1944. 65 minutes. *Producers:* (uncredited) Julien Duvivier & Charles Boyer. *Associate Producer:* Roy William Neill. *Executive Producer:* Howard Benedict. *Directors:* Reginald LeBorg & (uncredited) Julien Duvivier. *Screenplay:* Roy Chanslor & Ernest Pascal. *Story Idea:* Jean Levy-Strauss. *Photography:* George Robinson & Paul Ivano. *Camera Operators:* Fleet Southcott & Walter Strenge. *Second Camera:* Edward Cohen. *Editor:* Paul Landres. *Special Effects:* Willis R. Cook. *Music:* Frank Skinner & Alexandre (Alexander) Tansman. *Song:* "Only Those Who Listen to a Dream" *by* Paul Webster. *Music Mixer:* Paul Neal. *Art Directors:* John B. Goodman, Abraham Grossman & Richard H. Riedel. *Set Decorators:* Russell A. Gausman & Victor A. Gangelin. *Assistant Director:* Seward Webb. *Sound Director:* Bernard B. Brown. *Technician:* William Hedgcock. *Sound Mixer:* Joe Lapis. *Re-recording & Effects Mixer:* Ronald K. Pierce. *Script Clerks:* Dorothy Wright & Johnny Bowman. *Gowns:* Vera West.

Gloria Jean (*Jane Broderick*), Alan Curtis (*Cliff Banks*), Frank Craven (*Clem Broderick*), Grace McDonald (*Betty*), Vivian Austin (*Phyllis*), Frank Fenton (*Sam Baker*), Minna Gombell (*Marie*), Selmer Jackson (*Warden*), Lew Wood (*Prison Guard*), Robert Homans (*Grogan*), Perc Launders (*Sergeant*), Harry Strang (*Sgt. Bronson*), Lane Chandler (*Patrolman*), Billy Wayne (*Bartender*), Gayne Whitman (*Radio Announcer*), Frank Hagney, Edgar Dearing, Bill Hale, Dale Van Sickel (*Motorcycle Cops*), Dorothy Vaughan (*Maggie*), Bill O'Brien (*Waiter*), Bob Reeves (*Cop*), Ken Terrell, Bud Wolfe (*Radio Patrolmen*), Carey Loftin, Frosty Royce, Johnny Daheim (*Stunts*), Kate McKenna, Bob Pepper, Lois Schoonover, Reba King, Tom Steele, Helen Thurston. *Deleted from final print:* Erville Alderson (*Man*).

> Gloria Jean plays the little lady in a manner so sweet and sublime that she makes Snow White look like a burglar.
> —*Bosley Crowther,* The New York Times, *February 3, 1945*

A delicate, sentimental fantasy-drama, stylistically enhanced by expressive visuals, *Destiny* was built over the foundation of the unused fourth episode of the whimsical Julien Duvivier omnibus *Flesh and Fantasy*. Padded out to 65 minutes, *Destiny* is a misfire but an interesting one, encapsulating the faults and strengths of its parent film. Ernest Pascal's scenario, a hard-luck tale about a two-time loser who's steered off his destructive course by an afflicted girl with extraordinary capabilities, is preachy and laden with bromides. As in *Flesh and Fantasy*, we are willing to overlook the banal story and concentrate instead on the arresting cinematic techniques of the French director and his cinematographer, Paul Ivano. Both men deserve a round of enthusiastic applause for the movie's most impressive set piece, the supernaturally induced rainstorm that consigns the villain to his well-deserved doom.

By the time Universal had decided what it wanted to do with the vignette, nearly a year had passed since *Flesh and Fantasy*'s theatrical release. The episode's star, Gloria Jean, was at first dismayed by the studio's decision to withhold her first dramatic performance. "They notified me that the episode was cut out, and that they intended to make a full-length feature out of it," she told the authors. "I was impressed with that. When they told me that, I didn't feel so bad any more. Reginald LeBorg, who directed the extra scenes, was always very nice to me, I liked him."

Roy Chanslor was hired to compose a new screenplay, building upon Pascal's original material. Reginald LeBorg was selected to take over the director's chores, studio leading man Alan Curtis was called back to appear in the newly developed scenes, and a small cast of additional players was assembled. LeBorg soon learned that a bit more was required of him than he thought. "I took over for Roy William Neill as associate producer, but he still got the title. There was no producer. I had to make all the producing decisions," the director groused.

Both Julien Duvivier and Charles Boyer relinquished all rights to the project for $25,000 apiece. First called *Faith*, then retitled *The Fugitive* while the picture was still in the works, it was finally released as *Destiny*, that often-applied but heretofore never-used moniker of many a Universal production. *Destiny* began production around August 30, 1944, and wrapped a day over the 12-day schedule.

Jean admitted:

> *Destiny* was a B-movie. The story of the blind girl didn't turn out as effective as it would have been if they'd kept it the way it was, in *Flesh and Fantasy*.... The funny part of it is, they took a lot of girls from *other* studios and tested them for the part of the blind girl [in *Flesh and Fantasy*]. Charles Boyer was the producer on that, and they [Boyer and other behind-the-scenes types] were talking one day and they said, "I dunno, we just can't find a girl that *really* looks blind." And one of the men on the set, cinematographer Paul Ivano, said, "You know, you're looking right *at* her, if you'd only give her a test. Gloria Jean." And Boyer said, "You're right, let's test Gloria for this!" I was 17 at the time. There was no [test] scene, they just shot close-ups. I was supposed to be blind, so they had me look a certain way. It was all big head shots. I didn't have to talk or do any acting or *any*thing.

Paul Ivano not only suggested Gloria for the role, he photographed her screen test, *and* he was the one who photographed her in the movie.

Jean recalled her initial reaction to the script:

> When I read the script, I thought, "Oh, if I could *only* do this movie, what a wonderful break it would be for me!" Lo and behold, a couple days later, [I was] in the commissary. Boyer walked up with a big smile on his face and said, "You ready to do the movie? You got the part." Can you imagine how thrilled I was? I almost fell out of my chair. Boyer said when Julien Duvivier, the director, looked at my test, he said, "My God, that's the girl we want."

As to whether Boyer was a hands-on producer or cooped himself up in his office (*à la* Ben Pivar), Jean responded, "[H]e was very interested in everything."

Destiny gets off to an exciting start with a rousing road chase with bank robber Sam Baker (Frank Fenton) and his stooge Cliff Banks (Alan Curtis) in a convertible, trying to outrace motorcycle policemen. Abandoning the car, the two outlaws take off on separate paths and disappear into the hills. Banks is forced to make good his escape by jumping off a bridge into a river (a thrilling sequence lifted from Universal's 1942 spy thriller *Saboteur*, directed by Alfred Hitchcock).

Roy Chanslor's expanded script provides some interesting insights into Curtis' troubled character. Through his chance encounters with various strangers (most of them female), we witness his dramatic personal catharsis. An attractive librarian named Betty (well-played by hoofer Grace McDonald) is taken into the hitchhiking fugitive's confidence after she picks him up on the roadside. The popular tune, "I'll See You in My Dreams," heard over the car radio, sets off a series of flashbacks. It seems that Cliff was an okay guy until he hitched up with Phyllis (Vivian Austin), an alluring torch singer, and her shifty pal, Sam Baker. Thanks to Baker, Cliff takes part in an armed robbery and is sent to San Quentin for three years. That flashback ends and Cliff leaves Betty behind to resume his flight.

Pressbook ad for *The Fugitive*, the original title of *Destiny*, which was initially produced as part of the omnibus film *Flesh and Fantasy*. Is that clear?

The sorry details surrounding Cliff's downfall unfold further when he encounters Marie (Minna Gombell), a world-weary but seemingly compassionate cafe worker. In a second series of flashbacks, we learn that Cliff's recent run-in with the law came as a result of yet another association with bad egg Baker. Marie proves to be treacherous; she alerts the cops to Cliff's whereabouts in the hopes of collecting the reward. He just barely gets away.

From this point, Duvivier's original footage dominates the remainder of the film. Cliff arrives in Paradise Valley, an idyllic farming community (an American version of Shangri-La). Stopping at a roadhouse, the weary young man meets folksy Clem Broderick (Frank Craven) and his daughter Jane (Gloria Jean). Blind since birth, Jane has developed amazing extrasensory powers: she's in perfect harmony with the natural elements and the valley's wildlife, and has had some success as a dowser (a person capable of locating underground water sources with a divining rod).

Yet for all her powers, Jane is unable to see through the scheming stranger. Embittered by the hard blows life has dealt him, Cliff has become immune to the faith and generosity of others, and coldbloodedly plots to take control of the Broderick farm. He accompanies Clem into the woods on the pretext of disposing of a marauding bear. Minutes later, two shots ring out. Cliff returns home alone. Forcing himself on the terrified Jane, Cliff is attacked by her faithful dog.

Summoning up her unearthly powers, Jane conjures up a raging storm. In a tour de force display of special effects and riveting camerawork, Cliff pursues Jane through the forest to the banks of the swollen river. All of the forces of nature align themselves with their blind comrade. Branches of trees strike out menacingly, blocking Cliff's path. Reaching the pier, Jane attempts to untie the rowboat but Cliff intervenes. He plunges into the raging torrent, is swept away and drowns.

On this bleak, pessimistic note, the Duvivier-directed playlet came to a close. (A neat "bridge" connecting this story to the Betty Field-Robert Cummings Mardi Gras episode of *Flesh and Fantasy* had the costumed revelers discovering Curtis' body on the river bank. It is there that the lonely Henrietta and the lost Michael meet, thus setting the next story in motion.) Settling for a contrived, uplifting finis, Chanslor dismisses the murder-drowning incidents as a dream (or perhaps a premonition of Cliff's destiny). Not only is the youth redeemed by saving Clem's life following a skirmish with the bear, but all criminal charges against him are dropped in a contrived ending after the pesky Sam Baker (unbelievably) exonerates him.

Production for this episode of *Flesh and Fantasy* was scheduled to begin in late October 1942. In November, Duvivier trotted his cast and crew up to Angelus Crest and the Malibu Lake area to shoot exterior scenes. Initial plans to film the entire episode outdoors were abandoned when a fire destroyed the desired location. The troupe labored through December, took time off for a Christmas recess, then resumed production, finally wrapping on January 26, 1943. Willis R. Cook's special effects department constructed a whirlpool in the studio tank for the uncomfortably realistic storm sequence. Though confined to a water depth of three and a half feet, the current proved powerful enough to capsize a ten-foot-long rowboat.

Gloria Jean at first agreed with this publicity notice, but then contradicted herself. "We went to Lake Sherwood," she told the authors, "and they filmed where I was down on the dock, actually *in* the water there, They had men with boats making the waves high, and wind machines — it's just amazing, the things they did."

Another intriguing effect devised by Cook's crew was a field of 1200 wildflowers that magically bowed to the blind girl as she strolled amongst them. A piece in *The Hollywood Reporter* revealed that the stunt was accomplished by having 12 men operate a piano-like keyboard which controlled the hundreds of flowers by means of invisible thread. "It was like puppets, but of course you couldn't see the strings or anything," the actress recalled. "As I walked, *allll* these flowers would bend forward. It was beautifully done. It was a lot of work for the prop men, I'll tell ya that!" Only a modest-size bed of flowers turns up in the final cut, leading one to assume that the stunt was reduced in scope just before shooting, or that Universal's rabid press boys were up to their old tricks again.

Seen today, *Destiny* uncomfortably walks a

narrow line between fanciful drama and unintentional parody. (One shudders at the thought of the beating this naive little picture would receive at a revival screening attended by a typical modern-day audience of smartass hipsters and jaded intellectuals.) The trite messages preached in *Destiny*— have faith in your fellow man, practice good will toward others, etc.— are delivered with naïve enthusiasm as though we are dealing with novel concepts here. The film draws a distinct contrast between the corrupt inhumanity of urban life and the euphoric, at-peace-with-oneself serenity of Paradise Valley. To his credit, Duvivier imbues these segments with a hauntingly surreal and otherworldly quality, capturing the feel and texture of a vintage French film. The differences in cinematic style and sensibilities are striking: Duvivier was the artist, LeBorg a talented craftsman.

While the Duvivier-Pascal vignette presents Cliff Banks as an incorrigible good-for-nothing, richly deserving of the watery fate that awaits him, the LeBorg-Chanslor footage characterizes the man in an entirely different light: A basically decent if gullible fellow caught up in a spiraling set of circumstances over which he has little control. The Cliff Banks of *Destiny* is ripe for redemption; the Cliff Banks of *Flesh and Fantasy*, on the other hand, is on a collision course with the devil.

It strains credulity to buy into Cliff's radical change from Hard Luck Joe to fiendish schemer. ("Who could change *that* much?" Jean agreed.) The blame here lies squarely on the shoulders of scenarists Chanslor and Pascal, who might have provided a more believable basis for this shocking development had they had fleshed out the character in less sympathetic terms. However, much of the empathy we are supposed to feel for Banks is lost in Alan Curtis' typically stilted performance. Ruggedly handsome but stoic and inflexible, Curtis, who achieved minor celebrity as a B picture lead through the '40s, brought an air of icy detachment to his screen performances. "You had to get friendly with him, then he was very nice. But he was a little arrogant," was Reginald LeBorg's less-than-glowing assessment of the man. Curtis was brought into the cast of *Flesh and Fantasy* in mid–November 1942 as a replacement for Warner Bros. brat-packer John Garfield. Evidently unhappy with his loan-out to Universal, Garfield withdrew his services and was suspended by Jack Warner.

Born in Chicago, Alan Curtis earned his bread and butter as an artists' and photographers' model before making his screen debut in 1936. MGM took notice and cast Curtis in the role of Joan Crawford's worthless beau whom she wisely forsakes for steamship magnate Spencer Tracy in the well-mounted soaper *Mannequin* (1937). Prominent parts followed in *Four Sons* (1940), *High Sierra* (1941), Abbott and Costello's *Buck Privates* (1941), *Hitler's Madman* (1943), and the noir classic *Phantom Lady* (1944). Yet, first-class stardom eluded Curtis. With the quality of his pictures in sharp decline, and two failed marriages (to actresses Priscilla Lawson and Ilona Massey) behind him, he died at age 43 on February 1, 1953, shortly after undergoing kidney surgery in New York. "Alan Curtis was wonderful to work with, and Frank Craven was a lovely man —*Destiny* had a nice cast," Jean told us.

As the angelic Jane, a role that required an unaffected naturalness and sensitivity to bring it off, Gloria Jean is excellent. In both her Duvivier-directed *Flesh and Fantasy* scenes and in the new ones shot for *Destiny*, the young soprano, groomed by Universal to fill Deanna Durbin's shoes whenever that high-priced songbird stepped out of line, gives a flawless rendition of the blind girl who "sees" more deeply than the sighted folks around her. The musical-comedy star hadn't appeared in a drama for Universal since she debuted in 1939's *The Underpup*. Teresa Wright was originally selected to play Jane, but she was forced to turn down the role when she was ordered to rest by her doctor. (Reportedly, Bonita Granville was also in the running for the role.)

Did she have any problem with the Gallic Duvivier during shooting?

> Everyone warned me, they said Julien Duvivier was a little strict, and "Gloria, you may not like him," because I was used to doing all of the "light" comedies and musicals. I *loved* Duvivier! He took me aside and he said, "I want to give you a little advice. *Don't act* in this movie. Because the minute you think you're acting, you're not going to be good." Well, that stuck in my mind. So I was impressed with him. As a director he was *wonderful. Really* wonderful. He knew exactly what

he wanted. [H]e had an accent, but I understood him. I thought Duvivier was just the very best.

In an interview Jean granted to *Classic Images* (September 2004), the actress recalled a particularly thorny incident during the shoot:

> In one scene, Alan Curtis and I were handling a hive of bees and we were terrified of being stung. The bees were drugged by a fog, but they would land all over me, including my face. I was supposed to be blind and couldn't blink. I was also supposed to be natural like it happened all the time. Alan really panicked until the scene was over.

Had *Destiny* wound up as a vignette in *Flesh and Fantasy* as originally intended, it would have rated on a par with the equally enchanting (and similarly ingenuous) Mardi Gras episode. Both are the stuff of which fairy tales are made. Gloria Jean summed it up best. "*Destiny* wasn't all that bad as a feature, but it *lost* something—you could see the difference in the end product."

Critics' Corner

Alan Curtis plays the lad with a scowl and a sneer so acid that it virtually corrodes the screen.—*The New York Times*, February 3, 1945, Bosley Crowther

Rating: ★★ After you've seen and heard the story of the long-suffering hero ... and the blind girl who exudes goodness and sweetness, you will more than likely feel like you've had three ice cream sodas, with whipped cream.... [A] melodrama with too little suspense and too much sentiment.—*The New York Daily News*, February 3, 1945, Wanda Hale

[Curtis and Jean] are exceptionally good. Some of the situations are deeply appealing....—*Harrison's Reports*, December 9, 1944

This unheralded gem is one of those exquisite film cameos which emerge all too rarely from the studios and, once seen, leave a haunting memory of something rare and beautiful.... *Destiny* is wholly unpretentious yet superb screen fare and has captured something of the quality of a *Lost Horizon* or, if one may dare to venture back 25 years, *The Miracle Man*.—*The Hollywood Reporter*, December 1, 1944

[T]he essence of melodrama and fantasy are combined and the result is an unusual film hardly to be classed in either category.... A nice job is done in blending the elements....—*The Motion Picture Herald*, December 9, 1944, M.R.Y.

1945

The House of Fear

Released March 16, 1945. 69 minutes. *Executive Producer:* Howard Benedict. *Producer-Director:* Roy William Neill. *Screenplay:* Roy Chanslor. *Based on the story* "The Five Orange Pips" *by* Sir Arthur Conan Doyle. *Photography:* Virgil Miller. *Camera Operator:* Edward Cohen. *Music Director:* Paul Sawtell. *Art Directors:* John B. Goodman & Eugene Lourie. *Director of Sound:* Bernard B. Brown. *Technician:* William Hedgcock. *Set Decorators:* Russell A. Gausman & Edward R. Robinson. *Editor:* Saul A. Goodkind. *Dialogue Director:* Ray Kessler. *Assistant Directors:* Melville Shyer & Mort Singer, Jr.

Basil Rathbone (*Sherlock Holmes*), Nigel Bruce (*Dr. John H. Watson*), Aubrey Mather (*Bruce Alastair*), Dennis Hoey (*Inspector Lestrade*), Paul Cavanagh (*Dr. Simon Merrivale*), Holmes Herbert (*Alan Cosgrave*), Harry Cording (*Capt. John Simpson*), Sally Shepherd (*Mrs. Monteith*), Gavin Muir (*Mr. Chalmers*), Florette Hillier (*Alison MacGregor*), David Clyde (*Alec MacGregor*), Wilson Benge (*Guy Davies*), Leslie Denison (*Sgt. Bleeker*), Alec Craig (*Angus*), Dick Alexander (*Ralph King*), Cyril Delevanti (*Stanley Rayburn*).

Walls of hate ... holding an orgy of murder....
—*Ad blurb for The House of Fear*

Another Holmes series entry that takes the dogged detective far from his Baker Street haunts, *The House of Fear* is moderately interesting but mostly unmemorable. Like other films in the series (*Sherlock Holmes Faces Death, The Scarlet Claw*), *House of Fear* is what Universal itself called a "timeless" entry, one that allows audiences to get the impression that it takes place in the earlier era of the original Conan Doyle stories: Dialogue and characters appear to have come right out of the Victorian age, automobiles and other twentieth century conveniences are seldom if ever seen, and no references to the current state of world politics are made. (The series' final reference to current events was *The Spider Woman*'s depiction of painted targets of Hitler et al. in a carnival shooting gallery.)

The House of Fear has as its basis the unsatisfying Conan Doyle tale, "The Five Orange Pips." In this story, young John Openshaw appears out of a fierce London rainstorm and lays out his story to Holmes. Openshaw explains that his uncle, Col. Openshaw, a quick-tempered man who was once a Florida slave owner, returned to England a few years after the Civil War and settled down to a reclusive life on a Sussex estate. One day the uncle received a letter containing orange pips (seeds); scrawled upon the inner flap of the envelope were the letters K.K.K. The uncle took the letter as a death threat, burned some of his papers, and soon died a mysterious death which was ruled a suicide. Some months later, Openshaw continues, his own father received a similar letter containing orange pips along with a letter that demanded the uncle's papers (the letter-writer doesn't know that the uncle burned them); a few days later, the father died, "accidentally." And now young Openshaw reveals that he, too, has received a letter. Holmes promises to investigate and, after sending Openshaw on his way, deduces that the letters are from the Ku Klux Klan; obviously the colonel, a former member, was in possession of incriminating documents. But before Holmes can act, word reaches him of John Openshaw's "accidental" death. Holmes vows to bring the killers to justice, but the bark upon which the Klansmen had sailed for home is lost at sea.

Screenwriter Roy Chanslor (later the author of such well-known Western novels as *Johnny Guitar* and *Cat Ballou*) apparently found little to work with in the Conan Doyle story, and went about adding his own plot elements. His script pivots around a private club whose members are being killed off, each victim receiving shortly in advance of his disappearance and death an envelope containing orange pips. Under the working title *The Murder Club*, the film was shot in May 1944 ("wrapping" three days over schedule on the 31st of the month), with exteriors photographed at Nagana Rocks and on the Hacienda lawn. Part of the all-purpose *Green Hell* set is seen as a cellar at the conclusion.

The film opens with a series of flashbacks. A dulcet-voiced narrator introduces us to the Good Comrades, an unusual seven-member club headquartered in Drearcliff House, a centuried castle-like mansion perched on a seaside cliff in Scotland. The club members enjoy a laugh when Ralph King (Dick Alexander) receives a letter containing seven orange pips; King is killed in a fiery car crash shortly thereafter. There's no laughter when Stanley Rayburn (Cyril Delevanti) receives six orange pips; his mangled body is later dragged out of the sea. Both deaths conform to the gruesome legend of Drearcliff House, where "no man ever goes whole to his grave."

The narrator of these flashbacks is Mr. Chalmers (Gavin Muir), an insurance underwriter who is telling the grim story to Holmes and Watson (Basil Rathbone and Nigel Bruce). Chalmers considers the deaths suspicious in that the Good Comrades have set themselves up as a tontine (with the death of each beneficiary, the insurance money is divided among the survivors). Intrigued, Holmes accepts the case.

Holmes and Watson journey to Scotland, arriving just in time to receive news of the death of a third member, who was incinerated. The four remaining Good Comrades are Bruce Alastair (Aubrey Mather), Dr. Simon Merrivale (Paul Cavanagh), Alan Cosgrave (Holmes Herbert) and John Simpson (Harry Cording). Holmes and Watson move into desolate Drearcliff House and begin their investigation. Cosgrave is the next to receive orange pips (four), and despite police protection from the newly arrived Inspector Lestrade (Dennis Hoey), he disappears; his blown-to-bits body is later found in the ruins of a dynamite shed. Simpson finds three pips in his envelope and pretty soon there's nothing left of him but a torso. MacGregor (David Clyde), a tobacconist in the nearby village, sends a note which indicates that he has stumbled upon a clue, but before Holmes can get to the man, he's shot and killed.

Acting on a hunch, Holmes has Watson exhume MacGregor's coffin shortly after his funeral: it's empty. This confirms some unspecified suspicion of Holmes' and he rushes back to Drearcliff where the body of Dr. Merrivale has

Holmes (Basil Rathbone) and Watson (Nigel Bruce) are poised to solve the mystery of the orange pips in *The House of Fear* (courtesy Dan Scapperotti).

cleared and Watson is rescued as Lestrade places the men under arrest for the murder of MacGregor.

Although a synopsis of *The House of Fear* may suggest an action-packed mystery, it's actually slow-moving and talkative. There's a high death rate, yes, but none of this mayhem can occur on-screen; the various "murders" cannot be depicted since they do not actually occur. The viewer is left with repetitive episodes in which a victim receives the orange pips and disappears, then a scene of Holmes discovering a body. This device, which begins to wear thin during the opening flashback sequence, later becomes exceedingly tiresome when it represents the only activity in the film.

Director Roy William Neill tries to compensate for the near-complete absence of action by whipping up some old-dark-house (or castle) atmosphere, but things soon begin to drag. The mystery is nicely bewildering at first, but after a few too many scenes in which corpses are identified by the process of elimination, what's *really* going on becomes pretty obvious. The proceedings come to an abrupt halt during a too-long comedy relief scene in which Nigel Bruce searches the castle during a violent rainstorm and skittishly engages in a one-sided gunfight with a suit of armor and moving shadows.*

just been found, crushed by a fallen boulder. Lestrade places the last surviving Good Comrade, Alastair, under arrest.

Watson discovers a clue, but before he can bring it to Holmes' attention he vanishes mysteriously. Holmes and Lestrade discover a hidden passage that leads to a secret room; in it, the two men find the six supposedly dead Good Comrades. To collect money from the insurance company, the men had faked their own deaths using the stolen and mutilated corpses of recently buried villagers, and framed Alastair. Alastair is

The Good Comrades' scurrilous plot doesn't hold up under scrutiny; it just doesn't stand to reason that the insurance pay-outs would, or *could*, be made as quickly as these guys

* *"The noise from a gunshot bothered [Bruce] and, whenever he had to fire a pistol, we found him involuntarily closing his eyes," the Holmes series' executive producer Howard Benedict revealed in Michael B. Druxman's* Basil Rathbone: His Life and His Films. *"Sometimes, it would be several takes before we could get a usable take."*

are supposedly being bumped off. The Six Little Indians fake their deaths one after another, in very rapid succession; does the insurance company pay off within hours of a death, even in the midst of a mad flurry of activity like this? And in *cash*, which seems to be the only way this scheme could work for the "dead" Good Comrades? These are questions that might tax the deductive abilities of even Mr. Sherlock Holmes!

Despite the dreary ambience (and iffy premise), *The House of Fear* still rests notches above some of the other Universal Holmes films. Rathbone's performance may seem to lack its characteristic zip at times, but for the most part he and Nigel Bruce are in good form. Dennis Hoey gets a bit more than usual to do this go-round as Lestrade, and for once he comes off funnier and livelier than Nigel Bruce. A dinner-table scene in which Lestrade becomes apoplectic upon receiving a hand-delivered letter (it's just a note, but he thinks the envelope contains orange pips) is particularly amusing.

If the *House of Fear* pressbook is to be believed, one of the lighter moments behind the scenes came at the expense of Nigel Bruce. Apparently the actor was kiddingly accused of trying to steal every scene he shared with Rathbone, and also of trying to usurp some of director Neill's functions (the news item describes Bruce as "attempting an Orson Welles"). The pay-off came one day at the rushes, when a bogus set of opening credits were projected on the screen:

Nigel Bruce Productions Present
The House of Fear
Produced by Nigel Bruce
Directed by Nigel Bruce
Original Story: Nigel Bruce
Photography: Nigel Bruce
Art Direction: Nigel Bruce
Musical Score: Nigel Bruce
Recording: Nigel Bruce
Sound Effects: Nigel Bruce
Properties: Nigel Bruce

According to the item, no one in the room laughed louder than Bruce.*

The series regulars aside, the balance of the *House of Fear* cast is pretty colorless. As Bruce Alastair, Aubrey Mather is meek and phlegmatic to the point of irritation — but nevertheless, there ought to have been at least *one* person in the group of his best friends unwilling to participate in a scheme that leaves Alastair framed for murder! Mather was on loan-out from Fox; look in the background during two of his scenes to see the wolf's-head cane from *The Wolf Man* leaning against a wall. Paul Cavanagh, in his second of three Holmes entries, is a bit too obvious a red herring. Holmes Herbert and Harry Cording have substantial roles, and it's good to see these veteran players finally getting a chance to play bigger, better-than-usual parts. Sally Shepherd, as a solemn housekeeper, adds yet more gloom to a film that was gloomy enough already.

Producer-director Neill's young daughter Patricia apparently had her eye on the role of a young Scottish girl, and was no doubt encouraged when her dad told her, "You are just right for the part, you are a good actress, you're the type, and I know you would give a good performance." But then came the splash of cold water: He told her he was casting someone else, because he didn't want her to get her acting break because she was the daughter of the producer of the movie. The role of Alison MacGregor went instead to Florette Hillier, an unknown whose regular job was at a defense plant.

Collaborating with Universal vet John B. Goodman on the film's eerie art direction was Eugene Lourie, the celebrated Russian-born set designer of *Grand Illusion–The Rules of the Game–Limelight* fame (and, in later years, a director of science fiction films). Additionally contributing to the film's desired atmosphere of spooky weirdness is Virgil Miller's cinematography, with its frequent use of odd (but often distracting) "tilted" shots. Recognizably re-used in the movie are European Street; sets also seen in *The Invisible Man's Revenge* (the barroom), *The Mummy's Ghost* and *Dead Man's Eyes*; and stock footage of the fiery crash of Dr. Kemp's car from *The Invisible Man*, "flipped" to make it look a little different this time around.

Truth be told, *The House of Fear* is a Sherlock Holmes exploit which doesn't offer much

**Interestingly, another short pressbook article mentions that the earlier Universal Holmes movies with wartime themes had not gotten the hoped-for reaction from devotees of Conan Doyle mysteries. It's a bit of a surprise to find in a Universal-Holmes pressbook an outright admission that certain of the earlier series entrants hadn't gone over well with some of the fans.*

beyond the usual Rathbone-Bruce-Hoey acting chemistry and the novelty of another story played strictly according to Conan Doyle (played to seem as though it's taking place in an earlier era); it's in no danger of ever being called anyone's favorite Holmes picture. But for a legion of mystery fans this is more than adequate compensation for the 69-minute investment.

Critics' Corner

[I]n *The House of Fear,* [Holmes] lets the guilty get away with too much crime before he levels the final revolver. And then his solution, when it finally comes, is attained more by good luck and opponents' blunders than by good and artful management on his part.—*The New York Herald-Tribune,* March 17, 1945, Otis Guernsey, Jr.

[I]t becomes painfully apparent that the fascination of the gentleman is spent.... Sherlock Holmes has certainly gone to the bow-wows in the clutches of Hollywood.—*The New York Times,* March 17, 1945, Bosley Crowther

Rating: ★★★ [O]ne of the better pictures in the series ... Universal maintains the high standard it set for itself with other pictures in this entertaining series of detective puzzles.—*The New York Daily News,* March 17, 1945, Kate Cameron

[*The House of Fear* is] in keeping with the present trend of stories dealing with mass murders and the gradual elimination of the cast in pictures.... Direction, by Neill, is clever, and cannily designed to reap the greatest harvest of suspense from the script.... The photography by Virgil Miller does much to heighten the eerie quality of the background against which the story is played.—*The Hollywood Reporter,* March 15, 1945

[B]elow par for the series.... There is nothing unusual about the production, most of it being repetitious of the previous pictures.... The action slows down considerably in spots, and the suspense usually found in pictures of this type is lacking.—*Harrison's Reports,* March 24, 1945

That's the Spirit

Released June 1, 1945. 87 minutes. *Executive Producer:* Howard Benedict. *Writers-Producers:* Michael Fessier and Ernest Pagano. *Director:* Charles Lamont. *Photography:* Charles Van Enger. *Music Score & Direction:* Hans J. Salter. *Art Directors:* John B. Goodman & Richard H. Riedel. *Dance Ensembles Stager:* Carlos Romero. *Numbers for Peggy Ryan & Johnny Coy Staged by* Louis De Pron. *Songs:* "No Matter Where You Are," "Evenin' Star" (Jack Brooks & Hans J. Salter), "Fella with a Flute," "Oh, Oh, Oh" (Sidney Miller & Inez James), "Nola" (Felix Arndt), "How Come You Do Me Like You Do?" (Roy Bergere & Gene Austin), "Baby, Won't You Please Come Home?" (Clarence Williams & Charles Warfield), "Bugle Call Rag" (J. Hubert Blake & Carey Morgan), "Ja-Da" (Bob Carleton), "Do You Ever Think of Me?" (Earl Burnett, John Cooper & Harry D. Kerr). *Director of Sound:* Bernard B. Brown. *Technician:* Charles Carroll. *Set Decorators:* Russell A. Gausman & Andrew J. Gilmore. *Editor:* Fred R. Feitshans, Jr. *Gowns:* Vera West. *Dialogue Director:* Monty Collins. *Assistant Director:* William Tummel. *Special Photography:* John P. Fulton. *Second Camera:* Harold I. Smith. *Rerecording & Effects Mixer:* Ronald K. Pierce. *Music Mixer:* Paul Neal.

Jack Oakie (*Steve Gogarty*), Peggy Ryan (*Sheila Gogarty*), June Vincent (*Libby Cawthorne Gogarty*), Gene Lockhart (*Jasper Cawthorne*), Johnny Coy (*Martin Wilde, Jr.*), Andy Devine (*Martin Wilde*), Arthur Treacher (*Masters*), Irene Ryan (*Bilson*), Buster Keaton (*L.M.*), Victoria Horne (*Patience*), Edith Barrett (*Abigail Cawthorne*), Rex Story (*Specialty*), Karen Randle (*The Dark Lady*), Harry Tyler, Billy Newell (*Detectives*), Jack Roper (*Ticket Taker*), Virginia Brissac (*Miss Preble*), Charles Sullivan, Sid Troy (*Men*), Monty Collins (*Bellhop*), Jack Shutta, Fred Kelsey (*Detectives*), Dorothy Christy (*Nurse*), Eddie Dunn, Ed Gargan (*Policemen*), Mary Forbes (*Woman*), Mabel Forrest, Genevieve Bell, Herbert Evans, Lloyd Ingraham, Nelson McDowell (*Guests*), Wheaton Chambers (*Doctor*), Herbert Heywood (*Doorman*), Bobby Barber (*Butcher*), Lou Wood (*Assistant Dance Director*), Brooks Benedict (*Assistant Stage Manager*), Mary McLeod, Gloria Marlen (*Secretaries*), Teddy Infuhr (*Page Boy*), Eddie Cutler, Charles Teske (*Dance Specialty*), Jerry Maren, Billy Curtis (*Specialty Midgets*).

> As often occurs in such pictures, the idea sounds better than it looks, mainly because the spirit is strong but the writing is weak.
> —*Bosley Crowther,* The New York Times, *June 2, 1945*

This is a pesky title: It's a musical comedy that revolves around a ghost, so it needs to be included in the book, but it's about as suitable as *The Mummy's Curse* would be in a book on musicals.

Jasper Cawthorne (Gene Lockhart) is a turn-of-the-century New York banker-bluenose who unrelentingly imposes his prudish will upon his long-suffering wife Abigail (Edith Barrett) and daughter Libby (June Vincent). He is unforgiving when Libby woos and weds an oafish vaudeville hoofer, Steve Gogarty (Jack Oakie). Libby is dangerously near death as her baby is born and Steve wishes aloud that if anything is to happen, it will happen to him. The Dark Lady (Karen Randle), a distaff Grim Reaper, overhears him as she's heading into the hospital's maternity ward and claims Steve instead.

In Heaven, Steve is convinced that stuffed-shirt Cawthorne will continue to dominate the unhappy family and asks for a chance to return to Earth and set things right. After an 18-year probationary period he is permitted to make the journey, materializing again on this side of the veil as a spirit invisible and inaudible to everyone except his now-grown daughter Sheila (Peggy Ryan) and, of course, the audience. Sheila has show biz in her blood and wants to become a singer-dancer in a show but Cawthorne has put his aristocratic foot down.

Acting with her mother's consent, Sheila joins the cast of a production being staged by Martin Wilde (Andy Devine), Steve's old partner. Cawthorne buys up all of Wilde's IOUs and blackmails him into firing her. Using a magic flute whose music brings out the kid in people, Steve creates a showdown situation in which Cawthorne is soundly told off by his family and even by members of the household staff. Cawthorne begins to see the error in his willful ways and cheerfully becomes a partner in the show instead. Sheila and her leading man (Johnny Coy) dance their way into each other's hearts while Steve, now joined by the spirit of Libby (who has died), returns to Heaven.

That's the Spirit is a minor entry in the heavenly-comedy sweepstakes that began with *Here Comes Mr. Jordan* in 1941. That successful Columbia film, Oscar-nominated for Best Picture and in other categories (and a winner for Best Writing), was followed by numerous similar movies, among them 1943's *Heaven Can Wait* (another Best Picture nominee) and *A Guy Named Joe*, 1945's *The Horn Blows at Midnight*, 1946's *A Matter of Life and Death* a.k.a. *Stairway to Heaven*, 1947's *Down to Earth* and, best and most famous of all, 1946's *It's a Wonderful Life* (*another* Best Picture contender). *That's the Spirit* is the least-known title on this formidable list, and deservedly so: It's an unimaginative little picture that merely latched onto what was then a money-making formula but then devoted too much of the running time to teenage singer-dancer Peggy Ryan and newcomer Johnny Coy. It's not a bad film, but the spirit of fun is eventually dampened by the sense of *deja vu* and the surfeit of song-and-dance numbers.

There are a few neat touches in the film, and it benefits from the efforts of special effects ace John P. Fulton. (Oakie's ghost is a forerunner of science-fiction's *4D Man* in the way he walks through closed doors and other obstacles; there's even a surprising and ambitious bit where Oakie walks across a busy street as cars and trucks run through him.) According to the press kit, director Charles Lamont consulted many books and past films for ideas for the Heaven set. Spun glass, a new material developed for war use and never employed before for cinematic effects, formed the "clouds" seen in the sequence, and vapor, which rose no more than eight inches above the ground, was Heaven's "floor."

It's unusual, and a little creepy, to see Death embodied in the film: Actress Karen Randle plays the Dark Lady, a silent wraith who turns up several times during the proceedings. She first appears early on, as newlywed Oakie carries June Vincent over a threshold, tripping as he enters. The two end up in a heap and are about to clinch when they see the raven-tressed, white-faced Dark Lady framed in the doorway; she regards them dispassionately for a few seconds before quietly moving away. Her unexpected appearance, and the eerie organ chord that accompanies it, are enough to raise a few goosebumps, which is more than Universal's straight horror films were doing at this point. This female harbinger of death turns up again at the hospital, as June Vincent is in danger of dying in childbirth, and again toward the end of the film when she boards a train behind Vincent and Gene Lockhart. The audience — or at least *this* audience — assumes that Scrooge Lockhart is about to get his comeuppance, but it's Vincent who soon dies, paving the way for the happy ending where she joins Oakie and they head off to Heaven.

A good cast meets the minor demands of the picture. Beefy Jack Oakie is especially appealing and likable as the title ghost, and there's even a bit of pathos in a scene where he moons over his grieving wife (Vincent) who can neither see him nor hear him. Peggy Ryan and Johnny Coy do an okay job of filling their singing-dancing-acting juvenile roles, while pros June Vincent, Gene Lockhart and Andy Devine go through their paces almost effortlessly. Lockhart is at the center of the film's funniest scene: At a dreary little dinner party he is singing "Evenin' Star" in his usual solemn fashion until Jack Oakie's flute works its magic. Soon Lockhart is

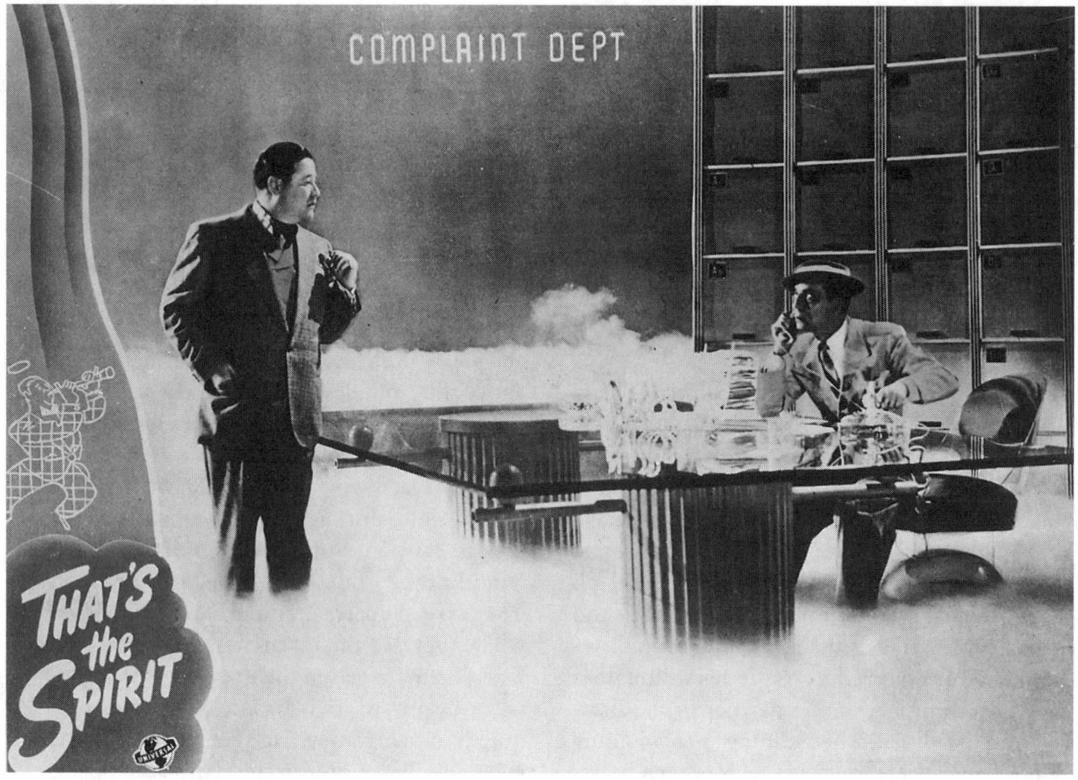

Jack Oakie confers with Buster Keaton in an out-of-this-world moment from *That's the Spirit* (courtesy John Cocchi).

belting out the oldtime song in swing fashion and his superannuated guests are raising the roof with their jukin' and jivin.' Irene Ryan, Granny on television's *The Beverly Hillbillies*, has a comic-relief role as a rubber-faced maid constantly alarmed by the sound of ghost Oakie's squeaky shoes.

Edith Barrett, playing the matriarch of the Cawthorne clan, was Mrs. Vincent Price at the time; when she and her husband lived at 53 West 53rd Street in Manhattan, they used to host Sunday afternoon tea parties attended by famous actors and actresses. Also "attending"—sort of—was Victoria Horne, who plays Patience in *That's the Spirit*. Horne was then a stock company player living in a tiny apartment on that building's top (fourth) floor, probably once a servant's quarters; the star-struck girl would shyly "crash" the parties by surreptitiously observing them on bended elbows from her window. On the set of *That's the Spirit*, Horne admitted this to Barrett, who gasped, "Oh, my ... why didn't you come down and join us?"

After Oakie died in 1978, his dedicated wife Horne devoted herself to keeping his memory alive, even writing a short 2001 book of anecdotes about their years together, *Life with Jack Oakie*. She told the authors,

> *That's the Spirit* was the happiest film to make. The entire cast looked forward to the entrance of Jack every day, he brought the most contagious happiness with him. On the last of shooting, Gene Lockhart presented him with a poem he wrote honoring him, and two of the lines are now engraved on Jack's plaque at Forest Lawn: "In a double-take, thou hast more than voice e'er spake."

Wifely devotion notwithstanding, the big name in *That's the Spirit* is of course Buster Keaton, that most brilliant of all silent screen comedians. Keaton's comedies are landmarks of the pre-talkie era, but by 1933 good fortune was no longer smiling upon the Great Stoneface: Talking pictures, alcohol and a series of martial mishaps had reduced the once-great funnyman to a has-been relegated to the Hollywood hinterlands. In 1944–45 he made appearances in Universal's *San Diego I Love You*, *That Night with You* and *That's the Spirit*, probably through his friendship with Ernest Pagano, who co-wrote and co-produced all three pictures. Keaton has little more than a cameo in *That's the Spirit* as L.M., head of Heaven's complaint department, keeping track of events back on Earth with what looks like one of our modern-day big-screen TVs. He wears his characteristic porkpie hat, with the ribbon changed from black to white, and plays, for the first and perhaps only time in his talkie career, a character who is sensible and articulate, if a bit irascible. Keaton seemed on the verge of regaining some of his lost popularity when the Dark Lady carted *him* off in 1966.

Friend and confidante of many of the 1940s Universal stars, Michael Fitzgerald, author of *Universal Pictures*, shared with the authors a few anecdotes told to him by *That's the Spirit* veterans:

> In the "Baby, Won't You Please Come Home?" number, Johnny Coy kept goofing up on purpose, and kept stopping the number. Peggy Ryan told him any errors would be covered in editing, and to continue until it was over. But he kept stopping. Finally one time when he stopped the shoot and bent over to tie his shoe, Peggy kicked him in the rear as hard as she could! ... June Vincent was pregnant at the time, and having a difficult pregnancy. That explains her weak eyes and fragile look — not makeup, but real. But since [late in the movie] her character is dying, it really works for the picture! It got to the point where she was too weak to go to the studio, so for a couple of scenes they came to *her* home to film. The final scene [Oakie and Vincent in a theater box], where she is dead (and *looks* it), was filmed in her own bedroom! ... When June saw *That's the Spirit* for the first time, she was down in San Diego with her wounded-in-action husband. The ending is so odd — she and Jack Oakie, now both dead, leave the theater together — that when the film ended, the entire audience was in shock. There was total silence!

Partially Heaven-set but hardly heaven-sent, *That's the Spirit* is a poor cousin to the bigger, better celestial fantasies of the '40s. According to Fitzgerald, it was the favorite picture of Peggy Ryan, Jack Oakie, June Vincent and Victoria Horne, and there certainly is *some* fun to be had, especially in the early going. But any fan lured by its supernatural element is apt to find it disappointingly derivative.

Critics' Corner

At its heaviest — Gene Lockhart and Andy Devine acting like boys of eight — the fantasy is both unfunny and mawkish. At its best — a flock of ancient socialites helplessly jiving Wagner's "Evenin' Star" — it has a weird, wild, death-dance vitality which shows how tame most deliberate surrealism is. — *Time,* June 18, 1945

[A] warm and tasty dish of entertainment with a seasoned group of players.... The film [is] sprinkled with several priceless lines.... — *The Film Daily,* May 16, 1945

[A] mild musical fantasy about show business.... The screenplay lacks [the] high comedy and emotional depth of a fantasy like *Here Comes Mr. Jordan*; accordingly, it is merely the conventional theatrical success story with a few camera tricks added to make it look different. — *The New York Herald-Tribune,* June 1945, Otis L. Guernsey, Jr.

The Frozen Ghost

Released June 29, 1945. 61 minutes. An Inner Sanctum Mystery, produced by arrangement with Simon and Schuster, Inc., Publishers. *Associate Producer:* Will Cowan. *Executive Producer:* Ben Pivar. *Director:* Harold Young. *Screenplay:* Bernard L. Schubert & Luci Ward. *Adaptation:* Henry Sucher. *Original Story:* Harrison Carter & Henry Sucher. *Photography:* Paul Ivano. *Musical Director:* Hans J. Salter. *Art Directors:* John B. Goodman & Abraham Grossman. *Sound Supervisor:* Bernard B. Brown. *Technician:* William Hedgcock. *Set Decorators:* Russell A. Gausman & Ray L. Jeffers. *Editor:* Fred R. Feitshans, Jr. *Dialogue Director:* Edward Dein. *Assistant Director:* Fred Frank. *Camera Operator:* William Dodds. *Property Master:* William Nunley. *Gowns:* Vera West. *Stand-Ins:* June Davis, Norma Holm.

Lon Chaney, Jr. (*Alex Gregor*), Evelyn Ankers (*Maura Daniel*), Milburn Stone (*George Keene*), Douglass Dumbrille (*Police Insp. Brant*), Martin Kosleck (*Rudi Poldan/Dr. Feldon*), Elena Verdugo (*Nina Coudreau*), Tala Birell (*Valerie Monet*), Arthur Hohl (*Skeptic*), Leyland Hodgson (*Doctor*), Pauline Drake (*Girlfriend*), Bobby Barber (*Fat Man*), Polly Bailey (*Gray-Haired Woman*), Jan Bryant (*Bobby-Sox Girl*), Charles Jordan, Eddie Acuff (*Reporters*), Dennis Moore (*Announcer*), William Haade (*Cop*), Jan Jacobson (*Organist*), Eddie Bruce (*Audience Member*), Bud Wolfe (*Cab Driver*), David Hoffman (*Inner Sanctum*), Ken Terrell (*Double for Martin Kosleck*).

It is impossible to find anything favorable to say about *The Frozen Ghost.*
— *Bert McCord,* The New York Herald-Tribune, *July 1945*

The fourth Inner Sanctum entry, *The Frozen Ghost*, was apparently conceived with little confidence. A couple of versions of the script were circulating around Universal's story department for some time. Reginald LeBorg intended to shoot the film back-to-back with the series opener *Calling Dr. Death* in 1943, but the production was postponed.

Filming on *The Frozen Ghost* finally got underway on June 19, 1944, on a 12-day schedule. Though it officially wrapped on July 1, *The Frozen Ghost* wasn't released until a year later (it ended up heading a dismal all-horror double bill with *The Jungle Captive*).

LeBorg's departure from the series had caused a rift between him and Lon Chaney, Jr. "At the beginning Chaney thought I would be his pal, and when after three Inner Sanctums I wanted to do a musical — a Deanna Durbin picture or something — he said to me, 'You traitor! We were supposed to do big things together!' I told him, 'We'll get together again, don't worry!'" LeBorg and Chaney finally did get together again —12 years later on the set of *The Black Sleep* (1956).

Harold Young, the director of *The Mummy's Tomb,* took the reins, but he didn't have the know-how to turn a rickety script into a cohesive thriller. The film opens with a shot of a publicity poster announcing "The Fascinating Maura ... The Hypnotic Subject of the Mysterious Gregor the Great." The camera closes in on the portrait on the poster which dissolves seamlessly into a live shot of the young woman who is in a state of trance. She is Maura Daniel (Evelyn Ankers), assistant to hypnotist Alex Gregor (Lon Chaney, Jr.), who is in the midst of doing a broadcast of their popular radio show. An audience participation segment is interrupted when a drunkard (Arthur Hohl) in the crowd denounces the act as a phony. Gregor invites the abusive heckler on stage, and is in the process of placing him in a trance when the man keels over and dies. Although a heart attack is listed as the cause of death, Gregor insists he's a murderer for subconsciously "willing" the man's demise.

Despondent, Gregor breaks off his engagement to Maura, gives up the act and takes a job at friend Valerie Monet's (Tala Birell) wax museum, where recent murders are graphically depicted (hardly the best setting to make him forget about his "crime"). The jealous Monet mistakes Alex's casual friendship with her niece Nina (Elena Verdugo) for romance and bitterly confronts the hypnotist. Gregor blacks out, only to discover when he recovers that Valerie has mysteriously disappeared. Police Insp. Brant (Douglass Dumbrille) investigates but cannot find the body; the eternal pessimist, Gregor is once again convinced he is responsible. This time the police start taking him seriously.

Unbeknownst to Gregor, there's a conspiracy afoot between the hypnotist's business manager, George Keene (Milburn Stone), and Rudi Poldan (Martin Kosleck), a disgraced plastic surgeon who works in Valerie's museum as a sculptor. Hoping to drive the hypnotist insane in order to gain control of his estate, the pair have put Monet into a state of suspended animation. But Rudi botches the job and Monet dies as a result of his negligence.

When Nina learns what has been going on, Rudi overpowers and drugs her. In a desperate attempt to unravel the mystery, Gregor places Maura into a state of deep hypnosis in order to unleash her psychic powers. Maura points an accusing finger at George, who is quickly nabbed by Brant. Gregor and Maura rush down to the wax museum's furnace room where Rudi is about to plunge Nina into the flames. The plastic surgeon loses his footing and suffers the fiery fate intended for the girl.

Except for the diversion of the offbeat *Strange Confession*, the Inner Sanctum films alternated between standard whodunits (*Calling Dr. Death*, *Dead Man's Eyes*) and pseudo-supernatural melodramas (*Weird Woman*). *The Frozen Ghost* strikes a balance between both but succeeds as neither. The script is a shapeless mess of genre bromides (hypnosis, a wax museum setting, murder, conspiracy, suspended animation and a mad plastic surgeon) without any attempt at basic plot construction — hell, there's barely a plot, just "ingredients." The picture represents the sort of movie factory grind work in which no one puts in their best effort. The film's one minor distinction is that for once the fantastic elements in the storyline appear genuine with Gregor the Great actually managing to imbue his subjects with extra-sensory gifts.

The Inner Sanctum films found a commercial niche during the war years, serving as brand-

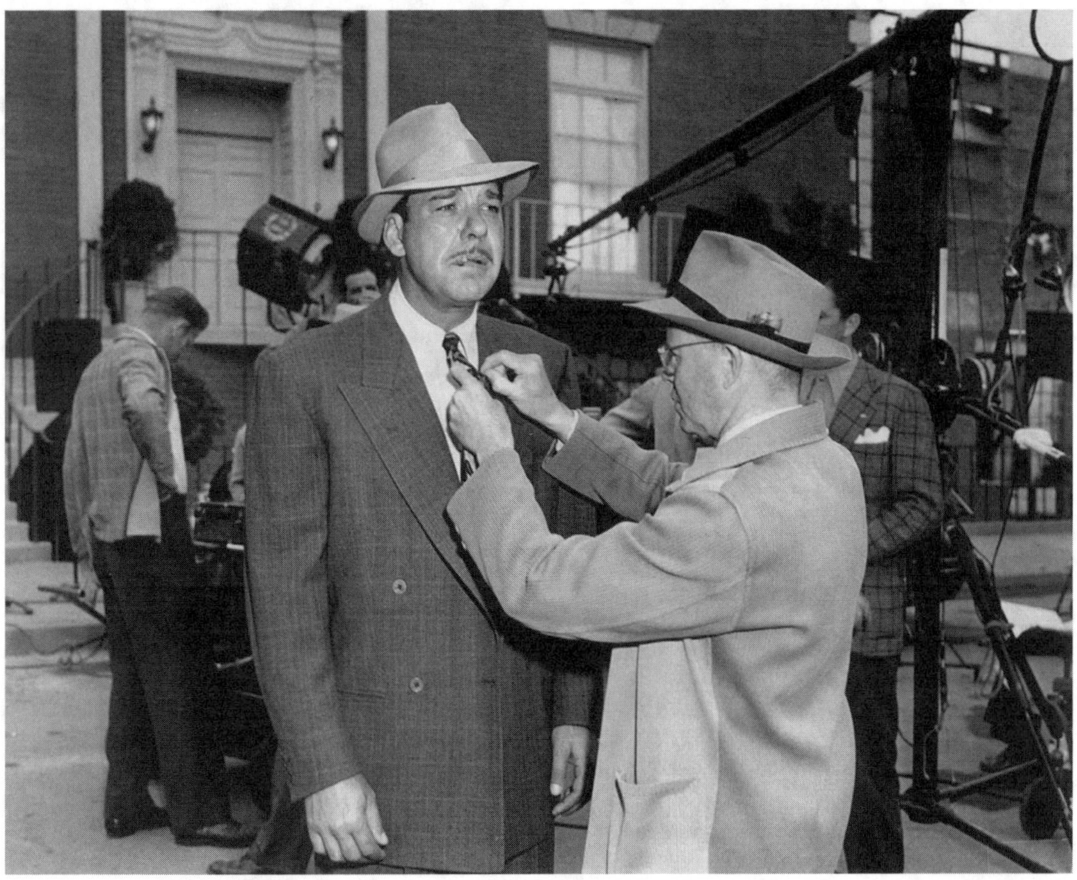

An uncharacteristically dapper Lon Chaney, Jr., gets a wardrobe adjustment before the cameras roll on *The Frozen Ghost*.

name fillers for A pictures. If *The Frozen Ghost* is the weakest of the lot, it's because it is such a by-the-numbers film. It slavishly follows the established formula of the series: A procession of attractive females mystifyingly vie for Chaney's affections, a persevering detective with a talent for barking up the wrong tree heads up the dead-end investigation as the best friend of the hero is exposed as the heavy in the last reel. The stylistic hallmark of the series, yards of stream-of-consciousness dialogue slopping up the soundtrack, is played against Paul Sawtell's endlessly recycled, radio-style spook music. (Sawtell moved on to Columbia's B unit where his Inner Sanctum musical cues got a new lease on life in several of William Castle's Whistler mysteries.)

Apart from a few tilted camera shots in the first scenes, Harold Young directs with an eye for efficiency rather than flair. The one major visual effect of Chaney's supposedly lethal hypnotic "stare" was achieved with utmost economy, merely a camera closing in on a photographic plate of the actor in one of his typically anguished Inner Sanctum poses.

Again, the major culprits of *The Frozen Ghost* are script writers Bernard L. Schubert and Luci Ward, who pad the film with such inanities as the fruitless search for Monet's barely concealed corpse which lies in a wax tableaux but somehow everyone fails to notice. This is followed by another utterly pointless scene of mayhem as a terrified Nina barely escapes death at the hands of the knife-throwing Rudi. Moments later, Gregor finds himself the target in yet another attack although this time his search for the culprit leads him to Rudi, who nonchalantly feigns innocence. With this, Gregor shrugs off the flagrant attempt on his life and simply leaves. This go-nowhere scene which arrives after three-

***The Frozen Ghost* was almost unanimously panned by the film critics. Left to right: Tala Birell, Milburn Stone, Chaney Jr., and Martin Kosleck.**

quarters of an hour of mostly numbing dialogue is so unmotivated and desultory it hardly brings any relief from the air of tedium. The next time we see Nina, she's in a state of catalepsy without benefit of any word of explanation. In keeping with the film's tone of dreary monotony, Rudi and George's guilt is matter-of-factly divulged in yet another dull dialogue exchange long before the wrap-up.

Lon Chaney is once again the woebegone hero, a martyr in the *Dead Man's Eyes* mode who spends most of his time sulking in a one-note performance. The actor no doubt found the Inner Sanctum series a welcome opportunity to shed his monster image in the hope of proving his mettle as a romantic leading man but the cruel joke is that these kinds of roles were just as beyond him as playing Dracula was two years earlier. Still, it's hard not to sympathize with any actor saddled with lines such as, "I killed that man ... I know I did.... Everywhere I go I see death, death, death, death, death, death, death, death, death!!"

Given the quality of her recent studio assignments, Evelyn Ankers' disengaged performance is forgivable. As she wrote in Doug McClelland's *The Golden Age of the 'B' Movie* (Charter House, 1978):

> In June and July, 1944 I was working on two pictures at once, *Bowery to Broadway* and *The Frozen Ghost*, a B. I remember it well because I was about six months pregnant with my beautiful daughter, Diana Dee. The Universal executives didn't know about my condition, and I wanted to keep working and receive my salary as long as possible.... And I knew they would fire me as soon as they found out.
>
> Tala Birell, who was also cast in *The Frozen Ghost*, did not know, however, and she couldn't understand why they had hired such a portly leading lady. The cameraman's assistant used to mark

our ultimate feet positions on the set floor in chalk outlines, and when he drew my feet he put two tiny baby feet between them. Believe it or not, poor Tala could never figure out why he marked mine like that, or why we all laughed so much each time she asked.

Milburn Stone's smooth, unaffected charm is again on display; in fact, he's a more appealing character than our tiresome hero. Douglass Dumbrille, a talented actor who couldn't overcome his unsympathetic demeanor, plays the usual B-movie detective who doesn't seem to have a clue. It's strictly a stock character except it's more poorly written than most; Dumbrille spends an inordinate amount of time inspecting the furniture and other accoutrements. ("Mme. Monet might have had okay tastes in paintings but I like 'em snappier!" is one of his wittier lines.) The supporting players, Tala Birell and Elena Verdugo, are good enough, but the real star of *The Frozen Ghost* is Martin Kosleck as the mad Rudi.

Kosleck came onto the set of *The Frozen Ghost* fresh from a nine-week personal appearance tour promoting Paramount's *The Hitler Gang* (1944) in which he played the Fuhrer's right-hand man Joseph Goebbels. Universal was intent on grooming Kosleck as a new horror star; the script of *The Frozen Ghost* even had him talking to his waxworks, an obvious reference to Lionel Atwill in *Mystery of the Wax Museum* (1933). "I liked Universal studios because I had wonderful parts," he told the authors. "I had my own dressing room on the lot and I felt very, very important. It wasn't a factory then."

Tala Birell, however, was far less pleased. She received her theatrical training on the Viennese stage where she, like Kosleck, worked under Max Reinhardt. The blonde actress signed a long-term contract with Carl Laemmle, Jr., in the '30s, and was promoted as another Garbo or Dietrich. Her hopes for a major career were quickly dashed and it wasn't long before Birell ended up playing supporting roles in program quickies.

Kosleck recalled participating in a particularly grim scene in *The Frozen Ghost*. "Tala Birell was shot dead or something, and I had to pull her out of the room. She was put on rollers and she just said, 'God! Can you imagine what we would have thought in Berlin!'" The indignant actress no doubt had the same reaction a year earlier when filming PRC's *The Monster Maker*, which found her being confronted in her bedroom by J. Carrol Naish's pet gorilla.

Universal was delighted with Kosleck's work and exercised their option on his contract, slating him to appear in two additional films with Chaney. The pair were reunited in *The Mummy's Curse*, which would be their last film together. Kosleck admits to having shed few tears over their premature parting, having found his frequently inebriated costar difficult and unpleasant. (Though released later, *The Frozen Ghost* was shot two months before the Mummy film.) "The director [Harold Young] apparently liked me and I had a lot of closeups. Chaney always came in and said, 'That's enough.' He hated me and I returned it. He was the star and he just wanted me out of the way."

Chaney regarded the Inner Sanctum series as his starring vehicles, and wasn't pleased when Kosleck got better notices than he for *The Frozen Ghost*. By the time the pair got together on *The Mummy's Curse*, an all-out feud was brewing. Chaney particularly relished stalking the diminutive Kosleck in the climactic moments of that film. Said Kosleck, "He enjoyed that thoroughly! I remember it well, I was pushed around. Why they had him as a star is beyond me. He was roaring drunk!"

Except for an occasional kind word for Kosleck, the critical verdict on *The Frozen Ghost* was hostile. In an uncharacteristically venomous mood, *The Hollywood Reporter* ribbed Universal by publishing the choicest barbs from a sampling of scathing reviews. Not accustomed to courting favor with the highbrows, especially for their programmers, Universal undauntedly put another Inner Sanctum project on the drawing boards.

The Frozen Ghost was the last released film Evelyn Ankers made under her Universal contract; her subsequent pictures like *Queen of Burlesque* (1946) and *The Texan Meets Calamity Jane* (1950) were forgettable. In the '60s, she and her actor husband Richard Denning relocated to Hawaii, where Denning enjoyed a recurring role as the governor on television's *Hawaii Five-O*. Ankers was offered the role of the governor's wife but the actress declined. "She wanted no part of it," Denning told the authors. "She had more fun when we'd go to Honolulu. I'd go there and be working on a *Five-O* and, of course, Evie would be in seventh heaven because now she was in Honolulu. Which is the *big* city—she'd be in her car, shopping all over town for everything. That was much more fun for her than working!" In fact, Ankers had been turning down roles for years (including a part in the 1956 Roger Corman thriller, *Day the World Ended,* despite pleas from the film's executive producer and family friend, Alex Gordon). In 1980, after the long-running *Five-O* series was finally terminated, Denning remarked, "Evelyn and I are looking forward to the '80s as a new era—retirement and pensions. We hope it beats working."

But this "new era" of bliss was not to be. Evelyn developed cancer shortly afterwards, but bravely determined to win her battle with the dreaded disease. By 1985 she seemed well on her way to a remarkable recovery. She had regained all lost weight, walked three miles a day, and felt and looked terrific; she frequently wrote to her Hollywood friends from her Maui home, emphasizing that she was on the road to good health. The inevitable finally occurred on August 28, 1985, when the veteran actress succumbed in her home.

If Evelyn Ankers only appeared in *The Wolf Man*, she still would have ranked among the leading "Scream Queens" of vintage horror movies, perhaps second only to Fay Wray. In interviews, she always professed to feeling uncomfortable in her own profession. As it turned out, her career was chosen for her by a willful stage mother. Ankers always projected poise and breeding (even when playing working girls), a musical Mid-Atlantic voice and a blood-curdling scream that still ranks with the best of them. Unfortunately, Universal never saw fit to develop a character for her quite as memorable as Gwen Conliffe. Her subsequent horror roles grew increasingly one-dimensional, reaching the point where she put in mere "appearances" in *The Invisible Man's Revenge*, *Son of Dracula* and the lamentable *Jungle Woman*. Evelyn Ankers, nevertheless, occupies a special role in the history of the American horror movie and in the hearts of thousands of fans who will always remember the girl with the half moon-shaped earrings.

Critics' Corner

[S]cares mildly without discovering any new wrinkles in the horror potential of a wax museum.... The goose-pimple trade will be as puzzled as thrilled no doubt by the heavy-handed plot that never quite convinces.—*The Hollywood Reporter*, June 13, 1945

Rating: ★ *The Frozen Ghost* will leave you stone cold, but not from fear.... There is no ghost, there is no mystery, and there is no suspense.—*The New York Daily News*, July 1945, Wanda Hale

You either sit down with your mouth hanging open or you wonder why you didn't stay home.—*The New York Post*, July 1945, Archer Winsten

When an uninspired cast is coupled with an uninteresting plot, the result is bound to add up to rather unexciting film fare, a fact proved conclusively in *The Frozen Ghost*....—*The New York Times*, July 28, 1945, Joelyn R. Littauer

The Jungle Captive

Released June 29, 1945. Reissued as *Wild Jungle Captive*. 63 minutes. *Associate Producer:* Morgan B. Cox. *Executive Producer:* Ben Pivar. *Director:* Harold Young. *Screenplay:* M. Coates Webster & Dwight V. Babcock. *Photography:* Maury Gertsman & (uncredited) Charles Van Enger. *Music Director:* Paul Sawtell. *Art Directors:* John B. Goodman & Robert Clatworthy. *Sound Director:* Bernard B. Brown. *Technician:* Robert Pritchard. *Re-recorder & Effects Mixer:* Ronald K. Pierce. *Music Mixer:* Paul Neal. *Set Decorators:* Russell A. Gausman & Andrew J. Gilmore. *Editor:* Fred R. Feitshans, Jr. *Assistant Directors:* Howard Christie, Harry Jones & Charles S. Gould. *Dialogue Directors:* Willard Holland & Phil Brown. *Camera Operator:* Harold Smith. *Second Camera:* Wallace Chewning. *Assistant Cameraman:* Phil Lathrop. *Key Grip:* Fred Buckley. *Costumes:* Vera West.

Otto Kruger (*Mr. Stendahl*), Vicky Lane (*Paula Dupree, the Ape Woman*), Amelita Ward (*Ann Forrester*), Phil Brown (*Don Young*), Jerome Cowan (*Police Insp. W.L. Harrigan*), Rondo Hatton (*Moloch*), Eddie Acuff (*Bill*), Ernie Adams (*Jim*), Charles Wagenheim (*Fred*), Eddy Chandler (*Motorcycle Cop*), Jack Overman (*Detective*), Billy Murphy (*Johnny*), Pat Gleason (*Tom*), Bob Pepper (*Policeman*), Dale Van Sickel (*Double for Rondo Hatton*), Billy Jones. Deleted from final print: Walter Tetley.

> Paula, the Ape Woman ... looks like an over-sized woodchuck with a hangover.
> —*Bert McCord,* The New York Herald-Tribune, *July 7, 1945*

Nobody expected the Ape Woman sequels to shoot for the moon plot-wise ... but by the same token, probably no one would ever have anticipated that the follow-ups to the lively and imaginative *Captive Wild Woman* would be quite *this* lame. The apple of Dr. Walters' eye rolls even farther from the tree in *The Jungle Captive,* a grab-bag of horror movie cliches that's exasperating in its repetitious scenes and obvious padding. It hasn't got the jaw-dropping effect of *Jungle Woman* (the ultimate in junky Universal horror), although common sense and logical plot progression are in short supply this time around as well.

The Jungle Captive is one of those pictures where a better story went on behind the camera than anything that happened out in front. Betty Bryant, recently signed by Universal to a term contract, was originally chosen to play the female lead, but this Australian actress (known only for her role in the Aussie-made *Forty Thousand Horsemen* [1940]) apparently had some funny ideas about how the picture business worked. On August 30, 1944, one day before production began, she appeared in the office of associate producer Morgan B. Cox and informed him that she didn't know whether she could find a babysitter to stay with her two year old on certain nights she was scheduled to work. On the first day of shooting she was unprepared, and on the second day she arrived 40 minutes late, just in time for a reprimand from director Harold Young.

To quiet the actress' maternal apprehensions, her physician Dr. Irving L. Ress, Hollywood's "obstetrician to the stars," was summoned. In private, Dr. Ress emphatically told Cox that there was nothing about motion pictures or motion picture people that he could admire. According to Ress, all the men in the movie business were concerned primarily with "making" any and all women in any way connected with the industry. Bryant was drawn into the argument and Ress nearly succeeded in creating a scene.

Over the next several days this embarrassing situation continued, with Ress hanging around the set, creating disturbances, careening around the darkened lot in his car and, in the words of Cox in a 16-page September 12 memo), "acting more like a thwarted lover than a reputable doctor." Cox concluded in his memo that Bryant, slightly ill throughout much of this ordeal and genuinely apologetic for the entire situation, was a victim of circumstances over which she had little control. Of course the boom was inevitably lowered on the hapless actress, and she was bumped. (In his September 9 *Los Angeles Times* column, Edwin Schallert sugar-coated the incident, reporting that Bryant had gotten ill and "has to go in the hospital for observation and treatment.") Amelita Ward replaced her in the picture, which ran two days over schedule (wrapping on September 16), probably as the result of the turmoil created by the mysterious Dr. Ress.

The film opens at the Medical Building, in a typically big but (as ever) unnamed major city. Stendahl (Otto Kruger), a biochemist, is conducting a revolutionary experiment, using electric current and blood transfusions to revive the heart of a dead rabbit (shades of *Life Returns*). To the delight of his young assistants Ann (Amelita Ward) and Don (Phil Brown), the procedure is a success.

The scene switches to the city morgue, where ugly bruiser Moloch (Rondo Hatton) appears out of the night with a note of release for the body of Paula the Ape Woman. When the attendant (Charles Wagenheim) becomes suspicious, Moloch attacks him from behind, choking him to death.* Stealing a morgue wagon, he transports the body of the Ape Woman out onto a desolate stretch of highway where he now places the cadaver in his own car and sends the wagon hurtling off a cliff. Moloch drives on, arriving at last at his destination, a lonely country house on nearby Old Orchard Road.

A surgical smock found near the wreckage of the wagon brings Inspector Harrigan (Jerome Cowan) of the Homicide Squad to Stendahl's offices. The glib policeman determines from laundry marks that the smock once belonged to Don, and casually questions the young intern before leaving.

When Stendahl asks Ann to accompany him on an errand, the pair end up at the Old

**Actor Wagenheim made a sideline career out of being choked and/or murdered: In addition to being strangled to death by Rondo Hatton in* The Jungle Captive*, he was fatally choked by George Zucco in* Halfway to Shanghai *(1942), as well as shot to death by Zucco in* Dark Streets of Cairo *(1940) throttled by Karloff in* House of Frankenstein*, and strangled by Hatton a second time in* The Brute Man*. Then in 1979, in the living room of his Hollywood apartment, he was beaten to death in real life!*

Pressbook ad for the last of the Ape Woman thrillers.

Orchard Road house. It was Stendahl who masterminded the theft of the Ape Woman's body, and now he planes to use Ann's blood in his efforts to restore life to the Ape Woman. As Stendahl siphons off her blood, Ann hovers dangerously near death, prompting a sympathetic reaction from Moloch. (It's obvious from the dialogue, and from little bits of "business" on Moloch's part, that Stendahl and Moloch are eventually going to go the Dr. Vollin-Bateman route over Stendahl's treatment of Ann, which is exactly what happens.)

As the Ape Woman returns to life, Stendahl realizes that he must now engineer her metamorphosis back into a woman if he hopes to claim that he has restored life to a human. Moloch is dispatched to steal the records of Dr. Walters (*Captive Wild Woman*) from Dr. Fletcher (*Jungle Woman*); in a later dialogue exchange we learn that Moloch killed Dr. Fletcher during the robbery.

Now using Ann's glandular secretions, Stendahl is able to change the Ape Woman into the beautiful Paula (Vicky Lane). But Paula's brain has somehow been damaged, and she now has only the instincts of an animal. Stendahl plans to transplant Ann's brain into Paula's head.

Paula escapes from the house and strays into the nearby woods. Moloch, panicked by her disappearance, drives to the Medical Building to notify Stendahl, and gets into an argument with Don. Don notices that Moloch is wearing a fraternity pin which he had given to Ann, and trails Moloch as he returns to the country house. Stendahl and Moloch get the drop on Don, and he becomes a bound and helpless spectator as Stendahl prepares to operate on the Ape Woman. When Don tells Moloch that Stendahl is planning to remove Ann's brain, the giant brute becomes enraged and Stendahl is forced to shoot him to death. The Ape Woman decides to add to the confusion, rising from the operating table and throttling the startled scientist. The Ape Woman is menacingly advancing on the unconscious Ann when Inspector Harrigan and his men, led to the house by a clue found in Stendahl's office, burst in and shoot her down.

It may be that *The Jungle Captive*'s sole purpose in our world is to serve as a bad example. A cinematic hero sandwich made up of jagged chunks and butt-ends, its time-tested ingredients include the mad doctor, scientific laboratories, life-restoring experiments, a dumb-brute assistant, a monster, Jekyll-and-Hyde transformations, young hero, swooning ingenue, etc. Naturally, nearly every such horror thriller falls back on some of these basics, but these screenwriters seem to be trying to cram a few too many chestnuts into this turkey. Tellingly, even the name of the film is cribbed from words in the earlier series titles. Had the series lasted longer, additional installments would no doubt have been called *Captive Woman*, *Wild Captive*, *Wild Woman* and *Woman Captive*, at which point it could have gone no further. (This amazing practice extended even to *The Jungle Captive*'s re-release title, *Wild Jungle Captive*.)

The Ape Woman gets the sort of treatment heretofore reserved for the latter-day Frankenstein's Monster: She remains comatose and helpless throughout most of the picture, while the human members of the cast gobble up the running time with their comings and goings. There isn't enough plot here for an hour television show, so the picture struggles to make it to feature length with a series of scenes that go nowhere. We get our first taste of this in the opening reel, as a talkative nerd of a delivery boy flirts with Amelita Ward; later we're treated to not one, not two, but three foiled escape attempts (two by the Ape Woman and one by Don) which add nothing to the picture but extra minutes. After seeing Rondo Hatton steal the Ape Woman's body, we sit through scenes of Inspector Harrigan trying to pin the crime on Don. After witnessing the Ape Woman's first escape, we watch Moloch search the empty house for her.

Adhering to the dictates of the party-poopers at the Breen Office, Paula remains demurely clothed throughout the film: As the Ape Woman she wears what looks like a surgical gown, and as Paula she's clad in a low-cut print dress that Stendahl and Moloch must have enjoyed putting on her. The Ape Woman's makeup here is slightly modified from the one seen in the earlier films, and an improvement. It's sleeker and more bestial-looking, and for the first and only time in the series the Ape Woman has a dangerous, almost frightening look about her. But this "female Wolf Man" makeup is squandered in a picture where she spends most of her time lying around dead.

The acting never rises above the script. It's always good to see an old pro like Otto Kruger in action, but he's generally better than he is here. Kruger's mad scientist is an arrogantly cold fish; he's also saddled with the kind of dialogue that drips with mildew (the unimportance of a single life in the furtherance of science, a mini-tirade against the doctors who laughed at his theories, and so on). His character even names his guard dog Satan, underlining the fact that he's working too darn hard at being the Villain.

The acting skills of former MGM contractee Vicky Lane, who plays Paula and the Ape Woman, also go untested since (like Acquanetta in *Captive Wild Woman*) she isn't permitted a peep of dialogue; she does, however, get standout "and" billing. She later married Tom Neal, star of *The Brute Man*, and they no doubt spent many an evening comparing notes on Rondo Hatton. Amelita Ward, who plays Ann, *also* goes thespically unchallenged, spending most of the movie snoozing on a lab table; it's amusing that a sick girl (Betty Bryant) was bounced from the picture and a healthy girl (Ward) replaced her in the role of a sick girl. Two years before she acted opposite the Ape *Woman*, Ward was signed to play the leading lady in Monogram's *The Ape **Man***— but, before cameras rolled, was replaced by Louise Currie.

When actor Leo Gorcey and his wife Penny began down the road to divorce, Penny realized that she could get a bigger settlement out of the East Side Kids–Bowery Boys star if she caught him doing the nasty with a girlfriend. Two private eyes hired by Penny tailed Leo and "the other woman" to the Gorcey home, waited an appropriate length of time, smashed down the door with a sledgehammer — and got the surprise of their lives when Gorcey reached for his Smith & Wesson and began blasting away at them. Meanwhile, neighbors may have gotten the surprise of *their* lives seeing "other woman" Amelita Ward, naked, bolting out of a window and making her getaway over a six-foot fence! Ward went on to become the next Mrs. Gorcey, retired from acting and, according to her son Leo Gorcey, Jr. (in his 2003 book *Me and the Dead End Kid*), became "a sloppy drunk" who "[tried] to get into the *Guinness Book of World Records* for the most number of simultaneous affairs while married." (Some of bisexual beauty Amelita's flings were with Jr.'s nannies!) "She was out to match the Dead End Kid, blow for blow, drink for drink, affair for affair," wrote Gorcey Jr. "Dad was sleeping with his nemesis."

On the other end of the Beauty Meter, *The Jungle Captive* also marked the second Universal horror film appearance of Rondo Hatton. The grim-looking actor with the man-in-the-moon profile, who caught the fancy of '40s audiences in *The Pearl of Death*, is seen again as a homicidal henchman, but with one major renovation: In *The Jungle Captive*, he gets *no* body padding, and *lots* of dialogue. And the whole Hatton mystique so artfully built up in the Sherlock Holmes film goes right out the window. His presentation in *The Jungle Captive* makes it clear that he's no giant (he's not much taller than the women in the movie), no muscleman and, really, not even *all* that ugly: In his other horror movies, other characters react to him as though his face is heart-stoppingly scary, but here some characters don't even give him much of a second look. (The trailer, in which the movie's title is shortened to simply *Jungle Captive*, plays up Moloch as much or perhaps even more than it does the Ape Woman.)

Even roles as rudimentary as Moloch are completely beyond Hatton's depth; a non–English speaker, trained to recite those same lines phonetically, and with no awareness of what they meant, couldn't have done much worse and conceivably might have done *better*! Hatton was back to mute roles by the time *The Spider Woman Strikes Back* went into production, but the damage had been done; audiences now knew that the little guy with the Dumbo ears was more pitiable than petrifying. (In the *Los Angeles Times* review of *Jungle Captive*, the critic wrote, "Rondo Hatton drew only giggles from the audience kids.")

Hatton was probably the farthest thing from an actor that was ever maneuvered in front of a Universal camera, but here again the real-life story eclipses his negligible on-screen accomplishments. An only child, Hatton was born in 1894 in Hagerstown, Maryland, and grew up in Hagerstown and in Tampa, Florida, where he attended Hillsborough High School. Photos of a youthful Hatton depict a lean, big-eared but good-looking teenager; the accompanying article (written by latter-day exploitation director

Paula Dupree (Vicky Lane) in all her hirsute glory.

Fred Olen Ray) indicates that Hatton at that time was a hit with the girls as well as an all-around high school athlete. Serving his country in World War I, he was exposed to German poison gas in a battle near Paris. As a result, he contracted the rare metabolic disease acromegaly. As all fans of *Tarantula* (1955) already know, it's a disfiguring ailment that manifests itself gradually: The skin thickens, facial features become exaggerated, and feet, hands and many internal organs become enlarged. The ailment is also characterized by excessive body odor, an unpleasant side effect which we can only hope Hatton (and his co-stars!) were spared.

Returning to Florida, Hatton found work as a writer for Tampa newspapers; his first marriage went to pot as his acromegalic condition worsened. Visiting the set of the Florida-made film *Hell's Harbor* (1930), Hatton was offered the part of a burly saloon proprietor by director Henry King. Years later, when Hatton and his second wife relocated to Hollywood, Rondo looked up the director and got another movie bit part, as a henchman in King's 1938 *In Old Chicago*. Hatton plays similarly small parts in numerous films during this late '30s–early '40s including *Alexander's Ragtime Band* and *Chad Hanna* (two more Henry King–directed features), *The Hunchback of Notre Dame*, *The Moon and Sixpence* (as a leper), *The Ox-Bow Incident* and more. His appearance in *The Pearl of Death* led to other Universal horror films and even to a short-lived series of his very own, as an American verison of *Pearl*'s Hoxton Creeper. Hatton was paid a flat $1,250 for his work in *The Jungle Captive*, a distinct improvement over the $408.35 he pulled in for his week-and-a-day's work on *Pearl*, and fatter paychecks lay ahead as Universal continued to groom him for bush-league stardom.

Hatton had to have been pleased with his belated "star" status (or at least with the extra bucks), but one has to wonder what crossed his mind whenever his real-life looks were cruelly commented upon in these films. Sensitivity is at a record low in *The Jungle Captive*, in a scene where Stendahl becomes annoyed with Moloch for showing sympathy toward Ann. "No offense, Moloch, but with that face you're not exactly a Casanova, you know," Stendahl deadpans, then adds insult to injury by indicating the dead body of the Ape Woman and suggesting, "*This* is more in your line!" You'd think that Hatton would have balked at this dialogue, if not to preserve his own dignity, then for the sake of his current wife. ("Universal was starring him and exploiting him, which was sort of too bad," recalls Hatton's *Brute Man* co-star Jane Adams.)

Stendahl's not only insensitive, he's also pretty mixed up. There's no explanation as to why he needs the body of the Ape Woman for his life-restoring experiment; using this freak as an experimental subject would only cheapen and sensationalize his work. And since Moloch killed the morgue attendant to get the body, you'd think that the Ape Woman would be the *last* person he'd want to present to the scientific community.

Using the Ape Woman's body also entails a maddening multi-step process for poor Stendahl. First he has to steal the body and return it to life. To transform her into Paula, he needs to steal Dr. Walters' medical records, which prompts a second murder. Now, since Paula's brain is damaged, he has to crack open Ann's skull and use *her* brain. So even if he could somehow miraculously sidestep the issue of the two murders (placing all the blame on Moloch, perhaps), the new Paula would have the brain of Ann and publicly charge Stendahl with *her* mutilation and murder! (All the talk of unneeded brain switches brings to mind the latter-day Frankenstein series, especially *House of Frankenstein*.)

Stendahl could have avoided all this to-do by restoring life to some poor dead slob who could really *use* it, but this common-sense approach never occurs to him. Stendahl's the Rube Goldberg of Universal mad scientists; despite his standing as an endocrine researcher, an electrolytic researcher and a clinical pathologist, not once in the whole movie does anyone extend him the courtesy of calling him "Doctor."

There's also some unintentional humor when Stendahl decides that he must remove Ann's brain and place it in the head of Paula. Clearly the man has never before performed any such operation, so he sends Moloch to steal Dr. Walters' papers. The instructions are typewritten on a single index card, and using this as a guide, first-time surgeon Stendahl expects to successfully transplant the girl's brain. (The card, seen in a closeup, reads in part, "A light mallet should be employed and the chisel should be held with the point directed to the nose, so that a slip would not enter either the eye or the brain.") This ridiculous scene, with Stendahl approaching the operation with the hopeful enthusiasm of an amateur chef or a home handyman, pretty well encapsulates the naivete of the entire picture.

Economy was the order of the day once again, with recognizable stock footage from earlier Universal films turning up throughout the picture. The shot of the Ape Woman in the morgue drawer is an optically darkened clip from the climax of *Jungle Woman*, while a shot of the Ape Woman's hand transforming (seen twice) is lifted from *Captive Wild Woman*. Additionally, the morgue wagon which crashes in flames is actually an alternate take of Dr. Kemp's car crash from *The Invisible Man*. A lot of the same old music cues come into play yet again, from *The Wolf Man* and *The Invisible Man's Revenge* to, appropriately enough, *The Pearl of Death* (the Creeper theme).

Phil Brown not only co-starred in *The Jungle Captive*, he worked without credit as one of its dialogue directors. Toward the end of his long life, he was an attraction at autograph shows where he traded on the fact that in *Star Wars* (1977) he'd played Luke Skywalker's scowling Uncle Owen. Buyers of his photos also got a Xerox copy of his old résumé—from which *Weird Woman* and *The Jungle Captive* had been strenuously crossed out! "They were both pretty low on my scale," he told the authors. "But it was money, and I had a wife and two very small children." He recalled his *Jungle Captive* antagonists Otto Kruger and Rondo Hatton as pleasant men, but admits that he felt sorry for Kruger, who proved by his appearance in the movie that he had lost his footing on the Hollywood ladder: "To be playing that crazy doctor in *Jungle Captive* was quite a comedown."

At the end of *The Jungle Captive*, Phil Brown uses the same tactic that Basil Rathbone did at the end of *The Pearl of Death*, employing psychology to turn Hatton against his master. (And again, as in *Pearl*, the empty-handed Hatton boldly/stupidly stalks a man with a gun — with the same predicable result.) The later Hatton film *House of Horrors* had the same denouement and *The Brute Man*, with a slight variation, tried it a fourth time. Universal's screenwriters were clearly at the end of their frayed rope.

Speaking of associate producer Morgan B. Cox, as we were, oh, about six pages ago, his name was eventually given to an award handed out by the Screen Writers Guild, and one of its many winners over the years was Michael A. Hoey, writer-son of actor Dennis Hoey. According to Michael, Cox was so active WGA–wise (serving on committees, etc.) that eventually that award was named for him. But Cox was also a very irascible guy who raised hell in boardrooms and made a lot of enemies, to the extent that one of the first recipients of the award began his acceptance speech by saying, "I didn't *like* Morgan Cox, but he's done some wonderful work within the Guild...."

Hoey continues:

> It became a sort of running gag. Whenever somebody got that award, if it was an oldtimer he usually started his acceptance speech with "I didn't *like* Morgan Cox" and, if it was a newcomer, with, "I never knew Morgan Cox." And at *this* point [2006], I'm sure "I never *heard* of Morgan Cox" has to have been spoken quite a few times along the line!

Ironically enough, the only veteran of *The Jungle Captive* ever to make a splash in the real world: The actress who got the boot, Betty Bryant. In 1963 she co-founded a charitable organization called the Foundation for the Peoples of the South Pacific, which has grown into a global network with member organizations in over 60 nations. For this achievement, Bryant received a humanitarian service award from Hillary Clinton in 2000.

Critics' Corner

I have come to the unalterable conviction that I just don't like motion pictures in which a fanatical doctor disinters werewolves, wolf-men, troglodytes and the like to bring them back to life with dire results to countless innocent victims. In the language of The Two Black Crows, "even if they were good. I wouldn't like them." But there is no danger of that in the case of *Jungle Captive....*—*The New York Herald-Tribune*, July 7, 1945, Bert McCord

The Ape Woman is a triumph of make-up over imagination.... The Jekyll/Hyde transformation stuff is too old to be of much interest, but it is still horrible.—*The Hollywood Reporter*, June 13, 1945

Vicky Lane plays the brainless woman with monosyllabic finesse and ... she grunts and growls as though she thought the whole business to be as stupid as it actually is.—*The New York Times*, July 7, 1945, Joelyn R. Littauer

[W]orthless and gruesome....—American Legion Auxiliary, 1945

A really horrific and expert score has been tailored to fit the macabre proceedings. It is far and away the best thing about the film.—National Film Music Council, 1945

Morbid and insidious, the horror film is definitely harmful for immature minds and of little or no entertainment value.—Daughters of the American Legion (Western Committee), 1945

A hideous horror picture, evidently designed to break down our humanitarian tendencies and to make war and its atrocities more easy to take.—Zeta Phi Eta, 1945

[This] cheap shocker is not fit for human consumption.—L.A. Sec. National Council of Jewish Women, 1945

Jungle Captive is superior to *Jungle Woman*, but only in the way that one punctured lung is superior to two.—"Dr. Cyclops," *Fangoria* #181, April 1999

The Woman in Green

Released July 27, 1945. 68 minutes. *Executive Producer:* Howard Benedict. *Producer-Director:* Roy William Neill. *Original Screenplay:* Bertram Millhauser. *Based on the characters created by* Sir Arthur Conan Doyle. *Photography:* Virgil Miller. *Musical Director:* Mark Levant. *Art Directors:* John B. Goodman & Martin Obzina. *Set Decorations:* Russell A. Gausman & Ted Von Hemert. *Editor:* Edward Curtiss. *Special Photography:* John P. Fulton. *Sound Director:* Bernard B. Brown. *Technician:* Glenn E. Anderson. *Dialogue Director:* Raymond Kessler. *Assistant Director:* Melville Shyer. *Production Manager:* Charles Stallings. *Camera Operator:* Ross Hoffman. *Second Camera Operator:* Wallace Chewning. *Special Effects:* Chris Guthrie. *Property Master:* Willard Nunley. *Gowns by* Vera West. *Re-recording and Effects Mixer:* Ronald K. Pierce. *Music Mixer:* Paul Neal. *Basil Rathbone's Stand-In:* Maurice Marks. *Nigel Bruce's Stand-In:* Captain George Hill.

Basil Rathbone (*Sherlock Holmes*), Nigel Bruce (*Dr. John H. Watson*), Hillary Brooke (*Lydia Marlowe*), Henry Daniell (*Prof. Moriarity*), Frederic Worlock (*Dr. Onslow*), Paul Cavanagh (*Sir George Fenwick*), Mary Gordon (*Mrs. Hudson*), Matthew Boulton (*Insp.*

Gregson), Tom Bryson (*Cpl. Williams*), Eve Amber (*Maude Fenwick*), Sally Shepherd (*Crandon*), Percival Vivian (*Dr. Simnell*), Harold DeBecker (*Shabby Man*), Olaf Hytten (*Norris*), Tommy Hughes (*Newsman*), Kay Harding (*Victim*), Leslie Denison (*Bar Man*), John Burton (*Waring*), Violet Seaton (*Mowbray*), Arthur Stenning (*Porter*), Norman Ainslee (*Electrician*), Tony Ellis (*Carter*), Ivo Henderson, Colin Hunter (*Constables*), Boyd Irwin (*Short-Tempered Officer*), Alec Harford (*Commissioner*), William H. O'Brien (*Pembrook House Waiter*), Eric Mayne (*Mesmer Club Member*), Eddie Parker (*Stunt Double for Henry Daniell*).

Once in Her Arms — No Man Could Refuse Her Love — or His Life!
— *Poster blurb for* The Woman in Green

The popular and ever-profitable Sherlock Holmes series had reached its third year of production, proving to be one of the studio's smartest investments. On December 23, 1944, Universal exercised its option on the rights to the Sir Arthur Conan Doyle short stories, again dealing directly with the late author's son, Denis P.S. Conan Doyle. The studio hyped up the occasion by announcing it was upgrading the series, increasing the budgets to "top proportions" and regarding each story as a "separate and individual production."

Seasoned readers of trade journals and press releases saw through this sham. The Holmes films were dependable moneymakers, and to tamper with the formula would be folly. Unsurprisingly, the budgets remained fixed and so did the series' status as supporting features. Not only didn't the films improve, but a general air of tiredness began to manifest itself; clearly, Roy William Neill's Holmes unit was running low on inspiration.

As the director would comment about the series, "Having to make each story different, and yet use the same set of characters, poses our most difficult production problem. But we still have to adhere to a circumscribed pattern: Detective meets antagonist. Antagonist gets the upper hand. Detective foils antagonist. Justice triumphs. Sherlock Holmes never fails his audience."

Although the Holmes unit seemed approaching the point of burn-out, oddly they returned with a tried-and-true formula for their next production. Written by series regular Bertram Millhauser, the new yarn resurrected (without explanation) Prof. Moriarity for one final showdown. Now heading up a blackmail ring, the king of crime hatches a bizarre murder scheme, employing hypnotism and a cool blond seductress to lure wealthy dupes. With the casting of that iciest of actors, Henry Daniell, as the criminal mastermind, the picture had all the earmarks of a compelling mystery.

The Breen Office saw things differently. Millhauser's script, titled *Invitation to Death*, submitted on December 21, 1944, was deemed to be in flagrant violation of the Production Code. The shocking, brutal depiction of the murders and mutilations of eight- and nine-year-old girls would have been much too strong for wartime audiences weaned on Andy Hardy. Alarmed that the film would "lower the moral sensibilities of the audience" and might even influence the weak-minded to imitate the crimes it depicted, the purity squad judged the script unacceptable.

Millhauser hammered out a revised script and not only was it approved, but it inspired a letter of congratulations for the "excellent manner in which the revisions were made." The major change in the new draft involved upping the age of the victims from elementary school age to about 20 years old. Satisfied that the addition of a dozen or so years on victims' ages would uphold public morality, the Breen Office gave their go-ahead. Other minor adjustments included the deletion of Moriarity's disguise as a Church of England minister, a nude silhouette of the leading lady in the shower, and a reference to hypnotism as a "holy science."

With all the bugs finally ironed out of the script, pre-production got underway. Series veteran Hillary Brooke was signed on January 6, 1945, landing one of her juiciest screen roles as Moriarity's sultry accomplice. Exactly one week later, shooting began on the production which was retitled *The Woman in Green*. Neill brought the shooting to a close on February 5.

The Woman in Green begins with the dreary narrative of Scotland Yard Insp. Gregson (Matthew Boulton), recalling a series of ghastly crimes dubbed the "Finger Murders," in which the victims, all young girls, had a single finger hacked off their dead bodies. When a full-scale investigation fails to turn up a lead, Sherlock Holmes (Basil Rathbone) and Dr. Watson (Nigel Bruce) are consulted. Holmes discounts the widely accepted theory that a maniac is responsible, instead believing a cold, calculating intelligence is at work.

Maude Fenwick (Eve Amber) pays the detective an urgent call at his Baker Street digs after making a gruesome discovery: The severed finger of a young girl, apparently belonging to the most recent murder victim. Miss Fenwick confesses that she saw her father, the eminent Sir George Fenwick (Paul Cavanagh), burying the body part under cover of night.

Holmes, Watson and Gregson pay a call on Fenwick, only to find him dead from a bullet wound. Holmes insists that Fenwick was murdered for learning the secret behind the crimes, and further deduces that the scheme is a blackmail ploy hatched by none other than Prof. Moriarity (Henry Daniell). Holmes' investigation points to a female accomplice, the beautiful Lydia Marlowe (Hillary Brooke), who judiciously selected Fenwick as their target. After being romanced by Lydia, Fenwick was placed in a hypnotic trance and was duped into believing he had committed murder after discovering the missing finger in his pocket. Confronting Fenwick with the evidence, Moriarity made a sizable blackmail demand.

An assassination attempt is made on Holmes' life. When the culprit turns out to be a discharged soldier (Tom Bryson) acting under hypnotic suggestion, the detective is positive his theory is correct. Lured to the Mesmer Club, a social gathering of hypnotists, Holmes strikes up a conversation with Lydia. She entices Holmes to her penthouse apartment where on Moriarity's orders, he is placed under hypnosis. Moriarity commands his rival to walk along a narrow ledge many stories above the street. But before Moriarity can give Holmes the order to jump, Gregson and a detail of policemen burst onto the scene. Holmes confesses that he was shamming hypnosis after replacing the woman's sedative with a drug that made him impervious to pain (a groaner of an explanation if ever there was one). Moriarity attempts to escape by leaping across to the next building, but loses his balance and falls to his death.

Director Roy William Neill explained the allure of the Sherlock Holmes series: "The Holmes pictures are different from the usual run of mysteries. They're neither psychological, horror, nor sex dramas. They're cops and robbers yarns that depend on pure deduction."

That said, the storyline of *The Woman in Green* seems comprised of at least as much horror and even sex as it is of pure Holmesian deduction. The horror element is in the form of the "Finger Murders." ("A series of the most atrocious murders since Jack the Ripper," says Insp. Gregson, Lestrade's fill-in for this outing. "A ghoul who hacks off a part of his victim's body and carries it away with him ... a loathsome souvenir of his butchery.") It soon becomes apparent that the mad-killer-on-the-loose angle is a mere piece in an intriguing mosaic that includes hypnotism, blackmail, mind-controlled assassins, a sleek and deadly femme fatale plus the irrepressible and seemingly indestructible Prof. Moriarity. The result is Universal's busiest storyline since *House of Frankenstein*. If the patchy story becomes understandably untidy in the telling, its occasional dull stretches are even more problematic.

Neill's direction is sturdy but rather mannered. The film's most striking visual set piece, Brooke's lulling her victims into hypnotic submission via a floating flower in a tabletop pool, relies more on photographic effects than any ingenuity on the part of the director. Surprisingly, the film's one on-camera murder scene, a terrified girl meeting up with the "Finger Murderer" in a dark alley, gets little help from Neill who frames the action in an uninteresting long shot. While this might have been the result of the studio kowtowing to pressure from the censors, it's rather flaccid filmmaking from a director who had staged some gripping scenes of violent death only months earlier in *The Scarlet Claw* and *The Pearl of Death*.

With the exception of a bland and conspicuously American actress (Eve Amber) in the supporting cast, Neill again maintains a convincingly British atmosphere although the Holmes stories never quite fell into the category of the drawing room mystery (they were, in fact, "adventures"). Except for the working class victims of the "Finger Murderer," *The Woman in Green* is very much an upper-crust affair which is not without its charms. Holmes leaves the sanctity of his Baker Street lodgings mostly to circulate in London's posh supper clubs, to pursue his investigations at Sir George's manor home or to take in the lofty atmosphere of the Mesmer Club. When the action momentarily shifts to a seedy waterfront hotel where Fenwick is dumped after his hypnosis session with Lydia, the sense of corruption is almost palpable. As is often the case with the Holmes series, there is the subtle assumption of crime as a lower-class pursuit. Although the detective readily mixes with the commonality in nearly all his cinematic adventures, it's hard to shake off his admonition of archvillain Giles Conover in *The Pearl of Death*, "I don't like the *smell* of you, either. That underground smell, the sick sweetness of decay." In *Sherlock Holmes and the Secret Weapon*, Holmes delivers to Moriarity his most cutting insult: "In the end, I always thought you'd turn out to be just another thug." It would seem that Holmes regards crime in the upper echelons as a betrayal of class.

Holmes' line takes on the ring of prophesy in *The Woman in Green*. Once the Napoleon of crime, Moriarity now seems like one of the bottom-feeders of the underworld. While earlier episodes had him engaged in such high-profile ventures as trying to heist the Crown Jewels and consorting with the Axis, here he's been reduced to picking up fast money in a particularly seedy blackmail racket. The script makes no secret that the characters are getting on in years. At one point, Holmes self-deprecatingly notes his age.

At no point is this sense of tiredness more evident than when the detective and Moriarity square off in Holmes' Baker Street flat midway through the picture. The ever unflappable Holmes looks up from his violin-playing without turning a hair, offering his old adversary a chair so they may resume their ongoing battle of wits. The wit, as it turns out, is in short supply and the two spar without much of a verbal payoff. Indeed, Moriarity only issues a lame, half-hearted threat on the life of Watson before departing for the foggy London streets.

While the script is by no means perfect, *The Woman in Green* at least shows a certain sophistication in plotting, playing a game of bait-and-switch almost before the storyline has time to establish itself. The gruesome history of the "Finger Murderer" is dispensed with within the first few minutes, leading the audience to anticipate a variation of *The Scarlet Claw* with Holmes bent on unmasking a madman at large. The issue gets quickly sidetracked after the detective's chance encounter with Sir George and Lydia at a tango bar, and when the narrative follows the couple to the woman's flat it becomes apparent that the story is taking an unexpected turn. By the time the film ends, the "Finger Murders" have faded so far into the background that the issue of whether it's actually Moriarity committing the act or one of his henchmen isn't even addressed. *The Woman in Green* is one of those rare murder movies in which the mystery is the motivation rather than who's actually doing it.

Watson's antics again hit the level of comic desperation. When the doctor denounces all hypnotic subjects as "weak-minded morons" to the stuffy president of the Mesmer Club (series semi-regular Frederic Worlock), we know it won't be long before he falls under the irresistible spell of the hypnotist himself. The scene as originally written has Watson dropping his trousers on command. The enforcers of the Production Code, however, insisted that the scene be modified; the final version has Watson meekly rolling up a single pant leg to his knees, sparing us the charnel house vision of Nigel Bruce in his skivvies.

The ninth entry in the series, *The Woman in Green* can be forgiven for the occasional moment of *déjà vu*, such as Holmes grimly promising retribution over the prostrate body of the "Finger Murderer"'s latest victim. In this case, however, it's the second time the body on the slab happens to be contract actress Kay Harding, the doomed Marie in *The Scarlet Claw*, now in an non-speaking bit part. Also, one would think that an enterprising writer would arrange for a more imaginative death for Moriarity. After falling to his death in his last two appearances (George Zucco in 20th Century–Fox's 1939 *The Adventures of Sherlock Holmes* and Lionel Atwill in *Sherlock Holmes and the Secret Weapon*), the professor plummets yet again in *Woman in Green*. One would think that the master criminal of the century would have the good sense to stay off rooftops considering his track record.

Mark Levant does only a so-so job in his capacity as music supervisor. He provides a ruminative, singsong ditty well-suited to the stuck-

Dr. Watson (Nigel Bruce) makes a fool of himself while under the spell of a hypnotist (Frederic Worlock) in *The Woman in Green* (courtesy Dan Scapperotti).

in-the-groove requirements of the hypnosis scenes; at other times, he seems to have plumb run out of Salter, Skinner and Sawtell's musical chestnuts. This is not a sin in itself but the soundtrack is supplemented with nondescript musical filler so lacking in the studio's trademark style that at times the film doesn't *sound* like a Universal picture.

Millhauser's screenplay is stronger in concept than it is in execution. There are holes in the plot that Neill couldn't quite fill (he worked without credit on many of the Holmes scripts). Four murders had been already committed before the trap is set for Fenwick, yet he is only implicated in the most recent crime. Was Fenwick the only blackmail victim? There's no indication that

Moriarity ensnared other victims in his scheme, so why did he butcher four girls needlessly? And why would Moriarity go through the trouble of finding and hypnotizing a rifle-toting sharpshooter from Her Majesty's army to do away with Holmes when a drive-by shooter or a knife in the detective's back would have served just as well?

The cast is uneven. The perennially smooth red-herring Paul Cavanagh tries his hand as a murder victim as Sir George Fenwick. Sally Shepherd, the frozen-face housekeeper of *The House of Fear* (1945), returns to form as Brooke's maid and Mary Gordon is once again on hand as Mrs. Hudson. Stuntman Eddie Parker can be seen doubling for Henry Daniell as he breaks away from his police escort in the final reel, only to drop from sight as he attempts to leap to an adjacent ledge.

Dennis Hoey's Lestrade is conspicuous in his absence. Matthew Boulton's Insp. Gregson narrates the opening of the film as if auditioning to be Lestrade's permanent replacement. (Perhaps the producers were correctly concluding that Watson was providing enough comedy to sustain the series.) Hoey was particularly busy in this stage of his career, having signed on to play a meaty dual role in the Columbia fantasy *A Thousand and One Nights* (1945), Dennis' son Michael's favorite film of his dad's. His non-participation in *The Woman in Green* might have been due to a scheduling conflict.

The choice of Boulton to play the inspector was particularly well-suited, the actor being no stranger to murder-and-dismemberment stories. In *Woman in Green*, the "Finger Murderer" takes away a finger. As the police inspector in the Broadway and London stage productions of *Night Must Fall*, as well as in the 1937 film version, Boulton investigates the psychopathic killer who hides his victim's head in a hat box.

Henry Daniell and Hillary Brooke, the two standouts in the cast, more than make up for the film's deficiencies. "I enjoyed playing the femme fatale," Miss Brooke remarked. "As a matter of fact, I enjoyed playing any part but because I was tall and blond I worked with a great many comedians. It was great fun and I did have a marvelous time."

She told Michael B. Druxman in his book *Basil Rathbone: His Life and His Films*:

> We had a scene in the picture where [Basil and I] were in a cocktail lounge. For some reason, the sequence was taking a long time to shoot, so, to break the monotony, we pretended we were getting drunk ... slurring our speech and the like ... with the scene ending by both of us sliding under the table and "passing out." The only complainer on the set was Henry Daniell ... invariably getting upset when things were delayed. He was a great Moriarity though.

It was an opinion shared by Basil Rathbone. In his autobiography *In and Out of Character*, the actor wrote: "There are other Moriaritys but none so delectably dangerous as that of Henry Daniel [*sic*]." Since this testimonial was made at a time after George Zucco's retirement from the screen and Lionel Atwill's death, one wonders if Rathbone was motivated to give a kind word to his old friend Daniell, whose career was slumping badly.

While brimming with possibilities and more than marginal genre accoutrements, *The Woman in Green* doesn't quite earn its place on the Sherlock Holmes series' A list. Holmes devotees will find minor points of interest. It's the only film in the series in which the detective's brother, Mycroft, is referenced, albeit briefly. Sherlockians also will note their hero nervously turning down drugs in Lydia's apartment (cannabis, as she describes it). Unfortunately, the chilling "Finger Murders" material peters out too early in the game and the ensuing plot elements of blackmail and hypnosis seem implausible even by 1945 standards. Still, it's a good, rough-around-the-edges adventure that makes fitting use of Hillary Brooke's elegant villainy and marks Rathbone's final cinematic joust with the redoubtable Prof. Moriarity.

Critics' Corner

Because it presents a little more of Baker Street and of the detective's philosophy than has been usual lately, *The Woman in Green* is one of the better Sherlock Holmes mystery thrillers.... Henry Daniell makes a perfect Professor Moriarty — suave, self possessed and confronting Holmes in a cooly audacious duel of wits.— *The New York Herald-Tribune*, June 16, 1945, Otis L. Guernsey, Jr.

Rating: ★★½ It's a good one, suspense is high, atmosphere is gory and the conversations between Holmes and his man, Watson, are as amusing as ever.— *The New York Daily News*, June 16, 1945, Wanda Hale

An acceptable, swift-moving melodrama ... Lovers of melodrama will derive much enjoyment. As directed by Roy William Neill, [the picture] moves swiftly to the solution of the plot. The Sir Arthur Conan Doyle characters have inspired Bertram Millhauser to pen a skillful script.—*The Film Daily*, June 19, 1945

Strange Confession

Released October 5, 1945. 62 minutes. Re-released as *The Missing Head*. An Inner Sanctum Mystery, produced by arrangement with Simon and Schuster, Inc., Publishers. *Producer:* Ben Pivar. *Director:* John Hoffman. *Screenplay:* M. Coates Webster. *Based on the play* "The Man Who Reclaimed His Head" *by* Jean Bart. *Photography:* Maury Gertsman. *Music Director:* Frank Skinner. *Art Directors:* John B. Goodman & Abraham Grossman. *Director of Sound:* Bernard B. Brown. *Technician:* Jess Moulin. *Set Decorators:* Russell A. Gausman & Andrew J. Gilmore. *Editor:* Russell Schoengarth. *Gowns:* Vera West. *Dialogue Director:* Willard Holland. *Assistant Directors:* Seward Webb & Harry Jones. *Camera Operator:* John Martin. *Rerecording & Effects Mixer:* Ronald K. Pierce. *Music Mixer:* Paul Neal.

Lon Chaney, Jr. (*Jeff Carter*), Brenda Joyce (*Mary Carter*), J. Carrol Naish (*Roger Graham*), Milburn Stone (*Stevens*), Lloyd Bridges (*Dave Curtis*), Addison Richards (*Dr. Williams*), Mary Gordon (*Mrs. O'Connor*), George Chandler (*Harper*), Gregory Muradian (*Tommy Carter*), Wilton Graff (*Brandon*), Francis McDonald (*Jose Hernandez*), Jack Norton (*Jack, Boarder*), Christian Rub (*Mr. Moore*), Leyland Hodgson (*Jason, Graham's Butler*), Ian Wolfe (*Frederick, Brandon's Butler*), Wheaton Chambers (*Mr. Reed*), Edward Mahler (*Tommy as an Infant*), Carl Vernell (*Chemistry Student*), Jack Perrin (*Patrolman*), William Desmond (*Vendor/Dock Extra*), Arthur Thalasso (*Dock Extra*), Charles Jordan (*Boarder*), Jody Gilbert (*Mrs. Todd*), David Hoffman (*Inner Sanctum*), Eric Mayne (*Bearded Man on Stage*), Beatrice Roberts, Ella Ethridge, Jack Davidson, James Carlisle, Broderick O'Farrell, Tony Santoro, Carlyle Blackwell, Jr., Lois Austin, Ann Lawrence, Dorothy Reisner, Gene Garrick, Sam Woolfe.

The credits list *Strange Confession* as being based on a composition—fourth grade, perhaps?
—*Thomas M. Pryor,* The New York Times, *November 8, 1945*

The penultimate entry in the Inner Sanctum sweepstakes, *Strange Confession* is a standalone entry in the murder-mystery series: There's a well-provoked murder, no mystery, and for once we're spared the burden of multiple reels of Lon Chaney, Jr., Suspect, anguishing under police scrutiny. What *Strange Confession is*, is a straightforward, well-done B-grade domestic drama cum domestic tragedy—and a refreshing change of pace. In some ways it might be the best of the six-film series.

As a church bell chimes midnight, Jeff Carter (Lon Chaney, Jr.) roams the dark streets of New York carrying a large valise. Dazed, he makes his way to the residence of prominent attorney Brandon (Wilton Graff), who dimly remembers former classmate Jeff as a chemistry whiz. The unbalanced Jeff opens the valise to display what's inside; Brandon reacts with horror. Now Jeff tells the lawyer his incredible story.

In flashback, we see Jeff and his wife Mary (Brenda Joyce) enjoying a spartan, "Ralph and Alice Kramden"–style Christmas dinner in their cheap boarding house apartment. Jeff is a brilliant chemist who cares nothing about money; to him it's more important to help suffering humanity, so he lets his boss Roger Graham (J. Carrol Naish) have all the credit and the monetary rewards his discoveries garner. Graham, a Grade-A heel, takes every advantage of Jeff, but he presses his luck when he insists on marketing an untested drug. Jeff and Graham argue and Jeff tenders his resignation. ("Well, that's gratitude for you," Graham sulks.) Graham blackballs Jeff, who ends up working as a pharmacist in a small drugstore.

Finding that he can't get along without Jeff, Graham appears at the Carter home, where Jeff has his "lab" sets up in a corner of the bathroom(!). Graham offers him his old job back at his own terms, and Jeff stubbornly turns him down. After Graham leaves, Mary justifiably berates her husband; she's tired of looking at that sink, that stove, that icebox and these four walls. Jeff sees the light and agrees to accept Graham's offer.

Now a top-salaried chemist, Jeff works to develop a drug called Zymurgine, a powder to be used in the treatment of colds, influenza and pneumonia. He tells Graham that he needs a mold from a certain South American plant in order to perfect the formula; this sits well with Graham, who's got his eye on Mary. Jeff and his assistant Dave (Lloyd Bridges) are sent south of the border to continue their work while Graham platonically wines and dines Mary.

When an influenza epidemic hits New

Lon Chaney, Jr., finally gets his well-earned revenge on J. Carrol Naish as Brenda Joyce tries to intervene in *Strange Confession.*

York, Graham takes advantage of the situation, manufacturing and marketing Zymurgine using one of Jeff's unproven, discarded formulae. Jeff, who has no knowledge of what's going on back home, perfects the stuff in South America and sends Graham the formula, but Graham already has the untested Zymurgine in production and doesn't care to start over again. Tommy (Gregory Muradian), the Carters' little boy, develops influenza and Mary gives him store-bought Zymurgine, which doesn't help. Tommy buys the farm.

Carrying a grudge and a gun, Mary calls on Graham intending to kill him for marketing a useless drug. Graham easily disarms her, and appears to be preparing to Have His Way With Her, just as Jeff appears in the doorway. Newly returned from South America and apprised of Tommy's death, Jeff has gone bananas. Snatching a handy bolo knife from a wall display, he attacks Graham and hacks off his head.

The flashbacks at an end, we return to Jeff and lawyer Brandon; the cops (and Mary) arrive just as Jeff finishes telling his story. Brandon, sympathetic to Jeff's plight, consoles Mary with a promise to defend him in court as the police place Jeff in custody.

Strange Confession is a remake of Universal's *The Man Who Reclaimed His Head,* the 1934 melodrama with Claude Rains, Joan Bennett and Lionel Atwill. Modernization of the story and a shift in locale were required in tailoring the property to the talents of Lon Chaney and to the Inner Sanctum mode, and screenwriter M. Coates Webster responded with a workable update.*

Cast against type (as usual), Lon Chaney does a creditable job in the leading role. Like

**The mind boggles at the thought of a faithful remake of* Reclaimed *with Chaney as the pacifist. Which wouldn't have been possible, anyway; this was early 1945, wartime, and, movie protagonist-wise, NO PACIFISTS NEED APPLY.*

most of his other Inner Sanctum protagonists, Chaney's Jeff Carter is a sensitive genius with the look of an out-of-shape bouncer (and, inexplicably, a toup with a Dracula-like hairline!). But this time Chaney nearly pulls it off because *this* genius is so different from all his others. Jeff Carter may be quite the bright and serious boy in the laboratory, but outside of work he's a lovable, Ralph Kramden–ish lug, loyal husband and good father, and not his usual Inner Sanctum character (the socially awkward egghead wallowing in misery). There are some scenes which don't play well, like Chaney's *Leave It to Beaver*–style exchanges with his son, but for the most part he handles the role convincingly. Outside of his portrayal of Larry Talbot, this may well be his best work in a Universal Horror.

What could have been the most memorable and dramatic part of the film, the attention-grabbing opener where Jeff (with mystery valise) barges into the lawyer's home, doesn't come off. In the equivalent scene in *The Man Who Reclaimed His Head*, Rains seems convincingly unbalanced as he appears at the lawyer's home, these early scenes capturing a mood of hidden horror; Chaney just acts like a simpleton, and when he rambles on and on about the strange things that can happen in a brilliant mind, you don't realize at first that it's his own mind he's talking about. (In both films Rains and Chaney are supposed to come across as insane at this point, although it's interesting that, after committing their murders, both men still have enough savvy to immediately go out and find a good mouthpiece!) In *Reclaimed*, there was a certain logic in the way Rains convinced himself that Lionel Atwill had stolen his mind, a certain justice in the way in which he took it back. In a streamlined, modernized B like *Strange Confession*, however, the decapitation of J. Carrol Naish seems thoroughly ghoulish and poorly motivated. Chaney spouts the same sort of dialogue that Rains did ("Why, it's just like he'd taken my head — my mind and brain, and used it...!"), but his climactic attack on Naish is an act of butchery that no subsequent amount of babble could justify.

Supporting performers are competent but unremarkable. J. Carrol Naish does well as the heel, although his character is perhaps a bit too oily and obvious; it's difficult to believe that even a sucker like Chaney could fail to spot Naish for the pint-sized snake in the grass he clearly is. The role of a fat-cat horndog might not seem like it'd be up Naish's alley but, if the Robert Mitchum bio *Baby I Don't Care* is to be believed, it was *perfect* casting; according to author Lee Server, Mitchum's few actor-friends, "denizens of the night brought together by their taste for booze and other substances," included "brawling roisterer" J. Carrol "Joe" Naish, "a rabid and surprisingly successful womanizer."

Strange Confession gives Naish a villainous sidekick, played by Milburn Stone, so here Chaney is being double-teamed by two old Inner Sanctum tormentors (Naish from *Calling Dr. Death*, Stone from *The Frozen Ghost*). Lloyd Bridges gives a likable "class clown" performance as Chaney's friendly assistant — "Ed Norton" to Chaney's "Ralph" — and it's fun to see this future TV star bringing up the rear in an Inner Sanctum cheapie. "I enjoyed working with Chaney very much," Bridges told the authors. "Of course, I'd been a great admirer of his father's. Chaney Jr. was very sweet, very nice. The picture might not have been too much to brag about, but he was a very pleasant man to work with."

The oddest pressbook item this time around described how a lavish dinner scene was dropped from the *Strange Confession* script at Chaney's insistence. Dispatches from Nice, France, had told of riots breaking out when a large plate of caviar was shown on screen during a recent showing of an American film; Chaney supposedly feared that a big display of food might offend his Gallic admirers. This silly little story is probably just another pack of pressbook lies, although there is a good, true story to be told as long as we're on the subject of Chaney and chow. Chaney apparently was haunted by the specter of poverty, and could not put out of his mind the days when he and his wife Patsy were struggling and had no money for food. In a 1943 news item he explained:

> When I got some money, I bought me hundreds of cans and some apparatus for using them. I've canned foods of all kinds. I've gone out in the ocean and caught tuna fish and canned them. I've shot game and canned it. It makes me feel better to see all that food, because a fellow never can tell how long his luck's going to run in the movies.

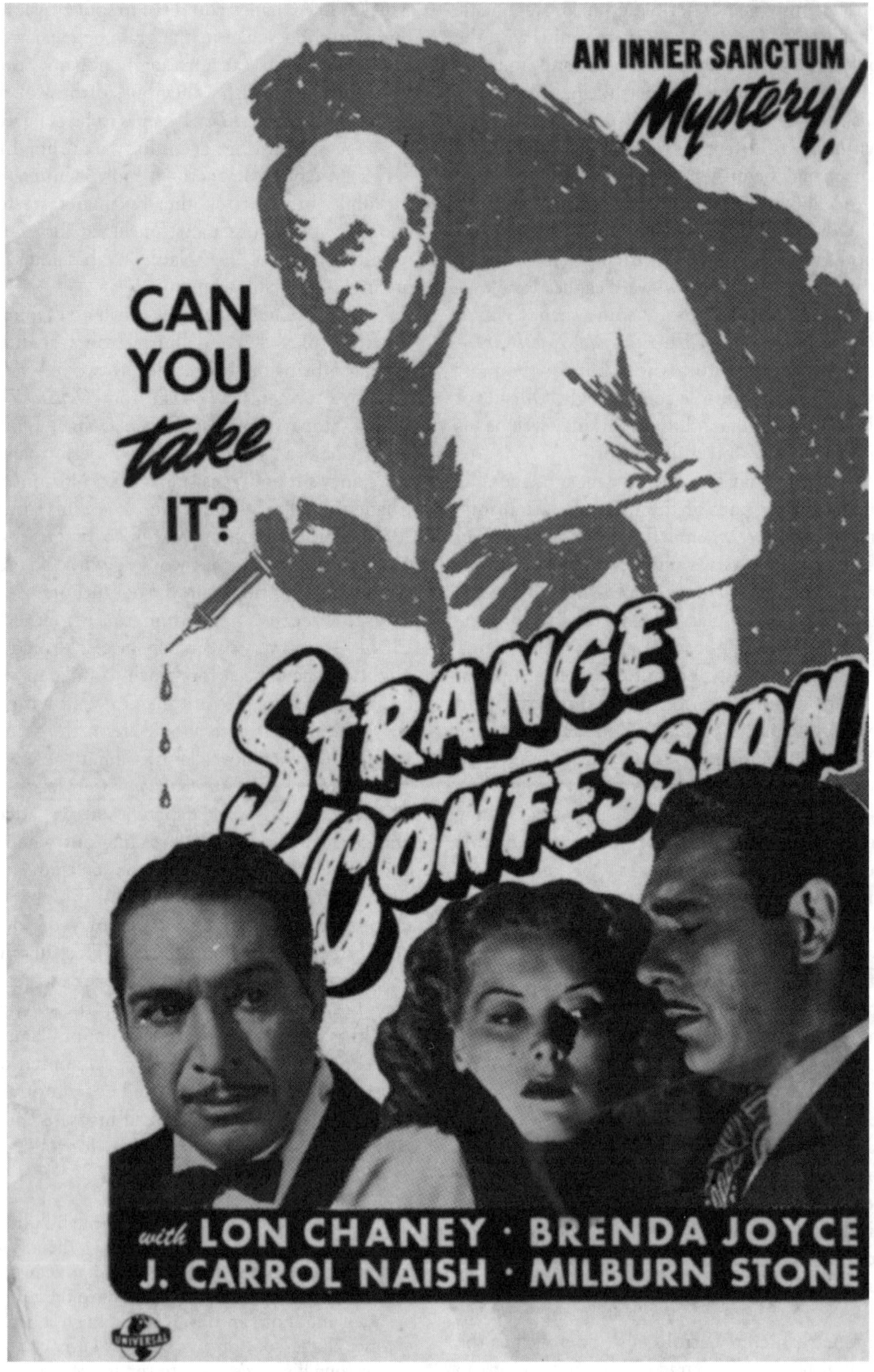

Pressbook ad.

Chaney's fear of hunger persisted; a fishing and hunting pal of Chaney's used to tell the story that, between Los Angeles and Chaney's ranch in San Diego, the actor had several freezer-lockers full of frozen food.

Strange Confession went into production on February 1, 1945, shooting on Universal's New England Street, the New York Street and on a *Gung Ho!* set. It was the first directorial stint for John Hoffman, a former montage technician who had worked on such films as *Boom Town* (1940), *Cover Girl* (1944) and *A Song to Remember* (1945). The film wrapped on February 14, five days over schedule, and the next Inner Sanctum, *Pillow of Death*, was hustled into production only a few days later, as if there were people out there waiting for these things. Over at Columbia a series of films based on the *I Love a Mystery* radio program had recently gotten underway, and the first entry (also titled *I Love a Mystery*—and also involving a disembodied head) had recently been released. Perhaps Universal was anxious to crank out as many Inner Sanctums as possible before the combined efforts of the two studios created a glut on the market.

Strange Confession was reissued by Realart in 1953 as *The Missing Head*, then seemed to drop from the face of the Earth. It was never part of television's famous *Shock* packages and no pirated prints seemed to be extant. The true explanation for the movie's disappearance may never be known; for what it's worth, the possibly apocryphal Story That Went Around was that Universal had made the decision to remake *The Man Who Reclaimed His Head* without rechecking their contract with Jean Bart, writer of the original play. The contract allowed for only one version of the play to be filmed, and so Universal had inadvertently stepped outside their legal rights in making *Strange Confession* at all; consequently, *Strange Confession* was caught in a legal tangle.

In the original *Universal Horrors*, we predicted that the movie might never again see the light of day because the cost of cutting through all the red tape would probably exceed the profit that could be made off of a home video release. To the surprise of Lon Chaney, Jr., fans everywhere, in 1997 the entire Inner Sanctum series made its home video bow as a trio of VHS double-bills—*Dead Man's Eyes* and *Pillow of Death*, *Weird Woman* and *The Frozen Ghost*, *Calling Dr. Death* and, yes, *Strange Confession*. A DVD release of all six movies as a two-disc set ("*Inner Sanctum Mysteries*: The Complete Movie Collection") followed in September 2006.

Critics' Corner

[A] program picture that needs all the help it can get.... A primary demerit is the old-fashioned, faltering screenplay that tells a story almost completely devoid of excitement.—*The Hollywood Reporter*, September 28, 1945, Jack D. Grant

Rating: ★★½ There's a little too much domesticity in the film for thriller fans.... [S]uspense is moderately good.... [G]ood performances from all principals.—*The New York Daily News*, November 1945

Slow to start, and slower to progress.... The usual action is lacking; the stress is all on character. Excellent acting by Lon Chaney, Brenda Joyce and J. Carrol Naish helps to maintain this emphasis.—*The Motion Picture Herald*, October 6, 1945, Thalia Bell

Well cast and, although slow-moving, is an interesting character study.—Daughters of the American Revolution (Eastern Committee), 1945

Direction is sure and Lon Chaney's characterization of a distraught man is excellent. Music is absolutely in tune with changing moods. Very good.—General Federation of Women's Clubs (Eastern Committee), 1945

Pursuit to Algiers

Released October 26, 1945. 65 minutes. *Producer-Director:* Roy William Neill. *Executive Producer:* Howard Benedict. *Original Screenplay:* Leonard Lee. *Based on the characters created by* Sir Arthur Conan Doyle. *Photography:* Paul Ivano. *Editor:* Saul A. Goodkind. *Assistant Director:* Seward Webb. *Musical Director:* Edgar Fairchild. *Art Directors:* John B. Goodman & Martin Obzina. *Sound Director:* Bernard B. Brown. *Technician:* Robert Pritchard. *Set Decorators:* Russell A. Gausman & Ralph Sylos. *Makeup:* Jack P. Pierce. *Dialogue Director:* Raymond Kessler. *Gowns:* Vera West.

Basil Rathbone (*Sherlock Holmes*), Nigel Bruce (*Dr. John H. Watson*), Marjorie Riordan (*Sheila Woodbury*), Rosalind Ivan (*Agatha Dunham*), Morton Lowry (*Sanford*), Leslie Vincent (*Nikolas*), Martin Kosleck (*Mirko*), Rex Evans (*Gregor*), John Abbott (*Jodri*), Gerald Hamer (*Kingston*), Wee Willie Davis (*Gubec*), Frederic Worlock (*Prime Minister*), Gregory Gaye (*Ravez*), Wilson Benge (*Clergyman*), Sven Hugo Borg (*Johansson*), Dorothy Kellogg (*Fuzzy-Looking Woman*), Tom P. Dillon (*Restaurant Proprietor*), Olaf Hytten (*Stimson*), Alan Edmiston (*Furtive Man*), James Craven (*Customer*), Ashley Cowan (*Steward*), George Leigh (*Reginald Dene*), James Carlisle, Sayre Dearing (*Aides*).

With some apprehension, we allowed Sherlock a taste of one of nature's noblest gifts — a kiss....
—*Roy William Neill on* Pursuit to Algiers

Hollywood treated few of its aging detectives well. *Pursuit to Algiers,* the tenth but not the last of the Sherlock Holmes adventures, proved that the series was on its last legs. A depressingly unambitious programmer, it not only pits the great detective against unworthy adversaries, but also relegates him to the thankless duty of serving as bodyguard to a visiting monarch. A hangdog air hovers over the whole production. In short, *Pursuit to Algiers* is arguably the weakest entry in the series.

The set-up of the story is more intriguing than the plot itself. Contemplating a holiday in Scotland, Holmes and Watson (Basil Rathbone and Nigel Bruce) saunter down a foggy London lane where they are accosted by a couple of seemingly innocuous passersby. One plants a newspaper on Holmes, insisting that he dropped it. Another draws the pair into a dingy fish-and-chips bar. Stepping into the pub, Holmes becomes aware that he is being pitched a series of clues by the waiters as well as the diners; the newspaper and menu, he notes, are rife with leads. The detective deduces that he is being directed to a particular address and dashes out to find the clandestine meeting place.

After this attention-grabbing opening, the plotline of *Pursuit to Algiers* takes a nosedive. The entire charade was cooked up by the ministers of a tiny European country whose monarch was recently killed in a motor accident (actually a well-disguised assassination plot). The heir to the throne, the young Prince Stephen, who is vacationing in England, now faces a similar fate, possibly while en route to his homeland. Over Watson's protests, Holmes agrees to escort the newly installed monarch as far as Algiers.

A snag in the plan forces Holmes to proceed with the prince on a two-passenger plane while Watson reluctantly boards an ocean liner to meet his partner in Algiers. Not long into the voyage, Watson hears a bulletin describing the fatal crash of Holmes' plane. Barely recovered from the blow, Watson is asked by the ship's steward Sanford (Morton Lowry) to minister to a stricken passenger. The patient is none other than Holmes, who explains that his plan to fly to Algiers was ditched for security reasons, and that he and the prince will arrive at their destination on that very ship. The detective introduces Watson to the prince Nikolas (Leslie Vincent), who is traveling under the guise of the doctor's nephew.

Keeping a watchful eye out for potential assassins amongst his fellow passengers, Holmes is immediately suspicious of American nightclub singer Sheila Woodbury (Marjorie Riordan). The songbird takes a romantic interest in young Nikolas and is visibly shaken by the detective's presence. The sharp-eyed Holmes observes that the girl is never without her music case and deduces that she is carrying the recently nabbed Duchess of Brookdale's emeralds. After a confrontation, Sheila admits she found the gems in her music case and has become an unwitting accomplice in a scheme to smuggle them out of the country. Holmes gladly takes the emeralds off her hands and promises Sheila that she will receive the sizable reward.

An unscheduled stop brings three additional passengers on board: The unctuous, heavyset Gregor (Rex Evans) and his traveling companions, the wiry Mirko (Martin Kosleck) and a giant mute named Gubec (Wee Willie Davis). Holmes recognizes Mirko as a famous carnival knife-thrower wanted by the police. He deduces that the three are on board to assassinate Prince Stephen. Mirko is outwitted by Holmes when he attempts to stab the detective as he sleeps in his berth. Holmes shrewdly uncovers a deadly explosive planted in a party favor meant for Nikolas.

As the ship anchors in Algiers, the desperate trio makes one final attempt on the prince's life. Breaking into Holmes' cabin, they subdue the sleuth and whisk Nikolas aboard a small craft. The prince's official reception party arrives to find Holmes bound and gagged. Holmes assures them that the culprits have been apprehended on shore, and tells them that young Nikolas was actually a decoy. The real Prince Stephen is Sanford, disguised as the steward throughout the voyage.

Pursuit to Algiers may have been conceived as a thinking man's thriller. Leonard Lee's generally humorless, dialogue-heavy script scrupulously eschews action; the confrontations be-

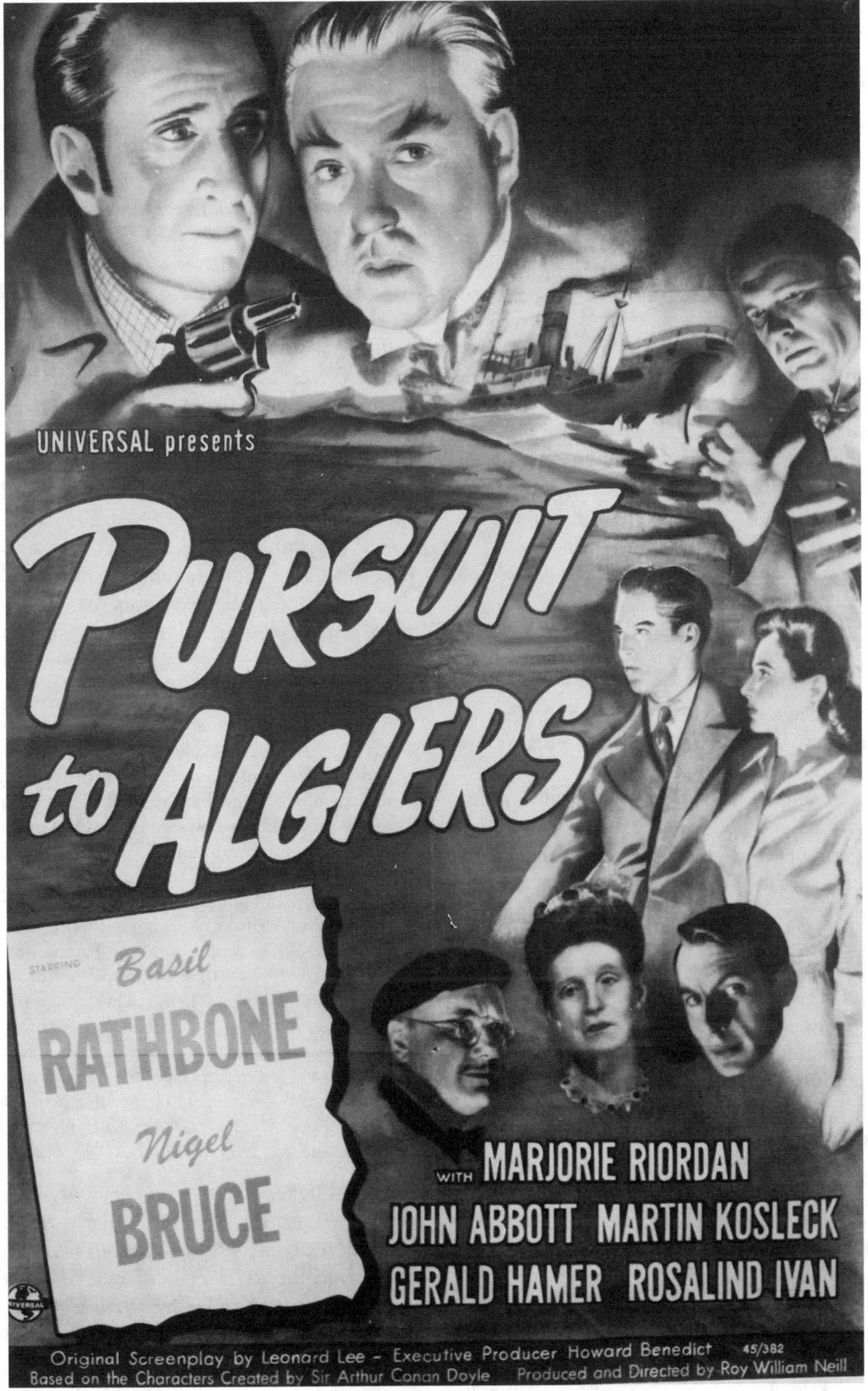

Poster art (courtesy Dan Scapperotti).

tween Holmes and his adversaries are genteel and matter-of-fact, and there's an undramatic twist ending. It's the kind of picture that could only be brought off with a lot of style. Unfortunately, *Pursuit to Algiers* has precious little to offer.

The ocean liner setting is a novelty but it's an obvious studio mock-up. (British movie producer Richard Gordon, upon recently seeing the movie, noted that the ship looked more like a dumpy *King Kong*–type freighter!) Director Roy William Neill wisely avoids the flatly lit, "sun-drenched" ship's deck and crams as much moody night footage into the picture as possible. A scene in which the ship passes through a fog bank gives the film a much-needed visual lift. But this is all window dressing for a banal, uninteresting screenplay. Except for recovering a cache of stolen jewels in an unrelated subplot, Holmes' investigative skills remain sadly under-used. For the remainder of the screen time, he is merely a bodyguard for the prince's decoy.

The picture is a throwback to the detective's earliest adventures which pitted Holmes against foreign agents and fifth columnists. But at least then the series had more zip. *Pursuit to Algiers* is so mannered, even the villains are rounded up off camera.

In spite of the movie's leanings toward international intrigue, all of the standard mystery programmer conventions are employed, to little effect, including the usual lineup of red herrings. John Abbott and Gerald Hamer skulk about conspiratorially only to be revealed as a pair of harmless archaeologists in the last reel. Marjorie Riordan's secret is unveiled halfway through the movie. Rosalind Ivan as a nosy eccentric can't be taken for anything but comic relief. The heavies are such a brazen lot — they practically conduct business out in the open — that these secondary characters are little more than excess baggage. Rex Evans, the leader, may be counted on to goad Rathbone into a genial verbal sparring match after each botched assassination attempt but, lacking the intended wit, their exchanges are merely tedious.

An uninspired choice to play the oily, treacherous Gregor, Evans is best remembered by horror fans as the pie-eyed tavern keeper who blew up the dam at the climax of Neill's *Frankenstein Meets the Wolf Man*. While pursuing an acting career, Evans ran a Hollywood art gallery, probably a necessity considering his usually minuscule roles. His husky build and allegedly sparkling repartee suggested a bargain basement Sydney Greenstreet, especially with Martin Kosleck at his side. (Kosleck lost out to Peter Lorre for the Joel Cairo role in the 1941 classic *The Maltese Falcon*.) Evans ranks down there with Arthur Margetson (*Sherlock Holmes Faces Death*) as one of the detective's least colorful foes.

Evans is easily upstaged by the dependable Kosleck, whose performance as the petulant knife-throwing psycho is the highlight of the film. Knives became the official weapon of choice for the actor during his stint at Universal, having cut, slashed and stabbed his way through the Holmes film, *The Frozen Ghost* and *The Mummy's Curse*. There's a delightful scene in *Pursuit to Algiers* wherein Rathbone is all apologies after smashing Kosleck's wrist with a porthole cover after a foiled murder attempt.

Off-camera, the two actors shared a common respect and affection for one another. Kosleck told us:

> I adored Basil. He was the most wonderful guy to work with. I remember I had an interview for a part in *The Mad Doctor* [1941], and I thought I had to give an audition, but he was in the producer's office when I came in. He got up and shook my hand. He had seen me as Dr. Goebbels in my first American film [1939's *Confessions of a Nazi Spy*], and he said, "You don't have to give an audition." And I got the part right then and there through his kindness. Working with him was just beautiful. We walked around the Paramount lot and discussed how to play scenes. We were always together on *Pursuit to Algiers*. There was a friend of mine in it who was not talented, only stuck-up [Leslie Vincent]. He got the part in the film through my influence. Basil took me aside and said, "Martin, how can you live with a person like that — a person who has *no talent*!" He's now a millionaire and lives in Hawaii.

Rathbone, of course, is always a pleasure to watch and listen to, even under these less-than-ideal circumstances. If *Pursuit to Algiers* is to be remembered by Conan Doyle devotees at all, it is for providing Holmes with his first and only screen kiss. Neill wrote in a 1945 article:

> With some apprehension, we allowed Sherlock a taste of one of nature's noblest gifts — a kiss — in *Pursuit to Algiers*, first of the Holmes product on

> [*sic*] Universal's 1945-46 season. It was the first kiss he had ever experienced, either in fiction or on celluloid. Marjorie Riordan is the lady who brushed his cheek lightly, in gratitude for his rescuing her from a precarious situation and Holmes worshippers accepted the salute with good grace.

In the supporting ranks, strongman Wee Willie Davis as Evans' mute henchman is barely noticeable, but Rosalind Ivan (who was so memorably odious as the harpy wives of Charles Laughton and Edward G. Robinson in 1944's *The Suspect* and 1945's *Scarlet Street*, respectively) contributes a few bright moments as an irritatingly enthusiastic tourist.

But the real star of *Pursuit to Algiers* is Nigel Bruce. Unlike most of the other writers in this series, Leonard Lee allotted the actor generous screen time, not for playing him up as a buffoon, but to reveal a more charismatic side to Watson's personality. This trait is especially evident in the scenes he shares with young Marjorie Riordan. The troubled girl and the good doctor become fast friends as the sea journey progresses. The songstress even coaxes Watson to accompany her as she entertains the guests, thus giving Bruce the opportunity to make his screen singing debut performing the old Scotch ballad, "Loch Lomond."

Bruce's acting career began back in 1919 when he made his stage debut in England. Coming to America, he got his first Broadway break in Noël Coward's "This Was a Man" in 1929. Five years later, Bruce answered the call of Hollywood and became a prominent member of the British colony. The archetype of the proud and hearty English gentleman, Bruce landed good roles in scores of features including *Stand Up and Cheer!* (1934), *Treasure Island* (1934), *Becky Sharp* (1935), *She* (1935) and *The Charge of the Light Brigade* (1936), before attaining cinematic immortality in the role of Dr. Watson in 1939's 20th Century–Fox production, *The Hound of the Baskervilles*. One of the actor's most unlikely roles was that of Lord Albert Esketh, Myrna Loy's belligerent husband in the Fox disaster film *The Rains Came* that same year. His acting career continued to flourish after the Sherlock Holmes series ended in 1946. Shortly before his death from a heart attack on October 8, 1953, at the age of 58, Bruce had a featured part in Hollywood's first 3-D spectacle, *Bwana Devil*.

Pursuit to Algiers was announced under the title *The Fugitive*. This tag is inappropriate enough for one to suspect the script was subjected to a last-minute overhaul, or possibly just cranked out after another Holmes project was ditched. Apparently, Universal or Roy Neill regarded *Pursuit to Algiers* as a missed opportunity. *Terror by Night*, the next Sherlock Holmes caper, is a thinly disguised remake. The action unreels on a Scotland-bound train with the detective guarding a fabulous jewel instead of an imperiled monarch, only the ingredients came together with splendid results. *Pursuit to Algiers* is, by comparison, an uninspired dry run.

Critics' Corner

As all moviegoers know by now, the twentieth-century adventures of these Sir Arthur Conan Doyle characters are marked by whodunit melodrama rather than the keen mental conflicts which made them famous. Holmes himself seems to sense the deterioration from time to time in the excellent Basil Rathbone characterization, and one of the lines in *Pursuit to Algiers* allows him to be positively nostalgic.... "The late Professor Moriarty," remarks Holmes in tribute to his former adversary, "was a virtuoso on the bassoon."—*The New York Herald-Tribune*, October 27, 1945, Otis L. Guernsey, Jr.

[T]his unerring accuracy of Holmes ... has now become so dependable that his pictures have virtually no suspense. All that is left is to sit there and chuckle at Dr. Watson's ... wretched jokes and sniff at the enemies.—*The New York Times*, October 27, 1945, Bosley Crowther

[B]elow par for the series.... The story is a rather contrived affair, sometimes difficult to follow, and its development does not adhere to logic.... The performances of Rathbone and Bruce are standard, but the others in the cast are not shown to good advantage; at times, their acting is amateurish.—*Harrison's Reports*, October 27, 1945

Neill's direction keeps the matters on the move, and he obtains expected performances from Basil Rathbone as Holmes and Nigel Bruce as Watson.—*The Hollywood Reporter*, 1945

[H]as many exciting moments.... [A] good detective film.—*The Motion Picture Herald*, October 27, 1945, M.R.Y.

House of Dracula

Released December 7, 1945. 67 minutes. *Executive Producer:* Joseph Gershenson. *Producer:* Paul Malvern. *Director:* Erle C. Kenton. *Screenplay:* Edward T. Lowe. *Story:* George Bricker & Dwight V. Babcock. *Photography:* George Robinson. *Editor:* Russell Schoengarth. *Music Director:* Edgar Fairchild. *Art Directors:* John

B. Goodman & Martin Obzina. *Sound Director:* Bernard B. Brown. *Technician:* Jess Moulin. *Set Decorators:* Russell A. Gausman & Arthur D. Leddy. *Gowns:* Vera West. *Makeup:* Jack P. Pierce & Joe Hadley. *Hair Stylist:* Carmen Dirigo. *Assistant Director:* Ralph Siosser. *Special Photography:* John P. Fulton. *Stand-in for Lon Chaney, Jr.:* Walter DePalma. *Stand-in for John Carradine:* Arthur W. Stern.

Lon Chaney, Jr. (*Lawrence Stewart Talbot/The Wolf Man*), John Carradine (*Count Dracula*), Martha O'Driscoll (*Miliza Morelle*), Lionel Atwill (*Inspector Holtz*), Onslow Stevens (*Dr. Franz Edlemann*), Jane Adams (*Nina*), Ludwig Stossel (*Seigfried*), Glenn Strange (*The Frankenstein Monster*), Skelton Knaggs (*Steinmuhl*), Joseph E. Bernard (*Brahms*), Fred Cordova, Carey Harrison (*Gendarmes*), Dick Dickinson, Harry Lamont (*Villagers*), Carey Loftin (*Onslow Stevens' Stunt Double*), Sailor Vincent (*Ludwig Stossel's Stunt Double*), Boris Karloff (*The Frankenstein Monster [in* Bride of Frankenstein *footage]*). Cut from final print: Gregory Muradian (*Johannes*), Beatrice Gray (*Johannes' Mother*).

My blood has been contaminated
by the blood of Dracula.
—*Dr. Edlemann (Onslow Stevens) in*
House of Dracula

Horror characters stretched out way beyond their potential stalk the *House of Dracula* in Universal's final monster rally.

The seventh installment in the Frankenstein series and the fourth entry for both Dracula and the Wolf Man, *House of Dracula* is a continuation of the everything-*and*-the-kitchen-sink spookery presented in the previous year's *House of Frankenstein*; in many ways, this sequel is almost a remake of that film. The Universal staff was out of fresh ideas, although this last in the studio's monster saga does feature some ingratiatingly macabre touches and a new Jekyll-Hyde–inspired character who manages to steal the spotlight from his classic colleagues.

The first hint that yet another monster rally was in the offing came via the April 1944 Hollywood trade papers, while *House of Frankenstein* was still in production. The announcement was that the title of this new film would be *The Wolf Man vs. Dracula*, and that Ford Beebe had been assigned to produce and direct. A *Wolf Man vs. Dracula* script remains an elusive item, although examination of a December 4, 1944, letter from spoilsport Joseph Breen to Universal's Maurice Pivar gives the strong impression that this script is quite different from that of *House of Dracula*; it may in fact be different altogether. Breen's letter makes reference to the script's inclusion of folk songs, a stake driven into a body (Dracula's?) with accompanying "ear-splitting screams," and a scantily clad character named Yvonne.

By February 1945, the film was being called *House of Dracula*, a new or much-revised script obviously having been written; Beebe was still listed as producer-director. And, for a time, Universal was announcing that Dracula would be played by Bela Lugosi. But by the time the film went into production in September, the producer-director chores were divvied up between Paul Malvern and Erie C. Kenton, the men who made *House of Frankenstein,* and John Carradine was back in the vampire cape. According to the pressbook, the actor's shoulder-length hair (his trademark "Buffalo Bill hairdo") was cut on the orders of Malvern before the start of shooting; he was also made-up to look older than he did in *House of Frankenstein*.

Count Dracula (Carradine), tiring of his undead existence, pays an unexpected pre-dawn visit on renowned surgeon Franz Edlemann (Onslow Stevens) in his castle home in seaside Visaria. (No clue as to how Dracula survived his on-camera disintegration in *House of Frankenstein* is provided—nor will there be any explanation for the returning Larry Talbot.) Proving to Edlemann that he is a vampire by showing him his coffin, hidden in Edlemann's own basement, the count urges the scientist to take on his case and discover a cure for the curse of vampirism.

Together with his nurses Miliza (Martha O'Driscoll) and humpback Nina (Jane Adams), Edlemann has been cultivating a tropical plant which produces mold that can be used to soften bones, a revolutionary alternative to surgery. Edlemann sets his work aside to concentrate on Dracula's plight. When Larry Talbot (Lon Chaney, Jr., still sporting his Inner Sanctum mustache) arrives at the castle seeking a consultation, Miliza explains that the doctor is occupied. Talbot, frantic with worry, runs out.

Later that night, Edlemann receives a phone call from Inspector Holtz (Lionel Atwill) of the Visaria gendarmery: Talbot has turned himself in, claiming to be a werewolf. As Edlemann, Miliza and Holtz look on, the moon shines through the barred window of Talbot's jail cell and he undergoes the transformation (the only time in the series that anyone witnesses it). The Wolf Man rattles the bars and then, perhaps realizing that the onlookers would like to talk, slumps down to the floor and goes to sleep(!). Edlemann, a workaholic, decides to take on Talbot's case as well.

Glenn Strange as the Frankenstein Monster in the monster rally *House of Dracula*.

At Edlemann's castle, Talbot reacts to some bad news with yet another anxiety attack, running outside and leaping off a cliff and into the pounding sea. Thinking that Talbot may have been washed through a sea-level cave entrance, Edlemann descends via bosun's chair into the cave to rescue him. There the good doctor discovers not only his pessimistic patient but also the body of the Frankenstein Monster (Glenn Strange) and the skeleton of Dr. Niemann (quicksand and the long arm of coincidence have deposited them here). Edlemann, apparently feeling that his plate is not yet full enough, soon has the Monster on an operating table in his lab and is weighing the plusses and minuses of reviving him.

Edlemann continues to treat Dracula, oblivious to the fact that the count has now got the hots for Miliza. Deciding to stick with being a vampire, the count turns the (operating) tables on Edlemann during a blood transfusion: He hypnotizes Edlemann, then reverses the flow of blood, maliciously infusing the doctor with some of his own poisonous plasma. Unaware of what has transpired, Edlemann revives in time to race to Miliza's room and ward off the hovering Dracula with a crucifix. The vampire flees to the castle basement and the sanctuary of his coffin just as the dawn breaks. Edlemann drags the coffin nearer to a window and opens it, fatally exposing Dracula to the rays of the rising sun.

Edlemann soon becomes aware of the vampiric blood in his veins and unselfishly redoubles his efforts to cultivate more mold for the coming operation on Talbot, which he eventually performs. (By the time he's done, he's wiped enough mold on his own apron for six more operations!) But that night he transforms into a gaunt, black-eyed killer who tears out the throat of his own servant Seigfried (Ludwig Stossel). Talbot, recovering from the operation, sees enough through the window of his bedroom to know that Edlemann is the murderer, but he naturally sympathizes with Edlemann and keeps the knowledge to himself.

Boldly stepping out into full moonlight to gauge the success of Edlemann's surgery, Talbot is elated to find that the operation has been proved a success and that the curse of werewolfery has been lifted. But Edlemann, again turning into the mad killer, hurries to the lab and revives the Monster. Talbot, Miliza and Inspector Holtz arrive on the scene just as Edlemann strangles Nina. The Monster goes into action, clobbering a gendarme, while Edlemann throws Holtz against a piece of machinery that sparks and electrocutes him (the same death scene Atwill had in *The Ghost of Frankenstein*). Talbot reluctantly shoots and kills Edlemann, then topples a huge rack filled with bottles of chemicals which burst into flames. Talbot and Miliza flee the castle in one of the movie's last original shots, the rest being footage from *The Ghost of Frankenstein* in which the Monster staggers around the burning room and is finally consumed. THE END fades to black and, for the first and only time in the Frankenstein series, the cast was apparently not worth repeating.

Universal must have thought that Edward T. Lowe's *House of Frankenstein* screenplay was worth repeating, though, because his *House of Dracula* script is basically a rehash. Once again Dracula is a warm-up act, dispatched much too quickly considering that this is a film with his name in the title. Larry Talbot (but not the Wolf Man) vies with a mad doctor and a hunchback for audience attention throughout most of the remaining footage, and the Monster remains in a coma until he's required to run amok in the curtain closer.

Despite the title, the house is not Dracula's although the count certainly makes himself at home there, moving into the basement armor room, bag and baggage. As in *House of Frankenstein*, John Carradine's soft-spoken Dracula is less Continental count than Kentucky colonel: Dignified and courtly, he has all the style and panache we hear ascribed to Lugosi's creaky portrayal. Carradine told *Fangoria*:

> When they asked me to play Dracula, I said yes, if you let me make him up and play him the way Bram Stoker described him — as an elderly, distinguished gentleman with a drooping mustache. [Universal] didn't like a big mustache, so I had to trim it and make it a very clipped, British mustache. It wasn't really in character.

Despite the juvenile qualities of the *House* movies, Carradine's remains one of the better vintage movie Draculas, easily outshining the ossified Lugosi as well as Christopher Lee's red-eyed track star. He's certainly not the right "type" for the role, exuding that Southern style charm, but the fact that he's still able to put it over attests to his masterful playing of the role. Carradine brings just the right balance of sinister elegance and sexual magnetism to *House of Dracula*: He's at his best in the creepy scene in which he exerts his hypnotic influence over piano-playing Martha O'Driscoll, and her rendition of "Moonlight Sonata" turns into a macabre dirge that sounds like something out of *The Twilight Zone*. It's a pity that Carradine never had the opportunity to play Dracula in an appropriate vehicle; aside from the two *House* films, he later played the role in *Billy the Kid Versus Dracula* (1966), in which he was pitted against the young gunslinger (Chuck Courtney); *Las Vampiras* (1969), a Mexican-made, Spanish-language stinker where he was confined to a cage throughout the film; and in the R-rated *Nocturna* (1979), in which the tax man turns the count's castle into a disco.

It's unclear how Dracula has managed to live for hundreds of years and yet be such a hopeless bungler. In both the 1931 *Dracula* and in *House of Dracula*, he keeps his coffin in a hiding place that's known to his enemies; it's such a poor strategy, antagonizing people who know where you lie helpless 12 hours out of every day. The count would also have been well-advised to invest a few dollars in a wristwatch: In *Dracula* and the two *House* films, he makes his Big Move at five minutes before dawn, giving himself exactly enough time to incite people to chase him back to the coffin he then must climb into!

There are actually two "vampires" in *House of Dracula*, and for years a fuss has been made over the wrong one: There's been something of a tendency among fans to make too much of Onslow Stevens' performance as the vampiric Edlemann. There's really very little that's remarkable about it. Stevens tackles the role with a striking lack of restraint, falling back on a lot of hoary horror clichés. His character does steal the show but that's no trick considering that, monster-wise, once he comes on, he's the only show in town: By then, we've already seen the last of Dracula and the Wolf Man, and the Monster is in his usual coma. Stevens' performance is almost anachronistically broad, with the actor chewing the scenery, leering hammily and doing everything but twisting the end of his mustache. Stevens' best moment as the "Hyde side" of Edlemann might be his last, as (shot by Larry Talbot) a look of gratitude and relief appears on his face, reminiscent of the finish of *WereWolf of*

John Carradine made a superb count in *House of Dracula* with Martha O'Driscoll. The movie's "circa 1880" setting makes it a prequel to the Lugosi *Dracula*!

London ("Thanks ... thanks for the bullet..."). Even though his characters ("Edlemann & Hyde") are the center of attention from start to finish, Stevens wound up with fifth billing, below even Lionel Atwill.

Stevens fares better as the human Edlemann, although this character's insistence on sticking labels on the monsters' maladies becomes annoying. Edlemann isolates the "peculiar parasite" in Dracula's blood that causes his vampiric condition, and also determines why Talbot changes into a werewolf; for some fans, these authors included, learning that our favorite supernatural characters merely have cut-and-dried medical afflictions goes against the grain. (For the record, Talbot becomes the Wolf Man because he has a metabolism that's "like a steam engine without a balance wheel.") This science-meets-the-supernatural touch may have struck a false note in *House of Dracula* but it worked well in such future films as *The Werewolf* (1956), *I Was a Teenage Werewolf* (1957) and especially *The Vampire* (1957), the latter starring John Beal as a small-town doctor with a very Edlemann-like predicament.

Chaney, looking about ten years older than he did in the then-four-year-old *The Wolf Man* (that demon rum!), gives a good performance as Talbot, but by this fourth Wolf Man installment he's clearly on autopilot. Little is seen of Talbot's Wolf Man self this time around, reportedly because of a shortage of yak hair but more probably to satisfy Breen Office regulations (the Wolf Man couldn't kill anyone in a film where Talbot survives to the end). Glenn Strange is his usual dopey-looking "prop" Monster, laid out on an operating table throughout most of the film anticipating his mild climactic tantrum.

Leading ladies Martha O'Driscoll and Jane Adams go through their paces without creating much of an impression; there really are no acting opportunities for either actress in the film.

O'Driscoll is at her best in scenes of tenderness with Chaney, as throughout the film there is a hint of blossoming romance between the two. In one scene she wears what looks like a Little Red Riding Hood outfit—highly appropriate for The Girl in a werewolf movie! Adams is her usual simpering self, although there is some pathos in her unrequited love for Onslow Stevens. Emaciated English actor Skelton Knaggs and the fat, frumpy, Germanic Ludwig Stossel are seen as brothers, indicative of the kind of thought that went into this picture.

The screenplay is a derivative one, lifting scenes and ideas from many earlier chillers. Again, the film is in large part a remake of *House of Frankenstein*, but apart from this major influence there are other noticeable "steals." The Carradine–Martha O'Driscoll piano scene is clearly presaged by a similar sequence in *Dracula's Daughter*—another movie in which a Dracula sought a cure from the curse of the vampire. Edlemann's cat Bartholomew reacts almost hysterically to his transformation just as Henry Hull's similar looking house pet does in *WereWolf of London*; Edlemann's hallucinogenic dream, with its Freudian overtones, plays like a take-off on a scene in the MGM *Dr. Jekyll and Mr. Hyde* (1941). Also noticeable are traces of the 1931 *Dr. Jekyll and Mr. Hyde*: A weird montage following Edlemann's initial transformation; a scene where "vampire" Edlemann approaches a door upon which someone is knocking, but (from the other side) we see human Edlemann open it; and the increasingly large shadow of "vampire" Edlemann filling the front wall of a hotel as he runs from a mob.

A September 20, 1945, draft of the script (titled, what else?, *Destiny*) includes many of the kind of script-to-screen changes that make for interesting reading. Early on there's a short scene where Edlemann examines a seven-year-old boy whose leg he has healed. (The scene was filmed, with Gregory Muradian playing the boy and Beatrice Gray, mother of future kid actor Billy Gray, as his peasant mom. It ended up on the cutting room floor, although there's still a reference to it in the finished film.) According to the script, the "pagan" piano tune Dracula compelled Miliza to play should be heard faintly every time the vampire exerts his hypnotic influence over her. "Vampire" Edlemann's hands have webbed fingers and vulture-like claws. The dream sequence is longer and more elaborate, with scenes of the Monster killing Miliza and hurling villagers around. Steinmuhl is a belligerent braggart-extrovert who angrily harangues the townspeople. It's also noteworthy that the script puts an approximate date on these goings-on, describing a "period of about 1880" even though one character mentions X-rays, not discovered until the turn of the twentieth century. But it seems nitpicky to complain about something like that in a movie in which Larry Talbot can be spotted thumbing through a copy of *Newsweek* magazine!

Released only a few months before the second Universal horror cycle sputtered to a close, *House of Dracula* represents one of the last Universal credits for most of the people involved. It was the final horror film for burly Lon Chaney, Universal's Master Character Creator. Chaney, whose hard drinking and boisterous hijinks won him few friends on the lot, was dropped from the studio payroll shortly after *House of Dracula* wrapped, and was forced to work as a freelancer. With horror films temporarily out of vogue, Chaney scrambled for jobs, taking roles in a long string of minor films before science fiction and monster pictures came back into style in the 1950s. By that time the actor's drinking problem had worsened to the point where many producers would only entrust him with non-speaking brute-man roles, and Chaney took some big steps backwards in his horror film career.

The actor transformed into the *green-eyed* monster one day on the set of *Spider Baby* (1964), according to writer-producer Jack Hill. Hill told the authors:

> I don't remember how the subject of Boris Karloff came up, but Lon said of Karloff, "He's not a damn bit better than *I* am." So he was kinda jealous of Karloff. It wasn't a big, extended [tirade], it just came up in conversation for some reason, and he was definitely resentful.* Of course, the

**Not too many years later, however, a* Castle of Frankenstein *writer caught up with Chaney and, in a brief interview, asked him which of his horror co-stars he most enjoyed working with. After some hemming and hawing, the always unpredictable Lon finally threw out one name: "Karloff is a friend of the family."*

thing that Lon didn't seem to understand, is that he was an alcoholic, and was considered almost unemployable. He didn't seem to realize that, when somebody gets that kind of reputation, it makes a big difference. Boris of course was *not* [an alcoholic], Boris was just absolutely, 100 percent "there." And, I have to say, Lon was, too, when I worked with him on *Spider Baby*. For *Spider Baby*, he went on the wagon. [*100 percent on the wagon?*] Well ... *pretty* much. I mean, virtually.

There are other sad stories connected with the cast of *House of Dracula*. Onslow Stevens died in 1977, a victim of abuse in the Van Nuys, California, nursing home where he had been under care for a heart ailment. A coroner's inquest jury ruled that the 70-year-old actor died "at the hands of another other than by accident" in the convalescent hospital. Director Erle C. Kenton was forced to retire from the picture business due to Parkinson's disease, which killed him on February 6, 1980, at age 83.

Diminutive tyrant Jack P. Pierce, Universal's grumpy Guardian of the Greasepaint, was dropped by the studio in 1947 to make way for the more modern methods of makeup ace Bud Westmore. Pierce ended up working on low-budget claptrap like *The Brain from Planet Arous* and *Teenage Monster* in the '50s, and later found a home as makeup man on television's *Mr. Ed.* Frank Taylor, writing in the calendar section of the August 11, 1968, *Los Angeles Times*, bitterly described Pierce's funeral as "a sad affair," with mourners hardly filling a solid row of pews:

A minister who had never met Pierce was bravely trying to eulogize him, but said little more than a few prayers and some kind words. In the audience of twenty-four people, only three were makeup artists. His union brothers sent flowers but most found it inconvenient to say farewell in person.... Hollywood bid farewell by staying away.

Even Universal's familiar European Street, seen in numerous horror films dating back to the original *Frankenstein*, came to an ignominious end: In 1986, the set was gutted by a blaze which fire investigators report was set deliberately. It took firefighters nearly a half hour to control the blaze, which spread quickly because so much of the set was dry old wood and foam rubber. Universal officials estimated the damage at $2,500,000.

Saddest of all these tales is the story of Lionel Atwill, who died of bronchial cancer six months after *House of Dracula* completed production. Things had finally begun to look up again for the much put-upon British actor in the mid '40s: The sex scandal finally seemed behind him, he was newly wed to Paula Pruter, a young woman, and at age 60 he became the father of a baby boy. But in February 1946, Atwill, too sick to continue to work, dropped from the cast of the Universal serial *Lost City of the Jungle*; he was replaced by a double and the chapterplay wrapped without him. Reginald LeBorg, longtime friend to Atwill, visited the ailing character star in his Pacific Palisades home:

I saw him once when he was very sick with cancer, at the end, about a week before he died. He must have lost 30 pounds, and he was pale, and he was lying in bed. He was very bitter — he knew he was going. He wanted to live because of the son — and he loved Paula. It was very tragic because, instead of being quiet and giving up his soul, he became mad at the world.

The Maddest Doctor of Them All died April 22, 1946; *House of Dracula* was his final feature. You can hear him hacking off-camera in one scene.

Not unexpectedly, economy rears its ugly head at several points during *House of Dracula*. Footage from *Bride of Frankenstein* turns up in the dream sequence, and much of *The Ghost of Frankenstein*'s fiery climax is reused as Edlemann's castle burns. The laboratory where Edlemann revives the Monster is a spartan, barn-like set, the cheapest mad lab in the series; one of the machines Edlemann uses while playing Mr. Fix-It with the Monster is the console that turned Virginia Bruce into the Invisible Woman (it has also appeared in other Frankenflicks); the sea-level cave contains a temple staircase from *The Mummy's Hand*. The music is a pastiche of past favorites, including *Son of Frankenstein* (heard over the Universal spinning-globe logo rather than the expected fanfare), *Black Friday, Man Made Monster, The Wolf Man, The Ghost of Frankenstein, Frankenstein Meets the Wolf Man, House of Frankenstein, The Scarlet Claw* and *The Invisible Man's Revenge*. In one clever musical touch, a drum roll heard after Talbot's jail cell transformation into the Wolf Man very much resembles an animal growl. This segues into recycled *Son of Frankenstein* music, performed in

"That creature is Man's responsibility," insists Onslow Stevens as he prepares to revitalize the Monster. Lon Chaney, Jr., and Jane Adams beg to differ.

such a way that it sounds like a barking dog is in the orchestra.

Sloppy storytelling mars this, one of the final scripts of Edward T. Lowe, whose writing career dated back to the nickelodeon days. (The following year, he retired and burned all his scripts, clippings and movie mementos in what he called "the great cleansing"!) Edlemann doesn't believe in vampires until Dracula shows him his coffin, which for some reason is all the proof the doctor needs. It's strange that Edlemann knows everything about Dracula's history, even recognizes the Dracula crest, but has never even heard of the Wolf Man. Stranger still is the creature Edlemann becomes after he's infused with the blood of Dracula: He casts no reflection in a mirror, which indicates that he's a vampire, and yet sunlight has no effect upon him. With neither nightfall nor moonlight triggering his transformations, the repeat viewer eventually realizes that Edlemann becomes the mad killer at the scriptwriter's whim, whenever the picture needs a dash of action. The way all the monsters happen to turn up, one after another, at Edlemann's door (or cave) gives the picture the same sort of atmosphere of silliness as a *Munsters* episode.

But for all of its many failings, the film has an agreeably creepy, low-key atmosphere as well as a number of exciting highpoints. Carradine's early scenes as Dracula are a delight, and the scene where he hypnotizes Miliza at the piano is a gem. There's a clever, innovative touch in the transfusion scene, with the images of Dracula and Edlemann blurring and running together while we still see nurse Nina in focus in a corner of the picture.

A highlight of the film is Edlemann's murder of poor Seigfried, as well as the ensuing chase scene with the vampiric Edlemann dashing through the Visarian streets with the angry mob at his heels. Doubling Onslow Stevens in these scenes is stunt great Carey Loftin, who arrived in Hollywood in 1935 and racked up an amazing total of screen credits over the next 55 years (including doubling Karloff in *House of Frankenstein*). He told the authors he came to the *House of Dracula* set with a hangover and, informed by the makeup man that he (Loftin) would be in the makeup chair for a while, fell asleep.

> I got comfortable and I actually took a nap. I was lying back and it felt nice and cool when he was putting this stuff on me. I thought it'd be regular makeup. When he got through, he sat me up and I looked at myself [in the mirror], I saw that I was a light green. I thought, "Oh, boy, I shouldn't have taken this job! I should've let somebody else do it. I don't *feel* good!" Then I found out it was makeup [*laughs*]!

In addition to the green makeup, Loftin also remembers having long fingernails in the scene where he fights with Sailor Vincent (Ludwig Stossel's stunt double) in the runaway wagon. In preparation for the fall from the wagon, Loftin had donned his hip pads but had *not* taped them to his body the way he should have, because he didn't want to have hairs yanked from his legs by the tape when work was finished. "I learned a lesson there," Loftin told the authors. "The runaway wagon cut across a cobblestone street, and when it cut across the curbing, that was our cue to kick ourselves out. Well, one of my hip pads slid up and, oh, *man*, [hitting the street] really took a big chunk of skin off. There were all these cowboys around the director and the camera, and Sailor got up and said to 'em, 'Why didn't one of you guys speak up and take that [stunt job]? Nothin' to it.' I said, 'Sailor! Speak for your*self*!' That day I learned, never mind pullin' some hairs out of your legs after you're done. When you do somethin' like that, you gotta tape those pads *down*, so they don't move. Tape 'em so they're there where they'll work."

Loftin also shared a memory of *House of Dracula* star Chaney:

> There was a *real* nice guy. He had the first real house trailer that I know of when he built a house on the back end of a big pick-up. He had a pot-bellied stove in there, he had a shake roof on it—it was *real* heavy. In 1942 I was down in Texas and I looked down the highway and I saw this trailer comin,' and I told my wife, I said, "*There* is Lon Chaney." She asked, "How do you know?" and I said, "No one else has anything like that." I forced him off the road, I got out of my Packard coupe and he came out, bare from the waist up. He was goin' to somewhere in Texas to do some huntin' and fishin,' but he was so overloaded he said he'd already fixed like a dozen flat tires [*laughs*]! He had the shake roof and the pot-bellied stove, he had his food and, of course, his booze, and it was super-heavy, *way* too heavy for the tires that he had.

Universal released *House of Dracula* on December 7, 1945, on a double-bill with the Western *The Daltons Ride Again*, also with Lon Chaney, Jr., and Martha O'Driscoll. Many critics brushed it off as yet another kiddie-oriented fright flick, and Universal's three classic monster series, intertwined and hopelessly cheapened, came to a simultaneous end ... a future encounter with Bud Abbott and Lou Costello notwithstanding.

Critics' Corner

[S]trange and weird characters cause thrills and chills in their presentation of the story.... This film fulfills the requirements for a satisfactory horror picture.—*The Motion Picture Herald*, December 8, 1945, M.R.Y.

Universal is still substituting quantity for imagination in horror shows.—*The New York Herald-Tribune*, December 22, 1945, Otis L. Guernsey, Jr.

A mighty good show ... the realms of pseudoscience interestingly invaded, and the squeamish proceedings given steady pace under the knowing direction of Erle C. Kenton.—*The Hollywood Reporter*, November 29, 1945, Jack D. Grant

Frankenstein's little boy doesn't die easily. And, unfortunately, neither does this type of cinematic nightmare.—*The New York Times*, December 22, 1945, Thomas M. Pryor

This is ... an entertainment that is more ludicrous than terrifying.... The more discriminating patrons will be either amused or bored.... Much happens, but nothing that will surprise anyone.—*Harrison's Reports*, December 1, 1945

It has plenty of suspense, dark dungeons and satisfactory performances by the entire cast.—*The Motion Picture Exhibitor*, 1945

Rating: ★½ [P]ositively guaranteed not to scare the pants off of anybody.... Unfortunately, the film hasn't the capacity for being funny, either, as is often the case when synthetic horror becomes too rambunctious.—*The New York Daily News*, December 22, 1945, Dorothy Masters

Pillow of Death

Released December 14, 1945. 66 minutes. An Inner Sanctum Mystery, produced by arrangement with Simon and Schuster, Inc., Publishers. *Director:* Wallace Fox. *Producer:* Ben Pivar. *Screenplay:* George Bricker. *Original Story:* Dwight V. Babcock. *Photography:* Jerome Ash. *Camera Operator:* Russ Hoffman. *Special Photographic Effects:* John P. Fulton. *Assistant Director:* Melville Shyer. *Editor:* Edward Curtiss. *Art Directors:* John B. Goodman & Abraham Grossman. *Set Decorators:* Russell A. Gausman & Leigh Smith. *Musical Director:* Frank Skinner. *Dialogue Director:* George Bricker. *Sound Director:* Bernard B. Brown. *Technician:* Jess Moulin. *Sound Editor:* Carl Elmendorf. *Makeup:* Jack P. Pierce. *Gowns:* Vera West.

Lon Chaney, Jr. (*Wayne Fletcher*), Brenda Joyce (*Donna Kincaid*), J. Edward Bromberg (*Julian Julian*), Rosalind Ivan (*Amelia Kincaid*), Clara Blandick (*Belle Kincaid*), George Cleveland (*Sam Kincaid*), Wilton Graff (*Capt. McCracken*), Bernard B. Thomas (*Bruce Malone*), J. Farrell MacDonald (*Sexton*), Victoria Horne (*Voice of Vivian Fletcher*), Harry Strang, Lee Phelps. *Deleted from final print:* Fern Emmett (*Mrs. Williams*), Arthur Hohl (*Mr. Williams*).

The must-miss movie of 1945.
—*Leonard Maltin's* Movies on TV

The final film in the Inner Sanctum series, *Pillow of Death* titillated postwar audiences with spiritualists, an alleged haunted house, spectral voices and, appropriately enough, in this series' last gasp, murder by suffocation. As had been the case in *Weird Woman* and *The Frozen Ghost*, the supernatural elements are counterfeit, and are exploited for the sole purpose of attracting horror fans. J. Edward Bromberg's cherubic seer is somewhat ambiguous. Although the police have made use of his gift of extrasensory perception in murder investigations, the séances he stages couldn't be phonier. The "phantom voice" of the killer's victim is written off in the end as nothing more than a guilt-inspired hallucination. All of the ingredients for a taut, even chilling melodrama are here, but *Pillow of Death* is so absurd and indifferently produced, it squanders any potential it may have had.

The stately home of wealthy Belle Kincaid (Clara Blandick) and her curmudgeon brother Sam (George Cleveland) is where most of the story's activity takes place. Belle, a student of the occult, consults regularly with psychic investigator Julian Julian (J. Edward Bromberg) to conjure up the spirits of long-dead Kincaids. When her niece Donna (Brenda Joyce) takes a romantic interest in her (Donna's) employer, attorney Wayne Fletcher (Lon Chaney, Jr.), Belle gets in touch with Fletcher's wife, Vivian, who's also an occultist.

Fed up with Vivian's devotion to metaphysics, and attracted to his secretary, Wayne decides to ask his wife for a divorce. Returning home after a late night at the office, Fletcher is met at the door by Capt. McCracken (Wilton Graff) and Julian. Vivian has been murdered; the cause of death is asphyxiation. Julian insists Vivian contacted him *after* she died: "She was that rare individual," Julian opines. "A natural medium for communication with the spirit world." When Wayne's alibi doesn't stand up under scrutiny, he is arrested, but is soon released on a writ of *habeas corpus*.

Despite Donna's objections, Belle and her cousin Amelia (Rosalind Ivan) stage a séance in an effort to reach Vivian's spirit. Wayne reluctantly attends. During the proceedings, a ghostly voice resembling Vivian's brands her husband as her murderer. Enraged by the accusation, Wayne discovers Bruce Malone (Bernard B. Thomas), Donna's persistent beau, hiding in the shadows, and accuses the young man of conspiring with Julian to frame him for murder.

Alone that night, Wayne is haunted by Vivian's voice (Victoria Horne). In a low-keyed, eerily effective set piece, Jerome Ash's camera follows a semi-hypnotized Fletcher into a local cemetery right up to Vivian's crypt. When her voice fades away, Wayne goes into hysterics. His anguished cries arouse the ire of the sexton (J. Farrell MacDonald), who insists that he leave the grounds at once.

The next morning, Amelia discovers Sam's body; he has been suffocated in the same manner as Vivian Fletcher. Wayne confesses to McCracken that he heard Vivian's voice. A check is made of the crypt, revealing that her body has been snatched.

Belle is the next victim of the mysterious Pillow Killer. Julian comes under McCracken's suspicion when the policeman learns that the seer was once a stage ventriloquist. He is taken into custody. Her mind unhinged by the Kincaid murders and Julian's incarceration, Amelia traps Wayne and Donna in a closet. She is about to pump it full of gas when Julian, whom Mc-

Cracken has released for lack of evidence, intervenes and saves the couple's lives.

Conducting their own investigation, Wayne and Donna stumble upon Vivian's corpse, hidden in the Kincaid cellar. Bruce appears and admits he stole the body in order to trick Fletcher into admitting his guilt.

Later that evening, Donna hears Wayne's voice coming from Sam's bedroom and investigates. She is horrified to find Fletcher holding an imagined "conversation" with Vivian. "Donna can't hear me, but she knows," Vivian's disembodied voice warns Wayne. "At last she realizes that you are a psychopathic killer. Isn't it too bad that you can't have her and all that Kincaid money, now that we are out of the way?"

At Vivian's prompting, Wayne attacks Donna and attempts to suffocate her with a bed pillow. McCracken and Bruce storm into the room and overpower him. Obeying his wife's instructions to follow her, the crazed attorney leaps out of the second-story window to his death.

Pity the staunch souls at the Breen Office who came into daily contact with scores of wretched scripts and producers just begging for their censorial approval. In the case of *Pillow of Death*, the Breen watchdogs kept a tight rein on the sex-violence elements of the story. In a January 3, 1945, letter to Universal editorial head Maurice Pivar, the Breen people emphasized their displeasure with the murderer's method of doing away with his victims on the grounds that it could be too easily imitated by the more impressionable viewer. Pointing out several lines of offensive dialogue ("Someone smothered her with a pillow while she dozed," "Then you put the pillow over my face and held it there"), the Breen Office recommended that the script be amended. As a result, all three murders committed by Wayne take place off-screen, thus satisfying the Breen Office if not thrill-seeking patrons. (A scene showing a pillow lying over the dead Sam Kincaid's face was also deemed unacceptable.)

The Breen Office deemed Wayne's "suicide" acceptable for the reason that he was crazed when he committed the act. Yet it really isn't a suicidal act; the "voice" of Vivian beckons her husband out the window to his death. The same ending caps the classic episode, "The Hungry Glass," of Universal's TV series *Thriller*, where William Shatner is beckoned to jump out the window by the ghost of his wife, floating in midair outside. In his deranged state of mind, Shatner (*à la* Chaney in *Pillow of Death*) doesn't realize that jumping out of the window will mean his end.

The allegedly adulterous relationship between Donna and Wayne also came under fire; producer Ben Pivar was instructed to "cool it" as much as possible. On January 8, the Breen Office sent the studio a follow-up letter, insisting that the italicized words in the following dialogue be eliminated from the script: "I'm going to do something *about us*," and "Don't *let your conscience* bother *you* about Vivian." The line "I'll be very gentle with the pillow" also had to go. (One can only speculate how the board of censors must have reacted to such intensely incendiary melodramas as *Double Indemnity* and *The Postman Always Rings Twice* if *Pillow of Death* got such a working over!) Pivar saw to it that the script alterations were made and, after a few more weeks of bellyaching, George Bricker's scenario was finally approved. The Breen people, however, got in one last dig, expressing apprehension as to how political censor boards may react to the film, particularly the *modus operandi* of the killer.

Director Wallace Fox began shooting the first scenes of *Pillow of Death* on February 26, 1945, just two weeks after production wrapped on *Strange Confession*. Fox shot the eerie cemetery-crypt scene outside the Shelby home, while the Hacienda set was used for the exterior of the Kincaid mansion. Once again, the old *Phantom of the Opera* Stage was pressed into service for various interior shots. A labor strike on the lot held up production for a few days, causing *Pillow of Death* to wrap on March 13, two days beyond the allotted 12-day schedule.

The brother of actor-director-producer Edwin Carewe, Wallace Fox's long career dates back to the early '20s. Although his directing and producing credits lean heavily towards run-of-the-mill B-Westerns and vintage television (*Annie Oakley*, *The Gene Autry Show*, *Ramar of the Jungle*), three exceptions stand out: *Pillow of Death* and a pair of Bela Lugosi shockers, both released by Monogram in 1942, *The Corpse Vanishes* and *Bowery at Midnight*. While not nearly as abysmal as the pictures Bela made for Ed

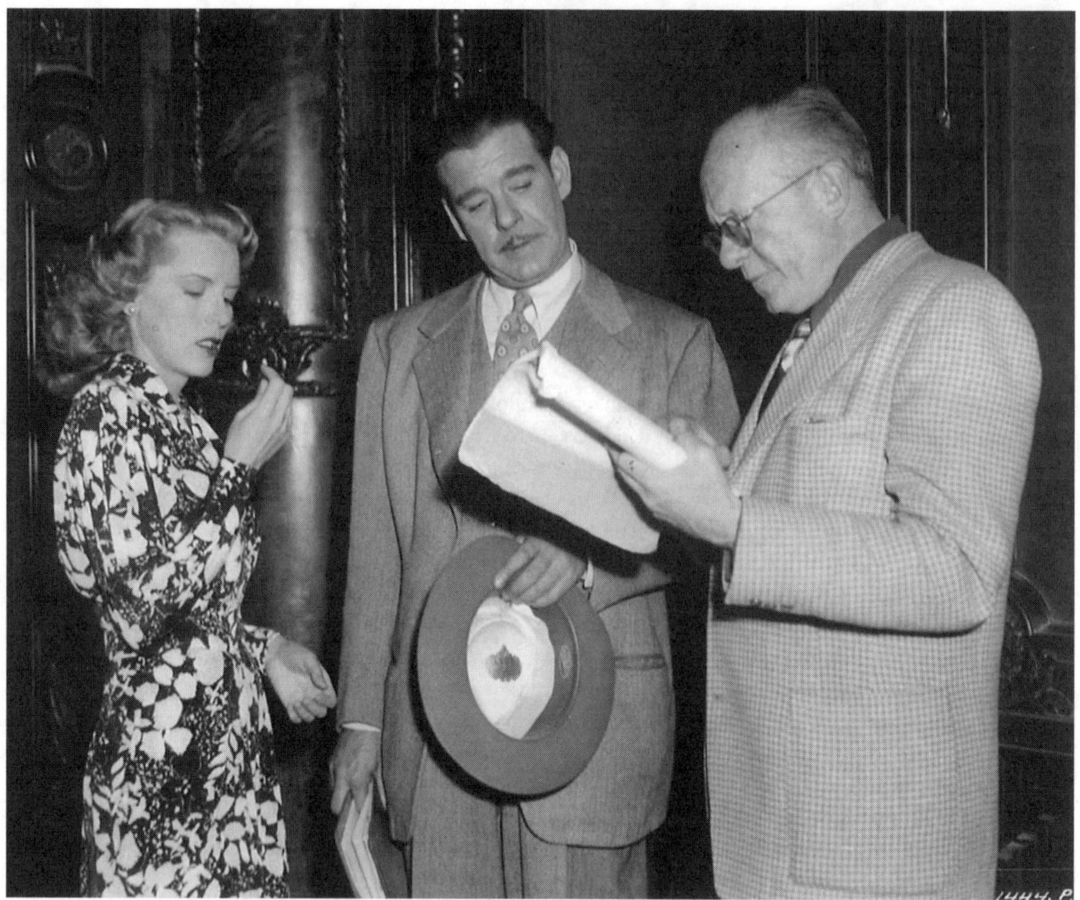

Lon Chaney, Jr., and Brenda Joyce are briefed before stepping in front of the cameras on the set of *Pillow of Death*.

Wood, these bottom-drawer penny dreadfuls with their deliriously over-the-top storylines and no-holds-barred theatrics, rank a close second.

Assigned to portray Chaney's ill-fated wife Vivian, Victoria Horne suffered the ultimate indignity for an actress: Her entire performance ended up on the cutting room floor. Bricker's screenplay had called for Horne to play host to fellow occultists Arthur Hohl and Fern Emmett in a scene that was later scrapped. The fact that the actress spent a day working closely with John P. Fulton is a good indication that Vivian Fletcher made at least one phantasmic appearance in the original script.

Asked by the authors if she could recollect any of her lost scenes in *Pillow of Death*, Horne recalled a quip made by her late actor-husband, Jack Oakie, at the time the picture was released: "Mommy dear," he said, "beauty is favored in motion pictures. That's why they put the camera on Lon Chaney and used only your voice."

Tediously paced and uninspired on every level, *Pillow of Death* pretty much encapsulates the chronic ailments that had stymied the Inner Sanctum series: A fairly intriguing tale demolished by ludicrous plotting, unbelievably bad dialogue, and aimless direction, with no effort to elevate the material above the level of Class B status. Worse yet, the films placed their most exploitable asset, Lon Chaney, Jr., at a disadvantage by putting him in roles unsuited to his working class persona.

With the possible exception of Fletcher's nocturnal prowl through the graveyard, and the surprise climax, all of the shock scenes fizzle. As mentioned previously, the mayhem occurs off-camera, for censorial reasons perhaps, but also to preserve the anonymity of the killer. It would have been intriguing to have the *camera* stalk each victim, as when Bela Lugosi smothered a servant in *Invisible Ghost* (1941) in subjective shots, but that effective little trick probably never occurred to Bricker nor Fox. Several sequences run far too long. In a vain attempt to build suspense and drive home the point that the Kincaid manse is infested with spirits, most of the cast shuffle up to the attic to investigate some strange sounds (rattling chains, weird guffaws, etc.); presumably it's the ghost of old Uncle Joe stirring up trouble again. After an interminable stretch, the source of the disturbance is revealed to be a mischievous raccoon!

The discovery of Belle Kincaid's corpse is arguably the worst shock scene ever staged for a Universal horror film. The scene opens in the corridor outside a suite of bedrooms. An off-pitch shriek of horror comes from behind a door. Amelia staggers out, announces that Belle has been murdered, and collapses into the arms of Donna and Julian (who is suffering from a bad case of "pillow head"). Just plain *awful*.

Pillow of Death dispenses with the seer-in-the-crystal-ball prologue and doesn't bother to reinstate Chaney's "stream of consciousness" asides (which had been previously abandoned in *Strange Confession*). For once, Chaney is actually *guilty* of the crimes of which he has been accused; we're not counting *Strange Confession*, as Chaney was the victim, driven to justifiable homicide. Wayne Fletcher murders his wife in cold blood, then slays Sam and Belle while acting on a psychopathic impulse, much as Bela Lugosi did in *Invisible Ghost*. Stilted throughout most of the movie, Chaney comes to life in the climax, assuming a Lennie-like *Of Mice and Men* stance as the authorities (and his own conscience) close in on him. Unfortunately, it's too little, too late. Contract player Chaney would have gotten his regular weekly salary — Universal charged to the production of *Pillow of Death* $10,000 for his services.

It was becoming the fashion at Universal during this period in the mid–'40s for the leading man to be unmasked as the culprit in question. In 1944's *Phantom Lady*, Ella Raines puts her life in jeopardy attempting to clear her boss Alan Curtis of murdering his wife. She seeks the aid of Curtis' good friend Franchot Tone, who turns out to be the real killer. Similarly, in the underrated Roy William Neill thriller *Black Angel* (1946), alcoholic pianist Dan Duryea helps June Vincent track down the murderer of his wife (whom Vincent's husband has been charged with killing), only to learn that he himself killed her in a drunken rage.

Unlike the average horror film heroine, Brenda Joyce is surprisingly unsympathetic as Donna; she's spoiled and self-centered, and expresses no outward remorse over having been at least indirectly responsible for the destruction of a marriage. And she doesn't act the least bit upset over the deaths of her aunt and uncle. Joyce was one of the actresses who replaced Maureen O'-Sullivan as Jane in the Johnny Weissmuller Tarzan movies being produced around this time by RKO-Radio studios.

The supporting characters in *Pillow of Death* are, for the most part, stagy and irritatingly eccentric. As the contentious Belle, Clara Blandick (Dorothy's Auntie Em in 1939's *The Wizard of Oz*) is a dour old crone with a one-sided disposition. On April 15, 1962, the aging actress, plagued by crippling arthritis and failing eyesight, took an overdose of sleeping pills, then (in homage to *Pillow of Death*, perhaps) tied a plastic bag around her head so that she'd die of asphyxiation. George Cleveland (Gramps of TV's *Lassie*) gets off a funny line or two as crusty old Sam Kincaid, whose only joy in life is appeasing his appetite. Bernard B. Thomas' snoopy next-door neighbor can be summed up in just one word: exasperating. If he isn't emerging from secret hiding places in the Kincaid house (he seems to know more about the layout of the place than the people who inhabit it), the callow youth is seen peering through windows, sneaking around corners, or making a general nuisance of himself. Bruce goes to any length to prove Fletcher's guilt — including stealing the corpse of the man's wife — for which he goes unpunished! To cap it off, the weasel gets the girl in the final clinch. On a more positive note, there's the formidable Rosalind Ivan, walking away with the acting honors as Amelia, a poor relation from England who is reduced to serving her family as a domestic after falling on hard times.

Whether he's attuning himself to metaphysical vibes or slipping into or out of psychic trances, J. Edward Bromberg's unctuous, overfed

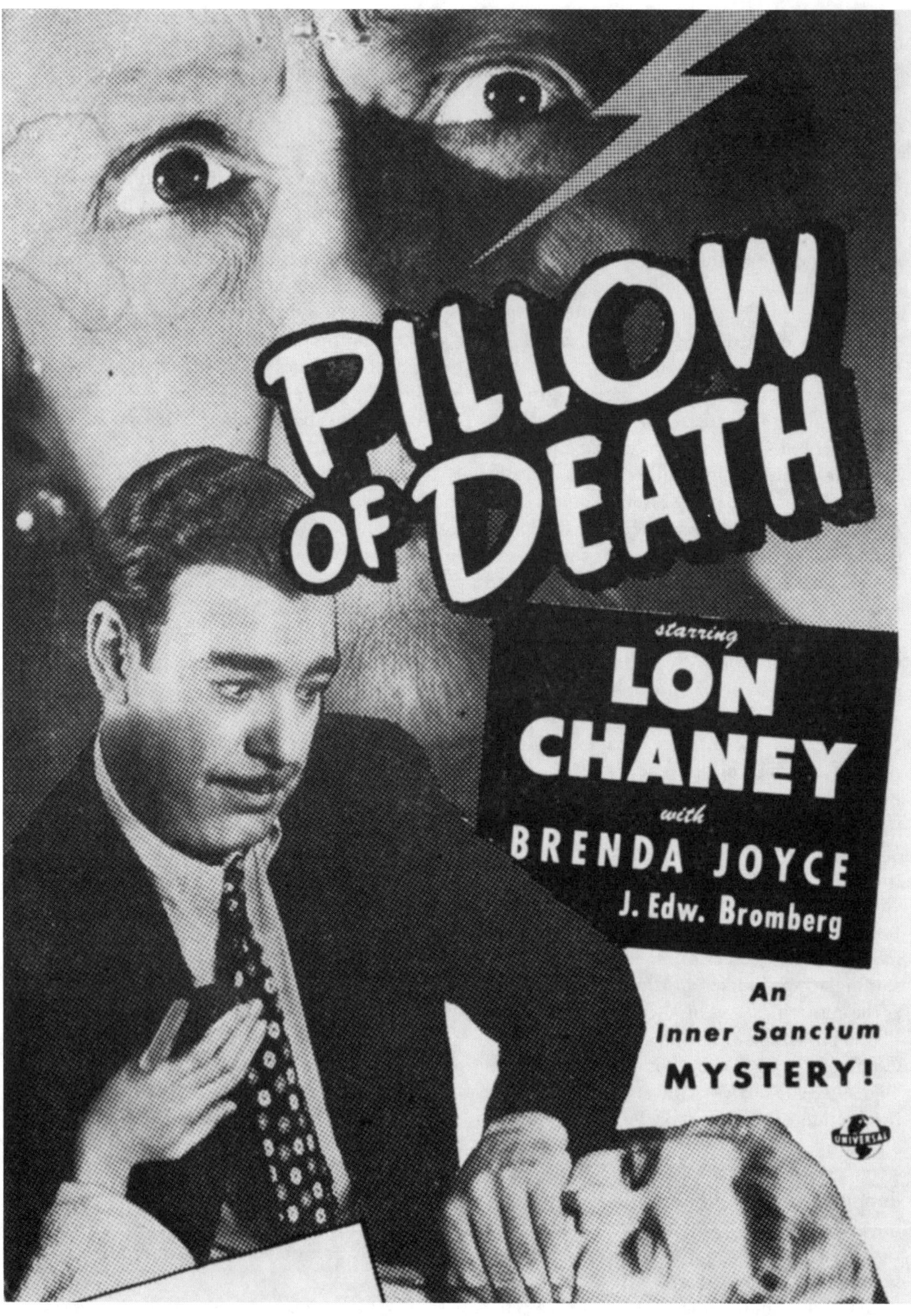

Atmospheric pressbook ad for the last of the Inner Sanctums.

Julian is disagreeably "odd." (Nils Asther invested infinitely more charm and suavity to a similar role in *Night Monster.*) Born abroad but raised in the Bronx, the actor began his career as a silk salesman, candy manufacturer and laundry worker. He studied acting under Leo Bulgakov of the Moscow Art Theater before landing two different parts in the Provincetown Theater production of "Princess Turandot." Bromberg joined the Group Theater and was part of Eva Le Gallienne's repertory company before establishing himself as a familiar character actor under the 20th Century–Fox banner in the late '30s. On occasion, the actor returned to the Broadway stage, most notably in the play "Jacobowsky and the Colonel" with Louis Calhern. Hounded by the McCarthy witch hunt posse, Bromberg suffered a fatal heart attack at the age of 47 on December 6, 1951, while appearing in the London stage production "The Biggest Thief in Town." Decades later, his son authored a book based on his father's life and premature death.

Pillow of Death predictably racked up more than its share of bad notices upon its release in December 1945 (it was double-billed with the all-star monster rally *House of Dracula* in many situations). The picture did garner at least *one* favorable review (from Jack D. Grant of the overly indulgent *Hollywood Reporter*), several lines of which bear repeating here:

> Few screen mysteries succeed in mystifying and by smartly turning just that trick *Pillow of Death* lifts itself out of the ordinary.... This offering is one of the better Inner Sanctum mysteries and owes much to the pace and movement maintained in the direction by Wallace Fox. There are also a number of top grade performances. Lon Chaney does a thoroughly believable job.

Makes you wonder if Mr. Grant saw the same picture as the rest of us.

Critics' Corner

It's an old plotline that Universal is pursuing with dogged earnestness and studied banality, so perhaps the charitable act ... would be to dismiss the subject without further ado.—*The New York Times*, January 26, 1946, Thomas M. Pryor

[N]ot much is left unexplained at the finale which really packs a punch.... [O]ne of the better Inner Sanctum mysteries....—*The Hollywood Reporter*, December 11, 1945, Jack D. Grant

Rating: ★½ There's more stimulation in a cup of coffee than in Rialto's newest bid for chills—and coffee's cheaper.... [J. Edward] Bromberg is supposed to look suspicious and mysterious, which he manages rather badly.—*The New York Daily News*, January 26, 1946, Dorothy Masters

It may serve as a supporting feature in theatres whose audiences like chilling murder mystery stories, regardless of whether or not they make any sense.—*Harrison's Reports*, December 15, 1945

1946

Terror by Night

Released February 1, 1946. 60 minutes. *Producer-Director:* Roy William Neill. *Executive Producer:* Howard Benedict. *Screenplay:* Frank Gruber. *Adapted from a story by* Sir Arthur Conan Doyle. *Photography:* Maury Gertsman. *Editor:* Saul A. Goodkind. *Musical Director:* Milton Rosen. *Art Directors:* John B. Goodman & Abraham Grossman. *Set Decorators:* Russell A. Gausman & Carl Lawrence. *Assistant Director:* Melville Shyer. *Dialogue Director:* Raymond Kessler. *Sound Director:* Bernard B. Brown. *Technician:* Jack A. Bolger, Jr. *Makeup:* Jack P. Pierce. *Hair Stylist:* Carmen Dirigo. *Gowns:* Vera West.

Basil Rathbone (*Sherlock Holmes*), Nigel Bruce (*Dr. John H. Watson*), Alan Mowbray (*Maj. Duncan-Bleek/Col. Sebastian Moran*), Dennis Hoey (*Insp. Lestrade*), Renee Godfrey (*Vivian Vedder*), Frederic Worlock (*Prof. William Kilbane*), Mary Forbes (*Lady Margaret Carstairs*), Skelton Knaggs (*Sands*), Billy Bevan (*Train Attendant*), Geoffrey Steele (*Roland Carstairs*), Leyland Hodgson (*Train Conductor*), Boyd Davis (*Insp. McDonald*), Janet Murdoch (*Mrs. Shallcross*), Gerald Hamer (*Alfred Shallcross*), Harry Cording (*Mock*), Bobby Wissler (*Mock Jr.*), Charles Knight (*Guard*), Gilbert Allen (*Steward*), Colin Kenny (*Constable*), Tom Pilkington (*Baggage Car Attendant*).

I think what Roy William Neill did with *Terror by Night* ... was remarkable.
—*Michael A. Hoey, movie producer and son of Dennis Hoey*

The placid shipboard intrigues of *Pursuit to Algiers* paved the way for this second, far superior mystery-in-motion, *Terror by Night.* Set aboard a roaring express train, this eleventh entry in the waning Sherlock Holmes series has a locale every bit as claustrophobic as its predecessor's, but it skillfully overcomes this handicap through savvy editing, taut direction by the accomplished Roy William Neill, and a story that keeps moving. Tailored to a compact 60 minutes, *Terror by Night* is rhythmically paced and wastes little time reaching its destination.

The concise screenplay was written by Frank Gruber, a prolific writer of pulp fiction since 1927. Gruber's screenwriting credits eventually rivaled his literary output in terms of volume. (Westerns and action dramas were his specialty, but his most significant credit was the 1944 adaptation of Eric Ambler's novel *The Mask of Dimitrios,* a dark, somber Warner Bros. drama starring Peter Lorre, Sydney Greenstreet and Zachary Scott.) In *Terror by Night,* Gruber spices up a banal fabulous-jewel-heist theme with several interesting touches — the express train setting (first and foremost), an air pistol that shoots poisonous darts, a Creeper-like henchman who obviously relishes his work and, best of all, the architect of the heist, an old protagonist of Sherlock Holmes, Prof. Moriarity's second-in-command, Col. Sebastian Moran. Adding to the fun are the other passengers, an oddball collection of Brits and Scots enacted by the cream of the series stock company.

Holmes (Basil Rathbone) and Watson (Nigel Bruce) are commissioned to protect one of the world's most famous jewels, the Star of Rhodesia, on a rail journey from London to Edinburgh. As in 1944's *The Pearl of Death,* this jewel also has a bloodstained heritage. Its current owner, the haughty Lady Margaret Carstairs (Mary Forbes), has the precious stone taken right out from under her nose by the detective's sleight-of-hand (Holmes replaces it with a counterfeit).

Lady Margaret's son Roland (Geoffrey Steele) is found murdered in their compartment. Though there are no visible signs of foul play, Holmes deduce that Carstairs has been poisoned. The imposter jewel is missing from its case. Insp. Lestrade (Dennis Hoey), also on board, launches an investigation in his typically stumbling manner. With the aid of an old school chum, Maj. Duncan-Bleek (Alan Mowbray) of the Twelfth Indian Lancers, Watson sets out to ensnare the guilty party.

Holmes detects certain similarities between this robbery and others in his experience and determines that it was perpetrated by Col. Sebastian Moran, "the most sinister, ruthless and diabolically clever henchman of our late and unlamented friend, Professor Moriarity. His specialty was spectacular jewel robberies." Though Holmes has never met the colonel face to face, he's nearly met death at his hands on three different occasions. The colonel takes another crack at eliminating Holmes by having his diminutive henchman push the detective out of the speeding train. Holmes struggles to maintain his grip on the door as his assailant (whose features are obscured) tries to dislodge him. Seconds before the roaring train enters a tunnel, Holmes kicks through a window and unlocks the latch. First-rate editing, dizzying camera shots of rushing landscapes, and an accompanying musical cue from the oft-used *Son of Frankenstein* score, contribute to the tension.

A stooped figure emerges once more from a false-bottom coffin in the baggage compartment. It is Moran's underling Sands (Skelton Knaggs). He enters Duncan-Bleek's compartment and addresses the jovial Englishman as Col. Moran! The pair quietly sneaks into Lestrade's compartment and conveniently finds him examining the real gem. Sands knocks the inspector unconscious and picks up the precious stone, but is immediately shot dead by Moran with an air pistol.

Insp. McDonald (Boyd Davis) of the Edinburgh Police and his men board the train and arrogantly take charge. A brief interrogation of Duncan-Bleek convinces the inspector he is indeed Moran. But before McDonald can take him into custody, Moran grabs a revolver and holds everyone at bay. Watson overpowers his "old chum" with a swift blow from behind, and, in the ensuing struggle in the dark, Moran is apparently bagged and dragged from the train by McDonald and his men.

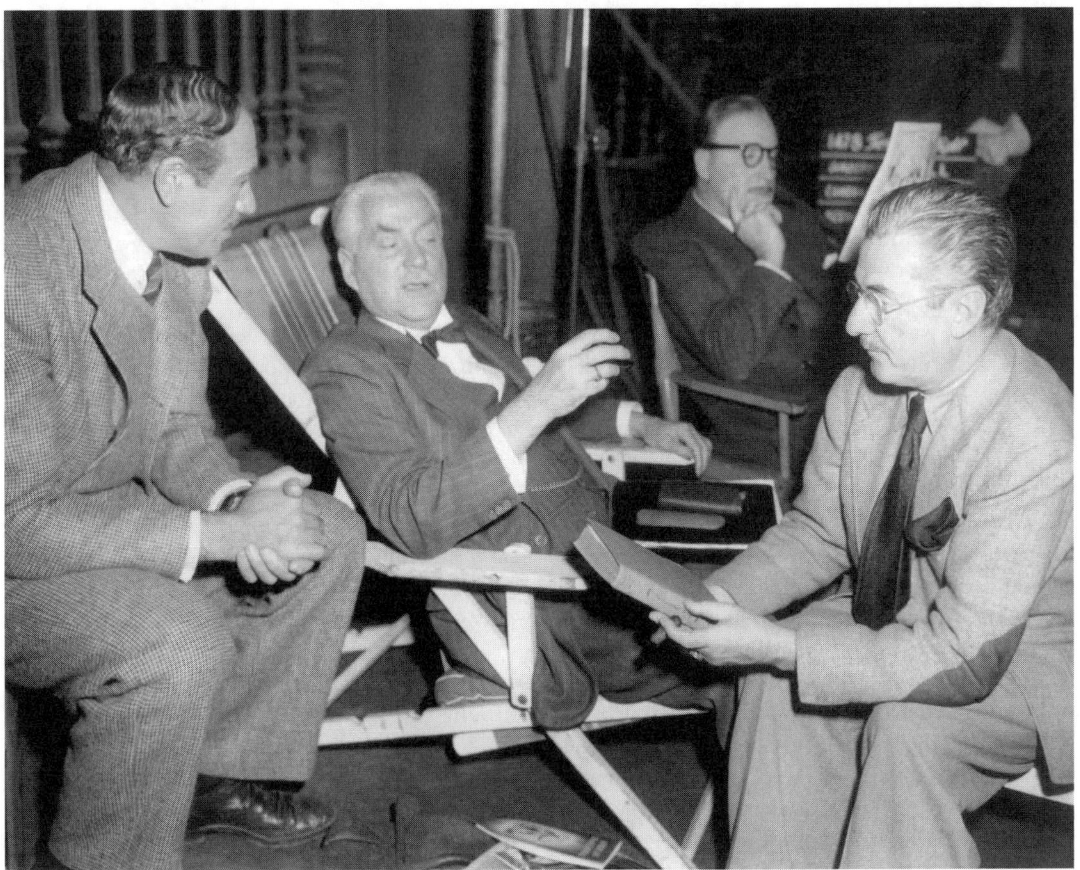

Rare on-the-set shot of *Terror by Night* director Roy William Neill (far right) with Dennis Hoey, Nigel Bruce and Alan Mowbray (courtesy Photofest).

Much to Watson's surprise, Moran hasn't been taken off the train after all, but lies, disarmed, in an adjoining seat. Holmes explains that McDonald and his men were imposters, summoned to rescue their leader. Lestrade surprisingly grasped the situation and, during the fight, pulled his coat over his head, tricking the phony policemen into thinking he was the colonel. Outside on the train platform, Lestrade reveals his identity and carts "McDonald" and the other members of Moran's gang off to the station house. The Star of Rhodesia, now stained with the blood of several more victims, is reclaimed.

Under the guidance of the unit's executive producer, Howard Benedict, *Terror by Night* went into production in October 1945. The belt-tightening practices so prevalent in the past few Holmes adventures is even more evident here: The film borrows extensively from the studio's library of stock shots of bustling train stations (including a stock shot or two borrowed from 1933's *Rome Express* that was also used in 1934's *The Black Cat*), speeding locomotives and barren landscapes fading into the distance. Nevertheless, these nifty bits of celluloid, inserted into the new footage by former serial director-turned-film editor Saul A. Goodkind, provide the narrative with a sense of urgency, and doubtlessly perk up what could have been a static presentation.

Terror by Night shares some basic similarities with its immediate predecessor, *Pursuit to Algiers*. Both stories are set on modes of transportation that inspire mystery and intrigue. Deception plays an important role in both pictures (here, Holmes substitutes a phony jewel; in *Pursuit to Algiers*, a phony prince). Lastly, the villains in both films are, on the surface, genteel, cultivated gentlemen who leave the dirty work to their seedy toadies.

Red herrings are found in almost every Sherlock Holmes movie. In *Terror by Night*, we have an interesting lot. There's Vivian Vedder (Renee Godfrey, the wife of director Peter Godfrey), barely concealing her Cockney origins behind a veneer of respectability, who is supposedly escorting her mother's body to Scotland for burial. Holmes unmasks her as an accomplice of Col. Moran; the coffin she brought on board has a secret compartment that concealed Sands.

The passenger list also includes a cantankerous mathematics professor named William Kilbane (Frederic Worlock). Holmes recalls that Col. Moran is known to be an aficionado of the subject, but this amounts to a false lead. Nigel Bruce and Worlock have a wonderful scene wherein the "ever helpful" Watson attempts to interrogate the grouchy prof, only to have the tables turned when the defensive Kilbane accuses *Watson* of the crime and has the bumbling medico pleading his innocence. Another amusing bit has Watson probing into the affairs of the mild-mannered Shallcross couple (Janet Murdoch and the dependable Gerald Hamer). When Mr. Shallcross reluctantly confesses to having committed the theft, the triumphant Watson calls in Holmes and Lestrade, only to wither with embarrassment when the item *they* stole turns out to be a teapot nabbed from a tourist hotel.

Alan Mowbray delivers a smooth performance as Moriarity's trusted successor. He is quite above suspicion throughout, indulging in flighty banter with Watson, even taking a stab at solving the mystery himself. But, once his cover is blown, he is as treacherous as any of Holmes' previous arch-rivals. (As in *Sherlock Holmes and the Voice of Terror*, the gullible Watson is [rather implausibly] duped into believing yet another imposter is a friend from his halcyon days.) Despite Mowbray's belated villainous turn, one comes away from *Terror by Night* with the impression that so infamous a character as Col. Sebastian Moran ought to have been given the same "royal treatment" (in terms of production value) afforded the likes of Prof. Moriarity, Adrea Spedding and Giles Conover. Mowbray was no stranger to the world of Arthur Conan Doyle. A veteran of hundreds of films and television shows, the portly performer essayed the role of Inspector Lestrade in 1933's *A Study in Scarlet*, and had a supporting role as a Scotland Yard man disapproving of the Baker Street sleuth in the 1932 Fox film *Sherlock Holmes*. In the last years of his life, Mowbray found himself in a role not to his liking: the father-in-law of Douglass Dumbrille, his close friend and fellow movie villain, who took Mowbray's young daughter as his wife, despite Mowbray's objections.

As Col. Moran's ill-fated backstabber, Skelton Knaggs is slime personified. The emaciated English actor, a former Shakespearean mime, is a familiar pockmarked face in many '40s horror films. Apart from his Universal credits, he was also seen to gruesome advantage in such genre works as *The Lodger* (1944), *The Picture of Dorian Gray* (1945), *Dick Tracy Meets Gruesome* (1947), *Master Minds* (1949) and the Val Lewton trio, *The Ghost Ship* (1943), *Isle of the Dead* (1945) and *Bedlam* (1946). Knaggs died at a youthful age of cirrhosis of the liver in 1955.

Terror by Night was the swan song of series stalwart Dennis Hoey as Inspector Lestrade (although he did play the character on the radio series with Rathbone and Bruce for about a year of its run). Always a day late and a dollar short, the short-sighted police official was the perfect foil for the brilliant detective, and Hoey captured the character's smug superiority and thick-headedness to perfection. The London-born actor planned to make teaching his avocation but his excellent singing voice made him a natural for the stage. Hoey's first professional appearance was in the 1919 play "Shanghai." He scored a success in the role of Ali Ben Ali in the London production of "The Desert Song." In the mid–'20s, Hoey came to America to co-star on Broadway in two musical operettas.

Hoey's motion picture debut, the 1927 silent movie *Tiptoes* with Dorothy Gish and Will Rogers, was filmed on his home soil. Then followed a decade of featured appearances in numerous "quota quickies," British films financed by American movie companies in order for *their* Hollywood films to be allowed to play in English theaters. Among these low-budget quickies were 1936's *Mystery of the Mary Celeste* with Bela Lugosi (Hammer's first chiller) and *The Murder in the Red Barn* starring the flamboyant British horror star Tod Slaughter. The strangest film of the lot however was 1936's *Uncivilised.* Shot in Queensland, Australia, it featured the

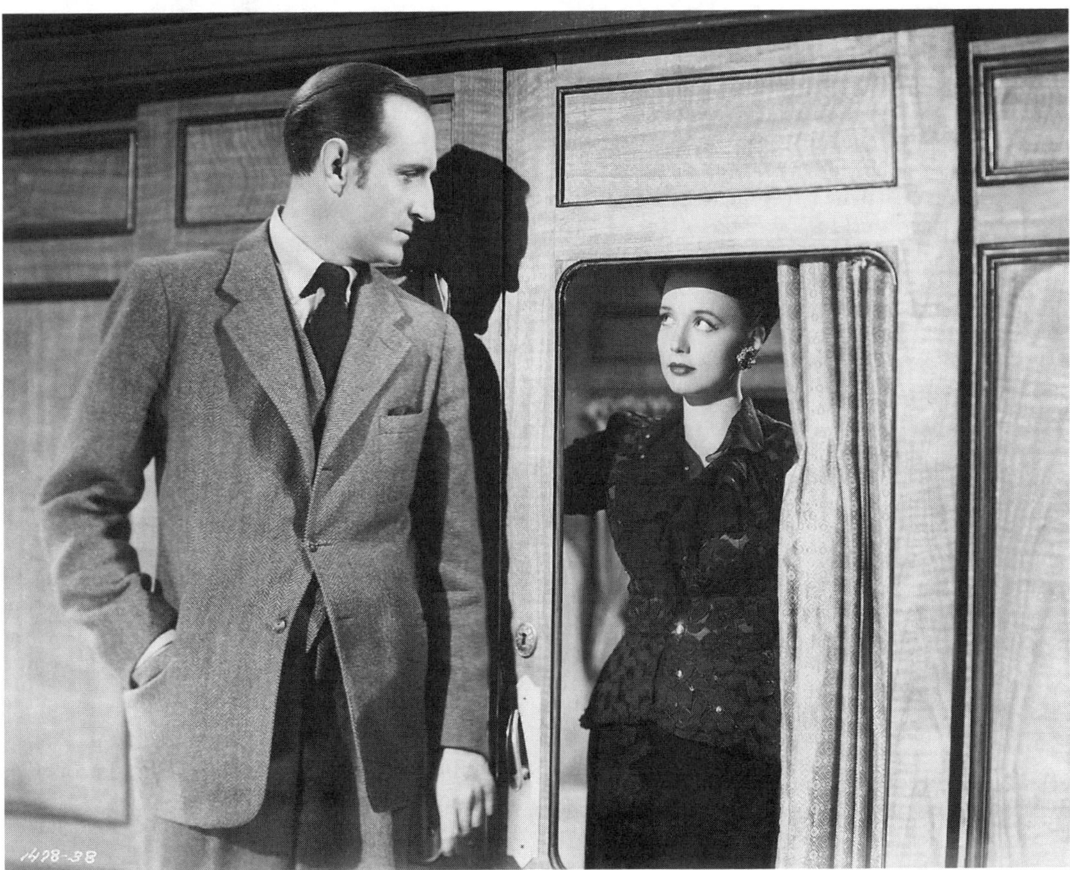

The mysterious Vivian Vedder (Renee Godfrey) is just one of the red herrings in *Terror by Night* with Basil Rathbone as Sherlock Holmes.

urbane Hoey as a bare-chested white jungle man named Mara who is the leader of an aboriginal tribe.

Hoey's son, filmmaker Michael A. Hoey, provided us with some interesting insights about his dad's return to America in the early '40s. "We came over just about the time the War was starting, and I think a couple of things combined to bring us over: *One* was that he had an offer to appear in a play on Broadway, and *two,* he saw the storm clouds brewing [over Europe]. We lived in New York for about four, five years. He was quite successful—he toured with Katharine Hepburn in a Theater Guild production of "Jane Eyre," playing Rochester. But she found [the play] "The Philadelphia Story" during the tour, and she decided she'd rather take that to Broadway than "Jane Eyre." Who knows what effect [being on Broadway in "Jane Eyre"] might have had on his career! At any rate, he got a lot of notice and offers, and I guess when they played in Los Angeles, he decided it was time to come out here. That was around the beginning of 1941. And he started working immediately, playing Englishmen.

> My father's first assignment in a Hollywood picture was a small scene in 20th Century–Fox's *A Yank in the R.A.F.* [1941]. He had a good run in Hollywood, as many as seven pictures a year. That was terrific in those days, and nowadays it would be *impossible* for an actor to get that many films a year. He was very well-known at 20th Century–Fox and did a number of films there in the early to mid–40s: In addition to *A Yank in the R.A.F.*, he was in two other Tyrone Power films, *Son of Fury* and *This Above All* [both 1942]; in *Bomber's Moon* and *They Came to Blow Up America* [both 1943] he played German officers. Fox director Henry King liked him a lot, and so did John Cromwell, who directed him in *Son of Fury* and *Anna and the King of Siam* [1946].

Michael continued:

> [M]y father got very typecast at Universal. My dad was on a non-exclusive contract to Universal, playing Lestrade. They only used him in two or three other [non–Holmes] pictures — but his character in those other pictures was, like, always Lestrade, even though they might have called him by another name! In *Frankenstein Meets the Wolf Man*, he plays a Scotland Yard inspector and even wore the same bloody wardrobe — Lestrade's bowler hat and the raincoat! Then he did a film called *She-Wolf of London* and it was the same thing, a Scotland Yard inspector, only at least he was not wearing the same clothes in *that* one.
>
> My father was still interested in writing and directing, and in fact wrote a story about the famous Drury Lane Ghost which supposedly haunts that London theater. He wrote a treatment which he thought he could sell to Universal for the Sherlock Holmes series. It would have been a natural but, unfortunately, his timing was off; by the time he did this, they were sort of winding down the series.... Then in 1946 he came up with a book by Anthony Gilbert, adapted it into a play, took it back to New York, and actually got some producers interested in it. The play, which was called "The Haven," was a "living room mystery": one set, five or six characters. He didn't direct it, he hired someone else to do that, but he *did* play the lead.... It should have been a hit. It was a ... well, it was a bomb [*laughs*]. It lasted about five performances, and then it closed.... Ironically, only a year or two later, there was an *enormous* success on Broadway called "An Inspector Calls" by J.B. Priestley, which was in effect the same idea. But there was a much more philosophical bent to the story, it wasn't just a straight murder mystery.

As to why his father retired prematurely from acting, Michael Hoey commented,

> He left Hollywood because he remarried — he married a woman of some wealth, I must say! A woman who lived in New York, and also had a home in Tampa, Florida. He continued to work in New York through (I would guess) around the mid–'50s. Someone sent me ... an [episode of TV's] *Omnibus* that was done around '56, a study of the great detectives of literature [and in it] they had my father play Sir Arthur Conan Doyle, which I thought was kind of fun.

Dennis Hoey passed away in the Sunshine State on July 25, 1960.

Terror by Night rates high marks in Michael Hoey's book, particularly the cleverly inventive way Roy Neill and his team overcame the cramped setting:

> They probably just had the one train corridor set and one or two compartment sets and a dining car, but [Neill] made it look so real that you never for a moment stopped believing that you were on a moving train throughout the entire film. The other thing I love is the opening montage of preparation, as they're getting ready to leave Euston Station. You see the coal being loaded on board the locomotive, you see baggage going into the baggage car, you see the food being brought on for the dining car and you see the passengers getting on board. *Murder on the Orient Express* [1974] opens with *exactly* the same montage. I don't want to say they stole it, but they were *influenced* by what they must have seen in this Sherlock Holmes film because it's almost shot for shot, the same idea. The music is building and driving, and as the train is getting ready to leave the station you get this sense of immediacy and excitement. Then Watson is late getting there, the train is pulling out before Watson suddenly shows up, and he has to jump on board. It was all very exciting, it got the feeling of motion going. It's the shortest of the Holmes films, but in my opinion it's probably the best one.

A minor entry to be sure, *Terror by Night* combines all of the right ingredients in properly measured doses and emerges as a better-than-average, late-in-the-game Sherlock Holmes entry. As in the case of two of its predecessors, *Sherlock Holmes and the Secret Weapon* and *The Woman in Green*, the black-and-white film fell victim to the colorization craze of the late '80s. Worse yet, an avalanche of dupey public domain prints made the rounds of local cable stations across the country. But thanks to the advances made in film restoration over the past decade, *Terror by Night* and the other titles in the Universal Holmes series can be savored in all their glory once again.

Critics' Corner

The latest criminal doings involving Sherlock Holmes and Dr. Watson have been poorly conceived and only loosely put together.... [T]he plot is nearly suspenseless and there is a great lack of imagination in the direction.... [T]he modern Sherlock Holmes has rarely sunk to lower levels of excitement.... — *The New York Herald-Tribune*, February 9, 1946, Otis L. Guernsey, Jr.

[T]he action is pretty exciting and, for the most part, mystifying. — *Harrison's Reports*, January 26, 1946

There is not a great deal of difference between one Sherlock Holmes film and the next, but the little there is weighs in favor of *Terror by Night*. That is because this episode ... is told in a tight continuity and with flavorsome atmosphere.... Obviously, Hitchcock's *The Lady Vanishes* inspired the author of the script, but that's not a bad inspiration.—*The New York Times*, February 9, 1946, Bosley Crowther

Rating: ★★½ [A] little more exciting than most Sherlock Holmes murder mysteries. And it's just as amusing as most of them but less believable if one must be analytical.—*The New York Daily News*, February 9, 1946, Wanda Hale

The Spider Woman Strikes Back

Released March 22, 1946. 59 minutes. *Director:* Arthur Lubin. *Producer:* Howard Welsch. *Original Screenplay:* Eric Taylor. *Photography:* Paul Ivano. *Cameraman:* William Dodds. *Editor:* Ray Snyder. *Assistant Director:* Fred Frank. *Art Directors:* John B. Goodman & Abraham Grossman. *Musical Director:* Milton Rosen. *Set Decorators:* Russell A. Gausman & Ralph Warrington. *Dialogue Director:* Joan Hathaway. *Sound Director:* Bernard B. Brown. *Technician:* Robert Pritchard. *Makeup:* Jack P. Pierce. *Hair Stylist:* Carmen Dirigo. *Gowns:* Vera West.

Gale Sondergaard (*Zenobia Dollard*), Brenda Joyce (*Jean Kingsley*), Kirby Grant (*Hal Wentley*), Milburn Stone (*Commissioner Moore*), Rondo Hatton (*Mario*), Hobart Cavanaugh (*Bill Stapleton*), Guy Wilkerson (*Lem*), Norman Leavitt (*Tom*), Horace Murphy (*Angry Older Rancher*), Hans Herbert (*Angry German Rancher*), Guy Beach, Bill Sundholm. *Deleted from final print:* Ruth Robinson (*Mrs. Wentley*), Adda Gleason (*Martha*), Lois Austin (*Jinnie Hawks*), Tom Daly (*Sam Julian*), Eula Guy (*Molly Corvin*), Eva Mudge.

Mistress of Menace!
—*Poster blurb for* The Spider Woman Strikes Back

The Spider Woman Strikes Back has attained the status of a camp classic over the years. This lurid little B boasts sinister seductress Gale Sondergaard at her deliciously wicked best, Rondo Hatton as a deaf mute in cahoots with the lethal lady and a rubbery subtropical plant with papier-mâché leaves that subsists on spiders and human blood, and goes by the vampiric-sounding name of Drochenema.

Actually, *The Spider Woman Strikes Back* is no worse than the average shocker released in this particularly dismal period, the tail-end of the second great horror cycle. It's slow-paced and repetitious (giving one the impression that it runs longer than its trifling 59 minutes), and the story is trite and silly, with more than its share of absurd dialogue (a few lines would have done George Bricker and M. Coates Webster proud). Still, *The Spider Woman Strikes Back* doesn't merit the scathing reactions it has gotten over the years from Gale Sondergaard and its director Arthur Lubin, who, deep into his golden years, had all but forgotten he had made the picture!

When Universal decided to launch a Spider Woman series in March 1945, with Ford Beebe acting as both associate producer and director, it would have been safe to assume that the studio planned to revive the Adrea Spedding character from 1944's *The Spider Woman*. Sondergaard played the part to the hilt, and turned out to be one of Sherlock Holmes' worthier adversaries. And the climax of *The Spider Woman*, with Adrea Spedding marching off to Scotland Yard in the custody of Insp. Lestrade, fairly cried out for a sequel—with or without Mr. Holmes' participation. But this promising prospect was not meant to be. Beebe was soon relieved of the assignment; his duties as a producer were assumed by Howard Welsch while Arthur Lubin (who happened to be in-between film projects) was handed the directorial reins.

In late May, Gale Sondergaard flew in after an Eastern hospital tour to begin preparations for *The Spider Woman Strikes Back*. She ought to have saved herself the trouble, as production was delayed for over four months (possibly, script alterations were made during this period which may have resulted in the elimination of Adrea Spedding and any reference to the Sherlock Holmes adventure). Shooting finally began on October 1 with the Providencia Ranch and the Shelby Home figuring prominently in the plot's action. Complying with the urgings of the Breen Office, Lubin minimized the picture's grislier aspects. The fiery deaths of Sondergaard and Hatton were staged so as not to suggest suicide. The final scenes were shot on October 18, three days over schedule.

Jean Kingsley (Brenda Joyce) arrives in the small Nevada cattle farming community of Domingo (population: a patriotic 1492) to act as companion to wealthy Zenobia Dollard (Gale Sondergaard). Zenobia had lost her vision after a visit to South America. Jean is driven out to the

Rondo Hatton and Gale Sondergaard, up to their necks in villainy in *The Spider Woman Strikes Back.*

Dollard estate by local rancher Hal Wentley (Kirby Grant), a former beau, who can't speak highly enough of the philanthropic Zenobia. (Had we not known in advance that Zenobia is the title menace, all of this adoration would have definitely aroused our suspicions.)

At the candlelit Dollard home, Jean meets Zenobia's manservant Mario (Rondo Hatton), a deformed deaf mute. In a well-executed shot, the blind woman enters the dimly lit parlor from the shadows. Zenobia's kindliness puts Jean at ease; she has Mario bring the tired young woman a glass of warm milk. Jean drinks it and retires for the evening.

It doesn't take long for Jean to discover that something foul is afoot. A letter arrives at the house for Betty Sanders, Zenobia's former companion, who purportedly left her employer on short notice to get married. When Jean sends her predecessor a letter, it is returned by the post office: Betty's current whereabouts are a mystery. Jean's health takes a sudden turn. She is plagued by headaches and loss of appetite and awakens each morning drawn of strength.

The cause of Jean's problems soon becomes apparent: Zenobia has been drugging her milk and then, after Jean retires, withdrawing a considerable amount of blood from her veins. In her basement laboratory, Zenobia nurses huge carnivorous plants; brought in from South America, they resemble oversized Venus flytraps, with wavy tendrils and hungry blossoms. By feeding the specimens a diet of live spiders and human blood, Zenobia is able to distill from the plants an elusive poison that she has been using to eliminate the cattle belonging to the local ranchers.

After a child becomes ill and dies from drinking milk taken from the poisoned livestock, panic-stricken farmers, fearing financial ruin, begin to desert Domingo. Hal calls in Commissioner Moore (Milburn Stone) of the U.S. Department of Agriculture to investigate the area for poison weeds.

Becoming increasingly suspicious of Zenobia and Mario, Jean observes the blind woman alone in the dining room and catches sight of her feeding a spider an ensnared moth. Realizing Jean knows the truth about her feigned blindness, Zenobia plans to add the young woman to her list of victims.

Introducing Jean to her lethal specimens, Zenobia brags of her scheme to reclaim the land once belonging to the Dollard family of farmers. "The poison from Drochenema's beautiful flowers leaves no trace. Feed it, Jean, let it drink," she says, handing the woman a vial of blood. "With your own strength, you've made it strong. You're going to die, Jean, like the others. But it won't be really dying, because you'll live on in this beautiful plant."

Discovering that Hal and Moore are on to her, Zenobia orders Mario to destroy all of the evidence. Within moments, the lab is transformed into a raging inferno. Mario tries to save Zenobia, who has become entangled in the plants' tendrils; both perish in the flames. Hal is able to get Jean out of harm's way seconds before the house is leveled by explosions.

An examination of Eric Taylor's screenplay reveals additional scenes that don't appear in the final cut of *The Spider Woman Strikes Back*. It is a good bet that these episodes were actually filmed, not just discarded from the script prior to the start of production, as the main title credits list five players who don't turn up in the film. Universal historian Michael Fitzgerald once spotted in *The Big Reel* an ad for a 16mm print of this movie that purportedly included "footage not in the TV versions." Is it possible that there exists out there in lost footage limbo an unabridged print containing scintillating sequences featuring Ruth Robinson, Adda Gleason and Eula Guy? The possibility is extremely remote: Unless footage was censored at the time pictures such as *Frankenstein* and *Dracula* were theatrically released, Screen Gems had no reason to tamper with the prints in their inventory, especially a title as inconsequential as *The Spider Woman Strikes Back*.

Based on a reading of the screenplay, the deletion of these episodes was a good idea; most of them are thuddingly repetitive and would have slowed down the pace of an already well-padded movie. Several of these scenes feature townspeople extolling Zenobia's virtues while others concern Hal's efforts to dispel Jean's suspicions toward her new employer. When a little boy dies after drinking the poisoned milk, the saintly Zenobia sends the family a check for $100 to cover funeral expenses! Jean complains to Hal about strange tapping sounds coming from inside her closet; he dismisses them as probably the result of a faulty ventilator. One little episode that's missing from the final cut would have *improved* the story's continuity. After Jean learns that Zenobia is feigning blindness, she rushes up to her room and starts to pack. Suddenly the whole door frame of her closet moves slowly inward. Zenobia appears from out of the shadows; Jean screams and faints. When she awakens, Jean finds herself in the laboratory, held prisoner by the Spider Woman and her loyal manservant. Curiously, the film's cheery coda does not appear in the script (which concludes with Hal and Jean fleeing the exploding Dollard estate).

The Spider Woman Strikes Back was for years a thorn in Gale Sondergaard's side. She eventually resigned herself to the film's notoriety and her intimate association with the role with a keen sense of humor. She told an interviewer:

> They thought they would do a series starring me as the Spider Woman and it had nothing to do with the other one. Well, I almost had hysterics at one time out of just hating it so, I remember. It came out, and people still talk about it, think it's great. And I'm all right.... I've seen it, and it isn't anything to be ashamed of, but I didn't like it when I did it.

Gale Sondergaard's career did indeed survive her starring turn in *The Spider Woman Strikes Back*. She was cast in 20th Century–Fox's lavish non-musical version of *The King and I, Anna and the King of Siam*, in the role of Lady Thiang, released that same year, and was once again recognized by the Academy of Motion Picture Arts and Sciences with a nomination in the category of Best Supporting Actress. She ultimately lost the Oscar to Anne Baxter for her performance as the tragic Sophie in *The Razor's Edge* (1946). Sondergaard once remarked to an interviewer:

> I've played a variety of roles, more, in fact, than anyone I know.... Most of those movies were fun to do. I don't consider that I really ever did anything that was "horrible." That's why when interviewers want to come and talk about horror films, I say, "I wasn't in any."

Arthur Lubin shared his thoughts about *The Spider Woman Strikes Back* with us in May 1988: "That was a horrible picture. It was always a joy to have Gale Sondergaard. She, was a charming, charming woman." The director added that Sondergaard had been a guest at his home in the Hollywood Hills not long before she passed away in August 1985.

A "guilty pleasure" for some, an unmitigated bore for others, *The Spider Woman Strikes Back* was further proof that Universal's preeminence in the business of making slick, entertaining shockers was over. The whole film has a depressing, claustrophobic aura about it. The gloomy old house setting is milked dry of all its potential. There are endless shots of Brenda Joyce flitting through darkened hallways as a sullen Rondo Hatton lurches closely behind. Instead of creating suspense, these bits of business irritate us by their repetitiveness and lack of imagination.

There is only the slightest similarity between the character Sondergaard portrays in *The Spider Woman Strikes Back* and Adrea Spedding. Zenobia Dollard's kinky preoccupation with spiders is a gratuitous touch, included only to give the title some validity. On a figurative level, however, this association works: Like a spider, she spins a web of deceit and destruction. She even uses poison to overcome her victims. Gale keeps a pretty tight rein on her performance and only occasionally succumbs to some good old-fashioned camping. The mere sight of the exquisitely wicked Sondergaard dropping spider snacks into the gaping blossoms of the vampire plants, her face beaming with perverted joy, is enough to warm a horror fan's heart.

Another look at Hatton as Mario, Sondergaard's deaf-mute manservant.

Rondo Hatton's appearance in *The Spider Woman Strikes Back* amounts to little more than window dressing. Portraying a deaf mute was a change of pace for the actor (he uses signing to communicate with Sondergaard). But aside from poisoning cattle and making Brenda Joyce feel so insecure that she chooses to dress in a closet, Hatton has little to do. (In trying to recall the actor for us, Lubin mistakenly referred to Hatton as a dwarf rather than a victim of acromegaly.) To add insult to injury, Gale Sondergaard, in an interview with writer David Del Valle, admitted that she thought Hatton's deformed features were the product of Jack Pierce's makeup wizardry. Poor Rondo gives the sentiment, "I get no respect," new meaning.

Any proposal to extend their new Spider Woman capers beyond *The Spider Woman Strikes Back* never materialized. By discarding their first conception of the character and featuring her equally dangerous but one-dimensional replacement in a tiring, uninspired formula thriller, Universal sabotaged what might have been an intriguing new series.

Critics' Corner

I went to see *The Spider Woman Strikes Back* feeling absolutely sure that the sleek brunette would be metamorphosed into a fat, furry black widow who would crawl slowly toward the helpless heroine sleeping quietly amidst a frenzied fanfare of incidental music. Actually, she does no such thing.... [T]he best she can do is indulge in a little amateur horticulture and kill off a few cows.—*The New York Herald-Tribune*, March 23, 1946, Bert McCord

Rating: ★★ Plot, though obvious, offers possibilities for thrills never achieved under careless production.... Good performances are practically impossible under the circumstances....—*The New York Daily News*, March 23, 1946, Dorothy Masters

[A]s uninhibited as its predecessors, and the formula is just the same.... Gale Sondergaard exudes evil all over the screen....—*The New York Times*, March 23, 1946, Edmond J. Bartnett

An indifferent program picture. Although it is supposed to be a horror melodrama, it is doubtful if it will have a frightening effect on any one [*sic*].... It belongs on the lower-half of a mid-week double bill.—*Harrison's Reports*, March 16, 1946

Gale Sondergaard gives a good performance and is chiefly responsible for maintaining the tone of the picture.... [T]his film has moments of suspense. The original screenplay ... effectively presents thriller entertainment.—*The Motion Picture Herald*, March 23, 1946, M.R.Y.

House of Horrors

Released March 29, 1946. 66 minutes. *Producer:* Ben Pivar. *Director:* Jean Yarbrough. *Screenplay:* George Bricker. *Original Story:* Dwight V. Babcock. *Photography:* Maury Gertsman. *Camera Operator:* John Martin. *Art Directors:* John B. Goodman & Abraham Grossman. *Musical Director:* Hans J. Salter. *Set Decorators:* Russell A. Gausman & Ralph Warrington. *Editor:* Philip Cahn. *Assistant Director:* Ralph Slosser. *Property Master:* Robert Murdock. *Sound Director:* Bernard B. Brown. *Technician:* Robert Pritchard. *Makeup:* Jack P. Pierce. *Gaffer:* John Brooks. *Rondo Hatton's Stand-in:* Ed Cushing. *Gowns:* Vera West.

Robert Lowery (*Steven Morrow*), Virginia Grey (*Joan Medford*), Bill Goodwin (*Police Lt. Larry Brooks*), Martin Kosleck (*Marcel DeLange*), Alan Napier (*F. Holmes Harmon*), Howard Freeman (*Hal Ormiston*), Joan Fulton [Shawlee] (*Stella McNally*), Virginia Christine (*Daisy Sutter*), Byron Foulger (*Mr. Samuels*), Janet Shaw, Tom Quinn (*Taxi Cab Drivers*), Jack Parker (*Elevator Boy*), William Newell (*Tomlinson*), Oliver Blake (*Janitor*), William Ruhl (*Ellis*), Syd Saylor (*Jerry*), Clifton Young, Kernan Cripps (*Detectives*), Terry Mason (*Clarence*), Stephen Wayne (*Speed*), Danny Jackson (*Office Boy*), Mary Field (*Nora*), Charles Wagenheim (*Walter*), Perc Launders (*Smith*). And introducing Rondo Hatton as *The Creeper*.

Out of the murk of the river...
Out of the clammy mist... Rises a new
fiend of horror... The Creeper!
—*Trailer blurb for* House of Horrors

On November 8, 1944, *The Hollywood Reporter* noted that producer Ben Pivar was in the midst of developing an entire new series of horror characters. The enterprising producer had recently been relieved of all lower budget pictures on his shooting schedule so that he could concentrate his efforts on higher bracket product. One of Pivar's objectives, according to the trade paper, was to star Rondo Hatton as that lumbering brute "The Creeper" in a round of top-budget movies, beginning with *House of Horrors*.

Either this bit of wishful thinking was cooked up by the boys in the publicity department or Pivar fell out of favor with the head honchos, for when *House of Horrors* went into production in September 1945 (under the shooting title *Murder Mansion*), nearly a year after its initial announcement, it was given the same B budget as the producer's past productions since he joined the organization in the late '30s. Up until the day he left Universal, Pivar never surpassed his rank as a purveyor of B-picture entertainment.

Although Universal insisted (via the film's main title and various publicity materials) that it was "introducing" Rondo Hatton as the Creeper, the brooding, acromegalic actor had already played the role (The Hoxton Creeper) in the Sherlock Holmes thriller *The Pearl of Death*. In *House of Horrors*, the Creeper's moniker might have been altered, his country of origin changed from the British Isles to America, even some of his behavioral traits modified, but under the skin he's that same psychopathic serial killer, snapping spines like match sticks at the slightest provocation.

The Breen Office had more reason than ever to exercise its powers when George Bricker's shooting script came under its scrutiny in August 1945. After all, *Murder Mansion* was a tale about a crazed murderer who preyed on buxom young women (and cynical critics) in an avant-garde setting. No objectionable artwork would be tolerated. Excessive gruesomeness including lurid screams and "gurgling" sounds (!) would not pass muster, nor was the Creeper allowed to leer at women with sexual desire. And, for heaven's sake, that "flashily dressed blonde" strolling around the waterfront at midnight must in no way suggest a prostitute!

Initial shooting of *House of Horrors* began on Tuesday, September 11, on the appropriately murky art studio set. B-movie stalwart Kent Taylor was originally selected to play the part of Police Lt. Larry Brooks, but on the fourth day of production (Saturday, September 15), before Taylor had appeared in a single scene, he was replaced by Bill Goodwin. In a curious postscript, years later, Taylor told an interviewer that he did indeed play the role but then, dissatisfied with the picture and the way it exploited Rondo Hatton, demanded that he (Taylor) be taken off the film. The original Assistant Director's Daily Reports put the lie to Taylor's dubious story, and Virginia Grey confirmed this, telling us that Goodwin was the only one to play Brooks. In another casting switch, an unbilled William Newell took over the role of Detective Tomlinson from Milburn Stone.

Rondo Hatton's eerie nocturnal prowlings were shot on such familiar back lot sets as the New York Street and Waterfront Street. Fully recovered from her torturous ordeal as the mud-packed Princess Ananka in *The Mummy's Curse*, Virginia Christine made a brief but memorable appearance as the shapely blond prostitute who got her back wrenched by the touchy killer. Christine's scene was shot on gloomy Tenement Street over a two-day stretch (Saturday, September 15–Monday, September 17). She vaguely recalled her participation in the picture:

> I needed the money [*laughs*]—all actors need money! It was a very short scene. They had a cat following me down the street. And in order to get the cat to follow me, they put some anchovies or sardines on the back of my heel [*more laughs*]! And that's all I remember about that film — absolutely all.

(Note: The curious puss didn't make it into the final cut.)

After a day of shooting odds and ends on a number of sets, director Jean Yarbrough closed down production on September 25, 1945, one day over schedule.

Although Hatton may have garnered audience attention as the picture's main "attraction," *House of Horrors* is unquestionably stolen by Martin Kosleck as Marcel DeLange, a classically impoverished Greenwich Village artist whose surrealist sculptures have made him (according to one hostile critic) "the laughingstock of New York art circles." Marcel is about to drown his sorrows in the waters of the murky river when he spots a limp figure (Rondo Hatton) crawling its way out of the drink. Studying the exhausted man's misshapen features, the artist gets an inspiration ... "The perfect Neanderthal Man!" Before long, the ecstatic Marcel is elbows-deep in clay, creating another "deathless masterpiece." He doesn't turn a hair when he discovers that his saturnine model is none other than the Creeper, a murderous brute whom the police believe had drowned while escaping their dragnet.

Late that night, without provocation, the Creeper steals out of Marcel's studio and nonchalantly slays a hooker (Virginia Christine). Police Lt. Larry Brooks (Bill Goodwin) recognizes the killer's brutal methods and comes to the conclusion the fugitive is still at large.

Underrated and unappreciated (at least in his own eyes), Marcel prays for the day when he can strike a blow against the critical establishment whom he believes is responsible for his lack of success. Now with the Creeper in his corner, Marcel's day of vindication is at last at hand. "Soon the whole world will recognize my genius," he muses modestly. It isn't long before some of the Big Apple's most respected art critics are found dead behind their typewriters. (In the case of Howard Freeman's laughably effete Hal Ormiston, the police find the rotund columnist sprawled across his kitchen floor dressed in one of the most garish evening robes ever to be drafted from a studio wardrobe department.) Only critic Joan Medford is spared. Sporting Hedda Hopper–style hats, Virginia Grey plays the part in a style more befitting a society reporter on a big city daily. The savvy art critic lifts a rough sketch of the Creeper from Marcel's work table and dashes off with it to her newspaper's engraving plant.

Incensed that Joan lifted the sketch, Mar-

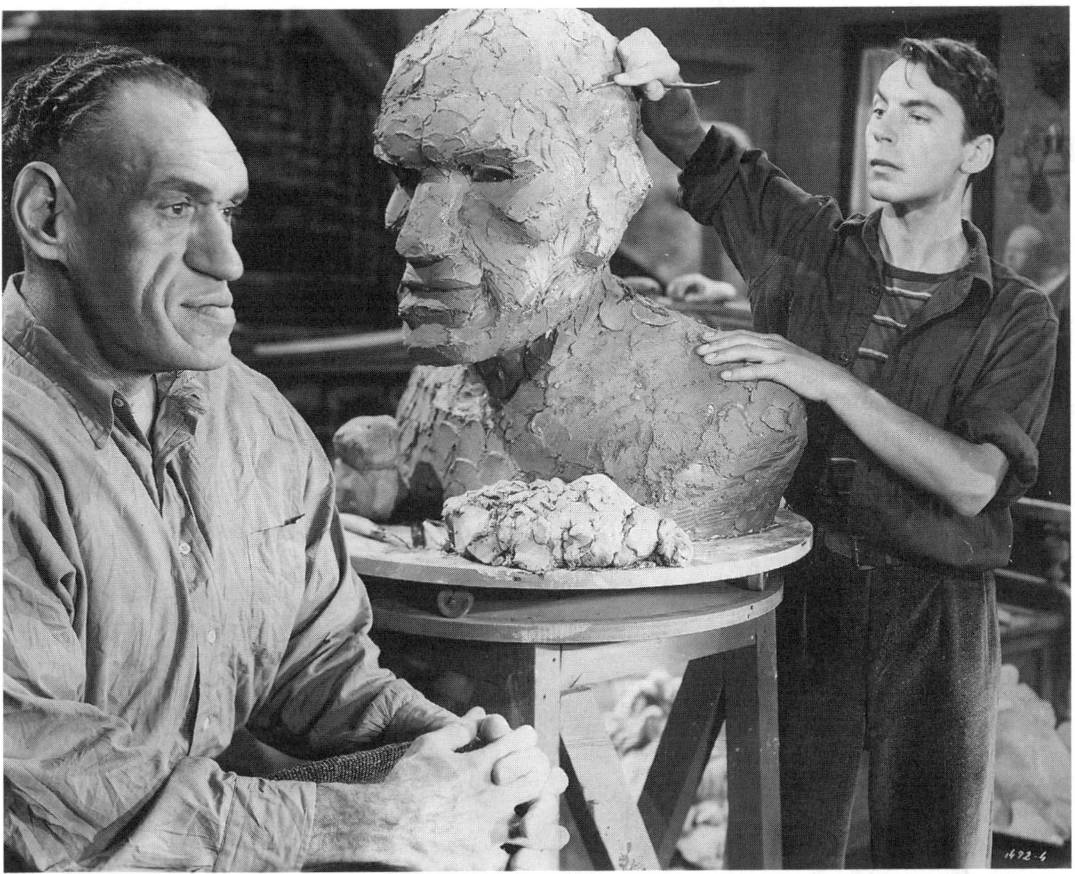

Marcel de Lange (Martin Kosleck) works on his "crowning achievement," a bust of the Creeper (Rondo Hatton), in *House of Horrors.*

cel sends the Creeper to the studio of her boyfriend, hot-headed commercial artist Steven Morrow (Robert Lowery). Instead of finding the art critic there, the Creeper encounters Morrow's model, Stella McNally (Joan Fulton). A victim of being in the wrong place at the wrong time, the poor girl meets the fate intended for Joan. (Contract player Joan Fulton eventually changed her last name to Shawlee and was pretty active in pictures during the '50s and '60s. She is probably best remembered as the leader of the all-girl band in 1959's laugh hit *Some Like It Hot.*)

Returning to Marcel's studio, the Creeper watches from a hiding spot as his friend and the snoopy Joan engage in a heated conversation. Marcel accuses her of betraying him. "My devoted friend is my symbol of strength, of power. Through him I shall destroy all my enemies — including you," he boasts. "Marcel, you're mad! Things like this just don't happen!" Joan counters. (Obviously, she hasn't seen many B horror pictures.) Joan shakes the artist's security by reminding him his signature on the Creeper's sketch puts his neck squarely in the noose. Then Marcel shrugs off her threat: he plans on telling the police he had no knowledge of his model's identity. (The chances that investigators are going to believe the Creeper knocked off Marcel's antagonists without the artist planting the idea in his head first are pretty slim.)

Understandably irked by Marcel's disloyalty, the Creeper strangles him to death and destroys the finished bust. Stalking Joan like a predatory cat, the Creeper is seconds away from adding her to his list of victims when a shot fired through the window by Lt. Brooks puts the maniacal killer in the prison hospital.

Rondo Hatton's one-note screen persona had pretty much been milked dry by the time *House of Horrors* rolled around, but that didn't stop Universal from finding further avenues to exploit at the unfortunate actor's expense. Whether or not Hatton resented this crass commercialism by a money-hungry Hollywood studio is debatable, though it might perhaps be fairer to say that Hatton exploited his own ugliness in these and other pictures. After all, no one forced him to accept work in films. After many years of playing bit parts (in the 1938 20th Century–Fox spectacular *In Old Chicago*, the actor was prominently cast as ruffian Brian Donlevy's bodyguard, Rondo), Hatton may have even been pleased to suddenly find himself a star of Universal attractions. Whatever his innermost feelings were, according to Martin Kosleck and Phil Brown, he was a pleasant, cooperative co-worker.

However positive Hatton's traits were as an individual, there is no getting around the fact that he was a terrible actor with virtually no range. In pictures such as *House of Horrors*, *The Jungle Captive* and *The Brute Man*, he is incapable of mouthing even the most mundane dialogue. Photographer Maury Gertsman's effective use of silhouettes and low angles in capturing Hatton's grotesqueness heighten the chill factor of the picture, but even his efforts are jettisoned whenever Rondo deadpans abysmal dialogue like, "You're my friend, shake," or, "You're going to tell the police about me, huh?"

Virtually every character in the film is a cliché: The flippant female art critic, the wiseguy Irish policeman, the dumb blonde model, the rugged, All-American boyfriend whose career as commercial artist is limited to painting calendar girls, and the starving surrealist who lives from one sale to the next. Even broader depictions are etched by Alan Napier and Howard Freeman as the churlish art critics. Their critiques are little more than character assassinations, befitting a scandal sheet and not an art column. And no one on the Universal payroll wrote clunker lines with the audacity of George Bricker. ("I have often wondered why a man would want to snap a woman's spine.")

Yet, despite these pitfalls, *House of Horrors* rates as the best shocker in this last gasp of Universal Horrors. It boasts creepy, atmospheric, film-noirish settings, evocative camerawork and is seldom dull. For a studio hack director with only two genre credits, *The Devil Bat* (1940) and *King of the Zombies* (1941), Jean Yarbrough conveys a properly unhealthy mood in the scenes set in Marcel's candlelit studio, its inventory overcrowded with all sorts of aberrations in clay. (Sharp-eyed buffs will spot the headpiece belonging to one of the rockmen from the serial *Flash Gordon Conquers the Universe* passing itself off as one of the sculptor's crazy creations.)

The suspenseful climax of *House of Horrors* finds the Creeper gravely wounded by a single police bullet. By not polishing off the murderer, Universal left the door wide open for a sequel. But instead of picking up the story where it left off, the studio decided to fill in the details of the killer's life and career by producing a *pre*quel, the creepy but lamentable *The Brute Man*. Though its justification for the Creeper's existence and motivation to kill is rather inept (the Creeper, we learn, was a love-scorned college student who, through his own impetuosity, caused a lab explosion that triggered the disfigurement of his face and affected his reason), *The Brute Man* does shed light on what makes this nasty killer tick.

These belated revelations, however, come too late to help first-time viewers of *House of Horrors* understand where the Creeper is coming from. Aside from some sketchy details provided by the police (he murdered at least one woman before the cops traced him to the river's edge), we know nothing about him and presume he is just some loathsome denizen of New York's violent night world. Bricker doesn't give us a clue as to his reason for committing these sordid crimes (other than an apparent lust to kill). The murder of the prostitute (which has all the earmarks of a Jack the Ripper–type killing) raises even more questions. Since there was no passion or profit motive, we can only guess that the Creeper murders innocent women because they express revulsion towards him. (When Marcel brings up the death of the hooker to his morose houseguest, the Creeper's only response is a faintly apologetic, "She screamed.")

The Creeper's alliance with Marcel is a partnership of brains and brawn. Once the pair bond, Marcel's festering desire to even the score with his persecutors becomes a reality. The Creeper is only too happy to oblige. This unholy alliance is well illustrated in a fine moment wherein Marcel, after having read aloud a

Rondo Hatton, Virginia Grey, Bill Goodwin and Robert Lowery share a light-hearted moment. In July 1946, Lowery prepared to embark on a 16-city tour to organize Robert Lowery fan clubs!

scathing critique of his work by art critic Holmes Harmon (Alan Napier), boasts of how he would love to tear the bitchy critic apart. The camera holds on a closeup of Marcel's violently gesturing hands, then pans over to the Creeper's, idly kneading a mound of clay. Without uttering a word, the killer rises from his chair and stalks off into the night.

Martin Kosleck walks away with the acting honors in the film's most challenging role (and unjustly received the lowest salary of all the principals—$1,334). The slightest bit of overacting on his part would have destroyed the credibility of the characterization. The actor was proud of his performance in *House of Horrors*. ("I get more fan mail on that ... I loved that part.") Kosleck was working on the Universal lot one day when he was approached by a producer (Ben Pivar most likely; Kosleck could not recall) and asked if he'd like to audition for a part in a forthcoming production. "He gave me a script to study during the lunch hour for an audition. I gave a completely memorized audition and got the part immediately." The scene that Martin was required to enact was the poignant little monologue Marcel speaks to his cat. A lifelong animal lover, Kosleck fondly remembered how well the scrawny little alley cat behaved in front of the camera, particularly in the scene where the feline performer was required to nestle close to his dead master's body at the film's finale.

Playing a succession of Nazi madmen and leering psychotics didn't sour Kosleck's outlook on Hollywood film acting. He loved to work and considered every role a challenge. The sensitive, cultured actor spent his childhood in the idyllic forests of Pomerania in Germany. His father hailed from a proud family of Russian aristocrats whose heritage dated back to the thirteenth century. Though he developed a passionate interest in art, Martin's burning desire was to become an actor.

Kosleck's artistic talents paved the way for his settlement in California in 1932. His canvases won him the acclaim of the West Coast critical establishment and the Hollywood community as well (one of his early champions was Albert Einstein). Plum roles in productions staged by the Pasadena Playhouse led to a screen test at Warner Bros. for the second lead in *Confessions of a Nazi Spy* in 1939. Francis Lederer got the part but Kosleck was awarded a featured role, that of Nazi propagandist Joseph Goebbels. The die was cast. For the next five decades, Martin Kosleck's screen image was forever linked to the beasts spawned by the Third Reich.

Kosleck alternated his appearances in propaganda pictures with featured parts in B horror films and mystery thrillers, earning him a reputation as one of Tinsel Town's most reliable baddies. Paramount's stylish 1941 melodrama *The Mad Doctor*, a modern-day Bluebeard tale, offered Martin an exceptionally strong role as homicidal psychiatrist Basil Rathbone's part-time lover and full-time henchman. Playing the part of a Fascist in Universal's 13-chapter serial *The Great Alaskan Mystery* (1944) won Kosleck entry into the portals of Hollywood's nightmare factory. His performances for the studio cemented his celebrity as one of the screen's beloved bogeymen.

Frequent television appearances, successful engagements on Broadway, and a sprinkling of movie credits (most notoriously, the 1964 cheapie *The Flesh Eaters*) kept the actor happily occupied through the late '70s. Poor health forced him into retirement long before he was ready to settle down. When asked by the authors if he harbored any unfulfilled acting goals, Kosleck responded, "I yearned to play Hamlet." On January 16, 1994, less than 24 hours before the Northridge earthquake shook Los Angeles, the octogenarian passed away in a Santa Monica hospital following abdominal surgery, leaving behind his long-time companion (and *Flesh Eaters* castmate) Christopher Drake.

In 1994, New York's *The Village Voice*, a popular arts-and-politics weekly with avant-garde leanings, cited *House of Horrors*, of all things, in a column focused on the National Endowment for the Arts and artist-critic relationships. In her tongue-in-cheek analysis of a film she clearly felt beneath her, staff critic Elizabeth Hess described Marcel DeLange's bizarre creations as "large Picassoid statues, the kind you might see dumped in front of restaurants on West Broadway." As for the members of the Fourth Estate portrayed in the movie, the *Voice* columnist opined that "Holmes Harmon epitomizes the ivory-tower critic who has praise for his friends and venom for those who break from tradition." Distressed by the intrusion of politics in matters relating to the NEA, Hess observed that "Harmon apparently isn't obligated to play by any rules — ethical, legal or otherwise — but members of the NEA's member council are..." She closes her column with the thinly veiled threat, "Where is the Creeper when we need him?"

Perhaps Marcel DeLange wasn't so crazy, after all.

Critics' Corner

Universal's newest horror creation is not in the best of taste.... [A] glandular and mental case, an ugly Neanderthal-featured brute of a moron called "The Creeper," who goes about strangling people at the drop of a suggestion.... The door for sequels is left wide open at the end, since the detective, after shooting the killer, says: "We have to get this man to a hospital." This is one door which should be closed at once.—*The New York Herald-Tribune*, February 23, 1946, Otis L. Guernsey, Jr.

Rating: ★★½ It's a spine-chiller, guaranteed to scare those who scare easily.—*The New York Daily News*, February 23, 1946, Wanda Hale

If you like this sort of thing, the picture is in the approved shuddery tradition and gets its story told quickly. Rondo Hatton is properly scary....—*The New York Times*, February 23, 1946, Edmond J. Bartnett

[T]here is little about the proceedings to horrify one unless the fact that the murders are committed by a half-witted giant can be considered horrendous rather than unpleasant. Discriminating audiences will find the far-fetched plot hard to take.—*Harrison's Reports*, March 9, 1946

Rondo Hatton, whose Neanderthal features suffice without the aid of makeup ... and his ape-like appearance on the screen brings a gasp to the audience.... Maury Gertsman's photographic direction makes the most of the ominous situations by clever use of lights, shadows and camera angles.—*The Motion Picture Herald*, March 9, 1946, George H. Spires

Night in Paradise

Released May 3, 1946. 84 minutes. *Director:* Arthur Lubin. *Producer:* Walter Wanger. *Associate Producer:*

Alexander Golitzen. *Screenplay:* Ernest Pascal. *Based on the novel* Peacock's Feather *by* George S. Hellman. *Adaptation:* Emmet Lavery. *Photography:* Hal Mohr & W. Howard Greene (Technicolor). *Technicolor Director:* Natalie Kalmus. *Associate:* William Fritzsche. *Special Photography:* John P. Fulton. *Art Directors:* John B. Goodman & Alexander Golitzen. *Editor:* Milton Carruth. *Music Score & Director:* Frank Skinner. *Song:* "Night in Paradise" *by* Jack Brooks & Frank Skinner. *Set Decorators:* Russell A. Gausman & Edward R. Robinson. *Assistant Director:* Fred Frank. *Dialogue Director:* Joan Hathaway. *Sound Director:* Bernard B. Brown. *Technician:* William Hedgcock. *Makeup:* Jack P. Pierce. *Costumes:* Travis Banton.

Merle Oberon (*Princess Delarai*), Turhan (*Aesop [Jason]*), Thomas Gomez (*King Croesus*), Gale Sondergaard (*Queen Attossa*), Ray Collins (*Leonides*), George Dolenz (*Frigia Ambassador*), John Litel (*Archon*), Ernest Truex, Jerome Cowan, Marvin Miller (*Scribes*), Douglass Dumbrille, Moroni Olsen, Francis McDonald (*High Priests*), Paul Cavanagh (*Cleomenes*), Richard Bailey (*Lieutenant*), Wee Willie Davis (*Salabaar*), Roseanne Murray (*Marigold*), Hans Herbert (*Priest*), Julie London, Barbara Bates, Daun Kennedy, Ruth Valmy, Karen X. Gaylord, Kathleen O'Malley, Karen Randle, Kerry Vaughn, Audrey Young, Patricia Alphin (*Palace Maidens*), Eula Morgan, Art Miles, Al Choals, Myrtle Ferguson, Frank Hagney (*Townspeople*), James Hutton (*Delarai's Messenger*), Juli Lynne (*Song Specialty*), Jean Trent (*Iris*), Jane Adams (*Lotus*), John Merton (*Sailor*), Dan Stowell (*Sentinel*), Pedro de Cordoba (*Magus*), Harry Cording (*Captain*), Ann Everett, Dorothy Tuomi, Marguerite Campbell, June Frazer (*Flower Girls*), Colin Campbell (*Goatman*), Nikki Kerkes, Mercedes Mockaitis (*Special Water Girls*), Harlan Miller (*Slave*), Denny Burke (*Contortionist*), Neal Young (*Nobleman*), Joe Bernard (*Old Man*), John Berkes, Al Ferguson, Pietro Sosso (*Beggars*), Dick Alexander, Earle Ozman (*Temple Guards*), Rex Evans (*Chef*), Jack Overman (*Man*), Wade Crosby (*Rough Man*), Charles Bates, Clyde Flynn, Joel Goodkind, Jimmy Fresco, Mickey Fresco, Juan Estrada, Robert Espinosa, Louis Montoya (*Boys*), Kit Guard (*Man in Crowd*), Maxine Hoppe (*Handmaiden*), Alex Harford (*Man on Statue*).

[*Night in Paradise*] is a pretty face with naught behind it....
—The New York Herald-Tribune, *June 6, 1946*

This fanciful tale about the semi-legendary Greek writer Aesop warrants inclusion in this book only for the fleeting appearance of Gale Sondergaard as a sorceress. Otherwise, it's a lightweight costumer that enabled Universal to strut its highbrow pretensions by luring a top Hollywood star (Merle Oberon) through its gates. *Night in Paradise* was the brainchild of Walter Wanger, the hotshot producer who had previously made films in collaboration with some of Hollywood's top directors (Ford, Hitchcock, Capra et al.) but, having fallen on hard times, settled down at Universal in 1942. *Night in Paradise* was Wagner's second attempt at bringing a Technicolor version of the George S. Hellman novel *Peacock's Feather* to the screen; the first (featuring RKO star Ann Harding) was scrapped in the mid–'30s. He revived the project just as his stock at Universal was sliding—Wanger's high-budget *Salome, Where She Danced* (1945) drew disastrous notices. Wanger wanted to borrow Ava Gardner from MGM, but Universal insisted on his casting Merle Oberon in the starring role. The cameras rolled on *Night in Paradise* a full decade after its inception, but the finished film languished in post-production at the studio for nearly a year. It was not released until the spring of 1946. A bonafide bomb, the picture reportedly cost Universal over $1.5 million dollars to produce; it lost the studio nearly $800,000.

The storyline is an obvious fabrication, occasionally cribbing a detail or two from the legend of Aesop, alleged author of scores of time-honored fables, whose very existence has been the source of speculation through the ages. (It became the fashion to credit Aesop with all manner of traditional stories and bits of folk wisdom, many of which must actually have come down from ancient times.)

The action is set in Lydia, circa 560 B.C. The all-powerful King Croesus (Thomas Gomez) incurs the wrath of Queen Attossa (Gale Sondergaard) when he selects Princess Delarai (Merle Oberon) of Persia as his bride. Jilted in love and bilked of a fortune in gold by the greedy Croesus, the Frigian queen appeals to the gods to double her powers of sorcery so that she may avenge this personal affront. Attossa spirits herself in disembodied form to the king's magnificent palace and taunts him mercilessly. Driven near mad, Croesus is advised by Aesop (Turhan Bey) to use reason to battle the queen's sorcery. Aesop, a slave turned famed storyteller, has just arrived from the Isle of Samos in a shaggy, simian-looking disguise (reminiscent of Lugosi's Ygor) to plead the case of his freedom-loving countrymen.

Aesop develops a fascination for Delarai, who reveals herself to be a beautiful but vain and heartless creature. Enraged by the wise man's perceptive ability to see into her soul, she brands him an "insolent ape" and scoffs at his prediction that she will one day beg for his love. Leonides (Ray Collins), Croesus' schemy chamberlain, and the mocking Attossa prey on the king's jealousies to discredit Aesop.

Aesop foils a trap set by Delarai and Leonides by arriving at the bride-to-be's sleeping chamber sans disguise. Calling himself Jason, a "dear friend" of Aesop, the strapping young man sweeps Delarai off her feet. But a scar reveals Jason's true identity. "People don't accept wisdom without age," Aesop laments, and tells the princess that his sole purpose was to humble her pride and reject her, not to fall in love with her. When Leonides and his men break into the chamber as planned, Aesop is nowhere to be found. Croesus accuses his chamberlain of betraying him and orders his execution, but withdraws the order in the nick of time.

Determined to ruin Aesop, Leonides and the high priest (Douglass Dumbrille) convince the king that the gods want war between Lydia and Samos. Forsaking his disguise, Aesop assumes the role of Lydian ambassador and consults the oracle in the Greek temple of Delphi. He finds the high priests to be a corrupt lot whose Apollian "revelations" can be swayed with the right amounts of gold. Delarai, who has sneaked off to the ancient city to find Aesop, is discovered hiding in the temple by the high priests, who condemn the lovers to be hurled from the cliffs overlooking the rocky shoreline. Since no rescue is possible, the writers fall back on a trite *deus ex machina* resolution by having the couple miraculously whisked away by the benevolent Attossa right from under the noses of their executioners.

A Maria Montez vehicle without Maria Montez, *Night in Paradise* is among the last of Universal's tongue-in-cheek costume extravaganzas of the '40s. Overripe and meretricious, it is every bit as vulgar as any in the studio's stable of exotic big budgeters in the *Arabian Nights* school. These outings were spirited, good-natured hokum at best, but *Night in Paradise* adds a pompous, pseudo-literary veneer to the shopworn formula. The result is unsurprisingly disappointing—a talking heads epic with little verve and even less wit. Serving up a gossamer plot woven around a production of elephantine gaudiness, *Night in Paradise* is resounding proof that if there is anything worse than kitsch, it's *boring* kitsch.

Art director Alexander Golitzen's credit as associate producer is a tip-off to the film's visual style. *Night in Paradise* has all the earmarks of a set designer's movie. The film unreels amid the plaster mock-ups of Grecian temples and painted powder-blue backdrops. Obvious, stage-bound "exterior" sets are consistent with the production's artificial texture; reality rears up suddenly via the exterior footage seen late in the film. *Night in Paradise* straddles the fence between ham-fisted burlesque and standard Hollywood costumer conventions. Writer Ernest Pascal, whose talents were well-suited for the grimly allegorical *Flesh and Fantasy*, contributes a murky, convoluted script that defies comprehension: a veritable Rubik's cube of obscure motivations, muddled characterizations and dreary palace intrigues. To make all this seem palatable, the film is steeped in jarring, modern-day dialogue, includes street-smart actors like Jerome Cowan (playing a scribe!) in its cast, and shamelessly offers a torchy, '40s-style number for good measure. Even less appealing is the tasteless, prepubescent sexual tone that passes for humor. Except for Oberon and Sondergaard, the female cast members are restricted to a procession of smiling, curvaceous handmaidens; their male counterparts are hardly more dignified, drooling and gawking at all this mammary splendor on cue.

At center stage, of course, is Turhan Bey's Aesop, who is more than a little reminiscent of Jean Marais in *Beauty and the Beast* (1946). After years of being groomed as an exotic romantic lead, he spends the better part of his screen time under the shaggy mange of Jack Pierce's unflattering makeup. Bey's brief emergence as his youthful, ever-unctuous self is anticlimactic. Spouting pearls of wisdom at every turn, Bey, Hollywood's bargain basement version of Charles Boyer, comes off looking ridiculous in the poorly conceived role.

According to Turhan Bey, *Night in Paradise*'s failure to ignite the box office was a foregone conclusion. "After the second week I knew it was going to be a terrific flop, and I think everybody else knew it, too," he told the authors. "So you can imagine that *that* was a little de-

Merle Oberon and Thomas Gomez revel in the gaudy splendor of the Technicolor fantasy *Night in Paradise.*

pressing. I think the thing that made me a little dubious about what Arthur Lubin was doing was that he treated us more or less like robots. When we came to the set, everything was already there; our movements were already laid out for us. Nobody could say, 'Look, couldn't I do it *this* way?' or 'I would feel much better doing it a different way.' To make a change was impossible, because everything was already set up. I had never encountered this before; in all the B pictures I worked on, nobody ever did this."

In regards to the horrific makeup design Jack Pierce foisted on the handsome actor, Bey remarked:

> It was at least an hour that Jack Pierce spent on me. It wasn't as difficult as it might look; the wig was easy, but the beard had to be done very carefully, each hair on its own, not just a beard pasted on. I really am proud to say that I got along very well with Jack Pierce, because Jack was not a man who took a liking to everybody. Oh, no, not at all! He never was temperamental or anything, but to get him to laugh, you had to be very close. This I had the pleasure of being with him. He was definitely the specialist in horror makeups. He was never rude, but I never saw him really warm up to anybody, and some people were a little scared of him. And nobody ever dared to come late to Jack Pierce — even the big stars. When Jack said, "Be here at five-thirty," you had to *be* there!

Merle Oberon's performance has all the smirky condescension of a A-player slumming in a B production. (Some sources reported that Louise Allbritton was originally slated for the role.) The elegant Miss Oberon fails to bring much sympathy to a scheming, self-centered character but at least cameraman Paul Ivano does her beauty full justice in several rapturous close-ups. Of his glamorous co-star, Turhan Bey recalled,

> I enjoyed working with her very much, but I doubt that she enjoyed working with me! This

was at a time, unfortunately, when I was often late on the set. Thomas Gomez, whom I loved, gave me hell every time I came late — he was very, very strict with me [*laughs*]! But I appreciated that; he was right, and he openly told me his mind.

Blustery Thomas Gomez gets into the spirit of the thing, playing to the rafters like a would-be Charles Laughton. Character actor Ray Collins' contribution as the corrupt chamberlain isn't far removed from his standard crooked politician roles, except that he's never hammed it up as broadly as he does here. His performance is embarrassing to watch. Gale Sondergaard is very much in her element as the sorceress Attossa. The actress, who was once up for the Wicked Witch role eventually played by Margaret Hamilton in *The Wizard of Oz* (1939), may have regarded this assignment as an inglorious consolation prize. Her first scene, set in a windswept mountaintop lair, has the vengeful queen gleefully exhibiting her occult skills, briefly adding some badly needed mayhem to the poky plot. But Sondergaard's appearance unfortunately amounts to little more than a cameo, though her few scenes are imaginatively handled. Materializing enigmatically in a flame, or in the mirror-like surface of a wall ornament, she goads Gomez into fulfilling her own mischievous ends. John P. Fulton displays his resourcefulness on several occasions, most notably in a dazzling bit wherein Sondergaard, appearing as a reflection in a pond (*à la* the 1940 *The Thief of Bagdad*), hands Bey a vial of poison. But such momentary diversions don't go far in relieving the tedium of this tinseled turkey of a movie.

Night in Paradise did little to bolster the career of its director, Arthur Lubin, who offered us these vague recollections of the production:

Night in Paradise was a fairy tale based on one of Aesop's fables. It was a silly story, it didn't make sense, but it was a very lavish production for Universal to make in those days. That production cost, I think, under a million dollars. Today, it would cost about five or ten million. [*Note: The late director made these comments in 1988. Needless to say, by twenty-first century standards, the budget for such an extravaganza would total quite a few million more!*] It was a little longer than the average production for Universal, about ten weeks. I was under contract to Universal and, in those days, when a director finished a picture they assigned him immediately to something that was ready to go so they didn't lose his salary by having him sit around. Walter Wanger was the producer. I had made a previous picture for him (*Eagle Squadron* [1942]), and he liked me. It was a big picture, and I brought it in on time. And the studio said, "Well, Lubin's available. Let's put him into *Night in Paradise*."

Night in Paradise became a bitter pill for Arthur Lubin to swallow as the film's release hastened his departure from Universal. Playing no small part in the termination of Lubin's contract was Turhan Bey, who, ironically, was given his first big break by the veteran director a few years before. Lubin told us:

Turhan Bey and I did not get along too well together. His rise to fame was too quick for him to handle, and he got very, very difficult. He was impossible! He didn't have me fired, but the studio didn't pick up my contract. He complained that I was giving Miss Oberon too many closeups, and not enough to him. He was just an unknown boy when he came to Universal studios. He was sent out from my lawyers in New York to me. I was the first one to make a screen test of him. The studio signed him and his rise was fabulous, but it went to his head.

Turhan Bey got in the final word in this friendship-gone-sour postscript when he told us, "The only picture that ever hurt *me* was a picture that Arthur Lubin directed." He was laughingly referring to *Night in Paradise*, of course.

Critics' Corner

The lavish Technicolor settings ... surround some of the most nonsensical screen doings of the year.... There are no high points in the script ... and so many low ones that it is difficult to choose a nadir among them.—*The New York Herald-Tribune*, June 6, 1946

Rating: ★★★ *Night in Paradise* is the spoofingest artistry of the season — expansive, expensive and luscious in Technicolor. Merle Oberon in cold-catching costumes is such superlative décor that neither Croesus ... nor Aesop ... rates anything more than casual attention.... [T]he cast fails to make the most of a fine opportunity for creating fun.—*The New York Daily News*, June 6, 1946, Dorothy Masters

It is an amusing entertainment of its kind, somewhat different because if its occasional use of modern slang, and of the tongue-in-cheek mannerisms of the players. But on the whole it offers little that is unusual, and its appeal will be directed mainly to those who have not tired of the numerous similar phantasies that have been shown in the past two years.—*Harrison's Reports*, April 13, 1946

Mr. Wanger tells this fable against a background of sumptuous settings in which beautiful maidens romp barefooted and in which Merle Oberon ... luxuriates in a milk bath that is second only to Cecil B. DeMille's washing of Claudette Colbert in *Cleopatra*.... [The cast] disport themselves with an air of self-conscious silliness. In short, *Night in Paradise* is an extravaganza which is more ridiculous than entertaining.—*The New York Times*, June 6, 1946, Thomas M. Pryor

[A] feast of beauty.... [T]he sets and the costuming is worth the price of anybody's admission to a theater, and in addition to that, there is narrative of engaging enough kind, animation in plenty, and a judicious leavening of the whole with humor.... The screenplay ... is a trim job.—*The Motion Picture Herald*, April 13, 1946, William R. Weaver

The Cat Creeps

Released May 17, 1946. 58 minutes. *Associate Producer:* Will Cowan. *Executive Producer:* Howard Welsch. *Director:* Erle C. Kenton. *Screenplay:* Edward Dein, Jerry Warner & (uncredited) Gertrude Walker. *Original Story:* Gerald Geraghty. *Photography:* George Robinson & (uncredited) Elwood Bredell. *Camera Operators:* Edward Coleman & Richard Towers. *Editor:* Russell Schoengarth. *Art Directors:* Jack Otterson & Abraham Grossman. *Music Director:* Paul Sawtell. *Assistant Directors:* Melville Shyer & Fritz Collings. *Set Decorators:* Russell A. Gausman & T.F. Offenbecker. *Sound Director:* Bernard B. Brown. *Technician:* William Hedgcock. *Gowns:* Vera West. *Director of Makeup:* Jack P. Pierce. *Hair Stylist:* Carmen Dirigo. *Assistant Camera:* Walter Bleumel & Philip Lathrop.

Noah Beery, Jr. (*Pidge "Flash" Laurie*), Lois Collier (*Gay Elliot*), Paul Kelly (*Ken Grady*), Fred Brady (*Terry Nichols*), Douglass Dumbrille (*Tom McGalvey*), Rose Hobart (*Connie Palmer*), Jonathan Hale (*Walter Elliot*), Iris Clive (*Kyra Goran*), Vera Lewis (*Cora Williams*), William B. Davidson (*James Walsh*), Arthur Loft (*Sampler*), Jerry Jerome (*Polich*).

In Its Eyes—A Murderer's Secret!
—*Poster blurb for* The Cat Creeps

By the mid–'40s, the popularity of horror films was apparently waning, and nearly all of Universal's one-time competitors had begun dropping out of the race. Universal kept plugging away, maybe just out of simple force of habit, but by 1946, nearly everything that had once been right about the company's horror films was now depressingly, demoralizingly wrong. The great stars like Karloff and Lugosi were long gone, and even "second-team" players Chaney, Atwill, Zucco and Carradine were names out of the studio's past. The very best a 1946 audience could expect from a Universal chiller was a Gale Sondergaard or a Martin Kosleck; even Poverty Row horror films usually boasted better name stars than these. The classic Universal monsters were also on ice, girding themselves for encounters with Abbott and Costello; Rondo Hatton, the little man with the big head, was their one monster character of the year. The folks writing and directing the studio's horrors were now just workaday hacks. Indeed, how much real difference is there between a cheap, dreary Universal like *The Spider Woman Strikes Back* or *The Cat Creeps* and a Monogram, PRC or Republic horror film from that same period? Horror film fans had truly been seduced and abandoned by the New Universal.

Emblematic of their new brand of below-par programmers, *The Cat Creeps* is a throwaway horror-whodunit that Universal called a chiller on the shaky basis of its setting (a lonely mansion) and some inane spook-talk about cats. Apart from the title and an old-dark-house backdrop, the film bears no relation to the 1930 version of *The Cat Creeps* nor to that film's antecedent, 1927's *The Cat and the Canary*.

Long-shrouded in mystery, the questionable "suicide" of Eric Goran becomes the object of scrutiny once again as the result of a letter written to the daily newspaper *The Morning Chronicle*. The letter writer, elderly crackpot Cora Williams, insists that Goran's death was a case of murder for money—$200,000—and insists that the investigation be reopened. Enclosed with the letter is a $1,000 bill which has been out of circulation since the time of Goran's death. Newshawk Terry Nichols (Fred Brady) balks at tackling the assignment because it appears that Walter Elliot, his girlfriend's father and a Senate hopeful, may be drawn into the scandal. When Nichols' corrupt bosses threaten to turn the assignment over to a notorious muckraking reporter, Nichols reconsiders.

Nichols calls on Elliot (Jonathan Hale) to warn him that the case is being reopened. Elliot's daughter Gay (Lois Collier) can't understand why her boyfriend has accepted the job of tying her father in with murder, and tells him off. After Nichols leaves, Elliot phones his lawyer Tom McGalvey (Douglass Dumbrille) to make hasty arrangements for a visit to Mrs. Williams at her island home on lonely Key Towers.

Converging at the mainland waterfront for a midnight trip to the island are Elliot, Gay, McGalvey, McGalvey's secretary Connie Palmer (Rose Hobart) and unscrupulous private eye Ken Grady (Paul Kelly). Nichols and his friend Pidge Laurie (Noah Beery, Jr.), a news photographer, turn up at the scene and insist upon accompanying the group to the island. Elliot reluctantly consents.

The seven arrive at Key Towers in a striking long shot: The landing dock, the launch and its passengers in the foreground, the spooky mansion and a bright full moon looming over them in the distant background. It's an eerily atmospheric moment that shows that Universal was still capable of doing *some*thing right. The group tramps through jungly undergrowth to the mansion and then everyone disperses in different directions. In an upstairs bedroom, Mrs. Williams (Vera Lewis) is attacked by an unseen figure who is (of course) one of the seven newcomers to the island. The mystery man (woman?) also sets fire to the launch, making a hasty retreat to the mainland impossible.

Mrs. Williams is not dead, but is in bad shape; in her "big scene," she revives long enough to reach out for Connie with clawing movements, babbling something about her "cat creeping." There's plenty of arguing and finger pointing, Pidge is kicked in the face by the unseen assailant, and a second attempt on Mrs. Williams' life is successful. (Pidge: "This is one island I'm giving back to the Japs!") Kyra (Iris Clive), a strange young woman who claims to be Eric Goran's daughter, mysteriously appears on the scene, carrying a cat and explaining that she has been "beckoned" by the dead Mrs. Williams. This odd character, who seems to have mystically stepped in out of *Cat People* (1942), also insists that the spirit of Mrs. Williams now possesses her housecat. Connie, a cat hater whose nerves are fairly shot by now to begin with, faints at the implication.

Lois Collier reacts to some unseen horror in the pseudo-supernatural chiller *The Cat Creeps.*

Amidst torrents of talk talk talk (this script should have been saved for a radio spook show), Gay is roughed up by the mystery figure and Connie and Grady are killed by him. With the roster of suspects now reduced to just two — Elliot and McGalvey — Nichols sets a trap which closes around McGalvey. Coming out on the losing end of a fistfight with Nichols, McGalvey confesses to murders both old and new. He admits to having killed Eric Goran, a crooked lawyer, in hopes of stealing the man's $200,000 but, since Goran had craftily hidden the money, McGalvey ended up with nothing. Connie and Grady learned of McGalvey's crime and bled him white with blackmail for years, so they had to go, too. In the conventional end to this conventional movie, Pidge finds the money in Mrs. Williams' birdhouse, Kyra turns out to be an actress imported by Nichols, Elliot can run for the Senate without fear of scandal, Nichols and Gay clinch and the cat has kittens.

The Cat Creeps went into production on January 3, 1946, with Howard Welsch and Will Cowan divvying producers' responsibilities, Erle C. Kenton directing and George Robinson acting as director of photography. (An uncredited Elwood "Woody" Bredell replaced Robinson during the latter stages of production.) The film's screenplay had already been subjected to the sharp scrutiny of the Breen Office, who offered their by-now tiresome caveats against character-choking and excessive gruesomeness. Additionally, the Breen letter advised that Connie's two uses of the word "witch" be carefully pronounced ("there can be no possible confusion with the unacceptable word 'bitch'"), and that scenes of cruelty to the titular cat be scrupulously avoided. Universal complied with all of the censor's suggestions: The word "witch" was struck from Connie's dialogue, and the Assistant Director's Daily Report officially records that the cat received the same hour-long lunch privileges as the human members of the cast. Scenes of choking were also carefully avoided, although in its haste to comply with that requirement, the film carelessly neglects even to *tell* its audience how Mrs. Williams and Connie are killed.

The Cat Creeps is filled with plot glitches of this sort. Although the entire story revolves around the 15-year-old murder of one Eric Goran, we are told nothing about the man until the last minutes of the picture. No one explains what Elliot's connection with Goran was, why Elliot fears the reopening of the case or how Goran, a mouthpiece for bootleggers, happened to hide $200,000 in the rooftop birdhouse of an old lady's island mansion. We learn via the wrap-up that Connie has been blackmailing McGalvey for years, yet an earlier scene showed McGalvey and Connie working together in a relatively business-like and convivial office environment. The "trap" that Nichols sets for the killer is childish and inconclusive; caught in it, McGalvey confesses to the string of murders for no reason whatsoever. The topper: Kyra turns out to be a follies stripper brought to the island by Nichols, who apparently felt that importing some weird chick to talk about cats and souls was the key to cracking the case—and he's right! What the writers of *The Cat Creeps* lacked in imagination, they compensated for with sheer nonsense. For most of the running time, the only highpoints are shots of shadows on walls (a man in a hat, a cat, etc.) and scenes in which the cat walks into rooms, always accompanied by the same hard-on-the-ears series of musical "meows."

Probably the oddest element in the picture is the strange character played by Iris Clive (a minor-and-*then*-some actress who did nothing else but Westerns). "Kyra Goran" seems to appear supernaturally on the island, full of prattle about spirits and cats. Parallels with characters from Val Lewton's *Cat People* are immediately apparent: Kyra initially speaks in an unrecognizable tongue (think Elizabeth Russell in her brief *Cat People* restaurant scene) and makes obtuse references to a cat-worshipping race. Since *The Cat Creeps* was co written by Edward Dein, who claimed to have been an uncredited collaborator on *Cat People*, it seems safe to assume that the Kyra character was part of his contribution. Dein apparently was influenced by having worked with Lewton (*Jungle Woman*, another Universal that carries Dein's name, also boasts several Lewtonesque touches), but was never able to successfully apply what he learned at the RKO B-unit to Universal pictures. There was no point in keeping the Ape Woman off camera throughout *Jungle Woman*, and the introduction of the Kyra character into *The Cat Creeps* only makes a silly picture sillier.

Like several of the Inner Sanctums, the *Cat Creeps* story builds around a group of basically ordinary people in a realistic environment; audiences instinctively know that in this type of set-up, any "supernatural" element that crops up will eventually be exposed as ersatz. There's never any doubt that Kyra will turn out to be a simple red herring; the picture gives this away frequently by showing her conspiratorially schmoozing with Nichols, with whom she's clearly in cahoots. Yet the mature, cosmopolitan characters played by Rose Hobart, Jonathan Hale and Douglass Dumbrille appear to swallow her fantastic claims whole-hog. The cat frightens Hobart into agreeing to confess, and Dumbrille and Hale start following the fleabag around the house expecting it to lead them to the money. It's almost as ridiculous as a later, slightly similar "chiller," the English-made *Shadow of the Cat* (1961).

Apart from the bizarre Kyra character, every other plot ingredient in *The Cat Creeps* has been pre-tested in scores of features: An obnoxious newsman-hero, a swooning ingenue, a gloomy house, fleeting shadows, clutching hands and bickering suspects who all go off in different directions just before the next mysterious event. ("Out one door and in the other — it's all so confusing!" Pidge grumbles, nicely encapsulating the whole movie.) Fred Brady and company respond to screams by bounding up a staircase not once, not twice but three separate times (always viewed from the same top-of-the-stairs camera angle); every hinge in the place gets a frequent workout. These elements were old hat before pictures began to talk yet the makers of *The Cat Creeps* trundle them out for another go-round; their only concern was exposing just enough film to call it a movie before dumping it onto the public.

The biggest deficit in a movie groaning under the weight of deficits is the exasperating and unfunny performance of the central player, Fred Brady. Brady's Terry Nichols is a never-empty well of condescending, humorless banter. Newsman-heroes have always tended to be an irritating breed in horror films, with Lee Tracy (*Doctor X*) and Wallace Ford (*The Mysterious Mr. Wong*) springing to mind as perhaps the worst offenders, but Brady, who looks like a cross between Donald O'Connor and Howdy Doody, also rates a spot on that lamentable list. He is a bland and unappealing actor even in his rare serious moments, and it comes as no surprise that his Hollywood acting career was a short one. Prior to *The Cat Creeps*, Brady was a radio writer and performer, and after his inauspicious movie-acting fling he was a screenwriter on *Champagne for Caesar* (1950), *Hollywood Story* (1951), *Never Wave at a WAC* (1952) and *Taxi* (1953).

The character of Pidge, his shutterbug-sidekick, is equally obnoxious, but top-billed Noah Beery, Jr., a breezier and more personable actor, comes across far better than Brady. ("Pidge" was Beery's real-life nickname.) Lois Collier, cute as ever, gives her usual near-miss performance. The creeping cat of the film's title was played by "Smoky," who caused some minor delays by fixing its gaze on the microphone rather than its trainer (the problem was solved with catnip). Like Fred Brady, Smoky too has gone on to great obscurity.

Paul Kelly, Douglass Dumbrille and Jonathan Hale are their old dependable selves, but truth be told these are all actors better taken in small doses rather than as the stars of a movie. Kelly ran the gamut in Universal murder mysteries: In *The Cat Creeps* he was a murder suspect and then a murder victim, in *The Missing Guest* he solved the murder mystery and in *Dead Man's Eyes* he *was* the murderer. As he was in real life: In 1927, high on Scotch, he beat to death the equally drunk husband of his actress-girlfriend Dorothy Mackaye. At the end of a highly publicized trial, Kelly was sentenced to one to ten years but served just over two. For trying to cover up the crime, Mackaye got one to three years but served less than ten months. They married in 1931; her play *Women in Prison*, based on her experiences, became the 1933 Barbara Stanwyck movie *Ladies They Talk About.*

The Cat Creeps wrapped up one day over schedule, with director Kenton pocketing a cool $5,000 for his 13 days of work. Double-billed in the spring of 1946 with *She-Wolf of London*, the combo no doubt had folks limping out of theaters with a "We shoulda stayed home tonight" attitude.

The film is an eminently forgettable one, not only for fans but even for its cast and crew. Rose Hobart remembers only that she enjoyed working with Paul Kelly, and Edward Dein, who wrote the picture, could recall nothing at all about the experience. Even today, the mention of the title prompts horror buffs to think instantly of the 1930 *The Cat Creeps*— a lost film which few if any of them has ever seen!

The Cat Creeps would probably rank with Universal's worst horror films but for a few minor highlights: The spooky shot of the boat arriving at the island, the murder of Paul Kelly and the violent climactic fistfight (both Brady and Dumbrille come away from the brawl with nasty facial gashes). But a minute of worthwhile footage does not compensate for nearly an hour of tiresome gab and endless pussy-footing. *The Cat Creeps* represents just one more nail in the coffin of Universal Horrors.

Critics' Corner

A well developed tale which engages the interest of all. — Daughters of the American Revolution (Eastern Committee), 1946

[I]t is a routine little thriller, with feeble attempts

at comedy.... The cat gives a pretty good performance but it gets mediocre support.... Incidentally, this film bears no resemblance to Universal's *Cat Creeps* of some years back, except that it also has the same title and is also shown on a screen.—*The New York Times*, May 18, 1946, Bosley Crowther

Rating: ★ [T]he least effective murder mystery that has been made in years. Running three minutes short of an hour, the film has the appearance of having been thrown together in about the same length of time.... [T]he performances, if possible, are worse than the production.—*The New York Daily News*, May 18, 1946, Wanda Hale

Direction of Erle C. Kenton is paced in a manner to give each point full opportunity to register, and the performances are evenly weighted, one against the other for suspense.—*The Motion Picture Herald*, April 13, 1946, William R. Weaver

Its production ... is exactly what the tight-knitted mystery subject deserved. Nor are faults to be found with the casting or the suspenseful direction of the practiced Erle C. Kenton.... Fred Brady undertakes the assignment of the brash reporter, somehow managing to suggest more of a song and dance man than a real news mugg.—*The Hollywood Reporter*, April 5, 1946, Jack D. Grant

There is nothing either frightening or mysterious about the law-breaking in *The Cat Creeps*, and it is not quite silly enough to be laughable.—*The New York Herald-Tribune*, May 18, 1946, Otis L. Guernsey, Jr.

She-Wolf of London

Released May 17, 1946. 61 minutes. *Director:* Jean Yarbrough. *Producer:* Ben Pivar. *Screenplay:* George Bricker. *Original Story:* Dwight V. Babcock. *Photography:* Maury Gertsman. *Camera Operator:* John Martin. *Editor:* Paul Landres. *Art Directors:* Jack Otterson & Abraham Grossman. *Assistant Director:* Ralph Slosser. *Musical Director:* William Lava. *Set Decorators:* Russell A. Gausman & Leigh Smith. *Dialogue Director:* Raymond Kessler. *Sound Director:* Bernard B. Brown. *Technician:* Joe Lapis. *Makeup:* Jack P. Pierce. *Gowns:* Vera West.

Don Porter (*Barry Lanfield*), June Lockhart (*Phyllis Allenby*), Sara Haden (*Martha Winthrop*), Jan Wiley (*Carol Winthrop*), Dennis Hoey (*Insp. Pierce*), Martin Kosleck (*Dwight Severn*), Eily Malyon (*Hannah*), Lloyd Corrigan (*Latham*), Frederic Worlock (*Constable Ernie Hobbs*), David Thursby, Olaf Hytten, James Finlayson, Warren Jackson (*Constables*), William H. O'Brien (*Bobby*), Jimmy Aubrey *(Cabby)*. *Deleted from final print:* Joan Wells (*Phyllis as a Child*), Clara Blandick (*Mrs. McBroom*).

She done me in ... the Wolf Woman!
—*Lloyd Corrigan in* She-Wolf of London

She-Wolf of London is the kind of chiller horror fans love to hate. It is one of those deceptive little ditties that tease us for an hour or so with tantalizing horror effects and grim atmospherics, only to come toppling down like a house of cards with the disclosure that the forces of the supernatural weren't responsible for the mayhem after all, just a greedy guardian attempting to gain control of an estate. We've seen it all before; it's an old trick that doesn't improve with age.

In the case of *She-Wolf of London*, there's absolutely no reason why George Bricker and Dwight V. Babcock could not have conceived the tale as a bonafide horror story rather than a predictable whodunit. They had the resources of Hollywood's premier horror factory at their disposal, yet the writers settled on a musty, old-fashioned murder melodrama that merely exploits the plot's supernatural angle rather than building upon it in a creative way. (Interestingly enough, in the 1913 two-reel short, *The Werewolf*, produced by Universal, the title character is actually a she-wolf.)

By adapting the title from one of Universal's early horror classics, the studio got more bang for its buck (just as it did for the 1946 release, *The Cat Creeps*). With *House of Dracula* presently making the rounds of the neighborhood grind houses, the monster rally days of Universal's Second Golden Age of Horror were effectively over. All that remained were the Rondo Hatton Creeper movies (no elaborate makeup jobs there) and eerie old house thrillers such as *She-Wolf of London* and *The Spider Woman Strikes Back* (again, no painstaking makeup effects). More than ever, economy was the order of the day.

Heralded in the trades more than a year before it went before the cameras, *She-Wolf of London* was hardly an example of the top flight fare Ben Pivar was promised after his promotion by the studio in November 1944. Signing on *House of Horrors* director Jean Yarbrough, Pivar obtained the services of June Lockhart, Don Porter, Sara Haden, Jan Wiley, Forrester Harvey and Una O'Connor to fill his cast. O'Connor was dropped from the roster in favor of Eily Malyon; Forrester Harvey passed away suddenly on the evening of December 14, 1945, before any of his scenes were shot. Undoubtedly, he was slated for

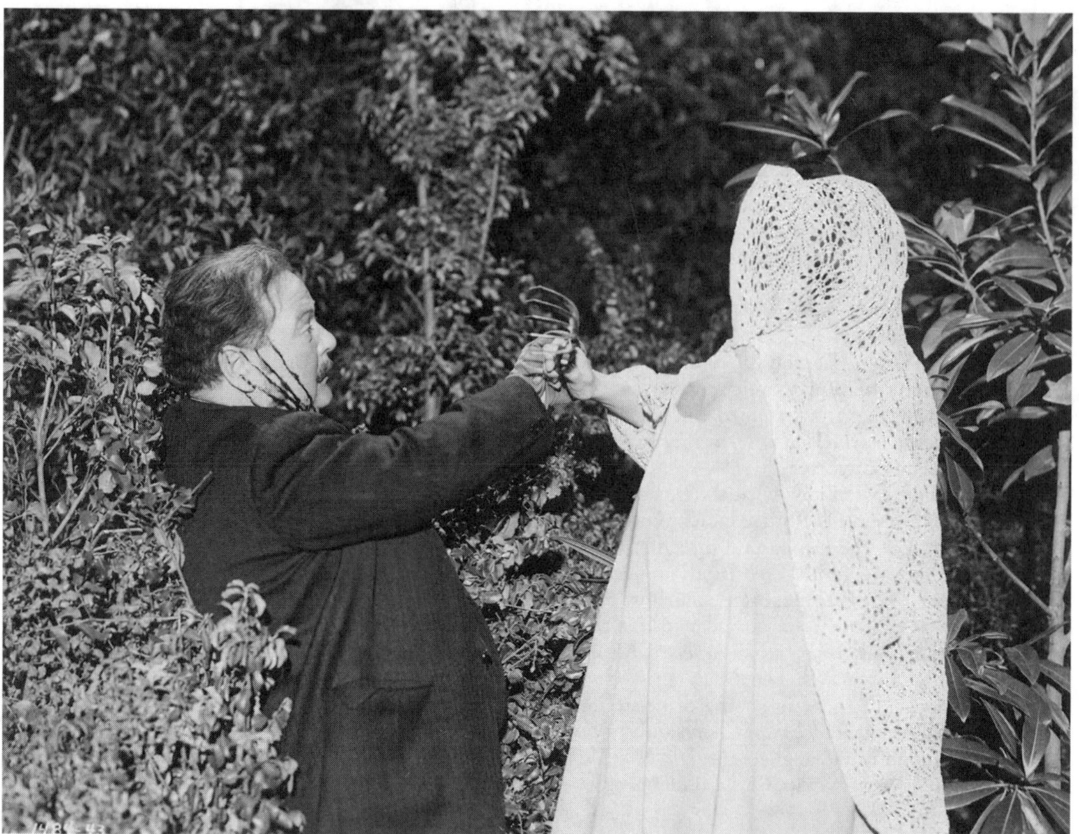

Latham (Lloyd Corrigan) is slashed to death by the title character in *She-Wolf of London.*

the role of Scotland Yard man Latham, which was ultimately filled by jovial character actor and former director Lloyd Corrigan. If Forrester Harvey *had* survived the making of the movie, he would have played a role similar to Mr. Twiddle in *The Wolf Man* (the head police investigator's assistant, who is prone to believing in werewolves).

The basic premise of *She-Wolf of London* had real potential. In turn-of-the-century London, Phyllis Allenby (June Lockhart) lives in dread fear of an ancient curse cast on her family by wolves. When a series of violent attacks occur in a nearby park, Phyllis is convinced that she is responsible. Plagued by nightmares, the troubled young woman awakens each morning to find her shoes muddied, her nightgown torn, and her hands and arms streaked with dried blood.

Residing with Phyllis is her aunt, Martha Winthrop (Sara Haden), and her cousin, Carol (Jan Wiley). Phyllis is ignorant of the fact that neither woman is her blood relative, and that the palatial home they all share actually belongs to her. It is to the film's detriment that scribe Bricker tips his hand and reveals this crucial bit of information much too soon. Armchair sleuths, not deceived by *She-Wolf of London*'s horrific come-on, must have smelled a rat when dear old Aunt Martha, eyebrow arched, announces that Phyllis "is the only heir."

A young boy is found mangled to death (his terrified scream rates amongst the most chilling in the annals of horror). Upon learning the news, Phyllis becomes hysterical and goes into seclusion, breaking off her engagement to barrister Barry Lanfield (Don Porter). Barry, Martha and Carol can't make Phyllis realize that she is letting her imagination run away with her.

Latham (Lloyd Corrigan), a Scotland Yard investigator, firmly believes the attacks are being committed by a "She-Wolf," and does a house-to-house check of the well-to-do neighborhood. Late that night, a veiled figure emerges from the home and disappears into the fog-enshrouded park. Latham becomes separated from his men and comes face-to-face with the murderer. By the time the bobbies find him, he is bleeding to death from wounds received in the attack.

Launching his own investigation, the ever-suspicious Barry stations himself outside Phyllis' house. He watches as Carol, a veil covering her head, emerges and walks into the park. Minutes later, Dwight Severn (Martin Kosleck), Carol's secret sweetheart, is almost clawed to death by a cloaked figure. The next day, Barry confronts Carol with his suspicions that she is the serial killer. Appalled by his accusations, Carol volunteers to accompany Barry to the police in an effort to get to the bottom of the grisly business.

Taking a cue from Alfred Hitchcock's *Suspicion* (1941), Martha prepares a glass of warm milk and serves it to the nerve-wracked Phyllis. She drains the glass and slips into a paralyzed state. Beaming malevolently, Martha confesses to Phyllis that she doctored the milk (as she'd been doing all along), and now plans to kill the helpless girl. Realizing only too well that Phyllis' marriage to Barry will make the young woman eligible to claim her inheritance (thus costing Martha the home she has managed for years), Martha set out to implicate Phyllis in the attacks that she herself committed. Drawing a knife, Martha is about to plunge it into the prostate girl's body when Hannah (Eily Malyon), the housekeeper, intervenes. Martha pursues Hannah to the head of the staircase, but stumbles and plummets down the steps. The knife deeply embedded in her own bosom, Martha dies moments before Barry, Carol and the authorities arrive on the scene.

Dusting off the Hacienda set as a stand-in for the Winthrop home and terrace, and flooding an area of the Providencia Ranch with "bee smoke" to simulate a misty London Park, Yarbrough began shooting *She-Wolf of London* on December 8, 1945, wrapping up production on the 21st, three days over schedule.

Don Porter's recollections of the last hours of shooting sounds like something out of Charles Dickens:

> The scene in the buggy was a process shot. It took *hours*; they never got the process right. They closed the set so people couldn't get away and go to all the Christmas parties on the other sets. We damned near starved to death. We smuggled in some sandwiches and finally they got the process right. I was focused and got the words right. The director said, "Cut! Print! That's a wrap!" and before I could get out of the buggy and help June, the set was cleared ... everybody left! The "bee smoke" that they used [in the park scenes] made it very difficult to talk. If you had a scene, they'd roll that stuff in at about ankle-height, then it would rise. Trying to do lines and keep from choking was a little difficult.

It doesn't take a detective (much less a moviegoer with half a brain) to pick out the real culprit in *She-Wolf of London* from among the red herrings. Sara Haden's early revelation that she really isn't Phyllis' aunt, but an old family domestic who has been living comfortably off the girl's assets, is a dead giveaway. Add to this her disclosure that she was once Phyllis' father's sweetheart and the case is solved before it has begun. On top of that, the sharp-eyed viewer could clearly make out the (hairless) features of a female face in the scene where the She-Wolf stalks Lloyd Corrigan (whether it was actually Haden under the white veil isn't discernible). *New York Times* film critic Thomas M. Pryor probably felt he wasn't ruining anyone's good time when he identified the "diabolical old crone" as the She-Wolf in his sarcastic review!

The Allenby Curse is given rather short shrift in the release print of *She-Wolf of London.* (In England, the picture was distributed under the apt title *The Curse of the Allenbys.*) Such unanswered queries as to why the Allenbys were accursed in the first place might have been explained in an episode cut from the final print. Set in Allenby Hall in the late nineteenth century, the missing scene(s), featuring seven-year-old Joan Wells as the young Phyllis and Clara Blandick as her nanny Mrs. McBroom, would have undoubtedly shed more light on this less-than-pressing matter.

For a tightly-budgeted B, *She-Wolf of London* is well-mounted. Jean Yarbrough makes the most of his limited resources and manages some real atmosphere in the prowling wolf-woman scenes. William Lava's broody musical score, heavy on portentous strings, and Maury Gertsman's faultless photography and lighting effects contribute to the overall aura of foreboding. (Gertsman isn't above incorporating such stylis-

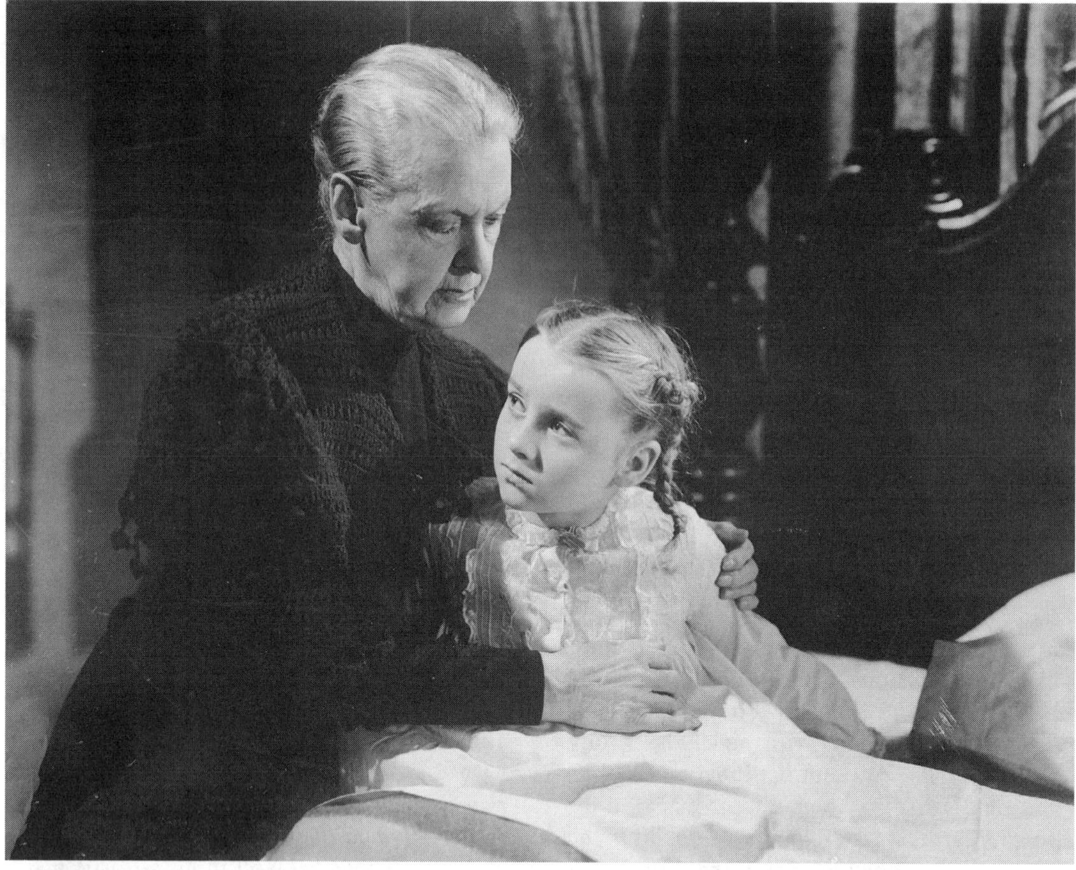

In a flashback scene excised from the release print of *She-Wolf*, Clara Blandick comforts Joan Wells (as the young Phyllis Allenby).

tically obvious little tricks as tilted camera effects and distorted lenses to alleviate the flat narrative.)

As ever, George Bricker demonstrates his woeful deficiencies as a screen writer. Lloyd Corrigan's seasoned detective theorizes, on the flimsiest of evidence, that a werewolf is afoot in modern London. In a failed attempt at cheering Phyllis, Barry rattles off several graphic passages from Shakespeare's "The Merchant of Venice" with the aplomb of a thespian. "The newspapers are full of it!" Carol gasps in reference to the latest She-Wolf attack. And, as a defeated Phyllis awaits Scotland Yard's arrival, dear Aunt Martha comfortingly coos, "The police will ask you hundreds of questions."

As poor, neurotic Phyllis, June Lockhart's character is too whiny to generate much audience sympathy. The only child of acting couple Gene and Kathleen Lockhart, June had her first taste of show business when she made her Metropolitan Opera debut at the age of eight as a ballerina. By the time *She-Wolf of London* came around, the young actress had the good fortune to act opposite Bette Davis (in *All This, and Heaven Too* [1940]) and Gary Cooper (in *Sergeant York* [1941]). June Lockhart recalled with a laugh for the authors:

> Oh, *She-Wolf of London* was fun to do. If I'm remembering right, I was just submitted for it by my agent. I did it, and — I was not very good in it. But the following year, I was the hot ingénue on Broadway in a wonderful comedy, so I guess what I needed [in *She-Wolf*] was a good direction. Well, I guess the director ... was a good one, but the film was of the genre that they did at Universal — I think it only took two weeks to shoot. That was so early in my experience, I was still learning the technique of film acting. There were a lot of English people in it who were friends of my father's — so there again, it was not strange or un-

usual or awkward. Don Porter was my leading man, and he was a dear.

The Broadway experience Lockhart referred to was the 1947 comedy "For Love or Money," with John Loder. The play itself was mediocre by all accounts, but the actress got a standing ovation opening night and immediately became the talk of the Great White Way. She went on to win a Tony, the Donaldson Award, the Theatre World Award and the Associated Press citation for Woman of the Year for Drama.

Don Porter and Jan Wiley contribute mature, no-nonsense performances but Sara Haden indulges in the kind of broad, wicked witch theatrics that are more apt to draw chuckles than chills. Haden has the same problem as Gale Sondergaard. She just can't help but exude venom, even when she's being nice. (The actress is best remembered for her frequent appearances as kindly Aunt Polly in the Mickey Rooney Andy Hardy movies.) As Jan Wiley's lover, an impoverished artist, Martin Kosleck is (refreshingly) out-of-character. (Not only is he on the outside of the mayhem looking in, Kosleck even walks away with one of the female leads in tow!) He recalled the experience with amusement, regarding his part in the film as a "consolation prize" for having played so many heavies.

Curious as it may seem, *She-Wolf of London*'s uninspired plotline could also be found in several other horror productions over the years, most notably *Devil Bat's Daughter* (1946), which, coincidentally, was reviewed by *Variety* on the same day as the Universal film. Former Miss America Rosemary LaPlanche plays the orphaned daughter of a scientist who is reputed to have been a vampire; the poor girl is troubled by nightmares, implicated in a murder and (of course) begins to believe that *she's* a vampire. It turns out that the girl's guardian (Michael Hale) has been spiking her nightly tonic with hallucinatory drugs and is guilty of perpetrating the crimes. Universal alumnus Griffin Jay penned the tepid screenplay for this PRC turkey. In the 1951 Columbia potboiler, *The Son of Dr. Jekyll*, Louis Hayward plays the hardheaded scion determined to vindicate his infamous parent. He attempts to duplicate the senior Jekyll's experiments; soon afterward, a string of attacks disturb the once-peaceful community. In a fiery climax, it is revealed that young Jekyll's guardian (Alexander Knox), who has been stealing from the estate, was responsible for the recent deaths as well as for the killings blamed on Dr. Jekyll himself. And, in 1957, Jack Pollexfen (who cowrote the story for *The Son of Dr. Jekyll*) wrote and produced *Daughter of Dr. Jekyll*, which is practically a remake of *She-Wolf of London*. Janet Jekyll (played by Gloria Talbott in the same irritatingly despondent style as Lockhart) returns to the ancestral stamping grounds and learns from her guardian (Arthur Shields) that her father was *the* Dr. Jekyll. Distressed by this bit of unwelcome news, she sinks into a deep depression and tries to break her engagement to stolid beau John Agar. Talbott blames herself for a shocking series of nocturnal murders, basing her suspicions on nightmares and blood-splattered nightclothes. As might be expected, Shields is behind the mystery: He has been doping Talbott's tonic and then committing the murders himself (the twist here is that he actually *becomes* a werewolf-like Mr. Hyde). As before, the motive for all of this mayhem is to gain control of the Jekyll estate and fortune.

Although by no means a good film, at least *Daughter of Dr. Jekyll* does deliver a red-blooded monster, which is more than can be said for either *She-Wolf of London* or its half-baked cousins.

Critics' Corner

Rating: ★★½ There's a lot of malevolent atmosphere to evoke suspense ... along with clues enough to anticipate a satisfactory violent climax.... [T]he film does a fancy job tight-rope walking until everything is keyed for a jump in the right direction.—*The New York Daily News*, April 6, 1946, Dorothy Masters

All that remains to be said ... about this latest release from Universal's bottom-drawer is that it certainly doesn't justify the effort expended in its behalf.—*The New York Times*, April 6, 1946, Thomas M. Pryor

It is boresome and long-drawn out, and it is given more to talk than to action. The plot, which has been done many times, is obvious, for the spectator is never really in doubt as to the murderer's identity.... Unlike the title indicates [*sic*], there is nothing about either the action or the characters that is horrifying or terrifying.—*Harrison's Reports*, April 13, 1946

Jean Yarbrough ... is most adroit in turning suspicions from [Haden to Wiley to Malyon]. It was a difficult task to balance these strange acts by other characters and at the same time maintain the mood of the period piece. Yarbrough does both with a master hand.... Lloyd Corrigan is a joy as usual.—*The Hollywood Reporter*, April 5, 1946, Jack D. Grant

Dressed to Kill

Released June 7, 1946. 72 minutes. *Producer-Director:* Roy William Neill. *Executive Producer:* Howard Benedict. *Screenplay:* Leonard Lee. *Adaptation:* Frank Gruber. *Based on a story by* Sir Arthur Conan Doyle. *Photography:* Maury Gertsman. *Editor:* Saul A. Goodkind. *Musical Director:* Milton Rosen. *Song:* Jack Brooks. *Art Directors:* Jack Otterson & Martin Obzina. *Director of Sound:* Bernard B. Brown. *Technician:* Glenn E. Anderson. *Set Decorators:* Russell A. Gausman & Edward R. Robinson. *Assistant Director:* Melville Shyer. *Dialogue Director:* Raymond Kessler. *Makeup:* Jack P. Pierce. *Hair Stylist:* Carmen Dirigo. *Gowns:* Vera West.

Basil Rathbone (*Sherlock Holmes*), Nigel Bruce (*Dr. John H. Watson*), Patricia Morison (*Hilda Courtney*), Edmond Breon (*Julian Emery*), Frederic Worlock (*Col. Cavanaugh*), Carl Harbord (*Insp. Hopkins*), Patricia Cameron (*Evelyn Clifford*), Tom P. Dillon (*Det. Thompson*), Harry Cording (*Hamid*), Mary Gordon (*Mrs. Hudson*), Ian Wolfe (*Scotland Yard Commissioner*), Holmes Herbert (*Ebenezer Crabtree*), Olaf Hytten (*Alfred*), Cyril Delevanti (*John Davidson*), Leyland Hodgson (*Tour Guide*), Topsy Glyn (*Kilgour Child*), Wally Scott (*Joe Cisto*), Sally Shepherd (*Tobacconist*), Marjorie Bennett (*Antique Shop Assistant*), Frank Baker (*Photographer*), Guy Bellis (*Doctor*), Wilson Benge (*Minister*), Lillian Bronson (*Minister's Wife*), Boyd Irwin (*Detective*), Guy Kingsford (*Undercover Convict*), Anita Sharp-Bolster (*Teacher*), Charlie Hall (*Cab Driver*), Alexander Pollard (*Auction Clerk*), Ted Billings, Tiny Jones (*Pub Extras*).

So fearfully awkward having a dead body lying about, don't you agree, Mr. Holmes?
—*Patricia Morison in* Dressed to Kill

Artistically, the Sherlock Holmes series was running out of gas, but the faithful still flocked to each new adventure in spite of the repetition of plots and the formula characters. The ever-loyal audience and the customary low budgets assured a profit for Universal but the twelfth entry, *Dressed to Kill*, was to be the last. Unsurprisingly, the film turned out to be another second-drawer outing, not without charm but certainly lacking in invention.

Julian Emery (Edmond Breon), a well-bred country-club Londoner, pays a call on his good friend Dr. Watson (Nigel Bruce). Emery recounts how he was attacked the night before by a housebreaker who absconded with a music box from his sizable collection. The bewildered Emery points out that the crook made off with a box of only marginal value, passing up others worth a small fortune. Sherlock Holmes (Basil Rathbone) suspects that the crime was something more than just a petty theft. When Emery is found murdered in his apartment the next day, the detective initiates a full-scale investigation.

Holmes traces the stolen music box to an auction gallery and learns that it was one in a set of three manufactured at Dartmoor Prison. When it turns out that the prisoner who made the boxes is serving a stretch for stealing a duplicate set of Bank of England plates from which five-pound notes are printed, Holmes deduces that the boxes contain a message to the prisoner's accomplices revealing the whereabouts of the missing plates.

The gang includes Hilda Courtney (Patricia Morison), a slinky, mink-clad brunette, the dapper Col. Cavanaugh (Frederic Worlock) and Hamid (Harry Cording), who works double-duty as their chauffeur and assassin. The trio find themselves competing with Holmes for possession of the complete set of music boxes.

The conspirators nab the detective, shackle him to an overhead pipe and attempt to dispatch him with poison gas but Holmes escapes in short order. Obtaining the last piece of the puzzle, Holmes concludes that the tune played by the boxes conceals a coded message. Assigning a letter to each note, the hiding place of the bank plates is revealed: a bookcase in the memorial home of writer Dr. Samuel Johnson. Holmes and the police catch the gang red-handed as they are about to make off with the goods, bringing the detective's last (Universal) adventure to a close.

Dressed to Kill is far from an underrated picture, but its few agreeable qualities are usually glossed over by reviewers. The film is small-scale and ungimmicky; in fact, it is the most rudimentary of the last group of Sherlock Holmes thrillers. It lacks the stylish visuals of *The Woman in Green* and avoids the novelty settings of *Pursuit to Algiers* (an ocean liner) and *Terror by Night* (a Scotland-bound train). In *Dressed to Kill*, Holmes rarely strays from his old, familiar environs, picking up obscure clues from musical boxes and half-forgotten dance hall ditties. The mystery is commonplace and unspectacular, but there is a certain appeal in the film's simplicity (in many of Conan Doyle stories, the detective never even leaves his drawing room). The early reels promise a cozy and reassuring entertainment, but the film soon gets stuck in a rut of clichés. Indeed, *Dressed to Kill* is the most derivative of the Sherlock Holmes adventures; virtually every turn of the plot has been cribbed from a previous entry.

As in *The Pearl of Death*, Holmes and his adversaries are in a dead heat, competing for piecemeal clues concealed in *objets d'art*, all of which fall into the hands of unsuspecting collectors. As in *Sherlock Holmes and the Secret Weapon*, the detective is confounded with a seemingly unbreakable code. Hilda Courtney, like Adrea Spedding (the Spider Woman), is quite adept at using smoke bombs and poison gas against her rivals, and like so many other Holmes villains, has mastered the art of disguise. Following the example of killer Alastair Ramson (*The Scarlet Claw*), she gets rid of a bothersome witness, in this case a little girl, by trussing her up and leaving her in a closet.

Watson is as inept as ever, but his baby talk somehow provides Holmes with the decisive clue: A mere quote of Dr. Samuel Johnson tips off the detective as to the location of the stolen bank plates. The typically over-zealous Holmes outsmarts himself by falling into Courtney's clutches, but her method of disposing of him proves so clumsy and ill-conceived, the detective practically walks away from it. The whole production seems as tired as the overused *Son of Frankenstein* music cues on the soundtrack.

Patricia Morison, the perfect choice for the role of the ruthless Hilda Courtney, is a disappointing femme fatale thanks to a script that offers her few opportunities. When her big confrontation scene with Holmes finally arrives, she's up against some pretty limp dialogue and an understandably bored sparring partner. More impressive is her disarmingly accurate turn as a frumpy Cockney charwoman who gets the best of Holmes in a particularly witty scene. The actress recalled her experiences making the film with Gregory Mank:

> Of course, Nigel Bruce — we called him "Willy" — was an absolute darling! It was a lot of fun. Basil and "Willy" broke for tea every afternoon on the set — the whole crew and everybody! The tea tray would come in with a silver service and everything.
>
> Universal, in those days, was like a nice little country club. There wasn't that terrible big Black Tower, and there was the commissary, like a little country restaurant. I remember, I was all made up for the old Cockney woman in my *Dressed to Kill* disguise, and I went into the commissary to have lunch as a test how good my makeup was. And the maitre d' said, "All the extras sit at the counter!"

Leonard Lee's pastiche script accommodates the studio's low-budgetary requirements and is so uncinematic it probably would have worked just as well as one of Rathbone and Bruce's Sherlock Holmes radio plays. The main titles fails to mention the specific Conan Doyle story the script was based on, although the likely contender is the very first Holmes adventure, "A Scandal in Bohemia." (Typical of the series, the movie borrows only a single plot incident.) In the course of the tale, Holmes diverts his female adversary, the elusive and beautiful Irene Adler, by setting a small fire; in the movie, the tables are turned with Courtney outfoxing Watson with a similar ruse.

Director Roy William Neill's prowling camera manages to enliven the dialogue-heavy script in one or two scenes. Ironically, he saves one the detective's most effective entrances for the last installment. Under the wistful strains of "Danny Boy" emanating from Holmes' violin, the film establishes the setting with a close-up of the number "221B" above the front door of Mrs. Hudson's Baker Street residence. This is followed by a quick cut to the interior as the camera ascends the staircase and then cutting yet again to an overhead shot of the detective's lonely study. Within moments, the two familiar figures, Holmes and Watson, are quietly reflecting on the latter's most recently published adventure (interestingly, "A Scandal in Bohemia"). The scene gives way to a brief poignant moment, giving the calculating detective his only chance in the series to romantically reflect on the elusive Irene Adler. One of Conan Doyle's most intriguing characters, the New Jersey–born Adler, often only referred to as "*the* woman," was the only female who stirred the detective's romantic longings in the entire run of Holmes adventures. The pensive scene is in stark contrast to the character's introduction in the first film, *Sherlock Holmes and the Voice of Terror*, which found Holmes very much in command of the situation, urgently arriving at the British Intelligence headquarters.

Patricia Morison attained her greatest fame on the stage as a musical star but her elegant villainy in *Calling Dr. Death* and *Dressed to Kill* made a strong impression as well. Her alluring, vaguely exotic personality was perfect for the movies although she never found a suitable star vehicle. (She would have made an ideal Katherine Caldwell in *Son of Dracula.*)

Rathbone's unshakable identification with Sherlock Holmes caused him much personal anguish as well as costing him some choice film roles (he lost out to George Sanders as Lord Henry Wotton in MGM's *The Picture of Dorian Gray* [1945]). Determined to salvage his movie career, the proud actor terminated the series by bowing out of it. Although the studio's contract with the Conan Doyle estate wouldn't lapse for another three years, it was very likely Universal would have pulled the plug on the series in any event. Artistically, the series had plainly run its course, and now with the world entering the dawn of the Atomic Age, Sherlock Holmes seemed more than ever a holdover from another era. Furthermore, with the studio's merger with International Pictures, the death knell was sounding for all programmer features on the production slate. The Sherlock Holmes series would have been an obvious casualty.

The picture's release hardly caused a stir and most critics seemed more interested in griping about the inappropriateness of the title. One wonders where these critics were looking when the sleek, elegantly coiffured Patricia Morison dispassionately extracted her ermine from under the body of poor old Emery (played to perfection by Edmond Breon), and then coldbloodedly stepped around the corpse. A very felicitous title, indeed, and far better than its original appellation, *Prelude to Murder*. (In England, the picture was released as *Sherlock Holmes and the Secret Code.*)

In a cruel twist of fate, the termination of the series did not profit Roy William Neill. He went on to direct Peter Lorre in a slick but intriguing film noir, *Black Angel* (1946), only to die (a heart attack) a few months after its release while visiting relatives in England in October 1946. "I can see traces of the Roy Neill I knew in the Columbia days in the skillful composition and staging of his scenes," Neill's sound man at Columbia, Edward Bernds, remarked in reference to the Holmes series. "I'm glad that he had a chance to exercise some of his skill, or you can call it artistry, without Columbia's tyrannical production office goading him to speed up, to get the scheduled day's work done any way he could."

In less than a decade, Basil Rathbone had gone from being regarded as one of Hollywood's most versatile players to being branded as a one-part actor. Dispirited, he found temporary salvation on the stage. In 1947, he had the great good fortune to be cast in the Henry James–inspired "The Heiress," which won him a Tony Award for Best Actor. However, the future did not look promising. The American theater was entering one of its most creative periods but the actor, who was most at home in classic and period roles, had difficulty fitting into a world where Tennessee Williams and Arthur Miller were the up-and-coming masters. Probably motivated by commercial considerations, Rathbone donned the deerstalker for the last time, reprising Conan Doyle's master detective in a play written by his wife, Ouida. Simply titled "Sherlock Holmes," the play was doomed to failure. The production opened on Broadway on October 30, 1953, and closed the following day.

Rathbone eventually returned to acting in motion pictures, appearing in the Bob Hope comedy, *Casanova's Big Night* (1954). On the set, he told a visiting reporter:

> I wasn't happy with what I had gotten myself into in Hollywood. After I had played Sherlock Holmes in 14 pictures and on 200 broadcasts, I decided it was time to call a halt. I was on a treadmill and I had to get off.

With barely concealed bitterness, Rathbone would write in 1955:

> Mickey Spillane and his ilk killed Sherlock Holmes. His accomplice was the people of today, the tempo of today, which greatly prefers violence and bloodshed in its mysteries to the art of conversation, to descriptive passages and carefully arrived-at deduction. The mysteries of Sherlock Holmes gave you these. Mickey gives you the violence of the .45.

Holmes (Basil Rathbone) and Watson (Nigel Bruce) round up a trio of murderous counterfeiters (Frederic Worlock, Patricia Morison, Harry Cording) in the climax of *Dressed to Kill*.

> I should have known better than to take my production of "Sherlock Holmes" to Broadway. During our tryout period in Boston, the house was never more than half full. I wondered why. I got to studying the audience from the wings. And then it hit me. Not one person in the house was under 45.... There just wasn't enough bloodshed and violence in "Sherlock Holmes" for younger people. There was talk, but no shooting; no "gats" and "dolls" and lips blood-stained from kissing. That sort of thing just wasn't Conan Doyle's dish of tea. I'm afraid it isn't mine, either.

The actor enjoyed a great success with his touring one-man show, "An Evening with Basil Rathbone" yet he often took jobs that were beneath him. In 1959, he took part in a revue called "Fun Time," which *The Hollywood Reporter* called the year's "shabbiest, most shameful show-biz shambles." Comic Jack E. Leonard was originally set to co-star, but the producer Jules Pfeiffer, the iconic comic strip artist and later playwright, fired him and took over the part himself. According to the *Reporter*,

> Pfeiffer reshuffled Rathbone's John Gielgud–type reading act from next-to-closing to the opening spot, cut the actor from 30 minutes to ten [and] gave the pit band the downbeat to play "Cow Cow Boogie" during Rathbone's soliloquies!

The *Reporter* described the show as resembling "something out of the Grand Guignol"—a genre in which Rathbone *also* acted, according to his actor-friend Booth Colman. Colman told the authors:

> When he [returned to Hollywood], he was old and tired and working in some [stage show] they did here, in the Santa Monica High School, I believe. It was a terrible comedown for him. I can only gather that he needed the money.... It was awful, a Grand Guignol play with the side of someone's face being fried in a pan and all that. It was *unfitting* to see him doing that stuff. I was so sorry that he felt he had to.

Throughout the remaining years of his life, and in the decades which followed, the Basil Rathbone Sherlock Holmes series remained in practically constant circulation. By the late '40s, they made the rounds on the Realart reissue circuit but Universal would prove to be a remarkably inept custodian of one of their most valuable war-era franchises. Rather than retaining the rights to the series, the studio sold the entire lot for some quick cash in the early '50s. As a result, all television prints were struck from negatives from which all traces of the studio that made them, including opening logos and closing titles, were crudely cut. A few titles even fell into the public domain, making them accessible to video bootleggers and colorization companies. In the '60s, the series' national syndicators packaged the films, accompanying them with introductions by Basil Rathbone himself.

Although this prized series was often cavalierly treated by various licensees or shown in unbecomingly murky, sometimes unwatchable prints, their enduring charms have not been lost on generations of film fans. Until the popular BBC television series with Jeremy Brett in the '90s, Basil Rathbone was virtually unrivaled as the quintessential screen incarnation of Sir Arthur Conan Doyle's master detective.

Critics' Corner

As compared to the recent episodes in this serial ... *Dressed to Kill* stands out like a drum major. Though no doubt, Sir Arthur Conan Doyle deserves credit for the story.... Leonard Lee's screenplay is a smooth, slick job.... The acting is uniformly good. Rathbone and Bruce have something with a bit more meat on it.... [R]ecommended highly to mystery addicts.—*The New York Herald-Tribune*, May 25, 1946, Joe Pihodna

Rating: ★★½ [A] welcome addition to the Sherlock Holmes series. A tricky story, plausible mystery and a solution achieved by logic make *Dressed to Kill* entertaining film fare ... good suspense ... good performances.—*The New York Daily News*, May 25, 1946, Dorothy Masters

It poses a puzzle worthy of the Doyle tradition and gives Dr. Watson a large, if unwitting share in pointing to the solution.... An attractive and engaging performance of the leading woman crook is the contribution of Patricia Morison.... There is simply a glimpse of Mary Gordon, yet without her none of the Holmes adventures would be complete.—*The Hollywood Reporter*, May 16, 1946, Jack D. Grant

Basil Rathbone and Nigel Bruce are up to usual form....—*Variety*, April 10, 1946

A cleverly worked out story of detection and characteristic performances by Basil Rathbone and Nigel Bruce ... make this a film which should please detective fans. It is exciting and suspenseful with a plot that unfolds slowly.—*The Motion Picture Herald*, May 5, 1946, M.R.Y.

The Time of Their Lives

Released August 16, 1946. 82 minutes. *Producer:* Val Burton. *Executive Producer:* Joseph Gershenson. *Director:* Charles T. Barton. *Original Screenplay:* Val Burton, Walter DeLeon & Bradford Ropes. *Additional Dialogue for Abbott and Costello:* John Grant. *Photography:* Charles Van Enger. *Editor:* Philip Cahn. *Art Directors:* John B. Goodman & Richard H. Riedel. *Musical Director:* Milton Rosen. *Special Photography:* David S. Horsley & Jerome Ash. *Assistant Director:* Seward Webb. *Camera Operator:* Harold Smith. *Sound Director:* Bernard B. Brown. *Sound Technician:* Jack A. Bolger, Jr. *Set Decorators:* Russell A. Gausman & Ruby R. Levitt. *Dialogue Director:* Morgan Farley. *Gowns:* Rosemary Odell. *Hair Stylist:* Carmen Dirigo. *Makeup:* Jack P. Pierce.

Bud Abbott (*Cuthbert Greenway/Dr. Ralph Greenway*), Lou Costello (*Horatio Prim*), Marjorie Reynolds (*Melody Allen*), Binnie Barnes (*Mildred*), John Shelton (*Sheldon Gage*), Gale Sondergaard (*Emily*), Lynne Baggett (*June Prescott*), Jess Barker (*Tom Danbury*), Robert Barrat (*Maj. Andre Putnam*), Donald MacBride (*Lt. Mason*), Ann Gillis (*Nora O'Leary*), William Hall (*Conners*), Rex Lease (*Sgt. Makepeace*), Selmer Jackson (*Prof. Dibbs*), Vernon Downing (*Leigh*), Marjorie Eaton (*Bessie*), Wheaton Chambers (*Bill*), Myron Healey, John Crawford, Kirk Alyn, Scott Thomson (*Dandies*), Harry Woolman (*Motorcycle Rider*), Walter Baldwin (*Bates*), Harry Brown (*Sergeant #2*), George M. Carleton (*Museum Guard*), Boyd Irwin (*Cranwell*).

Something NEW from BUD and LOU!
—*Poster blurb for* The Time of Their Lives

Well, it isn't exactly *Blithe Spirit*, but *The Times of Their Lives* is one of Abbott and Costello's best outings. The story is solid, the look and tone of the film is right, and much of the time it's funny when it wants to be.

The picture was shot when the boys' relationship was at one of its lowest ebbs and their basic formula was beginning to wear thin. Costello wanted to strike out on his own and try his hand at roles rich in Chaplinesque pathos, leaving Abbott in the awkward position of being a supporting player in one of his own vehicles. In *Little Giant* (1946), the team hardly shared any scenes at all, much to the bewilderment of

The whimsical comedy *The Time of Their Lives* was a welcome departure for Abbott and Costello (flanking Gale Sondergaard) and their fans.

ardent admirers. The film was profitable but less so than the two's earlier attractions.

The Time of Their Lives continued the pattern, but it's a far more imaginative undertaking. It was the team's last feature before the studio's restructuring, and the first to be directed by Charles T. Barton, who stayed on to helm over a half-dozen of the duo's pictures. Beginning his career in vaudeville and stock companies, Barton got his first movie break in two-reel comedies. He became an assistant director for William Wellman, worked on *Wings* (1927), and finally became a full-fledged director at Paramount and later Universal. He kicked off the team's series of monster-comedies with *Abbott and Costello Meet Frankenstein* (1948) and carried on with the much inferior *Abbott and Costello Meet the Killer, Boris Karloff* (1949).

Abbott and Costello's movies were usually afforded leisurely production schedules (by Universal's B standards) to accommodate the boys' legendary gin rummy sessions and their apathy about learning lines. The studio didn't seem to care as long as A&C continued to make money. *The Time of Their Lives*, which was shot under the title *The Ghost Steps Out*, had a 48-day schedule, spanning March 6 to April 30, 1946.

The bickering Bud and Lou put as much distance between themselves as they could off-camera, and even gave up their card playing. But the production was still faced with a major obstacle. According to *Bud and Lou* (Lippincott, 1977) by Bob Thomas, three weeks into shooting, Costello phoned Barton with an ultimatum. Unless he switched roles with Abbott, he was off the picture. It was a ridiculous demand even if a single frame hadn't been shot, but with half the film in the can already, it was totally unreasonable. The comedian stubbornly sat it out for two weeks while the frantic company shot around him as much as possible. Finally coming to his senses, Lou returned to the set without explanation and completed the film.

The most charitable excuse was that Lou didn't know a good script when he saw one. For someone eager to develop his character, Costello could have done, and had done, a lot worse than *The Time of Their Lives.* The story opens during the American Revolution. Tinker Horatio Prim (Lou Costello) receives a letter of commendation from George Washington. He proudly delivers it to his girlfriend Nora (Ann Gillis), a servant girl in the house of wealthy landowner Tom Danbury (Jess Barker). Nora discovers that her master is actually a traitor to the cause, but before she can act, Danbury abducts her and hides Horatio's letter in the secret compartment of a clock. Danbury's fiancée Melody Allen (Marjorie Reynolds) and Horatio learn of Danbury's treason and set out to rescue Nora, but are pursued by American soldiers. Mistaking the pair for traitors, the troops shoot them down on the spot, dumping their bodies into a well on Danbury's estate. Maj. Putnam (Robert Barrat) curses their souls to be forever imprisoned on the grounds unless evidence of their innocence is uncovered.

More than 150 years later, the spirits of Horatio and Melody still haunt the grounds. By this time, Sheldon Gage (John Shelton) has rebuilt Danbury Manor, even recovering most of the original furnishings. When the ghosts get wind of this, they frantically search the house to find Washington's letter to Horatio which will free their souls. Horatio's pranks on Gage and his houseguests send them into a panic. A favorite target is Dr. Ralph Greenway (Bud Abbott), a descendant of Cuthbert Greenway, who was Danbury's butler and the ghost's rival for Nora's affections.

Sheldon's girlfriend June Prescott (Lynne Baggett) suggests holding a séance to make contact with the spirits. Emily (Gale Sondergaard) the housekeeper, who happens to be a psychic, reaches not only Horatio and Melody, but the ghost of Tom Danbury as well. The hiding place of Washington's letter is finally revealed, but there's a hitch: The clock is now in the possession of a New York City museum. Greenway manages to steal it but is pursued by the police. After a harrowing car chase, Washington's letter is finally found, freeing the spirits of Horatio and Melody forever.

The Time of Their Lives presented Abbott and Costello with one of the best scripts of their careers. The boys' "usual" featured a loose storyline upon which they could hang their familiar but expertly delivered routines, occasionally interrupted by a musical act. It was a safe, predictable format. This time around, however, they had a well-developed plot that afforded them few opportunities for slapsticky diversions. Veteran Abbott and Costello gagster John Grant inserted additional material into the script, but his contribution is probably limited to the slap-in-the-face antics that slow the movie down.

Much of the rest of the picture works extremely well, including some clever bits which required the expert trick work of David Horsley and Jerome Ash to bring off. Costello's ghost, still not used to walking through walls, gets stuck between rooms until he gets a helping hand from Reynolds. In another scene, Costello and Reynolds walk "through" each other, swapping clothes in the process.

The latter scene is of particular interest in light of a 1955 *Hollywood Reporter* article, purportedly written by Bud and Lou. In discussing their philosophy of screen comedy, the pair stipulated: "One of the things we wouldn't touch with a ten-foot pole is girls' dresses, wigs and bustles as laugh-getters." Arguing it would be a subversive influence on impressionable young boys, the pair added, "There's enough homosexuality around without comics doing it." For the record, Costello appeared in female garb in any number of the team's films, including *Lost in a Harem* (1944), *Here Come the Co-eds* (1945), *Mexican Hayride* (1948) and *Abbott and Costello Meet the Killer, Boris Karloff.*

The real highlight of *The Time of Their Lives* is the séance scene, which manages to be both funny and genuinely chilling at the same time. An ancient incantation recited by Sondergaard whisks the spirits into the circle. In a startling, creepy moment, actor Jess Barker's (playing Tom Danbury) spectral voice is heard coming from Sondergaard's lips. As he did in *Abbott and Costello Meet Frankenstein* (1948), director Barton plays the supernatural scenes straight, displaying a genuine talent for the macabre. Barton, who was under contract to the studio through most of the '40s, was never given a full-fledged horror assignment. It's rather a pity, considering directors with little affinity for the genre (Jean Yarbrough and Harold Young come immediately to mind) routinely headed up the studio's monster shows.

Despite the separation of the team, it's worth noting that the script provides both with partners to play off their comedy. With charm to burn, Paramount loan-out Marjorie Reynolds is well up to the task of acting opposite Lou, in a far more substantial role than the usual token love interest in an Abbott and Costello movie. Reynolds had an odd career, starting off enacting the stock girl reporter role in Boris Karloff's Mr. Wong series, working her way up to dancing opposite Fred Astaire in *Holiday Inn* (1942) and portraying the female lead in Fritz Lang's *Ministry of Fear* (1944).

Binnie Barnes finds herself playing the straight woman to Bud Abbott who, for once, ends up on the receiving end of most of the physical gags, getting bullied, slapped around, and generally abused. While the film presents the comic in a slightly different light and he gets to play a respectable character for once (a psychiatrist, no less), Bud, having difficulty shaking off his old persona, still looks as if he should be playing craps on a street corner.

Gale Sondergaard is impeccably typecast as the pickle-faced housekeeper, receiving more than her share of barbs. Most quotable is Barnes' line, "Haven't I seen you in *Rebecca*?," which perfectly encapsulates the Sondergaard image. Not to be outdone is Costello, doing a double-take in his first encounter with the actress: "What well did she come out of?!"

There are some interesting faces in the supporting cast. Kirk Alyn, who played Superman in the Columbia serials dons a powdered wig to play a dandy in a short scene with two other serial stars, Myron Healey and John Crawford. Marjorie Eaton, the old crone in *Zombies of Mora Tau* (1957), is briefly seen as a maid and Robert Barrat, the butler in *Secret of the Blue Room*, is the Army officer who summons the supernatural forces to invade the Danbury homestead. Ann Gillis, Costello's girlfriend who greets him at the pearly gates in the last scene, probably had her most conspicuous role as Becky Thatcher in *The Adventures of Tom Sawyer* (1938). She was later seen as the effusive mom, singing "Happy Birthday" to her deadpan astronaut son, Gary Lockwood, on a spacecraft television monitor in Stanley Kubrick's *2001: A Space Odyssey* (1968).

The Time of Their Lives doesn't quite hold up to the conclusion; in fact, the last third doesn't seem to belong to the rest of the movie. The business of Abbott walking out of the museum with the concealed clock protruding from underneath his coat is typical movie nonsense, and the climactic car chase is second-drawer slapstick. One is left wondering how an obscure Yankee army officer ever became empowered to invoke such a potent curse. Also, Costello and Reynolds' supernatural powers seem to fluctuate from scene to scene. Supposedly, ordinary mortals cannot hear them, yet Costello "spooks" Abbott by tooting into his stethoscope.

The Time of Their Lives has been described as an Abbott and Costello movie for people who don't like Abbott and Costello. The team's departure from their established formula is an auspicious success even if the film didn't set the box office on fire. Nor did it make much headway in courting respect from the gentry of movie critics who either ignored or dismissed it as just another juvenile romp. In the end, the studio probably wished they had rewritten the script with Abbott replacing Reynolds for a more conventional teaming. Not surprisingly, the boys went back to basics in their next picture, *Buck Privates Come Home* (1947). While this was a far more profitable venture, *The Time of Their Lives* is deservedly remembered for presenting Abbott and Costello at their offbeat best.

Critics' Corner

While *The Time of Their Lives* won't win any prizes, credit for a new departure should go to the trio of writers. By allowing the comedians to go their separate ways, the writers have greatly improved their pictures.—*The New York Herald-Tribune*, November 1946 , Joe Pihodna

It has some bright moments when the comedy runs high, provoking hearty laughs, but on the whole the gags are familiar and at times too long and drawn out.—*Harrison's Reports*, August 17, 1946

This one's a picnic for Abbott and Costello fans. Replete with trowelled-on slapstick, corned-up gags and farcical plot, *The Time of Their Lives* won't shock the patrons with any unfamiliar novelties.... [T]he trick photography is handled with flawless technique.—*Variety*, August 14, 1946

By long odds, it is the best A&C show to date.... Marjorie Reynolds is the loveliest leading lady who ever chanced on the same screen with Abbott and Costello.... Charles Barton, justifying the confidence placed in him by [producers] Gershenson and Burton, directs to mark up a personal smash.—*The Hollywood Reporter*, August 12, 1946

The Brute Man

A Universal Picture. Released by Producers Releasing Corporation on October 1, 1946. 58 minutes. *Producer:* Ben Pivar. *Director:* Jean Yarbrough. *Screenplay:* George Bricker & M. Coates Webster. *Original Story:* Dwight V. Babcock. *Photography:* Maury Gertsman. *Editor:* Philip Cahn. *Art Directors:* John B. Goodman & Abraham Grossman. *Music Director:* Hans J. Salter. *Music:* Hans J. Salter & Frank Skinner. *Director of Sound:* Bernard B. Brown. *Technician:* Joe Lapis. *Set Decorators:* Russell A. Gausman & Edward R. Robinson. *Gowns:* Vera West. *Hair Stylist:* Carmen Dirigo. *Director of Makeup:* Jack P. Pierce. *Dialogue Director:* Raymond Kessler. *Assistant Directors:* Ralph Slosser & Harry Jones.

Rondo Hatton (*The Creeper*): Tom Neal (*Clifford Scott*), Jan Wiley (*Virginia Rogers Scott*), Jane Adams (*Helen Paige*), Donald MacBride (*Police Capt. M.J. Donelly*), Peter Whitney (*Police Lt. Gates*), Fred Coby (*Hal Moffat*), JaNelle Johnson (*Joan Bemis*), Beatrice Roberts (*Nurse*), Oscar O'Shea (*Mr. Haskins*), John Gallaudet, Pat McVey (*Detectives*), Peggy Converse (*Mrs. Obringer*), Joseph Crehan (*Police Commissioner Salisbury*), John Hamilton (*Prof. Cushman*), Lorin Raker (*Mr. Parkington*), Charles Wagenheim (*Pawnbroker*), Tristram Coffin (*Police Lieutenant/Radio Announcer*), Jack Parker (*Jimmy*), Jim Nolan (*Police Radio Announcer*), Margaret Hoffman (*Mrs. Hart*), Alan Foster (*Jeweler*), Cy Schindell, Warren Jackson (*Policemen*), Martin Skelly (*Cab Driver*), Danny Jackson (*Newsboy*), Rodney Bell, Perc Launders, John Roche (*Men*), Karen Knight, Norma Gilchrist (*Women*), Mary Ann Bricker (*Child*), Jim Clark, Joyce Stuart, Carl Anders, Gabrielle Windsor, Paula Gray, Larry Wyle (*Students*).

STREET BALLY of huge man with padded shoulders and chest, securely chained and being led by uniformed "officer" with rifle, is a natural for this picture. It's simple, inexpensive and effective. Card copy: "We have captured 'THE BRUTE MAN' ... see him at the Rivoli.
—Brute Man *pressbook tip for exhibitors*

Like the Universal horror cycle itself, the careers of all the great Universal horror stars ended quite ignobly. An emaciated Bela Lugosi strutted his stuff in Ed Wood movies; Karloff hobbled (or wheelchair-ed) around the superheated sets of el cheapo Mexican productions; Lon Chaney, Jr., spent his last days, sick and bloated, working in the lowest of low-budget indies; Basil Rathbone donned a Beatles-style wig and strummed a guitar in *Autopsia de un Fantasma* (1968); and John Carradine kicked around at the bottom of the barrel for much of the last two-thirds of his movie career.

Rondo Hatton's bogeyman career lasted only a scant two years, but even within that short time he managed to adhere to what would become the classic pattern. After a high of *The Pearl of Death*, a fine B-film in which his mute character The Hoxton Creeper made a tremendous impact, the Glutton of Glands instantly went downhill in lesser movies like *The Jungle Captive* and *The Spider Woman Strikes Back*. But even these thoroughly inferior Universals take on a veneer of comparative respectability measured against his final film, *The Brute Man*.

The Brute Man can be looked upon as an unofficial prequel to an earlier Hatton film: *House of Horrors* picks up where *The Brute Man* leaves off, with Hatton's already-notorious Creeper character returning to continue his well-publicized murder kick. If this was indeed Universal's intention, then *The Brute Man* probably holds the distinction of being filmdom's very first prequel (*Another Part of the Forest*, the 1948 prequel to 1941's *The Little Foxes*, is generally listed as the first prequel).

Although Hatton was signed to play (what else?) the title role in *The Brute Man* on December 5, 1944, production did not commence until nearly a year later. By the time cameras rolled in November 1945, Hatton had been joined in the cast by second-feature stalwart Tom Neal and leading ladies Jan Wiley and Jane Adams. Jean Yarbrough assumed directing chores, working from a screenplay that was below par even for minor-league screen scribes George Bricker and M. Coates Webster.

A big-city police manhunt is on for the killer of Hampton University Prof. Cushman. The culprit is the Creeper (Hatton), a hulking, deformed man who walks to the suburban home of Joan Bemis (JaNelle Johnson) and watches from hiding as the socialite escorts departing guests to their car. (Surprisingly, there are a few nice crane shots here.) After the guests have gone, the Creeper speaks to Joan from the shadows, identifying himself as Hal Moffat—a name Joan dimly recognizes. When he steps out into the light and Joan sees his face for the first time, she backs away stammering in hor-

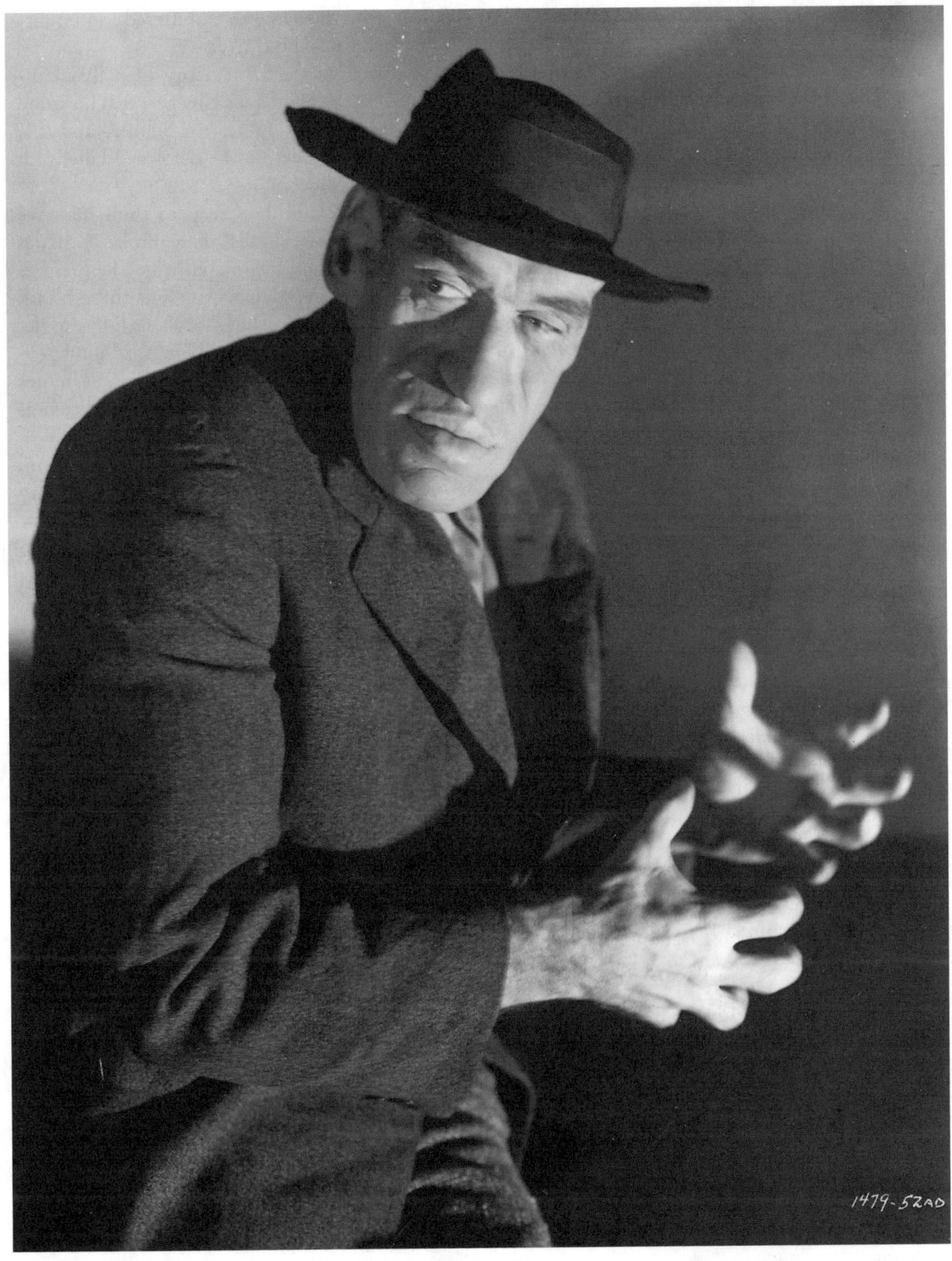

***The Brute Man*, a prequel to *House of Horrors*, was Rondo Hatton's swan song. (Some swan!) The film was released by PRC after his February 1946 death.**

ror. The Creeper lurches forward and strangles her.

The Creeper later finds himself hemmed in by police in a slum neighborhood. Scaling a fire escape, he breaks into the apartment of Helen Paige (Jane Adams), a piano teacher. Helen, who does not flinch at the Creeper's ugliness, accepts his story that he is being chased by a gang, and stalls the policemen who barge in and search her rooms. The Creeper gets away.

The next morning, at a local market, delivery boy Jimmy (Jack Parker) is listening to a radio broadcast concerning the Creeper as his boss Mr. Haskins (Oscar O'Shea) arrives. A note slid under the door during the night orders groceries delivered to 23 Waters Street, and Haskins dispatches Jimmy with the parcel. 23 Waters Street turns out to be a dilapidated storage area below the nearby waterfront pier, with the river lapping at the door; it's beyond belief that this dismal hovel (which must be underwater at high tide!) would have a mailing address, but it does, and Jimmy knows right where to find it! He spies on the Creeper from the shack next door (which doesn't have an address), but the Creeper catches on and kills his nosy new neighbor.

At Police Headquarters, Capt. Donelly (Donald MacBride) and Lt. Gates (Peter Whitney) treat the Creeper's murder spree as a joke. Grudgingly investigating Jimmy's disappearance, they find the boy's body at the Waters Street "address." The Creeper takes his time making an unobserved getaway through the pilings.

A press clipping found in the shack leads Donelly to believe that the Creeper is Hal Moffat, Hampton University Class of 1930. Further investigation leads the flatfoot to Moffat's old classmates Cliff Scott (Tom Neal) and Virginia Rogers (Jan Wiley), now man and wife and silver-haired (even though the characters would only be in their thirties!). Cliff narrates flashbacks which depict Moffat (Fred Coby) as a handsome young college gridiron hero here involved in a four-pointed romantic triangle with Cliff, Virginia and Joan Bemis. Cliff tricked Moffat into giving a wrong answer during an exam, and Prof. Cushman (John Hamilton) ordered the football star to remain after class. Hotheaded Hal had a fit of pique and shattered a beaker of chemicals which exploded in his face. His glands and nerves — and facial features — affected by the blast, an embittered Moffat disappeared from the University.

After hearing Scott's story, Donelly is convinced that Moffat is the Creeper, that his mind has been affected by his experience — and that the Scotts are next on the deformed killer's hit list.

Meanwhile, the Creeper's thoughts have turned to love. He kills a pawnbroker (Charles Wagenheim) and steals a pin which he presents to Helen Paige. Helen turns out to be blind, which explains a lot, but she takes a liking to her attentive new beau. She tells him that blind people are excellent judges of character, and invites the four-time murderer to drop by as often as he likes.

This toe-tapper of a movie just goes on and on, from bad to worse to worse yet. Donelly and Gates play gin rummy while the police commissioner (Joseph Crehan) implores them to do something about the Creeper case. Helen gives a piano lesson to a brat who's more interested in boogie-woogie. The Creeper tries to figure out a way to get Helen the money for a sight-restoring operation, the last thing in the world you'd think he would want her to have. As the movie seems to be entering its third hour, you look at the clock and realize that it's only been playing for 25 minutes.

The Creeper appears at the Scott home and demands their money, but Scott outfoxes the dimwitted killer and shoots him. The Creeper chokes Scott to death and escapes. He presents the jewels to Helen, telling her to pawn them and use the money for her operation. Helen is picked up by the police when she tries to hock the hot rocks. Donelly tells the blind girl that her boyfriend is the Creeper, knocking her conceit about the judgment of blind people into the proverbial cocked hat. When the Creeper reads in the paper that Helen is cooperating with the cops, he determines to add her to his corpse parade. He returns to her apartment and silently advances on the unsuspecting piano-playing girl, strangling mitts extended. Suddenly Donelly, Gates and uniformed policemen spring from their hiding places and the killer is quietly wrestled out of the room, a wrap-up that makes *Dracula*'s anticlimax look like an E-ticket thrill ride. For helping them lay their trap, the police arrange for Helen to have her operation.

Dark and morbid, *The Brute Man* stands out like a black mark even on a list of Universal's bad films because it weaves into its seamy story autobiographic details of Hatton's actual life. Hatton's character is seen in flashbacks as a handsome young football hero, which is precisely what Hatton *was*, at the University of Florida, before acromegaly set in. Finding actors playing "themselves" is not uncommon (fans call these *films à clef*): We have John Barrymore (*The Great Profile*), Bette Davis (*The Star*), Hedy Lamarr (*The Female Animal*), Judy Garland (*I Could Go On Singing*) and more. The fact that *The Brute Man* was a "re-imagining" of Hatton's private life, one not overburdened with good taste, could not have been missed by the unfortunate actor.

Hatton was probably the worst actor ever to labor in the Universal horror vineyards, and *The Brute Man* finds him at his most garrulous. Despite his newspaper background and the reminiscences of people like Martin Kosleck, who remember him as an intelligent guy, it's difficult to see this side of Hatton's personality in his performances. He speaks in a rasping monotone, slurs his lines, gropes for words and often seems on the verge of losing his train of thought entirely; at one point in *The Brute Man* he says yes while shaking his head no. It's the kind of acting that wouldn't be acceptable even at a pre-production cast get-together and table reading, much less in the movie itself. "He had an awful time remembering his lines," Jane Adams told the authors; for Greg Mank, she elaborated, "The progressive state of Rondo's disease made it very difficult for him to remember his script and always be responsive."

"So pathetic to work with — almost autistic," Adams told interviewer Jack Gourlay. "But a nice, thoughtful person."

Truth be told, Adams' performance as the blind Helen is nearly as embarrassing — and things are made worse by situations and dialogue that invite comparison to the Monster-Hermit interlude in *Bride of Frankenstein*, scenes as close to entertainment perfection as a Universal Horror ever came! Like the Monster, the Creeper is on the run from hunters (the police) when he is drawn by the sound of music and takes refuge in Helen's home; the Hermit and Helen don't immediately mention their blindness; when they do, the lines and even the delivery are similar (Hermit: "You must please excuse me, but I am blind"; Helen: "You see, I am blind"). The Hermit perceives that the Monster is bloody and exclaims, "You're *hurt*, my poor friend!"; Helen hears the Creeper groan and says, "Hal, you're *hurt*!" And both the Hermit and Helen imprudently latch onto the idea that this very strange intruder is a good candidate for future companionship. There's also a scene of the Creeper morosely examining his misshapen mush in a mirror, then breaking the glass with his fist, reminiscent of the Monster looking at his reflection in the surface of the waterfall pool, then lashing out at the image, in *Bride*. Elsewhere in the movie, Virginia gets her first glimpse of the Creeper in her vanity table mirror *à la* Valerie Hobson spying the Monster's entrance ... again in *Bride*. One hopes that *The Brute Man* wasn't some Universal B-unit genius' idea of a Creeper-centric version of *Bride of Frankenstein* ("The Creeper Demands a Mate!").

As for the other cast members, Tom Neal was "a strong, healthy, happy-go-lucky ex-football player, ex-boxer who had a physique that cried for female attention and got it," reminisced actress Barbara Payton in her 1963 autobiography (titled *I Am Not Ashamed* and crammed with 190 pages of reasons why she ought to have been). The reliable Neal is adequate here, although his "middle-age" makeup probably fooled no one. His Hollywood career collapsed after he beat the bejesus out of actor Franchot Tone, his rival for Payton's romantic attentions, in a 1951 dust-up; he became a landscaper, went bankrupt, shot and killed his wife and pulled down a six-year prison stretch. He died of heart failure in 1972, at the age of 58. Pert and pretty Jan Wiley, who plays Neal's wife, does an equally professional job but has very few scenes and almost nothing to do in them; it isn't surprising that, when asked about *The Brute Man* not long before her 1993 passing, she said she hardly remembered it. Fred Coby, who in the flashbacks plays Hal Moffat pre-deformity, was an excellent choice looks-wise as he has a face that actually resembles one that *could* morph into that of the Creeper. JaNelle Johnson, playing the Creeper's first on-screen victim, was the wife of actor George Dolenz, the mother of future Monkee Micky Dolenz and the grandmother of actress Ami Dolenz, a blonde cutie who in recent years has racked up a number of schlock horror credits.

What makes *The Brute Man* a bit of an endurance test, more than the performances of Hatton and Adams, is its unremitting dismal atmosphere. The film is a bleak world of a deformed killer, helpless victims, a lonely blind girl, dark tenements and squalid waterfronts. There's too heavy an emphasis on the Creeper character, and no hero, just Cliff (strangled by the Creeper with scarcely a struggle) and policemen Donald MacBride and Peter Whitney, who don't seem to take the case seriously. There's tedious comedy relief from the tedious drama in the by-play between MacBride and Whitney, but there's nothing funny about a police force that can't catch a disfigured killer even after the discovery of his Waters Street hovel; at that point, the Creeper is homeless, presumably walks the streets at all times, has nowhere to eat or drink, and could probably give Dick Tracy villain "B.O. Plenty" a run for his money, and still the cops can't pick up his trail. The task of stretching the story out to feature-film running time licks everybody; even at 58 minutes the film is as padded as Rondo's suit jacket. Perhaps as much as half of *The Brute Man* is time-killing stuff like petty arguments in the police inspector's office, banter between the grocery store delivery boy and the store owner, a five-minute no-dialogue scene of the Creeper sneaking into the Scott home, etc.

Brute Man's central portion, where the Creeper's origin (and his poor motive for murder) are revealed in comic book-style flashbacks, is a short reprieve from the general boredom; these scenes were shot on the thirteenth and final day of shooting, November 30, 1945. It's worth noting that the origin of Dr. Doom, archnemesis of comicdom's Fantastic Four, is too similar to the Creeper's to safely chalk up to coincidence.

For a film that has eventually proves to have almost nothing going for it, *The Brute Man* has a surprisingly effective opening. A police radio announcer broadcasts news of a killing, sparking a mini-montage of careening stock-footage squad cars. Now, in low-key, low-angle photography, we see the Creeper prowling the dark streets, conscious of the wailing police sirens but nevertheless unhurried. The sound of jukebox music replaces the sirens on the soundtrack as he approaches the Collegiate Cafe, a student hangout where, in striking contrast to the bleak atmosphere that's building, several dozen young people are juking and jiving to swing music. As the record ends, the ape-like grotesque saunters up to the window and peers wistfully inside. But his reverie is short: One by one, every head in the cafe turns and the students gape in voiceless horror at the deformed onlooker. The Creeper plods away grimly; the silent, slack-jawed students remain rooted in place. It's an atmospheric, mood-evoking opener — and nothing else in the film comes close to it.

The Brute Man ended up being released not by Universal but through PRC. In the face of their coming merger with International Pictures, Universal adopted a policy of no-more-B's and *Brute Man* became a casualty of that edict. The sale came at a propitious time for PRC, whose schedule had lagged behind due to the organization of Eagle-Lion on their old lot; according to a *Variety* news item, PRC paid Universal $125,000 for the picture. Sad to say, by 1946 the quality of the Universal Horrors had dipped to the point that *The Brute Man* is in fact a bit below the horror average of that Poverty Row studio (*The Devil Bat, The Monster Maker, Bluebeard, Fog Island, Strangler of the Swamp*, etc.). Even in '46, attentive fright film fans could divine that it was a Universal-made movie via the presence of Universal's Creeper character (with Hatton in the role), familiar music from *The Wolf Man, The Invisible Man's Revenge* and *Black Friday*, even the opening cast-crew listings which reuse the behind-the-credits images seen in *House of Horrors* (a walking–Creeper shadow, distorted to look like a midget's; a low-light, low-angle closeup of the actor; and a more proportionate walking–Creeper shadow).

Rondo Hatton, 51, shuffled off his mortal coil on February 2, 1946 (two months after the completion of *The Brute Man*), felled by a heart attack brought on by his glandular condition. Had he lived, it's not hard to picture him drifting back into bit or extra parts, or perhaps playing a Tor Johnson–esque part or two in '50s horror cheapies. Actually, his acting talent (what's in a word?) being what it was, he might not even have had *those* opportunities.

Hatton's remains were shipped to Tampa, Florida, and interred under the auspices of the American Legion. He didn't live to see either of his starring films in a theater; his passing preceded the release of both *House of Horrors* and *The Brute Man.*

In 2002, a half-century-plus following Hatton's death, David Colton of the Classic Horror Film Boards (www.monsterkid.com) inaugurated the Rondo Hatton Classic Horror Awards, a.k.a. "The Rondos," an on-line poll in which fans of the classic horror pick the best of the preceding year's genre books, magazines, DVD releases, conventions, etc. Winners receive — get this — a small (fist-sized) Rondo Hatton bust, designed and sculpted by Kerry Gammill and modeled after Marcel DeLange's stylized sculpture of the Creeper seen in *House of Horrors.* Model maker Tim M. Lindsey does the castings in resin and Gammill handles the final paint job. The twenty-first century finds the least of Universal's horror stars now representing the finest in genre achievement (see www.rondo award.com).

Critics' Corner

Rating: ★ [A] crude production ... compiled of bits from various B thrillers....—*The New York Daily News,* January 22, 1947, Wanda Hale

Ordinary program fare ... has its moments to recommend it to undiscriminating patrons who go in for this type of picture. Others, however, will find it tiresome, for it suffers from triteness in plot and in treatment.... It has suspensive situations here and there ... but the whole effect is artificial and "stagey;" in fact, some of the action and dialogue may provoke laughs, instead of serious response.—*Harrison's Reports,* October 1, 1946

The Brute Man scores high on improbability.... The basic idea is inspired by Rondo Hatton, a bit actor [with] a misshapen, enormous head and jaw.... It is his only fortune, for otherwise he is neither able to act or read lines with any degree of skill.... Just as clothes don't make a gentleman, so a face doesn't make both a villain and continuous thrills. All this picture has is a face, handicapped by encircling improbabilities.—*The New York Post,* January 22, 1947, Archer Winsten

[A] taut little melodrama.... [T]he film utilizes the standard suspense-rousing devices, but in its category, it stands favorably.... [Director] Jean Yarbrough ... keeps things moving briskly.—*The Motion Picture Herald,* October 26, 1946, Mandel Herbstman

Epilogue

Back in the '80s, writer Curt Siodmak noted to the authors the parallel between time, history and horror movies:

> When we made those pictures throughout the Second World War, we couldn't show an American with a machine gun mowing down 5000 Japanese. Nobody would have believed it; it wouldn't work. So we had the Gothic stories...
>
> When the war ended, the bottom fell out of the horror business. Then, when we began testing the atomic bomb, it all started again.

Siodmak may well have been quoting conventional wisdom at the time. In the late '40s, Universal (now Universal-International), along with the major Hollywood studios, may have been unwilling to take a box office risk with Gothic horror but the classic monster characters never really left the scene. In 1948, New York–based Realart Pictures (as well as a minor producing-distributing outfit called Film Classics, Inc.) negotiated for the reissue rights for Universal's library of features. As a result, Universal's monster line-up, along with Deanna Durbin, Abbott and Costello, W.C. Fields and many more of the studio's star personalities continued to play at neighborhood theaters, usually on double bills, until 1954.

Absent from the screen for several seasons in a major venue, however, the Universal Monsters finally got the benefit of an enthusiastically mounted production in *Abbott and Costello Meet Frankenstein* (1948). Lou Costello reportedly said that his kid could have written a better script, a judgment that borders on heresy considering the esteem in which the film is now held. Horror aficionados, unsurprisingly, often cite *Meet Frankenstein* as Abbott and Costello's best although, in truth, it wasn't especially typical of the team's pictures which often relied on their time-tested vaudeville routines (most of which found their way into the boys' previous film, 1948's *The Noose Hangs High*, released by Eagle-Lion). Visually, it turned out to be the best of the team's outings, boasting excellent sets and well-executed matte paintings. Added embellishments were a flamboyant Frank Skinner score and highly acceptable renderings of the original Jack Pierce makeup designs (facial appliances substituting for the usual greasepaint, yak hair and collodion, a mercy for the poor actors who used to suffer under it).*

The writers had only to go as far as the last batch of Frankenstein scripts for inspiration; the brain-switching contrivances that had beset the Monster was already approaching parody. With Dracula subbing for the traditional mad scientist and the ever-sympathetic Larry Talbot turned into a hero of sorts, the storyline of transplanting Lou Costello's brain into the head of the Monster practically wrote itself. Best of all, the material afforded Lou the opportunity to play his famous "scare take" to the hilt although some of the film's funniest moments have Lon Chaney, Jr., playing straight man to Costello, deadpanning through all his torturous Wolf Man bromides ("With each full moon..."). Glenn Strange, whose heavily lidded eyes and ponderous gait made him the most fearsome of the Universal Frankensteins, again is mostly comatose until the last reel. Bela Lugosi, who hadn't played Dracula on the screen since the early '30s, never looked more relaxed and less undead, and gets

**Pierce was dropped from the studio payroll in 1946 in a particularly coldhearted executive decision.*

Bela Lugosi relaxes between takes on the set of *Abbott and Costello Meet Frankenstein.*

into the spirit of the script though plastered under pancake makeup to hide his considerable aging. The new slant for the comedy team proved profitable for all concerned and the film remains a brisk, bright and perfectly timed burlesque.

Unfortunately, the novelty of the situation wore off quickly. The studio quickly followed *Meet Frankenstein* with *Abbott and Costello Meet the Killer, Boris Karloff* (1949) which turned out to be one of Bud and Lou's glummest outings. As middle age began creeping up on the team, their trademark rapid-fire delivery began to pall. Further installments of their "Meet the Monsters" cycle had sporadic bright spots but relied more heavily on slapstick as they turned their attentions to juvenile audiences.

Screen horror remained a stubbornly dormant genre in the first few years of the '50s. The best Universal could do was to release a pair of unambitious back lot Gothic thrillers to serve as classier-than-usual supporting features. The first of these, *The Strange Door* (1951, directed by Joseph Pevney), had its basis in a Robert Louis Stevenson short story, "The Sire de Maletroit's Door." This was followed by the Nathan Juran–directed *The Black Castle* (1952), a hodgepodge storyline which tossed in occasional swordplay, a premature burial angle and a particularly lively pool of alligators. Otherwise, the slender horror content of both pictures was provided by Boris Karloff who was surprisingly cast as sympathetic characters. *The Black Castle* also featured Lon Chaney, Jr., in another mute henchman role. (Like some of the titles covered in this book, horror films are often so classified on the basis of who's in 'em.)

Apart from the hand-me-down sets (*The Black Castle* makes particularly good use of the old *Tower of London* structures), both films had as their centerpiece the vigorous performances of their leading heavies. On that basis, *The Strange Door* has the advantage of Charles Laughton as the petulant, half-mad nobleman who has imprisoned his brother in the family dungeon for twenty years and engineers a disastrous marriage for the poor sod's daughter. Though at the lowest ebb of his career (he was only a year away from *Abbott and Costello Meet Captain Kidd*), the actor makes the most of his role and then some. Pevney's unwillingness to rein in his star doesn't do the actor any favors; if Laughton's jaw-dropping technical bravura is on full display, so too is his gleeful hamming. Stephen McNally, on the other hand, does his best as the disfigured nobleman in *The Black Castle*. More than capable in hard-bitten contemporary roles, McNally as a purple-prose spouting period character is clearly ill at ease. Still, it took more than a single performance to save these humorless and visually flat ventures.

As science fiction began to emerge as the new genre of the fantastic with George Pal reigning on the Paramount lot and even Howard

Hawks entering the fray with the groundbreaking *The Thing from Another World* (1951) for RKO, Universal saw the box office potential in a new array of creatures customized to suit the paranoia of the atomic age. As in decades past, the studio created their own signature style, largely created by the technicians and craftsmen working with limited budgets and no-name casts. Unlike the horror boom of the '30s, this new wave of thrillers didn't have the benefit of pre-sold literary properties to choose from, neither did they have visionary directors James Whale, Edgar Ulmer, or Karl Freund, on the payroll. Instead, they used journeymen filmmakers, the most stylish of whom was Jack Arnold, with Mercury Theater veteran William Alland heading up the productions.

Of course, the earliest of these films proved to be the most memorable but the fact that the studio employed the latest Hollywood gimmick, 3-D, to lure audiences, proved they were hedging their bets with the fledgling genre. *It Came from Outer Space* (1953) marked the first Alland-Arnold collaboration but it was with *Creature from the Black Lagoon* (1954) that the studio found their last classic monster personality in the Gill Man, the evolutionary link between man and fish.

The studio continued cranking out science fiction monstrosities such as the popular *Tarantula* (1955) but when the lavish Joseph Newman–directed space opera *This Island Earth* (1955) did only moderate business, the studio was forced to do some rethinking. Alland alerted studio brass that Columbia had spent considerably less money on *It Came from Beneath the Sea* (1955) than Universal was spending on their own standard sci-fi offerings and yet Columbia had come up with a movie with the same sort of box office potential. Part of the reason for this, Alland maintained, was Columbia's extensive use of stock footage. From then on, Alland's Universals were built around library shots, beginning with 1956's *The Mole People* (borrowed from the 1953 British film *The Conquest of Everest*) and continuing with 1957's *The Deadly Mantis* and *The Land Unknown*. Despite the budget-cutting, the studio happily allowed producer-director Albert Zugsmith to go the distance with *The Incredible Shrinking Man* (1957), based on the Richard Matheson novel, lavishing it with a smart production and sophisticated approach to the subject matter.

With the growing competition from television, movie attendance continued to decline to the lowest point in history. Hard-hit Universal-International suffered huge losses, and for many weeks during the spring of 1958, not a single picture was in production on the studio's soundstages. In the meantime, Hammer Films of England single-handedly revived the Gothic horror tradition by revisiting the works of Bram Stoker, Mary Shelley and even Nina Wilcox Putnam. Universal now found themselves in the ironic position of licensing and importing what was once their highly marketable properties after turning their back on them for over a decade. With a conspicuous lack of pride, the studio's new horror line consisted entirely of a slate of rushed-out bottom-of-the-bill features to accompany these new attractions; audiences found relatively opulent British Technicolor horrors such as *Horror of Dracula, The Mummy, Blood of the Vampire* (a non–Hammer) and *The Brides of Dracula* paired up with the dreary back lot black-and-whites *The Thing That Couldn't Die, Curse of the Undead, Monster on the Campus* and *The Leech Woman*, respectively. Trade papers referred to the Universal pictures as "horror quickies," probably because they were made so cheaply, they looked more like TV episodes than feature films from a major studio.

However bleak the times, 1957 proved to be a significant year in the history of the Universal horror film as the company sold their backlog of genre features released from 1931 to 1946 to television. Overnight, a whole new audience, many of whom had never *heard* of Karloff and Lugosi, became addicted to these movies. Not even Screen Gems, the Columbia Pictures television subsidiary that packaged the features under the title *Shock*, could have anticipated the tremendous public response that greeted these films as they made their debut on the airwaves in the autumn of 1957. Ninety American cities saw their own versions of *Shock Theater*, many of which garnered top ratings. (The New York City edition gave such nightly institutions as *The Jack Paar Show* and *The Late Show* a run for their money.) Out of this phenomenon emerged a subculture of horror show hosts, kitschy farceurs hired by local stations to boost the appeal of the

John Bromfield falls victim to the Gill Man (Tom Hennesy) in *Revenge of the Creature*, second film in the Black Lagoon series.

less attractive items in the package. Most of these jesters were fly-by-nighters, but at least one, Philadelphia's Roland (soon to become New York City's Zacherley), attracted a devoted following, branched out into the raucous world of rock 'n' roll and continues to be a mainstay at horror movie conventions.

While Universal ferociously marketed their monster characters throughout the years, licensing merchandise and releasing classic titles to the home video market, they had little confidence in their potential as far as producing and releasing new films. In the '60s the genre was sloughed off to studio television producers with *The Mun-*

sters and the *Thriller* series. When Frank Langella became the toast of Broadway with his romantic interpretation of Count Dracula in a well-mounted production of the old Hamilton Deane–John L. Balderston chestnut in 1977, Universal thought that Gothic horror, played straight, might have box office legs after all. But as many a producer of Hollywood musicals have learned, Broadway success doesn't always cross over to strip mall movie theaters. (Why are studio executives so slow to catch on that the two centers cater to entirely different markets?) The 1979 *Dracula* turned out to be a flavorful Victorian vampire piece despite its mixed reception and near-crippling faults, chiefly due to the mismatching of the director to the material. John Badham's flash-in-the-pan fame rested on his 1977 megahit *Saturday Night Fever* but his fitful handling of *Dracula* resulted in several jarring continuity errors in the final cut. Even the "teaser" ending in which the destroyed vampire's airborne cape blows in the wind like a bat in flight seemed presumptuous, paving the way for a sequel which never came. Despite the picture's lack of closure, it has the assets of a sumptuous production, steady pacing which never gets too bogged down in drawing room palaver, and a sweeping John Williams score. All in all, a noteworthy entry in the burgeoning *Dracula* catalogue.

By the '90s, the demographic-conscious studio was targeting younger audiences and designed their classic monster productions accordingly. Stephen Sommers' *The Mummy* (1999) and the inevitable *The Mummy Returns* (2001) owe more to Indiana Jones than the '30s–'40s thrillers which spawned them. Although the first film showed a plucky and adventurous spirit and an engaging romantic team in Brendan Fraser and Rachel Weisz, the video game mentality caught up with the series and ultimately caused its undoing. That the titled monster was no longer a bodily presence intermingling with the actors but an obviously transposed CGI effect took away a lot of the fun for those who had fond memories of Karloff and Chaney Jr. Unsurprisingly, such considerations seemed to escape the notice of general audiences, as did the cartoonish look of the major effects sequences; both films racked up impressive box office totals.

Repeating history, Universal decided the most profitable way to exploit their famous monster franchises was to serve them up *en masse*. In a nod to their World War II–vintage monster rallies, Universal produced a television movie, *House of Frankenstein 1997*, where again the Frankenstein Monster, Dracula and the Wolf Man were packed in a single tent in the course of a contemporary crime story. The studio raised the ante with the much ballyhooed *Van Helsing*, the intended summer blockbuster of 2004 which recast the monster characters in their proper nineteenth century surroundings. The ultimate Hollywood "roller coaster ride," the movie consists of nonstop action and CGI set pieces, rich period detail and is often brilliantly executed. But the piling on of so much dazzling pyrotechnics with scant attention to script or characterizations left most of the audience either numb or over-stimulated. With even the targeted younger audience reacting with indifference, *Van Helsing* performed below expectations despite massive hype and endless sales tie-ins.

While it seems likely that Universal's monster characters are here to stay in some form or another in spite of their spotty ticket sales in recent mainstream movies, interest in the studio's catalogue of Golden Age features as a whole may be dwindling. Surely such perennials as *Frankenstein*, *Dracula*, *The Invisible Man* and even *The Wolf Man* still have a long shelf life ahead of them, but what about their numerous sequels and spinoffs? Without the Mad Ghoul's visage plastered on kid's lunchboxes or Paula the Ape Woman tote bags in the offing, what is to become of these lesser known B titles? While cyberspace buzzes with vague news of colorization schemes, and dozens of fan sites devoted to horror movie minutiae are flourishing, common sense dictates that the *Horror Island*s and *Mad Doctor of Market Streets* of the world are doomed to live only as long as Baby Boomers maintain their collection of gray market video copies. A sad realization for horror fans perhaps, but for movies which were thought to be completely disposable 70 or so years ago, they've had an incredible run which their makers could have hardly foreseen. On a loftier plane, our assumption that *Frankenstein* and *Dracula* have attained a kind of literary permanence will be put to the ultimate test, the *cruelest* test, the test of time. And the clock is already ticking away.

Appendices

Containing I. Exclusions, Borderline Inclusions, Odds and Ends; II. Universal Serial Horrors; III. Universal Horror Oscars; IV. Screen Gems Shock *Television Packages.*

I. Exclusions, Borderline Inclusions, Odds and Ends

The following is a series of capsule reviews of movies that some readers may have expected to find in the main section of this book — movies which include some minor horror, science fiction or fantasy elements, but not enough that we could bring ourselves to make them subjects of full writeups. Also included are movies that were either misleadingly advertised by Universal as horror movies upon their original release, and/or were later sold by TV stations in the false guise of horror movies. There's even a review of a horror-comedy short and a couple writeups of non-horror productions with the great Universal horror stars in memorable or amusingly offbeat roles.

Ali Baba and the Forty Thieves (1943) The second (and best) of Universal's Technicolor desert adventure fantasies, loosely based on the beloved Arabian Nights fairy tale. Edmund L. Hartmann's script sidelines the posturing Maria Montez in favor of the action-oriented story of the son (Scotty Beckett) of the slaughtered caliph (Moroni Olsen) who joins a troupe of bandits and grows up to reclaim the throne. Scene-stealing villain Kurt Katch hisses venomously as Mongol conqueror Hulagu Khan but the acting limitations of Jon Hall and Turhan Bey are more evident than usual. Frank Puglia is fine as a traitorous royal who forces his daughter (Montez) into marrying the Khan. Even Andy Devine is bearable as Ali's guardian and protector. Rousing Edward Ward score. Directed with flair by Arthur Lubin.

Arabian Nights (1942) First of a series of six gaudy, brilliantly Technicolor fantasies that won tremendous favor with escapism-hungry moviegoers during the war years, and established Maria Montez and Jon Hall as a romantic screen team. The script, a rather loose affair, deals with two brothers (Hall and Leif Erickson) who battle one another for the title of caliph and the pampered hand of a dancing girl, Montez's Sherazade (*sic*). Despite occasional flare-ups of action, swordplay and harrowing scenes of torture, director John Rawlins treats the material as burlesque, favoring comics Billy Gilbert (in drag at one point), Shemp Howard (as Sinbad the Sailor) and John Qualen (as Aladdin) over the wooden leads. Edgar Barrier is thanklessly cast as the secondary villain, charmingly mischievous Sabu leads a climactic charge to save the day, and scheming Turhan Bey gets his comeuppance on the rack. Acquanetta and Elyse Knox appear briefly as virgins! "A" producer Walter Wanger (*The Trail of the Lonesome Pine* [1936], *Stagecoach* [1939], *Foreign Correspondent* [1940]) in his slumming mode. Garnered four Oscar nominations. A guilty pleasure if ever there was one.

Black Angel (1946) When her husband is charged with the murder of a sultry blonde blackmailer, lounge singer June Vincent teams with down-and-out songwriter Dan Duryea to find the culprit as the minutes tick off to the execution date. Director Roy William Neill's final film which he co-produced with Tom McKnight, a frequent advisor on the Holmes series; *House of Fear* writer Roy Chanslor tackled the script. The director bookends the film with two uncharacteristically flashy scenes: A dynamic opening shot in which the camera climbs up the studio miniature of a Wilshire Boulevard apartment, and the climactic flashback murder scene shot through a distorted lens to capture the killer's alcoholic fury. The rest is a deliberately plotted, finely polished noir as Vincent dogged pursues false leads and sizes up suspects in a posh nightclub managed by chain-smoking Peter Lorre. Based on the novel by Cornell Woolrich, the film suffers in comparison with *Phantom Lady* (1944) with which it shares several key plot points. The acting accolades go to Duryea who makes a surprisingly sympathetic hero. Ava Gardner, originally slated to star, was replaced by June Vincent.

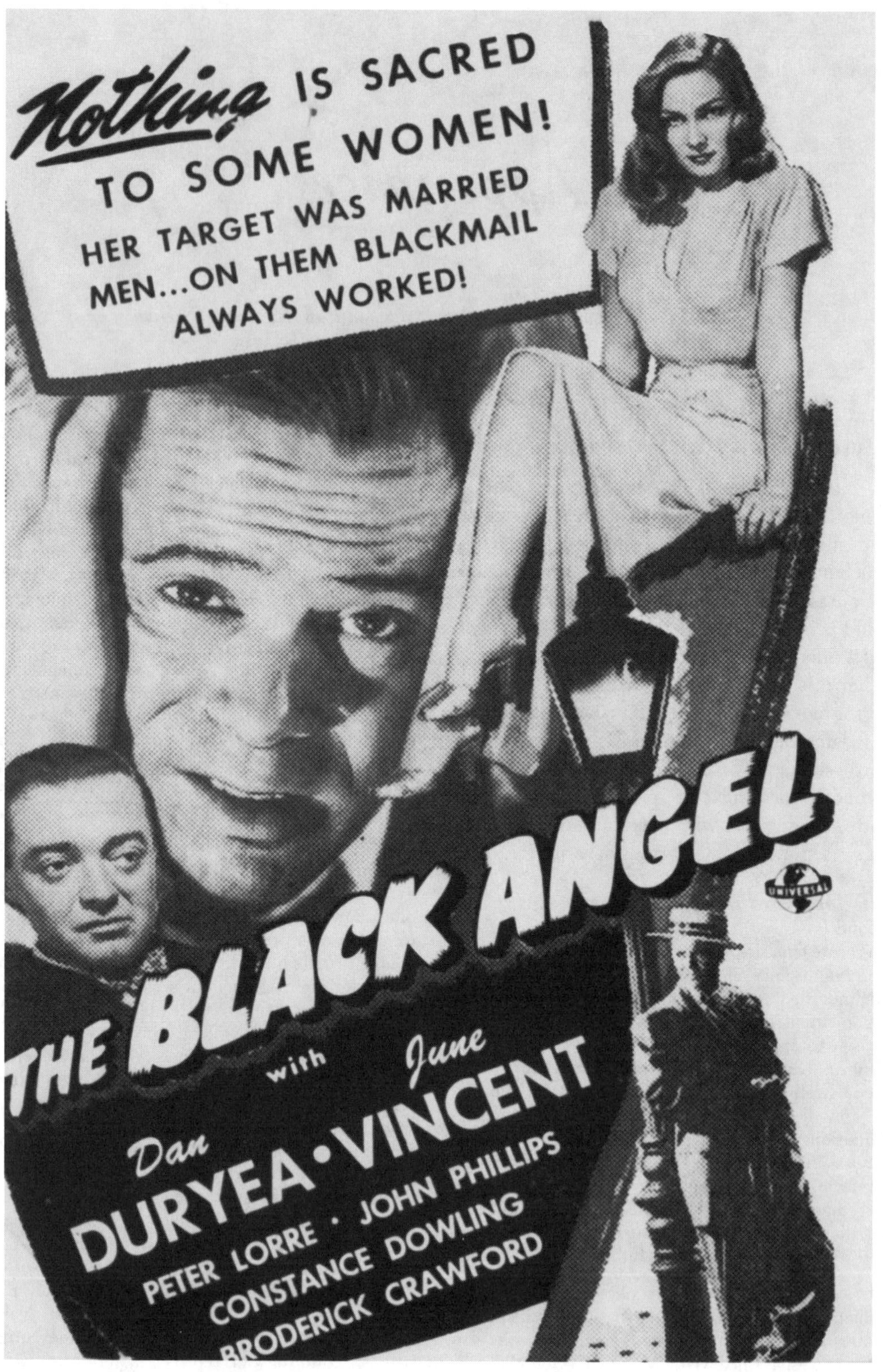

Shortly before his death, Sherlock Holmes specialist Roy William Neill directed this interesting film noir. (There's no *The* in the on-screen title.)

Boo (1932): How come nitrate disintegration is never around when you *need* it? An amazing example of the kind of stuff audiences were apparently once willing to sit still for, *Boo* is a short that incorporates and manipulates clips from three horror features in *Fractured Flickers* style, but has probably never come within a thousand miles of eliciting a single laugh from any audience member. Calling itself "A Universal Brevity" on-screen, it's narrated by a New Yawk–sounding Pete Smith wannabe who runs off at the mouth as we watch some kooky-looking chap consume a lobster-and-milk dinner while reading the novel *Dracula.* After he falls asleep, his resultant nightmare is comprised of clips from the 1922 *Nosferatu* (the narrator repeatedly calls that movie's vampire "Dracula"), the 1930 *The Cat Creeps* and the 1931 *Frankenstein* (the narrator pronounces it Franken*steen*). Sometimes the footage is run back and forth to make a character repeat an action many times. *Many,* many times. During one *Cat Creeps* scene featuring the Cat, the narrator babbles, "Here comes Dracula in disguise, but we'd know him anywhere; you can always recognize him by the fourth toe on his left foot," a good example of the general level of wit. You have to wonder why Universal used *Nosferatu* clips and called that vampire Dracula when they had their own *Dracula* movie to draw from; was the permission of Bela Lugosi perhaps withheld? Among the actors seen in the stock footage are Max Schreck in *Nosferatu,* Helen Twelvetrees and Lawrence Grant in *The Cat Creeps* and Boris Karloff, Mae Clarke and Edward Van Sloan in *Frankenstein. Boo* is included amongst the bonus material on Universal's DVD of the 1931 *Frankenstein* and the only thing that can be said in its favor is that it's the one and only place we can now go to see clips from *The Cat Creeps,* a lost film. "The moral of this story is, you can milk a cow, but a lobster is very ticklish." Directed by Albert DeMond.

Cobra Woman (1944) The charge of a South Sea island missionary (Maria Montez) is abducted to Cobra Island where her evil twin arranges human sacrifices to the local gods. Arguably the highpoint of Montez's Technicolor kitsch cycle with the graceless star in a good girl/bad girl dual role. Jon Hall provides the heroics, Sabu and a pet chimpanzee the comedy relief, as Lon Chaney, Jr., glumly looks on as a deaf strongman. Snickering aside, it's a well-packaged Saturday matinee romp which, at 70 minutes, doesn't have much chance of out-staying its welcome. Like a good studio soldier, director Robert Siodmak coasts through the camp with straight-faced efficiency. Did he realize his glory days at Universal were just ahead of him?

Cracked Nuts (1941) With an eye on the nickels burning holes in the pockets of kids in the Hootervilles, Pixleys and Crabwell Corners of this great nation, the Universal B-unit churned out this mirthless slapstick comedy dud. Mischa Auer is a down-and-out con man who installs sidekick Shemp Howard inside a robot suit in hopes of passing it off as a real mechanical man and swindling New York patent attorney William Frawley. But Frawley's broke, too, so the *two* of them team up to defraud rube Stuart Erwin, recent winner of a $5000 contest. "Ivan the Robot" has an oversized head with a sad face (resembling Auer) and a small toupee glued on top. Frawley's black servants (Mantan Moreland and Hattie Noel) react stereotypically to Ivan, of course. Once Noel gets over her fear, however, she starts making Ivan do her housework for her (she calls him Mr. Franken-tin), then puts a sheet over him and has him pose as a ghost in hopes of scaring Moreland out of his craps-shooting habit. More "fun" is derived from Moreland calling Ivan a zombie; turning Caucasian with fear; and, in the "ghost" scene, pulling a knife on Ivan and wildly slashing him! The movie ends in deranged fashion with a scene in which Shemp (still in the robot suit) smashes a plate glass store window and steals a blonde mannequin with which he's fallen in love(?!), cueing a high-speed (fast-motion), sirens-blaring police pursuit. The Hooterville kids could have made a better, smarter movie. Directed by Edward F. Cline.

Danger on the Air (1938) One of the better Crime Club entries, released on July 1, 1938. Those youthful *Black Doll* co-stars, Donald Woods, Nan Grey and William Lundigan, are reunited in this spirited murder mystery romp. This time out, Woods portrays Benjamin Butts, an ambitious radio sound engineer who launches his own investigation when a soft drink sponsor with a roving eye (Berton Churchill) is found dead in the office of a broadcast station. Deadly cyanogen gas is pegged as the murder weapon. Otis Garrett directs in an agreeably breezy fashion. Grey contributes a particularly ingratiating performance. Based on the novel *Death Catches Up with Mr. Kluck* by Xantippe, a pseudonym — we hope!

Danger Woman (1946) Dullish physicist Don Porter, one of the masterminds of the A-bomb, attempts to harness nuclear power for industrial applications. Years earlier, while Porter was off splitting atoms, his missus [Patricia Morison] *also* split. Now she arrives back on the scene, and so does a bevy of enemy agents trying to pilfer his secrets. This is Universal's follow-up to Morison's memorable turn as a femme fatale in *Dressed to Kill* but she hardly does anything to merit her title description in this rarely-seen programmer. One of the first Hollywood movies out of the gate to incorporate atomic energy into its plot although it mainly functions as a classic Hitchcock MacGuffin, setting the wheels of the plot in motion without having any thematic interest. Any film of this vintage featuring players such as Milburn Stone and Samuel S. Hinds waxing earnestly about The Bomb at least has some novelty value. The action rarely strays from the hero's living room as he smokes a pipe and grimly furrows his brow while his enemies steal everything that isn't nailed down. Directed by Lewis D. Collins.

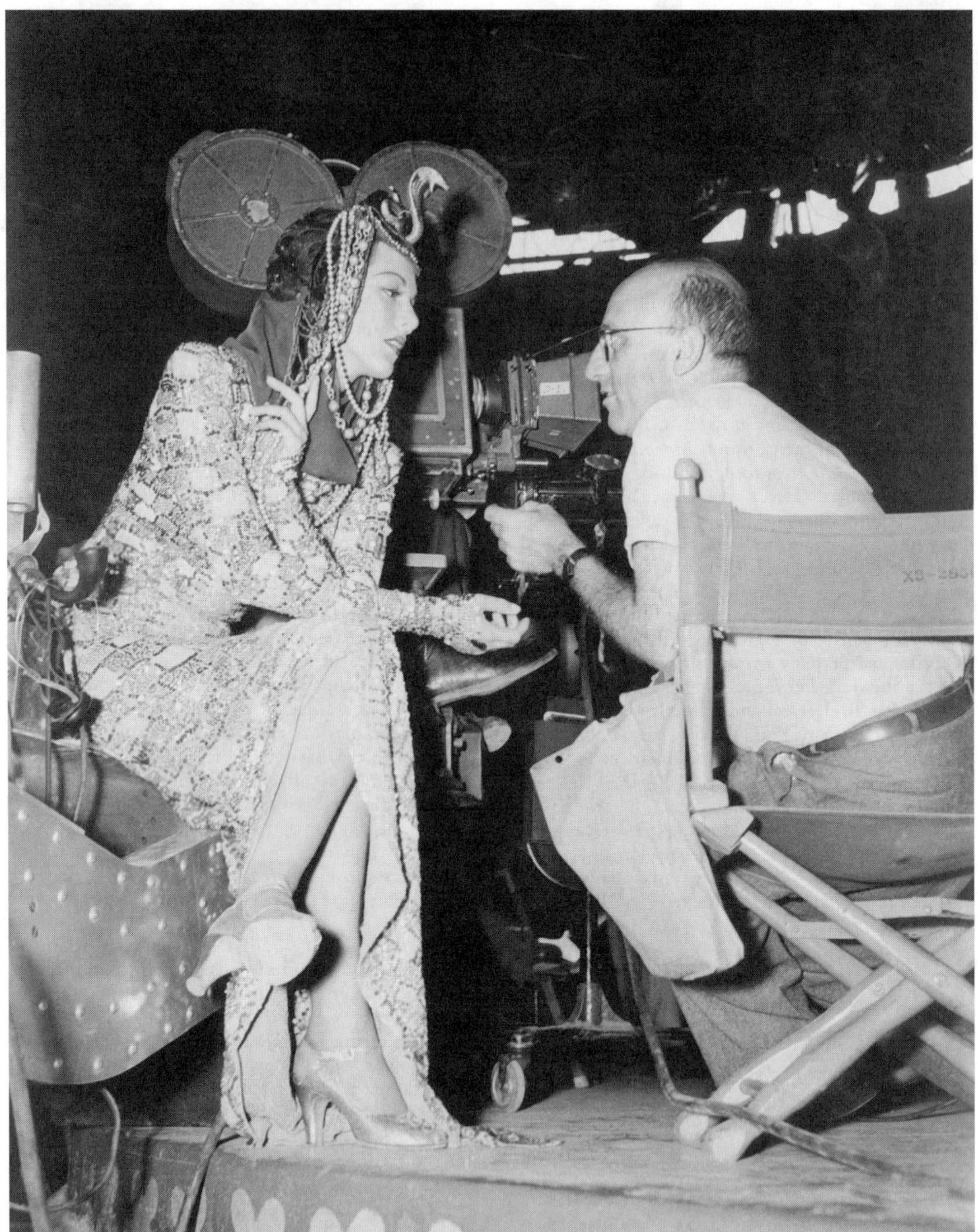

Maria Montez and director Robert Siodmak chat during a *Cobra Woman* shooting break (courtesy Photofest).

Dark Streets of Cairo (1940) Released on the heels of *The Mummy's Hand,* this exotic crime meller can almost qualify as a companion piece even without a shambling monster. When the "Seven Jewels of the Seventh Pharaohs" are unearthed in an archaeological dig, an Egyptian crime lord hopes to make a killing by palming off a counterfeit set as the originals. Soon the bodies of all those who stand in his way are found floating down the Nile. George Zucco is the fez-wearing heavy who fronts as an antiques dealer

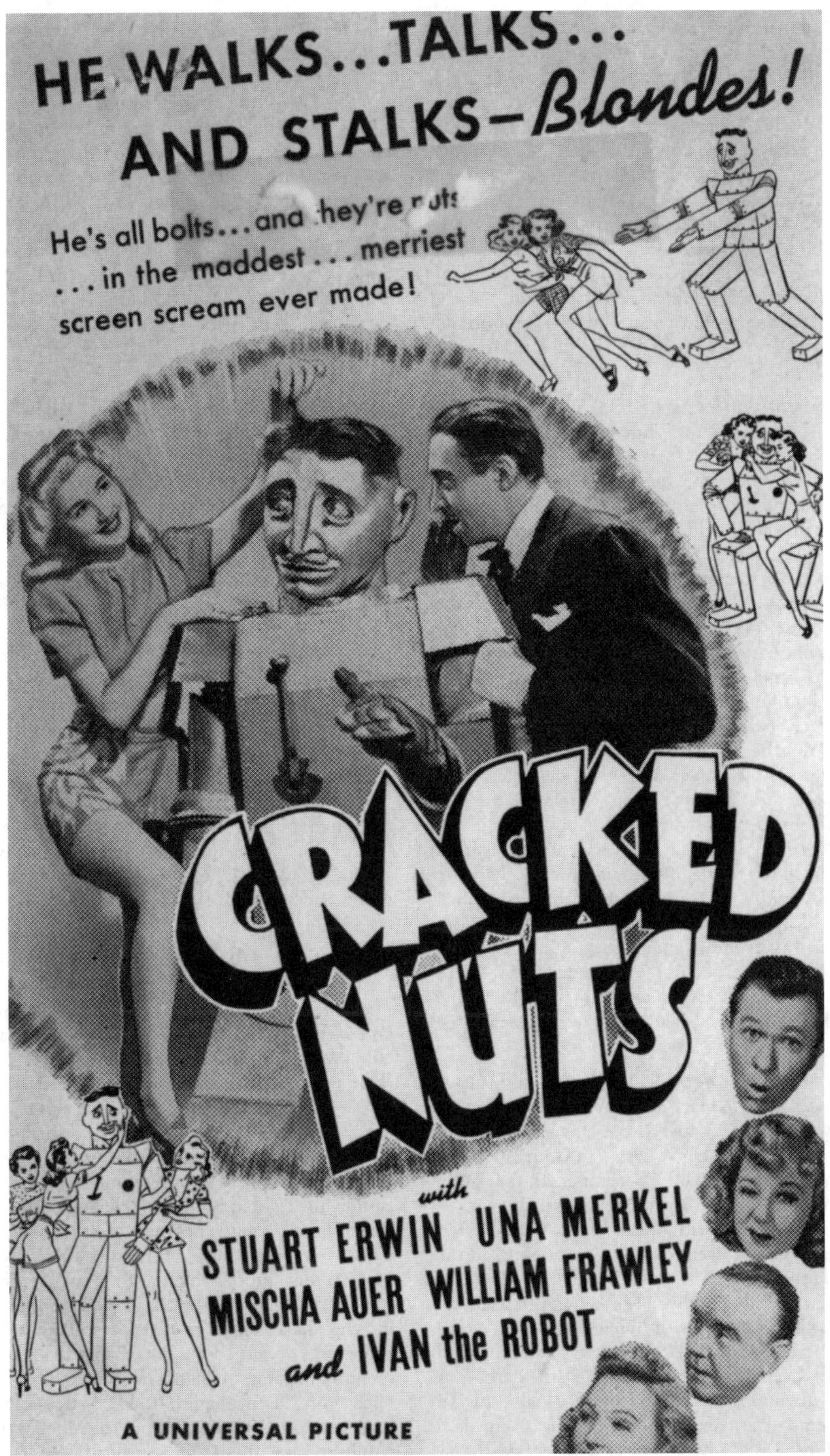

One of the wackier examples of '40s screwball comedy, *Cracked Nuts*.

amid the bustling street bazaars of Cairo with his *Mummy's Hand* henchman Siegfried Arno again at his side. Fairly strong stuff compared to the typically tepid studio programmer but the grim undercurrent runs afoul of Eddie Quillan's comic relief Brooklyn loudmouth. (Where's Wallace Ford when we need him?) Ralph Byrd (Dick Tracy of the Republic serials) is the nominal hero while former silent film star Rod LaRocque, playing a gentleman police inspector, is buried in the supporting cast. Among the familiar pleasures are the slightly redressed European Street, stock shots from *The Mummy,* and an abundance of *Son of Frankenstein* music cues. With Sigrid Gurie and Katherine DeMille. Directed by Leslie Kardos (László Kardos).

Destination Unknown (1933) The 1908 English play "The Passing of the Third Floor Back" was the story of a stranger who moves into a London rooming house and has such a quiet, positive influence on the lives of other boarders that it can only be described as ... Christ-like. Could it be...? Critics were quick to note the similarities when the same sort of story took place aboard a ship in director Tay Garnett's *Destination Unknown.* The rum-running ship *Prince Rupert* is crippled on a windless sea with 5000 cases of liquor but only one barrel of water, and all the problems *that* can cause. Amidst much bickering, back-stabbing and violence, a light in the form of a cross appears in a below-decks passage — but it turns out to be a stowaway (Ralph Bellamy) carrying a lantern. The mysterious, no-name Stowaway reveals that the sherry barrels are actually full of water, reforms the reformable and redeems the redeemable in ways that can only be described as ... well, *you* know. "Rush" of *Variety* liked the movie until the Stowaway character appeared, and then everything "dropped with a thud.... Idea was to picture a strong moral lesson, but it made this evening audience laugh." Another, better-known "Third Floor Back" redux was MGM's *Strange Cargo* (1940) with Ian Hunter as the divine buttinski. With Pat O'Brien, Alan Hale, Russell Hopton.

Drums of the Congo (1942) Universal didn't have to be asked twice to make an important contribution to the war effort: In between the Japanese attack on Pearl Harbor (December 7, 1941) and Germany's declaration of war on the U.S. (December 11), the studio began production on this tale of Axis skullduggery in the African interior, with Stuart Erwin (usually seen in movies as a sad-eyed, bumbling bumpkin) in the top male slot as sharp-shootin' he-man jungle guide Congo Jack. And, no, it isn't a comedy. American Intelligence is competing with "foreign agents" to be the first to locate the spot in Africa where a new ore, Vioo Mezi, has been discovered; it glows in the dark, is as hard as diamonds and would be invaluable in the manufacture of armaments. Don Terry is on our side, Ona Munson is a lady doctor, Erwin is her assistant and, giving a bit of a Kharis flavor to the proceedings, the baddies include Peggy Moran (in *Mummy's Hand* pith helmet and jodhpurs) and Turhan Bey. It turns out that the ore is a fragment from a stone that, according to the natives, "fell from the Moon" hundreds of years ago — but, disappointingly, no *Invisible Ray* footage of Rukh examining the meteor is used as stock. What stock there *is*, is mostly of the unpleasant jungle-critters-fighting-to-the-death variety. Seen as natives are, at the dawn of her career, teenage Dorothy Dandridge and, in the twilight of *his* career, Jules Bledsoe, one of the world's great black baritones and the originator of the role of Jim in the stage "Show Boat," pre–Paul Robeson. In that show, he sang "Old Man River"; here he sings "River Man." What range! Directed by Christy Cabanne.

East of Borneo (1931) The Spanish *Dracula* gang goes native as producer Paul Kohner, director George Melford, cinematographer George Robinson, actress Lupita Tovar (and *more*) reunite for this offbeat jungle adventure. White woman Rose Hobart contends with a boa constrictor, a leopard and every danger in the stock footage archive during an arduous trek to Marudu, a small kingdom at the foot of a volcano. She has come to find her runaway husband (Charles Bickford), now the hard-drinking court physician to a turban-topped prince (Georges Renavent) from the perfect-English, "silk pajamas" school of Third World Villainy. The sight of a native forced to swim for his life in a crocodile-infested river distresses Hobart but puts a grin on the face of Renavent, who complains to Bickford, "You outdo yourself to amuse a woman, she repays you with hysterics!" Renavent, the last of his line, announces that the volcano will erupt and destroy the kingdom upon his death. Sure enough, when he tries to rape Hobart and she shoots him, the lava starts spurting right on schedule, as though a hack screenwriter had planned it. "The whole premise was idiotic," Hobart told the authors.

Eyes of the Underworld (1942) The opening credits of this B crime drama are interrupted at the midpoint by a shot of Lon Chaney, Jr., looking sour and raising a fist behind the superimposed words "'Benny' as Characterized by Lon Chaney." "Benny" rhymes with Lennie and, yup, that's pretty much who he plays (*again*). Richard Dix stars as an ex-con, now the police chief of a city where auto theft is on the rise because of wartime cutbacks on the domestic use of steel and rubber. Dix's onetime cellmate "Benny" is now his devoted but dumb chauffeur. At the end, during a brawl with members of the car-heist gang, Chaney is shot a couple times but that only makes him madder, prompting him to jump over the hood of a car and continue fighting. (Dix, shot once during the melee, ends up in the hospital but Chaney, shot twice, doesn't!) As usual, Chaney looks genuinely out-of-control in the fight scene; as Reginald LeBorg once wrote, "Lon Chaney, Jr., had a streak of violence in his personality. In roles that called for it, his rage could become almost uncontrollable." Don Porter, co-star of *Eyes*, confirmed this when he told the authors, "Chaney was a big, hulking, nice guy unless you got into a screen fight with him. Then you had to be a little careful because he got very serious about it." *Eyes* ends on a comedy note with Lon mistakenly entering a hospital maternity ward, then running back out in a mad panic. The film, substandard and *then* some, inauspiciously marked Roy William Neill's return to Hollywood after several years of directing abroad. The working title? What else? *Destiny*! Claude Rains and Bela Lugosi were named as Chaney's costars in early trade paper announcements.

Gambling Ship (1939) "Blown Up Boats! Tapped Wires! Planted Bombs! Trapped Crooks!" These were a few of the colorful ad lines used to lure audiences into theaters to see this chapter in the still-going-strong Crime Club series. Irving Pichel (*Dracula's Daughter*'s cadaver-complected henchman Sandor) plays the ruthless head of a gambling syndicate known as the Professor, so named on account of his penchant for using mathematics to plot his illegal activities. Pichel's rival, philanthropist-businessman Selmer Jackson, refuses to sell him his gambling ship *Casino Del Mar*; before long, Jackson is killed in a speedboat explosion. The dead man's daughter (Helen Mack) takes over the operation of her father's high seas enterprise. She and undercover investigator Robert Wilcox prove Pichel's guilt and foil the racketeers as they prepare to blow up a shipful of orphans, no less. *Variety*'s reviewer described this film as a "dawdling cheapie with a light cast which topples to the status of a 'C' programmer." Pichel's performance, on the other hand, was assessed as "excellent." Directed by Aubrey H. Scotto.

Gift of Gab (1934) Karloff and Lugosi, both sadly underused by Universal in 1933–1934, were easily slotted into this farrago which seems to have been a studio round-up of any contractee who happened to be available. Ostensibly, it tracks the rise and fall of a shady street peddler (Edmund Lowe) who (implausibly) crashes into the big time as a loudmouth radio personality, quickly self-destructs, then redeems himself in the last reel. The thin storyline is loosely organized around popular musical and broadcast acts of the day (Ethel Waters, Ruth Etting, Gene Austin, etc.); Boris and Bela send up their "Boogie Men" image in a fleeting mystery skit with Paul Lukas serving as the corpus delicti. A joke without a punchline, the horror icons barely get in their brief snippets of dialogue before being shunted offstage. Brash American humor wasn't Karl Freund's forte and the director is utterly flummoxed in his attempt to turn Lowe into anything remotely resembling a sympathetic hero. It's dated in the extreme, but at least Gloria Stuart, radiant as ever, emerges with her dignity intact.

Graft (1931) According to The Books, it was while 43-year-old Boris Karloff was at Universal making this big-city newspaperman-vs.-gangsters comedy that director James Whale got a gander at him in the commissary and asked if he'd be willing to screen test for the part of the Frankenstein Monster ("Your face has startling possibilities"). Hence the inclusion of *Graft* in this appendix, since here we see Karloff sporting the look that intrigued Whale and led to Hollywood history being made. We should mention, however, that Karloff's vague memory was that Whale had seen him in the play "The Criminal Code" and/or the 1931 movie version and *that's* what prompted the offer. And we should mention that *Motion Picture* magazine (April 1932) says that Carl Laemmle, Jr., saw Karloff in *Five Star Final* (1931), and *that* led to the Monster role. And we should mention that Bela Lugosi claimed that *he* suggested Karloff for the job. And we should mention that ... oh, never mind, you get the point. *Graft*, although made at Universal, has a Whirlwind Pictures logo (a sparking pinwheel) and stars Regis Toomey as a wet-behind-the-ears cub reporter and Sue Carol (later the agent-wife of Alan Ladd) as The Girl. Fourth-billed Karloff has one of his most sizable pre–*Frankenstein* talkie roles as gangland torpedo Joe Terry, who kidnaps a young woman, shoots and kills a district attorney, brawls with Toomey aboard a yacht and is generally "where the action is" for nearly the entire 54-minute running time. At the authors' suggestion, *Graft* was recently included in the week-long (February 3–9, 2006) "Karloffest" at the Film Forum movie theater in Manhattan, possibly its first public showing in the 75 years since its initial release. Directed by Christy Cabanne.

Great Expectations (1934) Director Stuart Walker's warm-up act to *Mystery of Edwin Drood.* It's quite tastefully done but the definitive 1948 David Lean film has reduced this version of the Dickens classic into something of a curiosity. Phillips Holmes' underwhelming performance as Pip doesn't help but Henry Hull's Magwitch and Jane Wyatt's Estella offer fine compensation. Comparing this 1934 adaptation with what she calls "the *great Great Expectations*," Wyatt, told the authors, "But, you know, ours really wasn't a bad picture, not bad at all. But that was the first time I ran into drugs — Phillips Holmes. He wasn't showing up and there were all sorts of whisperings about him going on, that the trouble was that he was on some kind of drugs. He was so attractive and so good looking."

Green Hell (1940) James Whale's swan song at Universal is sadly deserving of its dud reputation. A group of adventurers trekking through the Amazon in search of Inca treasure have their hands full managing hostile natives as well as their own jealousies. The studio intended this as a high-toned jungle thriller with a name cast and enhanced production values. Unfortunately, the director never works up an adventurous spirit and the hothouse dramatics offer only dead weight. Francis Marion's script bears much of the blame. So much waste, so little fun. With Douglas Fairbanks, Jr., Joan Bennett, George Sanders, Vincent Price.

Hellzapoppin' (1941) Wall-to-wall delirium prevails as Ole Olsen and Chic Johnson produce a Broadway-bound musical revue. In real life, the pair

Graft **featured Boris Karloff in one of his pre–*Frankenstein* underworld roles. Seen with him in this shot are Dorothy Revier, Regis Toomey and Sue Carol (courtesy Bill Chase).**

had been toiling on the Midwest "vodvil" circuit for a quarter of a century before setting their sights on the Great White Way in the mid–'30s. Odds were that their new show would be a bust, so the tireless clowns tossed in everything they could think of, from gags-with-whiskers to references to then-current entertainment styles. Olsen and Johnson would later claim that the show had no script, and that their boisterous cast was instructed to just make things up as they went along. "Hellzapoppin'" bombed in Boston, but was a surprise hit in the Big Apple (opening on September 22, 1938), despite mixed reviews. It ran on Broadway for over three years and was considered one of the musical theater's biggest hits. The screen version is 84 of the most excruciating minutes ever committed to film. Mile-a-minute gags (few of them even remotely funny) poke fun at Hollywood — gaudy water ballets, overblown production numbers (including one appropriately set in Hades), even a cameo appearance by the Frankenstein Monster (reportedly played by stuntman Dale Van Sickel). As funny as a six-car pileup. With injuries. Contributing to this lunatic free-for-all are Martha Raye, Hugh Herbert, Robert Paige, Jane Frazee, Mischa Auer and the Harlem Congeroo Dancers.

Inside Information (1939) A clash between traditional and modern scientific police investigation methods is the unlikely theme of this Crime Club entry. Dick Foran is the rookie who locks horns with gruff captain Harry Carey, when the young cop tries to promote state-of-the-art policing techniques (including a "camera gun" to catch the culprits in action) over the seasoned vet's old-fashioned strong-arm methods. The rivalry comes to a head when Foran tries to solve a string of daring jewel robberies blueprinted by master thief Addison Richards, using the new methods he has learned at the police academy. The movie was based on the unpublished story "47th Precinct" by Burnet Hershey and Martin Mooney, the latter a real-life New York City crime reporter who went to prison for refusing to reveal some of his news

The Frankenstein Monster, reportedly played by stuntman Dale Van Sickel, makes a cameo appearance in the Olsen & Johnson free-for-all *Hellzapoppin'* (courtesy George Chastain).

sources, and did his first screenwriting job in the pokey! *Inside Information* is strictly cops-and-robbers tomfoolery with none of the occasional dark undercurrents of such Crime Club pictures as *The Black Doll, The Last Warning* and *The Witness Vanishes*. Directed by Charles Lamont.

The Lady in the Morgue (1938) Preston Foster and Frank Jenks are back as gumshoes Crane and Doc in the third of the Crime Club series, released on April 22, 1938. Taking its cue from the Jonathan Latimer novel of the same name, this confusing yarn has the wisecracking, dame-chasing investigators attempting to establish the identity of a blond suicide victim whose body mysteriously disappears from the city morgue. All of the ingredients for a crackerjack mystery thriller are here, but somewhere along the line, this inconsequential meller misses the mark. Supporting cast includes Patricia Ellis and B mystery fixture Thomas E. Jackson. Directed by Otis Garrett.

The Last Express (1938) "Unusually baffling" was how *New York Post* movie critic Archer Winsten described this obscure Crime Club entry. In his October 11, 1938, summation, Winsten reported, in tongue-in-cheek fashion, that *The Last Express* "packs into its brief span problems that would be properly answered in footage equal to *Marie Antoinette*." In addition to sorting through the usual array of murder suspects and incriminating evidence, ace detective Kent Taylor has to locate the whereabouts of an ancient deserted subway. Dorothea Kent, Greta Granstedt and Don Brodie round out the cast. Directed by Otis Garrett.

The Last Warning (1938) A mysterious blackmailer known as the Eye keeps Crane and Doc guessing in the last of the sleuthing team's Crime Club outings. Director Albert S. Rogell sustains an irreverent, lighthearted approach to the material throughout. Preston Foster, Frank Jenks, Joyce Compton, Kay Linaker, Raymond Parker and a young Albert Dekker seem to be enjoying themselves as much as the viewer. (The poolside scenes, according to Linaker, were shot at Rogell's home.) Based on Jonathan Latimer's grimly titled novel *The Dead Don't Care*. Do not confuse 1938's *The Last Warning* with Universal's 1929 chiller of the same name; directed by Paul Leni, the latter, an early talkie, was remade in 1939 as *The House of Fear*.

Love Birds (1934) Neither ZaSu Pitts or Slim Summerville was what you'd call easy on the eyes and yet they had long careers before both separately and as a team. Most of their pairings were at Universal and RKO; a list of these comedy credits, presented in this order, tells a story surely not told in any of the movies themselves: *Her First Mate, Out All Night* (both 1933), *Their Big Moment* (1934), *Little Accident* (1930), *The Unexpected Father* (1932), *They Just Had to Get Married* (1933), *Niagara Falls* (1941). If it seems like it's taking us a long time to get around to discussing the genre element in *Love Birds*, it's because we've never seen it and know only that there's a scene involving a comic ghost. Mainly it's a movie about a farmer (Summerville) and a teacher (Pitts) who co-own a desolate rancho where a gold tooth inlay found in the sand leads to a gold rush. Directed by William A. Seiter.

The Love Captive (1934) Shades of 1960's *The Hypnotic Eye* without the gore. Another extremely obscure Universal production with a tried-and-true genre element: Hypnotism. Suave Nils Asther portrays Dr. Alexis Collender, an unctuous charmer who weaves a hypnotic spell over his lovely subjects. When Alice Trask (Gloria Stuart) succumbs to Collender's power, her lover, Dr. Ware (Paul Kelly), plots to save her. Andre Sennwald, writing for *The New York Times*, described this film in his June 8, 1934, review as "a giddy contribution to the dizzy heat-wave season." Directed by Max Marcin.

The Man Who Cried Wolf (1937) Stage star Lawrence Fontaine (Lewis Stone) likes to cry *wolf*: He falsely confesses to every homicide that takes place in his city. But Fontaine's actually a *fox*: Secretly planning to bump off an old enemy, he's establishing a reputation as a crank so that police won't believe that one *truthful* confession. Well, now he's one sorry old *goat*: His own unsuspecting son is wrongly accused of that killing and condemned to die, and the authorities scoff at Fontaine's claim that *he* did it! Perhaps the Warners stock company could have energized the material but under Lewis R. Foster's direction it's leaden and morose. Included in Screen Gems' 1957 *Shock* TV package, and aired on *Creature Features*–type series for decades afterwards, *Man Who Cried Wolf* has the distinction of being the only movie ever to have a TV audience of impatient kids expecting Lewis Stone to transform into a werewolf. In 2006, however, those now grown-up kids might be interested to learn that this was written as a vehicle for Boris Karloff, then shelved when his Universal contract was dissolved. When it was later put back on the drawing boards, Lionel Barrymore and then his brother John were considered for the title role before Stone stepped in. With Tom Brown, Barbara Read, Jameson Thomas.

Mystery of Life (1931) After *Dracula*, what was Universal's next "monster movie"? The average Universaholic would say *Frankenstein* but the answer is actually this documentary which, more than a quarter-century before the studio's *The Land Unknown*, features dinosaurs! Subtitled "A Drama of Life as Told by Clarence Darrow," the film features lawyer-lecturer Darrow and a zoology professor, Dr. Parshley, discussing some of the theories which support evolution. They begin by rapping about the amoeba and the sea anemone, then move on to dinosaurs. According to *The American Film Institute Catalog: Feature Films, 1931–1940*, "Mechanical reconstructions of various dinosaurs, including a pterodactyl and tyrannosaurus rex, are animated against a recreation of their contemporary environment." The E-ticket thrill ride continues with a chat about somebody or other's theory of embryology and up-close looks at the embryos of fish, turtles, pigs, etc. At one point Darrow indicates the Tree of Life and quips, "We put ourselves on top because we made the tree. Try and make the ape believe we belong there." *Variety* thought the film's box office prospects were good since Darrow was then America's greatest one-man stage draw, but added, "It hurts that Dr. Parshley isn't any prettier to look at than Darrow." Directed by George Cochrane.

Mystery of the White Room (1939) Murder in a metropolitan hospital is the theme of this standard B mystery in the Crime Club series, released on March 17, 1939. Head surgeon and unlikely loverboy Addison Richards is stabbed to death when the lights black out during an operation. Once again, a non-professional (a doctor, played by Bruce Cabot) solves the crime, while the police fumble foolishly under crusty Thomas E. Jackson's direction. *Kong* series alumni Cabot, Helen Mack and Frank Reicher are reunited in this barely passable whodunit which squanders the interesting hospital setting. In a scene prefiguring *Dead Man's Eyes*, acid-blinded hospital attendant Frank Puglia's sight is restored via the transplanted corneas "donated" by the murder victim so that he might identify the guilty party. Based on the novel *Murder in the Surgery*, written by real-life medico James G. Edwards. Directed by Otis Garrett.

Nightmare (1942) The wife of a murdered British bureaucrat seeks the help of a Chicago gambler in London to help dispose of the body. Fleeing from the cops *and* a murder rap, the pair find themselves in even more jeopardy, falling into a hornet's nest of Nazi spies. Except for the B-list cast and the blah denouement, this *faux* Hitchcock suspenser could almost be mistaken for the real thing. The script is a virtual checklist of the director's tried-and-true ingredients: The catchy one-word title, the basic situation of a mismatched couple on the lam and a liberal dose of macabre humor (the corpse that refuses to stay put). It all simmers quite agreeably into a deft lightweight wartime thriller. Brian Donlevy and Diana Barrymore make a smart romantic team. With Henry Daniell, Gavin Muir and, in a brief appearance, Hans Conreid. Directed by Tim Whelan.

Phantom Lady (1944) When architect Alan Curtis is charged with the necktie strangulation of his unfaithful wife, his secretary (Ella Raines) sets out to find the one witness who can clear him: The nameless, sad-eyed title character whom everyone swears never existed in the first place. Unlike Robert Siodmak's 1944 *The Suspect* (set in turn-of-the-century London) and the Norman Rockwellesque *The Strange Affair of Uncle Harry* (1945), *Phantom Lady* is classic big city film noir and one of the director's grittiest movies. The spare and unplotty script provides ample opportunity to convey much of what the audience needs to know in purely visual terms (including the picture's most famous scene of Raines teasing Elisha

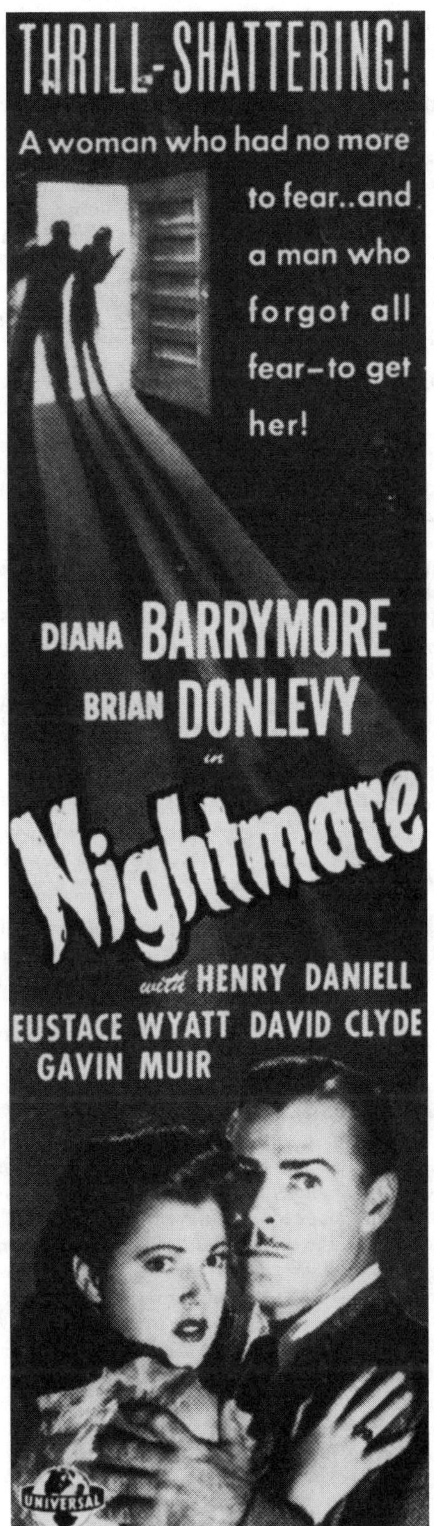

Pressbook ad for *Nightmare*, a shaky-A with Hitchcockian pretensions.

Cook, Jr., into an orgiastic drum solo). Siodmak nails the New York City atmosphere, from the Broadway glitter and posh Upper East Side apartments to the garbage can-strewn back alleys and seedy jazz joints. The only flaw is how Raines could have failed to spot the culprit at once. As the best friend of the condemned man, Group Theater–trained Franchot Tone beat the Method crowd to the punch with a twitchy, tremulous performance that has "psychopath" stamped all over it. Universal Horror regular Fay Helm is superb as the tragic wannabe bride at the center of Raines' search. From a story by Cornell Woolrich (writing under the name William Irish).

Postal Inspector (1936) Laughably heavyhanded paean to the United States Postal Service, buoyed (no pun intended) by riveting newsreel footage of the killer flood that swept through Pittsburgh in the spring of 1936. Ricardo Cortez (who can't help but ooze slime even when he's on the *right* side of the law) is the fiercely dedicated civil servant who lives to put mail fraud perps behind bars. Matters hit a bit closer to home when his treasury agent younger brother (Michael Loring) and future sister-in-law (Patricia Ellis) get mixed up in a million dollar treasury theft. Fulfilling his Universal contract after a featured role in *Dracula's Daughter* got nixed, Lugosi, as the brains behind the heist, gets a glimpse of the undistinguished movie assignments that were right around the corner. An unbilled Hattie McDaniel is embarrassingly typecast as the pandering maid of blond songbird Ellis, who warbles, "We'll have bluebirds on all our wallpaper decorating our dreams...." Return to sender! Directed by Otto Brower.

Remember Last Night? (1935) Universal belatedly rang down the curtain on Prohibition with this madcap whodunit which starts off with possibly the most rollicking drinking party in movie history. But the revellers — all Long Island socialites — find a corpse on their hands while tending to their morning-after hangovers. *Remember Last Night?* (based on the novel, *The Hangover Murders*) is often compared to *The Thin Man* (1934) for its sophisticated, inebriated wit. While it lacks the star power of William Powell and Myrna Loy, it's a far more of a technical dazzler due to James Whale's elegant direction. The camera cranes and dollies through the sumptuous sets (Grecian-themed with classic art deco accoutrements) while the smart ensemble cast handles the rapid-fire dialogue with aplomb. The macabre touches include Gustav von Seyffertitz's gaunt hypnotist, *The Devil-Doll*'s Rafaela Ottiano's blind woman who can see and E.E. Clive's gallows humor coroner's photographer. Leading lady Constance Cummings alternately refers to herself as the Bride of Frankenstein and Dracula's Daughter. With Edward Arnold, Robert Young, Sally Eilers, Robert Armstrong.

Shadow of a Doubt (1943) Alfred Hitchcock's own personal favorite among his many films. A fascinating study of evil on an intimate level, and a welcome departure from the wartime propaganda themes that diverted the director's attention during this early Hollywood period. In the story (by "Our Town" author Thornton Wilder), the peace and complacency of small-town America is shattered as prodigal son Uncle Charlie takes up residence with his sister and her family. He's really the Merry Widow Murderer, a serial killer who disposes of rich widows and lives off their fortunes. Joseph Cotten barely conceals the seething mania beneath his surface charm. Teresa Wright and Patricia Collinge are excellent as his loving niece and his sister respectively. Hitch wisely checks his bag of cinematic tricks, concentrating instead on mood and characterization. With Macdonald Carey, Henry Travers, Wallace Ford and Hume Cronyn as the next-door nerd. *Shadow of a Doubt* was "remade" twice in 1958 — once, officially, by Universal-International as *Step Down to Terror,* a cheap knock-off with Charles Drake as the mysterious stranger Johnny Walters, and then a disguised remake in United Artists' *The Return of Dracula* with Count Dracula (Francis Lederer) stepping in for Uncle Charlie!

She Gets Her Man (1945) Of all the films in this Also of Interest section, this one will probably be of the *least* interest, but let it not be said that we withheld the news of a mad serial killer movie from our readership. In this Joan Davis–William Gargan comedy, poisoned blowgun darts are the murder weapons du jour, the city authorities are baffled, and the daughter of the city's late police chief "Ma Pilkington" is summoned in the hopes that she has some of her mom's detective skills and daring. Faster than you can say *Destry,* she turns out to be a hick-town klutz (Davis) who immediately becomes an object of scorn. But with the help of local uniformed cop Leon Errol, she (of course) blunders her way to a solution and unmasks the killer. The method of murder brings to mind the 1939 *The House of Fear* (also starring Gargan) and *The Strange Case of Doctor Rx*; tried-and-true "scare comedy" sight gags come into play in a scene of Davis searching a darkened theater; and some of the antics have a vaguely surreal, Olsen & Johnson-ish flavor. If only it was funny! Directed by Erle C. Kenton.

The Sun Never Sets (1939) Rowland V. Lee's oddball comic strip salute to The Empire. Members of the British Colonial Office, stationed in Africa, suspect a mysterious entomologist (Lionel Atwill) is using propaganda broadcasts to persuade the locals to switch their allegiance to the Nazis. Long-winded with tedious soap opera diversions, but who could resist another round of Basil Rathbone confronting his frequent nemesis, Atwill? The wrap-up in which the frozen, statue-like corpses of the heavies are found in a bunker that has been hit by heavy aerial bombardment is truly bizarre. With Douglas Fairbanks, Jr. and Virginia Field.

The Witness Vanishes (1939) Universal wrapped up the Crime Club series on a satisfactory note with

Postal Inspector **was a strange amalgam of gangsters, government agents, bad pop songs — and Bela Lugosi!**

this minor programmer, released on September 22, 1939. Set in London, a welcome change of pace, the trite though mildly diverting story deals with a series of revenge killings, allegedly committed by wacky old Lucius Marplay (Barlowe Borland), former newspaper magnate, who has escaped from a sanitarium years after being railroaded there by his unscrupulous business associates. Marplay's enemies are mysteriously eliminated one by one *after* their obituaries appear in his paper. The lone survivor of this murder spree, Mark Peters (Edmund Lowe) turns out to be the real culprit; he took advantage of Marplay's notoriety to get rid of his (Peters') partners-in-crime. Wendy Barrie, Bruce Lester, Forrester Harvey, and Walter Kingsford (in a distasteful role as the office flirt) round out the cast. Inspired by James Ronald's magazine serial "They Can't Hang Me!" (the movie's original working title). A cozily familiar melodrama, agreeably scripted and well paced, *The Witness Vanishes* is an apt closing act to an almost forgotten mystery series. Directed by Otis Garrett.

Zanzibar (1940) At the end of World War I, Germany was forced to sign the Treaty of Versailles, a peace document calling for them to disarm, to make reparations for the damage they caused (especially in France and Belgium), etc. Buried in the fine print, Article 246 stipulated that they also hand over the stolen skull of Mkwawa, the sultan of the Hehe people, who had revolted against the Germans in 1898 and subsequently committed suicide to avoid capture; the long-awaited opportunity to bury Mkwawa's skull in his grave would give the Hehe the last ha-ha on the Germans. Years of stalling, excuses and "Skull, Skull, Who's Got the Skull?" eventually resulted in Universal's *Zanzibar*, which finds the skull enshrined by East African natives in a temple, regarded as sacred, and sought by both the British and the Germans as the world builds toward a new conflict (WWII). Working undercover on behalf of the good guys are big game hunter Lola Lane and her party, while the baddies are represented by rats Eduardo Ciannelli and Henry Victor. The temple set from *Green Hell* (later seen in *The Mummy's Hand*) houses the skull, which for no apparent reason has glowing eyes and produces an electronic hum; true to local legend, removing it from the temple immediately cues a volcanic eruption and a great deal of short-notice urban renewal, *a la* the finale of Universal's *East of Borneo* (1931), whence much of this climactic footage came. After mentally substituting the Ark of the Covenant for the skull, compare the plots of this movie and *Raiders of the Lost Ark* (1981), and then ask yourself if it's likely that Spielberg and/or Lucas ever saw *Zanzibar*. We vote aye. Directed by Harold D. Schuster.

II. Universal Serial Horrors

This is a list of every Universal sound serial that features "fantastic" film elements. Edited feature versions of some of these serials were made and distributed by Universal, but we have refrained from listing these "features" in the main section of the book. This appendix is intended only as a quick reference guide for readers interested in delving deeper into Universal's non-feature SF–horror output.

The Ace of Scotland Yard (1929). Director: Ray Taylor. Cast: Craufurd Kent, Florence Allen, Herbert Prior, Albert Priscoe, Monte Montague, Grace Cunard. Touted by Universal as the first talking serial, this sequel to the silent chapterplay *Blake of Scotland Yard* (1927) was issued in both sound and silent versions. A valuable ring is targeted by thieves in this borderline-horror mystery. 10 episodes.

Tarzan the Tiger (1929). Director: Henry MacRae. Cast: Frank Merrill, Natalie Kingston, Lillian Worth, Al Ferguson. Based on the Edgar Rice Burroughs novel *Tarzan and the Jewels of Opal*, this profitable follow-up to the silent serial *Tarzan the Mighty* (1928) pits the Ape Man against slave traders, jewel thieves and (more pertinently) a spell-casting queen and ugly beastmen. It was issued in silent and sound editions, the latter version boasting only music, sound effects and a few lip-synched lines of dialogue. 15 episodes.

The Jade Box (1930). Director: Ray Taylor. Cast: Jack Perrin, Louise Lorraine, Francis Ford, Wilbur S. Mack. Members of an Oriental cult vie with our heroes for possession of a jade box containing a vial that holds the secret of invisibility. Silent and sound versions. 10 episodes.

Detective Lloyd (1932). Director: Henry MacRae. Cast: Jack Lloyd, Wallace Geoffrey, Muriel Angelus, Lewis Dayton. Detective Lloyd battles international crooks and the priests of the Temple of Amenhotep II for possession of a valuable amulet. A death ray and possibly even a ghost figure into this English-made serial (England's *only* talkie serial), which was known over there as *The Green Spot Mystery*. Photographed by Desmond Dickinson, whose later career ranged from the Olivier *Hamlet* (1948) to most of Herman Cohen's gory English shockers! A 66-minute feature version, *Lloyd of the CID*, was also issued. 12 episodes.

The Jungle Mystery (1932). Director: Ray Taylor. Cast: Tom Tyler, Cecilia Parker, William Desmond, Philo McCullough, Noah Beery, Jr., Sam Baker. Zungu, a half-man, half-ape creature (played by Baker), buys this forgotten little epic a spot on this list. Lots of jungle hijinks with everybody seeking a large ivory cache; the ape-man is friendly, and helps our heroes. 12 episodes.

Phantom of the Air (1933). Director: Ray Taylor. Cast: Tom Tyler, Gloria Shea, LeRoy Mason, Hugh Enfield, William Desmond, Walter Brennan. The MacGuffin this time around is the Contragrav a device which overcomes the effects of gravity; villain

Mason's efforts to steal it are thwarted by "The Phantom," Desmond's remote-controlled plane. 12 episodes.

Perils of Pauline (1934). Director: Ray Taylor. Cast: Evalyn Knapp, Robert Allen, James Durkin, John Davidson, Frank Lackteen, Pat O'Malley. In Indo-China, an ivory disc engraved with the formula for a deadly gas is sought by Knapp, who's good, and Davidson, who isn't. A walking mummy, unfriendly natives and a henchman named Fang are also on hand. 12 episodes.

The Vanishing Shadow (1934). Director: Louis Friedlander [Lew Landers]. Cast: Onslow Stevens, Ada Ince, Walter Miller, James Durkin, William Desmond. After an evil political group hounds a man to death through a smear campaign, the man's son (Stevens) vows to get revenge. His arsenal of science fiction-style weapons includes a destroying ray, a vest of invisibility and a robot. Stevens was plenty steamed at Universal for sticking him in this one. 12 episodes.

Ace Drummond (1936). Directors: Ford Beebe & Cliff Smith. Cast: John King, Jean Rogers, Noah Beery, Jr., Guy Bates Post, Arthur Loft, Lon Chaney, Jr. The archvillainous Dragon strives to thwart a globe-girdling airplane service; heroic Ace Drummond (King) strives to thwart the Dragon; atomic ray guns come into play. With a character name like Ivan, Chaney has to be playing a bad guy. King sings "Give Me a Ship and a Song," no doubt a highpoint. Based on the newspaper feature by Eddie Rickenbacker. 13 episodes.

Flash Gordon (1936). Director: Frederick Stephani. Cast: Larry "Buster" Crabbe, Jean Rogers, Charles Middleton, Priscilla Lawson, John Lipson, Richard Alexander, Frank Shannon. The best-known (but not the best) of all sci-fi serials is also the most expensive (a reported $350,000) serial ever made. Flash (Crabbe), Dale Arden (Rogers) and Dr. Zarkov (Shannon) rocket to the planet Mongo, which is on a collision course with Earth. There, in the course of 13 increasingly juvenile episodes, they encounter monkey-men, shark-men, hawk-men, a dragon-dinosaur (played by Glenn Strange), and various other misfits, all under the baleful eye of the despicable space dictator Ming the Merciless (Middleton). Includes sets and props from *Just Imagine* (1930), *The Mummy, Bride of Frankenstein* and *Dracula's Daughter*. For kids of all ages; others need not apply. An 82-minute feature, *Rocket Ship*, was fashioned; feature-version titles include *Spaceship to the Unknown, Space Soldiers* and *Atomic Rocketship*. Based on the comic strip by Alex Raymond.

Tim Tyler's Luck (1937). Directors: Ford Beebe & Wyndham Gittens. Cast: Frankie Thomas, Frances Robinson, Al Shean, Norman Willis, Earl Douglas, Anthony Warde. Talk about a recipe for a successful Saturday matinee serial: Darkest Africa, lions, gorillas, a panther, an elephant, quicksand, an ivory-poaching villain named Spider Webb, a futuristic-looking armored tank—and, perhaps best of all, a hero (Frankie Thomas) not much older than the kids in the audience! Thomas told the authors that a frequent visitor to the back lot sets was Deanna Durbin, who loved the "jungle" atmosphere, animals, etc. 12 chapters.

Radio Patrol (1937). Directors: Ford Beebe & Cliff Smith. Cast: Grant Withers, Catherine Hughes, Mickey Rentschler, Adrian Morris. Here's a unique ploy: International crooks who want the formula for a new, flexible bulletproof glass kill the inventor and try to adopt his little son. There's hypnosis somewhere in here too. Based on the King Features syndicate comic strip. 12 episodes.

Flash Gordon's Trip to Mars (1938). Directors: Ford Beebe & Robert Hill. Cast: Larry "Buster" Crabbe, Jean Rogers, Charles Middleton, Frank Shannon, Beatrice Roberts, Richard Alexander, Donald Kerr. Who's stealing the earth's nitrogen? Flash (Crabbe), Dale (Rogers) and Zarkov (Shannon) trace the culprits to Mars, where the usual pattern of captures and escapes develops. Clay People, Tree People, a Queen of Magic (Roberts) of course, our old friend Ming (Middleton) provide menace. Includes a tinted sequence. Late in 1938, a feature version, *Mars Attacks the World*, was thrown together practically overnight to take advantage of the publicity surrounding Orson Welles' Mercury Theatre's notorious radio enactment of *The War of the Worlds* and the panic in the streets it caused. The TV feature version was called *Deadly Ray from Mars*. 15 episodes.

Buck Rogers (1939). Directors: Ford Beebe & Saul A. Goodkind. Cast: Larry "Buster" Crabbe, Constance Moore, Jackie Moran, Jack Mulhall, Anthony Warde, Henry Brandon. Buck (Crabbe) and his sidekick Buddy (Moran) go into suspended animation following an Arctic air crash, reawakening 500 years later to find that the world has been taken over by Killer Kane (played by cheap-thug specialist Warde). Based on novels and a comic strip. All the accouterments of a Flash Gordon serial: spaceships, antigravity devices, ray guns, robots, ad absurdum. Feature versions: *Planet Outlaws* and *Destination Saturn*. 12 episodes.

The Phantom Creeps (1939). Directors: Ford Beebe & Saul A. Goodkind. Cast: Bela Lugosi, Robert Kent, Regis Toomey, Dorothy Arnold, Edward Van Sloan, Eddie Acuff. Boris Karloff made his last serial in 1931 but here's Poor Bela still plugging away. As the antisocial Dr. Zorka, Lugosi manufactures a divisualizer belt, a death ray, a mechanical spider and a big, dopey-looking robot; in Chapter 12 he tries to destroy the world by dropping little bombs out of a biplane. Van Sloan's a baddie, too. Karloff is briefly seen in a snippet from *The Invisible Ray*. Also released as a 75-minute feature. 12 episodes.

It's hard to believe that the studio responsible for so many great monster makeups failed so miserably in the robot department. Case in point: *The Vanishing Shadow.*

Flash Gordon Conquers the Universe (1940). Directors: Ford Beebe & Ray Taylor. Cast: Larry "Buster" Crabbe, Carol Hughes, Charles Middleton, Frank Shannon, Anne Gwynne, Roland Drew. Who's sprinkling Purple Death dust on the planet Earth? Could it be Ming the Tireless (Middleton)? Flash (Crabbe), Dale (Hughes) and Zarkov (Shannon) take another one of their intergalactic jaunts to combat Ming a third and last time. Goodbye and good riddance. Three featurizations too many: *Peril from the Planet Mongo, Space Soldiers Conquer the Universe* and *Purple Death from Outer Space.* 12 episodes.

The Green Hornet (1940). Directors: Ford Beebe & Ray Taylor. Cast: Gordon Jones, Keye Luke, Anne Nagel, Wade Boteler, Philip Trent. The Hornet (Jones) and Kato (Luke), do-gooders forced to work outside the law, use their super-speed car and a gas gun in the war on crime. Anne Gwynne and Alan

Set visitor Gloria Jean poses with Ed Wolff (*another* risible robot!) during the making of *The Phantom Creeps.*

Pressbook ad for the second Flash Gordon serial.

Ladd have small parts. Based on the popular radio serial. 13 episodes.

The Green Hornet Strikes Again (1940). Directors: Ford Beebe & John Rawlins. Cast: Warren Hull, Keye Luke, Wade Boteler, Anne Nagel, Eddie Acuff. More of the same. Hull's a better Hornet than Jones, but this is still pretty rough going; the '60s television series starring Van Williams and Bruce Lee is a lot slicker and more entertaining all around. 13 episodes.

Junior G-Men (1940). Directors: Ford Beebe & John Rawlins. Cast: Billy Halop, Huntz Hall, Gabriel Dell, Bernard Punsley, Roger Daniels, Phillip Terry. The Dead End Kids team with G-man Terry to battle the Order of the Flaming Torch, an anarchist group. Scientific innovations include deadly new high explosives, a wireless detonator and an aerial torpedo. 12 episodes.

Sea Raiders (1941). Directors: Ford Beebe & John Rawlins. Cast: Billy Halop, Huntz Hall, Gabriel Dell, Bernard Punsley, Hally Chester, William Hall, Edward Keane, Reed Hadley. The Sea Raiders, foreign agents led by Keane and Hadley, are saboteurs who run afoul of a band of pugnacious juveniles. SF ingredients include a secret torpedo boat. 12 episodes.

Don Winslow of the Navy (1942). Directors: Ford Beebe & Ray Taylor. Cast: Don Terry, Walter Sande, Wade Boteler, Paul Scott, John Litel, Peter Leeds, Anne Nagel, Claire Dodd. A two-way television turns up in this story of Naval Intelligence officer Winslow (Terry) fighting to frustrate the evil plans of the Scorpion, a wily saboteur. One of Beebe's last serial assignments before his long-due promotion to features. 15 episodes.

Gang Busters (1942). Directors: Ray Taylor & Noel Smith. Cast: Kent Taylor, Irene Hervey, Ralph Morgan, Robert Armstrong, Richard Davies, Joseph Crehan. Archcrook Professor Mortis (Morgan) seemingly recruits his gang from the dead, using a death-simulating drug and an anti death treatment. A slightly ghoulish premise and an attractive cast make this one sound like more fun than it probably is. Based on the radio show. 13 episodes.

Junior G-Men of the Air (1942). Directors: Ray Taylor & Lewis D. Collins. Cast: Billy Halop, Gene Reynolds, Lionel Atwill, Frank Albertson, Richard Lane, Huntz Hall, Gabriel Dell, Turhan Bey. All the usual serial gadgetry, plus the added enticement of Atwill as the Japanese head of a sabotage ring. 13 episodes.

The Great Alaskan Mystery (1944). Directors: Ray Taylor & Lewis D. Collins. Cast: Milburn Stone, Marjorie Weaver, Edgar Kennedy, Samuel S. Hinds, Martin Kosleck, Ralph Morgan, Joseph Crehan, Harry Cording. Another great B cast in a story of Americans battling fascists for Morgan's Peratron, a device capable of transmitting matter through space. Released in England as *The Great Northern Mystery*. 13 episodes.

Jungle Queen (1945). Directors: Ray Taylor & Lewis D. Collins. Cast: Edward Norris, Eddie Quillan, Douglass Dumbrille, Lois Collier, Ruth Roman, Tala Birell. While the Nazis attempt to sic an African tribe on the Allies, Americans Norris and Quillan fight to keep the peace. Lothel (Roman), the supernatural Queen of the Jungle, uses her powers to help the Yanks defeat the German agents. The level of care that went into this thing is evident from watching the first scene of Chapter 1: Goose-stepping German soldiers menacingly march through the streets of some major city as comical "Spring Byington Goes Shopping"–type sitcom music plays on the soundtrack. It's tough to imagine *any* kid being so easily entertained that he'd sit still for this one. 13 episodes.

The Master Key (1945). Directors: Ray Taylor & Lewis D. Collins. Cast: Milburn Stone, Jan Wiley, Dennis Moore, Addison Richards, Byron Foulger. Scientist Foulger's machine, the Orotron, extracts gold from sea water and triggers the expected clashes between lawmen and Nazis. "Lash" LaRue plays Migsy. 13 episodes.

Lost City of the Jungle (1946). Directors: Ray Taylor & Lewis D. Collins. Cast: Russell Hayden, Jane Adams, Lionel Atwill, Keye Luke, Helen Bennett. Warmonger Sir Eric Hazarias (Atwill) hopes to spark World War III using Meteorium 245, a metal defense against the A-bomb. Atwill died during production, adding to the depressing atmosphere of an already tepid serial. 13 episodes.

The Mysterious Mr. M (1946). Directors: Lewis D. Collins & Vernon Keays. Cast: Richard Martin, Pamela Blake, Dennis Moore, Jane Randolph, Danny Morton. The villainous Mr. M uses Hypnotrene, a drug which produces a hypnotic effect, in his campaign to steal the newest submarine equipment. Universal's last serial. 13 episodes.

III. Universal Horror Oscars

The following Universal thrillers were nominated for Academy Awards in the categories listed. **Winners are shown in bold.**

MUSIC—SCORING

Frank Skinner, *The House of the Seven Gables* (1940)
Edward Ward, *Phantom of the Opera* (1943)

CINEMATOGRAPHY

Hal Mohr, W. Howard Greene, *Phantom of the Opera* (1943)

Rosalind Russell presented the winners with their Oscars.

Atmospherically styled sets such as this earned Alexander Golitzen, John B. Goodman, Russell A. Gausman and Ira S. Webb Oscars for 1943's *Phantom of the Opera* (Photofest).

Art/Set Direction

Alexander Golitzen, John B. Goodman, Russell A. Gausman, Ira S. Webb, *Phantom of the Opera* (1943)

Carole Landis presented the winners with their Oscars.

Alexander Golitzen, John B. Goodman, Russell A. Gausman, Ira S. Webb, *The Climax* (1944)

Special Effects

John P. Fulton, Bernard B. Brown, William Hedgcock, *The Invisible Man Returns* (1940)

John P. Fulton, John Hall, *The Invisible Woman* (1940)

John P. Fulton, Bernard B. Brown, *Invisible Agent* (1942)

Sound

Gilbert Kurland, *Bride of Frankenstein* (1935)

Bernard B. Brown, *Phantom of the Opera* (1943)

IV. Screen Gems *Shock* Television Packages

For most Baby Boomers, their introduction to the classic Universal horror films of the '30s and '40s came via late night *Shock* telecasts in the late '50s and early '60s. Within the safe confines of their homes, impressionable youngsters all across the country got their first glimpse of the famed monster characters that thrilled their parents' generation.

Containing 52 features, the original *Shock* catalogue, upon first glance, may surprise the uninitiated. Incredibly, the collection didn't include *Bride of Frankenstein* nor *House of Frankenstein*, nor did it boast such inescapably macabre fare as *Black Friday*, *Captive Wild Woman*, *The Mummy's Curse* nor *The Invisible Man's Revenge*. What it *did* include was an inordinate number of

B movies (i.e. *Chinatown Squad, The Spy Ring, Reported Missing, Destination Unknown,* etc.) that do not classify as horror films by the furthest stretch of the imagination (unless your definition of "shock" takes in such allied emotions as fear, mystery, dread, tension, and intrigue).

This vintage horror film package made such an impact on late night TV viewers that, a year later, Screen Gems assembled a second batch of creepies and called it (what else?) *Son of Shock.* This streamlined roster of 21 chillers contained many of the Universal thrillers that should have been included in the initial package, plus a generous selection of penny-dreadfuls from the vaults of Columbia studios ... the Karloff Mad Scientists series (from *The Man They Could Not Hang* to *The Boogie Man Will Get You*), *Night of Terror* with Lugosi, *Island of Doomed Men* and *The Face Behind the Mask* starring Peter Lorre and, on the distaff side, Rose Hobart playing the devil's emissary in *The Soul of a Monster.*

Unless one happened to find stills or write-ups about these films in then-current editions of *Famous Monsters, World Famous Creatures, Monster Parade, Monsters and Things* and *Journal of Frankenstein,* sensationalized newspaper and TV magazine advertisements promoting upcoming telecasts provided unforgettable first impressions of the screen delights to come.

Here is a listing of the movies that comprised the *Shock* and *Son of Shock* TV packages. When available, we've provided a come-on line taken off the TV section print ad itself, or the thumbnail synopsis provided by Screen Gems that appeared in *TV Guide* listings of the period.

For maximum effect, read these tempting titillaters through the eyes of an awestruck, horror-happy 11-year-old....

How many of these gems do *you* remember?*

The Original *Shock* TV Package

Films not covered in this book are provided with cast names.

Dracula (1931) *His fangs ruled an empire of Night.* (Ad line)

Frankenstein (1931) *The famous monster science couldn't control.* (Ad line)

Murders in the Rue Morgue (1932) *Gorilla kidnaps girl from deranged chemist.* (Ad line)

The Mummy (1932) *Ghoul hunts princess to share his tomb.* (Ad line)

Secret of the Blue Room (1933) *Suitors vanish in night of medieval terror.* (Ad line)

The Invisible Man (1933) *The phantom scientist who mocked all Nature's laws.* (Ad line)

The Black Cat (1934) *Newlyweds are the bait as fiends clash by night.* (Ad line)

Secret of the Chateau (1934) *A bookshop owner is confronted by two men who offer to sell him the original Gutenberg Bible.* (*TV Guide* synopsis)

Mystery of Edwin Drood (1935) *Based on Dickens' tale of shocking fiends and unsolved murder.* (Ad line)

The Raven (1935) *Sadist plots revenge with torture.* (Ad line)

The Great Impersonation (1935) *Dead man returns to plot mass murder.* (Ad line)

WereWolf of London (1935) *Botanist becomes a slave to mad cravings.* (Ad line)

Chinatown Squad (1935) With Lyle Talbot, Valerie Hobson, Andy Devine. *An agent for Chinese revolutionists is murdered in a Chinatown café. An ex-policeman attempts to solve the crime.* (*TV Guide* synopsis)

The Invisible Ray (1936) *Rivals for killer ray threaten Paris.* (Ad line)

Dracula's Daughter (1936) *Her fiendish love leads to a chamber of horrors.* (Ad line)

Night Key (1937) *A man invents a new type of burglar alarm, but it is stolen by his former partner. The inventor devises a scheme to gain revenge on the thief.* (*TV Guide* synopsis)

The Man Who Cried Wolf (1937) *Maniac's cunning puts wrong man in death-chair.* (Ad line)

Reported Missing (1937) With William Gargan, Jean Rogers, Dick Purcell. *When an airliner crashes while using a new invention, a hearing is set up to investigate the cause of the accident. At the hearing, the inventor makes statements which cast reflections on the pilot of the plane.* (*TV Guide* synopsis)

The Spy Ring (1938) With William Hall, Jane Wyman, Leon Ames. *An inventor is killed after he comes up with a device that transforms a machine-gun into an effective anti-aircraft device.* (*TV Guide* synopsis)

The Last Warning (1938) *When a mysterious character known as "The Eye" sends a man a series of extortion notes, a detective and his assistant are hired to solve the case.* (*TV Guide* synopsis)

Son of Frankenstein (1939) *The Monster's revenge leads to the boiling lava pit.* (Ad line)

Mystery of the White Room (1939) *A doctor is stabbed to death when the lights go out in an operating room during surgery. One of the suspects is the doctor's nephew.* (Ad line)

The Witness Vanishes (1939) *Grisly death comes by appointment as maniac prowls.* (Ad line)

The Invisible Man Returns (1940) *Phantom defies science to uncover man's innermost secrets.* (Ad line)

**The authors take no responsibility for the highly imaginative—and often inaccurate—synopses and ad lines!*

Whodunits and even espionage thrillers found their way into the *Shock* television package. Here are Walter Kingsford, Edmund Lowe and Wendy Barrie in a scene from *The Witness Vanishes*, last of the Crime Club movies.

Enemy Agent (1940) With Richard Cromwell, Helen Vinson, Robert Armstrong. *The head of an enemy spy ring has one of his men photograph secret material.* (*TV Guide* synopsis)

The Mummy's Hand (1940) *He waited 3000 years for vengeance.* (Ad line)

Man Made Monster (1941) *Electronic death shot from his dynamo fingers.* (Ad line)

A Dangerous Game (1941) With Richard Arlen, Jean Brooks, Andy Devine. *A detective is assigned to investigate a large insurance benefit paid to a man who is in a mental institution.* (*TV Guide* synopsis)

Horror Island (1941) *Pirate castle a trap for treasure hunters.* (Ad line)

Sealed Lips (1941) With William Gargan, June Clyde, Ralf Harolde. *A switch in witness chair puts a killer at large.* (Ad line)

The Wolf Man (1941) *Son of noble family turns into beast-on-the-prowl.* (Ad line)

The Mad Doctor of Market Street (1942) *Depraved scientist poses as God to enslave a nation.* (Ad line)

The Strange Case of Doctor Rx (1942) *Poison dart-thrower preys on murder court.* (Ad line)

Night Monster (1942) *Woman psychiatrist terrorized by unworldly strangler.* (Ad line)

Mystery of Marie Roget (1942) *Steel fingers crush beauty's last breath.* (Ad line)

The Mummy's Tomb (1942) *Ancient curse raises death from the tomb.* (Ad line)

Nightmare (1942) *Wartime saboteurs set a murder trap.* (Ad line)

Destination Unknown (1942) With William Gargan, Irene Hervey, Sam Levene. *A Dutch spy working for the Allies contacts an enemy agent in an attempt to learn the whereabouts of the St. Petersburg jewels.* (*TV Guide* synopsis)

Frankenstein Meets the Wolf Man (1943) *World's most hideous monsters in ghastly duel to death.* (Ad line)

The Mad Ghoul (1943) *Crazed surgeon operates on paralyzed victims.* (Ad line)

Son of Dracula (1943) *Bullets couldn't stop fiendish vampire.* (Ad line)

Calling Dr. Death (1943) *Nerve doctor's brain-wave hunts killer.* (Ad line)

The Mummy's Ghost (1944) *Ghoul returns from dead to reclaim mummified sweetheart. (Ad line)*

Weird Woman (1944) *Her voodoo terror brought death.* (Ad line)

Dead Man's Eyes (1944) *Eyes live on to brand killer.* (Ad line)

The Frozen Ghost (1945) *Hypnotist duels with unearthly forces in wax museum murder.* (Ad line)

Pillow of Death (1945) *A well-to-do lawyer murders his wife after falling in love with a beautiful young heiress.* (*TV Guide* synopsis)

House of Horrors (1946) *Strangler traps girl reporter.* (Ad line)

She-Wolf of London (1946) *Razor-clawed death laid to wolf-curse.* (Ad line)

The Spider Woman Strikes Back (1946) *Poison fiend and man eating plant threaten country.* (Ad line)

The Cat Creeps (1946) *Cat cry signals mystery isle murders.* (Ad line)

Danger Woman (1946) *Vile murder threatens atom danger.* (Ad line)

The *Son of Shock* TV Package

Behind the Mask (Columbia, 1932) With Boris Karloff, Jack Holt, Constance Cummings. *Mysterious Mr. X kills to protect the secrets of his dope ring.* (Ad line)

Night of Terror (Columbia, 1933) With Bela Lugosi, Wallace Ford, Sally Blane. *Man buried alive in plan to trap fiend.* (Ad line)

The Black Room (Columbia, 1935) With Boris Karloff, Marian Marsh, Robert Allen. *A prophesy of death drives fiend to grisly murders.* (Ad line)

Bride of Frankenstein (1935) *Chemistry gone mad! A lab lunatic unleashes a female monster.* (Ad line)

The Man Who Lived Twice (Columbia, 1936) With Ralph Bellamy, Marian Marsh, Isabel Jewell. *A notorious killer's appearance is changed by surgery.* (*TV Guide* synopsis)

The Man They Could Not Hang (Columbia, 1939) With Boris Karloff, Lorna Gray, Robert Wilcox. *Mechanical heart restores fiend to life.* (Ad line)

The Man With Nine Lives (Columbia, 1940) With Boris Karloff, Roger Pryor, Jo Ann Sayers. *Icehouse madman seeks human guinea pigs for frozen sleep.* (Ad line)

Black Friday (1940) *Medico on a murder binge after brain transplant.* (Ad line)

Before I Hang (Columbia, 1940) With Boris Karloff, Evelyn Keyes, Bruce Bennett. *Madman returns from gallows to conduct secret fountain-of-youth experiments.* (Ad line)

Island of Doomed Men (Columbia, 1940) With Peter Lorre, Rochelle Hudson, Robert Wilcox. *A racketeer runs an island empire where former convicts work for him.* (*TV Guide* synopsis)

The Devil Commands (Columbia, 1941) With Boris Karloff, Amanda Duff, Anne Revere. *Brainwave machine reduces man to robot.* (Ad line)

The Face Behind the Mask (Columbia, 1941) With Peter Lorre, Evelyn Keyes, Don Beddoe. *Outwardly he was calm — but raging hatreds seethed within him.* (Ad line)

An interesting variation on the Jekyll-Hyde theme, *The Man Who Lived Twice*, starring Ralph Bellamy and Marian Marsh, was one of the 12 Columbia chillers included in the *Son of Shock* TV package.

The Ghost of Frankenstein (1942) *Scientists war to control Monster when it strips its gears.* (Ad line)

The Boogie Man Will Get You (Columbia, 1942) With Boris Karloff, Peter Lorre, Jeff Donnell. *A string of corpses are kept in the wine cellar of a colonial inn which houses a demented professor who is trying to create a "superman."* (*TV Guide* synopsis)

Captive Wild Woman (1943) *A gorilla turned into a beautiful girl makes a much too-human mistake.* (Ad line)

The Soul of a Monster (Columbia, 1944) With Rose Hobart, George Macready, Jeanne Bates. *Medico becomes slave to a fiend when he forfeits soul.* (Ad line)

The Invisible Man's Revenge (1944) *A man with a persecution complex becomes invisible and sets out to haunt people.* (*TV Guide* synopsis)

House of Frankenstein (1944) *Touring horror troupe brings monsters back to life!* (Ad line)

The Mummy's Curse (1944) *Jealous mummy stalks swampland for reincarnated princess.* (Ad line)

The Jungle Captive (1945) *Ape woman, restored to life, wages lethal battle against brain graft.* (Ad line)

House of Dracula (1945) *Assorted fiends raise the roof...* (Ad line)

Index

Numbers in ***bold italics*** indicate photographs or illustrations.